Russia:
ALL 89 REGIONS

TRADE
AND INVESTMENT
GUIDE

PUBLISHER:

CTEC PUBLISHING LLC

PROJECT PARTICIPANTS:

COUNCIL FOR TRADE
AND ECONOMIC COOPERATION (US-RUSSIA)

K.C. HENNESSEY ASSOCIATES LLC (USA)

CENTREINVEST GROUP

PRESIDENT PUBLISHING CENTER

Russia:
ALL 89 REGIONS

TRADE
AND INVESTMENT
GUIDE

2004

OFFICIAL SOURCES

INDEPENDENT ANALYSIS

The publisher of
RUSSIA: ALL 89 REGIONS. TRADE AND INVESTMENT GUIDE
wishes to thank the following organizations, which have contributed
to the making of this Guide:

The Federation Council of the Federal Assembly of the Russian Federation
Executive authorities of 89 constituent entities of the Russian Federation
The Main Territorial Administration of the President of the Russian Federation
The Russian Union of Industrialists and Entrepreneurs (Employers)
The Chamber of Industry and Commerce of the Russian Federation
The World Bank
The US Department of Commerce
The U.S. National Association of Manufacturers (NAM)
The UN Development Program

SUMMARY

R ussia: All 89 Regions. Trade and Investment Guide is the first Russian and international guide of its kind targeted at Russian and foreign users offering basic information in one volume and illustrating the economic, industrial, resource, foreign trade, and investment potential of all 89 regions of Russia.

The Guide is a unique product of consistent joint effort of Russian and American business circles, and its publication was possible thanks to active support of legislative and executive authorities of the two countries and a number of leading international organizations.

Before work on the Guide began, the authors made sure there was a widespread demand in Russia and abroad for a directory describing the business climate in each region, particularly among potential business partners seeking a close-up view of the Russian regions and the country as a whole.

In the context of Russia's increasingly active integration with the global economy, the country's leadership and the leaders of the Russian regions seek to substantially increase the role of the regions in developing foreign economic and investment ties as one of the main drivers for economic growth. The Guide represents an opportunity for Russia's regions to present their economic potential and specific investment projects to a broad audience within the financial and business community.

The Guide also takes into account the growing interest among foreign businessmen in Russia's regional markets and direct dealing with them. They need comprehensive and objective information on the business environment in Russia's regions, their resource base, focus of industrial development, investment potential, and exports and imports of goods and services. The Russia: All 89 Regions. Trade and Investment Guide will serve them well in that regard.

In addition to the general information on the regions (geography, climate, and population), the Guide also contains information on economic growth trends for the past 7–10 years, including gross regional product volumes and industry breakdown, growth statistics and projections for core and traditional industry sectors, lists and volumes of goods produced, exported and imported, and each region's foreign economic relations and their geography. The investment appeal of each region is substantiated by specific indicators, including data on capital investment, inward foreign investment trends, enterprises with foreign investment operating in the region, local legislation on investor exemptions and privileges, and attractive investment projects available in the region. The regions provided information on approximately a thousand investment projects for inclusion in the Guide. This information may be of interest to investors throughout the world.

Primary information provided by the regions was carefully verified, classified, and supplemented. The Guide's structure complies with the internationally accepted standards for economic information.

The Guide includes an overview of the main economic events that have taken place in Russia and summary macroeconomic data for the first half of 2003.

Readers of the Guide will find an introductory article by Arkady Volsky, President of the Russian Union of Industrialists and Entrepreneurs (Employers), entitled Why Invest in Russia? (A Case in Favor). Other useful features of the Guide include information on the Russian tax system and the federal legislation on foreign investment, a list of international and overseas credit institutions represented in Russia, a list of the largest banks operating in the regions, and an analysis of 1H 2003 results of economic development of the Russian Federation. The Guide also features an explanatory note on how to use the Guide, subject indexes and references, economic maps of the regions, and contact details for the regional administrations, investment project initiators, foreign trade entities, and banks.

The Guide will be published every two years in the Russian and English languages in paper and CD-ROM format. Each new edition will be followed up by updates describing the most important economic developments arising in the regions. Accordingly, the publication of the Guide marks the emergence of a nationwide regional information support system that will be developed and improved.

The main sources of data are: official information provided by the administrations of Russia's regions, official publications of the

State Statistics Committee of the Russian Federation, data from regional statistical offices, estimates of regional experts, and independent expert analyses.

The Guide's authors would welcome comments and suggestions from readers as regards the structure and content of the Guide. Any such comments and suggestions will be incorporated into future editions.

LADIES AND GENTLEMEN:

I t is a great pleasure for me to present this Guide to Russia's regions to our domestic and overseas business partners. The modern Russia is a federative state composed of 89 regions. The Federation Council, a chamber of the Federal Assembly of the Russian Federation, or, as it is commonly known, the Chamber of the Regions, supports and encourages projects that provide information support with respect to regional economic interests and initiatives and assistance to our overseas partners in order for them to promote business relationships on a regional level. Mutually beneficial cooperation is contingent upon the availability of objective and reliable information on the foreign trade and investment potential of the cooperating parties. The Guide will be a good reference and information provider for them.

Speaking during a meeting of the State Council of the Russian Federation at the beginning of 2003, Russian President Vladimir Putin made it clear that regions' increasing role and activities are of paramount importance in promulgating Russia's foreign economic interests and promoting her industrial potential.

The publishers of this Guide were motivated by a determination to meet the demand in domestic and overseas business circles for first-hand information on the economic, investment and trade potential of Russia's regions, and the efforts of the regional authorities to create a legal and practical framework conducive to enhancing Russia's competitive position on the market for investment. Moreover, they have succeeded in compiling that information into a single volume. I hope that this marks only the beginning of a major and important project.

Russia's territorial, resource, and intellectual potential is enormous. History and fate have bestowed upon Russia a unique geopolitical and geo-economic position. This Guide provides a unique social and economic insight into each of our 89 regions.

I wish to draw the attention of potential domestic and overseas business partners to the investment projects listed at the end of the presentation for each region. These projects represent real opportunities for investment; they are supported by the regional authorities and federal authorities alike. They represent a clear illustration of the principle that whatever is good for investors is good for the nation. A wealth of opportunity is there for the taking by any investor who is serious about doing business and will want to expand their presence and influence in Russia's vast market.

Sergei Mironov,
CHAIRMAN OF THE FEDERATION COUNCIL
OF THE FEDERAL ASSEMBLY OF THE RUSSIAN FEDERATION

If Russia is to achieve the goals of growth and investment President Putin has set, Russia's regions will need to attract large volumes of investment – foreign as well as local – for the next decade and beyond. Russia's 89 regions offer a diverse blend of investment opportunities and challenges. Opportunities range from agriculture in the black earth regions in the South, to minerals and natural resources in the Northeast and Siberia, to heavy manufacturing in the industrial heartland along the Volga River and in the Urals, to high tech opportunities in the science cities of Siberia. Others include fisheries, forestry, shipbuilding, oil and gas in the Far East.

The challenges confronting Russia, as it seeks to increase investment levels, are equally great. Russia's regions would benefit immensely from modernizing their legal and judicial, banking and capital market systems. Russia's small and medium enterprises, a source of economic growth and job creation in many countries, need to be strengthened with new sources of commercial finance, modern technology, and better marketing opportunities. Russia has more skilled scientists and engineers than almost any country except the United States, but Russia's regions need to develop new, market-oriented ways to convert their knowledge and scientific skills into wealth by commercializing technology. Acting locally, but with an eye on global opportunities, will enhance the attractiveness of Russia's regions and its enterprises to both domestic and international investors. To achieve this, Russia's regional governments need to develop a modern, efficient, business-friendly approach to attracting investment, enforcing the rule of law, and establishing honest, transparent governance.

Under President Putin's leadership, Russia has already made great strides in meeting many of these challenges. But the job is not yet finished. The World Bank is proud to have been Russia's partner in development for the past twelve years. We have worked closely with federal, regional and local officials on a broad range of issues, including those affecting the investment climate. The World Bank stands ready to continue the support and cooperation that will enable Russia to succeed in her quest to transform her human, technological and natural resources into sustainable growth across its economy. We look forward to maintaining and strengthening our relationship with all levels of government and with the business community. It is, after all, the business community – foreign as well as local – that must seize the opportunities and invest with confidence in the Russian economy, in sectors of their choice.

I am pleased that the enormous effort expended in research and preparation of this catalog of the investment climate and opportunities across Russia will provide support to an investment drive that would benefit both the people of Russia and investors alike. The catalog, a clear, comprehensive, and incisive guide to the business conditions in each of Russia's regions, will help to provide prospective investors, both in Russia and abroad, with much of the basic information they will need to start investigating the opportunities available in Russia's regions. Solid and dependable information is the foundation on which informed investment decisions are based. Russia will be well served by the publication of this catalogue.

I wish you well.

James Wolfensohn,
PRESIDENT OF THE WORLD BANK

I welcome the publication, Russia: All 89 Regions. Trade and Investment Guide, as a tool for Americans and Russians to develop bilateral trade and investment. President Bush is committed to farther strengthening U.S.-Russian commercial relations, and I know these ties will help build economic growth and mutual understanding. In order to encourage business partnerships across Russia, I have held meetings with a number of Russia's Governors and Deputy Governors, and the Department of Commerce has established a network of representatives in 10 regions to collaborate with local governments and businesses, as well as American companies.

American companies with investments in Russia report that sales are growing, potential markets are expanding, and there are plans to increase their activities. American executives say that a major factor in their decisions to make or expand investments in Russia is whether a regional government is supportive of current and potential business partners. Some cities and regions are successfully attracting trade and investment through tax holidays, streamlining licensing and inspection requirements, eliminating conflicts between local and federation laws, and developing infrastructure supporting manufacturing and distribution industries.

Some Russian companies are demonstrating that it is possible to upgrade management and increase value by adopting codes of business conduct and good corporate governance standards. The business community in Russia is benefiting from passage of a new arbitration code and publication of a corporate governance code by the Russian Government. The Commerce Department's Good Governance Program is working with several Russian, American, and international organizations to promote better business practices and professional ethics, to strengthen corporate governance, and to improve commercial dispute resolution mechanisms. Under the auspices of the Russian-American Business Dialogue, the Commerce Department is working with the International Finance Corporation and the Russian Federal Commission for Securities Markets to publish a practical corporate governance manual for Russian companies.

During encounters with small business owners in Russia, I have been impressed by their entrepreneurship, as well as by their efforts to overcome a heavy regulatory burden. The success of Russia's federal and regional governments in eliminating unnecessary regulation will affect the growth rate of small businesses in Russia – and whether they can create jobs and deliver goods and services to consumers. We offer assistance to Russia's small businesses through the Department's Special American Business Internship Training Program's business internships, as well as our Business Information Service for the Newly Independent States (BISNIS) Program's market information, sales leads, and business consulting.

Best wishes to Americans and Russians in their efforts to develop trade and investment throughout Russia. The Department of Commerce is prepared to assist through Commercial Service and BISNIS staff located across Russia.

Donald L. Evans,
THE U.S. SECRETARY OF COMMERCE

The National Association of Manufacturers (NAM) looks forward to an intensified trade and investment relationship with Russian companies and public entities as Russia negotiates and enacts the market-opening reforms that will be required for it to join the World Trade Organisation. It is our hope and expectation that the Russia: All 89 Regions. Trade and Investment Guide can play a very useful role in bringing our members together with potential customers throughout Russia.

The NAM is comprised of 14,000 manufacturing companies, 10,000 of which are small and medium-sized firms. Our members make the highest-quality consumer, intermediate, and capital goods in the world – products that embody some of the most cutting-edge technology available today. Many of our members eagerly look forward to competing for sales on an even playing field in the emerging Russian economy.

To help foster improved U.S.-Russian economic ties, we support permanent normal trade relations as part of the process of Russia joining the WTO. We plan to be a forceful advocate for Russian accession to the WTO that includes a robust market-opening package lowering Russian barriers to imports from the United States.

As our economic links deepen, the NAM also looks forward to more extensive contacts with the Council for Trade and Economic Cooperation and the Russian Union of Industrialists and Entrepreneurs.

Jerry Jasinowski,
PRESIDENT OF THE U.S. NATIONAL
ASSOCIATION OF MANUFACTURERS

WHY INVEST IN RUSSIA? (A CASE IN FAVOR)

It should by now be evident to the international business community that Russia's economy is on the rise. It is approaching a dynamic equilibrium, whereby macroeconomic stabilization is accompanied by stabilization at the microeconomic level. Russia has made important strides on the path to market and political reform, which has not gone unnoticed by the global business community. The European Union and the United States recognized Russia as a market economy in 2002. Leading global rating agencies believe that the country has established a solid legal framework for business, improved the executive branch, and significantly enhanced the investment climate. S&P upgraded Russia's credit rating twice in 2002, putting it within reach of the "investment grade" that is common for most European countries. This is yet more evidence that investment risks are at their lowest today. To summarize, Russia is becoming increasingly attractive for foreign partners and for greater investment into various sectors of its economy. I would like to offer some of the reasons why I believe this is the case.

A STABLE POLITICAL SYSTEM

Russia's political system reforms implemented over the past few years have centralized governmental authority while harmonizing the roles and responsibilities of the federal government and the regions for the long run. The structure of federal and regional executive bodies is being continuously improved. In 2003–2004, in accordance with Presidential Decree No. 824 of July 23, 2003 On Measures For the Conduct of the Administrative Reform in 2003–2004 the government will perform the reform to restrict the state's meddling in business entities' activities, and to eliminate excessive government regulation.

NATURAL RESOURCES

Russia's natural resources are truly tremendous and unique. The country accounts for over 12% of global oil reserves and has around 230–240 trillion cubic meters of natural gas. Russia ranks fourth in the world by iron ore and coal output. It has the world's largest timber reserves, yielding an annual 700 million cubic meters of timber output with no negative effect on the environment. The competitive advantage bestowed on Russia by nature opens up wide-ranging opportunities for economic development and the establishment of strong trade ties with the global community.

ECONOMIC GROWTH

Russia has experienced sustainable economic growth since 1999, with GDP increasing by almost 20% over the past four years. The rise was mainly driven by accelerated growth in exports and trade. Economic growth has featured a strong increase in real household incomes and consumption.

During 2000–2002, Russians saw their income grow by almost a third. At 13%, Russia's personal income tax is Europe's lowest. Rising demand for labor amid a growing economy has noticeably reduced unemployment.

LEGAL PROTECTION OF FOREIGN INVESTMENT

In 2003, the Law on Foreign Currency Regulation has been amended in order to create an even more favorable environment for investments in the Russian economy and the development of international relations. The existing Law on Foreign Investment provides foreign investors with comprehensive and unconditional protection of their rights under the provisions of the civil legislation. Moreover, Russia's investment legislation is undergoing constant enhancement. In the space of the past two years, corporate and anti-monopoly legislation has been amended, and new Tax, Land, and Civil Procedural Codes free of discriminatory provisions against foreign investment and foreign business in general have been adopted.

In 2003, a new version of the Customs Code was adopted in line with international customs regulation standards. The new version envisages the deregulation of export proceed flows, the streamlining of customs procedures, and the establishment of a public advisory council tasked with protecting the interests of importers and exporters in the context of the State Customs Committee's regulation drafting activities.

STABLE PUBLIC FINANCES

Foreign debt repayments have ceased to be the determining factor influencing economic development and the government's budget policy.

Russia is on schedule with all of its foreign dept principal and interest repayments. In terms of debt burden, it is ranked among the moderately indebted countries, as the ratio of external borrowings to GDP has dropped to 41%, and federal budget spending on debt servicing has fallen to 12%. The government's pursuit of a policy of settling the debts of the former USSR has successfully resolved the issue of the foreign debt "repayments peak" in 2003.

TRADE BALANCE SURPLUS

In the current tense world market context, Russia's sizeable export potential makes it less dependent on the global situation. A strong current account and considerable international reserves (over $60 billion as of August 2003) are encouraging foreign investor interest in Russian financial instruments. Over the past year, foreign demand for Russian Eurobonds has grown significantly, signaling an increase in foreign investor confidence in Russia. Global financial institutions are striving to get long on Russian financial instruments, seeing them as a safe haven amid high global market volatility.

RUSSIA'S ACCESSION TO INTERNATIONAL TRADE ORGANIZATIONS

Russia is seeking to achieve a position in global trade consistent with its resource, industrial, investment, and scientific potential, and to become an equal and dependable player on the world market. WTO accession talks have seen a noticeable revival since mid-2000. The country has achieved a breakthrough in harmonizing its legislation with WTO standards and principles. We view Russia's accession to the WTO as an important element of her global economic integration.

LOW TAXES

The reduction of the tax burden is boosting corporate revenues and contributing to better transparency. Under the existing Tax Code, corporate profit tax has been reduced from 35% to 24%. The government is designing a host of measures aimed at further alleviation of the tax burden on manufacturing and service industries. The unified social tax rate will be slashed from 35% to 25% by 2005, the sales tax will be scrapped, and the export and capital construction VAT recovery procedure simplified by 2004.

FOREIGN INVESTMENT GROWTH

Leading global financial institutions recognize Russia's increasing investment appeal. At the beginning of 2003, cumulative foreign investment in Russia reached approximately $40 billion. According to the World Bank, foreign investment grew 38.7% in 2002 to $19.8 billion. At the same time, direct investment rose a mere 0.6% to $4.2 billion. These proportions of foreign direct financing hardly measure up to the potential opportunities opening up in Russia's economy. Russia has the capacity to absorb an annual $15–20 billion worth of direct investment, and all of the prerequisites for this are in place. Russian capital is being repatriated in what is perhaps the most telling sign of the improvement in the country's investment climate.

Some 10,000 foreign-owned companies are doing business in Russia at present. The high quality of their products and services combined with relatively cheap resources provide them with competitive advantages and good earnings opportunities. While opening a business in Russia was clearly a risky venture in the post-crisis years, a majority of companies have proven far-sighted by hanging on in the Russian market and reaping handsome rewards. The foreign companies with the best track record operating in Russia include BP, Cargill, Kraft, Lucent Technologies, Procter & Gamble, Hewlett-Packard, International Paper, ICN Pharmaceuticals, PepsiCo, Gillette, RJ Reynolds, General Motors, 3M, and numerous others.

These are just some of many persuasive reasons in favor of investing and doing other business in Russia. The stereotype of Russia as a global outcast is out of date. The role of Russia's regions in international affairs can and must be expanded. The Russian government is striving to provide maximum support and targeted assistance to promoting the regions' interests overseas. The publication of Russia: All 89 Regions. Trade and Investment Guide will help both the foreign and Russian business communities to get a better idea of Russia, its economic, resource, trade, and investment potential, as well as each region's capacities to select the most attractive offers and projects. I am confident that the Trade and Investment Guide will help promote reforms in Russia, and strengthen and expand cooperation between Russia's regions and the global community.

Arkady Volsky,

PRESIDENT OF THE RUSSIAN UNION OF INDUSTRIALISTS
AND ENTREPRENEURS (EMPLOYERS)

▲Delta

is proud to be official airline
sponsor of the
"Russia: All 89 Regions Trade
and Investment Guide"

MAKE LINES DISAPPEA

> ## PRINT YOUR OWN BOARDING PASS @ DELTA.COM/NYC

Now at delta.com/nyc, you can check in online, select your seat and print your boarding pass before you even go to the airport. Or handle it all quickly at any of our kiosks once you get there. Don't worry if you're not sure what to do, you'll find our terminal staffed with friendly, knowledgeable greeters to speed you on your way. So chances are, if you hate lines, you're going to love flying Delta.

▲ Delta Air Lines

RUSSIAN UNION OF INDUSTRIALISTS AND ENTREPRENEURS (EMPLOYERS)

The Russian Union of Industrialists and Entrepreneurs (Employers), a nationwide organization representing the interests of business in Russia, sees its mission as one of consolidating the efforts of Russian industrialists and entrepreneurs aimed at improving the business environment and raising the status of Russian business at home and abroad while maintaining a balance between the interests of society, government and business.

ARKADY VOLSKY,
PRESIDENT
OF THE RUSSIAN
UNION OF INDUSTRIALISTS
AND ENTREPRENEURS
(EMPLOYERS)

" The Union's committees and working groups, which set the tone for the Russian business community with regard to key economic issues, carry out important work as regards planning structural reform and economic modernization in Russia. The Union's proposals in such areas as taxation, customs and labor legislation, and judicial reform have already been incorporated into a variety of federal laws. The Union's viewpoints are taken into consideration with respect to reforms in key areas such as government and administration, the pension system, land relations, and currency and tax regulation. For us, it is crucial that these transformations should improve the investment climate in Russia, spark economic growth, create jobs, and raise incomes. The Union's guiding principle is that the interests of business are best defended by defending the interests of society as a whole."

Arkady Volsky

THE UNION TODAY:
- around 80% of Russia's GDP produced by enterprises represented by the Union;
- more than 320,000 representatives of industrial, scientific, financial and commercial organizations in all regions of Russia;
- 17 committees and working groups actively working on economic reforms in Russia;
- more than 100 sector and region specific unions and associations representing key sectors of the economy;
- regional associations of industrialists and entrepreneurs, representative offices and representatives of the Union in all 89 regions of Russia;

- coordination unions of industrialists and entrepreneurs in all seven federal districts of Russia set up for the purpose of enhancing collaboration between businesses in the districts.

COMMITTEES:
- corporate governance – Ruben Vardanyan (Rosgosstrakh)
- international business – Mikhail Khodorkovsky (YUKOS)
- tax and budget policy – Kakha Bendukidze (United Heavy Machinery)
- social relations and employer functions – Oleg Yeremeev (Russian Employers' Association Coordination Board)
- financial and capital markets – Alexander Mamut (Troika Dialog)
- land reform – Oleg Kiselev (Media-Sotsium)
- industrial policy – Vladimir Yevtushenkov (AFK Sistema)

WORKING GROUPS:
- WTO accession and customs legislation reform – Alexei Mordashov (Severstal Group)
- railway reform – Oleg Deripaska (Rusal)
- energy reform – Ruben Vardanyan (Rosgosstrakh)
- gas industry reform – Boris Titov (Interkhimprom)
- administrative reform – Alexander Shokhin (Renaissance Capital)
- judicial reform – Mikhail Friedman (Alfa Bank)
- pension reform – Igor Jurgens (Russian Union of Industrialists and Entrepreneurs)
- small and medium enterprise – Dmitry Zimin (VimpelCom)
- ecology working group within the Committee on Tax and Budgetary Policy – Nikolai Tonkov (NTM Holding)
- corporate ethics commission – Boris Titov (Interkhimprom)

РСПП

TEL.: (095) 748 41 57
FAX: (095) 748 41 56
E-MAIL: pr_dep@rspp.net
HTTP://www.rspp.biz;
www.rspp.com.ru

![U.S.-RUSSIA BUSINESS COUNCIL]

Working to
expand and enhance
the U.S.-Russian commercial relationship

The U.S.-Russia Business Council is a Washington-based trade association that represents the interests of nearly 300 member companies operating in the Russian market. The Council's mission is to expand and enhance the U.S.-Russian commercial relationship. The Council represents the interests of its members in a variety of ways: issue advocacy with both the U.S. and Russian governments; information and analysis to support business decisions; providing access to, and networking opportunities with, government officials and Russian private-sector representatives; and company-specific problem solving and new business development. Through a range of activities, the Council contributes to stability and the development of a free market in Russia and supports Russia's integration into the global economy.

1701 Pennsylvania Avenue, NW, Suite 520, Washington, DC 20006
[Tel] 202.739.9180 [Fax] 202.659.5920 info@usrbc.org
www.usrbc.org

Insuring National Development

Central Bank of Russia`s licence No. 2790-g

119121, Moscow, 3rd Neapolimovskyi per. 13/5, bldg. 1
phone: + 7 (095) 246-89-89, fax: + 7 (095) 246-37-88

VNESHECONOMBANK   ВНЕШЭКОНОМБАНК

state dimension

COUNCIL FOR TRADE AND ECONOMIC COOPERATION RUSSIA-USA (CTEC)

BORIS
PETROVICH
ALEXEEV,
PRESIDENT

YOUR BUSINESS PARTNER IN MOSCOW

Established in 1992 in Moscow as a Russian legal entity, the Council for Trade and Economic Cooperation Russia-USA (CTEC) is a non-commercial, non-governmental association for businesses from both countries. In terms of the goals and activities set forth in its charter, the CTEC is the successor to the US-USSR Trade & Economic Council (ASTEC), which played a major role in the past in developing trade and economic relations between the two countries. As a legally and financially independent organization, the Council works in close collaboration with the Russian Union of Industrialists and Entrepreneurs.

EFFECTIVE SOLUTIONS FOR RUSSIAN-US CORPORATE COLLABORATION

The Council aims to foster trade, economic, and investment cooperation between the US and Russia at the corporate level. Alongside its work aimed at establishing and developing business contacts, the Council attaches great importance to assisting companies and organizations from various countries in the implementation of specific business collaboration projects.

EXPERIENCED PROFESSIONALS AT YOUR SERVICE

The Council hosts trade and economic forums and conferences, organizes group and individual business programs for Russian and American businessmen, provides various types of advisory and information services, engages in publishing activity aimed at fostering business links with the Russian regions, and provides practical assistance with the following:

- Identification of potential partners for cooperation
- Implementation of trade and economic projects
- Assistance in attracting investment into new and ongoing projects
- Organizing marketing of goods and services and establishing business links with the Russian regions
- Organizing exhibitions, presentations, and other publicity events
- Passport and visa support.

3, NAB. T. SHEVCHENKO, 121248, MOSCOW; TEL: (095) 243 5470, 243 5494; FAX: (095) 258 8380
E-MAIL: ctec@sovintel.ru; HTTP://www.ctec.ru

Russia:
ALL 89 REGIONS

TRADE
AND INVESTMENT
GUIDE

HOW TO USE THIS GUIDE

The Guide contains basic information on the economic, industrial, resource, foreign trade, and investment potential of each of Russia's 89 regions.

Economic maps present data on each region's principal extraction and processing industries and major transport routes and infrastructure facilities. The most common map symbols are not shown in individual map legends; instead, they are explained on the general map legend page.

Conventional symbols for natural resources reflect the approximate location of mining enterprises rather than mineral deposits.

To facilitate quick search and selection of investment projects by financing type and project documentation criteria, special symbols explained on the general map legend page have been added to the text.

Subject indexes and references are provided to enable search by industry sector, mineral resource, production, export, and import data, and goods and services to be produced and provided as a result of investment project implementation.

Each search item is referenced to a region name, page number, and section or table number.

GENERAL REGION
DESCRIPTION STRUCTURE

ECONOMIC MAP

**A WORD FROM THE HEAD
OF REGIONAL ADMINISTRATION**

GENERAL INFORMATION
Geography
Climate
Population

ADMINISTRATION

ECONOMIC POTENTIAL
1997–2002 gross regional product (GRP). Industry breakdown
Major economic growth projections
Industrial output in 1997–2002 for major sectors of economy
Fuel and energy balance (output and consumption per resource)
Transport infrastructure
Main natural resources: reserves and extraction in 2002

TRADE OPPORTUNITIES
Main goods produced in the region
Exports, including extra-CIS
Imports, including extra-CIS
Major regional export and import entities

INVESTMENT OPPORTUNITIES
Investments in 1992–2002 (by industry sector),
    including foreign investments
Capital investment
Major enterprises (including enterprises with foreign investment)
Most attractive sectors for investment
Current legislation on investor tax exemptions and privileges
Regional entities responsible for raising investment
Federal and regional economic and social development programs

INVESTMENT PROJECTS

RUSSIAN FEDERATION

CONSTITUENT ENTITIES
OF THE RUSSIAN FEDERATION

REPUBLICS

01 Adygeya
02 Altai
03 Bashkortostan
04 Buryatia
05 Dagestan
06 Ingushetia
07 Kabardino-
　Balkaria
08 Kalmykia
09 Karachayevo-
　Cherkessia
10 Karelia
11 Komi
12 Mariy El
13 Mordovia
14 Sakha (Yakutia)
15 North Ossetia –
　Alania
16 Tatarstan
17 Tyva
18 Udmurtia
19 Khakassia

20 Chechen
　Republic
21 Chuvashia

TERRITORIES

22 Altai
23 Krasnodar
24 Krasnoyarsk
25 Maritime
26 Stavropol
27 Khabarovsk

REGIONS

28 Amur
29 Arkhangelsk
30 Astrakhan
31 Belgorod
32 Bryansk
33 Vladimir
34 Volgograd
35 Vologda
36 Voronezh
37 Ivanovo

38 Irkutsk
39 Kaliningrad
40 Kaluga
41 Kamchatka
42 Kemerovo
43 Kirov
44 Kostroma
45 Kurgan
46 Kursk
47 Leningrad
48 Lipetsk
49 Magadan
50 Moscow
51 Murmansk
52 Nizhny Novgorod
53 Novgorod
54 Novosibirsk
55 Omsk
56 Orenburg
57 Oryol
58 Penza
59 Perm
60 Pskov

61 Rostov

62 Ryazan

63 Samara

64 Saratov

65 Sakhalin

66 Sverdlovsk

67 Smolensk

68 Tambov

69 Tver

70 Tomsk

71 Tula

72 Tyumen

73 Ulyanovsk

74 Chelyabinsk

75 Chita

76 Yaroslavl

FEDERAL CITIES

77 Moscow

78 St. Petersburg

AUTONOMOUS

REGION

79 Jewish

AUTONOMOUS

DISTRICTS

80 Aginsky Buryatsky

81 Komi-Permyatsky

82 Koryaksky

83 Nenetsky

84 Taimyrsky

(Dolgano-Nenetsky)

85 Ust-Ordynsky

Buryatsky

86 Khanty-

Mansiysky – Yugra

87 Chukotsky

88 Evenkiysky

89 Yamalo-Nenetsky

According to Article 65 of the Constitution of the Russian Federation, the Russian Federation is comprised of 21 Republics, 6 Territories, 49 Regions, two Federal Cities, one Autonomous Region, and 10 Autonomous Districts.

CONSTITUENT ENTITIES OF THE RUSSIAN

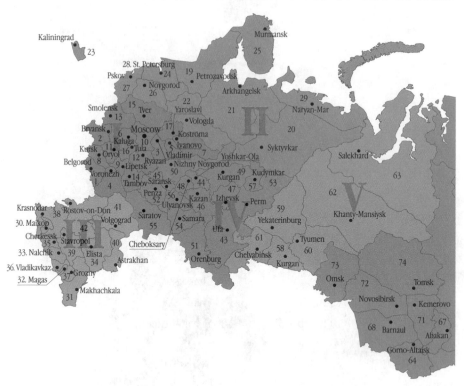

FEDERATION

FEDERATION AND FEDERAL DISTRICTS

The list of the Federal Districts has been approved by Decree of the President of the Russian Federation No. 849 of May 13, 2000 On Plenipotentiary Representative of the President of the Russian Federation in a Federal District (as amended on June 21, 2000).

The numbers of the constituent entities of the Russian Federation in sequential order according to the Constitution of the Russian Federation appear in square brackets (see pages 24–25).

MAP LEGEND

	Sea
	River, lake
PSKOV	Regional capital
Plussa	Town
TAMBOV REGION	Region
FINLAND	Country
BARENTS SEA	Sea
Lake Seliger Volga	Lake, river
Dolgy island	Island, peninsula
Cape of Kanin Nos	Cape
⚓	Seaport
✈	International airport
✈	Interregional airport
︎	Fishing port
●—•—▲	Oil pipeline
○—○—△	Gas pipeline
———	Railroad
———	Highway

INVESTMENT PROJECT CONVENTIONAL SYMBOLS

- ● Loan
- ■ Equity
- ★ Leasing
- ❖ Joint venture
- ◆ Business plan
- ▲ Feasibility study
- ▼ Investment proposal
- ◗ Project documentation

I. CENTRAL FEDERAL DISTRICT

1. Belgorod Region [31]
2. Bryansk Region [32]
3. Vladimir Region [33]
4. Voronezh Region [36]
5. Ivanovo Region [37]
6. Kaluga Region [40]
7. Kostroma Region [44]
8. Kursk Region [46]
9. Lipetsk Region [48]
10. Moscow Region [50]
11. Oryol Region [57]
12. Ryazan Region [62]
13. Smolensk Region [67]
14. Tambov Region [68]
15. Tver Region [69]
16. Tula Region [71]
17. Yaroslavl Region [76]
18. Moscow [77]

REGIONS OF THE CENTRAL FEDERAL DISTRICT

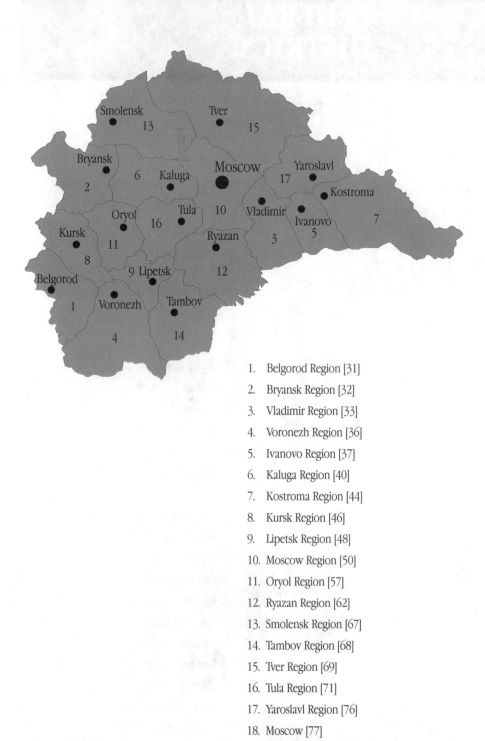

Smolensk 13

Tver 15

Bryansk 2

6 Kaluga

Moscow

Yaroslavl 17

Kostroma

Oryol 16 Tula 10 Vladimir 3 Ivanovo 5 7

Kursk 11 8

Ryazan

Belgorod 1 9 Lipetsk Voronezh Tambov 12

4 14

1. Belgorod Region [31]

2. Bryansk Region [32]

3. Vladimir Region [33]

4. Voronezh Region [36]

5. Ivanovo Region [37]

6. Kaluga Region [40]

7. Kostroma Region [44]

8. Kursk Region [46]

9. Lipetsk Region [48]

10. Moscow Region [50]

11. Oryol Region [57]

12. Ryazan Region [62]

13. Smolensk Region [67]

14. Tambov Region [68]

15. Tver Region [69]

16. Tula Region [71]

17. Yaroslavl Region [76]

18. Moscow [77]

01. BELGOROD REGION [31]

E C O N O M I C   M A P

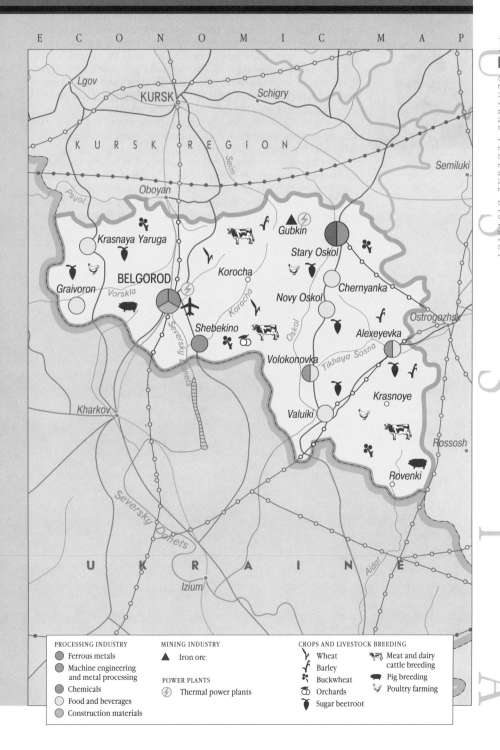

PROCESSING INDUSTRY
- ● Ferrous metals
- ● Machine engineering and metal processing
- ● Chemicals
- ○ Food and beverages
- ● Construction materials

MINING INDUSTRY
- ▲ Iron ore

POWER PLANTS
- ⚡ Thermal power plants

CROPS AND LIVESTOCK BREEDING
- Wheat
- Barley
- Buckwheat
- Orchards
- Sugar beetroot
- Meat and dairy cattle breeding
- Pig breeding
- Poultry farming

The Belgorod Region is endowed with well-developed industrial and agricultural sectors and abundant natural resources. The Region accounts for some 80% of the iron ore reserves of the Kursk Magnetic Anomaly, or more than 40% of Russia's total reserves of iron ore. Belgorod citizens are hard working people who make effective use of the Region's resources and renowned black earth soil.

Mining, metals, and the agroindustrial sector are the flagships of the Region's economy. The Region extracts one third of Russia's iron ore output and produces top grade steel and rolled metal. The Region boasts advanced machine engineering, chemicals, processing, light industry, and building materials sectors. It produces between five and fifteen per cent of Russia's grain, sugar, oil, and butter output, and a considerable share of the nationwide total output of meat and dairy products. The pursuit of a policy of establishing vertically integrated agricultural enterprises and attracting major investors has made the Belgorod Region an acknowledged leader in per capita output of livestock and tillage products and exports to other regions.

In terms of residential housing construction, two thirds of which is private, the Region leads the country and considerably exceeds the average nationwide per capita housing construction rate.

The Region is implementing important social welfare programs involving the extensive construction of social and cultural facilities and new educational establishments, including new premises for Belgorod State University.

The Region has completed construction work on its gas supply network and is currently implementing a major road construction and urban development program.

The investment policy pursued by the Administration and Government of the Belgorod Region aims to create conditions conducive to expanding manufacturing and increasing profitability. The Region's strong investment appeal has been confirmed several times by independent rating agencies.

Yevgeny Savchenko,
GOVERNOR OF THE BELGOROD REGION

1. GENERAL INFORMATION

1.1. GEOGRAPHY

The Belgorod Region covers a total area of some 27,100 square kilometers. The Region is located in the Central Black Earth Zone in the south of European Russia on the south-western and southern slopes of Mid-Russian Heights, and is drained by the Dnieper and Don rivers. To the south and to the north, it borders the Lugansk, Kharkov, and Sumy Regions of Ukraine, to the north and to the north-west – the Kursk Region, and to the east – the Voronezh Region.

1.2. CLIMATE

The Region is located in the forest-steppe temperate continental climate zone. The specific character of the Region's agriculture is largely determined by its fertile soils: about 80% of the Region lies under black earth soils, the most productive for agriculture.

Air temperatures in January temperature average –8°C, rising to +20°C in July. Average annual precipitation is 500 mm, and 550 mm in the northern and the western parts of the Region. The average growing season lasts 190 days.

1.3. POPULATION

According to preliminary 2002 census results, the Belgorod Region's population is 1,512,000 people. The average population density is 56 people per square kilometer. The economically active population totals 717,000. Official 2002 unemployment was 0.9%.

Demographically speaking, some 59% of population is of statutory working age, some 18% are below the statutory working age, and 23% are above the statutory working age.

The major urban centers of the Region and their population (2002 data) are Belgorod (337,600), Stary Oskol (216,000), Gubkin (85,400), and Shebekino (46,400).

Population							TABLE 1
	1992	1997	1998	1999	2000	2001	2002
Total population, '000	1,406	1,476	1,482	1,490	1,495	1,499	1,512
Economically active population, '000	693	644	655	720	725	738	717

2. ADMINISTRATION

4, pl. Revolyutsii, Belgorod, Belgorod Region, 308005
Phone: (0722) 22 4247; fax: (0722) 33 6705
E-mail: admin@regadm.bel.ru
http://www.beladm.bel.ru

NAME	POSITION	CONTACT INFORMATION
Yevgeny Stepanovich SAVCHENKO	Governor of the Belgorod Region	Phone: (0722) 22 4247 Fax: (0722) 33 6705 E-mail: admin@regadm.bel.ru
Oleg Nikolaevich POLUKHIN	Deputy Governor of the Belgorod Region, Chief of Staff of the Governor	Phone: (0722) 32 0230 Fax: (0722) 27 3259 E-mail: rukap@regadm.bel.ru
Vladimir Filippovich BOROVIK	First Deputy Head of the Belgorod Regional Government, Head of the Finance and Budgetary Policy Department	Phone: (0722) 22 3191 Fax: (0722) 32 1388 E-mail: findept@regadm.bel.ru
Vladimir Fedorovich ZOTOV	Deputy Head of the Belgorod Regional Government, Head of the Economic Security and Industry Department	Phone: (0722) 33 6288 Fax: (0722) 22 5795 E-mail: ekdept@regadm.bel.ru
Alexei Ivanovich ANISIMOV	Deputy Head of the Belgorod Regional Government, Head of the Agroindustrial Sector Department	Phone: (0722) 22 5541 Fax: (0722) 22 5674 E-mail: apkdept@regadm.bel.ru

I

CENTRAL FEDERAL DISTRICT

NAME	POSITION	CONTACT INFORMATION
Nikolai Dmitrievich GOLOVIN	Deputy Head of the Belgorod Regional Government, Head of the Fuel and Energy Sector and Housing and Communal Services Reform Department	Phone: (0722) 22 4777 Fax: (0722) 32 0374 E-mail: tekdept@regadm.bel.ru
Alexander Alexandrovich SUKHAREV	Deputy Head of the Belgorod Regional Government, Head of the Construction and Transport Department	Phone: (0722) 32 1748 Fax: (0722) 33 6710 E-mail: strdept@regadm.bel.ru

3. ECONOMIC POTENTIAL

3.1. 1997–2002 GROSS REGIONAL PRODUCT (GRP). INDUSTRY BREAKDOWN

The Belgorod Region's 2002 gross regional product reached $1,896.1 million, a 3% increase on 2001 levels (in comparable prices). Industrial production and agriculture, the main sources of growth, accounted for 33% and 19% of GRP, respectively.

GRP trends in 1997–2002   TABLE 2

	1997	1998	1999	2000	2001	2002
GRP in current prices, $ million	2,921.2	1,953.6	1,370.6	1,576.5	1,823.3	1,896.1

GRP industry breakdown in 1997–2002, % of total   TABLE 3

	1997	1998	1999	2000	2001	2002
GRP	100.0	100.0	100.0	100.0	100.0	100.0
Industry	34.5	38.6	39.0	34.6	32.5	33.0
Agriculture and forestry	10.4	8.8	15.9	19.8	18.1	19.0
Construction	10.5	9.8	8.5	7.9	8.7	5.4
Transport and communications	5.2	5.2	5.8	6.7	6.3	5.9
Trade and public catering	11.3	11.7	11.7	11.9	11.9	12.2
Other	22.7	20.5	14.0	13.8	16.9	18.9
Net taxes on output	5.4	5.4	5.1	5.3	5.6	5.6

3.2. MAJOR ECONOMIC GROWTH PROJECTIONS

The Belgorod Regional Administration is currently working on comprehensive measures aimed at securing the economic development of the Region. The following is an outline of the priorities identified for the coming years.

Industry: stepping up output growth; expanding markets via corporate restructuring and increased output of competitive products; increasing and revamping production capacities through loans and direct investments; and reducing costs and deploying energy-saving technologies.

Agriculture: stepping up output growth through agroindustrial sector reform; increasing agricultural investment through the integration of agricultural enterprises and increased cooperation with economically stronger companies and commercial entities. This is to be achieved through better labor incentives and the creation of conditions conducive to the introduction of advanced technologies in livestock breeding and crop cultivation.

Plans are afoot for the construction of new facilities, the upgrading of standard poultry farms, and the creation of integrated enterprises for beef and pork production. A program is currently underway for the development of pig-breeding based on cooperation with foreign companies. The program envisages the use of high yield hybrid livestock and European farming techniques.

Construction: improving output and restructuring existing construction facilities and creating new facilities based on modern efficient technologies used in industrial and residential construction.

Trade: expanding regional and international trade contacts within the Russian Federation and abroad.

Transportation: road haulage services are expected to grow following the opening of 1,000 kilometers of new paved roads in 2003; the creation of modern road haulage operators is planned.

3.3. INDUSTRIAL OUTPUT IN 1997–2002 FOR MAJOR SECTORS OF ECONOMY

The Belgorod Region is a combined agrarian and industrial region. Its key industries are ferrous metals, food and beverages, machine engineering, and metal processing. These account for a combined total of 71.8% of the Region's industrial output.

Ferrous metals. Ferrous metals accounts for 37.1% of total industrial output. The Region's ore dressing sector is represented by OAO Lebedinsky Ore Dressing Plant and OAO Stoylensky Ore Dressing Plant, both of which use strip mining, OAO KMARuda Plant, which operates deep mining, and OAO Oskolsky Electrometallurgical Plant. In 2002, the sector produced 32.8 million tons of concentrate and sintering ore, or 40% of the nationwide total.

Food and beverages. This sector accounts for 22.5% of total industrial output. Its main lines

Industry breakdown of industrial output in 1997–2002, % of total						TABLE 4
	1997	1998	1999	2000	2001	2002*
Industry	100.0	100.0	100.0	100.0	100.0	100.0
Ferrous metals	41.7	42.4	46.1	46.0	38.9	37.1
Food and beverages	17.0	18.4	20.9	20.1	23.2	22.5
Machine engineering and metal processing	12.9	12.0	9.6	11.6	12.3	12.2
Energy	13.7	12.5	8.5	8.8	10.7	11.0
Construction materials	7.4	7.3	6.8	7.5	8.0	8.9
Flour, cereals, and mixed fodder	2.4	2.2	2.0	1.8	2.8	3.1
Chemicals and petrochemicals	3.3	3.6	4.5	2.3	2.1	1.3
Forestry, timber, and pulp and paper	0.6	0.6	0.4	0.9	1.2	1.3
Light industry	0.5	0.5	0.5	0.3	0.4	0.4

*Estimates of the Belgorod Regional Administration

of specialization are sugar, meat, dairy, and vegetable products of various degrees of processing, vegetable oil, and mixed fodder. Major companies include ZAO Alekseevsky Dairy Preserves Plant, OAO Slavyanka Confectionery, OAO Efirnoye,OAO Belmyaso, OAO Belgorod Dairy Plant, ZAO Kristall-Bel, and OAO Gubkinsky Meat Processing Plant.

Machine engineering and metal processing. The sector accounts for 12.2% of total industrial output. Machine engineering and metal processing enterprises focus on the Region's ore dressing sector (mining machines, equipment repairs). The sector also includes enterprises from other sectors that have enjoyed fast growth in recent years (boiler manufacturing, chemicals processing, and equipment manufacturing).

Energy. The sector accounts for 11% of total industrial output. The Region has several power stations: the Gubkinskaya Thermal Power Station (36 MW), the Belgorodskaya Thermal Power Station (25.6 MW), an isolated generating plant in Shebekino (17 MW), and others. Their total installed capacity is 167 MW.

3.4. FUEL AND ENERGY BALANCE (OUTPUT AND CONSUMPTION PER RESOURCE)

Local power plants supply only 5% of the power the Region consumes. The rest is supplied from the Kursk and Voronezh power networks.

Demand for gas and oil products is fully met with supplies imported from outside the Region. The main oil products supplier is OAO Belgorodnefteproduct, a subsidiary of NK YUKOS.

Fuel and energy sector production and consumption trends, 1997–2002						TABLE 5
	1997	1998	1999	2000	2001	2002
Electricity output, billion kWh	0.4	0.4	0.4	0.4	0.5	0,5
Electricity consumption, billion kWh	10.1	10.0	10.6	9.9	10.0	10.1
Natural gas consumption, million cubic meters	1,368.5	1,005.8	1,731.5	1,689.2	1,538.3	1,336.7

3.5. TRANSPORT
INFRASTRUCTURE

Roads. The Region has 9,600 kilometers of roads, including 8,500 kilometers of paved highway. The Moscow – Crimea highway crosses the Region. The Region hosts some 31 road haulage enterprises. Agriculture produce, construction materials, and passengers are carried by road. A program was launched in 2001 with a view to opening 1,000 kilometers of new roads in 2003.

Railroads. The Region has 695 kilometers of railroads. Passenger routes connect the Region to Moscow and St. Petersburg, Crimea, and the Caucasus. Some 61% of all freight shipments and 59% of all passenger traffic in the Region is carried by rail.

Airports. Belgorod has air links to 15 cities in the CIS. The Belgorod Airport has international status and is capable of handling international flights. It receives about 30,000 passengers annually.

Gas pipelines. The Belgorod Region is crossed by the Stavropol – Moscow, Schebelinka – Belgorod – Kursk – Bryansk, and Schebelinka – Kupyansk – Valuyki – Alekseevka – Ostrogozhsk gas pipelines. The Region has the most extensive natural gas supply network not only in the Black Earth Zone, but in the whole of Russia.

3.6. MAIN NATURAL
RESOURCES: RESERVES
AND EXTRACTION IN 2002

Minerals and raw materials. The Region boasts major reserves of raw materials and minerals. It accounts for 80% of the total explored mineral resources of the Kursk Magnetic Anomaly, or 40% of all explored iron ore deposits in Russia. Predicted and recoverable iron ore resources amount to 40 billion tons, and quartzite resources stand at 180 million tons. The Region's potential reserves of minerals and raw materials are sufficient to supply existing ore mining plants and those under construction for a period of 150–200 years.

Deposits of construction materials such as chalk, sand, and clay, have been discovered in the Region. There are also indications of the presence of gold, graphite, and rare metals deposits. The Region is also believed to have deposits of platinum and hydrocarbons.

Land resourses. Agricultural lands occupy 2,713,400 hectares, over 70% of which are black earth soils.

4. TRADE OPPORTUNITIES

4.1. MAIN GOODS
PRODUCED IN THE REGION

Rolled ferrous metals and steel. Output for 2002: concentrated and sintering ore – 32.8 million tons, iron ore – 10.9 million tons, hot briquetted iron – 904,000 tons, steel – 2.2 million tons, and rolled ferrous metals – 2.1 million tons.

Construction materials. Output for 2002: sawn timber – 15,300 cubic meters; cement – 3.8 million tons; walling – 271 million conventional bricks.

Agriculture. Output for 2002: grain crops – 2 million tons; sunflower seed – 159,800 tons; sugar beet – 2 million tons; milk – 707,000 tons; cattle and poultry meat (live weight) – 200,000 tons; animal butter – 10,300 tons.

4.2. EXPORTS, INCLUDING EXTRA-CIS

Ferrous metals (ores and iron concentrates and ferrous metals) and construction materials (cement) are the Region's main exports (preliminary data from customs statistics).

The Region's 2002 foreign trade turnover was $1,106.7 million, 20% down on 2001. Extra-CIS exports rose by 3%; CIS exports were down by 32%. In 2002, the Region exported $501.2 million worth of goods (86.3% of the 2001 level), with $322.6 million (114%) of exports going outside the CIS, and $178.6 million (60%) to CIS countries. Ferrous metals account for 64% of exports. The bulk of the Region's exports goes to Ukraine, Hungary, Poland, Bulgaria, the Czech Republic, Italy, Israel, Germany, and Slovakia.

4.3. IMPORTS, INCLUDING EXTRA-CIS

In 2002, the Region's imports totaled $605.5 million (75.3% of the 2001 level), including $432.0 million (71.3%) from CIS countries, and $173.5 million (87.5%) from outside the CIS (preliminary data from customs statistics). In 2002, the Region's major imports were agricultural goods (53%), ferrous metals (28%), machinery and equipment (17%), and chemicals (1.5%). The major exporters to the Region are Ukraine, Moldova, Germany, Brazil, Cuba, the USA, and France.

Major regional export and import entities		TABLE 6
ENTITY	ADDRESS	PHONE, FAX, E-MAIL
OOO Kontakt Science and Production Enterprise	38, ul. Krasina, Belgorod, Belgorod Region, 308004	Phone: (0722) 32 6730 E-mail: contact@senergy.ru http://www.contact.bel.ru
OOO Belvneshtrans	42, ul. Kirova, Belgorod, Belgorod Region, 308001	Phone: (0722) 27 1736, 30 2442 E-mail: BVT@belgtts.ru

5. INVESTMENT OPPORTUNITIES

5.1 INVESTMENTS IN 1992–2002
(BY INDUSTRY SECTOR),
INCLUDING FOREIGN INVESTMENTS

The following main factors determine the investment appeal of the Belgorod Region:
- Its favorable geographical location close to major markets;
- Its developed transport and industrial infrastructures and reliable communications;
- Its rich natural resources (iron ores deposits and black earth soils);
- Legislation providing for tax privileges and guaranteed investors' rights;
- Its qualified workforce.

5.2. CAPITAL INVESTMENT

Industry and agriculture account for the lion's share of capital investment.

Capital investment by industry sector, $ million						TABLE 7
	1997	1998	1999	2000	2001	2002
Total capital investment	676.0	538.5	283.7	328.5	462.5	325.5
Including major industries (% of total)						
Industry	32.2	56.4	51.6	51.5	58.4	38.6
Agriculture and forestry	4.6	5.0	4.8	6.9	16.4	22.7
Construction	3.2	0.5	0.4	1.6	0.6	0.3
Transport and communications	5.0	2.4	6.4	6.0	4.0	7.1
Trade and public catering	0.8	0.3	0.3	1.2	0.5	0.6
Other	54.2	35.4	36.5	32.8	19.5	30.7

Foreign investment trends in 1996–2002						TABLE 8
	1996–1997	1998	1999	2000	2001	2002
Foreign investment, $ million	122.1	156.0	46.0	35.0	40.0	104.2
Including FDI, $ million	0.4	4.7	8.3	4.5	9.3	4.1

5.3. MAJOR ENTERPRISES
(INCLUDING ENTERPRISES
WITH FOREIGN INVESTMENT)

The Belgorod Region hosts numerous enterprises with foreign investment in sectors such as industry, construction, agriculture, wholesale and retail trade, and public services.

Major companies with foreign investment include ZAO Ruslime (Russian-Spanish) – chalk production; OOO Onken (Russian-German) – food; OAO Belgorod Fish Fodder Experimental Plant (Russian-British) – fish fodder; OOO Domat (Russian-Bulgarian) – food; and OAO Belgorod Dairy Plant (Russian-Italian) – food.

5.4. MOST ATTRACTIVE
SECTORS FOR INVESTMENT

Recent years have witnessed a growing influx of investment into industry and agriculture and commercial and residential construction. The Region's per capita residential construction (two thirds of which consists of private projects) rate is 1.8 times higher than the nationwide average, placing the Region near the top of the national league table for residential construction.

5.5. CURRENT LEGISLATION
ON INVESTOR TAX
EXEMPTIONS AND PRIVILEGES

In 2000, the Belgorod Region passed a Law On Investment in the Belgorod Region, which provides for tax benefits for investors. The Law seeks to foster investment activity, creates a most favored status for investors, and provides additional guarantees for organizations involved in investment projects.

Tax exemptions are granted to organizations that invest own or raised funds into projects selected through tenders by the Belgorod Regional Administration.

Tax incentives are available to legal entities registered and doing business within the Belgorod Region and participating in investment projects approved by the Belgorod Regional Administration.

Largest enterprises of the Belgorod Region			TABLE 9
COMPANY	SECTOR	2002 SALES, $ MILLION*	2002 NET PROFIT, $ MILLION*
OAO Oskolsky Electrometallurgical Plant	Ferrous metals	352.4	–26.0
OAO Lebedinsky Ore Dressing Plant	Ferrous metals	251.7	–17.0
OAO Stoylensky Ore Dressing Plant	Ferrous metals	178.2	11.7
OAO Belgorod Energy Machine Engineering Works	Machine engineering and metal processing	79.9	8.9
OAO KMAruda Plant	Ferrous metals	21.9	0.1
ZAO Starooskolsky Auto-Tractor Electric Equipment Works	Machine engineering and metal processing	28.0	1.9

*Data of the Belgorod Regional Administration

Regional entities responsible for raising investment		TABLE 10
ENTITY	ADDRESS	PHONE, FAX, E-MAIL
GU Fund for Residential and Mortgage Development	22, ul. Ostrovskogo, Belgorod, Beogorod Region, 308007	Phone: (0722) 31 0711 E-mail: belfond@mail.belgorod.ru

5.6. FEDERAL AND REGIONAL ECONOMIC AND SOCIAL DEVELOPMENT PROGRAMS FOR THE BELGOROD REGION

Federal targeted programs. In 2002, the Region had some 36 federal targeted programs underway, most of which had a social orientation. These include Science and Higher Education Integration, 2002–2006, Youth of Russia, 2001–2005, and The Elderly, 2002–2004.

The sub-programs included in the State Targeted Housing Program for 2002–2010 have been accorded priority status. If fulfilled, they will have a profound social effect, not only by providing the inhabitants of the Region with housing, but also by creating jobs in the construction sector and at enterprises involved in the production of construction materials.

In 2002, from all financing sources combined, the targeted programs in the Belgorod Region received some $51.6 million in funding, including $19.8 million from the federal budget, $19.1 million from the regional budget, and $12.7 million from non-budgetary sources.

Regional programs. In 2002, 40 programs were underway in the Region. Priority regional programs include The Belgorod Regional Program for Agricultural Machinery Development, 2001–2003, The Belgorod Regional Program for Energy Conservation, 2002–2005, The Belgorod Regional Program for Telephone Network Expansion, 1998–2003, and others.

Eight of the current regional programs are focused on goals related to the improvement of public health in the Region.

In order to satisfy the housing needs of its citizens, the Region adopted in 2002 a targeted Program for Development of Mortgage Lending in the Belgorod Region for 2003–2007. The Program envisages acquisition, on a preferential basis, of houses and flats by citizens dwelling within the Belgorod Region and financing of purchased flats and houses in the form of housing subsidies from the regional budget.

Other important regional programs include the programs for road construction and rural development. Under the said programs, work was being conducted in 167 neighborhoods in 2002. The Program 1000, launched in 2002, seeks to build 1,000 kilometers of paved road in 2003.

6. INVESTMENT PROJECTS

Industry sector and project description	1) Expected results 2) Amount and term of investment 3) Form of financing[1] 4) Documentation[2]	Contact information
1	2	3

ENERGY

01R001

Expansion of the Gubkinskaya Thermal Power Station (construction of a thermal power station with three combined-cycle plants).
Project goal: to provide reliable heat energy supply to industrial and residential users.

1) 510 MW capacity
2) $360 million/4 years
3) E, L, Leas.
4) Investment proposal

OAO Belgorodenergo
42, ul. Kommunisticheskaya,
Belgorod, Belgorod Region, 308870
Phone: (0722) 30 4059, 30 4050, 30 4116
Fax: (0722) 30 4555, 30 4077
E-mail: tts@belgorodenergo.ru, mail@belgorodenergo.ru
http://www.belgorodenergo.ru
Yevgeny Fedorovich Makarov, CEO
Vladimir Anatolyevich Bulanin,
Head of the Thermo-Technical Department

01R002

Construction of a gas-turbine unit at the Luch Thermal Power Station.
Project goal: to setup combined electrical and heat energy production for the central heating system of the city of Belgorod.

1) 60 MW capacity
2) $25 million/2.5 years
3) E, L, Leas.
4) FS

OAO Belgorodenergo
42, ul. Kommunisticheskaya,
Belgorod, Belgorod Region, 308870
Phone: (0722) 30 4059, 30 4050, 30 4116
Fax: (0722) 30 4555, 30 4077
E-mail: tts@belgorodenergo.ru, mail@belgorodenergo.ru
http://www.belgorodenergo.ru
Yevgeny Fedorovich Makarov, CEO
Vladimir Anatolyevich Bulanin,
Head of the Thermo-Technical Department

01R003

Construction of a gas-turbine unit at the Zapadnaya Thermal Power Station.
Project goal: to setup combined electrical and heat energy production for the central heating system of the city of Belgorod.

1) 90 MW capacity
2) $50 million/3.5 years
3) E, L, Leas.
4) Investment proposal

OAO Belgorodenergo
42, ul. Kommunisticheskaya,
Belgorod, Belgorod Region, 308870
Phone: (0722) 30 4059, 30 4050, 30 4116
Fax: (0722) 30 4555, 30 4077
E-mail: tts@belgorodenergo.ru, mail@belgorodenergo.ru
http://www.belgorodenergo.ru
Yevgeny Fedorovich Makarov, CEO
Vladimir Anatolyevich Bulanin,
Head of the Thermo-Technical Department

FOOD AND BEVERAGES

01R004

Reconstruction of a sugar plant.
Project goal: to raise daily sugar beet processing output.

1) 3,000 tons per day
2) $53.1 million/5 years
3) L
4) FS

ZAO Kristall-Bel
18, ul. Stroitelnaya, pos. Chernyaka,
Belgorod Region, 309561
Phone: (07232) 55 431
Fax: (07232) 55 291
Yury Ignatyevich Rudakov, CEO

---

[1] L – Loan, E – Equity, Leas. – Leasing, JV – Joint Venture
[2] BP – Business Plan, FS – Feasibility Study

1	2	3

AGRICULTURE

01R005

Development of poultry production. Project goal: to increase output.	1) Up to 200,000 tons per year 2) $200 million/1 year 3) L 4) FS	Economic Security and Industry Department of the Regional Administration 72, ul. Frunze, Belgorod, Belgorod Region, 308000 Phone: (0722) 33 6288, 33 6300, 25 4467, 25 4326 Larisa Vladimirovna Kovalyova, First Deputy Head of the Department

01R006

Development of pork production. Project goal: to increase output.	1) Up to 130,000 tons per year 2) $100 million/1 year 3) L 4) FS	Economic Security and Industry Department of the Regional Administration 72, ul. Frunze, Belgorod, Belgorod Region, 308000 Phone: (0722) 33 6288, 33 6300, 25 4467, 25 4326 Larisa Vladimirovna Kovalyova, First Deputy Head of the Department

ECONOMIC MAP

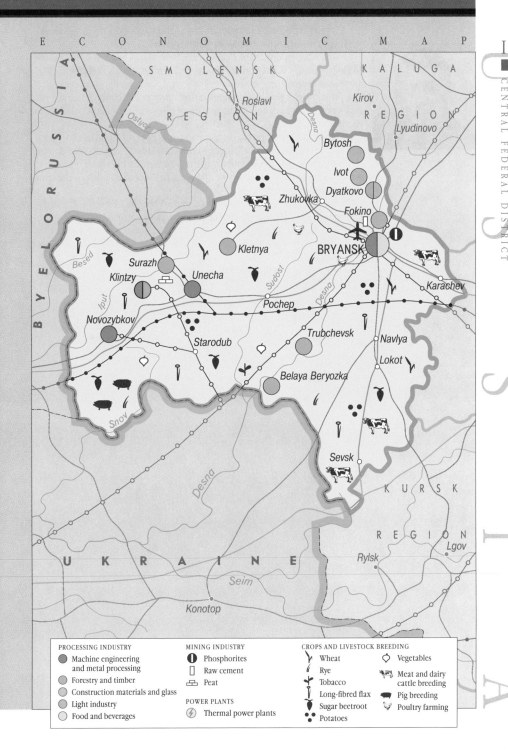

PROCESSING INDUSTRY
- ● Machine engineering and metal processing
- ● Forestry and timber
- ● Construction materials and glass
- ● Light industry
- ● Food and beverages

MINING INDUSTRY
- ❶ Phosphorites
- ▯ Raw cement
- ⛩ Peat

POWER PLANTS
- ⚡ Thermal power plants

CROPS AND LIVESTOCK BREEDING
- Y Wheat
- ⅄ Rye
- ⊥ Tobacco
- ⌁ Long-fibred flax
- ● Sugar beetroot
- ∴ Potatoes
- ◇ Vegetables
- 🐂 Meat and dairy cattle breeding
- 🐖 Pig breeding
- 🐓 Poultry farming

The Bryansk Region was first settled in prehistoric times prior to the foundation of Kievan Rus. Thanks to its unique geopolitical location at the border of Russia, Ukraine, and Belarus, the Bryansk Region is Russia's gateway to Europe. The Region enjoys a well-developed transport infrastructure with trunk railroads and highways, oil and gas pipelines, and an international airport.

The Regional Administration's investment policy aims to encourage investment in the real sector of the economy to boost the Region's economic growth and ensure its stable technological and social development.

One of the ways to accomplish this goal is to cooperate with partners seeking to invest in the Bryansk Region's economy.

We understand that the Region's investment appeal depends on factors having a positive impact on the investment climate, but also on practical steps augmenting these factors.

The Bryansk Regional Administration's investment policy is focused on high-tech production and the attraction of investment primarily into socially significant projects.

Thanks to our research, development, and operating potential, we are currently implementing a wide spectrum of investment projects. The core of our investment policy is to employ the most advanced high-tech projects, which increase the profitability of upgraded facilities and underpin the competitiveness of our output.

We invite investors to participate on mutually beneficial terms in the implementation of research and development initiatives, the introduction of new technologies, and the upgrading of operations with a high return on investment.

Yury Lodkin,
HEAD OF ADMINISTRATION (GOVERNOR)
OF THE BRYANSK REGION

1. GENERAL INFORMATION

1.1. GEOGRAPHY

The Bryansk Region covers a total area of 34,900 square kilometers in the western part of the East European Plain. To the west, it borders Belarus (the Gomel and Mogilev Regions), to the north – the Kaluga and Smolensk Regions, to the east and southeast – the Oryol and Kursk Regions, and to the south – Ukraine (the Chernigov and Sumy Regions).

1.2. CLIMATE

The Bryansk Region is located in the mild continental climate zone.

Average air temperature in January is –8°C, rising to an average of +19°C in July. Annual precipitation reaches 530–654 mm.

1.3. POPULATION

According to preliminary 2002 census results, the total population of the Bryansk Region was 1,379,000 people. The Region's average population density is 39.5 people per square kilometer. The economically active population amounts to 644,000 people. In 2002, the official unemployment level stood at 2.1%.

Demographically speaking, some 57.9% are of statutory working age, 18.4% are below the statutory working age, and 23.7% are beyond the statutory working age.

The Bryansk Region's major urban centers (2002 data) are Bryansk with 431,600 inhabitants, Klintsy with 66,200 inhabitants, Novozybkov with 43,500 inhabitants, and Dyatkovo with 34,300 inhabitants.

Population								TABLE 1
	1992	1997	1998	1999	2000	2001	2002
Total population, '000	1,459	1,469	1,460	1,451	1,438	1,425	1,379
Economically active population, '000	729	646	633	698	664	654	644

2. ADMINISTRATION

33, pr. Lenina, Bryansk, Bryansk Region, 241002
http://www.bryanskobl.ru

NAME	POSITION	CONTACT INFORMATION
Yury Yevgenyevich LODKIN	Head of Administration (Governor) of the Bryansk Region	Phone: (0832) 66 2611 Fax: (0832) 41 3895 E-mail: advis@bryanskobl.ru
Valery Filippovich RODOMANOV	First Deputy Head of Administration (Governor) of the Bryansk Region for Economic Policy	Phone: (0832) 66 3785 E-mail: advis@bryanskobl.ru
Petr Yefimovich ONENKO	First Deputy Head of Administration (Governor) of the Bryansk Region for Foreign Economic Relations, Investment Activity, Communications, and Energy	Phone: (0832) 74 1148 E-mail: onenko@brynskobl.ru
Boris Moiseevich KOPYRNOV	First Deputy Head of Administration (Governor) of the Bryansk Region for Agriculture, Food Policy, Natural Resources, and Ecology	Phone: (0832) 74 9837
Lyudmila Anatolyevna TYULYAGINA	Deputy Head of Administration (Governor) of the Bryansk Region, Head of the Financial Department of the Bryansk Region	Phone: (0832) 74 2029
Alexei Alexeevich IZOTENKOV	Head of the Economic Policy Committee of the Bryansk Regional Administration	Phone: (0832) 74 2025 Fax: (0832) 66 4855 E-mail: econ@bryanskobl.ru
Mikhail Semenovich KOBOZEV	Chairman of the Industry and Transport Committee of the Bryansk Regional Administration	Phone: (0832) 74 2708

3. ECONOMIC POTENTIAL

3.1. 1997–2002
GROSS REGIONAL
PRODUCT (GRP).
INDUSTRY BREAKDOWN

The Bryansk Region's 2002 gross regional product reached $1,224.6 million, or 10.9% up on 2001. Per capita GRP in 2001 was $775, rising to $889 in 2002.

3.2. INDUSTRIAL OUTPUT IN 1997–2002
FOR MAJOR SECTORS OF ECONOMY

The leading industrial sectors of the Bryansk Region are machine engineering and metal processing, processing industries (including flour milling, cereals, and mixed fodder), construction materials (including glass industry), forestry, and timber and pulp paper. These account for a combined 82.4% of total industrial output.

GRP trends in 1997–2002						TABLE 2
	1997	1998	1999	2000	2001*	2002*
GRP in current prices, $ million	1,933.6	1,199.7	731.7	929.8	1,104.4	1,224.6

*Estimates of the Bryansk Regional Administration

GRP industry breakdown in 1997–2002, % of total						TABLE 3
	1997	1998	1999	2000	2001*	2002*
GRP	100.0	100.0	100.0	100.0	100.0	100.0
Industry	21.8	18.9	21.8	22.7	19.4	18.5
Agriculture and forestry	13.2	17.3	21.6	21.4	18.5	16.7
Construction	4.9	4.3	4.2	5.4	5.9	5.8
Transport and communications	18.9	19.6	17.6	16.7	17.7	18.5
Trade and public catering	10.2	10.6	11.7	11.5	10.6	11.6
Other	24.2	22.6	16.2	15.7	22.1	22.5
Net taxes on output	6.8	6.7	6.9	6.6	5.8	6.4

*Estimates of the Bryansk Regional Administration

Industry breakdown of industrial output in 1997–2002, % to total						TABLE 4
	1997	1998	1999	2000	2001	2002*
Industry	100.0	100.0	100.0	100.0	100.0	100.0
Machine engineering and metal processing	37.5	33.5	33.5	35.9	39.9	29.9
Food and beverages	18.8	20.4	20.9	19.0	22.0	24.9
Construction materials	9.7	10.6	10.0	11.1	9.1	11.3
Energy	10.1	10.0	7.1	7.1	3.9	10.1
Flour, cereals, and mixed fodder	4.3	3.9	4.6	2.8	1.1	6.7
Forestry, timber, and pulp and paper	5.6	4.9	6.1	7.9	5.6	6.3
Glass and porcelain	5.0	5.5	7.2	7.8	7.3	3.3
Light industry	4.1	3.2	3.7	3.7	5.1	3.3
Chemicals and petrochemicals	1.5	0.6	1.1	1.0	1.0	1.0
Ferrous metals	–	0.9	0.8	1.1	0.7	0.8
Non-ferrous metals	0.6	1.7	1.5	0.02	–	–

*Estimates of the Bryansk Regional Administration

Machine engineering and metal processing.
The sector accounts for 29.9% of total industrial output.
The leading enterprises in the sector are OAO Bryansk
Machine Engineering Plant, OAO Bryansk Arsenal, OAO
Raditsky Machine Engineering Plant, and OAO Klintsov-
sky Crane Truck Factory. The Region has an important
military industrial sector, consisting namely of ZAO
Gruppa-Kremny (semiconductor instruments and inte-
gral microchips), FGUP Bryansk Electromechanical Plant,
FGUP Elektrodetal (electric equipment), OAO Monolit
(module heat generators GUT-100), and ZAO Termotron
Factory (railway transport safety equipment).

Food and beverages. The food and beverages
sector accounts for 24.9% of the Region's total industrial output. The largest enterprises in the sector are OAO
Bryankonfi and OAO Bezhitsky Food Factory (confectionery), OAO Bryansk Meat Plant, OOO Bryansk Meat
Processing Plant (sausage and delicatessen), OAO
Bryansk Dairy Plant (whole milk products), TnV
Starodubsky Cheese (cheese and whole milk products),
and OAO Bryanskspirtprom (liquors and spirits).

Construction materials. The sector
accounts for 11.3% of total industrial output. The
major enterprise in the sector is OAO Maltsov
Portland Cement, with a production capacity of
three million tons of cement per year.

Forestry, timber, and pulp and paper. The
sector accounts for 6.3% of total industrial output.
Enter-prises in the sector produce commercial timber, lumber, furniture, and carpentry articles. The

largest enterprises in the sector are OAO Seletsky
Timber Processing Plant (woodfiber laminates and
plywood), OAO Dyatkovo-DOZ (chipboards and furniture), OAO Brasov Furniture Factory (furniture),
and ZAO Proletary (industrial cardboard).

Agriculture. The Bryansk Region's agricultural
lands total 1.9 million hectares, of which 1.2 million
hectares are plowed fields. Livestock farming, namely
cattle and poultry, is also well developed. The tillage
sector specializes mainly in cereals (rye, wheat), potato, flax, vegetables, and sugar beet. Grain and sugar
beet output has been rising in recent years.

3.3. FUEL AND ENERGY BALANCE (OUT-
PUT AND CONSUMPTION PER RESOURCE)

The Bryansk Region is an energy deficient region.
The Region's total energy output accounts for less than
6% of overall consumption. Rural gas networks are currently being expanded at a very rapid rate: natural gas is
increasingly replacing solid fuels such as coal and peat.

3.4. TRANSPORT INFRASTRUCTURE

Roads. The Region has more than 6,000 kilometers
of public highway. A number of federal highways cross
the Region, including the Moscow – Kiev highway (with
access to the St. Petersburg – Kiev – Odessa route), the
Bryansk – Kobrin highway (with access to the Moscow –
Minsk – Brest route), and the Oryol – Roslavl highway.

Railroads. The Bryansk Region has 1,019 kilometers of railroads. Six railroads pass through the
Region linking it with other regions of Russia and the
rest of Europe. The Region has three major railroad

Fuel and energy sector production and consumption trends in 1997–2002						TABLE 5
	1997	1998	1999	2000	2001	2002*
Electricity output, billion kWh	0.3	0.3	0.3	0.3	0.2	0.2
Peat output, '000 tons	38.8	45.4	23.0	31.9	14.5	7.7
Electricity consumption, billion kWh	3.5	3.3	3.3	3.4	3.5	3.6
Natural gas consumption, million cubic meters	2,801.2	2,681.3	2,633.5	2,673.5	2,851.1	2,804.6
Peat consumption, '000 tons	38.8	45.4	23.0	31.9	14.5	7.7

*Estimates of the Bryansk Regional Administration

junctions: Bryansk 1 passenger station, Bryansk 2
shunting yard, and Unecha sectional station. A railroad
customs checkpoint that meets international standards
is currently under construction at Troyebortnoye.

Airports. A new international airport capable of handling Tu 154 class aircraft was opened
at Bryansk in 1994.

Oil and gas pipelines. The Druzhba oil pipeline
and several gas pipelines cross the Bryansk Region.

3.5. MAIN NATURAL RESOURCES:
RESERVES AND EXTRACTION IN 2002

The Region's principal natural resources are
phosphorites, raw concrete, glass sands, carbonates,
chalk, sand used in construction and the manufacturing of silicate goods, and forestry resources.

Mineral resources. The Region has deposits of
ferrous metals, titanium and zirconium placers, and
phosphorites (around 40 deposits with reserves totaling 127.2 million tons). The Region has numerous
deposits of mineral resources used in construction,
including clays (1 million tons), sands (construction
sand – 77.6 million cubic meters; and glass sand – 47.1
million cubic meters), chalk, limestone, marl, tripoli
(7.2 million cubic meters), construction stone, and
sand and gravel mixture (5.9 million cubic meters).
The Region's fuel resources mainly consist of peat bogs.

Forestry. Forests cover some 1.2 million hectares,
or one third of the Region's territory. Coniferous forests
account for 53% of the total forested area. Annual timber production totals 1.4 million cubic meters.

4. TRADE OPPORTUNITIES

4.1. MAIN GOODS
PRODUCED IN THE REGION
In 2002, the Bryansk Region produced:
Forestry, timber, and pulp and paper.
Woodfiber laminates – 338,000 conventional square meters (8.5% of the 2001 levels); chipboard – 107,600 conventional cubic meters (107%); paper – 21,300 tons (101%); cardboard – 50,000 tons (110%).

Machine engineering. Diesel shunters – 28 shunters (112%); autograders – 435 pieces (59.3%); timber processing equipment – 100 pieces (71%).

Construction materials. Concrete – 3,591,300 tons (104.9%); wall materials – 190.7 million conventional bricks (100.9%); window glass – 3,488,900 square meters (114.1%).

Light industry. Fabrics – 3,563,000 square meters (99.4%); wool thread – 1,300 tons (121.5%).

Food and beverages. Confectionery – 47,300 tons (108.2%); sausage – 14,300 tons (124.3%); whole milk products – 55,300 tons (168.6%); fat cheeses – 9,900 tons (110%).

4.2. EXPORTS,
INCLUDING EXTRA-CIS
1999 extra-CIS exports totaled $36 million and CIS exports reached $27.3 million. The corresponding figures for 2000 were $46 million and $34.7 million, $75.6 million and $41.3 million for 2001, and $126.1 million and $38.6 million for 2002.

The bulk of the Region's exports is represented by machine engineering and equipment ($84.9 million in 2002), and timber and lumber ($4.1 million), trucks ($2 million), and metal cutting tools ($1.4 million). Major importers of the Region's products include Germany, Italy, Kazakhstan, and Ukraine.

4.3. IMPORTS,
INCLUDING EXTRA-CIS
Extra-CIS imports amounted to $55 million in 1999, while CIS imports reached $50.6 million. The corresponding figures for 2000 were $48.6 million and $82.4 million, $64.3 million and $117.6 million for 2001, and $96 million and $116.2 million for 2002. The Bryansk Region's imports are mainly represented by machinery and equipment ($52.5 million in 2002), alcoholic and alcohol-free beverages ($14.5 million), paper and cardboard ($9.2 million), furniture ($8.7 million), synthetic detergents ($7.9 million), and rolled ferrous metals ($6.1 million). The Region's main trading partners for imports are Germany, Italy, Turkey, Ukraine, Belarus, Moldova, and Poland.

4.4. MAJOR
REGIONAL EXPORT
AND IMPORT ENTITIES
Due to the specific features of trade in the Bryansk Region, mainly industrial companies perform export and import operations.

Major regional export and import entities		TABLE 6
ENTITY	ADDRESS	PHONE, FAX, E-MAIL
OAO Bryansk Machine Engineering Factory	26, ul. Ulyanova, Bryansk, Bryansk Region, 241015	Phone: (0832) 55 8220, 55 0030, 55 8385 Fax: (0832) 55 8398 E-mail: post@bmz.bryansk.ru http://www.bmz.bryansk.ru
OAO Bezhitsky Steel Casting Plant	1, ul. Staleliteynaya, Bryansk, Bryansk Region, 241038	Phone: (0832) 57 8917, 57 6307 Fax: (0832) 57 1948
OAO Bryansk Arsenal	98, ul. Kalinina, Bryansk, Bryansk Region, 241000	Phone: (0832) 66 1794, 66 1725 Fax: (0832) 46 1794 E-mail: arsenal@online.bryansk.ru
ZAO Kremny Marketing	103, ul. Krasnoarmeyskaya, Bryansk, Bryansk Region, 241037	Phone/fax: (0832) 41 4214 E-mail: km@online.bryansk.ru
OAO Bryansk Wheel Tractor Plant	1, ul. Staleliteynaya, Bryansk, Bryansk Region, 241038	Phone: (0832) 57 8977, 57 0664, 57 1228 Fax: (0832) 57 1345 E-mail: rtd@gala.net
Belarussian Goods Trading House	4, Kharkovskaya, Bryansk, Bryansk Region, 241035	Phone: (0832) 73 6506, 73 6604, 73 6508

5. INVESTMENT OPPORTUNITIES

5.1. INVESTMENTS IN 1992–2002 (BY INDUSTRY SECTOR), INCLUDING FOREIGN INVESTMENTS

The following main factors determine the investment appeal of the Bryansk Region:

- Its favorable geographic location and developed transport links;
- Its developed transport infrastructure;
- Its high industrial potential;
- Its natural resources.

5.2. CAPITAL INVESTMENT

Transport and communications account for the majority of capital investments with 19.7%.

Capital investment by industry sector, $ million						*TABLE 7*
	1997	1998	1999	2000	2001	2002
Total capital investment	163.8	128.1	66.3	107.4	126.8	131.3
Including major industries (% of total)						
Industry	13.4	13.8	14.3	14.4	16.2	16.4
Agriculture and forestry	5.8	8.1	10.2	5.9	5.7	6.2
Construction	3.9	1.8	2.4	2.2	1.1	3.5
Transport and communications	27.0	33.3	21.2	13.0	12.2	19.7
Trade and public catering	0.5	1.0	1.0	0.6	1.1	1.3
Other	49.4	42.0	50.9	63.9	63.7	52.9

Foreign investment trends in 1996–2002						*TABLE 8*
	1996–1997	1998	1999	2000	2001	2002
Foreign investment, $ million	5.5	0.6	2.9	6.3	9.1	0.5
Including FDI, $ million	5.5	0.1	1.4	1.5	7.4	0.2

5.3. MAJOR ENTERPRISES (INCLUDING ENTERPRISES WITH FOREIGN INVESTMENT)

The Bryansk Region's major enterprises with foreign investment are OOO Rino Mastroto Group CIS (Italy), OOO Avista (Ukraine), OOO Logistic Center (Ukraine), OOO Suzemka Leasing (Ukraine), OOO Trend Plus (Poland), OOO Agira (Latvia), OOO Parus (Latvia), OOO Koneks (Moldova), OOO Platabo (Moldova), OOO Demandr (Belarus), OOO Vladiplus (Belarus), OOO ARGO (Lithuania), and OOO AUD-NER (Lithuania).

5.4. MOST ATTRACTIVE SECTORS FOR INVESTMENT

According to the Bryansk Regional Administration, machine engineering, forestry, timber, pulp and paper, light industry, food and beverages, and radio electronics are the most attractive sectors for investment.

5.5. CURRENT LEGISLATION ON INVESTOR TAX EXEMPTIONS AND PRIVILEGES

In 1996, the Region passed the a Law of the Bryansk Region On Investment Activity and Investor Tax Exemptions and Guarantees in the Bryansk

Largest enterprises of the Bryansk Region	*TABLE 9*
COMPANY	SECTOR
OAO Bryanskenergo	Energy
OAO Bryansk Machine Engineering Plant	Machine engineering and metal processing
OAO Bryansk Arsenal	Machine engineering and metal processing
OAO Maltsovsky Portland Cement	Construction materials
OAO Dyatkovo-DOZ	Forestry, timber, and pulp and paper
ZAO Melrukk	Flour, cereals, and mixed fodder
OAO Druzhba Trunk Oil Pipelines	Transport

I

CENTRAL FEDERAL DISTRICT

Region. The Law provides a regulatory, economic, and social framework for investment activity in the Region, and aims to increase the investment inflow and protect investors' rights, interests, and property regardless of the form of ownership.

Pursuant to the Law:

• All investors enjoy equal rights to carry out investment activity;

• Investors are granted income tax exemptions from the regional tax component;

• Enterprises of any legal form engaged in the creation of new or reconstruction and renovation of existing production facilities and carrying out investment projects are exempted from the region-al tax component of property tax on the newly installed or renovated portion of the property;

• Enterprises of any legal form are granted an exemption from land tax (rent) on land plots utilized within the investment project period;

• Investors are protected for a period of three years following the signing of an investment agreement from the effect of any new laws, regulations or rules that would impair the terms of investment;

• Investors are eligible under the applicable legislation for compensation for losses, including lost earnings, arising due to illegal actions or negligence by regional officials.

Regional entities responsible for raising investment		*TABLE 10*
ENTITY	ADDRESS	PHONE, FAX, E-MAIL
OOO Co-Invest Bryansk	5, per. Kanatny, Bryansk, Bryansk Region, 241000	Phone/fax: (0832) 44 6975, 44 6631 E-mail: coinvest@online.bryansk.ru
OOO Fintrust	Office 811, 103, ul. Krasnoarmeyskaya, Bryansk, Bryansk Region, 241037	Phone/fax: (0832) 72 2149 E-mail: fintrust@032.ru
Regional Investment Consultancy Center OAO GPIstroimash	15, ul. Institutskaya, Bryansk, Bryansk Region, 241035	Phone: (0832) 55 0136 E-mail: gpi@gpi.bryansk.ru
Economic Policy Committee of the Bryansk Regional Administration	33, pr. Lenina, Bryansk, Bryansk Region, 241002	Phone: (0832) 74 2025 Fax: (0832) 46 4855 E-mail: econ@bryanskobl.ru

5.6. FEDERAL AND REGIONAL ECONOMIC AND SOCIAL DEVELOPMENT PROGRAMS FOR THE BRYANSK REGION

Federal targeted programs. Since 2002, measures for social and economic development of the Bryansk Region have been included into the federal targeted program for the Elimi-nation of Differences in the Social and Economic Development of the Regions of the Russian Federation (2002–2010 and through 2015). The program aims to narrow gaps in the social and economic development of Russia's regions and to reduce the number of regions that lag behind the nationwide average level of social and economic development. The Federal Law On the Federal Budget for 2002 allocated $1.4 million to fund the program in the Bryansk Region. The Federal Law On the Federal Budget for 2003 stipulates a funding limit of $1.38 million.

Regional programs. The Region has drafted and is implementing a program for the protection of the rights of depositors and shareholders at financial institutions for 2003–2005. The program aims to create and maintain a register of shareholders and depositors in the Region; to publish information on violations of shareholders' and depositors' rights; to compensate damages inflicted to depositors by financial institutions; to consult with depositors on the procedures to be followed in protecting their rights; and to finance the Bryansk Regional Public State Fund for the protection of the rights of depositors and shareholders.

The regional targeted program for the Conversion of the Military Industrial Complex Enterprises of the Bryansk Region, 2002–2005 aims to launch production of new competitive products, to renovate the production facilities of the military industrial complex, and to retrain its personnel.

6. INVESTMENT PROJECTS

Industry sector and project description	1) Expected results 2) Amount and term of investment 3) Form of financing[1] 4) Documentation[2]	Contact information
1	2	3

MACHINE ENGINEERING AND METAL PROCESSING

02R001 ●		
Production of timber sawing machinery. Project goal: to expand operations.	1) 145 saw frames per year, revenue of $1.8 million per year 2) $1.9 million/2.8 years 3) L 4) Investment proposal	OAO Novozybkovsky Machine Engineering Plant 61, ul. Lenina, Novozybkov, Bryansk Region, 243020 Phone: (08343) 33 858, 33 503, 20 788 Fax: (08343) 34 826 E-mail: skala@online.debryansk.ru Alexander Emmanuilovich Metsger, CEO

02R002 ● ◆		
Upgrading of steel melting facilities at OAO Bryansk Machine Engineering Plant. Project goal: to increase output of rolled steel and metal goods.	1) 6,000 tons per year, revenue of $3.8 million 2) $16.1 million/5.7 years 3) L ($13.5 million) 4) BP	OAO Bryansk Machine Engineering Plant 26, ul. Ulyanova, Bryansk, Bryansk Region, 241015 Phone: (0832) 55 0030 Fax: (0832) 55 8399 E-mail: post@bmz.032.ru Anatoly Alexandrovich Zadorozhny, Executive Director

02R003 ● ◆		
Serial production of asphalt spreaders. Project goal: to expand and upgrade production of asphalt spreaders.	1) 120 spreaders per year, revenue of $8.9 million per year 2) $1.5 million/3.1 years 3) L ($1 million) 4) BP	OOO Raditsky Machine Engineering Plant 7, bul. Schorsa, Bryansk, Bryansk Region, 241031 Phone: (0832) 62 6486, 62 6114, 62 6444 Fax: (0832) 71 2826 E-mail: ramz@online.debryansk.ru Alexei Nikiforovich Zaikin, CEO

FORESTRY, TIMBER, AND PULP AND PAPER

02R004 ● ◆		
Manufacturing of furniture accessories and equipment for its production. Project goal: to expand operations and upgrade production of furniture accessories, hardware, equipment and production lines, and pneumatic instruments.	1) Revenue of $0.3 million per year 2) $1.3 million/2 years 3) L ($1.2 million) 4) BP	OAO Metallist 58, ul. Sovetskaya, Karachev, Bryansk Region, 242500 Phone: (08335) 21 481 Fax: (08335) 21 787 Vyacheslav Vasilyevich Lyudkevich, CEO

02R005 ● ◆		
Reconstruction of a plywood production shop. Project goal: to expand operations.	1) 20,000 cubic meters 2) $5 million/6 years 3) L 4) BP	OAO Seletsky Timber Processing Plant 3, ul. Dzerzhinskogo, Belaya Berezka, Trubchevsky District, Bryansk Region, 242250 Phone/fax: (08352) 24 949 Alexei Nikolaevich Vlasov, CEO

[1] L – Loan, E – Equity, Leas. – Leasing, JV – Joint Venture
[2] BP – Business Plan, FS – Feasibility Study

1	2	3

CONSTRUCTION MATERIALS

02R006

Construction of foam glass production facilities. Project goal: to produce foam glass.

1) 6,750 cubic meters per year, revenue of $0.5 million per year
2) $1 million/5 years
3) L
4) BP, FS

OAO Kvartsit
1a, ul. Pervomayskaya, Bytosh,
Dyatkovsky District, Bryansk Region,
242670
Phone/fax: (08333) 21 293
Fax: (08333) 21 895
E-mail: kvarzit@mail.ru
Viktor Ivanovich Novikov, CEO

LIGHT INDUSTRY

02R007

Production of wool fabric.
Project goal: to produce
competitive goods.

1) 3 million running meters per year; revenue of $5.7 million per year
2) $1.5 million/2 years
3) L
4) BP

OAO Klinta
3, ul. Voroshilova, Klintsy,
Bryansk Region, 243146
Phone: (08336) 44 093
Fax: (08336) 43 155, 40 204, 43 071
Mikhail Yuryevich Davydov, CEO

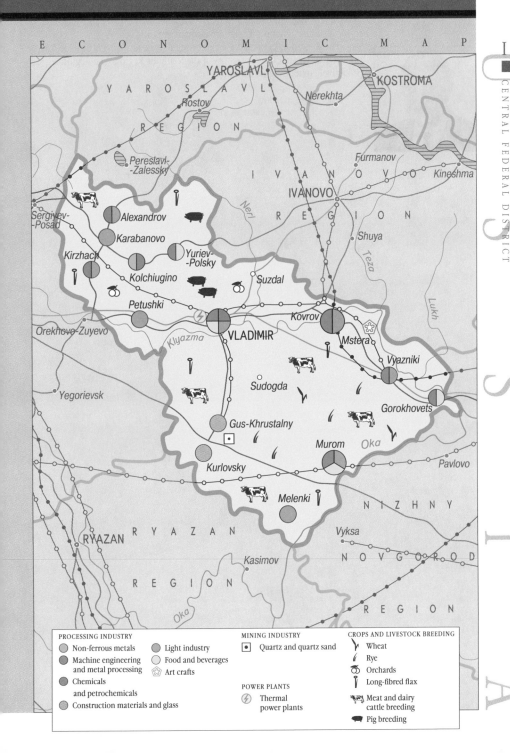

ECONOMIC MAP

PROCESSING INDUSTRY
- Non-ferrous metals
- Machine engineering and metal processing
- Chemicals and petrochemicals
- Construction materials and glass
- Light industry
- Food and beverages
- Art crafts

MINING INDUSTRY
- Quartz and quartz sand

POWER PLANTS
- Thermal power plants

CROPS AND LIVESTOCK BREEDING
- Wheat
- Rye
- Orchards
- Long-fibred flax
- Meat and dairy cattle breeding
- Pig breeding

The Vladimir Region is one of the pearls of Russia's Golden Ring – the tourist route of ancient Russian cities. The Region has always attracted visitors from all over the world. Ancient architecture and abundant and diverse natural beauty are not the only attractions our land has to offer. The Vladimir Region is a region for beneficial economic cooperation.

Its favorable geographic location, strong research and development potential, well-developed transport infrastructure, the presence of branches of reputable Russian banks, and its favorable legislative base, all contribute to the Vladimir Region's foreign investment appeal.

The Region has enacted a series of regulatory acts, which provide for preferential treatment of investors in the Vladimir Region. The Region is proactively extending its economic ties.

Nikolay Vinogradov,
GOVERNOR OF THE VLADIMIR REGION

1. GENERAL INFORMATION

1.1. GEOGRAPHY

The Vladimir Region covers an area of 29,000 square kilometers in Central Russia. To the west and south-west, it borders the Moscow Region, to the south – the Ryazan Region, to the north – the Yaroslavl and Ivanovo Regions, and to the east and south-east – the Nizhny Novgorod Region.

1.2. CLIMATE

The Vladimir Region is located in the temperate continental climate zone. Air temperatures in January average –7.9°C, rising to an average of +19.5°C in July. Annual precipitation is 500 mm. The growing season lasts around 160–180 days on average.

1.3. POPULATION

According to preliminary 2002 census results, total population in the Region was 1,525,000 peo-

ple. The average population density is 52.6 people per square km. The economically active population amounts to 809,000 people. In 2002, the official unemployment level stood at 1.3%.

The demographic structure of the population is as follows: 59.6% are of working age, 16.6% are below the statutory working age, and 23.8% are beyond the working age.

As of 2002, the Vladimir Region's major urban centers were Vladimir with 316,300 inhabitants, Kovrov with 155,600 inhabitants, and Murom with 126,800 inhabitants.

Population							TABLE 1
	1992	1997	1998	1999	2000	2001	2002
Total population, '000	1,651	1,632	1,626	1,618	1,604	1,589	1,525
Economically active population, '000	896	791	771	810	810	809	809

2. ADMINISTRATION

21, pr. Oktyabrsky, Vladimir, Vladimir Region, 600000
Phone: (0922) 33 1552; fax: (0922) 25 3445
E-mail: post@avo.ru; http://www.avo.ru

NAME	POSITION	CONTACT INFORMATION
Nikolay Vladimirovich VINOGRADOV	Governor of the Vladimir Region	Phone: (0922) 33 1552 Fax: (0922) 35 3445
Yury Matveevich FEDOROV	First Deputy Governor of the Vladimir Region, State Secretary (Chief of Staff of the Regional Administration)	Phone: (0922) 23 7905 Fax: (0922) 23 5426
Vladimir Viktorovich VERETENNIKOV	First Deputy Governor of the Vladimir Region (in charge of economic and industrial policy)	Phone: (0922) 32 5061 Fax: (0922) 32 6482 E-mail: vice@obladm.vladimir.ru
Vyacheslav Pavlovich KUZIN	Deputy Governor of the Vladimir Region, Head of the Central Finance Department of the Vladimir Regional Administration	Phone: (0922) 32 6554 Fax: (0922) 23 6055 E-mail: finupr@obladm.vladimir.ru
Vera Alexandrovna SHAMOTA	Head of Department of Foreign Economic Relations of the Vladimir Regional Administration	Phone: (0922) 33 1848 Fax: (0922) 23 6825 E-mail: dvs570@obladm.vladimir.ru
Valery Alexeevich KRETININ	Head of the Economic Department of the Vladimir Regional Administration	Phone: (0922) 32 6153 Fax: (0922) 32 6482 E-mail: economy@obladm.vladimir.ru
Vitaly Bronislavovich LONSKY	Head of the Industry Management Department of the Vladimir Regional Administration	Phone: (0922) 32 6300 Fax: (0922) 32 6524 E-mail: uprom@obladm.vladimir.ru

3. ECONOMIC POTENTIAL

3.1. 1997–2002 GROSS REGIONAL PRODUCT (GRP). INDUSTRY BREAKDOWN

The 2002 gross regional product amounted to $1,715.4 million, which represents 11.3% growth year-on-year. Transport and agriculture accounted for the bulk of the growth. Per capita GRP totaled $970 in 2001 and $1,125 in 2002.

3.2. MAJOR ECONOMIC GROWTH PROJECTIONS

The Plan of Actions of the Vladimir Regional Administration in the Social and Economic Sphere for 2002–2003 and the Conceptual Framework for Industrial Development in the Vladimir Region in 2003 provide an economic development blueprint for the Region and set the following objectives:

GRP trends in 1997–2002						TABLE 2
	1997	1998	1999	2000	2001*	2002*
GRP in current prices, $ million	2,538.6	1,599.6	1,063.0	1,260.2	1,540.6	1,715.4

*Estimates of the Vladimir Regional Administration

GRP industry breakdown in 1997–2002, % of total						TABLE 3
	1997	1998	1999	2000	2001*	2002*
GRP	100.0	100.0	100.0	100.0	100.0	100.0
Industry	39.6	41.0	39.7	41.6	41.5	41.1
Agriculture and forestry	9.5	12.2	20.2	12.3	11.3	11.5
Construction	6.7	4.2	3.9	4.8	4.6	4.6
Transport and communications	10.0	9.0	4.2	6.5	7.1	7.7
Trade and public catering	11.3	12.2	11.3	9.7	9.7	9.8
Other	19.0	19.4	18.7	18.9	18.9	18.5
Net taxes on output	3.9	2.0	2.0	6.2	6.9	6.8

*Estimates of the Vladimir Regional Administration

• Improvement of regional law to encourage investment and raise financing for the most promising investment projects;
• Support of cooperation among local businesses and establishment of joint ventures with foreign companies;
• Assistance in promoting local companies' output to the domestic and international markets via presentation at exhibitions and fairs; added incentives to manufacturers to improve product quality and competitiveness;
• The Region has undertaken to increase real GRP by 4.3% in 2003, as follows: industry – 3.2%, agriculture – 3%, construction – 2%, transport and communications – 4%, and retail and public catering – 2%.

3.3. INDUSTRIAL OUTPUT IN 1997–2002 FOR MAJOR SECTORS OF ECONOMY

The leading industries are machine engineering and metal processing and food and beverages sectors. These account for a combined 60.7% of total industrial output.

Machine engineering and metal processing. This is one of the Region's top priority sectors. Its leading sub-sectors are electrotechnical industry and transport engineering, which together account for over 40% of the machine engineering output. Railway and tractor engineering account for 30% of total industrial output. The Region's main enterprises in the machine engineering and metals sector are: OAO Electropribor Vladimir Plant, OAO Vladimir Electric Motor Plant, OAO Vladimir Tractor Plant, GUP Vladimir Production Company Tochmash, GUP Vladimir Plant Etalon, and OAO Magneton, a research and manufacturing company.

Food and beverages. The food industry accounts for some 17.6% of total industrial output. Producers of meat, flour and cereals, and mixed fodder have been steadily increasing their output since 2002. The largest companies in the sector include OAO Vladimir Bakery, OAO Yuryev-Polsky Skimmed Milk Dairy, OAO Lanikskoye Milk, and OAO Gorokhovetsky Pischevik.

Glass and porcelain. The share of the sector in total industrial output is 6.4%. The sector is represented by 23 companies, which jointly employ some 17,000 people. The major companies in the sector include OAO Russian-American Glass Company, OAO Krasnoye Ekho, OOO Cut-Glass Plant, and ZAO

Industry breakdown of industrial output in 1997–2002, % of the total						TABLE 4
	1997	1998	1999	2000	2001	2002*
Industry	100.0	100.0	100.0	100.0	100.0	100.0
Machine engineering and metal processing	41.0	41.1	41.7	42.5	43.1	43.1
Food and beverages	10.4	11.4	16.5	17.0	17.3	17.6
Energy	19.0	18.9	11.2	10.5	10.0	10.2
Glass and porcelain	4.5	4.9	5.9	6.5	6.9	6.4
Light industry	5.5	5.6	5.8	5.9	5.9	6.0
Chemicals and petrochemicals	4.2	4.2	5.7	5.5	5.3	5.8
Non-ferrous metals	3.1	2.9	3.8	2.7	3.5	3.7
Construction materials	4.2	3.8	3.0	3.0	2.9	3.0
Forestry, timber, and pulp and paper	4.0	3.5	3.3	2.4	1.7	1.9
Flour, cereals, and mixed fodder	1.7	1.5	1.1	1.0	1.0	1.0
Ferrous metals	0.5	0.5	0.4	0.5	0.7	0.7
Fuel	0.3	0.2	0.2	0.2	0.2	0.2

*Estimates of the Vladimir Regional Administration

I

Symbol. The Vladimir Region produces 46% of Russia's total output of profiled tableware, 23% of glass packaging, and 21% of window glass.

Light industry accounts for 6% of total industrial output of the Vladimir Region. Companies in the Region account for nearly 14% of Russia's total output of linen fabric. The largest enterprises in the sector are OOO Karat Plus, OOO Children's Clothing, and OAO Gorodischenskaya Trimming Factory.

Chemicals. The chemicals sector accounts for some 5.8% of total industrial output in the Region. The most promising sub-sectors are glass fiber, plas-

tics, and fertilizers. Major companies include OAO Vladimir Chemical Plant, OAO Film Materials Plant, OAO Profile, OOO Research and Production Company Macrometer, and ZAO Membrany.

3.4. FUEL AND ENERGY BALANCE (OUTPUT AND CONSUMPTION PER RESOURCE)

The Region imports nearly all of its fuel from other regions of Russia. Electricity is supplied by power stations in the Leningrad and Kostroma Regions, while oil products arrive from the Nizhny Novgorod Region.

Fuel and energy sector production and consumption trends, 1997–2002						TABLE 5
	1997	1998	1999	2000	2001	2002*
Electricity output, billion kWh	1.9	2.1	1.9	1.9	2.1	2.0
Electricity consumption, billion kWh	5.7	5.6	5.8	6.1	6.3	6.3
Natural gas consumption, million cubic meters	2,300.0	2,200.0	2,500.0	2,600.0	2,600.0	2,800.0

*Estimates of the Vladimir Regional Administration

3.5. TRANSPORT INFRASTRUCTURE

Roads. The Vladimir Region is criss-crossed by some 8,000 km of paved public highways. The Region's federal highways are: Moscow – Nizhny Novgorod – Kazan and Moscow – Yaroslavl. The road network links the northern regions of European Russia with the Volga region, the Urals, and the eastern regions of the country.

Railroads. The Vladimir Region has 1,650 km of railroads, providing links to other regions of Russia along the following principal rail corri-

dors: Moscow – Nizhny Novgorod, Moscow – Yaroslavl, and Moscow – Kazan.

Airports. The nearest airport with the capacity to accept large passenger and cargo aircraft is located 50 km outside the Vladimir Region in the city of Ivanovo.

River transport. The Oka and Klyazma rivers drain the Vladimir Region. The river port of Murom is located on the left bank of the Oka. The inland waterway link to Moscow provides access to the East and West European markets.

3.6. MAIN NATURAL RESOURCES: RESERVES AND EXTRACTION IN 2002

The Region's principal natural resources are timber, peat, mineral resources (limestone, fire and brick clays, quartz sand and stone, and flux materials), ore, gypsum, and mineral water.

Timber. About half of the Region's territory is covered with forests (1,520,900 hectares). The total reserve of wood is 244 million cubic meters, 60% of which is coniferous wood. Some 90% of the estimated felling sector is currently in use.

Peat. The Vladimir Region has the largest peat reserves in Russia – 59 million tons – spread through 124 peat deposits. The main deposits are in the Gus-Khrustalny and Sobinsky Districts.

Limestone and quartz sand. The Region's sand reserves have been accorded the status of reserves of federal significance, since they provide the raw material basis for Russia's glass industry. Large reserves of clear quartz sands are found in the Gus-Khrustalny and Melenkovsky Districts. Limestone deposits are located in the Oksko-Tsninsky District and are estimated at 30 million tons. The limestone is used to produce construction masonry and lime.

4. TRADE OPPORTUNITIES

4.1. MAIN GOODS PRODUCED IN THE REGION

Machine engineering. Vehicles, railroad, and tractor equipment.

Glass. Profiled tableware, glass packaging, and window glass.

Light industry. Cotton cloth and linen fabric.

Timber, pulp and paper. Plywood and lumber.

Chemicals. Lavsan and polyethylene thermal film, membrane water filtering systems, and chemicals for use in the auto industry.

4.2. EXPORTS, INCLUDING EXTRA-CIS

The Vladimir Region's exports to non-CIS countries amounted to $74.4 million in 2000, and exports to CIS – $26.7 million; the respective figures for 2001 were $84 million and $32.2 million, and for 2002 – $102 million and $45.5 million.

Industrial output accounts for the highest share in the Region's exports at 42.3%. The Region's main exports are locomotives, rolling stock, railroad machinery, and hydraulic equipment. Major importers of the Region's products include Ukraine, Algeria, Kazakhstan, Italy, Iran, Germany, Lithuania, Uzbekistan, Cuba, and Cyprus.

4.3. IMPORTS, INCLUDING EXTRA-CIS

Imports from non-CIS countries amounted to $76.9 million in 2000, and imports from CIS countries, to $70.4 million. The respective figures for 2001 were $103.5 million and $92.2 million, and for 2002 – $153.8 million and $43.2 million. Machinery prevailed in the structure of imports, accounting for 30% of total imports. Among the main goods imported to the Region are electrical engines and generators, cars and trucks, alcoholic beverages, non-organic chemicals, rubber and rubber goods, paper, cotton, electricity, oil and oil products, and natural gas. The main exporters to the Region are Germany, Ukraine, Moldova, France, Italy, Uzbekistan, Georgia, Kazakhstan, and the Netherlands.

4.4. MAJOR REGIONAL EXPORT AND IMPORT ENTITIES

Due to the specific features of trade in the Region, mainly industrial companies perform export and import operations.

5. INVESTMENT OPPORTUNITIES

5.1 INVESTMENTS IN 1992–2002 (BY INDUSTRY SECTOR), INCLUDING FOREIGN INVESTMENTS

The following factors determine the investment appeal of the Vladimir region:

• Its advantageous geographic location in the most economically developed part of European Russia;

• Its developed transport infrastructure, including roads, railroad, and inland waterways;

• Its legislation supporting investment activity.

5.2. CAPITAL INVESTMENT

Industry together with transport and communications account for the largest share of capital investment at 48.9% and 18.3%, respectively.

5.3. MAJOR ENTERPRISES (INCLUDING ENTERPRISES WITH FOREIGN INVESTMENT)

In 2001, 60 entities with foreign investment were operating in the Vladimir Region. These companies account for some 17% of total industrial output. The largest companies with foreign investment are OAO Rusjam, OAO RASKO Russian-American Glass Company, OAO Intervladles, and ZAO Craft Foods Rus.

Capital investment by industry sector, $ million

TABLE 6

	1997	1998	1999	2000	2001	2002
Total capital investment	414.4	215.9	141.7	172.5	216.4	299.3
Including major industries (% of total)						
Industry	44.8	38.1	41.1	43.4	47.9	48.9
Agriculture and forestry	2.5	4.9	6.5	6.8	6.6	6.7
Construction	1.1	2.2	3.3	5.6	0.8	1.2
Transport and communication	9.1	15.9	11.0	21.2	19.4	18.3
Trade and public catering	2.8	5.5	2.6	0.7	0.7	0.9
Other sectors	39.7	33.4	35.5	22.3	24.6	24.0

Foreign investment trends in 1996–2002

TABLE 7

	1996–1997	1998	1999	2000	2001	2002
Foreign investment, $ million	32.0	199.2	44.5	21.3	22.1	75.1
Including FDI, $ million	26.1	37.4	38.5	10.5	1.3	18.9

Largest enterprises of the Vladimir Region

TABLE 8

COMPANY	SECTOR
PK Electrokabel Plant	Machine engineering
OAO ZID	Machine engineering
OAO Vladimirenergo	Energy
GUP Vladimir Production Company Tochmash	Machine engineering
OOO Autopribor Plant	Machine engineering
OAO Kolchuginsky Sergo Ordzhonikidze Non-Ferrous Metal Processing Plant	Machine engineering
OAO Murom Switch Plant	Machine engineering

5.4. MOST ATTRACTIVE SECTORS FOR INVESTMENT

According to experts and the regional administration, the food and beverage and glass sectors offer the most appeal for investors.

5.5. CURRENT LEGISLATION ON INVESTOR TAX EXEMPTIONS AND PRIVILEGES

The Region has passed a Law of the Vladimir Region On State Support of Capital Investment in the Vladimir Region, pursuant to which Russian and foreign investors in the Region enjoy various forms of state support, including tax exemptions and loans. The approval of an investment project by the Vladimir Regional Administration constitutes grounds for applying for state support.

5.6. FEDERAL AND REGIONAL ECONOMIC AND SOCIAL DEVELOPMENT PROGRAMS FOR THE VLADIMIR REGION

Federal targeted programs. Some 29 federal targeted programs worth a total of $14.5 million were drafted in 2002. Among the priority federal programs for 2003 are: The Elimination of Inequalities in the Social and Economic Development of the Regions of the Russian Federation (2002–2010 and through 2015), Land Reform in the Russian Federation, and The State Small Enterprise Support Program for 1996–1997 (extended through 2004).

Regional entities responsible for raising investment

TABLE 9

ENTITY	ADDRESS	PHONE, FAX, E-MAIL
Department of Foreign Economic Realations of the Vladimir Regional Administration	21, Oktyabrsky pr., Vladimir, Vladimir Region, 600000	Phone: (0922) 33 1848 Fax: (0922) 23 6825 E-mail: dvs@obladm.vladimir.ru

I

Regional programs. The Regional Targeted Program for the Development of the Export Base and External Economic Infrastructure, 2001–2005 has been accorded a top priority status. This program, which is worth some $0.05 million, has as its core objective the provision of organizational and information support to export-focused companies in the Vladimir Region.

The Regional Targeted Program of Attracting Foreign Investment to the Vladimir Region is also underway in the Region. This program has a budget of some $0.04 million.

6. INVESTMENT PROJECTS

Industry sector and project description	1) Expected results 2) Amount and term of investment 3) Form of financing[1] 4) Documentation[2]	Contact information
1	2	3

MACHINE ENGINEERING AND METAL PROCESSING

03R001 ● ▼		
Launching production on the basis of seven machine tools supplied by leading international supplier Mazak. Project goal: to extend the existing production and introduce new types of civilian industrial products.	1) Profit of $1.2 million per year 2) $4.7 million/1 year 3) L 4) Investment proposal	OAO Kovrov Electromechanical Plant 55, ul. Krupskoy, Kovrov, Vladimir Region, 601903 Phone: (09232) 93 546, 93 063, 93 005 Fax: (09232) 30 077, 39 106, 30 060 E-mail: kemz@kc.ru Igor Fedorovich Belousov, CEO Nikolai Vasilyevich Zhigalov, Deputy Director
03R002 ● ◆		
Arranging joint production of electromagnetic heat meters and regulators. Project goal: to expand production of heat meters for commercial use.	1) 1,000 items (meters and regulators) annually 2) $0.3 million/2 years 3) L 4) BP	State Unitary Company Vladimir Plant Etalon 40, ul. Verkhnyaya Dubrova, Vladimir, Vladimir Region, 600036 Phone: (0922) 24 1414, 24 8846 Fax: (0922) 24 1414 E-mail: root@etalon.elcom.ru Mikhail Ivanovich Kabanov, Director
03R003 ● ▼		
Organizing and expanding production of instruments to substitute imports and save resources. Project goal: to expand output of existing and introduce new types of water and gas meters.	1) Gas meters – 250,000 pieces annually, cold and hot water meters – 210,000 pieces annually 2) $2.4 million/2 years 3) L 4) Investment proposal	State Unitary Company VPO Tochmash 1a, ul. Severnaya, Vladimir, Vladimir Region, 600007 Phone: (0922) 23 0645, 27 3346 Fax: (0922) 23 7310, 27 3294, 27 3171, 23 0777 E-mail: pochta@tochmash.vtsnet.ru Yury Alexeevich Zambin, CEO
03R004 ● ▼		
Expanding battery production. Project goal: to increase output and assortment of batteries.	1) To increase output from 180,000 to 400,000 items per year 2) $3 million/5 years 3) L 4) Investment proposal	OAO V.A. Degtyarev Plant 4, ul. Trud, Kovrov, Vladimir Region, 601900 Phone: (09232) 91 757, 91 029, 91 215, 30 389 Fax: (09232) 58 757, 53 576 E-mail: zid@zid.ru Alexander Vladimirovich Tmenov, CEO

[1] L – Loan, E – Equity, Leas. – Leasing, JV – Joint Venture
[2] BP – Business Plan, FS – Feasibility Study

1	2	3

03R005

● ▼

Manufacturing detonation devices
for the mining and coal sectors.
Project goal: to expand current
production.

1) n/a
2) $7 million/7 years
3) L
4) Investment proposal

Federal State Unitary Company
Murom Instrument Production Plant
O/S No. 17 Murom,
Vladimir Region, 602267
Phone: (09234) 63 471, 60 452, 60 885
Fax: (09234) 60 252
E-mail: adm@flame.murom.ru,
root@pribor.mourom.elcom.ru
Nikolay Mikhailovich Bibnev, CEO

03R006

● ▼

Commencing production
of environmentally friendly initiation
devices, blow compositions,
and derivative products.
Project goal: to set up new production.

1) n/a
2) $2 million/1.5 years
3) L
4) Investment proposal

Federal State Unitary Company
Murom Instrument Production Plant
O/S No. 17 Murom,
Vladimir Region, 602267
Phone: (09234) 63 471, 60 452, 60 885
Fax: (09234) 60 252
E-mail: adm@flame.murom.ru,
root@pribor.mourom.elcom.ru
Nikolay Mikhailovich Bibnev, CEO

03R007

● ◆

Launching production of submersible
electric pumps to world standards.
Project goal: to produce competitive
products.

1) Annual revenues of $0.6 million;
   30,500 submersible electric
   pumps per year
2) $0.8 million /2.5 years
3) L
4) BP

OAO Bavlensky Plant Electrodvigatel
1, ul. Mira, Bavleny, Kolchugino
District, Vladimir Region, 601755
Phone: (09245) 31 235, 31 251,
31 206, 21 531, 31 330
Fax: (09245) 21 541, 22 287
E-mail: mail@bemz.kolch.elcom.ru
Georgy Semenovich Samok, CEO

CONSTRUCTION MATERIALS

03R008

● ▼

Building a ceramic brick
manufacturing plant in Kolchugino.
Project goal: to produce
competitive products.

1) 30 million bricks per year
2) $10 million/1.5 years
3) L
4) Investment proposal

OOO Mayak
21, Ulyanovskoye shosse, Kolchugino,
Vladimir Region, 701770
Phone: (910) 414 3141
Phone/fax: (09245) 24 565
Nikolai Alexeevich Scherbina,
Director

GLASS AND PORCELAIN

03R009

● ◆

Launching production of various types of
tempered glass (strengthened, flat, architectural)
and related goods.
Project goal: to increase the product range.

1) Total output of 507,500 square
   meters per year
2) € 2 million/3 years
3) L
4) BP

OOO Magistral
7, ul. Starykh Bolshevikov,
Gus-Khrustalny, Vladimir Region, 601500
Phone/fax: (09241) 23 586, 21 237
E-mail: bronja@magist.gus.elcom.ru,
maksjukov@magist.gus.elcom.ru
Yury Anatolyevich Maksyukov, CEO

HOTELS, TOURISM, AND RECREATION

03R010

■ ● ▼

Building a120-room three-star hotel
Russkoye Podvorye in Suzdal.
Project goal: to develop national hotel
quality standards and increase tourism.

1) 120 rooms
2) $2.8 million/1.5years
3) L, E
4) Investment proposal

OOO Vladimirinvesttour Company
75-B, ul. B. Moskovskaya,
Vladimir, Vladimir Region, 600006
Phone: (0922) 32 4446, 32 5445,
32 3863
Fax: (0922) 32 5386
E-mail: vit@vitour.ru
Vladimir Yuryevich Sharov, CEO

I

CENTRAL FEDERAL DISTRICT

1	2	3

03R011 ● ▼

		Murom District Administration
Building a tourist facility.	1) A total area of	1, pl. 1100-letiya Muroma,
Project goal: to increase tourism.	10,000 square meters	Murom, Vladimir Region, 602200
	2) $5.6 million/5 years	Phone/fax: (09234) 31 757
	3) L	E-mail: murom@murom.obladm.
	4) Investment proposal	vladimir.ru
		Valentin Afanasyevich Kachevan,
		Head of District

ECOLOGY, WASTE PROCESSING

03R012 ● ▲ ◆

		Murom District Administration
Building garbage sorting facilities.	1) 50,000 tons per year	1, pl. 1100-letia Muroma,
Project goal: industrial processing	2) $2.5 million/2 years	Murom, Vladimir Region, 602200
of household waste.	3) L	Phone/fax: (09234) 31 757
	4) BP, FS	E-mail: murom@murom.obladm.
		vladimir.ru
		Valentin Afanasyevich Kachevan,
		Head of District

04. VORONEZH REGION [36]

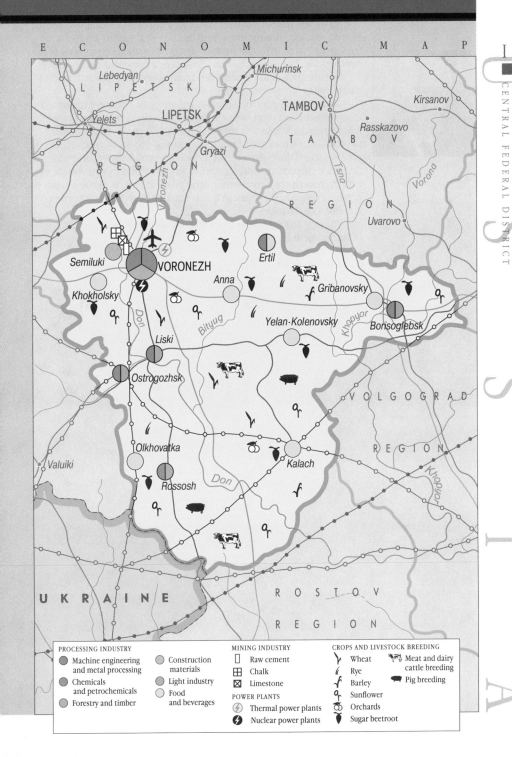

PROCESSING INDUSTRY

- Machine engineering and metal processing
- Chemicals and petrochemicals
- Forestry and timber
- Construction materials
- Light industry
- Food and beverages

MINING INDUSTRY

- Raw cement
- Chalk
- Limestone

POWER PLANTS

- Thermal power plants
- Nuclear power plants

CROPS AND LIVESTOCK BREEDING

- Wheat
- Rye
- Barley
- Sunflower
- Orchards
- Sugar beetroot
- Meat and dairy cattle breeding
- Pig breeding

The investment climate in the Voronezh Region has improved considerably over the recent years thanks in part to our research and development potential, for which Voronezh is one of the top ten Russian regions. More importantly however, over the years our industrialists, businessmen, and executives have learnt to become efficient and responsible managers. The time has come to look for equally businesslike and responsible partners with whom to develop and improve our Region's economy.

In ancient times, merchants risked their capital and sometimes their life steering caravans through virgin lands and bringing together peoples, countries, and cultures. In this information age, we face the same problems of risk minimization. The Voronezh Region has passed a number of laws guaranteeing the protection of investments and granting new privileges and preferential treatment to investors.

We are actively pursuing a policy of improving the investment climate and minimizing risk. As a result, over a thousand companies in the Region have established foreign trade links with partners from eighty countries. But the scope of this collaboration does not yet match our potential. The Region is expected to need $1.5 billion in investments over the next five years. We are committed to developing cooperation with producers of agricultural machinery and would welcome representatives of companies specialized in capital construction and gas network expansion. The Voronezh Region's agricultural sector offers extensive investment opportunities.

I hereby invite investors to set up mutually beneficial joint operations in the Voronezh Region.

Vladimir Kulakov,
HEAD OF ADMINISTRATION OF THE VORONEZH REGION

1. GENERAL INFORMATION

1.1. GEOGRAPHY

Located in the south-east of European Russia, the Voronezh Region covers a total area of 52,400 square kilometers. To the north, the Region borders the Lipetsk Region, to the north-east – the Tambov Region, to the west – the Volgograd Region, to the south-east – the Rostov Region, to the south-west –Ukraine, and to the west – the Belgorod Region.

1.2. CLIMATE

The Voronezh Region is located within the temperate continental climate zone. Air temperatures in January average –10.5°C, rising to +21.8°C in July. Annual precipitation reaches 450–550 mm.

1.3. POPULATION

According to preliminary 2002 census results, the total population in the Voronezh Region was 2,379,000 people. The average population density is 45.4 people per square kilometer. The economically active population totals 1,076,000 people. Official unemployment stood at 8.9% in 2002.

Demographically speaking, some 57.6% are of statutory working age, 16.9% are below the statutory working age, and 25.5% are beyond the statutory working age.

The Voronezh Region's major urban centers (2002) are Voronezh with 848,700 inhabitants, Borisoglebsk with 70,000 inhabitants, Rossosh with 63,000 inhabitants, and Liski with 56,000 inhabitants.

Population								TABLE 1
	1992	1997	1998	1999	2000	2001	2002
Total population, '000	2,471	2,496	2,482	2,472	2,456	2,437	2,379
Economically active population, '000	1,206	1,035	1,020	1,164	1,179	1,117	1,076

2. ADMINISTRATION

Voronezh Region Administration
1, pl. Lenina, Voronezh, Voronezh Region, 394018
Phone: (0732) 55 4534
E-mail: comadm@ns.comch.ru; http://admin.vrn.ru/

NAME	POSITION	CONTACT INFORMATION
Vladimir Grigoryevich KULAKOV	Head of Administration of the Voronezh Region	Phone: (0732) 55 2737 Fax: (0732) 52 0364
Sergei Mikhailovich NAUMOV	First Deputy Head of Administration of the Voronezh Region	Phone: (0732) 55 2615
Vladimir Georgievich KOBYASHEV	Deputy Head of Administration of the Voronezh Region, Chief of Staff of the Regional Administration	Phone: (0732) 55 3585
Ivan Ivanovich DUBOVSKOY	Deputy Head of Administration of the Voronezh Region, Head of the Main Agro-Industrial Division	Phone: (0732) 55 2864
Boris Anatolyevich KITAYEV	Deputy Head of Administration of the Voronezh Region for Regional Development	Phone: (0732) 55 1900
Alexander Nikolaevich TSAPIN	Deputy Head of Administration of the Voronezh Region, Chairman of the Regional Energy Commission	Phone: (0732) 55 1503
Leonid Ivanovich SELITRENNIKOV	Head of the Main Economic Development Division of the Administration of the Voronezh Region	Phone: (0732) 55 4512 Fax: (0732) 53 1720

3. ECONOMIC POTENTIAL

3.1. 1997–2002 GROSS REGIONAL PRODUCT (GRP). INDUSTRY BREAKDOWN

The 2002 gross regional product reached $2,399.1 million, a 9.6% increase on 2001 figures. Growth was mainly driven by the construction and transport sectors.

3.2. MAJOR ECONOMIC GROWTH PROJECTIONS

The 2003 industrial output is expected to increase by 4.2%, agriculture output is projected to grow by 2.8%, investments are expected to increase by 8.6%, and retail trade – by 5.5%. In 2003, manufacturing and services will be the main contributing factors to GRP growth.

GRP trends in 1997–2002						TABLE 2
	1997	1998	1999	2000	2001*	2002*
GRP in current prices, $ million	4,042.4	2,439.2	1,580.2	1,852.1	2,188.7	2,399.1

*Estimates of the Voronezh Regional Administration

GRP industry breakdown in 1997–2002, % of total						TABLE 3
	1997	1998	1999	2000	2001*	2002*
GRP	100.0	100.0	100.0	100.0	100.0	100.0
Industry	27.7	26.4	26.8	25.4	23.5	24.0
Agriculture and forestry	11.8	10.7	20.2	18.4	17.9	18.2
Construction	5.6	6.0	5.5	5.0	5.4	5.7
Transport and communications	12.9	9.3	9.6	14.2	10.4	11.5
Trade and public catering	12.9	16.0	15.5	11.1	13.6	12.4
Other industries	29.1	31.6	22.4	25.9	29.2	28.2

*Estimates of the Voronezh Regional Administration

3.3. INDUSTRIAL OUTPUT IN 1997–2002 FOR MAJOR SECTORS OF ECONOMY

The Voronezh Region's leading industries are machine engineering and metals, food and beverages, energy, and chemicals and petrochemicals. Together they account for over 80% of total output.

Machine engineering and metal processing. The sector accounts for 24% of total industrial output. Its main segments are aircraft manufacturing, machinery and machine tool production, agriculture machinery manufacturing, and excavators. The sector's largest companies include OAO VEKS, FGUP

Industry breakdown of industrial output in 1997–2002, % of total						TABLE 4
	1997	1998	1999	2000	2001	2002*
Industry	100.0	100.0	100.0	100.0	100.0	100.0
Machine engineering and metal processing	19.4	18.6	19.5	22.5	25.6	24.0
Food and beverages	18.7	20.1	23.9	26.7	24.9	23.8
Energy	26.8	24.1	17.9	18.0	18.1	19.1
Chemicals and petrochemicals	16.7	13.6	15.9	12.7	14.2	16.5
Construction materials	5.8	6.9	6.6	6.9	5.8	6.2
Forestry, timber, and pulp and paper	1.8	2.6	1.7	2.2	2.2	2.0
Ferrous metals	2.8	2.3	3.1	3.7	2.8	1.9
Flour, cereals, and mixed fodder	4.4	3.5	3.4	3.0	2.2	1.7
Light industry	1.2	0.9	1.2	1.1	0.9	0.8

*Estimates of the Voronezh Regional Administration

Voronezh Mechanical Engineering Plant, OAO Voronezh Aluminum Assemblies Plant, and OAO VZSAK.

Food and beverages. This sector accounts for 23.8% of total industrial output. The Voronezh Region is home to 12 sugar refineries, 15 meat factories, six flour mills, two groats mills, seven edible fat and oil companies, eight distilleries, five canned food factories, 34 dairies, 45 food plants, and over 120 bread factories and bakeries. OAO Voronezh Confectionery Factory is one of the largest companies in the Region.

Energy. The energy sector accounts for 19.1% of total industrial output. The industry is represented by two large companies: OAO Voronezhenergo and the Novovoronezhskaya Nuclear Power Station.

Chemicals and petrochemicals. The sector accounts for 16.5% of the Region's total industrial output. Its largest companies include OAO Minudobreniya and OAO Voronezhsintezkauchuk.

3.4. FUEL AND ENERGY BALANCE (OUTPUT AND CONSUMPTION PER RESOURCE)

Fuel and energy sector production and consumption trends, 1997–2002						TABLE 5
	1997	1998	1999	2000	2001	2002*
Electricity output, billion kWh	12.7	10.7	10.4	12.3	11.9	13.2
Electricity consumption, billion kWh	8.9	8.5	8.8	9.1	9.1	9.0
Natural gas consumption, million cubic meters	4,310.0	3,895.0	4,154.0	4,331.0	4,551.0	4,704.0

*Estimates of the Voronezh Regional Administration

3.5. TRANSPORT INFRASTRUCTURE

Roads. The Voronezh Region has more than 9,102 kilometers of paved public highway. The Region is linked to other regions of Russia by the following federal highways: Moscow – Voronezh – Rostov-on-Don, Tambov – Voronezh – Kursk – Belgorod, and Voronezh – Saratov. Over 40 transport companies with a total pool of 1,179 buses carry passengers within the Region.

Railroads. The Voronezh Region has 1,189 kilometers of railroads. The Region's railroad network is incorporated into the South-Eastern Railroad Network and represents one of the major transport routes linking the center of European Russia with the North Caucasus, the Volga area, Ukraine, and the eastern regions of the country.

Airports. The Region is served by an international airport. OAO Voronezhavia is the largest airline operating in the Region and the Central Black Earth Area. The company operates regular flights to CIS and non-CIS countries.

River transport. The Region has 573 kilometers of navigable waterways. The River Don links the Region to the Sea of Azov, the Caspian Sea, and the Black Sea.

The Region has two operational river ports at Liski and Voronezh. The port of Liski, located on the upper Don, handles bulk and high volume cargo transportation. The port has 12 self-propelled vessels, 38 barges, two floating cranes and seven port cranes. In addition, the port has its own railroad link. The port of Voronezh has nine self-propelled vessels, 25 barges, one oil station, and a dry dock.

Oil and gas pipelines. The Voronezh Region is crossed by several pipelines, including the Togliatti – Odessa ammonia pipeline, oil product pipelines (Nikolskoye – Voronezh, Voronezh – Liski, and Voronezh – Belgorod), and trunk gas pipelines (Stavropol – Moscow, Central Asia – Center, Urengoy – Novopskovskoye, and Petrovskoye – Novopskovskoye).

3.6. MAIN NATURAL RESOURCES: RESERVES AND EXTRACTION IN 2002

The Voronezh Region's main natural resources are minerals and raw materials, water, and forest resources.

Minerals and raw materials. The Region's minerals and raw materials include fire clays, molding sands, chalk, marls, limestone, zeolites, phosphorites, several spa and mineral water sources, and underground industrial and potable water deposits.

Water resources. The Voronezh Region is a zone of limited on-surface water resources. Rivers, lakes, reservoirs, ponds, and subterranean water sources represent the Voronezh Region's water resources. The Region's total surface water reserve covers 14,000 cubic kilometers. The Region has 2,557 water reservoirs and ponds with a total area of 30,400 hectares, and some 2,220 lakes with a total area of 76 square kilometers.

Forest resources. The total area of the Voronezh Region's forests is 626,000 hectares. Over the past five years, some 750 hectares of forest has been planted, including 110 hectares of roadside forest belts.

4. TRADE OPPORTUNITIES

4.1. MAIN GOODS
PRODUCED IN THE REGION
Energy. 2002 energy output was 13.2 billion kWh, a 10.9% increase compared to 2001 figures.

Steel. 2002 steel output was 11,100 tons, up by 11.6% on 2001 figures.

Sawn timber. 2002 sawn timber output was 51,000 cubic meters, 18.6% up on 2001 figures.

Construction lime. 2002 construction lime output was 238,200 tons, up by 27.9% on 2001 figures.

Varnish and paint. 2002 output of varnish and paint was 6,900 tons, a 80% increase on 2001 figures.

Granulated sugar. 2002 granulated sugar output was 478,000 tons, a 26% increase on 2001 figures.

Flour. 2002 flour output was 260,800 tons, up by 28.9% on 2001 figures.

Bread and bakery. 2002 output of bread and bakery products was down by 2% compared to 2001 at 139,400 tons.

4.2. EXPORTS, INCLUDING EXTRA-CIS
Exports to extra-CIS countries in 2000 reached $147.1 million, while exports to CIS countries totaled $35.3 million. The respective figures for 2001 were $178.2 million and $46 million, and for 2002 – $146.6 million and $49.4 million.

Main exports include food and raw materials for the food industry, petrochemicals, garments and footwear, ferrous and non-ferrous metals, and grain. Main export destinations include China (36.1% of total exports), Ukraine (16.1%), Turkey (9.5%), Kazakhstan (4.8%), and Germany (3.3%).

4.3. IMPORTS,
INCLUDING EXTRA-CIS
Imports from extra-CIS countries in 2000 reached $48.7 million, while imports from the CIS totaled $119.5 million. The respective figures for 2001 were $77.8 million and $102.6 million, and for 2002 – $150.2 million and $74.3 million.

Food and beverages, petrochemicals, energy, timber and timber products and machinery constitute the Region's main imports. Major exporters to the Region include Ukraine (30% of total imports), Germany (14.6%), China (6.3%), Cuba (6.2%), and Brazil (6.1%).

4.4. MAJOR REGIONAL
EXPORT AND
IMPORT ENTITIES
Due to the specific features of trade in the Region, mainly industrial companies perform export and import operations.

5. INVESTMENT OPPORTUNITIES

5.1. INVESTMENTS IN 1992–2002
(BY INDUSTRY SECTOR),
INCLUDING FOREIGN INVESTMENTS
The following factors determine the investment appeal of the Voronezh Region:
- Its good geographical location;
- Its natural resource potential;
- Its developed transport infrastructure;
- Its highly qualified workforce and cheap labor;
- Legislation supporting investment activities (guarantees of investors' rights and tax benefits for investors).

5.2. CAPITAL INVESTMENT
Industry (energy and machinery engineering) and transport and communications accounted for the bulk of investments in 2002.

Capital investment by industry sector, $ million						*TABLE 6*
	1997	1998	1999	2000	2001	2002
Total capital investment	580.1	377.4	228.5	293.7	328.7	471.2
Including major industries (% of total)						
Industry	24.2	22.9	23.2	23.7	26.0	37.6
Agriculture and forestry	4.4	3.7	6.0	6.7	7.8	6.9
Construction	2.2	2.2	1.8	1.8	1.4	0.9
Transport and communications	17.1	18.1	21.5	32.2	27.0	20.9
Trade and public catering	0.4	0.5	0.5	0.8	1.8	1.4
Other	51.7	52.6	47.0	34.8	36.0	32.3

Foreign investment trends in 1997–2002						*TABLE 7*
	1997	1998	1999	2000	2001	2002
Foreign investment, $ million	1.1	3.9	18.2	20.9	29.3	55.6
Including FDI, $ million	0.8	1.9	16.5	15.3	13.9	5.0

5.3. MAJOR ENTERPRISES (INCLUDING ENTERPRISES WITH FOREIGN INVESTMENT)

The largest companies with foreign investment are ZAO Lucent Technologies Svyazstroy (USA), OAO Voronezhplast (Czech Republic), OOO Microdesign (Germany), ZAO Be.Vo. (Netherlands), OAO Teleservice (USA), and OAO Voronezh Brewery (Sweden).

Largest enterprises of the Voronezh Region	*TABLE 8*
COMPANY	SECTOR
OAO VEKS	Machine engineering
FGUP Voronezh Mechanical Engineering Plant	Machine engineering
OAO Voronezh Aluminum Constructions Plant	Machine engineering
OAO VZSAK	Machine engineering
OAO Voronezhenergo	Energy
OAO Voronezh Confectionery Factory	Food and beverages
OAO Minudobreniya	Chemicals
OAO Voronezhsintzkauchuk	Chemicals

5.4. MOST ATTRACTIVE SECTOR FOR INVESTMENT

According to the Voronezh Regional Administration, the most attractive sectors for investors are high-tech manufacturing, agricultural production and processing, and trade and public catering.

5.5. CURRENT LEGISLATION ON INVESTOR TAX EXEMPTIONS AND PRIVILEGES

A new Regional draft Law On State (Regional) Support of Investment Activity in the Territory of the Voronezh Region has been developed and introduced to the Regional Duma. The Law regulates certain tax issues related to investment activities, namely:

• Tax benefits to investors in the form of partial or full exemption from tax and other payments to the regional budget, tax extensions, deferrals, tax credits, and investment tax credits;
• Benefits and privileges to investors with regard to land and other natural resources use, provided such provisions do not conflict with the legislation of the Russian Federation;
• Leasing to investors, on preferential terms, of buildings and other properties owned by the Regional Administration;
• Restructuring of debts to the regional budget, including those related to previously issued loans and credits;
• Information support for investment activities;
• Participation in the investment project development process;

• Participation in financing investment projects using regional budget funds in accordance with the applicable legislation;
• Provision on a tender basis of state (regional) guarantees to specific investment projects by means of the regional pledge fund's assets;
• Partial budget subsidies on loan interest to business entities implementing investment projects under the Voronezh Region's social and economic development programs and federal and regional targeted programs.

5.6. FEDERAL AND REGIONAL ECONOMIC AND SOCIAL DEVELOPMENT PROGRAMS FOR THE VORONEZH REGION

Federal targeted programs. A number of federal targeted programs is underway in the Voronezh Region, including the following priority programs: Upgrade of the Transport System of Russia, 2002–2010, Support to the Disabled, 2002–2006, Federal Program for the Development of Education, 2001–2005, Preventive Measures Against Social Diseases, 2002–2006, Creation of an Automated System for the State Land Cadastre Maintenance and State Records of Immovable Property, 2002–2007, Elimination of Social and Economic Differences Between the Regions of the Russian Federation, 2002–2010 and through 2015, and The Culture of Russia, 2001–2005.

Regional programs. The most important regional programs for the social and economic development of the Voronezh Region are: Soil Fertility Enhancement in the Voronezh Region,

Regional entities responsible for raising investment

TABLE 9

ENTITY	ADDRESS	PHONE, FAX, E-MAIL
ZAO Voronezh Regional Agency for Small & Medium Business Support	34, ul. Tsiuriupy, Voronezh, Vorinezh Region, 394000	Phone/fax: (0732) 53 1196, 53 0034, 55 6469 E-mail: vbrost@infobus.ru
State Fund for Small & Medium Business Support in the Voronezh Region	30, ul. Teatralnaya, Voronezh, Voronezh Region, 394000	Phone/fax: (0732) 51 2130, 51 9628 E-mail: vcpm@comch.ru
Swiss Fund for the Support of Economic Reform	72, ul. F. Engelsa, Voronezh, Voronezh Region, 394018	Phone/fax: (0732) 77 3041, 77 4025 E-mail: rsfund@comch.ru

2002–2005, Development of the Securities Market in the Voronezh Region, 2002–2006 (the program is to be approved by the Voronezh Regional Duma), Reforms in the Industrial Sector of the Penitentiary System and Support of Convict Labor Schemes, 2003, Social Support to the Disabled in the Voronezh Region, 2003–2005, and The Children of the Voronezh Region, 2003–2004.

6. INVESTMENT PROJECTS

Industry sector and project description	1) Expected results 2) Amount and term of investment 3) Form of financing[1] 4) Documentation[2]	Contact information
1	2	3

MACHINE ENGINEERING AND METAL PROCESSING

04R001 ● ◆		
Production of rolled metal grinders. Project goal: to increase sales of grinders.	1) Revenue of $11.3 million a year 2) $1.6 million/3 years 3) L ($0.8 million) 4) BP	OAO Voronezh Machine Tool Plant 48, pr. Truda, Voronezh, Voronezh Region, 394026 Phone: (0732) 21 0042 Fax: (0732) 16 4428 E-mail: vtf@stankozavod.com Nikolai Mitrofanovich Borodkin, CEO
04R002 ■ ● ★ ▲ ◆		
Development and serial production of boring rigs for well drilling (60 mm, 250/270 mm) and self-propelled mine cars of 30 tons carrying capacity. Project goal: to produce boring rigs and self-propelled mine cars using new technologies.	1) Boring rigs – 30 items a year, self-driven mine cars – 40 cars a year 2) $1.5 million/3.6 years 3) L, E, JV, Leas. 4) BP, FS	OAO Rudgormash 13, ul. Chebysheva, Voronezh, Voronezh Region, 394084 Phone: (0732) 45 4980, 44 7849, 49 9602 Fax: (0732) 49 7843, 37 5200 E-mail: market@rudgor.vsi.ru http://www.rudgormash.vrn.ru Anatoly Nikolaevich Chekmeniov, CEO

LIGHT INDUSTRY

04R003 ■ ● ★ ◆		
Technical upgrade. Project goal: to implement new technologies, replace the current product range, and implement international quality standards.	1) 7,100 pairs of footwear a year (revenue of $4.1 million a year) 2) $2.6 million/5 years 3) L, E, Leas. 4) BP	OAO Borisoglebovsky Trikotazh 1a, ul. Seredina, Borisoglebsk, Voronezh Region, 397160 Phone: (07354) 67 095 Fax: (07354) 67 089 Vladimir Viktorovich Lysenko, CEO

[1] L – Loan, E – Equity, Leas. – Leasing, JV – Joint Venture
[2] BP – Business Plan, FS – Feasibility Study

1	2	3

AGRICULTURE

04R004

Development of the agriculture sector.
Project goal: to provide services in terms
of soil cultivation, and the preparation,
drying, and sale of agriculture products,
and to implement high-tech tillage
techniques.

1) Revenues of $2.2 million a year
2) $0.7 million/3 years
3) L ($0.6 million)
4) BP

ZAO Pavlovskaya Machine
and Technology Station
8a, ul. Stroitelnaya, Pavlovsk,
Voronezh Region, 396430
Phone: (07362) 21 354
Fax: (07362) 29 260
E-mail: agrosnab@icmail.ru
Viktor Ivanovich Skutnev, CEO

04R005

Restoration of the Sputnik pig farm
at Prigorodny.
Project goal: to develop pork
production facilities.

1) 4,000 tons of pork a year
2) $2.5 million/20 months
3) L ($2 million)
4) BP

OAO Kalacheyevsky Meat Plant
23, ul. Promyshlennikov, Prigorodny,
Kalach, Voronezh Region, 397605
Phone: (07363), 44 255, 44 495
Fax: (07363) 44 391
E-mail:marketing@kmkmeat.ru
http://www.kmkmeat.ru
Nikolai Ivanovich Astanin, CEO

GENERAL COMMERCIAL MARKET ACTIVITIES SUPPORT

04R006

Development of a regional small business
financing system.
Project goal: to increase client base
of small businesses that cannot
access bank loans.

1) Issuing 3,000 loans per year
2) $0.6 million/3 months
3) L ($0.3 million)
4) BP

Voronezh Region State Fund
for Small Business Support
30, ul. Teatralnaya,
Voronezh, Voronezh Region, 394000
Phone/fax: (0732) 51 2130, 51 9628
E-mail: vcmp@comch.ru
Sergei Alexandrovich Sumenko, CEO

04R007

Creation of a pilot Small Business House
for the Central Black Earth Region.
Project goal: to create a unified complex
of 15 entities to provide a broad range
of support services to small businesses
(information, consulting, legal, finance,
leasing, insurance, and training) within
the Central Black Earth Region using
a unified information system network.

1) Revenues of $0.48 million a year
2) $0.6 million/1 year
3) L ($0.3 million), E
4) BP

Voronezh Region State Fund
for Small Business Support
30, ul. Teatralnaya,
Voronezh, Voronezh Region, 394000
Phone/fax: (0732) 51 2130, 51 9628
E-mail: vcmp@comch.ru
Sergei Alexandrovich Sumenko, CEO

04R008

Develop a business incubator within
the radio electronics industry.
Project goal: to expand the activities
of the business incubator.

1) Create 12 new jobs
2) $0.3 million/1 year
3) JV
4) BP

Voronezh Orbita Service Business
Incubator, 1, ul. Donbasskaya,
Voronezh, Voronezh Region, 394030
Phone: (0732) 77 4397, 77 4329, 77 6625
Fax: (0732) 77 6625
E-mail: mail@intercon.ru,
incubator@intercon.ru
Alexander Ivanovich Nekhayev, CEO

TRANSPORT

04R009

Development of freight road
haulage base.
Project goal: to develop the international
freight road haulage sector.

1) 120,000 tons of freight annually
2) $12 million/3 years
3) Leas.
4) BP

OOO PO Ilona
41, ul. Rostovskaya, Voronezh,
Voronezh Region, 394074
Phone: (0732) 77 2887
Fax: (0732) 77 7700
E-mail: ilonapo@online.ru
Igor Georgievich Shakin, CEO

05. IVANOVO REGION [37]

ECONOMIC MAP

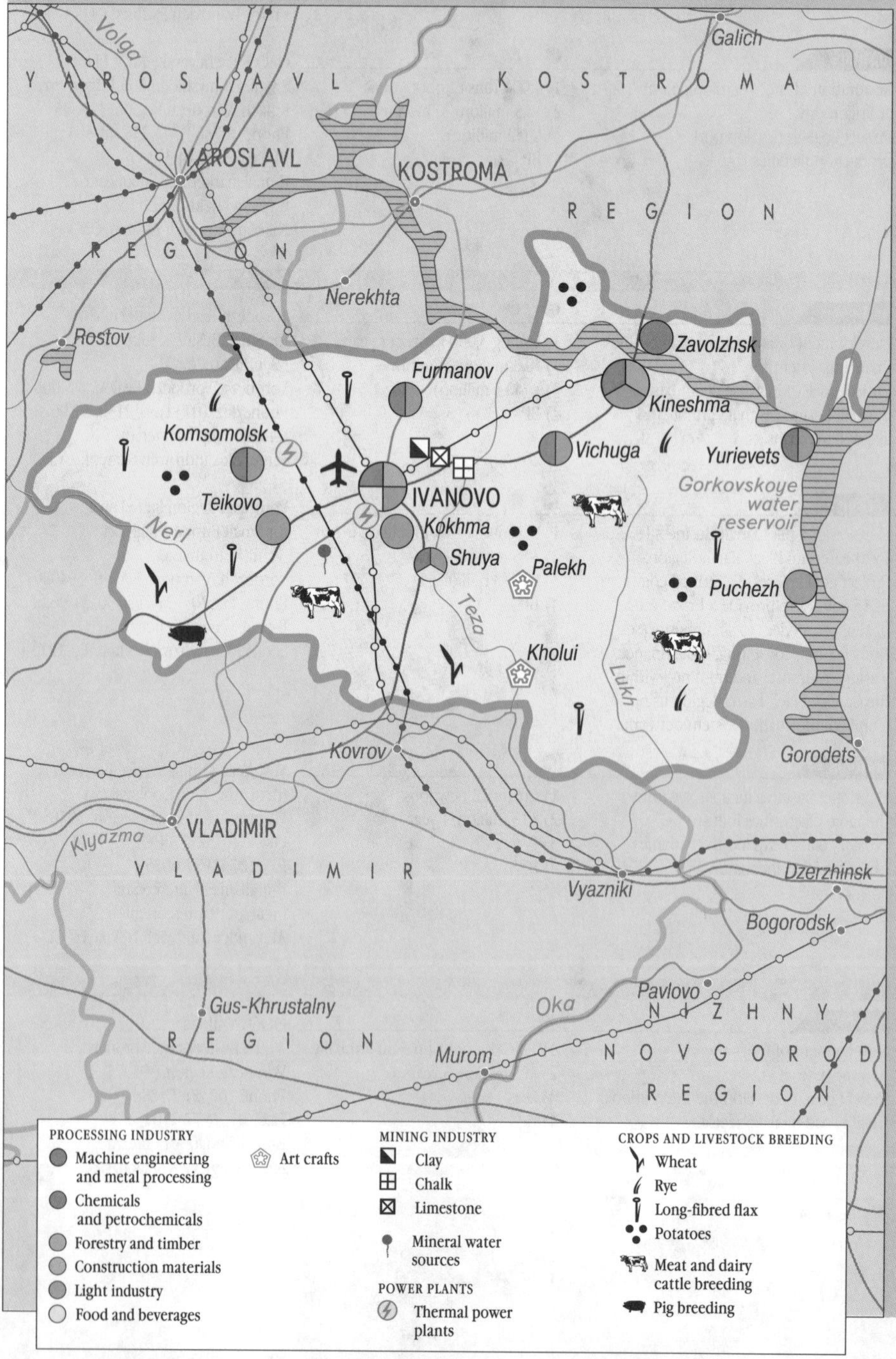
Volga
YAROSLAVL
YAROSLAVL
REGION
KOSTROMA
KOSTROMA
REGION
Galich
Nerekhta
Rostov
Zavolzhsk
Furmanov
Kineshma
Komsomolsk
Vichuga
Yurievets
Gorkovskoye water reservoir
Teikovo
IVANOVO
Kokhma
Shuya
Palekh
Nerl
Teza
Puchezh
Kholui
Lukh
Gorodets
Kovrov
VLADIMIR
Klyazma
VLADIMIR
REGION
Vyazniki
Dzerzhinsk
Bogorodsk
Pavlovo
Gus-Khrustalny
Oka
Murom
NIZHNY NOVGOROD REGION
PROCESSING INDUSTRY
Machine engineering and metal processing
Chemicals and petrochemicals
Forestry and timber
Construction materials
Light industry
Food and beverages
Art crafts
MINING INDUSTRY
Clay
Chalk
Limestone
Mineral water sources
POWER PLANTS
Thermal power plants
CROPS AND LIVESTOCK BREEDING
Wheat
Rye
Long-fibred flax
Potatoes
Meat and dairy cattle breeding
Pig breeding

The Ivanovo Region lies at the center of European Russia, 300 kilometers to the north-east of Moscow, at the crossroads of major transportation routes linking the Moscow and western regions with eastern and north-eastern regions of Russia. Besides highways and trunk railroads, the Region boasts river ports and an international airport.

Traditionally, the Region is one of Russia's leading industrial centers and is well known for its textiles and machine engineering sectors. Two thirds of the country's total cotton fabric output is still produced at factories in Ivanovo. Since time immemorial, Ivanovo has been known as the Russian Manchester.

According to experts, the Ivanovo Region's investment potential ranks 66th among the 89 regions of Russian Federation. The Region ranks 33rd in the regions' investment risk assessment.

Economists grade regional investment appeal on an eleven-notch scale. The Ivanovo Region is classified sixth, or 3B2, with insignificant potential and a moderate risk index (17 other regions of Russia are also classified 3B2). Russian experts believe that this grade, which implies capacity for gradual yet stable realization of long-term projects, is underestimated by foreign partners.

Expert estimates of the regional investment legislation are quite high due to its simplicity and clarity. We guarantee that potential investors will be immune from serious legal problems in the Ivanovo Region and that they will have no problem obtaining the privileges and guarantees granted by the law.

The Region possesses considerable scientific potential and a highly qualified workforce.

The regional economy is characterized by steady positive development trends, a factor that is of no small importance to the successful implementation of investment projects. Solvent consumer demand in the Region is also gradually rising.

Attracting foreign investment is one of the top priorities of the Ivanovo Regional Administration. Foreign investments in regional enterprises amounted to some $20 million over the past five years. The bulk of the investments was made by UK and Japanese companies.

Foreign investment in the Region is still at a trickle because the Region is not one of the regions most favored by foreign investors (those rich in natural resources, with large urban centers, or bordering with other countries). The Region's major industries, textile and machine engineering, require large-scale and long-term investments, and not every investor is ready to make the commitment. Nevertheless, some foreign companies, including such top league names as Komatsu and Sanek Ltd., are operating in the Region and enjoy the full support of the Regional Administration.

Today, the attitude towards foreign investors in Russian business circles has changed. The new generation of Russian manufacturers considers it quite acceptable to concede controlling stakes to partners on reasonable terms, and a thorough development of a business plan is no longer regarded as a foreigner's whim. We are ready and willing to resolve problems regarding property rights to production facilities and land plots under the provisions of the existing Russian legislation.

Vladimir Tikhonov,
HEAD OF ADMINISTRATION (GOVERNOR)
OF THE IVANOVO REGION

I

CENTRAL FEDERAL DISTRICT

1. GENERAL INFORMATION

1.1. GEOGRAPHY

Located in the center of European Russia, the Ivanovo Region covers a total area of 21,400 square kilometers. To the south, the Ivanovo Region borders the Vladimir Region, to the southeast – the Nizhny Novgorod Region, to the north – the Kostroma Region, and to the west – the Yaroslavl Region.

1.2. CLIMATE

The Region lies in the temperate continental climate zone. Air temperatures in January average –12°C, rising to +18°C in July. Annual precipitation averages 550 mm.

1.3. POPULATION

According to preliminary 2002 census results, the total population of the Ivanovo Region was 1,149,000 people. The Region's average population density is 53.7 people per square kilometer. The economically active population amounts to 573,000 people. The official unemployment rate stood at 1.4% in 2002.

Demographically speaking, some 59.4% of the population are of working age, 16% are below the statutory working age, and 24.6% are beyond the statutory working age.

As of 2002, the Ivanovo Region's major urban centers were Ivanovo with 432,200 inhabitants, Kineshma with 97,500 inhabitants, and Shuya with 64,700 inhabitants.

Population								TABLE 1
	1992	1997	1998	1999	2000	2001	2002
Total population, '000	1,289	1,253	1,242	1,232	1,219	1,205	1,149
Economically active population, '000	673	609	592	600	600	588	573

2. ADMINISTRATION

5, ul. Baturina, Ivanovo, Ivanovo Region, 153000
Phone: (0932) 41 9231
E-mail: aio@adminet.ivanovo.ru; http://www.ivadm@ivanovo.ru

NAME	POSITION	CONTACT INFORMATION
Vladimir Ilyich TIKHONOV	Head of Administration (Governor) of the Ivanovo Region	Phone: (0932) 41 7705
Alexander Yuryevich KANAEV	Vice Governor, First Deputy Head of Administration (Governor) of the Ivanovo Region for Economy and Industry	Phone: (0932) 41 6805 Fax: (0932) 41 0150 E-mail: kanaev@adminet.ivanovo.ru
Nikolai Vasilyevich ZIMIN	First Deputy Head of Administration (Governor) of the Ivanovo Region	Phone: (0932) 32 9781 Fax: (0932) 41 9231
Vladimir Nikolaevich GRIGORIEV	Deputy Head of Administration (Governor) of the Ivanovo Region in charge of Natural Resource Use and Property Relations, Head of the Representative Office of Administration of the Ivanovo Region at the Government of the Russian Federation	Phone: (0932) 41 7708 E-mail: grigoritv@adminet.ivanovo.ru
Vladimir Alexandrovich STARIKOV	Deputy Head of Administration (Governor) of the Ivanovo Region, in charge of Housing and Communal Services, Communications, and Transport	Phone: (0932) 32 7681 Fax: (0932) 32 7681
Vladimir Sergeevich SOKOV	Head of the Economic Development and Trade Department of the Ivanovo Region	Phone: (0932) 32 7348 Fax: (0932) 30 8966 E-mail: 005@adminet.ivanovo.ru
Georgy Viktorovich BOLSHAKOV	Head of the Investment and Tourism Department of the Ivanovo Region	Phone: (0932) 37 7567 Fax: (0932) 30 8966 E-mail: bolshakov@adminet.ivanovo.ru

3. ECONOMIC POTENTIAL

3.1. 1997–2002 GROSS REGIONAL PRODUCT (GRP). INDUSTRY BREAKDOWN

According to the Ivanovo Regional Administration, the 2002 gross regional product of the Region totaled $909.5 million, up 15.2 % on 2001. Per capita GRP in 2001 was $655, rising to $792 in 2002.

3.2. MAJOR ECONOMIC GROWTH PROJECTIONS

are set forth in the Ivanovo Region Development Strategy through 2010 developed by the Ivanovo Regional Administration. The Strategy sets the following objectives for 2003: 6.9% industry growth (including energy – 8%, light manufactur-

GRP trends in 1997–2002						TABLE 2
	1997	1998	1999	2000	2001*	2002*
GRP in current prices, $ million	1,386.4	902.9	508.5	643.2	789.6	909.5

*Estimates of the Ivanovo Regional Administration

GRP industry breakdown in 1997–2002, % of total						TABLE 3
	1997	1998	1999	2000	2001*	2002*
GRP	100.0	100.0	100.0	100.0	100.0	100.0
Industry	30.5	30.9	31.0	32.0	32.0	30.7
Agriculture and forestry	9.6	6.0	14.7	12.0	12.6	12.0
Construction	4.5	5.1	3.3	5.2	5.5	5.3
Transport and communications	7.9	7.2	7.0	7.2	7.3	7.6
Trade and public catering	11.8	8.6	11.9	11.9	12.6	11.8
Other	33.6	25.1	25.8	25.2	23.1	25.7
Net taxes on output	2.1	7.1	6.3	6.5	6.9	6.9

*Estimates of the Ivanovo Regional Administration

ing – 4–5%, chemicals – 8%, food and beverages – 3%, fuel – 9%), and 4% growth in agriculture.

3.3. INDUSTRIAL OUTPUT IN 1997–2002 FOR MAJOR SECTORS OF ECONOMY

The Ivanovo Region's leading industries include: light industry, energy, and machine engi-neering and metal processing. These sectors account for a combined 73.3% of total industrial output of the Region.

Light industry. The sector accounts for 36.2% of the Region's total industrial output. The sector's major companies are: OAO Shuya Cottons,

Industry breakdown of industrial output in 1997–2002, % of total						TABLE 4
	1997	1998	1999	2000	2001	2002*
Industry	100.0	100.0	100.0	100.0	100.0	100.0
Light industry	35.7	33.5	38.8	38.4	34.6	36.2
Energy	22.7	26.9	19.6	20.5	20.5	22.3
Machine engineering and metal processing	15.8	13.4	13.7	14.8	19.2	14.8
Food and beverages	12.6	12.8	14.5	12.0	10.4	13.0
Construction materials	3.5	3.7	2.7	2.7	3.6	4.1
Chemicals and petrochemicals	3.3	3.2	3.8	4.4	4.1	3.4
Forestry, timber, and pulp and paper	3.2	3.6	4.4	4.5	4.4	3.0
Fuel	0.1	0.1	0.1	0.1	0.1	0.1

*Preliminary data of the State Statistics Committee

CENTRAL FEDERAL DISTRICT

OAO Ivanovo Garment Factory, OAO Samtex, OAO Kokhmatextile, OAO Solidarnost, OAO Teikovo-Textile, and OAO Duet.

Energy. The sector accounts for 22.3% of the Region's total industrial output. The sector's largest company is the 650 MW OAO Komsomolskaya GRES.

Machine engineering and metal processing. The sector accounts for 14.8% of the Region's total industrial output. The largest companies in the sector include OAO Kranex Machine Building Company, OAO Avtoagregat, and OAO Avtokran.

Food and beverages. The sector accounts for 13% of the Region's total industrial output. The sector's major companies are OOO Limpopo, OAO Shuya Vodka, OAO Petrovsky Alcohol Plant, ZAO Ivanovo Brewery, OAO Krasnaya Zarya Confectionery Factory, and OAO Shuya Meat Plant.

3.4. FUEL AND ENERGY BALANCE (OUTPUT AND CONSUMPTION PER RESOURCE)

Fuel and energy sector production and consumption trends, 1997–2002						*TABLE 5*
	1997	1998	1999	2000	2001	2002
Electricity output, billion kWh	2.0	1.7	1.3	1.4	1.2	1.3
Electricity consumption, billion kWh	4.2	4.0	4.0	4.3	4.3	4.3
Natural gas consumption, million cubic meters	2,030.9	1,298.2	1,188.2	1,302.2	1,408.4	1,926.3

3.5. TRANSPORT INFRASTRUCTURE

Roads. The Ivanovo Region has 5,700 kilometers of paved public highway. The Region's road network provides links to the Kostroma Region, the Nizhny Novgorod Region, the Vladimir Region, and the Yaroslavl Region.

Railroad. The Region has 580 kilometers of railroads, which form part of the Northern railroad network of Russia. The Region's railroad network links the Ivanovo Region to Moscow, St. Petersburg, Yaroslavl, Nizhny Novgorod, and Samara. Major routes include St. Petersburg – Samara, Ivanovo – Moscow, and Moscow – Kineshma.

Airports. The Region is served by an international airport at Ivanovo. The airport is currently under reconstruction and not in use.

River transport. The Ivanovo Region's main navigable waterways are along the Volga river. Their total length is 220 kilometers. The Region's waterways provide access to the Caspian, Baltic, and White Seas.

Oil and gas pipelines. The Ivanovo Region is crossed by the Gorky – Polotsk oil pipeline and the Gorky – Yaroslavl gas pipeline (440 kilometers in total).

3.6. MAIN NATURAL RESOURCES: RESERVES AND EXTRACTION IN 2002

The Ivanovo Region's principal resources are construction materials (including clays, sands, and silicate products), mineral resources, and recreational resources.

Construction materials. Main resources are clays and loams (reserves of 51.8 million cubic meters), sand for silicate products (81.6 million cubic meters), gravel and sand (121.4 million cubic meters), peat (89 million tons), and sapropel (72 million cubic meters).

Mineral water. The Region has reserves of underground mineral water (1 gram/liter mineralization) and sodium sulphate curative and table water (1–5 gram/liter mineralization). Explored underground water reserves are estimated at 653,500 cubic meters per day, including mineral water at 296,000 cubic meters per day.

Recreational resources. The Region is considered to be one of the most environmentally pristine areas of Russia and has a huge recreational potential, including water and forest resources, beautiful landscapes, and curative water sources. The Ivanovo Region is part of Russia's Golden Ring and has an abundance of historic and cultural sites in its territory.

4. TRADE OPPORTUNITIES

4.1. MAIN GOODS PRODUCED IN THE REGION

The Region's 2002 output was as follows:

Light industry. Cotton fabric – 1,622 million square meters, linen fabric – 20 million square meters, wool fabric – 1.02 million square meters.

Energy. 1,335.2 million kWh.

Machine engineering and metals. Truck cranes – 1,261 units, excavators – 156 units, buses – 21 units.

Chemicals. Paint and varnish – 3,400 tons, synthetic dyes – 1,200 tons.

Construction materials. Lumber – 33,200 cubic meters, non-ore construction materials – 1,154,000 cubic meters, round timber – 77,300 cubic meters.

Food and beverages. Vegetable oil – 65,600 tons, ethyl alcohol – 1,537,000 decaliters, liquors and vodka – 655,700 decaliters, meat, including category one products – 279 tons.

4.2. EXPORTS, INCLUDING EXTRA-CIS

Extra-CIS exports amounted to $46.4 million in 2000, while exports to the CIS reached $12.3 million. The respective figures for 2001 were $51.8 million and $21.7 million, and $59.5 million and $23.2 million for 2002.

The Region's main exports include cotton fabric, linen fabric, excavators, and electric appliances. Main export destinations are the USA, Iran, Latvia, Germany, Ukraine, Uzbekistan, and Turkmenistan.

4.3. IMPORTS, INCLUDING EXTRA-CIS

Imports from extra-CIS countries amounted to $27.5 million in 2000, while imports from the CIS totaled $170.9 million. The respective figures for 2001

were $30.5 million and $145.6 million, and $36 million and $110.4 million for 2002.

The Ivanovo Region's key imports include cotton fiber, raw agricultural products, plastics, and oil processing products. Italy, Denmark, Germany, and Latvia are the main exporters to the Ivanovo Region.

4.4. MAJOR REGIONAL EXPORT AND IMPORT ENTITIES

Owing to the specific features of trade in the Region, export and import transactions are mainly performed by industrial enterprises.

5. INVESTMENT OPPORTUNITIES

5.1. INVESTMENTS IN 1992–2002 (BY INDUSTRY SECTOR), INCLUDING FOREIGN INVESTMENTS

The following factors determine the investment appeal of the Ivanovo Region:

- Its favorable geographical location;
- Its developed transport infrastructure;
- Its significant industrial potential;

- Legislation fostering investment activities in the Region;
- Its qualified workforce.

5.2. CAPITAL INVESTMENT

Industry and construction account for the lion's share of capital investment in the Ivanovo Region. In 2002, together they accounted for a combined 57.7% of total investment.

Capital investment by industry sector, $ million						TABLE 6
	1997	1998	1999	2000	2001	2002
Total capital investment	151.8	154.0	44.1	76.6	78.9	85.5
Including major industries (% of total)						
Industry	36.8	38.5	22.8	26.3	27.2	27.3
Agriculture and forestry	6.0	8.0	13.6	10.5	11.1	10.3
Construction	0.6	7.0	20.6	25.7	22.7	30.4
Transport and communications	16.4	7.0	5.3	5.7	6.3	7.5
Trade and public catering	1.5	2.2	2.9	3.2	0.5	0.4
Other	38.7	37.3	34.8	28.6	32.2	24.1

Foreign investment trends in 1996–2002						TABLE 7
	1996–1997	1998	1999	2000	2001	2002
Foreign investment, $ million	6.0	0.1	0.3	3.2	0.2	1.0
Including FDI, $ million	4.7	0.1	0.3	3.2	0.2	1.0

5.3. MAJOR ENTERPRISES (INCLUDING ENTERPRISES WITH FOREIGN INVESTMENT)

The Ivanovo Region hosts 188 companies with foreign investment representing 12 countries worldwide. The largest companies with foreign investment are ZAO Ivanovo Brewery, OAO Ivanhoe Garment Factory, OAO Kranex Machine Engineering Company, and OAO Avtoagregat.

5.4. MOST ATTRACTIVE SECTORS FOR INVESTMENT

According to the Ivanovo Regional Administration, machine engineering, textiles and garment

manufacturing, timber processing, and construction materials offer the greatest investment appeal.

5.5. CURRENT LEGISLATION ON INVESTOR TAX EXEMPTIONS AND PRIVILEGES

The Ivanovo Region has passed the following legislative acts regulating investment activities in the Region:

- Law On State Support to Investment Activities in the Ivanovo Region;
- Law On Support to Investment Activities in the Ivanovo Region in Form of the Capital Investment;

Largest enterprises of the Ivanovo Region		*TABLE 8*
COMPANY	SECTOR	
OAO Ivenergo	Energy	
OAO Slavneft-Ivanovonefteprodukt	Fuel	
OAO Shuya Cottons	Light industry	
OAO Tomna Kineshma Textile Factory	Light industry	
OAO Kokhmatextile	Light industry	
OAO Samtex	Light industry	
OAO Avtokran	Machine engineering	
OAO Kranex Machine Engineering Company	Machine engineering	
OAO Frunze Zavolzhsky Chemical Plant	Chemicals	
OAO Krasnaya Zarya Confectionery Factory	Food and beverages	
ZAO Ivanovo Brewery	Food and beverages	

• Decree of the Legislative Assembly of the Ivanovo Region On the Protection of Foreign Investments in the Ivanovo Region.

The current legislation establishes the following forms of state support:

• Tax exemptions to investors;

• Participation of the Ivanovo Regional Authorities in the development, expert assessment, and implementation of targeted programs and specific investment projects;

• Guarantees to investors against unfavorable changes in the legislation;

• Tax deferrals and credits for the regional component of taxes paid by investors.

5.6. FEDERAL AND REGIONAL ECONOMIC AND SOCIAL DEVELOPMENT PROGRAMS FOR THE IVANOVO REGION

Federal targeted programs. The Program for the Elimination of Inequalities in the Economic and Social Development of the Regions of the Russian Federation, 2002–2010 and through 2015 is the top priority for the Ivanovo Region. The purpose of the program is to close the gap in economic and social development between the most economically advanced and backward regions by 2010 by a factor of 1.5, and by 2015 by a factor of 2.0. A budget of $0.7 million will be allocated from the federal budget to finance the program in 2003.

Regional entities responsible for raising investment		*TABLE 9*
ENTITY	ADDRESS	PHONE, FAX, E-MAIL
Economic Development and Trade Department of the Ivanovo Regional Administration	5, ul. Baturina, Ivanovo, Ivanovo Region, 153000	Phone: (0932) 41 9231 E-mail: aio@adminet.ivanovo.ru http://www.ivadm@ivanovo.ru

Funding is provided under a federal targeted investment program for construction projects conducted under the following federal targeted programs: Prevention and Countermeasures against Social Diseases, 2002–2006, Environment and Natural Resources of Russia, 2002–2010, and Culture of Russia, 2001–2005.

Regional programs. The Ivanovo Region has implemented a number of regional programs in various areas, including industry, agriculture and food, environ-mental protection, law and order, health care, and public welfare. As of January 1, 2003, some 31 regional programs were underway in the Region. The following programs have been accorded top priority: Development of Donor Activity and Blood Transfusion Institutions in the Ivanovo Region, 2001–2003, and Environmental Improvement of the Ivanovo Region through 2005.

The Region's targeted programs received $6.4 million in funding from all levels of the budget and non-budgetary funds in 2002.

6. INVESTMENT PROJECTS

Industry sector and project description	1) Expected results 2) Amount and term of investment 3) Form of financing[1] 4) Documentation[2]	Contact information
1	2	3

OIL

05R001 ● ◆		
Oil production facilities. Project goal: oil processing.	1) 100,000 tons annually 2) $5.5 million/1.5 years 3) E (minimum $3.8 million) 4) BP	OAO Frunze Zavolzhsky Chemical Plant 1, ul. Zavodksaya, Zavolzhsk, Ivanovo Region 155410 Phone: (09333) 21 565, 24 240 E-mail: office@chem-pl.ivanovo.ru Vladimir Anatolyevich Shpilyovy, Director

MACHINE ENGINEERING AND METAL PROCESSING

05R002 ● ◆		
Production of Kineshma motorcycle side-car and its modifications. Project goal: to produce and sell the Kineshma side-car.	1) 20,000 units annually 2) $19.9 million/2.5 years 3) L ($4.7 million) 4) BP	OAO Avtoagregat 1, ul. 2 Shuyskaya, Kineshma, Ivanovo Region, 155815 Phone: (09331) 57 607 Fax: (09331) 20 765 E-mail: root@kineshma.ru http://www.kineshma.ru Valery Ardalyonovich Smyshlyayev, CEO

05R003 ● ◆		
Production of disc brake pistons. Project goal: to meet demand for disc brake pistons.	1) 11 million pistons a year 2) $1.7 million/15 months 3) L ($1.5 million) 4) BP	OAO Avtoagregat 1, ul. 2 Shuyskaya, Kineshma, Ivanovo Region, 155815 Phone: (09331) 57 607 Fax: (09331) 20 765 E-mail: root@kineshma.ru http://www.kineshma.ru Valery Ardalyonovich Smyshlyayev, CEO

FOOD AND BEVERAGES

05R004 ■ ● ★ ◆		
Facilities for vegetable production, storage, and processing. Project goal: to meet local demand for vegetables.	1) Profit of € 1.5 million a year (full loan repayment in 3 years) 2) € 3.1 million/6 months 3) L, E, Leas. 4) BP	OGUP Ivanovo Food Corporation Office 516, 44, ul. Suvorova, Ivanovo, Ivanovo Region, 153012 Phone: (0932) 32 5564 Fax: (0932) 30 4931 Vladimir Dmitrievich Voronoy, Director

[1] L – Loan, E – Equity, Leas. – Leasing, JV – Joint Venture
[2] BP – Business Plan, FS – Feasibility Study

I

CENTRAL FEDERAL DISTRICT

1	2	3

TRANSPORT INFRASTRUCTURE

05R005   ■ ❖ ▲ ◆

Reconstruction and development of the Ivanovo international airport. Project goal: to increase passenger and freight turnover.

1) Total area of the airport – 288 hectares; capacity of 400 passengers an hour
2) $1.8 million/5 years
3) JV, E
4) BP, FS

OAO Zolotoye Koltso Aviation Company, GA Airport
Ivanovo, Ivanovo Region, 153009
Phone/fax: (0932) 23 5979, 23 4485, 29 2943
Konstantin Sergeevich Onischenko, CEO

ECOLOGY, WASTE PROCESSING

05R006   ■ ● ◆ ▲

Facilities for industrial processing of solid household and industrial waste at Ivanovo and in the Ivanovo Region. Project goal: waste disposal.

1) n/a
2) $5 million/1.5 years
3) L, E
4) BP, FS

OOO Sokol
3, ul. Kalinina, Ivanovo, Ivanovo Region, 153002
Phone/fax: (0932) 41 3259
E-mail: sokol@i1.ru
Sergei Vyacheslavovich Cheremokhin, Director

I

CENTRAL FEDERAL DISTRICT

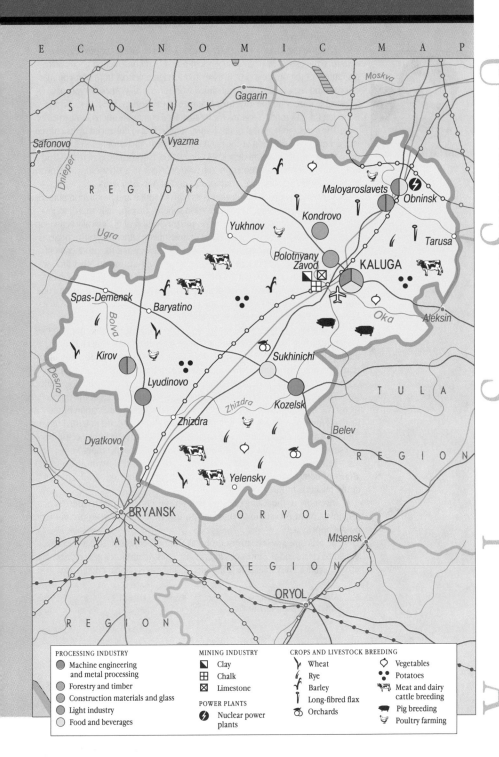

ECONOMIC MAP

RUSSIA

CENTRAL FEDERAL DISTRICT

SMOLENSK

Gagarin

Safonovo

Vyazma

REGION

Dnieper

Ugra

Maloyaroslavets

Kondrovo

Obninsk

Yukhnov

Tarusa

Polotnyany Zavod

KALUGA

Spas-Demensk

Baryatino

Oka

Aleksin

Kirov

Sukhinichi

Lyudinovo

Bolva

Zhizdra

Kozelsk

TULA

Desna

Zhizdra

Belev

REGION

Dyatkovo

Mtsensk

BRYANSK

Yelensky

ORYOL

BRYANSK

REGION

ORYOL

REGION

PROCESSING INDUSTRY
- Machine engineering and metal processing
- Forestry and timber
- Construction materials and glass
- Light industry
- Food and beverages

MINING INDUSTRY
- Clay
- Chalk
- Limestone

POWER PLANTS
- Nuclear power plants

CROPS AND LIVESTOCK BREEDING
- Wheat
- Rye
- Barley
- Long-fibred flax
- Orchards
- Vegetables
- Potatoes
- Meat and dairy cattle breeding
- Pig breeding
- Poultry farming

Thanks to its economic sustainability, structural balance and social stability, the Kaluga Region is among the top Russian regions in terms of investment potential development trends. Its favorable business climate has seen a number of investors launch new production facilities and achieve good results on the Russian market. The high reliability of our Region as a partner was noted in a Bulletin of the US Chamber of Commerce in Russia, which proclaimed the Region a corruption-free zone.

In 1999–2002, major foreign corporations invested some $354.7 million in the Region's economy.

Effective regulation of property relations, laws ensuring tax privileges to investors, the existence of an independent market for construction goods, state guarantees of the protection of Russian and foreign investors from non-commercial risk, and the availability of a qualified workforce – all of these factors have a favorable impact on the investment climate in the Region. The Kaluga Region is among Russia's top ten regions for its advanced communications infrastructure.

The investment appeal of the Kaluga Region is also enhanced by its convenient geographical situation at the center of European Russia only 180 kilometers from Moscow. The Region's deposits of limestone, palygorskite clay, tripoli, and glass sand offer good investment potential. According to analyst estimates, investments in these deposits have a payback period of only four years.

A specific feature of our Region is its high scientific and production potential, for which reason investments in innovation spheres are especially welcome. Projects currently underway with a focus on the production of biologically active supplements serve as examples of this kind of investment. Other innovative projects are centered around the deployment of laser technology and the production of radiological pharmaceuticals used in the treatment of cancers and other illnesses. Other innovation projects worth citing include a project for the production of energy and resource efficient electrical equipment and automated transport control systems. The city of Obninsk, a unique scientific center located in the Kaluga Region, was the first Russian city to receive the status of city of science.

A technology park is currently being built in Obninsk. The objective is to create infrastructure for the development of high-tech enterprises. Federal budget funding has been allocated to finance the construction of utilities and communications infrastructure to prepare the technology park for use by investors. Craftway Corporation plans to build an electronic equipment plant in the technology park.

The Region also offers promising investment opportunities in the timber sector. We believe that the development and comprehensive utilization of the Region's mineral resource base and linen sectors also offer good potential returns for investors. Tourism and recreation represent yet another lucrative sector for investment. The Region is also interested in agricultural cooperation.

Representatives of foreign companies note that pressure on the internal affairs of companies on the part of the regulatory authorities is a feature of doing business in Russia.

Investors in the Kaluga Region will not be subject to such interference. Any investment project involving foreign investment undergoes preliminary public approval.

We welcome any investment proposal. Our only condition is that the capital should be clean, and the investor's intentions, good. An investor's gain represents a smaller gain for every Kaluga Region resident, and this is our paramount goal.

Anatoly Artamonov,
GOVERNOR OF THE KALUGA REGION

1. GENERAL INFORMATION

1.1. GEOGRAPHY

The Kaluga Region covers a total area of 29,900 square kilometers. The Region is situated in the central part of the East European Plain. To the north, it borders the Moscow Region, to the east – the Tula Region, to the south – the Bryansk and Oryol Regions, and to the west – the Smolensk Region.

1.2. CLIMATE

The Kaluga Region is situated in the temperate continental climate zone.

The average air temperature varies from –10°C in January to +18°C in July. Average annual precipitation totals 650 mm. The average growing season lasts 177–184 days.

1.3. POPULATION

According to preliminary 2002 census results, the total population of Kaluga Region was 1,041,000 people. The average population density is 34.8 people per square kilometer. The economically active population is 533,000 people. In 2002, registered unemployment stood at 6.6%.

Demographically speaking, some 60.2% of the total population are of working age, 16.8% are below the statutory working age, and 23.0% are beyond the statutory working age.

The Kaluga Region's major urban centers (2002 data) are Kaluga with 335,100 inhabitants, Obninsk with 105,800 inhabitants, Lyudinovo with 40,000 inhabitants, Kirov with 42,400 inhabitants, and Maloyaroslavets with 30,400 inhabitants.

Population								TABLE 1
	1992	1997	1998	1999	2000	2001	2002
Total population, '000	1,078	1,093	1,092	1,087	1,078	1,069	1,041
Economically active population, '000	578	541	504	569	564	550	533

2. ADMINISTRATION

2, Pl. Stary Torg, Kaluga, Kaluga Region, 248600
Phone: (0842) 56 2357
E-mail: admgub@adm.kaluga.ru; http://www.admobl.kaluga.ru

NAME	POSITION	CONTACT INFORMATION
Anatoly Dmitrievich ARTAMONOV	Governor of the Kaluga Region	Phone: (0842) 56 2357 E-mail: admgub@adm.kaluga.ru
Viktor Fedorovich SAFRONOV	Vice Governor of the Kaluga Region	Phone: (0842) 57 6139 E-mail: admgub@adm.kaluga.ru
Leonid Vasilyevich BREDIKHIN	Deputy Governor of the Kaluga Region	Phone: (0842) 59 1544 E-mail: bredihin@adm.kaluga.ru
Nikolai Yevgenyevich SHUBIN	Director of the Regional Development Department of the Kaluga Region	Phone: (0842) 57 5690 Fax: (0842) 59 1576 E-mail: Shubin@adm.kaluga.ru
Marina Vyacheslavovna NEPARKO	Deputy Director – Head of Consumer Market Development Division of the Regional Development Department of the Kaluga Region	Phone: (0842) 59 1555 E-mail: neparko@adm.kaluga.ru
Alexei Zhorzhevich GOLOBORODKO	Head of the Department of International Economic Activity, Inter-Regional Relations, and Tourism of the Kaluga Region	Phone: (0842) 56 3152 E-mail: Goloborodko@adm.kaluga.ru
Alexander Alexeevich SAPEGIN	Head of the Industrial Sector Division of the Regional Development Department of the Kaluga Region	Phone: (0842) 57 9219 E-mail: sapegin@adm.kaluga.ru
Elena Vladimirovna MUZHICHKOVA	Head of the Commodities, Trade, and Services Market Division of the Regional Development Department of the Kaluga Region	Phone: (0842) 59 1565 E-mail: muzhichkova@adm.kaluga.ru

3. ECONOMIC POTENTIAL

3.1. 1997–2002 GROSS REGIONAL PRODUCT (GRP). INDUSTRY BREAKDOWN

The Kaluga Region's 2002 gross regional product was $1,274.7 million, 8.3% up on 2001. The growth was mainly industry driven: industry accounts for 37% of total GRP. GRP per capita in 2001 amounted to $1,100, rising to $1,224 in 2002.

3.2. MAJOR ECONOMIC GROWTH PROJECTIONS

According to the Kaluga Regional Administration, industrial output will reach $1,349.7 million in 2003 and $1,653.3 million in 2004. The Administration expects agricultural output to reach $298.9 million and $350.0 million, respectively.

GRP trends in 1997–2002						TABLE 2
	1997	1998	1999	2000	2001*	2002*
GRP in current prices, $ million	1,797.0	1,090.6	698.6	928.1	1,177.1	1,274.7

*Estimates of the Kaluga Regional Administration

GRP industry breakdown in 1997–2002, % of total						TABLE 3
	1997	1998	1999	2000	2001*	2002*
GRP	100.0	100.0	100.0	100.0	100.0	100.0
Industry	28.8	26.6	27.2	35.8	37.1	37.0
Agriculture and forestry	14.1	15.9	21.3	14.8	13.3	14.0
Construction	7.1	5.9	6.3	6.3	5.4	6.5
Transport and communications	5.8	8.0	5.6	6.4	7.2	7.5
Trade and public catering	10.0	10.8	10.3	8.7	8.5	10.0
Other	26.0	29.4	20.9	22.3	22.5	19.0
Net taxes on output	8.2	3.4	8.4	5.7	6.0	6.0

*Estimates of the Kaluga Regional Administration

3.3. INDUSTRIAL OUTPUT IN 1997–2002 FOR MAJOR SECTORS OF ECONOMY

The leading industries of the Kaluga Region are machine engineering and metal processing, food and beverages, forestry, and construction materials. These industries account for 79% of the Region's total industrial output.

Machine engineering and metals processing. The industry accounts for 36.7% of total industrial output. Its main sectors are automotive, aviation, energy and transport machinery, radioelectronics, and instruments. The largest enterprises are OOO Agrosovgaz, FGUP Remputmash, OAO Kaluga Turbine Factory, OAO Kaluga Engine, OAO PZ Tayfun, FGUP Kaluga Telegraph Equipment Plant,

Industry breakdown of industrial output in 1997–2002, % of total						TABLE 4
	1997	1998	1999	2000	2001	2002*
Industry	100.0	100.0	100.0	100.0	100.0	100.0
Machine engineering and metal processing	36.2	34.0	41.9	43.1	42.2	36.7
Food and beverages	20.5	21.9	21.9	22.0	21.4	22.7
Forestry, timber, and pulp and paper	10.1	10.4	12.8	13.0	12.6	12.2
Energy	17.3	19.2	10.5	7.7	8.6	11.0
Construction materials	7.5	7.8	6.3	7.3	7.0	7.4
Chemicals and petrochemicals	0.7	0.1	0.9	1.7	2.3	1.4
Light industry	2.1	1.7	1.9	1.5	1.7	1.3

*Estimates of the Kaluga Regional Administration

OAO Kaluga Automobile Electric Equipment Plant, OAO Kalugaputmash, and OAO Ventall Metal Constructions Plant.

Food and beverages. The sector accounts for 22.7% of total industrial output. Major sectors of the regional food industry include dairy and meat processing, corn and macaroni, confectionery, fermented, distilled and non-alcoholic beverages plants, and breweries. The largest industry enterprises are OOO Kaluga Beer Brewing Company, ZAO Kaluga Meat Processing Plant, OAO Kristall, ZAO Detchinsky Plant, and OAO Obninsk Dairy Plant.

Forestry, timber, and pulp and paper. This sector accounts for 12.2% of total industrial output. Its main products are paper and paper products, matches, chipboard, corrugated cardboard, and furniture. The leading enterprises are OAO Kondrovskaya Paper Company, OAO Troitskaya Paper Mill, OOO Gigiena Service, OAO Polotnyano-Zavodskaya Paper Mill, ZAO Plitspichprom, and ZAO Stora Enso Packaging.

Construction materials. This industry accounts for 7.4% of the Region's total output. Its main products are raw and processed timber, wall materials, concrete products, bricks, enamel baths, and ceramic tiles. Its largest enterprises are OAO Stroypolimerkeramika, ZAO Kirov Stroyfarfor, OOO Monolit Enterprise, OAO Kaluga Reinforced Concrete Plant, ZAO Azarovsky Wall Materials Plant, and ZAO Kaluga Construction Materials Plant.

3.4. FUEL AND ENERGY BALANCE (OUTPUT AND CONSUMPTION PER RESOURCE)
The Kaluga Region is an energy deficit region. Domestic energy output covers only 5% of demand.

Fuel and energy sector production and consumption trends, 1997–2002						TABLE 5
	1997	1998	1999	2000	2001	2002*
Electricity output, million kWh	144.8	119.0	109.0	137.0	148.5	147.5
Coal production, '000 tons	72.0	32.0	34.0	46.0	47.0	1.0
Electricity consumption, million kWh	3,614.2	3,615.7	3,808.7	3,916.7	3,980.7	3,991.4
Natural gas consumption, million cubic meters	1,799.0	1,732.0	1,720.0	1,645.0	1,791.0	1,760.0

*Estimates of the Kaluga Regional Administration

3.5. TRANSPORT INFRASTRUCTURE
Roads. The region has 6,564 kilometers of public paved highway. Two federal highways cross the Region: Moscow – Kiev and Moscow – Ivantsevichi.

Railroads. The Kaluga Region has 1,188 kilometers of railroads. Five rail routes cross the Region: Moscow – Bryansk, Vyazma – Bryansk, Tula – Kaluga – Vyazma, Tula – Kozelsk – Zanoznaya – Smolensk, and Sukhinichi – Roslavl. These routes link the Region to Ukraine, Moldova, and other European countries.

Airports. The Region has four airports at Grabtsevo (Kaluga), Shaykovka (the Kirov District), Yermolino (the Borovsk District), and Oreshkovo (Vorotynsk).

River transport. The Region's navigable section of the Oka River from Kaluga to Tarusa has a total length of 101 kilometer. Navigation is open for 170–200 days in the year.

Gas pipelines. Some 1,069 kilometers of trunk gas pipelines cross the Kaluga Region. OOO Mostransgaz is responsible for gas transportation in the Region.

3.6. MAIN NATURAL RESOURCES: RESERVES AND EXTRACTION IN 2002
Non-ore minerals. The bulk of the Kaluga Region's natural resources consists of refractory clays, palygorskit and bentonite clays, brown coal, glass sands, phosphorite, tripoli, peat, construction sands, chalk, and gypsum.

Forest resources. Forests cover a total area of 1,352,100 hectares. The predominating species are birch, asp, pine, and spruce.

Water resources. The Region's largest rivers are the Oka, the Ugra, the Zhizdra, and the Bolva. 47 reserves of underground water have been found in the Region with a total output of 987,000 cubic meters per day.

4. TRADE OPPORTUNITIES

4.1. MAIN GOODS PRODUCED IN THE REGION
Machine engineering. Steam turbine output in 2002 was 129,800 kWh, electric cables – 10,206 kilometers, printed circuits – 2,988,000 pieces, cash registers – 120,000 pieces, shunting and industrial locomotives – 9 vehicles, and railroad construction and repair machinery – 82 items.

Food and beverages. In 2002, the Region produced 3,100 tons of meat, 11,800 tons of sausages, 633.6 tons of butter, 59,400 tons of dairy products, 50,800 tons of flour, and 60,000 tons of bread and bakery. 2002 also saw an increase in distillery output by 1,351,000 decaliters (19%), beer – 19,175,000 decaliters (up 23%), and non-alcoholic beverages – 550,000 decaliters (270%).

Chemicals. In 2002, 6,800 items of thermo-plastic pipe and pipeline elements were produced, together with 2,300 plastic articles and 668,000 pairs of polymer footwear.

4.2. EXPORTS, INCLUDING EXTRA-CIS

In 2000, non-CIS exports amounted to $59.9 million and CIS exports, to $24.9 million. The respective figures for 2001 were $58.1 million and $57.1 million, and $34.3 million and $34 million for 2002.

The Region's core exports include machine engineering goods, electric equipment, wood, paper, and cardboard. The Region's main trading partners for exports are Ukraine (28% of total exports), Kazakhstan (20%), Germany (6.4%), Japan (6%), India (3.3%), and Italy (3%).

4.3. IMPORTS, INCLUDING EXTRA-CIS

In 2000, extra-CIS imports amounted to $88.6 million, and CIS imports, to $39.1 million. The respective figures for 2001 were $101.4 million and $34.4 million, and $159.6 million and $48.5 million for 2002.

In 2002, as in previous years, core imports included electric equipment, transport vehicles, laboratory and medical equipment, and food. 2002 also saw a dramatic increase in food industry imports: meat and meat product imports rose by a factor of 1.3 and canned meat imports were up 23 times.

Major regional export and import entities		*TABLE 6*
ENTITY	ADDRESS	PHONE, FAX, E-MAIL
OAO Kaluga – MOPR	11, ul. Parallelnaya, Kaluga, Kaluga Region, 248217	Phone/fax: (0842) 52 9493
GUP KO Kaluga Food Corporation	5, ul. Vilonova, Kaluga, Kaluga Region, 248620	Phone/fax: (0842) 57 5879, 57 5495
OAO Kalugaglavsnab	2, ul. Azarovskaya, Kaluga, Kaluga Region, 248017	Phone/fax: (0842) 59 1070, 55 0013
OAO Kaluga – Plazma	13, pr. 2 Akademichesky, Kaluga, Kaluga Region, 248033	Phone/fax: (0842) 72 9942

5. INVESTMENT OPPORTUNITIES

5.1. INVESTMENTS IN 1992–2002 (BY INDUSTRY SECTOR), INCLUDING FOREIGN INVESTMENTS

The following main factors determine the investment appeal of the Kaluga Region.

- Its favorable geographic location (proximity to the economic and financial center of Russia);
- Its developed transport infrastructure;
- Its high scientific and industrial potential (an advanced scientific research center in Obninsk);
- Legislation providing support for investment projects;
- Its highly qualified work force.

5.2. CAPITAL INVESTMENT

Transport and industry account for the lion's share of capital investment.

5.3. MAJOR ENTERPRISES (INCLUDING ENTERPRISES WITH FOREIGN INVESTMENT)

The Kaluga Region currently hosts some 250 enterprises with foreign investments, including 48 affiliates and a number of foreign representative offices. The largest enterprises with foreign investments operate in the forestry, timber, and paper sector: ZAO Stora Enso Packaging (Finland) and AO Politronic (Finland); the food and beverages sector:

Capital investment by industry sector, $ million						*TABLE 7*
	1997	1998	1999	2000	2001	2002
Total capital investment	292.2	172.5	114.9	188.2	247.9	255.2
Including major industries (% of total):						
Industry	19.0	40.5	49.1	37.0	35.8	48.0
Agriculture and forestry	12.9	6.9	4.1	4.0	3.0	2.2
Construction	3.0	2.2	2.0	1.6	2.0	1.9
Transport and communications	15.1	22.0	22.0	30.7	33.3	14.7
Housing and communal services	36.2	18.2	9.0	14.2	14.3	14.6
Other	13.8	10.2	13.8	12.5	11.6	18.6

Foreign investment trends in 1996–2002

TABLE 8

	1996–1997	1998	1999	2000	2001	2002
Foreign investment, $ million	2.3	65.4	102.9	80.7	103.0	37.2
Including FDI, $ million	1.7	65.2	92.1	74.2	31.5	35.4

OOO Kaluga Beer Brewing Company; and the machine engineering sector: ZAO Kaluga-Shon-Zarya (Germany), and OOO Agrisovgaz (the Netherlands).

5.4. MOST ATTRACTIVE SECTORS FOR INVESTMENT

According to the Region's Administration, machine engineering and metal processing, food and beverages, and forestry, timber, and pulp and paper are the most appealing sectors for investors.

5.5. CURRENT LEGISLATION ON INVESTOR TAX EXEMPTIONS AND PRIVILEGES

The Kaluga Region has passed legislation with a view to creating a favorable investment climate in the Region:

• The Law On State Support to Investment Activity in the Kaluga Region (defines the forms of tax exemptions and state guarantees, investment credits, and deferrals of regional tax);

Largest enterprises of the Kaluga Region

TABLE 9

COMPANY	SECTOR	2001 SALES, $ MILLION*	2001 NET PROFIT, $ MILLION*
OOO Kaluga Beer Brewing Company	Food and beverages	90.8	20.3
OOO Agrisovgaz	Machine engineering	62.0	1.2
ZAO Stora Enso Packaging	Forestry, timber, and pulp and paper	42.7	2.1
FGUP Remputmash	Machine engineering	35.1	0.6
ZAO Kaluga Meat Processing Factory	Food and beverages	35.1	4.1
OAO Kaluga Turbine Factory	Machine engineering	34.3	4.8
ZAO Detchinsky Plant	Food and beverages	25.6	-0.04
ZAO Plitspichprom	Forestry, timber, and pulp and paper	25.2	2.6
OAO Ventall Metal Plant	Machine engineering	21.7	0.3
OAO Kirov Plant	Machine engineering	20.6	2.3
OAO Kaluga Automotive Electrics Plant	Machine engineering	20.2	0.7
OAO Kristall	Food and beverages	19.9	5.3
OOO NPP AVTEL	Machine engineering	18.2	5.6
OAO Stroypolimerkeramika	Construction materials	17.9	2.2

*Data of the Kaluga Regional Administration

Regional entities responsible for raising investment

TABLE 10

ENTITY	ADDRESS	PHONE, FAX, E-MAIL
GU Regional Development Agency of the Kaluga Region	Office 507, 45, ul. Plekhanova, Kaluga, Kaluga Region, 248001	Phone/fax: (0842) 74 0257 E-mail: rda@kaluga.ru
NP Investment Technology Center (Invest-Center)	Office 63, 51, ul. Lenina, Kaluga, Kaluga Region, 248016	Phone/fax: (0842) 56 4964 E-mail: investcenter@kaluga.ru http://www.investcentr.ru
Kaluga Chamber of Commerce and Industry	9, Pl. Stary Torg, Kaluga, Kaluga Region, 248600	Phone/fax: (0842) 56 4797 E-mail: market@cci kaluga.ru
Obninsk Science and Technology Center	4, ul. Gorkogo, Obninsk, Kaluga Region, 249033	Phone: (08439) 95 644 Fax: (08439) 98 057 E-mail: okst@obninsk.org
Academic and Business Center of the Morozov Project FRIDAS	Office 220, 129, pr. Lenina, Obninsk, Kaluga Region, 249020	Phone: (08439) 34 643 Fax: (08439) 40 888

I

CENTRAL FEDERAL DISTRICT

• The Laws On Exemptions from Regional Tax Components in 2003 and On the Regional Budget for 2003 (create a framework for granting tax exemptions to enterprises involved in investment activity).

5.6. FEDERAL AND REGIONAL ECONOMIC AND SOCIAL DEVELOPMENT PROGRAMS FOR THE KALUGA REGION

Federal targeted programs. In 2002, $23.9 million was allocated from the federal budget to finance federal targeted programs in the Region. The funds went to finance 26 federal targeted programs plus eight extra-program projects from the federal targeted investment program.

Regional programs. The Kaluga Regional Administration has formulated some 49 regional programs for the development of industry, agriculture, environmental protection, healthcare, education, law enforcement, and public welfare.

The regional government is currently implementing a regional targeted program for State Support to the Development of Small Enterprise in the Kaluga Region, 2001–2003. The program aims to improve the legal, economic, and organizational framework for sustainable development of small enterprise in the Region.

6. INVESTMENT PROJECTS

Industry sector and project description	1) Expected results 2) Amount and term of investment 3) Form of financing[1] 4) Documentation[2]	Contact information
1	2	3

MINING

06R001		Kaluga Regional Department of Natural Resources and Environmental Protection of the RF Ministry of Natural Resources 2a, per. Starichkov, Kaluga, Kaluga Region, 248620 Phone: (0842) 57 3025 Fax: (0842) 72 4711 E-mail: geolkom@kaluga.ru Leonid Petrovich Nemenko, Department Head
Launch of a new enterprise for the extraction and sale of construction lime, expanded clay aggregate, polygorskite clay, and brick loam from a non-metal deposit. Project goal: to introduce raw building materials to the market.	1) Output of 530,000 cubic meters of brick, 320,000 cubic meters of expanded clay aggregate, 230,000 tons of palygorskite clay, and 240,000 cubic meters of crushed lime rock 2) $2.6 million/5 years 3) E (up to 100%) 4) Investment proposal	

06R002		ZAO International Consortium for Ecological Reconstruction Office 427, 18, ul. K. Libkhnekhta, Kaluga, Kaluga Region, 248002 Phone: (0842) 55 7980 Fax: (0842) 56 8496 E-mail: gelios@kaluga.ru Vyacheslav Nikolaevich Kanareykin, CEO
Launch of facilities for the production of peat briquettes using raw materials extracted from a peat deposit. Project goal: to expand business.	1) Output of 32,000 tons per year 2) $1.7 million/1.5 years 3) JV 4) Investment proposal	

06R003		Kaluga Regional Department of Natural Resources and Environmental Protection of the RF Ministry of Natural Resources 2a, per. Starichkov, Kaluga, Kaluga Region, 248620 Phone: (0842) 57 3025 Fax: (0842) 72 4711 E-mail: geolkom@kaluga.ru Leonid Petrovich Nemenko, Department Head
Launching of a new enterprise for the extraction and sale of dressed glass sand from a sand deposit. Project goal: to penetrate the market for dressed glass sand.	1) Output of 120,000 tons per year 2) $1.8 million/1.5 years 3) JV 4) Investment proposal	

[1] L – Loan, E – Equity, Leas. – Leasing, JV – Joint Venture
[2] BP – Business Plan, FS – Feasibility Study

1	2	3

MINING

06R004

■ ● ❖ ◆

Launch of an enterprise for the extraction and sale of refractory clay from a clay deposit.
Project goal: to penetrate the market for refractory and ceramic clay.

1) Output of 400,000 tons per year
2) $2.6 million/5 years
3) E, L, JV
4) Investment Proposal

Kaluga Regional Department
of Natural Resources and
Environmental Protection of the RF
Ministry of Natural Resources
2a, per. Starichkov, Kaluga,
Kaluga Region, 248620
Phone: (0842) 57 3025
Fax: (0842) 72 4711
E-mail: geolkom@kaluga.ru
Leonid Petrovich Nemenko,
Department Head

06R005

❖ ◆

Development of a deposit of high-quality tripoli for the production of adsorbents.
Project goal: to provide raw materials for local adsorbent producers.

1) 30,000 tons
2) $1.3 million/1–1.5 years
3) JV
4) BP

ZAO Sorbent
114, ul. Lenina, Kaluga,
Kaluga Region, 248600
Phone/fax: (0842) 56 1773, 57 3023
E-mail: sorbent@postklg.ru
Oleg Nikolaevich Khmyz, CEO

MACHINE ENGINEERING AND METAL PROCESSING

06R006

❖ ◆

Construction of a machine tool assembly facility.
Project goal: to penetrate the market for molds, press tools, and other tools of various degree of complexity.

1) 250 items per year
2) $1.8 million/1 year
3) JV
4) BP

OAO Kaluga Electronic Goods Plant
18, ul. Azarovskaya, Kaluga,
Kaluga Region, 248631
Phone: (0842) 55 0024
Fax: (0842) 51 1746, 51 1631
E-mail: avtoelektronika@kaluga.ru
Andrei Vilenovich Perchan, CEO

06R007

■ ◆

Construction of a facility for the production of industrial turbo-cooling machines.
Project goal: to penetrate the market for energy efficient and environmentally friendly turbo-cooling machines.

1) Up to 170 machines per month
2) $2.2 million/3 years
3) E
4) BP

OAO Specialized Radio
Equipment R&D Bureau
57, Grabtsevskoye shosse, Kaluga,
Kaluga Region, 248009
Phone/fax: (0842) 53 8570
E-mail: sktbr@kaluga.ru
Alexander Nikolaevich Tokaev, CEO

06R008

■ ● ▲

Upgrading of fixed assets and reconstruction of an operating locomotive plant.
Project goal: to penetrate the market for locomotives and new generation diesel locomotives.

1) 30 main line locomotives and 10 diesel tug trains per year
2) $5.1 million/3 years
3) E, L
4) FS

OAO Lyudinovsky Locomotive
Construction Plant
1, ul. K. Libkhnekht, Lyudinovo,
Kaluga Region, 249400
Phone: (08444) 20 257
Fax: (08444) 25 259
Petr Friedrikhovich Baum, CEO

06R009

● ▲

Launch of magnetic card vending machine production at an operating instrument plant.
Project goal: to expand the product range.

1) n/a
2) $3.2 million/4 years
3) L
4) FS

OAO Maloyaroslavets Instrument Plant
8, ul. Radischeva, Maloyaroslavets,
Kaluga Region, 249091
Phone: (08431) 26 782, (095) 333 8598
Fax: (08431) 26 762
E-mail: mpz@kaluga.ru
Vladimir Pavlovich Galygin, CEO

06R010

■ ● ◆

Launch of manufacturing of sugar production facilities.
Project goal: to introduce new machinery to the market.

1) Eight sugar production lines
2) $4.4 million/4 years
3) E, L
4) BP

OOO STANIS
Appt. 252, 49, pr. Marksa,
Obninsk, Kaluga Region, 249034
Phone/fax: (08439) 40 688
E-mail: stanis1@obninsk.com
Tatyana Mikhailovna Shimanskaya,
Project Manager

I

CENTRAL FEDERAL DISTRICT

1	2	3

06R011 ● ◆

		OOO Research and Production
Launch of stainless steel fuel ramp production.	1) 70,000 ramps per year	Company Autoelectronics-Elkar
Project goal: to introduce a product with	2) $1.6 million/1 year	18, ul. Azarovskaya, Kaluga,
improved consumer qualities to the market.	3) L	Kaluga Region, 248631
	4) BP	Phone: (0842) 51 1803, 51 1864
		Fax: (0842) 51 1746
		Nikolai Vasilyevich Tsilin, CEO

06R012 ■ ● ◆

		OOO Obninsk Science
Construction of facilities for the production	1) 16 hospitals for 400 patients	and Technology Center
of units for radiation decontamination	per year	4, ul. Gorkogo, Obninsk,
and sterilization of medical instruments	2) $1.0 million/3 years	Kaluga Region, 249033
and materials.	3) E, L	Phone: (08439) 95 644
Project goal: to introduce a product with	4) BP	Fax: (08439) 98 057
improved consumer qualities to the market.		E-mail: ocst@obninsk.org
		Yevgeny Afanasyevich Pashin, CEO

06R013 ● ◆

		OAO Research and Production Company
Construction of facilities for the production	1) Up to 20 items per year	Kaluga Instrument Plant Taifun
of thermal electrical direct current sources	2) $0.5 million/3 years	18, Grabtsevskoye shosse,
for cathode protection of trunk oil pipelines.	3) JV, L	Kaluga, Kaluga Region, 248009
Project goal: to expand the product range.	4) BP	Phone: (0842) 59 4389
		Fax: (0842) 52 2266
		E-mail: tfn@kaluga.ru
		Vladimir Sergeevich Nemychenkov,
		CEO

06R014 ■ ● ▼

		OAO Research and Production Company
Upgrading of fixed assets and construction	1) Up to 20,000 per year	Kaluga Instrument Plant Taifun
of electronic voltage converter facilities.	2) $6.2 million/4 years	18, Grabtsevskoye shosse, Kaluga,
Project goal: to expand the product range.	3) E, L	Kaluga Region, 248009
	4) Investment Proposal	Phone: (0842) 59 4389
		Fax: (0842) 52 2266
		E-mail: tfn@kaluga.ru
		Vladimir Sergeevich Nemychenkov, CEO

06R015 ■ ● ▲

		OAO Signal Instrument Plant
Construction of facilities for the production	1) 40 frequency converter	121, pr. Lenina, Obninsk,
of industrial energy converters at	per year, 10 mining machine	Kaluga Region, 249035
an operating instrument plant.	control units per year, and	Phone: (08439) 79 195
Project goal: to expand the product range.	50 welding machines per year	Fax: (08439) 79 361, 79 549
	(2004 revenue of $1.1 million)	E-mail: alarm@kaluga.ru
	2) $0.5 million/1 year	Valentin Yakovlevich Rodionov, CEO
	3) E, L	
	4) FS	

FORESTRY, TIMBER, AND PULP AND PAPER

06R016 ■ ● ▼

		Regional Development
Construction of facilities for the production	1) 1,000 tons per year	Department of the Kaluga Region
of industrial carbon from low quality timber	2) $0.9 million/1 year	2, pl. Stary Torg, Kaluga,
and lumber waste at regional timber	3) E, L	Kaluga Region, 248000
companies.	4) Investment Proposal	Phone: (0842) 57 5690
Project goal: to expand the product		Fax: (0842) 57 5857
range and utilize waste.		E-mail: otdinvest@adm.kaluga.ru
		Nikolai Yevgenyevich Shubin,
		Director

1	2	3

06R017 ■ ▼

Launching of laminated chipboard production.
Project goal: to penetrate the market
for woodchip materials.

1) 100,000 cubic meters per year
2) $0.6 million/1.5 year
3) E (up to 100%)
4) Investment Proposal

Regional Development
Department of the Kaluga Region
2, pl. Stary Torg, Kaluga,
Kaluga Region, 248000
Phone: (0842) 57 5690
Fax: (0842) 57 5857
E-mail: otdinvest@adm.kaluga.ru
Nikolai Yevgenyevich Shubin,
Director

HEALTHCARE

06R018 ■ ▲

Expansion and reconstruction
of a sanatorium.
Project goal: to increase the number
of vacationers.

1) Increase the number
   of beds by 80
2) $1.5 million/3 years
3) E
4) FS

ZAO Vyatichi Sanatorium
17, ul. Mira, Kremenki, Zhukovsky
District, Kaluga Region, 249185
Phone/fax: (08432) 50 811, 50 800
Phone/fax: (095) 195 9442
E-mail: kaluga@vyatichi.ru
Inna Ivanovna Kursakova, CEO

I

CENTRAL FEDERAL DISTRICT

07. KOSTROMA REGION [44]

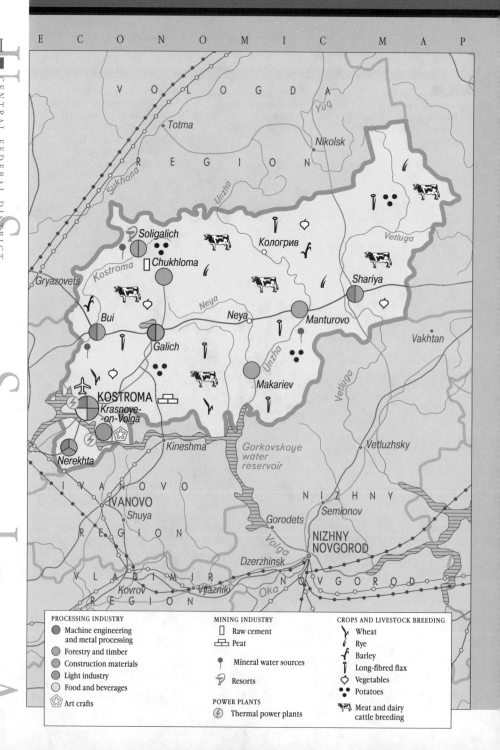

ECONOMIC MAP

PROCESSING INDUSTRY
- Machine engineering and metal processing
- Forestry and timber
- Construction materials
- Light industry
- Food and beverages
- Art crafts

POWER PLANTS
- Thermal power plants

MINING INDUSTRY
- Raw cement
- Peat
- Mineral water sources
- Resorts

CROPS AND LIVESTOCK BREEDING
- Wheat
- Rye
- Barley
- Long-fibred flax
- Vegetables
- Potatoes
- Meat and dairy cattle breeding

The Kostroma Region is the quintessential natural, cultural, and historical pearl of Central Russia, a region in which business life has always been very active and people have always been hard-working and cooperative.

With the help of this Guide we hope to attract attention to the issues involved in reviving the ancient land of Kostroma. We have all of the prerequisites for the development of comprehensive links with Russian and foreign businesses. These include an ecologically pure environment and enormous natural resources combined with a developed industrial infrastructure. Just some of the potentially lucrative areas for investment in our Region include the deployment of new timber processing technology to utilize the Region's innumerable timber reserves, participation in the revival of the traditional textiles sector, upgrading of the machine engineering sector, development of oil and sapropel deposits, and processing of berries and mushrooms.

I guarantee investors a most favorable investment environment based on a fully-fledged investment legislation base.

Victror Shershunov,
HEAD OF ADMINISTRATION (GOVERNOR)
OF THE KOSTROMA REGION

I

CENTRAL FEDERAL DISTRICT

1. GENERAL INFORMATION

1.1. GEOGRAPHY

The Kostroma Region covers a total area of 60,100 square kilometers. The Region is located in the north-eastern part of the Central Federal District. To the south, it borders the Ivanovo Region, to the northwest and north – the Vologda Region, to the northeast and east – the Kirov Region, and to the southeast – the Nizhny Novgorod Region.

1.2. CLIMATE

The Kostroma Region enjoys a moderate continental climate. Air temperatures in January average –13°C, rising to an average of +18°C in July. Annual precipitation totals 560 mm. The growing season lasts around 160–170 days.

1.3. POPULATION

According to preliminary 2002 census results, the total population of the Kostroma Region was 738,000 people. The average population density is 12.3 people per square kilometer. The economically active population totals 388,000 people. Official unemployment stood at 1.5% in 2002, while the actual rate was 6.4%.

Demographically speaking, some 59.2% are of statutory working age, 17.7% are below the statutory working age, and 23.1% are beyond the statutory working age.

The major urban centers of the Kostroma Region (2002 data) are: Kostroma with 279,400 inhabitants, Sharya with 40,500 inhabitants, and Buy with 33,700 inhabitants.

Population								TABLE 1
	1992	1997	1998	1999	2000	2001	2002
Total population, '000	806	795	791	787	781	774	738
Economically active population, '000	400	363	365	390	387	380	388

2. ADMINISTRATION

15, ul. Dzerzhinskogo, Kostroma, Kostroma Region, 156007
Phone: (0942) 31 3472; fax: (0942) 31 3395
E-mail: info@kos-obl.kmtn.ru
http://www.region.kostroma.net

NAME	POSITION	CONTACT INFORMATION
Viktor Andreevich SHERSHUNOV	Head of Administration (Governor) of the Kostroma Region	Phone: (0942) 31 3472 Fax: (0942) 31 3395 E-mail: shershunov@kos-obl.kmtn.ru
Yury Fedorovich TSIKUNOV	First Deputy Head of Administration of the Kostroma Region in charge of Construction, Transport, and Communications	Phone: (0942) 31 3516 E-mail: tsikunov@kos-obl.kmtn.ru
Alexander Kuzmich AVEROCHKIN	First Deputy Head of Administration of the Kostroma Region in charge of Economic Development	Phone: (0942) 31 6276 E-mail: averochkin@kos-obl.kmtn.ru
Tamara Vasilyevna GRISHINA	First Deputy Head of Administration of the Kostroma Region, Head of the Agroindustrial Sector Department	Phone: (0942) 55 1631 E-mail: grishina@kos-obl.kmtn.ru
Oleg Alexandrovich LEBEDEV	Deputy Head of Administration of the Kostroma Region in charge of Housing and Communal Services, and Energy	Phone: (0942) 31 5327 E-mail: lebedev@kos-obl.kmtn.ru

3. ECONOMIC POTENTIAL

3.1. 1997–2002 GROSS REGIONAL PRODUCT (GRP). INDUSTRY BREAKDOWN

The Kostroma Region's 2002 gross regional product amounted to $913.4 million, 10.7% up on 2001. Per capita GRP was $1,066 in 2001, and $1,238 in 2002.

3.2. MAJOR ECONOMIC GROWTH PROJECTIONS

The main goal of the Regional Administration for the medium term (through to 2005) is to achieve balanced development in all sectors of the regional economy by deploying idle economic resources and improv-

GRP trends in 1997–2002						*TABLE 2*
	1997	1998	1999	2000	2001*	2002*
GRP in current prices, $ million	1,436.3	899.6	580.0	646.1	825.0	913.4

*Estimates of the Kostroma Regional Administration

GRP industry breakdown in 1997–2002, % of total						*TABLE 3*
	1997	1998	1999	2000	2001*	2002*
GRP	100.0	100.0	100.0	100.0	100.0	100.0
Industry	26.4	28.3	29.3	29.7	30.4	30.4
Agriculture and forestry	18.8	18.9	21.0	19.8	19.0	19.0
Construction	7.2	7.4	6.4	5.9	6.8	6.4
Transport and communications	8.9	7.0	7.3	8.0	8.3	8.6
Trade and public catering	9.5	9.7	12.1	11.6	10.2	10.1
Other	25.4	24.2	17.3	19.0	19.9	20.2
Net taxes on output	3.8	4.5	6.6	6.0	5.4	5.3

*Estimates of the Kostroma Regional Administration

ing and enhancing production efficiency. Investment policy is focused on the development of efficient sectors of economy producing deep processed goods.

3.3. INDUSTRIAL OUTPUT IN 1997–2002 FOR MAJOR SECTORS OF ECONOMY

The Kostroma Region's major industrial sectors are energy, forestry, timber and pulp and paper, and machine engineering and metal processing. These account for a combined 66.9% of total industrial output.

Energy. Energy accounts for 30.4% of total industrial output. The largest enterprises in the sector are OAO Kostroma GRES (97% of total energy produced in the Region) and OAO Kostromaenergo

Industry breakdown of industrial output in 1997–2002, % of total						*TABLE 4*
	1997	1998	1999	2000	2001	2002*
Industry	100.0	100.0	100.0	100.0	100.0	100.0
Energy	49.5	42.3	29.0	29.9	32.0	30.4
Forestry, timber, and pulp and paper	11.5	12.9	19.5	17.0	16.8	19.3
Machine engineering and metal processing	12.3	10.3	14.0	15.2	16.8	17.2
Food and beverages	8.8	11.8	11.0	10.1	10.8	11.6
Light industry	4.2	5.0	7.7	5.1	5.0	5.3
Chemicals and petrochemicals	0.9	1.5	2.7	3.1	2.6	2.9
Construction materials	4.6	4.2	3.9	3.6	3.2	2.8
Ferrous metals	0.2	0.1	0.7	4.5	3.1	2.3
Fuel	0.2	0.1	0.2	0.1	0.2	0.2

*Estimates of the Kostroma Regional Administration

(3%). The total installed capacity of the Kostroma energy system is 3.8 GW.

Forestry, timber, and pulp and paper. The sector accounts for 19.3% of total industrial output. The timber industry accounts for the lion's share of the sector's output at 76.5%. The industrial enterprises of the Region produce a diversified product mix. The major part of the output is exported from the Region: 41% of commercial timber, 25% of sawn timber, 86% of chipboard, 65% of fiber board and 85% of glued plywood. Forestry, timber, and pulp and paper output accounts for more than 50% of the Region's exports.

The largest enterprises in the sector are OAO Fanplit, OAO Plywood Factory, OOO Sharyaplit, OOO Sharya Timber Factory, OAO Kostromamebel, and ZAO Aleksandrovbumprom.

Machine engineering and metal processing. The sector accounts for 17.2% of total industrial output. The machine engineering sector carries out a full spectrum of metal thermal treatment, cutting, and welding activities; the manufacture and maintenance of complex electronic units and modules; the assembly and testing of complex systems; and the assembly of complex instrument units. Enterprises in the sector produce cranes, excavating machines, equipment for the oil and gas industry, timber processing and cutting machines, spinning machines, inland waterway vessels, and consumer goods.

The largest enterprises in the sector are OAO Motordetal Kostroma Plant, OAO Galich Autocrane

Factory, OAO Kalorifer Factory, OAO Ship Machinery Factory, OAO Stromneftemash, and OAO Pegas.

Food and beverages. The sector accounts for 11.6% of total industrial output. Enterprises in this sector produce bread and bakery products, confectionery, butter, cheese, dairy products, cereals, and macaroni products.

The largest enterprises in the sector are OAO Russian Bread, ZAO Chistiye Klyuchi, FGUP Kostroma Distillery, and OOO Kostroma Dairy.

Light industry. The sector accounts for 5.3% of total industrial output. The Region is one of major suppliers of linen fabric in Russia (40.4 million square meters produced in 2002). The Kostroma Region makes about 30% of the fabric produced in the Russian Federation. Up to 90% of output is delivered outside the Region; about 35% of linen output is exported.

The largest enterprises in the sector are OOO Ivan Zvorykin Linen Factory, ZAO Kostroma Grand Linen Manufacture, OAO Orbita, OAO Nerta, OAO Nerekhtskaya Linen Mill, and OAO Remennaya Tesma.

Hotels and tourism. The Kostroma Region is a part of the Golden Ring of Russia, an internationally renowned travel route.

3.4. FUEL AND ENERGY BALANCE (OUTPUT AND CONSUMPTION PER RESOURCE)

The Region consumes about 28% of the energy it produces. Surplus energy is supplied to UES of Russia and to neighboring regions.

Fuel and energy sector production and consumption trends, 1997–2002						*TABLE 5*
	1997	1998	1999	2000	2001	2002*
Electricity output, billion kWh	13.1	14.1	13.2	12.7	13.3	11.6
Heat energy output, '000 Gcal	4,926.0	4,634.0	4,495.0	4,376.0	4,481.0	4,645.0
Electricity consumption, billion kWh	3.1	3.2	3.3	3.3	3.2	3.2
Natural gas consumption, million cubic meters	3,723.0	3,669.4	6,511.1	3,549.8	3,859.1	3,748.0

*Estimates of the Kostroma Regional Administration

3.5. TRANSPORT INFRASTRUCTURE

Roads. The Kostroma Region has 5,507 kilometers of paved public highway.

Railroads. The Region has 640 kilometers of railroads. The Moscow – Vladivostok railway line passes from the west to the east of the Region. The Region is connected by rail to Vologda, Cherepovets, and Yaroslavl in the west, and to Kirov and Yekaterinburg in the east.

Airports. An airport serves the city of Kostroma.

River transport. The Region's navigable section of the River Volga is 120 kilometers long. The Kostroma, Unzha, and Vetluga, tributaries of the Volga, are navigable and suitable for timber floating during the high water period in the spring.

River ports. A river port serves the city of Kostroma.

3.6. MAIN NATURAL RESOURCES: RESERVES AND EXTRACTION IN 2002

Fuel resources. The Region's peat reserves amount to 575 million tons. Some 48 of the Region's 1,500 peat bogs are developed. This creates an opportunity to expand development to new peat bogs (including an opportunity for the Region's peat enterprises to resume production of lump or briquette peat). The Region has also oil shale deposits.

Non-ore minerals. The Region has reserves of gravel-sand material (176 million cubic meters), sand, clay, and loam (35.8 million cubic meters), and limestone. Considerable reserves of high quality raw cement have been discovered in the Soligalichsky District. Limestone from the Belinskoye and Turovskoye deposits, clay from the Borovinskoye deposit and sand from the Borisyevskoye deposit can be used to make Grade 500 Portland Cement. The Region's limestone deposits supply raw material to OAO Soligalichsky Lime Plant, which produces lime powder and construction lime.

Water resources. The Region has twelve chloride and sulfate mineral water springs. They are used in the food industry and also form, along with cura-tive mud, the basis for the Region's recreational resources. The Region has two unique lakes, Galichskoye and Chukhlomskoye, with a total sapropel reserve of more than 500 million cubic meters.

Timber resources. Forests cover 4,667,200 hectares of the Region's territory. The annual timber output is 9.3 million cubic meters.

4. TRADE OPPORTUNITIES

4.1. MAIN GOODS
PRODUCED IN THE REGION

Energy. In 2002, the Region produced 11.6 billion kWh (1.7 billion kWh down on 2001).

Forestry, timber, and pulp and paper. In 2002, the Region produced industrial timber– 2,270,000 cubic meters (268,000 cubic meters down on 2001); sawn timber – 373,600 cubic meters (104,100 cubic meters down on 2001); fiber board – 12,004,000 square meters (1,297,000 square meters up on 2001).

Machine engineering and metal processing. In 2002, the Region produced 55 excavating machines (53 down on 2001); 862 timber-processing machines (87 up on 2001); 40 metal cutting machines (5 up on 2001); 569 cranes (13 down on 2001);

Food and beverages. In 2002, the Region produced meat – 6,904 tons (29 tons up on 2001); full fat cheese – 3,391 tons (102 tons up on 2001); flour – 28,800 tons (3,700 tons down on 2001);

4.2. EXPORTS, INCLUDING EXTRA-CIS

In 2000, the Region's extra-CIS exports totaled $66.5 million, with CIS exports totaling $3.3 million. The corresponding figures were $76.7 million and $14.9 million for 2001 and $68.5 million and $14.3 million for 2002.

The bulk of the Region's exports consists of timber and timber products (accounting for 43.8% of exports in 2002), machinery and equipment (13.4%), and linen and cotton fabric (10.8%).

4.3. IMPORTS, INCLUDING EXTRA-CIS

In 2000, imports from outside the CIS totaled $16.6 million, with CIS imports coming to $2.7 million. The corresponding figures were $12.6 million and $1.5 million for 2001, and $45.1 million and $2.3 million for 2002.

Machine engineering products (73.4% of all 2002 import), metals and metal products (4.1%), and flax fiber (3.4%) constitute the bulk of the Region's imports.

4.4. MAJOR REGIONAL EXPORT
AND IMPORT ENTITIES

Owing to the specific nature of the Region's export and import activities, export and import transactions are performed mainly by industrial enterprises.

Major regional export and import entities		*TABLE 6*
ENTITY	ADDRESS	PHONE, FAX, E-MAIL
OAO Kostroma Motordetal Factory	105, ul. Moskovskaya, Kostroma, Kostroma Region, 156604	Phone: (0942) 53 1331 Fax: (0942) 53 2721
OOO Ivan Zvorykin Linen Plant	7, ul. Tkachey, Kostroma, Kostroma Region, 156603	Phone: (0942) 51 4500 Fax: (0942) 51 4500
OOO Fanplit	2, ul. Komsomolskaya, Kostroma, Kostroma Region, 156961	Phone: (0942) 31 2208, 31 2145 Fax: (0942) 31 2316
OAO Manturovo Plywood Factory	2b, ul. Matrosova, Manturovo, Kostroma Region, 157400	Phone: (09446) 27 370 Fax: (09446) 27 348
OAO Forestry Holding Company Buylesprom	2, ul. 1 Maya, Buy, Kostroma Region, 157040	Phone: (09435) 20 420, 20 315 Fax: (09435) 20 370
ZAO Ekokhimmash	1, ul. Chapayeva, Buy, Kostroma Region, 157040	Phone: (09435) 24 897 Fax: (09435) 21 745
Committee for Foreign and Inter-Regional Trade Relations of the Kostroma Regional Administration	15, ul. Dzerzhinskogo, Kostroma, Kostroma Region, 156006	Phone: (0942) 31 2001, 31 8745 Fax: (0942) 31 8733 E-mail: kves@kosnet.ru

5. INVESTMENT OPPORTUNITIES

5.1. INVESTMENTS IN 1992–2002 (BY INDUSTRY SECTOR), INCLUDING FOREIGN INVESTMENTS

The following factors determine the investment appeal of the Kostroma Region:

- Its favorable geographical location (proximity of large markets);
- Its well-developed transport infrastructure;
- Laws supporting investment activity (guarantees for investor rights and preferential tax treatment for investors);
- Its qualified work force;
- Cheap energy resources.

5.2. CAPITAL INVESTMENT

Industry accounts for the majority of capital investment (54.2%).

Capital investment by industry sector, $ million						TABLE 7
	1997	1998	1999	2000	2001	2002
Total capital investment	232.5	167.1	129.7	164.8	166.0	184.1
Including major industries (% of total)						
Industry	36.8	41.6	51.1	58.9	51.6	54.2
Agriculture and forestry	3.7	4.9	3.6	4.2	4.9	5.6
Construction	1.8	1.7	1.8	2.0	1.1	1.0
Transport and communications	24.4	18.4	18.2	14.2	9.9	18.2
Trade and public catering	0.8	0.5	0.7	0.6	2.2	1.8
Other	32.5	32.9	24.6	20.1	30.3	19.2

Foreign investment trends in 1996–2002						TABLE 8
	1996–1997	1998	1999	2000	2001	2002
Foreign investment, $ million	0.5	1.9	1.9	4.7	0.9	0.1
Including FDI, $ million	0.5	1.9	1.5	4.3	0.9	0.1

5.3. MAJOR ENTERPRISES (INCLUDING ENTERPRISES WITH FOREIGN INVESTMENT)

Largest enterprises of the Kostroma Region		TABLE 9
COMPANY	SECTOR	2001 NET PROFIT, $ MILLION*
OAO Kostroma GRES	Energy	9.1
OAO Kostromaenergo	Energy	n/a
OAO Fanplit	Forestry, timber, and pulp and paper	5.5
OAO Kostroma Motordetal Factory	Machine engineering	0.9
OAO Kostroma Jewelry Factory	Jewelry	0.8
OAO Manturovo Plywood Factory	Forestry, timber, and pulp and paper	0.6
OAO Galichsky Autocrane Factory	Machine engineering	0.6
ZAO Chistye Klyuchi	Food and beverages	0.5
OAO Elektrosvyaz	Communications	0.1
OAO Krasnoselsky Yuvelirprom	Jewelry	0.001

*Data of the Kostroma Regional Administration

5.4. CURRENT LEGISLATION ON INVESTOR TAX EXEMPTIONS AND PRIVILEGES

The Region has enacted the following Laws of the Kostroma Region: On Investment Activity in the Kostroma Region and On the Development Budget of the Kostroma Region. These Laws provide partial exemptions from regional taxes until full project payback to industrial enterprises registered in the Region. Regulations have been drafted governing guarantees offered by the Region with respect to investment project implementation and establishing the rules of competitive tenders for financing priority investment projects.

Regional entities responsible for raising investment		*TABLE 10*
ENTITY	ADDRESS	PHONE, FAX, E-MAIL
Economy and Economic Reform Department of the Kostroma Regional Administration	15, ul. Dzerzhinskogo, Kostroma, Kostroma Region, 156006	Phone: (0942) 31 3583, 31 3186 Fax: (0942) 31 1444 E-mail: komecon@kos-obl.kmtn.ru
Committee for Foreign and Inter-Regional Trade Relations of the Kostroma Regional Administration	15, ul. Dzerzhinskogo, Kostroma, Kostroma Region, 156006	Phone: (0942) 31 2001, 31 8745 Fax: (0942) 31 8733 E-mail: kves@kosnet.ru
Chamber of Industry and Commerce of the Kostroma Region	Office 15, 38, ul. Kalinovskaya, Kostroma, Kostroma Region, 156013	Phone/fax: (0942) 55 6262

5.5. FEDERAL AND REGIONAL ECONOMIC AND SOCIAL DEVELOPMENT PROGRAMS FOR THE KOSTROMA REGION

Federal targeted programs. Utility and engineering service facilities are being built and revamped in the Region under the federal targeted program for The Elimination of Inequalities in the Social and Economic Development of the Regions of the Russian Federation, 2002–2010 and through 2015. A number of programs are being implemented with a view to improving the environmental situation in the Region, protecting historical and cultural conservation areas, and raising standards of living.

Regional programs. The Kostroma Regional Administration has developed key factors for social and economic development of the Kostroma Region for 2003. To achieve the projected goals, the Region implements the following regional targeted programs: Human Resources for the Agroindustrial Sector of the Kostroma Region, 2001–2005 with a total $17,800 budget; Development of the Fishing Industry of the Kostroma Region, 2001–2005 with a $15,700 budget; Enhancement of Soil Fertility of the Kostroma Region, 2002–2005, a $15,700 budget; Linen Industry Development of the Region, 2001–2006 with $116,400 in funding; Stable Development of Tourism in the Kostroma Region, 2000–2005 with a $3.1 million budget.

6. INVESTMENT PROJECTS

Industry sector and project description	1) Expected results 2) Amount and term of investment 3) Form of financing[1] 4) Documentation[2]	Contact information
1	2	3
MACHINE ENGINEERING AND METAL PROCESSING		
07R001 ■ ● ★ ◆		OAO Pegas
Production of engine control microprocessor system components. Project goal: to produce electromagnetic sprayers, electrical units, and throttle sensor elements.	1) 250,000 electrical units per year, 1,800,000 sprayers, and 500,000 sensors 2) $1.8 million/1.5 years 3) Leas., L, E 4) BP	23, ul. P. Scherbiny, Kostroma, Kostroma Region, 156961 Phone: (0942) 22 9663, 22 9655 Fax: (0942) 54 6653 E-mail: pegas@kosnet.ru Vladimir Mikhailovich Kobzev, CEO Nadezhda Anatolyevna Sharova, Deputy Director for Economy

[1] L – Loan, E – Equity, Leas. – Leasing, JV – Joint Venture
[2] BP – Business Plan, FS – Feasibility Study

I

1	2	3

07R002 ■ ● ★ ◆

		OAO Motordetal Kostroma Plant
Production of pistons for VAZ and ZMZ. Project goal: to launch a unit for the production of modern engine pistons, and arrange production and sales of piston spare parts.	1) 900,000 pistons per year 2) $5 million/2 years 3) L, Leas., E 4) BP	105, ul. Moskovskaya, Kostroma, Kostroma Region, 156001 Phone: (0942) 33 1193 Fax: (0942) 53 2721 Sergey Vasilyevich Radaev, Director of Sales and Development

FORESTRY, TIMBER, AND PULP AND PAPER

07R003 ■ ●

		Forestry Department of the Kostroma Regional Administration
Construction of a pulp and paper plant. Project goal: to produce bleached pulp and printing paper.	1) Up to 410,000 tons of bleached coniferous and deciduous pulp per year and up to 400,000 tons of bleached and unbleached paper per year 2) $896 million/n/a 3) L, JV, E 4) Investment memorandum	20, ul. Lenina, Neya, Kostroma Region, 156013 Phone: (0942) 31 3381, 31 4664 Fax: (0942) 31 4664 Gennady Nikolaevich Yurzov, Department Head

TRANSPORT

07R004 ● ★ ▼

		OAO Sharya Transport Company
Acquisition of machinery for the transportation of timber and JV Crono-Star's finished goods. Project goal: to provide for raw material supply and dispatch of finished goods.	1) Purchase of 30 product-range transport vehicles 2) $1.6 million/6 months 3) L, Leas. 4) Investment proposal	18, ul. Ivana Shatrova, Sharya, Kostroma Region, 157605 Phone: (09449) 20 941, 20 243 Fax: (09449) 20 941 Irina Nikolaevna Krylova, Head of the Planning and Economic Department

08. KURSK REGION [46]

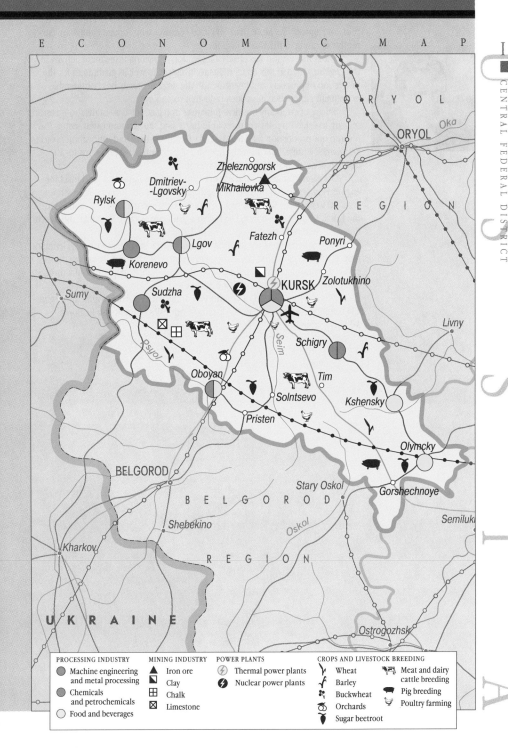

PROCESSING INDUSTRY	MINING INDUSTRY	POWER PLANTS	CROPS AND LIVESTOCK BREEDING	
⬤ Machine engineering and metal processing	▲ Iron ore	⚡ Thermal power plants	Ɏ Wheat	🐄 Meat and dairy cattle breeding
⬤ Chemicals and petrochemicals	◼ Clay	⚡ Nuclear power plants	⌇ Barley	🐖 Pig breeding
◯ Food and beverages	⊞ Chalk		❋ Buckwheat	🦃 Poultry farming
	⊠ Limestone		🍏 Orchards	
			❦ Sugar beetroot	

I am pleased to have this opportunity to introduce one of the most attractive and wealthy regions of the Central Federal District of the Russian Federation – the Kursk Region, and its main city, Kursk, which is a historical, cultural, scientific, and industrial center.

A unique combination of abundant natural resources, high industrial and scientific potential, and a qualified workforce make the Kursk Region's economy and enterprises attractive for investment.

The lion's share of capital investment in the Region goes to energy, transport, and agriculture. More than 100 joint ventures with foreign capital are currently operating in the Kursk Region.

The Kursk Region has enacted legislation regulating investment activity in the Region, which grants equal rights to investors, as well as guarantees for the protection of property and investments. The Region already has considerable investment experience in various industrial sectors.

We are open to any business initiatives and guarantee assistance to investors seeking to establish joint ventures in industry and the agrioindustrial sector, to revamp our production facilities, to carry out investment and innovation projects and joint scientific, educational, and cultural programs, and programs for the development of small and medium enterprise.

Our Region offers great trade opportunities. Ferrous metals and machine engineering and metal processing goods produced in our Region are in strong demand worldwide. Ball bearings, electric motors, and generators produced in the Kursk Region are exported to Bulgaria, Hungary, Poland, Romania, the Czech Republic, Argentina, and Egypt.

Our main partners for imports include Austria, Belgium, Germany, Denmark, Italy, the Netherlands, the US, Turkey, France, and Switzerland. These countries export ferrous metals, raw rubber, agricultural machinery, paper manufacturing equipment, and food to the Kursk Region.

We view the creation of conditions conducive to the development of mutually beneficial trade as one of the foremost priorities of the Kursk Regional Administration.

Alexander Mikhailov,
GOVERNOR OF THE KURSK REGION

1. GENERAL INFORMATION

1.1. GEOGRAPHY

The Kursk Region covers a total area of some 29,800 square kilometers at the center of the European part of the Russian Federation. To the north, the Region borders the Bryansk Region, to the east – the Oryol and the Lipetsk Regions, to the south – the Voronezh and the Belgorod Regions, and to the west – Ukraine.

1.2. CLIMATE

The Kursk Region is located within the temperate continental climate zone.

Air temperatures in January average –8.6°C, rising to +19.3°C in July. Annual precipitation reaches 580 mm. The average growing season lasts 175–200 days.

1.3. POPULATION

According to preliminary 2002 census results, the Kursk Region's population was 1,236,000 people. The average population density is 41.5 people per square kilometer. The economically active population amounts to 645,000 people. Official unemployment stood at 1.6% in 2002.

Demographically speaking, some 57.9% are of statutory working age, 17.5% are below the statutory working age, and 24.6% are beyond the statutory working age.

The Kursk Region's major urban centers (2002 data) are Kursk with 412,600 inhabitants, Zheleznogorsk with 99,000 inhabitants, and Kurchatov with 49,000 inhabitants.

Population								*TABLE 1*
	1992	1997	1998	1999	2000	2001	2002
Total population, '000	1,331	1,339	1,332	1,324	1,312	1,299	1,236
Economically active population, '000	661	580	582	624	650	623	645

2. ADMINISTRATION

House of Soviets, Krasnaya pl., Kursk, Kursk Region, 305002
Phone: (07122) 26 262; fax: (0712) 56 6573
E-mail: glava@region.kursk.ru, press@region.kursk.ru; http://www.region.kursk.ru

NAME	POSITION	CONTACT INFORMATION
Alexander Nikolaevich MIKHAILOV	Governor of the Kursk Region	Phone: (07122) 26 262, 27 818 Fax: (0712) 56 6573
Alexander Sergeevich ZUBAREV	First Deputy Governor of the Kursk Region, Chairman of the Regional Government	Phone: (07122) 25 192 Fax: (0712) 56 2982
Nikolai Ivanovich OVCHAROV	Deputy Governor of the Kursk Region, Chairman of the Property Management Committee	Phone: (0712) 56 6563
Gennady Pavlovich PLOKHIKH	Deputy Governor of the Kursk Region, Chairman of the Foreign Economic Relations Committee	Phone: (07122) 22 086 Fax: (0712) 55 4309
Anatoly Vasilyevich MIKHILEV	Deputy Chairman of the Kursk Regional Government for Agroindustrial Sector, Natural Resourses, and Geology	Phone: (07122) 27 310 Fax: (0712) 56 8030
Vladimir Ivanovich TRUNOV	Deputy Chairman of the Kursk Regional Government for Industry, Fuel and Energy Sector, Transport and Communications	Phone: (07122) 23 383 Fax: (0712) 56 6641
Nina Vasilyevna TKACHYOVA	Deputy Chairman of the Kursk Regional Government for the Region's Social and Economic Development and Investment Policy, Licensing, and Pricing	Phone: (07122) 26 464 Fax: (0712) 56 7614

CENTRAL FEDERAL DISTRICT

3. ECONOMIC POTENTIAL

3.1. 1997–2002 GROSS REGIONAL PRODUCT (GRP). INDUSTRY BREAKDOWN

The Kursk Region's 2002 gross regional product reached $1,480.6 million, 12.3% up on 2001. Per capita GRP totaled $1,014 in 2001 and $1,198 in 2002.

3.2. MAJOR ECONOMIC GROWTH PROJECTIONS

The Comprehensive Program for Social and Economic Development of the Kursk Region through 2002–2005 approved by a regional law in February 2002 sets forth the Region's economic development priorities. It sets the following strategic goals: to attract investments to the Region, to raise the efficiency of the Region's economy, and to boost trade and economic cooperation with other regions of Russia and abroad.

Over the coming years, the Region plans to increase output in energy, machine engineering and metals processing, petrochemicals, light industry, and food and beverages through higher labor productivity and better training, expansion into new markets, technical upgrading and enhancement of industrial production facilities, and the creation of new agricultural facilities.

The Program also provides a blueprint for growth in retail trade and consumer services.

GRP trends in 1997–2002						TABLE 2
	1997	1998	1999	2000	2001*	2002*
GRP in current prices, $ million.	2,490.9	1,701.7	967.8	1,135.8	1,318.9	1,480.6

*Estimates of the Kursk Regional Administration

GRP industry breakdown in 1997–2002, % of total						TABLE 3
	1997	1998	1999	2000	2001*	2002*
GRP	100.0	100.0	100.0	100.0	100.0	100.0
Industry	38.7	37.5	36.1	32.8	32.7	33.7
Agriculture and forestry	8.5	11.2	16.6	20.4	18.4	17.5
Construction	8.9	8.4	6.8	6.4	6.8	6.5
Transport and communications	7.4	6.1	4.8	6.0	5.8	6.0
Trade and public catering	12.3	11.7	12.3	12.2	13.0	12.6
Other	17.9	17.4	15.7	15.0	17.2	17.9
Net taxes on output	6.3	7.7	7.7	7.2	6.1	5.8

*Estimates of the Kursk Regional Administration

3.3. INDUSTRIAL OUTPUT IN 1997–2002 FOR MAJOR SECTORS OF ECONOMY

The Kursk Region's major industrial sectors are energy, machine engineering and metals processing, ferrous metals, and food and beverages. These sectors account for 76.1% of the Region's total industrial output.

Energy. Energy accounts for 31.7% of total industrial output. Electricity is generated by GP Kursk Nuclear Power Station.

Machine engineering and metal processing. The Region's machine engineering and metal processing sector accounts for 16.2% of total industrial output. The Region produces accumulators, bearings, automation devices, mobile units and power plants, geological mining and drilling equipment, spare parts for agricultural machinery, motor units, metal-cutting machine tools, and press-forging plants. The largest enterprises are ZAO Accumulator, OAO Elevatormelmash, ZAO Kursk Bearings Company, OAO Pribor, and OAO Elektroagregat.

Ferrous metals. The sector produces 14.9% of total industrial output. The largest enterprise is OAO Mikhailovsky Ore Dressing Plant.

Food and beverages. The sector's output consists of meat and dairy products, canned fruit and vegetables, confectionery, and sugar. It accounts for 13.3% of total industrial output. The largest enterprises are OAO Kurskmakaronprom, ZAO Konditer-Kursk, OAO Konfi, OAO Krasnaya Polyana+, and OGUP Poultry Farm Kurskaya.

Chemicals and petrochemicals. The sector accounts for 5.8% of total industrial output and produces general mechanical rubber goods, chemical fibers, polymer, and composite products. The largest enterprise is ZAO Kurskrezinotekhnika.

Industry breakdown of industrial output in 1997–2002, % of total						_TABLE 4_
	1997	1998	1999	2000	2001	2002*
Industry	100.0	100.0	100.0	100.0	100.0	100.0
Energy	33.3	31.1	22.5	22.3	23.3	31.7
Machine engineering and metal processing	14.3	13.1	14.7	18.2	19.8	16.2
Ferrous metals	10.9	13.6	16.0	13.9	12.7	14.9
Food and beverages	15.7	15.8	17.6	15.6	14.8	13.3
Chemicals and petrochemicals	12.0	13.5	14.5	14.5	12.3	5.8
Forestry, timber, and pulp and paper	2.4	2.4	4.4	4.8	4.8	4.8
Light industry	2.2	2.2	2.7	2.9	2.8	2.9
Construction materials	2.9	2.8	2.4	2.3	2.7	2.4
Flour, cereals, and mixed fodder	3.5	3.1	3.0	3.4	3.3	2.0
Glass and porcelain	0.4	0.4	0.4	0.5	0.6	0.6

*Estimates of the Kursk Regional Administration

3.4. FUEL AND ENERGY BALANCE (OUTPUT AND CONSUMPTION PER RESOURCE)

The Kursk Region is rich in energy resources. The Kurskaya Nuclear Power Station fully meets the Region's electricity needs, and 70% of the electricity output is exported to other regions of Russia and the CIS.

3.5. TRANSPORT INFRASTRUCTURE

Roads. The Kursk Region has some 5,300 kilometers of paved public highway. The following highways cross the Region: Moscow – Simferopol, Kursk – Borisoglebsk, and Trosna – Lemeshi.

Fuel and energy sector production and consumption trends, 1997–2002						_TABLE 5_
	1997	1998	1999	2000	2001	2002
Electricity output, billion kWh	19.5	20.0	23.0	23.1	18.7	20.5
Electricity consumption, billion kWh	7.4	7.6	7.9	8.1	7.1	7.4
Natural gas consumption, million cubic meters	1,764.9	1,214.6	1,239.2	1,247.6	1,212.0	1,791.7

*Estimates of the Kursk Regional Administration

Railroads. The Kursk Region has 1,100 kilometers of railroad. The Region is crossed by two trunk railroads: Moscow – Kharkov and Voronezh – Kiev.

Airports. The Kursk International Airport links the Region with other cities in Russia and the CIS.

Oil and gas pipelines. The Kursk Region is crossed by six trunk gas pipelines and two oil pipelines.

3.6. MAIN NATURAL RESOURCES: RESERVES AND EXTRACTION IN 2002

The natural resources of the Kursk Region are iron ore deposits of the Kursk Magnetic Anomaly, plus deposits of dolomite, copper-nickel ore, bauxite, non-ore construction minerals, phosphorite, peat, and mineral water.

Minerals. The Region is home to the world's largest iron ore deposit – the Kursk Magnetic Anomaly. Ore is mined at the Mikhailovskoye, Kurbakinskoye, Dichnyansko-Reutetskoye, Lev-Tolstovskoye, Shchig-rovskoye and Zapadno-Ostapovskoye deposits. These deposits contain gold, uranium, germanium, gallium, titanium, zirconium, nickel, manganese, lead, zinc, copper, and aluminum ores.

Non-ore deposits are also found in the Region, along with explored deposits of chalk, phosphorite, molding sand, and ceramic clay.

The Region has 247 peat deposits with reserves totaling 50 million tons spread over 11,918 hectares.

The Region also has considerable oil deposits.

Land resources. The Kursk Region has 3 million hectares of land, of which 2.3 million hectares is agricultural. The prevailing types of soil are black earth (70%) and gray forest soil.

Water resources. The Don and the Dnieper rivers flow through the Kursk Region. The Region also has mineral water reserves with a potential output of 1 million decaliters per year.

4. TRADE OPPORTUNITIES

4.1. MAIN GOODS
PRODUCED IN THE REGION
Ferrous metals. 2002 iron ore production was 15.1 million tons, while iron ore pellets output was 6.5 million tons.

Machine engineering and metal processing. In 2002, the sector produced mobile electric power plants with a total capacity of 113,000 kW, 964,000 car accumulators and batteries, and 74,000 general-purpose accumulators and batteries.

Food and beverages. In 2002 the sector processed 20,000 tons of meat products, 8,000 tons of sausage, 29,000 tons of whole milk products, 143,000 tons of flour, 96,000 tons of cereals, 15,000 tons of confectionery, 18,000 tons of pasta, and 555,000 decaliters of vodka and liquors.

Chemicals and petrochemicals. 2002 output: general mechanical rubber goods – 1,784 tons, thermoplastic pipes and pipeline components – 408 tons, and synthetic fiber and yarn – 2,095 tons.

Pharmaceuticals. OAO ICN Pharmaceuticals produced 44 million packages of cardio-vascular drugs in 2002, plus 47 million packs of analgesic, antipyretic, and antiphlogistic drugs.

4.2. EXPORTS, INCLUDING EXTRA-CIS
2002 extra-CIS exports totaled $54 million, and CIS exports reached $57.1 million. The corresponding figures for 2001 were $48.5 million and $52 million, and for 2002 – $60.3 and $34 million.

The bulk of the Region's 2002 exports were comprised of ore (2.5 million tons), rolling bearings ($2.5 million), electric motors and generators (759 units) and household washing machines (1,960 items). The Region's main export partners are Bulgaria, Hungary, Poland, Ukraine, Romania, Slovakia, the Czech Republic, Estonia, Argentina, Egypt, and Kazakhstan.

4.3. IMPORTS, INCLUDING EXTRA-CIS
Imports from extra-CIS countries amounted to $40.7 million in 2000. Imports from CIS countries totaled $139.2 million (in 2001 – $35.8 million and $151.3 million; and in 2002 – $23.7 million and $83.2 million, respectively).

The main goods imported into the Kursk Region in 2002 included ferrous metals (39,000 tons), synthetic rubber (137 tons), pipes (31,000 tons), plastics and plastic products ($6.5 million), agricultural harvest machines ($1.8 million), paper manufacturing equipment ($4 million), paper and cardboard ($9 million), and food and beverages. The Region's main import partners are Austria, Belgium, Germany, Denmark, Italy, Latvia, Moldova, the Netherlands, Poland, South Korea, Saudi Arabia, the United States, Turkey, Ukraine, France, and Switzerland.

Major regional export and import entities		*TABLE 6*
ENTITY	ADDRESS	PHONE, FAX, E-MAIL
ZAO GRINN Corporation	35, ul. Dimitrova, Kursk, Kursk Region, 305000	Phone/fax: (0712) 56 2398
OAO Kurskglavsnab	3, ul. 1st Stroitelnaya, Kursk, Kursk Region, 305025	Phone: (0712) 57 7159
OOO Intershina	150, pr. Kulakova, Kursk, Kursk Region, 305018	Phone: (0712) 51 0880

5. INVESTMENT OPPORTUNITIES

INVESTMENTS IN 1992–2002
(BY INDUSTRY SECTOR),
INCLUDING FOREIGN INVESTMENTS
The following factors determine the investment appeal of the Kursk Region:
- Its favorable geographical location (proximity to industrial centers of Russia and Ukraine);
- Its developed transport infrastructure;
- Its high industrial and scientific potential;
- Regional legislation granting tax exemptions and privileges to investors;
- Its highly qualified workforce;
- Cheap energy;
- Abundant natural resources.

5.2. CAPITAL INVESTMENT
The bulk of capital investment goes to industry, transport, and agriculture.

5.3. MAJOR ENTERPRISES
(INCLUDING ENTERPRISES
WITH FOREIGN INVESTMENTS)
More than 100 joint ventures with foreign capital are registered in the Kursk Region. These include JV ZAO Matis (Czech Republic), OOO Olip Obuks (Italy), OAO ICN Pharmaceuticals (international), the Kursk Brewery, a subsidiary of Sun Interbrew Holding Company (international), and others.

Capital investment by industry sector, $ million

TABLE 7

	1997	1998	1999	2000	2001	2002
Total capital investment	478.7	289.7	169.5	192.9	210.8	308.2
Including major industries (% of total)						
Industry	49.0	58.8	54.3	47.1	48.8	63.3
Agriculture and forestry	4.0	5.3	6.1	5.9	7.2	6.5
Construction	2.8	5.3	2.1	1.4	2.1	1.1
Transport and communications	8.0	6.1	16.5	11.1	11.5	6.7
Trade and public catering	3.9	0.5	2.1	9.6	9.6	2.3
Other	32.3	24.0	18.9	24.9	20.8	20.1

Foreign investment trends in 1997–2002

TABLE 8

	1997	1998	1999	2000	2001	2002
Foreign investment, $ million	1.3	14.0	11.0	7.5	24.0	4.0
Including FDI, $ million	1.3	13.4	10.7	7.5	4.3	3.4

Largest enterprises of the Kursk Region

TABLE 9

COMPANY	SECTOR
OAO Mikhailovsky Ore Dressing Plant	Ferrous metals
ZAO Accumulator	Machine engineering and metal processing
OAO Elevatormelmash	Machine engineering and metal processing
ZAO Kursk Bearings Company	Machine engineering and metal processing
OAO Pribor	Machine engineering and metal processing
OAO Elektroagregat	Machine engineering and metal processing
OAO Elektroapparat	Machine engineering and metal processing
OAO Schetmash	Machine engineering and metal processing
OAO Korenevsky Low Voltage Devices Plant	Machine engineering and metal processing
OAO Kurskagromash	Machine engineering and metal processing
ZAO Kurskrezinotekhnika	Chemicals and petrochemicals
OOO Izoplit-ZhSK	Construction materials
ZAO Seim	Light industry
ZAO GOTEK	Packaging
OOO Kursk Leather	Light industry
OAO ICN Pharmaceuticals	Chemicals and pharmaceuticals
OAO Krasnaya Polyana+	Food and beverages
OGUP Poultry Farm Kurskaya	Food and beverages

5.4. MOST ATTRACTIVE SECTORS FOR INVESTMENT

According to the Kursk Regional Administration, communications, machine engineering, chemicals and pharmaceuticals, food, agriculture, and trade and public catering are the most attractive industries for investment.

5.5. CURRENT LEGISLATION ON INVESTOR TAX EXEMPTIONS AND PRIVILEGES

The Kursk Region has enacted a Law On Investment Activity in the Kursk Region dated March 12, 2002, which provides a legal and economic framework for investment activity within the Region, accords equal rights to investors and provides guidelines for regulating investment activity.

I

CENTRAL FEDERAL DISTRICT

The Law provides for exempting investors from regional tax components.

The Law was accompanied by a Decree of the Governor of the Kursk Region On the Approval of the Guidelines for the Conclusion and Implementation of Investment Agreements in the Territory of the Kursk Region with a view to improving the procedure for concluding investment agreements.

Regional entities responsible for raising investment		*TABLE 10*
ENTITY	ADDRESS	PHONE, FAX, E-MAIL
Committee for Economy and Development of the Kursk Region	House of Soviets, Krasnaya pl., Kursk, 305002	Phone: (07122) 23 554 Fax: (0712) 56 8005
Kursk Regional Fund for Small Enterprise Support	6, Krasnaya pl., Kursk, 305000	Phone: (07122) 20 198

5.6. FEDERAL AND REGIONAL ECONOMIC AND SOCIAL DEVELOPMENT PROGRAMS FOR THE KURSK REGION

Federal targeted programs. The Kursk Region is participating in the implementation of 33 federal targeted programs financed in the amount of $125.8 million. Top priority has been accorded to the following programs: Housing, 2002–2010, Energy Efficient Economy, 2002–2005 and through 2010, Soil Fertility Enhancement, 2002–2005, Ecology and Natural Resources, 2002–2010, the Russian Federation Mineral Natural Resources Development Program, 1994–2000, etc.

Regional programs. The Kursk Regional Administration has drafted and is implementing more than 20 regional targeted programs for the development of industry, the agroindustrial sector, environmental protection, public welfare, and health-care. These include: The Development of the Land Reform, The Social and Economic Development in the Kursk Region, 2000–2005, Roads in the 21st Century, Energy Conservation in the Kursk Region, 2002–2005, The Development of Tourism in the Kursk Region, 2000–2004, etc. The total allocations for these programs amount to $31.5 million.

The Region is also carrying out a Comprehensive Program for Social and Economic Development of the Kursk Region, 2002–2005. The Program aims to make the Region more attractive for investment and to enhance the efficiency of the Region's economy. The Program is to be financed through private sector initiatives and allocations from the regional budget and non-budgetary funds. The Program aims to enhance the Region's industrial and agricultural output, to attract capital investment, and to increase tax collections to the federal and regional budgets

6. INVESTMENT PROJECTS

Industry sector and project description	1) Expected results 2) Amount and term of investment 3) Form of financing[1] 4) Documentation[2]	Contact information
1	2	3

08R001	● ★ ◆	OAO Elektroagregat
Establishment of production of standby power plants. Project goal: to produce ergonomic light and compact electrical installations.	1) 700 items per year 2) $0.7 million/3 years 3) L ($0.3 million), Leas. 4) BP	5-a, ul. 2nd Agregatnaya, Kursk, Kursk Region, 305038 Phone: (07122) 60 550 Fax: (0712) 50 1766, 50 1799 E-mail: Agregat@kursknet.ru Nikolai Sergeevich Shevchenko, CEO

[1] L – Loan, E – Equity, Leas. – Leasing, JV – Joint Venture
[2] BP – Business Plan, FS – Feasibility Study

1	2	3

08R002 ● ★ ◆

Establishment of production
of electric generators.
Project goal: to produce electric generators
to supply consumers with a cheap
source of energy.

1) 700 items per year
2) $1.9 million/3 years
3) L ($1.3 million), Leas.
4) BP

OAO Elektroagregat
5-a, ul. 2nd Agregatnaya, Kursk,
Kursk Region, 305038
Phone: (07122) 60 550
Fax: (0712) 50 1766, 50 1799
E-mail: Agregat@kursknet.ru
Nikolai Sergeevich Shevchenko,
CEO

08R003 ● ★ ◆

Establishment of production
of electric power plants.
Project goal: to develop and launch
batch production of electric power plants.

1) 2,000 items per year
2) $1.3 million/3 years
3) L ($0.6 million), Leas.
4) BP

OAO Elektroagregat
5-a, ul. 2nd Agregatnaya, Kursk,
Kursk Region, 305038
Phone: (07122) 60 550
Fax: (0712) 50 1766, 50 1799
E-mail: Agregat@kursknet.ru
Nikolai Sergeevich Shevchenko,
CEO

08R004 ● ◆ ▲

Development and manufacturing
of household electronic gas meters.
Project goal: to provide a reliable system
for controlling gas consumption.

1) 100,000 items per year
2) $14.7 million/1.5 years
3) L
4) BP, FS

FGUP Kursky Plant Mayak
8, ul. 50 Let Oktyabrya, Kursk,
Kursk Region, 305016
Phone/fax: (07122) 22 813
Fax: (07122) 20 690
Alexander Mikhailovich Bannikov,
Chief Engineer

FOOD AND BEVERAGES

08R005 ● ★ ◆

Upgrading of OAO Cheremisinovsky
Butter Plant's production facilities.
Project goal: to produce dairy
products and hard cheese.

1) Profit of $0.2 million per year
2) $0.9 million/0.5 year
3) L, Leas.
4) BP

OAO Cheremisinovsky Butter Plant
69, ul. Pochtovaya, Cheremisinovo
Village, Kursk Region, 306440
Phone: (07159) 21 574
Fax: (07159) 21 571
Petr Ivanovich Perepelkin, CEO

HOTELS, TOURISM, AND RECREATIONAL

08R006 ■ ● ◆

Completion of construction work
at the Korennaya Pustyn Historical
and Cultural Center.
Project goal: to revive a cultural
and spiritual center of Russia.

1) n/a
2) $1.9 million/1.5 years
3) L ($0.6 million), E
4) BP

Korennaya Pustyn Historic
and Cultural Center
61, ul. Sovetskaya, Svoboda Village,
Zolotukhinsky District,
Kursk Region, 306050
Phone: (07151) 41 182, 41 183
E-mail: Korennaya@yandex.ru
Vyacheslav Nikolaevich Lysykh,
CEO

09. LIPETSK REGION [48]

E C O N O M I C   M A P

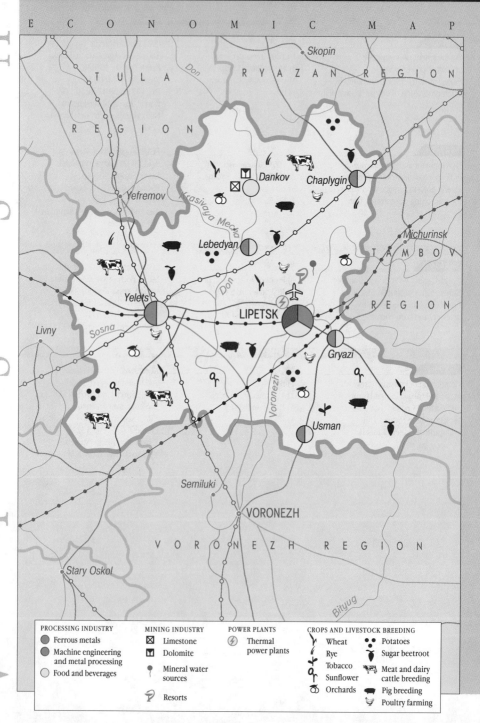

PROCESSING INDUSTRY	MINING INDUSTRY	POWER PLANTS	CROPS AND LIVESTOCK BREEDING	
● Ferrous metals	⊠ Limestone	⚡ Thermal power plants	Wheat	Potatoes
● Machine engineering and metal processing	⛉ Dolomite		Rye	Sugar beetroot
○ Food and beverages	● Mineral water sources		Tobacco	Meat and dairy cattle breeding
			Sunflower	Pig breeding
	℞ Resorts		Orchards	Poultry farming

The Lipetsk Region is among the few regions of Russia whose economy does not depend on federal subsidies. Situated at the center of European Russia at the crossroads of major transport routes, the Region boasts strong research, development, and production potential and an advanced infrastructure.

The Region is home to enterprises in the ferrous metals, machine engineering, energy, construction materials, and other sectors successfully operating in a market economy environment.

The Lipetsk Region's agricultural sector is steadily growing. The Region boasts a developed network of processing companies focused on the processing of grain, sugar beet, milk, meat, and fruit juices. The Region's agricultural output enjoys a substantial market share, particularly in the children's food sector, and its high quality is appreciated throughout Russia and the CIS.

We are ready and willing to engage in mutually beneficial collaboration and welcome any business proposals from foreign and domestic investors.

Oleg Korolev,
HEAD OF ADMINISTRATION OF THE LIPETSK REGION

I

CENTRAL FEDERAL DISTRICT

1. GENERAL INFORMATION

1.1. GEOGRAPHY

The Lipetsk Region covers a total area of 24,100 square kilometers. The Region is situated in the central part of the East European Plain. To the north-west, the Region borders the Tula Region, to the north – the Ryazan Region, to the east – the Tambov Region, to the south and south-east – the Voronezh Region, to the south-west – the Kursk Region, and to the west – the Oryol Region.

1.2. CLIMATE

The Lipetsk Region enjoys a temperate continental climate. The average air temperature in January is −10°C, rising to +19°C in July. Average annual precipitation is 500–600 mm.

1.3. POPULATION

According to preliminary 2002 census results, the total population in the Region was 1,213,000 people. The average population density is 50.3 people per square kilometer. The economically active population amounts to 611,000 people. Official unemployment in 2002 stood at 0.7%.

Demographically speaking, some 52% are of working age, 24% are below the statutory working age, and 24% are beyond the statutory working age.

As of 2002, the Lipetsk Region's major urban centers were Lipetsk with 506,000 inhabitants, Yelets with 116,700 inhabitants, Gryazi with 48,500 inhabitants, Dankov with 23,800 inhabitants, and Lebedyan with 21,400 inhabitants.

Population								TABLE 1
	1992	1997	1998	1999	2000	2001	2002
Total population, '000	1,234	1,249	1,248	1,245	1,240	1,235	1,213
Economically active population, '000	615	580	572	616	603	602	611

2. ADMINISTRATION

House of Soviets, pl. Lenina, Lipetsk, Lipetsk Region, 398014
Phone: (0742) 77 6596; fax: (0742) 27 2923
E-mail: glava@admlr.lipertsk.ru; http://www.admlr.lipetsk.ru

NAME	POSITION	CONTACT INFORMATION
Oleg Petrovich KOROLEV	Head of Administration of the Lipetsk Region	Phone: (0742) 77 6596, 27 2565
Petr Tikhonovich GORLOV	First Deputy Head of Administration of the Lipetsk Region	Phone: (0742) 27 2923
Tatyana Alexandrovna GLUKHOVKINA	Deputy Head of Administration of the Lipetsk Region for Economy, Finance, Investment, Trade, and International Relations	Phone: (0742) 27 1337
Nikolai Fedorovich TAGINTSEV	Deputy Head of Administration of the Lipetsk Region for the Agroindustrial Sector	Phone: (0742) 77 9968
Yury Ivanovich ALTUKHOV	Deputy Head of Administration of the Lipetsk Region for Administration, Legal Issues, and Transport	Phone: (0742) 27 6309
Stanislav Nikolaevich KRUPNOV	Deputy Head of Administration of the Lipetsk Region for Construction, Fuel and Energy, Housing and Communal Services, and Natural Resources	Phone: (0742) 27 7448
Vladimir Vasilyevich LAVRENTIEV	Deputy Head of Administration of the Lipetsk Region for Industry and State Property Management	Phone: (0742) 77 1535
Vladimir Mikhailovoch PODGORNY	Chief of the Investment and International Relations Department	Phone: (0742) 27 5583

3. ECONOMIC POTENTIAL

3.1. 1997–2002 GROSS REGIONAL PRODUCT (GRP). INDUSTRY BREAKDOWN

The 2002 gross regional product amounted to $1,965.4 million, which constitutes 12.4% growth year-on-year. The growth was achieved thanks to an increase in industrial output. In 2001, per capita GRP was $1,415, rising to $1,619 in 2002.

3.2. MAJOR ECONOMIC GROWTH PROJECTIONS

The blueprint for economic development in the Lipetsk Region is set forth in the Program for Social and Economic Development of the Lipetsk Region in 2003, which aims to achieve the following objectives:

GRP trends in 1997–2002						TABLE 2
	1997	1998	1999	2000	2001*	2002*
GRP in current prices, $ million	2,631.6	1,702.4	1,292.3	1,714.7	1,749.1	1,965.4

*Estimates of the Lipetsk Regional Administration

GRP industry breakdown in 1997–2002, % of total						TABLE 3
	1997	1998	1999	2000	2001*	2002*
GRP	100.0	100.0	100.0	100.0	100.0	100.0
Industry	45.7	41.3	53.4	58.8	50.5	53.1
Agriculture and forestry	10.1	10.7	11.9	10.2	10.5	9.2
Construction	6.9	6.0	3.8	4.2	5.7	6.4
Transport and communications	6.6	6.1	5.3	5.8	5.6	5.4
Trade and public catering	12.6	12.6	11.3	9.3	10.2	9.6
Other	18.1	23.3	14.3	11.7	17.5	16.3

*Estimates of the Lipetsk Regional Administration

Industry: to ensure sustainable output growth by increasing product competitiveness and sales, facilitate maximum capacity utilization, enhance investment, and expand local cooperation;

Agriculture: to increase output, improve land quality, provide financial assistance to agricultural producers through merchandise credits, subsidized bank interest, and using single and double warehouse receipts for grain collateral;

Construction: to introduce advanced technologies and resource efficient techniques and methods of production;

Transport: to create prerequisites for a stable and safe transport system that meets the transportation needs of the public and industry;

Trade: to ensure retail trade growth and develop trade links with other Russian regions.

3.3. INDUSTRIAL OUTPUT IN 1997–2002 FOR MAJOR SECTORS OF ECONOMY

The leading industrial sectors of the Lipetsk Region are ferrous metals, food and beverages, machine engineering, and metal processing. They account for 88.2% of total industrial output.

Ferrous metals. Ferrous metals dominate in the Region's industrial structure with 61% of total

industrial output. Among the main enterprises within the sector are OAO Novolipetsky Metal Works and OAO Lipetsk Metal Works Svobodny Sokol.

Food and beverages. This sector accounts for 14.7% of total industrial output. Major food and beverages and food processing companies are OAO Lebedyansky Experimental Canning Plant, OAO Lipetskhlebmakaronprom, ZAO Dankovsky Meat Processing Plant, OAO Lipetsk-moloko, and OAO Lipetsk Frozen Food Plant. Children's food and juices are produced in the Region.

Machine engineering and metal processing. The sector accounts for 12.5% of total industrial output. Major companies within the sector are ZAO Stinol, OAO Hydraulic Drive, OAO Energia, and OAO Lemaz.

Energy. The energy sector accounts for 7.2% of total industrial output. The main energy company is OAO Lipetskenergo.

3.4. FUEL AND ENERGY BALANCE (OUTPUT AND CONSUMPTION PER RESOURCE)

The Lipetsk Region is an energy deficit region. The energy sector meets 48% of the Region's demand for electricity, and 100% of its demand for heat.

Industry breakdown of industrial output in 1997–2002, % of total						TABLE 4
	1997	1998	1999	2000	2001	2002*
Industry	100.0	100.0	100.0	100.0	100.0	100.0
Ferrous metals	55.6	55.0	60.5	65.1	57.3	61.0
Food and beverages	10.5	12.1	13.5	11.6	10.2	14.7
Machine engineering and metal processing	12.7	11.8	12.3	10.9	14.3	12.5
Energy	13.8	13.8	7.9	6.7	7.4	7.2
Construction materials	3.2	2.8	1.9	2.0	2.3	1.9
Chemicals and petrochemicals	1.0	1.3	0.8	0.8	0.8	0.5
Light industry	0.4	0.4	0.5	0.5	0.6	0.5
Forestry, timber, and pulp and paper	0.1	0.1	0.1	0.1	0.1	0.1

*Estimates of the Lipetsk Regional Administration

Fuel and energy sector production and consumption trends, 1997–2002						TABLE 5
	1997	1998	1999	2000	2001	2002*
Electricity output, billion kWh	3.5	3.5	3.7	3.7	3.9	4.3
Electricity consumption, billion kWh	9.6	8.3	8.6	8.8	8.4	8.9
Natural gas consumption, million cubic meters	n/a	4,188.3	4,323.6	4,371.3	4,325.9	4,468.2

*Estimates of the Lipetsk Regional Administration

3.5. TRANSPORT INFRASTRUCTURE

Roads. The Region has 5,157 kilometers of public highway. Lipetsk has highway links with all adjacent regions and federal main routes such as the Moscow – Rostov-on-Don and Moscow – Volgograd federal highways.

Railroads. The Lipetsk Region has 752 kilometers of railroads, more than 50 railway stations, and two large railway junctions at Yelets and Gryazi.

Airports. The Lipetsk Region has an airport capable of accepting all types of aircraft.

Gas pipelines. The Stavropol – Moscow gas pipeline passes through the Region.

3.6. MAIN NATURAL RESOURCES: RESERVES AND EXTRACTION IN 2002

The Region's principal natural resources are mineral raw materials, timber, and water.

Mineral resources. The Region has explored and is developing deposits of the following construction materials: dolomite, lime, clay, sand, peat, iron and brown ore, brown coal, and phosphorite. The largest dolomite deposit is the Dankovskoye with reserves in excess of 700 million tons, and the largest fluxing limestone deposits are the Studenovskoye and Sitovskoye. Limestone is produced industrially at the Rozhdestvenskoye, Olshanskoye, and Khmelnitskoye deposits. The Region has deposits of expanded-clay loam, ceramic clay, and molding, silicate, and building sand. The Region's peat reserves exceed 90 million cubic meters.

Timber. Forests cover 200,000 hectares. Pine and deciduous trees prevail.

Water resources. The Ranova, Don, and Voronezh rivers and their tributaries drain the Region. The Region has mineral water springs and therapeutic peat mud. The Lipetsk resort is located at the site of mineral water springs and therapeutic mud fields.

4. TRADE OPPORTUNITIES

4.1. MAIN GOODS PRODUCED IN THE REGION

In 2002, the Region produced:
Coke. 4.4 million tons;
Steel. 8.6 million tons;
Finished ferrous metal rolls. 8 million tons;
Tractors. 656 tractors;

Cultivator tractors. 2,300 cultivators;
Refrigerators and freezers for household use. 1.1 million refrigerators and freezers.

4.2. EXPORTS, INCLUDING EXTRA-CIS

The Lipetsk Region's exports to extra-CIS countries amounted to $1,032.8 million in 2000, and exports to CIS – to $20.8 million. The respective figures for 2001 were $891.6 million and $32.1 million, and for 2002 – $1,148.3 million and $69.7 million.

The main types of goods exported by the Region are ferrous and non-ferrous metals and machines. Major importers of the Region's products include the UK, Malaysia, the USA, Turkey, and Ukraine.

4.3. IMPORTS, INCLUDING EXTRA-CIS

2000 imports from extra-CIS countries amounted to $120.9 million, and imports from CIS countries – to $40.1 million. The respective figures

for 2001 were $178.4 million and $44.8 million, and for 2002 – $213.4 million and $40.7 million.

The bulk of 2002 regional imports was represented by machinery, timber and timber goods, food and beverages and food feedstock. The main exporters to the Region are the UK, Malaysia, the USA, Turkey, and Ukraine.

4.4. MAJOR REGIONAL EXPORT AND IMPORT ENTITIES

Due to the specific features of trade in the Region, mainly industrial companies perform export and import operations.

5. INVESTMENT OPPORTUNITIES

5.1. INVESTMENTS IN 1992–2002 (BY INDUSTRY SECTOR), INCLUDING FOREIGN INVESTMENTS

The following factors determine the investment appeal of the Lipetsk Region:
- Its advantageous geographic location at the center of European Russia;
- Its developed transport infrastructure;

- Legislation providing support for investment activities (protection of investor rights and preferential tax treatment);
- Its highly qualified workforce.

5.2. CAPITAL INVESTMENT

Industry and transport accounted for the majority of capital investment in 2002.

Foreign investment trends in 1997–2002						*TABLE 6*
	1997	1998	1999	2000	2001	2002
Foreign investment, $ million	3.8	14.8	12.3	1.4	81.3	10.7
Including FDI, $ million	0.5	6.4	12.2	1.3	2.9	10.5

Capital investment by industry sector, $ million						*TABLE 7*
	1997	1998	1999	2000	2001	2002
Total capital investment	525.6	239.3	151.1	213.7	253.5	332.9
Including major industries (% of total)						
Industry	42.0	25.4	34.3	35.7	56.4	44.2
Agriculture and forestry	7.9	9.2	12.5	10.8	8.2	8.9
Construction	1.0	0.7	0.8	0.8	0.8	0.5
Transport and communications	12.8	20.7	16.7	14.1	14.4	9.3
Trade and public catering	1.0	0.8	0.8	0.9	0.7	0.4
Other	35.3	43.2	34.9	37.7	19.5	36.7

5.3. MAJOR ENTERPRISES (INCLUDING ENTERPRISES WITH FOREIGN INVESTMENT)

The Region has registered over 100 companies with foreign investment, including OOO Zolotoy Petushok Invest, OAO Progress, OAO Komtez, and OAO G.T.E.-Yelets.

5.4. MOST ATTRACTIVE SECTORS FOR INVESTMENT

According to the Lipetsk Regional Administration, the most appealing sectors for investors are

metals, machine engineering and metal processing, food and beverages, and construction.

5.5. CURRENT LEGISLATION ON INVESTOR TAX EXEMPTIONS AND PRIVILEGES

With a view to fostering a favorable investment climate in the Lipetsk Region, the Administration has passed the following laws: On the Provision of Guarantees for Investment Projects of Regional Companies and Organizations and On Support to Investment in the Lipetsk Region's Economy.

I

CENTRAL FEDERAL DISTRICT

Largest enterprises of the Lipetsk Region

TABLE 8

COMPANY	SECTOR
OAO Lipetskenergo	Energy
OAO Novolipetsky Metal Works	Metals
OAO Lipetsk Metal Works Svobodny Sokol	Metals
ZAO Stinol	Machine engineering
OAO Lemaz	Machine engineering
OAO Lipetskhlebmakaronprom	Food and beverages
ZAO Dankovsky Meat Processing Plant	Food and beverages
OAO Lipetskmoloko	Food and beverages
OAO Lipetsk Frozen Food Plant	Food and beverages

Regional entities responsible for raising investment

TABLE 9

ENTITY	ADDRESS	PHONE, FAX, E-MAIL
Investment and International Relations Department of the Lipetsk Regional Administration	1, pl. Sobornaya, Lipetsk, Lipetsk Region, 398014	Phone: (0742) 27 5583 Fax: (0742) 74 2920 E-mail: diir@admlr.lipetsk.ru

5.6. FEDERAL AND REGIONAL ECONOMIC AND SOCIAL DEVELOPMENT PROGRAMS FOR THE LIPETSK REGION

Federal targeted programs. The Region is implementing federal targeted programs for social and economic development, with the priority accorded to the following programs: Children of Russia, 2003–2006, with its sub-programs Disabled Children, Orphans, and Talented Children; Urgent Tuberculosis Prevention Measures in Russia, 1998–2004, Preventive Vaccines, 1999–2000 and through 2005, Culture of Russia, 2001–2005, The Elderly, 2002–2005, and Forests of Russia, 1997–2000 and through 2010.

Regional programs. The regional programs currently being implemented in the Lipetsk Region aim to improve healthcare, education, social policy, culture, sports, environmental rehabilitation, housing and communal services, agriculture, and transport. The priority regional programs include: The Program for Improving the Position of Women in the Lipetsk Region, 2002–2005, State Guarantees on Free Medical Services in the Lipetsk Region, 2002–2005, and Job Creation in the Lipetsk Region, 2002–2005. A total budget of $1,367 million was allocated to fund federal and regional programs in 2002.

6. INVESTMENT PROJECTS

Industry sector and project description	1) Expected results 2) Amount and term of investment 3) Form of financing[1] 4) Documentation[2]	Contact information
1	2	3

MACHINE ENGINEERING AND METAL PROCESSING

09R001		
Launching of production of the construction and finishing machines. Project goal: to increase the product range and output.	1) Market share increase to 30% 2) $5.0 million/n/a 3) JV 4) BP	OAO Lebedyansky Construction and Finishing Machinery Plant 87, ul. Shakhraya, Lebedyan, Lipetsk Region, 399620 Phone: (07466) 52 415, 52 107, 52 384, 55 230 Fax: (07466) 52 413 Alexander Ivanovich Roldugin, CEO

09R002		
Launching of additional facilities to manufacture high precision bearings. Project goal: to increase output.	1) Revenue of $2.2 million per year 2) $1.0 million/1 year 3) JV 4) BP	ZAO Lipetsk Machine Plant 66, ul. Sovetskaya, Lipetsk, Lipetsk Region, 398636 Phone: (0742) 77 4270 Fax: (0742) 77 4673 Alexander Vasilyevich Melnikov, CEO

09R003		
Upgrading of fixed assets at an existing alkaline battery producer. Project goal: to increase output, reduce costs, and improve the ecological situation.	1) $7 million 2) $6.8 million/1.5 years 3) L, Leas., JV 4) BP	OAO Energiya 1, pos. Electric, Yelets, Lipetsk Region, 399775 Phone: (07467) 74 003, 27 740, 21 498 Fax: (07467) 41 612 E-mail: elchemi@gw-el.lipetsk.su Vladimir Alexandrovich Arkhipenko, CEO

09R004		
Upgrading of fixed assets at an existing lithium battery producer. Project goal: to increase output and reduce production costs.	1) $5 million 2) $1 million/1.5 years 3) L, Leas., JV 4) BP	OAO Energiya 1, pos. Electric, Yelets, Lipetsk Region, 399775 Phone: (07467) 74 003, 27 740, 21 498 Fax: (07467) 41 612 E-mail:elchemi@gw-el.lipetsk.su Vladimir Alexandrovich Arkhipenko, CEO

CONSTRUCTION MATERIALS

09R005		
Completion of construction of a facing brick, tile, and drainage pipe plant. Project goal: to introduce ceramic building materials to the market.	1) Output of 20.4 million items per year 2) $2.7 million/n/a 3) JV 4) BP	OAO Inter-Firm Construction Materials Agroindustrial Company 19a, ul. Nekrasova, Usman, Lipetsk Region, 399340 Phone: (07472) 41 276 Fax: (07472) 41 315 E-mail: mafis@freemail.ru http://www.lipetsk.ru/~wwwus/maf Anatoly Alexandrovich Brusentsev, CEO

I

CENTRAL FEDERAL DISTRICT

---

[1] L – Loan, E – Equity, Leas. – Leasing, JV – Joint Venture
[2] BP – Business Plan, FS – Feasibility Study

1	2	3

09R006 ❖ ◆

Construction of new facilities for the production of extra light rocky gravel. Project goal: to introduce new building materials to the market.

1) Output of 50,000 cubic meters per year
2) $5.0 million/n/a
3) JV
4) BP

OAO Orgtechstroy
4, ul. Sovetskaya, Lipetsk,
Lipetsk Region, 398600
Phone: (0742) 77 1456
Fax: (0742) 77 1498
Oleg Ivanovich Mazur, CEO

09R007 ❖ ◆

Construction of a plant for the production of construction materials and sidewalk tiles at operating facilities. Project goal: to increase output and product range.

1) Output of 17.4 million bricks annually
2) $4.2 million/n/a
3) JV
4) BP

OOO Pressed Wall Unit
and Sidewalk Tile Production Plant
TECHNO-SERICK
5a, ul. Soyuznaya, Lipetsk,
Lipetsk Region, 399059
Phone: (0742) 74 0532
E-mail: n.ivchenko@mrg.lipetsk.ru
Sergei Nikolaevich Sologubov, CEO

FOOD AND BEVERAGES

09R008 ● ★ ◆

Construction of a plant for the production of vegetable oil and vegetable seed fodder. Project goal: to expand business.

1) Output of 50,000 tons of oil per year
2) $5.0 million/n/a
3) L, Leas.
4) BP

OAO Lebedyansky Elevator
1, ul. Privokzalnaya, Lebedyan,
Lipetsk Region, 399612
Phone: (07466) 55 386
Fax: (07466) 52 450
E-mail: vitas@gw-le.lipetsk.su
Igor Gennadyevich Bychkov, CEO

09R009 ★ ◆

Launching of new facilities at an existing brewery. Project goal: to produce a new kind of beer and increase output.

1) Output of 2.5 million decaliters per year
2) $21.5 million/7 years
3) Leas.
4) BP

ZAO Rosinka Plant
11, pr. Universalnaya, Lipetsk,
Lipetsk Region, 398032
Phone: (0742) 31 7997
Fax: (0742) 31 8769
E-mail: root@rosinka.lipetsk.su
Igor Vladimirovich Tenkov, CEO

09R010 ● ★ ◆

Upgrading of fixed assets of an existing tobacco factory. Project goal: to increase output and improve product quality.

1) Output of 10 billion items per year
2) $6 million/5 years
3) L, Leas.
4) BP

OAO Usman-Tobacco
2, ul. Tolstogo, Usman,
Lipetsk Region, 399370
Phone: (07472) 41 677, 40 552,
22 731
Fax: (07472) 41 689
Viktor Mikhailovich Boev, CEO

09R011 ■ ● ★ ◆

Launching of new starch production facilities at an existing enterprise. Project goal: to increase product range.

1) Processing facilities for 200 tons of potatoes and 80 tons of corn per day
2) $6.5 million/n/a
3) E, L, Leas.
4) BP

OAO Chaplyginsky Starch Plant
187, ul. Engelsa, Chaplygin,
Lipetsk Region, 399900
Phone: (07475) 21 432
Fax: (07475) 21 840
Yury Alexeevich Telyakov, CEO

09R012 ● ★ ❖ ▲

Launching of new instant coffee production facilities at an existing food factory. Project goal: to increase product range and output.

1) Output of 120 tons per year
2) $3.6 million/1 year
3) L, Leas., JV
4) FS

OAO Gryazinsky Food Factory
4, ul. Tchaikovskogo, Gryazi,
Lipetsk Region, 399053
Phone: (07461) 20 317
Fax: (07461) 20 361
E-mail: gpk@gr-gr.lipetsk.su
Vladimir Lukich Azarenkov, CEO

1	2	3

09R013 ● ★ ❖ ▲

Launching of facilities for the production of fast food macaroni at an existing food factory.
Project goal: to increase product range and output.

1) Output of 300 tons per year
2) $0.8 million/8 months
3) L, Leas., JV
4) FS

OAO Gryazinsky Food Factory
4, ul. Tchaikovskogo, Gryazi,
Lipetsk Region, 399053
Phone: (07461) 20 317
Fax: (07461) 20 361
E-mail: gpk@gr-gr.lipetsk.su
Vladimir Lukich Azarenkov, CEO

09R014 ● ★ ❖ ◆

Upgrading of fixed assets at an operating meat processing plant.
Project goal: to increase output and product quality.

1) n/a
2) $1.2 million/n/a
3) L, Leas., JV
4) BP

OAO Usmansky Meat Processing Plant,
56, ul. Privokzalnaya, Usman,
Lipetsk Region, 399340
Phone/fax: (07472) 21 964
Petr Fedorovich Andrianov, CEO

HOTELS AND TOURISM

09R015

Construction of an international business class hotel in Lipetsk.
Project goal: to increase the range and quality of services.

1) 50 beds
2) $5.0 million/n/a
3) JV
4) BP

OAO Orgtechstroy
4, ul. Sovetskaya, Lipetsk,
Lipetsk Region, 398600
Phone: (0742) 77 1456, 74 5698
Fax: (0742) 48 5331
Oleg Ivanovich Mazur, CEO

HEALTHCARE

09R016 ❖ ◆

Construction of a radiation unit at the Lipetsk Cancer Center.
Project goal: to increase the range of medical services.

1) 500 beds
2) $9.9 million/n/a
3) JV
4) BP

Healthcare Department
of the Lipetsk Region,
6, ul. Zegelya, Lipetsk,
Lipetsk Region, 398050
Phone: (0742) 77 9796
Fax: (0742) 27 3279
E-mail: Uzalo@lipetsk.ru
Vasily Khristoforovich Muruzov,
Department Head

CHEMICALS AND PETROCHEMICALS

09R017 ● ★ ❖ ◆

Launching of facilities for the production of a new type of plastic bags, modern polyethylene and polypropylene film packaging, and disposable dishes.
Project goal: to increase output and product range.

1) To increase output fivefold
2) $1.0 million/2 years
3) L, Leas., JV
4) BP

OOO Company VIS
6a, ul. Frunze, Lipetsk,
Lipetsk Region, 398059
Phone/fax: (0742) 27 3624
Yury Eduardovich Vilkevich, CEO

10. MOSCOW REGION [50]

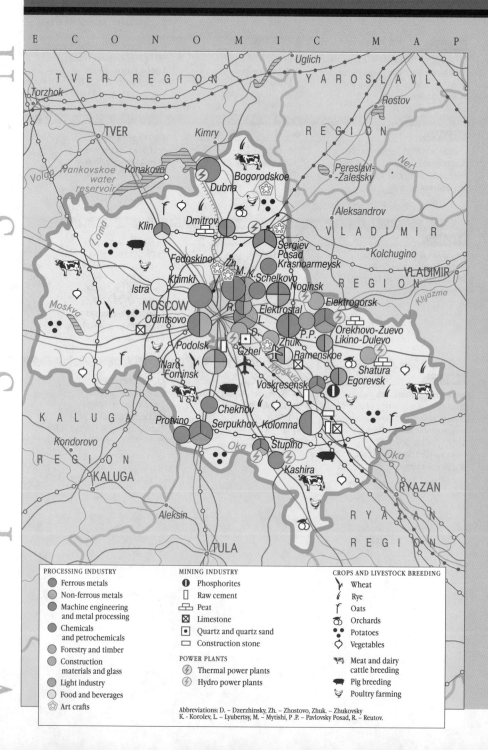

ECONOMIC MAP

RUSSIA

TVER REGION

YAROSLAVL REGION

VLADIMIR REGION

KALUGA REGION

RYAZAN REGION

TULA

Torzhok
Uglich
Rostov
Kimry
Pereslavl-Zalessky
Nerl
Tver
Vankovskoe water reservoir
Konakovo
Bogorodskoe
Volga
Dubna
Aleksandrov
Klin
Dmitrov
Sergiev Posad
Kolchugino
Lama
Fedoskino
Krasnoarmeysk
VLADIMIR
Zh.
M.K.
Schelkovo
Istra
Khimki
Noginsk
Klyazma
Moskva
MOSCOW
Elektrogorsk
R.
Elektrostal
Odintsovo
L.
Orekhovo-Zuevo
Likino-Dulevo
Podolsk
D.
Zhuk.
P.P.
Gzhel
Ramenskoe
Naro-Fominsk
Shatura
Egorevsk
Moskva
Voskresensk
Chekhov
Kondorovo
Protvino
Serpukhov
Kolomna
KALUGA
Oka
Stupino
Oka
Kashira
Aleksin
RYAZAN
RYAZAN REGION

PROCESSING INDUSTRY

- Ferrous metals
- Non-ferrous metals
- Machine engineering and metal processing
- Chemicals and petrochemicals
- Forestry and timber
- Construction materials and glass
- Light industry
- Food and beverages
- Art crafts

MINING INDUSTRY

- Phosphorites
- Raw cement
- Peat
- Limestone
- Quartz and quartz sand
- Construction stone

POWER PLANTS

- Thermal power plants
- Hydro power plants

CROPS AND LIVESTOCK BREEDING

- Wheat
- Rye
- Oats
- Orchards
- Potatoes
- Vegetables
- Meat and dairy cattle breeding
- Pig breeding
- Poultry farming

Abbreviations: D. – Dzerzhinsky, Zh. – Zhostovo, Zhuk. – Zhukovsky, K. - Korolev, L. – Lyubertsy, M. – Mytishi, P .P. – Pavlovsky Posad, R. – Reutov.

T he past three years have marked a period of clear economic growth in the Moscow Region spearheaded by the implementation of the Regional Government's targeted programs aimed at boosting industry, infrastructure, and the social sphere.

Recent economic reforms have had a profound impact on all sectors of the Region's economy. Three quarters of the Region's industrial and construction companies have now been privatized, including some 600 companies with foreign investment. These companies account for 70% of the Region's total industrial output.

The Moscow Regional Government is focused on encouraging the development of existing enterprises and the establishment of small and medium enterprises. The Region's economic development strategy aims to develop the machine engineering, food and beverages, and light industry sectors, and to introduce advanced technologies.

The Government's investment policy is reflected in the regional Law On Investment Activity in the Moscow Region, which summarizes all of the rules of the game for investors. The Law aims to provide a vehicle for raising investment and ensuring continuous interfacing with investors throughout project implementation. With this in mind, the Regional Government has established the Regional Investment Advisory Council with active investor participation.

For several years now, the Moscow Region has been working with numerous landmark international companies, including IKEA (Sweden), Auchan (France), Mars, PepsiCo (USA), Ehrmann (Germany), and many others. This collaboration highlights the economic appeal and dynamism of the Moscow Region. The Region currently has investment proposals worth some $63 million related to more than 300 companies and organizations in the research and development and industrial sectors on its books. Investors in the Region enjoy multi-optional proposals for the combined use of some 340,000 square meters of available operating facilities. We strive to make our relations with investors and trading partners mutually beneficial. The Regional Government sees its role as one of resolving social and economic issues and creating a friendly environment to provide investors with opportunities to invest in high-return projects.

This Guide will act as a round table of sorts uniting all concerned parties – the Administration, regional companies, and potential investors from across the globe. This is a very useful and constructive initiative.

I wish its organizers and participants every success.

Boris Gromov,
GOVERNOR OF THE MOSCOW REGION,
CHAIRMAN OF THE GOVERNMENT
OF THE MOSCOW REGION

I

CENTRAL FEDERAL DISTRICT

1. GENERAL INFORMATION

1.1. GEOGRAPHY

The Moscow Region covers a total area of 46,000 square kilometers. The Region is located in the center of European Russia in the basins of the Volga, the Oka, the Klyazma, and the Moskva rivers. To the north and north-west, the Region borders the Tver Region, to the west – the Smolensk Region, to the north-east – the Yaroslavl Region, to the east – the Vladimir Region, to the south-east – the Ryazan Region, to the south – the Tula Region, and to the south-west – the Kaluga Region. The specific feature of the Moscow Region is that it has Moscow, the capital of the Russian Federation, within its borders.

1.2. CLIMATE

The Moscow Region enjoys a temperate continental climate. The average air temperature in January is −6.7°C, rising to +19°C in July. The average annual precipitation is 450–650 mm. The growing season lasts for 130–140 days.

1.3. POPULATION

The 2002 census preliminary results revealed a total population of 6,627,000 people in the Region. The average population density is 144.1 people per square kilometer. The economically active population amounts to 3,434,000 people. The 2002 official unemployment level is 1.1%.

Demographically speaking, some 60.9% are of working age, 15.5% are below the statutory working age, and 23.6% are beyond the statutory working age.

As of 2002, the Moscow Region's major urban centers are: Podolsk with 181,500 inhabitants, Mytischi with 159,200 inhabitants, Lyubertsy with 156,900 inhabitants, Kolomna with 150,100 inhabitants, Balashikha with 148,200 inhabitants, Elektrostal with 146,100 inhabitants, Korolev with 143,100 inhabitants, Khimki with 141,300 inhabitants, Odintsovo with 134,700 inhabitants, Serpukhov with 131,200 inhabitants, Orekhovo-Zuevo with 122,300 inhabitants, Noginsk with 118,000 inhabitants, Sergiev Posad with 113,800 inhabitants, Schelkovo with 113,700 inhabitants, Zheleznodorozhny with 104,100 inhabitants, and Zhukovsky with 101,900 inhabitants.

Population								TABLE 1
	1992	1997	1998	1999	2000	2001	2002
Total population, '000	6,660	6,532	6,517	6,500	6,464	6,436	6,627
Economically active population, '000	3,688	3,292	3,226	3,482	3,531	3,443	3,434

2. ADMINISTRATION

6, Staraya Ploschad, Moscow, 103070
Phone: (095) 206 6042, 206 6862; fax: (095) 928 9812
E-mail: amo@mosreg.ru; http://www.mosreg.ru

NAME	POSITION	CONTACT INFORMATION
Boris Vsevolodovich GROMOV	Governor of the Moscow Region, Chairman of the Government of the Moscow Region	Phone: (095) 923 2413, 206 6278
Vasily Yuryevich GOLUBEV	First Deputy Chairman of the Government of the Moscow Region for Industry and Agriculture	Phone: (095) 206 0206, 924 5324
Alexander Vasilyevich GORNOSTAEV	Deputy Chairman of the Government of the Moscow Region for Housing and Communal Services and Construction	Phone: (095) 206 9145
Nikolai Mikhailovich REPCHENKO	Deputy Chairman of the Government of the Moscow Region for Economy, Finance, and Investment Policy	Phone: (095) 206 6095, 206 0154
Vyacheslav Borisovich KRYMOV	Minister of Economy of the Government of the Moscow Region	Phone: (095) 915 0463
Alexei Viktorovich KUZNETSOV	Minister of Finance of the Government of the Moscow Region	Phone: (095) 152 8911, 152 8908
Vladimir Ivanovich KOZYREV	Minister of Industry of the Government of the Moscow Region	Phone: (095) 229 6162

NAME	POSITION	CONTACT INFORMATION
Tigran Alexandrovich KARAKHANOV	Minister of External Economic Relations of the Government of the Moscow Region	Phone: (095) 727 1352
Alexei Felixovich BODUNKOV	Minister of Property Relations of the Government of the Moscow Region	Phone: (095) 958 2400
Petr Dmitrievich KATSYV	Minister of Transport of the Government of the Moscow Region	Phone: (095) 785 8021
Nikolai Alexeevich SAVENKO	Minister of Agriculture and Food of the Government of the Moscow Region	Phone: (095) 299 9102

I

3. ECONOMIC POTENTIAL

3.1. 1997–2002 GROSS REGIONAL PRODUCT (GRP). INDUSTRY BREAKDOWN

According to preliminary estimates, the 2002 gross regional product amounted to $9,488 million, which constitutes 7% growth year-on-year in comparable prices. The growth was achieved mainly thanks to an increase in industrial output. Per capita GRP amounted to $1,288 in 2001 and $1,432 in 2002.

GRP trends in 1997–2002						TABLE 2
	1997	1998	1999	2000	2001	2002*
GRP in current prices, $ million	13,462	10,322	6,309	6,883	8,292	9,488

*Estimates of the Moscow Regional Government

GRP industry breakdown in 1997–2002, % of total						TABLE 3
	1997	1998	1999	2000	2001	2002*
GRP	100.0	100.0	100.0	100.0	100.0	100.0
Industry	27.1	25.1	31.3	30.1	32.9	34.1
Agriculture and forestry	6.2	5.7	6.8	6.8	5.6	4.8
Construction	10.2	10.2	7.7	8.8	8.5	8.0
Transport and communications	14.2	15.4	7.3	8.6	8.6	8.8
Trade and public catering	14.6	14.3	11.9	9.8	9.9	10.1
Other	17.2	14.5	20.9	23.0	22.7	22.4
Net taxes on output	10.5	14.8	14.1	12.7	11.8	11.8

*Estimates of the Moscow Regional Government

According to the Moscow Regional Government, the following sectors account for the bulk of regional budget revenue: industry – 32%, retail and public catering – 13%, transport – 7%, and construction – 5%.

3.2. MAJOR ECONOMIC GROWTH PROJECTIONS

The focus area for regional development is structural reform of its economy through operational upgrade, launching of new operating facilities in subsidized municipalities, and the transition to production of finished goods that are competitive at both domestic and international markets.

The blueprint for economic development in the Moscow Region is set forth in the Conceptual Framework for Social and Economic Development, 1997–2005, adopted by the Moscow Regional Duma on June 25, 1997. The Framework stipulates the following areas for development:

Industry: attract strategic investors; build a legal and tax regime ensuring investment stability in such sectors as energy, chemicals, petrochemicals, furniture manufacturing, cryogen machine engineering, instrument engineering, including diamond instruments, and companies undergoing conversion and introducing dual purpose technology. These sectors will provide for further development based on self-financing and industrial diversification.

Agriculture: maintain specialized seed and cattle breeding enterprises, revive and expand all types of cooperation, including farms, processing and sales agricultural companies, and credit and insurance companies, using modern organizational structures, such as agricultural firms and concerns; stimulate competition, provide financial aid to strengthen and develop various companies; develop the processing sector by constructing mini-plants, mini-facilities, and mini-bakeries using own raw material, expand the product range and improve the quality of finished goods, and develop the sales network and sales market; provide milk-cattle breeding with concentrated fodder, improve the range and quality of crops grown in the Region; refurbish agricultural machinery through leasing; develop a system of short- and long-term mortgage lending, insurance of producers, and pledging of agricultural produce.

Trade: develop the infrastructure of the Moscow Region's markets, including warehousing, wholesale markets, and trade exchanges, and arrange stocking of locally produced agricultural produce;

Transport: gradually develop the transport infrastructure for better serving consumers and assist in strengthening the material and technical base of transport companies.

Construction: accelerate construction of priority social facilities; utilize local resources to expand output of building materials; implement a program for the development of roadside and airport services; introduce a system of construction project assessment in relation to compliance with ecological and safety requirements.

Residential construction: transition to a proactive investment policy focused on social issues and envisaging extension of the sources of financing, an increase in the share of extra budgetary investment, upgrade of operating facilities in construction, and re-focusing on output of assemblies and materials compliant with modern to construction requirements.

Housing and communal services: gradual transition to a new system of housing rent and payment for communal services to offer protection to low income population, introduce energy saving technology, materials and assemblies, introduce individual water, heat, and gas consumption metering, develop inter-district water supply systems; complete gas network extension in rural areas; gradually reconstruct residential buildings, and introduce alternative communal services.

Information and communications: integrate existing information systems and resources to create a unified information and telecommunication system with access to overseas information systems and develop an automated system of land and municipal construction registers.

Research and development policy: create a favorable regulatory base and investment environment for research and development companies engaged in high-tech innovative activities; encourage the development of new technologies in energy and resource saving, environmental protection, land plotting, construction, agriculture, and medical equipment; develop and implement a program for "science city" development (the cities of Dubna and Korolev).

External economic relations: develop partnership relations with foreign companies and regions of industrially developed countries, search for new prospective sales markets; increase the role of foreign trade in economy restructuring and develop conditions for steady economic growth.

Property management: develop favorable conditions and mechanisms for national capital accumulation and transformation into real investment, assist in the implementation of investment programs involving national corporate capital, support investment activity of medium-sized and small enterprise, and gradually increase foreign investment.

Investment policy: create conditions conducive to capital inflow, increase efficiency of corporate and private funds; develop modern organizational and legal forms of capital raising, such as international consortia, venture funds, or leasing companies; develop state insurance of foreign investors against non-commercial risks.

Tax policy: steadily reduce profit tax and abolish value added tax.

Small enterprise: create conditions conducive to the development of a legal framework for small enterprise base, including tax optimization; develop the small enterprise support infrastructure.

3.3. INDUSTRIAL OUTPUT IN 1997–2002 FOR MAJOR SECTORS OF ECONOMY

The leading industrial sectors of the Moscow Region are machine engineering and metal processing, food and beverages, chemicals and petrochemicals, building materials, forestry, timber, and furniture. Their combined output accounts for 76% of the Region's total industrial output.

Machine engineering and metal processing. The sector accounts for 26.8% of total industrial output. The Region's machine engineering sector is represented by nearly all types of operations. Moscow Region enterprises produce machines and equipment for ferrous metals, energy, construction, transport, agriculture, and light industry sectors (Mytischi, Lyubertsy, Podolsk, Kolomna, Dmitrov, Yegoryevsk), as well as radio electric and space equipment (Korolev, Reutov), and nuclear machinery (Electrostal, Podolsk). The Region also boasts enterprises in the optical-mechanical sector (Krasnogorsk, Sergiev Posad, and Lytkarino).

2002 output increased 15.1% year-on-year. Excavator output increased 60%, subway carriages – 50%, elevators – 29.5%, cars – 3.9%, and trucks – 2.4%. The major companies within the sector are: OAO Machine Engineering Plant (Electrostal), OAO KhK Kolomna Plant, OOO ROSTAR, OAO Demikhovsky Machine Engineering Plant , ZAO Metrovagonmash, OAO Machine Engineering Plant ZiO-Podolsk, ZAO Podolskabel, OAO Electrostal Heavy Machinery Plant,

Industry breakdown of industrial output in 1997–2002, % to total						TABLE 4
	1997	1998	1999	2000	2001	2002
Industry	100.0	100.0	100.0	100.0	100.0	100.0
Machine engineering and metal processing	32.8	26.4	32.3	30.4	29.6	26.8
Food and beverages	18.2	20.8	20.3	20.3	22.8	26.7
Chemicals and petrochemicals	11.0	8.8	10.4	9.6	9.2	8.2
Construction materials	8.3	8.0	7.0	8.1	7.6	8.0
Forestry, timber, and pulp and paper	4.9	5.5	6.3	6.4	6.6	6.3
Non-ferrous metals	2.0	1.8	2.4	6.3	5.9	5.2
Light industry	6.1	5.5	5.0	5.6	5.5	4.3
Energy	8.1	14.9	8.5	4.2	4.2	4.3
Ferrous metals	3.4	3.1	2.9	4.1	3.7	3.4
Fuel	0.2	0.1	0.2	0.1	0.1	0.1

I

CENTRAL FEDERAL DISTRICT

and OAO Chekhov Energy Machine Engineering Plant. ZAO Metrovagonmash has recently launched serial output of new generation subway carriages.

Food and beverages. The sector accounts for 26.7% of total industrial output. 2002 output grew 18.2% year-on-year: cheese production increased 27.4 times, mayonnaise – 7 times, dairy products – 1.8 times, confectionery – 1.3 times, non-alcoholic beverages – 1.2 times, pasta – 1.3 times, sausage – 1.2 times, and semi-finished meat products – 1.3 times. The upgrading of production facilities has enabled food and beverages and food processing companies to expand their product range and improve the quality of their output. The leading companies within the sector are OOO Mars, ZAO Klin Meat Processing Plant, ZAO Klin Brewery, OAO Istra Bakery, OAO Kolomna Experimental Meat Processing Plant, OAO Ramensky Meat Processing Plant, OAO Sergiev Posad Meat Processing Plant, OAO Podolsk Experimental Flour Mill, and OAO Noginsk Bakery.

Chemicals and petrochemicals. The share of the sector in total industrial output is 8.2%. The sector is focused on the production of mineral fertilizers, insecticides, plastic, chemical fiber, paint, and varnish. 2002 output grew 8.7% year-on-year thanks to an increase in synthetic resin and plastic production (19.2%) and increased output of plastic goods (56.4%). The leading companies are located in Voskresensk, Schelkovo, Klin, Serpukhov, Orekhovo-Zuevo, and Sergiev Posad. The major companies are OAO Mineral Fertilizers, ZAO Sergiev Posad Paint and Varnish Plant, OAO Mosstroiplastmass, OAO Chemical Fiber, OAO Carbolate, ZAO Eletroizolit, OAO Odintsovo Paint and Varnish Plant, OAO Phosphate, and OAO Stupino Glass Plastic Plant.

Construction materials. The sector accounts for 8% of total industrial output. The Moscow Region is the largest producer of building materials in the Central Federal District. Some 1,000 companies, including small enterprises, are engaged in the production of building materials. The Region produces nearly all types of main building materials and goods. 2002 output grew 19.3% year-on-year. The following materials saw considerable output growth: asbestos and cement sheeting (15.1%), ceramic facing tiles (68.9%), cement (9.4%), reinforced concrete assemblies and parts (24.3%), and foam fillers (13.9%).

Forestry, timber, and pulp and paper. The sector accounts for 6.3% of total industrial output. The largest furniture producers are OAO MK Shatura and ZAO Electrogorskmebel. OAO MK Shatura is the largest Russian producer of home and office furniture with a market share of some 12%. 2002 sales exceeded $103 million. The company sells its products at over 500 retail outlets in Russia and CIS.

ZAO Electrogorskmebel is a large company with diversified operations comprising a laminated board plant, a furniture factory, and chipboard and resin plants. ZAO Electrogorskmebel's trademark is well known in 75 of Russia's regions and across the CIS. Its main output is kitchen furniture. The company also produces wardrobes, furniture for halls and living rooms, desks, computer desks, etc. The company annually exports furniture to Germany, Belgium, and Austria.

Light industry. The share of this sector in total industrial output is 4.3%. The Region specializes in the production of cotton, wool, and silk fabric and knitwear.

The light industry sector is represented by 160 companies employing a total of 57,700 people. In 2002 (compared to 2001 figures), carpet and carpet goods production increased by 42.2%, silk fabric – by 7.9%, and clothes output grew as well. At the same time, footwear output fell by 10%, knitwear – by 11.6%, and cotton fabric – by 11.3%. Leading companies are situated in Balashikha,

Ramenskoye, Orekhovo-Zuevo, Pavlovsky Posad, Noginsk, Naro-Fominsk, Lyubertsy, Serpukhov, and Voskresensk. The largest companies are OAO GK Oretex, ZAO Textile Firm Oka, ZAO Textile Firm Kupavna, ZAO Narfomshelk, ZAO Lyubertsy Carpets, OAO Pavlovo-Posadsky Kamvolshik, ZAO Serpukhov Textile, OAO Yegoryevsk Cotton Fabric Factory, ZAO Voskresensk Technotkan, and ZAO Ivanteevka Knitwear.

Electricity. Electricity accounts for 4.3% of total industrial output. 2002 electricity output amounted to 21.6 billion kWh (95.2% of 2001 output). The Region operates the Kashirskaya and Shaturskaya GRES; TPS 22 (Dzerzhinsky), TPS 17 (Stupino), GRES 3 (Electrogorsk), and others.

Ferrous metals. The sector accounts for 3.4% of total industrial output. 2002 output increased by 11.1% year-on-year. Cold rolled steel strip output grew 2.8 times, steel net – 1.2 times, finished rolled steel – 1.2 times. One of the largest companies is OAO Electrostal Metal Plant.

Agriculture. The Region's agricultural sector has suburban specialization and intensive agriculture, and boasts the best tillage and livestock rearing efficiency in the Central Federal District. Livestock rearing is the leading sector, with dairy and beef cattle rearing, pig breeding, and poultry the leading subsectors. The Region's stock of poultry totals 40 million heads of chickens. The Region's agricultural companies supply some 3% of Russia's total output of milk and some 2% of its total meat output. Fodder dominates the tillage sector. Fodder crops cover three fifths of the total area under crops. Grain cultivation, which accounts for a quarter of crop output in the south of the Region, is developing steadily, as is potato cultivation and market gardening (mainly in the district adjoining Moscow). The average yield is: grain – 1,500 kg per hectare, potato – 12,100 kg per hectare, and vegetables – 18,100 kg per hectare.

Construction. In 2002, 3.2 million square meters of housing were put into use, which constitutes 14% growth year-on-year. The 2003 plan envisages the construction of 2.9 million square meters of living space from various sources of financing.

Transport. Transport is a leading sector of the Region's economy, employing some 6% of its total workforce and concentrating over 20% of fixed assets.

Road transport plays the leading role in the Region's transportation system. Some 5 million passengers are transported by road every year, making road transport the major form of passenger transit in the Region. The community shuttle fleet exceeds 4,700 buses and operates 1,300 local routes over a total route network exceeding 32,000 km. State company Mostransavto, whose fleet is scattered throughout most of the Region, is the passenger road transport operator in the Moscow Region.

Trucks account for some 70% of total freight transportation in the Region. Transport branches of

OAO Mosoblavtotrans operate a fleet of 4,000 vehicles. Commercial companies and individual truck owners have a pool of 76,000 trucks at their disposal.

According to the Moscow Regional Government, 2002 passenger turnover grew 11.4% year-on-year, and freight turnover amounted to 85.7% of the previous year's figure.

Wholesale and retail. The Moscow Region boasts some 489 wholesale companies, 40,000 retail outlets, 2,900 public catering facilities, 313 retail consumer markets, and 6,400 household service companies. Retail sales account for the largest share of turnover. Moscow is the major supplier of the Region. The Moscow Region satisfies 15% of Moscow's demand for food.

2002 retail turnover amounted to over $4.8 billion, 6% more than the year before. In accordance with the The Provincial Ring Program, major shopping centers have been established along the Moscow Ring Road: Auchan, Veimart, IKEA, Mega, Crocus City, and Gulfstream. An investment project for building wholesale and retail outlets and a network of distribution centers along the second ring road is underway.

Small enterprise. Small business is widely spread in retail, construction sector, and information technology. At the same time, small enterprise is weak in such important industrial areas as transport, communications, agriculture, and social and household services.

At the moment, the Moscow Region has over 47,000 small enterprises employing 263,400 people. All in all over 429,000 people, including individual entrepreneurs, are engaged in small enterprise. Some 30% of them work in industry, 23% – in retail and public catering, 14% – in construction, 7% – in transport, and 4% – in research and development.

Tourism. The Moscow Region has high potential for attracting tourists over and above that enjoyed by many European states. The Region has more than 7,000 historical and cultural sites, more than 200 mansions, 97 museums, 26 folk art centers, and 22 historical cities.

The Moscow Region operates over 300 tourist centers and motels, recreational centers belonging to organizations, and 270 tourist agencies. Some 73 hotels service tourist and guests of the Region. Dozens of tourist and excursion routes cross the Region.

Recreational and resort facilities. Recreation is a major business in the Moscow Region. The main driver for the development of the recreational and resort facilities is demand in the capital for recreation and resort facilities in the country. The Moscow Region has everything necessary to expand various types of recreation and rehabilitation centers, and its recreational resources range from its favorable temperate climate to its picturesque landscape.

The Region runs 150 rehabilitation centers, 160 desease prevention and treatment centers, 160 recreational centers and lodgings, and 470 summer camps for children.

3.4. FUEL AND ENERGY BALANCE (OUTPUT AND CONSUMPTION PER RESOURCE)

The Moscow Region is an energy deficit region. Electricity consumption exceeds output by 1.4–1.5 times.

3.5. TRANSPORT INFRASTRUCTURE

The Moscow Region enjoys a developed transport infrastructure. The railroad density exceeds the average for the country 8–10-fold and the density of paved public highway is 15% higher than the nationwide average and is twice as high as the Central Federal District's.

Fuel and energy sector production and consumption trends, 1997–2002						TABLE 5
	1997	1998	1999	2000	2001	2002*
Electricity output, billion kWh	19.0	19.5	20.0	20.6	22.7	21.6
Electricity consumption, billion kWh	27.4	27.4	27.6	30.2	33.0	34.3
Natural gas consumption, million cubic meters	11,230.0	9,146.0	8,580.0	8,870.0	10,265.0	10,127.0

*Estimates of the Moscow Regional Government

Roads. The Region has 12,500 kilometers of paved public highway. Some 18 federal highways with a total length of 2,400 kilometers cross the Region. The Region's federal road network is comprised of 13 radial highways originating in Moscow and two cement-paved ring roads – the small Moscow circle 50 kilometers from the center of Moscow and the large Moscow circle 80 kilometers from the Moscow Ring Road.

Radial roads link the capital to major Russian cities, and five of them lead to the border of the Russian Federation. The ring highways provide transport links within the Region and lift the transport burden off Moscow and main segments of the radial routes.

In recent years, the share of intercity and international transportation in the total transportation flow in the Moscow Region increased to 10%.

The growing intensity of transport flows exceeds the throughput capacity and technical parameters of major highway sections. In order to increase highway throughput, the united board of the Moscow and the Moscow Region administrations has developed a plan for the development of radial and circle highways within a 50-kilometer radius around Moscow.

Railroads. The Moscow Region is served by four branches of the Moscow Railroad and a branch of the Oktyabrskaya Railroad operating 2,178 kilometers of railroads, 12 locomotive and five carriage depots, and 200 railway stations. The railroad network comprises eleven main routes linked to the Region's ring railroad.

Transportation to and from Moscow plays a leading role in the Region's railroad structure.

The program for strengthening railroad infrastructure and upgrading the rolling stock of the Moscow railroad has been allocated a budget of $84.1 million for 2000–2003.

Airports. The Region is served by three local and two international airports providing freight and passenger transportation. The Vnukovo and Sheremetyevo airports are under Moscow's jurisdiction, while Domodedovo, Bykovo, and Myachkovo officially belong to the Moscow Region.

River ports. The Moscow water transport junction operates five ports, including the Northern, Southern, and Western ports located in Moscow and two regional ports in Serpukhov and Kolomna. Moreover, the Northern Port manages a cargo area, including the Dmitrov Terminal located at the Moscow Canal and the Great Volga terminal.

The main water routes of the Region are the Moscow Canal, the Moskva river, and the Oka river. The system of locks and hydro junctions on the Moskva and Oka rivers provides access to the Volga navigation system. The Moscow – Volga Canal ensures access to five seas: the Sea of Azov, the Baltic Sea, the White Sea, the Caspian Sea, and the Black Sea. The length of the Region's waterways is 580 kilometers. The Region's canals are up to 4 meters deep, and thus are suitable for any type of modern river vessels.

Oil and gas pipelines. Single thread oil pipelines Ryazan – Moscow and Yaroslavl – Moscow, a three-thread trunk pipeline called the Moscow Ring, and a two-thread trunk pipeline Ryazan – Moscow cross the Region. Two circles of oil product mainlines comprised of an aviation kerosene pipeline, gasoline pipeline, and diesel pipeline, all laid in circles, and a natural gas pipeline with multiple bends go through Yakhroma, Noginsk, Serpukhov, and Solnechnogorsk.

3.6. MAIN NATURAL RESOURCES: RESERVES AND EXTRACTION IN 2002

The main natural resources of the Moscow Region are cement raw materials, fire resistant, fusible, and non-fusible clay, facing stones, phosphorus, dolomite, mineral wool raw materials, construction stone, carbonate construction and lime pre-treatment rock, expanded clay aggregate, construction and silicon sand and gravel, quartz sand, fresh underground water and mineral springs, therapeutic mud, peat, and sapropel. All in all, the Region has discovered 871 deposits of mineral resources, of which it currently operates 375, including 22 deposits of construction stones and 23 deposits of clay and loam. The Region is rich in some 1,700 peat deposits.

Underground water. The Region features intensive protracted exploitation of its underground fresh water located in the coal water-bearing strata. Considerable water reserves are concentrated in the north-western and western parts of the Region, and their stratified formation enables the building of water reservoirs. The Ruza-Zvenigorod and Sestri-no-Istra water reservoirs play the main role in the Region's water reserve maintenance. The Region has explored 252 underground water deposits with a total exploitation reserve of 8,824,000 cubic meters per day. Underground water meets 85% of total demand for water.

Sand and gravel. The Region is rich in 69 deposits of sand and gravel with a total reserve of 793 million cubic meters, including 39 operating deposits with reserves of 605 million cubic meters.

Forests. Forests cover over 2 million hec-tare, including 41% of areas suitable for felling, which are continuously decreasing.

4. TRADE OPPORTUNITIES

4.1. MAIN GOODS
PRODUCED IN THE REGION

The main types of industrial output as of 2002:

Food and beverages. Bread – 410,000 tons, con-fectionery – 124,000 tons, ethanol – 1.4 million decali-ters, vodka and liquor – 13.9 million decaliters, canned fruit and vegetables – 600 million conventional cans, meat, including category one sub-products – 72,100 tons, dairy products – 511,000 tons, dry milk and powder mix for infants – 8,100 tons, and flour – 401,000 tons.

Machine engineering and metal processing. 2,800 elevators, 23 sections of mainline locomotives, 301 railway carriages, 114 subway carriages, 243,800 low yield electrical motors, 700,600 lead automotive batteries, 12,100 household sewing machines, 97,800 kitchen appliances, and 214,000 vacuum cleaners.

Automotive products. 19,400 cars and 1,600 buses.

Chemicals and petrochemicals. Mineral fer-tilizers – 460,000 tons, synthetic resin and plastic – 129,600 tons, paint and varnish – 61,500 tons.

Pharmaceuticals. Medicines – $117.9 million.

Construction materials. Cement – 2.5 mil-lion tons, 116 million asbestos and cement sheets (roofing), reinforced concrete assemblies and goods – 1,208,000 cubic meters, bricks – 604 million, tiles – 5.8 million square meters, ceramic toilet accessories – 764,000, linoleum – 8.3 million square meters;

Forestry, timber, and pulp and paper. Chip-board – 572,000 cubic meters.

Light industry. Cotton fabric – 187 million square meters, wool fabric – 12.5 million square me-ters, silk fabric – 16.3 million square meters, hosiery – 27.7 million pairs, and footwear – 1.7 million pairs.

Glass and porcelain. 52.3 million porcelain majolica tableware goods.

4.2. EXPORTS, INCLUDING EXTRA-CIS

1999 exports to extra-CIS countries reached $1,624.9 million. Exports to the CIS totaled $136.2 million. The corresponding figures for 2000 were $1,860.7 million and $219.1 million, $1,233 million and $359.4 million for 2001, and, according to the Moscow Regional Government, $1,100 million and $200 million for 2002.

The main types of goods exported by the Region in 2002 were: machine engineering products ($501.7 million), ferrous and non-ferrous metals ($303.2 million), petrochemicals ($166 million), min-eral fertilizers, and cement. Major importers of the Region's products include China (2002 export amounted to $148.1 million and constituted 2.4 times growth year-on-year), Ukraine ($143.5 million, 1.2 times drop), India ($117.5 million, 1.3 times growth), the USA ($90.1 million, 1.1 times growth), and Germany ($79.2 million, 1.5 times drop).

4.3. IMPORTS,
INCLUDING EXTRA-CIS

1999 imports from extra-CIS countries reached $1,013.7 million. Imports from CIS coun-tries totaled $363.2 million. The corresponding figures for 2000 were $1,496.8 million and $612.5 million, $2,039.7 million and $484.6 million for 2001, and, according to the estimates of the Moscow Regional Government, $2,700 million and $400 million for 2002.

The bulk of 2002 regional imports was repre-sented by machinery ($984.8 million), food and beverages ($627.2 million), and petrochemicals ($545 million). The main import partners are: Germany ($616.6 million), Italy ($229 million), Poland ($204.1 million, 1.7 times growth year-on-year), Ukraine ($177.5 million, 1.1 times drop), and China ($163.3 million, 1.9 times growth).

4.4. MAJOR REGIONAL
EXPORT AND IMPORT ENTITIES

Due to the specific features of trade in the Region, mainly industrial companies perform export and import operations.

5. INVESTMENT OPPORTUNITIES

5.1. INVESTMENTS IN 1992–2002 (BY INDUSTRY SECTOR), INCLUDING FOREIGN INVESTMENTS

The following factors determine the investment appeal of the Moscow Region:

- Its advantageous geographic location (nearly all of Russia's transit routes pass through the Moscow Region);
- Its developed transport infrastructure;
- Its considerable industrial, agricultural, and research and development potential;
- Legislation supporting investment activities;
- Its highly qualified workforce (high professional level of employees in the research and development sector and high general level of education);

- Favorable climate and availability of recreation facilities.

The investment climate in the Moscow Region is gradually improving: Moody's has increased the Region's foreign currency credit rating from B3 to B2. At the same time, the Region enjoys the sovereign foreign currency credit rating of B2. The rating outlook is stable.

5.2. CAPITAL INVESTMENT

Industry, transport, and communications account for the lion's share of capital investment.

Total foreign investment in the Region's economy amounts to some $3 billion. The bulk of investment is channeled to the food and beverage sector, reaching some $380 million in 2001–2002.

Capital investment by industry sector, $ million						*TABLE 6*
	1997	1998	1999	2000	2001	2002
Total capital investment	2,445	2,109	1,505	1,808	1,806	1,909
Including major industries (% of total)						
Industry	22.8	33.7	25.6	21.7	34.9	37.3
Agriculture and forestry	3.3	4.2	4.7	3.9	4.5	4.8
Construction	3.5	16.0	2.9	2.9	4.5	4.1
Transport and communications	22.3	16.7	34.2	47.9	24.1	16.0
Trade and public catering	1.2	0.9	3.9	2.7	6.5	5.6
Other	46.9	28.5	28.7	20.9	25.5	32.2

Foreign investment trends in 1997–2002						*TABLE 7*
	1997	1998	1999	2000	2001	2002
Foreign investment, $ million	74.5	708.7	443.8	290.6	372.7	690.0
Including FDI, $ million	72.1	637.1	390.0	204.9	312.7	589.1

5.3. MAJOR ENTERPRISES (INCLUDING ENTERPRISES WITH FOREIGN INVESTMENT)

The Region has registered more than 1,000 companies with foreign investment. Major companies with foreign investment include OOO KRKA-RUS (medicines), ZAO ODIKHEL (paint and varnish), OOO ROSTAR (aluminum cans), and others.

Such renowned investors as Saint Gobain, Auchan, Michelin, and Royal Canine have invested in the Moscow Region. Nestle, IKEA, PepsiCo, Mars, and FM Logistic are expanding their operations in the Region. The following major companies operate branches in the Region: British Petroleum, BMW, DaimlerChrysler, Danone, and Ehrmann.

According to the Moscow Regional Government, the output growth rates of companies with

foreign investment are twice as high as those of domestic companies.

5.4. MOST ATTRACTIVE SECTORS FOR INVESTMENT

Food and beverages, construction materials, trade and public catering, housing and communal services, and healthcare are the most appealing sectors for investors.

5.5. CURRENT LEGISLATION ON INVESTOR TAX EXEMPTIONS AND PRIVILEGES

The investment policy of the Moscow Regional Government is based on the Social and Economic Development Conceptual Framework for the Moscow Region, 1997–2005.

The Region has adopted the following laws related to investment activity: On Guarantees for Investment Activity in the Moscow Region, On Tax Privileges in the Moscow Region, and On Moscow Region's Debt. These

Largest enterprises of the Moscow Region	TABLE 8
COMPANY	**SECTOR**
OAO Electrostal, Electrostal	Ferrous metals
OAO Machine Engineering Plant ZiO-Podolsk, Podolsk	Boilers
OAO Podolsk Non-Ferrous Metal Plant, Podolsk	Secondary non-ferrous metals
ZAO Stupino Metal Company, Stupino District	Aluminum, magnum, and titanium roll
ZAO Metrovagonmash, Mytischi	Machine engineering
ZAO Klin Meat Processing Plant, Klin	Food and beverages
ZAO Klin Brewery, Klin District	Food and beverages
ZAO PBKM Naro-Fominsk, Naro-Fominsk District	Metal goods
OAO MSZ, Electrostal	Rare metals
OOO Ehrmann, Ramensky District	Food and beverages
OOO ROSTAR, Dmitrov District	Metal goods
OOO Nestle Zhukovsky Ice Cream, Zhukovsky	Food and beverages
OOO Campina, Stupino District	Food and beverages

laws aim to facilitate investment activity and develop procedures for granting tax privileges.

The Region has developed a draft investment policy framework through 2010 and a draft law On Investment Activity in the Moscow Region. The draft law envisages various forms of state support for investors, such as budget credits, state guarantees, investment tax credits, and investment tax privileges.

With a view to attracting investment into subsidized districts, the Region has prepared a legal initiative to grant tax privileges to organizations (including foreign entities) carrying out investment activity in specific districts. The initiative envisages tax exemptions from land tax on land plots used for the construction of manufacturing, social, or cultural facilities.

Regional entities responsible for raising investment		TABLE 9
ENTITY	**ADDRESS**	**PHONE, FAX, E-MAIL**
Ministry of External Economic Relations of the Moscow Region	10, ul. Sretenka, Moscow, 107045	Phone: (095) 727 1352 Fax: (095) 727 1349 E-mail: ictcamo@orc.ru
OAO Moscow Regional Investment Trust Company	Building 1, 9/1/1, per. Armyansky, Moscow, 101990	Phone: (095) 540 1203 Fax: (095) 207 8647
OAO Mortgage Corporation of the Moscow Region	130, Mozhaiskoye shosse, Odintsovo, Moscow Region, 143000	Phone: (095) 596 3421, 596 2398 Fax: (095) 596 3410 E-mail: iipoteka@online.ru
International Association of Business Cooperation	8 floor, IABC Office, 1, ul. Leningradskaya, Khimki, Moscow Region, 141400	Phone: (095) 572 3078, 572 4104 Fax: (095) 575 4562 E-mail: info@iabc.ru

5.6. FEDERAL AND REGIONAL ECONOMIC AND SOCIAL DEVELOPMENT PROGRAMS FOR THE MOSCOW REGION

Federal targeted programs. The Moscow Region is implementing several federal targeted programs. The Region has joined the federal targeted program Prevention and Elimination of Social Deceases, 2002–2006 and its subprograms Preventive Vaccination and Urgent Measures for the Prevention of Tuberculosis in Russia.

The Region is implementing the federal targeted program Upgrade of Russia's Transport System, 2002–2010, which aims to develop the Moscow air transport junction and the regional airport network.

The federal targeted program Energy Efficient Economy, 2002–2005 and through 2010 aims to construct a hydro accumulating power station in the Moscow Region and create a 2.6 Gcal/h demonstration central heating unit in Krasnoznamensk.

The program also envisages an upgrade. of heating systems by introducing non-channel network laying technology, automating central and private heating units, utilizing effective heat insulation materials and designs, diagnosing pipeline conditions, and transition to closed heat supply systems in Zhukovsky, Dubna, Mytischi, Dmitrov, and Korolev. The Region intends to develop energy effective heating systems for state companies and organizations based on new generation heliocollectors (Moscow Cardiology Center, Bykovo).

Regional programs. Some 44 regional targeted programs currently underway play an important role in the implementation of the Moscow Regional Government's economic and social policy. In 2003, regional budget funds will be allocated to the implementation of 34 regional targeted programs in various spheres of the economy: industry, agriculture, environmental rehabilitation, education, culture, healthcare, sports, social policy, and others.

To attract foreign investment, the Moscow Region is developing an investment portfolio for the retail sector (the Programs for the Development of Consumer Sales and Service Market in the Moscow Region through 2008, and Construction of Multipurpose Trade and Entertainment Centers to European Standards in the Cities of the Moscow Region, 2003–2007); environment and natural resources (Development of a Network of Companies Collecting, Utilizing, and Recycling Tractors and Vehicles and Large-Sized Metal Constructions in the Moscow Region, 2003–2007, Collection and Recycling of Lead Acid Batteries and Lead Bearing Waste in the Moscow Region, 2003–2010); transport and communications (Development of the Moscow Aviation Junction Infrastructure, 2002–2020, Development of Communications and Telecommunication Systems in the Moscow Region, 2003–2007, and Development of the Transport System in the Moscow Region, 2004–2007).

Emphasis is given to the Moscow Regional investment Program for the Development of Consumer Sales and Service Market in the Moscow Region through 2008, which aims to improve living standards by providing consumers with quality goods and services at affordable prices and to European standards. The Program is comprised of several sub-programs:

The sub-programs for transport infrastructure development have major objectives of constructing parking lots for trucks, warehouse terminals, repair shops, gas stations, etc.;

The sub-programs for trade network development aim to locate wholesale and small batch companies along highways and in the Regional cities, develop retail facilities (super- and minimarkets and discount stores), develop a network of specialized stores selling household appliances, furniture, clothes, footwear, children's goods, and expand services (trade and entertainment centers, restaurants, cafés, hotels, hairdressing salons, laundries, and tailors');

The sub-program for tourism, recreation, and resort development aims to reconstruct and develop the existing lodgings and rehabilitation centers, construct a network of hotels and motels, and develop the infrastructure of public and children's parks.

The program of the Moscow Regional Government for the Assistance in the Reform of Military Industrial Companies Located in the Moscow Region, 2003–2006 has been approved.

To solve the problem of energy supply, the Moscow Region has developed an Energy Development Program for the Moscow Region through 2010. The Program aims to upgrade the sector, increase output of cheap electricity to improve energy supply reliability, and build prerequisites for further economic growth.

The Moscow Regional Tourism Committee has developed a regional targeted program for the Development of Tourism in the Moscow Region, 2002–2005. The Program aims to make tourism a profitable industry of the Regional economy, develop tourism infrastructure, create a balanced market for tourist services, and meet demand for tourist and recreational services.

The Region has prepared a draft targeted program for the Support and Development of Small Enterprise, 2003–2004. Among the measures for the development of small enterprise are the improvement of the legislative and regulatory base, the implementation of effective business projects, the development of a network of municipal funds for the support of small enterprise and large cooperatives, and the development of exhibitions and fairs.

In order to reduce the number of programs and improve their quality, the Moscow Regional Government has issued a resolution limiting the number of regional targeted programs. The resolution lists 17 programs to be developed in the first half of 2003 and implemented as of 2004.

CENTRAL FEDERAL DISTRICT

6. INVESTMENT PROJECTS

CENTRAL FEDERAL DISTRICT

I

Industry sector and project description	1) Expected results 2) Amount and term of investment 3) Form of financing[1] 4) Documentation[2]	Contact information
1	2	3

NON-FERROUS METALS

10R001 ● ▲

Company upgrade and technical refurbishment. Project goal: to ensure the company's stable operation through an increase in sales of competitive goods, expanded sales markets and profit growth.	1) 6,000 series alloy bars – 300 tons per month, alloy profiles – 200 tons per month, rolled aluminum alloy sheets – 500 tons per month, forged and pressed goods – 100 tons per month, 2) $8 million/6 months 3) L 4) FS	OAO Stupino Metals Company 19, ul. Pristantsionnaya, Stupino, Moscow Region, 142800 Phone: (096) 644 7027 (from Moscow and the Moscow Region – (264) 47 027) Fax: (095) 262 1416 E-mail: info@smk.ru Vladimir Vasilyevich Prokofyev, CEO

CHEMICALS AND PETROCHEMICALS

10R002 ■ ● ❖ ◆

Production of carbon-carbon composite materials. Project goal: to supply aviation, energy, automotive, metal, and chemical companies with composite materials.	1) Revenue of up to $0.9 million per year 2) $3.4 million/4 years 3) L, JV, E 4) BP	OOO NPP Teplotekhnika Appt. 6, pr. Lenina, Krasnoarmeysk, Moscow Region, 141292 Phone: (096) 537 2542 (from Moscow and the Moscow Region – (253) 72 542) Fax: (095) 941 1276 Georgy Georgievich Smirnov, Director

MACHINE ENGINEERING AND METAL PROCESSING

10R003 ■ ● ❖ ◆

Comprehensive production of photoelectric systems. Project goal: to produce high quality premium-class solar and electronic silicon.	1) Net profit of $1.2 million per year 2) $3.8 million/9 months 3) L, JV, E 4) BP	Federal State Unitary Company NPO Machine Engineering 33, ul. Gagarina, Reutov, Moscow Region, 143966 Phone: (095) 302 1185, 302 3194 Fax: (095) 302 2001 E-mail: smpc@npomash.ru Herbert Alexandrovich Yefremov, CEO

10R004 ■ ● ❖ ◆

Comprehensive production of 12 MW photoelectric systems. Project goal: to develop advanced solar energy systems based on photoelectric crystal silicon transformers.	1) Revenue of up to $90 million per year 2) $20 million/13 months 3) L, JV, E 4) BP	Federal State Unitary Company NPO Machine Engineering 33, ul. Gagarina, Reutov, Moscow Region, 143966 Phone: (095) 302 1185, 302 3194 Fax: (095) 302 2001 E-mail: smpc@npomash.ru Herbert Alexandrovich Yefremov, CEO

10R005 ● ◆

Serial production of equipment to sort and utilize industrial, construction, and household waste. Project goal: to produce waste utilization equipment.	1) n/a 2) $7 million/21 months 3) L 4) BP	ZAO ROSSKETMASH 35, ul. Gagarina, Reutov, Moscow Region, 143966 Phone/fax: (095) 302 5488, 528 1466 Yemelyan Davydovich Kamen, CEO

[1] L – Loan, E – Equity, Leas. – Leasing, JV – Joint Venture
[2] BP – Business Plan, FS – Feasibility Study

1	2	3

10R006

Technical upgrade and expansion
of electrical and technical equipment output.
Project goal: to supply federal and industrial
targeted programs of the RF Ministry
of Atomic Energy with competitive electrical
and technical equipment.

1) n/a
2) $1.6 million/2.5 years
3) L
4) BP

OAO Protvino Experimental
Plant Progress
3, ul. Zheleznodorozhnaya,
Protvino, Moscow Region, 142280
Phone: (096) 774 0644
(from Moscow and the Moscow
Region – (27) 74 0644)
Fax: (096) 774 1611 (from Moscow and
the Moscow Region – (27) 74 1611)
E-mail: office@progress.serpuhov.su;
Oleg Fedorovich Makarov, CEO

10R007

Production of ceramic tractive devices
for the cable sector.
Project goal: to produce extra-strong
ceramic pulling devices for cable sector
drawing machines.

1) 26,000 items per year, revenue of
up to $2.2 million per year
2) $2 million/18 months
3) L, E
4) BP

Federal State Unitary Company
NPO Luch
24, ul. Zheleznodorozhnaya,
Podolsk, Moscow Region, 142100
Phone: (095) 715 9449, 715 9258
Fax: (095) 239 1749
E-mail: sdi@luch.podolsk.ru
Ivan Ivanovich Fedik, CEO

10R008

Serial production of sorting and recycling
equipment for construction and household
waste recycling.
Project goal: to produce recycling equipment.

1) Revenue of up to $20 million
per year
2) $15 million/3 years
3) L
4) BP

ZAO ROSSKETMASH
35, ul. Gagarina, Reutov,
Moscow Region, 143966
Phone/fax: (095) 302 5488, 528 1466
Yemelyan Davydovich Kamen, CEO

FORESTRY, TIMBER, AND PULP AND PAPER

10R009

Production of export lumber.
Project goal: to produce lumber
to world standards.

1) Up to 15,000 cubic meters
per year
2) $1 million/4 months
3) L
4) BP

OOO ETOS-F
35, ul. Gagarina, Reutov,
Moscow Region, 143966
Phone: (095) 528 5737, 528 3341
Fax: (095) 528 7763
E-mail: businessgrad@rambler.ru
Felix Edmontovich Santuryan, CEO
Yury Sergeevich Kozlov,
Executive Director

10R010

Production of ecologically pure
chipwood-and-polymer products from
recycled materials.
Project goal: to produce ecologically safe,
water resistant chipboard substitute
from recycled materials.

1) Up to 5,000 tons per year,
revenue of up to $4.5 million
per year
2) $5 million/14 months
3) L, E
4) FS

ZAO ROSSKETMASH
35, ul. Gagarina, Reutov,
Moscow Region, 143966
Phone/fax: (095) 302 5488, 528 1466
Yemelyan Davydovich Kamen, CEO

10R011

Construction of a plant to produce board
and other goods from ecologically pure
chipwood-and-polymer materials.
Project goal: to produce ecologically safe,
water resistant board and other goods from
chipwood-and-polymer materials using
recycled raw materials.

1) Up to 8,000 tons per year,
revenue of up to $7.5 million
2) $8.2 million/15 months
3) L, E
4) BP, FS

OOO ECO-21
2-a, ul. Lenina, Korolev,
Moscow Region, 141070
Phone: (095) 516 5791
Fax: (095) 516 8819
Anatoly Borisovich Kostenkov,
Director

1	2	3

10R012   ■ ● ◆ ▲

Construction of a plant to produce board and other goods from ecologically pure chipwood-and-polymer materials.
Project goal: to produce ecologically safe, water resistant board and other goods from chipwood-and-polymer materials using recycled raw materials.

1) Up to 8,000 tons per year, revenue of up to $7.5 million
2) $8.2 million/15 months
3) L, E
4) FS, BP is being prepared

OOO ECOKAMESMASH
4, pr. Shkolny, Zhukovsky, Moscow Region, 140180
Phone: (095) 556 6215
Fax: (095) 556 8285
Nikolay Nikolaevich Motovkin, CEO

TRANSPORT INFRASTRUCTURE

10R013   ● ❖ ◆

Construction of a business-class airport facility in Yegoryevsk.
Project goal: to service business-class aircraft, arrange training of business class aviation professionals, and process freight.

1) Throughput capacity up to 40 aircraft per day
2) $46.6 million/2 years
3) JV, preferential L
4) BP

Multipurpose Aviation Sports Company Riak
PO. Box 1414, Shuvoye Airdrome, Shuvoye, Yegoryevsk District, Moscow Region, 140300
Phone/fax: (096) 403 1890, 403 6506 (from Moscow and the Moscow Region – (240) 31 890, 36 506)
Moscow Representative Office
Office 228B, Building 8, 88, Volokolamskoye shosse, Moscow, 125362
Phone/fax: (095) 491 8677
Sergey Alexandrovich Sokolov, CEO

AGRICULTURE

10R014   ● ❖ ▲

Construction of a mushroom growing compost plant.
Project goal: to produce compost and expand the network of mushroom growing companies.

1) Up to 36,400 tons per year
2) $3.4 million/8 months
3) L, JV
4) FS

ZAO Novoselki
Novoselki, Kashira District, Moscow Region, 142941
Phone: (096) 693 3437, 693 3436, 693 3431, 692 0001 (from Moscow and the Moscow Region – (269) 33 437, 33 436, 33 431, 20 001)
Phone/fax: (096) 693 3438 (from Moscow and the Moscow Region – (269) 33 438)
E-mail: novoselki@mtu-net.ru
Nikolay Nikolaevich Malakhov, CEO

10R015   ■ ● ★ ❖ ▲

Construction of a mushroom growing mycelium plant.
Project goal: to produce mycelium for mushroom growing and reduce mushroom growing costs.

1) Field mushroom mycelium – up to 750,000 liters per year; wood mushroom mycelium – up to 250,000 liters per year
2) $3.4 million/6 months
3) L, JV, E, Leas.
4) FS

ZAO Novoselki
Novoselki, Kashira District, Moscow Region, 142941
Phone: (096) 693 3437, 693 3436, 693 3431, 692 0001 (from Moscow and the Moscow Region – (269) 33 437, 33 436, 33 431, 20 001)
Phone/fax: (096) 693 3438 (from Moscow and the Moscow Region – (269) 33 438)
E-mail: novoselki@mtu-net.ru
Nikolay Nikolaevich Malakhov, CEO

10R016   ■ ● ❖ ◆

Introduction of an energy saving technology for mushroom growing.
Project goal: to produce mushrooms.

1) Up to 300 tons of mushrooms per year; commercial substratum of mushrooms of up to 1,000 tons per year
2) $1.6 million/6 months
3) L, JV, E
4) BP

OOO NPP Teplotekhnika
Appt. 6, 1, pr. Lenina, Krasnoarmeysk, Moscow Region, 141292
Phone: (096) 537 2542 (from Moscow and the Moscow Region – (253) 72 542)
Fax: (095) 941 1276
Georgy Georgievich Smirnov, Director

1	2	3

ECOLOGY

10R017

Construction of a plant for processing solid household waste biological mass to produce organic fertilizers, biological gas, and electricity.
Project goal: to process biological mass.

1) Biological mass processing – up to 60 tons per day
2) $7.5 million/18 months
3) L, E
4) FS, BP is being prepared

OOO ECO-21
2-a, ul. Lenina, Korolev,
Moscow Region, 141070
Phone: (095) 516 5791
Fax: (095) 516 8819
Anatoly Borisovich Kostenkov,
Director

10R018

Construction of an automobile and household appliance processing facility.
Project goal: to process discarded automobiles and household appliances.

1) Up to 12,000 tons of ferrous metal in bricks; up to 2,000 tons of non-ferrous metal in bricks
2) $3 million/14 months
3) L, E
4) FS, BP is being prepared

OOO ECO-21
2-a, ul. Lenina, Korolev,
Moscow Region, 141070
Phone: (095) 516 5791
Fax: (095) 516 8819
Anatoly Borisovich Kostenkov,
Director

10R019

Construction of an automotive tire and rubber waste processing facility.
Project goal: to process automotive tires and rubber waste.

1) Up to 8,000 tons per year, $3.8 million
2) $3.2 million/15 months
3) L, E
4) FS, BP is being prepared

OOO ECO-21
2-a, ul. Lenina, Korolev,
Moscow Region, 141070
Phone: (095) 516 5791
Fax: (095) 516 8819
Anatoly Borisovich Kostenkov,
Director

10R020

Building of a construction and reinforced concrete waste processing and building materials production facility.
Project goal: to process reinforced concrete and produce a wide range of building materials, including commercial road metal, artificial stone, small wall units, and foam concrete polystyrene.

1) Revenue of up to $3.5 million
2) $2.8 million/12 months
3) L, E
4) FS, BP is being prepared

OOO ECO-21
2-a, ul. Lenina, Korolev,
Moscow Region, 141070
Phone: (095) 516 5791
Fax: (095) 516 8819
Anatoly Borisovich Kostenkov,
Director

10R021

Construction of a solid household and large waste sorting and primary processing facility.
Project goal: to process solid household and large waste.

1) Revenue of up to $4.5 million
2) $3.2 million/15 months
3) L, E
4) FS, BP is being prepared

OOO ECOKAMESMASH
4, pr. Shkolny, Zhukovsky,
Moscow Region, 140180
Phone: (095) 556 6215
Fax: (095) 556 8285
Nikolay Nikolaevich Motovkin, CEO

10R022

Construction of a biological mass processing plant for solid household waste to produce organic fertilizers, biological gas and electricity.
Project goal: to process biological mass after sorting solid household waste.

1) Organic fertilizers – up to 50 tons per day, biological gas – up to 6,000 cubic meters per day, generating capacity – 2,000 kWh
2) $7.5 million/18 months
3) L, E
4) FS, BP is being prepared

OOO ECOKAMESMASH
4, pr. Shkolny, Zhukovsky,
Moscow Region, 140180
Phone: (095) 556 6215
Fax: (095) 556 8285
Nikolay Nikolaevich Motovkin, CEO

10R023

Construction of an automobile and household appliance processing facility.
Project goal: to process discarded automobiles and household appliances.

1) 12,000 tons of ferrous metal in bricks (revenue of $0.5 million); 2,000 tons of non-ferrous metal in bricks ($2 million)
2) $3 million/14 months
3) L, E
4) FS, BP is being prepared

OOO ECOKAMESMASH
4, pr. Shkolny, Zhukovsky,
Moscow Region, 140180
Phone: (095) 556 6215
Fax: (095) 556 8285
Nikolay Nikolaevich Motovkin, CEO

I

CENTRAL FEDERAL DISTRICT

1	2	3

10R024 ■ ● ▲ ◆

Recultivation of solid waste dumb facility Narcomvod in Zhukovsky.
Project goal: to prevent waste from filtrating into the Moskva river and combustible facility products from getting into the air.

1) Revenue of $3.5 million per year
2) $6.2 million/18 months
3) L, E
4) FS, BP is being prepared

OOO ECOKAMESMASH
4, pr. Shkolny, Zhukovsky,
Moscow Region, 140180
Phone: (095) 556 6215
Fax: (095) 556 8285
Nikolay Nikolaevich Motovkin, CEO

10R025 ■ ● ▲ ◆

Construction of an automotive tire and rubber waste processing facility.
Project goal: to process automotive tires and rubber waste.

1) Up to 8,000 tons per year, Revenue of up to $3.8 million per year
2) $3.2 million/15 months
3) L, E
4) FS, BP is being prepared

OOO ECOKAMESMASH
4, pr. Shkolny, Zhukovsky,
Moscow Region, 140180
Phone: (095) 556 6215
Fax: (095) 556 8285
Nikolay Nikolaevich Motovkin, CEO

SCIENCE AND INNOVATION

10R026 ● ▲ ❖

Development and serial production of small-sized communication satellites on the basis of a unified space platform.
Project goal: to launch serial production of small-sized communication satellites to be used as a space segment of satellite communication and broadcasting systems.

1) Revenue of up to $14.4 million per year
2) $56 million/3 years
3) L, JV
4) FS

Federal State Unitary Company
NPO Machine Engineering
33, ul. Gagarina, Reutov,
Moscow Region, 143966
Phone: (095) 302 1185, 302 3194
Fax: (095) 302 2001
E-mail: smpc@npomash.ru
Gerbert Alexandrovich Yefremov, CEO

10R027 ● ◆

Construction of a proton-ion ray therapy center on the basis of an acceleration facility.
Project goal: to treat cancer patients with resistive types of tumor.

1) Up to 2,000 patients per year
2) $8 million/7 years
3) L
4) BP

Federal State Unitary Company
R&D Institute of High
Energy Physics
1, ul. Pobedy, Protvino,
Moscow Region, 142281
Phone: (096) 774 2579 (from Moscow and the Moscow Region – (27) 74 2579)
Fax: (096) 774 2824 (from Moscow and the Moscow Region – (27) 74 2824)
Yury Mikhailovich Antipov,
Project Manager

10R028 ▲ ❖

Development and introduction into medical practice of intellectual laser 3D complex topology object synthesis systems methodology for treating bone pathologies.
Project goal: to treat bone pathologies.

1) Revenue of up to $100 million
2) $151 million/11 years
3) JV
4) FS

Laser and Information Technology
Research and Development Institute
of the Russian Academy of Sciences
1, ul. Svyatoozerskaya, Shsatura,
Moscow Region, 140700
Phone: (096) 452 5995 (from Moscow and the Moscow Region – (245) 25 995)
Fax: (096) 452 2532 (from Moscow and the Moscow Region – (245) 22 532)
E-mail: panch@lazer.ru;
Vladislav Yakovlevich Panchenko,
Director

1	2	3

10R029 ● ▲ ◆

Launching of production and introduction into medical practice of Perfocor medical unit. Project goal: to produce technological and medical lasers.	1) 30 units per year 2) $3 million – small series; $14 million – large series/1 year 3) L 4) BP, FS	Laser and Information Technology Research and Development Institute of the Russian Academy of Sciences 1, ul. Svyatoozerskaya, Shatura, Moscow Region, 140700 Phone: (096) 452 5995 (from Moscow and the Moscow Region – (245) 25 995) Fax: (096) 452 2532 (from Moscow and the Moscow Region – (245) 22532) E-mail: panch@lazer.ru; Vladislav Yakovlevich Panchenko, Director

10R030 ■ ● ◆ ❖

Construction of a laboratory for research and certification of materials for energy equipment. Project goal: to research and certify materials used in energy equipment.	1) Up to $1.5 million per year 2) $3.6 million/3 years 3) L, JV, E 4) BP	OOO NPP Teplotekhnika Appt. 6, pr. Lenina, Krasnoarmeysk, Moscow Region, 141292 Phone: (096) 537 2542 (from Moscow and the Moscow Region – (253) 72 542) Fax: (095) 941 1276 Georgy Georgievich Smirnov, Director

I

CENTRAL FEDERAL DISTRICT

11. ORYOL REGION [57]

ECONOMIC MAP

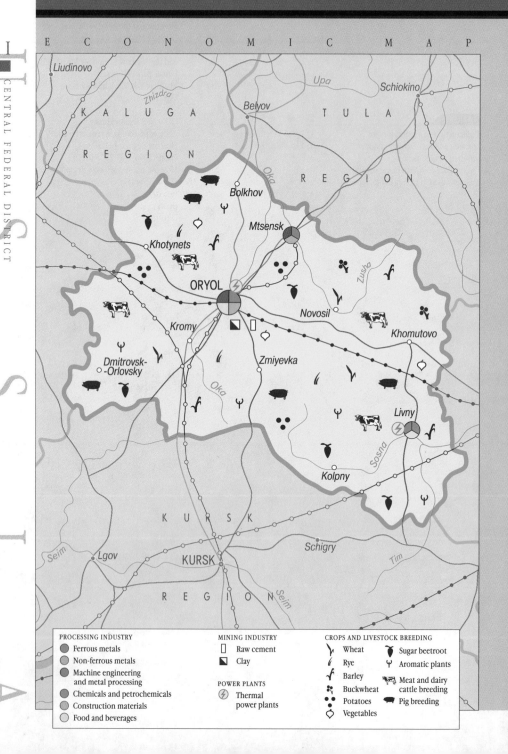

PROCESSING INDUSTRY		MINING INDUSTRY		CROPS AND LIVESTOCK BREEDING	
●	Ferrous metals	▯	Raw cement	⑂ Wheat	❦ Sugar beetroot
●	Non-ferrous metals	◣	Clay	⸜ Rye	⑂ Aromatic plants
●	Machine engineering and metal processing			⼂ Barley	🐄 Meat and dairy cattle breeding
●	Chemicals and petrochemicals		POWER PLANTS	⁂ Buckwheat	🐖 Pig breeding
●	Construction materials	⚡	Thermal power plants	⁙ Potatoes	
●	Food and beverages			◇ Vegetables	

Liudinovo, Zhizdra, Belyov, Upa, Schiokino, KALUGA REGION, TULA REGION, Oka, Bolkhov, Mtsensk, Khotynets, Zusha, ORYOL, Novosil, Khomutovo, Kromy, Zmiyevka, Dmitrovsk-Orlovsky, Oka, Livny, Sosna, Kolpny, KURSK, Lgov, Seim, Schigry, Tim, KURSK REGION, Seim

The Oryol Region is situated in the European part of Russia in the Mid-Russian Uplands. Its unmatched natural environment, excellent climate, ancient history, and people have all won the Region the accolades of granary of Russia, land of high moral and patriotic standards, and fountain of talent and genius.

We believe that our Region has all of the prerequisites to make a vigorous breakthrough in its economic development. Today, our Region boasts intensive agriculture and is a recognized testing area for advanced agricultural technology. The Region has a developed and diverse industrial economy: machine engineering, electronics, and metal processing, and industrial infrastructure: roads, railroads, and advanced telecommunications.

The Region is home to several major agricultural holdings and dozens of agricultural companies, which together with private farmers produce crops, engage in sales and marketing, process raw food, and supply fuel and fertilizers.

The Oryol Region is completing the construction of its gas network and implementing the Slavic Roots program, under which more than 5,000 cottages have already been built in rural areas. Farmers and employees of agricultural companies are entitled to housing loans against long-term produce supply contracts.

Thousands of small and medium enterprises operate in our Region, supported by a specially established Development Center. The issue of attracting investment is a priority for our Region, as it is for every region in Russia. Examples of successful investment projects in the Region include the joint establishment with foreign partners of high-tech enterprises, which are rare in Russia as yet. These include food production facilities, tile manufacturing plants, diamond cutting outfits, and refrigeration unit manufacturing and assembly plants. Every year, private investors bring nearly twice as much investment to the Region as the total regional budget expenditure.

Oryol is a city with high research and development potential and is home to several universities. We used to have branches of Moscow graduate schools. Today, however, Oryol boasts its own high-standing Classical, Technical, and Agrarian Universities, an Institute of Culture and Arts, and Institutes of Law and Commerce. Oryol also hosts the Academy of Government Communications and a regional Public Service Academy. Every seventh Oryol inhabitant is a student.

Stability, equitable treatment, and creativity are the underlying principles underpinning the strategy and tactics of the Regional authorities. The Oryol Region's potential — fertile black earth soil, industrial enterprises, universities, and, most important, its qualified workforce — open up wide prospects for cooperation, initiative, and enterprise. We are committed to introducing new technologies and methods and to creating conditions conducive to achieving mutual understanding between manufacturers and investors as to the benefits and appeal of partnership.

Yegor Stroev,
GOVERNOR OF THE ORYOL REGION

I

CENTRAL FEDERAL DISTRICT

1. GENERAL INFORMATION

1.1. GEOGRAPHY

Located in south-western Russia at the heart of the Mid-Russian Uplands, the Oryol Region covers a total area of some 24,700 square kilometers. To the north, the Region borders the Kaluga and Tula Regions, to the west – the Bryansk Region, to the south – the Kursk Region, and to the east – the Lipetsk Region.

1.2. CLIMATE

The Oryol Region is located within the temperate continental climate zone.

Air temperatures in January average –9°C, rising to +19°C in July. Annual precipitation reaches 490–590 mm. The average growing season lasts 175–185 days.

1.3. POPULATION

According to preliminary 2002 census results, the Oryol Region's population was 861,000 people. The average population density is 34.9 people per square kilometer. The economically active population is 464,000 people. Official unemployment stood at 1.4% in 2002.

Demographically speaking, some 58.7% are of the statutory working age, 17.2% are below the statutory working age, and 24.1% are beyond the statutory working age.

The Oryol Region's major urban centers (2002 data) are Oryol with 333,600 inhabitants, Livny with 52,000 inhabitants, and Mtsensk with 43,000 inhabitants.

Population								TABLE 1
	1992	1997	1998	1999	2000	2001	2002
Total population, '000	903	909	906	902	897	891	861
Economically active population, '000	454	387	395	447	445	434	464

2. ADMINISTRATION

1, pl. Lenina, Oryol, Oryol Region, 302001
Fax: (0862) 41 2530
E-mail: post@adm.orel.ru; http://www.adm.orel.ru

NAME	POSITION	CONTACT INFORMATION
Yegor Semenovich STROEV	Governor of the Oryol Region	Phone: (0862) 47 5300
Vitaly Alekseevich KOCHUEV	First Deputy Governor of the Oryol Region for Social and Economic Development, Finance and Investment Policy, and Enterprise Support	Phone: (0862) 47 5394
Igor Viktorovich SOSHNIKOV	First Deputy Governor of the Oryol Region for the Fuel and Energy Sector, Industry, Transport, Communications, Housing and Public Utilities, Architecture and Urban Planning, Food Processing, and the Agroindustrial Sector	Phone: (0862) 47 5255
Nikolai Nikolaevich TSIKOREV	Deputy Governor of the Oryol Region for Industrial Development and Reform Strategy, Labor and Employment, and Pricing Policy	Phone: (0862) 47 5275
Vyacheslav Vladimirovich PANARIN	Head of the Department for Enterprise, Investment and Innovation, Foreign Trade, and Inter-Regional Relations of the Oryol Regional Administration	Phone: (0862) 41 3618 E-mail: panarin@adm.orel.ru

3. ECONOMIC POTENTIAL

3.1. 1997–2002 GROSS REGIONAL PRODUCT (GRP). INDUSTRY BREAKDOWN

The Oryol Region's 2002 gross regional product amounted to $1,167.8 million, 13.3% up on 2001 levels. The growth was largely agriculture driven. Per capita GRP totaled $1,158 in 2001 and $1,356 in 2002.

3.2. MAJOR ECONOMIC GROWTH PROJECTIONS

The Oryol Regional Administration's primary goals in the coming years are to create a favorable investment climate and to ensure the comprehensive development of the Region. All industrial sectors are expected to grow.

GRP trends in 1997–2002						*TABLE 2*
	1997	1998	1999	2000	2001*	2002*
GRP in current prices, $ million	1,437.1	1,025.2	721.4	904.9	1,030.6	1,167.8

*Estimates of the Oryol Regional Administration

GRP industry breakdown in 1997–2002, % of total						*TABLE 3*
	1997	1998	1999	2000	2001*	2002*
GRP	100.0	100.0	100.0	100.0	100.0	100.0
Industry	26.1	23.5	21.5	23.2	22.7	21.0
Agriculture and forestry	15.1	14.7	19.3	21.4	20.0	21.2
Construction	6.6	4.9	6.4	5.9	6.6	6.3
Transport and communications	7.6	11.7	10.7	8.8	8.6	8.2
Trade and public catering	12.5	10.9	11.0	11.5	13.8	14.4
Other	25.6	28.3	19.9	17.2	18.1	19.1
Net taxes on output	6.5	6.0	11.2	12.0	10.2	9.8

*Estimates of the Oryol Regional Administration

Industry: enhancement of production through enterprise restructuring and reform, better labor productivity, development of new markets, and the improvement of product quality;

Agriculture: revamping and expansion of food processing enterprises, diversifying of the product mix, development of livestock breeding and poultry farming, introduction of advanced technologies, and upgrading of rural public utilities;

Construction: utilization of idle capacities, and manufacturing of new types of construction materials: roof sheeting, heat insulation materials, metal and plastic pipe, and sanitary equipment.

3.3. INDUSTRIAL OUTPUT IN 1997–2002 FOR MAJOR SECTORS OF ECONOMY

The Oryol Region's major industrial sectors are machine engineering and metal processing, food and beverages, energy, ferrous metals, and construction materials. These sectors account for 88.1% of the Region's total industrial output.

Machine engineering and metal processing. The Region's machine engineering and metal processing sector accounts for 30.2% of total industrial output. Leading products produced in the Region include technological equipment for automatic load-ers, construction equipment, utilities equipment, and agricultural machinery. The largest enterprises are ZAO OPK-Dormash, OAO Mtsensky Communal Services Machinery Plant, OAO Mtsensky Foundry, OAO Livgidromash, OAO Avtoagregat, OOO Frigoreks-Eurasia, OAO Livnynasos, OAO Pogruzchik, ZAO ORLEKS, and OAO Prompribor.

Food and beverages. The food sector accounts for 17.5% of total industrial output. The largest enterprises are OOO Livny-Sugar, OOO Otradino Sugar Refinery, OAO Oryoloblkhleb, OOO Livny Confectionery, OAO Ethanol, OAO Kristall, OAO Livny Meat Agricultural Company, and OAO Oryol Dairy.

Energy. The energy sector accounts for 15.1% of total industrial output. Electricity is supplied by the Orlovskaya Thermal Power Station and Livenskaya Thermal Power Station.

Ferrous metals. Ferrous metals production accounts for 12.9% of total industrial output. The sector produces cold drawn steel, steel cord, steel rope, pipe, and fastening elements. The largest enterprises are OAO OSPAZ and OAO Mezhgosmetiz-Mtsensk.

Construction materials. The sector accounts for 12.4% of total industrial output. The largest enterprise is ZAO Velor.

Industry breakdown of industrial output in 1997–2002, % of total						*TABLE 4*
	1997	1998	1999	2000	2001	2002*
Industry	100.0	100.0	100.0	100.0	100.0	100.0
Machine engineering and metal processing	23.9	23.1	26.5	26.4	28.3	30.2
Food and beverages	26.1	25.8	29.6	22.0	19.7	17.5
Energy	16.7	17.0	11.3	10.0	12.2	15.1
Ferrous metals	6.6	8.3	5.4	12.5	7.4	12.9
Construction materials	6.8	8.6	9.1	11.2	11.5	12.4
Flour, cereals, and mixed fodder	4.9	4.1	2.9	3.7	5.1	n/a
Light industry	7.7	5.7	5.4	3.9	4.8	3.6
Chemicals and petrochemicals	2.3	1.9	2.3	2.0	2.1	2.0
Forestry, timber, and pulp and paper	1.5	1.4	1.6	1.5	1.9	1.6
Non-ferrous metals	1.4	1.8	1.1	3.6	3.3	1.4
Glass and porcelain	0.2	0.2	0.2	0.1	0.1	n/a

*Estimates of the Oryol Regional Administration

Fuel and energy sector production and consumption trends, 1997–2002						*TABLE 5*
	1997	1998	1999	2000	2001	2002*
Electricity output, billion kWh	1.5	1.5	1.5	1.3	1.3	1.3
Electricity consumption, billion kWh	2.9	3.0	3.0	3.0	3.0	2.9
Natural gas consumption, million cubic meters	1,377.2	1,528.0	1,552.0	1,569.0	1,623.0	1,602.0

*Estimates of the Oryol Regional Administration

Agriculture. Agriculture accounts for 21.2% of total industrial output. The prevailing crops are grain (rye, wheat, buckwheat, barley, pea), sugar beet, potato, vegetables, oil crops, meat, milk, selection seed, and livestock.

3.4. FUEL AND ENERGY BALANCE OF THE REGION (OUTPUT AND CONSUMPTION PER RESOURCE)

The Oryol Region is an energy deficient region. The Oryol Region's power stations supply 45% of total electricity consumption. The remainder is imported from the Kursk, Tula, Lipetsk, and Bryansk Regions.

All gas and petrochemicals consumed in the Oryol Region are imported.

3.5. TRANSPORT INFRASTRUCTURE

Roads. The Oryol Region has 4,033 kilometers of paved public highway. The following highways cross the Region: Moscow – Oryol – Kharkov – Simferopol, Moscow – Kiev, Oryol – Tambov, and Oryol – Bryansk. Some 80% of freight is transported by road.

Railroads. The Oryol Region has some 590 kilometers of railroads. The major trunk railroads are Moscow – Kharkov – Crimea – Caucasus and Riga – Voronezh – Saratov.

Oil and gas pipelines. The Oryol Region is crossed by one oil and three international gas pipelines.

3.6. MAIN NATURAL RESOURCES: RESERVES AND EXTRACTION IN 2002

The main natural resources of the Oryol Region are iron ore, non-metal construction materials, and land.

Construction materials. The Region has deposits of the following construction materials: mineral pigments (93,000 tons), raw cement (32 million cubic meters), building stone (44 million cubic meters), mason sands (75.6 million cubic meters), clay for expanded clay production (3 million cubic meters), and chalk (11.6 million tons).

Other natural resources. The Oryol Region also has deposits of limestone, dolomite, kaolin (raw material for porcelain and insulation porcelain production), phosphorites, tripoli (57 million cubic meters), and peat.

Minerals. The Oryol Region is rich in iron ore (Kursk Magnetic Anomaly deposits hold some 117.6 million tons) and brown coal.

Land resources. Agricultural lands cover 2.086 million hectares of the Region's territory, including 1.663 million hectares (79.7%) of tillage.

Water resources. The Region has 2,100 water courses with a total length of 9,154 kilometers. The water resources of the Oka and the Zusha rivers are exploited for power generation.

4. TRADE OPPORTUNITIES

4.1. MAIN GOODS
PRODUCED IN THE REGION
Machine engineering and metal processing.
In 2002, the Region's enterprises produced 84,000 pumps, 231 bread ovens, 970 urban communal services machines, 214 construction loaders, 8.522 million capacitors, 6.521 million semiconductor devices, 6.959 million optical electronic devices, and 1.349 million electronic chips.

Food and beverages. 2002 meat processing output totaled 6,768 tons, animal fats output totaled 1,920 tons, cheese output totaled 3,764 tons, milk output reached 42,000 tons, bread output totaled 75,000 tons, sugar output totaled 39,000 tons, vegetable oil output totaled 1,919 tons, pasta output totaled 1,745 tons, and vodka and liquors output was 796,000 decaliters.

Construction materials. In 2002, the Region's enterprises produced 104 million conventional bricks, 145,000 cubic meters of prefabricated reinforced-concrete units, 6.364 million square meters of ceramic wall tiles, 4.484 million square meters of ceramic floor tiles, and 607,000 cubic meters of non-metal construction materials.

Ferrous metals. 2002 output included 38,000 tons of steel cable, 35,000 tons of steel wire, 4,594 tons of steel cord, 6,369 tons of steel pipes, 9.688 million square meters of steel mesh, and 19,000 tons of welding electrodes.

4.2. EXPORTS,
INCLUDING EXTRA-CIS
2000 extra-CIS exports totaled $66.2 million. CIS exports reached $17.1 million. The corresponding figures for 2001 were $107.6 million and $23.6 million, and $183.4 million and $33 million for 2002.

The bulk of the Region's exports consisted of ferrous and non-ferrous metals and derived products –

53.4% of exports (scrap metal, iron and steel scrap, rolled section, steel shapes, wire, copper, aluminium and derived products); machinery – 29.9% (vacuum fluid pumps, communal services machinery, motor graders, loaders, mechanical and electrical equipment, vehicles, optical devices); petrochemicals – 6.3% (raw rubber, rubber and rubber products, polymer materials, plastics and plastic products). The Region's main partners for exports are the Netherlands (31% of exports), Iraq (12.3%), Ukraine (10%), Kazakhstan (5.9%), the USA (5.8%), Germany (5.3%), Austria (3.9%), Uzbekistan (3.2%), Latvia (3.5%), and Japan (3.1%).

4.3. IMPORTS,
INCLUDING EXTRA-CIS
Imports from extra-CIS countries amounted to $103.6 million in 2000. Imports from CIS countries totaled $17.8 million. The corresponding figures for 2001 were $87.4 million and $28 million, and $151.1 million and $39.5 million for 2002.

Machinery accounted for 38.5% of imports (electrical and mechanical machinery and equipment, optical tools, vehicles, and railroad cars); petrochemicals – 28.2% (polymer materials, plastics, raw rubber, rubber and rubber products, essential oils and cosmetics, colorants, pigments, soap, detergents, and other chemical products); food and raw foods – 20.1%; furniture, cotton, knit fabrics and knitwear, ceramics, footwear, paper, and cardboard. The Region's main partners for imports are France (26.7% of imports), Italy (20.4%), Moldova (17.6%), Ukraine (15.6%), Germany (8.2%), and Spain (2.6%).

4.4. MAJOR REGIONAL
EXPORT AND IMPORT ENTITIES
Owing to the specific nature of the Oryol Region's export and import activities, export and import transactions are performed mainly by industrial enterprises.

5. INVESTMENT OPPORTUNITIES

5.1. INVESTMENTS IN 1997–2002
(BY INDUSTRY SECTOR),
INCLUDING FOREIGN INVESTMENTS
The following factors determine the investment appeal of the Oryol Region:
- Its favorable geographical location (proximity to Russia's industrial centers and high potential consumer demand);
- Its developed transport infrastructure;
- Legislation supporting investment activity (tax exemptions and privileges to investors);
- Its highly qualified workforce;
- Its cheap energy;
- Its natural resources.

5.2. CAPITAL
INVESTMENT
The bulk of fixed capital investment goes to industry transport, and communications.

5.3. MAJOR ENTERPRISES
(INCLUDING
ENTERPRISES WITH
FOREIGN INVESTMENT)
The Oryol Region hosts numerous enterprises with foreign investment, including OOO Oryol Coca-Cola Bottlers, ZAO Velor, OOO Frigoreks-Eurasia, ZAO EKO-MAL, OAO Oryol Winery, OOO SP Orita-Seramenti, OOO CP UFUK, ZAO OR-Zenner, OOO Orsteel, and OOO Lavrovo-Saxony.

Capital investment by industry sector, $ million

TABLE 6

	1997	1998	1999	2000	2001	2002
Total capital investment *Including major industries* (% of total)	225.5	160.9	126.6	173.5	192.9	181.0
Industry	17.5	16.5	31.1	44.0	29.4	25.0
Agriculture and forestry	9.0	8.1	11.4	14.8	15.8	7.0
Construction	6.4	9.1	6.9	4.9	6.7	3.0
Transport and communications	18.5	21.8	14.6	13.3	16.1	13.0
Trade and public catering	2.5	18.0	1.6	7.5	4.9	n/a
Other	46.1	26.5	34.4	15.5	27.1	n/a

Foreign investment trends in 1997–2002

TABLE 7

	1997	1998	1999	2000	2001	2002
Foreign investment, $ million	40.0	33.0	17.0	43.0	18.5	11.1
Including FDI, $ million	40.0	33.0	17.0	40.3	18.0	9.9

Largest enterprises of the Oryol Region

TABLE 8

COMPANY	SECTOR
ZAO OPK Road Machinery	Machine engineering and metal processing
OAO Livnynasos	Machine engineering and metal processing
OAO Livgidromash	Machine engineering and metal processing
OAO Avtoagregat	Machine engineering and metal processing
OAO Mtsensky Communal Services Machinery Plant	Machine engineering and metal processing
OAO Mtsensky Foundry	Machine engineering and metal processing
ZAO ORLEKS	Machine engineering and metal processing
OAO Prompribor	Machine engineering and metal processing
ZAO Mtsensky Vtortsvetmet Plant	Non-ferrous metals
OAO OSPAZ	Ferrous metals
OAO Gamma	Light industry
OAO Oryoloblkhleb	Food and beverages
OAO Etanol	Food and beverages

5.4. MOST ATTRACTIVE SECTORS FOR INVESTMENT

According to the Oryol Regional Administration, energy, non-ferrous metals, food, and agriculture are the most attractive industries for investment.

5.5. CURRENT LEGISLATION ON INVESTOR TAX EXEMPTIONS AND PRIVILEGES

The Oryol Regional Law On Investment Activity in the Oryol Region provides a legal and economic basis for investment activity in the Region and establishes regulatory procedures. The Law grants investors exemptions from certain regional tax components.

5.6. REGIONAL ENTITIES RESPONSIBLE FOR RAISING INVESTMENT

The Regional Administration Department for Enterprise, Investment and Innovation and Foreign Trade and Inter-Regional Relations is responsible for raising investment in the Oryol Region.

5.7. FEDERAL AND REGIONAL ECONOMIC AND SOCIAL DEVELOPMENT PROGRAMS FOR THE ORYOL REGION

Federal targeted programs. The Oryol Region is currently participating in 26 federal programs financed to a total of $44 million. The most important programs include the Federal Program for the Development of Education, 2001–2005, the federal targeted programs for the Elimination of

Inequalities in Social and Economic Development of the Regions of the Russian Federation, 2002–2010 and through 2015, Soil Fertility Enhancement, 2002–2005, Ecology and Natural Resources, 2002–2010, Modernization of Russia's Transport System, 2002–2010, and others.

Regional programs. The Oryol Regional Administration has drafted and is implementing ten regional targeted programs for the development of the economy, healthcare, and public welfare: Job Creation in the Oryol Region, 2001–2003, Working Conditions and Industrial Safety, 2001–2005, Development of Tourism in the Oryol Region, 2001–2005, and others. A total of $14.2 million has been allocated to finance the regional targeted programs.

6. INVESTMENT PROJECTS

Industry sector and project description	1) Expected results 2) Amount and term of investment 3) Form of financing[1] 4) Documentation[2]	Contact information
1	2	3
OIL		
11R001 ● ▲		OAO Northern Oil
Construction of a new oil refinery with facilities for processing fuel oil into diesel fuel. Project goal: to satisfy demand for oil products.	1) 3 million tons per year 2) $100.7 million/n/a 3) L ($84.9 million) 4) FS	Office 15, 21, ul. Vorontsovskaya, Moscow, 109004 Phone: (0862) 43 5370 Phone/fax: (095) 913 9752 E-mail: reception@orel.nordoil.ru Sergei Mikhailovich Nesterenko, CEO
ENERGY		
11R002 ● ▼		OAO Oryolenrgo
Renovation of the Livenskaya thermal power station's main facilities. Project goal: to increase capacity and to reduce production costs.	1) To increase installed capacity of the thermal power station from 12 to 42 MW, annual electricity output from 57 to 273 million kWh, and thermal energy output from 243,000 to 454,000 Gcal 2) $23.6 million/n/a 3) L 4) Investment proposal	2, pl. Mira, Oryol, Oryol Region, 302030 Phone: (0862) 25 0839, 25 4824 Fax: (0862) 25 8392 E-mail: secr@orlen.elektra.ru Vitaly Petrovich Fomichev, Chief Engineer
11R003 ● ▲		OAO Oryolenrgo
Revamping of energy plants at the Oryol Thermal Power Station. Project goal: to increase capacity, reduce production costs.	1) To increase electricity output by 33% and thermal energy output by 17% 2) $37.8 million/n/a 3) L 4) FS	2, pl. Mira, Oryol, Oryol Region, 302030 Phone: (0862) 25 0839, 25 4824 Fax: (0862) 25 8392 E-mail: secr@orlen.elektra.ru Vitaly Petrovich Fomichev, Chief Engineer
11R004 ■ ● ▲		OAO Energomashkorporatsia
Construction of small gas turbine thermal power stations in the Region. Project goal: to increase electricity output in the Region and to reduce production costs.	1) To increase by 30% electricity and heat energy supply to the regional market 2) $18 million/n/a 3) E, L 4) FS	Direction of the Gas Turbine Thermal Power Station Under Construction 34, ul. Saltykova-Schedrina, Oryol, Oryol Region, 302000 Phone: (095) 792 3908 Phone/fax: (0862) 43 6969 Vyacheslav Viktorovich Vakurov, Director

[1] L – Loan, E – Equity, Leas. – Leasing, JV – Joint Venture
[2] BP – Business Plan, FS – Feasibility Study

1	2	3

FERROUS METALS

11R005 ■ ● ▲

		OAO OSPAZ
Creation of copper-plated welding wire production facilities at a currently operating enterprise. Project goal: to diversify product mix.	1) Total output of 7,200 tons per year 2) € 1 million/n/a 3) E, L 4) FS	105, ul. Razdolnaya, Oryol, Oryol Region, 302025 Phone/fax: (0862) 46 1152, 46 2052 E-mail: vvk.pko@steel.orel.ru Valery Vasilyevich Kalmykov, CEO

11R006 ■ ● ▲

		OAO OSPAZ
Creation of production facilities for zinc-coated steel wire for aggressive environment at a currently operating enterprise. Project goal: to increase production, improve products quality, and expand exports.	1) Annual net profit of $1.1 million 2) $5 million/n/a 3) E, L 4) FS	105, ul. Razdolnaya, Oryol, Oryol Region, 302025 Phone/fax: (0862) 46 1152 E-mail: vvk.pko@steel.orel.ru Valery Vasilyevich Kalmykov, CEO

11R007 ■ ● ▲

		OAO OSPAZ
Creation of facilities for production of mesh works from zinc coated wire at an existing enterprise. Project goal: to increase output, raise quality, and diversify product mix.	1) Annual net profit of $1.0 million 2) $2.3 million/n/a 3) E, L 4) FS	105, ul. Razdolnaya, Oryol, Oryol Region, 302025 Phone/fax: (0862) 46 1152 E-mail: vvk.pko@steel.orel.ru Valery Vasilyevich Kalmykov, CEO

11R008 ■ ● ▲

		OAO OSPAZ
Renewal of main facilities for fastener and calibration equipment production at an operating enterprise. Project goal: to upgrade production facilities and manufacture competitive products.	1) Annual net profit of $0.9 million 2) $6.1 million/n/a 3) E, L 4) FS	105, ul. Razdolnaya, Oryol, Oryol Region, 302025 Phone/fax: (0862) 46 1152 E-mail: vvk.pko@steel.orel.ru Valery Vasilyevich Kalmykov, CEO

11R009 ● ★ ▲

		OAO Mezhgosmetiz-Mtsensk
Creation of additional facilities for copper based welding wire output (equipment purchase) at the active enterprise. Project goal: to increase output.	1) To increase output by 50% 2) $1.0 million/n/a 3) L, Leas. 4) FS	98A, ul. Sovetskaya, Mtsensk, Oryol Region, 303000 Phone/fax: (08646) 22 363 Vladimir Petrovich Kostyuchenko, CEO

CHEMICALS AND PETROCHEMICALS

11R010 ● ▲ ❖

		OAO Livnyplastic
Creation of production facilities for polystyrol and polypropylene film and food packages at an active chemicals enterprise. Project goal: to diversify product mix and produce food packaging.	1) Pre-tax profit of $0.6 million per year 2) $3.8 million/n/a 3) L ($3.2 million), JV 4) FS	2A, ul. Gaidara, Livny, Oryol Region, 303858 Phone: (08677) 31 580 Phone/fax: (08677) 32 545 E-mail: lplastik@rekom.ru Leonid Ivanovich Goncharov, CEO

11R011 ● ▲

		OAO Livnyplastic
Creation of facilities for the production of food packaging materials on the basis of a currently active chemical enterprise. Project goal: to introduce children's food packaging materials to the market.	1) n/a 2) $0.6 million/2 years 3) L 4) FS	2A, ul. Gaidara, Livny, Oryol Region, 303858 Phone/fax: (08677) 33 406 E-mail: Livnyplast@liv.orel.ru Leonid Ivanovich Goncharov, CEO

1	2	3

MACHINE ENGINEERING AND METAL PROCESSING

11R012 ■ ● ▲

Renovation of main facilities of an active enterprise for road construction and communal services machinery.
Project goal: to increase output, produce new products, and raise production profitability.

1) n/a
2) $5.7 million/n/a
3) E, L ($3.3 million)
4) FS

OAO Mtsensky Factory Kommash
Kommash Micro-District,
Mtsensk, Oryol Region, 303036
Phone: (08646) 22 249
Fax: (08646) 23 839
E-mail: kommash@orel.ru
Viktor Leonidovich Sasin, CEO

11R013 ● ▲

Creation of facilities for the production of equipment for bottle manufacturing at an operating factory.
Project goal: to diversify product mix.

1) n/a
2) $5.8 million/n/a
3) L
4) FS

OAO Oryol Glass Machinery Factory
6, ul. Gertsena, Oryol,
Oryol Region, 302030
Phone: (0862) 25 8980
Fax: (0862) 25 6198
Alexander Ivanovich Arkhipov, CEO

11R014 ■ ● ▲

Renewal of fixed assets of an operating enterprise producing glass shaping machinery.
Project goal: to increase output and diversify product mix.

1) Total annual revenue of $3.5 million
2) $1.1 million/n/a
3) E, L ($0.9 million)
4) FS

OOO Flax Factory
6, ul. Mashinostroitelnaya, Oryol,
Oryol Region, 302008
Phone: (0862) 22 1621
Fax: (0862) 75 6870
E-mail: flas@orel.ru
Stanislav Leonidovich Tubolevsky, CEO
Gennady Alexeevich Uglanov, Technical Director

11R015 ● ▲

Creation of facilities for manufacturing of chicken cage batteries at an active enterprise.
Project goal: to introduce a new product to the market and diversify product mix.

1) n/a
2) $2.7 million/n/a
3) L
4) FS

OAO Oryoltekhmash
155, ul. Moskovskaya, Oryol,
Oryol Region, 302006
Phone: (0862) 25 1172, 25 1054
Fax: (0862) 25 1054
E-mail: oreltekmash@rekom.ru
Alexey Petrovich Litvinov, CEO

CONSTRUCTION MATERIALS

11R016 ● ▲

Construction of new production facilities for heat insulating materials on the basis of foamed concrete.
Project goal: to introduce heat insulating materials to the market.

1) n/a
2) $18.4 million/n/a
3) L
4) FS

OAO Oryolstroy
7, pl. Mira, Oryol,
Oryol Region, 302030
Phone: (0862) 25 0523,
42 7368
Fax: (0862) 25 0531
Vladimir Vladimirovich Sobolev, CEO

11R017 ● ▲

Construction of new production facilities for attic windows for residential house building.
Project goal: to introduce house building goods to the market.

1) n/a
2) $9.8 million/n/a
3) L
4) FS

OAO Oryolstroy
7, pl. Mira, Oryol,
Oryol Region, 302030
Phone: (0862) 25 0523,
42 7368
Fax: (0862) 25 0531
Vladimir Vladimirovich Sobolev, CEO

11R018 ● ◆

Construction of a plant for ceramic brick production.
Project goal: to introduce ceramic bricks to the market.

1) Total output capacity of 10 million pieces per year
2) $3 million/n/a
3) L
4) BP

OAO Oryolstroy
7, pl. Mira, Oryol,
Oryol Region, 302030
Phone: (0862) 25 0523,
42 7368
Fax: (0862) 25 0531
Vladimir Vladimirovich Sobolev, CEO

I

CENTRAL FEDERAL DISTRICT

1	2	3

11R019 ❖ ▲

Construction of a plant for ceramic brick production on the basis of a high-melting infusible clays deposit. Project goal: to introduce ceramic bricks to the market.	1) Total output of 30 million pieces per year 2) $30.3 million/n/a 3) JV 4) FS	ZAO Stroytransgaz-Oryol 29, ul. Moskovskaya, Oryol, Oryol Region, 302030 Phone/fax: (0862) 47 0315, 47 0314 Vladimir Georgievich Merkulov, CEO

GLASS AND PORCELAIN

11R020 ● ▲

Creation of production facilities for food, chemical, medical, and perfume packages output. Project goal: to diversify product mix.	1) n/a . 2) $3.3 million/n/a 3) L 4) FS	OAO Oryolsteklo 19, ul. Poselkovaya, Oryol, Oryol Region Phone: (0862) 25 5050 Anatoly Petrovich Dontsov, CEO

FOOD AND BEVERAGES

11R021 ● ▲

Creation of a liquor production line at an active enterprise. Project goal: to increase output.	1) n/a 2) $3.4 million/n/a 3) L 4) FS	OAO Krystall 77, ul. 2nd Kurskaya, Oryol, Oryol Region, 302004 Phone/fax: (0862) 25 0536 Anatoly Mikhailovich Fokin, CEO

11R022 ● ▲

Construction of a plant for the production of ecologically pure fruit and berry products. Project goal: to introduce ecological food to the market.	1) Output of 10 tons per hour 2) $10.2 million/n/a 3) L ($7.2 million) 4) FS	UPKh Naugorskoye Bolotovskiye Dvory, Oryol District, Oryol Region, 302503 Phone/fax: (0862) 41 7925 Alexander Nikolaevich Drogaytsev Acting Director

11R023 ● ★ ◆

Construction of a beer brewery. Project goal: to introduce beer to the market.	1) Capacity of 20 million liters per year 2) $7.3 million/n/a 3) L, Leas. 4) BP	OAO Oryol Beer Association 1, pl. Lenina, Oryol, Oryol Region, 302001 Phone: (0862) 41 3618 Fax: (0862) 47 5341 E-mail: panarin@adm.orel.ru Vyacheslav Vladimirovich Panarin, Head of the Department for Investment Activity of the Governor's Office and the Administration of the Oryol Region

11R024 ● ▲

Construction of the second phase of facilities for a low fat turkey meat plant. Project goal: to increase low fat turkey meat output.	1) Total output of 2,400 tons per year 2) $6 million/n/a 3) Credit 4) FS	OAO APK Oryol Niva 10, ul. Polesskaya, Oryol, Oryol Region, 302028 Phone: (0862) 47 5228 Fax: (0862) 43 4527 E-mail: orpol@niva.orel.ru Anatoly Sergeevich Sudorgin, CEO

11R025 ● ◆

Construction of a malt plant for beer malt output. Project goal: to introduce beer malt to the market.	1) Total capacity of 20 thousand tons per year 2) $6.1 million/n/a 3) L 4) BP	OAO Oryol Beer Association 1, pl. Lenina, Oryol, Oryol Region, 302001 Phone: (0862) 41 3618 Fax: (0862) 47 5341 E-mail: panarin@adm.orel.ru Vyacheslav Vladimirovich Panarin, Head of Department for Investment Activity of the Governor's Office and the Administration of the Oryol Region

1	2	3

HOUSING, SOCIAL, AND COMMUNAL SERVICES

11R026

Renewal of main facilities of the Mtsensk thermal and power sector.
Project goal: to improve heat supply to the city's buildings.

1) n/a
2) $4.1 million/n/a
3) L
4) FS

OOO Oryolregiongaz
30, ul. Lenina, Oryol,
Oryol Region, 302028
Phone: (0862) 43 2100
Fax: (0862) 43 1996
E-mail: mrg57@orel.ru
Larisa Vasilyevna Udalova, CEO

COMMUNICATIONS

11R027

Development of cellular communication networks and Internet services.
Project goal: to increase the number of subscribers and improve communication quality.

1) To double the number of subscribers
2) $7.1 million/n/a
3) E
4) BP

OAO Rekom
27A, ul. Oktyabrskaya, Oryol,
Oryol Region, 302028
Phone: (0862) 43 4548
Fax: (0862) 48 0908
http://www.rekom.ru
Alexander Nikolaevich Prikazchikov, CEO

TRADE

11R028

Expansion and upgrade of trade and industrial complex Agrocombinat-Oryol.
Project goal: to increase output of production workshops at the complex, update product mix, raise productivity, and improve retail trade services.

1) To increase pre-tax profit by $2.7 million per year
2) $1 million/12 months
3) L ($0.8 million)
4) FS

TPK Agrokombinat-Oryol
287, ul. Komsomolskaya, Oryol,
Oryol Region, 302010
Phone: (0862) 72 6390
Fax: (0862) 72 6381
E-mail: TPK@agkom.orel.ru
Yelena Petrovna Lidinfa,
Director

SCIENCE AND INNOVATION

11R029

Construction of facilities for heat insulating materials production on the basis of foamed glass using a new production unit.
Project goal: to start commercial implementation of a new technology and production unit, and produce low cost heat insulating materials (2–2.5 times less expensive than peer products).

1) One unit of 10,000 cubic meters per year
2) $0.7 million/6 months
3) L
4) FS

Oryol State Technical University
29, Naugorskoye schosse,
Oryol, Oryol Region, 302020
Phone: (0862) 42 0024
Fax: (0862) 41 6684
E-mail: admin@ostu.ru
Vyacheslav Alexandrovich Golenkov,
Rector

12. RYAZAN REGION [62]

E C O N O M I C   M A P

MOSCOW REGION

Orekhovo-Zuyevo

VLADIMIR

Oka

Gus-Khrustalny

Murom

Yegorievsk

REGION

Kolomna

Oka

Melenki

Vyksa

Spas-Klepiki

Kasimov

Solotcha

RYAZAN

Oka

Moksha

Mikhaylov

Shilovo

Sasovo

Pronya

Shatsk

Korablino

Ranova

Tsna

Pavelets

Ryazhsk

Skopin

Morshansk

Dankov

LIPETSK

TAMBOV

Lebedyan

Don

Michurinsk

REGION

REGION

LIPETSK

PROCESSING INDUSTRY

- Machine engineering and metal processing
- Chemicals and petrochemicals
- Construction materials
- Light industry
- Food and beverages

Art crafts

MINING INDUSTRY

- Raw cement

POWER PLANTS

- Thermal power plants

CROPS AND LIVESTOCK BREEDING

- Wheat
- Barley
- Tobacco
- Orchards
- Potatoes
- Sugar beetroot
- Meat and dairy cattle breeding
- Pig breeding
- Poultry farming

The Ryazan Region occupies a well-deserved place among Central Russia's regions. The Region boasts advanced industrial, construction, agricultural, energy, communications, education, medicine, cultural, and folk craft sectors. The Region's industry is comprised of electricity generation, oil refining and chemicals sectors, machine engineering and metals processing, radio electronics, and instrument making.

Ryazan is not a particularly rich Region in terms of natural resources that could help solve all of its economic and social issues. What we do have, however, are deposits of limestone, marl, refractory and fusible clay, sand, and other mineral resources. Our most valuable resources include glass and quartz sand, phosporite, gypsum, brown ore, coal, and materials used for mineral dyes. A thick layer of high quality peat is one of the Region's most important natural resources.

Over the past five years, the Region's economy has demonstrated stable growth trends. Its industrial development growth index of 5–7% a year and improved figures in other spheres have been achieved thanks to high capacity utilization and increased capital investment.

Industrial revival in the Region has led to a four-fold increase in foreign trade turnover in recent years, peaking at over $1 billion in 2002. The Region has maintained a positive trade balance for several years now and raised exports of machinery and equipment, radio electronics and instruments, and oil products. More than 450 legal entities are engaged in foreign trade operations in the Region.

In spite of these obvious successes, we are not fully satisfied with our industrial growth rates. Social and political measures are only effective if accompanied by strong economic levers, and first and foremost, financial injections. The Region is taking measures aimed at preventing inflation, achieving targets, channeling revenues into the regional and local budgets, and adopting the regional budget on a timely basis to secure the Region's macroeconomic stability.

Owing to the increasing obsolescence of fixed assets installed dozens of years back, the Region sees the task of attracting major investment, including long-term financing, as one of paramount importance.

Many companies in the Region with well-established sales channels and market niches are unable to maintain their current output levels, let alone increase output, due to a lack of financing.

The Ryazan Region is beginning to carry out social and economic development planning in a medium-term perspective in the light of the need to source long-term financing for budget programs. Interest in our Region is growing, as witnessed by increasingly broad inter-regional relations. The Ryazan Region is open for bona fide mutually beneficial cooperation.

Vyacheslav Lyubimov,
HEAD OF ADMINISTRATION OF THE RYAZAN REGION

CENTRAL FEDERAL DISTRICT

1. GENERAL INFORMATION

1.1. GEOGRAPHY

Located in the center of European Russia, the Ryazan Region covers a total area of some 39,000 square kilometers. To the north, the Ryazan Region borders the Vladimir Region, to the north-east – the Nizhny Novgorod Region, to the east – the Republic of Mordovia, to the south-east – the Penza Region, to the south – the Tambov and Lipetsk Regions, to the west – the Tula Region, and to the north-west – the Moscow Region.

1.2. CLIMATE

The Ryazan Region is located within the temperate continental climate zone. Air temperatures in January average –10°C, rising to +20°C in July. Annual precipitation reaches 500 mm.

1.3. POPULATION

According to preliminary 2002 census results, the Ryazan Region's population was 1,228,000 people. The average population density is 31.5 people per square kilometer. The economically active population is 583,000 people. Official unemployment stood at 1.4% in 2002, while the actual rate was 8.1%.

Demographically speaking, some 57.9% are of the statutory working age, 16.2% are below the statutory working age, and 25.9% are beyond statutory working age.

The Ryazan Region's major urban centers (2002 data) are Ryazan with 521,700 inhabitants and Kasimov with 36,000 inhabitants.

Population							TABLE 1
	1992	1997	1998	1999	2000	2001	2002
Total population, '000	1,346	1,319	1,308	1,298	1,285	1,271	1,228
Economically active population, '000	670	588	568	602	613	595	583

2. ADMINISTRATION

30, ul. Lenina, Ryazan, Ryazan Region, 390000
Phone: (0912) 27 4507
E-mail: kan2@adm1.ryazan.su, laf@adm1.ryazan.su; http://www.gov.ryazan.ru

NAME	POSITION	CONTACT INFORMATION
Vyacheslav Nikolaevich LYUBIMOV	Head of Administration of the Ryazan Region	Phone: (0912) 27 2125
Nikolai Vasilyevich MUZHIKHOV	First Deputy Head of Administration of the Ryazan Region for the Housing and Communal Services and Energy Sectors	Phone: (0912) 29 6340
Nikolai Iosifovich TASKIN	First Deputy Head of the Administration of the Ryazan Region, Chairman of the Ryazan Region State Property Management Committee	Phone: (0912) 21 5730
Anatoly Fedorovich GOVOROV	Deputy Head of Administration of the Ryazan Region in charge of Territories, Local Authorities, Public Relations, Information, and Human Resource Policies	Phone: (0912) 27 1803
Sergei Viktorovich SALNIKOV	First Deputy Head of Administration of the Ryazan Region in charge of the Agroindustrial Sector and Food Industry	Phone: (0912) 44 0954
Vladimir Ivanovich KOKOREV	First Deputy Head of Administration of the Ryazan Region in charge of Economy	Phone: (0912) 21 2738
Vladimir Ivanovich KUTENTSIN	Deputy Head of Administration of the Ryazan Region in charge of Industrial Policy	Phone: (0912) 27 4508
Alexander Mikhailovich ZHDANOV	Head of the Department of Foreign Economic Relations and Investment of the Ryazan Regional Administration	Phone: (0912) 21 7562

3. ECONOMIC POTENTIAL

3.1. 1997–2002 GROSS REGIONAL PRODUCT (GRP). INDUSTRY BREAKDOWN

The Ryazan Region's 2002 gross regional product reached $1,659.1 million, 10% up on 2001 levels. The growth was due to an increase in services. Per capita GRP totaled $1,186 in 2001 and $1,351 in 2002.

3.2. INDUSTRIAL OUTPUT IN 1997–2002 FOR MAJOR SECTORS OF ECONOMY

The leading sectors of the Ryazan Region are machine engineering and metal processing and energy. These sectors account for 33.4% of the GRP.

GRP trends in 1997–2002						TABLE 2
	1997	1998	1999	2000	2001	2002*
GRP in current prices, $ million	2,459.3	1,451.6	930.9	1,136.4	1,508.3	1,659.1

*Estimates of the Ryazan Regional Administration

GRP industry breakdown in 1997–2002, % of total						TABLE 3
	1997	1998	1999	2000	2001	2002*
GRP	100.0	100.0	100.0	100.0	100.0	100.0
Industry	34.8	36.1	31.7	28.0	27.2	26.9
Agriculture and forestry	21.2	17.7	24.4	23.0	15.2	14.7
Construction	6.1	5.8	5.2	9.1	8.0	7.6
Transport and communications	2.2	2.0	1.7	1.5	4.9	6.3
Trade and public catering	8.7	10.3	11.4	12.0	10.2	11.3
Other	18.6	22.1	20.3	20.9	19.3	17.7
Net taxes on output	8.4	6.0	5.3	5.5	15.2	15.5

*Estimates of the Ryazan Regional Administration

Industry breakdown of industrial output in 1997–2002, % of total						TABLE 4
	1997	1998	1999	2000	2001	2002*
Industry	100.0	100.0	100.0	100.0	100.0	100.0
Machine engineering and metal processing	16.9	21.3	22.1	28.1	27.6	18.1
Energy	45.2	37.0	25.9	24.1	23.6	15.3
Fuel	9.1	10.2	10.3	9.6	9.2	9.4
Food and beverages	10.4	10.2	13.6	11.4	12.5	6.7
Construction materials	7.5	8.8	9.1	10.1	8.9	5.8
Light industry	3.7	4.2	5.0	4.3	4.6	5.3
Chemicals and petrochemicals	0.9	1.8	2.6	2.4	3.2	2.6
Non-ferrous metals	1.3	1.3	3.8	3.1	2.9	1.6
Forestry, timber, and pulp and paper	1.1	1.1	1.2	1.7	1.8	1.3
Ferrous metals	0.2	0.2	0.2	0.3	0.5	0.2

*Estimates of the Ryazan Regional Administration

Machine engineering and metal processing. The sector accounts for 18.1% of total industrial output. The largest enterprises are OAO SASTA, OAO Tyazhpressmash, OAO SAAZ, OAO Kombayn Firm, GUP Ryazan Instrument-Making Plant, and OAO Krasnoye Znamya Plant. The sector employs around 40,000 people.

Energy. The sector accounts for 15.3% of total industrial output. The largest enterprises are OAO Ryazanskaya Hydroelectric Power

Station, OAO Novo-Ryazanskaya Thermal Power Station, and OAO Ryazanenergo.

Light industry. The sector accounts for 5.3% of total industrial output. The largest enterprise is OOO Ryazanvest.

Chemicals and petrochemicals. The sector accounts for 2.6% of total industrial output. The largest enterprises are OAO Ryazan Synthetic Fiber, and ZAO Ryazan Cardboard and Ruberoid Plant.

3.3. FUEL AND ENERGY BALANCE (OUTPUT AND CONSUMPTION PER RESOURCE)

The Ryazan Region imports the bulk of its fuel (oil, petrochemicals, and natural gas).

Electricity is produced at four power stations with an overall capacity of 3.6 GW.

About half of the generated electricity is consumed in the Region; the rest is exported to adjacent regions (the Nizhny Novgorod, Penza, and Tula Regions).

Fuel and energy sector production and consumption trends, 1997–2002						TABLE 5
	1997	1998	1999	2000	2001	2002*
Electricity output, billion kWh	14.0	11.9	11.1	12.5	12.5	11.7
Electricity consumption, billion kWh	5.4	5.5	5.5	5.6	5.5	6.0
Natural gas consumption, million cubic meters	3,643.6	3,204.2	3,438.3	3,681.4	4,194.8	3,565.6

*Estimates of the Ryazan Regional Administration

3.4. TRANSPORT INFRASTRUCTURE

Roads. The Ryazan Region has more than 8,700 kilometers of paved public highway. Its main highways are Moscow – Volgograd, Moscow – Samara, and Ryazan – Ryazhsk – Aleksandro-Nevsky.

Railroads. The Ryazan Region has some 1,100 kilometers of railroads. The Region is crossed east – west and north – south by major trunk railroads linking the center of Russia with the Volga Region, the Urals and Siberia: Moscow–Ryazan – Samara, Moscow – Ryazan – Volgograd, Ryazan – Vladimir, and Tula – Ryazhsk – Penza.

River transport. The ports of Ryazan and Kasimov are located on the Oka River. The major shipping operator is the Oka Shipping Company. The total length of the Ryazan Region's navigable inland waterway system is 690 kilometers.

3.5. MAIN NATURAL RESOURCES: RESERVES AND EXTRACTION IN 2002

The main natural resources of the Ryazan Region are limestone, clay, mason and glass sand, peat, brown coal, timber, phosphorites, brown iron ore, and mineral dye raw materials.

Peat and brown coal. The Ryazan Region has 23 explored deposits of brown coal (301.6 million tons) and 1,062 peat deposits (222 million tons).

Forest resourses. The Region's forested area covers some 1.123 million hectares. The Region's Oka Biosphere Reserve is a nature reserve of international importance.

Construction materials. The Ryazan Region has 25 explored deposits of clay and loam (reserves totaling 160 million cubic meters), 19 deposits of mason sands (116 million cubic meters), and 4 deposits of carbonate strata for construction lime (118,000 cubic meters).

4. TRADE OPPORTUNITIES

4.1. MAIN GOODS PRODUCED IN THE REGION

Industrial production in the Ryazan Region in 2002 totaled:

Machine engineering and metal processing. Metal-cutting machine tools (1,000 items), cash registers (13,100 items).

Chemicals. Synthetic fiber and yarn (22,700 tons).

Petrochemicals (primary processing). 10.2 million tons.

Construction materials. Insulating and roofing materials (102 million square meters).

Food and beverages. Whole milk products output of 95,700 tons; meat, including category one meat products, 9,300 tons; full fat cheese,

6,200 tons; vodka and liquors, 767,000 decaliters; ethyl alcohol, 3.3 million decaliters.

Light industry. Silk cloth (4.3 million square meters).

4.2. EXPORTS, INCLUDING EXTRA-CIS

2001 extra-CIS exports reached $521.9 million. CIS exports totaled $25.5 million. The corresponding figures for 2002 were $938.6 million and $26.9 million.

The bulk of the Region's exports consists of petrol, lubricants, viscose fiber, instruments and control systems, radar equipment, machine tools, and silk cloth. The Region's main extra-CIS trading partners for exports are Estonia, Latvia, and China.

4.3. IMPORTS, INCLUDING EXTRA-CIS

Imports from extra-CIS countries reached $92.2 million in 2001. Imports from CIS countries totaled $18.1 million. The corresponding figures for 2002 were $148.9 million and $32.6 million.

The bulk of the Region's imports consists of gas condensate, pesticides, raw sugar, and frozen meat. The Region's main trading partners for imports are Switzerland, Kazakhstan, the Netherlands, Germany, and Hungary.

4.4. MAJOR REGIONAL EXPORT AND IMPORT ENTITIES

Owing to the specific nature of the Ryazan Region's export and import activities, export and import transactions are performed mainly by industrial enterprises.

5. INVESTMENT OPPORTUNITIES

5.1. INVESTMENTS IN 1992–2002 (BY INDUSTRY SECTOR), INCLUDING FOREIGN INVESTMENTS

The following factors determine the investment appeal of the Ryazan Region:

- Its favorable geographical location and proximity to large markets;
- Its developed transport infrastructure;
- Its considerable industrial potential;
- Its unique and comfortable recreation, vacation, and health spa facilities.

5.2. CAPITAL INVESTMENT

The bulk of fixed capital investment goes to industry, transport, and communications.

5.3. MAJOR ENTERPRISES (INCLUDING ENTERPRISES WITH FOREIGN INVESTMENT)

The Ryazan Region hosts 129 companies with foreign capital, including 50 companies wholly owned by foreign investors.

Capital investment by industry sector, $ million						TABLE 6
	1997	1998	1999	2000	2001	2002
Total capital investment	297.3	174.2	105.3	210.6	322.3	167.9
Including major industries (% of total)						
Industry	37.5	43.1	42.7	29.8	10.0	42.7
Agriculture and forestry	3.5	5.4	7.0	3.9	3.4	8.1
Construction	0.5	1.5	1.2	1.5	1.4	2.6
Transport and communications	21.8	17.1	20.7	18.6	16.3	31.0
Trade and public catering	5.5	2.1	1.2	1.0	0.8	0.5
Other	31.2	30.8	27.2	45.2	68.1	15.1

Foreign investment trends in 1996–2002						TABLE 7
	1996–1997	1998	1999	2000	2001	2002
Foreign investment, $ million	11.6	4.8	1.3	1.3	1.6	0.1
Including FDI, $ million	11.6	4.0	1.3	1.3	1.6	0.1

Largest enterprises of the Ryazan Region	TABLE 8
COMPANY	SECTOR
OAO Ryazanskaya Hydroelectric Power Station	Energy
OAO Ryazan Oil Refinery	Fuel
OAO Skopinsky Avtoagregatny Zavod	Machine engineering
OAO Ryazanenergo	Energy
OAO Novo-Ryazanskaya Thermal Power Station	Energy
ZAO Ryazan Cardboard and Ruberoid Plant	Chemicals
OAO Viscose	Chemicals

5.4. MOST ATTRACTIVE SECTORS FOR INVESTMENT

According to the Ryazan Regional Administration, electronics, instrument manufacturing, agriculture, and construction are the most attractive sectors for investment.

5.5. CURRENT LEGISLATION ON INVESTOR TAX EXEMPTIONS AND PRIVILEGES

The Ryazan Region has passed a Law On Investment Activity in the Ryazan Region.

Regional entities responsible for raising investment		*TABLE 9*
ENTITY	ADDRESS	PHONE, FAX, E-MAIL
OOO Ryazan Investment Agency	27, ul. Lenina, Ryazan, Ryazan Region, 390000	Phone: (0912) 21 0790 Fax: (0912) 27 5220 E-mail: ralcm@ralcm.ru www.ralcm.ru
ZAO Ryazanvneshservis	52, ul. Sobornaya, Ryazan, Ryazan Region, 390000	Phone: (0912) 77 3682, 28 9533
OOO Rinvestbank	7, ul. Griboedova, Ryazan, Ryazan Region, 390006	Phone: (0912) 24 0888, 24 1026
OOO Ryazan Chamber of Commerce and Industry	14, ul. Gorkogo, Ryazan, Ryazan Region, 390023	Phone: (0912) 28 9903 Fax:(0912) 28 9902 E-mail: RyazanCCI@rtpp.ryazan.su www.rtpp.webservis.ru

5.6. FEDERAL AND REGIONAL ECONOMIC AND SOCIAL DEVELOPMENT PROGRAMS FOR THE RYAZAN REGION

Federal targeted programs. Some 32 federal targeted programs are currently underway in the Ryazan Region, most of which are focused on public welfare.

The subprograms being conducted under the federal targeted program Housing, 2002–2010 have been allocated priority status. The program seeks to significantly improve public welfare by providing residential housing and creating jobs in the construction and construction materials sectors.

2002 residential construction amounted to 225 houses with the total floorspace of some 30,000 square meters. Annual budget allocations for this program totaled around $2.1 million.

Regional programs. The Ryazan Region is implementing more than 100 regional programs. The most important ones include Rural Public Welfare Development, Development of the Agroindustrial Sector, and Development of Material and Technical Support to Regional Educational Institutions. The Region is also carrying out a regional targeted program for the Development of the Regional Gas Supply Network. The program aims to revamp housing estates and connect them to gas supply networks.

In 2002, household gas supply facilities were introduced to 11,900 apartments, eleven boilers were switched to gas, and 118 heat supply plants were installed. The budget savings resulting from the switch to natural gas heating totaled $4.8 million.

6. INVESTMENT PROJECTS

Industry sector and project description	1) Expected results 2) Amount and term of investment 3) Form of financing[1] 4) Documentation[2]	Contact information
1	2	3

OIL

12R001 ● ■ ▲

Creation of facilities for deep fuel oil processing at an operating refinery. Project goal: to expand production of lubricating materials to substitute imports.

1) 60,000 tons per year (sales of $30 million)
2) $55.7 million/1.5 years
3) L
4) FS, BP

ZAO Ryazan Experimental Petrochemicals Plant
20, Ryazhskoye shosse, Ryazan, Ryazan Region, 391000
Phone/fax: (0912) 24 3326, 24 3327, 24 3120
E-mail: roznhp@post.rzn.ru
Yury Konstantinovich Rygalin, CEO
OOO Unikoil
4, ul. I. Franko, Moscow, 121108
Phone/fax: (095) 796 9047
E-mail: unikoil@unikoil.ru
http://www.unikoil.ru
Alexey Ernestovich Avilov, President

CONSTRUCTION MATERIALS

12R002 ● ▲

Introduction of a robotic welding line for welding construction steel structures. Project goal: to reduce costs, expand production, and improve quality of construction steel structures.

1) 1.8 million tons constructions per year
2) €0.37 million/2 years
3) L
4) FS

OOO Industrial Engineering Company Steel and Aluminum Works
14, Ryazhskoye shosse, Ryazan, Ryazan Region, 390011
Phone/fax: (0912) 21 0169, 44 0333
E-mail: goloktionov@psk-sak.ryazan.ru
Vladimir Borisovich Goloktionov, CEO

HOTELS AND TOURISM

12R003 ■ ● ❖ ◆

Construction of a medieval estate in historical surroundings as a tourist attraction. Project goal: to expand the tourism market.

1) Annual revenue of $85,000
2) $1.5 million/n/a
3) E, L, JV
4) BP

Public Cultural Institution Ryazan Historical and Architectural Memorial Museum
15, the Kremlin, Ryazan, Ryazan Region, 390000
Phone: (0912) 27 6065
Fax: (0912) 27 5455
E-mail: root@riamz.ryazan.ru
Lyudmila Dmitrievna Maksimova, Director

MACHINE ENGINEERING AND METAL PROCESSING

12R004 ■ ● ◆

Establishment of production of flat color plasma TV panels. Project goal: to introduce laser-technology color TV panels and monitors to the market.

1) 3,000 items per year (at the first stage)
2) $150 million/2 years
3) E, L ($125.5 million)
4) BP

OAO Plazma
24, ul. Tsiolkovskogo, Ryazan, Ryazan Region, 390023
Phone: (0912) 44 9002
Fax: (0912) 44 0681
Vladislav Georgievich Samorodov, CEO

[1] L – Loan, E – Equity, Leas. – Leasing, JV – Joint Venture
[2] BP – Business Plan, FS – Feasibility Study

1	2	3

12R005 ■ ● ▲

| Launch of production of equipment for dental color analysis. Project goal: to introduce an original compact device to the market. | 1) 10,000 items per year
2) $0.6 million/2 years
3) E, L
4) FS | OOO Pramed
34, ul. Shevchenko, Ryazan,
Ryazan Region, 390026
Phone/fax: (0912) 76 0382
E-mail: ramed@pochtamp.ru
Andrei Semenovich Likhvantsev, CEO |

12R006 ■ ● ▲

| Launch of production of equipment for non-invasive measurement of inter-cranial pressure in infants. Project goal: to introduce a new product to the market. | 1) 10,000 items per year
2) $0.5 million/2 years
3) E, L
4) FS | OOO Ramed
34, ul. Shevchenko, Ryazan,
Ryazan Region, 390026
Phone/fax: (0912) 76 0382
E-mail: ramed@pochtamp.ru
Gennady Konstantinovich Piletsky, CEO |

13. SMOLENSK REGION [67]

ECONOMIC MAP

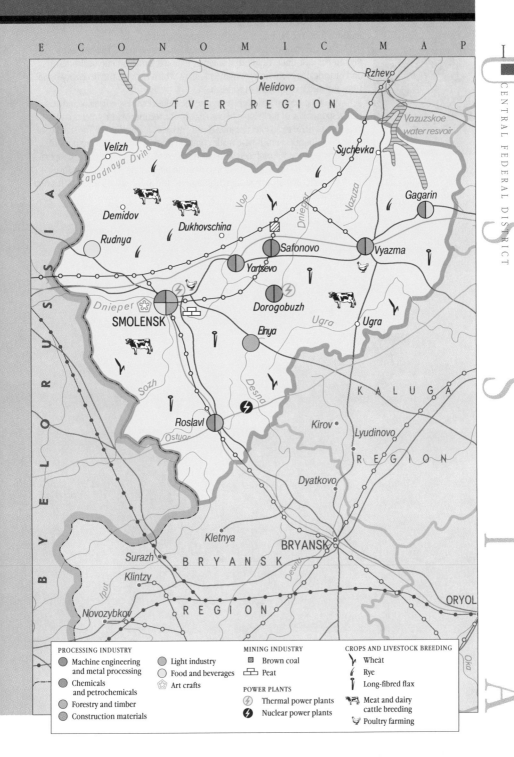

PROCESSING INDUSTRY

- Machine engineering and metal processing
- Chemicals and petrochemicals
- Forestry and timber
- Construction materials
- Light industry
- Food and beverages
- Art crafts

MINING INDUSTRY

- Brown coal
- Peat

POWER PLANTS

- Thermal power plants
- Nuclear power plants

CROPS AND LIVESTOCK BREEDING

- Wheat
- Rye
- Long-fibred flax
- Meat and dairy cattle breeding
- Poultry farming

The Smolensk Region's unique geographical location is one of the main resources we are eager to develop to the fullest extent possible. The Smolensk Region has strong potential for a mutually beneficial cooperation. Highways and trunk railways linking Western Europe to Central Russia cross the Region. The Region's major transshipment facilities, which are equipped with storage facilities, provide freight handling services. The Region's industry is a stable, and dynamically developing system that covers different branches, the main sectors being nuclear and heat energy, jewelry, machine and instrument engineering, timber, chemicals, light industry, food and beverages and construction materials.

The agroindustrial sector boasts considerable resources. The Smolensk Region has vast tracts of idle arable lands, national parks, unique health resorts, and historical and cultural monuments, all of which provide the necessary conditions for the development of tourism.

All of the Region's partners recognize the industriousness, reliability, and business responsibility of the people of our Region. The security of investments and conditions conducive to an effective investment payback are guaranteed. The stability of the local authorities, which have made common purpose with socially responsible and active businesses, combined with our readiness for mutually profitable cooperation, represent the key to successful implementation of all projects and initiatives.

We welcome all investors who come to the Smolensk Region with bona fide intentions!

Viktor Maslov,
HEAD OF ADMINISTRATION OF THE SMOLENSK REGION

1. GENERAL INFORMATION

1.1. GEOGRAPHY

The Smolensk Region covers a total area of 49,800 square kilometers. It is located in the central part of the East European Plain. To the south-west, west, and north-west, the Region borders the Republic of Belarus, to the north – the Pskov and Tver Regions, to the north-east – the Moscow Region, to the east – the Kaluga Region, and to the south-east – the Bryansk Region.

1.2. CLIMATE

The Smolensk Region has a moderate continental climate.

Air temperatures in January average –9.4°C, rising to +17°C in July. Annual precipitation reaches 691 mm.

1.3. POPULATION

According to preliminary 2002 census results, a total population in the Region was 1,051,000 . The Region's average population density is 21.1 people/km².

The number of economically active people totaled 561,000 in 2002. The official unemployment rate in the Region in 2002 was 0.9%.

Demographically speaking, some 60.3% are of working age, 16.8% are below the statutory working age, and 22.9% are beyond the statutory working age.

The Smolensk Region's major urban centers are Smolensk with 325,500 inhabitants, Vyazma with 59,000 inhabitants, Roslavl with 57,300 inhabitants, Yartsevo with 56,000 inhabitants, and Safonovo with 51,900 inhabitants.

Population								_TABLE 1_
	1992	1997	1998	1999	2000	2001	2002
Total population, '000	1,158	1,162	1,153	1,143	1,128	1,114	1,051
Economically active population, '000	586	521	526	567	565	556	561

2. ADMINISTRATION

1, ul. Lenina, Smolensk, Smolensk Region, 214008
Phone: (08122) 36 611; fax: (08122) 36 851
E-mail: Invest@admin.smolensk.ru; http://www.admin.smolensk.ru

NAME	POSITION	CONTACT INFORMATION
Viktor Nikolaevich MASLOV	Head of Administration of the Smolensk Region	Phone: (08122) 36 611 Fax (08122) 36 851
Alexander Viktorovich SCHELOKOV	First Deputy Head of Administration of the Smolensk Region in charge of Operational Management, Financing, and Funds	Phone: (08122) 36 519, 36 029 Fax: (08122) 34 386
Andrei Valentinovich UKRAINSKY	Deputy Head of Administration of the Smolensk Region in charge of Investment, Securities Market, and Foreign Economic Relations	Phone: (08122) 36 165 Fax: (08122) 36 175
Yury Palladyevich VASEV	Head of the Economic Development Department of the Smolensk Region	Phone: (08122) 36 125 Fax: (08122) 36 718
Nadezhda Semenovna IVANOVA	Head of the Budget and Tax Division of the Economic Development Department of the Smolensk Region	Phone: (08122) 33 686 Fax: (08122) 36 718
Valery Mikhailovich KAMYSHEV	Head of the Analysis and Forecasting Division of the Economic Development Department of the Smolensk Region	Phone: (08122) 36 666
Sergei Nikolaevich KUDRYAVTSEV	Head of the Foreign Economic Relations Division of the Smolensk Region	Phone: (08122) 68 526 Fax: (08122) 37 146

CENTRAL FEDERAL DISTRICT

3. ECONOMIC POTENTIAL

3.1. 1997–2002 GROSS REGIONAL PRODUCT (GRP). INDUSTRY BREAKDOWN

The Smolensk Region's GRP amounted to $1,382.5 million in 2002, a 6.7% increase on 2001. The increase was mainly accomplished via growth in industrial output, which accounts for 32.8% of total GRP. Per capita GRP in 2001 equaled $1,162, rising to $1,316 in 2002.

3.2. MAJOR ECONOMIC GROWTH PROJECTIONS

The Region's economic potential is based on industry, with its 250 large and medium-sized enterprises. Most of these are located in Smolensk and in the towns of Vyazma, Gagarin, Roslavl, Safonovo, Yartsevo, and Dorogobuzh. Goods produced in Smolensk are well

GRP trends in 1997–2002						TABLE 2
	1997	1998	1999	2000	2001*	2002*
GRP in current prices, $ million	1,928.6	1,239.6	874.7	1,063.1	1,295.3	1,382.5

*Estimates of the Smolensk Regional Administration

GRP industry breakdown in 1997–2002, % of total						TABLE 3
	1997	1998	1999	2000	2001*	2002*
GRP	100.0	100.0	100.0	100.0	100.0	100.0
Industry	32.0	36.9	37.8	31.7	31.5	32.8
Agriculture and forestry	11.9	10.3	10.7	11.5	12.1	10.9
Construction	5.8	4.6	3.9	11.1	9.7	7.2
Transport and communications	8.7	10.1	8.5	8.5	9.2	10.5
Trade and public catering	13.9	12.6	11.3	15.7	16.9	17.5
Other	27.7	25.5	24.4	15.6	15.3	12.4
Net taxes on output	–	–	3.4	5.9	5.3	8.7

*Estimates of the Smolensk Regional Administration

known outside Russia, as witnessed by awards from international fairs and competitions. More than 40 enterprises in the Region are exporters, including GUP Kristall, OAO Smolenskaya Linen Mill, ZAO Smolenskaya Linen Factory, ZAO Smolenskaya Hosiery Factory, and OAO Sitall. The Region's enterprises have the technical and labor potential to cooperate successfully on a European level.

3.3. INDUSTRIAL OUTPUT IN 1997–2002 FOR MAJOR SECTORS OF ECONOMY

Jewelry. Jewelry is the leading industry in the Region, yielding some 26% of its total industrial output. GUP Kristall is the world's largest cut diamond producer. The Smolensk Region, the diamond-cutting

Industry breakdown of industrial output in 1997–2002, % of total						TABLE 4
	1997	1998	1999	2000	2001	2002*
Industry	100.0	100.0	100.0	100.0	100.0	100.0
Jewelry	11.5	20.7	34.1	35.5	28.0	26.0
Energy	31.2	27.6	18.2	16.8	19.4	23.9
Machine engineering and metal processing	18.4	15.0	13.6	16.3	19.7	19.3
Food and beverage	14.4	14.3	13.2	10.2	9.7	9.9
Chemicals and petrochemicals	11.4	9.9	10.3	9.6	9.8	8.3
Construction materials	5.1	4.4	4.0	4.7	4.8	4.9
Light industry	2.8	2.3	2.4	3.0	2.9	2.7
Forestry, timber, and pulp and paper	1.3	1.2	1.4	1.4	1.1	1.7

*Estimates of the Smolensk Regional Administration

center of Russia, is home to nine diamond processing enterprises with some 5,000 employees. Annual cut diamond output totals some $300 million.

Energy. The energy sector accounts for some 23.9% of the Region's total industrial output. The Region's energy majors are the Smolenskaya Nuclear Power Station and OAO Smolenskenergo, which includes the Dorogobuzhkaya TPS, Smolenskaya GRES, Smolenskaya TPS 2, and 10 local branches. The industry provides employment for 12,000 people.

Machine engineering and metal processing. The machine engineering and metal processing sector accounts for 19.3% of the Region's total industrial output. The machine engineering sector comprises energy machinery and electric machinery enterprises, instrumentation plants, and road and communal services machinery companies. The sector features unique production facilities and technologies. The sector provides jobs for some 40,000 people.

Food and beverages. The Smolensk Region's food and beverage enterprises process local agricultural produce. The sector includes dairy, meat processing, flour milling, bakery, and alcoholic beverages enterprises, and accounts for some 9.9% of the Region's total industrial output. The largest enterprises include OAO Rosa, OAO Bakhus, OAO Sahko, OAO Smolmyaso, and OAO Khlebopek.

Chemicals and petrochemicals. The chemicals sector accounts for some 8.3% of the Region's total industrial output. OAO Dorogobuzh is one of Russia's leading manufacturers of mineral fertilizers and chemical synthesis products.

3.4. FUEL AND ENERGY BALANCE (OUTPUT AND CONSUMPTION PER RESOURCE)

The Region's considerable energy resources fully serve its electricity needs. Electricity output amounted to 22.7 billion kWh in 2002 (19.7 billion kWh was exported outside the Region).

Fuel and energy sector production and consumption trends, 1997–2002						TABLE 5
	1997	1998	1999	2000	2001	2002*
Electricity output, billion kWh	19.7	17.5	22.4	22.9	23.7	22.7
Electricity consumption, billion kWh	5.8	5.5	5.6	5.7	5.9	3.0

*Estimates of the Smolensk Regional Administration

3.5. TRANSPORT INFRASTRUCTURE

Roads. The Region has 8,862 km of paved roads. The Region's territory is criss-crossed by highways of national economic significance: Moscow – Minsk, Oryol – Vitebsk, and Moscow – Warsaw. Road haulage companies such as OAO Transit, OAO Smoltransmoloko, and ZAO Smolenskekspeditsiya provide reliable freight transportation services.

Railroads. The Smolensk Region has 1,260 km of railroads and two important railroad junctions, Vyazma and Roslavl, complete with modern loading/unloading, sorting, and warehouse facilities. The Region provides links to other regions of Russia, as well as the CIS and Baltic States and the rest of Europe. The Region's main rail corridors are Moscow – Smolensk – Minsk and Bryansk – Smolensk – Vitebsk.

3.6. MAIN NATURAL RESOURCES: RESERVES AND EXTRACTION IN 2002

The Region's principal natural resources are minerals and raw materials, forestry, and water.

Minerals and raw materials. Around 30 kinds of natural minerals are found in the Region, including low-heating-value brown coals (1.5 billion tons), peat (450 million tons), dolomite, chalk, limestone, and sapropel (150 million cubic meters).

Forest resources. Forests cover more than 43% of the Region's territory (34% coniferous forests, including 22% of fir, while deciduous forests have birch, aspen, alder, oak, rowan, hazel, snowball trees, linden, and poplar trees). The annual felling output is 3 million cubic meters; the total forest area is 2,121,500 hectares.

Water resources. An extensive river network covers the area. The Region is drained by three large rivers: the Dnepr, the Volga, and the Western Dvina. Around one hundred lakes cover an area of roughly 70 square km.

4. TRADE OPPORTUNITIES

4.1. MAIN GOODS PRODUCED IN THE REGION

Energy. The Region's output amounted to 22.7 billion kWh in 2002, 4% less than in 2001.

Mineral fertilizers. Output of mineral fertilizers in 2002 was up 18% year-on-year at 457,900 tons.

Large electric machinery. Output of large electric machinery was 980 pieces in 2002, 18% down on 2001.

Household refrigerators and freezers. Output of household refrigerators and freezers reached 53,900 pieces in 2002 (up 21% on 2001).

4.2. EXPORTS, INCLUDING EXTRA-CIS

In 2000, exports to extra-CIS countries amounted to $399.6 million, while exports to CIS were only $12.7 million, in 2001, these figures were respectively $405.2 million and $14.6 million, and in 2002, respectively $387.2 million and $14 million.

The bulk of the Region's exports is made up of jewelry, including precious and semi-precious stones and precious metals ($289.5 million), followed by chemicals ($71.3 million), machinery and equipment ($14.4 million), vehicles ($4.5 million), textiles ($3.6 million), and lumber and timber ($3.3 million). Major importers of the Region's products include Belgium, Israel, Panama, Switzerland, Lithuania, and Belarus.

4.3. IMPORTS, INCLUDING EXTRA-CIS

In 2000, imports from extra-CIS countries reached $83.5 million, and imports from CIS countries amounted to $23.8 million ($112.2 and $21.3 million in 2001, $156.5 and $18 million in 2002, respectively).

The bulk of the Region's imports is represented by machinery and equipment ($73.9 million), chemicals ($21.9 million), food and beverages products ($17.7 million), ferrous metals and articles ($11 million), and vehicles ($4.9 million). The bulk of the Region's non-CIS imports are from Bulgaria, Germany, Austria, France, Poland, Italy, Belgium, Spain, Belarus and Ukraine.

4.4. MAJOR REGIONAL EXPORT AND IMPORT ENTITIES

Due to the nature of the Region's exports and imports, export and import operations are conducted mainly by industrial enterprises.

5. INVESTMENT OPPORTUNITIES

5.1. INVESTMENTS IN 1992–2002 (BY INDUSTRY SECTOR), INCLUDING FOREIGN INVESTMENTS

The following factors determine the investment appeal of the Smolensk Region:

• Favorable geographical location on the crossroads of routes linking Moscow to Western Europe;

• A developed transport infrastructure;

• Legislation providing support for investment projects (guarantees of investor rights and the provision of tax incentives to investors);

• A highly qualified, comparatively low-cost labor force;

• Developed processing facilities;

• Abundant natural resources.

5.2. CAPITAL INVESTMENT

The transport and manufacturing sectors (energy and machine engineering) accounted for the lion's share of capital investment in 2002.

5.3. MAJOR ENTERPRISES (INCLUDING ENTERPRISES WITH FOREIGN INVESTMENT)

The Region's largest enterprises with foreign investment are GUP Kristall, JV Smolensk-Tashe, and OAO Yukar-Grafit. OAO Sitall produces glass bottles in cooperation with The Coca-Cola Company. Russian-Chinese joint venture Vyazma Sea-Lion manufactures dry-cleaning equipment. The European Bank for Reconstruction and Development and ZAO Fayans are currently implementing a joint sanitary ware-manufacturing project.

Foreign investment trends in 1996–2002						*TABLE 6*
	1996–1997	1998	1999	2000	2001	2002
Foreign investment, $ million	49.8	26.6	9.9	10.9	9.9	11.8
Including FDI, $ million	4.7	0.2	0.1	0.04	–	–

Capital investment by industry sector, $ million						*TABLE 7*
	1997	1998	1999	2000	2001	2002
Total capital investment	182.5	101.2	197.0	229.0	269.7	269.7
Including major industries (% of total):						
Industry	28.5	47.6	12.8	17.3	19.0	28.8
Agriculture and forestry	2.1	4.9	1.6	1.9	1.5	2.1
Construction	2.3	0.5	1.2	0.8	1.1	0.8
Transport and communications	26.4	15.4	73.9	66.7	62.6	50.0
Trade and public catering	0.3	0.5	0.2	0.3	0.4	0.5
Other	40.4	31.1	10.3	13.0	15.4	17.8

Largest enterprises of the Smolensk Region	*TABLE 8*
COMPANY	SECTOR
The Smolenskaya Nuclear Power Station	Energy
OAO Smolenskenergo	Energy
GUP Kristall	Jewelry
OOO Kristalldiam	Jewelry
OAO Dorogobuzh	Chemicals
FGUP PO Avangard	Chemicals
OAO Rosa	Food and beverages
OAO Bakhus	Food and beverages
OAO Gnezdovo	Construction materials
ZAO Fayans	Construction materials
OAO Khlebopek	Food and beverages
OAO Smolensky Timber Plant	Forestry and timber
OAO Smolensky Aircraft Plant	Machine engineering
ZAO Smolensky Auto Equipment Plant AMO ZIL	Machine engineering
FGUP SPO Analitpribor	Machine engineering
ZAO Smolensk Hosiery Factory	Light industry
OAO Charm	Light industry

I

CENTRAL FEDERAL DISTRICT

5.4. MOST ATTRACTIVE SECTORS FOR INVESTMENT

In 2002, capital investments rose by 7.5%. Investment projects are currently underway in the Vyazemsky, Smolensky, and Safonovsky Districts, and in the towns of Smolensk and Desnogorsk. The timber sector's investment growth rate, which has risen by the factor of 11.4, is the highest in the Region. The investment growth rate was also on the increase in machine engineering and metal processing (27%), building materials (27%), forestry (260%), and construction (53%). Investment into new equipment in the housing sector grew by 65%.

5.5. CURRENT LEGISLATION ON INVESTOR TAX EXEMPTIONS AND PRIVILEGES

The Smolensk Region has passed the following laws with a view to creating a favorable investment climate in the Region: On Tax Exemptions for External Investors (the law provides exemptions from regional and local tax components, and extends guarantees of the protection of investors' rights); On Tax Exemptions for Investors in the Smolensk Region (the law provides certain exemptions for investors: property tax, regional land tax component, and transport tax, and reduces the profit tax rate by four percentage points); On the Development Budget of the Smolensk Region (the law provides for the extension of interest-bearing, and repayable government guarantees, budget loans, and budget investment from the regional budget); On State Support of Investment Activity in the Smolensk Region (provides greater opportunities for state support to enterprises).

Regional entities responsible for raising investment		*TABLE 9*
ENTITY	ADDRESS	PHONE, FAX, E-MAIL
Smolensk Chamber of Commerce and Industry	12, ul. Marksa, Smolensk, Smolensk Region, 214000	Phone: (0812) 23 7450; fax: (0812) 23 7432 E-mail: smolcci@keytown.com
OOO Kovaleva & Co Appraisal Agency	AO Vita Administrative Building, 3-rd Micro District, Desnogorsk, Smolensk Region, 214018	Phone: (0812) 23 1782 Fax: (0812) 23 5353 E-mail: kovaleva1@sci.smolensk.ru
OOO Rosexpertiza	Building 3, 7, Tikhvinsky per. Moscow, 127055	Phone: (095) 721 3883; fax: (095) 721 3894 E-mail: rosexp@online.ru
OAO Tsentr Delo	10/2, pr. Gagarina, Smolensk, Smolensk Region, 214000	Phone: (0812) 29 1507; fax: (0812) 29 1648 E-mail: centrd@sci.smolensk.ru

5.6. FEDERAL AND REGIONAL ECONOMIC AND SOCIAL DEVELOPMENT PROGRAMS FOR THE SMOLENSK REGION

Federal targeted programs. A number of federal targeted programs for economic and social development of the Smolensk Region are underway, including: Modernization of Russia's Transport System, 2002–2010; Culture of Russia, 2001–2005; Housing, 2002–2010, with its subprograms State Housing Certificates, Provision of Housing for Refugees and Forced Migrants in the Russian Federation, Reforms and Modernization the Housing Sector in the Russian Federation, and Housing for Radiation Disaster Relief Participants, The Senior Generation, 2002–2004; Social Assistance for Disabled Citizens, 2003–2005, The Children of Russia, 2003–2006, with its subprograms Prevention of Child Neglect and Juvenile Delinquency,

Disabled Children, and Gifted Children; The Prevention and Fighting of Social Diseases, 2002–2006, including the following subprograms: Vaccine Measures, Diabetes, and Arterial Hypertension Prevention and Treatment; and The Enrichment of Russia's Soil, 2002–2006. The programs are financed from the federal budget, regional budget, local budgets, and non-budgetary funds.

Regional programs. The Smolensk Region's regional programs are focused on healthcare, education, social policies, culture, sports, the environment, housing, agriculture and transport, including the top priority programs The Program for Suppurt and Development of Scientific Activities in the Smolensk Region, 2002–2005, and Increasing the Soil Fertility in the Smolensk Region, 2002–2005.

In 2002, some $111.5 million was allocated for federal and regional targeted programs.

6. INVESTMENT PROJECTS

Industry sector and project description	1) Expected results 2) Amount and term of investment 3) Form of financing[1] 4) Documentation[2]	Contact information
1	2	3
MINING		
13R001 ● ★ ◆		OAO Smolensktorf
Acquisition of equipment for production of higher quality peat at lower cost. Project goal: peat cutting.	1) 12,000 tons of peat per year (revenue of $0.5 million per year) 2) $0.4 million/3.5 years 3) L, Leas. 4) BP	12, ul. Chaplina, Smolensk, Smolensk Region, 214014 Phone: (0812) 23 3710, (0812) 55 9774 Fax: (0812) 23 3710 Nikolai Ivanovich Shabrov, CEO
CHEMICALS AND PETROCHEMICALS		
13R002 ● ★ ◆		FGUP PO Avangard
Production of multi-purpose polymer composite cisterns for liquid gas (propane-butane) storage and transportation. Project goal: production of competitive goods in compliance with European standards.	1) 100 cisterns per year (revenue of $6.5 million per year) 2) $10 million/4 years 3) L, Leas. 4) BP	78, ul. Oktyabrskaya, Safonovo, Smolensk Region, 215500 Phone: (0814) 24 2045, 23 2563, 23 0024 Fax: (0814) 23 2655, 23 4707 E-mail: avangard@sci.smolensk.ru Leonid Mikhailovich Krishnev, CEO
MACHINE ENGINEERING AND METAL PROCESSING		
13R003 ● ★ ◆		ZAO Roslavl Auto Equipment Plant AMO ZIL
Launch of 4-section fuel pumps production on the basis of existing equipment. Objective: to produce an article that will be able to compete successfully with similar European products.	1) 40,000 fuel pumps a year (revenue of $10.6 million per year) 2) $3.7 million /3.2 years 3) L, Leas. 4) BP	196, ul. Michiurina, Roslavl, Smolensk Region, 216500 Phone/fax: (08134) 51 511, 31 219, 31 212 Fax: (08134) 20 016, 20 457, 31 212, (095) 992 1210 E-mail: raaz@sci.smolensk.ru Vladimir Filippovich Savchuk, CEO

[1] L – Loan, E – Equity, Leas. – Leasing, JV – Joint Venture
[2] BP – Business Plan, FS – Feasibility Study

| 1 | 2 | 3 |

FORESTRY, TIMBER, AND PULP AND PAPER

13R004 ● ★ ◆

Creation of new modern production facilities for large-format plywood. Project goal: production of competitive goods.

1) 30,000 cubic meters a year (revenue of $27.2 million per year)
2) $11 million/2.5 years
3) L, Leas.
4) BP

OAO Smolensk Timber Mill
430th km, Micro District Pronino,
Smolensk, Smolensk Region, 214022
Phone: (0812) 62 8909, 62 8037, 62 8236
Fax: (0812) 62 8037
E-mail: dokcm@keytown.com
Vladimir Nikolaevich Petchenko,
CEO

CONSTRUCTION MATERIALS

13R005 ● ★ ◆

Acquisition and installation of Italian Sacmi equipment with low energy requirements; and replacement of pressure equipment and glaze and pattern application unit. Project goal: production of large-format ceramic tiles.

1) 3 million square meters of ceramic tiles per year (revenue of $18 million per year)
2) 13.1 million/3 years
3) L, Leas.
4) BP

OAO Smolensky Building
Materials Combine
Gnezdovo Micro District,
Smolensk, Smolensk Region, 214034
Phone: (0812) 22 5285, 22 5755
Fax: (0812) 22 5479
Alexander Petrovich Volodin,
CEO

13R006 ● ★ ◆

Equipment acquisition and installation, reconstruction of production, warehouse and administrative facilities, and transport links and power supply system repairs. Project goal: to produce foam mortar goods and structures.

1) 160,000 cubic meters per year (revenue of $11.3 million per year)
2) $16.5 million/1.5 years
3) L, Leas.
4) BP

ZAO Kristall-Atomstroy Holding
64, ul. 25 Sentyabrya, Smolensk,
Smolensk Region, 214031
Phone: (0812) 51 2827
Fax: (0812) 51 2827, 61 1238
E-mail: kaholding@mail.ru
Igor Vladimirovich Kadnikov,
CEO

GLASS AND PORCELAIN

13R007 ● ★ ◆

Acquisition of equipment made by Germany's Netch-Thuringia. Project goal: to produce sanitary stoneware to world standards of design and quality.

1) Wash basins – 50,000, footstalls – 50,000, flushing cisterns – 100,000, toilet bowls – 100,000 per year (revenue of $3.5 million)
2) $1.9 million/2.5 years
3) L, Leas.
4) BP

OAO Smolensky Building
Materials Combine
Gnezdovo Micro District, Smolensk,
Smolensk Region, 214034
Phone: (0812) 22 5285, 22 5755
Fax: (0812) 22 5479
E-mail: gnezdovo@keytown.com
Alexander Petrovich Volodin,
CEO

LIGHT INDUSTRY

13R008 ● ★ ◆

Acquisition and installation of modern cotton spinning, weaving, and finishing equipment. Project goal: to improve quality of cotton fabrics and articles.

1) 1,322,000 running meters of cotton fabric per year; (revenue of $2 million per year)
2) $1.75 million/2.8 years
3) L, Leas.
4) BP

UMP Yartsevsky Cotton Factory
16, ul. Leninskaya, Yartsevo,
Smolensk Region, 215800
Phone: (08143) 41 794
Fax: (08143) 42 762
E-mail: xbk@sci.smolensk.ru
Vladimir Yuryevich Mazin,
CEO

13R009 ● ★ ◆

Modernization of spinning and finishing production facilities to improve linen quality. Project goal: to produce high class linen.

1) 6 million running meters of vest, suit, and dress materials, 650,000 running meters of linen fabrics, 1.74 million running meters of napery and bed linen per year
2) $4.5 million/1 year
3) L, Leas.
4) BP

OAO Smolenskaya Linen Mill
2/8, ul. Novo-Moskovskaya, Smolensk,
Smolensk Region, 214001
Phone: (0812) 22 0582
Fax: (0812) 29 9360
E-mail: Textil@sci.smolensk.ru
Nina Vasilyevna Belyakova,
CEO

1	2	3

FOOD AND BEVERAGES

13R010

Launch of a mixed fodder expanding and granulating line.
Project goal: to produce expanded and granulated mixed fodder.

1) 60,000 tons per year
(revenue of $8 million per year)
2) $1.3 million/2.4 years
3) L, Leas.
4) BP

OAO Gnezdovozernoprodukt
14, ul. Zadorozhnaya, Gnezdovo,
Smolensk, Smolensk Region, 214525
Phone (0812) 22 5851, 22 5451, 22 5753
Valery Viktorovich Molotkov,
CEO

AGRICULTURE

13R011

Completing the construction of a poultry factory (completion and reconstruction of 20 poultry houses, hatches, slaughterhouse, and processing area, and acquisition of equipment and vehicles).
Project goal: to increase the output of poultry meat and to enhance product quality.

1) 5,200 tons of poultry meat per year
(revenue of $45 million per year)
2) $6.7 million/1 year
3) L, Leas.
4) BP

OOO PO Optifud-Vyazma
Kaidakovo Village, Vyazemsky District,
Smolensk Region, 215101
Phone: (08131) 42 933
Fax: (08131) 42 933
Valery Nikolaevich Lukyanenko,
CEO

13R012

Acquisition and installation of new equipment, expansion of manufacturing capacity and efficiency enhancement.
Project goal: to reconstruct the poultry farm, raise agricultural production output (eggs, poultry meat).

1) Eggs – 140 million per year;
poultry meat – 860 tons per year
(revenue of $8 million per year)
2) 0.6 million/2 years
3) L, Leas.
4) BP

ZAO Prigorskoye
Prigorskoye Village, Smolensky District,
Smolensk Region, 214518
Phone: (0812) 23 6276
Fax: (0812) 27 0787
Yury Danilovich Skabaro,
CEO

HOTELS, TOURISM, AND RECREATION

13R013

Construction of a modern four-star hotel complex in Smolensk with a hotel, a conference hall, a business centre, a restaurant, an indoor swimming pool, and a parking lot.
Project goal: to develop the tourist services market.

1) 120 rooms (revenue
of $4 million per year)
2) $11.6 million/n/a
3) E, L, Leas.
4) BP

Smolensk Region Department
of Cultural Policy and Tourism
1, pl. Lenina, Smolensk,
Smolensk Region, 214008
Phone: (0812) 29 8512
Fax: (0812) 29 8514
E-mail: kult@admin.smolensk.ru
Viktor Mikhailovich Mikhnenkov, CEO

ECOLOGY AND WASTE TREATMENT

13R014

Construction of a household waste sorting and pressing complex.
Project goal: to utilize household waste.

1) 450,000 cubic metres of solid
household waste per year
(revenue of $2.5 million)
2) $1.6 million/2.5 years
3) E, L, Leas.
4) –

City Cleansing Municipal Enterprise
65b, ul. Tikhvinka, Smolensk,
Smolensk Region, 214019
Phone: (0812) 29 7466, 55 6057
Phone/fax: (0812) 55 6057
Gennady Anatolyevich Filipenkov,
Director

13R015

Acquisition of equipment produced by Russian manufacturers.
Project goal: to implement a comprehensive waste utilization management system.

1) 120,000 tons of solid waste
per year, 60,000 tons
of assorted waste per year
(revenue of $1.9 million per year)
2) $3.6 million/6 years
3) E, L, Leas.
4) BP

OOO Kontsern Vtorichniye Resursy
Office 319, 22, ul. Tenishevoy,
Smolensk, Smolensk Region, 214018
Phone/fax: (0812) 29 8508
E-mail: apolis@sci.smolensk.ru
Pavel Viktorovich Darulis,
CEO

TRANSPORT

13R016

Acquisition of haulage vehicles.
Project goal: to increase the range of services provided by road haulage companies to building and extraction industrial enterprises.

1) 10 million ton-kilometers per
year (revenue of $1.4 million)
2) 0.7 million/2.4 years
3) L, Leas.
4) BP

OAO Smolstrom-Service
23a, ul. Engelsa, Smolensk,
Smolensk Region, 214014
Phone/fax: (0812) 55 2363
Vyacheslav Fedorovich Kosykh,
CEO

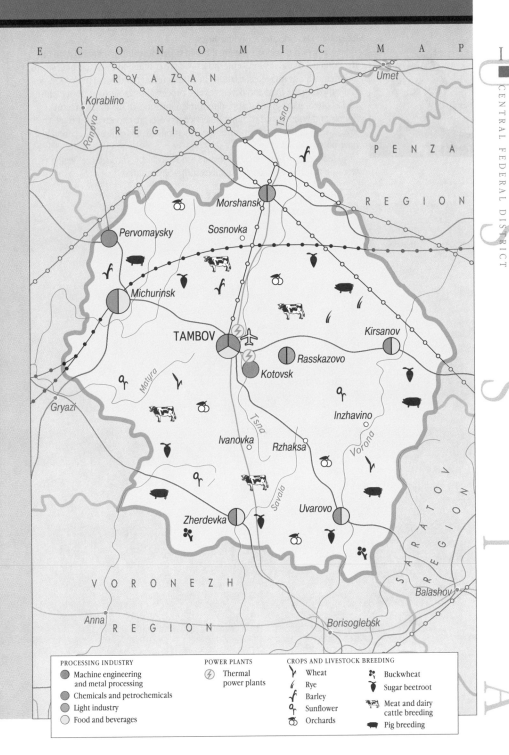

ECONOMIC MAP

RUSSIA

CENTRAL FEDERAL DISTRICT

PROCESSING INDUSTRY
- Machine engineering and metal processing
- Chemicals and petrochemicals
- Light industry
- Food and beverages

POWER PLANTS
- Thermal power plants

CROPS AND LIVESTOCK BREEDING
- Wheat
- Rye
- Barley
- Sunflower
- Orchards
- Buckwheat
- Sugar beetroot
- Meat and dairy cattle breeding
- Pig breeding

The Tambov Region has always been open to business cooperation, its inhabitants being equally adept at working and trading. Today, in addition to a highly qualified workforce and developed transport infrastructure and communications, the Region boasts considerable industrial and scientific potential. The Region also offers considerable investment opportunities and favorable conditions for profitable investment, the construction of new and expansion of existing industrial facilities, and the development of arable land.

The Region is actively encouraging domestic and foreign investment and expanding its trade and economic links.

Many of the Region's potential business partners still lack information on the potential of the Region's enterprises. We are committed to establishing strong and mutually advantageous relations in all spheres. Agroindustrial projects, especially those in the food and beverages and processing sectors, have been identified as offering the greatest appeal to foreign investors in the medium term. Energy and housing and communal service projects are expected to attract investments in the long term, after the structural reforms of Russia's economy have been completed.

A direct link to potential investors is now available through the Region's web-site at http://www.regadm.tambov.ru/inv/invest.shtml.

Oleg Betin,
HEAD OF ADMINISTRATION OF THE TAMBOV REGION

1. GENERAL INFORMATION

1.1. GEOGRAPHY

The Tambov Region covers a total area of 34,000 square kilometers. The Region is located within the Central Black Earth Region. To the north, the Region borders the Ryazan Region, to the east – the Penza Region and the Saratov Region, to the south – the Voronezh Region, and to the west – the Lipetsk Region.

1.2. CLIMATE

The Tambov Region is located within the temperate continental climate zone.

Air temperatures in January average −11.5°C, rising to +20°C in July. Annual precipitation reaches 370 mm. The average growing season lasts about 160 days.

1.3. POPULATION

According to preliminary 2002 census results, the total population of the Tambov Region is 1,180,000 people. The average population density is 34.7 people per square kilometer. The economically active population amounts to 576,000. In 2002, official unemployment stood at 2.7%.

Demographically speaking, some 57% are of statutory working age, 21% are below the statutory working age, and 22% are beyond the statutory working age.

The Tambov Region's major urban centers are Tambov with 294,300 inhabitants (2002) and Michurinsk with 115,500 inhabitants.

I

CENTRAL FEDERAL DISTRICT

Population								TABLE 1
		1992	1997	1998	1999	2000	2001	2002
Total population, '000		1,312	1,304	1,293	1,283	1,270	1,256	1,180
Economically active population, '000		621	541	504	592	583	543	576

2. ADMINISTRATION

14, ul. Internatsionalnaya, Tambov, Tambov Region, 392017
Phone: (0752) 72 1043; fax: (0752) 72 2518
E-mail: post@regadm.tambov.ru; http://www.regadm.tambov.ru

NAME	POSITION	CONTACT INFORMATION
Oleg Ivanovich BETIN	Head of Administration of the Tambov Region	Phone: (0752) 72 1061 Fax: (0752) 72 2518
Vladimir Ivanovich ANDREEV	First Deputy Head of Administration of the Tambov Region	Phone: (0752) 72 1230
Alexander Yakovlevich DUBOVIK	First Deputy Head of Administration of the Tambov Region, Head of the Regional Agriculture and Food Department	Phone: (0752) 72 3155
Kirill Viktorovich KOLONCHIN	Deputy Head of Administration of the Tambov Region, Head of the Regional Economic Development Department	Phone: (0752) 72 6661
Vladimir Alexandrovich TITARENKO	Deputy Head of Administration of the Tambov Region	Phone/fax: (0752) 72 4581, 72 0653
Petr Petrovich CHERNOIVANOV	Deputy Head of Administration of the Tambov Region, Head of the Regional Business Development and Consumer Market Department	Phone: (0752) 72 6307
Ivan Tikhonovich SCHEGLOV	Deputy Head of Administration of the Tambov Region, Chairman of the Regional Property Management Committee	Phone: (0752) 71 1511
Lyubov Petrovna TRETYAKOVA	Head of the Tambov Regional Finance Department	Phone: (0752) 72 1250

3. ECONOMIC POTENTIAL

3.1. 1997–2002 GROSS REGIONAL PRODUCT (GRP). INDUSTRY BREAKDOWN

Gross regional product was $1,231.4 million in 2002, 11.5% up on 2001. The growth was mainly driven by the trade, industry, and agricultural sectors. Per capita GRP was $879 in 2001 and $1,044 in 2002.

3.2. MAJOR ECONOMIC GROWTH PROJECTIONS

The blueprint for economic development in the Region is set forth in the Tambov Regional Law On the Program for the Development of the Tambov Region's Industry, 2002–2004. According to the blue-

GRP trends in 1997–2002						TABLE 2
	1997	1998	1999	2000	2001*	2002*
GRP in current prices, $ million	1,543.3	1,066.8	728.5	919.7	1,104.5	1,231.4

*Estimates of the Tambov Regional Administration

GRP industry breakdown in 1997–2002, % of total						TABLE 3
	1997	1998	1999	2000	2001*	2002*
GRP	100.0	100.0	100.0	100.0	100.0	100.0
Industry	26.2	22.5	22.3	20.1	18.6	18.1
Agriculture and forestry	13.0	14.0	19.5	17.1	23.0	22.0
Construction	5.4	5.4	4.0	3.8	4.8	5.1
Transport and communications	6.3	4.7	7.9	8.4	7.4	7.6
Trade and public catering	20.8	23.8	23.7	24.4	21.6	22.0
Other	21.7	23.4	15.8	19.9	18.4	18.7
Net taxes on output	6.6	6.2	6.8	6.3	6.2	6.5

*Estimates of the Tambov Regional Administration

print, a 4.3% increase in industrial output is expected in 2003 (including energy – 3.7%, chemicals and petrochemicals – 2.6%, machine engineering and metal processing – 2.3%, and food – 5.9%), accompanied by a 2% increase in agricultural output, a 5.5% increase in retail trade turnover, and an 8.5% increase in capital investment.

3.3. INDUSTRIAL OUTPUT IN 1997–2002 FOR MAJOR SECTORS OF ECONOMY

The leading industry sectors in the Tambov Region are energy, chemicals and petrochemicals, machine engineering and metals processing, and

the food industry. These sectors account for a combined 88.2% of total industrial output.

Machine engineering and metal processing. The sector accounts for 32.8% of total industrial output. The Region hosts some 258 enterprises, the largest being OAO Tambovpolimermash, OAO Komsomolets, PK Milorem, and OAO Pervomayskkhimmash.

Food and beverages. The sector accounts for 21.9% of total industrial output. The food and beverages industry includes 173 enterprises employing around 14,000 people. Major enterprises are OAO Kristall, OAO Nikiforovsky Sugar Plant,

Industry breakdown of industrial output in 1997–2002, % of total						TABLE 4
	1997	1998	1999	2000	2001	2002*
Industry	100.0	100.0	100.0	100.0	100.0	100.0
Machine engineering and metal processing	23.4	20.7	21.9	27.8	32.6	32.8
Food and beverages	23.4	25.9	29.1	26.8	24.4	21.9
Energy	20.7	21.1	16.1	15.5	16.6	19.9
Chemicals and petrochemicals	19.5	20.3	21.3	18.2	15.0	13.6
Light industry	2.6	2.3	3.8	3.6	3.6	3.2

*Estimates of the Tambov Regional Administration

OAO Talvis, OAO Tamola, OAO Tambovmyaso-
produkt, and OAO Tambovsky Bread Plant.

Energy. The sector accounts for 19.9% of total
industrial output. The energy sector includes 18 enterprises with a total work force of around 6,800 people. The
major power stations are the Tambovskaya Thermal Power Station and the Kotovskaya Thermal Power Station.

Chemicals and petrochemicals. The sector accounts for 13.6% of total industrial output. The Region
hosts some 14 enterprises employing 12,600 people. Major

enterprises include OAO Pigment, PK Kotovsky LKZ,
FGUP Kotovsky Plastics Plant, and OAO Tambovmash.

Light industry. The sector accounts for
3.2% of total industrial output. Major enterprises
include OAO Morshanskaya Manufaktura, OAO
Trikotazhnaya Nit, and OOO PF Raskom.

3.4. FUEL AND ENERGY BALANCE (OUT-
PUT AND CONSUMPTION PER RESOURCE)

The Region imports most of its fuel and
energy consumption.

Fuel and energy sector production and consumption trends, 1997–2002						TABLE 5
	1997	1998	1999	2000	2001	2002*
Electricity output, billion kWh	1.2	1.3	1.4	1.4	1.6	1.8
Electricity consumption, billion kWh	4.2	4.1	4.2	4.1	3.8	4.0
Natural gas consumption, million cubic meters	1480.9	1,264.9	1,313.3	1,287.3	1,411.2	1,999.7

*Estimates of the Tambov Regional Administration

3.5. TRANSPORT
INFRASTRUCTURE

Roads. The Region has 5,100 kilometers of
paved public highway. A total of 1.1634 million tons
of freight was carried by road in 2002. Major highways crossing the Region are Moscow – Volgograd –
Astrakhan, Tambov – Oryol, Tambov – Voronezh,
and Tambov – Ryazan.

Railroads. The Region has 736 kilometers
of railroads.

The South-East Railroad links the Region to the
Belgorod, Voronezh, Lipetsk, Kursk, Volgograd, Penza,
Saratov, Tula, and Rostov Regions.

Airports. The Tambov Airport is capable of
servicing charter flights.

Oil and gas pipelines. The Druzhba trunk oil
pipeline and the Sibir and Saratov – Tambov gas
pipelines cross the Tambov Region.

3.6. MAIN NATURAL RESOURCES:
RESERVES AND EXTRACTION IN 2002

Some 317 mineral deposits have been discovered in the Tambov Region, including 170 deposits
of minerals used in construction materials, 52 fresh
water sources, and 8 mineral water sources.

Construction materials. Ilmenite-rutile-zirconi-
um sands (887 million cubic meters), loams (62.7 million cubic meters), limestone (49 million cubic meters).

Minerals and mineral water. Phosphorites (248.0 million tons), sapropel (1.4 million tons),
subterranean fresh water (1 million cubic meters
per day), and subterranean mineral water (1,200
cubic meters per day).

Forests. The Region has 342,800 hectares
of forest, including 248,600 hectares of forests fit
for harvesting. The Region's total timber reserves
amount to 52 million cubic meters.

4. TRADE OPPORTUNITIES

4.1. MAIN GOODS
PRODUCED IN THE REGION

In 2002, the Tambov Region produced:

Machine engineering and metals.
Electric motors for automation and mechaniza-
tion, buses (362 pieces).

Chemicals and petrochemicals. Paint and varnish (52,200 tons), dyes (9,200 tons), synthetic resins
and plastics (11,100 tons), mineral wool (257,500 cubic
meters), linoleum (120,000 square meters).

Construction materials. Prefab concrete
(57,800 cubic meters), wall materials.

Light industry. Woolen fabric (2,579,000
square meters), knitwear, non-woven materials
(3,626,000 square meters).

Food industry. Full-fat cheese (5,300 tons), granulated sugar (575,000 tons), cigarettes (6,357 million items).

4.2. EXPORTS, INCLUDING EXTRA-CIS

2000 extra-CIS exports amounted to $22.2 mil-
lion, with CIS exports totaling $12.7 million. The respec-
tive figures for 2001 were $25.1 million and $18.2 million, and for 2002 – $31.5 million and $16.6 million.

The Region's main exports are organic chemicals, extracts and dyes, varnishes, paints, fermented goods and proteins, bearings, general mechanical rubber goods, technical equipment, metal
products, rawhide, and tobacco.

The Region's main export destinations are
Kazakhstan, Ukraine, Belarus, Germany, Latvia,
Moldova, Mongolia, Turkey, and Estonia.

4.3. IMPORTS, INCLUDING EXTRA-CIS

2000 extra-CIS imports amounted to $17 million, with CIS imports totaling $31.2 million. The respective figures for 2001 were $50 million and $17.9 million, and $54.8 million and $14.9 million for 2002.

The Region's main imports are raw sugar (43% of total imports), raw tobacco, raw chemicals, oil products, rubber, paper, ferrous metals (steel, cast iron), and machine engineering tools and equipment.

4.4. MAJOR REGIONAL EXPORT AND IMPORT ENTITIES

Due to the specific nature of exports and imports in the Tambov Region, export and import transactions are largely conducted by industrial enterprises.

5. INVESTMENT OPPORTUNITIES

5.1. INVESTMENTS IN 1992–2002 (BY INDUSTRY SECTOR), INCLUDING FOREIGN INVESTMENTS

The following factors determine the investment appeal of the Tambov Region:
- Its favorable geographical location;
- Its developed transport infrastructure;
- Legislation supporting investment.

5.2. CAPITAL INVESTMENT

The bulk of capital investment is concentrated in manufacturing, transport, and communications.

5.3. MAJOR ENTERPRISES (INCLUDING ENTERPRISES WITH FOREIGN INVESTMENT)

The Tambov Region hosts some 38 enterprises with foreign investment, including four wholly foreign owned companies: ZAO TAMAK (Germany), ZAO IZOROK (Germany), OOO MRKS-Les (Switzerland), and OOO Tambovsky Hardware Plant (Cyprus).

5.4. MOST ATTRACTIVE SECTORS FOR INVESTMENT

According to the Tambov Regional Administration, the agroindustrial sector is the most attractive sector for investment.

Capital investment by industry sector, $ million						TABLE 6
	1997	1998	1999	2000	2001	2002
Total capital investment	220.2	125.7	76.8	89.8	117.3	108.3
Including major industries (% of total):						
Industry	17.7	19.7	21.7	20.4	23.8	23.2
Agriculture and forestry	5.0	7.6	10.1	9.5	8.5	10.1
Construction	2.7	0.5	0.6	1.0	0.7	1.4
Transport and communications	30.8	21.1	21.0	24.9	20.0	24.4
Trade and public catering	1.2	1.4	1.3	1.4	1.2	0.5
Other	42.6	49.7	45.3	42.8	45.8	40.4

Foreign investment trends in 1996–2002						TABLE 7
	1996–1997	1998	1999	2000	2001	2002
Foreign investment, $ million	–	0.2	1.9	9.5	20.0	4.9
Including FDI, $ million	–	0.2	1.7	9.5	16.6	3.5

Largest enterprises of the Tambov Region	TABLE 8
COMPANY	SECTOR
OAO Tambovenergo	Energy
OAO Tambovnefteprodukt	Fuel
GUP Michurinsk Division of the South-Eastern Railroad of the Ministry of Railways of the Russian Federation	Transport
OAO Pigment	Chemicals
OOO Tambov Regional Gas Distribution Company	Natural gas

TABLE 9
Regional entities responsible for raising investment

ENTITY	ADDRESS	PHONE, FAX, E-MAIL
Tambov Regional Agency for Investment Technologies and Industrial Development (RAIR-Tambov Agency)	118, ul. Sovetskaya, Tambov, Tambov Region, 392000	Phone: (0752) 71 1388 Fax: (0752) 71 1320 E-mail: rair@tmb.ru

5.5. CURRENT LEGISLATION ON INVESTOR TAX EXEMPTIONS AND PRIVILEGES

The Tambov Regional Law On State Support of Investment Activity in the Tambov Region provides tax exemptions to banks, and insurance and other financial institutions engaged in investment activity. Investors investing own funds are eligible for a 4% profits tax rebate and a full exemption from property tax for the project payback period. These tax exemptions can be extended for an additional two year period in case of priority investment projects.

5.6. FEDERAL AND REGIONAL ECONOMIC AND SOCIAL DEVELOPMENT PROGRAMS FOR THE TAMBOV REGION

Federal targeted programs. The Region has underway a number of federal targeted programs focused on social welfare, development of agroindustrial policy, environmental improvement, and healthcare. The top priority program is The Elimination of Inequalities in Social and Economic Development of the Regions of the Russian Federation, 2002–2010 and through 2015.

Annual financing of the program amounts to $0.8–1.0 million from the federal budget and to $0.5 million from the regional budget and non-budgetary funds.

The Region is also implementing The Housing Program. The program goal is to stabilize residential construction by 2010. Annual program financing is $3.1 million from the federal budget and to $3.1 million from the regional budget and non-budgetary funds.

The Rural Social Development through 2010. Program's goal is to develop the social sphere and civil engineering infrastructure of rural areas. The program has been assigned a total financing of $588.3 million (federal budget).

Regional programs. More than 30 regional programs are now being implemented in the Region with a total financing of $22 million. The Small Enterprise Development and Support Program, 2002–2004 is the top priority regional program. The program goal is to create legislative and economic conditions conducive to the development of small enterprise. The program has been assigned $188,800 in financing from the regional budget.

6. INVESTMENT PROJECTS

Industry sector and project description	1) Expected results 2) Amount and term of investment 3) Form of financing[1] 4) Documentation[2]	Contact information
1	2	3
MINING		
14R001 ■ ❖ ▲		OAO Tsna 1 Industrial Mining Company
Development of an ilmenite-rutile-zirconium sand deposit and construction of an ore dressing plant. Project goal: to create a new enterprise.	1) 3.45 million cubic meters of sand annually 2) $40 million/3 years 3) E, JV 4) Preliminary FS	118, ul. Sovetskaya, Tambov, Tambov Region, 392000 Phone/fax: (0752) 71 1320 E-mail: rair@tmb.ru Anatoly Ivanovich Kakotkin, CEO
CHEMICALS AND PETROCHEMICALS		
14R002 ● ❖ ◆		OAO Kotovsky Paint and Varnish Factory
Maleic anhydride production at an existing petrochemicals enterprise. Project goal: to introduce a new product to the market and implement new technology.	1) 40,000 tons annually 2) $83.7 million/2 years 3) L, JV 4) BP	2, ul. Zheleznodorozhnaya, Kotovsk, Tambov Region, 393190 Phone: (07541) 23 903, 21 612 Fax: (07541) 24 985 E-mail: info@paints.ru, bpp@point.ru Vladimir Yuryevich Sazonov, CEO

[1] L – Loan, E – Equity, Leas. – Leasing, JV – Joint Venture
[2] BP – Business Plan, FS – Feasibility Study

1	2	3

CHEMICALS AND PHARMACEUTICALS

14R003

Development and implementation of respiratory protection systems for industrial personnel at enterprises with potentially hazardous environment. Project goal: to increase output and saturate the market with cheap and high-quality products.

1) 150,000–180,000 systems annually
2) $0.5 million/3.5 years
3) L, Leas.
4) BP

FGUP TambovNIKhI
19, Morshanskoye shosse, Tambov,
Tambov Region, 392680
Phone: (0752) 56 0680, 56 0914
Fax: (0752) 53 7904
E-mail: agr@pub.tmb.ru
Boris Viktorovich Putin,
CEO

MACHINE ENGINEERING AND METAL PROCESSING

14R004

Manufacturing a new generation of environmentally friendly refrigerator and air conditioning equipment. Project goal: to introduce a new product to the market and substitute imported products.

1) n/a
2) $25 million/4 years
3) L ($15 million)
4) BP

OAO Michurinsky Plant Progress
113, Lipetskoye Shosse, Michurinsk,
Tambov Region, 393773
Phone: (07545) 21 022, 21 160
E-mail: progres@mich.ru
Vladimir Anatolyevich Dmitriev,
CEO

14R005

Production of electronic weighing scales at an existing enterprise for use in retail in Russia. Project goal: to increase output and expand product range.

1) Annual output of 30,000 electronic weighing scales
2) $0.63 million/2 years
3) L, Leas.
4) BP

OAO Tulinovsky Tool Plant TVES
1, ul. Pozdnyakova, Tulinovka Village,
Tambovsky District,
Tambov Region, 393511
Phone: (0752) 66 7044, 66 7043,
66 7244; fax: (0752) 71 2605, 66 7241
E-mail: Abramov@tves.com.ru
Yevgeny Ivanovich Solodkov,
CEO

LIGHT INDUSTRY

14R006

Production of import replacing film coating materials. Project goal: to increase output and product variety, improve quality, increase exports.

1) Annual capacity of 12 million square metes
2) $6.6 million/5 years
3) L, JV
4) BP

OAO Iskozh
1a, ul. Oktyabrskaya, Kotovsk,
Tambov Region, 393170
Phone: (07541) 23 718, 24 332
Fax: (07541) 33 470
E-mail: iskozh@tmb.ru
Alexander Dmitrievich Butskikh,
CEO

FOOD AND BEVERAGES

14R007

Construction of a fruit, vegetable, and berry deep-freezing unit at an existing enterprise. Project goal: to increase product variety.

1) More than 8,000 tons annually
2) $1.9 million/4 years
3) L ($1.5 million), Leas.
4) BP

OAO Tambovsky Khladokombinat
1a, ul. Klubnaya, Tambov,
Tambov Region, 392000
Phone/fax: (0752) 72 0639
Andrei Ivanovich Gnatyuk,
CEO

AGRICULTURE

14R008

Apple-tree saplings growing. Project goal: to increase output.

1) 100,000 saplings annually
2) $0.6 million/5 years
3) L
4) BP

Michurinsk State Agricultural University
101, ul. Internatsionalnaya,
Michurinsk, Tambov Region, 393760
Phone: (07545) 53 137
Fax: (07545) 52 635
E-mail: mgau@mich.ru
Anatoly Ivanovich Zavrazhnov,
Provost

1	2	3

OTHER

14R009 ● ★ ▲

Construction of an oil pressing shop at existing enterprise for production of oil for use in the paint industry, and refined edible oil.
Project goal: to increase product variety and increase output.

1) 130 tons of oil daily
2) $82 million/2 years
3) L, Leas.
4) FS

OAO Kotovsky Paint and Varnish Factory
2, ul. Zheleznodorozhnaya, Kotovsk,
Tambov Region, 393190
Phone: (07541) 23 903, 21 612
Fax: (07541) 24 985
E-mail: info@paints.ru, bpp@point.ru
Vladimir Yuryevich Sazonov,
CEO

I

CENTRAL FEDERAL DISTRICT

15. TVER REGION [69]

ECONOMIC MAP

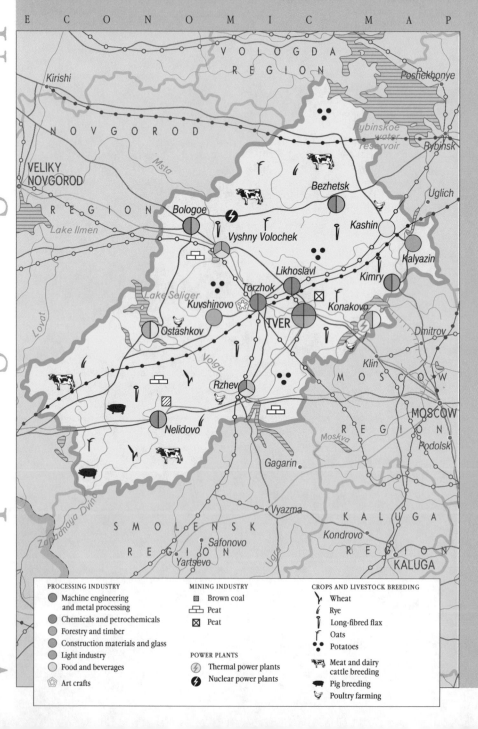

VOLOGDA
REGION

Kirishi

Poshekhonye

NOVGOROD

Rybinskoe
water
reservoir

Rybinsk

VELIKY
NOVGOROD

Uglich

REGION

Lake Ilmen

Bezhetsk

Bologoe

Kashin

Vyshny Volochek

Kalyazin

Likhoslavl

Lake Seliger

Torzhok

Kimry

Kuvshinovo

Konakovo

Ostashkov

TVER

Lovat

Volga

Dmitrov

Klin

MOSCOW

Rzhev

MOSCOW

Nelidovo

REGION

Moskva

Podolsk

Gagarin

Zapadnaya Dvina

Vyazma

KALUGA

SMOLENSK

Kondrovo

REGION

Safonovo

REGION

Yartsevo

Ugra

KALUGA

Msta

PROCESSING INDUSTRY

- ● Machine engineering and metal processing
- ● Chemicals and petrochemicals
- ● Forestry and timber
- ● Construction materials and glass
- ● Light industry
- ○ Food and beverages

- ✿ Art crafts

MINING INDUSTRY

- ▨ Brown coal
- ⌂ Peat
- ⊠ Peat

POWER PLANTS

- ⚡ Thermal power plants
- ⚡ Nuclear power plants

CROPS AND LIVESTOCK BREEDING

- ⋎ Wheat
- ⫟ Rye
- ⫯ Long-fibred flax
- ⫧ Oats
- ⁝ Potatoes
- 🐄 Meat and dairy cattle breeding
- 🐖 Pig breeding
- 🐓 Poultry farming

The Russian people entered the new millennium with the hope of returning their country to the ranks of the strong and prosperous. Achieving this requires us to join forces to build a civilized market economy. The time has come to invest in the Russian regions, whose potential is virtually unlimited and investment prospects have not yet been truly appreciated.

The Tver Region is the largest region in Central Russia. Situated between the two Russian capitals of Moscow and St. Petersburg, the Region links the country's two most developed economic areas – the Central and North Western Districts.

Recent years have seen a turning point in the Region's economy: output in key industrial sectors is growing and new technologies and management principles are being introduced. And this is just the beginning. Ahead we see an economic leap forward for which the Tver Region has all necessary prerequisites, including a qualified workforce, developed transport infrastructure, reliable legal framework, and sound financial institutions. The Region has accumulated considerable experience in the area of international cooperation.

The Regional Administration is focused on the revival and development of the Region, on raising living standards through the creation of conditions conducive to business initiative and enterprise, and on establishing an appealing investment image for the Upper Volga in the eyes of Russian and international investors.

Vladimir Platov,
GOVERNOR OF THE TVER REGION

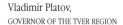

CENTRAL FEDERAL DISTRICT

1. GENERAL INFORMATION

1.1. GEOGRAPHY
The Tver Region covers a total area of 84,200 square kilometers. To the south, the Tver Region borders the Smolensk and Moscow Regions, to the west – the Pskov and Novgorod Regions, to the north – the Vologda Region, and to the east – the Yaroslavl Region.

1.2. CLIMATE
The Tver Region enjoys a continental climate. Air temperature in January temperature averages –4.4°C, rising to an average of +21.6°C in June. Annual precipitation reaches 500 mm.

1.3. POPULATION
According to preliminary 2002 census results, the population of the Tver Region amounts to 1,473,000 people. The average population density is 17.5 people per square kilometer. The economically active population totals 910,000 people. Official unemployment stood at 4.8% in 2002.

Demographically speaking, some 59% are of statutory working age, 16% are below the statutory working age, and 25% are beyond the statutory working age.

The Region's major population centers are (2002 data): Tver with 409,400 inhabitants, Rzhev with 67,400 inhabitants, Vyshny Volochek with 58,800 inhabitants, and Kimry with 57,900 inhabitants.

Population							TABLE 1
	1992	1997	1998	1999	2000	2001	2002
Total population, '000	1,661	1,637	1,626	1,614	1,595	1,575	1,473
Economically active population, '000	848	746	744	790	778	774	910

2. ADMINISTRATION

44, ul. Sovetskaya, Tver, Tver Region, 170000
Phone: (0822) 32 1051; fax: (0822) 42 5508
E-mail: tradm@tversu.ru; http://www.region.tver.ru

NAME	POSITION	CONTACT INFORMATION
Vladimir Ignatyevich PLATOV	Governor of the Tver Region	Phone: (0822) 32 1051
Anatoly Alexeevich BOCHENKOV	Deputy Governor of the Tver Region in charge of Industry	Phone: (0822) 32 2846
Anatoly Sergeevich KLEYMENOV	Deputy Governor of the Tver Region in charge of Economic Policy in the Tver Region	Phone: (0822) 32 8210

3. ECONOMIC POTENTIAL

3.1. 1997–2002 GROSS REGIONAL PRODUCT (GRP). INDUSTRY BREAKDOWN
The Tver Region's 2002 gross regional product amounted to $1,926.4 million, up 12% on 2001. Per capita GRP was $1,090 in 2001 and $1,307 in 2002.

3.2. INDUSTRIAL OUTPUT IN 1997–2002 FOR MAJOR SECTORS OF ECONOMY
The Tver Region's major industrial sectors are machine engineering, energy, food, light industry, forestry and paper, and chemicals. These account for a combined 88.4% of total industrial output.

GRP trends in 1997–2002					TABLE 2
	1997	1998	1999	2000	2001	2002*
GRP in current prices, $ million	2,660.6	1,825.6	1,146.4	1,377.5	1,717.3	1,926.4

*Estimates of the Tver Regional Administration

GRP industry breakdown in 1997–2002, % of total						*TABLE 3*
	1997	1998	1999	2000	2001	2002*
GRP	100.0	100.0	100.0	100.0	100.0	100.0
Industry	35.2	30.5	31.2	32.1	30.9	31.9
Agriculture and forestry	10.0	10.7	14.7	13.6	13.7	11.7
Construction	8.7	8.2	7.7	8.8	8.9	10.2
Transport and communications	6.5	7.1	8.6	10.0	11.8	11.8
Trade and public catering	7.3	9.3	11.7	11.1	11.7	11.9
Other	26.3	27.3	16.4	17.2	16.6	16.3
Net taxes on output	6.0	6.9	9.7	7.2	6.4	6.2

*Estimates of the Tver Regional Administration

Machine engineering and metal processing. The sector accounts for 32.8% of total industrial output. The main products produced by the sector are passenger rail cars, scoop excavators, tower cranes, fire-fighting equipment, and machine tools. The sector also includes steel structure welding enterprises and producers of industrial equipment and instruments.

Energy. Energy accounts for 25.3% of total industrial output. The largest enterprises in the sector are the 2 GW Kalininskaya Nuclear Power Station and the 2.4 GW OAO Konakovskaya Hydroelectric Power Station.

Light industry. Light industry accounts for 7.3% of total industrial output. In 2002, the sector produced approximately 69 million running meters of cotton fabric and worsted cloth, 7,500 tons of flax fiber, 2.5 million pieces of white linen garments and outer knitwear, and approximately 3.8 million square meters of imitation leather. The Tver Region provides approximately 40% of Russia's total flax fiber output.

Forestry, timber, and pulp and paper. The sector accounts for 6.4% of total industrial output. The sector is represented by about 90 enterprises (27 timber enterprises, 30 forestry enterprises, and 33 carpentry and furniture enterprises). The Region's timber companies produce over 430,000 cubic meters of sawn timber, 62,000 cubic meters of glued plywood, and 480,000 square meters of window and doorframes. In 2002 they produced approximately 13 million square meters of fiberboard and over 92,000 cubic meters of chipboards, 5,300 tons of paper, and 33,600 tons of paperboard.

Chemicals and petrochemicals. The chemicals sector accounts for 4% of total industrial output. Enterprises in the sector produce polyester fibers, fiberglass plastic and fiberglass plastic items, thermoplastic sheeting, polymer films, printing resins, and offset printing inks.

Fuel. The fuel sector accounts for 0.1% of total industrial output. The sector is represented by 13 peat enterprises. In 2002, the sector's marketable output reached $1.9 million.

Industry breakdown of industrial output in 1997–2002, % of total						*TABLE 4*
	1997	1998	1999	2000	2001	2002*
Industry	100.0	100.0	100.0	100.0	100.0	100.0
Machine engineering and metal processing	21.0	21.2	23.8	27.6	32.7	32.8
Energy	42.2	38.1	26.3	24.5	22.6	25.3
Food and beverages	10.7	11.8	13.9	12.8	12.5	12.6
Light industry	5.7	5.9	7.9	8.1	8.0	7.3
Forestry, timber, and pulp and paper	5.3	6.1	7.2	7.7	6.1	6.4
Chemicals and petrochemicals	3.3	3.7	6.0	5.6	4.8	4.0
Construction materials	3.3	2.5	3.4	3.2	3.1	3.2
Glass and porcelain	2.7	2.7	3.2	2.8	2.7	2.2
Flour, cereals, and mixed fodder	2.0	1.7	3.3	2.7	2.6	1.9
Ferrous metals	0.2	0.3	0.3	0.3	0.3	0.2
Fuel	0.3	0.3	0.3	0.2	0.1	0.1

*Estimates of the Tver Regional Administration

Fuel and energy sector production and consumption trends, 1997–2002						TABLE 5
	1997	1998	1999	2000	2001	2002*
Electricity output, billion kWh	17.9	20.7	22.8	22.3	23.1	24.4
Electricity consumption, billion kWh	6.2	6.3	6.4	6.4	6.5	6.4
Natural gas consumption, million cubic meters	3,439.5	3,794.5	3,772.8	1,739.5	3,581.4	4,206.0

3.3. FUEL AND ENERGY BALANCE (OUTPUT AND CONSUMPTION PER RESOURCE)

The Region has an extensive power generation system that fully covers the Region's demand for energy. The Region exports more than two thirds of its domestic energy output.

3.4. TRANSPORT INFRASTRUCTURE

Roads. The Region has 14,987 kilometers of paved public highway. Two international highways, Moscow – St. Petersburg and Moscow – Riga, cross the Region, connecting it with the Baltic States and Scandinavia.

Railroads. The Tver Region's has 1,806 kilometers of railroads. The following sectors of the Oktyabrskaya Railroad pass through the Region: Moscow – St. Petersburg, Moscow – Riga, Rybinsk – Bologoye – Pskov – Riga, and Moscow – Sonkovo – St. Petersburg.

Airports. Tver is served by a category one airport, which can handle large capacity cargo aircraft.

River ports. Tver has the largest river port in the upper Volga, with freight terminals capable of handling river-sea class vessels with a draft of up to four meters.

3.5. MAIN NATURAL RESOURCES: RESERVES AND EXTRACTION IN 2002

The Tver Region enjoys considerable natural resources, including sandy gravel, mortar sands and silicate sands, fusible and refractory clay, limestone, peat, sapropel, fresh underground waters, and lignite.

Peat. The Region's peat reserves are estimated at 2,051 million tons. Some 43 peat fields with a total area of 300,000 hectares are developed commercially.

Water resources. The Region has more than 500 large lakes, including Lake Seliger. The Region also has approximately 1,000 large and medium-sized rivers with a total length of over 17,000 kilometers. The Volga and the Western Dvina rise in the Region. The Region has nine artificial reservoirs, the largest being the Ivanovskoye, Rybinskoye, and Uglichskoye Reservoirs.

Forest resources. Forests cover 5.3 million hectares, or 62.9% of Region's territory. Timber reserves are estimated at 147.8 million cubic meters, including the commercial reserves of approximately 100 million cubic meters.

4. TRADE OPPORTUNITIES

4.1. MAIN GOODS PRODUCED IN THE REGION

In 2002 the Tver Region produced:

Energy: 24.4 billion kWh.

Machine engineering and metal processing: rail passenger cars – 521; construction lifters – 147; flax pullers – 297; excavators – 602.

Glass and porcelain: porcelain, household tableware and majolica – 22.3 million pieces

Forestry, timber, and pulp and paper: commercial timber – 499,000 dense cubic meters; sawn timber – 212,000 cubic meters; plywood – 29,100 cubic meters; chipboard – 41,400 cubic meters; and solid fiberboard – 7.3 million cubic meters.

Major regional export and import entities		TABLE 6
ENTITY	ADDRESS	PHONE, FAX, E MAIL
OAO Tverskaya Manufaktura Partnership	15, pr. Kalinina, Tver, Tver Region, 170001	Phone/fax: (0822) 42 2122, 42 2505, 42 4966
OAO Pozhtekhnika	34, Leningradskoye shosse, Torzhok, Tver Region, 172060	Phone: (08251) 51 179 Fax: (08251) 51 784
ZAO Rozhdestvenskaya Manufaktura	47, ul. Spartaka, Tver, Tver Region, 170647	Phone: (0822) 42 2552 Fax: (0822) 42 2531
OAO Tverskoy Excavator	11, ul. Industrialnaya, Tver, Tver Region, 170000	Phone: (0822) 33 2744, 33 3230 Fax: (0822) 33 3038
ZAO Vyshnevolotsky Textile	1, ul. Krasnaya, Vyshny Volochek, Tver Region, 171151	Phone: (08233) 11 397 Fax: (08233) 12 740

Light industry: cotton fabric and worsted cloth – 69 million running meters; flax fiber – 7,500 tons; knitwear – 2.5 million pieces, imitation leather – 3.8 million square meters.

4.2. EXPORTS, INCLUDING EXTRA-CIS

2000 exports to extra-CIS countries reached $86.5 million. Exports to the CIS totaled $15 million. The corresponding figures for 2001 were $77.6 million and $35 million, and $89.1 million and $31.4 million for 2002.

The Region's main exports include railroad cars, excavators and loaders, special purpose cars, fire-fighting and electrical equipment, geophysical instruments, cotton fabric and yarn, hide, timber, and timber products.

4.3. IMPORTS, INCLUDING EXTRA-CIS

2000 imports from extra-CIS countries reached $54.8 million. Imports from CIS countries totaled $30 million. The corresponding figures for 2001 were $94.4 million and $27.9 million, and $107.2 million and $12.1 million for 2002.

The Region's main imports are processing equipment, cotton fiber, facing tiles, clothes and footwear, and food and beverages.

5. INVESTMENT OPPORTUNITIES

5.1. INVESTMENTS IN 1997–2002 (BY INDUSTRY SECTOR), INCLUDING FOREIGN INVESTMENTS

The main factors determining the investment appeal of the Tver Region are:
- Its favorable geographical location (proximity to markets and high consumption potential);
- Its developed transport infrastructure;
- Laws supporting investment activity;
- Its highly qualified workforce;
- Its natural resources: timber, peat, natural construction materials, and mineral and fresh water sources.

5.2. CAPITAL INVESTMENT

Industry accounts for the largest share of capital investment (57.1%).

Foreign investment trends in 1996–2002						*TABLE 7*
	1996–1997	1998	1999	2000	2001	2002
Foreign investment, $ million	24.4	4.9	4.0	7.9	24.3	9.1
Including FDI, $ million	0.5	4.4	2.0	3.8	19.4	5.0

Capital investment by industry sector, $ million						*TABLE 8*
	1997	1998	1999	2000	2001	2002
Total capital investment	364.8	320.3	245.8	346.8	374.4	446.1
Including major industries (% of total):						
Industry	31.8	29.5	22.5	18.0	30.2	57.1
Agriculture and forestry	3.2	4.1	2.4	1.7	2.9	2.4
Construction	23.8	2.2	0.6	0.4	1.5	1.4
Transport and communications	19.8	34.9	54.0	64.0	49.7	24.5
Trade and public catering	3.7	0.6	0.5	0.8	0.6	0.5
Other	17.7	28.7	20.0	15.1	15.1	14.1

Largest enterprises of the Tver Region	*TABLE 9*
COMPANY	SECTOR
OAO Tver Rail Car Building Plant	Machine engineering
OAO Tverskoy Excavator	Machine engineering
OAO Tver Energy System	Energy
OAO Konakovskaya GRES	Energy
OAO BSK-Stroymekhanizatsiya	Construction

5.3. MOST ATTRACTIVE SECTORS FOR INVESTMENT

According to experts and the Tver Regional Administration, the most attractive sectors for investment are forestry, timber, pulp and paper, food, glass, printing, light industry, machine engineering and metals processing, and construction materials.

5.4. CURRENT LEGISLATION ON INVESTOR TAX EXEMPTIONS AND PRIVILEGES

The Tver Region has enacted a Law On State Support to Investment Activity in the Tver Region. The law governs the rights of business entities implementing investment projects to obtain state support and investment guarantees. The Region has also developed and implemented mechanisms for providing investment tax credits and Regional Administration's guarantees for loans allocated from the federal budget, commercial bank loans, and loans from private investors.

The Region has set up an Investment Advisory Committee to consider issues related to the provision of state support in the form of tax privileges.

Enterprises are eligible for an investment tax credit pursuant to the regulations on subsidies allocated from the regional budget to compensate interest on loans obtained to finance investment projects.

5.5. FEDERAL AND REGIONAL ECONOMIC AND SOCIAL DEVELOPMENT PROGRAMS FOR THE TVER REGION

Federal targeted programs. The Region is conducting a number of large-scale programs. The program for the Economic and Social Development of the Tver Region, 1998–2005 aims to achieve extensive reforms of the regional economy. The Program includes priority projects for the construction and revamping of energy facilities, and the development of transport infrastructure, machine engineering enterprises, production and processing facilities, environmental protection, and tourism.

The Forests of Russia, 2001–2005 program aims to ensure the maintenance of forestry resources and timely reproduction of commercially valuable species.

Regional programs. The Tver Regional Administration is developing and implementing programs for the development of the industrial and agro-industrial sectors, and the improvement of law and order and public health and welfare. The Region has approved and is implementing some 40 regional programs with total financing of $22.3 million.

One of the most important regional programs currently underway is the Program for the Creation of a Favorable Environment for the Attraction of Investment into the Economy of the Tver Region, 2001–2003. The program aims to foster a favorable environment for attracting investment into the economy of the Region, to improve the business environment to ensure sustainable economic growth, and improve local living standards.

The aim of the Program for Mortgage Lending in the Tver Region, 2002–2005 is to create an efficient market-based home purchasing system based on private savings, subsidies, and long-term mortgage lending. The goal is to stimulate the Region's housing market and the economy as a whole.

The program for the Development of the Linen Sector of the Tver Region, 2001–2005 aims to revive and stabilize the scientific, technical and production resources of the linen sector by expanding the area under seed, purchasing fertilizers and pesticides, and setting up a strategic flax seed reserve.

The Region is also implementing a program for the Development of Dairy and Beef Farming in the Tver Region, 2001–2005 and a program for the Stabilization and Development of Poultry Farms in the Tver Region, 1999–2000 and through 2005.

6. INVESTMENT PROJECTS

Industry sector and project description	1) Expected results 2) Amount and term of investment 3) Form of financing[1] 4) Documentation[2]	Contact information
1	2	3
CHEMICALS AND PETROCHEMICALS		
15R001 ● ◆		OAO Tverstekloplastik
Production of fiberglass pipes with couplings using rotary molding. Project goal: to manufacture new types of products.	1) 700 km of pipes annually 2) $11.3 million/2–3 years 3) L ($10 million) 4) BP	45, ul. P. Savelyevoy, Tver, Tver Region, 170039 Phone: (0822) 55 3552, 55 3591 Fax: (0822) 55 3331 E-mail: marketing@tsp.tver.ru Nikolai Ivanovich Lyutov, CEO

[1] L – Loan, E – Equity, Leas. – Leasing, JV – Joint Venture
[2] BP – Business Plan, FS – Feasibility Study

1	2	3

15R002 ● ◆

Production of textured and smooth drawn polyester filament. Project goal: to produce filament using new technologies.	1) 4,600 tons of textured polyester filament annually, 1,200 tons of smooth drawn filament annually 2) $10.5 million/3.5 years 3) L 4) BP	OAO Tverskoy Poliefir 1, pl. Gagarina, Tver, Tver Region, 170000 Phone: (0822) 33 3398, 33 9783 Fax: (0822) 33 9372, 33 9373 Boris Vasilyevich Marischuk, CEO

CHEMICALS AND PHARMACEUTICALS

15R003 ● ❖ ◆

Production of highly efficient bioactive bandage material. Project goal: production of bandage material.	1) Up to 2 million pieces annually 2) $3 million/2 years 3) L ($2 million), JV 4) BP	OOO NFP KhimMedService 14, ul. Ozernaya, Tver, Tver Region, 170008 Phone: (0822) 43 1687, 49 2308 E-mail: npshimmed@yandex.ru Roman Vladimirovich Vasilyev, Director

15R004 ■ ◆

Construction of a pharmaceuticals factory. Project goal: to produce pharmaceuticals.	1) 30,000 flasks of injection powder per shift, 1.4 million of standard pills per shift 2) $7 million/2–3 years 3) E ($6.9 million) 4) BP	OAO Novozavidovsky Mounted Assemblies Plant 3A, ul. Nekrasova, Novozavidovsky, Konakovsky District, Tver Region, 171271 Phone: (095) 539 2029, (08242) 22 092 Fax: (08242) 22 341 Victor Vasilyevich Sukhov, CEO

15R005 ■ ◆

Establishment of production of immunity agents. Project goal: to satisfy the demand for immunity agents.	1) n/a 2) $11.2 million/2–3 years 3) E ($11.1 million) 4) BP	OAO Novozavidovsky Mounted Assemblies Plant 3A, ul. Nekrasova, Novozavidovsky, Konakovsky District, Tver Region, 171271 Phone: (095) 539 2029, (08242) 22 092 Fax: (08242) 22 341 Victor Vasilyevich Sukhov, CEO

MACHINE ENGINEERING AND METAL PROCESSING

15R006 ● ★ ❖ ▼

Production of welded solebars for cargo carts. Project goal: to develop and produce welded solebars for cargo carts.	1) 10,000 pieces annually 2) $6.1 million/2–3 years 3) L, Leas., JV 4) Investment proposal	OAO Centrosvar 47, ul. P. Savelyevoy, Tver, Tver Region, 170039 Phone: (0822) 55 3433, 55 3592 Fax: (0822) 55 3538 Konstantin Fedorovich Pauchenkov, CEO

15R007 ● ◆

Technical revamping of OAO Tverskoy Rail Car Building Plant to produce a new generation of rail cars. Project goal: to produce and sell a new generation of rail cars (non-compartment sleepers, compartment sleepers, special wagons), to increase sales.	1) 605 pieces annually 2) $30 million/2–3 years 3) L 4) BP	OAO Tverskoy Rail Car Building Plant 45b, Peterburgskoye shosse, Tver, Tver Region, 170003 Phone: (0822) 50 4923, 55 5222 Fax: (0822) 55 9152 E-mail: sdir@dir.tvz.ru Vladimir Ivanovich Savin, CEO

15R008 ■ ● ◆

Restructuring of OAO Zavidovsky Experimental Mechanical Factory. Project goal: to create facilities for manufacturing new products: hydraulic lifters mounted on ZIL Bychok trucks.	1) 230 items per year 2) $2.6 million/2–3 years 3) L, E 4) BP	OAO Zavidovsky Experimental Mechanical Factory 7, ul. Parkovaya, Novozavidovsky, Konakovsky District, Tver Region, 171270 Phone: (08242) 22 196 Vyacheslav Ivanovich Kvasov, CEO

CENTRAL FEDERAL DISTRICT

1	2	3

15R009 ■ ◆

Creation of a pilot production facility for metal coating of 10–30 mm pipes. Project goal: to produce 10–30 mm pipes.	1) 100,000 running meters 2) $1 million/2–3 years 3) E ($0.9 million) 4) BP	OAO Novozavidovsky Mounted Assemblies Plant 3A, ul. Nekrasova, Novozavidovsky, Konakovsky District, Tver Region, 171 2712 Phone: (095) 539 2029, (08242) 22 341, 22 092 Victor Vasilyevich Sukhov, CEO

FORESTRY, TIMBER, AND PULP AND PAPER

15R010 ■ ● ◆

Modernization and technical revamping of OAO Nelidovsky Wood-Processing Works. Project goal: to construct production facilities for dry veneer sheet and window frames.	1) 45,000 cubic meters of dry veneer sheet, and 50 cubic meters of window frames annually. 2) $2.4 million/3 years 3) L, E 4) BP	OAO Nelidovsky Wood-Processing Works 7, ul. Zavodskaya, Nelidovo, Tver Region, 172523 Phone: (08266) 31 106, 31 105, 31 207 E-mail: neldok@chat.ru Valery Vasilyevich Lebedev, CEO

CONSTRUCTION MATERIALS

15R011 ■ ● ◆

Launch of production of Geokar peat insulating blocks. Project goal: to construct a mini-plant for production of insulating blocks.	1) 2,880,000 cubic meters annually 2) $54 million/2–3 years 3) L, E ($18 million) 4) BP	ZAO Bezhetsky Pilot and Experimental Plant 78, ul. Kashinskaya, Bezhetsk, Tver Region, 171980 Phone: (08231) 20 592, 21 804 Fax: (08231) 21 886 E-mail: boez@bezh.dep.tver.ru; Nikolai Sergeevich Savostov, CEO

15R012 ▼ ❖

Expansion of production facilities at ZAO Tver Reinforced Concrete Plant 4. Project goal: to increase reinforced concrete output.	1) 2,000 square meters of prefab reinforced concrete blocks 2) $1 million/2–3 years 3) JV (the stake of $0.5 million) 4) Investment proposal	ZAO Tver Reinforced Concrete Plant 4 Lazurnaya Industrial Zone, Tver, Tver Region, 170017 Phone: (0822) 49 2746, 49 7188 Fax: (0822) 49 7845, 33 7311 E-mail: ZHBI@online.tver.ru Alexander Sergeevich Rybakov, Director

15R013 ● ▲

Reconstruction of a production line for the production of environmentally friendly board with improved strength for household and civil construction. Project goal: to produce insulating mineral fiberboards made of basalt rocks for housing construction.	1) 100,000 cubic meters of boards annually 2) $1.5 million/2–3 years 3) L 4) FS	OAO Izoplit Complex Izoplit, Konakovsky District, Tver Region, 171277 Phone: (08242) 65 478, extension 518, 511 Fax: (08242) 65 478, extension 570 Victor Nikolaevich Romanov, Director

LIGHT INDUSTRY

15R014 ● ★ ❖ ◆

Production of trim film for automobile passenger compartments and furniture. Project goal: at the first stage, to introduce low-price and high-quality products to the market; at the second stage, to reinforce market position and increase production volumes.	1) 1 million square meters of automotive trim film and 1 million square meters of furniture film annually; 2) $1.6 million/2–3 years 3) L ($1.3 million), JV, Leas. 4) BP	OAO Iskozh-Tver 13, ul. Industrialnaya, Tver, Tver Region, 170000 Phone/fax: (0822) 32 1431, 33 0798, 33 3890 E-mail: iskog@tvcom.ru Timur Lyutianovich Kravets, CEO

15R015 ● ◆

Technical revamping of the enterprise. Project goal: to produce linen yarn knitwear.	1) 373,200 pieces annually 2) $2 million/2–3 years 3) L 4) BP	ZAO Kimrsky Linen Knitwear 66, ul. Lenina, Kimry, Tver Region, 171510 Phone: (08236) 31 771, 32 054 Fax: (08236) 32 132 Galina Grigoryevna Artamonova, CEO

1	2	3

FOOD AND BEVERAGES

15R016 ● ◆ ▲

Potato production and processing and construction of a distillery.
Project goal: to stabilize potato production and ensure sales for agricultural producers.

1) 460,000 decaliters of rectified spirit annually
2) $10.5 million/2–3 years
3) L ($7.5 million)
4) FS, BP

ZAO Soyuz-Agro
Zapolok Village, Redkino, Konakovsky District, Tver Region, 171260
Phone/fax: (08242) 65 476
Konstantin Konstantinovich Miskov, CEO

15R017 ● ◆

Catching and processing of freshwater fish at OAO Seliger.
Project goal: to reproduce, catch, and deep process freshwater fish at Lake Seliger.

1) 1.5 million of standard cans of fish annually, 600 kg of fish daily (smoke shop), up to 1,000 kg daily (salter shop), refrigerating facilities for 100 tons
2) $1.7 million/2–3 years
3) L
4) BP

OAO Seliger
1, ul. Uritskogo, Ostashkov, Tver Region, 172735
Phone/fax: (08235) 23 123
Vladimir Georgievich Petrov, CEO

15R018 ● ❖ ▲

Creation of distribution refrigerating facilities.
Project goal: to distribute food products and provide food storage services.

1) capacity – 5,300 tons of simultaneous storage
2) $7 million/2–3 years
3) L, JV
4) FS

OAO Tver Refrigerator
46/38, ul. Krasina, Tver, Tver Region, 170005
Phone/fax: (0822) 31 1661
Sergei Vladimirovich Kozlov, CEO

AGRICULTURE

15R019 ● ◆

Development of beef cattle breeding farms in the Tver Region.
Project goal: to breed Charolais and Limousin cattle and introduce new high quality meat products to the market.

1) 3,650 tons annually
2) $2.5 million/2–3 years
3) L
4) BP

GUP Tverskoye Cattle Breeding Farm
Avvakumovo, Kalininsky District, Tver Region, 170533
Phone/fax: (0822) 33 4640, 37 6322
Alexander Ivanovich Vorobyev, Head

15R020 ● ◆

Production and processing of brewing barley and construction of a malting house.
Project goal: to produce malt in order to provide additional market for brewing barley and to develop brewing.

1) 30,000 tons annually
2) $10.5 million/2–3 years
3) L
4) BP

ZAO Tver-Agro-Solod
Zapolok Village, Redkino, Konakovsky District, Tver Region, 171260
Phone/fax: (0822) 36 9210
Lidia Vasilyevna Betsenko, Director

15R021 ● ◆

Bezhetsky Linen pilot project.
Project goal: to recover linen production and develop linen-production facilities in the Tver Region.

1) 1,150 tons of long flax fiber annually, 1,350 tons of short flax fiber annually, 600 tons of hackled fiber annually, 650 tons of sorbents annually, 300 tons of linseed-oil annually
2) $5 million/2–3 years
3) L
4) BP

Agricultural Department of the Bezhetsky District Administration
40, ul. Bolshaya, Bezhetsk, Tver Region, 171980
Phone: (08231) 22 444, 22 232
Fax: (08231) 20 234
Nikolai Alexandrovich Shalonin, Head of the Agricultural Department of Bezhetsky District Administration

TRANSPORT INFRASTRUCTURE

15R022 ■ ◆ ▲

Construction of a by-pass toll highway around Vyshniy Volochek.
Project goal: to improve transport communications.

1) 46.3 km of road
2) $117 million/2–3 years
3) E ($58.5 million)
4) BP, FS

GU Moscow-St. Petersburg Highway Administration of the Ministry of Transport of the Russian Federation
62-A, prospekt Tchaikovskogo, Tver, Tver Region, 170002
Phone: (0822) 36 8790
Fax: (0822) 33 7643
E-mail: office@e95.tver.ru
Oleg Yuryevich Malikov, Department Head

I

CENTRAL FEDERAL DISTRICT

1	2	3

15R023 ● ▼

Reconstruction of the road network in the north-western part of the Tver Region. Project goal: to improve transport communications and produce sand and gravel mix.	1) 10 km of road; 50,000 cubic meters of mined rock annually 2) $1 million/2–3 years 3) L 4) Investment proposal	Administration of the Molokovsky District 15, ul. Lenina, Molokovo, Tver Region, 171680 Phone: (08275) 21 361, 21 152 Fax: (08275) 21 377 Nadezhda Alexandrovna Vorobyeva, Deputy Head of Administration, Head of the Economic Department

TRADE

15R024 ● ◆

Construction of an interregional wholesale market in Tver. Project goal: to increase sales.	1) Projected turnover of 339,500 tons annually 2) $10 million/n/a 3) L 4) BP	OAO Tver Interregional Wholesale Food Market 53, ul. Pobedy, Tver, Tver Region, 170037 Phone: (0822) 36 1363, 36 3320 Fax: (0822) 36 0854 Vladimir Khristianovich Rosenberg, CEO

15R025 ● ◆

Construction of a trade and exhibition center in Tver. Project goal: to expand trade and office areas.	1) 7,000 square meters 2) $7.3 million/4.2 years 3) L 4) BP	OAO Expo-Tver 6, ul. Pushkinskaya, Tver, Tver Region, 170000 Phone: (0822) 33 4598, 33 9170 Fax: (0822) 49 0556, 32 1513, 33 9667 E-mail: expotv@tvcom.ru http://www.expo.tver.ru Sergei Ivanovich Danilov, CEO

HOTELS, TOURISM, AND RECREATION

15R026 ■ ● ❖ ◆

Reconstruction of the Tver Kremlin. Project goal: to create a cultural and tourist center.	1) 15,000 square meters of buildings, 300,000 visitors annually, annual revenue of $4 million 2) $25 million/4–5 years 3) L ($12 million), E, JV 4) BP	OOO Komilfo Travel Agency 23/12, ul. Novotorzhskaya, Tver, Tver Region, 170000 Phone/fax: (0822) 48 1121, 49 0687, 42 6277 E-mail: komilf@tvcom.ru Natalya Gennadyevna Ivanova, Director

15R027 ● ▲

Building a water sports, recreation, and tourism center. Project goal: to create facilities for water sports and recreation with a developed infrastructure for yacht maintenance.	1) n/a 2) $1.2 million/2–3 years 3) L 4) FS	Non-Commercial Enterprise Upper Volga Yacht Club 1, Naberezhnaya Afanasiya Nikitina, Tver, Tver Region, 170026 Phone: (0822) 42 5697, 55 3830 E-mail: cafe@mail.ru Alexander Vladimirovich Terentyev, Director

15R028 ● ◆

Building a Moscow Sea water sports center. Project goal: to construct an world-class sports, historical, and cultural center.	1) Up to 550 tourists daily 2) $25 million/2–3 years 3) L 4) BP	NP SO Russian Ocean Sailing Club 35/2, ul. Mishina, Moscow, 125083 Phone: (095) 212 2345 E-mail: ushakov@rosc.ru, info@rosc.ru http://www.rosc.ru Alexey Borisovich Ushakov, Chairman of the Board of Directors

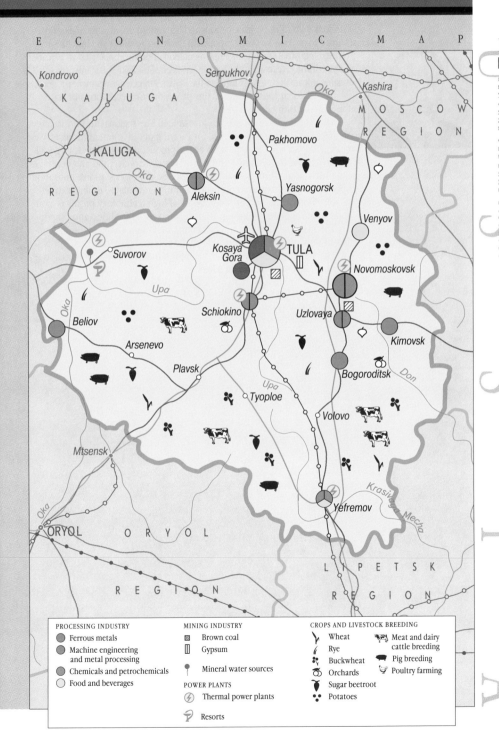

16. TULA REGION [71]

ECONOMIC MAP

PROCESSING INDUSTRY
- 🔴 Ferrous metals
- 🔴 Machine engineering and metal processing
- 🔴 Chemicals and petrochemicals
- ⚪ Food and beverages

MINING INDUSTRY
- ▨ Brown coal
- ▥ Gypsum
- • Mineral water sources

POWER PLANTS
- ⚡ Thermal power plants
- ♒ Resorts

CROPS AND LIVESTOCK BREEDING
- ⅄ Wheat
- ⎰ Rye
- ❀ Buckwheat
- ⬬ Orchards
- ⍭ Sugar beetroot
- ⁘ Potatoes
- 🐄 Meat and dairy cattle breeding
- 🐖 Pig breeding
- 🐓 Poultry farming

In today's world, the social and economic development of any region is inextricably linked with how efficient its investment policy is. The increased business activity in the Tula Region's economy in 2001–2003, improved financial performance of companies and organizations, a fall in the number of unprofitable companies, a favorable external economic situation, gradual growth in real income, and successful budget execution, have all contributed to facilitating investment processes in the Region.

State support to investors is primarily directed towards the implementation of projects with short payback periods and high return on investment. Priority is accorded to projects involving production facilities upgrading and installation of advanced industrial equipment, implementation of new technologies, and creation of jobs. For three years now, the Region has been subsidizing bank interest on investment loans for projects listed in the Region's targeted investment program.

The regional legislation contains provisions on other forms of state support to investment.

The Tula Region is in need of investment. The regional authorities are committed to providing assistance for carrying out investment projects. We welcome investments in such areas as the production of competitive goods and services for the domestic and international markets, food and beverages, deep processing of brown coal, reconstruction of power stations, utilization of power plant ash waste to produce aluminum raw materials and extract valuable components, export and import of high technology products, construction of residential housing, industrial and social facilities, and others.

The Regional Administration is committed to creating conditions conducive to investment and mutually beneficial trade relations.

The Tula Region, with its vast economic and investment potential, is open to all investors and trade partners.

Vasily Starodubtsev,
GOVERNOR OF THE TULA REGION

1. GENERAL INFORMATION

1.1. GEOGRAPHY

Located in the European part of Russia, the Tula Region covers a total area of 25,700 square kilometers. To the north, it borders the Moscow Region, to the north-east – the Kaluga Region, to the south – the Lipetsk Region, to the south-west – the Oryol Region, and to the east – the Ryazan Region.

1.2. CLIMATE

The Tula Region enjoys a moderate continental climate. Air temperatures in January average –9°C, rising to an average of +20°C in July. Average annual precipitation totals 500 mm.

1.3. POPULATION

According to preliminary 2002 census results, the total population of the Tula Region stood at 1,676,000 people. The average population ensity is 65.2 people per square kilometer. The economically active population totals 794,000 people. Official unemployment stood at 1.2% in 2002.

Demographically speaking, some 57.3% are of working age, 16% are below the statutory working age, and 26.7% are beyond the statutory working age.

The major urban centers of the Tula Region (2002 data) are Tula with 472,300 inhabitants, Novomoskovsk with 134,000 inhabitants, and Uzlovaya with 79,300 inhabitants.

Population							TABLE 1
	1992	1997	1998	1999	2000	2001	2002
Total population, '000	1,839	1,795	1,780	1,763	1,740	1,716	1,676
Economically active population, '000	930	813	802	822	831	828	794

2. ADMINISTRATION

2, pr. Lenina, Tula, Tula Region, 300600
Phone: (0872) 27 8436; fax: (0872) 20 6326
E-mail: admin@region.tula.ru; http://www.region.tula.ru

NAME	POSITION	CONTACT INFORMATION
Vasily Alexandrovich STARODUBTSEV	Governor of the Tula Region	Phone: (0872) 27 8436 Fax: (0872) 20 6326
Alexander Viktorovich LUNEV	Deputy Governor of the Tula Region for Economy and Structural and Investment Policy	Phone: (0872) 20 6504 Fax: (0872) 27 7217
Vitaly Alekseevich BOGOMOLOV	Deputy Governor of the Tula Region for Industrial Policy, Fuel and Energy Sector, Transport and Communications, Geological Exploration, and Natural Resources	Phone: (0872) 36 5425
Nikolai Tikhonovich MAKHRIN	Deputy Governor of the Tula Region, Head of the Agroindustrial Sector	Phone: (0872) 27 7698
Albert Ivanovich POPOV	Deputy Governor of the Tula Region for Construction, Roads, and Housing and Communal Services	Phone: (0872) 27 4749
Vladimir Grigoryevich ROTIN	Deputy Governor of the Tula Region for Small and Medium Business Support, Consumer Services, and Fisheries	Phone: (0872) 27 7138
Vladimir Ivanovich FADEEV	Director of the Economic Development Department of the Tula Regional Administration in charge of Investment Policy and Macroeconomic Analysis and Social and Economic Development Forecasting	Phone: (0872) 33 2149 Fax: (0872) 33 2149 E-mail: Fadeev@adm.tula.ru

I

CENTRAL FEDERAL DISTRICT

3. ECONOMIC POTENTIAL

3.1. 1997–2002 GROSS REGIONAL PRODUCT (GRP). INDUSTRY BREAKDOWN

The Tula Region's 2002 gross regional product amounted to $1,949 million, up 6.3% on 2001. Per capita GRP was $1,069 in 2001, and $1,163 in 2002.

3.2. MAJOR ECONOMIC GROWTH PROJECTIONS

The blueprint for the social and economic development of the Tula Region in 2003 is set forth in the Conceptual Framework for Economic Development of the Tula Region in 2003. In 2003, industrial output is projected to amount to $2,517 million

(100.2% on 2002 levels), agriculture and forestry output – to $556.9 million (111.3%), construction – $286.3 million (112.4%), transport and communications – $201.4 million (110.8%), trade and public catering, including wholesale industrial and technical goods trade – $402.7 million (113.8%).

3.3. INDUSTRIAL OUTPUT IN 1997–2002 FOR MAJOR SECTORS OF ECONOMY

The Tula Region's major industrial sectors are food and beverages, chemicals and petrochemicals, and machine engineering and metal processing. These accounted for a combined 64.4% of total 2002 industrial output.

GRP trends in 1997–2002						TABLE 2
	1997	1998	1999	2000	2001*	2002*
GRP in current prices, $ million	2,800.9	1,881.0	1,217.7	1,554.3	1,834.1	1,949.0

*Estimates of the Tula Regional Administration

GRP industry breakdown in 1997–2002, % of total						TABLE 3
	1997	1998	1999	2000	2001*	2002*
GRP	100.0	100.0	100.0	100.0	100.0	100.0
Industry	30.6	30.7	37.3	40.2	40.9	43.0
Agriculture and forestry	13.1	12.5	13.6	12.5	12.5	11.5
Construction	5.9	5.7	5.9	8.4	5.9	6.5
Transport and communications	6.1	7.6	6.7	6.9	7.2	6.1
Trade and public catering	11.2	9.3	11.0	9.6	9.5	10.7
Other	33.1	34.2	25.5	18.2	19.1	18.0
Net taxes on output	–	–	–	4.2	4.9	4.2

*Estimates of the Tula Regional Administration

Industry breakdown of industrial output in 1997–2002, % of total						TABLE 4
	1997	1998	1999	2000	2001	2002*
Industry	100.0	100.0	100.0	100.0	100.0	100.0
Food and beverages	11.7	12.4	15.0	13.8	16.2	22.9
Chemicals and petrochemicals	21.8	20.3	25.0	26.9	23.5	22.2
Machine engineering and metal processing	15.0	16.8	16.5	15.1	22.3	19.3
Ferrous metals	19.2	22.2	22.5	20.2	16.5	16.5
Energy	20.3	16.9	10.5	10.2	10.8	11.1
Construction materials	3.3	3.3	2.8	3.6	3.7	3.9
Light industry	1.4	1.7	2.0	1.7	1.6	1.5
Non-ferrous metals	0.3	0.3	0.8	0.7	0.6	0.7
Fuel	2.0	1.3	0.5	0.4	0.5	0.5

*Estimates of the Tula Regional Administration

Food and beverages. The sector accounts for 22.9% of total industrial output. The largest enterprises are OAO Taopin and OAO Tulaspirt.

Chemicals and petrochemicals. The sector accounts for 22.2% of total industrial output. Enterprises in the sector specialize in the production of synthetic rubber, plastics, synthetic fiber and filament, and industrial rubber. The largest enterprises are OAO Novomoskovskaya AK Azot, OAO Schekinoazot, and OAO Yefremovsky Synthetic Rubber Plant.

Machine engineering and metal processing. The sector accounts for 19.3% of total industrial output. Enterprises in the sector specialize in the production of food and light industry equipment, gas equipment, and agricultural equipment. Major enterprises include OAO Tula Combine Factory, OAO Aleksinsky Heavy Industrial Fittings Plant, OAO Kran-Uzlovsky Fedunets Machine Engineering Plant, and OAO Kireevsky Light Metal Assemblies Plant.

Ferrous metals. The sector accounts for 16.5% of total industrial output. Enterprises in the sector specialize in the production of cast iron and ferromanganese. The largest enterprises are OAO Tulachermet and OAO Kosogorsky Steel Works.

3.4. FUEL AND ENERGY BALANCE (OUTPUT AND CONSUMPTION PER RESOURCE)

The energy sector of the Tula Region is represented by two major enterprises: OAO Cherepetskaya GRES with an installed capacity of 1,425 MW and OAO Tulenergo Thermal Power Station with an installed capacity of 1,388 MW. Local power stations cover 62% of the total demand for energy (which was 10.3 billion kWh in 2002), with the Federal Wholesale Electricity Market (FOREM) covering the 38% deficit.

The Tula Region has no oil refineries; it is totally dependent on fuel imports from other regions of the Russian Federation.

OAO AK Tulaoblgaz covers local demand for natural gas (7.1 billion cubic meters in 2002) and liquefied gas (8,700 tons in 2002).

The Region's coal industry is represented by 60 enterprises, including seven coal production subsidiaries of OAO Tulaugol, and mine construction subsidiaries of OAO Mosbassshakhtostroy. The Tula Region is sixteenth amongst the regions of the Russian Federation in terms of coal output.

Fuel and energy sector production and consumption trends, 1997–2002						*TABLE 5*
	1997	1998	1999	2000	2001	2002
Electricity output, billion kWh	9.1	7.2	7.0	7.1	7.0	6.3
Coal output, million tons	2.1	1.3	0.9	0.8	1.0	0.8
Electricity consumption, billion kWh	10.4	9.9	10.1	10.5	10.6	10.3
Natural gas consumption, million cubic meters	6,942.0	5,810.0	6,217.0	6,459.0	6,648.0	7,137.0

3.5. TRANSPORT INFRASTRUCTURE

Roads. The Tula Region has some 7,200 kilometers of paved public highway, including 819 kilometers of federal highway. The Moscow – Simferopol and Moscow – Voronezh highways pass through the Region.

Railroads. The Tula Region has 1,106 kilometers of railroads. The Moscow Railroad passes through the Region, serving 423 industrial enterprises with spur links to the railroad. Passenger carriage accounts for 18% of total railroad traffic. The principal railway lines are Moscow – Tula – Oryol, Penza – Tula – Kaluga, and Tula – Bryansk.

3.6. MAIN NATURAL RESOURCES: RESERVES AND EXTRACTION IN 2002

The main natural resources of the Tula Region are brown coal, rock salt, strontium ores, and construction materials.

Brown coal. The Tula Region has 39 brown coal deposits with a total reserve of 1,552 million tons. Some 14 deposits are actively developed.

Rock salt and strontium ore. A 20 to 65 meter thick rock salt layer is found at a depth of 800–1,100 meters throughout the north of the Region, with 93–97% of the layer consisting of sodium chloride (NaCl). Rock salt reserves are estimated at 557 billion tons. The Tula Region has also around 20 strontium ore deposits with a total reserve of approximately 200 million tons.

Construction materials. Mason stone (744.8 million tons), soft clay (90.7 million tons), refractory clay (6.7 million tons), flux limestone (483.5 million tons), and gypsum (1,487.9 million tons).

4. TRADE OPPORTUNITIES

4.1. MAIN GOODS
PRODUCED IN THE REGION
In 2002, the Region produced:
Coal: 822,000 tons;
Chemicals and petrochemicals: mineral fertilizers – 678,000 tons, synthetic fiber and filament – 18,000 tons, synthetic resin and plastics – 89,100 tons, synthetic rubber – 56,000 tons, linoleum – 5.7 million square meters.
Ferrous metals: rolled ferrous metal products – 45,900 tons;
Food and beverages: ethanol – 7.1 million decaliters, distilled beverages – 519,000 decaliters, meat, including category one by-products, – 15,600 tons, whole milk products – 126,000 tons.

4.2. EXPORTS, INCLUDING EXTRA-CIS
In 2002, the Tula Region's foreign trade turnover amounted to $940.2 million, up 26.6% on 2001.

Exports, amounting to $750.8 million, account for 79.9% of foreign trade turnover and increased by 21.1% on 2001. Exports to extra-CIS countries amounted to $671.2 million (21.6% increase), while exports to CIS countries totaled $79.6 million (17.1% growth).

The main trading partners for export are Greece, Germany, the UAE, Ukraine, India, the USA, Italy, China, South Korea, Brazil, Poland,

Major regional export and import entities		*TABLE 6*
ENTITY	ADDRESS	PHONE, FAX, E MAIL
OAO Schekinoazot	Pervomaysky, Tula Region, 301212	Phone: (08751) 92 538, 92 938 Fax: (0872) 31 2266 E-mail: sninks@azot.tula.net
OOO TD Schekinokhimvolokno	Schekino, Tula Region, 301200	Phone: (0872) 35 0456, 36 5453 Fax: (0872) 36 7170
OAO Vanadium-Tula	1, ul Przhevalskogo, Tula, Tula Region, 300016	Phone: (0872) 46 6846 Fax: (0872) 45 7926
OAO Polema	19A, ul Przhevalskogo, Tula, Tula Region, 300017	Phone: (0872) 45 7067, 45 7542 Fax: (0872) 45 7703 E-mail: polema@tula.net
OAO Veap	4, ul. Mezhdunarodnaya, Venev, Tula Region, 301620	Phone: (08745) 52 378 Fax: (08745) 51 286
OAO Kosogorsky Metal Works	4, Orlovskoye shosse, Kosaya Gora, Tula, Tula Region, 300903	Phone: (0872) 33 9904, 24 3553 E-mail: plan@kmz.tula.net
ZAO Suvorovskaya Nit	Suvorov, Tula Region, 301400	Phone: (08763) 23 983, 23 908, 20 142 Fax: (08763) 23 908
OAO Tula Cartridge Plant	139, ul. Marata, Tula, Tula Region, 300035	Phone: (0872) 41 0593, 41 0352 Fax: (0872) 41 1174 E-mail: info@tcwammo.tula.ru
OAO AK Tulamashzavod	2, ul. Mosina, Tula, Tula Region, 300002	Phone: (0872) 32 1202, 32 7849, 36 9083 Fax: (0872) 27 2620 E-mail: lcenz@tula.net
OAO Oktava	24, ul. Kaminskogo, Tula, 300000	Phone: (0872) 20 0006, 20 0011, 20 0081 Fax: (0872) 36 0177 E-mail: otava@tula.net
OAO Tula Arms Plant	1A, ul. Sovetskaya, Tula, 300002	Phone: (0872) 32 1701, 32 1712, 32 1701 Fax: (0872) 27 3439 E-mail: toz@tula.net
OAO AK Novomoskov-skbytkhim	64, Komsomolskoye shosse, Novomoskovsk, Tula Region, 301670	Phone: (08762) 31 908, (095) 705 9966 Fax: (095) 705 9951 E-mail: info@procterandgamble. ru

Kazakhstan, Turkey, the Netherlands, Mexico, the Czech Republic, and Hungary.

Traditionally, the Tula Region's enterprises export a wide range of products, including: iron and ferroalloys, ferrous and non-ferrous metal products, synthetic rubber, polyamide threads, caprolactam, methyl alcohol, ammonia and nitrogen fertilizers, vanadium oxide and artificial diamond goods, detergents, optic devices, microphones, fittings, and machine engineering goods.

4.3. IMPORTS, INCLUDING EXTRA-CIS

Imports from extra-CIS countries amounted to $189.4 million in 2002, a 54% growth on 2001.

Imports from CIS countries totaled $148.3 million, or 86.5% growth on 2001 level.

The main goods imported by the Region are: ferments, malt, corn and raw sugar, manganese ore and concentrate, organic and non-organic chemicals, essential oils and coloring agents, plastic goods and ethylene polymer products, aluminum, copper, paper and cardboard, and pipes.

4.4. MAJOR REGIONAL EXPORT AND IMPORT ENTITIES

Owing to the specific nature of the Region's export and import activities, export and import transactions are performed mainly by industrial enterprises.

5. INVESTMENT OPPORTUNITIES

5.1. INVESTMENTS IN 1992–2002 (BY INDUSTRY SECTOR), INCLUDING FOREIGN INVESTMENTS

The following factors determine the investment appeal of the Tula Region:

- Its favorable geographical location (proximity to large consumer markets);
- Its qualified work force;
- Its well-developed transport infrastructure.

5.2. CAPITAL INVESTMENT

Industry, transport and communications account for the lion's share of capital investment.

5.3. MOST ATTRACTIVE SECTORS FOR INVESTMENT

Ferrous metals, food and beverages, chemicals and petrochemicals, machine engineering, and metal processing are the most attractive industries for investment.

5.4. CURRENT LEGISLATION ON INVESTOR TAX EXEMPTIONS AND PRIVILEGES

The Tula Region has passed a Law of the Tula Region On State Support to Investment Activity in the Tula Region, which provides for tax credits (on a competitive basis), government guarantees for investment loans, and land and non-residential property leasing assistance to investors operating in the Region.

5.5. FEDERAL AND REGIONAL ECONOMIC AND SOCIAL DEVELOPMENT PROGRAMS FOR THE TULA REGION

Federal targeted programs. A total of $10.2 million was spent on federal targeted programs in the Region in 2002. The federal targeted program for The Elimination of Inequalities in Social and Economic Development of the Regions of the Russian Federation, 2002–2010 and through 2015 has been accorded priority status in the Region. A budget of $1.6 million was allocated for this program by the federal government in 2003.

Capital investment by industry sector, $ million						TABLE 7
	1997	1998	1999	2000	2001	2002
Total capital investment *Including major industries* (% of total):	611.7	393.4	185.7	362.5	276.2	288.7
Industry	42.3	37.6	46.2	30.1	38.9	44.0
Agriculture and forestry	4.0	4.5	5.1	4.8	6.3	8.3
Construction	2.5	0.2	0.4	0.8	0.6	0.7
Transport and communications	17.5	22.4	26.8	50.2	33.2	17.2
Trade and public catering	1.2	1.4	0.8	1.7	1.7	–
Other	32.5	33.9	20.7	12.4	19.3	29.8

Foreign investment trends in 1997–2002						TABLE 8
	1997	1998	1999	2000	2001	2002
Foreign investment, $ million *Including FDI*, $ million	35.7 34.9	31.5 29.9	35.1 5.7	81.6 20.5	43.8 17.6	17.8 11.8

Largest enterprises of the Tula Region
TABLE 9

COMPANY	SECTOR
OAO Tulamashzavod Joint-Stock Company	Defense
OAO Tula Arms Plant	Defense
GUP Instrumentation Design Bureau	Defense
OAO Tulachermet	Ferrous metals
OAO Kosogorsky Steel Works	Ferrous metals
OAO Novomoskovskaya AK Azot	Chemicals
OAO Schekinoazot	Chemicals
OAO Yefremovsky Synthetic Rubber Plant	Chemicals
OAO Tula Combine Factory	Machine engineering
OAO Aleksinsky Heavy Industrial Fittings Plant	Machine engineering
OAO Kran-Uzlovsky Fedunets Machine Engineering Plant	Machine engineering
OAO Kireevsky Light Metal Assemblies Plant	Machine engineering
OAO Taopin	Food and beverages
OAO Tulaspirt	Food and beverages

Regional entities responsible for raising investment
TABLE 10

ENTITY	ADDRESS	PHONE, FAX, E-MAIL
Economic Development Department of the Tula Regional Administration	2, pr. Lenina, Tula, Tula Region, 300600	Phone: (0872) 33 2149 Fax: (0872) 20 6326 http://www.region.tula.ru

A federal targeted program for the Reform and Development of the Defense Sector, 2002–2006 is underway in the Region. The program aims to retool enterprises in the defense sector.

Regional programs. Some 25 regional programs for enterprise development, welfare, environmental rehabilitation, and public health are underway in the Region.

Top priority has been allocated to the Social Infrastructure Construction Project. A budget of $5.2 million was allocated to the project in 2003. The regional targeted program for the Rehousing of Residents of Tumbledown and Unfit Habitations in the Tula Region, 2002–2010 is financed by the Region. A budget of $7.9 million was allocated to the program in 2003.

6. INVESTMENT PROJECTS

Industry sector and project description	1) Expected results 2) Amount and term of investment 3) Form of financing[1] 4) Documentation[2]	Contact information
1	2	3

FERROUS METALS		
16R001 ■ ● ◆		OAO Novostal
Construction of a mining and smelting plant. Project goal: to supply pellets, steel billets, and rolled steel to the market.	1) Plant capacity: 2 million tons of metallized brickets per year 2) € 2,000 million/n/a 3) E, L 4) BP	1, ul. Shkolnaya, Tula-50, Tula Region, 300027 Phone/fax: (0872) 45 8504, 45 7421 E-mail: novostal@tula.net Marina Ivanovna Chevakina, Project Director

[1] L – Loan, E – Equity, Leas. – Leasing, JV – Joint Venture
[2] BP – Business Plan, FS – Feasibility Study

1	2	3

16R002 ■ ● ★ ◆

Upgrading of foundry production facilities.
Project goal: to enhance production efficiency and improve product quality.

1) 1,800 tons of steel output per year, 1,200 tons of iron output per year after the upgrading
2) € 2 million/5 years
3) E, L, Leas.
4) BP

ZAO Industriya Servis
3a, ul. Veresaeva, Tula, Tula Region, 300002
Phone/fax: (0872) 31 5356, 31 5912, 31 5025
E-mail: industry@tula.net
Alexander Alekseevich Dedikin,
CEO

CHEMICALS AND PETROCHEMICALS

16R003 ■ ▲

Renovation and extension of an operating synthetic rubber enterprise.
Project goal: to raise output and diversify the product mix.

1) n/a
2) € 21 million /n/a
3) E
4) FS

OAO Yefremovsky Synthetic Rubber Plant
2, ul. Stroiteley, Yefremov, Tula Region, 301840
Phone: (08741) 62 546,
25 161, 25 361, 66 745
Fax: (08741) 62 373
E-mail: ezsk@tula.net
Vladimir Anatolyevich Belikov,
CEO

16R004 ■ ● ◆

Launch of filled polymer production facilities at an operating enterprise.
Project goal: to raise sales and diversify the product mix.

1) 2,000 tons of plastics per year
2) $0.8 million/6 months
3) E, L
4) BP

OAO Khimvolokno
Schekino, Tula Region, 301240
Phone: (08751) 54 972, 96 127
Fax: (08751) 54 557
Phone/fax: (0872) 36 7170
Alexander Alexandrovich Bogoslavsky,
CEO

16R005 ■ ● ◆

Implementation of a new aluminum sulfate production technology at an operating enterprise.
Project goal: to reduce costs.

1) n/a
2) € 3 million/n/a
3) E, L
4) BP

OAO Schekinoazot
ul. Simferopolskaya, pos. Pervomaysky,
Tula Region, 301212
Phone: (08751) 92 517, 92 538
Fax: (0872) 31 2266
E-mail: stinks@azot.tula.net
Boris Alexandrovich Sokol,
CEO

MACHINE ENGINEERING AND METAL PROCESSING

16R006 ■ ● ◆

Production of a new type of combine harvester.
Project goal: to diversify the product mix.

1) 500 combine harvesters per year
2) € 11 million/5 years
3) E, L
4) BP

OAO Tula Combine Factory
31, ul. Scheglovskaya Zaseka, Tula,
Tula Region, 300004
Phone: (0872) 41 6693
Fax: (0872) 46 7311
E-mail: tkz@unc.net
Baranov Alexander Anatolyevich,
CEO

16R007 ■ ● ◆

Production of a new version of diesel engine.
Project goal: to supply a new version of diesel engine adapted to electric machinery.

1) 5,000 diesel engines per year
2) € 32 million/2 years
3) E, L
4) BP

OAO AK Tulamashzavod
2, ul. Mosina, Tula, Tula Region, 300002
Phone: (0872) 36 9385, 36 5102, 36 2201
Fax: (0872) 27 2620
E-mail: engine@tulamach.net, laser@tulamach.net
Albert Alexandrovich Pleshanov,
Project Director

16R008 ■ ● ◆

Development and production of a powerful industrial laser (capable of cutting tough materials more than 20 mm thick).
Project goal: to diversify product mix.

1) 7 lasers per year
2) € 1.1 million/1 year
3) E, L
4) BP

OAO AK Tulamashzavod
2, ul. Mosina, Tula, Tula Region, 300002
Phone: (0872) 36 9385, 36 5102, 36 2201
Fax: (0872) 27 2620
E-mail: engine@tulamach.net, laser@tulamach.net
Albert Alexandrovich Pleshanov,
Project Director

17. YAROSLAVL REGION [76]

ECONOMIC MAP

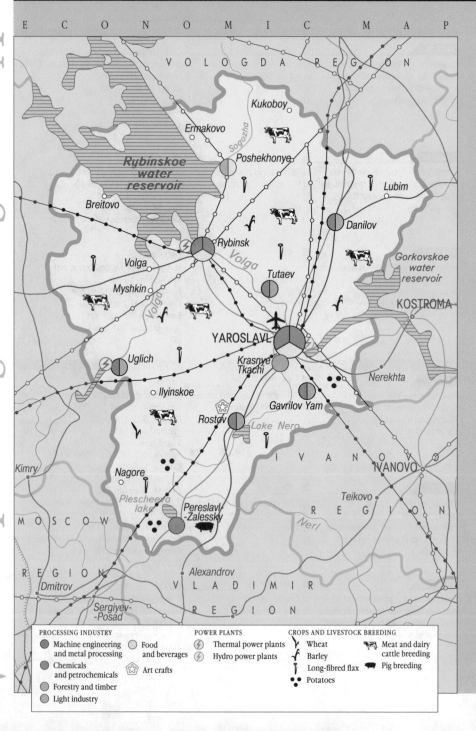

VOLOGDA REGION

Kukoboy

Ermakovo

Sogozha

Poshekhonye

Rybinskoe water reservoir

Lubim

Breitovo

Danilov

Volga

Rybinsk

Volga

Gorkovskoe water reservoir

Tutaev

Myshkin

Volga

KOSTROMA

YAROSLAVL

Uglich

Krasnye Tkachi

Nerekhta

Ilyinskoe

Gavrilov Yam

Rostov

Lake Nero

IVANOVO

Kimry

Nagore

IVANOVO

Plescheevo lake

Teikovo

Pereslavl-Zalessky

Nerl

REGION

MOSCOW

REGION

Alexandrov

VLADIMIR

Dmitrov

REGION

Sergiyev-Posad

PROCESSING INDUSTRY
- Machine engineering and metal processing
- Chemicals and petrochemicals
- Forestry and timber
- Light industry
- Food and beverages
- Art crafts

POWER PLANTS
- Thermal power plants
- Hydro power plants

CROPS AND LIVESTOCK BREEDING
- Wheat
- Barley
- Long-fibred flax
- Potatoes
- Meat and dairy cattle breeding
- Pig breeding

I n terms of economic and research and development potential, the Yaroslavl Region ranks third among the Central Russian regions. The Region is home to tens of thousands of companies. Over 300 large enterprises in the Region have federal importance. These include tire, motor, and shipbuilding plants and an oil refinery. The Region's external trade turnover exceeds $1 billion. The Region has preserved its rich cultural and historical heritage, and is often referred to as the pearl of Russia's Golden Ring tourist route.

The Regional Administration's information database contains over 200 investment projects and 100 targeted programs. The Region is implementing several major investment projects, the largest being the reconstruction of OAO Slavneft-Yaroslavlnefteorgsyntez. In summer 2002, the preliminary stage of the Program for Cooperation between the Yaroslavl Regional Administration and the Government of Moscow, which aims to attract investment into the Yaroslavl Region's economy, was completed. For half a year now, the Regional Administration together with municipalities have been working to arrange an investment program for a total of $150 million. The program identifies two focus areas: large-scale residential housing construction in Yaroslavl and Rybinsk, and the construction of hotels in Yaroslavl, Rybinsk, Rostov, Pereslavl-Zalessky, and Uglich. Since 2000, the Administration together with German company TRANSFORM has been implementing a project for the Establishment of Municipal Development Centers in eight regional municipal districts.

The consistency of the regional investment policy has enabled us to realize a number of major investment projects at OAO Kodak and OAO Slavich in Pereslavl-Zalessky, OAO R&D and Production Company Saturn, and OAO Rybinskheboproduct in Rybinsk, and OAO Kholodmash and OAO Ruskhleb in Yaroslavl.

The main objectives and tasks of the Yaroslavl Regional Administration are set forth in the program for social and economical development of the Region for 2000–2003 entitled From Survival to Prosperity.

The focus areas of regional development are utilization of information technologies, development of export-oriented production, and customization of machine engineering output for the Ukrainian and Belarussian markets. A program for the development of diesel production in the Yaroslavl Region carried out by four major local machine engineering companies jointly with machine engineering companies of Belarus, envisages a breakthrough to a new quality level of diesel manufacturing to world standards. Experts from the Institute of Software Systems of the Russian Academy of Science (Pereslavl-Zalessky) together with their Belarussian colleagues have created a unique super computer SKIF, which matches and in some characteristics exceeds modern super-computers, including those produced in the West. R&D and Production Company Saturn has entered into agreements with RAO UES and OAO Gazprom for the supply of gas turbine units of various capacities.

The Region has good prospects for the development of tourism and tourist infrastructure, including hotels, roads, public catering services, and medical and cultural facilities. In 2001, the Arena 2000 – Locomotive stadium, built to host large international competitions and other events, was opened in Yaroslavl.

Over the past several years, the Region has developed a totally new system of state regulation of investment activity. Its guidelines reflect federal policy, but they also incorporate specific features of the regional economy, geography, and culture.

Anatoly Lisitsyn,
GOVERNOR OF THE YAROSLAVL REGION

CENTRAL FEDERAL DISTRICT

1. GENERAL INFORMATION

1.1. GEOGRAPHY

The Yaroslavl Region covers a total area of some 36,400 square kilometers. The Region lies in the north of European Russia at the center of the East European Plain. The Region borders the Ivanovo, Kostroma, Moscow, Tver, Vladimir, and Vologda Regions. The River Volga, one of Russia's longest waterways, flows through the Yaroslavl Region. The Volga provides a navigable waterway between the Sea of Azov, the Baltic Sea, the Black Sea, the Caspian Sea, and the White Sea.

1.2. CLIMATE

The region is located within the temperate continental climate zone. Air temperatures average –6.1°C in January, rising to +21.6°C in July.

Annual precipitation reaches 580–690 mm. The average growing season lasts 150–170 days.

1.3. POPULATION

According to preliminary 2002 census results, total population in the Yaroslavl Region is 1,368,000 people. The average population density is 37.6 people per square kilometer. The economically active population is 728,000 people. Official unemployment stood at 1.8% in 2002.

Demographically speaking, some 59.4% are of working age, 16.5% are below the statutory working age, and 24.1% are beyond the statutory working age.

The region's major urban centers are Yaroslavl with 613,200 inhabitants and Rybinsk with 222,800 inhabitants.

Population							TABLE 1
	1992	1997	1998	1999	2000	2001	2002
Total population, '000	1,470	1,441	1,433	1,425	1,412	1,400	1,368
Economically active population, '000	774	679	676	732	747	728	728

2. ADMINISTRATION

3, pl. Sovetskaya, Yaroslavl, Yaroslavl Region, 150000
Phone: (0852) 72 8128; fax: (0852) 32 8414; http://www.adm.yar.ru

NAME	POSITION	CONTACT INFORMATION
Anatoly Ivanovich LISITSYN	Governor of the Yaroslavl Region	Phone: (0852) 72 8128 E-mail: gubern@adm.yar.ru
Nikolai Pavlovich VORONIN	Deputy Governor of the Yaroslavl Region	Phone: (0852) 21 0743, 30 3771 Fax: (0852) 30 3771
Sergei Alexandrovich BUROV	Deputy Governor of the Yaroslavl Region	Phone: (0852) 30 7435
Vladimir Alexandrovich KOVALEV	First Deputy Governor of the Yaroslavl Region for Regional Budget	Phone: (0852) 72 8455 Fax: (0852) 32 9442
Alexander Germanovich FEDOROV	First Deputy Governor of the Yaroslavl Region for Industrial Policy and Fuel and Energy Sector	Phone: (0852) 72 8215
Irina Ilyinichna SKOROKHODOVA	First Deputy Governor of the Yaroslavl Region	Phone: (0852) 72 8361
Artur Yuryevich SAZONOV	Deputy Governor of the Yaroslavl Region for Economy, Economic Analysis, Investment, and Business	Phone: (0852) 72 9035
Vladimir Nikitich KHRIASHCHEV	Deputy Governor of the Yaroslavl Region	Phone: (0852) 30 3133
Anatoly Pavlovich FEDOROV	Deputy Governor of the Yaroslavl Region, Director of the Finance Department of the Regional Administration	Phone: (0852) 72 8368
Mikhail Vasilyevich BOROVITSKY	Deputy Governor of the Yaroslavl Region, Director of the Agroindustrial Complex and Environmental Protection and Management Department of the Regional Administration	Phone: (0852) 72 8188

NAME	POSITION	CONTACT INFORMATION
Gennady Vladimirovich IVANOV	Deputy Governor of the Yaroslavl Region, Director of the State Property Management Department of the Regional Administration	Phone: (0852) 21 7248
Nikolai Ivanovich NEPRYAEV	Deputy Governor of the Yaroslavl Region, Director of the Department of State Regulation of Economic Activity of the Regional Administration	Phone: (0852) 72 6701
Irina Viktorovna ABROSIMOVA	Director of the Department of Economic Development, Investments, and International Cooperation of the Regional Administration	Phone: (0852) 72 9415 Fax (0852) 32 7835 E-mail: abro@adm.yar.ru

3. ECONOMIC POTENTIAL

3.1. 1997–2002 GROSS REGIONAL PRODUCT (GRP). INDUSTRY BREAKDOWN

The Yaroslavl Region's 2002 gross regional product reached $2,696.7 million, up 10.8% on 2001. Industrial production and services accounted for the bulk of the growth. Per capita GRP totaled $1,739 in 2001, and $1,971 in 2002.

3.2. MAJOR ECONOMIC GROWTH PROJECTIONS

A blueprint for economic development is given in the From Survival to Prosperity Program for the Development of Yaroslavl Region for 2000–2003. The following areas have been earmarked as priority:

Creating conditions conducive to enhanced production. Fostering and supporting the expansion of sales markets for products and services of local enterprises and organizations;

Expanding the share of services in GRP;

Conserving and developing the energy and natural resources of the region;

Developing the transport infrastructure;

Improving living, public health, and education standards, improving law enforcement, and enhancing the environmental situation;

Creating and maintaining a highly qualified workforce;

Supporting housing construction.

The social and economic development program provides the following outlook for 2003: industrial output up 3.7% (including food and beverage industry output up 15%, construction materials output up 5%, chemicals and petrochemicals output up 3.6%, fuel industry output up 3.8%), and agricultural output up 2%. Capital investment is expected to rise by 6.8%, with foreign trade turnover up 3.2% and retail turnover up 3.1%.

3.3. INDUSTRIAL OUTPUT IN 1997–2002 FOR MAJOR SECTORS OF ECONOMY

The leading industries of the Yaroslavl Region are machine engineering and metal processing, food and beverages, and chemicals and petrochemicals. Total industrial and service output in 2002 amounted to $2,218 million in manufacturer prices (net of excise taxes and VAT).

GRP trends in 1997–2002						TABLE 2
	1997	1998	1999	2000	2001*	2002*
GRP in current prices, $ million	3,390.0	2,283.5	1,470.8	1,665.6	2,434.0	2,696.7

*Estimates of the Yaroslavl Regional Administration

GRP industry breakdown in 1997–2002, % of total						TABLE 3
	1997	1998	1999	2000	2001	2002*
GRP	100.0	100.0	100.0	100.0	100.0	100.0
Industry	32.1	35.5	41.7	42.3	43.0	41.3
Agriculture and forestry	8.3	6.6	12.4	8.2	7.0	6.8
Construction	4.7	4.4	4.5	5.3	7.1	6.8
Transport and communications	9.8	9.2	7.3	7.5	7.9	7.9
Trade and public catering	16.5	15.4	12.0	11.2	7.9	7.8
Other	19.7	16.0	13.3	15.3	12.9	14.3
Net taxes on output	8.9	12.9	8.8	10.2	14.2	15.1

*Estimates of the Yaroslavl Regional Administration

Industry breakdown of industrial output in 1997–2002, % of total						_TABLE 4_
	1997	1998	1999	2000	2001	2002*
Industry	100.0	100.0	100.0	100.0	100.0	100.0
Machine engineering and metal processing	30.5	27.5	27.9	31.7	31.9	30.8
Food and beverages	12.5	15.6	17.4	17.8	19.7	22.6
Chemicals and petrochemicals	20.0	16.8	17.2	20.5	21.6	18.9
Energy	12.4	13.6	7.3	7.8	8.2	9.3
Fuel	14.4	14.1	18.9	10.9	8.1	9.0
Light industry	2.9	3.7	3.8	3.8	3.5	3.1
Forestry, timber, and pulp and paper	1.2	1.4	1.4	1.7	1.5	1.9
Construction materials	2.7	2.9	2.0	2.0	1.9	1.7

*Estimates of the Yaroslavl Regional Administration

Fuel and energy sector production and consumption trends, 1997–2002						_TABLE 5_
	1997	1998	1999	2000	2001	2002*
Electricity output, billion kWh	3.9	4.6	3.9	3.6	4.0	4.0
Oil products, '000 tons	7,716.0	7,624.0	9,768.0	10,826.0	11,485.0	11,780.0
Electricity consumption, billion kWh	6.4	6.3	6.6	6.8	6.9	7.1
Natural gas consumption, million cubic meters	2,378.1	2,398.2	2,399.1	2,522.4	3,119.5	3,214.4

*Estimates of the Yaroslavl Regional Administration

Machine engineering and metal processing. This industry accounts for 30.8% of total industrial output. The Region's machine engineering sector specializes in the production of diesel engines and fuel systems, aircraft engines, and electrical machinery. The sector is represented by 88 large and medium enterprises, the most prominent being OAO Yaroslavl Electric Machinery Plant, OAO Tutayevsky Motor Plant, OAO Saturn Aircraft Engine Factory (former OAO Rybinsk Motors), OAO Auto Diesel, OAO Vympel, OAO Gavrilov-Yamsky Machine Engineering Plant, and OAO Kholodmash.

Food and beverages. The industry accounts for 22.6% of total industrial output. The largest enterprises are GUP Butter and Cheese Production R&D Institute, OAO Ruskhleb, and ZAO Balkan Star.

Chemicals and petrochemicals. Chemicals and petrochemicals enterprises account for 18.9% of the Region's industrial output. The petrochemicals industry is represented by two large enterprises, OAO Slavneft-Yaroslavnefteorgsintez and Mendeleev Yaroslavl Oil Refinery. Other chemicals and petrochemicals enterprises are OAO Yaroslavl Tire Factory, OAO Slavich Company, OAO Lakokraska, OAO Russian Paints, and OAO Yaroslavl Industrial Carbon.

3.4. FUEL AND ENERGY BALANCE (OUTPUT AND CONSUMPTION PER RESOURCE)

The Yaroslavl Region has no natural fuel deposits of its own: all fuel consumed in the Region is imported from other regions of Russia. The Region's oil product requirements are fully met by its two oil refineries. Surplus petroleum products are exported to adjacent regions of Central Russia.

3.5. TRANSPORT INFRASTRUCTURE

The Yaroslavl Region has a well-developed transport network that includes the rail, road, water, and air transport. Geographically speaking, Yaroslavl is situated at a distance of only 250 km from Moscow.

Roads. The Yaroslavl Region has 7,000 km of paved public highways. The Moscow – Yaroslavl – Arkhangelsk and Yaroslavl – Kostroma federal highways which link the central and northern regions of Russia pass through the Yaroslavl Region. The Yaroslavl Region has highway links to the Ivanovo, Tver, and Vologda Regions. In 2002, some 26.9 million tons of freight was transported by road. The Region is currently working on the construction of a bridge over the Volga River.

Railroads. The Yaroslavl Region has 650 km of railroads. More than 18 million tons of freight was carried by rail within the Region in 2002. The Yaroslavl Region has direct rail links to Arkhangelsk and Vorkuta. The Region's railroads provide internal and transit connections between the central, northern, north-eastern, and eastern regions of the country. The main railroad junctions are the Yaroslavsky, Danilovsky, and Rybinsky.

Airports. The Yaroslavl Region is served by domestic and international passenger airlines. The possibility exists for the integration of the Region into European transport corridors such as the Helsinki – St. Petersburg – Moscow corridor, with outlets to the North, Siberia, and the Far East.

The Tunoshna Airport, which has been granted international status, is currently under reconstruction. The Tunoshna Airport will help ease the pressure on Moscow's airports, enable the development of the tourism sector, and reduce the time and cost of delivery of freight and passengers from the Yaroslavl Region and adjacent areas to CIS and non-CIS destinations.

River transport. The Yaroslavl Region's main navigable waterway is the Volga River, the main artery of the unified inland waterway system of European Russia. The Region's inland waterway transportation companies also use the lower courses of tributaries flowing into the Volga and the Rybinsk Reservoir. The total length of the Region's navigable inland waterway system is 818 km.

The main ports, Yaroslavl, Rybinsk, and Uglich, have modern cargo handling equipment and cargo operating systems. Annual water freight transport turnover exceeds 5 million tons. Navigation on the Region's waterways is open for 200–220 days a year.

3.6. MAIN NATURAL RESOURCES: RESERVES AND EXTRACTION IN 2002

The main natural resources of the Yaroslavl Region are peat and mineral resources (sapropel, gravel and sand material and limestone).

Peat. The Yaroslavl Region has over 900 peat deposits covering a total area of 80,000 hectares. The total reserves stand at around 360 million tons. The highest concentrations of deposits are located in the Neokuzsky, Rybinsky, Yaroslavsky and Pereslavsky Municipal Districts. A number of major peat deposits in the Region (the Solodikha, Bolshoye Nagoryevskoye, and Pykhanskoye) have been declared nature reserves and are not subject to development.

Mineral resources. The State Register of Mineral Reserves lists 28 deposits of gravel-sand material (239 million cubic meters in total); 13 deposits of sand (56 million cubic meters in total); six virgin deposits of travertine (204,000 cubic meters in total); one deposit of mineral pigments in the Rostov Region (38,000 cubic meters in total); 17 deposits of brick clay and loam (23 million cubic meters) plus one deposit of thinning sand (617,000 cubic meters); and four deposits of clay and loam for use in the production of keramzite gravel (8 million cubic meters in total). Total industrial grade deposits of minerals used to make construction materials exceed 325 million cubic meters.

4. TRADE OPPORTUNITIES

4.1. MAIN GOODS PRODUCED IN THE REGION

Machine engineering: electric motors; road construction machinery; buses; car engines and turbo jet engines; diesel internal combustion engines; electric motors and generators.

Food and beverages: alcoholic beverages; beer; dairy products; full fat cheese; flour.

Petroleum products and chemicals: tires; polymer film; photographic paper; synthetic resin; plastic. The Region's chemicals industry produces over 16% of all tires made in Russia, and more than 24% of its total output of paints and varnishes. Chemicals enterprises in the Region produce plastics, industrial carbon, rubber industrial goods, and photographic chemicals.

Forestry products: wood, timber.

4.2. EXPORTS, INCLUDING EXTRA-CIS

In 2000, the Region's extra-CIS exports totaled $822.2 million, and CIS exports totaled $47.4 million; the corresponding figures were $1,247.7 million and $66.5 million for 2001, and $258.4 million and $85.9 million for 2002.

The bulk of the Region's exports consists of machine engineering goods (38%) and fuel and energy products (37%).

The main machine engineering goods exported from the Region are road construction machinery, electric motors, friction gear, internal combustion engines, and construction equipment.

The main chemicals industry products exported from the region are polymer film, photographic paper, photographic materials, paint and varnish, pneumatic tires, industrial carbon, and rubber items.

The largest consumers of the Region's petroleum products are (2001 data): the Netherlands ($546.8 million), Finland ($22.9 million), Sweden ($6.1 million), Estonia ($3.1 million), and the UK ($2.9 million). The main consumers of the Region's chemicals products are CIS countries: Ukraine ($15.4 million), Kazakhstan ($2.9 million), Moldova ($1.8 million), and Uzbekistan ($1.5 million).

Machine engineering goods are exported to such countries as Latvia ($57.9 million), Ukraine ($23.2 million), Finland ($20.8 million), Kazakhstan ($6.4 million), Libya ($4.7 million), Iraq ($2.4 million), and Germany ($2.3 million).

4.3. IMPORTS, INCLUDING EXTRA-CIS

In 2000, imports from outside the CIS totaled $150.9 million, with CIS imports coming to $41 million; the corresponding figures were $210.4 million and $37.4 million for 2001, and $201.8 million and $31.3 million for 2002. The bulk of the Region's imports is constituted by machine engineering products (36.4%); food and edible feedstock (30.7%); and petrochemicals (14.5%).

The main machine engineering goods imported to the Region include equipment for the food and beverages industry, printing equipment, equipment for rubber and plastic processing, and lifting equipment. In 2001, the largest purchases of machine engineering products were made in Germany ($27.1 million), Italy ($13.9 million), the USA ($4.9 million), and Switzerland ($4.5 million).

The main food products imported into the Region are beef, bread grain, tobacco feedstock, and confectionery. Food products and feedstock are imported mainly from CIS countries: Kazakhstan, Kyrgyzstan, Moldova, Azerbaijan, and Ukraine.

The main chemical products imported by the Region are organic dyes, fragrant materials and mixes, polymer plate, sheet, and film, printing ink, varnish, and acyclic spirits and their derivatives. Chemical products are imported mainly from Germany, Switzerland, Sweden, Italy, Finland, the Netherlands, and Turkey.

Major regional export and import entities		*TABLE 6*
ENTITY	ADDRESS	PHONE, FAX, E MAIL
ZAO Yarterminal	7, ul. Saltykova-Schedrina, Yaroslavl, Yaroslavl Region, 150000	Phone/fax: (0852) 72 8466, 30 2832, 30 2682
GUP Rostek-Yaroslavl	95, ul. Svobody, Yaroslavl, Yaroslavl Region, 150049	Phone/fax: (0852) 45 1540

5. INVESTMENT OPPORTUNITIES

5.1. INVESTMENTS IN 1997–2002 (BY INDUSTRY SECTOR), INCLUDING FOREIGN INVESTMENTS

The main factors contributing to the investment appeal of the Yaroslavl Region are:
- Its good geographic location and access to large markets and links with other Russian regions and all countries worldwide;
- Its favorable industrial infrastructure (the most economically developed and advanced region of European Russia);
- Its well-developed transport infrastructure, including rail, road, water and air links; and
- Laws supporting investment activity.

5.2. CAPITAL INVESTMENT

The bulk of fixed capital investment goes to industry (62%), and transport and communications (15%).

5.3. MAJOR ENTERPRISES (INCLUDING ENTERPRISES WITH FOREIGN INVESTMENTS)

Some 300 enterprises with foreign investments from over 40 countries worldwide are registered in the Yaroslavl Region. The largest enterprises with foreign investments are OOO Bertelsmann Distribution Center, OOO Intertour, OOO Polygraph Print, OOO Pack-Plast, OOO Balkan Star Service, OOO Investmart, and OOO Upper Volga Corrugated Board Factory.

5.4. MOST ATTRACTIVE SECTORS FOR INVESTMENT

According to the Yaroslavl Regional Administration, the most attractive sectors for investment are the machine engineering, chemicals and petrochemicals industries, the food industry, construction, and transport.

Capital investment by industry sector, $ million						*TABLE 7*
	1997	1998	1999	2000	2001	2002
Total capital investment	448.2	290,0	245.6	288,4	496.4	354.4
Including major industries (% of total):						
Industry	53.0	40.8	58.6	55.7	41.4	62.0
Agriculture and forestry	3.4	4.7	3.5	3.3	2.2	3.4
Construction	1.8	1.8	1.0	3.7	0.9	1.7
Transport and communications	14.9	14.6	15.4	14.3	32.7	15.0
Trade and public catering	1.9	0.7	1.3	1.9	1.4	0.8
Other	25.0	37.4	20.2	21.1	21.4	17.1

Foreign investment trends in 1995–2002						*TABLE 8*
	1995–1997	1998	1999	2000	2001	2002
Foreign investment, $ million	127.6	76.7	40.1	7.7	14.1	29.0
Including FDI, $ million	67.1	11.5	4.6	3.7	3.9	2.6

Largest enterprises of the Yaroslavl Region	*TABLE 9*
COMPANY	SECTOR
OAO Autodiesel (Yaroslavl Engine Factory)	Machine engineering
OAO Slavneft-Yaroslavnefteorgintez	Petrochemicals
OAO Yarpivo	Food and beverages
OAO Balkan Star	Tobacco
OAO NPO Saturn	Machine engineering
OAO Yaroslavl Tire Factory	Chemicals
OAO Yaroslavl Electric Machinery Plant	Machine engineering
OAO Lakokraska	Chemicals
OAO Russian Paints	Chemicals
OAO Slavich Company	Chemicals
Branch of ZAO Kodak A/O	Chemicals
OAO Kholodmash	Machine engineering
OAO Vympel	Shipbuilding

I

5.5. CURRENT LEGISLATION ON INVESTOR TAX EXEMPTIONS AND PRIVILEGES

The Region has enacted a Law On State Support to Investment Activity in the Yaroslavl Region. The Law provides for preferential tax treatment from the moment of first sale of goods (works, services) until full project payback, up to a maximum of five years. Exemptions are granted for the regional tax component of property tax, land tax, and, partially, profits tax. Priority projects and programs are granted state support in the form of governmental guarantees, regional budget subsidies on bank loan interest, information support, and state participation in the development, expert examination, and implementation of programs.

According to the Law On Incentives for the Economic Development of the Yaroslavl Region, enterprises increasing their regional profit tax payments are entitled to growth subsidies from the regional budget of up to 80% of the profit tax increase.

5.6. FEDERAL AND REGIONAL ECONOMIC AND SOCIAL DEVELOPMENT PROGRAMS FOR THE YAROSLAVL REGION

Federal targeted programs. The Yaroslavl Region is participating in the implementation of 43 federal programs that target the development of industry, the agro-industrial complex, the social sphere, environmental protection, and law enforcement. The Region's federal programs were financed to the tune of around $89.2 million in 2002.

The most significant federal targeted programs underway in the Region are the Energy Efficient Economy Program, 2002–2005 and through 2010 and the Program for the Modernization of Russia's Transport System, 2002–2010.

The federal targeted program for the Modernization of Russia's Transport System, 2002–2010 aims to develop the national transport infrastructure. Under the program, construction work is underway on several facilities of major importance for the north-east of Russia and adjacent regions. In 2002, the Program was allocated financing to the tune of around $26.8 million, including around $15.9 million for the construction of a by-pass around Yaroslavl with a bridge over the Volga; approximately $4.5 million for the reconstruction of the Tunoshna Airport; and around $6.4 million for the reconstruction of a CHZ locomotive repair shop.

The federal targeted program Energy Efficient Economy, 2002–2005 and through 2010 has as its objective the reconstruction of existing and construction of new facilities for the fuel and energy industries. Under the program, work is underway on the revamping of equipment at OAO Slavneft-Yaroslavnefteorgsintez, the Region's major fuel industry enterprise. This project is being financed via a $200 million loan from the Japan Bank for International Cooperation. The project financing in 2002 reached some $41.4 million.

The federal targeted investment program envisages the construction and reconstruction of

Regional entities responsible for raising investment		TABLE 9
ENTITY	ADDRESS	PHONE, FAX, E-MAIL
Yaroslavl Office of the Fund for Small Enterprise Development Assistance in the Scientific and Technical Spheres OOO YarECOS-Invest	62, ul. Svobody, Yaroslavl, Yaroslavl Region, 150014	Phone: (0852) 21 9344, 21 8144 E-mail: garant@nord.net.ru
Autonomous Non-Profit Agency for the Development of Municipal Districts and Housing Lending	1/19, ul. Deputatskaya, Yaroslavl, Yaroslavl Region, 150000	Phone/fax: (0852) 72 5786 Email: goldyar@yandex.ru
Non-Profit Interregional Engine Ecology Innovation Technology Center	62, ul. Svobody, Yaroslavl, Yaroslavl Region, 150014	Phone: (0852) 21 9344, 21 8144 Phone/fax: (0852) 45 8974
OOO Soyuz-Audit	9, ul. Polushkina Roscha, Yaroslavl, Yaroslavl Region, 150003	Phone: (0852) 91 7802, 30 8403
NP Development Center	2, Uspenskaya pl., Uglich, Yaroslavl Region, 152610	Phone: (08532) 50 276 E-mail: soyuz@yaroslavl.ru
OOO Yaroslavl Insurance Group – Narodny Reserve Insurance Company	61a, prospekt Lenina, Yaroslavl, Yaroslavl Region, 150054	Phone: (0852) 45 9596
Non-Profit Investment Agency of Municipal Entities of the Yaroslavl Region	8, ul. Sovetskaya, Yaroslavl, Yaroslavl Region, 150000	Phone/fax: (0852) 303959 E-mail: Km1973@yandex.ru

22 industrial facilities in the Yaroslavl Region. In 2002, total financing exceeded $7.6 million.

Regional programs. A total of some $50.3 million has been allocated from the regional budget for 39 planned regional projects. The Yaroslavl Region is implementing programs in road building, public welfare, public health, law enforcement, and agro-industrial policy. The high-est priority for the Region is assigned to social programs, including: Resettlement of Citizens from Tumbledown and Damaged Housing in the Yaroslavl Region, 2003–2007, State Support to Young Families in Acquisition (Construction) of Housing, 2003–2005, Improvement and Development of Roads of the Yaroslavl Region, 2001–2003 and through 2010.

6. INVESTMENT PROJECTS

Industry sector and project description	1) Expected results 2) Amount and term of investment 3) Form of financing[1] 4) Documentation[2]	Contact information
1	2	3
CHEMICALS AND PETROCHEMICALS		
17R001 ● ★ ◆		
Manufacturing of new CMK Model tires at OAO Yaroslavl Tire Factory. Project goal: to expand production.	1) 400,000 per year 2) $3.6 million/n/a 3) L, Leas. 4) BP	OAO Yaroslavl Tire Factory 81, ul. Sovetskaya, Yaroslavl, Yaroslavl Region, 150040 Phone: (0852) 30 5433 Fax: (0852) 79 1004 E-mail: direct@yashz.ru http://www.yashz.yaroslavl.ru Alexander Ivanovich Andreev, CEO

[1] L – Loan, E – Equity, Leas. – Leasing, JV – Joint Venture
[2] BP – Business Plan, FS – Feasibility Study

1	2	3

17R002

Creation of electrographic toner production facilities. Project goal: to develop production of import-replacement goods.	1) 1,000 toners per year ($15 million) 2) $5 million/n/a 3) JV 4) BP	OAO Company Slavich 2, pl. Mendeleeva, Pereslavl-Zalessky, Yaroslavl Region, 152020 Phone: (08535) 21 543 Fax: (08535) 22 560, 21 281 E-mail: adm@slavich.ru http://www.slavich.ru Alexander Mikhailovich Dyma, CEO

MACHINE ENGINEERING AND METAL PROCESSING

17R003

Construction of the second stage of a wharf for building promising new generation boats. Project goal: to organize the manufacturing of a new series of boats for distribution to the domestic and foreign markets.	1) 5 Mirage and 8 Mongoose boats annually 2) $28.4 million/n/a 3) L 4) BP	OAO Vympel Shipyard 4, ul. Novaya, Rybinsk, Yaroslavl Region, 152912 Phone: (0855) 21 1931, 20 2301, 20 2400 Fax: (0855) 21 1877 mail: aovympel@yaroslavl.ru Victor Borisovich Doskin, CEO

17R004

Establishment of the production of electromagnetic fuel injectors for gasoline engines. Project goal: to manufacture goods consistent with international quality standards.	1) 1,000,000 items per year ($4.7 million) 2) $10.4 million/n/a 3) L, Leas. 4) BP	OAO GavrilovYamsky Machine Engineering Plant Agat 1, proyezd Mashinostroiteley, Gavrilov-Yam, Yaroslavl Region, 152240 Phone: (08534) 23 264 Fax: (08534) 20 964 E-mail: agat@gmzagat.ru Vladimir Nikolaevich Korytov, Director

FOOD AND BEVERAGES

17R005

Production of solid caramel, with and without filling. Project goal: to launch a new product, high-quality solid caramel.	1) n/a 2) $4.3 million/n/a 3) L, JV(50/50) 4) BP	OAO Ruskhleb 5 ul. Gromova, Yaroslavl, Yaroslavl Region, 151061 Phone/fax: (0852) 55 1371 E-mail: ruskhleb@yaroslavl.ru Alexander Mikhailovich Zaichenko, CEO

17R006

Renewal of obsolete equipment and increased output at lower production costs. Project goal: to produce competitive brands of beer.	1) 3.2 million decaliters per year ($1 million) 2) $1.6 million/n/a 3) L, Leas. 4) BP	OAO Rybinsk Brewery 48 ul. Rabochaya, Rybinsk, Yaroslavl Region 152900 Phone: (0855) 26 1905 Phone/fax: 26 1907, 26 3577 Denis Yuryevich Golovansky, CEO

17R007

Establishment of a separate flour milling unit based on Italian technology. Project goal: to organize the production of flour mixes corresponding to European quality standards; to increase production of superior quality flour by 10–15%.	1) 330 tons/day of flour mixes ($11.3 million per year) 2) $3.5 million/n/a 3) E, L, Leas. 4) BP	OAO Rybinskkhleboprodukt 1, Cheremkhovskaya Gavan, Rybinsk, Yaroslavl Region, 152900 Phone: (0855) 26 6403, 26 7322 Fax: (0855) 26 6359 E-mail: rhp@yaroslavl.ru Vladimir Andreevich Burau, CEO

1	2	3

17R008

Creation of a show farm and a service center for the production and sale of high quality dairy products based on Dutch technology and available cattle breeding facilities.
Project goal: to implement promising new dairy technologies and improve dairy product quality.

1) Increase milk output by 2,676,000 liters per year ($0.6 million)
2) $0.7 million/n/a
3) E (up to 49%), L
4) BP

OOO Novoye Schedrino
Administration building of SPK Molot, Safonovo Village, Yaroslavsky District, Yaroslavl Region, 150508
Phone/fax: (0852) 30 2481, 32 9405
E-mail: agronova@mail.ru
Yevgeny Ivanovich Veselov, Director

PRINTING

17R009

Production of printed matter.
Project goal: to produce printed matter: books, magazines, labels, and packaging.

1) n/a
2) $0.8 million/n/a
3) L
4) BP

OAO Rybinsky Printing House
8, ul. Chkalova, Rybinsk, Yaroslavl Region, 152901
Phone: (0855) 52 0934
Fax: (0855) 21 0357
E-mail: printing@yaroslavl.ru
Vladimir Vladimirovich Denisov, CEO

TRANSPORT INFRASTRUCTURE

17R010

Reconstruction of the Tunoshna Airport; creation of intermodal Tunoshna complex (runway renovation/extension; replacement of radio navigation and lighting equipment).
Project goal: to create an airport infrastructure consistent with international standards; to provide air links to adjacent regions (Ivanovo, Kostroma, Tver, and Vologda).

1) n/a
2) $16 million/n/a
3) E, L
4) BP

GUP Tunoshna Yaroslavl Regional Airport
26, Tunoshna, Tunoshna Airport, Yaroslavl District, Yaroslavl Region, 152202
Phone/fax: (0852) 43 1810
http://www.tunoshna.ru
Anatoly Mikhailovich Koval, Director

COMMUNICATIONS

17R011

Construction of Nordnet Digital Communications System.
Project goal: to provide high speed data transmission and telephony services; to provide Internet access.

1) Serving 16,000 telephone users and 2,500 Internet users annually ($36.5 million and $14.3 million)
2) $8 million/n/a
3) L
4) BP

OAO SeverTransCom
37, ul. Pobedy, Yaroslavl, Yaroslavl Region, 150048
Phone/fax: (0852) 72 1728, 72 1738, 72 1708
E-mail: info@ctk.ru
Valery Pavlovich Volkov, CEO

TRADE

17R012

Construction of a trade center at MUP Sennaya Ploshchad Cultural and Commercial Center.
Project goal: to develop the retail services market.

1) Retail space: 4,090 square m ($1.2 million)
2) $1.3 million/n/a
3) L
4) BP

MUP Sennaya Ploshchad Cultural and Commercial Center
16, ul. Lunacharskogo, Rybinsk 152934
Phone: (0855) 21 3780
Fax: (0855) 21 9463
E-mail: sploshad@mail.ru
Igor Mikhailovich Peshkov, Director

17R013

Construction of a trade and service center in the town of Gavrilov-Yam.
Project goal: to create conditions conducive to the emergence of SMEs; to provide services (car repair, consumer household services, and public catering).

1) Annual revenues of $0.2 million
2) $0.3 million/n/a
3) L
4) BP

OOO Gavrilov-Yam Trade and Service Center
1a, ul. Kirova, Gavrilov Yam, Yaroslavl Region, 152240
Phone/fax: (08534) 24 060, 24 086, 24 084
Irina Leonidovna Smirnova, CEO

1	2	3

HOTELS AND TOURISM

17R014

Creation of a small hotel chain in the cities of the Yaroslavl Region (Yaroslavl, Rostov Veliky, Uglich, and Pereslavl-Zalessky). Project goal: to raise hotel standards to European levels with a view to developing tourism.

1) Annual revenues of $1.9 million
2) $8.3 million/n/a
3) JV (100% foreign investment)
4) BP

Yaroslavl Regional Department of Culture and Tourism
9/4, ul. Revolutsionnaya, Yaroslavl, Yaroslavl Region, 150000
Phone/fax: (0852) 30 5642
E-mail: koptev@adm.yar.ru, prazdnik@region.adm.yar.ru
Vladimir Victorovich Prazdnikov, Deputy Director of Department

17R015

Construction of a 120 room Balkan four-star hotel in Yaroslavl. Project goal: to enhance the level of service in the hotel market.

1) 120 beds ($5.5 million per year)
2) $8.2 million/n/a
3) L
4) BP

OOO Balkan Star Service
22, ul. Pobedy, Yaroslavl, Yaroslavl Region, 150040
Phone/fax: (0852) 73 3789
E-mail: bstabak@yaroslavl.ru
Yury Pavlovich Kardakov, Director

I

CENTRAL FEDERAL DISTRICT

R U S S I A

CENTRAL FEDERAL DISTRICT

ECONOMIC MAP

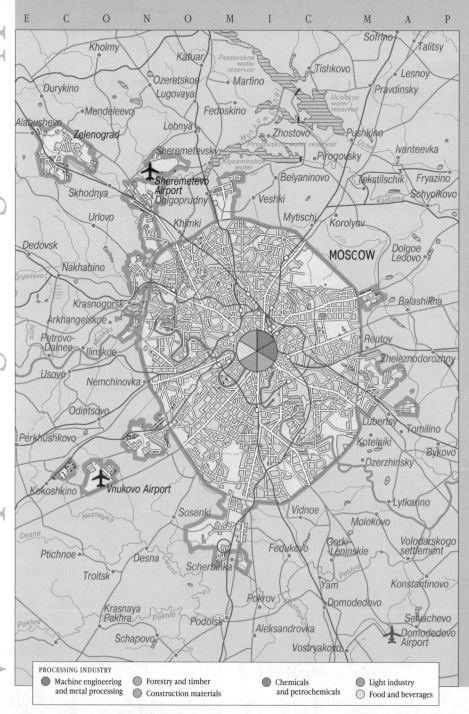

Kholmy
Katuar
Pestovskoe water reservoir
Tishkovo
Sofrino
Talitsy
Lesnoy
Durykino
Ozeretskoe
Marfino
Pravdinsky
Lugovaya
Uchiskoe water reservoir
Mendeleevo
Fedoskino
Alabushevo
Zelenograd
Lobnya
Zhostovo
Pushkino
Ivanteevka
Sheremetevsky
Pirogovskoe water reservoir
Pirogovsky
Skhodnya
Kiyazminskoe water
Belyaninovo
Tekstilschik
Fryazino
Sheremetevo Airport
Dolgoprudny
Veshki
Schyolkovo
Urlovo
Khimki
Mytischi
Korolyov
Kiyazma
Dedovsk
MOSCOW
Dolgoe
Ledovo
Nakhabino
Gryazeva
Balashikha
Krasnogorsk
Arkhangelskoe
Moskva
Petrovo-Dalnee
Ilinskoe
Reutov
Istra
Zheleznodorozhny
Usovo
Nemchinovka
Odintsovo
Lubertsy
Tomilino
Kotelniki
Perkhushkovo
Bykovo
Dzerzhinsky
Kokoshkino
Vnukovo Airport
Lytkarino
Neznayka
Sosenki
Vidnoe
Desna
Molokovo
Ptichnoe
Desna
Fedukovo
Gorki-Leninskie
Volodarskogo settlement
Troitsk
Scherbinka
Pakhra
Yam
Konstantinovo
Krasnaya Pakhra
Pokrov
Domodedovo
Selyachevo
Pakhra
Podolsk
Aleksandrovka
Domodedovo Airport
Schapovo
Vostryakovo

PROCESSING INDUSTRY
- Machine engineering and metal processing
- Forestry and timber
- Construction materials
- Chemicals and petrochemicals
- Light industry
- Food and beverages

I am pleased to have this opportunity to extend my greetings to potential investors and trading partners of the city of Moscow. Moscow today is the largest and most dynamically developing regional market in Russia. Major financial flows are channeled through the city, and it accounts for some 30% of domestic retail and 40% of wholesale trade. Moscow is engaged in extensive capital construction and is implementing comprehensive social programs and, in particular, small enterprise support programs.

Moscow is the absolute leader among Russia's regions in terms of foreign investment, which increased 49.3% year-on-year to reach $8.4 billion in 2002.

In recent years, the Moscow Government has focused on turning the capital into a financial, trade, and tourism center.

In order to achieve this goal, we have invested a considerable portion of the budget into the development of business infrastructure, and the construction and reconstruction of transport and communications and new high technology centers, as stipulated in Moscow General Development Plan through 2020.

This is borne out by budget figures and general information on the scope and structure of the investment programs of the Government of Moscow. I trust that this publication will contribute to the success of investor business initiatives in the Russian capital.

On my own behalf and on behalf of the Moscow Government, I wish you every success in your initiatives.

Yury Luzhkov,
MAYOR OF MOSCOW

CENTRAL FEDERAL DISTRICT

1. GENERAL INFORMATION

1.1. GEOGRAPHY

Moscow, the capital of the Russian Federation, has the twin status of federal city and a Russian region. Moscow covers an area of 1,080.4 square kilometers.

1.2. CLIMATE

Moscow enjoys a temperate continental climate. The average air temperature in January is −10°C, rising to +24°C in July. Average annual precipitation reaches 700 mm.

1.3. POPULATION

The preliminary 2002 census results revealed a total population of 10,317,000 people, including the 216,000 residents of Zelenograd. The economically active population amounts to 5,497,000 people. The 2002 official unemployment level was 1.4%.

Demographically speaking, some 59.9% are of working age, 15.8% are below the statutory working age, and 24.3% are beyond the statutory working age.

Population								TABLE 1
	1992	1997	1998	1999	2000	2001	2002
Total population, '000	8,865	8,547	8,537	8,538	8,537	8,546	10,317
Economically active population, '000	4,693	4,072	4,036	4,278	4,276	4,378	5,497

2. ADMINISTRATION

13, ul. Tverskaya, Moscow, 125032.
Phone: (095) 777 7777; fax: (095) 234 3295, 234 3297; E-mail: mayor@mos.ru; http://www.mos.ru

NAME	POSITION	CONTACT INFORMATION
Yury Mikhailovich LUZHKOV	Mayor of Moscow	Phone: (095) 292 7238 Fax: (095) 229 4887
Valery Pavlinovich SHANTSEV	Vice Mayor of Moscow, Head of the Moscow Economic Policy and Development Sector	Phone: (095) 292 0881, 290 7735 E-mail: mayor@mos.ru
Petr Nikolaevich AKSENOV	First Deputy Mayor of Moscow, Head of the Moscow Municipal Economy Sector	Phone: (095) 258 3760
Vladimir Iosifovich RESIN	First Deputy Mayor of Moscow at the Moscow Government, Head of the Moscow Architecture, Construction, Development, and Reconstruction Sector	Phone: (095) 925 4626 Fax: (095) 299 9656 E-mail: resin@kpr.mos.ru
Oleg Mikhailovich TOLKACHEV	First Deputy Mayor of Moscow, Head of the Property and Land Relations Sector, Head of Department	Phone: (095) 292 0663, 202 9181, 299 2048 E-mail: dgma@mos.ru
Lyudmila Ivanovna SHVETSOVA	First Deputy Mayor of Moscow, Head of the Social Sector	Phone: (095) 290 7196, 290 7197 E-mail: shw36@post.mos.ru
Viktor Alexeevich KOROBCHENKO	Chief of Staff of the Moscow Government, First Deputy Mayor of Moscow at the Moscow Government	Phone: (095) 229 1466 E-mail: zpkva@maria3.mos.ru
Mikhail Alexandrovich MEN	Deputy Mayor of Moscow at the Moscow Government	Phone: (095) 290 7178 E-mail: menn@post.mos.ru
Iosif Nikolaevich ORDZHONIKIDZE	Deputy Mayor of Moscow at the Moscow Government	Phone: (095) 229 6360 E-mail: dvsoin@mos.ru
Yury Vitalyevich ROSLYAK	Deputy Mayor of Moscow at the Moscow Government, Head of the Moscow Economic Policy and Development Department	Phone: (095) 200 5462 Fax: (095) 913 6001 E-mail: deprm@econ.mos.ru
	MINISTERS OF THE MOSCOW GOVERNMENT	
Yevgeny Vladimirovich YEGOROV	Minister of the Moscow Government, Head of the Small Enterprise Development Support Department	Phone: (095) 256 1787 E-mail: dmp@econ.mos.ru

NAME	POSITION	CONTACT INFORMATION
Yury Viktorovich KOROSTELEV	Minister of the Moscow Government, Head of the Finance Department	Phone: (095) 251 3526 E-mail: avdeev@depfin.econ.mos.ru
Vladimir Ivanovich MALYSHKOV	Minister of the Moscow Government, Head of the Consumer Market and Services Department	Phone: (095) 200 2449 Fax: (095) 200 3573 E-mail: dprms@maria2.mos.ru
Alexander Ivanovich BABURIN	Minister of the Moscow Government, Head of the Food Resources Department	Phone: (095) 924 7967, 925 0468 E-mail: prod@dpr.mos.ru
Alexander Ilyich MUZYKANTSKY	Minister of the Moscow Government, Head of the Information and Public Relations Department	Phone: (095) 202 6480 E-mail: zpmai@mos.ru
Yevgeny Alexandrovich PANTELEEV	Minister of the Moscow Government, Head of the Science and Industrial Policy Department	Phone: (095) 924 9889 Fax: (095) 299 8616 E-mail: kolom@dnpp.mos.ru
Leonid Arnoldovich BOCHIN	Minister of the Moscow Government, Head of the Environment and Ecology Department	Phone: (095) 202 8474 Fax: (095) 291 8343 E-mail: bochin@post.mos.ru

3. ECONOMIC POTENTIAL

3.1. 1997–2002 GROSS REGIONAL PRODUCT (GRP). INDUSTRY BREAKDOWN

Moscow accounts for some 9% of Russia's total gross domestic product. According to the Moscow Government, gross regional product amounted to $68,390.7 million in 2002, which constitutes 13.5% growth year-on-year. Retail and public catering account for the lion's share at 48.3%. The share of industrial output increased from 8% to 8.5% in 2002, mainly due to increased production of chemicals and machinery. The share of transport and communications grew from 7.9% to 9.8%. Per capita GRP amounted to $7,049 in 2001 and $6,628 in 2002.

3.2. MAJOR ECONOMIC GROWTH PROJECTIONS

Industry: The city has elaborated a comprehensive program for the industrial development of Moscow through 2004–2006. The program aims to renew and upgrade the industrial base, create and promote the production of advanced technologies, integrate the operations of industrial companies and small enterprises to produce innovative goods, strike a balance between industrial, social and eco-

GRP trends in 1997–2002						*TABLE 2*
	1997	1998	1999	2000	2001*	2002*
GRP in current prices, $ million	54,902.7	37,548.0	31,897.5	47,742.5	60,239.9	68,390.7

*Estimates of the Moscow Government

GRP industry breakdown in 1997–2002, % of total						*TABLE 3*
	1997	1998	1999	2000	2001*	2002*
GRP	100.0	100.0	100.0	100.0	100.0	100.0
Industry	13.6	13.0	9.8	7.9	8.0	8.5
Construction	7.7	7.7	5.1	5.2	5.3	4.1
Transport, communications	10.8	10.0	8.5	7.3	7.9	9.8
Retail and public catering	32.0	33.8	45.1	49.9	49.9	48.3
Other	22.9	24.1	19.9	18.5	17.8	18.2
Net taxes on output	13.0	11.4	11.6	11.2	11.1	11.1

*Estimates of the Moscow Government

nomic, and civil construction, develop industrial infrastructure, and improve regulations and laws related to the state regulation of industry.

Pursuant to the Moscow Government's forecasts, 2003 industrial growth will amount to 5% in comparable prices, including 3% in energy, 3% in fuel, 14.5% in chemicals and petrochemicals, 5% in machine engineering and metal processing, and 5% in the building materials sectors. Capital investment growth is expected to reach 3% and the consumer price index is expected to grow by 15%. In 2004, industrial output will increase by 5%, including 7% in building materials, 7% in chemicals and petrochemicals, 5.5% in machine engineering and metal processing, 4.5% in fuel, and 3% in energy and non-ferrous metals. Capital investment is expected to grow by 4%, while the consumer price index is expected to gain 12%.

Retail and consumer market: The priority consumer market areas are: the protection of consumer rights and support of enterprises, the development of wholesale and small batch trading, and the improvement in the retail sector regulatory and legal base.

In 2003, there are plans afoot to establish 530 new retail and public catering companies, reconstruct and upgrade 435 existing sales outlets and 23 markets, create regulations governing retail outlet zoning, and eradicate trade stand areas. According to the Moscow Government, in 2003, 2004, and 2005, retail turnover will increase by 4%, 5.5%, and 4%, respectively.

Wholesale: Moscow accounts for 40% of total wholesale turnover. A priority task of the Moscow Government is to set up a modern wholesale market infrastructure. The existing wholesale facilities will be employed to the maximum possible extent. In 2003–2004, the city will establish eight to nine wholesale food markets at existing vegetable storage facilities and set up four to five specialized meat and fish wholesale markets

at deep freeze storage facilities. Wholesale outlets will be zoned and developed in compliance with the Moscow General Development Plan through 2020.

Small enterprise: In 2003–2005, Moscow intends to focus on promoting small enterprise in urban economy sectors such as ecology, small-scale energy generation, and housing and communal services. According to the Moscow Government, in 2003 small enterprises will employ up to 2 million people, and their total share of GRP will grow by 30%.

Tourism: The Moscow Government has adopted and is implementing a special tourism development program through 2010. The blueprint for the comprehensive development of the Moscow Golden Ring tourism and recreation zone envisages the construction of a multifunctional and modern tourism infrastructure in the historical center of Moscow to service domestic and foreign tourists. Under the Moscow Golden Ring project, some 65 facilities will be reconstructed, restored, or built, and some 40 plots and areas will be turned into pedestrian zones. The project budget amounts to $2.3 billion.

The Moscow Government plans to reconstruct the Rossia Hotel (project cost – $235 million), the Ostankino Hotel (project cost – $20 million), and the Tourist Hotel (project cost – $42 million).

3.3. INDUSTRIAL OUTPUT IN 1997–2002 FOR MAJOR SECTORS OF ECONOMY

Industrial policy. The Moscow Government is pursuing an industrial policy aimed at encouraging the production and sale of competitive goods and the launch of new import substitutes and export-focused high technology products through the granting of privileges to manufacturers, partial subsidizing of bank interest expense, public listing of industrial enterprises, and expansion of trade links with other countries and other regions of Russia.

Industry breakdown of industrial output in 1997–2002, % of total

TABLE 4

	1997	1998	1999	2000	2001	2002*
Industry	100.0	100.0	100.0	100.0	100.0	100.0
Food and beverages	21.8	31.7	32.1	33.2	29.3	31.9
Machine engineering and metal processing	19.2	25.0	30.9	30.6	27.6	28.9
Energy	36.0	19.2	9.6	9.3	9.1	10.4
Construction materials	5.2	5.8	4.1	4.1	4.7	4.0
Chemicals and petrochemicals	2.9	4.6	4.7	5.5	5.1	2.8
Light industry	2.5	2.6	3.1	2.9	2.9	2.7
Forestry, timber, and pulp and paper	2.1	2.1	2.9	3.4	3.1	2.3
Fuel	3.4	2.2	2.2	1.7	9.7	1.7
Non-ferrous metals	0.6	0.8	1.5	1.0	0.9	1.5
Ferrous metals	0.8	0.9	1.1	1.2	0.8	0.9
Flour, cereals, and mixed fodder	1.3	1.2	1.9	1.9	1.2	0.8

*Estimates of the Moscow Government

The Moscow Government provides financial support to industrial enterprises in the form of reimbursable, interest-bearing budget loans (at no less than 25% of the Central Bank refinancing rate), partial subsidies for interest expense (no less than 75%) on commercial bank loans, budget subsidies to partially cover interest expense on corporate debt securities, and the restructuring of industrial companies' debt to the Moscow budget.

Moscow's industry spearheads the social and economic development of the Russian Federation. Some 5% of Russia's total industrial output and 11.5% of the country's consumer goods output is produced in Moscow. In 2001 and 2002, tax payments by Moscow industrial enterprises to the federal budget amounted to $2,351 million and $2,801 million, respectively. Moscow's share of total tax payments to the federal budget increased from 16.2% in 2001 to 22.2% in 2002.

Moscow has over 1,000 large and 13,000 small industrial companies. The industrial sector employs some 530,000 people, or 12% of the economically active population. Food and beverages and machine engineering and metal processing hold leading positions in the industrial sector. Their combined share in total industrial output was 60.8% in 2002.

Food and beverages. The sector accounts for 31.9% of total industrial output. Food and beverage companies in Moscow produce confectionery, meat and dairy products, pasta, oil and butter, vodka, and alcoholic beverages. The largest companies within the sector are: OAO Cherkizovsky Meat Processing Plant, OAO Tsaritsino, OAO Red October, OAO Tsaritsinsky Dairy Plant, ZAO Mikoyanovsky Plant, ZAO Moscow-Efes Brewery, OAO Margarine Plant, OOO Bakhus, OAO Confectionery Concern Babaevsky, OAO Ochakovsky Dairy Plant, OAO Ostankinsky Dairy Plant, OAO Ostankino Brewery, OAO Extra M, OAO Moscow Fat Plant, OOO Parmalat MK, OOO Pepsico Holdings, and ZAO Moscow Ochakovo Brewery and Non-Alcoholic Beverages Plant.

In 2002, the Moscow Government provided food and beverage companies with bank interest subsidies for a total of $3.8 million. In 2003, this amount will increase to $8.2 million.

Machine engineering and metal processing. The sector accounts for 28.9% of total industrial output. Machine engineering and metal processing output in 2002 reached 119.8% of the 2001 figure. The major companies within the sector are OAO Likhachev Plant (ZIL), ZAO Moskabelmet, OAO Mostochlegmash, OAO TVEL, OAO Avtoframos, and OAO Karacharovsky Mechanical Engineering Plant.

Energy. The energy sector accounts for 10.4% of total industrial output. 2002 electricity output was up 1.3% year-on-year. Moscow utilities companies generated 98 million Gcal of heat in 2002, of which 44.7 million Gcal was subsidized by the city. In 2002, the installed capacity of Moscow's thermal power stations increased by 130 Gcal/hour year-on-year following the expansion of the Matveevskaya, Nagatinskaya,

Chertanovo, Biryulovo, Tushino 3, Peredelkino, and Mitino local thermal stations. The leading company within the sector is OAO Mosenergo, which comprises four power stations, a hydroelectric power station, and 16 thermal power stations.

Chemicals and petrochemicals. The share of the sector in total industrial output is 2.8%. 2002 chemical output was 139.3% of the 2001 figure. Moscow's chemical companies produce synthetic resins and plastics, tires, and pharmaceuticals. The major companies are: ZAO International Potassium Company, OAO Moscow Tire Plant, OAO Gammakhim, and OAO Polimerbyt.

Light industry. The sector accounts for 2.7% of total industrial output. 2002 output was 109.8% of the 2001 levels. The light industry sector produces cotton and silk fabric, knitwear, and hosiery. The largest companies are: OAO Trekhgornaya Manufaktura, and ZAO Moscow Petr Alexeev Fine Fabric Factory.

Fuel. The sector accounts for 1.7% of total industrial output. 2002 fuel output was up 7.9% year-on-year. The largest company is OAO Moscow Oil Refinery.

Electronics. Moscow's electronics manufacturers produce electric batteries, radiotelephone equipment, automatic tools and equipment, integrated circuits, and computers. The largest companies within the sector are: OAO Angstrom, ZAO Danfoss, OAO Moscow Electric Lamp Plant, OAO Component Plant, and OAO Elma.

Retail and consumer market. In 2002, Moscow hosted more than 56,000 consumer market companies. In 2002, 1,935 new companies were established, including 1,035 retail, 350 public catering, and 420 public service companies. Some 814 enterprises were reconstructed, including 479 retail, 176 public catering, and 159 public service companies. Moscow accounts for some 30% of Russia's retail trade turnover. The year 2002 saw stable development of supply links with the Krasnodar and Stavropol Territories, the Moscow, Kaluga, Belgorod, Vologda, and Astrakhan Regions, and the Republics of Karelia, Tatarstan, Mordovia, and Udmurtia.

Several major international companies operate on the Moscow market. These include Metro, Spar, Ramenka, IKEA, Danone, and Auchan. Several new shopping malls opened in 2002, including Golden Babylon, A Million Small Things, Metro Cash & Carry, Atrium, Nizhny Novgorod Passage, and Panorama. Over 5,000 companies provide consumer services in Moscow. A fast food network comprised of Russian Bistro, Rostics, Yolki-Palki Taverns, McDonalds, Mu-Mu, and other companies, is rapidly growing.

Small enterprise. As of 2001–2002, small enterprise accounted for 10–12% of Moscow's GRP. Some 180,000 small enterprises operate in the city employing over 1.5 million people. The number of small enterprises in Moscow per thousand inhabitants (20.4) is close to the proportion typical of major world cities. Over 35% of Moscow's small

CENTRAL FEDERAL DISTRICT

Fuel and energy sector production and consumption trends, 1997–2002						*TABLE 5*
	1997	1998	1999	2000	2001	2002*
Electricity output, billion kWh	47.5	45.3	45.7	48.3	48.3	48.9
Electricity consumption, billion kWh	35.1	36.1	36.7	38.1	39.7	44.4
Natural gas consumption, million cubic meters	25.0	25.9	24.8	25.0	25.6	25.6

*Estimates of the Moscow Government

enterprises are engaged in retail sales and public catering, 15% – in construction, 12% – in manufacturing, and 10% – in research and development.

Tourism. Moscow is a major world tourist destination. According to the World Tourism Organization, by 2020 Russia may become one of the top ten most visited countries in the world. More than 200 of Moscow's architectural sites and monuments are registered with UNESCO.

2002 hotel revenue increased 20.9% to $541.8 million and tax payments amounted to $111.5 million, which constitutes 8.8% growth year-on-year. In 2002, Moscow's hotels hosted 3.5 million people, including 1 million foreign guests. Moscow's hotel network expanded thanks to the construction of the following new hotels: Hyatt (Ararat Park Hyatt Moscow), Tverskaya, Palace Hotel, Grand Hotel, Vinogradovo, Aurora-Luxe, Yekaterina, and Proton. The Golden Ring Hotel was reopened after reconstruction.

3.4. FUEL AND ENERGY BALANCE (OUTPUT AND CONSUMPTION PER RESOURCE)

Moscow enjoys surplus electricity generation capacities and exports some 18% of the electricity it produces.

As a result of a program for the development and improvement of the fuel and energy balance in 2002, the city fully meets its demand for natural gas, electricity, heat, and solid fuel.

In 2002, Moscow carried out a series of energy saving measures that resulted in total savings of 280,900 tons of conventional fuel.

3.5. TRANSPORT INFRASTRUCTURE

Roads. Moscow boasts a 4,604.4 kilometer road network, including 1,289.4 kilometers of highways. The city's transport infrastructure includes some 317 civil engineering facilities, including 68 bridges and 249 overpasses and flyovers.

In 2002, Moscow's 109 kilometer Ring Road (MKAD) was reconstructed; the road network area increased by 1.2 million square meters, and construction of the 53-kilometer third transport ring is in progress. Plans are afoot to increase the road network density from 5.3 kilometers to 8 kilometers per square kilometer and the highway network from 1,289.4 kilometers to 1,900 kilometers in 2003.

Moscow subway. Moscow has 265.6 kilometers of subway and 165 stations serviced by 4,221 cars. In 2002, the Moscow subway transported some 3.2 billion passengers. Subway revenues amounted to $184.8 million, $25.1 million up on 2001.

In 2003, as part of the Moscow subway development program through 2015, a sector of the Serpukhovsko-Timiryazevskaya Line from Annino to Dmitry Donskoy Boulevard stations and the stations Park Pobedy and Vorobyevy Gory were put into operation. The 2003–2005 development plan envisages the launch of the Butovo Light Metro Line (Chechersky Proyezd and Novokuryanovo stations) and a mini-subway (Kievskaya Line to Moscow-City); in 2006–2010, the Chkalovskaya – Trubnaya, Maryino – Zyablikovo, Park Pobedy – Kuntsevskaya, Krylatskoye – Strogino, Novogireevo – Novokosino, Vykhino – Zhulebino, Krasnogvardeyskaya – Brateevo, and Mitino – Strogino lines will be put into operation; in 2011– 2015, the Maryina Roscha – Likhobory, Park Pobedy – Olympic Village, and Rechnoy Vokzal – Ulitsa Dybenko lines will be launched.

Railroads. The Moscow railroad junction services over 2,000 trains daily. In 2002, the Moscow Railroad transported some 650 million passengers. In accordance with the Moscow General Development Plan through 2020, the Moscow Railroad will be fundamentally upgraded to create high-speed railroad routes and integrate with the international railroad system. The Moscow Government has plans to construct high-speed passenger lines to St. Petersburg, Smo-lensk, Nizhny Novgorod, and Kursk, with respective new terminals. High-speed lines will also be built to Yaroslavl, Kazan, Ryazan, Pavelets, and Kiev.

Airports. Moscow is served by Bykovo, Vnukovo, Sheremetyevo, and Domodedovo airports. In 2002, the Municipal Air Transport Development Framework through 2005 was approved. This document envisages the construction of a railroad linking Sheremetyevo to Moscow – Leningradsky Railway Station, plus other highway, railroad, and monorail links from the airports to the city center. In 2002, work began to establish a state unitary company Moscow Aviation Center to ensure the efficient use of aircraft for municipal purposes.

3.6. NATURAL RESOURCES: RESERVES AND EXTRACTION IN 2002

The city's principal natural resources are timber and recreational resources.

Timber. Forests and city parks cover 35,000 hectares. The restricted access Moose Island National Park and Bitsa Forest Natural Park account for 14.7% of the city's total forests and parks. City forests account for 22.1%, and other parks for 63.2%.

Recreational resources. The Moose Island National Park was established pursuant to Resolution No. 401 of the Government of the RSFSR of August 24, 1983, in Moscow and the Moscow Region area to preserve nature, optimize the use of natural resources, develop national culture, and create conditions conducive to rest and recreation. The Bitsa Forest Park, which is located in the South-Western District of Moscow, covers a total area of 2,200 hectares. The perimeter of the park stretches for 33.7 kilometers.

4. TRADE OPPORTUNITIES

4.1. MAIN GOODS
PRODUCED IN THE REGION
In 2002, Moscow produced:

Machine engineering and metal processing: 1,366 alternating current motors, 6,523,000 kWh of power transformers, 95 kilometers of power cables, 152 metal cutting machine tools, $2.7 million worth of computer facilities and spare parts, 53,200 personal computers, $22.7 million worth of automated tools and instruments and spare parts, 3,400 centrifugal pumps, 246 compressors, $17.7 million worth of medical equipment, 14 cranes with a lifting capacity of more than 5 tons, 3,900 elevators, 11,900 trucks, 728 buses, 1,200 household fridges, and 491,700 TV sets;

Chemicals and petrochemicals: 1,988,500 tons of automobile gasoline, 1,300 tons of synthetic dyes, 86,600 tons of synthetic rubber and plastic, 2.8 million tons of fuel oil, 2.2 million tires for agricultural machinery and motorcycles, 2.1 million tires for cars and trucks;

Ferrous metals: steel – 45,600 tons, steel roll – 57,500 tons, steel pipes – 49,400 tons, steel wire – 2,500 tons;

Construction materials: 163.5 million conventional bricks, 1.4 million cubic meters of reinforced concrete goods and assemblies, 5.6 million square meters of insulation and soft roofing materials;

Light industry: 32.7 million square meters of cotton fabric, 9.2 million square meters of wool fabric, 13.4 million square meters of silk fabric, 24.7 million pairs of hosiery, 4.3 million knitwear goods, 2.5 million pairs of footwear;

CENTRAL FEDERAL DISTRICT

Major regional export and import entities			*TABLE 6*
ENTITY	ADDRESS	PHONE, FAX, E MAIL	
ZAO Russian Oil Export	24, ul. Academika Pilyugina, Moscow, 117393	Phone: (095) 133 3404 Fax: (095) 777 5916	
GUP Foreign Trade Company Almazyuvelirexport	25/1, bulvar Zubovsky, Moscow, 119021	Phone: (095) 255 7881 Fax: (095) 255 7880 E-mail: almaz@mail.cnt.ru http://www.almaz.ru	
ZAO Energomashexport	25/A, per. Protopopovsky, Moscow, 129090	Phone: (095) 737 8600 Fax: (095) 288 7990 E-mail: info@powerm.ru	
OOO Gazexport	Building 1, 10, per. 3rd Golutvinsky, Moscow, 119180	Phone: (095) 230 9618, 230 9619 Fax: (095) 230 2410	
ZAO Magma	8, ul. Malaya Yakimanka, Moscow, 109180	Phone: (095) 238 3032, 238 3024 Fax: (095) 238 1333 E-mail: magma@rinet.ru	
OAO World Trade Center	12, nab. Krasnopresnenskaya, Moscow, 123610	Phone: (095) 256 6303, 253 2277 Fax: (095) 253 2481	
OAO Tekhsnabexport	26, per. Staromonetny, Moscow, 119180	Phone: (095) 239 4798 Fax: (095) 953 0820, 953 2412 E-mail: tenex@online.ru	
GP Russian Foreign Trade Company Zarubezhneft	Building 1, 9/1/1, per. Armyansky, Moscow, 101990	Phone: (095) 748 6500, 748 6446 Fax: (095) 748 6505, 956 1491 E-mail: nestro@nestro.ru http://www.zarubezhneft.ru	
ZAO Crok Incorporated	Building 3, 26, ul. Novoryazanskaya, Moscow, 107066	Phone: (095) 974 2274 Fax: (095) 974 2277 E-mail: croc@croc.ru	

Food and beverages: meat, including category one sub-products – 2,200 tons, sausage – 351,000 tons, fat – 973 tons, semi-finished meat products – 46,000 tons, butter – 2,400 tons, cheese – 3,900 tons, dairy products in terms of milk – 1,031,000 tons, lump sugar – 27,200 tons, flour – 564,800 tons, bread and bakery – 478,600 tons, confectionery – 244,500 tons, macaroni – 86,200 tons, margarine – 24,700 tons, vodka and liquors – 12.2 million decaliters, brandy – 1 million decaliters, grape wine – 2.5 million decaliters, sparkling wine – 2.4 million decaliters, beer – 78.4 million decaliters, non-alcoholic beverages – 31.7 million decaliters, mineral water – 2.3 million decaliters.

4.2. EXPORTS, INCLUDING EXTRA-CIS

1999 exports to extra-CIS countries reached $16,132 million. Exports to the CIS totaled $2,297 million. The corresponding figures for 2000 were $22,471 million and $2,482 million, $22,151 million and $2,264 million for 2001, and, according to the Moscow Government, $6,509 million and $424 million for 2002.

The main types of goods exported by Moscow in 2002 were (as percentage to total exports in dollar terms): machinery, including metal cutting machine tools, trucks, buses, and electronic goods – 19.4%, fuel and energy – 17.3%, ferrous and non-ferrous metals and metal goods, including rolled metal and steel pipes – 3.1%, petrochemical products, including synthetic rubber, plastic, and automobile tires – 2.3%, food and beverages, including confectionery, vodka and liquors, beer, and grape wine – 1.8%, tanning raw materials, fur, and fur goods – 0.7%, clothing and footwear – 0.4%, timber and timber goods – 0.2%.

Major importers of the city's products include Germany ($2,618.1 million), France ($1,031.7 million), China ($944.8 million), Italy ($870.7 million), and the USA ($697.4 million).

4.3. IMPORTS, INCLUDING EXTRA-CIS

1999 imports from extra-CIS countries reached $8,511 million. Imports from CIS countries totaled $892 million. The corresponding figures for 2000 were $9,187 million and $1,695 million, and $13,250 million and $1,231 million for 2001, and, according to the estimates of the Moscow Government, $12,924 million and $893 million for 2002.

The bulk of 2002 imports was represented by food and beverages (eggs, meat and meat products, milk, and grain), petrochemicals (caustic soda, paint and varnishes), machinery (trucks and bulldozers), timber (industrial timber, lumber, cardboard, and paper), building materials and goods (roofing and insulation materials, wall and other non-ore building materials). Major exporters to Moscow include Switzerland ($2,247.6 million), the Netherlands ($1,117.1 million), Israel ($428 million), China ($331.8 million), and the UK ($308.1 million).

5. INVESTMENT OPPORTUNITIES

5.1. INVESTMENTS IN 1997–2002 (BY INDUSTRY SECTOR), INCLUDING FOREIGN INVESTMENTS

Moscow is the largest city and main banking and stock exchange center of Russia. The city concentrates 80% of Russia's financial resources. Standard & Poor's has accorded a BB+ credit rating and a stable outlook to Moscow, which reflects the city's steadfast economic development.

Moscow has been divided into several large civil construction investment project zones: Business Moscow, Children's Wonder Park, Sports Moscow, and Historical Moscow.

The Moscow Government offers foreign partners effective options for participation in municipal investment projects: joint stock joint ventures; 100% foreign investment into the project, leasing, real estate investment contracts, foreign participation in

Capital investment by industry sector, $ million						TABLE 7
	1997	1998	1999	2000	2001	2002*
Total capital investment	9,220.5	6,607.3	3,895.5	5,553.3	6,451.6	5,840.5
Including major industries (% of total):						
Industry	11.3	8.4	12.5	9.9	9.1	8.5
Agriculture and forestry	–	0.1	0.1	0.1	–	–
Construction	7.2	2.4	1.3	2.1	2.8	2.1
Transport and communications	11.2	10.2	12.4	17.0	25.2	17.7
Retail and public catering	4.0	4.5	4.7	5.1	4.1	5.9
Housing	22.6	15.5	22.6	22.6	19.9	49.5
Other	43.7	58.9	46.4	43.2	38.9	16.3

*Estimates of the Moscow Government

Foreign investment trends in 1996–2002						*TABLE 8*
	1996–1997	1998	1999	2000	2001	2002*
Foreign investment, $ million	13,037	5,860	2,653	4,037	5,654	8,400
Including FDI, $ million	5,150	803	788	1,472	1,155	1,680

*Estimates of the Moscow Government

Largest enterprises of Moscow	*TABLE 9*
COMPANY	SECTOR
OAO Mosenergo	Energy
OAO Likhachev Plant (ZIL)	Automotive
OAO MTS	Telecommunications
OAO Rostelecom	Telecommunications
ZAO International Potassium Company	Chemicals
ZAO Khimmanagement	Chemicals
OOO Unilever	Food and beverages
OAO Russian Product	Food and beverages
OAO Red October	Confectionery
OAO Confectionery Concern Babaevsky	Confectionery
OAO Lianozovsky Dairy Plant	Meat and dairy
OAO Cherkizovsky Meat Processing Plant	Meat and dairy
OAO Moscow Plant Kristall	Liquor and vodka
ZAO Liggett-Dukat Ltd	Tobacco
OAO Moscow Oil Refinery	Oil refinery
State Unitary Company Moscow Lenin Subway	Railroad transport
OAO Aeroflot – Russian International Airlines	Air transport
ZAO SDR	Retail and public catering
OAO Housing Construction Company No. 2	Construction

I

real estate construction and execution of general contracts subject to the contractor arranging financing. In 2002, the Moscow Government actively participated in the operations of the Russian Regions' Advisory Council for International and External Economic Links.

The following factors determine the investment appeal of Moscow:
- Its extensive sales market and high consumer potential;
- Its developed industrial and transport infrastructure;
- Legislation supporting investment activities (protection of investor rights and preferential tax treatment);
- Its qualified workforce;
- The Government's track record of working with investors;
- The irreproachable reputation of the Moscow Government as regards foreign investor and business partner relations.

5.2. CAPITAL INVESTMENT

The housing and communal services, transport, and communication sectors account for the lion's share of capital investment.

According to the Moscow Government, in 2002 Moscow accumulated and raised 40-45% of total foreign investment in the Russian Federation. Foreign investment in Moscow reached $8.4 billion in 2002.

As of 2002, Moscow's major strategic investors were Germany ($1,860 million), the UK ($1,389 million), Luxembourg ($991 million), Cyprus ($838 million), and France ($719 million).

5.3. MAJOR ENTERPRISES (INCLUDING ENTERPRISES WITH FOREIGN INVESTMENTS)

As of January 1, 2003, Moscow and the Moscow Region hosted 6,318 companies with foreign investment, which accounted on average for more than 40% of the charter capital of these companies. 2002 output of companies with foreign investment amounted to $40 billion, some 1.4 times more than in 2001 in comparable prices.

The largest wholly foreign-owned companies are: Cargill, Kraft, Procter & Gamble, Hewlett Packard, Inter-national Paper, ICN Pharmaceuticals, PepsiCo, Gillette, RJ Reynolds, General Motors, 3M, McDonald's, Coca-Cola, British American Tobacco, Unilever, IBM, Mars, Motorola, GE Lucent Technologies, DHL, Pratt & Whitney, Wrigley's, Ford, United Technologies, Xerox, DuPont, Exxon, and Citibank.

5.4. MOST ATTRACTIVE SECTORS FOR INVESTMENT

According to Moscow Government experts, sectors closest to the end user such as retail, productions of food and beverages and consumer goods, telecommunications, housing construction, tourism and hotelliery, and the reconstruction of five-storey residential houses, are the most appealing for investors.

5.5. CURRENT LEGISLATION ON INVESTOR TAX EXEMPTIONS AND PRIVILEGES

The Moscow Government offers the following types of cooperation in implementing municipal programs:

- Investment in the privatization of municipal enterprises;
- Investment agreements on real estate management with proportional distribution of revenues;
- Investment project credits;
- Municipal tax privileges and federal exemptions on priority programs and city development areas, investment and tax credits with deferred tax payment, and credit and interest repayment by installments;
- Extension of investment tax credits on socially important investment programs;
- Municipal tax deferrals to allocate funds to investment programs and accumulate financial resources to purchase raw materials.

Investors participating in residential housing programs, the reconstruction of five-storey residential buildings, the construction of multi-level parking lots, the development of hotel and tourism facilities, and underground area utilization programs, are eligible for numerous privileges. Preferential treatment is also granted to investors in road construction projects.

The Moscow Government has developed and enacted a series of legislative and regulatory acts aimed at encouraging small enterprise: Resolution of the Moscow Mayor On Additional Measures to Streamline State Registration of Small Enterprises; Resolution of the Moscow Government On Support to Folk Arts and Crafts; Resolution of the Moscow Mayor On the Improvement of Relations between Supervising Authorities and Small Enterprises in Moscow; Resolution of the Moscow Government On a Comprehensive Program for the Development and Support of Small Enterprise in Moscow, 2001–2003.

5.6. FEDERAL AND REGIONAL ECONOMIC AND SOCIAL DEVELOPMENT PROGRAMS FOR MOSCOW

Federal targeted programs. Moscow is implementing dozens of social and econo mic programs. Top priority status has been accorded to The National Technology Base, 2002–2006 program, which aims to develop and produce new advanced materials ranging from traditional structural alloys with higher quantitative performance to advanced unbalanced and "intellectual" materials with new performance characteristics. The implementation of new technologies will enable Russia and Moscow to continue pursuing their lead in materials development.

The main objectives of the Energy Efficient Economy, 2002–2005 and through 2010 program as regards Moscow are as follows: transitioning to energy saving technology and machinery, ensuring a reliable supply of energy resources, reducing operating costs in the energy and transport sectors, cutting costs of end consumer processing and use of fuel and energy, and reducing pollution resulting from energy sector operations.

Sub-programs under the program envisage the reconstruction of oil refining facilities to increase the level of refining, increased output of high quality oil products and reduced operating costs; the optimization and rationalization of gas consumption; the completion of construction work and launch of waste ash processing units and creation of new thermal power station units (OAO Mosenergo's TPS 22).

Regional entities responsible for raising investment			*TABLE 10*
ENTITY	ADDRESS	PHONE, FAX, E-MAIL	
Science and Industrial Policy Department of Moscow	13, ul. Tverskaya, Moscow, 125032	Phone: (095) 924 9889 Fax: (095) 299 8616	
Economic Policy and Development Department of Moscow	13, ul. Tverskaya, Moscow, 125032	Phone: (095) 200 5462 Fax: (095) 913 6001	
Architecture, Construction, Development, and Reconstruction Center of Moscow	5, per. Nikitsky, Moscow, 103864	Phone: (095) 291 0865, 202 0911 Fax: (095) 956 8140	
Moscow Committee of External Economic Relations	13, ul. Tverskaya, Moscow, 125032	Phone: (095) 229 9509 Fax: (095) 725 0414 E-mail: hotel@dvs.mos.ru	

The efficiency of energy consumption in the residential sector will be raised with the help of non-costly measures eliminating inefficient use of electric equipment and engineering networks; the implementation of industrial energy saving technology with short payback period, and special investment projects in the residential and communal services sector.

The ecological effect of the program will range from increased energy efficiency of existing equipment to elimination of pollution.

Regional programs. Moscow is implementing dozens of regional programs that aim to support small enterprise and industrial companies and develop external trade, tourism, and hotel business. The Moscow Government has developed a comprehensive industrial activities program for 2004–2006 and a special purpose tourism development program through 2010. An energy saving program for 2001–2003, a targeted mid-term ecological program for 2003–2005, and many others are currently being implemented.

The Moscow General Development Plan through 2020 provides a framework for the city's urban development plans that aim to create a favorable urban environment conducive to ongoing growth, ensure ecological safety, and preserve the city's natural and cultural heritage. The General Development Plan takes into account Moscow's status as the capital of Russia and the links between the city and the Moscow Region. The General Plan includes the reconstruction of residential housing, the reorganization of industrial areas, the development of public, business, and cultural centers and tourism and recreational sites, the comprehensive aesthetic improvement of the city, the development and implementation of urban development plans of administrative areas, districts, and other territorial units of Moscow, as well as the expansion of the city.

The Small Enterprise Support Program, 2001–2003 is being successfully implemented. The major objectives of the program are: to eliminate red tape, provide registration and licensing assistance, provide financial support (leasing of equipment belonging to the Moscow Government, preferential taxation, and office rent privileges). By the end of 2003, between 50,000 and 100,000 small enterprises will have received state support.

The Moscow Government's Electronic Moscow Program focuses on the provision of information services to businesses and individuals and the development of new approaches to education, social assistance, and healthcare. The program will ensure the city's information security and a series of large-scale projects will be implemented: the Muscovite's Social Card project, the creation of a database of city inhabitants, and the introduction of electronic document processing. The program term is five years. The municipal budget allocated $619.8 million ($107 million in 2003) for the program, plus another $1,371.7million ($78.7 million in 2003) from extra-budgetary sources.

Moscow is implementing a municipal energy saving program for 2001–2003 with a focus on reducing fuel and energy consumption and cutting residential heating subsidies and budget expenses on energy consumed by social facilities. Over three years, the program will result in electricity and heat savings of $4.5 million and $0.9 million, respectively. One of social consequences of the program is the gradual transition to 100% coverage of electricity and heating costs by residents.

6. INVESTMENT PROJECTS

Industry sector and project description	1) Expected results 2) Amount and term of investment 3) Form of financing[1] 4) Documentation[2]	Contact information
1	2	3
CHEMICALS AND PETROCHEMICALS		
18R001 ● ▲		OAO Moscow Committee on Science
Establishment of a company and industrial output of chitosan at refurbished industrial facilities using the existing technology and regulations of ZAO SONAT. Project goal: to produce chitosan.	1) Up to 200 tons of chitosan per year 2) $3 million/1 year 3) L 4) FS	and Technology 6/3, per. Borisoglebovsky, Moscow 121069 Phone: (095) 203 9350; fax: (095) 201 2884 Vladimir Grigoryevich Sister, CEO

[1] L – Loan, E – Equity, Leas. – Leasing, JV – Joint Venture
[2] BP – Business Plan, FS – Feasibility Study

1	2	3

CHEMICALS AND PHARMACEUTICALS

18R002

■ ❖ ▼

Production of infusion solutions and containers for blood collection and storage. Project goal: to meet demand of Moscow and Moscow Region clinics for infusion solutions

1) n/a
2) $8.5 million/3 years
3) E, JV
4) Investment proposal

OAO Moscow Committee on Science and Technology
6/3, per. Borisoglebovsky, Moscow 121069
Phone: (095) 203 9350; fax: (095) 201 2884
Vladimir Grigoryevich Sister,
CEO

MACHINE ENGINEERING AND METAL PROCESSING

18R003

■ ● ❖ ▲

Technical upgrade of the Moscow Bearings Plant. Project goal: to improve product quality and produce new types of bearings through technical upgrade of the company.

1) Estimated profit of $20 million per year
2) $32.7 million/3 years
3) L, E, JV
4) FS

OAO Moscow Committee on Science and Technology
6/3, per. Borisoglebovsky, Moscow 121069
Phone: (095) 203 9350; fax: (095) 201 2884
Vladimir Grigoryevich Sister,
CEO

18R004

■ ● ❖ ▲

Technical upgrade of truck and bus manufacturing to make vehicles with engines compliant with the EURO 2 and EURO 3 environmental standards. Project goal: to launch production of a series of upgraded trucks and buses

1) n/a
2) $500 million/3 years
3) L, E, JV
4) Investment proposal

OAO Moscow Committee on Science and Technology
6/3, per. Borisoglebovsky, Moscow 121069
Phone: (095) 203 9350
Fax: (095) 201 2884
Vladimir Grigoryevich Sister,
CEO

18R005

❖ ▼

A city battery-powered mini-vehicle. Project goal: to arrange passenger transportation in areas prohibited for vehicles with internal combustion engines, such as parks, stadiums, golf courses, etc.

1) n/a
2) $3.5 million/3 years
3) JV
4) Investment proposal

OAO Moscow Committee on Science and Technology
6/3, per. Borisoglebovsky, Moscow 121069
Phone: (095) 203 9350; fax: (095) 201 2884
Vladimir Grigoryevich Sister,
CEO

18R006

■ ● ★ ❖ ▼

Development and production of small street cleaning vehicles with hybrid engines for Moscow communal services. Project goal: to produce small street cleaning vehicles.

1) Up to 200 items per year, revenue of up to $0.5 million per year
2) $1.5 million/2 years
3) L, E, JV, Leas.
4) FS

OAO Moscow Committee on Science and Technology
6/3, per. Borisoglebovsky, Moscow 121069
Phone: (095) 203 9350
Fax: (095) 201 2884
Vladimir Grigoryevich Sister,
CEO

18R007

❖ ▲

Development and production of test samples of digital cell interactive TV sets and launching of serial production in Russia. Project goal: to introduce new goods (base stations and subscriber kits).

1) Estimated profit of $1.4 million per year
2) $3.5 million/1 years
3) JV
4) FS

OAO Moscow Committee on Science and Technology
6/3, per. Borisoglebovsky, Moscow 121069
Phone: (095) 203 9350
Fax: (095) 201 2884
Vladimir Grigoryevich Sister,
CEO

TRANSPORT INFRASTRUCTURE

18R008

■ ● ❖ ▲

High-speed transport system Moscow-City – Sheremetyevo Airport. Project goal: to provide high-speed link from Sheremetyevo Airport and regional junctions to the city hubs.

1) Up to 27,500 passengers per hour
2) $720 million/5 years
3) L, E, JV
4) FS

OAO Moscow Committee on Science and Technology
6/3, per. Borisoglebovsky, Moscow 121069
Phone: (095) 203 9350; fax: (095) 201 2884
Vladimir Grigoryevich Sister,
CEO

1	2	3

TRADE

18R009

■ ▲

Construction of the Zelenogradsky production and trade center.
Project goal: to lease retail space.

1) Two pavilions with 57 sales units and a total area of 8,928 square meters, distribution center – 3,963 square meters, two warehouses – 7,143 square meters
2) $23.7 million/3 years
3) E
4) FS

OAO Moscow Committee on Science and Technology
6/3, per. Borisoglebovsky, Moscow 121069
Phone: (095) 203 9350
Fax: (095) 201 2884
Vladimir Grigoryevich Sister,
CEO

18R010

■ ▼

A trade and service center at the premises of OAO Sergo Ordzhonikidze Plant.
Project goal: to lease retail space.

1) Total area of the trade and service center of 40,965 square meters
2) $72.7 million/n/a
3) E
4) Investment proposal

OAO Moscow Committee on Science and Technology
6/3, per. Borisoglebovsky, Moscow 121069
Phone: (095) 203 9350; fax: (095) 201 2884
Vladimir Grigoryevich Sister,
CEO

18R011

■ ● ★ ▲

Trade and entertainment center Tushino Plaza.
Project goal: to lease retail space.

1) Total area of 88,160 square meters
2) $85 million/1 year
3) E, L, Leas.
4) FS

OAO Moscow Committee on Science and Technology
6/3, per. Borisoglebovsky, Moscow 121069
Phone: (095) 203 9350
Fax: (095) 201 2884
Vladimir Grigoryevich Sister,
CEO

HOTELS, TOURISM, AND RECREATION

18R012

■ ❖ ▲

Refurbishment of the Gostiny Dvor Hotel as part of comprehensive reconstruction of the Old Gostiny Dvor.
Project goal: to provide hotel services.

1) Area of 15,000 square meters, 122 rooms
2) $30 million/1.5 years
3) E, JV
4) FS

OAO Moscow Committee on Science and Technology
6/3, per. Borisoglebovsky, Moscow 121069
Phone: (095) 203 9350; fax: (095) 201 2884
Vladimir Grigoryevich Sister,
CEO

18R013

● ▲

Reconstruction of the Moskva Hotel.
Project goal: to provide hotel services.

1) Total area after reconstruction of 143,500 square meters; up to 800 rooms
2) $250 million/2 years
3) L
4) FS under development

OAO Moscow Committee on Science and Technology
6/3, per. Borisoglebovsky, Moscow 121069
Phone: (095) 203 9350
Fax: (095) 201 2884
Vladimir Grigoryevich Sister,
CEO

18R014

● ▲

Construction of a five-star hotel.
Project goal: to provide hotel services.

1) 300 rooms
2) $40 million/2 years
3) L
4) FS

OAO Moscow Committee on Science and Technology
6/3, per. Borisoglebovsky, Moscow 121069
Phone: (095) 203 9350; fax: (095) 201 2884
Vladimir Grigoryevich Sister,
CEO

18R015

■ ▼

Reconstruction of the Ostankino Hotel.
Project goal: to provide hotel services.

1) n/a
2) $20 million/2 years
3) E
4) Investment proposal

OAO Moscow Committee on Science and Technology
6/3, per. Borisoglebovsky, Moscow 121069
Phone: (095) 203 9350; fax: (095) 201 2884
Vladimir Grigoryevich Sister,
CEO

1	2	3
18R016 ● ❖ ▼		OAO Moscow Committee on Science
Reconstruction of the Pekin Hotel and Business Center. Project goal: to provide hotel services.	1) Increase in area from 25,900 square meters to 77,800 square meters 2) $200 million/3 years 3) JV, L 4) Investment proposal	and Technology 6/3, per. Borisoglebovsky, Moscow 121069 Phone: (095) 203 9350 Fax: (095) 201 2884 Vladimir Grigoryevich Sister, CEO
18R017 ■ ▲		OAO Moscow Committee on Science
Construction of a multifunctional auto sports center at the Nagatino flood-lands. Project goal: to construct an auto-racing track and an auto, technical, entertainment, and business center.	1) n/a 2) $100 million/1.5 years 3) E 4) FS	and Technology 6/3, per. Borisoglebovsky, Moscow 121069 Phone: (095) 203 9350 Fax: (095) 201 2884 Vladimir Grigoryevich Sister, CEO
18R018 ■ ▼		OAO Moscow Committee on Science
Reconstruction of the Severnaya Hotel. Project goal: to provide hotel services.	1) Total area of 14,200 square meters, 176 rooms 2) $22 million/2 years 3) E 4) Investment proposal	and Technology 6/3, per. Borisoglebovsky, Moscow 121069 Phone: (095) 203 9350; fax: (095) 201 2884 Vladimir Grigoryevich Sister, CEO
18R019 ■ ● ▼		OAO Moscow Committee on Science
Reconstruction of the Rossia Hotel. Project goal: to provide hotel services.	1) 1,800 rooms 2) $235 million/4 years 3) E, L 4) Investment proposal	and Technology 6/3, per. Borisoglebovsky, Moscow 121069 Phone: (095) 203 9350; fax: (095) 201 2884 Vladimir Grigoryevich Sister, CEO
18R020 ● ▼		OAO Moscow Committee on Science
Reconstruction of the Tourist Hotel. Project goal: to provide hotel services.	1) New construction area of 9,400 square meters, reconstruction area of 26,600 square meters 2) $42 million/2 years 3) L 4) Investment proposal	and Technology 6/3, per. Borisoglebovsky, Moscow 121069 Phone: (095) 203 9350 Fax: (095) 201 2884 Vladimir Grigoryevich Sister, CEO

BUSINESS INFRASTRUCTURE DEVELOPMENT

1	2	3
18R021 ■ ● ❖ ▼		OAO Moscow Committee on Science
Construction of a cultural and business center at Novinsky Boulevard. Project goal: to lease space.	1) n/a 2) $101.5 million/1 year 3) L, E, JV 4) Investment proposal	and Technology 6/3, per. Borisoglebovsky, Moscow 121069 Phone: (095) 203 9350; fax: (095) 201 2884 Vladimir Grigoryevich Sister, CEO

JOINT VENTURE GAZKOMPLEKTIMPEKS-PATTERANI

LYUDMILA
VIKTOROVNA
KASIMOVA,
CEO

Joint venture Gazkomplektimpeks-Patterani, a closed joint stock company, was established in 1995. The company is a multi-line enterprise, whose core activities include:

CONSTRUCTION OF FRAMELESS ARC INSTALLATIONS

- Based on the advanced US technology and equipment, the company produces and assembles unique durable frameless constructions of broad application: hangars, garages and parking lots, grain and vegetable storage facilities, horse riding halls, production facilities, warehouses, sports facilities, etc. A movable computerized

mini-plant performs an ongoing rolling of various panel and arc profiles made of zinc coated steel or aluminum. Due to its own equipment and teams of qualified staff the company is able to reduce to a minimum the time required for assembling. Light weight of installations enables the company to assemble various installations without building a deep foundation.

SUPPLIES OF EQUIPMENT

- The company supplies special equipment to fuel and energy enterprises. The company has an extensive experience and expertise of working in harsh geological and climatic conditions and supplies standard and large equipment to oil and gas companies for exploration of oil and gas fields.

TRANSPORTATION AND WAREHOUSING OF MATERIALS AND EQUIPMENT

- The company has its own storage facilities for materials and equipment in Podolsk with total area of over 26,000 square metes. The storage territory includes over 7,000 square meters of warehouses and some 400 meters of railroad branch.

CONSTRUCTION, DESIGN, AND ASSEMBLY

- Depending on a customer, the company may develop and implement any design projects and perform finishing and mounting of any objects, from a Moscow apartment re-design to construction of a residential block of flats in the Polar Circle. The company's designers, developers and builders boast some projects implemented, such as Iceberg 4-star hotel in Nadym, OOO VNIIGAZ's Guest House in Moscow, and a number of apartment interior design projects.

WHOLESALE AND RETAIL TRADE

- The company's branches in Moscow and Podolsk, which are equipped with modern trading equipment, offer the broadest range of goods and high quality of services.

The company has demonstrated eight years of strong success expanding its business and increasing volumes of work. Over the past three years the company's economic ratios have increased by 200–300%. These facts secure the company's future and allow us to expand our business into new areas and start new projects.

SECTION 6, 36, UL. GARIBALDI,
MOSCOW, RUSSIA, 117418
PHONE: (095) 719 9288, 719 9250
FAX: (095) 719 9260
E-MAIL: info@patterani.ru
HTTP://www.patterani.ru

EXPOCENTR – A GLOBAL BRAND

Closed joint stock company Expocentr (Expocenter) is one of the leading exhibition organizations in Eastern Europe and the largest of the more than one hundred exhibition organizations operating in Russia. In the almost fifty years since it was established, Expocentr has organized and hosted many thousand events of all sizes in Russia and abroad: international exhibitions and fairs, national and foreign exhibitions, specialist salons, and scientific and technical symposiums.

Each year, the Exhibition Complex at Krasnaya Presnya in Moscow hosts between sixty and eighty exhibitions and fairs of varying size and importance involving around 15,000 participant firms. Almost all of Expocentr's exhibitions and fairs are international events or events with an international input, owing to the specifics of the exhibition complex. Until recently, more than half of the companies with exhibition stands were foreign, although Russian companies have

During the exhibition season (which runs practically the whole year through with only short breaks), Expocentr receives more than 3.5 million visitors. The more industrially-oriented and scientific exhibitions tend to be visited mainly by economic and industrial experts from Moscow, the Moscow Region and many regions of Russia.

All exhibitions organized directly by Expocentr are carried out under the patronage of the Chamber of Commerce and Industry of the Russian Federation.

These include the Consumexpo fair (consumer goods) and Prodexpo (food and public catering equipment). Our "heavy exhibition artillery" consists of the international exhibitions Metals Processing, Forestry Machinery, Agricultural Machinery, Oil and Gas, Inlegmash (equipment for light industry enterprises), Chemicals, the electro-medical forums Healthcare and Healthcare Equipment, exhibitions devoted to

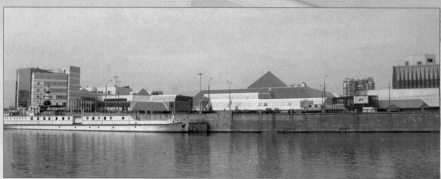

begun to take up a greater share of late. On average, Expocentr rents more than 400,000 square meters of exhibition space every year. Accordingly, each square meter of exhibition space is rented twelve or thirteen times a year. No other exhibition complex in Europe boasts such an intense use of its space. Nor does this intensity of use of exhibition space have any negative impact on the quality of the exhibitions or services or the content and significance of the accompanying scientific and practical programs.

Our experience has shown that between 30–50% and upwards of firms that participate in our exhibitions win profitable contracts as a result (although this is generally a trade secret).

the high technologies of today and tomorrow – Communications – Expocomm, Information Communication in Russia in the Twenty First Century, High Technologies of the Twenty First Century, Science – Scientific Instruments, Footwear – the World of Leather, etc.

Some of the top events organized by our business partners at Expocentr include travel and tourism and autosalon, and many other exhibitions and fairs.

Since 1975, Expocentr has been a member of the Union of International Fairs (UFI), the main exhibition organization on the international arena. Some of the exhibitions hosted by Expocentr have won praise from the UFI and other international organizations for their

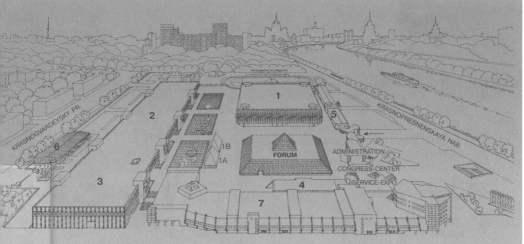

scale and quality. The Forestry Machinery exhibition was assessed highly by the European International Association of Producers of Timber Processing Equipment, which has included the exhibition into the list of events it supports. The International Car Manufacturers' Organization has officially registered the Russian Autosalon. Expocentr is the only Russian member of Interexpo, an international non-governmental association. Expocentr has been representing the Russian exhibition community at Interexpo since 1978.

Iran, Pakistan, Poland, Romania, Turkey, Finland, France, Czech Republic, Chile, Sweden, former Yugoslavia, etc.

All of the exhibitions organized by ZAO Expocenter enjoy the support of the federal ministries and government bodies, and the government of Moscow. The exhibition program is organized with the direct participation of the Chamber of Commerce and Industry of Russia, the Moscow Chamber of Commerce and Industry, industrial associations and industry unions, with a view to

Sixteen of the international festivals organized by Expocentr have been awarded prizes by the International Union of Exhibitions and Fairs. Our international exhibition partners include more than fifty firms and organizations with a solid reputation in the exhibition world, including the German Economic Committee on Exhibitions and Fairs, the Italian Association of Exhibitions and Fairs, Messe Dusseldorf International GmbH and East-West Partner (Germany), the Italian Foreign Trade Institute and major Italian companies Fiera Milano, Bologna Fiera, Interexpo, British company International Trade and Exhibitions GB, Ltd., American company I.J. Krause and Associates Inc., and firms and export companies in Austria, Belgium, Hungary, Denmark, Israel, Indonesia,

organizing traditional, internationally recognized exhibitions and concluding long-term contracts. Expocentr organizes the participation of Russian firms and organizations at 15–20 exhibitions and fairs abroad each year. Our direct contact service for foreign exhibitions is becoming ever more popular as Russian firms go from strength to strength financially and as the government puts in place mechanisms to help Russian firms in this area.

Apart from that, Expocentr has been the organizer by government decree of Russian stands at international exhibitions for many years now.

TRADE AND COOPERATION
THROUGH EXHIBITIONS!

F S U E

Marka Publishing and Trading Centre

Federal state unitary enterprise the Publishing and Trading Centre "Marka" of the Ministry for Communications and Informatization of the Russian Federation has been Russia's unique enterprise majoring in issuing and distributing means of denoting postage payment for 150 years.

Today MARKA provides Russia with postage stamps, imprinted envelopes and post cards on various themes. It issues about 70 subject stamps annually, more than 500 subject post cards and about 300 subject covers, produces various types of philatelic goods.

The overall print quantity of the product issued by MARKA amounts to 1,5 billion.

MARKA publishes the "Philately" and "Marka" magazines, which are very popular with stamp collectors.

Products of MARKA reflect the multi-national nature of the Russian Federation, cultural and historic heritage of the peoples living in the country, major domestic and foreign developments, achievements in all spheres of knowledge, flora and fauna.

4/6 BOLSHAYA GRUZINSKAYA STR., STROYENIE 9, MOSCOW, 123242, RUSSIAN FEDERATION
TEL.: +7 (095) 254 0328
FAX: +7 (095) 254 8584
E-MAIL: office@marka-art.ru
HTTP://www.marka-art.ru

MOSCOW TRAINING & MANUFACTURING ENTERPRISE No. 11 VOS

WE GIVE LIGHT

ALEXANDER
ALEXANDROVICH
MARKELOV,
CEO

Moscow Training & Manufacturing Enterprise No. 11 of the All-Russian Society for the Blind (VOS) was founded in 1959. More than half of the company's employees are visually challenged people who have undergone specially tailored training courses. In total, the enterprise, a limited liability company, employs more than a thousand people. In March 2003, we joined forces with our branch in Stavropol with a view to filling a market niche in the South of Russia.

OOO Moscow Training & Manufacturing Enterprise No. 11 of the All-Russian Society for the Blind boasts a strong reputation as a major developer and producer of electrical goods with serious advantages over its domestic peers in terms of price, reliability, quality, design and product range (150 different items).

In 2003, OOO Moscow Training & Manufacturing Enterprise No. 11 of the All-Russian Society for the Blind was awarded an ISO 9001 certificate with respect to its electrical goods output based on tests carried out by VNIIS, the Russian authority charged with certification of quality systems. In other words, the enterprise's output is now fully consistent with European standards.

The enterprise produces around 1.5 million articles per month, most of which have been awarded diplomas in the Hundred Best Products in Russia competition. OOO Moscow Training & Manufacturing Enterprise No. 11 of the All-Russian Society for the Blind is a three time laureate of the nationwide competition for the 1000 Best Enterprises in Russia of the Twenty First Century, and has been awarded a Russian Government diploma For High Social Effectiveness. And the list of the enterprise's achievements goes on.

The electrical goods manufactured by OOO Moscow Training & Manufacturing Enterprise No. 11 of the All-Russian Society for the Blind can be found in residential houses and offices alike, hence our developed dealership network throughout Russia – from St. Petersburg to Moscow to Vladi-vostok. We work directly with numerous construction and specialized assembly enterprises in the capital, the Moscow Region, Vladikavkaz, Saratov, Novokuznetsk, Surgut, etc.

Our products (all of which are patented) are made from fire resistant plastics, high quality bronze, and other Russian and imported advanced materials. Sockets and switches for concealed and open wiring; single, double and triple switches; dimmers; programmable long-distance switches; integrated units for plumbing units; sockets with child safety covers: this and more forms part of the enterprise's constantly expanding product range. However, this is not enough: the task of fully retooling our production facilities can only be achieved through investment. Our enterprise needs further financial investment to develop new products.

Over the past few years, our enterprise has increased its output several times over. By the end of 2003, we expect the enterprise's output in dollar terms to reach $1 million per month. This is thanks to the fact that our product assortment ranges from the simplest, least expensive articles to premium articles designed for the most discerning of customers.

52, UL. MOLODOGVARDEYSKAYA
MOSCOW, 123351, RUSSIA
TEL.: (095) 141 2441, 141 5525, 141 5454
FAX: (095) 140 9664
E-MAIL: upp11voc@mtu-net.ru

SVOBODA – A WORLD OF COSMETICS!

KLAVDIA MIKHAILOVNA CHIGARINA, CEO

Svoboda produces natural and ecologically safe personal hygiene and cosmetics products, including toilet soap, toothpaste, creams, haircare products, etc. The company employs more than 1,600 people at its research center and five production facilities: soap, cosmetics, toothpaste and shampoo, glycerin, and tube. Svoboda's research center develops and launches production of new types of cosmetics. All of Svoboda's products were developed in-house, and many are patented. Svoboda's high production standards and modern equipment enable the production of top quality cosmetics at affordable

- creams and gels of various types for various categories of skin
- Gamma hair dye
- Gamma Color hair tints
- Shampoo (Special Herb, etc.)
- Hair conditioners
- Shower gel
- Bath foam
- Chemical hair curling agents (Lokon)
- Toiletries for children and teenagers (Tik-Tak, Children's, Roller, etc.)
- Cosmetics (Night Violet, Nectar, Aloe, Business Woman, Milk and Honey, Green Tea, etc.)

prices. Svoboda is involved in business and creative partnerships with the leading perfume and cosmetics companies worldwide. Svoboda's mission is to produce cosmetic products for the mass market and to meet consumers' preferences using the latest scientific achievements. Our goal is to improve our customers' health, preserve their beauty, and prolong their youth.

OUR PRODUCTS

- toilet soap (Extra, Group 1, Children's, etc.)
- toothpaste (Parodontol, Carimed, Family, etc.)

- Luxury series (Diamond)
- Boxed cosmetic gift sets

Svoboda's products are sold throughout Russia and the CIS. Owing to the fierce competition, the company is constantly improving its distribution network. Svoboda has an extensive network of distributors in Russia and the CIS with warehouse facilities in many cities where customers can buy the entire product range at factory prices. The company is developing a chain of retail outlets in Moscow.

47, UL. VYATSKAYA, 127015 MOSCOW; TEL: (095) 285 1719, 285 82 09; FAX: (095) 285 0889
E-MAIL: max@svobodako.ru; HTTP://www.svobodako.ru

O A O
AVTOBAN
ROAD CONSTRUCTION COMPANY

Open Joint Stock Company Avtoban Road Construction Company boasts a highly qualified workforce and uses modern equipment and leading technologies to:
- build, repair and reconstruct highways in European Russia and Western Siberia;
- produce large-sized reinforced concrete articles;
- produce asphalt and cement mixes.

BLDG. 2, 8, 2 VERKHNE-MIKHAILOVSKY PR.,
MOSCOW, 117419, RUSSIA
TEL.: (095) 955 7135, 737 6138
FAX: (095) 733 9374
E-MAIL: avtoban1@mail.ru
HTTP://www.avtoban-dsk.com

O A O
YAKOR
INSURANCE COMPANY

Registered on May 27, 1991 by companies in the road construction sector. Charter capital – RUR 50 million. One of the company's core activities is insuring transportation enterprises:
- insurance of road and bridge construction work

- property insurance for transport companies
- insurance of land vehicles, aircraft, and marine and river vessels
- insurance of consignments, carriers, consignors, and vessel owners.

BUILDING 2, 5-7, PODSOSENSKY PEREULOK, 103062, MOSCOW
TEL./FAX: (095) 232 9962, 917 3200
E-MAIL: yakor@yakor.ru; HTTP://www.yakor.ru

NON-STATE
PENSION FUND OPEKA

Non-State Pension Fund Opeka is an experienced player in the market for non-state pension insurance (license No. 370 of August 30, 2000) and one of Russia's top ten non-state pension funds in terms of its development trends. Opeka has sufficient resources to participate in pension reform and provides employers with ready-made supplementary non-state pension insurance schemes. Opeka also offers private customers the opportunity to build up a private pension provision and invites legal entities and private individuals to establish long-term relationships with the fund.

BUILDING 2, 8, 2 VERKHNE-MIKHAILOVSKY PR., MOSCOW, 117419, RUSSIA
TEL.: (095) 954 1176; E-MAIL: opeka-npf@mail.ru

II. NORTH-WESTERN FEDERAL DISTRICT

REGIONS OF THE NORTH-WESTERN FEDERAL DISTRICT

19. Republic of Karelia [10]

20. Komi Republic [11]

21. Arkhangelsk Region [29]

22. Vologda Region [35]

23. Kaliningrad Region [39]

24. Leningrad Region [47]

25. Murmansk Region [51]

26. Novgorod Region [53]

27. Pskov Region [60]

28. St. Petersburg [78]

29. Nenetsky Autonomous District [83]

19. REPUBLIC OF KARELIA [10]

ECONOMIC MAP

Umba

Chupa

Lake Pyaozero

Kestenga

Lake Topozero

Kem

Kostomuksha

Ushkozero

Belomorsk

Nadvoitsy

Segezha

Lake Vigozero

Lake Segozero

White Sea-Baltic Canal

Medvezhegorsk

Lake Vodozero

Yoensu

Suoyarvi

Kondopoga

Sortavala

Martsialnye Vody

Pudozh

Pitkyaranta

Lakhdenpokhya

Priozyorsk

PETROZAVODSK

Vyborg

Lake Ladoga

Lake Onega

Kandalakshsky gulf

WHITE SEA

Onega gulf

Onega

Kem

ARKHANGELSK REGION

FINLAND

RUSSIA

PROCESSING INDUSTRY	MINING INDUSTRY	LIVESTOCK BREEDING
● Ferrous metals	▲ Iron ore	◤ Sea mammals (seal) catch
● Non-ferrous metals	◇ Marble	● Animal farming
● Machine engineering and metal processing	⊡ Quartz and quartz sand	🐄 Meat and dairy cattle breeding
● Forestry and timber	◇ Granite	
● Construction materials	⚬ Mineral water sources	POWER PLANTS
○ Food and beverages	⚓ Fishing ports	⚡ Thermal power plants
	⚓ Resorts	⚡ Hydro power plants

The Republic of Karelia is the first and so far the only region of the Russian Federation to receive the European Region of 2003 designation. This prestigious nomination means that the Commission of the European Communities of the European Parliament and the Council of Europe have recognized the international activity of Karelia in the Barents Sea region and its cross-border cooperation, openness, and readiness for mutually beneficial cooperation in all spheres of the economy and trade.

The Karelian economy is traditionally export-oriented. Some 70% of industrial output is exported, over half of which consists of forestry and paper industry products. Karelia's location at the border, relatively low transport costs, and rich and high quality forest resources create a favorable environment for competition. These sectors account for some 70% of all investments in the industry in the Republic.

The Republic of Karelia is situated on the Baltic Plate. The Republic boasts 238 prospected deposits of mineral resources. Another 640 deposits and occurrences of mineral resources have been recorded. The Republic has over 20 varieties of strategic raw materials: iron ore, titanomagnetite, non-ferrous and rare earth metals, and gold. However, the greatest investment potential for the immediate future lies in the Republic's deposits of building and trim stone. The Republic collaborates closely with major investors from Moscow, St. Petersburg, and other major cities within the framework of inter-regional ties in the quarrying and stone processing sectors. Karelia is uniquely positioned in this sphere thanks to the availability of a wide range of building and trim stone and its proximity to the central regions and cities of Russia. We are ready to supply these construction materials and to arrange all the necessary conditions for investors.

Of course, Karelia's potential is not limited to the forestry and minerals sectors. Our Republic's tourism potential is also great. This year, for the first time in decades, the number of tourists deciding to take their vacation within Russia has exceeded the number vacationing abroad. The flow of domestic vacationers is shifting from the south of the country to the more moderate climes of central and north-western Russia. Karelia is synonymous with world heritage sites such as Kizhi and Valaam. The northern Ladoga area of Karelia is also known as the "Karelian Switzerland". Its myriad rivers and lakes, and historical, cultural, geological, and recreational sites offer unique conditions for rest and recuperation.

I am confident that the opportunities for mutually beneficial collaboration are not limited to the above. The Government of the Republic of Karelia has declared 2003 its year of investment. Raising investment has been deemed the Republic's foremost priority for 2003. We are resolved to make full use of all available means to support investment, both Russian and foreign. The Investment Policy of the Government of the Republic of Karelia for 2003–2006 has been drafted with exactly that in mind. Its chief aim is to create a favorable and stable investment climate and conditions conducive to investment in the Republic.

Sergey Katanandov,
HEAD OF THE REPUBLIC OF KARELIA

1. GENERAL INFORMATION

1.1. GEOGRAPHY

Situated in the north-west of Russia, the Republic of Karelia covers a total area of 180,500 square kilometers. Karelia borders Finland to the west, the Leningrad and Vologda Regions to the south, the Murmansk Region to the north, and the Arkhangelsk Region to the east. The north-east shores of Karelia are washed by the White Sea. Some 723 kilometers of the western border of Karelia coincide with the international frontier between the Russian Federation and Finland.

1.2. CLIMATE

The Republic of Karelia is located in the Atlantic continental climate zone.

The average temperature ranges from –8.0°C in January to +16.4°C in July. Annual precipitation reaches 500–700 mm.

1.3. POPULATION

According to preliminary 2002 census results, the total population of the Republic of Karelia was 717,000 people. The average population density is 4 people per square kilometer. The economically active population totals 400,000 people. Official unemployment stands at 7.9% (2002); the actual rate is 8.7%.

Demographically speaking, some 63.2% are of statutory working age, 18.2% are below the statutory working age, and 18.6% are beyond the statutory working age.

The Republic's ethnic mix is 73.6% Russian, 10% Karelian, 7.0% Byelorussian, and 2.3% Finnish. The Republic's major urban centers (2002 data) are Petrozavodsk with 266,200 inhabitants, Kondopoga with 36,600 inhabitants, Segezha with 33,800 inhabitants, and Kostomuksha with 32,500 inhabitants.

Population							TABLE 1
	1992	1997	1998	1999	2000	2001	2002
Total population, '000	799	779	775	771	765	760	717
Economically active population, '000	437	393	388	417	394	395	400

2. ADMINISTRATION

19, pr. Lenina, Petrozavodsk, Republic of Karelia, 185028. Phone: (8142) 76 1586; fax: (8142) 76 4148
E-mail: government@karelia.ru; http://www.gov.karelia.ru

NAME	POSITION	CONTACT INFORMATION
Sergei Leonidovich KATANANDOV	Head of the Republic of Karelia	Phone: (8142) 76 9888
Pavel Viktorovich CHERNOV	Prime Minister of the Republic of Karelia	Phone: (8142) 76 4066
Ivan Mikhailovich SHURUPOV	Deputy Prime Minister of the Republic of Karelia, in charge of Economy, Agriculture, and Fishing	Phone: (8142) 78 2464
Alexander Semenovich KOLESOV	Deputy Prime Minister of the Republic of Karelia, Minister of Finance of the Republic of Karelia	Phone: (8142) 78 5335 Fax: (8142) 71 6456
Yury Ivanovich PONOMAREV	Deputy Prime Minister of the Republic of Karelia, Minister of Forestry, Natural Resources, and Ecology of the Republic of Karelia	Phone: (8142) 76 8163 E-mail: forest@karelia.ru
Alexander Pavlovich MUKHIN	Deputy Prime Minister of the Republic of Karelia, in charge of State Property, Construction and Architecture, and Housing and Utilities	Phone: (8142) 76 0626
Alexander Vladimirovich GRISHCHENKOV	Minister of Economic Development of the Republic of Karelia	Phone: (8142) 78 2734 Fax: (8142) 78 1039 E-mail: economy@karelia.ru
Sergey Ivanovich DENISOV	Minister of State Property of the Republic of Karelia	Phone: (8142) 78 2459 E-mail: mgs@karelia.ru

II

NORTH-WESTERN FEDERAL DISTRICT

NAME	POSITION	CONTACT INFORMATION
Gennady Vladimirovich KOLOSOV	Minister of Agriculture and Food of the Republic of Karelia	Phone: (8142) 78 5215
Alexander Valeryevich YEFIMOV	Chairman of the State Committee on Construction, Architecture, and Construction Industry of the Republic of Karelia	Phone: (8142) 76 5914 E-mail: gostroy@onego.ru
Yevgeny Yevgenyevich KOTKIN	Chairman of the State Committee on Physical Culture, Sports, and Tourism of the Republic of Karelia	Phone: (8142) 78 4166 E-mail: goscomsport@karelia.ru
Boris Grigoryevich ZHITNY	Chairman of the State Committee on Fishing of the Republic of Karelia	Phone: (8142) 78 2135 E-mail: fishcom@karelia.ru
Galina Stepanovna MIKHALEVA	Head of the Department of Foreign Economic Activity, Interregional Links and Cross-Border Cooperation, Trade, and Consumer Market of the Ministry of Economic Development of the Republic of Karelia	Phone: (8142) 78 2770
Yury Vladimirovich SMIRNOV	Chief of the Investment Policy Department	Phone: (8142) 78 3502

3. ECONOMIC POTENTIAL

3.1. 1997–2002 GROSS REGIONAL PRODUCT (GRP). INDUSTRY BREAKDOWN

The Republic of Karelia's 2002 gross regional product reached $1,214 million, or 2% up on 2001. Per capita GRP amounted to $1,562 in 2001 and $1,693 in 2002.

3.2. MAJOR ECONOMIC GROWTH PROJECTIONS

The Government of the Republic of Karelia has formulated short-term (through 2003), medium-term (through 2006), and long-term (through 2010) development programs for the Republic. The Ministry of Economic Development has for-mulated conceptual frameworks for the development of specific industries. The programs and conceptual frameworks set the following objectives:

Industry: sustainable development of the Republic's industrial companies, development of new energy and resource saving production facilities, increased competitiveness of Karelia producers' goods, and economic potential growth;

Agriculture: development of agricultural production, increased agricultural output, sustained rural population, and harmonious development of rural areas;

Construction: technical upgrade and preparation of the sector for the implementation of small

GRP trends in 1997–2002						TABLE 2
	1997	1998	1999	2000	2001*	2002*
GRP in current prices, $ million	1,706	1,153	821	1014	1,187	1,214

*Estimates of the Administration of the Republic of Karelia

GRP industry breakdown in 1997–2002, % of total						TABLE 3
	1997	1998	1999	2000	2001*	2002*
GRP	100.0	100.0	100.0	100.0	100.0	100.0
Industry	35.9	43.3	50.7	46.9	40.5	40.0
Agriculture and forestry	4.6	4.5	4.4	3.2	3.2	3.2
Construction	8.6	6.6	5.8	7.6	10.7	10.5
Transport and communications	17.8	15.4	12.8	16.2	14.9	15.0
Trade and public catering	15.3	15.8	12.5	12.2	10.4	11.0
Other	15.6	12.9	12.8	13.6	20.0	20.0
Net taxes on output	2.2	1.5	1.0	0.3	0.3	0.3

*Estimates of the Administration of the Republic of Karelia

Industry breakdown of industrial output in 1997–2002, % of total						TABLE 4
	1997	1998	1999	2000	2001	2002*
Industry	100.0	100.0	100.0	100.0	100.0	100.0
Forestry, timber, and pulp and paper	35.7	41.8	54.9	55.8	48.7	45.9
Ferrous metals	15.6	17.0	13.6	13.4	12.8	13.4
Food and beverages	10.5	10.1	7.8	6.7	13.8	13.0
Energy	18.3	13.9	7.4	7.6	9.1	11.3
Machine engineering and metal processing	8.5	6.9	6.5	7.8	5.9	6.3
Non-ferrous metals	4.4	5.5	5.2	4.0	5.3	5.6
Construction materials	3.9	2.3	2.1	2.7	2.7	3.0
Flour, cereals, and mixed fodder	1.7	1.5	1.6	1.3	1.2	0.7
Light industry	0.5	0.4	0.3	0.3	0.2	0.5

*Estimates of the Administration of the Republic of Karelia

and medium size investment projects regarding limited and individual construction;

Tourism: Enhancement of investment appeal, creation of an attractive image of the Republic on international markets, and establishment of developed tourism and recreational facilities in the Republic.

3.3. INDUSTRIAL OUTPUT IN 1997–2002 FOR MAJOR SECTORS OF ECONOMY

The Republic's leading industries are forestry, timber, pulp and paper, ferrous metals, food, and energy. These account for 83.6% of the total industrial output.

Forestry, timber, and pulp and paper. The Republic of Karelia is a major forestry, timber, and pulp and paper producing region. The sector accounts for 45.9% of total industrial output. The timber industry employs half of all industrial workers in the Repu-blic. More than 30 timber and paper plants and mills are located in the Republic. Major companies include: AO Segezha Pulp and Paper Plant, AO Kondopoga, OAO Zapkarelles, OAO Lahdenpohja Logging Enterprise, and OAO Karelia DSP.

Food and beverages. The food industry accounts for 13% of the Republic's total industrial output. The fishing industry provides the lion's share (57%) of food industry output. Other major food industry segments include bakery, dairy, and alcoholic beverages. Major enterprises in the sector include AO Petrozavodsk Meat Processing Plant,

OAO Petrozavodsk Dairy, OAO Karelrybflot, and OAO Karelia Fish Processing Plant.

Ferrous metals. Ferrous metals account for some 13.4% of total industrial output. The Republic hosts around 30 mining enterprises, with another 30 currently being established. Some 15 enterprises provide the bulk of output in the sector. These include OAO Karelian Pellet, OAO Karelnerud, Mosavtodor State Unitary Enterprise, and Pitkjaranta Mining Directorate State Unitary Enterprise. OAO Karelian Pellet is the fifth largest of Russia's 25 mining and ore dressing enterprises involved in ore extraction and iron ore concentrate production.

Energy. The Republic's major energy company is OAO Karelenergo. Karelenergo supplies 70% of the Republic's energy output. The installed capacity of the Karelian energy system is 913.8 MW. The Republic's largest HEPS at Petrozavodsk (280 MW) supplies 85% of Petrozavodsk's heat energy consumption. Four independent thermal power stations run by paper mills (combined capacity 204 MW) also operate in the Republic.

3.4. FUEL AND ENERGY BALANCE (OUTPUT AND CONSUMPTION PER RESOURCE)

Electricity accounts for the bulk of the Republic's fuel and energy output. Total electricity output in 2002 was 3.7 billion kWh. Major electricity consumers include the ferrous and non-ferrous metals sectors and the timber and paper industries. These

Fuel and energy sector production and consumption trends, 1997–2002						TABLE 5
	1997	1998	1999	2000	2001	2002*
Electricity output, billion kWh	4.3	4.7	4.3	4.3	4.3	3.7
Electricity consumption, billion kWh	6.5	6.6	7.3	7.3	7.5	7.5
Natural gas consumption, million cubic meters	245.3	394.7	393.7	362.3	388.8	426.5

*Estimates of the Administration of the Republic of Karelia

account for 63.6% of total consumption. The Republic of Karelia is an energy deficit region. OAO Karelenergo generates 57.1% of the energy consumed in the Republic, with the remaining 42.9% imported via FOREM (the Federal Wholesale Electricity Market) from the adjacent OAO Kolenergo and OAO Lenenergo energy systems.

3.5. TRANSPORT INFRASTRUCTURE

Roads. The Republic of Karelia has 7,786 kilometers of paved public highway. The northern transport corridor, which begins in the Perm Region and links Russia to the rest of Europe, passes through the Karelian towns of Segezha and Kostomuksha and onwards to Finland via the international border crossing near the town of Lutta. The Republic has another international border crossing at Vartsila. Other border towns provide basic border crossing services. The federal Kola highway, which links St. Petersburg to Murmansk via Petrozavodsk, carried 60.2 million tons of freight per kilometer in 2002.

Railroads. The Republic has 2,700 kilometers of railroads, with links to Murmansk, St. Petersburg, and Helsinki. In 2002, 12,940,000 tons of freight was carried by rail, 2.4% up on 2001.

Airports. The Republic is served by the Besovets International Airport at Petrozavodsk. In addition, the Republic has three airports, two airdromes and three landing strips for Lesavia aircraft landing. Upon completion, the Besovets International Airport will be capable of accepting all modern aircraft.

3.6. MAIN NATURAL RESOURCES: RESERVES AND EXTRACTION IN 2002

Forest resourses. Forests cover 49% of the Republic. Over half of the forests are pine species, one third is fir, and one tenth is deciduous. The total timber reserve is 910 million cubic meters. The standing reserve is 935 million cubic meters, including 823 million cubic meters of coniferous and 112 million cubic meters of deciduous. Mature and over-mature reserves stand at 435.8 million cubic meters, including 382.3 million cubic meters of coniferous (87.7%).

Minerals. The Republic's mineral resources include 238 explored deposits, including 25 types of ores, 378 peat deposits, 11 underground industrial and potable water reserves, and 2 mineral water deposits. Main mineral resources are: iron ore, titanium, vanadium, molybdenum, precious metals, diamonds, mica, construction materials (granites, diabases, and marble), ceramic feedstock (pegmatite, spar), apatite-carbonate ores, and alkaline amphibole asbestos.

Water resources. Water covers 25% of the Republic's area. Karelia has more than 60,000 lakes, including Europe's two largest lakes, Ladozhskoye and Onezhskoye. Major rivers include the Vodla, Vyg, Kovda, Kem, Suna, and Shuya. The Republic has 83,000 kilometers of inland waterways. Marshes covering some 18% of the Republic's territory contain more than 4 billion tons of peat reserves. Karelia's lakes and marshes form a major source of high quality fresh water (2,000 million cubic meters).

4. TRADE OPPORTUNITIES

4.1. MAIN GOODS PRODUCED IN THE REGION

Forestry, timber, pulp and paper – the Republic accounts for 23% of the paper manufactured in the Russian Federation, 9% of pulp output, and 7.3% of commercial timber output. In 2002, the Republic produced 4.9 million running meters of commercial timber, 684,000 cubic meters of sawn timber, 72,100 tons of pulp, 715,000 tons of paper (Karelia is the top paper producing region in Russia), and 63,100 tons of cardboard;

Iron ore – Karelia is a major producer of iron ore concentrate. It mines 10% of the iron ore mined in Russia;

Food and beverages – The 2002 fish and seafood catch was 78,400 tons, or up 15% on 2001. Some 17 operational trout farms in the Republic produced 2,400 tons of trout and fishpond material in 2002, or up 20% on 2001. Output of marketable fish in real terms, including canned fish, was 60,300 tons (up 25.4% on 2001). In 2002, the Republic produced 43,400 tons of bakery products, 770 million decaliters of distilled alcohol. Meat output topped 2,100 tons, butter output reached 424 tons, and whole milk output was 44,700 tons.

Machine engineering – Karelia is Russia's sixth largest producer of agricultural equipment. In 2002, the sector manufactured 1,500 tractors.

4.2. EXPORTS, INCLUDING EXTRA-CIS

Some 57% of the Republic's output (in dollar terms) is exported. In 2000, extra-CIS exports totaled $531.6 million and CIS exports totaled $7.2 million. The corresponding figures were $563.4 million and $6.2 million for 2001, and $513.7 million and $7.9 million for 2002. Some 76% of Karelia's foreign trade is conducted with European countries. Lumber accounts for over half of all exports, followed by iron ore pellets with 13-15%, paper and cardboard with 6-9%, and sawn timber with 5-7%. The Republic's main export destinations are Finland (32% of total exports), Germany (7%), the Netherlands (7%), and the UK (6%).

4.3. IMPORTS, INCLUDING EXTRA-CIS

Imports in 2002 amounted to $149 million (in dollar terms), up 5% on the previous year.

The Republic's major imports include: machine engineering goods (37%), paper, cardboard and related articles (22%), and petrochemicals (20%). Imports of paper and cardboard doubled in 2002, with import of ferrous and non-ferrous metals up 120%.

4.4. MAJOR REGIONAL EXPORT AND IMPORT ENTITIES

Due to specific character of the Republic's exports and imports, most export and import transactions are carried out by industrial enterprises. These include OAO Karelian Pellet, OAO Petrozavodmash, OAO Onezhsky Tractor Plant, OAO Segezha Pulp and Paper Plant, OAO Karellesprom, and others.

5. INVESTMENT OPPORTUNITIES

5.1. INVESTMENTS IN 1992–2002 (BY INDUSTRY SECTOR), INCLUDING FOREIGN INVESTMENTS

The following factors determine the investment appeal of the Republic:
- Its advantageous geographical position (close to the border with Finland);
- Its developed transport infrastructure (major commercial routes linking Russia and Europe cross the Republic);
- Its natural resources (forests and minerals);
- Its highly qualified workforce and high scientific potential;
- Laws supporting investment activity.

5.2. CAPITAL INVESTMENT

In 2002, the Government of the Republic of Karelia declared the raising of investments and further improvement of the investment climate as its major priorities. 2002 investments totaled $328.4 million. The bulk of capital investment goes to transport and industry.

5.3. MAJOR ENTERPRISES (INCLUDING ENTERPRISES WITH FOREIGN INVESTMENT)

Karelia hosts 184 registered enterprises with investments from Finland, or 57.3% of the total number of enterprises with foreign investments in the Republic. The Republic is currently negotiating investment projects with major western enterprises, including Stora Enso (Finland) and IKEA (Sweden), for the construction of a number of industrial facilities in Karelia.

5.4. MOST ATTRACTIVE SECTORS FOR INVESTMENT

According to expert estimates and the Government of the Republic, the most attractive sectors for investment are forestry and timber, mining industry, construction and construction materials, energy, fishing and fish processing, and tourism.

5.5. CURRENT LEGISLATION ON INVESTOR TAX EXEMPTIONS AND PRIVILEGES

Pursuant to the Law On Investment Activity in the Republic of Karelia, investors are granted:
- tax exemptions (worth a total of $0.7 million over the past two years);
- guarantees of the Government of the Republic of Karelia for loans taken out by Karelian enterprises to implement investment projects (the 2003 budget provides $7.71 million in financing for this purpose);
- direct soft loans from the budget (at one third of the Central Bank's refinancing rate);
- investment tax

Capital investment by industry sector, $ million						TABLE 6
	1997	1998	1999	2000	2001	2002*
Total capital investment	214.2	132.4	116.6	227.4	376.9	328.4
Including major industries (% of total)						
Industry	25.7	39.3	41.5	41.6	24.6	23.9
Agriculture and forestry	2.0	4.9	5.2	3.3	1.5	1.4
Construction	0.8	1.9	1.2	1.5	1.6	1.0
Transport and communications	38.4	18.7	19.9	36.3	52.1	60.9
Trade and public catering	0.6	8.8	5.0	2.8	2.2	2.2
Other	32.5	26.4	27.2	14.5	18.0	10.6

*Estimates of the Administration of the Republic of Karelia

Foreign investment trends in 1996–2002					TABLE 7
	1996–1997	1998	1999	2000	2001	2002*
Foreign investment, $ million	6.7	5.1	15.5	22.2	41.7	20.4
Including FDI, $ million	6.7	5.1	4.5	6.8	34.3	6.6

*Estimates of the Administration of the Republic of Karelia

Largest enterprises of the Republic of Karelia			*TABLE 8*
COMPANY	SECTOR	2001 SALES, $ MILLION*	2001 NET PROFIT, $ MILLION*
OAO Kondopoga	Pulp and paper	209.4	67.1
OAO Karelian Pellet	Mining and iron ore dressing	136.8	-6.7
OAO Segezha Pulp and Paper Plant	Pulp and paper	95.7	1.0
OAO Karelenergo	Electricity	89.2	3.4
OAO Nadvoitsk Aluminum Plant	Aluminum	55.2	4.2
OAO Pitkjaranta Pulp Factory	Pulp and paper	23.7	0.9
ZAO Petrozavodsk Paper Mill Equipment Plant	Heavy, energy, and transport machine engineering	23.4	2.3

*Data of the Administration of the Republic of Karelia

Regional entities responsible for raising investment		*TABLE 9*
ENTITY	ADDRESS	PHONE, FAX, E-MAIL
Chamber of Commerce and Industry of the Republic of Karelia	4, ul. Engelsa, Petrozavodsk, Republic of Karelia, 185000	Phone: (8142) 78 3040 Fax: (8142) 76 5478 E-mail: chamber@karelia.ru http://chamber.karelia.ru/
Fund for Small Enterprise Support and Development	4, ul. Engelsa, Petrozavodsk, Republic of Karelia, 185035	Phone: (8142) 78 2191 Fax: (8142) 78 2255 E-mail: e-mabusiness@onego.ru
Federal Investment Chamber	22-a, pr. Lenina, Petrozavodsk, Republic of Karelia, 185000	Phone: (8142) 78 3495
Karelia-Moscow Inter-Regional Marketing Center	40, ul. Volodarskogo, Petrozavodsk, Republic of Karelia, 185035	Phone: (8142) 53 2507 E-mail: mmc@onego.ru
OOO Perspektiva Center	37, ul. Kuzmina, Petrozavodsk, Republic of Karelia, 185035	Phone: (8142) 55 6818
Business Project Financial Company	4, ul. Kalinina, Petrozavodsk, Republic of Karelia, 185000	Phone: (8142) 55 0830
ZAO Petroinvest	5, ul. Kirova, Petrozavodsk, Republic of Karelia, 185000	Phone: (8142) 76 5964

5.6. FEDERAL AND REGIONAL ECONOMIC AND SOCIAL DEVELOPMENT PROGRAMS FOR THE REPUBLIC OF KARELIA

Federal targeted programs. The Government of the Republic of Karelia is implementing a number of federal targeted programs, including the following priority programs: Upgrade of Russia's Transport System, 2002–2010, Energy Efficient Economy, 2002–2005 and through 2010, Elimination of Differences in Social and Economic Development of Regions of the Russian Federation, 2002–2010 and through 2015, The Elderly, 2002–2004, Ecology and Natural Resources of Russia, 2002–2010.

Regional programs. The Republic of Karelia has adopted a number of regional programs for social and economic development through to 2010.

The majority of these programs are focused on social issues, including: The Elderly, 2003–2004, Children's Healthcare, 2002–2004, Fire Safety and Social Protection, 2002–2004.

The republican targeted program Exploitation of Underground Resources and Development of the Mining Industry of in the Republic of Karelia, 2000–2002–2010 is focused on the creation of a mining and geology management company to foster more efficient use of the Republic's mineral resources.

Under the Program Enhancement of Road Traffic Safety in the Republic of Karelia, 2003–2005 construction and upgrade of roads to the international frontier with Finland (sections of the Kem–Lonka, Priazha– Lemetti, and Kostomuksha– State Border roads); and completion of the construction of transit roads to the Leningrad, Vologda, and Arkhangelsk Regions are underway.

6. INVESTMENT PROJECTS

Industry sector and project description	1) Expected results 2) Amount and term of investment 3) Form of financing[1] 4) Documentation[2]	Contact information
1	2	3
MINING		
19R001 ● ★ ◆ ▲		ZAO Interkamen
Crude sledged stone products output from gabbro-diabase raw waste. Project goal: production of blocks from gabbro-diabase.	1) 7,000 square meters of paving blocks per year 2) $0.8 million/0.5 years 3) L, Leas. 4) BP, FS	5, ul. Kirova, Petrozavodsk, Republic of Karelia, 185035 Phone/fax: (8142) 78 0280 E-mail: inter@onego.ru Anatoly Semenovich Solovey, Director
ENERGY		
19R002 ■ ● ◆		OAO Karelenergo
Construction of a small hydro power station (130 MW). Project goal: to increase electricity output.	1) Electricity – 328 GWh per year 2) $150 million/3 years 3) E, L 4) BP	43, ul. Kirova, Petrozavodsk, Republic of Karelia, 185035 Phone: (8142) 78 2621, 78 2620, 76 5995 Fax: (8142) 76 5995 E-mail: beljakvv@karelen.elektra.ru sekr@karelen.elektra.ru; Valery Vasilyevich Beliakov, First Deputy General Director
FORESTRY, TIMBER, AND PULP AND PAPER		
19R003 ■ ● ▲		OOO Bumex Lahdenpohja Plywood Mill
Construction of a plywood timber mill. Project goal: production of competitive goods.	1) Capacity 70,000 cubic meters of plywood or 100,000 cubic meters of plywood timber per year 2) €30 million/1 year 3) E, L 4) FS	11, ul. Titova, Petrozavodsk, Republic of Karelia, 185035 Phone: (8142) 76 8022; fax: (8142) 76 034 E-mail: bumex@onego.ru Dmitri Alexandrovich Beliayev, Director
19R004 ■ ● ◆ ▲		OAO Suojarvi Kartontara
Fixed assets upgrade. Project goal: to extend the product range (class A cardboard with white coating), expand output, and improve quality.	1) Operating profit $0.95 million per year 2) $2.8 million/2.5 years 3) E, L 4) FS, BP	24, ul. Nuhi Idrisova, Suojarvi, Republic of Karelia, 186870 Phone: (81457) 21 158, 22 374 E-mail: skf@onego.ru Viktor Alexandrovich Patrakov, CEO
FOOD AND BEVERAGES		
19R005 ■ ● ◆		OOO Kivach Firm
Creation of a commercial fish complex with processing infrastructure. Project goal: to expand sales of fish.	1) n/a 2) $2 million/2 years 3) E, L 4) BP	1a, ul. Anokhina, Petrozavodsk, Republic of Karelia, 185000 Phone: (8142) 76 3181; fax: (8142) 76 2008 E-mail: kivach_ltd@onego.ru; Avtandil Afanasyevich Chaduneli, President

[1] L – Loan, E – Equity, Leas. – Leasing, JV – Joint Venture
[2] BP – Business Plan, FS – Feasibility Study

II

NORTH-WESTERN FEDERAL DISTRICT

20. KOMI REPUBLIC [11]

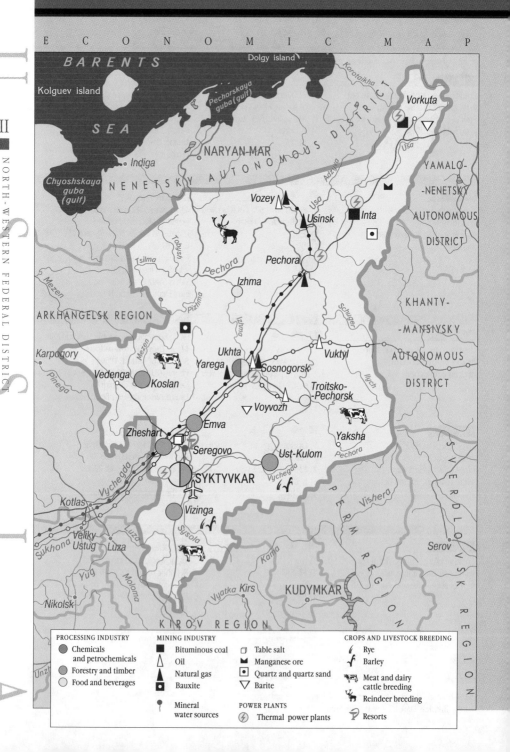

ECONOMIC MAP

BARENTS SEA

Kolguev island

Dolgy island

Pechorskaya guba (gulf)

Chyoshskaya guba (gulf)

Indiga

NARYAN-MAR

NENETSKY AUTONOMOUS DISTRICT

Korotaikha

Vorkuta

YAMALO--NENETSKY AUTONOMOUS DISTRICT

Tsilma

Tobysh

Pechora

Usa

Adzva

Usa

Vozey

Usinsk

Inta

Mezen

Pizhma

Izhma

Pechora

Schugor

KHANTY--MANSIYSKY AUTONOMOUS DISTRICT

ARKHANGELSK REGION

Karpogory

Mezen

Vedenga

Koslan

Ukhta
Yarega

Sosnogorsk

Vuktyl

Ilych

Pinega

Voyvozh

Troitsko-Pechorsk

Emva

Zheshart

Seregovo

Ust-Kulom

Yaksha

Pechora

SYKTYVKAR

Vychegda

Vizinga

Sysola

PERM REGION

Vishera

Serov

SVERDLOVSK REGION

Kotlas

Veliky Ustug

Luza

Sukhona

Vychegda

Luza

Kama

Yug

Moloma

Nikolsk

Vyatka Kirs

KUDYMKAR

KIROV REGION

Unzha

PROCESSING INDUSTRY	MINING INDUSTRY		CROPS AND LIVESTOCK BREEDING
Chemicals and petrochemicals	Bituminous coal	Table salt	Rye
Forestry and timber	Oil	Manganese ore	Barley
Food and beverages	Natural gas	Quartz and quartz sand	Meat and dairy cattle breeding
	Bauxite	Barite	Reindeer breeding
Mineral water sources	POWER PLANTS		Resorts
	Thermal power plants		

T he Komi Republic is one of the richest mineral resource regions of the north-west of Russia. The Republic is fourth in terms of oil, natural gas and coal output in Russia, and boasts extensive forest resources.

The social and economic development priorities of the Komi Republic are set forth in the comprehensive action plan for 2003, which establishes the primary objectives to be accomplished by the Republic. A State Geological Survey and Natural Resources Renewal Program is to be developed and implemented with the aim of expanding the Republic's explored natural reserves. Its main goal will be to increase the number of explored fuel deposits (oil, natural gas, gas condensate, and coking and power-generating coal).

Work is continuing on the development of the Komi Republic's mining sector: the Middle-Timan Bauxite Mine is under construction, as is a pit at the Khoilinsk Barite Deposit. Iron and manganese ore mining is underway at the Parnoksk Deposit. Vein quartz output is expanding together with titanium ore and gold mining output. The Government of the Republic intends to draft and implement a Conceptual Framework for the Development of the Komi Republic's Metal Mining Industry through 2010.

We believe that our future prospects and implementation of our plans are closely linked to opportunities for mutually beneficial trade and investment cooperation with Russia's regions and foreign countries alike.

We export fuel, oil products, timber, and pulp and paper products to 32 countries. Our main imports are food and beverages.

The Republic hosts over 150 foreign-owned companies with participation of investors from Austria, the UK, Germany, Cyprus, the USA, and Switzerland.

The efforts of the Republic's Administration aimed at creating a favorable investment climate in the Republic have earned the Republic a high credit rating and a large influx of foreign investment. According to preliminary estimates, foreign investment has risen more than fivefold on last year's level. We are available to do business with anyone who is ready to do business with us.

Vladimir Torlopov,
HEAD OF THE KOMI REPUBLIC

II

NORTH-WESTERN FEDERAL DISTRICT

1.GENERAL INFORMATION

1.1. GEOGRAPHY

Located in the north-east of European Russia and drained by the Pechora, Vychegda and Mezen rivers, the Komi Republic covers a total area of 416,800 square kilometers (2.4% of Russia's total area). The Republic extends some 1,275 kilometers from the south-west to the north-east.

To the west, the Republic borders the Arkhangelsk Region, to the north-west and north – the Nenetsky Autonomous District, to the east – the Yamalo-Nenetsky and Khanty-Mansiysky Autonomous Districts, to the south – the Perm Region, and to the south-west – the Kirov Region.

1.2. CLIMATE

The Komi Republic lies in the sub-Arctic and moderate continental climatic zones. Most of the Republic is subject to a moderate continental climate with long winters and short, cool summers.

Air temperatures in January average –17.1°C, rising to +19°C in July. Annual precipitation reaches 450–625 mm.

1.3. POPULATION

According to preliminary 2002 census results, the Komi Republic's total population is 1 million people. The average population density is 2.4 people per km^2. The economically active population amounts to 589,000 people, while the official unemployment rate was 2.7% as of 2002.

Demographically speaking, some 66.6% are of working age, 19% are below the statutory working age, and 14.4% are beyond the statutory working age.

The Republic's major urban centers are Syktyvkar with 230,000 inhabitants, Ukhta with some 103,500 inhabitants, Vorkuta with 87,400 inhabitants, and Pechora with 58,800 inhabitants (as of 2002).

Population							TABLE 1
	1992	1997	1998	1999	2000	2001	2002
Total population, '000	1,245	1,176	1,163	1,151	1,136	1,126	1,019
Economically active population, '000	693	616	583	618	594	596	589

2. ADMINISTRATION

9, ul. Kommunisticheskaya, Syktyvkar, Komi Republic, 167610
Phone: (8212) 28 5112; fax: (8212) 21 4384; e-mail: adm@rkomi.ru; http://www.rkomi.ru

NAME	POSITION	CONTACT INFORMATION
Vladimir Alexandrovich TORLOPOV	Head of the Komi Republic	Phone: (8212) 28 5112 Fax: (8212) 21 4384 E-mail: adm@rkomi.ru
Nikolai Valentinovich LEVITSKY	First Deputy Head of the Komi Republic, in charge of general economic issues	Phone: (8212) 28 5108 Fax: (8212) 24 0587
Pavel Anatolyevich ORDA	Deputy Head of the Komi Republic, in charge of industrial development issues	Phone: (8212) 28 5139 Fax: (8212) 24 5005
Alexei Yuryevich KABIN	Deputy Head of the Komi Republic, in charge of financial and economic activities	Phone: (8212) 28 5107 Fax: (8212) 24 6277
Ivan Yevgenyevich STUKALOV	Minister of Economic Development of the Komi Republic	Phone: (8212) 28 5128 Fax: (8212) 24 4305
Vyacheslav Mikhailovich GAIZER	Minister of Finance of the Komi Republic	Phone: (8212) 24 1453 Fax: (8212) 24 6407
Vyacheslav Sergeevich BIBIKOV	Minister of Architecture, Construction, Housing, and Energy of the Komi Republic	Phone: (8212) 28 5504 Fax: (8212) 24 3279
Gennady Fedorovich NIZOVTSEV	Minister of Agriculture and Food of the Komi Republic	Phone: (8212) 28 8371 Fax: (8212) 24 1127

NAME	POSITION	CONTACT INFORMATION
Vasily Pavlovich KUZNETSOV	Minister of Economic Relations of the Komi Republic	Phone: (8212) 24 4489 Fax: (8212) 24 1482 E-mail: minek@rkomi.ru
Alexander Pavlovich BOROVINSKIKH	Minister of Natural Resources and Environment of the Komi Republic	Phone: (8212) 24 5588 Fax: (8212) 24 0744
Vladimir Petrovich BASKAKOV	Minister of Industry of the Komi Republic	Phone: (8212) 24 0348

3. ECONOMIC POTENTIAL

3.1. 1997–2002 GROSS REGIONAL PRODUCT (GRP). INDUSTRY BREAKDOWN

In 2002, gross regional product totaled $3.16 million, a 3% growth year-on-year. Per capita GRP amounted to $2,726 in 2001 and $3,102 in 2002.

3.2. MAJOR ECONOMIC GROWTH PROJECTIONS

The Program for Social and Economic Development in the Komi Republic through 2005 developed by the Republic's Government sets the following objectives:

GRP trends in 1997–2002						*TABLE 2*
	1997	1998	1999	2000	2001	2002*
GRP in current prices, $ million	4,388.1	2,975.6	1,903.5	2,571.8	3,069.6	3,160.9

*Estimates of the Government of the Komi Republic

GRP industry breakdown in 1997–2002, % of total						*TABLE 3*
	1997	1998	1999	2000	2001	2002
GRP	100.0	100.0	100.0	100.0	100.0	100.0
Industry	36.0	35.0	50.0	49.0	39.4	n/a
Agriculture and forestry	3.0	2.0	2.0	2.0	1.7	n/a
Construction	10.0	8.0	5.0	8.0	8.2	n/a
Transport and communications	20.0	21.0	15.0	15.0	11.0	n/a
Trade and public catering	11.0	11.0	10.0	9.0	12.3	n/a
Other industries	20.0	23.0	18.0	17.0	27.4	n/a

Industry: production growth at an average annual rate of 4%; growth through increased oil and gas production and launch of new oil and gas fields, further development of metal mining industry, and growth in titanium ore and gold production;

Energy: maintaining stability in the sector and ensuring moderate production growth;

Agriculture: annual production growth at 6–13% (due to increased crop output);

Transport and communications: increase in subscriber line numbers; reconstruction and upgrade of equipment, and increase in international line capacity.

3.3. INDUSTRIAL OUTPUT IN 1997–2002 FOR MAJOR SECTORS OF ECONOMY

Industry plays the leading role in the Republic's economy and includes over 30 industrial sectors. One quarter of the Republic's economically active population is employed by industrial enterprises. Major sectors include: fuel (55.9% of total 2002 output), timber (23.6%), and energy (12.5%). Total 2002 output was $1,985 million. Increased output in the oil and paper sectors made a major contribution to the total output growth (+0.7%).

Industry breakdown of industrial output in 1997–2002, % of total						TABLE 4
	1997	1998	1999	2000	2001	2002*
Industry	100.0	100.0	100.0	100.0	100.0	100.0
Fuel	53.8	56.5	63.5	65.0	65.2	55.9
Forestry, timber, and pulp and paper	14.2	16.4	19.4	19.6	18.9	23.6
Energy	18.6	15.4	8.5	8.0	9.1	12.5
Food and beverage	4.2	4.4	3.1	2.9	2.6	3.5
Construction materials	3.0	2.3	1.6	1.3	1.2	1.4
Light industry	1.4	1.4	1.2	1.3	1.2	1.4
Machine engineering and metal processing	2.8	1.9	1.2	1.1	1.2	0.9
Non-ferrous metals	–	0.1	0.1	0.1	0.2	0.2
Chemicals, and petrochemicals	–	–	–	–	0.1	0.1
Ferrous metals	0.1	0.1	–	–	–	–
Flour, cereals, and mixed fodder	0.1	0.1	0.4	0.3	0.1	0.1

*Estimates of the Government of the Komi Republic

Oil. The Komi Republic occupies a strategic place in Russia in terms of oil production. Oil production and processing account for over 50% of total industrial output in the Republic. Subsidiaries of Russia's oil majors including OOO LUKoil-Komi, OAO Komineft, and OAO Severnaya Neft are active players in the Republic's oil industry.

Natural gas. The Republic's gas industry is represented by subsidiaries of OAO Gazprom. Severgazprom, the largest, controls the Republic's major gas fields. The Republic's largest gas processing company, the Sosnogorsk Gas Processing Plant, is the only natural gas and unstable condensate processing plant in the North-Western Federal District. Its annual output is 1,500 million cubic meters of natural gas and 1.25 million tons of unstable condensate. The plant's main products include: industrial carbon, gasoline, liquefied gas, stable gas condensate, and general mechanical rubber products.

Coal. The Republic currently has some eleven coalmines in operation with a total annual output of 23 million tons, and five concentrating mills. The industry's major companies are OAO Vorkutaugol, OAO Shakhtoupravlenie Intinskaya Coal Company, OAO Shakhta Vorgashorskaya, and OAO Shakhta Zapadnaya-Bis.

The Republic's **forestry, timber, and pulp and paper industry** includes felling, production of timber building materials and board, and veneer and furniture production. Major wood processing companies include: OAO Timber Industrial Company Syktyvkarsky LDK, OOO Syktyvkar Veneer Plant, OOO Wallboard Plant.

Energy. The Republic's energy system includes the power plants and grids of OAO AEK Komienergo (the Vorkuta TPS 1 and 2, Sosnogorsk TPS, Inta TPS), Pechora GRES, Syktyvkar Timber Industrial Complex TPS, and a number of smaller power stations. The total installed capacity of the Republic's energy system stands at 2,284 MW. Power production is mainly focused on the Republic's internal needs. Only 1% of the Republic's power output is exported.

3.4. FUEL AND ENERGY BALANCE (OUTPUT AND CONSUMPTION PER RESOURCE)

Power output in 2002 totaled some 8.8 billion kWh, a 1% increase compared to 2001. Heat output reached 20.1 million Gcal, or 5.8% up on the previous year. OAO Komienergo and Pechora GRES are the largest power producers in the Republic.

Oil production in the Republic in 2002 reached 9.6 million tons, with natural gas output reaching 3.4 billion cubic meters. Coal output in 2002 totaled some 12.9 million tons, including 8.2 million tons of coking coal, and 4.7 million tons of power-generating coal.

3.5. TRANSPORT INFRASTRUCTURE

At the end of 2002, the Republic's transport network comprised 1,700 km of railroads, 2,800 km of navigable inland waterways, 3,600 km of gas pipeline, 700 km of oil pipeline, and 5,300 km of public highway.

In terms of public highway and railroad density, the Republic is way behind most other regions of Russia.

In 2002, the Republic's transport system carried some 236.9 million passengers and 148.3 million tons of freight.

3.6. MAIN NATURAL RESOURCES: RESERVES AND EXTRACTION IN 2002

The Republic is unique in terms of the variety, quality and disposition of its natural resources. There are barite deposits, and bauxites, iron and manganese ores, and vein quartz are extracted. According to various estimates, the gross value of the Republic's total natural reserves stands at $11 trillion, or some 8% of Russia's total projected potential.

Oil resources. The Republic has some 258 oil fields suitable for industrial operation, or more than 50% of all of the oil fields of the Timano-Pechora Oil and Gas

Fuel and energy sector production and consumption trends, 1997–2002						TABLE 5
	1997	1998	1999	2000	2001	2002*
Electricity output, billion kWh	7.8	7.8	7.7	7.9	8.4	8.8
Oil output (including gas condensate), '000 tons	7,851.0	8,085.0	7,691.0	8,181.0	9,158.0	9,600.0
Natural gas output, million cubic meters	3,526.0	3,858.0	3,893.0	4,057.0	3,798.0	3,400.0
Electricity consumption, billion kW/h	6.8	6.9	6.8	7.0	7.1	7.0
Oil consumption, '000 tons (primary processing)	3,762.0	2,817.0	2,233.0	3,643.0	3,572.0	3,690.0
Oil products consumption, '000 tons	995.1	953.2	844.3	806.1	827.8	835.0
Natural gas consumption, million cubic meters	5,125.9	5,044.2	5,130.1	5,248.7	5,649.1	5,700.0

*Estimates of the Government of the Komi Republic

Province. Currently, the Republic's oil and gas companies operate around 40 hydrocarbon fields with total extractable industrial oil reserves of 468.6 million tons and 117.3 billion cubic meters of free gas. Total production in the Republic in 2002 amounted to 9.6 million tons of oil and 3.4 billion cubic meters of natural gas.

Gas reserves. The Republic accounts for some 53% of total gas reserves of the Timano-Pechora Oil and Gas Province. About 74% of the Republic's recoverable gas is located in 12 producing fields. The largest Vuktylskoye gas field provides about 90% of total natural gas output. Smaller gas fields, the Zapadno-Soplesskoye, Yugidskoye and Pechorogorodskoye, provide over 5% of total gas output.

Coal reserves. The Pechora coal basin offers a major industrial basis for the development of Russia's energy, metals and coke industries. Extrapolated coal reserves are estimated at over 240 billion tons, whereas explored reserves are around 9 billion tons. Three coal fields within the Pechora coal basin are currently being worked.

Forestry resources. The Komi Republic has the largest forest reserves in European Russia. By various estimates, the Republic's forest reserves amount to 2.8 billion cubic meters, of which 87% is coniferous. The Republic's natural environment has good potential for recreational, tourism, and curative purposes.

4. TRADE OPPORTUNITIES

4.1. MAIN GOODS PRODUCED IN THE REGION

Timber. During 2002, the total volume of timber shipped out of the Republic fell by 13.8% year-on-year to 5.4 million running meters. Paper output grew by 5.7% in 2002 to 528,000 tons, with board output rising 19.5% to 155,000.

Light industry. In terms of fabric production, the Republic occupies fifth position in Russia. Fabric output rose by 1.3% in 2002 to 79.9 million square meters.

Food and beverages. Total 2002 output fell by 3.5% year-on-year. Bread and bakery products output for the year fell by 6.6% to 59,500 tons, whole milk output was down 7.2% at 25,100 tons, and liquor output fell by 14.3% to 944,500 decaliters.

4.2. EXPORTS, INCLUDING EXTRA-CIS

Exports to non-CIS countries totaled $656.8 million in 2001; exports to CIS countries amounted to $61.6 million. The figures for 2002 were $581.2 million and $83.4 million, respectively. The Republic exports its products to 32 countries, with Poland, Germany and the Netherlands its principal export destinations. Fuel and oil products, timber and lumber, and pulp and paper constitute the bulk of the Republic's export.

4.3. IMPORTS, INCLUDING EXTRA-CIS

Imports from non-CIS countries in 2001 totaled $107.8 million, compared with $3.9 million from CIS countries. The same figures for 2002 were $135.6 million and $1.3 million, respectively. The bulk of the Republic's imports is represented by food and beverage products, including meat and sausage, canned meat, cheeses, and butter.

4.4. MAJOR REGIONAL EXPORT AND IMPORT ENTITIES

Due to specifics of the Komi Republic's economy, export and import activities are mainly conducted by the Republic's industrial enterprises.

II

NORTH-WESTERN FEDERAL DISTRICT

5. INVESTMENT OPPORTUNITIES

5.1. INVESTMENTS
IN 1992–2002 (BY INDUSTRY
SECTOR), INCLUDING
FOREIGN INVESTMENTS

The Komi Republic is one of the most investment friendly areas of the Russian Federation. The following factors determine the investment appeal of the Republic:

- Legislation supporting investment activities (guarantees for investors in terms of taxation and exemptions);
- Cheap energy;
- Large natural resource potential.

5.2. CAPITAL INVESTMENT

Capital investments in 2002 decreased by 18.2% compared to 2001. The most dramatic investment decrease was in the oil production, oil processing, and pulp and paper industries. At the same time, these industries retain leading positions in terms of capital investments. In the area of services, pipeline transportation is number one industry in terms of capital investment.

The Republic's principal investor countries in 2001 were Cyprus (30.1% of total foreign investment), Switzerland (25.4%), Finland (23.6%), Luxembourg (18.6%), Norway (1.2%), and the USA (0.6%). The principal investor countries in 2002 were Finland (73.4% of total foreign investment), Austria (11.5%), Cyprus (8.7%), Luxembourg (3.5%), and Belgium (2.5%).

5.3. MAJOR ENTERPRISES
(INCLUDING ENTERPRISES
WITH FOREIGN INVESTMENT)

The Republic hosts some 19,200 companies, of which more than 150 are companies with foreign investments. Investors from Germany, the USA, Austria, the UK, Cyprus, and Switzerland are the main foreign investors in the Republic. The Republic's largest companies, including companies with foreign participation, are: OOO LUKoil-Komi, OAO AEK Komienergo, OAO Tebukneft, ZAO Komiarktikoil, ZAO Bytech-Silour, OAO Severnaya Neft, ZAO Sever-TEK, OOO Severgazprom, and OOO Sosnogorsky GPZ.

Capital investment by industry sector, $ million						TABLE 6
	1997	1998	1999	2000	2001	2002*
Total capital investment	902.5	443.4	266.6	607.8	810.3	662.8
Including major industries (% of total):						
Industry	41.8	45.3	58.8	70.5	64.2	62.8
Agriculture and forestry	0.5	0.7	1.5	0.6	0.6	1.2
Construction	10.6	12.5	11.7	6.8	7.6	4.4
Transport and communications	31.6	22.8	18.1	16.5	18.6	24.5
Trade and public catering	0.3	0.9	0.6	1.3	0.8	1.1
Other	15.2	17.8	9.3	4.3	8.2	6.0

*Estimates of the Governmentof the Komi Republic

Foreign investment trends, 1996–2002						TABLE 7
	1996–1997	1998	1999	2000	2001	2002*
Total foreign investment, $ million	92.6	218.1	54.4	54.0	76.8	339.6
Including FDI, $ million	29.8	22.8	41.1	23.2	34.1	82.1

*Estimates of the Government of the Komi Republic

5.4. MOST
ATTRACTIVE SECTORS
FOR INVESTMENT

Companies in the fuel and energy and forestry sectors offer the strongest investment appeal. These account for 85% and 14%, respectively, of total investment in the Republic.

5.5. CURRENT LEGISLATION
ON INVESTOR TAX
EXEMPTIONS AND PRIVILEGES

The Republic's investment-related legislation continued to improve in 2002. The Komi Republic's Law On Investment Activity in the Komi Republic was significantly amended. The Republic's Govern-

Largest enterprises of the Komi Republic	*TABLE 8*
COMPANY	SECTOR
OOO LUKoil-Komi	Oil
OAO AEK Komienergo	Energy
ZAO Komiarktikoil	Oil
ZAO Bytech-Silour	Oil
OAO Severnaya Neft	Oil processing
OOO Severgazprom	Natural gas
OAO Neusiedler Syktyvkar	Pulp and paper

Regional entities responsible for raising investment		*TABLE 9*
ENTITY	ADDRESS	PHONE, FAX, E-MAIL
The Komi Republic UNIDO National Expert Group	59A, ul. Lenina, Syktyvkar, Komi Republic, 167000	Phone: (8212) 29 1136 Fax (8212) 29 1137 E-mail: post@rida.komi.com
The Komi Republic Chamber of Commerce and Industry	212, ul. Karla Marksa, Syktyvkar, Komi Republic, 167610	Phone: (8212) 24 5850 Fax: (8212) 24 5850 E-mail: palata@parma.ru

ment grants the following exemptions and privileges to investors within the Republic for the estimated project payback period (limited to three years): a lower profit tax rate, a property tax exemption, a land tax exemption, and a vehicle tax exemption. In addition, the Republic's Government may grant investment tax credits and government guarantees to investors.

5.6. FEDERAL AND REGIONAL ECONOMIC AND SOCIAL DEVELOPMENT PROGRAMS FOR THE KOMI REPUBLIC

Federal targeted programs. The Komi Republic is implementing a number of federal targeted programs, the major of which is the Federal targeted program Energy Effective Economy, 2002–2005 and through 2010. Under the Program, the Komi Republic will increase oil production by 2005 by launching new oil and gas fields, upgrade fixed assets, and put into operation new oil transportation facilities from newly developed oil fields.

Regional programs. The Komi Republic's Government has adopted a number of the Republic's development programs, in particular the program for Economic and Social Development of the Komi Republic, 1998–2005, and Development of the Komi Republic's Agroindustrial Complex for 2001–2005.

These programs are focused on the increase in the agriculture production and processing resource potential, ongoing restructuring of industrial sectors, and implementation of agriculture and land reforms. The programs focused on increasing efficiency of agricultural producers represent priority objectives for the Republic. These are: Reproduction of Food Fish and Restoration of Fish Breeding in the Komi Republic, 2003–2005, and Program for Horse Breeding in the Komi Republic, 2003–2005.

5. INVESTMENT PROJECTS

Industry sector and project description	1) Expected results 2) Amount and term of investment 3) Form of financing[1] 4) Documentation[2]	Contact information
1	2	3

OIL

20R001 ■ ● ★

Field facilities for construction at the Yuzhno-Shapkinsky oil and gas condensate field. Project goal: oil production.

1) 1.1 million tons of oil and gas condensate annually
2) $372.1 million/3 years
3) E, L, Leas.
4) Investment feasibility study

ZAO SeverTEK
p/o box 116, 4, ul. Lesnaya,
Usinsk, Komi Republic, 169710
Phone: (82144) 41 334
Fax: (82144) 41 249
E-mail: severtek@st.usinsk.ru
Viktor Vladimirovich Mikharev,
CEO

COAL

20R002 ● ■ ◆

Exposure of the second shaft level at the Vorkutinskaya mine. Project goal: to achieve projected production levels and reduce the cost of production.

1) 1.65 million tons annually
2) $2.8 million/2 years
3) L; participation in the project on a compensatory basis by supplying ready made goods
4) BP

OAO Vorkutaugol
62, ul. Lenina, Vorkuta,
Komi Republic, 169908.
Phone: (82151) 72 473, 75 441
Fax: (82151) 72 242
E-mail: oskid@ovu.vorkuta.com
Viktor Ivanovich Erkgardt, CEO

20R003 ● ■ ◆

Ventilation shaft No. 4 of the Komsomolskaya mine. Project goal: to achieve projected production levels and to provide ventilation, delivery of workers, materials, and cargos.

1) 2.3 million tons annually
2) $18.5 million/2 years
3) L, participation in the project on a compensatory basis by supplying ready made goods
4) BP

OAO Vorkutaugol
62, ul. Lenina, Vorkuta,
Komi Republic, 169908
Phone: (82151) 72 473, 75 441
Fax: (82151) 72 242
E-mail: oskid@ovu.vorkuta.com
Viktor Ivanovich Erkgardt, CEO

MINING

20R004 ● ★ ◆

Increase in barite production and processing. Project goal: Increase in barite ore production and processing.

1) 120,000 tons of ore annually
2) $3.1 million/2 years
3) L, Leas
4) Draft design, mining development plan

ZAO Khoylinsky Ore
Mining & Processing Plant
64, ul. Lenina, Vorkuta,
Komi Republic, 169908
Phone: (82151) 63 086
Fax: (82151) 75 310
E-mail: barit@vorkuta.com;
Igor Ivanovich Goncharov, CEO

20R005 ■ ● ★ ▲

Field facilities construction at the Parnoksky iron and manganese ore field. Project goal: iron and manganese ore production and processing.

1) Production of 80,000 tons of iron and manganese ore and 50,000 tons of manganese concentrate annually
2) $10 million/3 years
3) E; L, Leas., loan contingent on equipment supplies; project finance
4) FS

OAO Komi Manganese
1, ul. Trudovaya, Inta,
Komi Republic, 169840
Phone: (82145) 22 277
Fax: (82145) 24 882
Mikhail Nikolaevich Manusharov,
CEO

[1] L – Loan, E – Equity, Leas. – Leasing, JV – Joint Venture
[2] BP – Business Plan, FS – Feasibility Study

II

NORTH-WESTERN FEDERAL DISTRICT

1	2	3

20R006 ■ ● ★ ▲

Comprehensive development of the Yarega oil and titanium field. Project goal: comprehensive development of the Yarega heavy oil and titanium field with associated mineral resources.

1) Production and processing of 1.2 million tons of oil a year.; production of 1.2 million tons of titanium ore a year; production of 220,200 tons of titanium concentrate a year
2) $566.8 million/4 years
3) L; Leas; participation in the project on a compensatory basis by supplying ready made goods
4) FS

OAO Yarega Oil & Titanium Co. 1, ul. Lermontova, Yarega, Ukhta, Komi Republic, 169347 Phone: (82147) 54 200 Fax: (82147) 56 032 E-mail: ntitan@online.ru Alexander Alexandrovich Pranovich, CEO

20R007 ■ ● ▲

Construction of Salt Plant for production of Extra salt on the base of Seriogovskoye salt field. Project goal: production of high quality product, increase of product sales to European Russia.

1. 0,36 million tons of salt a year
2. $51.9 million/3.5 years
3. E; finance binding loan contingent on equipment supplies
4. FS

State Organization Directorate for Enterprises under Construction under the Komi Republic Economy Development Program, 108, ul. Internatsionalnaya, Syktyvkar, Komi Republic, 167000 Phone: (8212) 24 2742, 24 6772 Fax: (8212) 24 6219, 24 6772 E-mail: inform@admpro.parma.ru Andrey Vladimirovich Kiselev, Director

NON-FERROUS METALS

20R008 ■ ● ★ ▲

Construction of an alumina and aluminum plant in Komi Republic. Project goal: to supply raw material (bauxites) to Urals aluminum plants.

1) Annual production of alumina – 1.4 million tons; primary aluminum – 0.40–0.45 million tons; foundry and rolled products – 0.37 million tons; aluminum products (extruded sections, panels, sheets, bands, foils, rods and wires) – 0.23 million tons
2) $2.4 billion/8 years
3) E; corporate bonds issue; L, loan contingent on equipment supplies; Leas.
4) FS

OAO Siberian-Urals Aluminum Company 40, M/ Ordynka, Moscow, 113095 Phone: (095) 933 02 00, 933 02 07 Fax: (095) 933 0181 Vladimir Iliyich Skorniakov, First Vice-President

FORESTRY, TIMBER, AND PULP AND PAPER

20R009 ■ ● ★ ◆

Turbine generator-based power supply for a fibreboard plant in Yevma, Komi Republic. Project goal: to supply over 90% of the company's energy needs.

1) Decrease by 15–20% of energy costs of wallboard production
2) $2 million/1 year
3) E, L, Leas.
4) BP

OOO Wallboard Plant 35, ul. Vymskaya, Yevma, Knyazhpogostsky District, Komi Republic, 169200 Phone: (82139) 92 446, 91 219 Fax: (82139) 99 787 E-mail: ivd@edvp.ru, secretary@edvp.ru Andrey Borisovich Kochetkov, CEO

1	2	3

20R010 ■ ● ▲

Construction of a pulp plant in the Udorsky District of the Komi Republic. Project goal: to deepen the degree of chemical processing of surplus low quality wood, to increase the company's share of the market for commercial sulphate cellulose.

1) Annual production of commercial sulphate cellulose – 400,000 tons; viscose cellulose – 100,000 tons
2) $807.4 million/4 years
3) E; L; loan contingent on equipment supplies
4) FS

The Komi Republic Ministry of Industry, 157, ul. Internatsionalnaya, Syktyvkar, Komi Republic, 167610 Phone: (8212) 21 4399, 24 4037, 24 2646; Fax: (8212) 21 4399 E-mail: minprom@rkomi.ru Vladimir Petrovich Baskakov, Minister of Industry

20R011 ■ ● ◆

Facilities for the production of medium density laminated wooden fiber boards. Project goal: production of marketable products (wood fiber board, laminated floors, laminated wallboards, and ceiling panels).

1) 100,000 cubic meters a year
2) $46.95 million/2 years
3) E (up to 75–80%); L
4) BP

OOO Wallboard Plant 35, ul. Vymskaya, Yevma, Knyazhpogostsky District, Komi Republic, 169200 Phone: (82139) 92 446, 91 219 Fax: (82139) 99 787 E-mail: ivd@edvp.ru, secretary@edvp.ru; Andrey Borisovich Kochetkov, CEO

TRANSPORT INFRASTRUCTURE

20R012 ● ★ ◆ ▲

Construction of Arkhangelsk – Syktyvkar – Perm railroad line. Project goal: to enhance transport efficiency.

1) A significant decrease in cargo transportation distance (up to 800 km) from the Urals and Siberia to Arkhangelsk and Murmansk
2) $653.9 million/6.5 years
3) E, L, long-term development of natural resources along the future railroad line
4) BP, FS

OAO MK Belkomur 108, ul. Internatsionalnaya, Syktyvkar, Komi Republic, 167000 Phone: (8212) 44 7721 Fax: (8212) 44 7771 E-mail: belkomur@online.ru Valery Nikolaevich Nabatchikov, CEO

COMMUNICATIONS

20R013 ● ★ ◆

Construction of a Pechora-Inta optical fiber communication line. Project goal: upgrade of communication lines to ensure quality communication services between electronic telephone exchanges; increase, in the number of lines and quality of international communications services.

1) n/a
2) $1.0 million/2 years
3) L, loan contingent on equipment supplies; Leas
4) BP

OAO Svyaz RK 60, ul. Lenina, Syktyvkar, Komi Republic, 167610 Phone: (8212) 21 6050 Fax: (8212) 21 5170 E-mail: komisvyaz@parma.ru Vikenty Alexandrovich Kozlov, CEO

21. ARKHANGELSK REGION [29]

ECONOMIC MAP

BARENTS SEA

Amderma

Vaygach island

Dolgy island

Vorkuta

Korotaikha

Usa

Pechorskaya guba (gulf)

Kolguev island

Peschanoozerskoe

NARYAN-MAR

Pechora

KOMI

Usa

Adzva

Izhma

Cape of Kanin Nos

Cape of Svyatoy Nos

Chyoshskaya guba (gulf)

Ponoy

Tsylma

Pechora

REPUBLIC

Ukhta

Troitsko-Pechorsk

WHITE SEA

Mezenskaya guba (gulf)

Kuloy

Mezen

Mezen

Vychegda

Dvinskaya guba (gulf)

ARKHANGELSK

Karpogory

Vendinga

Pinega

Emva

Vychegda

SYKTYVKAR

Severodvinsk

Lomonosovo

Novodvinsk

Onezhskaya guba (gulf)

Onega

Savinsky

Plesetsk

Solvychegodsk

Koryazhma

Severnaya Dvina

Vaga

Kotlas

Susola

Onega

Nyandoma

Sukhona

Veliky Ustug

Vychegda

Velsk

Vyatka

Pudozh

Lacha lake

Lake Onega

Konosha

VOLOGDA REGION

KIROV REGION

Lake Vozhe

Totma

Nikolsk

KIROV

PROCESSING INDUSTRY

- Non-ferrous metals
- Machine engineering and metal processing
- Forestry and timber
- Construction materials
- Food and beverages
- Art crafts

MINING INDUSTRY

- Bauxite
- Fishing ports

POWER PLANTS

- Thermal power plants
- Resorts

CROPS AND LIVESTOCK BREEDING

- Rye
- Barley
- Potatoes
- Meat and dairy cattle breeding

I am happy to have this opportunity to present the Arkhangelsk Region, a northern maritime territory with huge potential where many of Russia's strategic interests meet.

Arkhangelsk has long been a world transport junction. We are continuing our efforts to strengthen the northern transport corridor and shipping route, the eastern leg of which is managed from Arkhangelsk.

The port of Arkhangelsk is Russia's oldest seaport, a port which today remains crucial to international trade and domestic shipping along the Arctic coast.

Forestry constitutes the basis of our economy. Every third cubic meter of Russia's exported lumber is produced here in the Arkhangelsk Region, plus one quarter of all domestically produced pulp.

The Arkhangelsk Region is rich in natural resources such as natural gas, oil, peat, bauxites, and a variety of ores. The Region's Lomonosov diamond deposit is well known throughout the world. Industrial extraction of diamonds is due to commence as soon as next year.

The Region possesses strong industrial potential and unique technical expertise. The defense enterprises at Severodvinsk, which not only build and repair nuclear submarines, but manufacture excellent civilian goods also, top the league table in this regard. Severodvinsk enterprises build fishing trawlers, motorboats, and screw propellers for ocean liners.

The city of Plesetsk is home to the only space launch site in Europe.

The Arkhangelsk Region declared the year 2002 as the year of enterprise to highlight yet another rapidly growing area of economy. Some 5,000 small and medium enterprises are registered in the Region (one sixth of which are manufacturing companies) and employ over 80,000 people.

The Regional Administration realizes that economic success is contingent on attracting investment. With that in mind, we are continuously striving to build a stable market infrastructure, facilitate private sector growth, enhance small business, and integrate European Russia's northern territories into the Barents region's social and economic system by attracting Russian and foreign investors.

We have something to be proud of and show to the world: our greatest wealth is our people. The strong character of a maritime people, wit, and the ability to consolidate efforts – all of these we possess in abundance. Northerners are talented and hard working people, and most importantly, reliable and fair business partners.

Anatoly Yefremov,
HEAD OF ADMINISTRATION OF THE ARKHANGELSK REGION

1. GENERAL INFORMATION

1.1. GEOGRAPHY

The Arkhangelsk Region covers an area of 587,400 square kilometers. Located in the north of European Russia, the Region borders the Republic of Karelia, the Komi Republic, the Vologda Region, and the Kirov Region. From the north, the Region is washed by the Barents Sea, the Kara Sea, and the White Sea.

1.2. CLIMATE

Owing to the proximity of the Arctic Ocean, the Arkhangelsk Region's climate features both continental and maritime influences. The average air temperature in January −11.9°C, rising to +18°C in July.

1.3. POPULATION

According to preliminary 2002 census results, the Region's total population was 1.3 million people.

The average population density is 2.3 people per square kilometer. The economic active population amounts to 767,000 people. In 2002, the official unemployment level stood at 2.6%.

Demographically speaking, some 63.3% of the population are of working age, 18.6% are below the statutory working age, and 18.1% are beyond the statutory working age.

As of 2002, the Arkhangelsk Region's major urban centers were: Arkhangelsk with 355,500 inhabitants, Severodvinsk with 201,500 inhabitants, Kotlas with 79,800 inhabitants, and Novodvinsk with 48,400 inhabitants.

Population								_TABLE 1_
		1992	1997	1998	1999	2000	2001	2002
Total population, '000		1,570	1,506	1,492	1,478	1,459	1,442	1,336
Economically active population, '000		820	739	729	758	761	759	767

2. ADMINISTRATION

49, pr. Troitsky, Arkhangelsk, Arkhangelsk Region, 163000. Phone: (8182) 65 3102; fax: (8182) 64 6511
E-mail: adm@dvinaland.ru; http://www.arkhadm.gov.ru

NAME	POSITION	CONTACT INFORMATION
Anatoly Antonovich YEFREMOV	Head of Administration of the Arkhangelsk Region	Phone: (8182) 65 3041
Alexander Yefimovich POLIKARPOV	First Deputy Head of the Regional Administration for Resource and Property Management, Chairman of the Regional Committee for State Property Management	Phone: (8182) 64 0531 E-mail: polikarpov@dvinaland.ru
Anatoly Yevgenyevich KOZHIN	First Deputy Head of the Regional Administration for Infrastructure Development	Phone: (8182) 20 8363 E-mail: kozin@dvinaland.ru
Viktor Nikolaevich PAVLENKO	First Deputy Head of the Regional Administration, Chief of the Regional Administration's Staff	Phone: (8182) 64 8884 E-mail: pavlenko@dvinaland.ru
Svetlana Pavlovna GORLANOVA	Deputy Head of the Regional Administration for Foreign Relations and Tourism Development, Chairman of the Foreign Relations and Tourism Development Committee	Phone: (8182) 64 6481 E-mail: intercom@dvinaland.ru
Vladimir Alexandrovich KOLOMENTSEV	Deputy Head of the Regional Administration for Economic Development, Director of the Economic Development Department	Phone: (8182) 64 6672 Fax: (8182) 64 6278 E-mail: econo@dvinaland.ru
Alexander Viktorovich MAXIMOV	Deputy Head of the Regional Administration for Transport and Communications, Director of the Transport and Communications Department	Phone: (8182) 65 3038 Fax: (8182) 65 6589 E-mail: transdep@dvinaland.ru
Alexei Fridrikhovich PAVLOV	Deputy Head of the Regional Administration, Director of the Forestry Department	Phone: (8182) 20 7301 Fax: (8182) 20 7301 E-mail: lesdep@dvinaland.ru

NAME	POSITION	CONTACT INFORMATION
Elena Alexandrovna RUBAN	Deputy Head of the Regional Administration for finance, Director of the Finance Department	Phone: (8182) 64 6242 Fax: (8121) 21 1811 E-mail: arhfindept@dvinaland.ru
Maxim Vyacheslavovich SHUBTSOV	Deputy Head of the Regional Administration for Fuel and Enegy, Director of the Fuel and Energy Department	Phone: (8182) 64 1133 Fax: (8182) 64 1336 E-mail: atek@atnet.ru
Ludmila Viktorovna VARAKINA	Deputy Director of the Economic Development Department of the Regional Administration, Chairman of the Investment and Foreign Trade Committee	Phone: (8182) 64 7058

3. ECONOMIC POTENTIAL

3.1. 1997–2002 GROSS REGIONAL PRODUCT (GRP). INDUSTRY BREAKDOWN

The 2002 gross regional product of the Arkhangelsk Region amounted to $2,179 million, or 0.8% less than in 2001. Per capita GRP was $1,631 in 2002 and $1,524 in 2001. Industry and trade dominate the GRP structure with 37.5% and 15.6%, respectively.

3.2. INDUSTRIAL OUTPUT IN 1997–2002 FOR MAJOR SECTORS OF ECONOMY

The Region's leading sectors are forestry, timber and pulp and paper. The Region accounts for a large share of Russia's total timber, pulp, and paper output. The Region is currently developing its fuel sector, machine engineering, metal processing, energy, and fishing industries.

GRP trends in 1997–2002						TABLE 2
	1997	1998	1999	2000	2001	2002*
GRP in current prices, $ million	3,612.9	2,258.3	1,494.1	2,078.4	2,197.3	2,179.0

*Estimates of the Arkhangelsk Regional Administration

GRP industry breakdown in 1997–2002, % of total						TABLE 3
	1997	1998	1999	2000	2001	2002*
GRP	100.0	100.0	100.0	100.0	100.0	100.0
Industry	33.9	33.0	40.9	45.8	36.4	37.5
Agriculture and forestry	4.9	5.8	6.9	5.0	4.8	4.7
Construction	5.5	4.7	4.1	7.1	7.6	7.1
Transport and communications	14.6	12.6	11.4	10.8	11.2	10.3
Trade and public catering	14.4	14.3	17.4	14.9	16.8	15.6
Other	26.7	29.6	19.3	16.4	23.2	24.8

*Estimates of the Arkhangelsk Regional Administration

Forestry, timber, and pulp and paper. The Arkhan-gelsk Region is one of the largest timber producing regions of Russia. While the sector accounts for over 46,3% of total industrial output. Over 200 enterprises engage in timber procurement; 26 companies located mainly in Arkhangelsk, Onega, and Mezen represent the timber-processing sector. The Region's timber mills operate at 70% of capacity. Three major pulp and paper combines operate in the region: the Arkhangelsk, Kotlas (the largest in Russia), and Solombala.

Fuel. Fuel production is concentrated in the Nenetsky Autonomous District (an administrative district within the Arkhangelsk region), which is rich in

oil and gas (a detailed description is provided in the chapter on the Nenetsky Autonomous District).

Machine engineering and metal processing. Machine engineering is represented by defense enterprises. The Region is home to the Russian State Center for Nuclear Shipbuilding, which specializes in building, repairing, and refurbishing submarines, ships, and vessels of all types and purposes. The Center also builds offshore drilling rigs, including floating jack-up rigs for oil and gas drilling off Russian's Arctic coast, fishing trawlers, components for floating fish processing plants, tugs, cutters, and screw propellers. The Region's leading enterprises are FGUP PO Sevmash and FGUP MP Zvezdochka.

TABLE 4

Industry breakdown of industrial output in 1997–2002, % of total	1997	1998	1999	2000	2001	2002*
Industry	100.0	100.0	100.0	100.0	100.0	100.0
Forestry, timber, and pulp and paper	38.9	42.7	52.7	50.9	48.9	46.3
Fuel	11.5	7.8	14.0	15.0	12.6	17.6
Machine engineering and metal processing	12.7	16.8	12.5	14.6	15.7	14.5
Energy	19.3	17.5	8.1	7.2	10.2	9.7
Food and beverage	10.0	7.7	7.8	6.9	8.4	8.1
Construction materials	3.2	2.3	1.4	1.3	1.5	1.3
Light industry	0.7	0.4	0.3	1.3	0.4	0.8
Non-ferrous metals	0.2	0.1	0.2	0.3	0.3	0.3
Chemicals and petrochemicals	0.3	0.2	0.2	0.1	0.2	0.3
Flour, cereals, and mixed fodder	0.2	–	0.5	0.4	0.3	0.2
Ferrous metals	0.1	0.1	0.1	0.1	0.1	0.1

*Estimates of the Arkhangelsk Regional Administration

Energy. The region has 16 power stations with a total generation capacity of 19.3 GW. The three largest power stations belong to OAO Arkhenergo, an RAO UES of Russia company (the Arkhangelsk Thermal Power Station and the Severodvinsk TPS-1 and TPS-2).

Food and beverages. This sector is represented mainly by fishing companies. Fish processing is performed by the Arkhangelsk and Pechora (the town of Naryan-Mar) fish-processing plants, plus several smaller businesses. A new fish-processing mini-plant with a capacity of five tons of fish per day was recently put into operation. Several production lines manufactured by EMF Lebensmitteltechnik-Anlagenbau (Germany) have been installed at the plant.

Defense. The Arkhangelsk Region is home to specialized defense companies with high output and strong scientific potential, and also hosts the strategically important First State Test Space Ship Launch Site of the Ministry of the Defense at Plesetsk. The Plesetsk space center has long been one of the busiest space launch sites in the world, and has vast potential for expanding launching services in the future.

3.3. FUEL AND ENERGY BALANCE (OUTPUT AND CONSUMPTION PER RESOURCE)

The region's power stations produced 6.1 billion kWh in 2002, while regional consumption amounted to 7.5 billion kWh. Some 1.6 million tons of conventional fuel was consumed for electricity production. The Region's power generation facilities are mostly coal and fuel oil fired (70.7%). The Region's largest electricity consumers are industrial companies (55.8% of total electricity consumption) and the residential sector (12.7%). Heat energy output totaled 21.7 million Gcal in 2001.

3.4. TRANSPORT INFRASTRUCTURE

Roads. Most internal freight and passenger traffic is carried by road. The Arkhangelsk – Moscow Highway (M-8) plays an important role in the regional economy, as it provides road access to the rest of Russia and abroad. The Arkhangelsk Region has 7,118 kilometers of paved public highway.

Railroads. The Region has 1,764 kilometers of railroad linking Arkhangelsk – Konosha – Vologda – Moscow, Kotlas – Konosha – Vologda, Arkhangelsk – Obozerskaya – Murmansk, Kotlas-Kargodogu – Kirov, and Arkhangelsk – Karpogory.

Airports. The Region's air transportation sector carries out passenger services, delivery of urgent freight to geological expeditions, and forestry protection functions. The airport at Arkhangelsk is currently undergoing reconstruction with a view to upgrading its capacity to enable it to service aircraft of up to 400 tons.

Seaports. The port of Arkhangelsk is Russia's oldest commercial port. Its docks are the second longest in the world after those of London. The port services commercial, oil, fishing, and other vessels, and has its own fleet of icebreakers, which keep waterways open year-round for Russian and foreign ships. The port's annual freight turnover is some 1 million tons, but can be increased to 8 million tons. The port services various types of freight, including containers, metals, carton, pulp, oil and oil products, and bulk goods.

3.5. MAIN NATURAL RESOURCES: RESERVES AND EXTRACTION IN 2002

Timber. The Arkhangelsk Region is rich in forests, which cover some 230,000 square km of its territory. Coniferous species prevail, with fir trees accounting for 55.7% and pine for 26.6% of total reserves. The commonest deciduous species are birch trees – 16.3% and aspen – 1.1%. The industrial reserve of timber is estimated at 1,580 million cubic meters.

The Region is also rich in **mineral resources.** The Region boasts an efficient mineral resource extraction and processing infrastructure. The Nenetsky Autonomous District produces oil and gas, while the Plesetsk District is home to bauxite extraction. Industrial production of dia-

monds is due to commence shortly at the Lomonosov deposit, which has the third largest proven reserves of diamonds in the world. The Region also has considerable deposits of limestone, dolomites, cement ingredients, gypsum and anhydrides, peat, sand, clay and fusible loams, construction stone, underground water, manganese, copper, zinc, lead, amber, and agates for jewelry.

Fuel and energy sector production and consumption trends, 1997–2002						TABLE 5
	1997	1998	1999	2000	2001	2002
Electricity output, billion kWh	5.5	5.6	5.5	5.7	6.3	6.1
Electricity consumption, billion kWh	6.6	6.6	6.9	7.1	7.4	7.5
Natural gas consumption, billion cubic meters	1,602.8	1,703.4	1,704.7	1,767.7	1,856.7	2,013.7

4. TRADE OPPORTUNITIES

4.1.MAIN GOODS PRODUCED IN THE REGION
Forestry. 2002 output of industrial lumber reached 8.3 million cubic meters, sawn timber – 1.9 million cubic meters, plywood – 66,000 cubic meters, paper – 320,600 tons, merchantable pulp – 727,900 tons, and carton – 674,300 tons.

Food and beverages. Fish and seafood form the basis of the local food industry. In 2002, the Region produced 123,500 tons of seafood and 2 million cans of fish. Companies in the Region produced 925,500 decaliters of alcoholic beverages and 267,000 decaliters of beer. Vegetable output is dominated by potatoes – 403,500 tons.

4.2. EXPORTS, INCLUDING EXTRA-CIS
The Arkhangelsk Region's export to extra-CIS countries amounted to $757.1 million in 2000; exports to CIS totaled $12.5 million. The figures for 2001 were $606.2 million and $14.6 million, respectively, and for 2002 – $625 million and $31.4 million. The Region's major exports are timber and pulp (48.6% of total exports), paper (18.2%), crude oil (18.1%), and vessels (12.1%). Major importers of the Region's products include Poland (11.2% of

total exports), Ireland (9.9%), Panama (9.8%), the Netherlands (9.8%), and Germany (8.6%).

4.3. IMPORTS, INCLUDING EXTRA-CIS
2000 imports from extra-CIS countries amounted to $93.9 million; imports from CIS countries totaled $10.1 million. The respective figures for 2001 were $108.7 million and $5.5 million, respectively, and for 2002 – $142.6 million and $5 million. Machinery dominates imports, accounting for 65% of the total in 2001. The Region's major imports include ship and submarine equipment (boilers, reactors, electrical equipment – 32.3% of total imports), ships and boats (23.9%), and metal goods (7.7%). The main exporters to the Region are the UK (25.3%), Finland (12.5%), Sweden (10.8%), and Germany (8.0%).

4.4. MAJOR REGIONAL EXPORT
AND IMPORT ENTITIES
Owing to the specific features of trade in the Region, export and import transactions are performed mainly by industrial companies, including OAO Kotlas Pulp and Paper Plant, OAO Arkhangelsk Pulp and Paper Plant, OOO Titan, and OAO North Sea Shipping Line.

5. INVESTMENT OPPORTUNITIES

5.1. INVESTMENTS IN 1992–2002
(BY INDUSTRY SECTOR), INCLUDING
FOREIGN INVESTMENTS
The following factors determine the investment appeal of the Arkhangelsk region:
  • Its developed transport infrastructure (a seaport, an international airport, and an international transport corridor);
  • Legislation providing support for investment (guaranteed investor rights, preferential taxation);

  • Its natural resources (local supplies of timber and mineral resources).
5.2. CAPITAL INVESTMENT
According to 2002 data, industry accounts for the lion's share of capital investment (77.7%). The bulk of capital investment is channeled into the fuel and timber sectors. Transport and communications account for 12.1% of total investment. In 2002, investment in these industries amounted to 75.6 million.

Capital investment by industry sector, $ million						TABLE 6
	1997	1998	1999	2000	2001	2002
Total capital investment	464.9	238.4	162.9	372.2	528.1	626.3
Including major industries (% of total):						
Industry	33.5	22.8	35.0	48.6	56.7	77.7
Agriculture and forestry	3.6	4.5	2.6	1.1	0.6	1.0
Construction	1.3	1.7	0.7	1.1	1.8	1.1
Transport and communication	41.1	38.7	36.3	24.2	24.1	12.1
Other	20.5	32.3	25.4	25.0	16.8	8.1

Foreign investment trends in 1996–2002						TABLE 7
	1996–1997	1998	1999	2000	2001	2002
Foreign investment, $ million	31.4	22.8	348.6	39.0	50.5	272.4
Including FDI, $ million	18.9	10.5	0.4	1.4	1.4	96.5

5.3. MAJOR ENTERPRISES (INCLUDING ENTERPRISES WITH FOREIGN INVESTMENT)

The Arkhangelsk Region is home to 181 companies with foreign investment, including 50 manufacturing enterprises. The Region's largest enterprises with foreign investment are JV Polyarnoe Siyanie, OAO Arkhenergo, OAO Arkhangelsk Pulp and Paper Plant, OAO Kotlas Pulp and Paper Plant, and ZAO Shalakusha Timber Processing. Wholly foreign-owned enterprises include OOO Sovdam (Germany), OOO Sofar (France, Latvia), ZAO Arctic Nenets Limited (Cyprus), ZAO Planet (Finland), and OOO Wood & Us (USA).

Largest enterprises of the Arkhangelsk Region	TABLE 8
COMPANY	SECTOR
OAO Kotlas Pulp and Paper Plant	Pulp and paper
OAO Arkhangelsk Pulp and Paper Plant	Pulp and paper
OAO Arkhenergo	Energy
FGUP PO Severodvinsk Machinery Company	Shipbuilding
FGUP PO Arctic	Shipbuilding
OAO North Sea Ship Line	Water transport

5.4. MOST ATTRACTIVE SECTORS FOR INVESTMENT

According to the experts and the Regional Administration, the forestry, timber processing, pulp and paper, and food and beverages sectors offer the strongest investment appeal. The defense sector conversion project also present certain interest. The project envisages the production of ice-class oil drilling rigs for use on the Barents Sea shelf and the construction of fishing trawlers.

5.5. CURRENT LEGISLATION ON INVESTOR TAX EXEMPTIONS AND PRIVILEGES

Investors conducting investment projects listed in the Region's investment program are eligible for tax privileges during the payback period of the project (up to a five year maximum) with respect to property and profit taxes.

Tax credits for investments are provided for the period specified in the legislation. Tax credits are activated as soon as the investor invests profit into the object specified by the investment tax credit agreement.

Regional entities responsible for raising investment		TABLE 9
ENTITY	ADDRESS	PHONE, FAX, E-MAIL
GUP Investment Company Arkhangelsk	12, ul. Voskresenskaya, Arkhangelsk, Arkhangelsk Region, 163000	Phone: (8182) 65 2127 Fax: (8182) 65 7544 E-mail: Progect@atnet.ru

II

N O R T H - W E S T E R N F E D E R A L D I S T R I C T

5.6. FEDERAL AND REGIONAL ECONOMIC AND SOCIAL DEVELOPMENT PROGRAMS FOR THE ARKHANGELSK REGION

Federal targeted programs. The Arkhangelsk Region is implementing a significant number of federal targeted programs, including the Program for Support of Social and Economic Development of the North, the most important program, which envisages development and support to small and medium size businesses in a number of the Region's areas regarded as areas of the Extreme North, assistance to industrial companies of the Arkhangelsk Region in terms of stabilization of their operations, exploration, prospecting, and use of diamond deposits in the Region, and steps to be taken in order to further develop the seaport of Arkhangelsk.

Regional programs. The current Economic and Social Development Program for the Arkhangelsk Region for 2001–2005 was developed by the Arkhangelsk Regional Administration together with representatives of businesses, research organizations, and public associations with a view to improving living standards in the Region. The Program takes a two-pronged sector and geographical approach to the task of developing the Region's economy and social system. The Program consists of 16 sub-programs broken down by sector and more than 24 programs of economic and social development for individual regional municipalities. To implement the industrial part of the program, the Region will need some $2.8 billion in financing.

6. INVESTMENT PROJECTS

Industry sector and project description	1) Expected results 2) Amount and term of investment 3) Form of financing[1] 4) Documentation[2]	Contact information
1	2	3
MACHINE ENGINEERING AND METAL PROCESSING		
21R001 ● ▲		State Unitary Company PO Sevmash
Output of high-pressure vessels for the oil and gas sector. Project goal: to produce and supply high-pressure vessels to Russian oil and gas companies.	1) Projected capacity of 80 vessels/year 2) $3.5 million/2 years 3) L 4) FS	58, Arkhangelskoe Shosse, Severodvinsk, Arkhangelsk Region, 164500 Phone: (81842) 94 717, 61 703, 94 601 Fax: (81842) 61 441 E-mail: spm@sevmash.ru David Guseinovich Pashaev, CEO
21R002 ● ▲ ◆		OAO Grumant Fleet
Building of fishing trawlers. Project goal: to renovate the regional trawler fleet.	1) 7 vessels 2) $42 million/3.5 years 3) L 4) FS, BP	15, Nikolsky Pr., Arkhangelsk, Arkhangelsk Region, 163020 Phone/fax: (8182) 23 31 70 E-mail: yagry@atnet.ru Alexander Pavlovich Antipin, CEO State Unitary Company MP Zvezdochka 12, Mashinostroitel Pr., Severodvinsk, Arkhangelsk Region, 164509 Phone: (81842) 79 360, 70 297 Fax: (81842) 72 850 E-mail: info@star.ru Nikolai Yakovlevich Kalistratov, CEO
FORESTRY, TIMBER, AND PULP AND PAPER		
21R003 ● ◆		OAO Solombala Timber Mill,
Launching of production of furniture plywood boards. Project goal: to expand exports and deepen processing.	1) Exports of 12,100 cubic meters of plywood boards 2) $1.2 million/4–6 months 3) L 4) BP	1/1, Dobrolyubov St., Arkhangelsk, Arkhangelsk region, 163012 Phone: (8182) 22 82 87, 22 01 03 Fax: (8182) 65 75 67 E-mail: sldk@sldk.ru Ivan Alexeevich Novikov, CEO

[1] L – Loan, E – Equity, Leas. – Leasing, JV – Joint Venture
[2] BP – Business Plan, FS – Feasibility Study

1	2	3

21P004 ● ◆

		ZAO Timber Mill No. 25
Construction of a timber mill.	1) 220,000 cubic meters/year	26, ul. Postysheva, Arkhangelsk,
Project goal: to increase	2) €14 million/n/a	Arkhangelsk Region, 163025
output of lumber.	3) L	Phone: (8182) 29 3100, 23 1358
	4) BP	Fax: (8182) 29 3062
		E-mail: general@lesz25.atnet.ru
		Mikhail Nikolaevich Papylev, CEO

21R005 ● ◆

		OOO Furniture Factory Severny Dom
Development and refurbishment	1) 10-fold increase in output	41/31, Zheleznodorozhnaya ul.,
of wood furniture production.	(turnover of $2.3 million/year)	Severodvinsk, Arkhangelsk
Project goal: to increase output.	2) $0.3 million/3 years	Region, 164521
	3) L ($0.1 million)	Phone/fax: (81845) 51 912
	4) BP	Fax: (81842) 68 690
		E-mail: sevdom@atnet.ru
		Vyacheslav Yanovich Enson, CEO

21P006 ● ▲

		OOO PKP Titan
Launching of coated paper production	1) Output of 150,000 tons/year	7, Primorskaya ul., Arkhangelsk,
at OOO Arkhangelsk Pulp and Paper Plant.	2) $217 million/n/a	Arkhangelsk Region, 163061
Project goal: to expand the range	3) L	Phone: (8182) 24 3510
of products.	4) FS	Fax: (8182) 20 5831
		E-mail: titans@atnet.ru
		Sergei Pavlovich Kozlov, CEO

21R007 ● ▲

		OOO PKP Titan
Production of components for European	1) Output growth by 6,000	7, Primorskaya ul., Arkhangelsk,
standard trays at OAO Shalakushsky	cubic meters/year	Arkhangelsk Region, 163061
Timber Plant.	2) $1.7 million/n/a	Phone: (8182) 24 3510
Project goal: to increase output	3) L	Fax: (8182) 20 5831
and improve quality (drying machine).	4) Preliminary FS	E-mail: titans@atnet.ru;
		Sergei Pavlovich Kozlov, CEO

21R008 ● ◆

		OOO Primorsky Timber Mill
Development of a modern wood-cutting	1) Output 18,200 cubic meters/year	27, Arkhangelskoe Shosse, Severo-
and wood-processing enterprise.	2) $14.5 million/n/a	dvinsk, Arkhangelsk Region, 164500
Project goal: to increase output	3) L ($14.5 million)	Phone: (81845) 50 273
and improve quality.	4) BP	Alexei Valeryevich Skalepov, CEO

21P009 ● ◆

		State Unitary Company
Development of new non-flammable	1) Total sales $27.3 million (2004–2010)	MP Zvezdochka
materials and introduction of modern	2) $4.1 million/10–12 months	12, pr. Mashinostroiteley, Severo-
furniture manufacturing technologies	3) L ($3.6 million)	dvinsk, Arkhangelsk Region, 164509
to existing operations.	4) BP	Phone: (81842) 79 360, 70 297
Project goal: to expand the range		Fax: (81842) 72 850
of output and improve quality.		E-mail: info@star.ru
		Nikolai Yakovlevich Kalistratov, CEO

GLASS AND PORCELAIN

21R010 ● ◆

		State Unitary Company Severny Reid
Production of decorative glass dishes	1) Output of 2 million products/year	46, ul. K. Marksa, Severodvinsk,
at State Unitary Company Severny Reid.	(Sales $1.9 million/year)	Arkhangelsk Region, 164514
Project goal: to increase output and range	2) $0.9 million/1 year	Phone: (81842) 38 960, 37 578
of products and improve product quality.	3) L ($0.9 million)	Fax: (81842) 38 758
	4) BP	E-mail: reid@atnet.ru,
		contact@reid.atnet.ru
		Sergei Iosifovich Barmin, CEO

II

NORTH-WESTERN FEDERAL DISTRICT

1	2	3

FOOD AND BEVERAGES

21R011 ● ★ ❖ ▲

Production of dry gluten and ethanol. Project goal: to improve the quality of flour, and increase output of ethanol for liquor sector.

1) Output of 6 tons of dry gluten and 2,000 decaliters of ethanol/day
2) $6.3 million/n/a
3) Joint Venture, L, Leas.
4) FS

OAO Arkhangelsk Bakery
Zharovihinsky Promuzel, Arkhangelsk,
Arkhangelsk Region, 163016
Phone/fax: (8182) 61 4444
Fax: (8182) 62 8440
E-mail: akhp@atnet.ru
Alexander Mikhailovich Lyalyakin
CEO

TRANSPORT INFRASTRUCTURE

21R012 ● ◆ ▲

Construction of the Nyuksenitsa – Arkhangelsk gas pipeline. Project goal: to provide regional companies and residential services with natural gas.

1) 4500 million cubic meters/year
2) $300 million/n/a
3) L
4) BP, FS

OAO Severgaz
7, Primorskaya ul., Arkhangelsk,
Arkhangelsk Region, 163061
Phone/fax: (8182) 20 6985, 20 6616
E-mail: severgaz@awah.ru,
severgaz@arh.ru;
Vladimir Viktorovich Gudovichev, CEO
Moscow representative office
30/7, ul. Petrovka, Moscow, 127006
Phone: (095) 200 1710
Fax: (095) 209 0723

21R013 ● ▼ ◆

Reconstruction of the Arkhangelsk airport. Project goal: to transform the airport into a world-class facility compliant with international standards, to accept large aircrafts of up to 400 tons.

1) Annual increase in freight turnover by 10%, passenger turnover by 7%
2) $66.2 million/8–9 years
3) L
4) Investment Proposal, FS, Master plan developed by ASTA (Germany)

OAO Arkhangelsk Airport
8, Talagi, Arkhangelsk,
Arkhangelsk Region, 163047
Phone: (8182) 21 5172, 21 5514
Fax: (8182) 64 0913
E-mail: arhap@atnet.ru
Yury Vasilyevich Vasilyev, CEO

21R014 ● ▲

Reconstruction of the Solovki airport. Project goal: to accept and service new types of aircraft (An 24 and Il 114).

1) Annual growth of passenger turnover by 17,000 people
2) $2.9 million/16 years
3) L
4) FS

Solovki Airport
2nd Arkhangelsk Aviation Group
Solovki, Solovki District,
Arkhangelsk Region, 164409
Phone (8182) 65 2544, 65 3038
Fax: 65 6589
E-mail: ludvik@dvinaland.ru
(Department of Transport and
Communication of the Arkhangelsk
Regional Administration).

21R015 ● ◆

Construction of the Karpogory – Vendinga railroad. Project goal: to service freight traffic between the Republic of Komi and the Arkhangelsk and Murmansk seaports (with subsequent construction of railroad links to the Urals, Siberia, Central Asia, Kazakhstan, and north-east regions of Russia).

1) Freight traffic of 17.7 million and 5.7 million tons northbound and southbound, respectively
2) $120.4 million/n/a
3) L ($103.8 million)
4) BP

OAO Belkomur
108, ul. Internatsionalnaya,
Syktyvkar, Republic of Komi, 167610
Phone: (8212) 44 7721, 44 7729
Fax: (8212) 44 7771
E-mail: belkomur@online.ru
Valery Nikolaevich Naboichikov, CEO
Brach of OAO Belkomur
17, ul. K. Libnekhta, Arkhangelsk,
Arkhangelsk region, 163061
Phone: (8182) 64 1195
Fax: (8182) 21 1770
E-mail: belkomur@arh.ru;
Vladimir Ivanovich Fedotov,
Branch Director

1	2	3

ECOLOGY

21P016 ● ▲

Reconstruction of common purification systems of the Solombala Pulp and Paper Mill, the city of Arkhangelsk, and the Arkhangelsk Hydrolysis Plant. Project goal: to improve the ecological situation in the region, and reduce water purification costs.

1). Compliance with environmental requirements
2) $7 million/3 years
3) L ($5 million)
4) FS

OAO Solombala Pulp and Paper Plant
4, ul. Kirovskaya, Arkhangelsk,
Arkhangelsk Region, 163059
Phone: (8182) 23 0525, 29 9624
Fax: (8182) 23 0494
E-mail: office@sppm.ru
Nikolai Piterimovich Lvov, CEO

JEWELRY

21P017 ● ◆ ▲

Extension of diamond cutting operations at Federal State Unitary Company MP Zvezdochka.
Project goal: to open up new opportunities in diamond-cutting, start jewelry production.

1) Output of 62,130 carat diamonds
   and 197,300 pieces of jewelry a year
2) $5.3 million/14–15 months
3) L
4) FS, BP, work project

Federal State Unitary Company
MP Zvezdochka
12, pr. Mashinostroiteley,
Severodvinsk,
Arkhangelsk region, 164509
Phone: (81842) 79 360, 70 297
Fax: (81842) 72 850
E-mail: info@star.ru
Nikolai Yakovlevich Kalistratov, CEO

II

NORTH-WESTERN FEDERAL DISTRICT

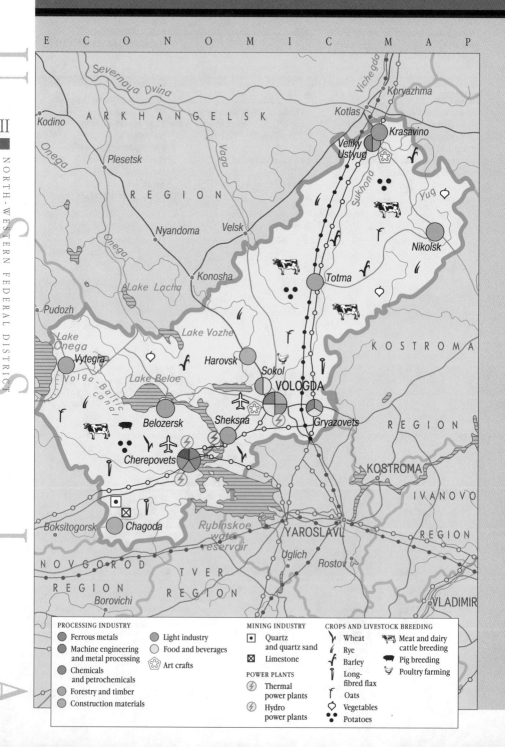

22. VOLOGDA REGION [35]

ECONOMIC MAP

I am pleased to be given this opportunity to introduce the Vologda Region, an industrial region in the north of Russia. The Vologda Region is a dynamically developing region located within the North-Western Federal District. All of its sectors – ferrous metals, chemicals, timber, machine engineering, transport, and agriculture – offer significant development potential.

While there is no doubt that the Region's stable economic growth trends can only strengthen, domestic and foreign investment and trade and economic cooperation with international business will accelerate this growth.

Regional legislation has been in place for over five years now that sets forth priority areas for investment and seeks to create a favorable investment climate. More and more companies in the Region are obtaining external investment or internal financing for technical upgrading and development.

The Region's social stability and commitment to partnership bode well for investors. Investors are understandably reluctant to invest in regions prone to industrial disputes and strikes. These manifestations of social tension have been absent from the Vologda Region for many years now. The Vologda Region is among Russia's top ten regions for minimum investment risk, and in terms of social risk factors, it is the third safest region in Russia.

Over the past three years, $1 billion has been invested into the regional economy, the bulk of which has come from domestic investors. The conclusion to be drawn is obvious: if domestic investors have faith in the Region, foreign investors will soon follow suit. And we already have several proposals. The Vologda Region's economy is becoming more and more attractive to business.

The Region is intensifying its participation in the economic integration of Russian regions and is becoming a center of business activity in the North-Western District and beyond thanks to the annual Russian Forests and Russian Flax international exhibitions and the Veliky Ustyug, Birthplace of Father Christmas project. We invite Russian and foreign partners to actively participate in these projects.

I am confident that learning more about the investment projects we offer will help build trust, respect, and mutually beneficial cooperation between the Vologda Region and other Russian regions, the CIS and beyond.

Vyacheslav Pozgalev,
GOVERNOR OF THE VOLOGDA REGION,
HEAD OF THE VOLOGDA REGIONAL GOVERNMENT

II

NORTH-WESTERN FEDERAL DISTRICT

1. GENERAL INFORMATION

1.1. GEOGRAPHY

Situated in the north of European Russia, the Vologda Region covers a total area of 145,700 square kilometers. To the north, the Region borders the Arkhangelsk Region, to the east – the Kirov Region, to the south – the Kostroma and Yaroslavl Regions, to the south-west – the Tver and Novgorod Regions, to the west – the Leningrad Region, and to the north-west – the Republic of Karelia.

1.2. CLIMATE

The Vologda Region enjoys a temperate continental climate.

The average air temperature in January is –7.7°C, rising to +20.1°C in July. Average annual precipitation exceeds 480 mm.

1.3. POPULATION

According to preliminary 2002 census results, the total population of the Vologda Region amounted to 1,270,000 people. The economically active population was 672,000 people. While 2002 official unemployment was 2.2%, the actual rate is 5.9%.

Demographically speaking, some 60.6% are of working age, 18.4% are below the statutory working age, and 21% are beyond the statutory working age.

The Region's major urban centers are Cherepovets with 312,200 inhabitants, Vologda with 292,800 inhabitants, Sokol with 43,000 inhabitants, Veliky Ustyug with 33,400 inhabitants, and Gryazovets with 16,200 inhabitants.

Population							TABLE 1
	1992	1997	1998	1999	2000	2001	2002
Total population, '000	1,358	1,339	1,334	1,328	1,319	1,311	1,270
Economically active population, '000	686	625	631	672	673	665	672

2. ADMINISTRATION

2, ul. Gertsena, Vologda, Vologda Region, 160035. Phone: 7 (8172) 72 0764. Fax: 7 (8172) 25 1554, 25 1454
E-mail: avo@vologda-oblast.ru; http://www.vologda-oblast.ru

NAME	POSITION	CONTACT INFORMATION
Vyacheslav Yevgenyevich POZGALEV	Governor of the Vologda Region, Head of the Vologda Regional Government	Phone: (8172) 72 2380
Nikolai Vladimirovich KOSTYGOV	First Deputy Governor of the Vologda Region for Economy, Finance, Social and Economic Development, and Municipal Relations	Phone: (8172) 25 0865
Alexei Nikolaevich PLEKHANOV	First Deputy Governor of the Vologda Region for Industry, Construction, Energy, Transport and Communications, Housing and Communal Services, Small and Medium Enterprise, Trade, and Interregional and External Relations	Phone: (8172) 72 6354
Sergei Mikhailovich GROMOV	First Deputy Governor of the Vologda Region for the Agroindustrial Sector and Food Resources	Phone: (8172) 72 0259
Galina Sergeevna IZOTOVA	First Deputy Governor of the Vologda Region, Head of the Financial Department in charge of Financial Bodies and Compliance with Uniform Budget Principles, Funding of Production and Social and Cultural Spheres, and Developing Financial Base for Comprehensive Social and Economic Development of the Region	Phone: (8172) 72 0232
Leonid Genrikhovich IOGMAN	Deputy Governor of the Vologda Region, Head of the Department of Economy	Phone: (8172) 72 8470
Anatoly Alexeevich PAK	Deputy Governor of the Vologda Region, Head of the Property Department	Phone: (8172) 72 0572

3. ECONOMIC POTENTIAL

3.1. 1997–2002 GROSS REGIONAL PRODUCT (GRP). INDUSTRY BREAKDOWN

The 2002 gross regional product amounted to $2,549.4 million, which constitutes 6.5% growth year-on-year. Per capita GRP amounted to $1,833 in 2001 and $1,953 in 2002.

3.2. INDUSTRIAL OUTPUT IN 1997–2002 FOR MAJOR SECTORS OF ECONOMY

The leading industrial sectors of the Vologda Region are ferrous metals, chemicals, machine engineering and metal processing.

Ferrous metals. This sector accounts for 60% of total industrial output. Major companies within

GRP trends in 1997–2002						TABLE 2
	1997	1998	1999	2000	2001*	2002*
GRP in current prices, $ million	3,409.5	2,422.8	1,886.8	2,433.5	2,394.2	2,549.4

*Estimates of the Vologda Regional Government

GRP industry breakdown in 1997–2002, % of total						TABLE 3
	1997	1998	1999	2000	2001*	2002*
GRP	100.0	100.0	100.0	100.0	100.0	100.0
Industry	47.8	53.3	55.1	58.4	45.5	44.5
Agriculture	7.8	7.1	9.5	7.1	8.6	8.3
Construction	6.2	6.1	5.1	5.5	6.1	6.4
Transport and communications	8.4	7.6	5.7	6.0	9.6	10.4
Trade and public catering	7.8	6.6	9.4	9.6	10.9	10.6
Other	21.5	18.6	11.9	11.9	16.2	15.7
Net taxes on output	0.5	0.7	3.3	1.5	3.1	4.1

*Estimates of the Vologda Regional Government

Industry breakdown of industrial output in 1997–2002, % of total						TABLE 4
	1997	1998	1999	2000	2001	2002*
Industry	100.0	100.0	100.0	100.0	100.0	100.0
Ferrous metals	58.7	55.8	65.6	66.3	58.5	60.0
Energy	10.9	10.2	6.7	6.3	8.2	8.6
Forestry, timber, and pulp and paper	5.9	5.8	7.7	6.3	7.6	7.4
Machine engineering and metal processing	6.1	5.2	3.4	3.5	4.7	7.3
Food and beverages	6.5	7.0	7.2	5.7	7.5	6.9
Chemicals and petrochemicals	7.6	11.8	5.6	8.7	9.6	6.5
Building materials	1.4	1.4	0.9	0.8	0.9	0.8
Flour, cereals, and mixed fodder	1.1	0.6	0.5	0.6	0.8	0.5
Light industry	0.7	0.6	1.1	0.7	0.7	0.7
Glass and porcelain	0.2	0.2	0.2	0.4	0.6	0.6
Non-ferrous metals	0.2	0.3	0.3	0.2	0.3	0.1

*Estimates of the Vologda Regional Government

II

NORTH-WESTERN FEDERAL DISTRICT

the sector are OAO Severstal (rolled ferrous metals) and OAO Cherepovets Steel Rolling Plant (graded cold-rolled steel, steel profile, and regular wire).

Forestry, timber, and pulp and paper. The share of this sector is 7.4% of total industrial output. Over a thousand companies operate in this sector, including 70 large and medium companies, some 300 small enterprises, and over 700 industrial shops on non-industrial companies. The main types of output are industrial timber, lumber, pulp, paper, cardboard, and timber fiber and plywood board. The Region recently launched new lumber facilities with a capacity of 150,000 cubic meters of lumber.

Machine engineering and metal processing. Comprised of 36 large and medium companies, this sector accounts for 7.3% of total industrial output. The main types of goods are rolling bearings, timber cutting machinery, agricultural machinery and equipment, and optical mechanical and electronic instruments.

Food and beverages. The Region hosts some 300 food and beverage companies. The sector accounts for 6.9% of total industrial output. The leading sub-sectors are meat processing, butter and cheese, and dairy products. Other developed sub-sectors include fisheries. Food companies in the Region produce the whole range of dairy and meat products.

Chemicals and petrochemicals. This sector accounts for 6.5% of total industrial output. Major companies within the sector are OAO Cherepovetsky Azot (ammonia and ammonia nitrate), OAO Ammophos (ammophos, diammonium phosphate, and diammophoska), and OAO Agro-Cherepovets (carbamide).

Light industry. The Region is home to some 200 light industry companies. The sector accounts for 0.7% of total industrial output. Among the largest companies are OAO Vologda Textile (flax fabric), OAO Severlen (flax fabric), and OAO Vologda Style (clothes).

Agriculture. Arable lands cover 10% of the Region's area. Dairy cattle rearing is the leading agricultural sector. The Region grows mainly rye and spring wheat, but also barley, oats, pea, potatoes, and vegetables. The Region's primary commercial crop is flax.

3.3. FUEL AND ENERGY BALANCE (OUTPUT AND CONSUMPTION PER RESOURCE)

The Vologda Region is an energy deficit region with some 50% of electricity imported from the adjacent Kostroma, Kirov, Tver, Yaroslavl, and Leningrad regional energy systems.

Fuel and energy sector production and consumption trends, 1997–2002						TABLE 5
	1997	1998	1999	2000	2001	2002*
Electricity output, billion kWh	5.3	5.6	6.2	6.2	5.8	6.1
Electricity consumption, billion kWh	10.6	11.5	12.0	12.5	12.5	12.6
Oil product consumption, '000 tons of conventional fuel	438.0	415.0	399.0	389.0	376.0	397.0

*Estimates of the Vologda Regional Government

3.4. TRANSPORT INFRASTRUCTURE

Roads. The Region has 13,500 kilometers of paved public highway. Two federal highways, Moscow – Arkhangelsk and Vologda – Novaya Ladoga, pass through the Region.

Railroads. The Vologda Region has 768 kilometers of railroads. Two main railroads, Moscow – Arkhangelsk and St. Petersburg – Yekaterinburg, cross the Region.

Airports. The Vologda airport is capable of accepting Yak 40 type of aircraft. The village of Kipelovo (77 kilometers south-west of Vologda) is equipped with a runway capable of accepting large aircraft of any type. The Cherepovets airport can accept Tu 134, Yak 42, An 12 and other aircraft up to 70 tons.

River transport. The Volga – Baltic waterway passes through the Region. Access to waterways enables companies in the western part of the Region to transport goods directly from their warehouses abroad by river-sea class vessels, thus avoiding expensive transshipping at the Baltic seaports. The Region has some 1,600 kilometers of inland waterways.

3.5. MAIN NATURAL RESOURCES: RESERVES AND EXTRACTION IN 2002

The Vologda Region's main natural resources are forests and water.

Forests. The Vologda Region is thickly forested, with 11.6 million hectares, or 79.6% of its area, under forest cover. Total timber reserves exceed 1.5 billion cubic meters, or 1.8% of Russia's total. The Region is one of Russia's leading regions in terms of timber output.

Water resources. The Region is extremely rich in water reserves, with 1,323 rivers, 4,240 lakes, and five water reservoirs.

Mineral resources. The Region has considerable reserves of non-ore minerals: sand, gravel, brick and roofing raw materials, flux limestone, dolomites, peat, and sapropel.

The Region has 590 explored deposits of sand, gravel, clay, and lime, over 2,000 peat deposits exceeding one square kilometer each (total reserve of over 5.5 billion tons), and 14 deposits of sapropel. The Vysokovskoe building sand deposit with reserves of 9,642,000 cubic meters is located in the Ust-Kubinsky District.

4. TRADE OPPORTUNITIES

4.1. MAIN GOODS PRODUCED
IN THE REGION
The main goods produced in the Region as of 2002 were:

Ferrous metals:
- Steel – 9.7 million tons;
- Iron – 7.7 million tons;
- Finished ferrous metal roll – 8.3 million tons;

Chemicals:
- Mineral fertilizers – 1,640,000 tons;

Machine engineering:
- Ball bearings – 30 million items;

Forestry and timber:
- Industrial timber – 5.7 million cubic meters;
- Lumber – 722,000 cubic meters;
- Plywood – 308,700 conventional cubic meters;
- Timber-fiber tight board – 24.8 million conventional square meters;

Light industry:
- Flax fabric – 10.4 million square meters;
- Knitwear – 1,194,600 items;

Food and beverages:
- Meat, including category one sub-products – 27,500 tons;
- Butter – 4,000 tons;
- Dairy products in terms of milk – 169,000 tons.

4.2. EXPORTS, INCLUDING EXTRA-CIS
The Vologda Region's exports to extra-CIS countries amounted to $1,505.4 million in 2000, with exports to the CIS totaling $12.8 million. The respective figures for 2001 were $1,099.4 million and $23.2 million, and for 2002, $1,254.7 million and $48.1 million.

The main types of goods exported by the Region are metals (4,284,200 tons) and chemical fertilizers (2,209,700 tons) produced in Cherepovets, Vologda's machine engineering output (6,778,500 bearings), and timber and plywood (2,699,400 cubic meters).

As of 2002, major importers of the Region's products included Switzerland (14% of total exports), China (8.6%), the USA (6.4%), South Korea (5.5%), Finland (5.2%), Germany (4%), Thailand and Turkey (3% each), Italy and Nigeria (2.8% each), Mexico (2.6%), the UK (2.4%), and Saudi Arabia (1.9%).

4.3. IMPORTS, INCLUDING EXTRA-CIS
2000 imports from extra-CIS countries amounted to $96.6 million, with imports from CIS countries totaling $30.2 million. The respective figures for 2001 were $117.5 million and $25.1 million, and for 2002 – $167.7 million and $22.4 million.

The bulk of the Region's 2002 imports was represented by machinery, ferrous and non-ferrous metals, and petrochemicals.

The main exporters to the Region as of 2002 were: Germany (13.8% of total exports), China (12.6%), Ukraine (11.1%), the UK (10%), France (9.9%), Canada (8.2%), the USA (6.8%), Italy (5.7%), Belgium (3.2%), and the Netherlands (2.9%).

Major regional export and import entities		TABLE 6
ENTITY	ADDRESS	PHONE, FAX, E-MAIL
The Vologda Chamber of Industry and Commerce	15, ul. Lermontova, Vologda, Vologda Region, 160035	Phone: (8172) 72 8180 Fax: (8172) 72 1480 E-mail: grant@vologda.ru

5. INVESTMENT OPPORTUNITIES

5.1. INVESTMENTS IN 1992–2002
(BY INDUSTRY SECTOR), INCLUDING
FOREIGN INVESTMENTS
The following factors determine the investment appeal of the Vologda Region:
- Its advantageous geographic location and proximity to sales markets;
- Its developed transport and industrial infrastructure;
- Legislation providing support for investment activities (protection of investor rights and preferential tax treatment);
- Organizational and financial support for investment projects and safety guarantees provided by the executive authorities;
- Highly qualified workforce.

5.2. CAPITAL
INVESTMENT
Industry accounts for the lion's share of capital investment (56%).

5.3. MAJOR ENTERPRISES
(INCLUDING ENTERPRISES
WITH FOREIGN INVESTMENT)
Some 250 companies with foreign investment are represented in the Region. Among the largest companies are OAO Severstal, OAO Pokrovsky Glass Plant, OAO Elektrosvyaz, ZAO Amko, OAO Kipelovo Timber Plant, OOO PLO Monzales, OAO Vologda Baby Food Plant, OOO Van Leer Vologda, OOO Estpeel, and ZAO Trading House TAT.

Capital investment by industry sector, $ million

TABLE 7

	1997	1998	1999	2000	2001	2002
Total capital investment	531.5	359.6	246.6	305.5	354.1	396.8
Including major industries (% of total):						
Industry	43.3	44.4	42.4	40.3	50.7	56.0
Agriculture and forestry	2.5	4.8	4.9	6.4	6.7	6.4
Construction	1.6	3.1	1.4	1.5	2.8	1.4
Transport and communications	22.7	21.1	29.2	30.4	22.2	22.2
Trade and public catering	0.7	1.2	1.3	1.6	1.3	2.3
Other	29.2	25.4	20.8	19.8	16.3	11.7

Foreign investment trends in 1996–2002

TABLE 8

	1996–1997	1998	1999	2000	2001	2002
Foreign investment, $ million	20.4	7.7	6.7	19.9	29.6	31.6
Including FDI, $ million	19.3	0.7	5.6	9.2	0.3	6.6

Largest enterprises of the Vologda Region

TABLE 9

COMPANY	INDUSTRY, SECTOR
OAO Vologdaenergo	Energy
OAO Severstal	Ferrous metals
OAO Cherepovets Rolled Steel Plant	Ferrous metals
OAO Ammophos	Chemicals
OAO Cherepovetsky Azot	Chemicals
ZAO Agro-Cherepovets	Chemicals
ZAO Vologda Bearing Plant	Machine engineering and metal processing
OOO SSM-Tyazhmash	Machine engineering and metal processing
OAO Dormash	Machine engineering and metal processing
OAO Sokol Pulp and Paper Plant	Forestry, timber, and pulp and paper
ZAO Cherepovets Plywood Furniture Factory	Forestry, timber, and pulp and paper
OAO Agroskon	Building materials
OOO Chagodoschensky Glass Plant and Co.	Glass and porcelain
OAO Pokrovsky Glass Plant	Glass and porcelain
OAO Severlen	Light industry
OAO Vologda Textile	Light industry
ZAO Vologda Dairy Plant	Food and beverages
ZAO Vologda Meat Processing Plant	Food and beverages

5.4. MOST ATTRACTIVE SECTORS FOR INVESTMENT

According to experts and the Vologda Regional Government, the most potentially appealing sectors for investors are forestry, chemicals, food and beverages, energy, and tourism.

5.5. CURRENT LEGISLATION ON INVESTOR TAX EXEMPTIONS AND PRIVILEGES

In order to foster investment, the Vologda Region has passed the law On State Regulation of Investment Activity in the Vologda Region, which provides general principles and guarantees as regards investment activity in the Region. The Region has established a legislative and regulatory base for providing privileges and guarantees to investors.

Tax exemptions provided by the regional tax legislation are seen as an important tool for channeling investment into the development, upgrading, and reconstruction of the Region's enterprises.

In addition to the above law the Region has adopted the following laws and regulations:

- On Terms and Conditions for the Provision of Regional Tax Exemptions, Privileges, and Deferrals;
- On Investment Tax Credit;
- On the Reduced Rate of Profit Tax for Certain Categories of Taxpayers;
- On Corporate Property Tax
- On Transport Tax.

Regional entities responsible for raising investment		TABLE 10
ENTITY	ADDRESS	PHONE, FAX, E-MAIL
Department of Economy of the Vologda Regional Government	2, ul. Gertsena, Vologda, Vologda Region, 160035	Phone: (8172) 72 8470 Fax: (8172) 72 2719 E-mail: de@vologda-oblst.ru
The Vologda Chamber of Industry and Commerce	15, ul. Lermontova, Vologda, Vologda Region, 160035	Phone: (8172) 72 1480 Fax: (8172) 72 3258 E-mail: grant@vologda.ru
OOO Financial Management Center	47, ul. Blagoveschenskaya, Vologda, Vologda Region, 160035	Phone (8172) 72 8818 Fax: (8172) 72 8818 E-mail: volwood@vologda.ru

5.6. FEDERAL AND REGIONAL ECONOMIC AND SOCIAL DEVELOPMENT PROGRAMS FOR THE VOLOGDA REGION

Federal targeted programs. In 2002, the Region funded some 24 federal targeted programs, with a total budget of $38,7 million.

Regional programs. The Regional Government develops and implements programs focused on agroindustrial sector, the development of healthcare and social welfare. The Region has accorded priority to the following programs: Assistance to Employ-ment in the Vologda Region, 2003–2005, Program for the Recovery of Insolvent Companies within the Agroindustrial Sector of the Vologda Region, 2001–2005, Social Monitoring, 2002–2006, and The Youth Policy, 2002–2004.

6. INVESTMENT PROJECTS

Industry sector and project description	1) Expected results 2) Amount and term of investment 3) Form of financing[1] 4) Documentation[2]	Contact information
1	2	3
ENERGY		
22R001 Reconstruction and technical renovation of the Krasavino Thermal Power Station using the combined cycle technology. Project goal: to increase electricity output.	1) Power capacity: 65 MW 2) $20 million/2 years 3) E, L 4) BP, FS	MUEP Krasavino Power and Heat Networks 148a, pr. Sovetsky, Krasavino, Velikoustyugsky District, Vologda Region, 162341 Phone/fax: (81738) 41 861 E-mail: kets@vologda.ru Alexander Vsevolodovich Shvetsov, CEO

[1] L – Loan, E – Equity, Leas. – Leasing, JV – Joint Venture
[2] BP – Business Plan, FS – Feasibility Study

1	2	3

CHEMICALS AND PETROCHEMICALS

22R002

Construction of a pilot plant for melamine production. Project goal: to introduce new technologies.

1) 360,000 tons a year
2) $2 million/2.5 years
3) L
4) BP

ZAO Agro-Cherepovets
10, Cherepovets, Vologda Region, 162610
Phone: (8202) 51 9281
Fax: (8202) 59 2272
Boris Vasilyevich Novikov, CEO

FORESTRY, TIMBER, AND PULP AND PAPER

22R003

Renovation of fixed assets. Project goal: to increase output and improve quality.

1) n/a
2) $5.2 million, n/a
3) L, Leas
4) BP

OOO Mezhdurechieles
14, ul. Naberezhnaya, Turovets, Mezhdurechensky District, Vologda Region, 161071
Phone: (81749) 22 537
Vladimir Valentinovich Kozlov, CEO

22R004

Development of sawn timber production. Project goal: to increase output and diversify product mix.

1) Processing capacity: 150,000 cubic meters of feedstock a year
2) $3.4 million/1.5 years
3) L
4) BP

OOO Vologodskie Lesopromysh-lenniki Holding Company
3, ul. Blagoveschenskaya, Vologda, Vologda Region, 160000
Phone/fax: (8172) 72 8817, 72 8818
E-mail: volwood@vologda.ru
Alexander Nikolaevich Churkin, CEO

22R005

Launch of edged sawn timber production. Project goal: to increase output and diversify product mix.

1) 28,000 cubic meters of edged sawn timber a year
2) $1.1 million/0.5 years
3) E, L
4) BP

OOO StaPo-Totma
Zadnyaya, Totemsky District, Vologda Region, 161300
Phone: (81739) 24 262, 24 263
Vasily Petrovich Yermolin, CEO

22R006

Launch of a pre-fabricated timber house production plant (using a technology supplied by Konito, Finland). Project goal: to bring a new product to the market.

1) 100 houses per year with average floor space of 250 square meters
2) $1.1 million/1 year
3) E, L ($0.9 million)
4) BP

OAO Vologda StaPo
3, ul. Blagoveschenskaya, Vologda, Vologda Region, 160035
Phone: (8172) 21 0722
Gennady Anatolyevich Shamraev, CEO

22R007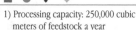

Construction of a new timber mill. Project goal: to bring timber goods to the market.

1) Processing capacity: 250,000 cubic meters of feedstock a year
2) $75.3 million/1.5 years
3) E, L, JV
4) BP, investment proposal

The Department of Economy of the Government of the Vologda Region
2, ul. Gertsena, Vologda, Vologda Region, 160035
Phone: (8172) 72 8470
Fax: (8172) 72 2719
Leonid Genrikhovich Eogman, Department Head, Deputy Governor of the Vologda Region

22R008

Construction of facilities for round timber processing and planed board output at idle premises of an operational enterprise. Project goal: to increase output and diversify product mix.

1) 40,000 cubic meters of processed round timber a year, output of up to 25,000 cubic meters of edged board
2) $1.1 million/2 years
3) L
4) BP

OAO Ustyugles Timber Holding Company
60, ul. Naberezhnaya, Veliky Ustyug, Vologda Region, 162340
Phone: (81738) 24 359, 21 375, 21 137
Fax: (81738) 24 482
Viktor Denisovich Golyshev, CEO

1	2	3

CONSTRUCTION MATERIALS

22R009

Construction of a ceramic decorative
bricks plant at the premises of
a house construction plant.
Project goal: to bring ceramic
bricks to the market.

1) 20 million a year
2) $4.1 million/1 year
3) E
4) BP

Department of Construction, Energy,
and Housing and Communal Services
of the Government
of the Vologda Region
2, ul. Gertsena, Vologda,
Vologda Region, 160035
Phone: (8172) 72 1222
Fax: (8172) 25 1098
Viktor Vladimirovich Ryabishin,
Department Head

LIGHT INDUSTRY

22R010

Renovation of fixed assets
of a textile factory.
Project goal: to increase output
and improve product quality.

1) n/a
2) $13.4 million, n/a
3) L
4) BP

OAO Vologda Textile
135-b, pr. Sovetsky, Vologda,
Vologda Region, 160012
Phone: (8172) 75 7949
Fax: (8172) 75 8639
Vladimir Alekseevich Shkolin, CEO

AGRICULTURE

22R011

Renovation of fixed assets
of a poultry farm.
Project goal: to increase output,
improve product quality, and reduce costs.

1) Eggs output: 152 million a year
   Poultry meat output: 720 tons a year
2) $2.1 million/1.5 years
3) L
4) BP

ZAO Malechkino
Malechkino, Cherepovets District,
Vologda Region, 162691
Phone/fax: (8202) 66 6921
Afanasy Dmitrievich Shasherin, CEO

TRADE

22R012

Construction of a new wholesale
market in Vologda.
Project goal: to expand and improve
the quality of wholesale services.

1. n/a
2. $1.2 million/6 years
3. L
4. FS

Department of Food Resources
of the Vologda Region
19, ul. Predtechenskaya, Vologda,
Vologda Region, 160000
Phone: (8172) 72 4622
Fax: (8172) 72 3194
E-mail: depprod@vologda.ru
Tamara Pavlovna Britvina,
Department Head

II

NORTH-WESTERN FEDERAL DISTRICT

23. KALININGRAD REGION [39]

ECONOMIC MAP

BALTIC

SEA

LITHUANIA

Klaypeda

Kurshskayaa kosa (spit)

Rybachy

Kurshsky gulf

Yantarny

Zelenogradsk

Svetly

Baltiysk

Polessk

Sovetsk

Myamunas

Neman

Krasnoznamensk

KALININGRAD

Gvardeysk

Chernyakhovsk

Pregolya

Mamonovo

Nesterov

Gusev

Bagrationovsk

Lyna

Lake Mamry

P O L A N D

Olshtyn

PROCESSING INDUSTRY
- ● Machine engineering and metal processing
- ● Forestry and timber
- ○ Food and beverages

MINING INDUSTRY
- ▲ Oil
- Peat
- ✦ Amber

POWER PLANTS
- Thermal power plants
- Fishing ports

CROPS AND LIVESTOCK BREEDING
- Potatoes
- Meat and dairy cattle breeding
- Pig breeding
- Poultry farming

The Kaliningrad Region is, figuratively speaking, a plenipotentiary of Russia in Europe. This westernmost region of Russia is completely separated from the rest of the country by international frontiers and the sea. The unique geopolitical position of the Region has an effect on its economy, on all aspects of the life of its people, and, of course, on our intentions.

Today, at a time when European countries are unifying, Russia also has a role to play in the process of European integration. In this context, the Kaliningrad Region is regarded by the country's leaders as a springboard for advancing cooperation. Our Region has the potential to fulfill this mission.

The Kaliningrad Region sits high on the list of the priorities of the federal government. A Federal Targeted Program for the Development of the Kaliningrad Region Through 2010 has been drafted and is being implemented. The Program comprises major strategic projects related to the Region's energy, transport, and telecommunications infrastructure. The Kaliningrad Region's geographical location makes it an ideal transportation hub linking Russia, Europe, and the Baltic states. An amendment to the Law on the Special Economic Zone in the Kaliningrad Region is pending, which will pave the way for the creation of an even more favorable investment climate in the Region.

The Kaliningrad Region boasts considerable natural resources. The Region is home to the world's largest commercial amber deposits, which account for over 90% of the world's total amber supply. The Region also boasts deposits of high-quality oil, brown coal, peat, rock salt, and construction materials. Industry is the leading sector of the Region's economy, accounting for 40% of its gross regional product.

The Region's natural environment is unique and unrivaled. Its mild maritime climate, mineral waters, therapeutic muds and sandy beaches attract vacationers to the Baltic Sea coast for both spa and recreational activities. The Region also has good prospects for the development of links and cooperation in various spheres of humanitarian affairs, including culture, education, healthcare, and ecology. We have gained considerable experience in this field.

The geopolitical position of the Kaliningrad Region encourages the development of cooperation, and the Russian Government supports us in all our initiatives. The people of the Kaliningrad Region are enterprising and hospitable. I am confident that no one who decides to invest in the westernmost region of the Russian Federation will have cause to regret such a decision.

Vladimir Yegorov,
HEAD OF ADMINISTRATION (GOVERNOR)
OF THE KALININGRAD REGION

II

NORTH-WESTERN FEDERAL DISTRICT

1. GENERAL INFORMATION

1.1. GEOGRAPHY

The Kaliningrad Region is the outermost western region of the Russian Federation, completely separated from the rest of the country by international frontiers and the sea. The Region covers an area of some 15,100 square kilometers.

To the north and to the east the Region borders Lithuania, to the south – Poland, and to the west lies the Baltic Sea. The city of Kaliningrad lies only 35 kilometers from the Polish border and 70 kilometers from the Lithuanian border. The nearest Russian regional center, Pskov, is 800 kilometers from Kaliningrad, while Moscow is 1,289 kilometers distant.

1.2. CLIMATE

The Region enjoys a transitional maritime-to-temperate continental climate. January air temperatures average –2 to –4°C, rising to +17–18°C in July. Annual precipitation varies between 650 mm and 940 mm.

1.3. POPULATION

According to preliminary 2002 census results, the Region's population was 955,000 people. The average population density is 63.2 people per square kilometer. The economically active population amounts to 488,000. Official 2002 official unemployment stood at 2.2%.

Demographically speaking, some 60.9% of population is of statutory working age, some 19.6% are below the statutory working age, and 19.5% are beyond the statutory working age.

The Region's largest cities had the following populations in 2002: Kaliningrad – 430,300, Sovietsk – 43,700 Chernyakhovsk – 43,300, Baltiysk – 31,800.

Population								*TABLE 1*
	1992	1997	1998	1999	2000	2001	2002
Total population, '000	894	936	943	951	949	947	955
Economically active population, '000	493	466	484	492	489	446	488

2. ADMINISTRATION

**1, ul. Dm. Donskogo, Kaliningrad, Kaliningrad Region, 236007. Phone: (0112) 46 7545, 45 5965
Fax: (0112) 46 3554 E-mail: ako@ako.baltnet.ru; http://www.gov.kaliningrad.ru**

NAME	POSITION	CONTACT INFORMATION
Vladimir Grigoryevich YEGOROV	Head of Administration (Governor) of the Kaliningrad Region	Phone: (0112) 46 7545
Vladimir Vilevich PIROGOV	Vice Governor of the Kaliningrad Region	Phone: (0112) 46 4558 E-mail: secretariat@vice-governov.kaliningrad.ru
Mikhail Aronovich TSYKEL	Vice Governor of the Kaliningrad Region, in charge of international relations and fuel and energy issues	Phone: (0112) 45 3510
Vitaly Petrovich ZHDANOV	Chief of the Central Department for Economic Development and Trade of the Administration of the Kaliningrad Region	Phone: (0112) 46 5406 E-mail: zhdanov@gov.kaliningrad.ru
Mikhail Yuryevich PLYUKHIN	Chairman of the Committee for the Development of the Special Economic Zone of the Administration of the Kaliningrad Region	Phone: (0112) 46 2737 E-mail: oez@gov.kaliningrad.ru
Valentin Fedorovich ZAKHAROV	Chairman of the Committee on Revenues and Investments of the Administration of the Kaliningrad Region	Phone: (0112) 46 6324 E-mail: invest@gov.kaliningrad.ru

3. ECONOMIC POTENTIAL

3.1. 1997–2002 GROSS REGIONAL PRODUCT (GRP). INDUSTRY BREAKDOWN

The Kaliningrad Region's 2002 gross regional product amounted to $1.259 billion. GRP growth for the year in comparable prices topped 6%. Industry forms the basis of the Region's economy, accounting for 40.6% of GRP in 2002. Per capita GRP in 2002 was $1,318.

3.2. MAJOR ECONOMIC GROWTH PROJECTIONS

The Kaliningrad Regional Administration has developed a Strategy for the Region's Economic and Social Development through 2010, which contains the following growth projections:

Industry: 8–12% annual industrial output growth on the back of increased machine engineer-

GRP trends in 1997–2002						TABLE 2
	1997	1998	1999	2000	2001*	2002*
GRP in current prices, $ million	1,402.1	883.1	658.6	929.6	1,082.4	1,258.8

*Estimates of the Kaliningrad Regional Administration

GRP industry breakdown in 1997–2002, % of total						TABLE 3
	1997	1998	1999	2000	2001*	2002*
GRP	100.0	100.0	100.0	100.0	100.0	100.0
Industry	30.4	30.6	33.9	37.7	41.5	40.6
Agriculture and forestry	6.7	7.2	8.9	7.8	7.1	5.9
Construction	9.0	5.3	4.9	6.4	6.6	7.3
Transport and communications	14.0	13.9	11.5	10.4	9.8	10.8
Trade and public catering	14.3	18.9	16.6	15.0	9.6	8.5
Other	21.8	20.5	20.4	17.8	20.8	22.5
Net taxes on output	3.8	3.6	3.8	4.9	4.6	4.4

*Estimates of the Kaliningrad Regional Administration

ing, light, forestry and timber and energy sectors output, including automotive production at ZAO Avtotor, the development of shipbuilding, and the production of equipment and household electric appliances.

Agriculture: Growth in output of 5–6% annually through improved tillage and stock-breeding efficiency;

Construction: 7% growth in output; introduction of new materials and structures, technical and technological revamping of facilities in the sector, application of modern methods and tools for raising capital to finance residential construction;

Transport and communications: 10–15% annual growth in services; continued renovation of major transportation routes and international border crossings with a view to increasing capacity and improving quality of services; development of sea links to ports at the Baltic sea and in St. Petersburg.

3.3. INDUSTRIAL OUTPUT IN 1997–2002 FOR MAJOR SECTORS OF ECONOMY

The Region's major industrial sectors are the food industry (represented mainly by the fishing) with 32.5%, machine engineering and metal processing with 25%, the fuel industry with 16.4%, timber, pulp and paper industry with 11.7%, and the power industry with 10%.

Food and beverages (fishing). The sector is mainly represented by meat and fish processing companies, and liquor and vodka producers. Starting in 1997, the fish-processing industry began to show signs of production growth. Output of refrigerated and canned fish has been rising for the past three years. The largest enterprises in the sector are OAO MariNPO, OAO Atlantrybflot and ZAO Kaliningrad Canned Fish Plant.

Machine engineering and metal processing. Currently, the Region carries out diversification of production in the industry. Over the past 2–3 years, companies within the machine engineering sector producing cars and sophisticated electric appliances started operations in the Region. ZAO Avtotor producing BMW and KIA cars represents the automotive industry. The plant's annual capacity is 10,000 cars, and the company has already been recognized as one of the best BMW assemblers. The company has received an ISO quality certificate. Also, the Region manufactures TV sets (OOO Telebalt) and spark plugs (OOO Brisk).

The Region's traditional companies are PSZ Yantar Shipbuilding Company, the Quartz Plant producing electronic goods, Gazavtomatika, JV OAO Baltkran, OAO Sistema, OAO Vagonostroitel, and OKB Fakel.

II

NORTH-WESTERN FEDERAL DISTRICT

Industry breakdown of industrial output in 1997–2002, % of total						TABLE 4
	1997	1998	1999	2000	2001	2002*
Industry	100.0	100.0	100.0	100.0	100.0	100.0
Food, flour, cereals, and mixed fodder	43.8	40.0	35.5	27.0	31.1	32.5
Machine engineering and metal processing	16.0	13.3	15.9	19.1	19.6	25.0
Fuel industry	7.8	8.9	18.7	25.5	20.4	16.4
Forestry, timber, and pulp and paper	7.1	9.2	10.1	12.1	13.0	11.7
Energy	18.0	18.3	9.1	9.2	9.8	10.0
Light industry	1.3	2.0	4.8	1.9	1.8	1.5
Construction materials	2.0	1.6	1.4	1.3	1.3	1.4

*Estimates of the Kaliningrad Regional Administration

Pulp and paper. The sector is represented by five enterprises: four pulp-and-paper mills and one paper mill. Raw materials are delivered mainly from the northern regions of Russia. The Region's facilities produce approximately 400,000 tons of pulp annually (11% of total Russian pulp output), 150,000 tons of paper, and 30,000 tons of paperboard. The largest enterprises are JV ZAO Cepruss, OOO Nemansky Paper Mill, and OAO Sovietsky Paper Mill.

Energy. The regional power company, OAO Yantarenergo (a subsidiary of UES of Russia), controls energy distribution in the Region. OAO Yantarenergo's installed capacity is 133 MW. Yantarenergo owns a 600 kW wind power station and a small 40 kW hydroelectric power station at Zaozernaya. Yantarenergo is currently engaged in the construction of Pravdinskaya HEP Station-3 with a capacity of 7.4 MW (one of the three planned HEP units with 1.14 MW capacity has already been put into operation).

Oil. Low sulfur (0.2%) oil is extracted from an offshore deposit in the Baltic Sea at a depth of 1,500–2,000 meters. The principal oil producer is OOO LUKoil-Kaliningradmorneft, the operator of the Kravtsovskoye deposit.

3.4. FUEL AND ENERGY BALANCE (OUTPUT AND CONSUMPTION PER RESOURCE)

The Kaliningrad Region is an energy deficient region. Local power stations operating on imported fuel oil and natural gas are able to provide only 8% of the Region's electricity needs, while the rest is supplied via Lithuania from Russia. The total 2001 electricity output of all Kaliningrad Region power stations amounted to 246 million kWh, with 67 million kWh produced by OAO Yantarenergo. Other power stations (belonging to industrial enterprises) produced 179.3 million kWh. Energy consumption in 2001 amounted to 2,980 million kWh.

Fuel and energy sector production and consumption trends, 1997–2002						TABLE 5
	1997	1998	1999	2000	2001	2002*
Electricity output, billion kWh	0.2	0.2	0.2	0.2	0.2	0.2
Oil output (including gas condensate), '000 tons	764.0	743.0	702.1	749.0	743.0	745.9
Natural gas extraction, million cubic meters	14.0	14.0	10.0	11.0	11.0	10.5
Electricity consumption, billion kWh	2.8	2.8	2.8	3.0	2.9	3.3
Natural gas consumption, million cubic meters	446.3	471.1	455.3	444.0	514.0	563.5

*Estimates of the Kaliningrad Regional Administration

3.5. TRANSPORT INFRASTRUCTURE

Roads. The Kaliningrad Region has some 4,600 kilometers of paved public highway. The Region's road network is utilized at 50% of its capacity. The Region has 23 functioning international border crossings (including six car crossings) and more than 20 regular traffic routes to the Baltic States, Poland, and Germany.

Railroads. The Kaliningrad Region has 640 km of railroad. The Region's railroads are linked with those of Lithuania and Poland. The city of Kaliningrad also has a European gauge rail link.

Sea ports. The Region's sea ports are the only Russian ice free ports in the Baltic. The total nominal transshipment capacity of the Region's sea ports amounts to some 14.8 million tons per year (approximately one third of Russia's total Baltic transshipment capacity). The port of Kaliningrad has an installed handling capacity of 16,420,000 tons of freight and a total of 8 kilometers of berthing facilities.

3.6. MAIN NATURAL RESOURCES: RESERVES AND EXTRACTION IN 2002.

Amber. The Region is home to the world's largest commercial amber deposits, which account for 90% of the world's total amber supply. Amber deposits are located in the north-western sector of the Sambiisk Peninsula. The amber field covers a total area of 300 square kilometers, and is around 25–30% explored. The amber reserves of the Sambiisk Peninsula are estimated at 283,000 tons. The largest deposit is at Palmikenskoye, between the villages of Sinyavino and Pokrovskoye.

Recoverable oil reserves are estimated at 275 million tons.

Peat bogs cover more than 1,000 square kilometers, or more than 7% of the Kaliningrad Region's total area. The thickness of the peat layer varies between 3-5 meters and 12 meters, with total peat reserves estimated at 3 billion cubic meters. Peat is used for agricultural purposes mainly as an organic fertilizer and as a biological fuel for boilers.

Coal reserves stand at some 50 million tons, while high grade rock salt reserves are estimated at several dozen million tons. The Region is also home to numerous explored deposits of building material reserves (sand, clay, and sandy gravels).

4. TRADE OPPORTUNITIES

4.1. MAIN GOODS PRODUCED IN THE REGION

Natural resources. 2002 amber output amounted to 207.9 tons (24.7% down on the previous year), and peat output was 20,000 tons (18.7% down on the previous year). Oil output amounts to approximately 740,000 tons annually.

Machine engineering and metal processing. In 2002 the Region produced 543,000 television sets (26% of total Russian output). Automotive output in 2002 rose by 16% to 5,700 cars. Enterprises in the sector produce and overhaul ships, cranes, loaders, and equipment for the fishing industry, in addition to electrical welding equipment, automation and control systems for main gas pipelines, commercial and paper-making equipment, and road construction machinery.

Pulp and paper industry. 2002 pulp output amounted to 119,000 tons, while paper output amounted to 69,600 tons.

Food and beverages. Alcoholic beverages output in 2002 amounted to 4.2 million decaliters (4.4% up on the previous year), beer output at 4.1 million decaliters (0.4% down on the previos year), canned food output at 179 million can equivalents (27.1% down on the previous year), and the fish catch at 360,000 tons (4.7% growth).

4.2. EXPORTS, INCLUDING EXTRA-CIS

Exports to extra-CIS countries in 2000 amounted to $432.3 million; exports to CIS countries totaled $9.3 million. The figures for 2001 were $389.3 million and $13.8 million, respectively, and for the first nine months of 2002 – $390 million and $18 million. The main goods exported from the Region in 2002 were: oil (35% of total exports), timber products (13%), and fish products (10%), and vessels (3.2%).

4.3. IMPORTS, INCLUDING EXTRA-CIS

Imports from extra-CIS countries in 2000 amounted to $764.3 million; imports from CIS countries totaled $44.7 million. The figures for 2001 were $960.6 million and $23.8 million, respectively, and for the first nine months of 2002 – $1,538 million and $40 million.

The main goods imported by the Region in 2002 were: food (15%, mainly meat and fish products), ferrous metals (5%), and plastics (3%).

4.4. MAJOR REGIONAL EXPORT AND IMPORT ENTITIES

Owing to the specific location of the Region, individuals, small retail companies and large, mainly industrial enterprises perform export and import transactions in the Kaliningrad Region. These include OOO LUKoil-Kaliningradmorneft, ZAO Avtotor, OOO Interfood, OAO Zapadnoye Parokhodstvo, etc.

5. INVESTMENT OPPORTUNITIES

5.1. INVESTMENTS IN 1992–2002 (BY INDUSTRY SECTOR), INCLUDING FOREIGN INVESTMENTS

The following factors determine the investment appeal of the Kaliningrad Region:
- Its favorable geographical location (frontiers with Poland and Lithuania, direct connection to Western Europe);

- The existence of a Special Economic Zone and legislation supporting investment activities (guarantees for investor rights, and preferential tax treatment for investors);
- Its developed transport infrastructure;
- Its natural resources (amber, peat, and oil).

II

NORTH-WESTERN FEDERAL DISTRICT

Capital investment by industry sector, $ million						TABLE 6
	1997	1998	1999	2000	2001	2002
Total capital investment	196.1	112.0	91.2	162.5	270.2	207.5
Including major industries (% of total):						
Industry	33.7	43.8	44.9	57.7	56.2	48.2
Agriculture and forestry	2.0	6.0	9.6	5.7	3.3	3.3
Construction	0.0	6.6	2.4	4.2	1.1	6.5
Transport and communications	15.4	20.6	15.4	17.5	18.6	21.5
Trade and public catering	0.4	2.4	2.0	1.5	0.6	2.3
Other	48.5	20.6	25.7	13.4	20.2	18.2

Foreign investment trends in 1995–2002						TABLE 7
	1995–1997	1998	1999	2000	2001	2002
Foreign investment, $ million	50.8	39.4	18.3	19.1	24.6	47.7
Including FDI, $ million	44.8	9.2	4.1	6.6	3.3	5.9

5.2 CAPITAL INVESTMENT

Industry accounts for the lion's share of fixed capital investments, with the fuel industry topping the league table.

5.3. MAJOR ENTERPRISES (INCLUDING ENTERPRISES WITH FOREIGN INVESTMENT)

The Kaliningrad Region hosts some 1,820 enterprises with foreign capital from 65 countries. These include: 746 wholly foreign owned enterprises, 498 enterprises with Lithuanian capital, 490 enterprises with Polish capital, and 312 enterprises with German capital. The largest enterprises with foreign investments are JV ZAO Cepruss, JV OAO Baltkran, and ZAO Avtotor.

5.4. MOST ATTRACTIVE SECTORS FOR INVESTMENT

According to experts and the Regional Administration's evaluations, the most promising sectors for investment are the fuel industry, timber, machine engineering, food and beverages, and light industry. Trading companies and consumer goods manufacturing outfits located in the Region's Special Economic Zone also offer good investment appeal.

5.5. CURRENT LEGISLATION ON INVESTOR TAX EXEMPTIONS AND PRIVILEGES

The Region enjoys the status of Special Economic Zone. This status was assigned to the Region by a Presidential Decree of 1991 and later secured in a federal law. Special Economic Zone regulations are effective throughout the Region's territory except for zones dedicated to military purposes.

Under the Special Economic Zone regulations, inhabitants of the Region are allowed to import goods duty-free, and companies registered there enjoy such privileges and incentives as:

• Duty and tax free imports to the Special Economic Zone (subject to import quota restrictions for certain goods);

• An exemption for resident companies from the regulations on the mandatory conversion of foreign currency earnings;

• Duty and tax free access to the Russian market (including the Customs Union with Belarus) for goods processed in the Special Economic Zone that meet local added value requirements.

• Reduced income tax and other privileges.

Largest enterprises of the Kaliningrad Region	TABLE 8
COMPANY	SECTOR
OOO LUKoil-Kaliningradmorneft	Oil production
ZAO Avtotor	Machine engineering
OAO PSZ Yantar	Shipbuilding
JV ZAO Cepruss	Pulp and paper
OAO SPPI-RVVK	Food and beverages (liquors and vodka)

In 2002, the Region approved a Law On State Support to Companies Engaging in Capital Investment in the Kaliningrad Region. The Law provides for the following forms of state support to companies introducing investments to the Kaliningrad Region:

- Tax incentives;
- Investment credits for the regional component of companies' property tax;
- Partial subsidies for loan interest;
- Provision of land plots free of charge;
- Provision of regional budget guarantees to investors for financing raised for investment purposes;
- Support to priority investment projects.

Regional entities responsible for raising investment		TABLE 9
ENTITY	ADDRESS	PHONE, FAX, E-MAIL
Investment company Barents Capital	16, ul. Pugacheva, Kaliningrad, Kaliningrad Region, 236000	Phone: (0112) 55 7171 E-mail: barents@triplus.ru

5.6. FEDERAL AND REGIONAL ECONOMIC AND SOCIAL DEVELOPMENT PROGRAMS FOR THE KALININGRAD REGION

Federal targeted programs. Currently, underway is The Federal Targeted Program for the Development of the Kaliningrad Region through 2010, which provides for the securing of a stable power supply in the Region through the revamping of existing and introduction of new power suppliers – the Kaliningrad Thermal Power Station-2 and solution of the gas problem by construction of the second gas pipeline.

Regional programs. The Region has developed The Strategy of Social and Economic Development of the Kaliningrad Region, which provides for:

- The development of the city of Kaliningrad as a major Russian traffic hub;
- The development of telecommunications infrastructure (upgrading of telecommunications facilities, the construction of a fiber optic telecommunication link from the city of Kaliningrad to St. Petersburg, the development of an intra-regional fiber optic digital communications network, and the construction of a new relay station;
- The renewal of the trawler fleet and increa-sed catch yields. The finalization of financial leasing procedures has been singled out as an important task;
- The finalization of financial leasing procedures.

6. INVESTMENT PROJECTS

Industry sector and project description	1) Expected results 2) Amount and term of investment 3) Form of financing[1] 4) Documentation[2]	Contact information
1	2	3
NATURAL GAS		
23R001 ■ ● ◆		ZAO Gas-Oil
Construction of an underground gas reservoir. Project goal: to reduce gas pipeline load.	1) Total volume 1,200 million cubic meters, effective volume 800 million cubic meters 2) $96.3 million/3 years 3) E, L 4) BP	14, ul. Nakhimova, Kaliningrad, Kaliningrad Region, 236010 Phone: (0112) 22 9407 Fax: (0112) 22 9446, 22 9450 E-mail: gasoil@gasoil.koenig.su Igor Vitalyevich Yarovoy, CEO

[1] L – Loan, E – Equity, Leas. – Leasing, JV – Joint Venture
[2] BP – Business Plan, FS – Feasibility Study

II

NORTH-WESTERN FEDERAL DISTRICT

1	2	3

ENERGY

23R002 ● ◆

Construction of the Kaliningrad Thermal Power Station-2.
Project goal: to expand power generating facilities.

1) 900 MW
2) $412.2 million/5.4 years
3) L
4) BP

OAO Kaliningradskaya TPS -2
2, per. Energetikov, Kaliningrad,
Kaliningrad Region, 236034
Phone: (0112) 46 3321
Fax: (0112) 43 2401, 59 3792
E-mail: Adm@tec2.yantar.elektra.ru
Yevgeny Ivanovich Chubakov, CEO

23R003 ● ◆

Revamping of the Thermal Power Station-1, Kaliningrad City.
Project goal: to reduce fuel cost per unit.

1) 45 MW (3 steam, 1 gas turbines)
2) $21.5 million/3 years
3) L
4) BP

OAO Yantarenergo
34, ul. Teatralnaya, Kaliningrad,
Kaliningrad Region, 236000
Phone: (0112) 43 6514
Fax: (0112) 43 6026
E-mail: adm@yantar.elektra.ru
Oleg Nikolaevich Gladkov, CEO

23R004 ● ◆

Revamping of a thermal power station at Gusev.
Project goal: to reduce fuel cost per unit.

1) 15 MW
2) $13.3 million/3 years
3) L
4) BP

OAO Yantarenergo
34, ul. Teatralnaya, Kaliningrad,
Kaliningrad Region, 236000
Phone: (0112) 43 6514
Fax: (0112) 43 6026
E-mail:adm@yantar.elektra.ru
Oleg Nikolaevich Gladkov,
CEO

23R005 ● ◆

Revamping of a hydroelectric power station at Svetly.
Project goal: to reduce fuel cost per unit.

1) 110 MW
2) $59.9 million/4 years
3) L
4) BP

OAO Yantarenergo
34, ul. Teatralnaya, Kaliningrad,
Kaliningrad Region, 236000
Phone: (0112) 43 6514
Fax: (0112) 43 6026
E-mail: adm@yantar.elektra.ru
Oleg Nikolaevich Gladkov, CEO

MACHINE ENGINEERING AND METAL PROCESSING

23R006 ● ◆

Construction of small trawlers at OAO PSZ Yantar.
Project goal: to increase production.

1) 10 vessels
2) $12.7 million/3 years
3) L
4) BP

OOO Rybflot-Kaliningrad
45, ul. Portovaya, Kaliningrad,
Kaliningrad Region, 236039
Phone: (0112) 47 2214
Vyacheslav Fedorovich Kolganov,
Director

23R007 ● ❖ ◆

Construction of a shipbuilding plant for small ships within OAO PSZ Yantar.
Project goal: to diversify vessel mix.

1) Annual output of 300 vessels
2) $10 million/3.5 years
3) L, JV
4) BP

ZAO Vestles
10, Transportny tupik, Kaliningrad,
Kaliningrad Region, 236002
Phone: (0112) 44 7200
Fax: (0112) 47 4268
Sergei Vladimirovich Zhavoronkov,
CEO

FORESTRY, TIMBER, AND PULP AND PAPER

23R008 ● ◆

Renewal of the plant's fixed assets.
Project goal: improvement of ecological situation, reduction of costs.

1) Lowering waste emission and discharge
2) $14.1 million/6.5 years
3) L
4) BP

OOO Nemansky CBK
3, ul. Podgornaya, Neman,
Kaliningrad Region, 238710
Phone: (01162) 22 927
Fax: (01162) 22 189
Mikhail Zaidullovich Kasimov, CEO

1	2	3

FOOD AND BEVERAGES

23R009 ■ ◆

Malt production.
Project goal: to construct a new
malt-house with elevator.

1) 80,000 tons per year
2) $30 million/3 tons
3) E
4) BP

OOO Nemansky Solod
240, ul. Dzerzhinskogo, Kaliningrad,
Kaliningrad Region, 236034
Phone/fax: (0112) 47 2717
Yury Pavlovich Testov, CEO

23R010 ● ◆

Production of long-life dairy products
and powdered milk.
Project goal: to diversify product mix
(construction of facilities on the basis
of existing enterprise for production
of long-life dairy products
and powdered milk).

1) n/a
2) $5 million/3 years
3) L
4) BP

OOO Agroneman
2a, ul. Sovkhoznaya, Michurinsky,
Gusevsky District,
Kaliningrad Region, 238031
Phone: (0112) 31 0022
Fax: (0112) 31 0299
Sergei Alexandrovich Kirillov,
Director

23R011 ● ◆

Production of vegetable oil.
Project goal: to construct facilities for oil
crop processing (rape seed, sunflower).

1) 2,500 tons annually
2) $5.1 mn/5.5 years
3) L
4) BP

Elita Farm
Sholokhovo Village, Kaliningrad
Region, 238640
Phone: (01158) 23 796
Sergei Mikhailovich Antipin,
Farm Director

AGRICULTURE

23R012 ● ◆

Leguminous crop production
and cultivation of winter wheat.
Project goal: to extend export
opportunities for forage beans
and winter rape.

1) n/a
2) $5.6 million/3 years
3) L
4) BP

ZAO Khlebnikovskoye
Krasnoznamensky District,
Khlebnikovo Village,
Kaliningrad Region, 238730
Phone: (01164) 22 335
Fax: (01164) 33 696
Alexei Ivanovich Smirnov,
Executive Director

23R013 ● ◆

Construction of greenhouse facilities.
Project goal: to cultivate vegetables
in closed environment.

1) 5,000 tons of vegetables annually
2) $5.7 million/3 years
3) L
4) BP

OOO Yantarnaya Niva
7, ul. Kaliningradskaya,
Sholokhovo settlement, Polessky
District, Kaliningrad Region, 238640
Phone: (01158) 23 796
Sergei Mikhailovich Antipin, Director

TRANSPORT INFRASTRUCTURE

23R014 ● ▲

Construction of a gas trunk pipeline
to the Kaliningrad Region.
Project goal: to supply gas to the Region and
to Kaliningrad Thermal Power Station-2.

1) 1,050 million cubic meters annually
2) $191.9 million/4 years
3) L
4) FS

ZAO Gas-Oil
14, ul. Nakhimova, Kaliningrad,
Kaliningrad Region, 236010
Phone: (0112) 22 9407
Fax: (0112) 22 9446, 22 9450
E-mail: gasoil@gasoil.koenig.su
Igor Vitalyevich Yarovoy, CEO

23R015 ■ ● ◆

Revamping of the Khrabrovo Airport.
Project goal: to achieve international
standards of air traffic services, and to
develop landing facilities, including
facilities for aircraft over 100 tons.

1) Additional 30–40 aircraft per day
2) $16.1 million/n/a
3) E, L
4) BP

GUP Kaliningradavia
Guryevsky District, Airport
Kaliningrad Region, 236315
Phone: (0112) 45 9420, 45 9580
Fax (0112) 45 9580
E-mail: postmaster@avia.gasinter.net
Victor Ivanovich Krishkovetz, CEO

1	2	3

23R016

Reconstruction of a container terminal at the Kaliningrad Sea Port.
Project goal: capacity extension.

1) 150,000 tons annually
2) $8.02 million/4 years
3) L
4) BP

OAO Commercial Sea Port
24, ul. Portovaya, Kaliningrad,
Kaliningrad Region, 236003
Phone: (0112) 57 2364
Fax: (0112) 44 6318
E-mail: kaliningrad@scport.ru
Valdimir Vladimirovich Kalinichenko,
CEO

23R017

Construction of a deepwater port at Baltiisk (12 deepwater terminals).
Project goal: to develop transportation and transshipment facilities.

1) 6.2 million tons annually
2) $163.6 million/7 years
3) E
4) BP

GU Kaliningrad Sea Port
Administration
24, ul. Portovaya, Kaliningrad,
Kaliningrad Region, 236003
Phone: (0112) 47 2217
Fax: (0112) 47 1483
Georgy Nikolaevich Sebov, Director

23R018

Road haulage.
Project goal: to renew the road-train fleet (purchase of 500 long-haul road trains on a leasing basis).

1) 500 road trains (haulers
   and semi-trailers)
2) $37.5 million/5 years
3) Leas.
4) BP

Regional Representative Office
of the International
Haulage Association
2a, ul. Yanalova, Kaliningrad,
Kaliningrad Region, 236023
Phone: (0112) 55 0321
Fax: (0112) 55 1142
E-mail: kaliningrad@kld.asmap.ru
Nikolai Mikhailovich Kudryashov,
Director of the Regional
Representative Office

ARKADY AKOPOVICH AVETISYANTS, CEO, Candidate of geological and mineral sciences, member of the Russian Academy of Natural Sciences, honorable worker of the gas industry, awarded a Services to the Fatherland Order, award of Excellence in the Ministry of the Gas Industry, laureate of the Nationwide People and Careers competition

KaliningradGazkomplektimpex is rightfully considered one of the most important components of the Kaliningrad Region's gas transportation and storage facilities. The Kaliningrad division of OOO Gazkomplektimpex (an OAO Gazprom subsidiary responsible for material and technical inventory logistics) is a modern and dynamic enterprise successfully operating in the following areas:

- transport servicing of import and export product flows;
- product storage;
- comprehensive customs clearance;
- telecommunications services (Internet access, digital telephony);
- marketing research.

KaliningradGazkomplektimpex provides top quality and timely services to foreign trade participants using modern goods, customs, storage and telecommunications terminals run by a highly-qualified team of professionals. Alongside conventional cargos, the company provides transshipment and customs clearance services with respect to drilling and prospecting equipment, oversized and bulky goods, wide-bore tube, pipeline laying equipment for gas pipeline divisions, and other equipment.

KaliningradGazkomplektimpex possesses:
- modern freight handling equipment capable of the rapid loading and unloading of con-

signments of up to 40 tons, including 20 foot and 40 foot high-capacity containers;
railway sidings capable of accommodating up to twenty railcars at a time;
- more than 8,500 square meters of roofed and insulated warehouse space, of which 4,500 square meters is heated;
- reliable 24-hour security systems to ensure the safe-guarding of clients' property.

As one of the leading multi-profile enterprises in the region, KaliningradGazkomplektimpex maintains industrial, business, financial and other links with dozens of firms, organizations and scientific establishments both within Russia and overseas. OAO Gazprom's decision to locate this multi-profile facility at the border between Russia and Europe was taken with a view to strengthening Russia's integration with the global economy. From the very outset, KaliningradGazkomplektimpex was designed to act as a link between Gazprom and Europe.

With that in mind, a 15 hectare site has been equipped with transport, energy, telecommunications and other links and utilities. The site will host production facilities and commercial and exhibition space to be used jointly by the Russian and foreign partners.

In the context of its business partnerships, KaliningradGazkomplektimpex strives to achieve broad and mutually beneficial collaboration focused on raising the company's industrial potential and profitability and on raising its technological level. Long-term collaboration in a context of stable business relationships is one of the core corporate values of KaliningradGazkomplektimpex.

1B, UL. TURUKHANSKAYA, 236009, KALININGRAD (REGION)
TEL.: (0112) 35 1113
FAX: (0112) 35 1123
E-MAIL: secretar@gazkomplekt.com
HTTP://www.gazkomplekt.com

24. LENINGRAD REGION [47]

ECONOMIC MAP

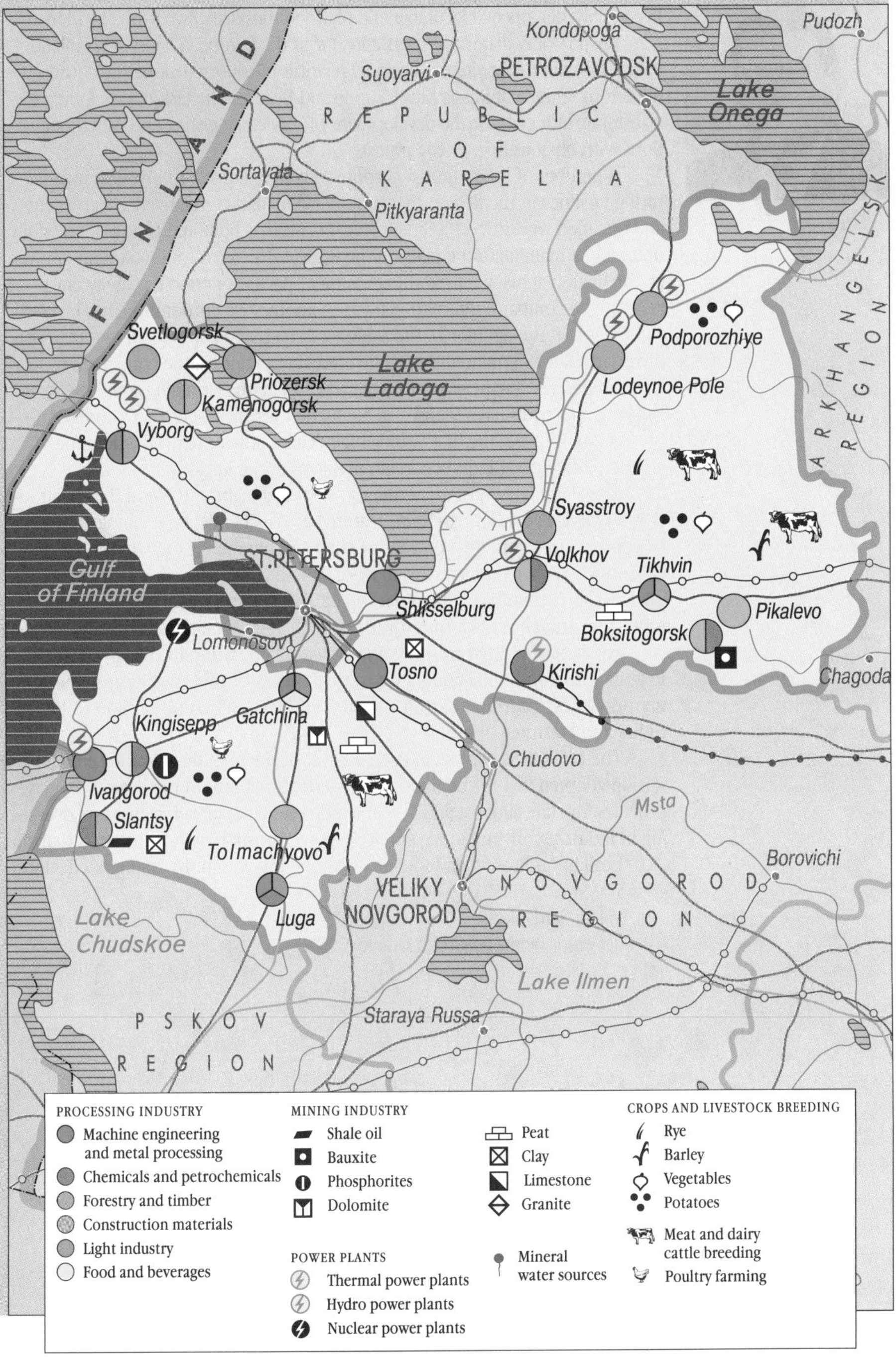
Kondopoga
Pudozh
PETROZAVODSK
Suoyarvi
Lake Onega
FINLAND
REPUBLIC OF KARELIA
Sortavala
Pitkyaranta
ARKHANGELSK REGION
Podporozhiye
Svetlogorsk
Lake Ladoga
Priozersk
Kamenogorsk
Lodeynoe Pole
Vyborg
Syasstroy
Gulf of Finland
ST.PETERSBURG
Volkhov
Tikhvin
Shlisselburg
Pikalevo
Lomonosov
Boksitogorsk
Tosno
Kirishi
Chagoda
Kingisepp
Gatchina
Chudovo
Ivangorod
Msta
Slantsy
Tolmachyovo
Borovichi
VELIKY NOVGOROD
NOVGOROD REGION
Luga
Lake Chudskoe
Lake Ilmen
Staraya Russa
PSKOV REGION
PROCESSING INDUSTRY
Machine engineering and metal processing
Chemicals and petrochemicals
Forestry and timber
Construction materials
Light industry
Food and beverages
MINING INDUSTRY
Shale oil
Bauxite
Phosphorites
Dolomite
Peat
Clay
Limestone
Granite
POWER PLANTS
Thermal power plants
Hydro power plants
Nuclear power plants
Mineral water sources
CROPS AND LIVESTOCK BREEDING
Rye
Barley
Vegetables
Potatoes
Meat and dairy cattle breeding
Poultry farming

T he Leningrad Region has achieved a lot in recent years in terms of economic development and finding solutions to social problems. The Region's industrial output has doubled since the 1990's, and the quality of the output has improved dramatically.

Economic success is contingent on a constant influx of investment. Over the past three years, Russian and foreign investors have put more than $3.4 billion in the Region's economy. Investment in 2001 exceeded $994 million, over half of which came from Russian companies.

We have identified a number of priority sectors for the Region's development that offer the greatest appeal for investors, with timber topping the league. In 2002, IKEA of Sweden opened its timber and plywood subsidiary Swedwood in Tikhvin.

Russia's only major transport corridor to the European Union via Finland passes through the Leningrad Region. Freight is transported along the corridor to numerous regions of Russia plus Ukraine and Belarus. The task of developing the transit corridor calls for the development of services, logistics, and other functions with obvious investment appeal.

A number of international corporations have chosen to invest in manufacturing facilities in the Region thanks to its wide market, relatively cheap energy, and qualified workforce. Phillip Morris, for one, has built and is now successfully operating a manufacturing plant in the Region. The terms of investment granted by the Region actually halved the investment payback period originally envisaged by the company. International Paper, another US corporation, has invested $65 million in the upgrade of the Svetogorsk Pulp and Paper Plant and plans to invest another $85 million. Danish investors are financing the construction of a corrugated cardboard plant in Vsevolzhsk, while the German corporations Henkel and Knauff have found a stable market for the goods they produce in the Region. In 2002, the first Ford vehicles came down the production line of an automobile plant built by foreign investors in the Region.

International corporations are also gaining a higher profile in the construction sector. Russian-German Joint Venture MC-Bauchemie, for example, has started construction work on a powder mixture and bitumen plant, while German concern Heidelberg Cement Group has acquired a 75% stake in a local cement plant and is currently building up its operations. Other foreign majors are currently preparing business plans for the construction of manufacturing plants.

We are committed to providing investors operating in the Leningrad Region with conditions conducive to the success of their business, including tax privileges, information transparency, and guaranteed protection of their rights and contractual terms.

The Law of the Leningrad Region On Investment Activity in the Leningrad Region adopted in 1997 embodies the investment appeal of the Region. The law provides for state support and investor protection measures for investors operating in industry, construction, communications, transport, agriculture, and tourism.

I call upon Russian and foreign investors to invest in the Leningrad Region.

Valery Serdyukov,
GOVERNOR OF THE LENINGRAD REGION

1. GENERAL INFORMATION

1.1. GEOGRAPHY

The Leningrad Region covers a total area of 84,500 square kilometers (not counting St. Peters-burg). The Region is situated in the north-west of Russia. To the north-west it borders Finland, to the west – Estonia, to the south and south-west – the Novgorod and Pskov Regions, to the east – the Vologda Region, and to the north – the Republic of Karelia.

1.2. CLIMATE

The Leningrad Region enjoys a temperate continental climate.

The average air temperature in January is −10°C, rising to +17°C in July. The average annual precipitation ranges between 550–850 mm.

1.3. POPULATION

Preliminary 2002 census results revealed a total population of 1,671,000 people in the Region. Average population density is 19.8 people per square kilometer. The economically active population amounts to 764,000 people. 2002 official unemployment level stood at 6.9%.

Demographically speaking, some 62.1% are of working age, 16.3% are below the statutory working age, and 21.6% are beyond the statutory working age.

As of 2002, the Leningrad Region's major urban centers were Gatchina with 82,900 inhabitants, Vyborg with 78,600 inhabitants, and Tikhvin with 66,600 inhabitants.

Population								TABLE 1
	1992	1997	1998	1999	2000	2001	2002
Total population, '000	1,666	1,671	1,674	1,674	1,667	1,659	1,671
Economically active population, '000	888	829	812	839	851	871	764

2. ADMINISTRATION

67, Suvorovsky prospekt, St. Petersburg, Leningrad Region, 193311
Phone: (812) 274 3563; fax: (812) 276 6431; http://www.lenobl.ru

NAME	POSITION	CONTACT INFORMATION
Valery Pavlovich SERDYUKOV	Governor of the Leningrad Region	Phone: (812) 274 3563
Vladimir Vladimirovich KIRILLOV	First Deputy Governor of the Leningrad Region	Phone: (812) 274 9189 Fax: (812) 274 9189
Alexei Ivanovich AKULOV	Deputy Governor of the Leningrad Region, Representative of the Leningrad Regional Government at the Government of the Russian Federation	Phone: (095) 291 3355
Alexander Alexandrovich BRAKHNO	Deputy Governor of the Leningrad Region	Phone: (812) 274 4280
Yury Ivanovich GOLOKHVASTOV	Deputy Governor of the Leningrad Region for Agricultural Sector	Phone: (812) 110 0052
Ivan Nikolaevich GRIGORYEV	Deputy Governor of the Leningrad Region for Regional Property Management	Phone: (812) 110 3372
Grigory Viktorovich DVAS	Deputy Governor of the Leningrad Region, Chairman of the Economic and Investment Committee	Phone: (812) 274 1446
Nikolai Ivanovich PUSTOTIN	Deputy Governor of the Leningrad Region for Social Development	Phone: (812) 274 9431
Alexander Ivanovich YAKOVLEV	Deputy Governor of the Leningrad Region, Chairman of the Finance Committee	Phone: (812) 274 4018, 274 5231
Alexander Yuryevich DROZDENKO	Deputy Governor of the Leningrad Region, Chairman of the Leningrad Regional Committee for State Property Management	Phone: (812) 315 7575, 314 6884

II

NORTH-WESTERN FEDERAL DISTRICT

3. ECONOMIC POTENTIAL

3.1. 1997–2002 GROSS REGIONAL PRODUCT (GRP). INDUSTRY BREAKDOWN

The 2002 gross regional product amounted to $3,059.3 million, which constitutes 10.4% growth year-on-year. The growth was achieved thanks to an increase in industrial output. Per capita GRP amounted to $1,669 in 2001 and $1,832 in 2002.

3.2. MAJOR ECONOMIC GROWTH PROJECTIONS

At the moment, there is no single document that provides the blueprint for economic development in the Region. The last conprehensive program for development of the Leningrad Region expired in 2002. The major directions for development are set forth in individual targeted programs for economic and social

GRP trends in 1997–2002						TABLE 2
	1997	1998	1999	2000	2001	2002*
GRP in current prices, $ million	3,269.9	2,274.2	1,669.8	2,109.6	2,770.2	3,059.3

*Estimates of the Leningrad Regional Administration

GRP industry breakdown in 1997–2002, % of total						TABLE 3
	1997	1998	1999	2000	2001	2002*
GRP	100.0	100.0	100.0	100.0	100.0	100.0
Industry	35.3	39.7	41.8	41.5	37.9	41.9
Agriculture and forestry	13.5	11.9	16.5	12.8	12.2	10.8
Construction	9.7	7.4	7.5	11.5	12.6	12.5
Transport and communications	4.8	6.2	6.8	7.8	6.9	7.5
Trade and public catering	9.8	9.6	7.8	7.8	8.2	7.3
Other	21.5	20.9	17.2	14.0	15.9	15.4
Net taxes on output	5.4	4.3	2.4	4.6	6.3	4.6

*Estimates of the Leningrad Regional Administration

development, which identify the following priorities: exploration and development of new mineral deposits, development of small enterprise, and improvement of operating technology and productivity in agriculture.

3.3. INDUSTRIAL OUTPUT IN 1997–2002 FOR MAJOR SECTORS OF ECONOMY

The leading industrial sectors of the Leningrad Region are food and beverages, forestry, timber, pulp and paper, fuel, and energy. Their combined share in total industrial output is 71.4%. Due to steadfast growth in industrial output, 1998–2002 output increased 1.9 times.

The Region hosts some 300 industrial enterprises, most of which are joint stock companies. Many production outfits in the Region are branches of St. Petersburg companies.

Food and beverages. The sector accounts for 25.3% of total industrial output. The major companies within the sector are ZAO Philip Morris Izhora (tobacco products), ZAO Veda (alcoholic beverages), ZAO Gatchina Mixed Fodder Plant, OAO Kingisepp Bakery, OOO Maleta, OAO Sosnov Dairy Plant, and OOO National Wine Terminal.

The sector is enjoying intensive development. 2002 output grew 1.6 times year-on-year. ZAO

Phillip Morris Izhora and ZAO Veda accounted for the bulk of the growth.

Forestry, timber, and pulp and paper. The sector accounts for 17.4% of total industrial output and comprises several related sub-sectors: lumber, timber, and pulp and paper. The sector is represented by some 770 companies, including 70–80 large and medium sized outfits, over 20 timber sawmills, some 20 furniture factories, three pulp and paper plants, and five cardboard factories. The Region's timber plants produce 12,000 cubic meters of veneer, 56,000 cubic meters of chipboards, up to 400,000 tons of pulp, up to 420,000 tons of paper, and up to 200,000 tons of cardboard.

The major company within the sector is OAO Svetogorsk, which produces office paper, cardboard for liquid food packages, industrial pulp, and offset paper. The company has completed full reconstruction of its main production lines and transferred to new chlorine-free pulp bleaching technology, which ensures a European-standard quality of output.

Other large companies include ZAO Tikhvin KLPKh, OAO Timber Chemical Plant, OOO Swedwood Tikhvin, ZAO Kamennogorsk Offset Paper Plant, OAO

Industry breakdown of industrial output in 1997–2002, % of total						TABLE 4
	1997	1998	1999	2000	2001	2002*
Industry	100.0	100.0	100.0	100.0	100.0	100.0
Food and beverages	11.1	10.3	9.6	16.8	24.0	25.3
Forestry, timber, and pulp and paper	12.5	14.0	20.0	20.5	18.0	17.4
Fuel	24.7	22.5	26.2	28.7	19.5	17.1
Energy	17.2	16.2	9.4	7.5	9.5	11.6
Machine engineering and metal processing	9.0	9.7	9.7	5.9	8.0	7.0
Non-ferrous metals	7.2	7.8	8.5	7.3	6.3	7.0
Chemicals and petrochemicals	7.9	8.9	6.4	4.3	4.9	5.7
Construction materials	5.0	4.3	3.2	3.4	4.5	4.8
Flour, cereals, and mixed fodder	3.0	3.4	4.0	3.4	3.2	0.9
Light industry	1.0	1.2	1.1	1.0	1.0	0.8
Ferrous metals	0.6	–	0.2	0.1	0.3	–

*Estimates of the Leningrad Regional Administration

Syassky Pulp and Paper Plant, OAO Priozerie Logging Plant, OAO Priozerie Furniture Plant, and OAO St. Petersburg Cardboard Printing Company (a major Russian producer of cardboard from recycled paper).

Fuel. The share of this sector in total industrial output is 17.1%. Among the largest companies are OOO PO Kirishinefteorgsintez, OAO Leningradslanets, and OAO Shale Plant. 2002 year-on-year growth was 1.6%.

OOO PO Kirishinefteorgsyntez is a major refinery with a refining capacity of over 17 million tons of oil per year. Its production capacities are fully utilized. The company is constructing a unit for deep oil processing. Upon the completion of the project, processing will reach 72–73% and the quality of kerosene and diesel output will meet world standards.

OAO Leningradslanets specializes on shale extraction. The company also produces lime tiles, spare parts for mining machinery, and other products.

OAO Shale Plant produces shale oil, electricity, and heat. In 2002, the plant launched coke tempering operations and now exports tempered coke and polymer resins.

Energy. Energy accounts for 11.6% of industrial output. Major companies include OAO Lenenergo, OAO Leningrad Nuclear Power Station with a capacity of 4,000 MW, and OAO Kirishi Thermal Power Station with a capacity of 2,080 MW.

Machine engineering and metal processing. The sector accounts for 7% of total industrial output. Major companies within the sector include OAO Vyborg Shipbuilding Plant (shipbuilding), OAO Burevestnik (accessories for vessels and fuel and energy companies), OAO Pirs (equipment for coal, mining, and chemical sectors), ZAO Priborstroitel (instrument engineering), OOO Helkama Forste Viipuri (freezing equipment), OAO Luzhsky Abrasive Plant (abrasive instrument output), OOO Caterpillar

Tosno (road construction machinery), OAO Krizo Plant (vessel electric equipment), OAO ToMeZ (residential service and road machinery), ZAO Ford Motor Company (vehicle engineering), and ZAO TZTM Titran (tractor engineering and metal assemblies).

Non-ferrous metals. The share of this sector is 7%. The largest companies are OAO Bauxitogorsk Alumina (production of alumina, hydrate, coagulate for water purification, metallographic and fire resistant materials), and OAO Metallurg, including branches Pikalevsky Alumina and Volkhov Aluminum (aluminum and chemicals).

Chemicals and petrochemicals. The sector accounts for 5.7% of total industrial output. 2002 output grew 8.3% year-on-year. The Region's chemicals and petrochemicals sector is represented by some 150 large and medium companies, including OOO Production Company Phosphorite (mineral fertilizers, food supplements, and other chemicals), OAO Henkel-ERA (detergents), OAO Volkhov Chemical Plant (household chemicals), OAO Khimik (solvents), State Unitary Company Morozov Plant (organic silicate paint and military goods), ZAO Polymer Foot-wear, ZAO Polymer-Faro (rubber covers and rubber goods), and others. Chemical units operate at OOO PO Kirishinefteorgsintez (raw materials for detergents), Volkhov Aluminum, (a branch of OAO Metallurg – mineral fertilizers, supplements for metal production, polyphosphate – raw material for detergents, and aluminum sulphate), and other companies.

Chemicals enterprises produce a wide range of products, most of which, such as synthetic resins, plastic, soda ash, sulphuric acid, mineral fertilizers, and bleaching materials, are experiencing output growth. OOO Production Company Phosphorite increased output of core products in 2002 through its investment program and the purchase of new machinery primarily for its ore-dressing unit.

II

N O R T H - W E S T E R N   F E D E R A L   D I S T R I C T

Construction materials. The sector accounts for 4.8% of total industrial output. Output growth in 2002 amounted to 31.4% year-on-year. Output of reinforced concrete assemblies, cement, wall tiles, and non-ore building materials increased considerably. The building materials sector includes open cast pits (ceramic and fire-resistant clay, limestone and dolomite, road-metal, sand, and gravel) and over 50 plants producing cement, asphalt, lime, clay, ceramic goods, roofing tiles, roll roofing materials, brick, concrete and reinforced concrete goods and assemblies, and various other building assemblies. The Tosno District's building material companies produce 60% of the total regional output of bricks and 100% of its wall and floor tiles output.

The major companies within the sector are OAO Nephrite-Ceramics, ZAO Quartz, ZAO Petroceramics, OAO Stroidetal Plant, OAO Tsesla, ZAO Kamennogorsk Open Cast Pit Management Company, ZAO Semiozersk Open Cast Pit Management Company, and OAO Tolmachevo Reinforced Concrete and Metal Assembly Plant.

Light industry. The sector accounts for 0.8% of total industrial output. 2002 output grew 16.1% year-on-year. The sector increased output of knitwear, fabric, and nonwoven fabric. The main companies include OAO Fanema, ZAO Luzhsky Knitwear, OOO Komatso, ZAO Volkhovchanka, ZAO Finskor, ZAO Nika, OAO Scanworkwear, and OAO Uzor.

Glass and porcelain (glass containers). In 2002, the first light bottle production line was launched at ZAO Veda-PAK with the capacity of 270 million bottles. The company utilizes advanced equipment and modern glass production technology. As well as light bottles, the company produces food jugs to world standards.

Agriculture. The Leningrad Region's agricultural sector continued to grow in 2002. Some 13 farms in the Region ranked among the 300 largest and most efficient agricultural companies in Russia. The most successful companies are ZAO Agro-Balt (grain, potato, meat and dairy products), Telman ASKhOZT (grain, potato and vegetables), ZAO Agrofirm Vyborzhets (greenhouse vegetables), ZAO Prinevskoe Livestock Breeding Plant, ZAO Cattle Breeding Farm Rapti, ZAO Gomontovo, ZAO Rabititsi, ZAO Poultry Factory Roskar, and ZAO Poultry Factory Sinyavskaya.

In 2002, farms in the Region harvested 60,300 tons of grain (108% of 2001), 762,900 tons of potato (97%), and 245,100 tons of vegetables in open fields and greenhouses (95.9%). The 2002 winter crop covered an area of 3,300 hectares (97%). In 2002, the Region's livestock breeding farms increased pork output by 13% year-on-year, and poultry output by 5%. Cattle output fell, however. In 2002, the average cow yielded 5,491 kg of milk (5% growth year-on-year), and at eight farms the average milk yield exceeded 8,000 kg. Livestock output increased 18%.

In spite of the stabilization trend and an increase in output of individual types of agricultural produce, the overall financial position of the Region's agriculture is unsatisfactory. In order to improve the situation, in 2002 the Regional budget allocated $7.3 million and the federal budget – $9 million to support agriculture. Federal and local funding helped develop a leasing system for the upgrade of agricultural machinery.

3.4. FUEL AND ENERGY BALANCE (OUTPUT AND CONSUMPTION PER RESOURCE)

Fuel and energy sector production and consumption trends, 1997–2002						TABLE 5
	1997	1998	1999	2000	2001	2002*
Electricity output, billion kWh	31.2	27.6	31.4	30.8	35.9	35.2
Electricity consumption, billion kWh	11.7	11.2	12.1	13.3	13.9	10.3
Natural gas consumption, million cubic meters	2,450.3	3,003.0	3,284.2	3,592.0	4,017.6	5,124.9

*Estimates of the Leningrad Regional Administration

3.5. TRANSPORT INFRASTRUCTURE

Roads. The Region has 10,440 kilometers of paved public highway, including 1,245 kilometers of federal highway. The road network comprises seven federal highways, including the Russia, Scandinavia, and St. Petersburg – Pskov highways, which link the Region to other Russian regions and provide access to the rest of Europe.

Railroads. The Leningrad Region has 3,200 kilometers of railroads. Freight turnover reaches 100 million tons per year. Branches of the state Unitary Company Oktyabrskaya Railroad account for 82% of total freight turnover and over 20% of passenger transportation.

Airports. The only airport that formerly serviced local flights has gone bankrupt and ceased operations. St Petersburg airport is now the only airport in the Region.

Sea and river transport. The Volga – Baltic canal passes through the Region linking Russia's internal waterways to St. Petersburg and the Baltic Sea ports. North West River Shipping Company transports over 40 million tons of freight per navigation season.

Sea and river ports. The Region boasts modern river ports at OAO Leningrad River Port and OAO Podporozhsky Port, both of which are equipped with advanced freight transshipment equipment, and seaports at ZAO Vyborg Seaport, ZAO Vysotsky Sea Trade Port, OAO Primorsky Port, and OAO Sea Trade Port Ust-Luga. The Region enjoys a well-developed vessel construction, maintenance, and repair infrastructure.

Oil and gas pipelines. Construction of the Baltic Pipeline System is a prospective project. The System focuses on a new direction for Russian oil exports from the Timano-Pechora, West Siberia, and Volga Regions and oil transit from the CIS, primarily from Kazakhstan. The project envisages construction of a new crude oil reloading terminal in Primorsk.

3.6. MAIN NATURAL RESOURCES: RESERVES AND EXTRACTION IN 2002

The main types of natural resources of the Leningrad Region are bauxite, phosphate rock, oil shale, molding and glass sand, carbonate minerals used for metal and cement production, and fire resistant and cement clay. The Region has explored 26 types of minerals, including 20 non-ore minerals used in construction and for mineral fertilizers. The state reserve balance lists 173 deposits of solid minerals, 46% of which are currently being developed.

Bauxite. Bauxite deposits were developed in the Region from 1931 onwards and served as the raw material base for OAO Bauxitogorsk Alumina. Currently the Region develops no bauxite deposits due to insufficient explored high quality reserves and complicated mining conditions. OAO Bauxitogorsk Alumina imports raw materials to utilize its operating capacities. It would be possible to provide the company with local raw materials through developing small low-profit deposits, primarily the Malogorsky, Yavasemsky, and Zadorsky deposits with combined reserves of some 5 million tons.

Phosphate rock. The Kingisepp deposit of shell phosphate with the reserve of 227 million tons (part of the deposit is difficult to access) represents the Region's reserves of phosphate rock. The deposit has been exploited by OAO Phosphorite since 1963 (in 2002 operating facilities of OAO Phosphorite were transferred to OOO Industrial Group Phosphorite). Annual extraction amounts to 1.9–2.5 million tons, while the company's operating capacity is 7 million tons. Phosphate powder obtained after material dressing is used mostly for agricultural needs and for chemicals (ammophos, super-phosphate, and thermal phosphate). Additional reserves of the raw material are located to the south of the Kingisepp deposit and in the Volosov District, where phosphate lies at a depth of 90–120m.

The Region has explored phosphate deposits in restricted areas, but their use is limited.

Combustible minerals (oil shale and peat). The Region has one deposit of oil shale – Leningradskoe – with proven reserves of 1,002 million tons. OAO Leningradslanets develops the deposit and extracts 1.1–1.5 million tons of shale per year, while the projected capacity is 2.3 million tons. Prospective shale bearing soil with estimated reserves of up to 1.3 billion tons is found in the eastern part of the Region.

The Region has explored 363 peat deposits with total reserves of 961 million tons. Peat is developed at 48 deposits.

Glass sand. Total reserves of sand deposits listed in the state reserve system (the Luzhskoe, Lipsky Mokh, and Zacherenie) amount to 7.6 million tons. OAO Phosphorite has accumulated 33 million tons of sand as phosphate dressing waste. To use this sand in glass production, it must be tested and a dressing plant built. Due to high demand for this raw material, the Region commenced intensive geological surveying in its south-western and eastern districts in 2000. 2001 glass sand output amounted to 289,000 tons.

Carbonate minerals. The Region has considerable reserves of limestone, dolomite, marl, lime tuff, and marsh deposits.

Limestone and dolomite deposits amount to 74.2 million tons. The Region develops three deposits: the Alexeevskoe, Kikerinskoe, and Vrudskoe; their combined output in 2001 reached 132,000 tons. Non-processed carbonate minerals are widely used for construction as construction stones, cement and lime ingredients, lime and dolomite powder, and flux and other materials (OAO Metallurg, OAO Tsesla, and others). Development of explored deposits of granite, gabbro (to produce road metal and facing materials), construction sand, and gravel is limited by complicated geological conditions, ecological restrictions, and large cost of infrastructure development.

Sapropel. The Region has discovered 215 million tons of sapropel in 230 lakes. Sapropel deposits of the Pendikovskoe Lake, Tosno District, Kolpanskoe Lake, and Gatchina District are prepared for industrial operations.

Other minerals. Geological surveying and estimation of iron and manganese deposits in the Gulf of Finland carried out in 1999–2001 has been completed, and balance reserves of the South and Central shelves have been identified. Prospective deposits of diamonds (the Luzhskaya and Podporozhskaya sites), gold, polymetal ore, oil and gas (the South Ladoga and Chagodinskaya sites), and geothermal sources of heat have been discovered.

Underground waters. The Region has three deposits of mineral waters that are not currently operated. The Region has a sufficient supply of underground waters for drinking and household purposes.

Forestry. Forests cover 6.1 million hectares. The following species of trees prevail: pine – 37%, fir tree – 29%, and birch – 26%. 2002 timber reserve amounted to 647 million cubic meters. Annual timber output is 12.3 million cubic meters, which harms neither forests nor their ecological condition.

4. TRADE OPPORTUNITIES

4.1. MAIN GOODS
PRODUCED IN THE REGION

2002 industrial output of major sectors amounted to:

Energy. Electricity – 35.2 billion kWh, heat – 11 million Gcal;

Fuel. Primary products of oil refining – 14.8 million tons, automotive gasoline – 1.6 million tons, fuel oil – 4.3 million tons, diesel fuel – 3.6 million tons, liquefied natural gas – 275,300 tons, and shale – 1.1 million tons;

Chemicals and petrochemicals. Synthetic resins and plastic – 10,800 tons, serum – 9,100 tons, plastic goods – 935 tons, benzyl – 20,100 tons, sulphuric acid – 826,800 tons, soda ash – 195,000 tons, mineral fertilizers – 273,000 tons, rubber footwear – 1,023,000 pairs, detergents – 32,100 tons, bleaches – 415 tons, microbiological protein – 5,600 tons;

Machine engineering and metal processing. 11 vehicles with special purpose cabins, truck tanks and truck and trailers, high pressure pipelines with diameter of 100 mm and over – 652 tons, flexible cable – 29 km, 60 forge and pressing machines, 86 centrifugal pumps, 12,600 industrial pipeline valves, gate valves, and accessories;

Forestry, timber, and pulp, and paper. Cut timber – 2.5 million dense cubic meters, industrial timber – 2.1 million dense cubic meters, lumber – 166,400 cubic meters, plywood – 13,600 cubic meters, commercial pulp – 94,900 tons, chipboard – 83,000 conventional cubic meters, paper – 362,300 tons, and cardboard – 114,300 tons;

Construction materials. Cement – 1.8 million tons, 175.3 million conventional bricks, reinforced concrete goods and assemblies – 154,700 cubic meters, glazed wall tiles – 6.3 million square meters, floor tiles – 1.9 million square meters, facade tiles – 683,100 square meters, 47.4 million roofing slates, non-ore construction materials – 11.1 million cubic meters;

Light industry. 8.2 million square meters of fabric, 3.2 million items of knitted wear, 1,400 long and mid-length coats, 131,100 pairs of trousers, 305,800 coats, 100,000 pairs of footwear;

Food and beverages. Fish, including canned fish – 6,900 tons, meat, including category one sub-products – 2,100 tons, canned meat – 7.2 million conventional cans, sausage – 3,400 tons, butter – 689 tons, dairy products in terms of milk – 47,100 tons, cheese, including goat cheese – 129 tons, flour – 12,400 tons, macaroni – 5,200 tons, bread and bakery – 63,600 tons, confectionery – 3,600 tons, vodka and liquor – 4.6 million decaliters, 39.1 billion cigarettes, tea – 46,300 tons.

4.2. EXPORTS, INCLUDING EXTRA-CIS

1999 exports to extra-CIS countries reached $1,093.5 million. Exports to the CIS totaled $22.3 million. The corresponding figures for 2000 were $2,070.9 million and $27.7 million, $2,066.7 million and $48.7 million for 2001, and $1,504 million and $56 million for 2002.

The main types of goods exported by the Region are: fresh and frozen fish (2002 exports amounted to 2,800 tons), vodka (28,390 decaliters), cement (159,000 tons), gasoline (1,127,100 tons), kerosene (452,000 tons), diesel fuel (2,657,900 tons), fuel oil (5,833,100 tons), calcium fertilizers (22,900 tons), unprocessed timber (3,319,800 cubic meters), processed timber (84,100 tons), pulp (58,200 tons), paper and unbleached cardboard (127,900 tons), craft-paper and cardboard (36,500 tons), ferrous metals (94,600 tons), waste and scrap ferrous metals (91,400 tons), aluminum and aluminum goods (28,400 tons), rolling bearings ($1.6 million), and 1,400 electric motors and generators. The major importers of the Region's products are: Switzerland (47% of total exports in 2002), Sweden (13.6%), Finland (11.6%), Estonia (5.9%), the Netherlands (3.9%), Ukraine (2.7%), and Norway (2.3%).

4.3. IMPORTS, INCLUDING EXTRA-CIS

1999 imports from extra-CIS countries reached $362.1 million. Imports from CIS countries totaled $12.2 million. The corresponding figures for 2000 were $438.4 million and $21.6 million, $793.9 million and $13.7 million for 2001, and $596 million and $10 million for 2002.

The bulk of 2002 regional imports was represented by frozen meat (72,100 tons), poultry (78,800 tons), instant coffee (3,500 tons), beer, wine, and vermouth (968,600 decaliters), strong alcoholic beverages (90,580 decaliters), non-organic chemicals (132,300 tons), tanning and dying extracts and lacquer (8,700 tons), essential oils and essence (1,200 tons), plastic and plastic goods (9,800 tons), polyethylene (2,200 tons), synthetic rubber (1,600 tons), ferrous metals (8,200 tons), 184 railroad and tram carriages, 257 buses, 7,600 cars, 611 trucks, vessels ($20.8 million), and furniture ($3.6 million). The main import partners are the USA (17.7% of total imports in 2002), Germany (11.7%), Brazil (10.2%), Finland (9.7%), the UK (5.4%), Italy (4.2%), Sweden (3.5%), and the Netherlands (3.2%).

4.4. MAJOR REGIONAL EXPORT
AND IMPORT ENTITIES

Due to the specific features of trade in the Region, mainly industrial companies perform export and import operations.

5. INVESTMENT OPPORTUNITIES

5.1. INVESTMENTS IN 1992–2002 (BY INDUSTRY SECTOR), INCLUDING FOREIGN INVESTMENTS

The following factors determine the investment appeal of the Leningrad Region:

- Geographic location (borders with Finland, and Estonia, and direct access to the Baltic Sea);
- Well-developed transport infrastructure;
- Legislation providing support for investment activities;
- Qualified workforce;
- Natural resources.

5.2. CAPITAL INVESTMENT

Industry, transport, and communications account for the lion's share of capital investment.

5.3. MAJOR ENTERPRISES (INCLUDING ENTERPRISES WITH FOREIGN INVESTMENT)

The Region has registered some 800 companies with foreign investment.

Major companies with foreign investment include ZAO Veda-PAK (Gibraltar), OOO Penoplex-Kirishi (British Virgin Islands), and OOO MC Bauchemi Russia (Ireland).

Companies with 100% foreign ownership include OAO Henkel-ERA (Germany), ZAO Kappa St. Petersburg (Netherlands), OOO Swedwood Tikhvin (Netherlands), OOO Caterpillar Tosno (USA, Switzerland), ZAO Phillip Morris Izhora (USA), ZAO Ford Motor Company (USA), OOO Helkama Forste Viipuri (Finland), and OOO Kraft Foods (Germany).

Capital investment by industry sector, $ million						_TABLE 6_
	1997	1998	1999	2000	2001	2002
Total capital investment _Including major industries_ (% of total):	819.3	412.3	509.6	684.0	998.4	633.0
Industry	41.0	41.0	69.0	49.0	39.0	50.6
Agriculture and forestry	1.0	0.3	0.2	1.0	1.0	6.8
Construction	3.0	2.0	1.0	0.3	1.0	2.7
Transport and communications	30.0	33.0	17.0	39.0	49.0	22.4
Other	25.0	23.7	12.8	10.7	10.0	17.5

Foreign investment trends in 1997–2002						_TABLE 7_
	1997	1998	1999	2000	2001	2002
Foreign investment, $ million	170.4	190.7	288.3	305.6	327.0	148.3
Including FDI, $ million	75.6	90.6	236.2	205.5	238.2	115.3

5.4. MOST ATTRACTIVE SECTORS FOR INVESTMENT

According to experts and the Regional Government, forestry, timber, pulp and paper, machine engineering and metal processing, food and beverages, transport, and communications are the most appealing sectors for investment.

5.5. CURRENT LEGISLATION ON INVESTOR TAX EXEMPTIONS AND PRIVILEGES

The Leningrad Region's legislation governing investment activity comprises legislative acts and legal acts of executive regional authorities.

The law On Investment Activity in the Leningrad Region set forth a set of state support measures and protections for investors performing investment activities in industry, construction, communications, transport, agriculture, and tourism. It envisages additional state guarantees to investors provided by the Leningrad Regional Government and exemptions from local taxes.

For instance, the law stipulates tax reductions with respect to the following local taxes for the payback period of the project but no longer than the period set forth in the project's business plan: tax on property acquired or created for the investment project, tax on profit received as a result of investments, tax on profits from property and funds received by the investors free of charge to implement the investment project.

The law of the Leningrad Region On State Guarantees of the Leningrad Region on Investment Loans provides a mechanism for the provision by the Leningrad Region of state guarantees to facilitate investment activity and attract funds to the Region's economy and sets forth terms and conditions for the provision of state guarantees on investment loans.

The law of the Leningrad Region On Tax and Investment Tax Credits provides for investment tax credits to taxpayers engaged in research and development or design and testing work, as well as tech-

Largest enterprises of the Leningrad Region	TABLE 8
COMPANY	SECTOR
OAO Leningrad Nuclear Power Station, OAO Lenenergo, OAO Kirishi Power Station	Energy
OAO Luzhsky Abrasive Plant, ZAO Ford Motor Company, OAO Vyborg Shipbuilding Plant, OAO Burevestnik, OAO Pirs, ZAO Priborostroitel, OOO Helkama Forste Viipuri, OOO Caterpillar Tosno, OAO Krizo Plant, OAO ToMeZ, ZAO TZTM Titan	Machine engineering and metal processing
OOO PO Kirishinefteorgsintez, OAO Leningradslanets, OAO Shale Plant	Fuel
OAO Henkel-ERA, OOO PG Phosphorite, OAO Volkhov Chemical Plant, OAO Khimik, State Unitary Company Morozov Plant, ZAO Polymer Faro	Chemicals and petrochemicals
OAO Svetogorsk, OAO St. Petersburg Cardboard Printing Company, OAO Timber and Chemical Plant, OOO Swedwood Tikhvin, ZAO Kamennogorsk Offset Paper Plant, OAO Syassky Pulp and Paper Plant, OAO Priozerie Logging Plant, OAO Priozerie Furniture Plant	Forestry, timber, pulp, paper, and printing
ZAO Phillip Morris Izhora, ZAO Veda, OOO Maleta, OAO Sosnov Dairy Plant, OOO National Wine Terminal	Food and beverages
OAO Nefrit Ceramics, ZAO Quartz, ZAO Petroceramics, OAO Stroidetal Plant, OAO Tsesla, ZAO Kamennogorsk Open Cast Pit Management Company, ZAO Semiozersk Open Cast Pit Management Company, OAO Tolmachevo Reinforced Concrete, Metal Assembly Plant	Construction materials
OAO Fanema, ZAO Luzhsky Knitwear, OOO Komatso, ZAO Volkhovchanka, ZAO Finskor, ZAO Nika, OAO Scanworkwear, OAO Uzor	Light industry
OAO Bauxitogorsk Alumina, OAO Metallurg and its branches, Pikalevsky Alumina and Volkhov Aluminium	Non-ferrous metals

nical upgrade, expansion, reconstruction, implementation, and innovation, including creation of new or improvement of existing technology, development of new types of raw materials, and performance of socially important orders for the Leningrad Region. The Leningrad Regional Government is entitled to provide investment tax credits to taxpayers with respect to corporate profit tax and local taxes.

The Region has passed several resolutions of the Leningrad Regional Government and the Governor regulating investment activity, such as the Resolution of the Leningrad Regional Government On the Approval of Methodology to Compute the Investment Payback Period for the Purpose of Preferential Tax Treatment in the Leningrad Region, and the Resolution of the Leningrad Regional Government on the Provision of Tax and Investment Tax Credits.

In addition to the above documents directly related to investment activity, the Leningrad Regional Government has developed several regulatory acts on municipal construction, land, property, and other issues.

5.6. FEDERAL AND REGIONAL ECONOMIC AND SOCIAL DEVELOPMENT PROGRAMS FOR THE LENINGRAD REGION

Federal targeted programs. The Region is implementing several federal targeted programs, including Ecology and Natural Resources of Russia 2002–2010, Elimination of Inequalities in the Social and Economic Development of the Regions of the Russian

Federation 2002–2010 and through 2015, Upgrade of Russia's Transport System 2002–2010, and Energy Effective Economy 2002–2005 and through 2010.

Under the Upgrade of Russia's Transport System program, the Region intends to construct a ring-road around St. Petersburg and build and reconstruct access to newly built and upgraded ports in the Gulf of Finland. This will help improve efficiency of the ports in the northern part of the Gulf of Finland and provide road access to the strategically important port of Kronstadt. The conditions of highways along the Russia's western border and in the Leningrad and Pskov Regions will also be improved.

Regional programs. The Region is implementing the following regional programs of primary importance:

The regional targeted program Development and Utilization of Mineral and Resource Base in the Leningrad Region 2003–2005. The main objectives of the program are to ensure a balance between extraction and reproduction of the most popular minerals, to facilitate exploration, geological surveying, and development of new deposits in an environmentally friendly way, geological and ecological research and implementation of new technology for the development and processing of mineral resources, economical evaluation of effects of mining on the environment, and land recultivation and processing of mining and mineral processing waste in the Leningrad Region, and to provide information support to management decisions aimed at rational use and protection of mineral resources. The program financing amounts to $2.1 million from the local budget, including $0.7 million for 2003.

The Regional targeted program For the Reform of Regional Finance Management in the Leningrad Region 2003–2005 aims to mobilize financial resources to secure the Region's further social development, improve the quality of budget services provided to the Region's population (provided the cost of budget services will go down), improve the standard of living of the Region's population, create conditions and new incentives conducive to further economic development of the Region, and maintain the Region's favorable investment climate.

The Regional targeted program Development and Support to Small Enterprise in the Leningrad Region 2003–2005. The main objectives of the program are to accelerate development of small enterprise and ensure accessibility of loans for small enterprise. A budget of $4 million has been allocated for the program from the local budget, including $0.8 million in 2003, $1.5 million in 2004, and $1.7 million in 2005.

The comprehensive regional program Development of Agricultural Sector in the Leningrad Region 2001–2005 aims to increase economic viability and competitiveness of produce, decrease debts and improve financial and economic performance of most agroindustrial companies, improve the technical level of operations and labor productivity, and raise profits of agricultural companies. The local budget allocated $44 million for the program.

Regional entities responsible for raising investment		*TABLE 9*
ENTITY	ADDRESS	PHONE, FAX, E-MAIL
St. Petersburg office of ZAO PricewaterhouseCoopers Audit	19/21, ul. Dostoevskogo, St. Petersburg 191126	Phone: (812) 326 6969 Fax: (812) 326 6699
Joint Venture ST-Inter	Office 613, 111, Grazhdansky prospect, St. Petersburg 194265	Phone: (812) 531 1367 Fax: (812) 532 4874 E-mail: st@stinter.spb.su
ZAO United Consulting Group	64, Ligovsky prospect, St. Petersburg 191040	Phone: (812) 325 4860 Fax: (812) 325 4863 E-mail: postmaster@inkasbank.spb.su
ZAO AGRIConsult	36, Voznesensky prospect, St. Petersburg 190000	Phone/fax: (812) 310 8245 E-mail: agricons@mail.wplus.net
ZAO Kiptan Consulting	P.O. Box 191, Appt. 1, 27, Griboedov Channel Quay, St. Petersburg 191186	Phone: (812) 314 7278 Fax: (812) 314 7276 E-mail: kiptan@spb.cityline.ru
ZAO Consulting Firm Projects, Investments, Consulting	6 floor, 21, ul. Kuybysheva, St. Petersburg 197045	Phone/fax: (812) 230 1719, 421 3189 E-mail: pic@pop.convey.ru

6. INVESTMENT PROJECTS

Industry sector and project description	1) Expected results 2) Amount and term of investment 3) Form of financing[1] 4) Documentation[2]	Contact information
1	2	3
MINING		
24R001 ■ ● ❖ ▲		OAO Luzhsky Ore Dressing Plant
Technical upgrade of OAO Luzhsky Ore Dressing Plant Project goal: to increase output of moulding sand	1) n/a 2) $3 million/1 year 3) L, E, JV 4) FS in preparation	Razyezd 131 km, Luga, Leningrad Region, 188260 Phone: (81272) 68 096, 23 842 Andrei Vladimirovich Shashnev, Project Coordinator

[1] L – Loan, E – Equity, Leas. – Leasing, JV – Joint Venture
[2] BP – Business Plan, FS – Feasibility Study

II

NORTH-WESTERN FEDERAL DISTRICT

1	2	3

FORESTRY, TIMBER, AND PULP AND PAPER

24R002 ● ◆

Launching of production of patterned lumber, matched board, window casings, and baseboards.
Project goal: to provide materials for construction and furniture sectors.

1) n/a
2) $1.3 million/1 year
3) L $1.0 million
4) BP

OOO PF Priozersk-Les
5, ul. Zavodskaya, Priozersk,
Leningrad Region, 188760
Phone: (81279) 23 787
Fax: (81279) 24 546
Valery Vasilyevich Kiselev, Director

24R003 ■ ● ❖ ▲

Production of packaging cardboard.
Project goal: to produce packaging cardboard for companies producing construction goods, detergents, and other consumer goods.

1) 30 million square meters per year
2) $5 million/1 year
3) L, E, JV
4) FS in preparation

OOO Aeroportstroi+
10, ul. Sadovaya, Annino, Anninskaya
Volost, Lomonosov District,
Leningrad Region, 188505
Phone: (812) 595 4503, 595 4504
Anatoly Fedorovich Kosmynin,
Director

AGRICULTURE

24R004 ● ▼

Technical upgrade of poultry houses.
Project goal: to increase output.

1) Up to 150 million eggs per year
2) $1.4 million/1 year
3) L
4) Investment proposal

ZAO Nevskaya Poultry
Leskolovo, Vsevolzhsky District,
Leningrad Region, 188668
Phone/fax: (81270) 54 140
Konstantin Yevgenyevich Smirnov,
Financial Director

24R005 ● ▼

Construction of a fruit and berry processing shop.
Project goal: to expand product range.

1) Net profit – $0.25 million per year
2) $1.5 million/1 year
3) L
4) Investment proposal

ZAO Skreblovo
Skreblovo, Luzhsky District,
Leningrad Region, 188273
Phone: (81272) 58 323, 58 382, 58 373
Alexander Fedorovich Grebnev,
Director

24R006 ■ ● ❖ ◆

Merger of four major agricultural companies of the Leningrad Region – ZAO PZ Prinevskoe, ZAO Vsevolzhskoe, ZAO Telman Plemkhoz, and SPK PZ Detskoselskoe.
Project goal: to produce, store, conduct pre-sale preparation, process, and sell vegetables and potato.

1) n/a
2) $3.5 million/1 year
3) L, E, JV
4) BP

ZAO PZ Prinevskoe,
ZAO Vsevolzhskoe,
ZAO Telman Plemkhoz,
and SPK PZ Detskoselskoe
Vsevolzhsk, Leningrad Region, 180000
Phone: (812) 248 0194
Vladimir Ivanovich Oleinik,
Project Coordinator

24R007 ■ ● ❖ ◆

Production of dry brewer's spent grains from brewing waste of OAO Lenkhleboproduct.
Project goal: to strengthen the fodder base of agricultural companies, provide the cattle breeding sector with valuable feed, and the fodder sector with cheap raw material, and solve the breweries' waste utilization problem.

1) Estimated revenue –
  $0.2 million per year
2) $0.8 million/1 year
3) L, E, JV
4) BP

OAO Lenkhleboproduct
87/2, Nevsky prospect,
St. Petersburg, 191036
Phone: (812) 277 5030
Oleg Pavlovich Goncharov, CEO

TRANSPORT INFRASTRUCTURE

24R008 ■ ● ❖ ◆ ▲

Construction of a terminal for reloading exported liquid ammonia and methanol at the west bank of the Vysotsky Island in the Vyborg District.
Project goal: to reload liquid ammonia and methanol from railroad transport onto sea vessels.

1) Up to 4 million tons of liquid ammonia and methanol per year
2) $72 million/2 years
3) L, E, JV
4) FS, BP

ZAO Baltkhim-Export
Office 1–16, 3, ul. Smolnogo,
St. Petersburg, 193311
Phone: (812) 276 4294, 276 4296
Fax: (812) 279 0906
Valery Ivanovich Semenyak,
Project Coordinator

1	2	3

24R009 ■ ● ❖ ▲

Construction of a port at Batareynaya Bay in the Lomonosov District and oil product pipeline system Kirishi-Batareynaya. Project goal: to receive oil products by railroad and pipeline from oil refineries and reload them onto sea vessels.

1) 7.5 million tons of oil products per year
2) $520 million/2 years
3) L, E, JV
4) FS

OAO Oil Company Surgutneftegaz
37, ul. Podkovyrova,
St. Petersburg, 197022
Phone: (812) 329 3400
Fax (812) 329 3407
Vladimir Leonidovich Bogdanov, CEO

20R010 ■ ● ❖ ◆ ▲

Construction of a container terminal in Vistino of the Kingisepp District. Project goal: to reload general freight and containers.

1) Up to 9 million tons of freight per year
2) $361.8 million/2 years
3) L, E, JV
4) FS, BP

ZAO Tekhnoimpex
Vistino, Kingisepp District
Leningrad Region, 180000
Phone: (812) 314 5396, 275 2808
Alexey Alexandrovich Konev,
Project Coordinator

24R011 ■ ● ❖ ▲

Construction of a freight sea terminal at Ermilovskaya Bay of the Vyborg District. Project goal: to construct a modern seaport to service commercial export.

1) Freight turnover – up to 8 million tons per year
2) $253.3 million/2 years
3) L, E, JV
4) FS in preparation

ZAO Morskoe
5, ul. Dimitrova, Vyborg,
Leningrad Region, 188900
Phone: (81278) 31 859
Fax: (81278) 30 739
Alexander Sergeevich Shlykov,
Project Coordinator

24R012 ■ ● ❖ ▲

Construction of a sea freight reloading center for general freight in Primorsk of the Vyborg District. Project goal: to reload general and container freight.

1) Up to 5 million tons of freight per year
2) $158 million/2 years
3) L, E, JV
4) FS in preparation

ZAO Primorsk Sea Freight Center
10, Moskovsky prospect, Vyborg,
Leningrad Region, 188900
Phone: (812) 315 0582, 314 5396
Alexay Terentyevich Kobets,
Project Coordinator

24R013 ■ ● ❖ ▲

Construction of a sea freight reloading terminal for ammonia and carbamide and port infrastructure. Project goal: to process domestic raw materials and exported finished goods.

1) Liquid ammonia – 680,000 tons per year; granulated carbamide – 750,000 tons per year
2) $349.7 million/3 years
3) L, E, JV
4) FS in preparation

ZAO North Gas Refinery
5, Detsky prospect,
St. Petersburg,196084
Phone/fax: (812) 118 3257
Viktor Viktorovich Marmulev, CEO

24R014 ■ ● ❖ ▲

Construction of a regional distribution and accumulation freight center. Project goal: to receive oil products by railroad and pipeline transport from oil refineries and reload them onto sea vessels.

1) Reloading of a total of 2.5 million tons of non-hazardous freight per year
2) $50 million/2 years
3) L, E, JV
4) FS in preparation

OOO Freight Reloading Station
Industrial Site of OAO Phosphorite,
Kingisepp, Leningrad Region, 188452
Phone: (81275) 29 703, 29 635
Gennady Semenovich Kalika, CEO

II

NORTH-WESTERN FEDERAL DISTRICT

25. MURMANSK REGION [51]

ECONOMIC MAP

BARENTS SEA

Rybachy Peninsula

Nikel
Zapolyarniy

MURMANSK
Kildinstroy

Kharlovka

Cape Svyatoy Nos

Tuloma

Lake Imandra

Olenegorsk

Voronya

Monchegorsk

Kirovsk

Iokanga

Kovdor
Apatity

Kandalaksha

Krasnoschele

Ponoy

Varzuga

Lesozavodsky

Umba

Kandalakshsky gulf

Pyalitsa

Kestenga

Lake Topozero

WHITE SEA

Ushkozero

Dvinskaya guba (gulf)

Kem

Onezhskaya guba (gulf)

Belomorsk

Severodvinsk ARKHANGELSK

Nadvoitsy

Onega

Segezha
Lake Vygozero

PROCESSING INDUSTRY		MINING INDUSTRY	POWER PLANTS
Non-ferrous metals	Construction materials	Nickel ore	Thermal power plants
Machine engineering and metal processing	Food and beverages	Copper ore	Nuclear power plants
Chemicals and petrochemicals		Bauxite	Hydro power plants
Forestry and timber		Apatite	Coordinated hydroelectric system
		Micas	
		Iron ore	LIVESTOCK BREEDING
		Fishing ports	Reindeer breeding

O ver the past few years, the Murmansk Region has been a continuous focus of attention. This is due not only to the prospects for the development of oil and gas in the Arctic zone, but also to the newly opened opportunities of transcontinental transport corridors along the Northern Sea Route. The vast natural resources of the Kola Peninsula, the developed industrial and social infrastructure of the Murmansk Region, and the favorable market conditions prevailing in the Region are well known both within Russia and abroad.

The Murmansk Region is a major industrial center. Its major sectors are mining, non-ferrous metals, and fisheries. The Region produces nickel, copper, cobalt, raw and dressed ore, and aluminum. Fishing companies produce a wide range of fish products: canned, frozen, fresh, smoked, and dried fish, and balyk. Ship-repair and fishing equipment manufacturing and packaging sectors have emerged in the Region to serve its core sectors.

The Murmansk Seaport plays a special role as the starting point of the Northern Sea Route linking Russia to Scandinavia, the UK, Canada, and the USA.

Insufficient information on investment activity, investment projects carried out by companies in the Region, and research and development in new technology and new materials has in the past acted as a deterrent for investors and trading partners. In order to overcome this drawback, the Regional Government has issued a Catalog of Investment and Innovation Proposals. This publication represents a step in the implementation of the Region's program for social and economic development. Numerous companies and organizations in the Murmansk Region are currently implementing development projects. The Regional executive and local authorities are assisting in the implementation of a number of proposals and projects and facilitating the establishment of inter-regional and international economic links.

Investment and innovation projects form the basis of the Economic Development Framework for the Murmansk Region through 2015, which was adopted by the Regional Government in 2001 and is currently being implemented.

I wish every success to all potential investors in their search for new ideas and partners and in developing their business, and I hope that the projects and proposals set forth herein will be of interest to them.

Yury Yevdokimov,
GOVERNOR OF THE MURMANSK REGION

II

NORTH-WESTERN FEDERAL DISTRICT

1. GENERAL INFORMATION

1.1. GEOGRAPHY

Situated in Russia's north-west on the Kola Peninsula, the Murmansk Region covers a total area of 144,900 square kilometers. To the west, the Region borders Norway and Finland, to the south – the Republic of Karelia, and to the north, east, and south-east the Region is washed by the Barents and White Seas.

1.2. CLIMATE

The Murmansk Region has an arctic maritime climate.

The average air temperature in January is –5.3°C, rising to +14.1°C in July. The average annual precipitation is 350–1,000 mm.

1.3. POPULATION

According to preliminary 2002 census results, the population of the Murmansk Region totaled 893,000 people. The average population density is 6.2 people per square kilometer. The economically active population amounts to 580,000 people. 2002 official unemployment was 12.8%.

Demographically speaking, some 68.2% are of working age, 16.9% are below the statutory working age, and 14.9% are beyond the statutory working age.

As of 2002, the Region's major urban centers were Murmansk with 336,700 inhabitants, Severomorsk with 77,800 inhabitants, and Apatity with 68,300 inhabitants.

Population							TABLE 1	
	1992	1997	1998	1999	2000	2001	2002
Total population, '000	1,165	1,051	1,034	1,018	1,001	988	893
Economically active population, '000	639	563	568	583	583	577	580

2. ADMINISTRATION

75, pr. Lenina, Murmansk, Murmansk Region, 183038
Phone: (8152) 48 6200; fax: (8152) 45 1054. E-mail: obl.admin@murman.ru; http://gov.murman.ru

NAME	POSITION	CONTACT INFORMATION
Yury Alexeevich YEVDOKIMOV	Governor of the Murmansk Region	Phone: (8152) 48 6201 Fax: (8152) 47 6503
Alexander Anatolyevich SELIN	First Deputy Governor of the Murmansk Region	Phone: (8152) 48 6210
Sergei Alexandrovich NIKITAEV	First Deputy Governor of the Murmansk Region, Head of the Finance Department of the Murmansk Region	Phone: (8152) 68 1281
Vladimir Nikolaevich MOTLOKHOV	Deputy Governor of the Murmansk Region, Head of the Economic Department of the Murmansk Region	Phone: (8152) 48 6204
Viktor Alexandrovich MILLER	Deputy Governor of the Murmansk Region, Head of the Construction, Architecture, and Residential and Communal Service Reform Department of the Murmansk Region	Phone: (8152) 48 6204
Sergei Alexeevich SUBBOTIN	Deputy Governor of the Murmansk Region for Economic Security	Phone: (8152) 48 6252
Vladimir Mikhailovich YEVSEEV	Deputy Head of the Economic Department of the Murmansk Region, Head of the Department of External Economic and Cross-Regional Relations	Phone: (8152) 47 7264
Alexander Nazarovich ALIMOV	Head of the Sub-Department of Enterprise and Innovation of the Economic Department of the Murmansk Region	Phone: (8152) 48 6319

3. ECONOMIC POTENTIAL

3.1. 1997–2002 GROSS REGIONAL PRODUCT (GRP). INDUSTRY BREAKDOWN

The 2002 gross regional product amounted to $2,250 million, which constitutes 11.4% growth year-on-year. Per capita GRP amounted to $2,043 in 2001 and $2,519 in 2002.

3.2. MAJOR ECONOMIC GROWTH PROJECTIONS

The Economic Development Strategy of the Murmansk Region through 2015 sets the following targets for the Region:

Mining: moderate growth (0.5–1%) in the mining sector through 2015, with a focus on output quality;

GRP trends in 1997–2002						TABLE 2
	1997	1998	1999	2000	2001	2002*
GRP in current prices, $ million	3,143.5	2,396.4	1,702.7	2,075.0	2,019.8	2,249.8

*Estimates of the Murmansk Regional Administration

GRP industry breakdown in 1997–2002, % of total						TABLE 3
	1997	1998	1999	2000	2001	2002*
GRP	100.0	100.0	100.0	100.0	100.0	100.0
Industry	41.0	40.4	47.6	50.8	45.6	42.5
Agriculture and forestry	1.1	0.2	0.9	0.6	1.1	1.0
Construction	4.6	4.1	3.8	3.8	7.1	6.7
Transport and communications	11.5	12.4	10.6	10.4	11.1	12.5
Trade and public catering	11.7	12.6	13.9	11.9	12.9	13.1
Other	30.1	30.3	23.2	22.5	22.2	24.2

*Estimates of the Murmansk Regional Administration

Fuel and energy: energy sufficiency in the Kola electricity system by 2015, export generation capacity of 500 MW and 3.0–3.5 billion kWh of electricity, construction of a second nuclear power plant KAES-2 (the first unit with generating capacity of 645 MW will be completed by 2010), development of new oil and gas fields, construction of new pipelines, commencement of natural gas extraction at the Shtokman field with estimated maximum production of 60 billion cubic meters;

Food and beverages (fisheries): a 20% increase in fish catch by 2015 and five-fold fish processing output growth;

Transport and communications: freight turnover increase to 47-50 million tons per year and the development of sea transport through the construction of new ice-breakers and large-capacity tankers, and the reconstruction of cargo ports of the Murmansk Region to expand throughput.

3.3. INDUSTRIAL OUTPUT IN 1997–2002 FOR MAJOR SECTORS OF ECONOMY

The leading industrial sectors of the Murmansk Region are non-ferrous metals, energy, food, and chemicals. Their combined share in total industrial output is 82.7%.

Non-ferrous metals. Metals account for 27.1% of total industrial output. The aluminum sector is rep-

resented by the Kandalaksha aluminum melting companies. The major enterprise is OAO Kandalaksha Aluminum Plant (a subsidiary of OAO SUAL). Copper, nickel, and cobalt are produced at OAO Severonickel (Monchegorsk) and OAO Pechenganickel (Zapolyarny) plants. The regional companies extract and dress nephelite, bauxite, and titanium ore.

Energy. The sector accounts for 21.8% of total industrial output. OAO Kolenergo services the whole of the Murmansk Region. The company consists of 17 hydroelectric power stations, two thermal power stations, two electricity grid companies, an experimental tidal power plant, and several other enterprises. The Kola Nuclear Power Station, which is comprised of four energy units, is independent of OAO Kolenergo.

Food and beverages. The share of this sector in total industrial output is 17.3%. Fisheries accounts for the lion's share of the sector with 81.1%. The Union of Fishing Companies Murmansk Trawler Fleet Consortium catches some 31.4% of the Region's fish output. The share of the Consortium in the food sector's total output is 25.5%.

Chemicals and petrochemicals. The sector accounts for 16.5% of total industrial output. Chemical companies utilize phosphate materials, natural gas, and waste from ferrous and non-ferrous metal processing. OAO Apatite, the largest phosphate production company

II

NORTH-WESTERN FEDERAL DISTRICT

Industry breakdown of industrial output in 1997–2002, % of total						*TABLE 4*
	1997	1998	1999	2000	2001	2002*
Industry	100.0	100.0	100.0	100.0	100.0	100.0
Non-ferrous metals	36.0	32.8	38.5	37.7	28.4	27.1
Energy	24.0	22.6	13.2	13.5	18.1	21.8
Food and beverages	13.3	17.1	19.4	18.0	18.8	17.3
Chemicals and petrochemicals	11.0	10.9	11.9	14.3	17.4	16.5
Ferrous metals	8.0	9.9	10.0	9.3	9.9	9.9
Machine engineering and metal processing	4.8	3.9	4.2	4.5	4.9	5.4
Construction materials	1.2	1.0	0.7	0.8	0.9	0.8
Flour, cereals, and mixed fodder	0.8	0.7	0.8	0.7	0.6	0.5
Forestry, timber, and pulp and paper	0.3	0.4	0.3	0.3	0.3	0.2
Light industry	0.3	0.3	0.2	0.2	0.3	0.2
Fuel	0.1	0.1	–	0.2	0.1	0.1
Glass and porcelain	–	–	–	–	0.3	–

*Estimates of the Murmansk Regional Administration

Fuel and energy sector production and consumption trends, 1997–2002						*TABLE 5*
	1997	1998	1999	2000	2001	2002
Electricity output, billion kWh	16.2	16.1	16.5	17.4	16.7	16.5
Electricity consumption, billion kWh	13.3	12.8	12.6	12.7	12.6	12.4

in Russia, supplies over two thirds of Russia's phosphate raw materials to the domestic and external markets.

3.4. FUEL AND ENERGY BALANCE (OUTPUT AND CONSUMPTION PER RESOURCE)

The Murmansk energy system enjoys excessive capacities. The installed capacity of OAO Kolenergo is 2 GW. The Kola Nuclear Power Station generates some 60% of the Region's electricity. Its 2002 output reached 9.6 billion kWh of electricity and 90,000 Gcal of heat energy. OAO Kolenergo and the Kola Nuclear Power Station fully satisfy the Region's demand for electricity. Surplus electricity is exported to the Republic of Karelia, Finland, and Norway.

3.5. TRANSPORT INFRASTRUCTURE

In 2002, freight transportation grew by 1.6% to 33 million tons. Sea cargo turnover increased by 13.2% and railway cargo turnover by 1.4%. Road and air transport account for a considerable but decreasing share of freight transportation at 30% and 9.1%, respectively.

Roads. The Region has 4,200 kilometers of paved public highway. Annual freight turnover is 500 million tons.

Railroads. The Murmansk Region has 891 kilometers of railroads. Railroad routes provide access to Murmansk and the port of Murmansk, and link the Region to Central Russia.

Airports. The Region has two large airports – the Murmansk Airport at Murmashi and the Khibiny

Airport at Apatity. The Murmansk airport operates international routes to Kirkenes and Tromso in Norway, Rovaniemi in Finland, and Lulea in Sweden.

Sea transport. The 49 vessels of OAO Murmansk Ship Lines, including nuclear-powered ice-breakers, provide freight and passenger transportation services.

Seaports. The Murmansk Commercial Seaport is the largest Russian seaport above the Arctic Circle with year-round operations. The port ranks fourth in freight transshipment volumes among Russia's 42 ports. The port is the main processor of freight to the Far North and Arctic areas, and for extra-CIS exports. The port achieved a record freight processing volume of 9.7 million tons in 2001. Its through-put capacity is 12 million tons of freight per year.

3.6. MAIN NATURAL RESOURCES: RESERVES AND EXTRACTION IN 2002

The Kola Peninsula has more than 60 large deposits of various mineral resources. Currently, the Region extracts some 30 types of minerals, the most valuable being phosphorus, titanium, iron, aluminum, copper, nickel, and zirconium ore. The region is rich in mica, ceramics and building materials, facing stone, and semi-precious and decorative stones.

Oil and gas fields have been discovered under the Barents Sea, including the Shtokman gas condensate deposit with a reserve of 3 trillion cubic meters.

4. TRADE OPPORTUNITIES

4.1. MAIN GOODS
PRODUCED IN THE REGION

The Region produces 100% of Russia's total output of apatite and 12% of iron ore concentrate, 14% of refined copper, 43% of nickel, and 14% of edible fish products.

Metals. In 2002, the Region produced 7.6 million tons of iron ore and 4 million tons of apatite concentrate.

Forestry. Industrial timber output amounted to 87,700 dense cubic meters, and lumber to 21,900 cubic meters.

Food and beverages. In 2002 fish catch amounted to 680,000 tons, canned fish – 27 million conventional cans, meat – 5,600 tons, and bread and bakery products – 42,300 tons.

4.2. EXPORTS, INCLUDING EXTRA-CIS

The Murmansk Region's exports to extra-CIS countries amounted to $587.9 million in 2000, while exports to the CIS totaled $4.7 million. The corresponding figures for 2001 were $534.5 million and $5 million, and $470.9 million and $1

million for 2002. Some 45% of total industrial output was exported in 2002.

The Region trades with some 80 countries. The main types of goods exported by the Region in 2001 were non-ferrous metals and metal goods – 124,000 tons, apatite concentrate – 3,065,000 tons, fish – 205,000 tons, and raw timber – 67,900 cubic meters.

4.3. IMPORTS, INCLUDING EXTRA-CIS

2000 imports from extra-CIS countries amounted to $125.4 million, imports from CIS countries totaled $4.9 million. The corresponding figures for 2001 were $113.5 million and $7.4 million, and $89.7 million and $1.5 million for 2002.

The major exporters to the Region are Norway, Finland, the UK, Germany, Sweden, and the Netherlands.

4.4. MAJOR REGIONAL
EXPORT AND IMPORT ENTITIES

Due to the specific features of trade in the Murmansk Region, export and import operations are performed mainly by industrial aluminum and chemical companies.

5. INVESTMENT OPPORTUNITIES

5.1. INVESTMENTS IN 1992–2002
(BY INDUSTRY SECTOR),
INCLUDING FOREIGN INVESTMENTS

The following factors determine the investment appeal of the Murmansk Region:

• Its advantageous geographic location (the Region is situated at the crossroads of major sea routes and has sea and land borders with European countries);

• Its developed transport infrastructure (year-round operating seaport, advanced ice-breaker fleet);

• Legislation supporting investment activities (organizational and financial support to investment projects and executive authorities' guarantees of business safety);

• Its highly qualified workforce;

• Cheap electricity;

• Availability of natural resources.

5.2. CAPITAL INVESTMENT

Industry accounts for the lion's share of capital investment with 52.8%.

5.3. MAJOR ENTERPRISES (INCLUDING
ENTERPRISES WITH FOREIGN INVESTMENT)

As of 2001, the Region hosted 97 companies with foreign investment. The following companies are participating in the exploration and development of the Shtockman oil and gas field: OAO Gazprom, Conoco (USA), Total (France), Norsk Hydro (Norway), and Fortum (Finland).

Capital investment by industry sector, $ million						TABLE 6
	1997	1998	1999	2000	2001	2002
Total capital investment *Including major industries* (% of total):	412.8	182.4	223.6	255.6	376.3	296.4
Industry	58.8	55.6	52.2	46.2	57.4	52.8
Agriculture and forestry	0.3	1.3	1.7	3.0	1.3	2.0
Construction	3.2	1.0	0.7	1.6	0.8	0.9
Transport and communications	17.0	23.2	13.6	31.4	24.6	23.9
Trade and public catering	3.6	0.7	2.6	2.0	0.8	1.3
Other	17.1	18.2	29.2	15.8	15.1	19.1

Foreign investment trends in 1996–2002						*TABLE 7*
	1996–1997	1998	1999	2000	2001	2002
Foreign investment, $ million	6.3	9.6	14.6	44.0	12.4	20.2
Including FDI, $ million	4.9	2.2	8.2	29.3	2.3	2.3

5.4. MOST ATTRACTIVE SECTORS FOR INVESTMENT

Mining, fuel and energy, and transport and communications are the most potentially appealing sectors for investment.

The development of the oil and gas reserves of the Arctic shelf will necessitate the upgrading of the transport infrastructure, including pipeline transport.

5.5. CURRENT LEGISLATION ON INVESTOR TAX EXEMPTIONS AND PRIVILEGES

The Region has passed several laws regulating investment activity in the Region:
  • On Investment Tax Credits in the Murmansk Region;
  • On Investment Activity and Guarantees in the Murmansk Region;
  • On Economic Development Zones in the Murmansk Region.

Pursuant to the Law On Investment Tax Credits in the Murmansk Region, the Region provides investment credits for the regional component of profit or property tax. Investors performing investment projects listed in the Region's investment program enjoy preferential rights to investment tax credit.

In compliance with the Regional law, investors performing investment projects listed in the Region's investment program are eligible for state guarantees and tax privileges.

Tax privileges provide for reduced payments of local taxes and non-budgetary fund contributions for the project payback period (subject to granted privileges). Exemptions and privileges include:

Tax on property created or acquired during the implementation of an investment project;

Tax on profit from sales of products, works, and services, produced at the facilities created (acquired) during the implementation of an investment projectsor using a technology put into operation during the project;

Tax on profit from assets granted to an investor to implement the investment project.

Largest enterprises of the Murmansk Region	*TABLE 8*
COMPANY	SECTOR
OAO Kola Mining and Metal Company	Non-ferrous metals
OAO Kandalaksha Aluminum Plant	Non-ferrous metals
OAO Kovdor Ore Dressing Plant	Ferrous metals
OAO Olkon	Ferrous metals
OAO Kolenergo	Energy
OAO Apatite	Chemicals
OAO Kovdorslyuda	Construction
Union of Fishing Companies Murmansk Trawler Fleet Consortium	Fishery, food
OAO Khlebopek	Food and beverages
OAO Murmansk Bakery	Food and beverages

5.6. FEDERAL AND REGIONAL ECONOMIC AND SOCIAL DEVELOPMENT PROGRAMS FOR THE MURMANSK REGION

Federal targeted programs. The Region is implementing the federal targeted program for the Modernization of Russia's Transport System 2002–2010, which envisages the construction of a bridge over the Kola Bay to link the Region to Scandinavia, and the development of shipping transport and cargo port infrastructure.

The Murmansk Region is participating in the following programs: Energy Efficient Economy 2002–2005 and through 2010 and The Elimination of Inequalities in the Social and Economic Development of the Regions of the Russian Federation 2002–2010 and through 2015.

Regional programs. The Region has drafted more than ten targeted programs, including the priority Scientific and Technical Program for the Murmansk Region 2003, which aims to improve science and technology in basic sectors and life-sustenance systems in line with the economic development strategy approved by Resolution No. 251-PP of the Murmansk Region of December 20, 2001.

Regional entities responsible for raising investment		*TABLE 9*
ENTITY	ADDRESS	PHONE, FAX, E-MAIL
Northern Chamber of Industry and Commerce	10, per. Rusanova, Murmansk, Murmansk Region, 183766	Phone: (8152) 47 2999, 47 3459 Fax: (8152) 47 3978 E-mail: ncci@online.ru http://www.ncci.ru
Union of Industrialists and Entrepreneurs (Employers) of the Murmansk Region	2, ul. Sofyi Perovskoy, Murmansk, Murmansk Region, 183016	Phone: (8152) 45 3513 Fax: (8152) 45 0599 E-mail: sppmo@dionis.mels.ru http://www.sppmo.ru
Economic Department of the Murmansk Region	75, pr. Lenina, Murmansk, Murmansk Region, 183038	Phone: (8152) 45 1054 E-mail: obl.admin@murman.ru http://gov.murman.ru

II

N O R T H - W E S T E R N   F E D E R A L   D I S T R I C T

6. INVESTMENT PROJECTS

Industry sector and project description	1) Expected results 2) Amount and term of investment 3) Form of financing[1] 4) Documentation[2]	Contact information
1	2	3

MINING

25R001 ■ ● ▲		OAO Kovdor Ore Dressing Plant
Acquisition of equipment and machinery for ore extraction from deep pit layers. Project goal: to increase output through deeper pit extraction.	1) Total extraction of 12 million tons of ore per year 2) $6.3 million/n/a 3) E, L 4) FS	5, ul. Sukhacheva, Kovdor, Murmansk Region, 184141 Phone: (81535) 71 815, 76 013 Fax: (81535) 72 763 E-mail: Bbw@kovgok.ru Igor Vyacheslavovich Melik-Gaikazov, CEO

ENERGY

25R002 ■ ● ★ ▲		OAO Kolenergo
Construction of the Iokanskaya Hydroelectric Power Station. Project goal: to produce electricity from hydro resources.	1) n/a 2) $53.5 million/n/a 3) E, L, Leas. 4) FS	2, ul. Kirova, Murmashi, Murmansk Region, 184364 Phone/fax: (8152) 64 9017 E-mail: common@kolen.elektra.ru Yevgeny Georgievich Gorbunov, CEO

MACHINE ENGINEERING AND METAL PROCESSING

25R003 ■ ● ★ ▲		GTEP TEKOS
Construction of facilities for the production of foam polyurethanium thermal-insulated steel pipes for heat and hot water supply systems. Project goal: to penetrate the market of pipes for residential housing construction.	1) Up to 100 km of pipes per year 2) $1.1 million/1 year 3) E, L, Leas. 4) FS	15, ul. Promyshlennaya, Murmansk, Murmansk Region, 183034 Phone/fax: (8152) 43 5214 Igor Vyacheslavovich Saburov, Director

[1] L – Loan, E – Equity, Leas. – Leasing, JV – Joint Venture
[2] BP – Business Plan, FS – Feasibility Study

1	2	3

FOOD AND BEVERAGES

25R004 ❖ ▲		
Upgrading of fixed assets of a mayonnaise producer. Project goal: to extend product range.	1) n/a 2) $8.9 million/1 year 2) JV 2) Preliminary FS	OOO Sevtekchcenter South Moorage, Murmansk Fishing Seaport, Murmansk, Murmansk Region, 183001 Phone/fax: (8152) 28 6486 E- mail: sevteh@dionis.mels.ru Valery Ivanovich Levenets, CEO

TRANSPORT INFRASTRUCTURE

25R005 ■ ● ▲		
Construction of a reloading terminal for apatite concentrate and phosphorus fertilizers at the operating seaport. Project goal: to expand the range of transshipment services.	1) Capacity of 3 million tons per year 2) $9.4 million/3 years 2) E, L 2) FS	Federal State Unitary Company Kandalaksha Trade Seaport, 19, ul. Belomorskaya, Kandalaksha, Murmansk Region, 184040 Phone/fax: (81533) 92 141 Alexander Vasilyevich Strashny, General Manager

25R006 ● ◆		
Construction of a freight moorage at the operating seaport. Project goal: to expand the range of port services.	1) 300,000 tons of general freight 2) $22.3 million/2 years 2) L 2) BP	Murmansk Commercial Seaport Administration, 19, pr. Portovy, Murmansk, Murmansk Region, 183024 Phone/fax: (8152) 42 0232, 48 0021 Valery Viktorovich Nikulin, CEO

25R007 ■ ● ❖ ◆		
Establishment of an ice-breaker fleet to provide year-round transportation of oil, natural gas, gas concentrate, and other goods. Project goal: to increase the volume and range of port services.	1) 4 modern nuclear ice-breakers 2) $950.2 million/3 years 2) E, L, JV 2) BP	OAO Murmansk Sealines 15, ul. Kominterna, Murmansk, Murmansk Region, 183038 Phone: (8152) 48 1008, 48 1048, 45 4842 Fax: (8152) 45 5629 E- mail: postmaster@msco.ru Alexander Mikhailovich Medvedev, CEO, Andrei Alexeevich Smirnov, contact person

HOTEL BUSINESS, TOURISM, AND RECREATION

25R008 ■ ▲ ◆		
Construction of a tourist and entertainment center at the tourist hotel Khibiny. Project goal: to provide tourist services.	1) n/a 2) $1.0 million/5 years 2) E, L 2) BP	OOO Khibiny Recreation Center 25, ul. Leningradskaya, Kirovsk, Murmansk Region, 184230 Phone: (81531) 32 714 Natalia Vladimirovna Krotova, Director

SCIENCE AND INNOVATION

25R009 ❖ ▲		
Development of a fiber optical system for linear seismic exploration of off-shore oil and gas fields. Project goal: to create a pilot fiber optical receiver and recording system.	1) n/a 2) $1.3 million/3 years 2) JV 2) Research and development study, FS	Federal State Unitary Company Sevmorneftegeofizika 17, ul. K. Marksa, Murmansk, Murmansk Region, 183647 Phone/fax: (8152) 45 6049 E-mail: postmaster@smng.murmansk.ru Konstantin Alexandrovich Dolgunov, CEO

26. NOVGOROD REGION [53]

E C O N O M I C M A P

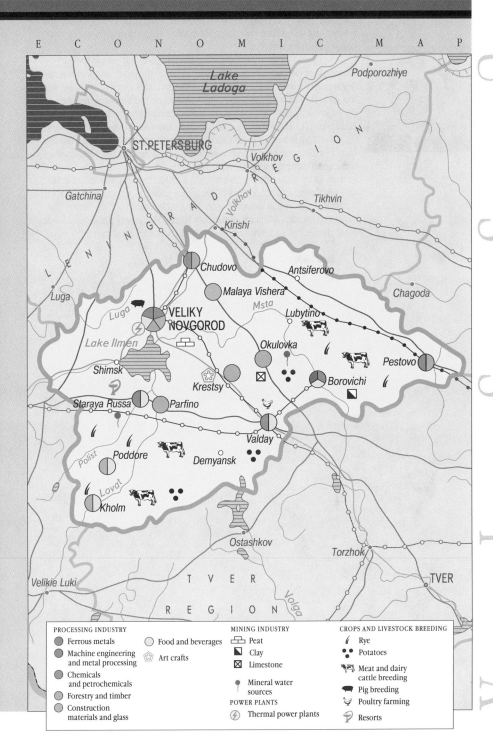

Lake Ladoga

Podporozhiye

ST.PETERSBURG

Volkhov

Gatchina

Tikhvin

Luga

Kirishi

Chudovo

Antsiferovo

Chagoda

Malaya Vishera

Msta

Lubytino

VELIKY NOVGOROD

Okulovka

Lake Ilmen

Pestovo

Shimsk

Krestsy

Borovichi

Staraya Russa

Parfino

Valday

Poddore

Demyansk

Polist

Lovat

Kholm

Ostashkov

Torzhok

TVER

Velikie Luki

T V E R

R E G I O N

Volga

PROCESSING INDUSTRY
- Ferrous metals
- Machine engineering and metal processing
- Chemicals and petrochemicals
- Forestry and timber
- Construction materials and glass
- Food and beverages
- Art crafts

MINING INDUSTRY
- Peat
- Clay
- Limestone
- Mineral water sources

POWER PLANTS
- Thermal power plants

CROPS AND LIVESTOCK BREEDING
- Rye
- Potatoes
- Meat and dairy cattle breeding
- Pig breeding
- Poultry farming
- Resorts

The Novgorod land is second to none in terms of its history, culture, and people. Novgorod was the birthplace of the Novgorod Republic, the first democratic system of government in the history of Russia. Trade and crafts prospered in this land, and the ancient river trade route "from Vikings to the Greeks" passed through Novgorod.

Novgorod's unique geographic location, considerable natural resources, stable social and political situation, dynamically developing research and development and education sector, highly qualified workforce, targeted approach to economic management, and favorable enterprise environment, all open up new opportunities for investors.

Novgorod's industry is expanding at a fast pace. Our Region has had to overcome numerous difficulties in order to get to the point we are at now. At the beginning of market reforms and during the period of systemic crisis, we were forced to find new solutions to complicated social and economic problems.

I know that hard work, a rational analysis-based approach, and radical out-of-the-box approaches, enabled the Region to find effective solutions in that difficult situation.

The Region has successfully sorted out complex tasks related to the development of a comprehensive market economy infrastructure, a competitive environment, small enterprise support, a favorable investment climate, and steady industrial growth. Today, we are faced with the strategic task of fostering innovation in all spheres of economic development. This implies taking an innovation-based approach to furthering growth in industrial, economic, and human resource potential. The Novgorod Regional Administration is committed to improving the Region's investment climate and attracting new foreign investment into the Region.

Mikhail Prusak,
GOVERNOR OF THE NOVGOROD REGION

1. GENERAL INFORMATION

1.1. GEOGRAPHY

Situated in north-western Russia, the Novgorod Region covers a total area of 55,300 square kilometers. To the north it borders and the Leningrad Region, to the west – the Pskov Region, to the south – the Tver Region, and to the east – the Vologda Region.

1.2. CLIMATE

The Novgorod Region enjoys a moderate continental climate. Air temperatures in January average –9.7°C, rising to an average of +16.9°C in July. Annual precipitation reaches 660 mm. The growing season lasts around 160–180 days.

1.3. POPULATION

According to preliminary 2002 census results, the total population of the Novgorod Region stood at 695,000. The average population density is 12.6 people per square kilometer. The economically active population is 355,200 people. Official unemployment stood at 1.3% in 2002; the actual rate was 5.8%.

Demographically speaking, some 59.6% are of statutory working age, 17.1% are below the statutory working age, and 23.3% are beyond the statutory working age.

The major urban centers of the Novgorod Region (2002 data) are Veliky Novgorod with 217,200 inhabitants, Borovichi with 58,800 inhabitants, and Staraya Russa with 40,700 inhabitants.

Population							TABLE 1
	1992	1997	1998	1999	2000	2001	2002
Total population, '000	751	738	737	734	727	720	695
Economically active population, '000	376	350	357	366	365	369	355

2. ADMINISTRATION

1, Sofiyskaya pl., Veliky Novgorod, Novgorod Region, 173005. Phone: (8162) 13 2287; fax: (8162) 13 1330
E-mail: niac@niac.ru; http://region.adm.nov.ru

NAME	POSITION	CONTACT INFORMATION
Mikhail Mikhailovich PRUSAK	Governor of the Novgorod Region	Phone: (81622) 74 779
Mikhail Denisovich SKIBAR	First Deputy Head of the Novgorod Regional Administration for Industry, Construction, Architecture, Foreign and Inter-regional Economic Relations	Phone: (81622) 78 380
Alexander Sergeevich BOYTSOV	Deputy Head of the Novgorod Regional Administration for the Agroindustrial Sector, Food Policy, Communal Services and Environment Protection	Phone: (81622) 74 775
Anton Vasilyevich ZEMLYAK	Deputy Head of the Novgorod Regional Administration	Phone: (8162) 13 2560
Nikolai Stepanovich IVANKOV	Deputy Head of the Novgorod Regional Administration for Housing and Communal Services, Fuel and Energy, and Forestry	Phone: (81622) 72 675
Nikolai Nikolaevich RENKAS	Deputy Head of the Novgorod Regional Administration for Healthcare, Education, and Social Policy	Phone: (81622) 74 766
Vladimir Grigoryevich ALFIMOV	Deputy Head of the Novgorod Regional Administration, Chairman of the Committee for State Property Management of the Novgorod Region (in charge of land use and transport)	Phone: (8162) 13 2222
Vladimir Nikolaevich PODOPRIGORA	Deputy Head of the Novgorod Regional Administration, Representative of the Novgorod Region at the Government of the Russian Federation	Phone: (095) 299 4004

NAME	POSITION	CONTACT INFORMATION
Arnold Alexandrovich SHALMUEV	Chairman of the Economic Committee of the Novgorod Regional Administration	Phone: (81622) 74 770
Irina Lvovna ZHELTOVA	Head of the Department for Construction and Investment Policy of the Novgorod Regional Administration	Phone: (81622) 76 040

3. ECONOMIC POTENTIAL

3.1. 1997–2002 GROSS REGIONAL PRODUCT (GRP). INDUSTRY BREAKDOWN

The Novgorod Region's 2002 gross regional product amounted to $1.044 billion, 8.8% up on 2001. Industrial production accounted for the bulk of the growth, providing 38.7% of total GRP. Per capita GRP was $1,333 in 2001 and $1,504 in 2002.

3.2. MAJOR ECONOMIC GROWTH PROJECTIONS

The blueprint for the social and economic development of the Region in 2003 is set forth in the Conceptual Framework for the Economic Development of the Novgorod Region in 2003. The industrial sector is expected to maintain growth through competitive output, penetration of new markets, expansion and renewal of production facilities, active pursuit of innovation, reduction of production costs, and utilization of resource saving technologies.

3.3. INDUSTRIAL OUTPUT IN 1997–2002 FOR MAJOR SECTORS OF ECONOMY

The Novgorod Region's major industrial sectors are chemicals and petrochemicals, forestry, timber and paper, food and beverages, and

GRP trends in 1997–2002						TABLE 2
	1997	1998	1999	2000	2001*	2002*
GRP in current prices, $ million	1,271.3	954.6	661.2	743.7	960.0	1,044.3

*Estimates of the Novgorod Regional Administration

GRP industry breakdown in 1997–2002, % of total						TABLE 3
	1997	1998	1999	2000	2001*	2002*
GRP	100.0	100.0	100.0	100.0	100.0	100.0
Industry	38.2	37.9	41.2	41.8	37.6	38.7
Agriculture and forestry	9.5	9.3	10.1	11.2	10.8	9.8
Construction	8.2	8.2	8.1	9.1	13.2	12.2
Transport and communications	6.5	5.5	4.4	5.2	5.9	6.0
Trade and public catering	13.5	16.0	15.2	11.8	13.2	14.4
Other	23.5	22.4	17.5	18.3	17.8	16.8
Net taxes on output	0.6	0.7	3.5	2.6	1.5	2.1

*Estimates of the Novgorod Regional Administration

machine engineering. These sectors account for a combined 79.1% of total industrial output.

Chemicals and petrochemicals. The sector accounts for 26.9% of the total industrial output. The largest enterprises are OAO Akron, OAO Fliderer-Chudovo, and OAO Novgorod Fiberglass Factory.

Food and beverages. The sector accounts for 20.9% of total industrial output. The major segments of the Region's food industry include processed and unprocessed meat, dairy and vegetable products, confectionery, macaroni, and alcoholic and non-alcoholic beverages. Major enterprises include OAO Laktis, OOO Nov-gorod Bacon, ZAO Dirol, OAO Novgorodsky Myasnoy Dvor, OAO Deka, OAO Alkon, and OOO Lakto-Novgorod.

Forestry, timber, and pulp and paper. The sector accounts for 18.9% of total industrial output. The largest enterprises in the sector are ZAO SP Chudovo RWS, OAO Parfinsky Plywood Factory, and OOO Amkor Rench Novgorod.

Machine engineering and metal processing. The sector accounts for 12.4% of total industrial output. The largest enterprises in the sector are OOO Elbor-Abraziv, OOO Elbor-Chiza, OAO Mstator, OAO Spektr, OOO Firma Vektor, OOO

Industry breakdown of industrial output in 1997–2002, % of total						*TABLE 4*
	1997	1998	1999	2000	2001	2002*
Industry	100.0	100.0	100.0	100.0	100.0	100.0
Chemicals and petrochemicals	31.4	34.4	34.2	31.6	29.9	26.9
Food and beverages	16.8	17.8	22.2	20.7	21.8	20.9
Forestry, timber, and pulp and paper	10.9	13.0	14.0	14.7	14.1	18.9
Machine engineering and metal processing	11.2	9.2	10.1	10.9	12.4	12.4
Energy	16.5	15.0	8.5	8.8	8.8	9.9
Ferrous metals	5.5	4.3	5.5	7.0	6.5	5.8
Construction materials	4.2	3.3	2.5	2.4	2.9	2.5
Flour, cereals, and mixed fodder	0.8	0.7	0.9	1.3	1.6	0.5
Glass and porcelain	0.9	0.7	0.9	0.8	0.4	0.4
Light industry	0.6	0.4	0.4	0.3	0.4	0.3
Fuel	0.1	–	0.1	–	0.1	0.1

*Estimates of the Novgorod Regional Administration

Fuel and energy sector production and consumption trends, 1997–2002						*TABLE 5*
	1997	1998	1999	2000	2001	2002*
Electricity output, billion kWh	0.8	0.9	0.9	1.0	0.9	0.8
Electricity consumption, billion kWh	2.9	2.9	2.9	3.1	3.1	3.1
Natural gas consumption, million cubic meters	2,576.0	2,615.0	2,638.9	2,633.5	2,641.9	2,654.9

*Estimates of the Novgorod Regional Administration

Bakaut, OAO Transvit, FGUP Automobile Repair Works No. 123, and OAO MK Splav.

Energy. The sector accounts for 9.9% of the total industrial output. The installed capacity of OAO Novgorodenergo Thermal Power Station, the largest enterprise in the sector, is 190 MW. Its thermal output reaches 630 Gcal/h.

Ferrous metals. The sector accounts for 5.8% of total industrial output. The largest enterprise in the sector is OAO Borovichi Refractory Materials Factory.

3.4. FUEL AND ENERGY BALANCE (OUTPUT AND CONSUMPTION PER RESOURCE)

Local power stations cover only 25% of total demand for energy in the Region.

3.5. TRANSPORT INFRASTRUCTURE

Roads. The Novgorod Region has some 9,000 kilometers of paved public highway. In 2002, some 1.3 million tons of freight was transported by road. Major freight routes link the Region to Finland, Germany, and Sweden.

Railroads. The Novgorod Region has 1,200 kilometers of railroad. The Moscow – St. Petersburg railway passes through the Region.

3.6. MAIN NATURAL RESOURCES: RESERVES AND EXTRACTION IN 2002

The Region's principle natural resources are non-metal minerals and fresh and mineral subterranean waters. Promising deposits of kimberlite diamond and oil and gas are being developed.

Non-metal minerals. 1,435 peat deposits, occupying a total area of 471,100 hectares and with total reserves of 1,716.6 million tons, have been discovered and explored in the Novgorod Region. The bulk of the peat reserve (69%) is contained in large deposits with an area of more than 1,000 hectares.

Some 83 refractory clay, limestone, quartz sand, and mineral pigment deposits have been explored in the Region.

Water resources. A total of 12 mineral water springs have been explored in the Novgorod Region. Most of the springs are operational. Chloride or chloride and sulfate water springs of varying cationic content are the most common. Sodium sulfate and bicarbonate (alkaline) water springs occur less frequently.

Forest resources. The Region has more than 3,489,500 hectares of forests, with deciduous forests covering more than a half of the Region's territory.

Recreational resources. The Novgorod Region's recreational resources include Lake Ilmen and Lake Seliger, mineral and radon springs, a curative mud resort at Staraya Russa, and the Valdai National Park with its campsites and recreation areas which attract Russian and foreign vacationers alike.

II

NORTH-WESTERN FEDERAL DISTRICT

4. TRADE OPPORTUNITIES

4.1. MAIN GOODS
PRODUCED IN THE REGION
Chemicals. 2002 chemical fertilizer output was 967,500 tons (in nutrient equivalent). Fiberglass output amounted to 3,450 tons.

Food and beverages. 2002 dairy output was 61,100 tons (in milk equivalent), 11.6% up on 2001. Meat output, including first grade by-products, reached 11,900 tons (4.4% up on 2001).

Timber. 2002 commercial timber output amounted to 1.44 million cubic meters, lumber output totaled 1.24 million cubic meters, and glued plywood output reached 136,200 square meters (9.3% up on 2001).

Machine engineering. The principal products of the sector are monitoring and metering instruments, antennae, car diagnostic equipment, steel pipeline fixtures, semiconductor instruments, transformers, relays, electronic chips, printed circuit boards, and dosers and fillers for liquid and paste foods.

4.2. EXPORTS, INCLUDING EXTRA-CIS
The Region's 1999 extra-CIS exports totaled $249.6 million. CIS exports reached $11.6 million. The corresponding figures were $259.7 million and $11.9 million for 2000, $287.8 million and $10.5 million for 2001, and $346.1 million and $28.4 million for 2002.

The bulk of the Region's exports consists of petrochemicals and timber. The Region major partners for exports are China (41.5% of total exports), Finland (21.1%), Estonia (4.8%), Belarus (4.6%), Mexico (4.4%), Latvia (3.1%), the USA (2.9%), Algeria (2.9%), and Poland (2.8%).

4.3. IMPORTS,
INCLUDING EXTRA-CIS
In 1999, the Region's extra-CIS imports totaled $100.4 million. CIS imports totaled $11.8 million. The corresponding figures were $56.7 million and $7.7 million for 2000, $106.6 million and $6.9 million for 2001, and $131.6 million and $29.6 million for 2002.

The bulk of the Region's imports consists of timber, petrochemicals, and metal engineering products. The Region's main trading partners for imports are Finland (24.3% of total imports), Germany (21.7%), Belarus (13.9%), France (8.2%), the USA (6.4%), Poland (5.7%), Denmark (5.0%), and Ukraine (3.9%).

4.4. MAJOR REGIONAL EXPORT
AND IMPORT ENTITIES
Owing to the specific nature of the Region's export and import activities, export and import transactions are performed mainly by industrial enterprises.

5. INVESTMENT OPPORTUNITIES

5.1. INVESTMENTS IN 1992–2002
(BY INDUSTRY SECTOR), INCLUDING
FOREIGN INVESTMENTS
The following factors determine the investment appeal of the Novgorod Region:
• Its favorable geographical location, proximity to Moscow and St. Petersburg and to EU countries and the Baltic States;
• Its developed transport infrastructure;
• Legislation supporting investment projects (tax incentives to investors).

5.2. CAPITAL INVESTMENT
The bulk of fixed capital investment goes to forestry, timber and paper, and food and beverages sectors.

5.3. MAJOR ENTERPRISES
(INCLUDING ENTERPRISES
WITH FOREIGN INVESTMENT)
The Region's largest enterprises with foreign investment are OOO Amkor Rench Novgorod, OAO Akron, ZAO Dirol, ZAO Cadbury, and ZAO Chudovo-RWS.

Capital investment by industry sector, $ million						TABLE 6
	1997	1998	1999	2000	2001	2002
Total capital investment	200.3	175.4	164.7	169.5	259.5	176.4
Including major industries (% of total):						
Industry	37.9	48.7	42.1	23.1	18.5	38.0
Agriculture and forestry	1.4	3.0	1.6	1.8	1.2	3.2
Construction	1.1	0.9	0.4	0.6	2.2	0.5
Transport and communications	22.3	24.1	46.3	61.6	71.5	43.7
Trade and public catering	2.6	1.2	0.5	0.7	0.6	1.6
Other	34.7	22.1	9.1	12.2	6.0	13.0

Foreign investment trends in 1996–2002						*TABLE 7*
	1996–1997	1998	1999	2000	2001	2002
Foreign investment, $ million	125.3	44.5	88.1	49.5	50.1	61.6
Including FDI, $ million	17.2	7.6	32.7	19.7	23.8	12.1

Largest enterprises of the Novgorod Region	*TABLE 8*
COMPANY	SECTOR
OAO Akron	Chemicals
OAO Fliderer-Chudovo	Chemicals
OAO Novgorod Fiberglass Factory	Chemicals
OAO Transvit	Machine engineering and metal processing
FGUP PO Quant	Machine engineering and metal processing
FPG Kontur	Machine engineering and metal processing
Novgorod GARO Plant Company	Machine engineering and metal processing
OAO Agrokabel	Machine engineering and metal processing
Starorussky Automobile Repair Works No. 123	Machine engineering and metal processing
ZAO SP Chudovo RWS	Forestry, timber, and pulp and paper
OAO Parfinsky Plywood Factory	Forestry, timber, and pulp and paper
OOO Amkor Rench Novgorod	Forestry, timber, and pulp and paper

5.4. MOST ATTRACTIVE SECTORS FOR INVESTMENT

According to the Regional Administration, timber, food, and machine engineering are the most attractive sectors for investment.

5.5. CURRENT LEGISLATION ON INVESTOR TAX EXEMPTIONS AND PRIVILEGES

The tax legislation of the Region includes Laws On Tax Privileges to Individuals and Organizations for 2003 and On Investment Activities in the Novgorod Region. The Novgorod Regional Duma passed the Decree On Most Favored Economic Status Zones, which provides for regional and local tax exemptions for commercial organizations engaged in non-trade related activities.

5.6. FEDERAL AND REGIONAL ECONOMIC AND SOCIAL DEVELOPMENT PROGRAMS FOR THE NOVGOROD REGION

Federal targeted programs. The Novgorod Regional Administration is implementing programs targeted at the industrial sector, public health and education, agroindustrial and youth policy, public welfare, and environmental protection.

Regional programs. The Region is implementing a comprehensive program for support and development of small business Small Business-Stage 4, 2001–2003. The program aims to improve the small business environment and the financial standing of small enterprises, create new jobs, and raise the share of small enterprise in total output.

The Region has developed and implements The Program for the Fisheries Development in the Region through 2005. The program's major goals are to stabilize and gradually increase fish breeding, catch and processing, to expand fish product range, and to ensure profits sufficient for enhanced development of the industry.

The Program for Soil Fertility Enhancement in the Region, 2002–2005 aims to increase crop yield, create strong fodder base, and provide agriculture products to the population of the Region.

Regional entities responsible for raising investment		*TABLE 9*
ENTITY	ADDRESS	PHONE, FAX, E-MAIL
Foreign Investment Department of the Novgorod Regional Administration	1, Sofiyskaya pl., Veliky Novgorod, Novgorod Region, 173005	Phone: (8162) 13 2486 Fax: (8162) 13 2502 E-mail: radm@novgorod.net
Invest-In Group of Companies	20, ul. Velikaya, Veliky Novgorod, Novgorod Region, 173003	Phone. (8162) 11 5190 Fax: (8162) 13 2039 E-mail: info@invest-in.ru

II

NORTH-WESTERN FEDERAL DISTRICT

6. INVESTMENT PROJECTS

Industry sector and project description	1) Expected results 2) Amount and term of investment 3) Form of financing[1] 4) Documentation[2]	Contact information
1	2	3

	ENERGY	

26R001 ● ❖ ◆ ▲

| Steam and gas power station construction. Project goal: to meet the Region's demand for electricity. | 1) Capacity – 650 MW, electricity output – 4.1 billion kWh per year
2) $608 million/4 years
3) E, JV
4) FS, BP | OAO Novgorodenergo
3, ul. B. St. Petersburgskaya, V. Novgorod, Novgorod Region, 173001
Phone: (81622) 74 116
Phone/fax: (81622) 78 182
E-mail: post@novgor.elektra.ru
Valery Ivanovich Sosinovich, Chief Engineer |

	HOUSING AND COMMUNAL	

26R002 ■ ❖ ◆ ▲

| Construction of a heating main pipeline. Project goal: to close inefficient boilers, and improve the environmental situation in the city. | 1) 11.5 km
2) $10.5 million/3 years
3) E, JV
4) FS, BP | OAO Novgorodenergo
3, ul. B. St. Petersburgskaya, V. Novgorod, Novgorod Region, 173001
Phone: (81622) 74 116
Phone/fax: (81622) 78 182
E-mail: post@novgor.elektra.ru
Valery Ivanovich Sosinovich, Chief Engineer |

	FORESTRY, TIMBER, AND PULP AND PAPER	

26R003 ■ ❖ ◆ ▲

| Production of joiner assemblies and furniture units. Project goal: to produce high quality wooden units to European standards (glued bar, furniture components, linear boards for door units, door units, and lumber). | 1) 300 cubic meters of glued bars per year; 220 cubic meters of furniture components per year; 100,000 meters of linear boards per year; 1,500 door units per year; 1,000 cubic meters of lumber per year
2) $1 million/1.5 years
3) E, JV
4) FS, BP | OOO Adok
5, ul. Oktyabrskaya, Antsiferovo, Khvoininsky District, Novgorod Region, 174580
Phone: (81667) 51 942
Fax: (81667) 51 942
Valentin Mikhailovich Efimov, CEO
OOO Dom-Service
5, Kovanko, Borovichi, Novgorod Region, 174400
Phone: (81664) 20 779, 23 100
Fax: (81664) 21 719
Valentin Mikhailovich Yefimov, CEO |

26R004 ■ ● ★ ❖ ◆

| Establishment of a company to produce chemical-thermal mechanical ground wood. Project goal: to produce bleached chemical-thermal mechanical ground wood from aspen timber. | 1) 100,000 tons per year; revenue – $40 million per year
2) $100 million/3 years
3) JV, E, L, Leas.
4) BP | ZAO BumPromMash
Office 1, 7, ul. Kooperativnaya, V. Novgorod, Novgorod Region, 173003
Phone/fax: (8162) 13 8580
E-mail: bshm@mail.natm.ru
Alexander Sergeevich Volkov, CEO |

[1] L – Loan, E – Equity, Leas. – Leasing, JV – Joint Venture
[2] BP – Business Plan, FS – Feasibility Study

1	2	3

CONSTRUCTION MATERIALS

26R005

Production of floor board units.
Project goal: to produce high quality
floor board.

1) 1,000 cubic meters per year
2) $1.3 million/1 year
3) JV
4) FS, BP

ZAO Business Partner
22, ul. Prusskaya, V. Novgorod,
Novgorod Region, 173015
Phone: (8162) 13 6878
Phone/fax: 13 6753
E-mail: delpart@mal.natm.ru
Viktor Petrovich Antyufeev,
First Deputy CEO

26R006

Construction of a workshop
for production of facing brick.
Project goal: to produce facing brick.

1) 26 million items per year (facing –
   20 million, common – 6 million)
2) € 5 million/3 years
3) JV
4) FS, BP

ZAO Business Partner
22, ul. Prusskaya, V. Novgorod,
Novgorod Region, 173015
Phone: (8162) 13 6878
Phone/fax: (8162) 13 6753
E-mail: delpart@mal.natm.ru
Viktor Petrovich Antyufeev,
First Deputy CEO

FOOD AND BEVERAGES

26R007

Construction of a coffee factory.
Project goal: to produce powder
and granulated instant coffee.

1) 2,400 tons per year
2) $9.5 million/3 years
3) JV
4) FS, BP

ZAO Bumprommash
Office 1, 7, ul. Kooperativnaya, V. Nov-
gorod, Novgorod Region, 173003
Phone/fax: (8162) 13 8580
E-mail: bshm@mail.natm.ru
Alexander Sergeevich Volkov, CEO

AGRICULTURE

26R008

Reconstruction of egg and poultry
production facilities.
Project goal: to increase egg output.

1) 165 million eggs per year,
   cost reduction by 15%
2) $4.4 million/1.5 years
3) E, JV
4) FS, BP

ZAO Gvardeets
Podberezye, Novgorod District,
Novgorod Region, 173502
Phone: (81622) 14 2692
Olga Vladimirovna Chizh,
Director

HOTEL BUSINESS, TOURISM, AND RECREATION

26R009

Construction of the Paraskeva tourist center.
Project goal: to provide
tourist and hotel services.

1) Revenue – $1.3 million per year
2) $1.8 million/1.5 years
3) E, JV, L
4) FS, BP

ZAO NovInTourService
14, ul. Andreevskaya, V. Novgorod,
Novgorod Region, 173004
Phone/fax: (8162) 66 4712
E-mail: nits@novgorod.net
Eduard Yevgenyevich Ni, CEO

26R010

Construction of the second unit
and reconstruction of the first
unit of the Intourist hotel.
Project goal: to provide tourist
and hotel services.

1) 309 hotel rooms
2) $10 million/1.5 years
3) E, JV
4) FS, BP

OAO Intourist-Novgorod
16, ul. Velikaya, V. Novgorod,
Novgorod Region, 173001
Phone: (8162) 27 4235
Fax: (8162) 27 4157
E-mail: nov@intourist.natm.ru
Igor Nikolaevich Tserkovny, CEO

II

NORTH-WESTERN FEDERAL DISTRICT

27. PSKOV REGION [60]

ECONOMIC MAP

LENINGRAD REGION

Slantsy

Luga

Chudovo

Gdov

Tartu

Lake Chudskoe

Lake Peypsi

Luga

Volkhov

Plussa

Plussa

VELIKY NOVGOROD

Msta

NOVGOROD

Lake Ilmen

E S T O N I A

PSKOV

Shelon

Staraya Russa

Pechyory

Dno

Porkhov

L A T V I A

Ostrov

R E G I O N

Polist

Novorzhev

Lovat

Velikaya

Bezhanitsy

Opochka

Pustoshka

Velikie Luki

T V E R

Sebezh

Lovat

Nevel

Tserkovische

Nelidovo

R E G I O N

B Y E L O R U S S I A

Polotsk

Zapadnaya Dvina

Zapadnaya Dvina

S M O L E N S K REGION

PROCESSING INDUSTRY
- Machine engineering and metal processing
- Forestry and timber
- Construction materials and glass
- Light industry
- Food and beverages

MINING INDUSTRY
- Peat
- Clay
- Limestone
- Mineral water sources

POWER PLANTS
- Thermal power plants

CROPS AND LIVESTOCK BREEDING
- Wheat
- Rye
- Long-fibred flax
- Potatoes
- Meat and dairy cattle breeding
- Pig breeding
- Poultry farming

- Resorts

The small region of Russia enjoys great economic potential. Its advantageous geographical location is compounded by a highly developed transport infrastructure, a modern customs infrastructure, a highly qualified workforce, and considerable production facilities. The regional authorities appreciate the importance of creating a favorable investment climate.

State support to investment activity in the Pskov Region takes several forms: an improved legislative framework, tax privileges to investors, price and tariff regulation, reduced administrative barriers, and the promotion of regional investment opportunities.

I am confident that the Pskov Region's economic potential can be successfully realized through mutually beneficial collaboration.

Yevgeny Mikhailov,
HEAD OF ADMINISTRATION OF THE PSKOV REGION

II

NORTH-WESTERN FEDERAL DISTRICT

1. GENERAL INFORMATION

1.1. GEOGRAPHY

Situated in the north-west of European Russia, the Pskov Region covers an total area of 55,300 square kilometers. To the west, the Region borders Estonia and Latvia, to the south – the Republic of Belarus and the Smolensk Region, to the east – the Novgorod and Tver Regions, and to the north – the Leningrad Region.

1.2. CLIMATE

The Region is located within the temperate continental climate zone with certain maritime influences. January air temperatures average –8°C, rising to +17°C in July. Annual precipitation reaches 550–600 mm.

1.3. POPULATION

According to preliminary 2002 census results, the Pskov Region's total population was 761,000 people. The average population density is 13.8 people per square kilometer. The economically active population amounts to 356,000 people. Official unemployment stood at 11% in 2002.

Demographically speaking, some 59.3% of the population are of statutory working age, 16.9% are below the statutory working age, and 23.8% are beyond the statutory working age.

The major urban centers of the Pskov Region (2002 data) are Pskov with 202,700 inhabitants, Velikiye Luki with 105,000 inhabitants, and Ostrov with 28,200 inhabitants.

Population								TABLE 1
	1992	1997	1998	1999	2000	2001	2002
Total population, '000	840	826	819	811	801	790	761
Economically active population, '000	419	349	362	397	377	375	356

2. ADMINISTRATION

23, ul. Nekrasova, Pskov, Pskov Region, 180001. Phone: (8112) 16 2203; fax: (8112) 16 0390
E-mail: sekretar@obladmin.pskov.ru; http://www.pskov.ru

NAME	POSITION	CONTACT INFORMATION
Yevgeny Eduardovich MIKHAILOV	Head of Administration of the Pskov Region	Phone: (8112) 16 4818 Fax: (8112) 16 0390 E-mail: sekretar@obladmin.pskov.ru
Vladimir Yakovlevich KUSHNIR	Deputy Head of the of the Pskov Regional Administration, Chairman of the Regional Administration Committee for State Property Management	Phone: (8112) 16 4393 Fax: (8112) 16 5210 E-mail: kgi.@obladmin.pskov.ru
Dmitry Vladimirovich SHAKHOV	Deputy Head of the of the Pskov Regional Administration in charge of Foreign Trade and Tourism	Phone: (8112) 16 5337
Anatoly Alexandrovich TULKIN	Deputy Head of the of the Pskov Regional Administration for Agriculture, Trade and Retail Markets	Phone: (8112) 16 9318
Anatoly Petrovich SALTYKOV	Deputy Head of the of the Pskov Regional Administration for Transport	Phone: (8112) 16 1921
Vladimir Alexeevich MOISEYEV	Deputy Head of the of the Pskov Regional Administration, Head of the Construction, Architecture and Housing and Communal Services Office of the Pskov Region	Phone: (8112) 16 9096
Vladimir Gavrilovich FEDULOV	First Deputy Chairman of the Regional Administration Committee for Economic Development and Industrial Policy	Phone: (8112) 16 4547
Valerian Borisovich KLENEVSKY	First Deputy Chairman of the Regional Administration Committee for Economic Development and Industrial Policy	Phone: (8112) 16 0571

3. ECONOMIC POTENTIAL

3.1. 1997–2002 GROSS REGIONAL PRODUCT (GRP). INDUSTRY BREAKDOWN

The Pskov Region's 2001 gross regional product was $705.4 million, 16% up on 2000. Per capita GRP in 2000 totaled $759, and $893 in 2001.

3.2. MAJOR ECONOMIC GROWTH PROJECTIONS.

The Pskov Regional Administration forecasts GRP growth of 28.4% by 2005, bringing annual GRP up to $1,123.8 million. Industry is likely to achieve the strongest growth rates (30%): output growth in the energy sector is projected at 70% by 2005, in machine engineering and metals processing – 27.4%, in the light industry – 22.7%, and in food and beverages – 20%.

3.3. INDUSTRIAL OUTPUT IN 1997–2002 FOR MAJOR SECTORS OF ECONOMY

The leading industries of the Pskov Region are food and beverages, machine engineering and metal processing, and energy. These account for a combined 74.1% of total industrial output.

Food and beverages. The food and beverages sector accounts for 30.1% of total industrial output. Meat processing accounts for the lion's share of total output in the sector. OAO Veliko-luksky Meat Factory, the largest producer in the sector, accounts for over 80% of total meat output of the Region.

GRP trends in 1997–2002						TABLE 2
	1997	1998	1999	2000	2001*	2002
GRP in current prices, million $	1,102.8	657.5	485.1	608.2	705.4	n/a

*Estimates of the Pskov Regional Administration

GRP industry breakdown in 1997–2002, % of total						TABLE 3
	1997	1998	1999	2000	2001*	2002
GRP	100.0	100.0	100.0	100.0	100.0	100.0
Industry	22.5	23.1	18.5	19.4	20.8	n/a
Agriculture and forestry	14.3	12.2	21.4	16.1	16.7	n/a
Construction	7.2	4.9	4.4	4.3	5.4	n/a
Transport and communications	12.8	13.2	14.4	19.1	17.0	n/a
Trade and public catering	10.6	13.4	14.0	15.4	15.3	n/a
Other	32.6	33.2	27.3	25.7	24.8	n/a

*Estimates of the Pskov Regional Administration

Dairies in the Region produce whole-milk products, yogurt, cheese, and mayonnaise. OAO Pskov City Dairy, one of the largest dairy producers in the Region, produces over 56 different products. OAO Lyubyatovo, a leading confectionery firm, produces crackers and snacks.

Machine engineering and metal processing. The sector accounts for 29.9% of total industrial output. The sector produces low yield electric motors for household devices, automotive relays, high-voltage equipment and insulators, transformer substations, cables, radiometric instruments, communications equipment, condensers, electric welding equipment, lifting and haulage machinery for timber logging, forest fire-fighting and pipeline repair equipment, and retail and refrigeration equipment.

Major enterprises in the sector include OOO Pskov Heavy Electric Welding Equipment, which manufactures equipment for welding pipes of various diameters, metal sheeting, and rails. ZAO

Tochlit performs precision casting operations. OAO Krasny Luch Glass Works produces glass and color filters for subway systems and railroads.

Energy. The sector accounts for 14.1% of total industrial output. The largest producer is OAO Pskovskaya GRES. Its two power units have a capacity of 430 MW. The planned commissioning of a third unit will increase the overall capacity to 600 MW.

3.4. FUEL AND ENERGY BALANCE (OUTPUT AND CONSUMPTION PER RESOURCE)

The Pskov Region enjoys a surplus of power output. Energy exports are set to increase once OAO Pskovskaya GRES puts its third power generation unit into operation.

3.5. TRANSPORT INFRASTRUCTURE

Roads. The Pskov Region has 10,000 kilometers of paved public highway, including highway links to Germany, the Baltic States, and the Republic of Belarus. Road transport accounts for 92% of total freight traffic and 97% of total passenger traffic.

Industry breakdown of industrial output in 1997–2002, % of total						TABLE 4
	1997	1998	1999	2000	2001	2002*
Industry	100.0	100.0	100.0	100.0	100.0	100.0
Food and beverages	22.7	23.5	29.4	28.1	28.8	30.1
Machine engineering and metal processing	31.5	30.9	31.6	31.4	32.3	29.9
Energy	24.2	24.3	15.3	13.3	15.2	14.1
Light industry	5.3	4.7	5.9	5.4	5.3	5.8
Construction materials	2.2	4.8	3.9	4.1	3.9	4.0
Forestry, timber, and pulp and paper	3.5	4.1	5.6	5.6	4.2	2.8
Ferrous metals	0.1	1.1	1.5	2.3	2.1	2.6
Flour, cereals, and mixed fodder	2.7	2.0	3.0	3.1	3.6	2.6
Fuel	0.1	0.1	n/a	3.5	1.1	2.5
Chemicals and petrochemicals	0.2	0.6	0.6	0.8	1.3	1.3
Glass and porcelain	0.8	0.4	0.5	0.5	0.8	1.2
Non-ferrous metals	0.1	0.1	0.2	0.4	0.1	0.1

*Estimates of the Pskov Regional Administration

Railroads. The Pskov Region has 1,055 kilometers of railroads. The Region has five international rail border checkpoints at its borders with Estonia (one), Latvia (two), and the Republic of Belarus (two).

Airports. The key operator is FGUP Pskovavia, which has airport facilities suitable for international flights. Cargo and passenger traffic is slight. Work on extending the runway to 2,500 meters is underway. This will enable the Pskov Airport to receive virtually any type of passenger and cargo aircraft and to serve as a reserve airport for GUAP Pulkovo International Airport at St. Petersburg.

Fuel and energy sector production and consumption trends, 1997–2002						TABLE 5
	1997	1998	1999	2000	2001	2002*
Electricity output, billion kWh	1.2	2.2	2.3	2.4	2.5	2.2
Electricity consumption, billion kWh	2.1	2.0	2.0	2.0	2.0	1.5
Oil consumption, '000 tons	424.5	434.2	408.0	362.8	349.4	415.0
Natural gas consumption, million cubic meters	528.1	1,074.7	1,085.0	1,105.7	1,189.5	1,134.6

*Estimates of the Pskov Regional Administration

3.6. MAIN NATURAL RESOURCES: RESERVES AND EXTRACTION IN 2002

The Pskov Region enjoys considerable mineral resources. Refractory and fusible clays, raw materials for mineral pigments, sapropel and curative muds are its most valuable resources.

Construction materials. The region boasts 133 deposits of mortar sand and sand gravel materials with 54 deposits under development. In 2001, their output totaled 1,410,000 cubic meters, with remaining reserves estimated at 157,000,000 cubic meters. The Region has 29 deposits of fusible clays, two of which are under development. 2001 output totaled 92,200 cubic meters, with remaining reserves estimated at 51,917,000 cubic meters.

2001 output at the Region's only refractory clay deposit was 106,000 tons, with reserves of 22,200,000 tons still available.

Peat. Three of the Region's 392 deposits of peat are under development. Total annual output is 61,200 tons (2001), with 675 million tons of reserves still available.

Oil shale. The 800 square kilometer Gdov deposit holds the bulk of the Region's oil shale reserves, which are estimated at 400 million tons.

Other resources. The Region possesses substantial forest resources (around 40% of its area is forested) and fish resources (the annual potential fish catch in the Region's rivers and lakes is estimated at 1,200 tons).

4. TRADE OPPORTUNITIES

4.1. MAIN GOODS
PRODUCED IN THE REGION
Food and beverages. 2002 output of bread and bakery products was 75,300 tons, confectionery – 9,700 tons, butter – 2,400 tons, and cheese – 5,800 tons.

Machine engineering and metal processing. The sector produces electric motors, electric welding equipment, alternating current and direct current motors, resistors, water heaters, and condensers. Consumer goods manufactured in the Region include refrigerators, radio sets, electric kettles, and electric stoves.

Textile. The Region is the fifth largest producer of knitwear in Russia. 2002 knitwear output was 8.3 million items.

Footwear industry. Footwear output reached 402,000 pairs in 2002.

4.2. EXPORTS, INCLUDING EXTRA-CIS
Exports to extra-CIS countries in 2000 amounted to $103.5 million, while exports to CIS countries totaled $4.7 million. The corresponding figures for 2001 were $534.5 million and $5 million, and $117.5 million and $5 million for 2002.

4.3. IMPORTS, INCLUDING EXTRA-CIS
Imports from extra-CIS countries in 2000 amounted to $71.4 million, imports from CIS countries totaled $6.2 million. The corresponding figures for 2001 were $162.4 million and $3.4 million, and $171.5 million and $3.4 million for 2002.

4.4. MAJOR REGIONAL EXPORT
AND IMPORT ENTITIES
Due to the specific nature of export and import operations in the Pskov Region, export and import transactions are largely carried out by industrial enterprises.

5. INVESTMENT OPPORTUNITIES

5.1. INVESTMENTS IN 1992–2002
(BY INDUSTRY SECTOR), INCLUDING
FOREIGN INVESTMENTS
The following main factors determine the investment appeal of the Pskov Region:
- Its favorable geographical location (highway and railroad links to Moscow and St. Petersburg, the Baltic States, and the ports of Murmansk and Kaliningrad);

- Legislation supporting investment activities (guarantees of investor rights, preferential tax treatment for investors);
- Its qualified workforce;
- Its cheap energy resources (electricity);
- Its natural resources.

5.2. CAPITAL INVESTMENT
Transport and industry account for the bulk of capital investment.

Capital investment by industry sectors, $ million	1997	1998	1999	2000	2001	2002
Total capital investment	159.7	97.9	59.2	87.0	96.0	51.3
Including major industries (% of total):						
Industry	24.7	13.8	17.2	10.4	13.8	16.7
Agriculture and forestry	2.0	4.3	4.2	6.4	7.0	5.6
Construction	3.3	0.3	0.5	0.9	1.2	1.8
Transport and communications	24.2	20.2	15.5	23.4	26.9	33.4
Trade and public catering	0.6	3.7	4.1	4.0	3.4	2.0
Other	45.2	57.7	58.5	54.9	47.7	40.5

TABLE 6

Foreign investment trends in 1996–2002	1996–1997	1998	1999	2000	2001	2002
Foreign investments, $ million	11.4	3.7	2.8	1.1	5.2	3.9
Including FDI, $ million	9.5	1.9	1.5	0.5	4.8	2.1

TABLE 7

II

NORTH-WESTERN FEDERAL DISTRICT

05.3. MAJOR ENTERPRISES (INCLUDING ENTERPRISES WITH FOREIGN INVESTMENT)

The Region hosts 79 enterprises with foreign capital. The largest are OOO Protek (Russia-Italy), OOO Italforma (Russia-Italy), OOO Faber-Luki (Russia-Italy), and OOO Gdov Canned Vegetables (Russia-Estonia). Wholly foreign owned enterprises include OOO Promstroy Engineering (Latvia), OOO Skywood (Estonia), OOO Hotel Planeta (Latvia), OOO Leskom (Estonia), OOO Baltko (Lithuania), and OOO Nex (Finland).

Largest enterprises of the Pskov Region			TABLE 8
COMPANY	SECTOR	2001 SALES, $ MILLION*	2001 NET PROFIT, $ MILLION*
ZAO Pskov Pischeprom	Food	11.7	0.007
OAO Avtoelektroarmatura	Machine engineering	11.6	0.5
OOO Pskov Meat	Food	9.4	0.4
ZAO Pskov Slavyanka Garments	Clothing	7.4	1.5
OAO Pskov Mechanical Drive Plant	Machine engineering	6.7	0.2
ZAO Pskov Dairy	Dairy	5.0	0.4
OAO Pskov Pleskava Radio Components Plant	Machine engineering	4.5	0.03
OAO Pskov Electric Machine Plant	Machine engineering	4.3	- 0.3
OAO Pskov Heavy Electric Welding Equipment	Machine engineering	3.9	- 0.1
OAO Impuls	Machine engineering	3.5	- 0.5
OAO Ostrovsky Dairy	Dairy	2.1	- 0.2

*Data of the Pskov Regional Administration

5.4. MOST ATTRACTIVE SECTORS FOR INVESTMENT

According to experts and the Pskov Regional Administration, trade and public catering, transport, construction, forestry and timber, and machine engineering and metal processing are the most attractive sectors for investment.

5.5. CURRENT LEGISLATION ON INVESTOR TAX EXEMPTIONS AND PRIVILEGES

The Pskov Regional Law On State Support to Investment Activity in the Pskov Region, adopted in 2001, provides for the following forms of state support to investment:

- Tax exemptions for actual payback term of an investment project (not exceeding the project's projected payback period);
- Reduction of the regional profits tax component to 10.5%; reduction of property tax to 0.01% (for property created, purchased and/or acquired as part of the deal);
- Exemption from tax on vehicles used to implement an investment project per a business plan;
- Exemption from the regional component of land tax (applicable to land plots acquired by an investor for the purpose of developing (establishing) a new enterprises as a complex of assets).

Regional entities responsible for raising investments			TABLE 9
ENTITY	ADDRESS	PHONE, FAX, E-MAIL	
Pskov Regional Development Agency	9, ul. Bastionnaya, Pskov 180004	Phone: (8112) 72 4420 Fax: (8112) 16 0041 E-mail: nikolai@ellink.ru	
Pskov Regional Chamber of Commerce and Industry	15A, ul. Sovetskaya, Pskov 180000	Phone: (8112) 16 3883 E-mail: info@cci.pskov.ru	

5.6. FEDERAL AND REGIONAL ECONOMIC AND SOCIAL DEVELOPMENT PROGRAMS FOR THE PSKOV REGION

Federal targeted programs. Since 2002, social and economic development measures for the Pskov Region have been included into the federal targeted program Elimination of Differences in the Social and Economic Development of the Russian Federation's Regions, 2002–2010 and through 2015. The program aims to reduce social and economic development gaps among the Russian Federation's regions and to reduce the number of under-developed regions. The Federal

Law On the 2002 Federal Budget provides for $2.1 million in financing for measures undertaken in the Pskov Region. The actual disbursement was $2.1 million. The Federal Law On the 2003 Federal Budget provides for $1.2 million in financing.

Regional programs. The Pskov Regional Administration has drafted and is currently implementing a regional targeted program for The Improvement of the Investment Climate in the Pskov Region, 2002–2003, which aims to develop an investment infrastructure in the Region. The program is focused on reforming the regional economic legislation, supporting regional investment

projects, attracting investment into efficient and competitive sectors to establish efficient enterprises, and raising financing for investment projects at the domestic and foreign capital markets.

Several regional targeted programs benefiting the social sector are also underway. High priority has been accorded to the program for the Computerization of the Education System in the Pskov Region, 2002–2005, The Regional Targeted Program for Residential Mortgage Lending in the Pskov Region, 2001–2006, the Pskov Region Job Creation Program, 2001–2003, and the Culture in the Pskov Region, 2001–2005 program.

6. INVESTMENT PROJECTS

II

NORTH-WESTERN FEDERAL DISTRICT

Industry sector and project description	1) Expected results 2) Amount and term of investment 3) Form of financing[1] 4) Documentation[2]	Contact information
1	2	3
MACHINE ENGINEERING		
27R001 ● ▲		ZAO Pskov Electric Motors
Establishment of additional facilities for production of asynchronous motors. Project goal: to increase output.	1) Output of 210,000 motors per year 2) $4 million/n/a 3) L ($3.2 million) 4) FS	26, Krasnogorskaya naberezhnaya Pskov, Pskov Region, 180021 Phone: (81122) 22 3231 Fax: (81122) 22 2260 Anatoly Nikolaevich Solovyov, CEO
HOTEL BUSINESS, TOURISM, AND RECREATION		
27R002 ◆		Pskov Regional Administration
Sale of the highly comfortable Intourist. Hotel, construction of which has not been completed. Project goal: to sell the business.	1) 167 rooms 2) $10 million/n/a 3) Sale of a hotel under construction 4) BP	23, ul. Nekrasova, Pskov, Pskov Region, 180000 Phone: (8112) 16 4393, 72 3867 Fax: (8112) 16 5210 Vladimir Yakovlevich Kushnir, Deputy Head of the Regional Administration
27R003 ◆		Pskov Regional Administration
Sale of the Podznoyevy Palaty culture and hotel complex, construction of which has not been completed. Project goal: to sell the business.	1) 1,000 tourists per year 2) $4 million/n/a 3) Sale of a hotel and culture complex under construction 4) BP	23, ul. Nekrasova, Pskov, Pskov Region, 180000 Phone: (8112) 16 4393, 72 3867 Fax: (8112) 16 5210 Vladimir Yakovlevich Kushnir, Deputy Head of the Regional Administration

[1] L – Loan, E – Equity, Leas. – Leasing, JV – Joint Venture
[2] BP – Business Plan, FS – Feasibility Study

28. ST. PETERSBURG [78]

ECONOMIC MAP

Lake Lembolovskoe
Pobeda
Lebyazhe
Lake Lubinskoe
Kuyvozi
Matoksa
Lake Royka
Voloyarvi
Yakovlevo
Roschino
Simagino
Verkhniei Oselki
Ushkovo
Leninskoe
Lake Bolshoe Simaginskoe
Vartemyagi
Lake Korgolovskoe
Lake Khepoyarvi
Zelenogorsk
Sestra
More
Repino
Solnechnoe
Beloostrov
Sertolovo
Toksovo
Okhta
Pesochny
Ukki
Kuzmolovsky
GULF OF FINLAND
Sestroretsk
Levashovo
Pargolovo
Lake Sestroretsky Razliv
Kornevo
Scheglovo
Vsevolozhsk
Lisy Nos
Kotlin island
Kronshtadt
Nevskaya guba (gulf)
Kirovskie islands
Dekabristov island
Kaltino
Lebyazhiye
Bolshaya Izhora
Oranienbaum
ST. PETERSBURG
Vasilevsky island
Bely island
Kanonersky island
Myaglovo
Lomonosov
Petergof
Strelna
Chyornaya
Volodarsky
Pulkovo Airport
Shushary
Ust-Izhora
Sverdlova name
Razbegaevo
Metallostroy
Pontonny
Saperny
Petrovskoe
Annino
Aleksandrovskaya
Pushkin
Kolpino
Gostilitsy
Ropsha
Russko-Vysotskoe
Pavlovsk
Krasny Bor
Lopukhinka
Dyatlitsy
Kipen
Taytsy
Fedorovskoe
Ulyanovka
Cheremykino
Vitino
Skvoritsy
Zaytsevo
Kommunar
Kaskovo
Starye Nizkovtsy
Bolshoe Rezino
Romanovka
Forsonovo
Syaskelevo
Gatchina
Semrino
Novolisino
Klopitsy
Voyskovitsy
Pogi

PROCESSING INDUSTRY
- Ferrous metals
- Non-ferrous metals
- Machine engineering and metal processing
- Chemicals and petrochemicals
- Forestry and timber
- Construction materials and glass
- Food and beverages

POWER PLANTS
- Thermal power plants
- Fishing ports

T oday, St. Petersburg is among the fastest growing regions of the Russian Federation. The City on the Neva, with its great history, rich traditions, and economic and spiritual potential, quite logically occupies a leading position in the new Russia.

Our efforts to restructure and revamp the city's industrial giants have begun to bear fruit in recent years. In 2002, the city's gross regional product rose by 5.7%, compared to the nationwide average of 4%. Industrial output grew by 31%, compared with a national average of only 3%. Experts say that these trends will continue to prevail in the coming years.

The City Government's policies aimed at supporting and developing small enterprise have also been quite successful. St. Petersburg currently hosts more than 90,000 small enterprises, providing jobs for some 600,000 people. Today, small businesses generate some 28% of the city's fiscal revenue.

Valentina Matvienko,
GOVERNOR OF ST. PETERSBURG

The 300th anniversary of the founding of St. Petersburg has stepped well outside the borders of Russia and turned into a celebration of international significance. Our jubilee has attracted guests from many countries throughout the world. The international significance of St. Petersburg – the second largest business center in Russia after Moscow, and the cultural capital of Russia – has grown and strengthened apace. St. Petersburg is now an interesting and prosperous place to live and work. Today's St. Petersburg is the target of very lucrative investments. We are committed to ensuring a favorable investment climate and to improving legislative framework. We are always ready for business cooperation and welcome any interesting mutually beneficial offers.

GOVERMENT OF ST. PETERSBURG

II

NORTH-WESTERN FEDERAL DISTRICT

1. GENERAL INFORMATION

1.1. GEOGRAPHY

St. Petersburg covers a total area of 1,439 square kilometers. The city is situated at the eastern edge of the Gulf of Finland.

1.2. CLIMATE

St. Petersburg is located within the temperate continental climate zone.

January air temperatures average –6.3°C, rising to +18.1°C in July. Annual precipitation averages 634 mm.

1.3. POPULATION

According to preliminary 2002 census results, St. Petersburg's total population was 4,669,000 people. The economically active population amounts to 2,468,000. As of 2002, the official unemployment rate was 0.9%.

Demographically speaking, some 61.6% are of statutory working age, 14.8% are below the statutory working age, and 23.6% are beyond the statutory working age.

Population							*TABLE 1*
	1992	1997	1998	1999	2000	2001	2002
Total population, '000	4,971	4,746	4,716	4,696	4,661	4,628	4,669
Economically active population, '000	2,644	2,346	2,316	2,426	2,417	2,437	2,468

2. ADMINISTRATION (as of October 5, 2003)

Smolny, St. Petersburg, 193060.
Phone: (812) 271 7413; fax: (812) 276 1827
E-mail: gov@gov.spb.ru; http://www.gov.spb.ru

NAME	POSITION	CONTACT INFORMATION
Alexander Dmitrievich BEGLOV	Acting Governor of St. Petersburg, Head of the Government of St. Petersburg	Phone: (812) 271 7413, 274 5924 E-mail: gov@gov.spb.ru
Alexander Ivanovich VAKHMISTROV	Deputy Governor of St. Petersburg, Chairman of the Committee for Construction	Phone: (812) 319 9030
Sergei Yuryevich VETLUGIN	Deputy Governor of St. Petersburg, Chairman of the Committee for Economic Development, Industrial Policy and Trade	Phone: (812) 315 5152 E-mail: ceip@gov.spb.ru
Mikhail Yuryevich KRYLOV	Deputy Governor of St. Petersburg, Chairman of the Committee for Finance	Phone: (812) 314 5674 E-mail: kef@uakef.spb.su
Valery Lvovich NAZAROV	Deputy Governor of St. Petersburg, Chairman of the Committee for Municipal Property Management	Phone: (812) 276 1557 E-mail: vg_kugi@gov.spb.ru
Alexander Vladimirovich PROKHORENKO	Deputy Governor of St. Petersburg, Chairman of the Committee for Foreign Relations	Phone: (812) 276 1204, 276 1113 E-mail: vg_extlinks@gov.spb.ru

3. ECONOMIC POTENTIAL

3.1. 1997–2002 GROSS REGIONAL PRODUCT (GRP). INDUSTRY BREAKDOWN

St. Petersburg's 2002 gross regional product was $10,559 million, 11.5% up on 2001. Per capita GRP in 2001 totaled $2,046, and $2,261 in 2002.

3.2. MAJOR ECONOMIC GROWTH PROJECTIONS

Recent trends suggest annual GRP growth of 5–5.8% through to 2005. Higher growth will be achieved through a greater focus on priority development areas in potentially competitive sectors that are likely to boost output of products and services.

GRP trends in 1997–2002						*TABLE 2*
	1997	1998	1999	2000	2001*	2002*
GRP in current prices, $ million	13,087.1	9,324.1	6,112.2	7,301.8	9,473.5	10,558.8

*Estimates of the St. Petersburg Government

GRP industry breakdown in 1997–2002, % of total						*TABLE 3*
	1997	1998	1999	2000	2001*	2002*
GRP	100.0	100.0	100.0	100.0	100.0	100.0
Industry	20.6	25.6	25.0	25.6	27.5	26.0
Construction	6.9	6.5	5.8	6.6	7.4	7.5
Transport and communications	18.8	16.4	14.0	16.1	14.1	14.3
Trade and public catering	22.8	20.1	22.5	21.5	20.6	21.7
Other	24.6	25.0	21.8	22.0	22.0	22.1
Net taxes on output	6.3	6.4	10.9	8.2	8.4	8.4

*Estimates of the St. Petersburg Government

As a main objective for the St. Petersburg's economy for 2003, the Government has set the task to maintain the existing economy growth rates through:
- Increased capital investment into key sectors of the city's economy from the St. Petersburg's budget (including the infrastructure development fund and other budget tools);
- Development of joint financing of priority projects from the budget and non-budgetary funds;
- Development of new territories, primarily around the Ring Road;
- Maintenance of St. Petersburg's positive image, increased inflow of tourists and payback of newly created cultural and entertainment installations and facilities for the built 300th anniversary of St. Petersburg;
- Development of transport transit capabilities of St. Petersburg, primarily the seaport and the transport logistics system.

3.3. INDUSTRIAL OUTPUT IN 1997–2002 FOR MAJOR SECTORS OF ECONOMY

St. Petersburg's leading industries are machine engineering and metals processing, and food and beverages. These account for a combined 68.3% of total industrial output.

Food and beverages. The sector accounts for 34.9% of total industrial output. The leading manufacturers are ZAO Krupskaya Confectionery, OAO Petmol, ZAO Parnas-M, ZAO St. Petersburg Piskaryovsky Plant, ZAO Liviz, ZAO Nevo Tobacco, OAO Petro, OAO Baltika Brewery, OAO Stepan Razin Combine, and OAO Vena.

Machine engineering and metal processing. Machine engineering accounts for 33.4% of total industrial output. 2002 machine engineering output for the light industry and food processing was up 122.9% year-on-year, diesel engines output was

Industry breakdown of industrial output in 1997–2002, % of total						*TABLE 4*
	1997	1998	1999	2000	2001	2002*
Industry	100.0	100.0	100.0	100.0	100.0	100.0
Food and beverages	26.3	28.5	34.6	34.8	34.5	34.9
Machine engineering and metal processing	34.4	34.0	36.8	34.9	35.0	33.4
Energy	16.3	13.6	7.6	7.9	9.9	11.7
Metals	3.6	3.6	3.4	4.5	5.0	4.7
Construction materials	3.5	2.8	2.5	2.7	2.6	3.0
Forestry, timber, and pulp and paper	2.9	3.0	3.5	3.0	2.5	2.4
Light industry	2.7	2.7	2.4	2.4	2.0	1.8
Chemicals and petrochemicals	3.9	3.0	1.7	1.6	1.2	1.2

*Estimates of the St. Petersburg Government

up 119.8%, electric welding equipment output rose 118.9%, lifting and haulage equipment output was up 113.8%, and plumbing and gas equipment output rose 108.2%. The largest machine engineering enterprises are OAO Izhorskie Plants, OAO Leningrad Metal Processing Plant, OAO Kirovsky Plant, OAO Nevsky Plant, and OAO Elektrosila.

St. Petersburg is Russia's shipbuilding center. OAO Baltiysky Plant, FGUP Admiralty Shipyard, and OAO Almaz Shipyard build nuclear ice-breakers, tankers, refrigerator ships, hovercraft, and racing and cruise yachts.

Energy. The energy sector accounts for 11.7% of total industrial output. Power is supplied to the city by municipal thermal power stations that are subsidiaries of OAO Lenenergo, or small power plants installed at industrial enterprises. Power is transmitted using the high-voltage power transmission lines and transformer substations of OAO Lenenergo.

Metals. The sector accounts for 4.7% of total industrial output. The largest enterprises are ZAO Metals Plant, ZAO Neva Met, ZAO Steel, ZAO LST Metal, ZAO Alloy, and OAO Kermet.

Forestry, timber, and pulp and paper. The sector accounts for 2.4% of total industrial output. 2002 output rose 10% year-on-year, with output expected to rise by 9–10% per annum in 2003–2005. The largest enterprises are OAO Ust-Izhorsky Plywood Factory, OAO Lenraumamebel, OAO MKO Sevzapmebel, OAO Svetoch, and ZAO PO Parus.

Chemicals and petrochemicals. The sector accounts for 1.2% of total industrial output. 2002 output was 7% up on 2001. The largest enterprises are OAO NPF Pigment (paint and varnish), OAO Krasny Treugolnik (industrial rubber), ZAO Petrospirt (basic organic synthesis), and OAO Plastpolymer (plastic).

3.4. FUEL AND ENERGY BALANCE (OUTPUT AND CONSUMPTION PER RESOURCE)

The energy sector meets 50% of St. Petersburg's total needs.

The city's heating supply system comprises over 560 boiler houses (primarily natural gas fired), which are subsidiaries of GUP TEK St. Petersburg.

Natural gas is supplied by St. Petersburg GGKH (PK) Lengaz, which operates eleven gas distribution stations and a 5,000 kilometer natural gas distribution network.

3.5. TRANSPORT INFRASTRUCTURE

Roads. St. Petersburg has 846 kilometers of paved public highway. The city has highway links to Moscow, Murmansk, and Pskov, and to the Finnish and Estonian borders.

Railroads. St. Petersburg has 1,258 kilometers of railroads.

Airports. St. Petersburg's FGUAP International Pulkovo Airport is located 15 kilometers north of the city center. The airport handles 2 million passengers a year.

Sea and river ports. St. Petersburg's seaport comprises the former Commercial Seaport, the Timber Port, the shipbuilding and repair docks, the river freight ports of Vasileostrovsky and Nevsky, and smaller ports at Lomonosovsky and Kronstadt.

3.6. MAIN NATURAL RESOURCES: RESERVES AND EXTRACTION IN 2002

Water resources. The city's surface fresh water resources are contained in the catchment area of the water system composed of Lake Ladoga, the Neva River, the Neva Inlet, and the Gulf of Finland. The city accommodates 40 rivers, delta arms, river branches, and canals, with a total length of 217.5 kilometers. The largest waterways are the Major Neva and the Minor Neva, the Major Nevka, the Middle Nevka and the Minor Nevka, the Fontanka River, the Karpovka River, the Okhta River, the Zhdanovka River, the Moika River, the Chornaya River, and the By-Pass Canal.

Fuel and energy sector production and consumption trends, 1997–2002						*TABLE 5*
	1997	1998	1999	2000	2001	2002*
Electricity output, billion kWh	7.6	7.8	8.0	8.2	9.3	7.7
Electricity consumption, billion kWh	15.7	16.6	15.6	16.6	19.0	20.0
Natural gas consumption, million cubic meters	n/a	8,268.4	8,306.3	8,548.4	8,939.7	10,171.6

*Estimates of the St. Petersburg Government

4. TRADE OPPORTUNITIES

4.1. MAIN GOODS PRODUCED IN THE REGION

Food and beverages. In 2002, the sector produced 26,300 tons of fishery products, including canned fish (22.1% up on 2001); 1,100 tons of meat, including category one by-products; 2.5 million cans of meat; 330,900 tons of whole milk output (measured in milk equivalent); 391,700 tons of flour; 302,700 tons of bread and bakery products; 118,100 tons of confectionery; 2.3 million decaliters of vodka and other alcoholic beverages; 237,900 decaliters of brandy; 326,100 decaliters of wine; 812,000 decaliters of sparkling wine; and 151.4 million decaliters of beer.

Energy. In 2002, the energy sector produced 7.7 billion kWh of electricity, and 33 million Gcal of thermal energy.

Machine engineering and metal processing. In 2002, the sector produced steam turbines with an aggregate capacity of 2.6 million kWh; hydraulic turbines with an aggregate capacity of 31.2 million kWh; generators for steam, gas and hydraulic turbines with an aggregate capacity of 2.6 million kWh; 629 large electric machines; 647,100 electricity meters; 4,600 tons of accumulators and lead-acid storage batteries; 25,900 cameras; and 48,800 vacuum cleaners.

Metals. In 2002, the sector produced 461,200 tons of steel (12.5% down on 2001); 406,400 tons of finished ferrous metal rolled products (up 36.7%); 29,300 kilometers of steel pipe (up 4.8%); 4,100 tons of cold-rolled steel strip (down 37%); 11,800 tons of steel wire (down 12.7%); and 8,200 tons of welding electrodes (down 4.7%).

Construction materials. In 2002, the sector produced 510,300 cubic meters of reinforced concrete structures and elements (16.4% up on 2001), and 5.5 million square meters of linoleum.

Forestry, timber, and pulp and paper. In 2002, the sector produced 41,600 cubic meters of sawn timber; 116,300 cubic meters of plywood (30.1% up on 2001); 508,600 square meters of door frames (up 48.5%); 98,400 square meters of prefabricated window frames (up 29.4%); 32,800 tons of paper (up 11.7%); and 11,000 tons of cardboard.

Chemicals and petrochemicals. In 2002, the sector produced 522 tons of polymer film; 148 tons of thermoplastic sheeting; 1,200 tons of synthetic resins and plastics; 8,900 tons of plastic goods; 29,800 tons of paint materials; 153,100 tires (15.7% up on 2001); and industrial rubber and asbestos products.

Chemicals and pharmaceuticals. In 2002, the sector produced 16.8 million ampoules and

17.1 million packages of cardiovascular drugs; 52.3 million packages of analgesics, antipyretics and anti-inflammatory drugs (19.2% up on 2001); 3.6 million packages of antiasthmatics and antihistamines; and 62.5 million ampoules and 11.6 million packages of vitamins.

Chinaware and earthenware. In 2002, the sector produced 4.9 million pieces of chinaware, earthenware and majolica.

4.2. EXPORTS, INCLUDING EXTRA-CIS

Exports to extra-CIS countries in 1999 amounted to $1,994.6 million, while exports to CIS countries totaled $139.9 million. The respective figures for 2000 were $2,404 million and $140.4 million, and $1,789.1 million and $157.7 million for 2001. 2002 exports were $1,144 and $125 million, respectively.

The city's main exports in 2002 were machine engineering goods (44%), ferrous and non-ferrous metals (23%), timber and timber products (12%), and petrochemicals (5%). St. Petersburg exports chiefly to China (15.8%), Germany (10.2%), Finland (8.6%), the USA (5.9%), Ukraine (4.2%), and Kazakhstan (4%).

4.3. IMPORTS, INCLUDING EXTRA-CIS

Imports from extra-CIS countries in 1999 amounted to $2,219.2 million; imports from CIS countries totaled $201.4 million. The respective figures for 2000 were $2,366.4 million and $232.2 million, and $3,802.9 million and $233.4 million for 2001. 2002 imports totaled $3,260 million and $144 million, respectively.

The city's main imports in 2002 comprised food and edible raw materials (46%), machine engineering goods (25%), and petrochemicals (12%). The city's main import partners are Germany (14.5%), Finland (10.5%), the USA (8.6%), Brazil (5.8%), Italy (4.3%), and Ukraine (3.3%).

4.4. MAJOR REGIONAL EXPORT AND IMPORT ENTITIES

Export and import operations are mainly carried out by industrial enterprises in St. Petersburg.

II

NORTH-WESTERN FEDERAL DISTRICT

5. INVESTMENT OPPORTUNITIES

5.1. INVESTMENTS IN 1992–2002 (BY INDUSTRY SECTOR), INCLUDING FOREIGN INVESTMENTS

The following key factors determine the investment appeal of St. Petersburg:

- Its favorable geographical location;
- Its developed transport infrastructure;
- Legislation supporting investment activities;
- Its qualified work force.

5.2. CAPITAL INVESTMENT

The bulk of capital investment is channeled to the transport sector (33.5%). The construction of the Ring Road and approach roads accounted for the bulk of capital expenditure, followed by construction projects implemented under the Railways

Ministry's investment program (specifically, construction and rehabilitation of railroad stations).

5.3. MAJOR ENTERPRISES (INCLUDING ENTERPRISES WITH FOREIGN INVESTMENT)

The city's largest enterprises with foreign investment are OOO OSKO, ZAO Pulkovo Freight Terminal, ZAO JT International, OOO OTIS LIFT, OAO Peterburgstroi Skanska, and ZAO Alcatel.

5.4. MOST ATTRACTIVE SECTORS FOR INVESTMENT

According to the St. Petersburg Administration, tourism, shipbuilding, transport infrastructure, communications, and food and beverages are the most attractive sectors for investment.

Capital investment by industry sectors, $ million

TABLE 6

	1997	1998	1999	2000	2001	2002
Total capital investment	1,960.3	1,356.1	1,324.9	1,275.9	1,746.6	2,023.6
Including major industries (% of total):						
Industry	35.8	27.5	32.1	33.8	28.9	19.7
Construction	5.3	9.2	11.0	11.1	8.9	4.6
Transport and communications	24.7	24.6	29.3	25.4	39.2	39.8
Trade and public catering	2.9	6.0	4.8	2,7	1.5	2.6
Other	31.3	32.7	22.8	27.0	21.5	33.3

Foreign investment trends in 1997–2002

TABLE 7

	1997	1998	1999	2000	2001	2002
Foreign investment, $ million	234.0	413.3	698.5	1,159.9	1,171.4	881.0
Including FDI, $ million	149.3	259.9	272.0	146.7	114.1	84.1

Largest enterprises of St. Petersburg

TABLE 8

COMPANY	SECTOR
AO Baltika Brewery, OAO Vena, ZAO Stepan Razin Combine, OAO Petro, ZAO Philip Morris Neva, ZAO Nevo Tobacco, ZAO JV Rothmans Nevo, OO Bravo International, ZAO Coca Cola St. Petersburg Bottlers, ZAO Neva Chupa Chups, ZAO Krupskaya Confectionery, ZAO Parnas-M, ZAO St. Petersburg Piskaryovsky Dairy, OAO Petmol, OAO Kirov Bakery, OAO Pekar, OAO Khlebny Dom, ZAO Nevskaya Cosmetics, ZAO Aist.	Food and beverages
OAO Severny Shipyard, OAO Baltiysky Zavod, FGUP Admiralty Shipyard, OAO Almaz Shipyard, OAO Izhorskiye Zavody, OAO Leningrad Metals Plant, OAO Turbine Blades, OAO Nevsky Zavod, OAO Elektrosila, OAO New Era, OAO Novaya Sila, ZAO Elektropult, OAO Kirovsky Zavod, OAO Zvezda, OAO Northern Cables, ZAO Elektrotyaga, OAO Rigel Accumulators, ZAO Baltelektro, OAO LOMO, OAO Leningrad Electromechanical Plant, OOO OTIS St. Petersburg, OAO Morion, OAO Podyomtransmash, OAO Oktyabrsky Electric Car Repairs, ZAO Wagonmash.	Machine engineering and metal processing
ZAO Metals Plant, ZAO Neva-Met, ZAO Steel, ZAO LST Metal, ZAO Alloy, OAO Kermet.	Metals
OAO Ust-Izhorsky Plywood, OAO Lenraumamebel, OAO MKO Sevzapmebel, OAO Svetoch, ZAO PO Parus, ZAO Prestige, OAO Paper, OAO Unipak.	Forestry, timber, and pulp and paper
OAO NPF Pigment, OAO Krasny Treugolnik, ZAO Petrospirt, OAO Plastpolymer.	Chemicals and petrochemicals

5.5. CURRENT LEGISLATION ON INVESTOR TAX EXEMPTIONS AND PRIVILEGES

The current Law On Tax Benefits (1995) offers tax privileges to investors making extensive investments into fixed assets. Under the terms of the Law, net book value of fixed assets put into operation over the previous four quarters is deductible from the tax base for the regional component of corporate property tax.

Other laws governing investor tax exemptions and privileges include the Law On the Procedure and Terms for the Provision and Cancellation of Tax Privileges (1997), the Law On Certain Aspects of Taxation in 2000–2003 (1999), and the Law On the Moratorium on Tax Rate Increases in St. Petersburg (2000).

Under international agreements concluded between St. Petersburg and foreign governments, any legal entity with foreign capital is exempt from the regional component of corporate profits tax, property tax, land tax, tax on advertising, and tax on motor vehicles for the period stipulated in the international agreement (up to a maximum of seven years).

Regional entities responsible for raising investment		*TABLE 9*
ENTITY	ADDRESS	PHONE, FAX, E-MAIL
The Fund for Federal and Regional Programs Attached to the Government of St. Petersburg	39 B, pr. Rimskogo-Korsakova, St. Petersburg, 190068	Phone: (812) 110 8337, 110 8442 Phone/fax: (812) 110 8336 E-mail: fond@robotek.ru http://www.abic.spb.ru
GU Investment Management	Room 254, 76, nab. r. Moiki, St. Petersburg, 190000	Phone: (812) 310 0205 http://www.stateinvest.spb.ru
The Fund for Construction Investment Projects	76, nab. r. Moiki, St. Petersburg, 190000	Phone: (812) 319 9550, 312 2661 E-mail: spfund@online.ru
The Hall of Investment Projects	2nd Floor, 11, pl. Ostrovskogo, St. Petersburg, 191011	Phone/fax: (812) 312 2430 E-mail: invhall@fisp.spb.ru
GU St. Petersburg Center for International Cooperation	21, nab. r. Fontanki, St. Petersburg, 191011	Phone: (812) 313 4900 Phone/fax: (812) 313 4901

5.6. FEDERAL AND REGIONAL ECONOMIC AND SOCIAL DEVELOPMENT PROGRAMS FOR ST. PETERSBURG

Federal targeted programs. Priority programs include the federal targeted science and technology program Science and Technology: Priority Areas for Research and Development, 2002–2006 ($0.2 million in federal funding slated for 2003), Electronic Russia, 2002–2010 ($54.5 million), Reform and Development of the Defense Industry, 2002–2006 ($3.1 million), Upgrading of the Russian Transport System, 2002–2010 ($28.7 million) with two sub-programs: Marine Transport and Inland Waterways, and Reform and Development of the Defense and Industrial Sector 2002–2006 ($3.1 million). In addition, the city is running programs related to social, cultural, and environmental protection as well as the protection of historic monuments.

Regional programs. The targeted program for State Support to Small Enterprise in St. Petersburg 2002–2004, aims to develop a comprehensive system of state support to small businesses in the city. The planned level of financing from the city of St. Petersburg is $5.3 million.

The targeted program for The Completion of Construction of the South-Western Sewage Disposal Plant slated for implementation in 2002–2016 has been launched with the aim of improving the environmental situation in the city and its suburbs. A total of € 249 million in funding is to be assigned to the program. Targeted programs for the Development of Tourism in St. Petersburg (2002–2005) and Street Lighting in St. Petersburg (2000–2003) are also currently underway. Some $3.8 million and $14.2 million in funding is to be assigned to the respective programs.

6. INVESTMENT PROJECTS

Industry sector and project description	1) Expected results 2) Amount and term of investment 3) Form of financing[1] 4) Documentation[2]	Contact information
1	2	3
HOTEL BUSINESS, TOURISM, AND RECREATION		
28R001 ■ ● ◆		State Russian Museum
Creation of a multifunctional computer center. Project goal: to diversify services for the population.	1) Sales of $3.3 million per year, income of $1.4 million per year 2) $12.6 million/1.5 years 3) E ($7.5 million), L ($5.1 million) 4) BP	4, ul. Inzhenernaya, St. Petersburg, 191011 Phone: (812) 313 4169, 314 5710 Fax: (812) 314 4153 E-mail: net@peterlink.ru, info@rusmuseum.ru http://www.rusmuseum.ru Alexander Alexandrovich Nikolenko, Head of the New Electronic Technologies Department

[1] L – Loan, E – Equity, Leas. – Leasing, JV – Joint Venture
[2] BP – Business Plan, FS – Feasibility Study

II

NORTH-WESTERN FEDERAL DISTRICT

1	2	3

28R002

Construction of a cultural and sports complex (Belvedere palace, 28 luxury suite hotel, a golf club, a horse riding center, tennis courts, and a cottage village). Project goal: to diversify services for the population, and to develop tourism.

1) n/a
2) n/a/3 years
3) L
4) Investment proposal

ZAO Peter Golf Sport Club
P.O. Box 143, St. Petersburg, 191040
Phone: (812) 314 4220
Fax: (812) 312 4617
E-mail: spbgolf@sovintel.spb.ru
Alexei Mikhailovich Rybin, CEO

28R003

Construction of a roofed water park in St. Petersburg (an aquapark, a hotel, a parking lot, and leisure infrastructure). Project goal: to diversify services for the population.

1) Total complex area –
   26,500 square meters
2) $34.5 million/1.5 years
3) L ($2.8 million)
4) BP

ZAO First Petersburg Aquapark
21, ul. Ordinarnaya,
St. Petersburg, 197022
Phone: (812) 346 1825
Fax: (812) 327 5348
E-mail: aquapark@omillioni.spb.ru
Elena Alexeevna Kurikova, Accountant

28R004

Ozero Dolgoye municipal recreation zone development and irrigation. Project goal: to diversify services for the population.

1) n/a
2) $1.5 million/1 year
3) L ($0.8 million)
4) BP

Territorial Directorate of the Primorsky District (Administration)
83, ul. Savushkina, St. Petersburg, 197374
Phone: (812) 430 0915, 430 0509, 430 0524
Fax: (812) 430 0814
Yury Lvovich Osipov, Head of the Territorial Directorate of the Primorsky District

28R005

Construction of the high standard Mikhailovsky Hotel. Project goal: to diversify hotel services.

1) Hotel of 60 suites, total
   area of 5,000 square meters
2) $12.5 million/2 years
3) E ($12.5 million)
4) BP

State Russian Museum
4, ul. Inzhenernaya, St. Petersburg, 191011
Phone: (812) 313 4169, 314 5710
Fax: (812) 314 4153
E-mail: net@peterlink.ru,
info@rusmuseum.ru
http://www.rusmuseum.ru
Alexei Alexandrovich Merkulov, Director

HOUSING AND SOCIAL

28R006

Construction of multifunctional residential complex on the Gulf of Finland shore. Project goal: to diversify services for the population.

1) Useful area of the complex –
   176,600 square meters
2) $92.1 million/3 years
3) E ($82.7 million), L ($8 million)
4) BP

ZAO Specialized Construction and Installation Association LenSpecSMU (Holding)
2, Bogatyrsky prospekt,
St. Petersburg, 197348
Phone: (812) 380 0525
Phone/fax: (812) 380 0529
E-mail: lenspecsmu@lenspecsmu.ru
http://www.lenspecsmu.ru
ZAO St. Petersburg World Financial and Trade Center (holding affiliate)
Office 115, ul. Kapitanskaya,
St. Petersburg, 199155
Phone: (812) 352 4298, 351 7015
Fax: (812) 352 2870
Pyotr Grigoryevich Mayorov, CEO

II

N O R T H - W E S T E R N   F E D E R A L   D I S T R I C T

1	2	3

TRANSPORT INFRASTRUCTURE

28R007 ● ◆

Creation of the St. Petersburg Taxi enterprise (purchase of 500 taxi cabs, construction of a technical service center, and a dispatch office).
Project goal: to diversify transport services for the population, and to develop transport infrastructure.

1) Revenues from passenger transportation of $0.2 million per 10 months
2) $20 million/3 years
3) L ($20 million)
4) BP

OOO Passenger Motor Transport Enterprise of the Taxi Association
137, ul. Babushkina, St. Petersburg, 193012
Phone: (812) 262 4227, 262 4218
Fax: (812) 262 5421
Mikhail Fedorovich Bogdanovsky, President of the Russian Urban Taxi Association
Mark Zalmanovich Kurtik, CEO of OOO Passenger Motor Transport Enterprise of the Taxi Association

II

N O R T H - W E S T E R N   F E D E R A L   D I S T R I C T

PETERSBURG JEWELERS ASSEMBLY

АЛЬФА

АРИНА

D·А·И·М·О·Н·D

КЛАД

КАРАТ

Роза

СТРАХОВАЯ ГРУППА МЕГАРУСС

АРДОС®

POMELNIKOV ARTSP

Ювелирный дом САДКО

ООО «СевЗапЮвелирпром»

КАСТ

Еstablished on October 26, 2001, St. Petersburg Jewelers Assembly now includes some sixteen leading makers of gold, silver and platinum jewels with precious and semi-precious stones, exclusive jewelers and gem cutters, and firms specializing in the sale of jewels and equipment used to make jewelry.

The Assembly's core objective is to revive the craft of jewelry in St. Petersburg and in Russia, to create a civilized jewelry market, and to offer protection to the commercial interests of jewelers.

Strong on exhibition activities, the Assembly has organized its own exhibition event – «Piter-Juvelir».

ЮВЕЛИРНЫЙ ДОМ КАХОЛОНГ САНКТ-ПЕТЕРБУРГ

РУССКИЕ САМОЦВЕТЫ
RUSSKIYE SAMOTSVETY CORPORATION

петроЗОЛОТО
ПРОИЗВОДИТЕЛЬ ИЗДЕЛИЙ С БРИЛЛИАНТАМИ

JUVELIRTÖRG ЮВЕЛИРТОРГ
АО "ЮВЕЛИРНАЯ ТОРГОВЛЯ СЕВЕРО-ЗАПАДА"

St. Petersburg:
Alfa Jewelry Factory - Pr. Energetikov 6. Tel/fax (812) 528 07 70
Adros SPB - Ul. Zhukovskogo 4. Tel/fax (812) 272 07 55
Arina - Ul. Ordzhonnikidze 42. Tel/fax (812) 378 66 57
Art SP - PO Box 11. Tel (812) 164 98 39 Fax (812) 164 09 41
Diamond Design - Ul. Podolskaya 35. Tel (812) 112 69 05 Fax (812) 317 80 79
Kast - Pl. Rastrelli 2. Tel (812) 274 23 59 Fax (812) 274 19 98
Kakholong - Ul. Ordzhonnikidze 42. Tel/fax (812) 378 60 24, 379 66 98, 379 67 98
V.A. Panasyuk **KLAD** - Nab. Reki Fontanki 90/1, room 015. Tel (812) 112 40 95 Fax (812) 112 46 30
SK Megaruss-D - Bolshoi Pr., PS, 29A, office 504. Tel/fax (812) 118 65 76, 118 65 86
Petrozoloto - Ul. Egorova 18, lit A. Tel (812) 103 39 28 Fax (812) 248 25 61
Roza - Nab. Reki Volkovki 9. Tel/fax (812) 166 44 78
Russian Gems - Pl. Karla Faberge 8. Tel (812) 528 01 03 Fax (812) 528 09 18
Sadko - Kondratevsky pr. 38. Tel. (812) 545 15 47, 545 15 37 Fax (812) 545 15 97
SevZapJuvelirprom - Ul. Dalya 10. Tel (812) 234 67 55 Fax (812) 234 97 05
North Western Jewelry Trading - Novosmolenskaya Nab. 1. Tel (812) 355 59 53 Fax (812) 355 59 39
14 Carats - Moskovsky Pr. 212. Tel/fax (812) 140 38 09

АССАМБЛЕЯ ЮВЕЛИРОВ САНКТ-ПЕТЕРБУРГА

UL. ORDZHONNIKIDZE 43, OFFICE 301, 196143 ST. PETERSBURG
TEL (812) 378 61 67 FAX (812) 127 87 00
E-MAIL: assembly@front.ru

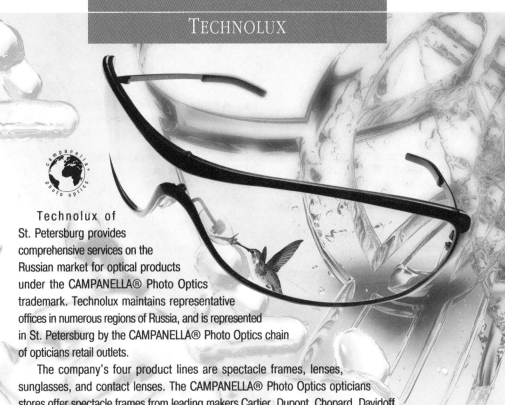

Technolux of St. Petersburg provides comprehensive services on the Russian market for optical products under the CAMPANELLA® Photo Optics trademark. Technolux maintains representative offices in numerous regions of Russia, and is represented in St. Petersburg by the CAMPANELLA® Photo Optics chain of opticians retail outlets.

The company's four product lines are spectacle frames, lenses, sunglasses, and contact lenses. The CAMPANELLA® Photo Optics opticians stores offer spectacle frames from leading makers Cartier, Dupont, Chopard, Davidoff, Chanel, Max Mara, and Kenzo, as well as more affordable brands such as Polaroid.

The company's exclusive offerings include hand made gold and gem encrusted spectacle frames. Technolux is licensed to sell gold spectacle frames in Russia.

The company's partner in the luxury spectacle frame segment is French company Bourgeois.

Technolux employs highly qualified providing medical services such as contact lens prescription, ophthalmological examinations, and lens grinding. Technolux uses modern equipment supplied by French company Essilor to provide top quality medical services and grind lenses to the most exacting specifications.

Technolux is developing a franchise network within Russia and is seeking to establish partner relationships with ophthalmological professionals throughout Russia.

CAMPANELLA® Photo Optics is open to people who respect true values, professionalism, and mutually beneficial financial collaboration.

Technolux was established in 1995.

CEO – Alexander Stanislavovich Slobozhan.

A crystal clear view of the world.

Кристальный взгляд на мир...

CAMPANELLA®
optics

SUVOROVSKY PROSPEKT 60, 193015 ST. PETERSBURG
TEL/FAX (812) 274 16 31, 274 75 69, 274 88 95, 274 66 09; INFORMATION HOTLINE: 971 71 77
E-MAIL: grand@campanella.ru;   HTTP://www.campanella.ru

Established in St. Petersburg in 1995, Baltimor's core activity is the production and retailing of high-quality food products.

Baltimor is Russia's top ketchup producer, with a 50% market share (GFK 2002 data), and controls 4% of the market for mayonnaise (AC Nielsen 2002 data). Baltimor has production facilities in Russia and Uzbekistan.

In 2002, the company's sales totaled $90 million.

TRADEMARKS AND PRODUCTS

Baltimor owns three brands: Baltimor, Stavropolye, and Eastern Gourmand.

Brand positioning:

Baltimor: premium quality in the medium to high price bracket.

Stavropolye: high quality in the medium price bracket.

Eastern Gourmand: good quality in the low price bracket.

Baltimor produces the following products under its three brands:

Baltimor:
- ketchup (more than 50 varieties)
- mayonnaise (around 10 varieties)
- mustard (four varieties)
- vinegar (three varieties)
- canned fruit and vegetables
- tomato paste

Stavropolye:
- ketchup (more than 10 varieties)
- light mayonnaise
- canned fruit and vegetables
- jam

Eastern Gourmand:
- ketchup (15 varieties)
- light mayonnaise

PRODUCTION

Baltimor operates four factories in Russia, which produce its full range of products: St. Petersburg, Moscow, Krasnodar, and Khabarovsk.

RAW MATERIALS

Baltimor produces its own raw materials (tomato and pumpkin paste) using top grade tomatoes and other vegetables.

We apply scrupulous quality control and selection procedures to raw materials bought from external suppliers.

Baltimor works exclusively with the leading global suppliers of raw materials to the food industry.

TECHNOLOGY AND RECIPES

Baltimor uses leading production technologies developed and operated by our teams of highly qualified specialists.

We use only original recipes which we develop in-house.

Baltimor is constantly striving to improve its recipes and packaging.

QUALITY

Baltimor has completed the transition from a quality control system to a quality management system.

The company includes an independent quality control department, which reports directly to senior management.

Quality control staff are present at all production facilities at all stages of the production process.

MARKET POSITION

Baltimor controls up to 50% of the Russian ketchup market and 4% of the mayonnaise market.

In Russia's major urban centers, our market share rises to 65% for ketchup and 8% for mayonnaise (2002 data from GFK and AC Nielsen).

CLIENTS

Baltimor has some 137 clients spread throughout Russia. Our main international clients include Metro, Migros, IKI, Auchan, Billa, Rimi, etc. We also export to China, South Korea, Mongolia, Germany, the US, Israel, Austria, Latvia, Ukraine, Kazakhstan, Georgia, Uzbekistan, and Kyrgyzia.

Baltimor also produces products for other companies (including the top international brands) under their own brands.

BALTIMOR, PL. KONSTITUTSII 2, 196247 ST. PETERSBURG
TEL./FAX: (812) 118 69 60   HTTP://www.baltimor.ru

REMTYAZHMASH

For more than 10 years now, Remtyazhmash has been engaged in the capital repair and upgrading of unique heavy machine tools. Remtyazhmash's machine tool plant enables the parallel mechanical finishing of a full range of large-sized components for the machine engineering sector and the manufacturing of non-standard equipment and metal constructions of all levels of complexity. One of the company's main advantages is its assembly workshop, which can house machine tools for assembly of any size. Remtyazhmash uses the ISO 9001 quality assurance system as certified by the reputable German firm AFAQ ASCERT. Remtyazhmash's main customers include the major European industrial groups CATTANEO, WILLIAM COOK, and SULZER, and Russia's KAMAZ, Electrosila, and others.

PR. OBUKHOVSKOI OBORONY 120, 192012 ST. PETERSBURG
TEL (812) 267 39 92, 267 72 19, FAX (812) 267 38 50
E-MAIL: remtm@remtm.spb.ru   HTTP://www.remtm.spb.ru
E-MAIL: spmo@spmo.spb.ru   HTTP://www.spmo.spb.ru

Founded in 1992, TALOSTO is one of Russia's largest producers of frozen foods. TALOSTO is made up of three factories specializing in the production of frozen meat, ice-cream, and pastry, a refrigerated truck fleet, a design bureau, and a livestock rearing outfit.

PERSONNEL

TALOSTO employs some 2,500 people at its factories in St. Petersburg and Volkhov and its subsidiaries in Moscow and Krasnodar.
TALOSTO is preparing to undergo ISO 9000 certification in 2004.

PRODUCTS AND TRADEMARKS

TALOSTO produces more than 100 varieties of ice-cream, upwards of 60 types of frozen food, and more than 30 types of frozen pastry and pastry foods. The company's daily output stands at 160 tons.

Meat dumplings are the company's main frozen food line, produced in three varieties: classical, ravioli, and pinzatti. TALOSTO produces meat dumplings under the trademarks «Bogatyrskie», «Zyryanskie», «Gladiator», and «Super». TALOSTO's main meat dumpling brand is called «Sam Samych».

TALOSTO also produces beef chops, meat balls, «Masteritsa» and «Blinov & Co.» pancakes, curd and fruit dumplings, and «No Worries» pastry and dough.

TALOSTO produces ice-cream in more than ten different formats: wafer tubes, lollies, choc-ices, blocks, sandwiches, mini-tubs, rolls, cakes, batch ice-cream in various flavors, and plastic packaged ice-cream. TALOSTO's main ice-cream brands are Oasis, Alibi, and Gold Ingot.

MARKET

TALOSTO has more than 50 partners in Russia and abroad. The company's products are sold throughout Russia and in Kazakhstan, Belarus, Kyrgyzia, Azerbaijan, Ukraine, Israel, Finland, Sweden, and Germany.

OFFICIAL RECOGNITION

In 1999, TALOSTO was acclaimed as Russia's best food enterprise. In 2001, TALOSTO was awarded the Commercial Prestige Cup in Madrid.

AWARDS 2001

Oasis Ice-cream named Product of the Year. Bogatyrskie meat dumplings named Product of the Year.
Sam Samych and Bogatyrskie meat dumplings and Oasis and Ingot ice-cream included in the 100 Best Russian Products.

AWARDS 2002

Brand of the Year title awarded to Sam Samych meat dumplings trademark.

UL. KUZNETSOVSKAYA 52, 196105 ST. PETERSBURG
TEL/FAX (812) 327 66 11
E-MAIL: spb@talosto.ru   HTTP://www.talosto.ru

«I foresee that sometime, and maybe in our own lifetime, Russians will astonish the most advanced nations by their accomplishments in science, their tirelessness in labor, and the greatness of their glory.»

Peter the Great

The mission of St. Petersburg Brand Publishing House is to provide information and image support to Russian companies. The company works closely with leading enterprises in St. Petersburg and the North-Western region, executive and legislative bodies, and business associations.

One of the company's key projects is the St. Petersburg Brand Business Encyclopedia. The Encyclopedia is rated highly and in high demand among Russian and foreign users thanks to its high quality binding, reliable and accurate information, and its well planned development strategy. The Encyclopedia is distributed via Russian and overseas Chambers of Commerce, and at major forums, exhibitions, and congresses held in the North-Western Federal District.

The company is working on the publication of the North-Western information directory, a convenient and necessary information publication for directors of Russian and foreign companies containing reliable and accurate information on the economic and investment situation in the North-Western District: the Republics of Karelia and Komi, the Arkhangelsk, Murmansk, Pskov, Novgorod, Kaliningrad, Vologda, and Leningrad regions, and the city of St. Petersburg.

The company employs a creative, committed and responsible work team that values professionalism and dedication. We strive to ensure that our work inspires the confidence, respect and approval of society, our business partners, and our clients.

OFFICE 342, 90, NAB. REKI FONTANKI, ST. PETERSBURG, 191180, RUSSIA
TEL: (812) 113 3576, 112 4096; TEL/FAX (812) 113 1928, 312 8437
E-MAIL: mail@peterbrand.sp.ru

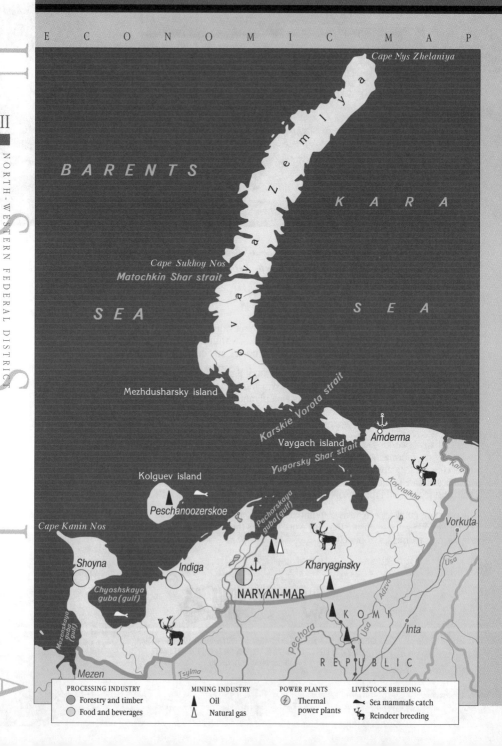

29. NENETSKY AUTONOMOUS DISTRICT [83]

ECONOMIC MAP

BARENTS

SEA

KARA

SEA

Cape Mys Zhelaniya

Novaya Zemlya

Cape Sukhoy Nos
Matochkin Shar strait

Mezhdusharsky island

Karskie Vorota strait

Vaygach island

Yugorsky Shar strait

Amderma

Kolguev island

Peschanoozerskoe

Pechorskaya guba (gulf)

Korotaikha

Kara

Cape Kanin Nos

Shoyna

Indiga

Kharyaginsky

Vorkuta

Chyoshskaya guba (gulf)

NARYAN-MAR

Usa

KOMI

Inta

Mezenskaya guba (gulf)

Pechora

Usa

Adzva

Mezen

Tsylma

REPUBLIC

PROCESSING INDUSTRY
● Forestry and timber
● Food and beverages

MINING INDUSTRY
▲ Oil
△ Natural gas

POWER PLANTS
⚡ Thermal power plants

LIVESTOCK BREEDING
🦭 Sea mammals catch
🦌 Reindeer breeding

Age old traditions combined with forward-looking progress – this must be the right way to describe the Nenetsky Autonomous District today. Our District is located at the extreme north-east of European Russia. Nearly all of its territory is located above the Arctic Circle.

The Nenets lands are extremely wealthy. But our riches are not limited to the oil and gas that have made the Nenetsky Autonomous District famous: we also have deposits of most of the elements listed on the periodic table. According to the latest survey, one single percentage point of the riches of the Nenets lands translated into industrial reserves is valued at as much as $500 billion.

To date, the District's development has been directly dependent on the oil industry. The oil sector provides revenues for the regional and local budgets, jobs for the local population, and fuel supplies to the District. This is why we welcome first and foremost projects by companies willing to invest in our natural resources, to improve our economy and welfare.

The sheer scale of our natural resources represents a magnet to investments and arouses justified interest in our region. With this in mind, appropriate legislative and economic levers have been devised and are being improved.

We are ready to consider any initiative from investors willing to invest in the north of the Timano-Pechora Region, with a specific focus on creating oil and gas transport infrastructure and constructing external transport facilities (pipelines, offshore oil terminals, etc.), as these investments will determine both the sequence and rate at which the deposits are developed.

Vladimir Butov,
HEAD OF ADMINISTRATION
OF THE NENETSKY AUTONOMOUS DISTRICT

II

NORTH-WESTERN FEDERAL DISTRICT

1. GENERAL INFORMATION

1.1. GEOGRAPHY

The Nenetsky Autonomous District covers a total area of some 176,700 square kilometers. The District lies in the furthest north-eastern part of European Russia. To the south the District borders the Komi Republic, and to the east, the Yamalo-Nenetsky Autonomous District. To the north and north-west, the District is washed by the White Sea, the Barents Sea, and the Kara Sea.

1.2. CLIMATE

The District is located within the mixed maritime and continental climate zone. Air temperatures in January average –22°C, rising to +12°C in July.

1.3. POPULATION

According to preliminary 2002 census results, the total population of the District amounted to 42,000 people. The average population density is 0.2 people per square kilometer. The economically active population stood at 23,000 in 2002. Official 2002 unemployment was 2.4%. Demographically speaking, some 63.7% of the population is of statutory working age, 23.1% are below the statutory working age, and 13.2% are beyond the statutory working age.

The District ethnic mix is as follows: 70% Russian, 15,6% Nenets, and 9,5% Komi.

The District's largest urban centers had the following populations in 2002: Naryan-Mar – 25,500, Iskateley – 7,100, and Amderma – 1,900.

Population							TABLE 1
	1992	1997	1998	1999	2000	2001	2002
Total population, '000	53	46	46	46	45	45	42
Economically active population, '000	n/a	25	24	25	24	24	23

2. ADMINISTRATION

20, ul. Smidovitcha, Naryan-Mar, Nenetsky Autonomous District, 166000
Phone: (81853) 42 113, Fax: (81853) 42 269. E-mail: nencit@atnet.ru

NAME	POSITION	CONTACT INFORMATION
Vladimir Yakovlevich BUTOV	Head of Administration of the Nenetsky Autonomous District	Phone: (81853) 42 113
Yury Ivanovich PADALKA	First Deputy Head of Administration of the Nenetsky Autonomous District	Phone: (81853) 43 062
Tatiana Gennadyevna SHLIAKOVA	Acting First Deputy Head of Administration of the Nenetsky Autonomous District	Phone: (81853) 42 257
Andrei Vladimirovich GETMAN	Deputy Head of Administration of the Nenetsky Autonomous District for Comprehensive Use of Natural Resources	Phone: (81853) 43 063
Svetlana Ivanovna KOZLOVA	Deputy Head of Administration, Head of the Financial Department of the Nenetsky Autonomous District	Phone: (81853) 42 032
Yury Anatolyevich KAZNACHEEV	Deputy Head of Administration of the Nenetsky Autonomous District, Head of the Agricultural Department	Phone: (81853) 42 263
Valentin Ivanovich CHIRKOV	Deputy Head of Administration of the Nenetsky Autonomous District for Industry, Transport, Communications, Energy, Housing and Construction	Phone: (81853) 42 208
Ninel Alekseevna SEMIASHKINA	Head of the Economy and Investment Department of the Nenetsky Autonomous District Administration	Phone: (81853) 42 125

NAME	POSITION	CONTACT INFORMATION
Vera Stepanovna SHKRIABINA	Head of the Investment Department of the Nenetsky Autonomous District Administration	Phone: (81853) 41 733

3. ECONOMIC POTENTIAL

3.1. 1997–2002 GROSS REGIONAL PRODUCT (GRP). INDUSTRY BREAKDOWN

The Nenetsky Autonomous District's 2002 gross regional product amounted to $432 million. 2001 per capita GRP totaled $9,600.

3.2. MAJOR ECONOMIC GROWTH PROJECTIONS

According to the District's economic growth projections, the District's industrial output will rise to $2.4 billion by 2005 (a fivefold increase on 2002). Considerable growth in industrial output (70.5%-77.9%) is expected in

GRP trends in 1997–2002						*TABLE 2*
	1997	1998	1999	2000	2001	2002
GRP in current prices, $ million	n/a	251.4	227.7	323.1	432.0	n/a

2003. Industrial output is expected to continue gro-wing in 2004–2005, but at a lower rate: 41.4%–44.6% year-on-year in 2004, and 33.7%–39.1% year-on-year in 2005.

The following measures are planned with a view to underpinning industrial output growth in the District:

Industry: growth in industrial output through the development of the fuel industry. A steep increase in oil and gas output is projected. Oil output is expected to top 20 million tons in 2005 (compared with 5.1 million tons in 2002);

Agriculture: the creation of conditions conducive to the effective operation of agricultural enterprises, improved living standards in rural areas, efficient use of budgetary funds allocated to the agroindustrial sector, the provision of feedstock to processing enterprises, and the securing of fish, meat and dairy supplies for the general public;

Construction: the implementation of new residential construction projects and social infrastructure projects;

Transport: creating transport infrastructure, and expanding the roads network. The foremost objective of the District Administration's Transport Committee is the construction of Naryan Mar – Usinsk highway (88 kilometers of a 300 kilometer highway are to be built).

The District also plans to revamp seaport and airport facilities and to construct an oil transportation system.

3.3. INDUSTRIAL OUTPUT IN 1997–2002 FOR MAJOR SECTORS OF ECONOMY

The District's major industrial sectors are the fuel industry, which accounts for 96.5% of total output, and the food industry (represented by fishing, dairy and meat-packing), which accounts for 2.3%.

Fuel industry. The Timano-Pechora Fuel and Energy Complex is under construction within the District for the purpose of developing its oil, gas and coal deposits. Some 12 hydrocarbon deposits have been earmarked for development. Oil and gas are extracted in the District by the following companies: OAO LUKoil Komi (49%) and TotalFinaElf (9%) at the Kharyaginskoye oil field; OOO Poliarnoye Sianie (23%) at the Ardalinskoye and Oshkotynskoye oil fields, OAO Severnaya Neft (8%) at the Sandiveyskoye, Khasireyskoye, and Cherpayuskoye oil fields, OAO Archangelskgeoldobycha (4%) at the Varandeyskoye and Toraveyskoye oil fields, OOO Bovel (3%) at the Tedinskoye oil field, ZAO Arcticneft (2%) and GFUP Arcticmorneftegas-razvedka (0.4%) at the Peschanoozerskoye oil and gas condensate field, OAO Pechoraneft (1%) at the Middle Khariaginskoye oil field, ZAO Kolvageoldobycha (0.2%) at the East

Industry breakdown of industrial output in 1997–2002, % of total						*TABLE 3*
	1997	1998	1999	2000	2001	2002*
Industry	100.0	100.0	100.0	100.0	100.0	100.0
Fuel	93.3	91.0	95.4	96.9	95.9	96.5
Food	3.5	5.7	4.0	2.4	3.0	2.3
Energy	1.8	2.7	0.5	0.6	0.8	1.0

*Estimates of the Nenetsky Autonomous District Administration

Khariaginskoye oil field, and OOO Pechorneftegazprom at the Vasilkovskoye oil and gas condensate field.

Food and beverages. The District specializes in meat, fish, dairy, and bakery products.

The largest enterprises in the sector are OAO Miasoprodukty, OAO Vita, and OAO Naryan-Mar bakery plant.

Forestry. OAO Pechorsky Les (timber plant), the oldest enterprise in the Far North of Russia, processes feedstock imported from other regions and exports its output.

Energy. The largest enterprise in the sector is GUP Naryan-Mar Power Station, which produces energy for Naryan-Mar and the township of Iskateley. The station accounts for 80% of the District's total energy output. Other townships and communities are supplied by local diesel power stations.

3.4. FUEL AND ENERGY BALANCE (OUTPUT AND CONSUMPTION PER RESOURCE)

Total 2002 electricity output in the District amounted to 90.1 million kWh. 2002 oil output increased by 8.6% to 5.1 million tons. Natural gas output amounted to 125 million cubic meters.

3.5. TRANSPORT INFRASTRUCTURE

Roads. The District has no developed road network and no land connection to other regions of Russia.

Airports. Air transport is the main means of transportation in the District. Naryan-Mar has air links with all townships and communities within the District and almost all regions of Russia. Air transportation services are provided by FGUP Naryan-Mar Joint Air Team. Naryan-Mar airport meets modern aviation requirements. The District's second largest airport, GUP Amderma Airport, can accommodate An 24, Tu 134, Tu 152, and Il 76 aircraft. Naryan-Mar airport services passenger flights to and from Moscow, St. Petersburg, Arkhangelsk, and Anapa.

Oil and gas pipelines. The Baltic Pipeline Consortium has laid trunk pipelines in the District over recent years.

3.6. MAIN NATURAL RESOURCES: RESERVES AND EXTRACTION IN 2002

Oil and gas resources. The District has 80 explored hydrocarbon fields, including 74 oil fields, five gas condensate fields and one gas field. A total of 38 fields containing 559 million tons of proven extractable reserves of oil and 523 billion cubic meters of natural gas have been prepared for commercial development. Six are already in commercial operation.

Minerals. The District has developed deposits of fluorite, agate, and amber. Copper, nickel, and cobalt deposits have also been found. Plans are afoot to commence gold and diamond mining in the District. The District also has deposits of other minerals including clay (over 4 million tons), sand, sand-gravel and pebble-gravel mixtures (some 4 billion cubic meters in more than 100 deposits), limestone (83 million cubic meters), and coal (over 10 billion cubic meters).

Fuel and energy sector production and consumption trends, 1997–2002						*TABLE 4*
	1997	1998	1999	2000	2001	2002*
Electricity output, billion kWh	0.1	0.1	0.1	0.1	0.1	0.1
Oil output (including gas condensate), '000 tons	3,264.0	3,353.0	3,914.0	4,516.1	4,702.0	5,103.0
Natural gas extraction, million cubic meters	162.0	n/a	116.0	126.0	121.0	125.0
Electricity consumption, billion kWh	0.1	0.1	0.1	0.1	0.1	0.1
Oil products consumption, '000 tons	25.0	44.8	23.5	32.5	46.7	26.6
Natural gas consumption, million cubic meters	87.0	71.0	99.0	100.0	92.0	120,0

*Estimates of the Nenetsky Autonomous District Administration

4. TRADE OPPORTUNITIES

4.1. MAIN GOODS PRODUCED IN THE REGION

Oil and gas. 2002 oil output amounted to 5.1 million tons, natural gas output – to 125 million cubic meters. The District is the second largest producer in the North-Western Federal District after the Komi Republic.

Food and beverages. Dairy output in 2002 amounted to 2,400 tons, bread and bakery – 3,100 tons, meat – 700 tons, sausage – 500 tons, and seafood and fish – 8,700 tons.

Mineral water. 2002 output amounted to 6,600 decaliters.

4.2. EXPORTS, INCLUDING EXTRA-CIS

The bulk of the District's exports comprise oil products. Oil exports in 2002 amounted to 1.5 million tons (29% of total output). Food represents a smaller share of the District's exports. In 2002, the District exported 2,583 tons of fish.

4.3. IMPORTS, INCLUDING EXTRA-CIS

The bulk of the District's imports consist's of oil equipment. The District also imports food and alcoholic beverages.

Major regional export and import entities		*TABLE 5*
ENTITY	ADDRESS	PHONE, FAX, E-MAIL
Social Fund for Support of Social Programs in the Nenetsky Autonomous District	2, ul. Lesozavodskaya, Naryan-Mar, Nenetsky Autonomous District, 166000	Phone: (81853) 40 883 Fax: (81853) 40 071 E-mail: provans@atnet.ru
Barentsev Information Center in the Nenetsky Autonomous District	1, ul. Studencheskaya, Naryan-Mar, Nenetsky Autonomous District, 166000	Phone: (81853) 40 684
SPK RK Andeg	10, ul. Saprygina, Naryan-Mar, Nenetsky Autonomous District, 166000	Phone: (81853) 45 304

5. INVESTMENT OPPORTUNITIES

5.1. INVESTMENTS IN 1992–2002 (BY INDUSTRY SECTOR), INCLUDING FOREIGN INVESTMENTS

The following factors determine the investment appeal of the Nenetsky Autonomous District:
- Its natural resources (considerable hydrocarbon reserves: oil, natural gas, gas condensate, minerals, including non-ferrous and precious metals, fish, and plant (algae) and hunting resources);
- Its favorable geographical location (at the northern coast of European Russia, in proximity to the Northern Sea Route);
- Legislation supporting investment activities (guarantees of investor rights, preferential tax treatment for investors, and organizational and financial support of investment projects).

5.2. CAPITAL INVESTMENT

Industry accounts for the lion's share of fixed capital investments, with the oil and gas sector topping the league table.

5.3. MAJOR ENTERPRISES (INCLUDING ENTERPRISES WITH FOREIGN INVESTMENT)

The Nenetsky Autonomous District hosts some 400 enterprises.

A number of foreign oil companies, including Conoco (USA), TotalFinaElf (France), and Norsk Hydro Sverige AB (Norway) are currently involved in oil field development projects together with Russian enterprises. The following joint ventures operate oil fields in the District: Russian-American OOO Poliarnoye Siyanie (Conoco, OAO Arkhangelskgeoldobycha, and OAO Rosneft), Russian-Finnish ZAO SeverTEK (Fortum (Finland), and OAO LUKoil-Komi).

5.4. MOST ATTRACTIVE SECTORS FOR INVESTMENT

According to the District Administration, the most attractive sectors for investment are the oil industry, transport, and construction.

Capital investment by industry sector, $ million						*TABLE 6*
	1997	1998	1999	2000	2001	2002
Total capital investment *Including major industries* (% of total):	82.4	60.7	33.0	167.3	496.0	557.4
Industry	89.0	89.8	77.1	91.6	96.1	95.9
Transport and communications	1.3	0.7	3.5	3.6	1.5	1.1
Other	9.7	9.5	19.4	4.8	2.4	3.0

Foreign investment trends in 1996–2002						*TABLE 7*
	1996–1997	1998	1999	2000	2001	2002
Foreign investment, $ million	68.8	18.9	31.5	69.3	192.6	247.8
Including FDI, $ million	0.3	0.2	31.5	69.3	192.6	94.4

		TABLE 8	
Largest enterprises of the Nenetsky Autonomous District			
COMPANY	SECTOR	2001 SALES, $ MILLION*	2001 NET PROFIT, $ MILLION*
OOO Poliarnoye Sianie	Oil production	151.5	37.9
ZAO Severgeoldobycha	Geological exploration	10.7	0.9
ZAO Arcticneft	Oil production	10.6	0.1
FGUP Naryan-Mar Joint Air Brigade	Air transportation	8.8	0.2
OAO Naryan-Marseismorazvedka	Geological exploration	8.2	0.4
GUP Naryan-Mar Power Station	Energy	1.7	0.2
OAO Miasoprodukty	Meat	1.6	0.04
OAO Artelecom	Communications	1.5	0.2

*Data of the Nenetsky Autonomous District Administration

5.5. CURRENT LEGISLATION ON INVESTOR TAX EXEMPTIONS AND PRIVILEGES

The Nenetsky Autonomous District has enacted a Law On Investment Activities in the Nenetsky Autonomous District, which governs the objectives, principles, and methods of investment regulation in the District.

The Law regulates issues relating to legal and financial support for investment activities, guarantees equal rights to investors, and facilitates investors' relations with the District authorities.

Tax exemptions are granted to investors placing their own or borrowed funds into the District's investment program projects, and to banks and financial institutions providing loans to investors.

Investors enjoy the following privileges:
• A reduction in the regional property tax component (for a period of up to five years);
• A full or partial exemption from the regional profits tax component;
• Regional tax exemptions.

		TABLE 9	
Regional entities responsible for raising investment			
ENTITY	ADDRESS	PHONE, FAX, E-MAIL	
Social Fund for Support of Social Programs in the Nenetsky Autonomous District	2, ul. Lesozavodskaya, Naryan-Mar, Nenetsky Autonomous District, 166000	Phone: (81853) 40 883 Fax: (81853) 40 071 E-mail: Provans@atnet.ru	
OAO Miasoprodukty	11, ul. Yubileinaya, Naryan-Mar, Nenetsky Autonomous District, 166000	Phone: (81853) 44 134 Fax: (81853) 44 131	

5.6. FEDERAL AND REGIONAL ECONOMIC AND SOCIAL DEVELOPMENT PROGRAMS FOR THE NENETSKY AUTONOMOUS DISTRICT

Federal targeted programs.

The Nenetsky Autonomous Region is implementing one of the major federal targeted programs, the Federal Targeted Program for the Economic and Social Development of Small Indigenous Nations of the North through 2010. Its aim is to ensure the sustainable development of small indigenous peoples in the Russian North through the development of traditional sectors of the economy, the improvement of living standards, the creation of infrastructure, and the improvement of social conditions.

The District also focuses much attention on the Federal Program for the Modernization of Russia's Transport System, 2002–2010. The program provides for the construction of the Naryan-Mar – Usinsk highway, and reconstruction of a runway at the

Naryan-Mar airport. The program aims to ensure year-round cargo delivery to the Nenetsky Autonomous District and better flight safety.

The Russia's Soil Fertility, 2002–2005 Federal Targeted Program aims to increase output of high-quality fodder for increased livestock yield.

Regional programs. The Nenetsky Autonomous District Administration is implementing a number of programs focused on development of industry, agriculture, environment, healthcare and social wel- fare. Currently, the district is implementing 12 re-gional programs with total financing of $2.6 million. Particularly, the program for the Development of Industrial Processing of Reindeer Products in the Nenetsky Autonomous District 2002–2005 aims to achieve more efficient processing of reindeer products through modernized production processes with a view to improving the quality of reindeer meat output. A budgetary loan of $0.2 million has been allocated to the program.

6. INVESTMENT PROJECTS

Industry sector and project description	1) Expected results 2) Amount and term of investment 3) Form of financing[1] 4) Documentation[2]	Contact information
1	2	3
FORESTRY, TIMBER, AND PULP AND PAPER		
29R001 ● ▲		
Revamping of a timber sawmill. Project goal: to increase sawn timber output.	1) up to 50,000 cubic meters annually 2) $4.2 million/2 years 3) L 4) FS	OOO Lesozavod 2, ul. Zavodskaya, Naryan-Mar, Nenetsky Autonomous District, 166000 Phone: (81853) 44 067 Fax: (81853) 44 091 E-mail:forest@atnet.ru; Alexander Vladimirovich Chernousov, CEO
FOOD AND BEVERAGES		
29R002 ●		
Revamping of the Naryan-Mar fish plant. Project goal: to process and store fish products.	1) Frozen fish output – up to 1,000 tons annually, smoked fish output – 60 tons per year 2) $2.9 million/2 years 3) L 4) BP under development	OAO Pechora Fish Plant 42, ul. 60 Let Oktiabria, Naryan-Mar, Nenetsky Autonomous District, 166000 Phone/fax: (81853) 42 591, 45 301 Irina Eduardovna Khozyainova, External Manager
TRANSPORT INFRASTRUCTURE		
29R003 ●		
Revamping of the Naryan-Mar seaport. Project goal: to increase seaport capacity and freight turnover.	1) Up to 500,000 of freight annually 2) $18.3 million/3 years 3) L 4) FS	GUP Naryan-Mar Commercial Seaport, 11, ul. Portovaya, Naryan-Mar, Nenetsky Autonomous District, 166000 Phone: (81853) 42 157, 42 925 Fax: (81853) 42 395 Sergei Ivanovich Chuporov, Director
29R004 ● ▲		
Construction of the Naryan-Mar – Usinsk public highway. Project goal: to connect the District to the Komi Republic and Russian federal and regional centers.	1) 80 km 2) $9 million/9 years 3) L 4) FS	Road Facilities Management Committee Office 47, 39, ul. Lenina, Naryan-Mar, Nenetsky Autonomous District, 166000 Phone/fax: (81853) 44 222 E-mail:dornao@atnet.ru Elek Leibovich Rybak, Chairman

II

NORTH-WESTERN FEDERAL DISTRICT

---

[1] L – Loan, E – Equity, Leas. – Leasing, JV – Joint Venture
[2] BP – Business Plan, FS – Feasibility Study

III. SOUTHERN FEDERAL DISTRICT

30. Republic of Adygeya [01]
31. Republic of Dagestan [05]
32. Republic of Ingushetia [06]
33. Republic of Kabardino-Balkaria [07]
34. Republic of Kalmykia [08]
35. Republic of Karachayevo-Cherkessia [09]
36. Republic of North Ossetia – Alania [15]
37. Chechen Republic [20]
38. Krasnodar Territory [23]
39. Stavropol Territory [26]
40. Astrakhan Region [30]
41. Volgograd Region [34]
42. Rostov Region [61]

REGIONS OF THE SOUTHERN FEDERAL DISTRICT

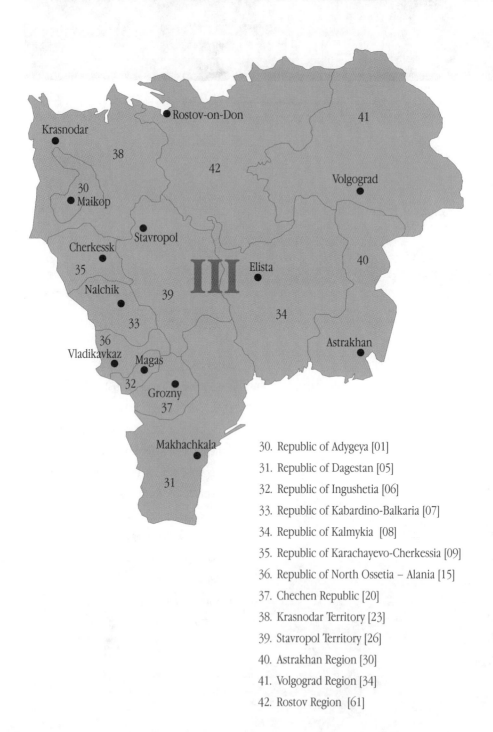

30. Republic of Adygeya [01]

31. Republic of Dagestan [05]

32. Republic of Ingushetia [06]

33. Republic of Kabardino-Balkaria [07]

34. Republic of Kalmykia [08]

35. Republic of Karachayevo-Cherkessia [09]

36. Republic of North Ossetia – Alania [15]

37. Chechen Republic [20]

38. Krasnodar Territory [23]

39. Stavropol Territory [26]

40. Astrakhan Region [30]

41. Volgograd Region [34]

42. Rostov Region [61]

30. REPUBLIC OF ADYGEYA [01]

ECONOMIC MAP

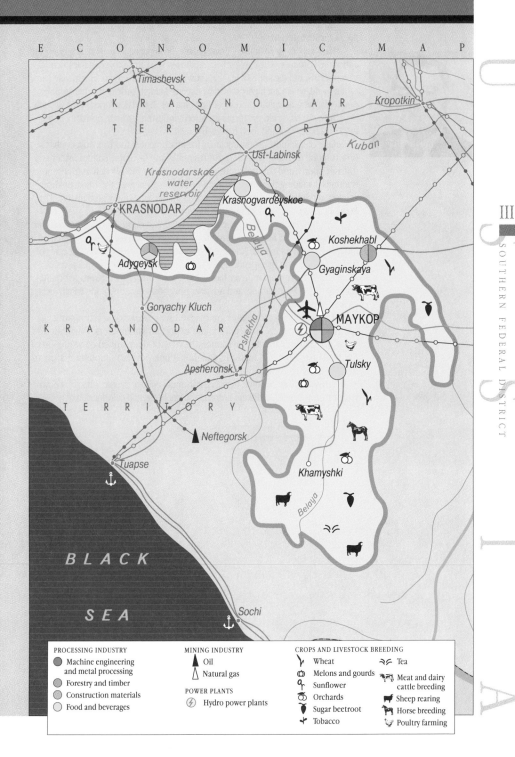

Timashevsk

Kropotkin

K R A S N O D A R

T E R R I T O R Y

Kuban

Ust-Labinsk

Krasnodarskoe water reservoir

KRASNODAR

Krasnogvardeyskoe

Koshekhabl

Gyaginskaya

Adygeysk

Belaya

Goryachy Kluch

K R A S N O D A R

Pshekha

MAYKOP

Apsheronsk

Tulsky

T E R R I T O R Y

Neftegorsk

Khamyshki

Belaya

Tuapse

BLACK

SEA

Sochi

PROCESSING INDUSTRY
- Machine engineering and metal processing
- Forestry and timber
- Construction materials
- Food and beverages

MINING INDUSTRY
- ▲ Oil
- △ Natural gas

POWER PLANTS
- ⚡ Hydro power plants

CROPS AND LIVESTOCK BREEDING
- Wheat
- Melons and gourds
- Sunflower
- Orchards
- Sugar beetroot
- Tobacco
- Tea
- Meat and dairy cattle breeding
- Sheep rearing
- Horse breeding
- Poultry farming

The Republic of Adygeya was established in 1991. Adygeya's rise to republican status within the Russian Federation has broadened its economic development capabilities, including direct contacts with Russian and foreign partners.

Adygeya's investment appeal stems from its political and social stability, legislative base guaranteeing protection of investor rights, qualified workforce, and last but not least, the commitment on the part of the Republic's authorities to mutually beneficial cooperation.

Adygeya is an agricultural region, and this fact determines its priority areas for investment.

Rich soils and a favorable climate enable the Republic to grow ecologically pure agricultural produce: wheat, sugar beet, sunflower seed, tobacco, vegetables, rice, watermelons, and the kinds of tea that grow in this most northern tea-growing part of the world, which are highly valued by experts. Market gardening, cattle farming, poultry farming, apiculture, and horse breeding are all well developed in the Republic.

Adygeya has good prospects for strong industrial growth, primarily in the food and beverages and food processing sectors.

One of the most promising areas for investment is tourism. Adygeya has second-to-none recreational and tourist resources and favorable conditions for eco-tourism, sports, and cultural tourism. Our land is enormously rich in tourist attractions, including the Great Azish and Dakhovskaya caves, the Khadzhokhsky canyon, the Bolshoy Rufabgo stream gorge, granite canyons, waterfalls, etc. The Republic also possesses vast hunting resources.

Our mountains boast unique microclimates and outstanding landscapes. Our local mineral waters have recognized healing properties and have long been used in the treatment of a range of illnesses. The curative mud deposits and karst caves of our Republic have a therapeutic effect for many kinds of respiratory illnesses.

The Belaya mountain river has become something of a pilgrimage destination for white-water rafting, and Adygeya now hosts the annual Inter Rally Belaya rafting competition.

The Republic's mountains are covered with snow for seven months of the year and are ideal for beginner and expert downhill skiers. Downhill skiing is a promising area for investment in view of the planned construction of the Maikop – Dagomys highway, which will link Adygeya's mountain areas to the Black Sea coast near Sochi.

Adygeya's main resource, however, is its multi-cultural people, who are renowned for their centuries-old traditions, hospitality, friendliness, and colorful culture.

Khazret Sovmen,
PRESIDENT OF THE REPUBLIC OF ADYGEYA

1. GENERAL INFORMATION

1.1. GEOGRAPHY

Located in southern Russia entirely within the borders of the Krasnodar Territory, the Republic of Adygeya has no borders with other Russian regions and covers an area of 7,800 square kilometers.

1.2. CLIMATE

The Republic is located within the temperate continental climate zone.

January air temperatures average 0°C, rising to +24°C in July. Annual precipitation averages 600 mm. The average growing season lasts 160 days.

1.3. POPULATION

According to preliminary 2002 census results, the Republic of Adygeya's total population was 447,000 people. The average population density is 57.3 people per square kilometer. The economically active population amounts to 204,000 people. As of 2002, the official unemployment rate was 13.5%.

Demographically speaking, some 57.8% are of statutory working age, 19.5% are below the statutory working age, and 22.7% are beyond the statutory working age.

The ethnic mix is 24.1% Adygeyan, 68% Russian, 3% Ukrainian, and 4.9% others.

The major urban centers of the Republic of Adygeya (2002 data) are Maikop with 162,400 inhabitants and Adygeisk with 14,700 inhabitants.

Population							*TABLE 1*
	1992	1997	1998	1999	2000	2001	2002
Total population, '000	440	449	450	449	448	446	447
Economically active population, '000	203	170	163	203	200	198	204

2. ADMINISTRATION

22, ul. Zhukovskogo, Maikop, Republic of Adygeya, 385000
Phone: (87722) 22 209; fax: (87722) 70 147; http://www.adygheya.ru

NAME	POSITION	CONTACT INFORMATION
Khazret Medjidovich SOVMEN	President of the Republic of Adygeya	Phone: (87722) 71 900 Fax: (87722) 70 147 E-mail: prezident@adygheya.ru
Nikolai Vasilyevich DEMCHUK	Vice President of the Republic of Adygeya	Phone: (87722) 70 250 Fax: (87722) 70 147 E-mail: vipresident@adygheya.ru
Khazret Yunusovich KHUADE	Prime Minister of the Republic of Adygeya	Phone: (87722) 25 234 Fax: (87722) 70 147 E-mail: premier@adygheya.ru
Tamara Nikolaevna MALAKHOVA	Deputy Minister of Economic Development and Trade of the Republic of Adygeya	Phone: (87722) 25 666 Fax: (87722) 22 612 E-mail: mineco@maykop.ru
Tatyana Nikolayevna KIRILLOVA	Minister of Finance of the Republic of Adygeya	Phone: (87722) 25 684 Fax: (87722) 22 717 E-mail: minfin@maykop.ru

3. ECONOMIC POTENTIAL

3.1. 1997–2002 GROSS REGIONAL PRODUCT (GRP). INDUSTRY BREAKDOWN

In 2002, the Republic of Adygeya's gross regional product was $238.8 million, 2.5% up on 2001. Per capita GRP in 2001 totaled $521, and $535 in 2002.

3.2. MAJOR ECONOMIC GROWTH PROJECTIONS

The creation of conditions conducive to the development and expansion of tourism is an economic development priority for the Republic of Adygeya. There is scope for the development of state-

III

SOUTHERN FEDERAL DISTRICT

of-the-art alpine skiing facilities on the Lagonak plateau in concert with the development of Krasnaya Polyana winter resort in the Krasnodar Territory.

3.3. INDUSTRIAL OUTPUT IN 1997–2002 FOR MAJOR SECTORS OF ECONOMY

The leading industries of the Republic of Adygeya are food and beverages, forestry and timber, pulp and paper, and machine engineering and metal processing.

Food and beverages. The sector produces canned meat, fruit and vegetables, confectionery, pasta, wine and vodka, and bakery products. Major producers are ZAO Maikop Confectionery, OAO Maikop Wine and Vodka, and OAO Maikop Pasta.

Forestry, timber, and pulp and paper. The sector comprises six large and medium-sized manufacturers producing commercial timber, sawn timber, parquet, veneer, cabinet furniture, chairs, and corrugated board. ZAO Paperboard Package is the largest manufacturer.

Machine engineering and metal processing. OAO Zarem Reducer Factory, the largest manufacturer in the sector, produces over 50 types of reducers.

Agriculture. Apiculture, horse breeding, and industrial poultry farming are developed. Grain, melons and gourds, sunflower, vegetables, sugar beet, tobacco, and tea are grown.

GRP trends in 1997–2002 TABLE 2

	1997	1998	1999	2000	2001*	2002*
GRP in current prices, million $	486.8	343.0	198.8	206.6	232.9	238.8

*Estimates of the Government of the Republic of Adygeya

GRP industry breakdown in 1997–2002, % of total TABLE 3

	1997	1998	1999	2000	2001*	2002*
GRP	100.0	100.0	100.0	100.0	100.0	100.0
Industry	16.6	14.1	17.5	18.8	18.1	15.8
Agriculture and forestry	19.6	25.9	25.3	22.6	24.4	25.6
Construction	6.0	6.1	6.9	7.3	7.7	8.1
Transport and communications	4.7	3.8	2.9	3.2	3.3	3.5
Trade and public catering	9.7	9.0	10.4	14.6	15.2	15.9
Other	29.8	33.1	29.6	25.8	24.5	24.7
Net taxes on output	13.6	8.0	7.4	7.7	6.8	6.4

*Estimates of the Government of the Republic of Adygeya

Industry breakdown of industrial output in 1997–2002, % of total TABLE 4

	1997	1998	1999	2000	2001	2002*
Industry	100.0	100.0	100.0	100.0	100.0	100.0
Food and beverages	48.9	50.8	51.3	45.9	47.8	43.9
Forestry, timber, and pulp and paper	13.7	14.2	22.2	23.6	22.5	22.8
Machine engineering and metal processing	10.6	8.9	9.9	11.1	11.4	12.8
Construction materials	6.7	7.2	6.5	8.2	6.8	8.3
Energy	7.9	7.4	3.6	3.2	3.8	4.0
Chemicals and petrochemicals	1.1	1.0	0.4	1.1	1.8	2.0
Light industry	0.6	0.2	0.7	1.1	1.0	1.0
Fuel	0.8	0.8	0.4	1.6	2.0	0.9
Flour, cereals, and mixed fodder	4.3	3.6	2.2	2.1	1.8	0.7

*Estimates of the Government of the Republic of Adygeya

3.4. FUEL AND ENERGY BALANCE (OUTPUT AND CONSUMPTION PER RESOURCE)

Adygeya is one of the energy deficient regions of the North Caucasus. Its own generation facilities cover 10-15% of total demand. A small 400 kW hydroelectric power station has been built and put into operation in the Republic. Adygeya shares its power system with the Krasnodar Territory. The Republic imports energy from the North Caucasus interconnected power system. The largest supplier of oil products to the Republic is the Adygeya Branch of OOO LUKoil-Yugnefteprodukt.

Fuel and energy sector production and consumption trends, 1997–2002						TABLE 5
	1997	1998	1999	2000	2001	2002*
Electricity output, billion kWh	0.1	0.1	0.1	0.1	0.1	0.1
Oil output (including gas condensate), '000 tons	0.9	0.7	0.7	0.8	1.3	1.0
Natural gas output, million cubic meters	209.0	198.0	170.0	184.0	189.0	147.0
Electricity consumption, billion kWh	0.7	0.7	0.7	0.8	0.7	0.6
Natural gas consumption, million cubic meters	590.0	563.0	604.0	621.0	608.0	605.0

*Estimates of the Government of the Republic of Adygeya

3.5. TRANSPORT INFRASTRUCTURE

Roads. The Republic of Adygeya has 1,537 kilometers of paved public highways. The Armavir – Tuapse highway, which links the town of Maikop with the seaport of Tuapse, passes through the Republic. Major road haulage operators include OAO Adygeya Avtotrans and Road Management Office of the Republic of Adygeya – Adygeya Avtodor.

Railroads. The Republic has 148 km of railroads. The Novosibirsk – Krasnodar and Armavir – Tuapse trunk lines and the Belorechenskaya – Maikop – Kamennomostsky branch line pass through the Republic.

The Republic of Adygeya has rail links with the Rostov Region, the Krasnodar Territory, the Stavropol Territory, and other areas in the North Caucasus.

Airports. The Khansky International Airport serves Moscow plus destinations in Armenia, Turkey, and Syria.

Gas pipelines. The Samurskaya – Sochi trunk gas pipeline passes through the Republic. Branches of OOO Kubangazprom and OAO Gazprom operate in the Republic.

3.6. MAIN NATURAL RESOURCES: RESERVES AND EXTRACTION IN 2002

The principal natural resources of the Republic of Adygeya are minerals, land, forests, and water (including mineral water and curative mud sources).

Mineral resources. Seven deposits of brick clays and loams, five deposits of sand-and-gravel, and two deposits of gypsum plaster have been explored in the Republic. The Republic possesses crushed stone reserves based on rock quarried at the Dakhovsky granite deposit. The Republic also has several deposits of mortar sand and high-quality limestone, which can be utilized in glass production.

Land resources. The Republic's soils are primarily leached or mildly leached black earth soils. Gray forest and rendzina soils, which are widely utilized in the cultivation of cereals, industrial crops, and fruit, occur across vast areas in the southern part of the Caucasus foothills.

Forest resources. Forests cover 285,700 hectares, or 36.6% of the Republic's total area. The main forest species are beech and oak. The Republic has valuable plantations of chestnut and walnut trees.

Water resources. The Republic of Adygeya is drained by two water basins: the underground Great Caucasus basin and the Azov-Kuban basin. Over 50 million cubic meters of water is drawn from underground sources in the Republic annually. The Republic's rivers and reservoirs contain substantial fish reserves.

4. TRADE OPPORTUNITIES

4.1. MAIN GOODS PRODUCED IN THE REGION

Machine tools. 2002 output was 30 machine tools.

Commercial timber. 2002 output was 24,400 cubic meters of dense timber.

Cardboard. 2002 output reached 50,700 tons.

Bricks. 16.5 million conventional bricks in 2002.

Granulated sugar. 2002 output was 49,800 tons.

Bread and bakery products. 2002 output was 16,400 tons.

Vegetable oils. 2002 output was 3,448 tons.

4.2. EXPORTS, INCLUDING EXTRA-CIS

Exports to extra-CIS countries in 1999 amounted to $1.4 million, while exports to CIS countries totaled $0.3 million. The corresponding figures were $1.5 million and $0.4 million for

2000, $95.2 million and $0.4 million for 2001, and $1.6 million and $0.3 million for 2002.

The Republic mainly exports food, agricultural and machine engineering goods, and timber and timber products. Key importers are Turkey, Iran, Lebanon, Congo, Ukraine, Kazakhstan, and Uzbekistan.

4.3. IMPORTS TO THE REGION, INCLUDING EXTRA-CIS

Imports from extra-CIS countries in 1999 amounted to $7.9 million, imports from CIS countries totaled $1.5 million. The corresponding figures were $7.5 million and $0.9 million for 2000,

$21 million and $1 million for 2001, and $9 million and $0.7 million for 2002.

The Region mainly imports equipment, construction materials, and agricultural and consumer goods. Key exporters to the Republic include Brazil, Turkey, and Austria.

4.4. MAJOR REGIONAL EXPORT AND IMPORT ENTITIES

Owing to the specific nature of export and import operations in the Republic of Adygeya, import and export transactions are mainly conducted by industrial enterprises.

5. INVESTMENT OPPORTUNITIES

5.1. INVESTMENTS IN 1992–2002 (BY INDUSTRY SECTOR), INCLUDING FOREIGN INVESTMENTS

The following key factors determine the investment appeal of the Republic of Adygeya:

- Its favorable geographical location;
- Its developed transport infrastructure;
- Legislation supporting investment activities (guarantees for investors' rights and preferential tax treatment for investors);
- Its qualified workforce;
- Its natural resources.

5.2. CAPITAL INVESTMENT

Industry and transport account for the bulk of capital investment.

Capital investment by industry sectors, $ million						*TABLE 6*
	1997	1998	1999	2000	2001	2002
Total capital investment	52.9	47.6	39.4	44.9	51.7	49.3
Including major industries (% of total)						
Industry	19.3	23.9	48.3	20.8	17.7	16.0
Agriculture and forestry	9.3	10.3	7.5	9.9	5.7	5.4
Construction	3.1	10.0	13.7	2.5	2.2	3.0
Transport and communications	4.2	6.0	2.8	22.7	24.1	18.9
Trade and public catering	3.7	43.3	4.2	11.9	0.4	0.9
Other	60.4	6.5	23.5	32.2	49.9	55.8

Foreign investment trends in 1996–2002						*TABLE 7*
	1996–1997	1998	1999	2000	2001	2002
Foreign investment, $ million	0.1	0.6	0.9	0.7	2.7	2.1
Including FDI, $ million	0.1	0.6	0.9	0.7	1.7	2.1

5.3. MAJOR ENTERPRISES (INCLUDING ENTERPRISES WITH FOREIGN INVESTMENT)

The Republic of Adygeya hosts 50 enterprises with foreign capital from the UK, France, Turkey, and Syria.

5.4. MOST ATTRACTIVE SECTORS FOR INVESTMENT

According to experts and the Government of the Republic of Adygeya, the agroindustrial, timber, and tourism sectors are most attractive for investment.

5.5. CURRENT LEGISLATION ON INVESTOR TAX EXEMPTIONS AND PRIVILEGES

The Law of the Republic of Adygeya On Investment Activity in the Republic of Adygeya governs investment activity in the Republic. The law sets forth a number of measures regarding state support and the protection of investors' rights in the Republic's industry, communications, agriculture, and transport sectors.

Largest enterprises of the Republic of Adygeya	TABLE 8
COMPANY	SECTOR
OAO Maikop Brewery	Food and beverages
ZAO Maikop Confectionery	Food and beverages
OAO Maikop Wine and Vodka	Food and beverages
OAO Maikop Pasta	Food and beverages
OAO Sugar Factory	Food and beverages
ZAO Paperboard Package	Timber
OAO Zarem Reducer Factory	Machine engineering
OAO Maikop Machine Engineering Plant	Machine engineering

Regional entities responsible for raising investment		TABLE 9
ENTITY	ADDRESS	PHONE, FAX, E-MAIL
Adygeya-Invest Investment and Finance Company	61, ul. Krasnooktyabrskaya, Maikop, Republic of Adygeya, 352706	Phone: (87722) 23 750 Fax: (87722) 22 677

III

SOUTHERN FEDERAL DISTRICT

5.6. FEDERAL AND REGIONAL ECONOMIC AND SOCIAL DEVELOPMENT PROGRAMS FOR THE REPUBLIC OF ADYGEYA

Federal targeted programs. A number of federal targeted programs are underway in the Republic, with top priority accorded to the Russia's South, 2002–2006 Federal targeted program.

Regional programs. The Program for the Social and Economic Development of the Republic of Adygeya, 2003-2007 is currently being drafted.

6. INVESTMENT PROJECTS

Industry sector and project description	1) Expected results 2) Amount and term of investment 3) Form of financing[1] 4) Documentation[2]	Contact information
1	2	3

	ENERGY	
30R001	● ◆	OAO Teuchezhskaya Hydro Power Station
Construction of the Teuchezhskaya Hydro Power Station at the Krasnodar Water Reservoir spillway. Project goal: to increase electricity output.	1) Capacity – 48 MW 2) $22.5 million/2 years 3) L 4) BP	22, ul Zhukovskogo, Maikop, Republic of Adygeya, 385000 Phone: (87722) 21 933 Fax: (87722) 70 141 Inver Yusufovich Natkho, CEO

	FORESTRY, TIMBER, AND PULP AND PAPER	
30R002	● ◆	OAO 24 DOK-M
Construction of timber processing facilities for coniferous and deciduous lumber at an operating timber company. Project goal: to increase output and exports.	1) Projected capacity of 500,000 square meters of door units per month 2) $30 million/1 year 3) L 4) BP	98, ul. Shosseinaya, Maikop, Republic of Adygeya, 385000 Phone/fax: (87722) 21 147 E-mail: dok24@mail.ru Nalby Khazretovich Pshepy, Executive Director

[1] L – Loan, E – Equity, Leas. – Leasing, JV – Joint Venture
[2] BP – Business Plan, FS – Feasibility Study

1	2	3

30R003

Upgrading of cardboard facilities at an operating paper company. Project goal: to expand output range (cardboard and paper for corrugated board production).

1) Three-fold output increase
2) $30 million/5 years
3) L
4) BP, preliminary FS

ZAO Cartontara
2, per. Profsoyuzny, Maikop,
Republic of Adygeya, 385000
Phone: (87722) 48 455
Fax: (87722) 48 820
E–mail: kartontara@maykop.ru
Vladimir Mikhailovich Samozhenkov, CEO

GLASS AND PORCELAIN

30R004

Construction of a glass plant for the production of jars and bottles. Project goal: to increase output and expand product range.

1) 144 million bottles per year and 96 million jars per year
2) $20.5 million/1.3 years
3) L
4) BP

OAO Adygeya Glass
4/3, ul. Dmitrova, Maikop,
Republic of Adygeya, 385000
Phone: (87722) 32 220
Fax: (87722) 35 825
E–mail: adg-glass@mail.ru
Asfar Dzhanchatovich Chermit, CEO

TRANSPORT INFRASTRUCTURE

30R005

Reconstruction of the Maikop International Airport, including construction of a new runway. Project goal: to increase freight and passenger throughput.

1) Revenue of up to $15.7 million per year
2) $25 million/4 years
3) L
4) BP, design and budget documentation

OAO Adygeya Airlines
Airport, Maikop,
Republic of Adygeya, 385000
Phone: (87722) 31 004
Fax: (87722) 31 656
E–mail: avlad@istnet.ru;
avlad@radnet.ru
Alexander Pavlovich Pedchenko,
General Director

31. REPUBLIC OF DAGESTAN [05]

ECONOMIC MAP

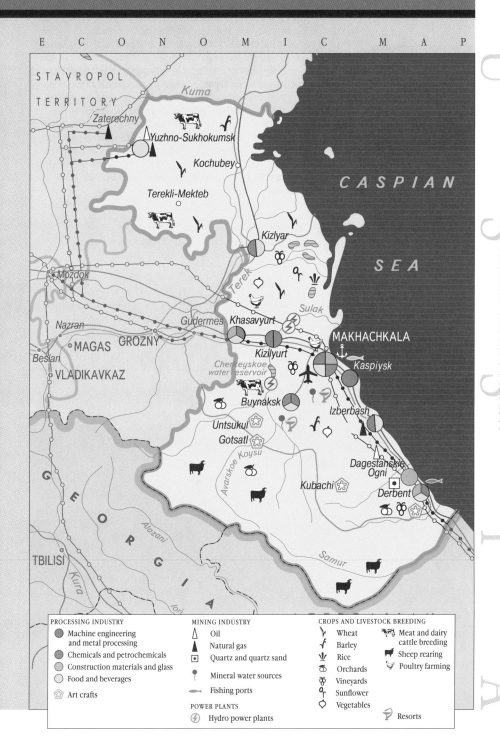

STAVROPOL
TERRITORY
Kuma
Zaterechny
Yuzhno-Sukhokumsk
Kochubey
Terekli-Mekteb

CASPIAN

Kizlyar

SEA

Terek

Mozdok

Sulak

Nazran
Gudermes   Khasavyurt
MAGAS   GROZNY
Kizilyurt   MAKHACHKALA
Beslan
VLADIKAVKAZ   Kaspiysk
Cherkeyskoe
water reservoir
Buynaksk
Izberbash
Untsukul
Gotsatl
G   Dagestanskie
Ogni
E   Avarskoe Koysu
Kubachi   Derbent
O   Kizilyurt
Alazani
R
G
TBILISI   I
Kura   A   Samur
Iori

PROCESSING INDUSTRY
- 🔴 Machine engineering and metal processing
- 🔴 Chemicals and petrochemicals
- ⚪ Construction materials and glass
- ⚪ Food and beverages
- ✿ Art crafts

MINING INDUSTRY
- △ Oil
- ▲ Natural gas
- ⊡ Quartz and quartz sand
- • Mineral water sources
- ⚓ Fishing ports

POWER PLANTS
- ⚡ Hydro power plants

CROPS AND LIVESTOCK BREEDING
- Y Wheat
- f Barley
- ⚭ Rice
- ☉ Orchards
- ⚭ Vineyards
- ⚘ Sunflower
- ◇ Vegetables
- 🐄 Meat and dairy cattle breeding
- 🐑 Sheep rearing
- 🦃 Poultry farming
- ⚕ Resorts

T he Republic of Dagestan has strong potential for the development of mutually beneficial partnerships in various economic sectors. Its geographical
location (the Republic is a strategic transport hub for the north-south traffic), rich natural resources, developed transport infrastructure, industrial, and
agricultural sectors, and considerable labor and intellectual resources, determine
the strong investment appeal of the Republic of Dagestan.

Positive economic development trends, accelerated growth in social and
economic indexes, and a stable political and social situation create considerable
scope for further improvement in the Republic's investment climate.

In recent years, the Republic's authorities and bodies of local self-governance have been increasingly focusing on attracting investment into the region.
With a view to creating a climate conducive to raising internal and foreign capital
and securing investor rights, the Republic of Dagestan has passed a Law On Investment and Investment Guarantees in the Republic of Dagestan and is taking
other measures aimed at improving the Republic's investment appeal.

In 2002, the Republic channeled its investment resources into the food and beverages, food processing, building materials, machine engineering and metals processing,
chemicals, and glass sectors, as well as agriculture, light industry, and folk arts and crafts.

The Republic offers various forms of cooperation and support to potential
partners who are sincerely interested in developing business links with the
Republic of Dagestan.

Magomedali Magomedov,
CHAIRMAN OF THE STATE COUNCIL
OF THE REPUBLIC OF DAGESTAN

III

SOUTHERN FEDERAL DISTRICT

1. GENERAL INFORMATION

1.1. GEOGRAPHY

Situated in the eastern part of the North Caucasus in the southern Russian Federation, the Republic of Dagestan covers a total area of 50,300 square kilometers. To the north, the Republic borders the Republic of Kalmykia, to the north-west – the Stavropol Territory, to the west – the Republic of Chechnya, and to the south – Azerbaijan. The Republic's international frontier with Georgia passes along the watershed ridge of the Great Caucasus.

1.2. CLIMATE

The Republic of Dagestan enjoys a temperate continental climate. The average air temperature in January is −3°C, rising to +24°C in July. The average annual precipitation is 200–400 mm. The growing season lasts for some 160–180 days.

1.3. POPULATION

According to preliminary 2002 census results, total population in the Republic was 2,584,000 people. The average population density is 51.4 people per square kilometer. The economically active population amounts to 916,000 people; the official unemployment level is 22.7%.

Demographically speaking, some 55.7% are of statutory working age, 31.5% are below the statutory working age, and 12.8% are beyond the statutory working age.

The Republic's ethnic mix is 27.5% Avar, 15.6% Darghin, 12.9% Kumyk, 11.3% Lezghin, 9.2% Russian, and 23.5% other ethnic groups.

As of 2001, the Republic's major urban centers were Makhachkala with 466,800 inhabitants, Derbent with 100,800 inhabitants, Khasavyurt with 86,600 inhabitants, Kaspiysk with 69,500 inhabitants, and Buinaksk with 55,400 inhabitants.

Population							TABLE 1
	1992	1997	1998	1999	2000	2001	2002
Total population, '000	1,890	2,073	2,094	2,120	2,143	2,160	2,584
Economically active population, '000	757	736	728	864	830	824	916

2. ADMINISTRATION

1, pl. Lenina, Makhachkala, Republic of Dagestan, 367005
Government: Phone (reception): (8722) 67 2017; fax: (8722) 67 3051
State Council: Phone: (8722) 67 3060; fax: (095) 705 9290, 705 9291
E-mail: soc35@minec.e-dag.ru; http://www.e-dag.ru

NAME	POSITION	CONTACT INFORMATION
Magomedali Magomedovich MAGOMEDOV	Chairman of the State Council of the Republic of Dagestan	Phone: (8722) 67 3059
Khizri Isaevich SHIKHSAIDOV	Chairman of the Government of the Republic of Dagestan	Phone: (8722) 67 1994
Mukhu Gimbatovich ALIEV	Chairman of the National Council of the Republic of Dagestan	Phone: (8722) 67 3055
Marat Sirazhutinovich ILYASOV	Minister of Economy of the Republic of Dagestan	Phone: (8722) 67 2008
Magomedsalikh Magomedovich GUSAEV	Minister of National Policy, Information, and External Relations of the Republic of Dagestan	Phone: (8722) 67 2117
Akhmed Ibragimkhalilovich IBRAGIMKHALILOV	Minister of Industry and Scientific and Technical Development of the Republic of Dagestan	Phone: (8722) 68 3122
Umalat Ilmutdinovich NASRUTDINOV	Minister of Agriculture and Food of the Republic of Dagestan	Phone: (8722) 67 1902
Ramazan Shakhbanovich MAMEDOV	Representative of the Republic of Dagestan to the President of the Russian Federation	Phone: (095) 916 0673, 916 1536 Fax: (095) 928 4112

3. ECONOMIC POTENTIAL

3.1. 1997–2002 GROSS REGIONAL PRODUCT (GRP). INDUSTRY BREAKDOWN

The 2002 gross regional product amounted to $1,356.3 million, which constitutes 25.6% growth year-on-year. In 2001, per capita GRP amounted to $500, rising to $526 in 2002.

3.2. MAJOR ECONOMIC GROWTH PROJECTIONS

The Republic's priorities in terms of social and economic development are: the development of legislation to provide a favorable investment climate, the reduction of local taxes and levies, the creation of a balanced and efficient budget system, the encour-

GRP trends in 1997–2002						TABLE 2
	1997	1998	1999	2000	2001*	2002*
GRP in current prices, $ million	1,492.3	860.6	537.0	758.2	1,079.8	1,356.3

*Estimates of the Government of the Republic of Dagestan

GRP industry breakdown in 1997–2002, % of total						TABLE 3
	1997	1998	1999	2000	2001*	2002*
GRP	100.0	100.0	100.0	100.0	100.0	100.0
Industry	12.8	13.8	19.8	18.3	18.3	18.4
Agriculture and forestry	17.4	18.3	25.1	27.1	28.6	28.6
Construction	19.2	8.7	7.4	7.9	7.9	7.4
Transport and communications	13.0	10.1	7.3	5.8	6.2	6.4
Trade and public catering	16.7	17.5	17.2	16.2	16.9	18.3
Other	20.9	31.6	23.2	24.7	22.1	20.9

*Estimates of the Government of the Republic of Dagestan

agement of structural changes in the economy, including restructuring of natural monopolies, the development of financial infrastructure and mid-term financial stability, and sustainable and accelerated economic growth through the utilization of internal competitive advantages and structural readjustments.

3.3. INDUSTRIAL OUTPUT IN 1997–2002 FOR MAJOR SECTORS OF ECONOMY

The leading industrial sectors of the Republic of Dagestan are food and beverages, fuel, energy, and machine engineering and metal processing. These account for a combined 84.7% of total industrial output.

Industry breakdown of industrial output in 1997–2002, % of total						TABLE 4
	1997	1998	1999	2000	2001	2002*
Industry	100.0	100.0	100.0	100.0	100.0	100.0
Food and beverages	22.8	25.5	29.9	24.1	24.9	35.0
Fuel	15.7	15.8	30.5	29.4	24.1	21.1
Energy	25.5	25.7	13.8	10.0	15.7	18.7
Machine engineering and metal processing	14.1	13.9	13.0	17.2	18.5	9.9
Construction materials	9.3	12.2	7.4	3.0	3.9	7.2
Chemicals and petrochemicals	2.7	2.2	2.1	1.9	3.7	2.4
Light industry	4.3	1.5	0.8	0.9	1.6	1.2
Forestry, timber, and pulp and paper	0.3	0.5	0.4	1.1	1.9	0.2

*Estimates of the Government of the Republic of Dagestan

Food and beverages. The sector accounts for 35% of total industrial output. The Republic produces canned food, wine, and fish products. The canned food sector is represented by a large number of companies and employs a large number of people. The Republic produces some 100 types of canned food, including canned vegetables, fruit, and fish. Major companies within the sector include OAO Makhachkala Bakery No. 1, ZAO Liquor and Vodka Plant, OAO Main Fishery Company Sulak Fishing, and OAO Makhachkala Meat Processing Plant.

Fuel. The sector accounts for 21.1% of total industrial output. The Republic is focused on high grade oil and gas development. The Republic has scope for increased oil and gas extraction through the development of the Inchkhe offshore oil and gas field and increased oil recovery. Deep drilling is the most promising development area. Major companies within the sector include OAO Dagneft and OOO Dagestangazprom.

Energy. The share of this sector in total industrial output is 18.7%. Most electricity is produced by hydro-electric power stations, the largest being the 1 MW Chirkeiskaya HEP Station. The leading companies within the sector are OAO Dagenergo and OAO Energy and Electrification.

Machine engineering and metal processing. This sector accounts for 9.9% of total industrial output. The main types of products are ships, aircraft, electrical equipment, pumps, diesel engines, computers, grinding machines, and equipment for the food sector. Major companies are: OAO Gadjiyev Plant, OAO Dagbyttekhnika, OAO Agroprommash, and OAO Sudremont.

3.4. FUEL AND ENERGY BALANCE (OUTPUT AND CONSUMPTION PER RESOURCE)

The Republic boasts an export-focused oil sector. Natural gas is mainly consumed internally within the republic as a highly efficient fuel in the industrial, agricultural, and residential sectors. The Republic fully meets internal demand for electricity and exports excess output to the unified energy system of North Caucasus.

Fuel and energy sector production and consumption trends, 1997–2002	1997	1998	1999	2000	2001	2002*
Electricity output, billion kWh	3.8	2.9	3.3	3.3	3.9	5.0
Oil extraction (including gas concentrate), '000 tons	367.6	359.8	360.5	326.5	345.0	337.2
Natural gas output, million cubic meters	657.7	669.6	747.7	739.2	571.9	589.8
Electricity consumption, billion kWh	2.5	2.5	2.7	2.7	2.8	2.9
Oil consumption, '000 tons	18.8	19.1	25.2	13.6	18.3	24.8
Natural gas consumption, million cubic meters	1,720.0	1,725.0	1,730.0	1,747.0	1,692.0	1,600.0

TABLE 5

*Estimates of the Government of the Republic of Dagestan

3.5. TRANSPORT INFRASTRUCTURE

The Republic of Dagestan enjoys a well-developed transport system that comprises road, railroad, sea, and air services.

Roads. The Republic has 7,283 kilometers of paved public highways. The Rostov – Baku international highway passes through Dagestan. The main route linking the Republic to other Russian regions is the Kizlyar – Astrakhan highway. Southbound traffic passes through Derbent, with northbound traffic routed through Kizlyar. Traffic to central lowland districts passes through Khasavyurt, to central foothill districts – through Izberbash, and to mountain areas – through Buinaksk. Makhachkala is the central transit junction.

Railroads. The Republic of Dagestan has 516 kilometers of railroads. The Republic is crossed by two major railroad sectors – an 277 kilometer electrified sector crosses the Republic from north to south from Gudermes to Samur, and a second 129 kilometer sector goes from Kizlyar to Artezian. A route from Sham-khal to Buinaksk links the foothill area to the Guder-mes-Samur route. The Moscow – Baku, Kiev – Baku, Makhachkala – Moscow, and Moscow – Tbilisi railroads are of paramount importance to the Republic. The Republic has completed the route from Karlanyurt to Kizlyar, which provides a gateway to Europe and Asia.

Airports. The Makhachkala International Airport serves many Russian cities and destinations in CIS and non-CIS countries, including the Middle East.

Sea transport. Due to changes in the Region's geopolitical situation and the internationalization of the Caspian Sea, the role of shipping routes linking the Republic to the Caspian states of Azerbaijan, Kazakhstan, Iran, and Turkmenistan and through the Volga – Don Canal to other countries, has increased.

Seaports. The Makhachkala seaport was accorded international status in 1993. Since then it has been providing immigration and customs services. Plans are afoot to reconstruct the port, which is the only ice-free Russian Caspian port.

Oil and gas pipelines. The Republic is developing pipeline transportation routes. It currently operates the Izberbash – Makhachkala – Grozny and Yuzhno – Sukhumsk – Grozny pipelines, and the Makat – North Caucasus and Mozdok – Kazimagomed trunk gas pipelines, in addition to local lines.

3.6. MAIN NATURAL RESOURCES: RESERVES AND EXTRACTION IN 2002

The Republic's principle natural resources are minerals, water, and fish.

Mineral resources and raw materials. The Republic extracts oil, natural gas, black coal, quartz glass sand, building materials (sand, lime, marl, dolomite, gypsum, marble, and gravel), oil shale, and iron and polymetal ore. The Republic has mineral water springs.

Water resources. The Republic has a dense river net comprised of the Terek, Sulak, and Samur rivers. Water reserves are used in the hydro energy sector, for irrigation, water supply, and timber transportation. The Republic has over 100 small lakes with a total area of some 150 square kilometers.

Fish resources. Dagestan is rich in fish resources. Its coastal waters supply such species as sprat, carp, sazan, Caspian roach, and chub. The Caspian area is a renowned breeding ground for valuable species such as sturgeon and salmon, and seals. Dagestan's numerous rivers are rich in trout, barbel, and bream.

4. TRADE OPPORTUNITIES

4.1. MAIN GOODS PRODUCED IN THE REGION

Main types of industrial output in 2002:

- Electricity – 5 billion kWh;
- Oil (including gas condensate) – 337,000 tons;
- Bread and bakery products – 179,000 tons;
- Vodka and liquor – 591,000 decaliters;
- Cognac – 650,000 decaliters.

4.2. EXPORTS, INCLUDING EXTRA-CIS

The Republic of Dagestan's exports to extra-CIS countries amounted to $111.1 million in 2000. Exports to the CIS totaled $21.8 million. The respective figures for 2001 were $74.4 million and $18 million, and $61.5 million and $12.3 million for 2001.

The main types of goods exported by the Republic are: oil products, electricity, fruit and vegetables, alcoholic and non-alcoholic beverages, and confectionery. Major importers of the Republic's products are Iran, Greece, the Czech Republic, Poland, Cyprus, Turkmenistan, Switzerland, China, and Azerbaijan.

4.3. IMPORTS, INCLUDING EXTRA-CIS

2000 imports from extra-CIS amounted to $3.7 million. Imports from the CIS totaled $19.8 million. The respective figures for 2001 were $5.1 million and $13.3 million, and $30 million and $15.3 million for 2002.

The bulk of the Republic's imports consists of consumer goods, food, machinery, agricultural machinery, and ferrous and non-ferrous metals. The main exporters to the Republic are Germany, Turkey, Iran, Georgia, Azerbaijan, and Ukraine.

4.4. MAJOR REGIONAL EXPORT AND IMPORT ENTITIES

Due to the specific features of trade in the Republic of Dagestan, export and import operations are performed mainly by industrial companies.

5. INVESTMENT OPPORTUNITIES

5.1. INVESTMENTS IN 1992–2002 (BY INDUSTRY SECTOR), INCLUDING FOREIGN INVESTMENTS

The following factors determine the investment appeal of the Republic of Dagestan:

- Its advantageous geographic location, proximity to large markets, and high consumer potential;
- Its cheap energy resources (electricity, oil, and natural gas);
- Its developed transport infrastructure;
- Legislation supporting investment activities (protection of investor rights and preferential tax treatment);
- Its qualified workforce;
- Its natural resources.

5.2. CAPITAL INVESTMENT

Industry and transport account for the biggest share of capital investment.

5.3. MAJOR ENTERPRISES (INCLUDING ENTERPRISES WITH FOREIGN INVESTMENT)

The Republic of Dagestan hosts some 130 companies with foreign investment, including Joint Venture Dagneftindustriya (USA), ZAO Inom (Turkey), JV Khazarturk International Company (Turkey), OAO Ornament (USA), JV OOO Safinat-Makhachkala (Malta), ZAO Caspiy-1 (USA), OOO Dagtelecom (Cyprus), and OOO SAPELLI (Turkey).

5.4. MOST ATTRACTIVE SECTORS FOR INVESTMENT

According to the Government of the Republic of Dagestan, the most potentially appealing sectors for investors are food and beverages, oil extraction and refining, defense, metals, agriculture, and tourism.

5.5. CURRENT LEGISLATION ON INVESTOR TAX EXEMPTIONS AND PRIVILEGES

The legal framework for investment in the Republic of Dagestan is based around the following laws and regu-

Capital investment by industry sector, $ million						TABLE 6
	1997	1998	1999	2000	2001	2002
Total capital investment	570.0	195.0	72.1	123.7	171.6	169.6
Including major industries (% of total)						
Industry	19.3	19.5	29.6	21.1	28.5	27.9
Agriculture and forestry	6.1	4.4	7.7	6.7	7.7	10.6
Construction	0,8	0.3	0.6	1.8	0.1	0.7
Transport and communications	37.2	25.3	19.8	22.9	17.9	37.3
Trade and public catering	–	–	0.2	–	–	–
Other	36.6	50.5	42.1	47.5	45.8	23.5

Foreign investment trends in 1992–2002						TABLE 7
	1992–1997	1998	1999	2000	2001	2002*
Foreign investment, $ million	26.1	10.0	0.4	2.1	1.0	2.0
Including FDI, $ million	26.1	10.0	0.4	2.1	1.0	2.0

*Estimates of the Government of the Republic of Dagestan

III

Largest enterprises of the Republic of Dagestan	TABLE 8
COMPANY	SECTOR
OAO Dagenergo	Energy
OAO Dagdiesel	Machine engineering
OAO Gadzhiyev Plant	Machine engineering
OAO Buinaksk Machinery Plant	Machine engineering
OAO Dagfos	Chemicals and petrochemicals
OAO Steklovolokno	Chemicals and petrochemicals
OAO Dagogni Glass Plant	Chemicals and petrochemicals
OAO Main Fishery Company Sulak Fishing	Food and beverages
OAO Makhachkala Meat Processing Plant	Food and beverages
OAO Caspian Garment Manufacturing	Light industry
OAO Dagtextile	Light industry

SOUTHERN FEDERAL DISTRICT

lations: On Investment and Investment Guarantees in the Republic of Dagestan, On the Development Budget of the Republic of Dagestan, Governmental Resolution of the Republic of Dagestan On the Implementation of Article 12 of the Law of the Republic of Dagestan On Investment and Investment Guarantees in the Republic of Dagestan, On Granting Budget Credits for the Purpose of Implementation of Highly Efficient Contracts for Production and Shipment of Goods, Including Exports, and the Resolution of the Kayakentsky District Assembly On Preferential Tax Treatment of External Investors Registered in the Kayakentsky District.

5.6. REGIONAL ENTITIES RESPONSIBLE FOR RAISING INVESTMENT

The Dagestan State Investment Fund was established by a resolution of the Government of Dagestan with the aim of attracting investment into the Republic's economy, providing expert assessments of investment projects and programs, accumulating proceeds from investment projects for reinvestment in the Republic's economy, maintaining a register of legal entities, and entering into investor agreements and contracts.

5.7. FEDERAL AND REGIONAL ECONOMIC AND SOCIAL DEVELOPMENT PROGRAMS FOR THE REPUBLIC OF DAGESTAN

Federal targeted programs. The Republic of Dagestan is implementing the following social and economic development programs: Russia's South, Upgrading of Russia's Transport System, 2002–2010, Russia's Culture, 2001–2005, The Elderly, 2002-2004, Children of Russia, 2003–2006, Federal Program for Education, 2001–2005, Prevention and Elimination of Social Deceases, 2002–2006, Improving Soil Fertility in Russia

2002–2005, Development of a Unified Educational Information Environment, 2001–2005, and The Elimination of Inequalities in the Social and Economic Development of the Regions of the Russian Federation, 2002–2010 and through 2015.

Regional programs. The Republic's regional programs are chiefly focused on rural electrification, extension of the gas network, healthcare, education, social policy, environmental rehabilitation, housing and communal services, agriculture, and transport.

6. INVESTMENT PROJECTS

Industry sector and project description	1) Expected results 2) Amount and term of investment 3) Form of financing[1] 4) Documentation[2]	Contact information
1	2	3
CHEMICALS AND PETROCHEMICALS		
31R001 ■ ● ◆		
Production of quality phosphates. Project goal: to produce phosphates.	1) 210,000 tons per year; revenue of $12.6 million per year 2) $4.6 million/2 years 3) L, E ($0.8 million) 4) BP	OAO Dagfos 3, ul. I. Shamilya, Kizilyurt, Republic of Dagestan, 368100 Phone: (87234) 21 064 Fax: (87234) 21 115 Khabib Gadzhievich Rapiguliev, CEO
MACHINE ENGINEERING AND METAL PROCESSING		
31R002 ■ ● ◆		
Production of electrical motors for household heaters, gas tank units for vehicles, diesel fuel heaters, an agricultural combine with replaceable units, agricultural model of MAI 890 aircraft, and autonomous heating unit BAT-250. Project goal: to produce competitive products.	1) 1 million electric motors per year; 18,700 gas tank units per year; 100,000 diesel fuel heaters per year; 5,000 multi-purpose machines per year; 50 MAI 890 aircraft per year; 500 autonomous heating units per year; revenue of $10.1 million per year 2) $1.1 million/2 years 3) L, E ($0.9 million) 4) BP	OAO KEMZ Concern 1, ul. Kutuzova, Kizlyar, Republic of Dagestan, 368800 Phone: (87239) 23 148 Fax: (87239) 22 277 Akhmet Ibragimovich Magometov, CEO
31R003 ● ◆		
Serial production of automatic radio direction finders. Project goal: to produce direction finders.	1) 10,000 instruments per year 2) $1.0 million/2 years 3) L 4) BP	OAO R&D Institute Saphir 2b, ul. Ataeva, Makhachkala, Republic of Dagestan, 367005 Phone: (8722) 67 8238 Fax: (8722) 67 8274 E-mail: Sapfir@dinet.ru Adil Abukovich Saidov, CEO
31R004 ■ ● ◆		
Serial production of cases for semiconductor instruments. Project goal: to launch production of competitive products.	1) 200 million items per year, revenue of $8.5 million per year 2) $2.3 million/2 years 3) L, E ($1.1 million) 4) BP	State Unitary Company Elmeer Mutsalaul, Republic of Dagestan, 367009 Phone: (872310) 10 3925, 10 4080 E-mail: saadi@dagnet.ru Arash Ibragimovich Saadulaev, CEO

[1] L – Loan, E – Equity, Leas. – Leasing, JV – Joint Venture
[2] BP – Business Plan, FS – Feasibility Study

1	2	3

31R005 ■ ● ◆

Production of electrical and mechanical wheel amplifier.
Project goal: to introduce a new product and satisfy demand for amplifiers.

1) 100,000 items per year, revenue of $18.9 million per year
2) $2.2 million/2 years
3) L, E ($1.4 million)
4) BP

OAO Aviaagregat
37, ul. Irchi Kazaka, Makhachkala,
Republic of Dagestan, 367030
Phone/fax: (8722) 62 0274
E-mail: agregat@dinet.ru
Gairbeck Abdulkerimovich Gamzatov, CEO

31R006 ■ ● ◆

Serial production of 6–7 generation TV sets.
Project goal: to produce competitive goods.

1) 50,000 TV sets per year, revenue of $6.5 million per year
2) $2.9 million/2 years
3) L, E ($0.9 million)
4) BP

OAO Electrosignal
87, ul. Lenina, Derbent,
Republic of Dagestan, 368600
Phone: (87240) 23 453
Fax: (87240) 25 803, 47 182
E-mail: d_elecs@dinet.ru
Dalgat Mardanovich Mirzabekov, CEO

31R007 ■ ● ◆

Production of upgraded welding instruments AC-1 and AC-2.
Project goal: diversification of operations.

1) 1,000 items per year, revenue of $2.4 million per year
2) $1.1 million/2 years
3) E, L ($0.6 million)
4) BP

OAO Dagdiesel Plant
1, ul. Lenina, Kaspiysk,
Republic of Dagestan, 368300
Phone: (87246) 32 426, 32 496
Fax: (87246) 67 181
Nikolai Stepanovich Pokorsky, CEO

TRANSPORT INFRASTRUCTURE

31R008 ● ◆

Reconstruction of the Makhachkala International Commercial Seaport.
Project goal: to increase freight turnover, and develop and reconstruct the dry dock and oil terminal.

1) n/a
2) $4.6 million/4 years
3) L
4) BP

Makhachkala Commercial Seaport
5, Portshosse, Makhachkala,
Republic of Dagestan, 367012
Phone: (8722) 67 2892
Fax: (8722) 67 2914, 67 2782
E-mail: mmtpru@yahoo.com
Abusupyan Magometovich Kharkharov,
Head of Seaport

31R009 ● ◆

Reconstruction of the airport of the State Unitary Company Dagestan Airlines.
Project goal: to create a major transport junction in the south of Russia.

1) n/a
2) $4.5 million/4 years
3) L
4) BP

State Unitary Company
Dagestan Airlines
Airport, Makhachkala,
Republic of Dagestan, 367016
Phone: (8722) 65 4920, 65 4930
Fax: (8722) 65 4925
Alexei Djabrailovich Djabrailov, CEO

OTHER

31R010 ■ ● ◆

Production of sparkling wine corks.
Project goal: to satisfy demand of alcoholic beverage plants.

1) 50,000 items per year, revenue of $1.5 million per year
2) $1.1 million/2 years
3) L, E ($0.3 million)
4) BP

OAO Dagtelecoms
109, ul. Akushinskogo, Makhachkala,
Republic of Dagestan, 367014
Phone: (8722) 66 2588
Fax: (8722) 66 2577
Muzakir Shikhsaidovich Shikhsaidov, CEO

32. REPUBLIC OF INGUSHETIA [06]

ECONOMIC MAP

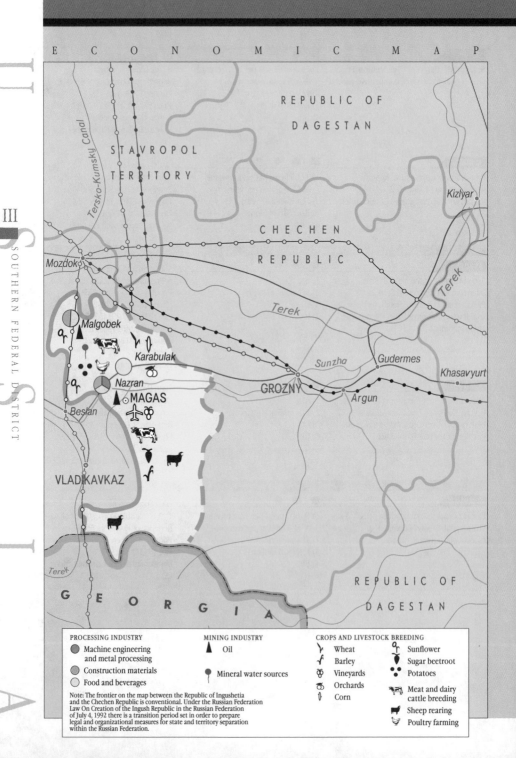

REPUBLIC OF DAGESTAN

STAVROPOL TERRITORY

Tersko-Kumsky Canal

Kizlyar

CHECHEN REPUBLIC

Mozdok

Terek

Malgobek

Karabulak

Sunzha   Gudermes

Khasavyurt

Nazran   GROZNY

MAGAS   Argun

Beslan

VLADIKAVKAZ

Terek

GEORGIA

REPUBLIC OF DAGESTAN

PROCESSING INDUSTRY
- Machine engineering and metal processing
- Construction materials
- Food and beverages

MINING INDUSTRY
- Oil
- Mineral water sources

CROPS AND LIVESTOCK BREEDING
- Wheat
- Barley
- Vineyards
- Orchards
- Corn
- Sunflower
- Sugar beetroot
- Potatoes
- Meat and dairy cattle breeding
- Sheep rearing
- Poultry farming

Note: The frontier on the map between the Republic of Ingushetia and the Chechen Republic is conventional. Under the Russian Federation Law On Creation of the Ingush Republic in the Russian Federation of July 4, 1992 there is a transition period set in order to prepare legal and organizational measures for state and territory separation within the Russian Federation.

The Republic of Ingushetia, the youngest republic within the Russian Federation, was established on June 4, 1992. Today, Ingushetia is a gigantic construction site in which thousands of Russian and foreign specialists work hand in hand. Magas, the capital of Ingushetia, is a rapidly growing city. The city is constructing an international airport, new highways, factories, a power station, and social infrastructure facilities. The Republic's market economy has been demonstrating high growth rates.

As President of the Republic of Ingushetia, I will do everything in my power to develop a favorable investment climate within the Republic and build mutually beneficial contacts with all Russian regions and foreign countries.

The Framework for Social and Economic Development states that in 2003 and over the next few years the main focus will be on the Republic's oil sector – the development of new fields, restoration of oil wells, construction of an oil refinery, and development of a petrochemical sector. Reforms in the agroindustrial sector will focus primarily on strengthening the production and technical base, improving infrastructure, and motivating enterprise. We place our hopes in the construction and building materials sectors. The Republic is faced with the task of creating its own procurement base to produce building materials, goods, and assemblies.

The Republic's authorities realize that these plans can only be implemented through the deployment of all economic management levers, including investment activity.

Murat Zyazikov,
PRESIDENT OF THE REPUBLIC OF INGUSHETIA

III

SOUTHERN FEDERAL DISTRICT

1. GENERAL INFORMATION

1.1. GEOGRAPHY

The Republic of Ingushetia covers a total area of 3,600 square kilometers. The Republic is situated in the south of the European part of Russia, in the center of the Caucasus mountain range. To the east and north-east, the Republic borders the Chechen Republic, to the west and north-west – the Republic of North Ossetia – Alania, and to the south and south-east – Georgia.

1.2. CLIMATE

The Republic of Ingushetia has a continental climate. The average air temperature in January is –5°C, rising to +21°C in July. The average annual precipitation reaches 1,200 mm.

1.3. POPULATION

According to preliminary 2002 census results, total population in the Republic was 469,000 people.

The average population density is 130.3 people per square kilometer. The economically active population amounts to 181,000 people. The 2002 official unemployment level was 11.1%.

Demographically speaking, some 60.4% are of working age, 29.9% are below the statutory working age, and 9.7% are beyond the statutory working age.

The Republic's ethnic mix is 83% Ingush, 11.2% Chechen, 4% Russian, and 1.8% other ethnic groups.

As of 2002, the Republic's major urban centers were Nazran with 126,700 inhabitants, Malgobek with 53,100 inhabitants, Karabulak with 27,700 inhabitants, and Magas with 100 inhabitants.

Population							*TABLE 1*
	1992	1997	1998	1999	2000	2001	2002
Total population, '000	202	308	313	317	355	460	469
Economically active population, '000	176	91	99	105	112	145	181

2. ADMINISTRATION

Presidential Administration, Magas, Republic of Ingushetia, 386101
Phone: (8732) 22 1651; phone/fax: (8734) 55 1155, (095) 334 2039
E-mail: admin@ingushetia.ru; http://www.ingushetia.ru

NAME	POSITION	CONTACT INFORMATION
Murat Magometovich ZYAZIKOV	President of the Republic of Ingushetia	Phone/fax: (095) 334 2039, (8734) 55 1155
Timur Akhmetovich MOGUSHKOV	Chairman of the Republican Government of the Republic of Ingushetia	House of Government, Magas, 386101 Phone: (8732) 22 5680 Fax: (095) 737 0073
Rashid Yakhyaevich GAISANOV	Minister of Economy of the Republic of Ingushetia	House of Government, Magas, 386101 Phone: (8734) 55 1225 Phone/fax: (8734) 55 1117 E-mail: economri@mail333.com
Enverkhadzhi Gasanovich KHALUKHAEV	Deputy Chairman of the Government of the Republic of Ingushetia, Minister of Finance	House of Government, Magas, 386101 Phone: (8734) 55 1117, 22 5141 Phone/fax: (8734) 55 1361 E-mail: mfri@mail333.com
Ibragim Solsaevich MALSAGOV	Minister of Construction of the Republic of Ingushetia	Pr. Respubliki, Government Quarter, Magas, 386102 Phone: (8734) 55 1335, 55 1450 Phone/fax: (8734) 55 1347
Magomed Beksultanovich TATVIEV	Deputy Chairman of the Government of the Republic of Ingushetia in charge of Industry, Transport, and Communications	House of Government, Magas, 386101 Phone: (8734) 55 1145

NAME	POSITION	CONTACT INFORMATION
Sultan Allaudinovich GIREEV	Deputy Chairman of the Government of the Republic of Ingushetia, Minister of Agriculture and Food	2, ul. Chechenskaya, Nazran, Republic of Ingushetia, 386100 Phone: (8732) 22 6207 Fax: (8732) 22 7305, 22 7067
Khasmagomet Visengereevich KHAMKHOEV	Chairman of the Committee for Natural Resources of the Republic of Ingushetia	122, ul. Seinaroeva, Ordzhonikidzevskaya, Republic of Ingushetia, 386200 Phone: (8732) 12 1326, 12 2275

3. ECONOMIC POTENTIAL

3.1. 1997–2002 GROSS REGIONAL PRODUCT (GRP). INDUSTRY BREAKDOWN

The 2002 gross regional product of the Re-public of Ingushetia amounted to $118.7 million, which constitutes a 27.1% fall year-on-year. Per capita GRP was $353 in 2001 and $252 in 2002.

3.2. MAJOR ECONOMIC GROWTH PROJECTIONS

According to major economic development forecasts for 2003, the Republic plans to:

Industry: promote its oil sector by developing new fields, rehabilitating temporarily closed wells, constructing an oil refinery, and developing petro-

TABLE 2

GRP trends in 1997–2002	1997	1998	1999	2000	2001*	2002*
GRP in current prices, $ million	182.3	109.8	83.9	214.0	162.9	118.7

*Estimates of the Government of the Republic of Ingushetia

TABLE 3

GRP industry breakdown in 1997–2002, % of total	1997	1998	1999	2000	2001*	2002*
GRP	100.0	100.0	100.0	100.0	100.0	100.0
Industry	5.5	11.4	19.6	11.8	15.1	16.2
Agriculture and forestry	16.5	14.9	12.9	3.8	5.2	11.9
Construction	22.6	13.1	8.1	8.4	8.3	7.9
Transport and communications, and trade and public catering	27.3	25.7	14.8	9.9	21.9	24.8
Other	28.1	34.9	44.6	66.1	49.5	39.2

*Estimates of the Government of the Republic of Ingushetia

chemical production through the attraction of domestic and foreign investment;

Agriculture: develop the agroindustrial sector through strengthening its operational and technical base, improving the existing infrastructure, promoting small enterprise, and creating jobs to reduce unemployment;

Construction: develop the construction and building materials sectors to establish the Repub-lic's building materials, construction goods, and assemblies industries.

3.3. INDUSTRIAL OUTPUT IN 1997–2002 FOR MAJOR SECTORS OF ECONOMY

The leading industrial sectors of the Republic of Ingushetia are fuel, energy, and building materials. These account for 88.6% of total industrial output.

Fuel. The sector accounts for 65.5% of total industrial output. OAO Ingushneftegazprom carries out oil and gas prospecting and develops oil fields in the Republic.

Energy. This sector accounts for 18.9% of total industrial output. The major company within the sector is OAO Ingushenergo.

Construction materials. The sector accounts for 4.2% of total industrial output. The largest enterprise is GUP Ingushskoye Karieroupravleniye.

Machine engineering and metal processing. The sector accounts for 4.1% of total industrial output. FGUP Nazran Low Yield Electric Engines Plant is the largest company within the sector.

Agriculture. Traditional agricultural sectors are cattle breeding and potato, sugar-beet, and grain cultivation. The Republic has all of the nec-

Industry breakdown of industrial output in 1997–2002, % of total

TABLE 4

	1997	1998	1999	2000	2001	2002*
Industry	100.0	100.0	100.0	100.0	100.0	100.0
Fuel	75.0	43.4	68.7	70.9	63.2	65.5
Energy	–	32.2	14.0	11.6	13.9	18.9
Construction materials	5.7	9.9	4.5	2.5	3.3	4.2
Machine engineering and metal processing	0.2	3.3	0.2	3.4	6.1	4.1
Food and beverages	12.9	7.6	10.4	9.9	8.5	3.9
Chemicals and petrochemicals	3.8	1.9	0.5	–	2.3	1.4
Forestry, timber, and pulp and paper	0.1	0.5	0.4	0.5	1.0	0.9
Printing	2.2	0.4	1.1	0.8	0.9	0.7
Light industry	0.1	0.7	–	0.4	0.8	0.5

*Estimates of the Government of the Republic of Ingushetia

essary conditions for vine and fruit cultivation. Cattle breeding for milk and meat and industrial poultry are well developed.

3.4. FUEL AND ENERGY BALANCE (OUTPUT AND CONSUMPTION PER RESOURCE)

Oil extraction is the largest fuel and energy subsector. The Republic exports some 170,000 tons of oil per year. The Republic has no electricity generation capacities. Electricity is supplied by North Caucasus power stations. Currently, construction of the 64 MW Ingushskaya Gas Turbine Power Station is underway.

3.5. TRANSPORT INFRASTRUCTURE

Roads. The Republic has 804 kilometers of paved public highway. The main federal route is the Baku – Mineralniye Vody – Rostov-on-Don –

Fuel and energy sector production and consumption trends, 1997–2002

TABLE 5

	1997	1998	1999	2000	2001	2002*
Oil output (including gas concentrate), '000 tons	107.0	124.9	136.6	164.2	187.9	145.5
Electricity consumption, billion kWh	0.3	0.3	0.3	0.4	0.4	0.4
Natural gas consumption, million cubic meters	201.7	389.5	405.3	459.7	490.7	592.2

*Estimates of the Government of the Republic of Ingushetia

Moscow highway. The Georgian Military Highway passes through the Grand Caucasian mountain ridge and crosses the Republic of Ingushetia.

Railroads. Total length of the Republic's railroad is 72 km. The Republic is crossed by the North Caucasian railroad, which provides access to Rostov-on-Don and Baku.

Airports. The Ingushetia airport is capable of accepting Boeing aircraft.

Oil pipelines. The Baku – Novorossiysk trunk oil pipeline passes through the Republic and transports the Republic's oil from the Caspian shore to the West.

3.6. NATURAL RESOURCES: RESERVES AND EXTRACTION IN 2002

The Republic's principal natural resources are mineral raw materials, timber, and water.

Mineral raw materials. Oil is the most important raw material, with reserves in excess of 20 million tons. The Republic's solid mineral resources are represented by non-ore construction materials, including marble (reserves of 6,542,000 cubic meters), dolomites (reserves of 60.2 million cubic meters), lime (reserves of 2,255,900 cubic meters), and high quality brick clay (over 30 deposits with reserves of 8,622,000 cubic meters).

Timber. This sector is represented by high-value tree species, including beech, oak, and plane. Timber reserves total 7 million cubic meters.

Water. Ingushetia enjoys vast natural reserves of thermal healing, mineral, and mountain spring water.

4. TRADE OPPORTUNITIES

4.1. MAIN GOODS
PRODUCED IN THE REGION

Oil products. In the first half of 2002, the Republic of Ingushetia produced 145,500 tons of oil products.

Bricks. In 2002, the Republic produced 18.3 million conventional bricks.

None-ore construction materials. In 2002, the Republic produced 350,500 cubic meters of construction materials.

Bread and bakery. In the first half of 2002, the Republic produced 2,100 tons of bread and bakery products.

Mineral water. In 2002, the Republic produced 1.9 million bottles of mineral water.

Confectionary. In 2002, the Republic produced 324 tons of confectionary goods.

4.2. EXPORTS,
INCLUDING EXTRA-CIS

The Republic's exports to extra-CIS countries amounted to $26.3 million in 2000, with exports to the CIS totaling $0.1 million. The respective figures for 2001 were $20.1 million and $0.5 million, and $18.7 million for 2002 to extra-CIS countries. In 2002, the Republic did not export its goods to CIS countries.

The main types of goods exported by the Republic are oil and gas condensate. Major importers of the Republic's products include Italy, the USA, Korea, France, and Azerbaijan.

4.3. IMPORTS, INCLUDING EXTRA-CIS

2000 imports from extra-CIS amounted to $2.4 million, with imports from the CIS totaling $0.2 million. The respective figures for 2001 were $3.7 and $0.5 million, and $0.1 and $0.1 million for 2002.

The main types of goods imported by the Republic of Ingushetia are energy, machinery, equipment, vehicles, and food. The main exporters to the Republic are Turkey, the United Arab Emirates, Saudi Arabia and Italy.

4.4. MAJOR REGIONAL
EXPORT AND IMPORT ENTITIES

Due to the specific features of trade in the Republic, mainly industrial companies perform export and import operations.

5. INVESTMENT OPPORTUNITIES

5.1. INVESTMENTS IN 1992–2002
(BY INDUSTRY SECTOR),
INCLUDING
FOREIGN INVESTMENTS

The following factors determine the investment appeal of the Republic of Ingushetia:

- Its advantageous geographic location (access to Caucasian and Middle Eastern markets);
- Its developed transport infrastructure;
- Its fertile soil and favorable climate;

- Legislation supporting investment activities (protection of investor rights and preferential tax treatment);
- Its qualified workforce;
- The availability of natural resources (oil reserves).

5.2. CAPITAL
INVESTMENT

Construction and industry account for the lion's share of capital investment.

III

SOUTHERN FEDERAL DISTRICT

Capital investment by industry sector, $ million						*TABLE 6*
	1997	1998	1999	2000	2001	2002
Total capital investment	121.0	41.4	25.9	33.8	49.8	57.1
Including major industries (% of total)						
Industry	11.5	26.5	3.2	37.9	32.2	12.6
Agriculture and forestry	0.9	0.5	1.7	2.2	2.0	11.1
Construction	26.0	1.7	6.1	4.2	37.0	35.9
Transport and communications	10.6	12.3	24.2	4.9	3.7	9.0
Trade and public catering	1.0	–	–	–	0.2	–
Other	50.0	58.9	64.8	50.8	24.9	31.4

		TABLE 7	
Largest enterprises of the Republic of Ingushetia			
COMPANY	SECTOR	2001 SALES, $ MILLION*	2001 NET PROFIT, $ MILLION*
State Unitary Company GO Ingushneftegazprom	Fuel	15.5	3.8
OAO Nazran Bakery	Food and beverages	1.3	0.5
OOO Khimreagent	Chemicals	0.9	0.3
State Unitary Company Nazran Low Yield Electric Motor Plant	Machine engineering	0.3	n/a
State Ingush Pit Management Company	Building materials	0.3	n/a
OAO Mineral Water Achaluki	Food and beverages	0.25	0.003

*Estimates of the Government of the Republic of Ingushetia

5.3. MOST ATTRACTIVE SECTORS FOR INVESTMENT

According to experts and the Government of the Republic of Ingushetia, the most appealing sectors for investors are oil, food and beverages, machine engineering and metal processing, building materials, and agroindustrial production.

5.4. CURRENT LEGISLATION ON INVESTOR TAX EXEMPTIONS AND PRIVILEGES

The Republic's Law On Tax Exemptions for Individual Categories of Taxpayers, which envisages privileges to companies investing in the Republic of Ingushetia, seeks to establish a favorable investment climate in the Republic.

		TABLE 8
Regional entities responsible for raising investment		
ENTITY	ADDRESS	PHONE, FAX, E-MAIL
Ministry of Economy of the Republic of Ingushetia	House of Government, Magas, Republic of Ingushetia, 386101	Phone: (8734) 55 1225 Phone/fax: (8734) 55 1117 E-mail: economri@mail333.com
Regional Enterprise Support and Competition Development Fund of the Republic of Ingushetia	12, pr. Bazorkina, Nazran, Republic of Ingushetia, 386101	Phone: (8732) 22 5898 E-mail: tppri@mail.ru

5.5. FEDERAL AND REGIONAL ECONOMIC AND SOCIAL DEVELOPMENT PROGRAMS FOR THE REPUBLIC OF INGUSHETIA

Federal targeted programs: The Republic of Ingushetia is implementing several federal targeted programs: Russia's South, 2002–2006, Improving Soil Fertility in Russia, 2002–2005, Upgrading the Transport System of Russia, 2002–2010, Federal Program for the Development of Education, 2002–2005, Prevention of and Fight against Social and Economic Diseases, 2002–2006, Children of Russia, 2001–2003, Social Support to the Disabled, 2000–2005, Housing, 2002–2010, and Youth of Russia 2001–2005.

Regional programs. A number of republican targeted programs is underway in the Republic. The priority status has been accorded to the following programs: Development of the Agroindustrial Sector of the Republic of Ingushetia (implementation period: 2003; budget for 2003: $9.1 million), Geological Prospecting, Production, and Replacement of Mineral and Ecologically Pure Spring Waters, 2002–2003 (2003 budget: $0.4 million), Geological Study of Subsoil Resources and Replacement of the Solid Mineral Base of the Republic of Ingushetia, 2002–2003 (2003 budget: $0.4 million), and Rehousing of Residents of Unfit Habitations, 2002–2010 (2003 budget: $0.2 million).

6. INVESTMENT PROJECTS

Industry sector and project description	1) Expected results 2) Amount and term of investment 3) Form of financing[1] 4) Documentation[2]	Contact information
1	2	3

<table>
<tr><td colspan="3" align="center">OIL</td></tr>
<tr>
<td>32R001
Construction of a refinery in Karabulak. Project goal: to meet demand for oil products in the Republic.</td>
<td>● ▲
1) Gasoline A-76, AI-93, AI-95, AI-98 – 27,200 tons, kerosene – 14,000 tons, diesel fuel – 16,900 tons, fuel oil – 39,900 tons, plant capacity – 120,000 tons, projected revenue – $18.7 million
2) $6.1 million/1.5 years
3) L
4) FS</td>
<td>OAO Ingushneftegazprom 75, ul. Nuradilova, Malgobek, Republic of Ingushetia, 386301 Phone: (8734) 22 3632, 22 3808 Fax: (8734) 22 3808 Girey Mussievich Myakiev, CEO</td>
</tr>
<tr><td colspan="3" align="center">MINING</td></tr>
<tr>
<td>32R002
Construction of a dolomite powder plant. Project goal: to produce dolomite powder and extend the construction sector's raw material base.</td>
<td>● ▼
1) 100,000 tons per year, annual revenue of $0.8 million
2) $3.1 million/1.2 years
3) L
4) Investment proposal</td>
<td>State Unitary Company Kavdolomite Promzhilbaza, Magas, Republic of Ingushetia, 386101 Phone/fax: (8732) 55 1241 Alikhan Yakhyaevich Barkhanoev, Director</td>
</tr>
<tr><td colspan="3" align="center">CONSTRUCTION MATERIALS</td></tr>
<tr>
<td>32R003
Production of finishing building materials via waste hyper-pressing. Project goal: to produce high quality building materials (brick, paving stones, and tiles) from crushed stone, lime, shell rock, road metal, slag, broken bricks, and other construction waste.</td>
<td>● ◆
1) 2 million paving stones, 3.6 million bricks, and 1.2 million facing tiles per year, projected revenue of $1.6 million
2) $1.5 million/9 months
3) L
4) BP</td>
<td>State Unitary Company Kavdolomite Promzhilbaza, Magas, Republic of Ingushetia, 386101 Phone/fax: (8732) 55 1241 Alikhan Yakhyaevich Barkhanoev, Director</td>
</tr>
<tr>
<td>32R004
Construction of facilities for cellular concrete wall blocks production. Project goal: production of small size cellular concrete wall blocks for use in various climate zones.</td>
<td>● ▼
1) Annual output of 180,000 cellular blocks and 4,600 square meters of concrete, expected revenues of $2.1 million.
2) $0.7 million/8 months
3) L
4) Investment proposal</td>
<td>GUP Ingushskoye Karieroupravleniye 1, ul. Im. Oskanova, Karabulik, Republic of Ingushetia, 386230 Phone/fax: (8734) 44 4250 Ruslan Khusenovich Ozdoev, Director</td>
</tr>
<tr><td colspan="3" align="center">GLASS AND PORCELAIN</td></tr>
<tr>
<td>32R005
Construction of a bottle plant. Project goal: to develop production of glass packages in the Republic of Ingushetia for alcoholic beverage and canning industries.</td>
<td>● ▼
1) Annual output of 60 million bottles, expected revenues of $3.6 million.
2) $6.4 million/2 years
3) L
4) Investment proposal</td>
<td>GUP Glass Plant Ul. 52 OGTB, Sagopshi, Malgobek District, Republic of Ingushetia, 386300 Phone: (8732) 26 0865, 24 1042 Savarbek Sultanovich Berkharoev, CEO</td>
</tr>
</table>

III

SOUTHERN FEDERAL DISTRICT

---

[1] L – Loan, E – Equity, Leas. – Leasing, JV – Joint Venture
[2] BP – Business Plan, FS – Feasibility Study

1	2	3

FOOD AND BEVERAGES

32R006 ● ▼

Construction of a mineral water bottling factory on the basis of the Sleptsovsk water deposit.
Project goal: production of mineral water for treatment of respiratory tract and metabolic diseases.

1) Annual output of 30.3 million bottles of mineral water, expected revenues of $3.9 million
2) $2.4 million/1.3 years
3) L
4) Investment proposal

Ministry of Economy,
Parliament House, Magas,
Republic of Ingushetia, 386101
Phone: (8732) 55 1281
Fax: (8732) 55 1117
E-mail: economri@mail333.com
Umalat Izrailovich Torshkhoev,
Director

HOUSING AND SOCIAL

32R007 ● ▼

Residential construction in the town of Magas.
Project goal: to provide housing to people of the Republic and to conduct efficient housing policy.

1) Total residential area of 10,980 square meters, expected revenues of $3.2 million per year
2) $0.7 million/1.5 years
3) L
4) Investment proposal

OOO Promstroy
3, ul. Chunskaya, Nazran
Republic of Ingushetia, 386100
Phone: (8732) 22 6903
Beslan Savarbekovich Shadyzhev,
Director

33. REPUBLIC OF KABARDINO-BALKARIA [07]

E C O N O M I C M A P

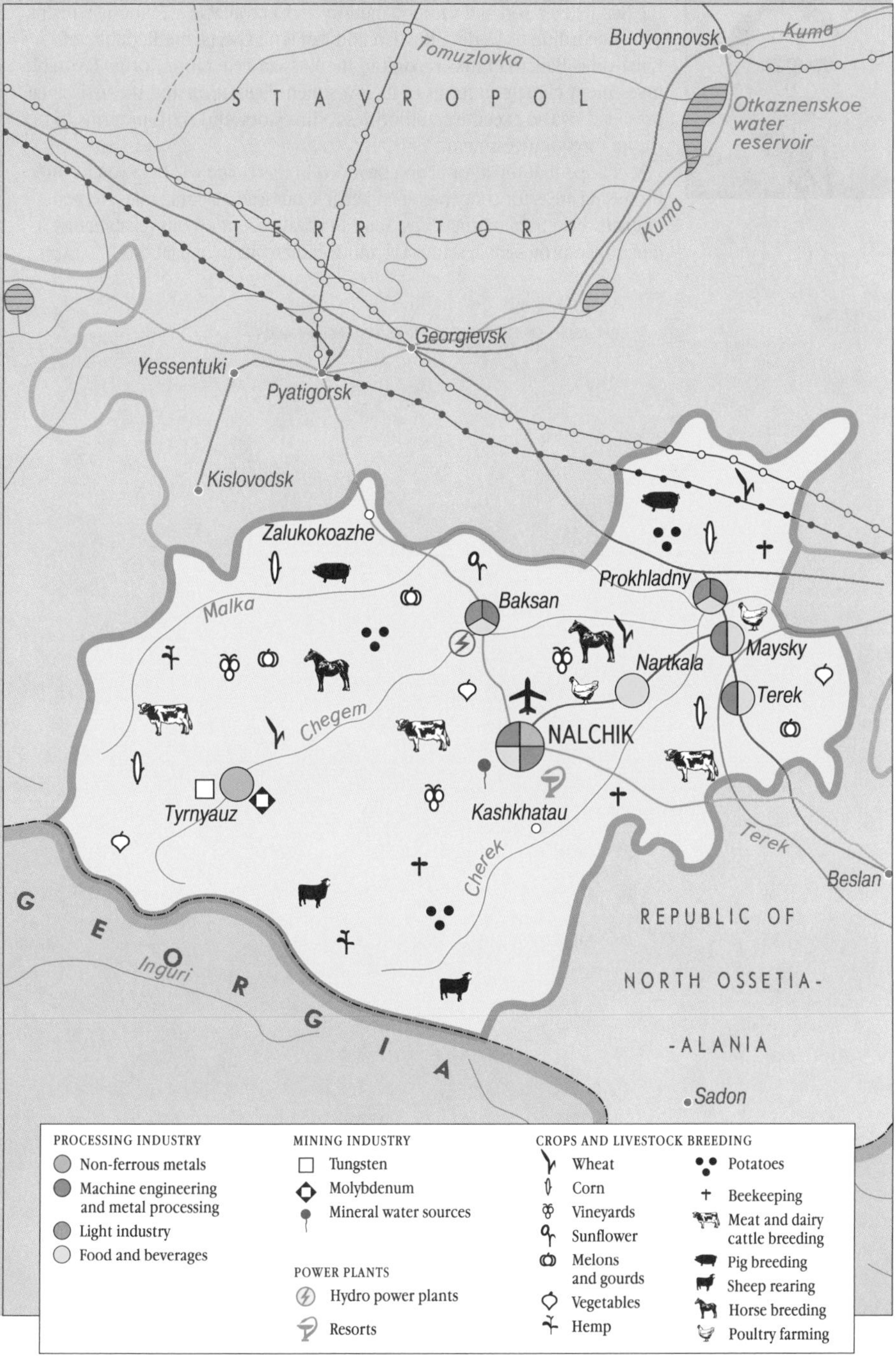

Budyonnovsk
Kuma
Tomuzlovka
S T A V R O P O L
T E R R I T O R Y
Otkaznenskoe water reservoir
Kuma
Georgievsk
Yessentuki
Pyatigorsk
Kislovodsk
Zalukokoazhe
Malka
Baksan
Prokhladny
Maysky
Nartkala
Terek
Chegem
NALCHIK
Tyrnyauz
Kashkhatau
Cherek
Terek
Beslan
REPUBLIC OF NORTH OSSETIA-ALANIA
Sadon
G E O R G I A
Inguri
PROCESSING INDUSTRY
Non-ferrous metals
Machine engineering and metal processing
Light industry
Food and beverages
MINING INDUSTRY
Tungsten
Molybdenum
Mineral water sources
POWER PLANTS
Hydro power plants
Resorts
CROPS AND LIVESTOCK BREEDING
Wheat
Corn
Vineyards
Sunflower
Melons and gourds
Vegetables
Hemp
Potatoes
Beekeeping
Meat and dairy cattle breeding
Pig breeding
Sheep rearing
Horse breeding
Poultry farming

The Republic of Kabardino-Balkaria is one of the major centers of the multi-profile economy of the North Caucasus. The Republic possesses unique natural, cultural, and industrial resources and is open to cooperation in various spheres.

The following chapter of the Investment Guide presents information on the Republic's economic, technological, and human resource potential. The Republic's advantageous geopolitical position at the crossroads of Russia's main southern transport arteries, favorable climate, rich mineral resource base, and qualified workforce, all are conducive to the development of mutually beneficial relations. Mount Elbrus – the highest mountain on the European continent – is the pearl of the Republic's resort and vacation industry and a profitable area for investment.

According to leading Russian and foreign experts, the Republic of Kabardino-Balkaria ranks second in the Russian Federation for its favorable investment climate in terms of its investment legislation and the assistance provided by the executive authorities to investors, and sixth in terms of per capita foreign investment.

I hope that the information provided in this Guide will help you identify promising areas for cooperation and enable our leading companies to create mutually beneficial partnerships. You can always count on our reliability, assistance, high professional standards, and commitment to obligations.

Valery Kokov,
PRESIDENT OF THE REPUBLIC OF KABARDINO-BALKARIA

III

SOUTHERN FEDERAL DISTRICT

1. GENERAL INFORMATION

1.1. GEOGRAPHY

The Republic of Kabardino-Balkaria covers a total area of 12,500 square kilometers. The Republic is located in the south of European Russia, on the northern slopes of the central Great Caucasus (Mount Elbrus – 5,642 meters) and the adjacent plains. To the north and the north-east, the Republic borders the Stavropol Territory, to the west – the Republic of Karachayevo-Cherkessia, to the east and south-west – the Republic of North Ossetia – Alania, and to the south – Georgia. Nalchik is the capital.

1.2. CLIMATE

Kabardino-Balkaria is located within the temperate continental climate zone, with average January temperatures ranging from −12°C in the mountains to −3°C in the plains, and average July temperatures ranging from +4°C to +23°C, respectively. Average annual precipitation is 600–650 mm.

1.3. POPULATION

According to preliminary 2002 census results, Kabardino-Balkaria has a population of 901,000 people. The average population density is 72.1 people per square kilometer. The economically active population totals 320,000. The actual 2002 unemployment rate was 16.2%.

Demographically speaking, some 57.9% are of statutory working age, 24.7% are below the statutory working age, and 17.4% are beyond the statutory working age.

The ethnic mix is 49.2% Kabardin, 30.7% Russian, and 9.6% Balkar.

The major urban centers of Kabardino-Balkaria and their population (2002 data) are Nalchik – 273,900, Prokhladny – 59,400, Baksan – 31,700, Tyrnyhauz – 26,700, Maisky – 25,200, and Terek – 18,500.

Population		1992	1997	1998	1999	2000	2001	2002
Total population, '000.		778	784	786	786	785	784	901
Economically active population, '000.		341	289	301	362	353	321	320

TABLE 1

2. ADMINISTRATION

27, pr. Lenina, Nalchik, Republic of Kabardino-Balkaria, 360028
Phone: (8662) 40 2142; fax: (8662) 47 7029; e-mail: udkm@kbr.net.ru

NAME	POSITION	CONTACT INFORMATION
Valery Mukhamedovich KOKOV	President of the Republic of Kabardino-Balkaria	Phone: (8662) 40 2142 Fax: (8662) 47 6174 E-mail: udkm@kbr.net.ru
Gennady Sergeevich GUBIN	Vice President of the Republic of Kabardino-Balkaria	Phone: (8662) 40 2154 Fax: (8662) 47 0434 E-mail: udkm@kbr.net.ru
Husein Dzhabrailovich CHECHENOV	Chairman of the Government of the Republic of Kabardino-Balkaria	Phone: (8662) 40 2970 Fax: (8662) 47 6183 E-mail: udkm@kbr.net.ru
Yury Kambulatovich ALTUDOV	First Deputy Chairman of the Government of the Republic of Kabardino-Balkaria	Phone: (8662) 47 4231 Fax: (8662) 47 4231 E-mail: udkm@kbr.net.ru
Nikolai Alexandrovich MASLOV	Deputy Chairman of the Government of the Republic of Kabardino-Balkaria, Minister of Property and Land of the Republic of Kabardino-Balkaria	Phone: (8662) 47 2308 Fax: (8662) 47 2308
Khasanby Vladimirovich SHEOZHEV	Minister of Economic Development and Trade of the Republic of Kabardino-Balkaria	Phone: (8662) 40 2038 Fax: (8662) 47 3495 E-mail: mineco@kbr.net.ru
Boris Magomedovich RAKHAEV	Minister of Finance of the Republic of Kabardino-Balkaria	Phone: (8662) 40 2038 Fax: (8662) 47 3558

NAME	POSITION	CONTACT INFORMATION
Sultan Belostanovich ABROKOV	Minister of Industry and Communications of the Republic of Kabardino-Balkaria	Phone: (8662) 47 3181 Fax: (8662) 47 3080
Aziratali Nokhovich AKHMETOV	Minister of Fuel and Energy of the Republic of Kabardino-Balkaria	Phone: (8662) 47 6181 Fax: (8662) 47 6181

3. ECONOMIC POTENTIAL

3.1. 1997–2002 GROSS REGIONAL PRODUCT (GRP). INDUSTRY BREAKDOWN

Kabardino-Balkaria's 2002 gross regional product was 7.5% up on 2001 at $828.6 million. 2001 per capita GRP was $984, and $921 in 2002.

3.2. MAIN ECONOMIC GROWTH PROJECTIONS

Industrial output is expected to grow by 8% year-on-year in 2003 (in monetary terms). Output growth projections by sector (in terms of physical output volumes) are as follows: medical 23%, food 18%, timber 7%, light industry 7%, machine engineering and metal processing 3%, and construction materials 2%. The first plant of the Nizhny-Cherkesskaya Power Station System (the Aushigerskaya Power Station) is to be put into operation in 2003, bringing electricity output in Kabardino-Balkaria to 250 million kWh a year.

GRP trends in 1997–2002						*TABLE 2*
	1997	1998	1999	2000	2001*	2002*
GRP in current prices, $ million	864.6	638.3	425.4	576.6	771.1	828.6

*Estimates of the Government of the Republic of Kabardino-Balkaria

GRP industry breakdown in 1997–2002, % of total						*TABLE 3*
	1997	1998	1999	2000	2001*	2002*
GRP	100.0	100.0	100.0	100.0	100.0	100.0
Industry	21.4	20.2	15.9	17.1	19.1	18.5
Agriculture and forestry	23.5	24.8	32.6	32.0	32.4	31.5
Construction	10.0	7.9	7.1	8.4	7.0	7.8
Transport and communications	6.0	4.6	3.4	3.1	5.0	4.0
Trade and public catering	10.5	11.6	13.9	13.2	13.0	14.0
Other	21.7	21.8	18.7	15.9	14.5	15.2
Net taxes on output	6.9	9.1	8.4	10.3	9.0	9.0

*Estimates of the Government of the Republic of Kabardino-Balkaria

3.3. INDUSTRIAL OUTPUT IN 1997–2002 FOR MAJOR SECTORS OF ECONOMY

The Republic's key sectors are food and beverages, machine engineering and metal processing, energy, and non-ferrous metals. These account for a combined 90% of total industrial output.

Food and beverages. The sector accounts for 39.9% of industrial output. The most advanced segments of the food sector are flour, brewing, distilling, starch, and fruit and vegetables. The Republic is a major supplier of mineral water (10% of total Russian output). More than 50 enterprises operate in the food sector, including OAO Nalchik Confectionery Factory, OAO Kabardino-Balkarian Mineral Waters, and OOO Prokhladnensky Distillery.

Machine engineering and metal processing. The machine engineering and metal processing sector accounts for 26.1% of total industrial output. Enterprises in the sector include OAO Nalchik Machine Engineering Plant, OAO Tersky Diamond Tools Plant, OAO Nalchik High Voltage Equipment Plant, OAO Nalchik Semiconductor Plant, and others.

Energy. The energy sector accounts for 16.4% of industrial output. The largest enterprise in the sector is the Baksanskaya Power Station.

Non-ferrous metals. The non-ferrous metals industry accounts for 5.9% of total industrial output. The largest enterprises are OAO Tyrnyauz Mining Plant, OAO Tyrnyauz Tungsten and Molybdenum Plant, and OAO Gidrometallurg. These

Industry breakdown of industrial output in 1997–2002, % of total						TABLE 4
	1997	1998	1999	2000	2001	2002*
Industry	100.0	100.0	100.0	100.0	100.0	100.0
Food and beverages	23.6	25.6	36.7	40.6	39.7	39.9
Machine engineering and metal processing	26.1	25.7	25.2	27.6	25.0	26.1
Energy	30.4	25.3	16.6	14.0	13.6	16.4
Non-ferrous metals	2.9	4.1	7.6	5.3	9.0	5.9
Light industry	4.0	3.5	3.4	3.8	4.0	4.1
Construction materials	7.3	7.6	6.1	5.0	4.8	3.6
Flour, cereals, and mixed fodder	1.8	1.4	2.0	1.2	0.6	0.6
Forestry, timber, and pulp and paper	1.5	2.6	0.5	0.4	0.3	0.5
Fuel	–	–	–	0.7	0.3	0.3
Chemicals and petrochemicals	0.1	0.6	0.1	0.5	1.9	0.1
Ferrous metals	–	0.1	0.2	0.1	–	–
Glass and porcelain	0.5	0.5	0.3	–	–	–

*Estimates of the Government of the Republic of Kabardino-Balkaria

three companies constitute a unified non-ferrous metals sector, which extracts and processes tungsten and molybdenum ores at the Tyrnyauz Field. Their output is used to build spacecraft and rocket shells and to produce heat resistant and high-strength alloys, and electrical vacuum devices.

Light industry. This sector accounts for 4.1% of total output. The sector includes knitwear, artificial leather, and carpet weaving enterprises.

Agriculture. In 2002, agriculture output rose by 6.7% year-on-year to $430 million. Tillage accounts for 62.6% and livestock for 37.4%. Wheat and corn, millet and sunflower seed, potatoes and vegetables, hemp, and melons and gourds are cultivated in the Republic. Beekeeping and viticulture are also common in the Republic. The livestock sector focuses on cattle, sheep, pig, horse and poultry.

3.4. FUEL AND ENERGY BALANCE (OUTPUT AND CONSUMPTION BY RESOURCE)

The Republic's energy sector has strong potential for development thanks to the significant hydropower resources contained in its mountain rivers. Eight rivers flow through Kabardino-Balkaria with a power potential ranging from 72 MW to 430 MW. The Republic currently operates the Baksanskaya Power Station (25 MW), four low yield power stations, and two isolated power generators at industrial facilities.

3.5. TRANSPORT INFRASTRUCTURE

Road transport plays the leading role in the sector. It accounts for more than 80% of freight transportation.

Roads. The Republic has 2,887 kilometers of paved public highway. The Caucasus Highway carries international, internal, and inter-regional traffic, and connects the Republic to Southern Russia, Azerbaijan, and Georgia.

Railroads. The Republic has 133 kilometers of railroad, with direct rail links to Moscow and other parts of Russia.

Airports. The Nalchik International Airport operates international flights to Turkey, Syria, Jordan, and the United Arab Emirates.

Oil and gas pipelines. The Republic has 6,261.9 kilometers of gas pipeline and 36 kilometers of oil pipeline.

Fuel and energy sector production and consumption trends in 1997–2002						TABLE 5
	1997	1998	1999	2000	2001	2002*
Electricity output, billion kWh	0.2	0.1	0.1	0.1	0.1	0.2
Oil output (including gas condensate), '000 tons	4.0	5.3	10.0	9.0	9.6	9.7
Electricity consumption, billion kWh	1.5	1.5	1.6	1.6	1.5	1.5
Oil consumption, '000 tons	135.7	149.2	100.0	133.0	149.2	110.9
Natural gas consumption, million cubic meters	1,269.6	1,278.5	1,349.6	1,375.2	1,335.9	1,346.7

*Estimates of the Government of the Republic of Kabardino-Balkaria

**3.6. MAIN
NATURE RESOURCES:
RESERVES AND
EXTRACTION IN 2002**

The main natural resources of Kabardino-Balkaria are molybdenum and tungsten ores, complex ores, gold, coal, mineral construction materials, and mineral water springs.

Molybdenum and tungsten ores. The Tyrnyhauz Field contains about half of the world's molybdenum and tungsten ore reserves.

Oil and natural gas. Kabardino-Balkaria occupies the western part of the Tersko-Caspian oil field. Potential recoverable hydrocarbon reserves are estimated at 32 million tons of fuel equivalent. Recoverable oil reserves (eight oil fields) stand at 7.3 million tons.

Mineral water. The Republic has more than 100 mineral water springs with narzan type springs being the most common.

Recreational resources. Nature reserves and national parks cover 15.2% of the Republic's territory. The largest include the Kabardino-Balkaria Natural Reserve, which covers a total area of 81,507,000 hectares, and the Elbrus Foothills National Park, which covers a total area of 100,400 hectares. Kabardino-Balkaria is home to unique wonders of nature such as the Chegem Gorge Cascade Waterfalls, the Blue Lakes, and the Karst potholes and caves of the Malkinskoye Gorge. The federal resort Nalchik is located in the Republic. Kabardino-Balkaria is a major winter sports destination in Russia. A modern winter sports and vacation resort has been created near Mount Elbrus. Mount Cheget and the Elbrus Foothills are equipped with cable-car runs.

4. TRADE OPPORTUNITIES

**4.1. MAIN GOODS
PRODUCED IN THE REGION**

Non-ferrous metals. In 2002, the Republic produced 3,300 tons of tungsten anhydride, 30% down on 2001. Tungsten and molybdenum concentrates are also produced.

Machine engineering and metal processing. Output in 2002: timber processing machines – 422 (79% up on 2001), diamond tools – 2,507,800 carats (18% up on 2001), power cables – 21,800 kilometers (2% down on 2001), wire – 550 tons (24% up on 2001), and voltage regulators – 244,500 (11.7% up on 2001).

Food and beverages. Output in 2002: bread and bakery products – 30,000 tons, vegetable oil – 1,800 tons, canned fruit and vegetables – 161 million standard jars, vodka and alcoholic beverages – 8.2 million decaliters, mineral water – 11.5 million decaliters, whole-milk products – 11,200 tons, and cheese – 1,200 tons.

4.2. EXPORTS, INCLUDING EXTRA-CIS

1999 exports to extra-CIS countries reached $16 million. Exports to the CIS totaled $9.8 million. The corresponding figures for 2000 were $6.6 million and $2.4 million, $3.2 million and $1.4 million for 2001, and $1.2 million and $1.9 million for 2002.

The main types of goods exported by the Republic include machine engineering goods (electric machinery and equipment – 33%), and food (confectionery, alcoholic and non-alcoholic beverages – 23.3%). Other exports include raw hide, fur, timber, and textiles.

The main trading partners for exports are Finland, Turkey, Kazakhstan, Ukraine, and Azerbaijan.

4.3. IMPORTS, INCLUDING EXTRA-CIS

1999 imports from extra-CIS countries reached $77.3 million. Imports from CIS countries totaled $10.7 million. The corresponding figures for 2000 were $5.5 million and $8.7 million, $3.3 million and $2.1 million for 2001, and $5.5 million and $2.1 million for 2002.

The Republic's main imports are food (milk and dairy products, fats and oils, oil seed, cereals – 32.3%), machine engineering goods (machinery and transport vehicles – 27.2%), chemicals (plastics and plastic goods, proteins, tanning substances and dyeing extracts, detergents – 9.9%), and metal processing goods (ferrous metal and aluminum products – 6.2%).

The main import partners in 2002 were Ukraine (20%), Germany (11.7%), Bulgaria (11.4%), Finland (8.1%), and Turkey (8.4%).

**4.4. MAJOR REGIONAL
EXPORT AND IMPORT ENTITIES**

Owing to the specific nature of the Republic's export and import activities, export and import transactions are performed mainly by industrial enterprises.

5. INVESTMENT OPPORTUNITIES

**5.1. INVESTMENTS IN 1992–2002
(BY INDUSTRY SECTOR),
INCLUDING
FOREIGN INVESTMENTS**

The following main factors determine the investment appeal of the Republic:

- Its favorable geographical location and proximity to major markets;
- Its developed transportation infrastructure;
- Laws supporting investment activity;
- Its highly qualified workforce;
- Natural and recreational resources.

5.2. CAPITAL INVESTMENT

Industry, construction, transport and communications account for the lion's share of capital investment.

Capital investment by industry sector, $ million						TABLE 6
	1997	1998	1999	2000	2001	2002
Total capital invested	164.9	114.9	57.2	85.4	104.4	124.0
Including major industries (% of total)						
Industry	29.9	45.3	41.4	15.1	17.7	33.0
Agriculture and forestry	3.0	2.9	2.8	2.0	1.9	2.1
Construction	0.4	0.4	0.5	32.4	33.6	24.0
Transportation and communications	5.8	5.8	5.6	19.3	15.8	17.3
Trade and public catering	6.6	0.7	0.7	6.1	10.6	7.1
Other	54.3	44.9	49.0	25.1	20.4	16.5

Foreign investment trends in 1992–2002						TABLE 7
	1992–1997	1998	1999	2000	2001	2002
Foreign investment, $ million	18.5	28.0	29.5	27.5	–	–
Including FDI, $ million	13.4	25.0	26.5	23.4	–	–

5.3. MAJOR ENTERPRISES (INCLUDING THOSE WITH FOREIGN INVESTMENT)

Major companies with foreign capital include OOO Kardif and Company (Russia, Italy), OOO Duman (Russia, Turkey), OOO Aquila (Russia, Italy), OOO Nalchik Wholesale and Retail Food Market (Russia, Serbia and Montenegro), and OAO Zikhy-Bosphorus (Russia, Turkey).

5.4. MOST ATTRACTIVE SECTORS FOR INVESTMENT

According to the Kabardino-Balkaria Government, the most promising sectors for investment are hotels and tourism.

5.5. CURRENT LEGISLATION ON INVESTOR TAX EXEMPTIONS AND PRIVILEGES

The following laws create a statutory framework for support to investment activity in the Republic:

The Law of the Republic of Kabardino-Balkaria On Investment Activity in the Republic of Kabardino-Balkaria provides for full and unconditional legal protection of Russian and foreign investors operating in the territory of Kabardino-Balkaria.

The Law of the Republic of Kabardino-Balkaria On Tax Privileges to Investors and Organizations Involved in Foreign Trade Activity or Import Replacement Manufacturing. Pursuant to the legislation

Largest enterprises of the Republic of Kabardino-Balkaria	TABLE 8
COMPANY	SECTOR
OAO Nalchik Machine Engineering Plant	Machine engineering and metal processing
OAO Nalchik High Voltage Equipment Plant	Machine engineering and metal processing
OAO Nalchik Semiconductor Plant	Machine engineering and metal processing
OAO Tersky Diamond Tools Plant	Machine engineering and metal processing
OAO Gidrometallurg	Non-ferrous metals
OAO Tyrnyauz Ore Dressing Plant	Non-ferrous metals
OAO Tyrnyauz Tungsten and Molybdenum Plant	Non-ferrous metals
OAO Kavklazkabel	Electrotechnical
OAO Nalchik Halva Plant	Food and beverages
OAO Kabardino-Balkaria Mineral Waters	Food and beverages
OOO ZET Chernorechensky Food Processing Plant	Food and beverages
OOO Narbek	Footwear

of the Russian Federation, the Law provides for tax benefits to investors, including foreign investors, conducting investment activity in the Republic, and to organizations involved in foreign trade or import replacement manufacturing. Organizations with foreign capital are eligible for full or partial exemption from regional tax components and duties and income tax.

		TABLE 9
Regional entities responsible for raising investment		
ENTITY	ADDRESS	PHONE, FAX, E-MAIL
Ministry of Economic Development and Trade of the Republic of Kabardino-Balkaria	27, pr. Lenina, Nalchik, Republic of Kabardino-Balkaria, 360028	Phone: (8662) 47 7420, 40 2038 Fax: (8662) 47 3495 E-mail: mineco@kbr.net.ru
Special Programs Administration of the Republic of Kabardino-Balkaria	7, ul. Kulieva, Nalchik, Republic of Kabardino-Balkaria, 360030	Phone: (8662) 40 4089 Fax: (8662) 40 4062 E-mail: aspkbr@yahoo.com

5.6. FEDERAL AND REGIONAL ECONOMIC AND SOCIAL DEVELOPMENT PROGRAMS FOR THE REPUBLIC OF KABARDINO-BALKARIA

Federal targeted programs. The Republic of Kabardino-Balkaria is implementing programs focused on housing and communal services, agriculture, resort and recreation and public welfare. The priority has been accorded to the Programs: Housing (2002–2010), Russian Ecology and Natural Resources Program (2002–2010), Soil Fertility Improvement Program (2002–2005), Rural Areas Social Development Program through 2010, Creation of an Automated State Land Cadastre and Real Estate Registration System (2002–2007) (with a $4.5 million budget, including $1.3 million from the federal budget), Seismic Safety in Russia (2002– 2010), Development of the Elbrus Foothills Region as an International Tourism, Mountain Climbing, and Alpine Skiing Center (1996–2005), Culture of Russia (2001–2005), The Elderly (2002–2004), Youth of Russia (2001–2005), and Children of Russia (2003–2006).

Regional programs. The Republic has a number of regional programs focused on
• Social and economic growth of the Republic: the Program for the Social-Economic Development of Kabardino-Balkaria in 2003–2006 with a $1,022.6 million budget; the Program for Social Development of Rural Communities in Kabardino-Balkaria through 2010 with a $333.5 million budget, including $50.3 million from the federal budget and $50.3 million from Republic's budget.
• Housing and communal services development and revamping: Reform and Upgrade of the Housing and Communal Services Sector of the Republic of Kabardino-Balkaria, 2002–2010 with total funding of $35.3 million, including $3.9 million from the federal budget and $16.9 million from the Republic's budget;
• Residential development: The Housing 2010 Program with a $940.8 million total budget, including $15.8 million from the federal budget and $47.2 million from the Republic's budget;
• Development of viticulture and winemaking: The Development of Viticulture and Winemaking in the Republic of Kabardino-Balkaria, 1999-2004, and other programs.

The Kabardino-Balkaria Health Resorts Development Program for 2002-2006 has been allocated $15.5 million in financing, including $3.3 million from the federal budget, and $1.8 million from the Republic's budget. The program seeks to boost the development of health resort infrastructure in the Republic.

6. INVESTMENT PROJECTS

Industry sector and project description	1) Expected results 2) Amount and term of investment 3) Form of financing[1] 4) Documentation[2]	Contact information
1	2	3
MINING		
33R001 Reconstruction of a tungsten and molybdenum concentrate plant. Project goal: to increase operations to a profitable level.	● ▲ 1) 1 million tons of concentrates a year 2) $30 million/2.5 years 3) L 4) FS	OAO Tyrnyauz Ore Dressing Plant 19, pr. Elbrussky, Tyrnyauz, Republic of Kabardino-Balkaria, 361600 Phone/fax: (86638) 42 926, 42 235 Satar Anuarovich Musukaev, CEO
MACHINE ENGINEERING AND METAL PROCESSING		
33R002 Creation of a new diamond stone-cutting tools plant using new technology. Project goal: to produce diamond stone-cutting tools.	● ▲ 1) Revenue – $3 million a year 2) $2.4 million/1.5 years 3) L 4) FS	OAO Tersky Diamond Tools Plant 1, per. Yubileiny, Terek Republic of Kabardino-Balkaria, 361200 Phone: (86632) 93 690, 91 176, 91 157 Fax: (86632) 93 251 Adalby Belolovich Tleuzhev, CEO
33R003 Creation of fluorescent light bulb assembly line. Project goal: manufacturing of fluorescent light bulbs using modern technologies.	● ◆ ▲ 1) Revenue in 2004 – $9.2 million, in 2005 – $14.9 million. 2) $12 million/3 years 3) L 4) BP, FS	OAO Nalchik Electrovacuum Plant 1, ul. Musukayeva, Nalchik Republic of Kabardino-Balkaria, 360024 Phone/fax: (8662) 91 4638 Albert Izatovich Kilchukov, CEO
LIGHT INDUSTRY		
33R004 Knitted sportswear and underwear production setup. Project goal: to make knitted wear matching the world standards.	● ◆ 1) Revenue up to $2.2 million a year 2) $1 million/1.5 years 3) L 4) BP	OOO Nalchik Knitwear 9, ul. Malbakhova, Nalchik, Republic of Kabardino-Balkaria, 360022 Phone: (8662) 95 2806 Fax: (8662) 95 1110 Felix Abubekirovich Abrokov, CEO
HOTEL BUSINESS, TOURISM, AND RECREATION		
33R005 Construction of the Priyut Odinnadtsati Hotel on Mount Elbrus. Project goal: to develop tourism (mountain-climbing, Alpine ski climbing, mountain skiing, etc.).	❖ ▲ 1) 125 beds, revenue up to $0.3 million a year 2) $2.0 million/15 months 3) JV 4) FS	Ministry of Resorts and Tourism of the Republic of Kabardino-Balkaria 2, ul. Kanukoeva, Nalchik, Republic of Kabardino-Balkaria, 360022 Phone: (8662) 42 0584; 49 9211 E-mail: mkit@mail.com Zaur Dalkhatovich Gekkiev, Minister
HEALTHCARE		
33R006 Establishment of public recreation, rehabilitation, and entertainment water-park in Nalchik resort area. Project goal: to provide health and recreational services to the public.	❖ ▲ 1) 1,000 persons a day, revenue of $3.9 million a year 2) $8 million/1.3 years 3) JV 4) FS	Ministry of Resorts and Tourism of the Republic of Kabardino-Balkaria 2, ul. Kanukoeva, Nalchik, Republic of Kabardino-Balkaria, 360022 Phone/fax: (8662) 42 0584, 49 9211 E-mail: mkit@mail.com Zaur Dalkhatovich Gekkiev, Minister

[1] L – Loan, E – Equity, Leas. – Leasing, JV – Joint Venture
[2] BP – Business Plan, FS – Feasibility Study

III

SOUTHERN FEDERAL DISTRICT

1	2	3

33R007 ❖ ▲

Renovation of the Mayak Sanatorium in the Nalchik resort area. Project goal: to renovate buildings, replace the utilities system, and improve room standards.	1) 150 beds, revenue up to $0.8 million a year 2) $1.7 million/2 years 3) JV 4) FS	Ministry of Resorts and Tourism of the Republic of Kabardino-Balkaria 2, ul. Kanukoeva, Nalchik, Republic of Kabardino-Balkaria, 360022 Phone: (8662) 42 0584; 49 9211 E-mail: mkit@mail.com Zaur Dalkhatovich Gekkiev, Minister

33R008 ❖ ▲

Renovation of the Pansionat Aushiger Sanatorium at Aushiger. Project goal: to renovate the sanatorium and improve room standards.	1) 100 beds, revenue up to $0.6 million a year 2) $1.5 million/18 months 3) JV 4) FS	Ministry of Resorts and Tourism of the Republic of Kabardino-Balkaria 2, ul. Kanukoeva, Nalchik, Republic of Kabardino-Balkaria, 360022 Phone: (8662) 42 0584; 49 9211 E-mail: mkit@mail.com Zaur Dalkhatovich Gekkiev, Minister

33R009 ❖ ▲

Renovation of the Narzan Sanatorium in the Nalchik resort area. Project goal: to renovate the sanatorium, replace utility systems, and improve room standards.	1) 250 beds, revenue up to $1.3 million a year 2) $1.8 million/20 months 3) JV 4) FS	Ministry of Resorts and Tourism of the Republic of Kabardino-Balkaria 2, ul. Kanukoeva, Nalchik, Republic of Kabardino-Balkaria, 360022 Phone: (8662) 42 0584; 49 9211 E-mail: mkit@mail.com Zaur Dalkhatovich Gekkiev, Minister

33R010 ❖ ▲

Renovation of the Nartan Sanatoriumin in the Nalchik resort area. Project goal: to renovate buildings, replace utilities system, and improve room standards.	1) 200 beds, revenue up to $1.1 million a year 2) $1.5 million/20 months 3) JV 4) FS	Ministry of Resorts and Tourism of the Republic of Kabardino-Balkaria 2, ul. Kanukoeva, Nalchik, Republic of Kabardino-Balkaria, 360022 Phone: (8662) 42 0584; 49 9211 E-mail: mkit@mail.com Zaur Dalkhatovich Gekkiev, Minister

III

SOUTHERN FEDERAL DISTRICT

34. REPUBLIC OF KALMYKIA [08]

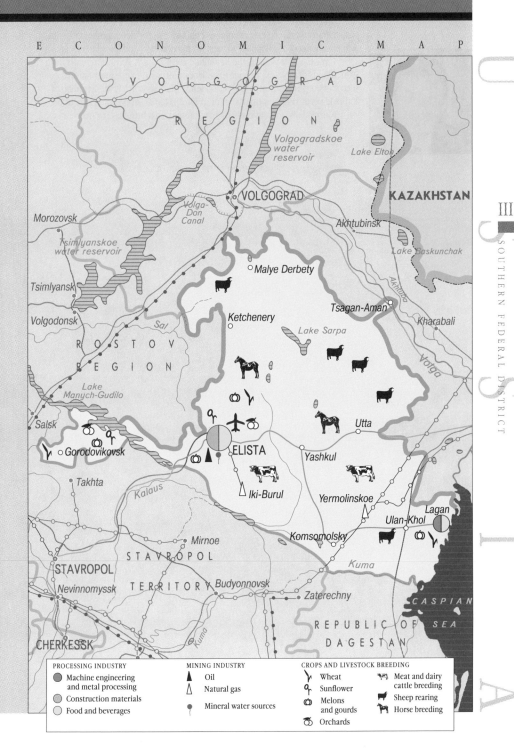

ECONOMIC MAP

VOLGOGRAD REGION

Volgogradskoe water reservoir

Lake Elton

KAZAKHSTAN

VOLGOGRAD

Morozovsk

Volga-Don Canal

Akhtubinsk

Lake Baskunchak

Tsimlyanskoe water reservoir

Akhtuba

Malye Derbety

Tsimlyansk

Ketchenery

Tsagan-Aman

Kharabali

Volgodonsk

Sal

Lake Sarpa

Volga

ROSTOV REGION

Lake Manych-Gudilo

Utta

Salsk

Gorodovikovsk

ELISTA

Yashkul

Takhta

Kalaus

Iki-Burul

Yermolinskoe

Lagan

Ulan-Khol

Mirnoe

Komsomolsky

STAVROPOL TERRITORY

Kuma

Zaterechny

CASPIAN SEA

STAVROPOL

Nevinnomyssk

Budyonnovsk

REPUBLIC OF DAGESTAN

CHERKESSK

Kuma

PROCESSING INDUSTRY
- Machine engineering and metal processing
- Construction materials
- Food and beverages

MINING INDUSTRY
- Oil
- Natural gas
- Mineral water sources

CROPS AND LIVESTOCK BREEDING
- Wheat
- Sunflower
- Melons and gourds
- Orchards
- Meat and dairy cattle breeding
- Sheep rearing
- Horse breeding

The unique geographic location of the Republic of Kalmykia, which is situated on the shores of the Caspian Sea at the crossroads of major transportation routes, determines its multifaceted investment appeal. The Republic's considerable reserves of hydrocarbons, the unique culture of the Kalmyk people, the Republic's exceptional steppe landscapes, access to the Caspian Sea, rich cattle breeding traditions, and political and economic stability, are some of the factors that predetermine the favorable investment prospects of our Republic.

The Republic's investment policy is focused on improving the investment legislative framework, creating conditions conducive to the development of business, and enhancing of the Republic's image on the domestic and international arena.

Over the past decade, the Republic's authorities and entrepreneurs have gained considerable experience in collaboration with major international companies and corporations. It is with confidence that we say that the Republic of Kalmykia is a competent participant in international economic cooperation.

Kalmykia is open to constructive international business cooperation!

Kirsan Ilyumzhinov,
PRESIDENT OF THE REPUBLIC OF KALMYKIA,
CHAIRMAN OF THE GOVERNMENT OF THE REPUBLIC OF KALMYKIA

III

SOUTHERN FEDERAL DISTRICT

1. GENERAL INFORMATION

1.1. GEOGRAPHY

Situated in the south-east of European Russia, the Republic of Kalmykia covers a total area of 76,100 square kilometers. To the north the Republic borders the Volgograd Region, to the west – the Rostov Region, to the southwest – the Stavropol Region, to the south – the Republic of Dagestan, to the east – the Astrakhan Region, and to the south-east is washed by the Caspian Sea.

1.2. CLIMATE

The Republic has a continental climate. The average air temperature in January is −2°C, rising to +26.9°C in July. The average annual precipitation ranges from 170 mm in the east to 400 mm in the west. The growing season lasts for some 180 days.

1.3. POPULATION

According to preliminary 2002 census results, the Republic's total population amounted to 292,000 people. The average population density is 3.8 people per square kilometer. The economically active population amounts to 141,700 people. 2002 official unemployment level stood at 2.8%; the actual rate is 19.1%.

Demographically speaking, some 59.8% are of working age, 25.3% are below the statutory working age, and 14.9% are beyond the statutory working age.

The Republic's ethnic mix is 45.4% Kalmyk, 37.7% Russian, 4% Dargyn, 2.8% Chechen, 1.9% Kazakh, and 8.4% other ethnic groups. As of 2002, the Republic of Kalmykia's major urban centers are: Elista with 104,300 inhabitants, Lagan with 15,200 inhabitants, and Gorodovikovsk with 10,400 inhabitants.

Population		1992	1997	1998	1999	2000	2001	2002
Total population, '000		327	318	317	316	314	314	292
Economically active population, '000		159	139	147	141	145	142	142

TABLE 1

2. ADMINISTRATION

House of Government, Elista, Republic of Kalmykia, 358000
Phone: (84722) 50 655, 61 388; fax: (84722) 62 880; e-mail: aris_rk@cityline.ru; http://kalm.ru

NAME	POSITION	CONTACT INFORMATION
Kirsan Nikolaevich ILYUMZHINOV	President of the Republic of Kalmykia, Chairman of the Government of the Republic of Kalmykia	Phone: (84722) 50 655, 61 388
Valery Petrovich BOGDANOV	Vice President of the Republic of Kalmykia	Phone: (84722) 52 714, 26 844
Alexei Maratovich ORLOV	First Deputy Chairman of the Republican Government, Permanent Representative of the Republic of Kalmykia to the President of the Russian Federation	Phone: (84722) 61 123
Anatoly Vasilyevich KOZACHKO	Deputy Chairman of the Republican Government for the Agroindustrial Sector	Phone: (84722) 60 156
Vladimir Borisovich SENGLEEV	Deputy Chairman of the Republican Government, Minister of Economy	Phone: (84722) 52 846
Valery Erdnievich BOVAEV	Deputy Chairman of the Republican Government, Minister of Industry and Trade	Phone: (84722) 61 056
Vyacheslav Nikolaevich GOLOVANOV	Minister of Investment Policy of the Republic of Kalmykia	Phone: (84722) 29 555

3. ECONOMIC POTENTIAL

3.1. 1997–2002 GROSS REGIONAL PRODUCT (GRP). INDUSTRY BREAKDOWN

The 2002 gross regional product amounted to $305.4 million, which constitutes 0.7% growth year-on-year. Per capita GRP amounted to $966 in 2001 and $1,045 in 2002.

3.2. MAIN ECONOMIC GROWTH PROJECTIONS

The Republic has accorded priority status to the development of its fuel and energy sector. Large reserves of hydrocarbons comparable to the Astrakhan field have been discovered in Kalmykia's sector of the Caspian lowlands.

GRP trends in 1997–2002						TABLE 2
	1997	1998	1999	2000	2001*	2002*
GRP in current prices, $ million	286.8	174.1	91.6	314.4	303.2	305.4

*Estimates of the Government of the Republic of Kalmykia

GRP industry breakdown in 1997–2002, % of total						TABLE 3
	1997	1998	1999	2000	2001*	2002*
GRP	100.0	100.0	100.0	100.0	100.0	100.0
Industry	16.8	15.4	25.0	11.8	10.9	9.9
Agriculture and forestry	15.7	-1.4	13.3	6.8	8.3	8.3
Construction	7.4	12.6	5.9	32.7	26.5	26.9
Transport and communications	2.1	5.5	4.6	2.0	2.4	2.7
Trade and public catering	5.4	6.7	5.6	3.1	4.0	4.0
Other	42.1	50.0	42.9	16.4	18.8	20.3
Net taxes on output	10.5	11.2	2.7	27.2	29.1	27.9

*Estimates of the Government of the Republic of Kalmykia

Industry breakdown of industrial output in 1997–2002, % of total						TABLE 4
	1997	1998	1999	2000	2001	2002*
Industry	100.0	100.0	100.0	100.0	100.0	100.0
Energy	36.7	45.3	28.3	21.4	25.2	47.6
Fuel	23.1	21.0	48.4	57.4	44.1	34.7
Food and beverages	7.9	5.5	5.7	5.8	8.0	8.7
Machine engineering and metal processing	5.5	4.4	2.3	2.0	2.2	3.2
Construction materials	9.1	14.9	7.7	7.9	14.3	2.1
Flour, cereals, and mixed fodder	3.8	3.5	3.9	3.3	3.2	1.3
Light industry	1.2	0.7	0.6	0.5	0.8	0.4
Forestry, timber, and pulp and paper	0.6	1.0	0.4	0.3	0.5	0.3
Chemicals and petrochemicals	–	–	–	0.3	0.5	–

*Preliminary data of the State Statistics Committee of Russia

In the processing sector, a program has been developed and is currently underway for the creation of major leather, fur, and top grade wool processing companies and the production of yarn and knitted wear.

Machine engineering companies are being upgraded. Investment proposals have been prepared for reconstruction of existing companies and construction of new facilities to produce refrigerators and warehouses.

In the construction materials sector, the Republic has developed investment proposals for the establishment of large-scale manufacturing of light concrete wall units, the upgrade of silicate brick manufacturing facilities, and the development of lime deposits to produce lime and cement.

The Republic has also developed investment projects for the creation of a new international communi-

Fuel and energy sector production and consumption, 1997–2002						TABLE 5
	1997	1998	1999	2000	2001	2002*
Electricity output, billion kWh	0.001	0.001	–	–	0.001	–
Oil output (including gas condensate), 000' tons	314.0	295.0	242.0	248.0	269.0	187.0
Natural gas extraction, million cubic meters	109.0	91.0	77.0	62.0	57.0	53.0
Electricity consumption, billion kWh	0.8	0.7	0.6	0.6	0.6	0.5
Natural gas consumption, million cubic meters	316.0	286.0	327.0	272.0	270.0	276.0

*Estimates of the Government of the Republic of Kalmykia

cations system, the construction of an international airport, and the establishment of an air freight carrier.

3.3. INDUSTRIAL OUTPUT IN 1997–2002 FOR MAJOR SECTORS OF ECONOMY

The leading industrial sectors of the Republic of Kalmykia are energy, fuel, and food and beverages. Their combined share in total industrial output is 91%.

Fuel. The sector accounts for 34.7% of total industrial output. The sector is represen-ted by OAO Kalmneft, OAO Kalmgaz, ZAO KalmTatneft, State Company Kalmnedra, ZAO Oil Company Kalmistern, ZAO Kalmpetrol, OOO Onyx Plus, and OAO Kalmneftegas.

Food and beverages. The sector accounts for 8.7% of total industrial output. The sector is represented by OOO Arshansky Meat Processing Plant, OOO Caspian Fish Processing Plant, and OOO Alaya.

Agriculture. The agriculture sector accounts for 8.3% of the Republic's GRP. Arable lands cover a total area of some 4.2 million hectares, including 669,400 hectares of land used for grain cultivation. Cattle breeding accounts for 72.7% of agricultural output, and tillage for 27.3%. Pasture cattle breeding is especially well developed. Fine-fleeced sheep breeding is the largest livestock sector with some 40% of total agricultural output.

3.4. FUEL AND ENERGY BALANCE (OUTPUT AND CONSUMPTION PER RESOURCE)

The Republic has no electricity generation capacities. The united energy system of the North Caucasus supplies electricity to the Republic. In order to meet local demand for electricity and heat, the Republic is currently constructing the Kalmykia Wind Power Station with a capacity of 22 MW and the Elista Steam Gas Power Station (320 MW).

2001 oil extraction fell by 14% compared to 1997, falling by a further 30% in 2002 to 187,000 tons. The reason behind this downwards trend is insufficient financing of well rehabilitation, well launching, and production intensification measures.

Natural gas output amounted to 53 million cubic meters in 2002, which constitutes a 51% fall on 1997 figures.

3.5. TRANSPORT INFRASTRUCTURE

Roads. The Republic has 2,367 kilometers of paved public highway. Its main highways are Volgograd – Elista – Stavropol, Elista – Astrakhan, and Mineralnye Vody – Kaspiysky. In 2002, the Republic's transport companies carried 916,900 tons of freight.

Railroads. The Republic of Kalmykia has 154 kilometers of railroads. The main railway route Saratov – Astrakhan – Grozny – Makhachkala – Baku passes through the Republic. In 2002, some 99,000 tons of freight was transported by rail. The Republic's railroad transportation sector is expected to take off with the construction of the Lagan – Ulan Khol – Elista railroad with an onwards link to Volgograd.

Airports. Elista is served by an international airport.

Oil and gas pipelines. The Caspian Pipeline Consortium's Tengiz – Novorossiysk oil pipeline, which was built to transport crude oil from the Tengiz and other adjacent fields in Kazakhstan and Russia to the Black Sea terminal at Novorossiysk, crosses the Republic of Kalmykia.

3.6. MAIN NATURAL RESOURCES: RESERVES AND EXTRACTION IN 2002

The main natural resources of the Republic of Kalmykia are oil, natural gas, industrial magnesium chloride (bischofite), and raw construction materials.

Oil and gas fields. The Republic has 39 discovered hydrocarbon fields, including 19 oil and ten gas fields, and five oil and gas and five gas condensate fields. The Republic's estimated reserves total 3 billion tons of oil and condensate and 2.5 trillion cubic meters of gas. Proven reserves reach 80 million tons of oil and 20 billion cubic meters of gas.

Construction materials. The Republic has as many as 17 deposits of brick clay and lime shell rock with reserves of 35 million cubic meters, eight deposits of construction and silicate sands with 50 million cubic meters of reserves, two clay and gypsum deposits, and an expended clay aggregate deposit with over 10 million cubic meters of reserves.

Natural gas. The Listinskoye field's nitric gas reserves with a nitrate content of 86.7% are estimated at 6.4 million cubic meters, with daily discharge of 39,100 cubic meters. The Krasnokhudskaya No. 1 well's carbonic gas reserves with carbon content of 97.5% are estimated at 800 million cubic meters, with daily discharge of 2,000 cubic meters.

Mineral water. Highly mineralized deposits of iodine-bromine, chloride-sulphate, and sodium water with a mineralization level of 1–15 g/l are spread throughout the Republic. The iodine content varies from 11 to 24 mg/l the bromine content, from 120 to 1,600 mg/l.

III

SOUTHERN FEDERAL DISTRICT

4. TRADE OPPORTUNITIES

4.1. MAIN GOODS
PRODUCED IN THE REGION
Agriculture. 2002 meat output totaled 850,000 tons, grain – 444,900 tons, sunflower seed – 14,800 tons, live cattle and poultry – 26,600 tons, milk – 59,400 tons, and 52 million eggs.

4.2. EXPORTS, INCLUDING EXTRA-CIS
The Republic's export to extra-CIS countries amounted to $179.4 million in 2000. Exports to CIS reached $16.8 million. The corresponding figures for 2001 were $114.4 million and $12.4 million, and $22.4 million and $2.6 million for 2002.

The main types of goods exported by the Republic (% of total exports) are food and raw food – 0.8%, fuel and energy – 37.3%, petrochemicals – 0.3%, metals – 14.3%, timber and timber goods – 1%, and machine engineering goods – 45.9%. Major importers of the Republic's products include the United Arab Emirates – 37.7%, Italy – 19.1%, and Kazakhstan – 12.7%.

4.3. IMPORTS,
INCLUDING EXTRA-CIS
2000 imports from extra-CIS countries amounted to $25.3 million. Imports from the CIS reached $22.1 million. The corresponding figures for 2001 were $38.6 million and $23.3 million, and $33.3 million and $12 million for 2002.

The bulk of 2002 imports consisted of (% of total imports): food and raw edible materials – 29.4%, fuel and energy – 42.6%, petrochemicals – 2%, metals – 14.4%, and machine engineering goods – 8.2%. The Republic's main import partners are Turkmenistan – 42.5%, Ukraine – 34.1%, and Georgia – 11.8%.

4.4. MAJOR REGIONAL
EXPORT AND IMPORT ENTITIES
Due to the specific features of trade in the Republic, mainly industrial companies perform export and import operations.

5. INVESTMENT OPPORTUNITIES

5.1. INVESTMENTS IN 1992–2002
(BY INDUSTRY SECTOR),
INCLUDING FOREIGN INVESTMENTS
The following factors determine the investment appeal of the Republic of Kalmykia:
- Its advantageous geographic location (proximity to large industrial centers);

- Its developed transport infrastructure (a transport network linking European countries to the Middle East, India, and China);
- Hydrocarbon fields;
- Highly qualified workforce and specialists.

5.2. CAPITAL
INVESTMENT

Capital investment by industry sector, $ million						TABLE 6
	1997	1998	1999	2000	2001	2002
Total capital investment	63.8	58.2	18.9	235.6	187.5	121.8
Including major industries (% of total)						
Industry	20.9	11.7	14.5	2.3	1.7	2.3
Agriculture and forestry	13.2	8.4	11.3	1.2	1.2	2.7
Construction	0.8	0.7	1.5	0.1	1.6	–
Transport and communications	25.4	56.9	47.8	95.1	87.9	85.5
Trade and public catering	0.6	0.3	–	–	0.4	–
Other	39.1	22.0	24.9	1.3	7.2	9.5

5.3. MAJOR ENTERPRISES
(INCLUDING ENTERPRISES
WITH FOREIGN INVESTMENT)
As of January 1, 2002, the Republic hosted 1,089 companies with foreign investment.

5.4. MOST ATTRACTIVE
SECTORS FOR INVESTMENT
The Republic has accorded priority status to the development of its agricultural processing sector.

Kalmykia has significant potential for the production of environmentally clean agricultural and food products.

5.5. CURRENT LEGISLATION ON INVESTOR
TAX EXEMPTIONS AND PRIVILEGES
The Government of the Republic of Kalmykia is consistently pursuing a policy of improving the Republic's investment climate. The Republic has introduced preferential taxation for investors and adopted the Republic of Kalmykia's Law On Investment Activity in the Republic of

Largest enterprises of the Republic of Kalmykia			TABLE 7
COMPANY	SECTOR	2002 SALES, $ MILLION*	2002 NET PROFIT, $ MILLION*
OAO Kalmgaz	Natural gas	0.7	0.05
OAO Aquaplus	Food and beverages	1.1	0.6

*Estimates of the Government of the Republic of Kalmykia

Kalmykia in the Form of Capital Investment, which envisages tax privileges to investors. The new draft law On Investment Activity in the Republic of Kalmykia aims to regulate issues related to investor rights protection, create an investment infrastructure, and develop an annual investment program. The Republic has established a system of continuous monitoring of promising investment projects, and created conditions conducive to the development of small enterprise, including safeguarding of interests, provision of incentives, and methodological and consulting assistance.

5.6. FEDERAL AND REGIONAL ECONOMIC AND SOCIAL DEVELOPMENT PROGRAMS FOR THE REPUBLIC OF KALMYKIA

Federal targeted programs. The Russia's South federal targeted program is of major importance to the Republic as one of its objectives is the construction of a highway route linking Astrakhan to Makhachkala via the Republic.

Regional programs. The Government of the Republic of Kalmykia has developed and approved a Republican targeted program for Development of the Republic of Kalmykia's Fishing Industry through 2005. The program aims to increase efficiency of natural resource use, ensure reproduction and protection of fish resources, reconstruct and revamp fish breeding farms, reconstruct the existing ponds, refurbish fixed assets of companies and fishing collective farms on the basis of broad implementation of science and technology solutions, and increase quality and expand product range.

The Republic is currently implementing a Presidential Program entitled The Revival of Traditional Pasture Livestock Breeding, 2001–2010, which aims to develop pasture breeding of the four traditional species of livestock in the Republic: cattle, horses, fat tail sheep, and camels.

As a result of implementation of the Development of the Milk Horse Breeding in the Republic of Kalmykia, 2001-2005 program, the Republic is expecting to increase output of the koumiss drink used for medical treatment purposes.

The Republic has underway the program for Development of the Tourism Activity in the Republic of Kalmykia 2001–2005.

6. INVESTMENT PROJECTS

Industry sector and project description	1) Expected results 2) Amount and term of investment 3) Form of financing[1] 4) Documentation[2]	Contact information
1	2	3

OIL		
34R001 Construction of an oil refinery. Project goal: to refine oil.	■ ● ▲ 1) Unleaded gasoline – 200,000 tons, aviation kerosene – 30,000 tons, diesel and boiler fuel – 250,000 tons, high quality wax and liquefied methane – 20,000 tons 2) $13.1 million/3 years 3) L, E 4) FS	Kalmykia Republican Department of Natural Resources and Environment of the RF Ministry of Natural Resources 4, ul. Lermontova, Elista, Republic of Kalmykia, 358000 Phone: (84722) 53 403 Bata Sodmanovich Khulkhachiev, Head of the Department

[1] L – Loan, E – Equity, Leas. – Leasing, JV – Joint Venture
[2] BP – Business Plan, FS – Feasibility Study

III

SOUTHERN FEDERAL DISTRICT

1	2	3

34R002

■ ● ▲

| Construction of a small oil refinery. Project goal: to refine oil. | 1) 100,000 tons per year
2) $22 million/10 months
3) L, E
4) FS | ZAO Kalmpetrol Oil Company
20, ul. Pushkina, Elista,
Republic of Kalmykia, 358000
Phone: (095) 733 9921,
(84722) 52 108
Fax: (095) 733 9921, (84722) 50 745
E-mail: kalmpetrol@elista.ru
Gennady Petrovich Kyukeev, CEO |

CONSTRUCTION MATERIALS

34R003

■ ● ▲

| Production of small-sized building blocks from cellular lime concrete. Project goal: to produce small-sized building blocks. | 1) 40,000 cubic meters per year
2) $0.6 million/3 years
3) L, E
4) FS | State Unitary Company Elista Building Materials Company
East Industrial Zone, Elista,
Republic of Kalmykia, 358000
Phone: (84722) 52 171
Andrei Meltovich Nemgirov,
Director |

LIGHT INDUSTRY

34R004

■ ● ◆

| Construction of the second unit of the Arschi Leather Plant. Project goal: to produce leather. | 1) Revenue of $3.6 million per year
2) $1.4 million/2 years
3) L, E
4) BP | OAO Arschi Leather Plant
North Industrial Zone, Elista,
Republic of Kalmykia, 358000
Phone: (84722) 20 657
Valery Kimovich Burlutkin, CEO |

FOOD AND BEVERAGES

34R005

■ ● ▲

| Construction of a baby food production unit. Project goal: to produce baby food. | 1) 15 tons per shift (milk equivalent)
2) $0.9 million/2 years
3) L, E
4) FS | State Unitary Company Kalmagropromstroiproject
15, ul. N. Ochirova, Elista,
Republic of Kalmykia, 358000
Phone: (84722) 64 221
Lyubov Erendzgenovna Kornusova,
Director |

34R006

● ◆

| Reconstruction of workshops at a meat cannery. Project goal: to produce canned meat. | 1) 2.5 million cans and 1,500 tons of sausage per year, revenue of $4.2 million per year
2) $0.7 million/6 months
3) L
4) BP | OAO Meat Cannery Arshan
Arshan, Republic of Kalmykia,
358000
Phone: (84722) 61 700, 60 794
Valery Alexeevich Dzhapov, CEO |

AGRICULTURE

34R007

● ▲

| Development of pasture cattle breeding. Project goal: to revive pasture cattle breeding in the Republic. | 1) Livestock – up to 3,700 tons per year (starting from 2006)
2) $3.2 million/6 years
3) L
4) FS | State Pasture Pedigree Company
83, ul. Y. Klykova, Elista,
Republic of Kalmykia, 358000
Phone: (84722) 52 989
Tseden Badmaevich Tyurbeev,
Director |

1	2	3

TRANSPORT INFRASTRUCTURE

34R008

Construction of a seaport at Lagan.
Project goal: to transport freight
and passengers.

● ▲

1) Turnover – 4,372 vessels per year;
   freight turnover – 20 million
   tons per year; passenger turnover –
   up to 22 million people per year
2) $703.1 million/2 years
3) L
4) FS

Ministry of Transport
of the Republic of Kalmykia
Office 406, City Chess Hall,
Shakhmat, Republic of Kalmykia,
358014
Phone: (84722) 20 732
Yury Sergeevich Olzeev,
Deputy Minister

34R009

Reconstruction of the Elista airport.
Project goal: to increase the airport's
throughput.

■ ● ◆

1) Up to 25,000 people per year;
   freight transshipment –
   up to 20 tons per year
2) $7.3 million/5 years
3) L, E
4) BP

Federal State Unitary Company Elista
United Aviation Detachment
Airport, Elista,
Republic of Kalmykia, 358000
Phone: (84722) 53 350
Yury Maximovich Kokuev,
Director

HOTEL BUSINESS, TOURISM, AND RECREATION

34R010

National tourist and entertainment
yurt center Jangarland.
Project goal: to provide tourist services.

■ ● ◆

1) Up to 67,000 people per year
2) $3.2 million/5 years
3) L, E
4) BP

Ministry of of Youth, Tourism, and
Sports of the Republic of Kalmykia
249, ul. Lenina, Elista,
Republic of Kalmykia, 358000
Phone: (84722) 53 383
Fax (84722) 62 970
E-mail: minmol@rambler.ru
Sheveldan Naranovich Dzhimbeev,
Minister

III

SOUTHERN FEDERAL DISTRICT

35. REPUBLIC OF KARACHAYEVO-CHERKESSIA [09]

ECONOMIC MAP

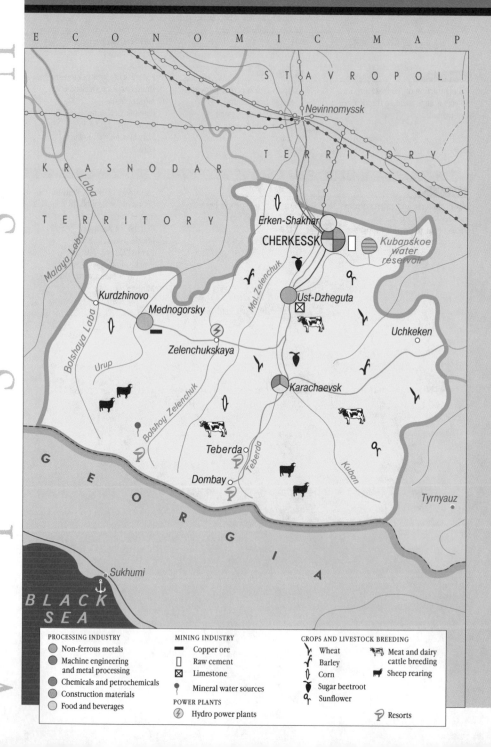

STAVROPOL

Nevinnomyssk

KRASNODAR

TERRITORY

Laba

Malaya Laba

TERRITORY

Erken-Shakhar

CHERKESSK

Kubanskoe water reservoir

Kurdzhinovo

Mednogorsky

Bolshaya Laba

Urup

Zelenchukskaya

Mol. Zelenchuk

Ust-Dzheguta

Uchkeken

Bolshoy Zelenchuk

Karachaevsk

Teberda

Teberda

Dombay

Kuban

Tyrnyauz

G E O R G I A

Sukhumi

BLACK SEA

PROCESSING INDUSTRY
- Non-ferrous metals
- Machine engineering and metal processing
- Chemicals and petrochemicals
- Construction materials
- Food and beverages

MINING INDUSTRY
- ▬ Copper ore
- ☐ Raw cement
- ⊠ Limestone
- ● Mineral water sources

POWER PLANTS
- ⚡ Hydro power plants

CROPS AND LIVESTOCK BREEDING
- Wheat
- Barley
- Corn
- Sugar beetroot
- Sunflower
- Meat and dairy cattle breeding
- Sheep rearing
- ⚓ Resorts

The Republic of Karachayevo-Cherkessia lies in the foothills of the North West Caucasus, near the silver-sloped Mount Elbrus. Covering a total area of 14,100 square kilometers, the Republic is populated by 440,000 people representing 89 different ethnic groups. Its mild climate, natural beauty, and the hospitality and warmth of its people have earned the Republic the reputation of an idyllic land of snowy mountains, azure lakes, fast-flowing mountain rivers, and lush Alpine meadows. Karachayevo-Cherkessia is the place of pilgrimage for everybody who likes and values the natural beauty. The Republic is famous not only for its natural beauty however, but also for its hard-working people who have turned it into a region with developed industry and agriculture.

Small-scale power stations have been built on the Kuban, Bolshoi Zelenchuk, and Maly Zelenchuk rivers. A thermal power station has also been launched in the Republic. Thousands of kilometers of power lines have been strung across the Republic to harness the abundant hydro resources of Karachayevo-Cherkessia. The Great Stavropol Canal delivers water from the Republic to the Stavropol Territory.

A network of roads connects the Republic to the Krasnodar and Stavropol Territories and the Mineralniye Vody Airport.

The welfare of the Republic's population depends on a favorable investment climate in the Republic. The Republic is currently conducting negotiations on the development of its timber and thermal and mineral water sectors and the exploration of its abundant deposits of ore, gold, coal, granite, marble, and other minerals.

The economic development of the Republic and improvement of living standards will underpin peace and law and order in the Northern Caucasus Region, and, consequently, contribute to the prosperity and prestige of the Russian state as a whole.

Mustafa Batdiyev,
PRESIDENT OF THE REPUBLIC
OF KARACHAYEVO-CHERKESSIA

III

SOUTHERN FEDERAL DISTRICT

384

1. GENERAL INFORMATION

1.1. GEOGRAPHY

Situated in southern Russia in the foothills and mountains of the Great Caucasus range, the Republic of Karachayevo-Cherkessia covers a total area of 14,100 square kilometers, with some 80% of it situated in the mountainous area. To the west, the Republic borders the Krasnodar Territory, to the north and north-east – the Stavropol Territory, to the east – the Republic of Kabardino-Balkaria, and to the south – Georgia.

1.2. CLIMATE

The Republic of Karachayevo-Cherkessia enjoys a temperate continental climate. The average air temperature in January is $-3.2°C$, rising to $+20.6°C$ in July. The average annual precipitation ranges from 550 mm in lowlands to 2,500 mm in the mountains. The growing season lasts some 150 days. Black earth soils, alpine-forest brown soils, and alpine-meadow soils prevail in the Republic.

1.3. POPULATION

According to preliminary 2002 census results, the population of the Republic totaled 440,000 people. The average population density is 31.2 people per square kilometer. The economically active population amounts to 168,000 people. While 2002 official unemployment level stands at 1.3%, the actual rate is 18.6%.

Demographically speaking, some 58.1% are of working age, 22.9% are below the statutory working age, and 19% are beyond the statutory working age.

The Republic's ethnic mix is 31.2% Karachay, 9.7% Cherkess, 42.4% Russian, 6.6% Abazin, 3.2% Nogay, and 6.9% other ethnic groups.

As of 2002, the Republic's major urban centers were Cherkessk with 116,400 inhabitants, Ust-Dzheguta with 31,300 inhabitants, and Karachaevsk with 29,900 inhabitants.

Population							TABLE 1
	1992	1997	1998	1999	2000	2001	2002
Total population, '000	428	434	434	433	431	431	440
Economically active population, '000	209	172	175	172	184	185	168

2. ADMINISTRATION

House of Government, pl. Lenina, Cherkessk, Republic of Karachayevo-Cherkessia, 369000
Phone: (87822) 57 354; fax: (87822) 55 346
E-mail: inform@karachay-cherkes.ru; http://www.karachay-cherkes.ru

NAME	POSITION	CONTACT INFORMATION
Mustafa Azret-Alievich BATDIYEV	President of the Republic of Karachayevo-Cherkessia	Phone: (87822) 54 011 Fax: (87822) 52 980
Vera Mikhailovna MOLDAVANOVA	Vice President of the Republic of Karachayevo-Cherkessia	Phone: (87822) 54 020
Ruslan Alievich KAZANOKOV	Chairman of the Government of the Republic of Karachayevo-Cherkessia	Phone: (87822) 54 008, 54 845
Zaur Chapaevich ADZHIEV	Deputy Chairman of the Republican Government for Coordination of Economic Development, Financial, Tax, and Customs Policy, Enterprise and External Economic Links, and Investment Policy	Phone: (87822) 54 257
Boris Khadzhi-Akhmatovich GOCHIYAEV	Deputy Chairman of the Republican Government for Coordination of Natural Resources, Food Policy, and the Agroindustrial Sector	Phone: (87822) 53 342
Anatoly Konstantinovich BARKOV	Deputy Chairman of the Republican Government for Coordination of Industry, Transport, Communications, Fuel, and Energy	Phone: (87822) 52 288

3. ECONOMIC POTENTIAL

3.1. 1997–2002 GROSS
REGIONAL PRODUCT (GRP).
INDUSTRY BREAKDOWN

The 2002 gross regional product amounted to $286.9 million, which constitutes 13.2% growth year-on-year. The growth was achieved thanks to the development of the machine engineering, chemicals, petrochemicals, and food and beverages sectors. Per capita GRP amounted to $588 in 2001 and $652 in 2002.

GRP trends in 1997–2002						*TABLE 2*
	1997	1998	1999	2000	2001*	2002*
GRP in current prices, $ million	468.8	288.4	183.3	206.0	253.4	286.9

*Estimates of the Karachayevo-Cherkessia Republican Government

GRP industry breakdown in 1997–2002, % of total						*TABLE 3*
	1997	1998	1999	2000	2001*	2002*
GRP	100.0	100.0	100.0	100.0	100.0	100.0
Industry	21.6	19.4	18.4	18.5	18.0	19.6
Agriculture and forestry	21.6	21.7	29.5	28.0	24.9	26.5
Construction	7.5	8.8	5.5	4.4	8.9	8.9
Transport and communications	2.6	3.8	2.9	3.2	3.5	3.7
Trade and public catering	9.7	12.0	12.5	14.1	13.9	14.3
Other	29.5	33.3	24.6	27.2	26.8	23.4
Net taxes on output	7.5	1.0	6.6	4.6	4.0	3.6

*Estimates of the Karachayevo-Cherkessia Republican Government

3.2. MAJOR ECONOMIC
GROWTH PROJECTIONS

The Republic of Karachayevo-Cherkessia is implementing the Program for the Social and Economic Development of the Republic of Kara-chaevo-Cherkessia, 1999–2000 and through 2005, which determines the following objectives:

The development, reconstruction, and technical refurbishment of processing enterprises in the metals and agricultural sectors and the development of recreational services and tourism;

Support to small enterprise in the light industry, food and beverages, building materials, construction, transport, and the residential and communal sectors;

Industrial infrastructure development; and

The reconstruction, technical upgrading, or diversification of major machine engineering, electrical, and radio industrial companies, including former military industrial enterprises.

As a result of this set of comprehensive measures, GRP is expected to grow to $330.4 million in 2003 (3.5% growth year-on-year), industrial output will increase to $173 million (6% growth), and agricultural output will reach $160.5 million (5% growth).

3.3. INDUSTRIAL OUTPUT IN 1997–2002
FOR MAJOR SECTORS OF ECONOMY

The leading industrial sectors of the Republic of Karachayevo-Cherkessia are chemicals and petrochemicals, food and beverages, building materials, and energy. Their combined share of total industrial output is 91.3%.

Chemicals and petrochemicals. The sector accounts for 27% of total industrial output. The sector produces paint and varnish, synthetic resins, formalin, synthetic glue, detergents, and industrial rubber goods. Major companies within the sector are OAO Resinotechnika and OAO Z.S. Tsakhilov Red Labor Banner Order Cherkessk Chemical Production Company.

Food and beverages. The sector accounts for 27% of total industrial output. The largest companies are OAO Erken-Shakharsky Sugar Mill, OOO Farm Saturn, OOO Firm Mercury, ZAO Visma, OAO Food Technologies, and OAO Caucasian Flora.

Construction material. The share of this sector is 20.8%. The companies produce Portland cement, sulphate cement, building and industrial lime, cement and sand units, roof and sidewalk tiles, and other goods for civilian and residential construction. Major companies include OAO Kavkazcement, ZAO Izvestnyak, and ZAO Strommekh.

Agriculture. The sector accounts for 26.5% of GRP. The Republic focuses on beef and dairy cattle breeding and sheep breeding. The Republic grows wheat, corn, barley, sugar beet, and sunflower.

III

SOUTHERN FEDERAL DISTRICT

Industry breakdown of industrial output in 1997–2002, % of total						*TABLE 4*
	1997	1998	1999	2000	2001	2002*
Industry	100.0	100.0	100.0	100.0	100.0	100.0
Chemicals and petrochemicals	20.5	22.0	33.3	36.9	31.7	27.0
Food and beverages	16.8	18.7	21.3	19.6	25.9	27.0
Construction materials	33.3	31.4	20.7	15.5	16.6	20.8
Energy	18.1	16.0	12.3	13.8	15.0	16.5
Machine engineering and metal processing	5.5	4.8	4.9	6.0	4.7	3.9
Non-ferrous metals	1.6	2.8	4.2	5.4	4.0	3.8
Forestry, timber, and pulp and paper	1.8	2.0	2.0	1.4	0.8	0.8
Light industry	1.0	1.2	0.4	0.4	0.6	0.5
Flour, cereals, and mixed fodder	0.5	0.6	0.5	0.5	0.3	0.3
Fuel	0.5	0.1	–	–	–	–

*Estimates of the Karachayevo-Cherkessia Republican Government

III

SOUTHERN FEDERAL DISTRICT

3.4. FUEL AND ENERGY BALANCE (OUTPUT AND CONSUMPTION PER RESOURCE)

The Republic meets its demand for electricity by purchasing electricity at the Federal Wholesale Electricity Market from the Stavropol and Nevin-nomysskaya Hydroelectric Power Stations and Stavropolenergo's Kuban HEPS system. Two units of the Zelenchukskaya HEPS launched in 1999 and 2002 with a total capacity of 160 MW are owned by RAO UES of Russia.

Fuel and energy sector production and consumption trends, 1997–2002						*TABLE 5*
	1997	1998	1999	2000	2001	2002*
Electricity output, billion kWh	0.02	0.02	0.06	0.1	0.1	0.2
Electricity consumption, billion kWh	1.5	1.4	1.4	1.2	1.2	1.2
Natural gas consumption, million cubic meters	536.7	526.3	490.7	544.9	519.9	929.9

*Estimates of the Karachayevo-Cherkessia Republican Government

3.5. TRANSPORT INFRASTRUCTURE

Roads. The Republic of Karachayevo-Cherkessia has 1,887 kilometers of public highway. The Military-Sukhumi highway, which links Karachayevsk, Teberda, and Dombai, begins in the Republic. Road transport accounts for some 76% of all freight turnover. Plans are afoot to design and construct a 430 kilometer road from Kislovodsk to Sochi, of which 157 kilometers will be laid in the Republic.

Railroads. The Republic has 51 kilometers of railroads. The railroad branch Cherkessk – Ust-Dzheguda crosses the Republic and forms part of the North Caucasian railroad network.

3.6. MAIN NATURAL RESOURCES: RESERVES AND EXTRACTION IN 2002

The main natural resources of the Republic of Karachayevo-Cherkessia are coal, lead, zinc, tungsten and molybdenum ore (the Ktiteberdin-skoye deposit), copper (the Urupskoye deposit), and building materials (quality marble at Teberda, granite, and quartz sand), and gold.

Recreational resources. The Republic's resorts and recreational areas located near Narzan mineral water springs and thermal springs, account for a large part of its economic potential. The Republic's unique nature and its mountains provide opportunities for the development of mountain climbing and tourism. Teberda, Dombai, and Arkhyz are renowned centers for downhill skiing and mountaineering.

4. TRADE OPPORTUNITIES

4.1. MAIN GOODS
PRODUCED IN THE REGION

Chemicals and petrochemicals. In 2002, the Republic produced 44,200 tons of paint and varnish, 10,000 tons of synthetic resins and plastic, 1,844,000 rubber belts, 233 tons of non-molded industrial rubber goods, and 679 tons of molded industrial rubber goods.

Construction materials. 2002 cement output reached 1.3 million tons, 5.5 million conventional bricks of wall materials, 54,700 tons of construction lime, 436,100 tons of industrial lime, 26,700 tons of gypsum, and 212,000 cubic meters of non-metal construction materials.

Food and beverages. In 2002, the Republic produced 414 tons of sausage, 11 tons of fat, 100 tons of butter, 219,000 conventional cans of canned meat, 61,600 tons of granulated sugar, 3,800 tons of yeast, 2,200 tons of bread and bakery products, 47 tons of confectionery, 53 tons of pasta, 48 tons of vegetable oil, 709,000 decaliters of vodka and liquor, 28,200 decaliters of fruit and berry wine, 151,000 decaliters of beer, 2.1 million decaliters of non-alcoholic beverages, and 10.7 million decaliters of mineral water.

Agriculture. In 2002, the Republic's enterprises produced 171,200 tons of grain, 162,200 tons of sugar beet, 4,900 tons of sunflower seed, 166,800 tons of potatoes, 64,300 tons of vegetables, 253 tons of meat (including sub-products), and 31,200 tons of dairy products.

4.2. EXPORTS, INCLUDING EXTRA-CIS

The Republic's exports to extra-CIS countries amounted to $0.5 million in 2000, and exports to CIS – $3.1 million. The corresponding figures for 2001 were $0.5 million and $3.9 million, and $0.8 million and $4.4 million for 2002.

The main types of goods exported by the Republic in 2002 were food and raw materials – $0.3 million, chemicals, including rubber – $3.2 million, and machinery, equipment, and transport vehicles – $0.2 million. Major importers of the Region's products include Greece, Bulgaria, Iran, Turkey, Kazakhstan, Moldova, Ukraine, and Georgia.

4.3. IMPORTS,
INCLUDING EXTRA-CIS

2000 imports from extra-CIS amounted to $1.9 million, and imports from CIS – $2.4 million. The corresponding figures for 2001 were $6.4 million and $2 million, and $5.2 million and $1.3 million for 2002.

The main types of goods imported by the Republic in 2002 were food and raw materials – $0.1 million, chemicals (rubber) – $1.4 million, textiles and footwear – $0.6 million, and machinery, equipment, and transport vehicles – $3.2 million. The main exporters to the Republic are Belgium, the Czech Republic, Finland, France, Germany, Italy, New Zealand, Armenia, Georgia, Kazakhstan, Ukraine, and Moldova.

4.4. MAJOR REGIONAL
EXPORT AND IMPORT ENTITIES

Due to the specific features of trade in the Republic of Karachayevo-Cherkessia, mainly industrial companies perform export and import operations.

5. INVESTMENT OPPORTUNITIES

5.1. INVESTMENTS
IN 1992–2002
(BY INDUSTRY SECTOR),
INCLUDING FOREIGN INVESTMENTS

The following factors determine the investment appeal of the Republic of Karachayevo-Cherkessia:

• Resorts in areas of unique natural beauty (the Teberda National Park);

• Considerable reserves of building materials;

• Mineral water springs with various chemical compositions and raw materials for the pharmaceuticals and perfume and cosmetics industries.

5.2. CAPITAL INVESTMENT

Energy accounts for the lion's share of capital investment (35% of total investment) owing to the construction of the Zelenchukskaya HEPS funded by RAO UES of Russia.

5.3. MAJOR
ENTERPRISES (INCLUDING
ENTERPRISES WITH
FOREIGN INVESTMENT)

The Republic hosts 39 large companies, most of which represent the food and beverages sector (13 companies), construction materials (eight companies), machine engineering (five enterprises), and electronic industry (four enterprises).

5.4. MOST ATTRACTIVE
SECTORS FOR INVESTMENT

Priority areas for investment include the Dombai – Teberda – Arkhyz vacation and recreation center, and the development of deposits of copper concentrate, iron ore, tungsten, clay, non-metal materials, Narzan mineral waters, and thermal waters.

III

SOUTHERN FEDERAL DISTRICT

Capital investment by industry sector, $ million						TABLE 6
	1997	1998	1999	2000	2001	2002
Total capital investment	98.8	55.5	23.5	22.6	46.7	46.4
Including major industries (% of total)						
Industry	40.0	21.3	44.1	24.9	48.8	36.5
Agriculture and forestry	3.9	4.3	9.5	13.7	12.8	23.3
Construction	3.9	0.1	0.7	0.2	0.1	2.3
Transport and communications	7.8	5.4	18.4	18.3	11.6	12.8
Trade and public catering	0.4	0.1	1.9	10.1	0.3	1.0
Other	44.0	68.8	25.4	32.8	26.4	24.1

Foreign investment trends in 1996–2002						TABLE 7
	1996–1997	1998	1999	2000	2001	2002
Foreign investment, $ million	0.1	3.0	–	0.1	–	–
Including FDI, $ million	0.1	3.0	–	0.1	–	–

Largest enterprises of the Republic of Karachayevo-Cherkessia	TABLE 8
COMPANY	SECTOR
OAO Zelenchukskaya HEPS	Energy
OAO Tsakhilov Cherkessk Chemical Production Enterprise	Chemicals and petrochemicals
OAO Resinotekhnika	Chemicals and petrochemicals
OAO Low Voltage Instrument Plant	Machine engineering
OAO Kholodmash	Machine engineering
OAO Kavkazcement	Construction materials
ZAO Izvestnyak	Construction materials
OOO Mercury Firm	Food and beverages
OOO Saturn Farm	Food and beverages

III

SOUTHERN FEDERAL DISTRICT

5.5. CURRENT LEGISLATION ON INVESTOR TAX EXEMPTIONS AND PRIVILEGES

Investors operating in the Republic of Karachayevo-Cherkessia are protected by the legislation of the Russian Federation. In 2003, the Government of the Republic of Karachayevo-Cherkessia plans to adopt the Law of the Republic of Karachayevo-Cherkessia On Investment Activity in the Republic of Karachayevo-Cherkessia.

5.6. FEDERAL AND REGIONAL ECONOMIC AND SOCIAL DEVELOPMENT PROGRAMS FOR THE REPUBLIC OF KARACHAYEVO-CHERKESSIA

Federal targeted programs. The Russia's South federal targeted program plays an important role in im-proving the economic and social efficiency of the Repub-lic. In 2002–2006, the following funding will be allocated under the Program: tourism, recreation and resort services – $7.8 million, communications and information – $0.1 million, healthcare, education and culture – $7.6 mil-lion, agroindustrial sector – $1 million, improvement of residential and communal infrastructure – $2 million, gas network expansion – $1.7 million, and industry – $0.5 million.

Regional programs. The Republican Govern-ment is financing several targeted programs. The major programs are The Development of Postal Services in the Republic of Karachayevo-Cherkessia, 1995–2005 (2002 financing amounted to $0.03 million), The Fight against Tuberculosis, 1999–2000 extended to 2004 ($0.08 million), The Development and Preservation of the Culture, Arts, and Cinematography of the Republic of Karacha-yevo-Cherkessia, 2001–2005 ($0.03 million), Diabetes, 2002–2004 ($0.25 million), So-cial Support to the Disabled in the Republic of Karachayevo-Cherkessia, 2002–2005 ($0.23 mil-lion), Prevention of Child Neglect and Juvenile Delinquency, 2002–2005 ($0.32 million), and Disabled Children, 2002–2004 ($0.02 million).

Regional entities responsible for raising investment		TABLE 9
ENTITY	ADDRESS	PHONE, FAX, E-MAIL
South Russian Investment Assistance Fund	Office 405, 406, pr. Lenina, Rostov-on-Don, 344038	Phone: (8632) 72 8708, 72 8732 Fax: (8632) 72 8767

6. INVESTMENT PROJECTS

Industry sector and project description	1) Expected results 2) Amount and term of investment 3) Form of financing[1] 4) Documentation[2]	Contact information
1	2	3

HOTELS AND TOURISM		
35R001 ■ ● ★ ◆		
Development of the Dombai-Teberda-Arkhyz vacation and recreation center, and reconstruction of old and construction of new roads. Project goal: to renovate and develop the Dombai-Teberda-Arkhyz center and expand tourism services.	1) Revenue of $30 million per year 2) $14.2 million/1 year 3) L ($7.1 million), Leas., E 4) BP in progress	State Committee on Physical Culture, Sports, and Tourism of the Republic of Karachayevo-Cherkessia 1, pl. Kirova, Cherkessk, Republic of Karachayevo-Cherkessia, 369000 Phone: (87822) 57 368, (87822) 65 025, 60 785 E-mail: gupkavkaz@mail.ru http://www.alanturism.com Murat Alibievich Laitanov, Chairman of the Committee; Kazbek Zaurovich Appoev, Head of Tourism Department

III

SOUTHERN FEDERAL DISTRICT

---

[1] L – Loan, E – Equity, Leas. – Leasing, JV – Joint Venture
[2] BP – Business Plan, FS – Feasibility Study

36. REPUBLIC OF NORTH OSSETIA – ALANIA [15]

ECONOMIC MAP

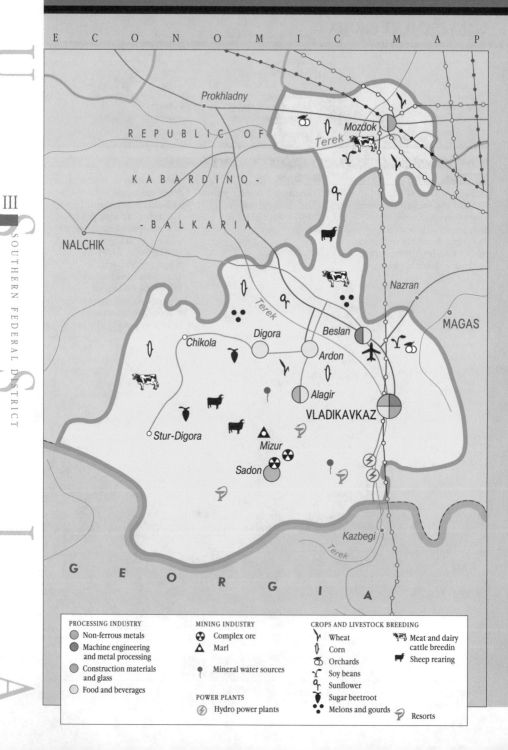

Prokhladny

REPUBLIC OF

KABARDINO-

-BALKARIA

NALCHIK

Mozdok

Terek

Nazran

MAGAS

Digora

Chikola

Beslan

Ardon

Alagir

VLADIKAVKAZ

Stur-Digora

Mizur

Sadon

Kazbegi

Terek

GEORGIA

PROCESSING INDUSTRY
- Non-ferrous metals
- Machine engineering and metal processing
- Construction materials and glass
- Food and beverages

POWER PLANTS
- Hydro power plants

MINING INDUSTRY
- Complex ore
- Marl
- Mineral water sources

CROPS AND LIVESTOCK BREEDING
- Wheat
- Corn
- Orchards
- Soy beans
- Sunflower
- Sugar beetroot
- Melons and gourds
- Meat and dairy cattle breedin
- Sheep rearing
- Resorts

Major social and economic development indicators and official statistics demonstrate that the Republic of North Ossetia – Alania has shaken off its erstwhile reputation as one of the most backward regions of Russia and is gradually taking its deserved place among Russia's regions.

Industrial output has grown by over a third over the past four years. Agriculture has improved considerably also, and the Republic has created the pre-requisites for full-on recovery of its agricultural output.

The Republic sees its task going forward as one of progressing from stabilization to sustainable and progressive social, economic, and cultural development.

The Republic's economic policy calls for steady growth in all industrial spheres, more efficient state property management, the development of small enterprise, enhanced budgetary and tax discipline, and improved legislation.

The Republic has laid the prerequisites for its economic development. Important social and economic decisions have been taken at the federal and regional levels. The federal government has approved the Russia's South federal targeted program, with a budget of over $31.5 million to be allocated to the Republic over a five-year period.

Several months ago, we adopted a regional program for comprehensive social and economic development in 2003 and through 2005.

As President of the Republic of North Ossetia – Alania, I promised to create a business friendly climate in the Republic, and I believe we have accomplished certain achievements in this area: businesses in dozens of areas of enterprise now enjoy lower tax rates than in any other region of Russia.

These measures, however, are not exhaustive. I propose maintaining an open and constructive dialogue between the Republic's authorities and business circles with a view to raising our relationship to a new level. The Republic needs to facilitate investment by introducing new legal acts and initiatives aimed at encouraging investment, lending, and banking activity.

According to the Republic's estimates, mid-term investment is expected to grow by 13–15% a year. The focus will be on resorts and tourism. We are current-ly completing the preparation of a program for resort, rehabilitation, and tourism development in the North Caucasus area.

I urge potential investors to have confidence in the Republic's undertaking to provide a favorable climate for industrial and other entrepreneurial activity.

Alexander Dzasokhov,
PRESIDENT OF THE REPUBLIC OF NORTH OSSETIA – ALANIA

1. GENERAL INFORMATION

1.1. GEOGRAPHY

The Republic of North Ossetia – Alania covers a total area of 8,000 square kilometers. The Republic is situated in the south of Russia on the northern slopes of the Great Caucasus range. To the north, the Republic borders the Stavropol Territory, to the north-east – the Chechen Republic, to the east – the Republic of Ingushetia, to the west – the Republic of Kabardino-Balkaria, and to the south – Georgia. Some 48% of its territory is covered by mountains.

1.2. CLIMATE

The Republic enjoys a temperate continental climate. January air temperatures average –1.2°C, rising to +25.3°C in July. Average annual precipitation reaches 500 mm. The growing season lasts for some 190 days.

1.3. POPULATION

According to preliminary 2002 census results, the Republic's population totaled 710,000 people. The average population density is 88.8 people per square kilometer. The economically active population amounts to 352,000 people. 2002 official unemployment stood at 1%. The actual rate is 16.7%.

Demographically speaking, some 57.3% are of working age, 21% are below the statutory working age, and 21.7% are beyond the statutory working age.

The Republic's ethnic mix is 53% Ossetin, 29.9% Russian, 5.2% Ingush, 2.2% Armenian, and 9.7% other ethnic groups.

As of 2002, the Republic of North Ossetia – Alania's major urban centers were Vladikavkaz with 315,100 inhabitants, Mozdok with 82,200 inhabitants, and Beslan with 53,300 inhabitants.

Population								TABLE 1
	1992	1997	1998	1999	2000	2001	2002
Total population, '000	694	664	662	663	670	677	710
Economically active population, '000	356	288	275	309	328	343	352

2. ADMINISTRATION

1, pl. Svobody, Vladikavkaz, Republic of North Ossetia – Alania, 362038
Phone: (8672) 53 3524; fax: (8672) 74 9248
E-mail: app-info@osetia.ru; http://alania.osetia.ru

NAME	POSITION	CONTACT INFORMATION
Alexander Sergeevich DZASOKHOV	President of the Republic of North Ossetia – Alania	Phone: (8672) 53 3516 Fax: (8672) 53 3747 http://president.osetia.ru/resp.htm
Mikhail Mikhailovich SHATALOV	Chairman of the Government of the Republic of North Ossetia – Alania	Phone: (8672) 53 3556 Fax: (8672) 74 3656
Konstantin Borisovich URTAEV	First Deputy Chairman of the Government of the Republic of North Ossetia – Alania, Minister of Finance	Phone: (8672) 53 3994 Fax: (8672) 74 8173
Valery Tazretovich BALIKOEV	Deputy Chairman of the Government of the Republic of North Ossetia – Alania, Minister of Economy	Phone: (8672) 53 6282 Fax: (8672) 53 7586
Vladimir Dzambolatovich TABOLOV	Head of the External Economic Relations Department of the Ministry of Economy of the Republic of North Ossetia – Alania	Phone: (8672) 53 3197 Fax: (8672) 74 6150 E-mail: vesrno@mail.ru
Nadezhda Petrovna KHOLINA	Head of the Department of Economic Analysis and Capital Construction Forecasting (in charge of investment activity)	Phone: (8672) 53 2957

3. ECONOMIC POTENTIAL

3.1. 1997–2002 GROSS REGIONAL PRODUCT (GRP). INDUSTRY BREAKDOWN

The 2002 gross regional product amounted to $545.4 million, which constitutes 14.3% growth year-on-year. The growth was achieved thanks to growth in machine engineering (up 27.5% on 2001), glass and porcelain (22.4%), chemicals (12%), timber, pulp, and paper (10.8%), food and beverages (7.1%), and energy (10.6%). Per capita GRP amounted to $706 in 2001 and $768 in 2002.

3.2. MAJOR ECONOMIC GROWTH PROJECTIONS

The Republic's Government has adopted a So-cial and Economic Development Program for the Republic of North Ossetia – Alania, 2002–2004. A priority area for the Republic's social and economic development is recreation and tourism, including the reconstruction

GRP trends in 1997–2002						TABLE 2
	1997	1998	1999	2000	2001*	2002*
GRP in current prices, $ million	586.2	418.1	309.5	415.6	477.2	545.4

*Estimates of the Government of the Republic of North Ossetia – Alania

GRP industry breakdown in 1997–2002, % of total						TABLE 3
	1997	1998	1999	2000	2001*	2002*
GRP	100.0	100.0	100.0	100.0	100.0	100.0
Industry	20.7	17.4	19.7	13.8	14.4	14.0
Agriculture and forestry	8.2	7.7	11.7	8.6	8.7	8.5
Construction	7.3	8.5	5.5	8.5	9.5	9.3
Transport and communications	7.1	6.1	4.7	3.7	4.0	4.1
Trade and public catering	16.0	18.3	21.0	18.0	19.8	19.1
Other	40.7	42.0	37.4	47.4	43.6	45.0

*Estimates of the Government of the Republic of North Ossetia – Alania

Industry breakdown of industrial output in 1997–2002, % of total						TABLE 4
	1997	1998	1999	2000	2001	2002*
Industry	100.0	100.0	100.0	100.0	100.0	100.0
Food and beverages	17.5	16.1	24.8	26.1	38.6	60.4
Non-ferrous metals	26.4	26.6	31.9	28.5	18.7	11.6
Energy	20.9	19.7	10.5	12.2	10.6	9.2
Machine engineering and metal processing	10.3	9.7	9.0	8.3	6.7	4.9
Glass and porcelain	4.3	4.7	4.2	4.2	4.3	3.4
Construction materials	8.6	6.9	5.0	3.9	6.1	2.8
Forestry, timber, and pulp and paper	2.7	2.9	2.8	3.9	4.3	2.4
Light industry	4.9	3.4	3.7	4.2	3.4	1.8
Chemicals and petrochemicals	1.1	1.4	1.7	2.3	2.1	0.7
Flour, cereals, and mixed fodder	1.8	0.7	1.4	2.5	1.5	0.4
Fuel	–	–	–	0.4	1.1	–
Ferrous metals	0.1	–	0.4	0.2	0.2	–

*Estimates of the Government of the Republic of North Ossetia – Alania

III

SOUTHERN FEDERAL DISTRICT

Fuel and energy sector production and consumption trends, 1997–2002						TABLE 5
	1997	1998	1999	2000	2001	2002*
Electricity output, billion kWh	0.4	0.3	0.3	0.3	0.3	0.3
Oil output (including gas concentrate), '000 tons	1.6	1.7	5.6	6.9	4.5	4.1
Electricity consumption, billion kWh	1.9	1.9	2.0	2.1	2.1	2.1
Natural gas consumption, million cubic meters	1,307.0	1,307.0	1,350.0	1,404.0	1,468.0	1,523.0

*Estimates of the Government of the Republic of North Ossetia – Alania

and upgrade of resorts, the construction of new resorts, the creation of state regulation mechanisms, a marketing, information, and human resource base, and the development of tourism infrastructure.

Agricultural objectives include the creation of a local food market, the launch of a system of state procurement for the Republic's food fund, extending business links with other regions, and greater penetration by the Republic's producers of other Russian and CIS markets.

3.3. INDUSTRIAL OUTPUT IN 1997–2002 FOR MAJOR SECTORS OF ECONOMY

The leading industrial sectors of the Republic of North Ossetia – Alania are food and beverages, non-ferrous metals, and energy. Their combined share of total output is 81.2%.

Food and beverages. The sector accounts for 60.4% of total industrial output. The main types of products are vodka, ethanol, cornstarch, syrup, glucose, dextrin, and corn oil. Major enterprises within the sector include State Unitary Company Vladikavkaz Liquor and Vodka Plant Terek, OAO Beslan Company, OAO Istok, OOO Atsamaz, ZAO Berd-Lavera, OAO Salyut, OAO Vladikavkaz Brewery and Non-Alcoholic Beverages Plant Daryal, and State Unitary Company Vladikavkaz Bakery and Macaroni Plant.

Non-ferrous metals. The sector accounts for 11.6% of total industrial output. The main types of goods produced include lead, zinc, sulphuric acid, copper vitriol, tungsten carbide, and hard and heavy alloys. The main companies operating in this sector include OAO Electrozinc, State Unitary Company Sadonsky Lead and Zinc Company, and OAO Pobedit.

Energy. The sector accounts for 9.2% of total industrial output. The Republic operates five hydroelectric power stations, including four stations that form part of OAO Sevkavkazenergo. Construction of a major HEP station is underway at Zaramagskaya.

Machine engineering and metal processing. The sector accounts for 4.9% of total industrial output. Enterprises in the sector focus on the production of automatic and pneumatic equipment for tractors, and radio and electronic goods, including resistors and electronic image converter tubes for night viewing devices. Major producers include OAO Magnet, OAO Electrocontactor, State Unitary Company Binom, State Unitary Company Gran, Federal State Unitary Company Razryad, OAO Topaz, OAO Ossetia Automobile Tractor Equipment Plant, and OAO Kristall.

Agriculture. Arable land covers 385,000 hectares, or 48.2% of the Republic's area, including 91,400 hectares of ploughed fields, 6,500 hectares of perennial crops, 21,600 hectares of hayfields, and 165,500 hectares of pastures. The Republic grows wheat, corn, sunflower, kenaf, soybean, sugar beet, and ether and oil-yielding crops. Dairy and beef cattle breeding is well developed.

3.4. FUEL AND ENERGY BALANCE (OUTPUT AND CONSUMPTION PER RESOURCE)

The Republic's hydroelectric power stations with a total capacity of 85.2 MW generate 350 million kWh of electricity per year, or 14% of the total amount of energy consumed in the Republic.

3.5. TRANSPORT INFRASTRUCTURE

Roads. The Republic has 2,300 kilometers of public highway. The Caucasus federal highway (Rostov-on-Don – Makhachkala), the Georgian Military Highway and the Trans-Caucasian highways pass through the Republic, providing access to Central Russia, the Caucasus states, Turkey, and Iran.

Railroads. The Republic has 144 kilometers of railroads. A section of North-Caucasian railroad and the Prokhladnaya – Mozdok – Gudermes branch line cross the Republic. In 2002, 1.9 million tons of freight was transported by rail.

Airports. The Republic is served by an international airport at Beslan, 20 kilometers from the capital.

Gas pipelines. The trunk gas pipelines Stavropol – Mozdok – Vladikavkaz – Tbilisi, Stavropol – Mozdok – Vladikavkaz – Yerevan, Stavropol – Mozdok – Grozny, and Stavropol – Mozdok – Beslan – Nalchik pass through the Republic. The total length of the Republic's trunk gas pipelines is 393.4 kilometers, plus 199 kilometers of branch pipeline, and 3,383.9 kilometers of distribution pipeline.

3.6. MAIN NATURAL RESOURCES: RESERVES AND EXTRACTION IN 2002

The Republic's main natural resources are oil, metal ores, dolomites, and mineral water springs.

Metal ore. The Republic is rich in zinc, lead, copper, and silver ores. The main deposits are the Sadonskoye, Zgidskoye, Arkhonskoye, and Kholstinskoye.

Non-metal mineral resources. The Republic has more than 40 deposits of granite (including the Tseiskoye, Buronskoye, Bugultinskoye, Daryalskoye, and Digorskoye), roofing shale, marble (the Dzhimarinskoye and Zaramagskoye), lime (the Melkhiorskoye, Baltiyskoye, Tarskoye, Chernorechenskoye, Fetkhuzskoye, and Bizskoye), dolomite, and marl.

Oil and natural gas. Oil fields are found in the northern part of the Republic, including the Zamankulskoye, Kharbizhinskoye, Akhlovskoye, and North Malgobekskoye fields with estimated total reserves of 56,800 tons of fuel, including 21,300 tons of oil and 35.5 billion cubic meters of natural gas.

Mineral water. The Republic has more than 300 sodium chloride, hydrocarbon chloride, sodium calcium, sulphate chloride, and hydrocarbon sulphate mineral water springs. Industrial reserves amount to some 15,000 cubic meters per day. The most valuable mineral waters are Karmadon, Ursdon, Fatima, Tib 1, and Tib 2.

Resorts and recreational reserves. The Republic has all the prerequisites for the development of tourism, mountain hiking, and downhill skiing. The Tamisk balneological resort and the Tseisky Canyon mountain recreational center are the most popular resorts. In the future, the Republic will be able to host up to 200,000 tourists, 600,000 visitors, and provide rehabilitation services to 50,000 people annually.

4. TRADE OPPORTUNITIES

4.1. MAIN GOODS
PRODUCED IN THE REGION
Food and beverages. Bakery and bread output in 2002 amounted to 23,000 tons, meat (including sub-products) – 2,200 tons, dairy products – 5,800 tons, and vegetable oil – 122 tons.

Agricultural products. 2002 output of grain totaled 250,100 tons, sunflower seed – 4,100 tons, 92.8 million eggs, 42,800 tons of vegetables, and 91,200 tons of potatoes.

4.2. EXPORTS, INCLUDING EXTRA-CIS
The Republic of North Ossetia – Alania's exports to extra-CIS countries amounted to $64.8 million in 2000. Exports to the CIS reached $2.3 million. The corresponding figures for 2001 were $63.5 million and $4.6 million, and $78.7 million and $11.8 million for 2002.

The main types of goods exported by the Republic of North Ossetia – Alania in 2002 were zinc and zinc goods ($55.7 million), boilers and equipment ($16 million), grain ($5.9 million), metals and metal ceramics ($1.2 million), lead and lead goods ($1.6 million), electrical machinery and equipment ($3.9 million), flour and cereals ($2.4 million), alcoholic and non-alcoholic beverages and vinegar ($2.4 million), instruments and cutlery ($0.6 million), dairy products, eggs, and honey ($0.6 million), salt, sulfur, and tiles ($0.4 million), mineral fuel, oil, and refinery products ($0.3 million), and fat, butter, and vegetable oil ($0.3 million).

Major importers of the Republic's products include Switzerland, Turkey, Slovakia, Spain, France, Ireland, Georgia, Kazakhstan, and Ukraine.

4.3. IMPORTS, INCLUDING EXTRA-CIS
2000 imports from extra-CIS countries amounted to $58.9 million. Imports from CIS countries reached $8.5 million. The corresponding figures for 2001 were $47.8 million and $20.2 million, and $35.8 million and $27.3 million for 2002.

The bulk of 2002 regional imports included ore, slag, and ash ($28.7 million), alcoholic and non-alcoholic beverages and vinegar ($13.6 million), fruit and nuts ($1.2 million), boilers and equipment ($6.9 million), zinc and zinc goods ($0.9 million), metal goods ($2.8 million), non-organic chemicals ($1.3 million), polymers, plastic, and plastic goods ($1.4 million), glass and glass goods ($0.5 million), furniture ($0.8 million), electrical machines and equipment ($1.1 million), and vegetables ($0.3 million). The main exporters to the Republic are Spain, France, and Ireland.

Major regional export and import entities		*TABLE 6*
ENTITY	ADDRESS	PHONE, FAX, E-MAIL
OAO Electrozinc	1, ul. Zavodskaya, Vladikavkaz, Republic of North Ossetia – Alania, 362001	Phone: (8672) 53 5930

5. INVESTMENT OPPORTUNITIES

5.1. INVESTMENTS IN 1992–2002
(BY INDUSTRY SECTOR),
INCLUDING
FOREIGN INVESTMENTS
The following factors determine the investment appeal of the Republic of North Ossetia – Alania:

• Its advantageous geographic location (Russia's southern gateway to the Caucasus and Asia, and the possibility of transit for Azerbaijani oil);
• Its mineral resources (multiple deposits of non-metal building materials and decorative stones), and balneological recreational resources;

Capital investment by industry sector, $ million						TABLE 7
	1997	1998	1999	2000	2001	2002
Total capital investment	105.8	69.9	38.2	58.9	76.9	57.6
Including major industries (% of total)						
Industry	16.9	10.5	14.6	13.3	18.1	28.2
Agriculture and forestry	9.5	1.7	4.4	3.0	2.9	4.0
Construction	1.8	0.5	1.1	1.7	0.2	0.2
Transport and communications	13.6	13.5	25.4	37.6	38.5	20.6
Trade and public catering	0.1	0.3	0.4	0.5	2.0	0.6
Other	58.1	73.5	54.1	43.9	38.3	46.4

Largest enterprises of the Republic of North Ossetia – Alania		TABLE 8
COMPANY	SECTOR	2002 SALES, $ MILLION*
OAO Beslan Company	Food and beverages	50.3
OAO Electrozinc	Non-ferrous metals	30.7
OAO Sevkavkazenergo	Electricity	24.8
OAO Pobedit	Non-ferrous metals	12.0
OAO Kristall	Machine engineering and metal processing	1.0
State Unitary Company Sadonsky Lead and Zinc Company	Non-ferrous metals	0.7
State Unitary Company Gran	Machine engineering and metal processing	0.4
OAO Magnet	Machine engineering and metal processing	0.3
Federal State Unitary Company Razryad	Machine engineering and metal processing	0.3
State Unitary Company Binom	Machine engineering and metal processing	0.2
OAO Topaz Plant	Machine engineering and metal processing	0.06

*Data of the Government of the Republic of North Ossetia – Alania

• Legislation supporting investment activities (protection of investor rights and preferential tax treatment).

5.2. CAPITAL INVESTMENT

Industry, transport, and communications account for the lion's share of capital investment.

5.3. MAJOR ENTERPRISES (INCLUDING ENTERPRISES WITH FOREIGN INVESTMENT)

The Republic has 68 registered companies with foreign investment from Turkey, Germany, etc.

5.4. MOST ATTRACTIVE SECTORS FOR INVESTMENT

According to the Republic's Government, the most potentially appealing sectors for investors are construction materials, mineral water, rehabilitation centers, tourism, mountaineering, and downhill ski resorts.

5.5. CURRENT LEGISLATION ON INVESTOR TAX EXEMPTIONS AND PRIVILEGES

With a view to creating a legislative and regulatory base for economic reform in the Republic of North Ossetia – Alania, the Republic's Government passed more than 20 laws in 1998–2002. The Republic passed a Law On Investment Activity in the Republic of North Ossetia – Alania, which aims to improve the Republic's investment appeal, create new sources of tax revenue, create new jobs, guarantee protection of investor rights, interests, and property, and foster a competitive environment. The law provides for state guarantees of foreign investor rights and provides various forms of support to investment activity, including preferential taxation and real estate and asset leasing privileges.

With a view to encouraging investment activity and promoting more efficient use of the Republic's investment resources, the Government of the Republic of North Ossetia– Alania has adopted several resolutions:

• On the Approval of the Provisions on Investment Project Tender Procedures and Criteria Applied to the Allocation of Investment Resources of the Republic of North

Regional entities responsible for raising investment		*TABLE 9*
ENTITY	ADDRESS	PHONE, FAX, E-MAIL
Small and Medium Enterprise Development Assistance Agency of the Republic of North Ossetia – Alania	8, ul. Lenina, Vladikavkaz, Republic of North Ossetia-Alania, 362038	Phone: (8672) 54 8365 E-mail: dolphin@osetia.ru

Ossetia – Alania, and on the Composition of the Investment Tender Committee of the Ministry of Economy of the Republic of North Ossetia – Alania;
• On the Investment Assistance Agency;
• On the Reorganization of the Investment Fund of the Republic of North Ossetia–Alania into the Fund for the Support and Development of the Republic of North Ossetia – Alania.

5.6. FEDERAL AND REGIONAL ECONOMIC AND SOCIAL DEVELOPMENT PROGRAMS FOR THE REPUBLIC OF NORTH OSSETIA – ALANIA

Federal targeted programs. The Republic received $21.3 million in 2002 under the Russia's South federal targeted program, including $5.7 million from the Regional Development Fund. The program envisages the launch of the Bozang metals mine with a view to developing the Republic's non-ferrous metal base. A project is underway for the commencement of production of modern materials with pre-determined characteristics using vacuum smelting at OAO Kristall.

Another top priority is to upgrade the Republic's oil industry. The Republic plans to reconstruct 18 wells to secure annual oil output of 213,000 tons.

The Republic is set to receive some $11.0 million in financial assistance under federal targeted programs in 2002–2004. The funding has been earmarked to finance social, children, culture and education, and youth projects. The Republic has accorded priority status to programs that seek to promote rational use of natural resources, improve land fertility, environmental rehabilitation, and seismological safety.

Regional programs. The Republic has developed and is implementing a program for the extension of trade, economic, scientific, technical, and social and cultural cooperation between the Republic of North Ossetia – Alania and the Mtskheta-Mtianetsky province of Georgia through 2005. The objective of the program is to establish joint ventures and implement joint investment projects, and provide joint regulation of the labor market and migration. Investments in 2002–2004 will amount to $30.5 million.

6. INVESTMENT PROJECTS

Industry sector and project description	1) Expected results 2) Amount and term of investment 3) Form of financing[1] 4) Documentation[2]	Contact information
1	2	3
MACHINE ENGINEERING AND METAL PROCESSING		
36R001 ● ◆		OAO Vladikavkaz-Gazoapparat
Reconstruction and technical upgrade of OAO Vladikavkaz-Gazoapparat. Project goal: to produce gas and electric ranges.	1) 160,000 gas and electric range per year, net profit of $4.3 million per year 2) $2.4 million/1 year 3) L 4) BP	P.O. Box 300, 9, Chermenskoye shosse, Vladikavkaz, Republic of North Ossetia – Alania, 362021 Phone: (8672) 76 7495, 76 1744, 76 2710 Fax: (8672) 76 7130, 76 8461 Valery Georgievich Sopoev, CEO

[1] L – Loan, E – Equity, Leas. – Leasing, JV – Joint Venture
[2] BP – Business Plan, FS – Feasibility Study

1	2	3

CONSTRUCTION MATERIALS

36R002   ● ◆ ❖

A polycarbonate plate plant in Vladikavkaz. Project goal: to produce polycarbonate plates.	1) 3,500 tons per year, revenue of €17.5 million per year 2) €2.4 million/1 year 3) L, JV 4) BP	ZAO Kavkazelektronstroi 20b, ul. Butaeva, Vladikavkaz, Republic of North Ossetia – Alania, 362011 Phone: (8672) 76 7470, 76 4071, 76 6450 Fax: (8672) 76 4071 Felix Tembolatovich Tsakhilov, President

LIGHT INDUSTRY

36R003   ● ❖ ◆ ▲

Technical upgrade of OAO Mozdok Patterns. Project goal: to produce curtains and curtain lace.	1) 20.1 million square meters of curtain and lace per year, revenue of $1.1 million per year 2) $1.5 million/3 months 3) L, JV 4) BP, FS	OAO Mozdok Patterns 1, ul. Fabrichnaya, Mozdok, Republic of North Ossetia – Alania, 363700 Phone: (86736) 32 743 Fax: (86736) 32 114 E- mail: uzor@Ossetia.ru Vladimir Vasilyevich Taridonov, CEO

FOOD AND BEVERAGES

36R004   ● ◆

Launch of production of hard cheeses. Project goal: to produce hard cheeses.	1) 200 tons per year; revenue of $0.6 million per year 2) $0.55 million/1 year 3) L 4) BP	Municipal Unitary Company Mozdok Dairy Plant 63, ul. Usanova, Lukovskaya, Mozdok District, Republic of North Ossetia – Alania, 363720 Phone/fax: (86736) 31 410, 25 228 Valery Alexandrovich Derbitov, Director

37. CHECHEN REPUBLIC [20]

ECONOMIC MAP

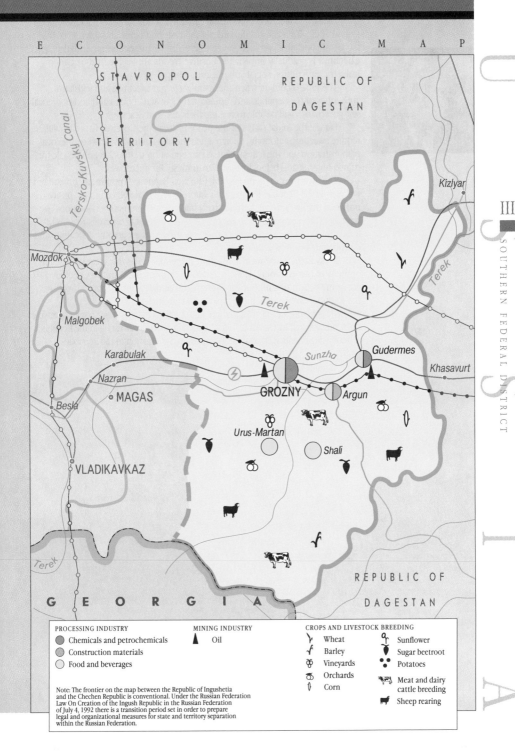

STAVROPOL

TERRITORY

REPUBLIC OF

DAGESTAN

Tersko-Kuvsky Canal

Kizlyar

Mozdok

Terek

Terek

Malgobek

Karabulak

Sunzha

Gudermes

Nazran

Khasavurt

Besla

MAGAS

GROZNY

Argun

Urus-Martan

Shali

VLADIKAVKAZ

Terek

GEORGIA

REPUBLIC OF

DAGESTAN

PROCESSING INDUSTRY
- 🔴 Chemicals and petrochemicals
- ⚪ Construction materials
- ⚪ Food and beverages

MINING INDUSTRY
- ▲ Oil

CROPS AND LIVESTOCK BREEDING
- Wheat
- Barley
- Vineyards
- Orchards
- Corn
- Sunflower
- Sugar beetroot
- Potatoes
- Meat and dairy cattle breeding
- Sheep rearing

Note: The frontier on the map between the Republic of Ingushetia
and the Chechen Republic is conventional. Under the Russian Federation
Law On Creation of the Ingush Republic in the Russian Federation
of July 4, 1992 there is a transition period set in order to prepare
legal and organizational measures for state and territory separation
within the Russian Federation.

For over ten years, my motherland, the Chechen Republic, has been ravaged by the hostilities of an undeclared war. The results of the referendum of March 23, 2003, which was proclaimed the Day of the Chechen Republic's Constitution, demonstrated that the Chechen people are in favor of peace, accord, and territorial integrity of Russia. It is clear that if we, the Chechen people, pursue the course of peace and stability, we have the potential to change the situation radically.

I see my task as one of restoring Chechnya to the Russian Federation's legal system after a long and painful ordeals and restoring peace and the rule of law.

Unbiased observers recognize that political and economic situation in Chechnya is gradually improving. Positive trends are visible in the economy, industry, agriculture, social sphere, and culture.

The time is coming when the lawfully elected executive and legislative authorities of the Republic and representatives of state bodies and bodies of local self-governance will be able to resume their day-to-day activities.

During the initial stages of the peace process, the Chechen Republic will require sweeping autonomy, an agreement dividing authority between the local administration and the federal center, compensation to the Chechen people for ruined housing and belongings, and an amnesty for guerrillas.

The investment potential of the Chechen Republic is enormous. Investment will enable the Republic to drastically improve its social and economic position provided the investments are effectively implemented in market conditions. We have all of the prerequisites to become one of the most prosperous regions of Russia thanks to our rich resource base, advantageous geographical location, and our people's business acumen.

Investment is the most important prerequisite for the successful development of our economy. The current level of investment in the Chechen economy is insufficient. But for foreign and domestic investors to invest in the Republic, we must achieve peace and stability!

My colleagues and I are committed to doing everything in our power to ensure that domestic and foreign investors who are interested in investing in the Republic's economy are encouraged by radical changes in the situation in the Republic.

Akhmat Kadyrov,
PRESIDENT OF THE CHECHEN REPUBLIC

1. GENERAL INFORMATION

1.1. GEOGRAPHY
The Chechen Republic is located in the south of the Russian Federation in the Northern Caucasus. To the west it borders the Republic of Ingushetia, to the north-west, the Republic of North Ossetia – Alania, to the east, the Republic of Dagestan, and to the north, the Stavropol Territory. The southern border of the Chechen Republic coincides with the international frontier between the Russian Federation and Georgia.

The Chechen Republic covers a total area of more than 16,000 square kilometers. The distance from the Chechen capital (Grozny) to Moscow is 2,007 kilometers.

In terms of relief, the Republic is divided into the northern plain (two-thirds of the Republic) and the mountains in the south (one third). Southern Chechnya consists of the foothills and slopes of the Great Caucasus mountain range. The north of the Republic is occupied by the Tersko-Kumskaya lowlands.

1.2. CLIMATE
The Republic's climate is continental, with average temperatures in January from –4°C in the plains to –12°C in the mountains, rising in July to +21°C and +25°C, respectively. Annual precipitation on average reaches 300–600 mm in the plains, and up to 1,500 mm in the mountains.

The climate in the mountain areas is suitable for curative purposes. The plains of Chechnya lie under steppe and semi-steppe soils and are utilized for agriculture. The soils are highly fertile, with black and brown earth and meadow brown soils predominating.

1.3. POPULATION
The preliminary 2002 census results revealed a total population in the Chechen Republic of 1,100,000 people. The official report at the Parliamentary Assembly of the Council of Europe mentioned 900,000 people. This figure evidently included the approximately 250,000 refugees who presently live in the Republic of Ingushetia and other Russian regions.

The Chechen Republic is essentially rural. The urban population accounts for 26.3%, and the rural, for 73.7%.

The capital of the Republic is Grozny with over 223,000 inhabitants (2002). The Republic has 340 towns and villages, including four major urban centers at Urus-Martan, Gudermes, Shali, and Argun.

As the security situation in the Republic normalizes and economic and public life recovers, the population will increase thanks to refugees returning home.

Experts estimate that around 130,000–140,000 refugees from Chechnya are currently living in the Republic of Ingushetia.

Demographically speaking, some 350,000–400,000 people are of the statutory working age, while there are only around 150,000 jobs. High birth rates in the Republic (6–8 children per family on average) mean that many people of statutory working age work at home.

According to the Russian Federation Government's estimates, the Republic has around 320,000 children, of whom 220,000 are of school age, and 100,000 are of pre-school age. The Republic has 170,000 pensioners.

2. ADMINISTRATION

Government House, 10, ul. Garazhnaya, Grozny, Chechen Republic, 364000

NAME	POSITION	CONTACT INFORMATION
Akhmat Abdulkhamidovich KADYROV	President of the Chechen Republic	Phone: (8712) 22 2009
Anatoly Alexandrovich POPOV	Chairman of the Government of the Chechen Republic	Phone: (8712) 22 2001 Fax: (8712) 22 2014
Adlan Abubakarovich MAGOMADOV	Deputy Chairman of the Government of the Chechen Republic, Plenipotentiary Representative of the Chechen Republic to the President of the Russian Federation	Office 1804, 19, ul. Novy Arbat, Moscow, 127025 Phone: (095) 203 6352 Fax: (095) 203 9314

3. ECONOMIC POTENTIAL

3.1. 1997–2002 GROSS REGIONAL PRODUCT (GRP). INDUSTRY BREAKDOWN
Before the Chechen crisis, the Republic enjoyed the strongest industrial potential in the Northern Caucasus thanks to its well-developed oil production and processing industries and agriculture. Industrial output accounted for 67% of total gross regional product. The Chechen Republic was largely self-sufficient for food and beverages.

By the early 1990's, heavy industry prevailed in the industrial breakdown with around 80% of total industrial output. The Republic's 12 major industries produced more than 1,000 articles.

The Republic's industry specialized mostly in oil production and processing (92% of total Russian output of aviation oil and engine fuel, bitumen, and paraffin), petrochemicals (synthetic ethyl spirit, polyethylene, etc.), microbiology, machine engineering and tools (oil equipment, pumps, electric tools, automobile trailers, and medical instruments), food and beverages, and the light industry.

Half of the Republic's industrial enterprises were located in Grozny, including all oil refineries and chemical plants, and most machine engineering and metal processing plants.

The two military campaigns in the Republic resulted in the destruction of its heavy industry and infrastructure, the collapse of its economic and social structures, and plummeting living standards.

The changed demographic and ethnic structure has left the Republic monoethnic. Russian-speaking specialists have left, and the rural population is now three times larger than the urban population.

3.2. MAJOR ECONOMIC GROWTH PROJECTIONS

The current economic growth projections call for the revival of the fuel and energy sector (oil production, electricity, heat supply to towns and villages), construction, agriculture, and food and beverages. Most industrial enterprises will be placed outside Grozny, resulting in substantial improvements in the environmental situation in the town.

Agriculture and processing industries based on local raw materials will take a leading place in the Republic's economy. The recovery effort will be centered on small and medium sized enterprises, rather than industrial giants, as these have the greatest job creation and tax revenue potential in the short-term.

3.3. INDUSTRIAL OUTPUT IN 1997–2002 FOR MAJOR SECTORS OF ECONOMY

The Republic's industrial recovery rates are not very high. 2002 output at operating enterprises was $223.1 million.

Of the major sectors of the economy, only the oil industry is developing rapidly. In 2001, the oil sector brought $41.1 million into the Republic's budget, or almost four times the planned $10-14 million. In 2002, 1.5 million tons of oil was produced, or 2.1 times as much as in 2001 and equal to the pre-war output of 1994.

The construction materials industry has strong growth potential thanks to high local demand. In 2002, 8.1 million conventional bricks were produced in the Chechen Republic.

The situation is also favorable for food and beverages growth, especially in sectors that use local rather than imported feedstock. In 2002, some 3,100 tons of bread was produced in the Republic, 12% more than in 2001.

Small and medium sized business has also begun to develop rapidly, with the emergence of numerous cafes, car repair shops, car washes, radio and TV repair shops, drycleaners, and other service enterprises.

In coming years, alcoholic beverages may become one of the most profitable sectors of the Chechen economy. The production facilities of the Republic's three distilleries at Grozny, Chervlenaya, and Naurskaya survived the wars almost completely intact. Chechnya's vineyards have the capacity to act as feedstock suppliers to the sector.

Agroindustrial sector. Chechnya enjoys favorable natural conditions for agriculture: fertile soils, a warm and humid climate, and natural meadow pasture lands.

According to the Ministry for Agriculture of the Chechen Republic, tillage stood at 360,000 hectares at its peak in the early 1990's, with 517,000 hectares under pasture, and collective gardens and vineyards comprising more than 20,000 hectares. In 2002, more than 240,000 hectares of land was under tillage.

The agroindustrial sector has strong growth potential. The past two years saw record grain harvests in the Republic: 240,000 tons in 2001 and 350,000 tons in 2002, with an average yield of 2,200 kilograms per hectare.

The Republic is self-sufficient for bread. Since October 1, 2001, bread baked at the state-owned bakery is sold at a fixed price of $0.13 per loaf.

The Republic's internal demand for grain is 150,000 tons a year. The Republic has the potential to sell surplus grain output in the future. The agricultural sector is funded and equipped from the federal budget on a non-repayable basis. The Ministry of Agriculture of Russia supplies the Republic with seeds, fertilizers, and machinery.

Some $9.4 million is to be allocated to agriculture in the Chechen Republic in 2003. The funds will be spent on the development of the grain, fruit and vegetables, and processing industries. A program for the recovery of these sectors has already been worked out.

Cattle farming is a special area of concern. Early in 2003, live pedigree cattle were brought into the Republic from state-owned stud farms in the Stavropol Territory, North Ossetia, and Voronezh. The project was funded under the Federal Targeted Program for the Economic and Social Recovery of the Chechen Republic in 2002 and Subsequent Years). State sector farms in Chechnya own around 1,500 heads of cattle, with more than 273,000 held in the private sector.

The Republic plans to fully restore livestock farming to pre-war levels within ten years.

Chechryba Fisheries Company has launched five fish hatcheries in the Republic.

3.4. TRANSPORT INFRASTRUCTURE

Chechnya enjoys an advantageous transport location in the Northern Caucasus as a transit territory for foreign relations with Caspian Sea states and Russian Black sea regions, Ukraine, European, and Trans-Caucasian countries. The Republic's main types of transport are railroad, automotive transport and pipelines (oil and gas).

The Chechen republic is crossed by the Trans-Caucasian Railroad from Baku to Rostov-on-Don, the Baku – Grozny – Novorossiysk – Rostov highway, and a section of the trunk oil pipeline Baku – Novorossiysk, which provides the only exit for Azerbaijani oil to world markets.

Railroad communications with Chechnya collapsed in August 1999. In 2002, rail traffic was resumed throughout the Republic's railroad network, and a new passenger service was launched on the Grozny – Gudermes – Moscow route. The Ministry of Railways of Russia allocated $1.9 million to restore passenger communications.

Currently, the Republic operates cargo and passenger rail transit traffic on the following routes Mozdok – Chervlennaya – Uzlovaya – Grozny, Chervlennaya – Uzlovaya – Kizlyar, Gudermes – Grozny, Grozny – Aldy, and Chervlennaya – Uzlovaya – Khasavyurt.

Chechnya has 560 kilometers of trunk gas pipelines linking the Republic to the Trans-Caucasian countries, the Stavropol Territory, and Dagestan. FGUP Chechengazprom was established in August 2000 to manage the gas pipeline. The company reports directly to the Ministry of Fuel and Energy of Russia. Under an agreement with the Itera group of companies and the state oil company of Azerbaijan (GNKA), FGUP Chechengazprom transports gas to the Republic of Azerbaijan through Chechnya. From 1996 to 2002, transit services for gas exports cost around $10 million.

Chechnya is also developing its communications infrastructure. A general plan for communications reconstruction up to 2005 has been drafted, and draft projects have been worked out for the near term. In 2001, the Russian Federation budget allocated $11.8 million to build a new communication network and to restore networks ruined during the war. A satellite communications network has been built with the capacity to service around 200 lines based on remote subscriber technology linked to the Moscow and Rostov-on-Don telecommunications networks. A fiber-optic cable was laid in the Republic on the Budennovsk – Kizlyar – Makhachkala route, and a digital fiber-optic line on the Kizlyar – Gudermes – Argun – Grozny route.

A state telecommunications enterprise, Elektrosvyaz, has been established in the Chechen Republic. In 2002, digital communication units were put in operation in Vedeno, Nozhay-Yurt, and Shatoy. Digital radio-relay lines are under construction in the mountain districts of Chechnya.

In the postal communications sector, 87% of the previously existing post offices are now operational.

3.5. MAIN NATURAL RESOURCES: RESERVES AND EXTRACTION IN 2002

The Republic's principal natural resources are oil (and gas condensate), natural gas, hydroelectric resources, construction materials, minerals, geothermal waters, soil, recreation resources, and zeolites.

Chechnya's light, low-sulphur oil is among the highest grade oils in the country. Reserves are estimated at 40–50 million tons, but are already largely depleted. Total explored reserves (to a depth of 4.5–5 kilometers) exceed 780 million tons. The Republic has 24 developed oil deposits, including 1,440 wells, of which only 550 are currently operational. The rest are either exhausted or damaged. In 2000, OAO Grozneftegaz was established as a subsidiary of state-owned Rosneft by a decree of the Russian Government On the Emergency Measures Aimed to Recover Oil and Gas Industry in the Chechen Republic. In 2002, Grozneftegaz produced 1.5 million tons of oil (compared with the 3–4 million tons produced annually in the Republic in the early 1990's). Around 80% of the oil output is exported.

Natural gas reserves exceed 60 billion cubic meters. Natural gas production in Chechnya in the early 1990's exceeded one billion cubic meters per year, but by 1998 had decreased to 118 million cubic meters.

The Chechen Republic has large reserves of unutilized mountain river hydroelectric resources and good geothermal potential. As early as the 1980's, plans were afoot to build three geothermal circulatory systems to supply heat to Grozny from the Petropavlovsky and Khankalsky geothermal springs. These projects were never implemented.

Several deposits of another valuable mineral, zeolite, have been discovered in the Republic with total reserves exceeding 5.5 billion tons. These deposits are not developed at present. The former Soviet Union extracted and consumed 170,000 tons of zeolites, utilizing them mainly in agriculture as a biologically active additive for cattle and poultry farming, a fertilizer enhancer, and a water consumption regulator for plants. Zeolites are also used in the petrochemicals industry as a catalyzer in various oil processing processes.

4. INVESTMENT OPPORTUNITIES

In 2000–2001, the Chechen Republic had the lowest investment attractiveness index and the highest risk ratio of all the 89 Russian regions. This had to do with the generally unstable situation in the Republic. However, the low level of investment in the Republic belies its resource potential, advantageous transport location, and geography.

According to experts from the Republic's government, the business and general investment climate in Chechnya will improve if military operations cease, the legal and legislative aspects of the

Republic's relationship with the federal center are resolved, crime and corruption are eradicated, and a legislative framework for business development and investor guarantees is implemented.

A lot of businesses and individuals are willing to invest in the Chechen economy under Russian state guarantees as the situation normalizes, specifically companies from the USA, Sweden, Turkey, Belgium, Saudi Arabia, and other countries, Chechen entrepreneurs from other Russian regions and CIS countries, and major Russian companies such as OAO NK Rosneft, OAO Gazprom, and RAO UES of Russia.

4.1. FEDERAL AND REGIONAL ECONOMIC AND SOCIAL DEVELOPMENT PROGRAMS FOR THE CHECHEN REPUBLIC

The Russian federal budget allocated some $274.2 million to carry out the Federal Targeted Program for the Economic and Social Recovery of the Chechen Republic in 2002 and Subsequent Years. In the context of a funding deficit, the Russian government has outlined three investment priorities for the coming years: to restore the fuel and energy sector (oil production and processing), agriculture, and education. The restoration of housing, communal services and large energy suppliers are other priorities for the allocation of funding from the federal budget. In the energy sector, the focus will be on the restoration of the Argun Thermal Power Station.

A general plan for the rebuilding of Grozny has been prepared and adopted. A comprehensive plan has also been elaborated to develop the economy and improve public welfare in the Chechen Republic.

Some $509.7 million has been allocated from the Russian federal budget to the Chechen Republic, of which $141.6 million has been earmarked for the funding of the federal targeted program for the recovery of the Republic; $22.3 million to the Republic's

ministries to construct facilities in their sectors; $119.6 million to restore the energy sector; and around $239.1 million to finance salaries and pensions.

Comparatively little investment flows into small enterprise in Chechnya from Chechen entrepreneurs and businessmen living in other Russian regions. In 2001, Chechen investors put around $10 million into the Chechen economy to restore food and beverages enterprises (a bakery, a sugar plant, and two distilleries), and to build and equip schools, hospitals, and a maternity hospital in Grozny.

Entrepreneurs from the Chechen diaspora make up the Regional Union of Industrialists and Entrepreneurs, which is member of the Russian Union of Entrepreneurs and Industrialists (Employers).

The Republic's government runs a committee on small and medium enterprise support. In March 2002, the Republic's government adopted a Decree On the Small and Medium Enterprise Development Support Program in the Chechen Republic. Some $20 million in financing is planned for 2002–2003, of which $5 million is to be allocated from the local budget and $0.4 million from the federal budget. The remainder will come from non-budgetary sources and the private sector.

The program seeks to bring down unemployment. Small and medium sized enterprises represent a stable source of income for many inhabitants of Chechnya, and provide tax revenues to the federal and local budgets. The Republic plans to spearhead its economic recovery and ensure the development of market relations through investment into small and medium enterprise, job creation in the sector, and by raising the share of local products and services.

The Ministry of Economic Development and Trade of the Russian Federation estimates the cost of full economic recovery in the Republic at $3 billion.

38. KRASNODAR TERRITORY [23]

ECONOMIC MAP

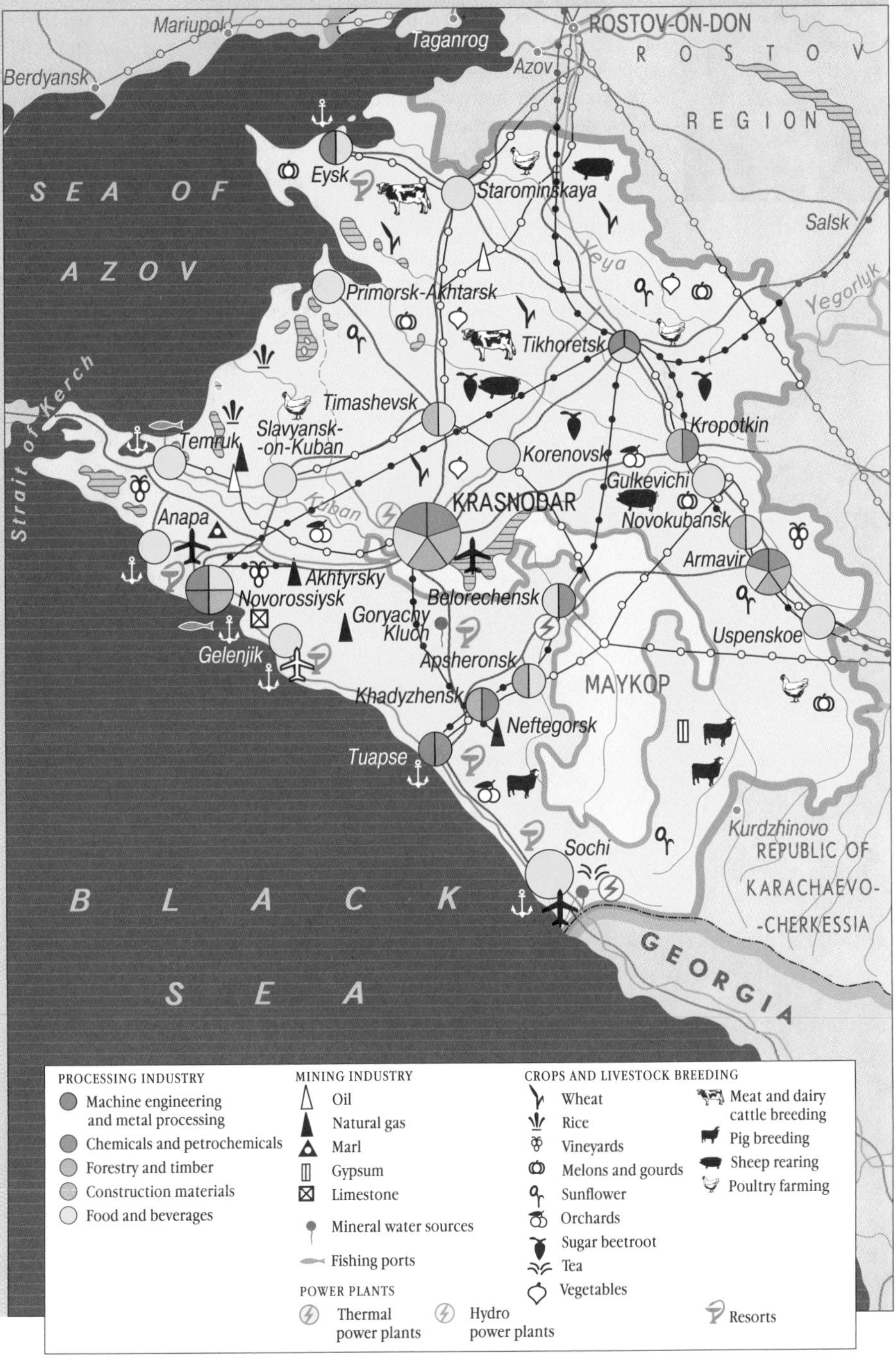

Places and labels on map:

Mariupol, Taganrog, ROSTOV-ON-DON, Berdyansk, Azov, ROSTOV REGION, Eysk, Starominskaya, Salsk, SEA OF AZOV, Primorsk-Akhtarsk, Yeya, Vegorluk, Tikhoretsk, Timashevsk, Kropotkin, Temruk, Slavyansk-on-Kuban, Korenovsk, Gulkevichi, Strait of Kerch, Anapa, Kuban, KRASNODAR, Novokubansk, Armavir, Akhtyrsky, Belorechensk, Novorossiysk, Goryachy Kluch, Uspenskoe, Gelenjik, Apsheronsk, MAYKOP, Khadyzhensk, Neftegorsk, Tuapse, Kurdzhinovo, REPUBLIC OF KARACHAEVO-CHERKESSIA, Sochi, BLACK SEA, GEORGIA

Legend

PROCESSING INDUSTRY
- Machine engineering and metal processing
- Chemicals and petrochemicals
- Forestry and timber
- Construction materials
- Food and beverages

MINING INDUSTRY
- Oil
- Natural gas
- Marl
- Gypsum
- Limestone
- Mineral water sources
- Fishing ports

POWER PLANTS
- Thermal power plants
- Hydro power plants

CROPS AND LIVESTOCK BREEDING
- Wheat
- Rice
- Vineyards
- Melons and gourds
- Sunflower
- Orchards
- Sugar beetroot
- Tea
- Vegetables
- Meat and dairy cattle breeding
- Pig breeding
- Sheep rearing
- Poultry farming
- Resorts

The Kuban, as the Krasnodar Territory is usually called, is one of the most important regions of Russia. Its advantageous geographical location, climate, and natural conditions are the objective reasons behind the exceptional attractiveness of the region. It is not without reason that the Kuban is called the Pearl of Russia, for its granaries and sanatoriums.

The Territory, which is served by international airports and a developed highway and railroad system, is the "sea gateway" to the southern border regions of Russia. The Kuban's subsoil abounds in oil, gas, mineral waters, and raw construction materials. Warm seas and unrivalled recreation facilities have made the Kuban one of the country's most popular resort and vacation regions.

Another natural asset of the Kuban is its four million hectares of highly fertile black earth lands that make its agroindustrial sector the largest producer and supplier of agricultural products in Russia. Other important sectors include the food processing industry, which accounts for half of total industrial output, fuel and energy, and construction.

The Territory is a region of high investment potential. It is not by accident that the Kuban holds tenth position in Russia in terms of investment volume and second in terms of investment legislation efforts. Comparable in size to a large European country, the Territory is ready to continue working effectively in this direction.

For any investor, stability and regional development standards are of utmost importance. The Krasnodar Territory meets these requirements. We invite Russian and foreign partners to engage in fruitful cooperation with our Territory. We guarantee our assistance in the advancement of your investment projects.

Alexander Tkachev,
HEAD OF ADMINISTRATION (GOVERNOR)
OF THE KRASNODAR TERRITORY

III

SOUTHERN FEDERAL DISTRICT

1. GENERAL INFORMATION

1.1. GEOGRAPHY

The Krasnodar Territory is situated on the Kubano-Azov lowland and the western part of the Caucasus mountain range, and covers a total area of 76,000 square kilometers. To the north and northeast, the Territory borders the Rostov Region, to the east – the Stavropol Territory, to the south – Georgia and the Republic of Karachayevo-Cherkessia, and to the south the Territory is washed by the Azov and the Black Seas.

1.2. CLIMATE

Most of the Krasnodar Territory enjoys a temperate continental climate, while at the Black Sea coast the climate is subtropical. Air temperatures in January average –5°C in the mountains and 0°C on the plains, rising to +13°C and +24°C, respectively, in July. Annual precipitation is 400 mm on the plains, and up to 3,200 mm in mountain areas.

The growing season lasts around 260 days. The plains are covered with black earth soil.

1.3. POPULATION

According to preliminary 2002 census results, the Territory's total population is 5,124,000 people. The average population density is 67.4 people per square km. The economically active population amounts to 2,052,000 people. While 2002 official unemployment stood at 0.7%, the actual rate is 10.7%.

Demographically speaking, some 58% are of working age, 19% are below the statutory working age, and 23% are beyond the statutory working age.

As of 2002, the Krasnodar Territory's major urban centers were Krasnodar with 644,800 inhabitants, Sochi with 328,800 inhabitants, Novorossiysk with 231,900 inhabitants, Armavir with 193,900 inhabitants, Yeisk with 84,600 inhabitants, and Kropotkin with 81,300 inhabitants.

Population								TABLE 1
	1992	1997	1998	1999	2000	2001	2002
Total population, '000	4,737	5,011	5,015	5,010	5,007	4,999	5,124
Economically active population, '000	2,270	2,154	2,088	2,334	2,335	2,290	2,052

2. ADMINISTRATION

35, ul. Krasnaya, Krasnodar, Krasnodar Territory, 350014
Phone: (8612) 62 5716; fax: (8612) 68 3542
E-mail: registry@kuban.ru; http://admkrai.kuban.ru

NAME	POSITION	CONTACT INFORMATION
Alexander Nikolaevich TKACHEV	Head of Administration (Governor) of the Krasnodar Territory	Phone/fax: (8612) 62 5716
Alexander Alexandrovich REMEZKOV	First Deputy Head of Administration of the Krasnodar Territory for Economy, Finance, and Control	Phone: (8612) 62 4554, 62 8088 E-mail: remezkov@hotbox.ru
Vitaly Vladimirovich PUSHKIN	First Deputy Head of Administration of the Krasnodar Territory for Agroindustrial Complex	Phone: (8612) 62 1042
Zoya Ivanovna ROSCHUPKINA	Deputy Head of Administration of the Krasnodar Territory, Chief of Staff of Administration of the KrasnodarTerritory	Phone: (8612) 62 4760, 68 5081
Oleg Konstantinovich BEZRODNY	Deputy Head of Administration of the Krasnodar Territory for Construction, Architecture, and Housing and Communal Services	Phone: (8612) 68 4711
Yury Alexandrovich BARZYKIN	Deputy Head of Administration of the Krasnodar Territory for the Development of Azov and Black Sea Coasts, Recreation, Rehabilitation, and Tourism, General Director of the Azov-Black Sea Coast Development Department	Phone: (8612) 62 5897 E-mail: admkurort@admkuban. krasnodar.ru
Alexander Sergeevich SIDORENKO	Deputy Head of Administration of the Krasnodar Territory for Liaison with Law Enforcement Agencies, Transport, Fuel, and Energy	Phone: (8612) 68 2751, 68 4513

NAME	POSITION	CONTACT INFORMATION
Viktor Mikhailovich BONDAR	Deputy Head of Administration of the Krasnodar Territory for Property Issues, Head of the Property Relations Department	Phone: (8612) 62 5126, 68 2862

3. ECONOMIC POTENTIAL

3.1. 1997–2002 GROSS REGIONAL PRODUCT (GRP). INDUSTRY BREAKDOWN

The Krasnodar Territory accounts for 2.1% of Russia's total GDP. The 2002 gross regional product

exceeded $7,246.2 million, which constitutes 13.7% growth year-on-year.

The positive GRP trend was the result of an increase in output of goods and services in the main sectors of the economy. Agriculture accounts for the lion's share of GRP at 17.3%.

GRP trends in 1997–2002						*TABLE 2*
	1997	1998	1999	2000	2001*	2002*
GRP in current prices, $ million	7,872.2	5,558.9	4,299.8	5,382.3	6,370.3	7,246.2

*Estimates of the Krasnodar Territory Administration

GRP industry breakdown in 1997–2002, % of total						*TABLE 3*
	1997	1998	1999	2000	200*1	2002*
GRP	100.0	100.0	100.0	100.0	100.0	100.0
Industry	15.1	17.9	16.4	15.7	15.6	15.6
Agriculture and forestry	14.4	11.4	11.6	17.7	18.6	17.3
Construction	9.9	10.0	16.0	16.1	15.5	17.4
Transport and communications	15.4	19.0	18.0	16.3	15.1	17.0
Trade and public catering	11.6	10.9	10.9	10.8	11.6	11.4
Other	n/a	n/a	n/a	16.9	17.7	15.3
Net taxes on output	n/a	n/a	n/a	6.5	5.9	6.0

*Estimates of the Krasnodar Territory Administration

3.2. MAJOR ECONOMIC GROWTH PROJECTIONS

The Krasnodar Territory Administration has developed a number of mid-term programs aimed at fostering economic growth. The priority programs are:

• The Program for Increasing Oil and Gas Extraction, which aims to utilize low yield fields to the maximum extent;

• The Conceptual Framework for the Development of the Krasnodar Territory's Seaports through 2020, which aims to expand operating ports, starting with Novorossiysk and Tuapse, and construct new port facilities at Sochi, Gelendzhik, and the Taman Peninsula.

3.3. INDUSTRIAL OUTPUT IN 1997–2002 FOR MAJOR SECTORS OF ECONOMY

The leading industrial sectors, represented by some 700 large and medium size companies and

over 4,000 small enterprises, are food and beverages, energy, fuel, machine engineering and metal processing, and construction materials. These account for over 80% of total industrial output.

Food and beverages. The food and food processing sectors hold the leading position, accounting for 43.1% of total industrial output.

The Territory has 16 sugar refineries, ten vegetable and fruit canning plants, seven fish canning plants, 42 dairy and 23 meat processing plants, seven butter and fat plants, two tea and two tobacco processing plants, 48 vineyards, eleven wine plants, four distillers, and 25 bakeries.

Major companies within the sector are: OAO Krasnodar Butter and Fat Plant, OAO Armavir Butter and Fat Plant, OAO Abrau-Durso, OAO Krasnodar Meat Plant, ZAO Krasnodar Fish Plant, Municipal Unitary Company Krasnodarptitsa, ZAO Anit Ltd., and Subsidiary No. 1 of ZAO Moscow Brewery and Soft Drink Plant Ochakovo.

Industry breakdown of industrial output in 1997–2002, % of total						TABLE 4
	1997	1998	1999	2000	2001	2002*
Industry	100.0	100.0	100.0	100.0	100.0	100.0
Food and beverages	37.7	43.3	48.8	42.8	45.2	43.1
Energy	20.1	17.0	12.0	13.4	14.1	13.5
Fuel	7.0	6.2	9.2	10.5	8.8	9.6
Machine engineering and metal processing	10.3	8.0	8.1	9.4	11.2	8.7
Construction materials	7.1	7.2	6.4	7.9	8.5	7.3
Forestry, timber, and pulp and paper	4.6	4.0	3.2	3.8	3.6	5.5
Flour, cereals, and mixed fodder	5.9	6.4	4.8	5.1	4.9	3.9
Chemicals and petrochemicals	1.8	3.0	3.6	3.3	2.3	2.1
Light industry	1.8	1.3	1.0	1.3	1.6	2.0
Glass and porcelain	0.5	0.5	0.5	0.6	0.6	0.5
Ferrous metals	0.2	0.3	0.3	0.2	0.2	0.1

*Estimates of the Krasnodar Territory Administration

Energy. This sector accounts for 13.5% of total industrial output. OAO Kubanenergo is the main energy generator and supplier. The energy system comprises the Krasnodar Power Station, three hydroelectric power stations, high-voltage transmission lines and transformer substations.

Fuel. This sector accounts for 9.6% of total industrial output. The Territory is home to three oil refineries, the largest being ZAO Krasnodareconeft Refinery and OAO Krasnodarneftegeofizika.

Machine engineering and metal processing. The sector accounts for 8.7% of total industrial output. Over 100 companies produce a wide range of machinery, including metal-cutting and lumber machines, automation tools, agricultural vehicles, electrical engines, compressors, pumps, refrigerators, and oil exploration and extraction equipment. Major companies within the sector are OAO AvtoKuban, OAO Krasnodar ZIP, OAO Molot, OAO Krasny Dvigatel, OOO Electro, and ZAO Agrostroimash.

Construction materials. The sector accounts for 7.3% of total industrial output. The Territory's four construction materials manufacturers – OAO Kuban Gypsum-Knauf, OAO Novokuban Ceramic Wall Materials Plant, ZAO Reinforced Concrete Goods Plant, and OAO Ceramic Goods Plant – are among Russia's top construction materials companies.

Timber and furniture. The sector accounts for 5.5% of total industrial output and is represented by 35 large and medium companies producing lumber, chipboard, parquet flooring, and home and office furniture. Industrial timber export amounts to 100,000 cubic meters per year. Major companies include OAO Krasnodar Furniture Firm, OAO Kuban Furniture, and OOO SBS-Furniture Company.

Agriculture accounts for some 17.3% of gross regional product and over 5% of Russia's gross agricultural product, including 10% of grain output, 19% of sugar beet output, and 15% of sunflower seeds output. The Territory has 4.4 million hectares of arable land, including 3.9 million hectares of ploughed fields, 77,000 hectares of orchards, and 35,000 hectares of vineyards.

Resorts and recreation. Over 1,300 recreation and tourism enterprises, which can accept some 220,000 people at a time, generate an estimated $333.5 million per year in the Krasnodar Territory. The Territory is home to all of Russia's major seaside resorts, including Sochi, Anapa, Gelendzhik, Tuapse, and Yeisk.

3.4. FUEL AND ENERGY BALANCE (OUTPUT AND CONSUMPTION PER RESOURCE)

The fuel and energy sector accounts for some 23% of total industrial output. Over the past three years, oil output has risen by 254,000 tons, or 16%, and natural gas – by 749 million cubic meters, or 39%. Primary oil refining reached 5.2 million tons in 2001, which constitutes 220% growth on 1998 levels.

3.5. TRANSPORT INFRASTRUCTURE

The transport sector accounts for 17% of the Territory's GRP.

Roads. The Territory has 10,400 kilometers of roads, including the following: Krasnodar – Novorossiysk, Krymsk-Port – Caucasus, and federal roads Krasnodar – Baku and Don (Moscow – Voronezh – Rostov-on-Don – Krasnodar – Novorossiysk).

Railroads. The Krasnodar Territory has 2,200 kilometers of railroads. The main route going through the Territory is the Krasnodar section of the North-Caucasus railroad. The main freight flow goes in the direction of the seaports. Freight is dominated by oil, oil products, timber, lumber, grain, sugar, construction materials, and equipment.

Fuel and energy production and consumption trends, 1997–2002						TABLE 5
	1997	1998	1999	2000	2001	2002*
Electricity output, billion kWh	6.9	6.8	7.1	6.9	6.4	6.1
Oil output (including gas concentrate), '000 tons	1,606.0	1,590.0	1,579.0	1,716.0	1,787.0	1,833.0
Natural gas extraction, million cubic meters	1,985.0	1,908.0	1,919.0	2,418.0	2,766.0	2,668.0
Electricity consumption, billion kWh	13.5	13.4	14.0	12.6	12.3	11.9
Oil consumption, '000 tons	3,476.0	2,335.8	4,153.9	4,815.0	4,991.0	5,185.0
Natural gas consumption, million cubic meters	n/a	3,681.0	3,973.0	4,723.0	4,273.0	5,738.6

*Estimates of the Krasnodar Territory Administration

Airports. The Krasnodar Territory has international-al airports at Krasnodar, Sochi, Anapa, and Gelendzhik.

Seaports. There are eight seaports in the Territory: Novorossiysk, Tuapse, Sochi, Anapa, Gelendzhik, Yeisk, Temryuk, Caucasus, and the Krasnodar river port. These account for up to 40% of the Russian Federation's ports freight turnover. Major shipping companies are OAO Novorossiysk Sea Ship Line, OAO Novoship, and OOO Barwel Novorossiysk.

Oil and gas pipelines. Sections of such major oil pipelines as Makhachkala – Grozny – Tuapse, oil pipelines of OAO Transneft, OAO Chernomortransneft, ZAO Caspian Pipeline Consortium, and the Lazarevs-koe – Tuapse – Nebug gas pipeline, all pass through the Territory. Plans are afoot to lay a gas pipeline from Tyumen to Turkey through the Territory.

3.6. MAIN NATURAL RESOURCES: RESERVES AND EXTRACTION IN 2002

The Territory is rich in over 60 types of mineral resources, including oil, natural gas, iodide-bromine waters, marble, lime, sandstone, iron and apatite ores.

Oil and gas. The Krasnodar Territory is the birthplace of Russia's oil sector. Some 68 oil fields currently provide 1.5-1.7 million tons of oil and up to 2 billion cubic meters of natural gas every year. Most of the fields are located in the western and central foothills (Abinsk, Seversk, and Apsheron districts).

Recreational resources. Its Mediterranean-type climate, warm seas, unique mineral water springs, and therapeutic mud make the Territory one of the most ecologically pure and popular recreational and tourism regions of the country.

4. TRADE OPPORTUNITIES

4.1. MAIN GOODS PRODUCED IN THE REGION

Food and beverages. The Territory's enterprises supply over one third of Russia's output of granulated sugar (2 million tons), some 40% of concentrated fruit juice output, 100% of canned meat for infants, and 6% of cheeses and canned dairy products. Other products include vegetable oil (320,000 tons) and canned fruit and vegetables (376 million conventional cans).

Wine, liquor, and tobacco. The Territory pro-duces 10 million decaliters of wine per year (including 2.5 million decaliters of sparkling wine and 4.8 million decaliters of grape wine). A favorite of the Russian mar-ket, the classic sparkling wine Abrau-Durso, is pro-duced at the Abrau-Durso Plant. All in all, the Territory produces over 120 brands of alcoholic beverages. 2002 tobacco output amounted to 37.1 billion items.

Agriculture. The 2002 gross grain yield totaled 8,481,200 tons, sunflower seed – 732,400 tons, sugar-beet – 4.2 million tons, dairy products – 436,000 tons, and meat (including by-products) – 88,800 tons.

Industry. In 2002, the Territory's enterprises pro-duced 6,300 tons of paints and varnish, 105,300 tons of mineral fertilizers, 7,000 electric mixers, 31,000

cubic meters of lumber, 33,300 tons of cardboard, 2.4 million tons of cement, 580 million conventional bricks of wall construction materials, 3 million square meters of fabric, and 9,757,000 pairs of footwear.

4.2. KEY EXPORTS, INCLUDING EXTRA-CIS

The Territory's foreign trade turnover amounted to $2 billion in 2002 (extra-CIS trade accounted for 91% and CIS trade for 9%). Major trade partners in-clude Turkey, Bulgaria, Italy, Greece, the Netherlands, Germany, Spain, and the USA. The Territory maintains close links with Ukraine, Kazakhstan, and Uzbekistan.

Exports to extra-CIS countries totaled $944.9 million in 2000, with exports to CIS countries totaling $50.8 million. The respective figures for 2001 were $912.6 million and $79 million, and $986.9 mil-lion and $96.3 million for 2002. The main goods exported by the Territory are crude oil, sunflower seeds, sugar, tobacco products, raw timber, and grain.

4.3. KEY IMPORTS, INCLUDING EXTRA-CIS

2000 imports from extra-CIS countries amounted to $501.4 million, while imports from CIS countries totaled $70.3 million. The respective figures for 2001 were $558 million and $69.2 million, and $872.7 million and $82.1 million for 2001. Imports from CIS accounted for 12% of total imports, and imports from extra-CIS, for 88%. The main goods imported by the Territory are raw sugar, fertilizers and pesticides, agricultural equipment, citrus plants, oil products, and medicine. The main exporters to the region are Ukraine, Germany, Italy, France, Turkey, China, Cuba, Greece, and the USA.

4.4. MAJOR REGIONAL EXPORT AND IMPORT ENTITIES

Due to the specific features of trade in the Krasnodar Territory, export and import operations are performed mainly by industrial companies.

5. INVESTMENT OPPORTUNITIES

5.1. INVESTMENTS IN 1992–2002 (BY INDUSTRY SECTOR), INCLUDING FOREIGN INVESTMENTS

The following factors determine the investment appeal of the Krasnodar Territory:

- Its advantageous geographic location;
- Its developed transport infrastructure (direct access to international sea routes through the Black Sea and the Mediterranean);
- Considerable potential of agricultural companies (rich raw material base for processing sector);

- Availability of unique recreational resources for tourism;
- Fertile arable lands producing a full spectrum of temperate crops and several types of subtropical crops;
- Availability of natural resources;
- Highly qualified workforce;
- Dynamic legislative base.

5.2. CAPITAL INVESTMENT

Transport accounts for the biggest share of capital investment at 89.1%, followed by food and beverages at 5.3%, and services (retail and public catering) at 4.5%.

Capital investment by industry sector, $ million						*TABLE 6*
	1997	1998	1999	2000	2001	2002
Total capital investment	1,716.4	1,225.0	1,064.2	1,945.8	2,172.5	2,140.0
Including major industries (% of total)						
Industry	21.5	24.1	13.8	9.2	9.6	11.1
Agriculture and forestry	7.0	5.5	5.5	4.3	5.2	5.8
Construction	9.1	3.6	2.3	2.4	4.0	4.5
Transport and communications	15.2	25.0	24.0	22.5	19.2	25.4
Trade and public catering	1.1	1.1	0.5	1.5	1.9	2.1
Other	46.1	40.7	53.9	60.1	60.1	51.1

Foreign investment trends in 1992–2002						*TABLE 7*
	1992–1997	1998	1999	2000	2001	2002*
Foreign investment, $ million	108.8	69.5	304.4	617.8	583.3	185.1
Including the construction						
of the Caspian oil pipeline, $ million	–	–	268.3	567.8	450.6	27.7
Including FDI, $ million	86.7	49.4	295.4	597.8	476.2	72.6

*Estimates of the Krasnodar Territory Administration

5.3. MAJOR ENTERPRISES (INCLUDING ENTERPRISES WITH FOREIGN INVESTMENT)

The Krasnodar Territory is home to 781 companies with foreign investment from 60 countries. Major companies are OAO Krasnodartabakprom, ZAO Sochi Pepsi-Cola Soft Drinks Plant, OAO Kuban Gypsum-Knauf, and JV Tetra-Pak Kuban. Investors from the USA account for 47.3% of total investment, the Netherlands – 29%, Cyprus – 14.4%, and the UK – 6.5%.

5.4. CURRENT LEGISLATION ON INVESTOR TAX EXEMPTIONS AND PRIVILEGES

In 1999, the Territorial Legislative Council passed the Krasnodar Territory's Law On State Support to Investment Activity in the Krasnodar Territory, which ensures various forms of state support to investment activity, including tax privileges, investment credits from the local budget, guarantees provided by the Territorial Administration, and reimbursement (subsi-

III

SOUTHERN FEDERAL DISTRICT

Largest enterprises of the Krasnodar Territory	*TABLE 8*

COMPANY	SECTOR
OAO Rosneft-Krasnodarneftegaz	Oil
OAO Philip Morris Kuban	Tobacco
OAO Kubanenergo	Energy
OAO Novorossiysk Commercial Seaport	Water transport
OOO Kubangazprom	Pipeline transport
OAO Tuapse Trade Seaport	Water transport
OOO SBS Firm	Timber
OOO Yugneftegaz	Fuel
OAO Kuban Airlines	Aviation
OAO Novoroscement	Construction materials

dizing) of portions of interests on loans issued from the territorial budget. Moreover, investors may rent land, use natural resources, and acquire the Territory's real estate on preferential terms.

Investors putting their own or borrowed funds into investment projects with the "approved" status are eligible for exemptions from local taxes. Domestic and foreign investors have equitable rights to tax privileges.

The Law envisages special tax incentives for banks and leasing companies providing loans for the implementation of projects with the "approved" status. The loan guarantee offered by the Administration is a major measure aimed at attracting private-sector investment.

Regional entities responsible for raising investment		*TABLE 9*
ENTITY	ADDRESS	PHONE, FAX, E-MAIL
Economic Development, Investment, and External Economic Relations Department of the Krasnodar Territory	35, ul. Krasnaya, Krasnodar, Krasnodar Territory, 350014	Phone: (8612) 62 5839, 53 4598 E-mail: depec@krasnodar.ru
GUP Economic Development Agency of the Krasnodar Territory	57, ul. Komsomolskaya, 4th floor, Krasnodar, Krasnodar Territory, 350063	Phone: (8612) 62 2253, 62 2294 E-mail: personal@istnet.ru
GU Investinformservice APK	36, ul. Rashpilevskaya, Krasnodar, Krasnodar Territory, 350000	Phone: (8612) 62 5212, 62 2219 E-mail: iKS@aris.krasnodar.ru
GUP Kubaninvest of the Krasnodar Territory	36, ul. Rashpilevskaya, Krasnodar, Krasnodar Territory, 350000	Phone: (8612) 69 4731, 69 4446, 69 4747 E-mail: kubaninvest@depinvest.ru
GUP Krasnodar Territory Audit and Control Center	2/1, ul. Korolenko, Krasnodar, Krasnodar Territory, 350038	Phone: (8612) 55 2860, 55 9268, 55 2869
GUP Expertise	242, ul. Selezneva, Krasnodar, Krasnodar Territory, 350058	Phone: (8612) 64 0935, 64 0936

5.5. FEDERAL AND REGIONAL ECONOMIC AND SOCIAL DEVELOPMENT PROGRAMS FOR THE KRASNODAR TERRITORY

Federal targeted programs. The major federal targeted program of economic and social development for the Territory is the Russia's South program, which is due to run through 2006. The Program aims to develop a modern tourism industry by creating resort infrastructure in Sochi, Anapa, Gelendzhik, and Temryuk, improving transport and engineering infrastructure, and improving the resort zone's energy supply. The program comprises some 90 projects for a total of $921.8 million, including 26 projects in the town of Sochi. The resort development component of the program is worth some $213.9 million. The federal budget has earmarked $37.8 million in funding for this program.

Regional programs. The Krasnodar Territory Administration is developing and implementing over 50 regional programs focused on social issues such as healthcare, education, and social welfare. A budget of $54.2 million has been allocated to these program from the federal budget to complement the $24 million allocated from the regional budget. The Territory has accorded priority status to the following programs:

- The Quality Program's objectives are to ensure the quality and safety of products supplied to the local consumer market and protect the population from low quality products that pose an environmental or health hazard. The Territory's budget allocated $0.3 million in financing the program in 2002.
- The Territory's budget allocated more than $2.5 million in 2002 to support the Educational Program in the Krasnodar Territory, 2001–2005

and computerization and establishing a unified local information network in the Territory.

- Other important local programs include: the comprehensive program Extending the Gas Supply Network of the Krasnodar Territory, Priority Areas for Research in the Agroindustrial Complex of the Krasnodar Territory, 2001–2005 (research and development on new agricultural vehicles), and Development of the Vine Sector of the Krasnodar Territory, 2001–2005.

Every year, the Krasnodar Territory Administration adopts a regional investment program aimed at developing housing and communal services and rural gas, heat, and water networks, and building social facilities. The program has a budget of $37.8 million for 2003.

6. INVESTMENT PROJECTS

Industry sector and project description	1) Expected results 2) Amount and term of investment 3) Form of financing[1] 4) Documentation[2]	Contact information
1	2	3
ENERGY		
38R001 ■ ● ★ ◆ ▲		OAO Kubanenergo
Reconstruction of the Krasnodar Thermal Power Station, installation of a steam-gas unit (450 MW). Project goal: to increase electricity and heat output.	1) Electricity output – 474 MW, heat output – 450 Gcal/h per year 2) $200 million/2 years 3) E, L ($80 million), Leas. 4) FS, BP	2, ul. Stavropolskaya, Krasnodar 350033, Krasnodar Territory Phone: (8612) 69 6359, 68 4905, 68 5913 Fax: (8612) 68 2493 E-mail: telet@kuben.elektra.ru Vitaly Yevgenyevich Spiridonov, CEO
38R002 ● ★ ▲		ZAO Neftegaztekhnologia-Energia
Construction of a distribution grid of heat gas reciprocating power stations at Slavyansk-on-Kuban. Project goal: to increase electricity and heat output.	1) Electricity revenues – $11.2 million, heat revenues – $1.1 million per year 2) $3.8 million/1.5 years 3) L, Leas. 4) FS	9, ul. Krasnaya, Slavyansk-on-Kuban 353560, Krasnodar Territory Phone: (86146) 22 286, 73 112 Fax: (86146) 22 273 E-mail: total@ngt-energy.ru; http://www.ngt-energy.ru Valentin Vasilyevich Eremenko, CEO Anatoly Konstantinovich Travnikov, Deputy CEO
CHEMICALS AND PHARMACEUTICALS		
38R003 ■ ● ◆ ▲		ZAO Roskarfarm
Production of crystalline beta-carotene and carotene-enriched food and medicine. Project goal: to increase output and product range.	1) Output of 10 tons of crystalline beta-carotene ($10.7 million) per year 2) $4.5 million/n/a 3) E, L ($2.5 million) 4) FS, BP	70, ul. Sedina, Krasnodar, 350000 Krasnodar Territory Phone: (8612) 55 0231, 75 1939 Fax: (8612) 75 1939 E-mail: roskarfarm@mail.ru Robert Vramovich Kazaryan, CEO

[1] L – Loan, E – Equity, Leas. – Leasing, JV – Joint Venture
[2] BP – Business Plan, FS – Feasibility Study

III

SOUTHERN FEDERAL DISTRICT

1	2	3

38R004 ■ ● ◆ ▲

Production of a new generation blood substitute. Project goal: to introduce new product to the market.	1) Output of 200,000 doses ($3.5 million) per year 2) $3.1 million/1 year 3) E, L 4) FS, BP	ZAO Plazma-M 1, Yeiskoe shosse, Krasnodar, 350031 Krasnodar Territory Phone: (8612) 69 7452, (812) 593 5313 Fax: (8612) 69 7452 E-mail: plazma-m@yandex.ru Anton Vladimirovich Kuzmenko, CEO

38R005 ■ ● ◆ ▲

Establishment of blood plasma replacing substance production. Project goal: to introduce a new product to the market.	1) Annual production of 12 million bottles 2) $9 million/1 year 3) E, L 4) FS, BP	ZAO Plazma-M 1, Yeiskoe shosse, Krasnodar, 350031 Krasnodar Territory Phone: (8612) 69 7452, (812) 593 5313 Fax: (8612) 69 7452 E-mail: plazma-m@yandex.ru Anton Vladimirovich Kuzmenko, CEO

38R006 ● ▲

Production of crystalline iodide (mineral resource base development). Project goal: to increase output.	1) Output of 175 tons per year 2) $5.2 million/3 years 3) L 4) FS	GUP Troitsk Iodide Plant Oil Production Site Troitskaya, Krymsk District, 353360 Krasnodar Territory Phone: (86131) 21 281 Semion Viktorovich Portnoy, Acting Director

FORESTRY, TIMBER, AND PULP AND PAPER

38R007 ■ ● ★ ◆

Construction of a furniture wood board plant. Project goal: to introduce a new product to the market.	1) Output of 100,000 cubic meters per year 2) $84 million/1.5 years 3) E, L, Leas. 4) BP	OAO Yug 1, ul. Zavodskaya, Mostovskoy, Krasnodar Territory, 352571 Phone: (86192) 51 400, 52 661 Fax: (86192) 52 540 E-mail: ug@mail.kuban.ru http://www.ug.kuban.ru Alexander Yakovlevich Marshalko, CEO

FOOD AND BEVERAGES

38R008 ■ ● ◆ ▲

Construction of a soybean processing plant with a capacity of 46,000 tons per year. Project goal: to introduce soybean products, including soy concentrate, fat-free soy flour, and non-refined soybean oil to the market.	1) Sales of $35.1 million per year 2) $23 million/1 year 3) E, L 4) FS, BP	ZAO Agrocomplex 1, ul. Stepnaya, Vyselki, Krasnodar Territory, 353100 Phone: (86157) 22 991, 48 797, 22 668, 21 945 Fax: (86157) 22 991, 25 544 E-mail: vslagro@krintel.ru Alexei Nikolaevich Tkachev, CEO

38R009 ■ ● ◆

Production of diet meat products and canned vegetables and meat for infants. Project goal: to introduce new products to the market.	1) Sales of $10 million per year 2) $14.8 million/2 years 3) E, L ($13.3 million) 4) BP	ZAO Tikhoretsky Meat Processing Plant 16, ul. Udarnikov, Tikhoretsk, 352121, Krasnodar Territory Phone: (86152) 22 888 Fax: (86196) 23 020, 22 908 Nikolai Vasilyevich Timoshenko, CEO

AGRICULTURE

38R010 ■ ● ▲

Upgrading of a poultry plant's fixed assets. Project goal: to increase output of chicken meat.	1) Sales of $10.5 million per year 2) $9 million/1.5 years 3) E, L 4) BP	OOO Lazurnoye 74, ul. Krasnaya, Dinskaya, Krasnodar Territory, 353200 Phone: (86162) 53 427, 52 500 Fax: (86162) 54 269 E-mail: lazur@dinsk.kuban.ru Valentin Nikolaevich Shepelev, Director

1	2	3

38R011 ■ ● ▲

Construction of fruit storage. facilities with regulated air parameters Project goal: to increase output.	1) Capacity of 5,000 tons of fruit annually 2) $3 million/1 year 3) E, L 4) FS	ZAO Agrocompany Giant Orchard 615, ul. Shkolnaya, Slavyansk-on-Kuban 353565, Krasnodar Territory Phone: (86146) 26 236, 26 232 Fax: (86146) 25 544 E-mail: info@sadgigant.ru Grigory Anatolyevich Klad, CEO

TRANSPORT INFRASTRUCTURE

38R012 ■ ● ◆ ▲

Construction of a deep-water wharf in the Tuapse Seaport to load oil and oil products to exporting tankers with a carrying capacity of 90-110,000 tons. Project goal: to increase freight processing and service new types of vessels.	1) Capacity of 7 million tons per year 2) $16.9 million/1.5 years 3) L, E 4) FS, BP	State Company Sea Administration of Tuapse Seaport 8, ul. Gorkogo, Tuapse, 352800 Krasnodar Territory Phone: (86167) 76 400 Fax: (86167) 76 403 E-mail: map@tuapseport.ru Bogdan Vasilyevich Vantsar, CEO

38R013 ● ◆ ▲

Construction of two wharfs in the Tuapse Seaport for transs-hipment of general freight. Project goal: to increase freight processing.	1) Capacity up to 1 million tons per year 2) $16.9 million/3 years 3) L 4) FS, BP	State Company Sea Administration of Tuapse Seaport 8, ul. Sovetov, Tuapse, 352800 Krasnodar Territory Phone: (86167) 76 400 Fax: (86167) 76 403 E-mail: map@tuapseport.ru Bogdan Vasilyevich Vantsar, CEO

38R014 ● ▲

Construction of a deep-water oil wharf in the Sheskharis Bay, Novorossiysk. Project goal: to increase freight processing and service new types of vessels.	1) Capacity of 15 million tons per year 2) $71.2 million/1.5 years 3) L ($70.8 million) 4) FS	State Company Sea Administration of Novorossiysk Seaport 19, ul. Sovetov, Novorossiysk, 353900 Krasnodar Territory Phone: (8617) 25 3251 Fax: (8617) 25 4530 E-mail: alekc@mapn.morflot.ru Yevgeny Gennadyevich Trunin, Head

---

38R015 ● ▲

Reconstruction of the Sochi seaport – construction of a car-ferry unit and a marina. Project goal: to extend range of services and increase freight processing.	1) Capacity of 200,000 tons of freight and 130,000 passengers per year; 100 yachts 2) $32.5 million/3 years 3) L 4) FS	State Company Sea Administration of Novorossiysk Seaport 19, ul. Sovetov, Novorossiysk, 353900 Krasnodar Territory Phone: (8617) 25 3251 Fax: (8617) 25 4530 E-mail: alekc@mapn.morflot.ru Yevgeny Gennadyevich Trunin, Head

---

HOTELS AND TOURISM

38R016 ■ ● ★ ❖ ▼

Creation and development of the Kras-naya Polyana mountain resort complex. Project goal: to improve efficiency of the Sochi resort area by using it in winter time too in addition to summer.	1) Maximum daily capacity is 25,000 people 2) $1,400 million/1–5 years 3) L, Leas., E, JV 4) Investment proposal	OAO Krasnaya Polyana 51, Kurortny prospect, 354000, Sochi Krasnodar Territory Phone/fax: (8622) 62 4521 E-mail: management@krasnayapolyana.com Vladimir Nasibulovich Sharafutdinov, CEO

III

SOUTHERN FEDERAL DISTRICT

1	2	3

38R017

Construction of a tourist and entertainment center at the Yugra Island in Tuapse.
Project goal: to increase sales and range of services.

1) Sales of $13.1 million per year
2) $58.6 million/2.5 years
3) E, L
4) FS, BP

Branch of OOO Yugra Island
Yugra Recreational Center, Olginka, Tuapse District, 352840, Krasnodar Territory
Phone: (86167) 99 610
Fax: (86167) 99610
E-mail: ostrov@ugrahotel.ru
http://www.ugra-island.ru
Yury Valeryevich Tokarev,
Head of Branch

38R018

Establishment of an ethnographic village at Kazak in the Abinsk District.
Project goal: to introduce new services to the market.

1) Sales of $0.4 million per year
2) $0.8 million/1 year
3) E, L
4) Investment proposal

Executive Committee
of the Abinsk District
31, ul. Internatsionalnaya,
Abinsk, 353320, Krasnodar Territory
Phone: (86150) 51 351
Fax: (86150) 52 700
Vladimir Panteleevich Radchenko,
Chairman of the Committee

MACHINE ENGINEERING AND METAL PROCESSING

38R019

Production of radio communication instruments in Krasnodar.
Project goal: to increase output of instruments.

1) Output of 5,000 units
   ($0.75 million) per year
2) $1 million/2 years
3) L, Leas.
4) FS

OAO R&D and Production
Company Rythm
5, ul. Moskovskaya, Krasnodar
350072, Krasnodar Territory
Phone: (8612) 52 1105, 55 8766
Fax: (8612) 52 3341
E-mail: ritm@mail.kuban.ru
Alexander Antonovich Lotto,
CEO

39. STAVROPOL TERRITORY [26]

ECONOMIC MAP

ROSTOV REGION

Salsk

Manych

Lake Manych-Gudilo

Yegorlyk

REPUBLIC

ELISTA

OF KALMYKIA

Kalaus

Chograyskoe water reservoir

Izobilny

Svetlograd

STAVROPOL

Armavir

Nevinnomyssk

Budyonnovsk

Zelenokumsk

Kuma

CHERKESSK

Zheleznovodsk

Mineralnye Vody

Kurdzhinovo

Essentuki

Georgievsk

REPUBLIC OF

Pyatigorsk

KARACHAEVO-

Kislovodsk

Prokhladny

-CHERKESSIA

Mozdok

Kuban

REPUBLIC OF

KABARDINO-

NALCHIK

Nazran

GROZNY

G

Sukhumi

Tyrnyauz

BALKARIA

MAGAS

E

Beslan

REPUBLIC OF

O

NORTH

VLADIKAVKAZ

R

OSSETIA-

G

-ALANIA

I

Rioni

A

PROCESSING INDUSTRY	MINING INDUSTRY	CROPS AND LIVESTOCK BREEDING	
● Machine engineering and metal processing	△ Natural gas	Ⴤ Wheat	◇ Vegetables
● Chemicals	▲ Oil	⚲ Vineyards	🐄 Meat and dairy cattle breeding
● Construction materials	🭬 Mineral water sources	↓ Corn	🐖 Sheep rearing
○ Food and beverages		•• Potatoes	🐖 Pig breeding
	POWER PLANTS	⚲ Sunflower	🦢 Poultry farming
	⚡ Thermal power plants	🍎 Orchards	⚲ Resorts
	⚡ Hydro power plants	▼ Sugar beetroot	
		Ⴑ Rape	

The Stavropol Territory is a region of high industrial and agricultural potential. It is also mineral resource rich, with deposits of natural gas, oil, rare earth metals, construction materials, and mineral water. The Stavropol Territory is home to the North Caucasus's largest thermal power stations, Stavropolskaya and Nevinnomysskaya, and is criss-crossed by oil and gas trunk pipelines. Its chief wealth and production resource is its soil. More than 40% of the Territory's land is covered with highly fertile black earth soil.

The Government of the Stavropol Territory is fully aware that continued economic growth would require the substantial development of trade, economic, and investment cooperation and an increase in capital investment into the upgrading of production facilities and the deployment of new technologies. Along with strengthening the Territory's own resources, foreign investment is recognized as having an important role to play. The Territory is home to more than four hundred enterprises with foreign investment.

Investors are drawn by the enormous potential of the domestic consumer market and access to qualified workforce. Much foreign investment is concentrated in the agriculture and mineral resource development and processing sectors.

Another type of investor – the portfolio investor – is found at OAO Arnest Household Chemicals Plant, which is partially owned by the European Bank for Reconstruction and Development and Pioglobal investment fund (holders of a $10 million stake).

We expect the agroindustrial sector, led by the food and beverages and food processing industries, to continue topping the league table for foreign investment in the medium term. The energy and housing sectors are likely to see their investment appeal factor rise in the future as a result of the structural reform drive in the Russian economy.

The year 2003 will mark the bicentennial of Kavkazskiye Mineralniye Vody, a unique spa resort of international renown. The Territory's rehabilitation and recreational centers were recognized as the country's top health resorts during the Sanatorium-2002 exhibition. We will continue to attract investment, including foreign investment, to upgrade our recreational and resort centers.

The Government of the Stavropol Territory is committed to creating conditions conducive to improving the investment climate and increasing foreign investment. To that end, the Government of the Stavropol Territory is taking the following proactive steps: developing new laws and mechanisms to economically encourage foreign investors in the Stavropol Territory; concluding by the Territory Government of investment agreements with major investors and assignment of Stavropol Territory Government officials as supervisors to investment projects; implementing a system of government guarantees for priority investment projects; creating a mechanism for extending tax incentives to investors engaged in priority projects; and implementing measures aimed at overcoming the information vacuum by informing potential investors of lucrative investment opportunities in the Stavropol Territory.

Alexander Chernogorov,
GOVERNOR OF THE STAVROPOL TERRITORY

1. GENERAL INFORMATION

1.1. GEOGRAPHY

Located in South-Western Russia's North Caucasus region between the Black Sea, the Caspian Sea, and the Sea of Azov, the Stavropol Territory covers a total area of 66,500 square kilometers. To the south, the Territory borders the Republic of North Ossetia – Alania, the Republic of Kabardino-Balkaria, the Republic of Karachayevo-Cherkessia, and the Chechen Republic, to the north – the Rostov Region and the Republic of Kalmykia, to the east – the Republic of Dagestan, and to the west – the Krasnodar Territory.

1.2. CLIMATE

Spread across the steppe and semi-desert zones, the Stavropol Territory enjoys a continental climate. Air temperatures in January average –5°C, rising to +25°C in July. Annual precipitation reaches 300–500 mm. The growing season in the Stavropol Territory lasts around 180 days on average. More than 40% of the Territory is covered with highly fertile black earth soil, with a further 52% lying under brown earth.

1.3. POPULATION

According to preliminary 2002 census results, total population in the Territory was 2.7 million people, of whom 1,164,000 people were economically active. The Territory's average population density is 40 people per square kilometer. While official unemployment stands at 0.9%, the actual rate is 10.3%.

Demographically speaking, some 57.8% are of working age, 20.5% are below the statutory working age, and 21.7% are beyond the statutory working age.

The Stavropol Territory's major urban centers (2002) are: Stavropol with 337,500 inhabitants, Pyatigorsk with 181,300 inhabitants, Nevinnomyssk with 131,700 inhabitants, Kislovodsk with 115,900 inhabitants, and Yessentuki with 88,200 inhabitants.

Population								TABLE 1
	1992	1997	1998	1999	2000	2001	2002	
Total population, '000	2,507	2,644	2,653	2,660	2,660	2,644	2,731	
Economically active population, '000	1,228	1,109	1,078	1,241	1,237	1,186	1,164	

2. ADMINISTRATION

1, pl. Lenina, Stavropol, Stavropol Territory, 355025
Phone: (8652) 35 1172; fax: (8652) 35 0638, 35 7694; e-mail: invest@stavropol.net; http://www.stavinvest.ru

NAME	POSITION	CONTACT INFORMATION
Alexander Leonidovich CHERNOGOROV	Governor of the Stavropol Territory	Phone: (8652) 35 2252
Valery Veniaminovich GAYEVSKY	First Deputy Chairman of the Government of the Stavropol Territory, Minister of Economic Development and Trade	Phone: (8652) 35 4471 Fax: (8652) 26 6813
Vladimir Fedorovich GARKUSHA	First Deputy Chairman of the Government of the Stavropol Territory, Minister of Agriculture	Phone: (8652) 35 0540 Fax: (8652) 35 7320
Vitaly Ivanovich MIKHAILENKO	Chief of Administration of Kavkazskiye Mineralniye Vody, a specially protected ecological and resort area of the Russian Federation, First Deputy Chairman of the Government of the Stavropol Territory	Phone: (87934) 70 250 Fax: (87934) 72 711
Gennady Mikhailovich KLYUSHNIKOV	Deputy Chairman of the Government of the Stavropol Territory, Minister of Industry, Transport, and Communications	Phone: (8652) 35 2132 Fax: (8652) 26 1526
Tatyana Alexandrovna POGORELOVA	Deputy Chairman of the Government of the Stavropol Territory, Minister of Finance	Phone: (8652) 35 9642
Vladimir Mikhailovich RYZHINKOV	Deputy Chairman of the Government of the Stavropol Territory, Minister of State Property	Phone: (8652) 35 0552

III

SOUTHERN FEDERAL DISTRICT

NAME POSITION	CONTACT INFORMATION
Alexander Nikolayevich ORESHKOV — Deputy Chairman of the Government of the Stavropol Territory, Minister of Housing and Communal Services, Construction, and Architecture	Phone: (8652) 35 5572 Fax: (8652) 35 8633

3. ECONOMIC POTENTIAL

3.1. 1997–2002 GROSS REGIONAL PRODUCT (GRP). INDUSTRY BREAKDOWN

In 2002, the Stavropol Territory's gross regional product reached $2,975.3 million, a 16.1% increase compared to 2001 figures. The growth resulted mainly from industry and services (trade and public catering) growth. Per capita GRP in 2001 totaled $969, in 2002 – $1,130.

3.2. MAJOR ECONOMIC GROWTH PROJECTIONS

The Conceptual Framework for Social and Economic Development of the Stavropol Territory through 2006 and the Federal Targeted Program for Economic and Social Development of the Stavropol Territory, 2003–2007 map out economic development in the Territory over the coming years and set the following objectives:

Industry: maintenance of output growth rates by opening new markets and fostering growth in solvent consumer demand; enterprise restructuring; expansion and renewal of production capacity through borrowing and direct investment; active pursuit of innovation; curtailment of production costs and active encouragement of resource saving technologies;

GRP trends in 1997–2002						TABLE 2
	1997	1998	1999	2000	2001*	2002*
GRP in current prices, $ million	4,381.6	2,960.8	1,651.9	2,098.8	2,562.1	2,975.3

*Estimates of the Stavropol Territory Government

Industry breakdown of industrial output in 1997–2002, % of total						TABLE 3
	1997	1998	1999	2000	2001*	2002*
GRP	100.0	100.0	100.0	100.0	100.0	100.0
Industry	20.9	19.4	20.5	20.2	20.4	22.0
Agriculture and forestry	17.9	18.2	16.4	16.1	15.9	14.7
Construction	6.3	8.5	6.4	11.3	9.8	9.5
Transport and communications	12.9	10.4	12.7	10.1	11.7	11.3
Trade and public catering	14.8	14.3	16.8	14.7	13.7	14.3
Other	21.7	26.0	21.4	21.3	23.3	21.8
Net taxes on output	5.5	3.2	5.8	6.3	5.2	6.4

*Estimates of the Stavropol Territory Government

Agriculture: growth in output, enhanced production efficiency through the deployment of innovative agricultural techniques, modern management methods, encouragement of investment in new processing capacity; and fostering of cooperation and integration in the agroindustrial sector;

Construction: creation of new and restructuring of existing construction capacity via the deployment of high-output technologies in the residential and industrial construction sectors;

Trade: the development of trade links with other regions of Russia and abroad;

Transport: growth in the road haulage sector, the creation of modern road haulage organizations, the encouragement of international and Trans-Caucasus transit traffic to and from other regions of Russia; and growth in air traffic through the reconstruction of the Territory's airports.

3.3. INDUSTRIAL OUTPUT IN 1997–2002 FOR MAJOR SECTORS OF ECONOMY

The Territory is home to over 350 major and medium sized enterprises. Its core industries are energy, food and beverages, chemicals and petrochemicals, and machine engineering and metals, which together make up a combined total of some 78.6% of the Territory's industrial output. The Stavropol Territory was judged to be among the top five regions of Russia in terms of output of competitive products during the Top 100 Products in Russia Competition in 2001.

Industry breakdown of industrial output in 1997–2002, % of total						TABLE 4
	1997	1998	1999	2000	2001	2002*
Industry	100.0	100.0	100.0	100.0	100.0	100.0
Energy	35.6	35.6	24.0	26.9	28.3	26.3
Food and beverages	24.8	25.4	28.9	24.4	24.1	22.6
Chemicals and petrochemicals	12.8	11.9	19.2	21.9	20.9	17.2
Machine engineering and metal processing	8.7	9.6	10.8	11.0	10.5	12.5
Fuel	4.2	4.8	4.9	5.8	5.5	6.6
Construction materials	4.3	4.4	4.6	3.1	2.4	2.9
Light industry	1.6	1.3	1.1	1.0	2.2	1.1
Forestry, timber, and pulp and paper	1.3	0.9	1.1	1.0	0.9	1.1

*Estimates of the Stavropol Territory Government

Energy. The energy sector accounts for some 26.3% of the Territory's total industrial output. The Territory's main power stations are the Stavropol GRES (2,400 MW – the largest in the North Caucasus), the Nevinnomysskaya GRES (1,340 MW), and the Kuban HEP system with its seven hydroelectric stations (465 MW).

Food and beverages. The food industry accounts for some 22.6% of total industrial output. Major sectors of the Territory's food industry include cereals and pasta, processed and unprocessed meat, dairy and vegetable products, and fermented, distilled, and non-alcoholic beverages.

Major companies include OAO Stavropolsky Preserves Factory, OAO Stavropolsky Dairy, OAO Pyatigorsk Meat Processing Plant, OAO Kholod, OAO Stavropol Sugar, ZAO Kavminvody, OAO Narzan, OOO Coca-Cola Stavropolye Bottlers, and OAO Syrodel.

Chemicals and petrochemicals. The chemicals and petrochemicals sector accounts for 17.2% of the Territory's total industrial output. The Territory's leading chemicals and petrochemicals enterprises are OAO Nevinnomyssky Azot, OAO Vneshtradeinvest, and OOO Stavrolen, all of which export products overseas.

Machine engineering and metal processing. This sector accounts for some 12.5% of the Territory's total industrial output. Major enterprises include OAO Stapri Piston Ring Factory, OAO Avtopritsep-Kamaz, ZAO Krasny Metallist, OAO Krast, OAO Pyatigorskselmash, OAO ArZIL, and OAO Spetsinstrument.

Fuel. Fuel production accounts for some 6.6% of the Territory's total industrial output. The Stavropol Territory is a region of developed oil and gas extraction and operation infrastructure. In 1998, the Praskoveysky Oil Refinery with annual oil processing capacity of 50,000 tons was launched. A mini oil refinery with annual processing capacity of 25,000 tons for the Zhuravskoye oil field is under construction and is to be launched in 2003. OAO Rosneft-Stavropolneftegaz is the largest enterprise in the sector.

Agriculture. The Territory's specific feature is its fertile soils. Most of the steppe land is arable and cultivated for crop growing.

3.4. FUEL AND ENERGY BALANCE (OUTPUT AND CONSUMPTION PER RESOURCE)

The Stavropol Territory has significant energy resources. The Territory's energy companies supply electricity within the Territory and to most other areas of the Southern Federal District. The potential capacity of the Territory's energy companies is over 4 GW. Its power stations are potentially capable of producing up to 25 billion kWh annually, while the Territory's own needs are only 12 billion kWh a year.

The Stavropol Territory is home to Europe's largest natural gas reservoir from which gas is pumped to Turkey via the Blue Stream pipeline.

3.5. TRANSPORT INFRASTRUCTURE

Roads. The Stavropol Territory has more than 7,400 km of paved public highway, with more than 150 road haulage companies assuring a stable road transportation sector. The Territory's road system links the ports of the Black Sea, the Sea of Azov, and the Caspian Sea to the rest of the Russian Federation and cross-border destinations.

Railroads. The Stavropol Territory has 1,500 km of railroad, providing links to other regions of Russia along the Kavkazskaya – Tikhoretskaya – Rostov-on-Don rail corridor. The Territory's principle freight corridor is the Kavkazskaya – Rostov-on-Don route. Plans are afoot to lay a 240 km rail corridor running from Budennovsk to Neftekumsk to Kobuchei, and onwards to the Trans-Caucasian republics and Central Asia.

III

SOUTHERN FEDERAL DISTRICT

Fuel and energy sector production and consumption, 1997–2002						TABLE 5
	1997	1998	1999	2000	2001	2002*
Energy output, billion kWh	18.2	17.7	16.3	18.3	17.9	17.2
Oil output (including gas condensate), '000 tons	847.2	907.7	920.2	1,021.7	1,079.0	1,014.9
Natural gas extraction, million cubic meters	360.1	329.6	321.6	375.7	393.4	414.1
Energy consumption, billion kWh	7.0	7.0	7.7	7.8	7.8	n/a
Oil consumption, '000 tons	n/a	11.3	13.9	–	0.07	n/a
Natural gas consumption, million cubic meters	n/a	8,355.6	7,468.4	8,405.1	8,335.8	n/a

*Estimates of the Stavropol Territory Government

Airports. The Stavropol Territory's two international airports are located at Mineralniye Vody and Stavropol, with passenger numbers averaging around 400,000 annually. The airports and the airport complex at Mineralniye Vody are currently under reconstruction with support from the Stavropol Territory Government under the Russian Transport System Modernization, 2002–2010 and Russia's South federal targeted programs. For these purposes, $3.6 million was allocated over the last four years. Following the completion of reconstruction work, the Territory's airports will be capable of accepting all types of aircraft.

Oil and gas pipeline. Major trunk underground oil and gas pipelines, including sections of the Caspian Pipeline Consortium and the Blue Stream gas pipeline system, were laid in recent years.

3.6. MAIN NATURAL RESOURCES: RESERVES AND EXTRACTION IN 2002

The Territory's principle natural resources are natural gas, oil, rare earth metals minerals used in construction materials, asbestos, Glauber's and edible salt, and curative mud. The Mineralniye Vody district is home to the renowned mineral water sources Narzan, Yessentuki, and Slavyanovskaya.

Oil and gas deposits. The Territory's largest natural gas fields are the Mirnenskoye, Sengileyevskoye, and Severo-Stavropolsko-Pelagiadinskoye.

The Territory's total natural gas output in 2002 reached 414.1 million cubic meters. In 2003, oil output is planned to reach 1.3 million tons, while gas output will total 410 million cubic meters. Extractable oil reserves total some 88 million tons, while natural gas reserves total 49 billion cubic meters.

Mineral thermal and fresh water. The Territory's mineral water reserves produce 12,450 cubic meters of mineral water a day. The mineral water bottling sector is currently operating at 11% capacity. Plans are afoot to produce daily in 2003: mineral water – 3,000 cubic meters, thermal water – 1,500 cubic meters, and fresh water – 283,000 cubic meters. Commercial reserves of mineral water are 27,000 cubic meters per day, thermal water – 12,000 cubic meters per day, and fresh water – 3.3 million cubic meters per day. In addition to that, reserves prepared for commercial use are: mineral water – 14,000 cubic meters per day, thermal water – 12,000 cubic meters per day, and fresh water – 1.6 million cubic meters per day.

Other minerals. The Territory has significant deposits of minerals used in the production of construction materials: clays for ceramic brick and tile production – 90 million cubic meters, clays for claydite production – 12 million cubic meters, sand and gravel mix – 290 million cubic meters, sand for construction purposes and silicate brick production – 125 million cubic meters, quartz sand for glass industry – 19 million cubic meters, shell rock – 32 million cubic meters, and sandstone – 11 million cubic meters.

The Territory has two deposits of glass sand with total reserves of over 10,000 cubic meters. The Territory also has ten promising fields of titanium and zirconium deposits.

Recreational resources. The Stavropol Territory has become recognized due to discovery of medical mineral water and mud sources in its territory. The world-renowned Kavkazskie Mineralniye Vody district is the site of a major spa and health resort center around Lake Tambukan with an abundance of mineral water sources. The Mineralniye Vody health resort center has over 100 sanatoriums and rest houses in its territory. The Territory's main resort towns are Pyatigorsk, Kislovodsk, Yessentuki, and Zheleznovodsk.

4. TRADE OPPORTUNITIES

4.1. MAIN GOODS PRODUCED IN THE REGION

Chemicals. Output of mineral fertilizers reached 782,700 tons in 2002, while output of paints and varnishes amounted to 14,500 tons.

Food and beverages. In 2002, bread and bakery output was 166,200 tons, vegetable oil – 58,900 tons, meat – 24,500 tons, grain – 6.3 million tons, whole milk – 552,700 tons, mineral water – 22.8 million decaliters, sparkling wine –

76,500 decaliters, ethyl alcohol – 650,600 decaliters, and brandy – 274,400 decaliters.

Medical goods. The region's enterprises produce special-purpose immunobiological medication, such as anti-toxic serum, vaccines, disbacteriosis medicines, and allergens. $4.2 million worth of medicinal goods was produced in 2002. FGUP Allergen is the leading manufacturer in the sector.

Perfumes and cosmetics. OAO Arnest is the sector's leader, supplying up to 40% of Russia's aerosol product requirements.

4.2. EXPORTS, INCLUDING EXTRA-CIS

Europe accounts for 40% of the Territory's total foreign trade turnover, followed by the CIS at 20%, North and South America at 15%, and Asia at 10%.

CIS and non-CIS exports accounted for 10% and 90% of the total, respectively. Petrochemicals and electricity constitute the bulk of the Territory's exports. Main exported goods include:

oil, mineral fertilizers, polyethylene, artificial sapphires, wheat, wool, and sunflower and rape seeds. Services, including telecommunications, education, and health care, account for up to 10% of the Territory's foreign trade turnover. Major importers of the Territory's products include Italy (15.5% of total exports), Ukraine (11.1%), the U.S. (10.6%), China (8%), and Germany (7.9%).

4.3. IMPORTS, INCLUDING EXTRA-CIS

The bulk of imports is represented by machinery, equipment, and vehicles (about 50% of total) and food products (20%). Italy, Ukraine, the USA, China, Germany, Kazakhstan, and France are major exporters to the Stavropol Territory.

4.4. MAJOR REGIONAL EXPORT AND IMPORT ENTITIES

Due to the specific features of the Stavropol Territory, export and import transactions are mainly conducted by industrial enterprises.

5. INVESTMENT OPPORTUNITIES

5.1. INVESTMENTS IN 1997–2002 (BY INDUSTRY SECTOR), INCLUDING FOREIGN INVESTMENTS

The following factors determine the investment appeal of the Stavropol Territory:
- Good geographical location and proximity to large markets;
- Cheap energy;
- Developed transport links and industrial infrastructure;
- Legislation providing a basis for the provision of tax incentives to investors and protection of investors' rights;
- Organizational and financial support for investment projects, and government guarantees of a safe business environment;

- Unique and agreeable conditions for recreation, tourism, and convalescence;
- A highly qualified workforce.

5.2. CAPITAL INVESTMENT

The transport and industry sectors account for the biggest share of capital investment.

5.3. MAJOR ENTERPRISES (INCLUDING ENTERPRISES WITH FOREIGN INVESTMENT)

The Stavropol Territory is home to more than 400 enterprises with foreign investment from some 52 countries worldwide. The largest companies in the Territory were set up with investments from the USA and European Union countries. In the food industry, the Stavropol Territory's largest companies with American investment are OOO Coca-Cola Stavropolye

III

SOUTHERN FEDERAL DISTRICT

Capital investment by industry sector, $ million						TABLE 6
	1997	1998	1999	2000	2001	2002*
Total capital investment	699.7	430.4	288.8	564.0	569.6	549.4
Including major industries (% of total):						
Industry	25.8	27.2	26.3	17.4	18.3	20.1
Agriculture and forestry	5.7	9.4	8.2	5.1	16.3	9.7
Construction	3.8	3.1	2.2	1.2	1.7	0.6
Transport and communications	16.2	15.8	25.4	51.9	33.5	50.0
Trade and public catering	2.7	3.1	2.4	1.4	3.3	2.1
Housing	29.5	32.4	27.6	14.9	15.5	4.6
Health care	3.1	1.2	1.4	2.7	4.9	4.3
Education	1.4	0.4	0.9	0.6	0.8	1.3

*Estimates of the Stavropol Territory Government

Foreign investment trends in 1997–2002						*TABLE 7*
	1997	1998	1999	2000	2001	2002*
Foreign investment, $ million	36.4	67.3	8.8	34.3	20.9	59.6
Including FDI, $ million	36.2	11.8	4.9	21.8	17.6	33.9

*Estimates of the Stavropol Territory Government

Bottlers (non-alcoholic beverages) and Heinz (children's food). A mineral water bottling plant producing Novoterskaya Tselebnaya mineral water was built in the Territory with investments from OAO Gazprom and Turkish partners.

A joint Russian-Norwegian enterprise Stav-TeleSot is the leading company in the Territory's mobile telecommunications sector, while Alcatel is the Territory's leading telecommunications equipment enterprise.

German investors have set up a subsidiary of Eurasia-Transit on the basis of Sovtransavto-Mineralniye Vody, the largest haulage company in the south of Russia.

5.4. MOST ATTRACTIVE SECTORS FOR INVESTMENT

According to the Stavropol Territory Government, companies in the chemicals and petrochemicals, food and beverages and food processing, and transport and communications sectors represent the strongest investment appeal. In a longer term, as structural reforms get underway, energy and housing will become priority sectors for investors.

5.5. CURRENT LEGISLATION ON INVESTOR EXEMPTIONS AND PRIVILEGES

The Stavropol Territory has passed the following laws: On the Attraction of Foreign Investment to the Territory's Economy, On State Support to

Investment Activity in the Stavropol Territory, and On State Support to Organizations Implementing Investment Projects by Using Loans Issued by the Stavropol Territory's Banks.

These laws provide a legal and economic framework for government support to investors, guarantee equitable protection of rights, and facilitate investor access to government bodies. Investors putting their own or borrowed funds into investment projects and investors successfully completing competitive tenders organized by the Stavropol Territory Government are eligible for tax exemptions.

Investors performing investment projects listed in the Territory's investment program are eligible, subject to approval from the Territory's Finance Ministry, for:

- Deferral of regional taxes;
- An investment credit for the regional profit tax component and regional taxes;
- Tax benefits for the regional land tax component;
- Exemptions for leased assets.

The Government of the Stavropol Territory is drafting the following laws for adoption by the Stavropol Territory Duma:

- On Innovation Activities in the Stavropol Territory;
- On State Support to Leasing Activities in the Stavropol Territory.

Regional entities responsible for raising investment		*TABLE 8*
ENTITY	ADDRESS	PHONE, FAX, E-MAIL
The Stavropol Territory Chamber of Commerce and Industry	Office 402, 384, ul. Lenina, Stavropol, Stavropol Territory, 355003	Phone: (8652) 94 5334
The Stavropol Business Information Center Public and State Fund	Office 410, 384, ul. Lenina, Stavropol, Stavropol Territory, 355003	Phone: (8652) 35 0078 Fax: (8652) 26 6886 E-mail: sbic@stavropol.net
Interleasing Invest Leasing Company	66, ul. Krasnoflotskaya, Stavropol, Stavropol Territory, 355003	Phone: (8652) 35 0397 Fax: (8652) 35 0250
Financial and Savings Company Investment and Financial Co.	458, ul. Lenina, Stavropol, Stavropol Territory, 355000	Phone: (8652) 35 2727 Fax: (8652) 35 2726
Invest-Center Investment and Financial Co.	23, ul. Lomonosova, Stavropol, Stavropol Territory, 355000	Phone: (8652) 94 5052 Fax: (8652) 35 6680
STEK Financial Company	458, ul. Lenina, Stavropol, Stavropol Territory, 355029	Phone: (8652) 35 3414 Fax: (8652) 35 2726
Strategia Financial Company	42, ul. Gorkogo, Stavropol, Stavropol Territory, 355006	Phone: (8652) 94 2102, 94 5199 Fax: (8652) 28 0993

5.6. FEDERAL AND REGIONAL ECONOMIC AND SOCIAL DEVELOPMENT PROGRAMS FOR THE STAVROPOL TERRITORY

Federal targeted programs. The major federal targeted programs are:

The Russia's South federal targeted program through 2006 aims to alleviate social tension in the region by creating conditions conducive to stable economic growth and the realization of the region's geo-strategic potential. The main objective of the program is to reinforce inter-regional cooperation. The program provides for a $320.9 million social and economic development budget for the Territory.

The federal targeted program for The Elimination of Inequalities in the Social and Economic Development of the Regions of the Russian Federation (2002–2010 and through 2015) aims to reduce regional gaps in key social and economic deve-lopment indicators by 2010, create conditions conducive to the development of enterprise, and improve the investment climate. A budget of $390.1 million has been allocated to this program from the federal budget.

The federal targeted program for The Economic and Social Development of the Stavropol Territory, 2003-2007. The main objective of the Program is to create a favorable environment for the accelerated development of the Territory's economy, to develop its advantages and strengths, to modernize and restructure the Territory's economy, and to solve the Territory's social problems, including increasing income and job creation. A total budget of $632.4 million has been allocated to this program, including: $147.9 million from the federal budget to complement the $107 million allocated from the Stavropol Territory's regional and municipal budgets and $37.8 million – from extra-budgetary sources and private financing initiatives.

The federal focused investment program providing for $8.5 million in financing for the Stavropol Territory in 2003, plays an important role in terms of the social and economic development of the Territory.

Regional programs. The Stavropol Territory Government is developing and implementing over 60 regional targeted programs focusing on industrial development, agricultural policy, environmental rehabilitation, law enforcement, healthcare, and public welfare.

Major programs include: Liquidation of the Consequences of the 2002 Natural Disaster in the Stavropol Territory ($95.6 million budget), The Territorial Targeted Program for Education Development in the Stavropol Territory, 2001–2004 ($76.5 million), and The Implementation of Information Systems for the Stavropol Territory Government, 2002–2005 ($44.6 million). Plans are afoot to allocate some $4.4 million for the implementation of The Stavropol Territory's Targeted Program for Small Business Support, 2001–2002. This program aims to increase the proportion of people employed by small businesses, as well as individual entrepreneurs, to 25% of the total economically active population (some 300,000 people). The small business share in the Territory's total GRP will increase to 14%–15%.

6. INVESTMENT PROJECTS

Industry sector and project description	1) Expected results 2) Amount and term of investment 3) Form of financing[1] 4) Documentation[2]	Contact information
1	2	3
MINING		
39R001	■ ◆	OOO Agropromenergo
Construction of an enrichment plant. Project goal: to expand quartz sand production and enrichment for use as feedstock for optical manufacturing.	1) 800,000 tons of quartz sand per year 2) $6.9 million/4 years 3) E 4) BP	3, ul. Zavokzalnaya, Blagodarny, Stavropol Territory, 356420 Phone: (86549) 23 390 Fax: (86549) 21 374 E-mail: A-Energi@mail.ru Ivan Petrovich Sadovschikov, CEO

[1] L – Loan, E – Equity, Leas. – Leasing, JV – Joint Venture
[2] BP – Business Plan, FS – Feasibility Study

III

SOUTHERN FEDERAL DISTRICT

1	2	3

MACHINE ENGINEERING AND METAL PROCESSING

39R002 ★ ❖ ◆

Acquisition and launch of new treatment facilities designed to manufacture metal-cutting tools.
Project goal: to manufacture world-class metal-cutting tools.

1) 4,800 items per year
2) $3.3 million/3 years
3) Leas., JV
4) BP

OAO Spetsinstrument
162/2, ul. Kalinina, Georgiyevsk,
Stavropol Territory, 357800
Phone/fax: (87951) 63 992,
64 119, 64 275
E-mail: instrum@georgievsk.ru
Alexander Nikiforovich Tolkachev, CEO

ENERGY

39R003 ■ ▲

Reconstruction of the Kislovodskaya thermal power station.
Project goal: to increase electricity output while cutting production costs by installing efficient and environmentally friendly equipment.

1) Electricity – up to 218 million kWh; Heat energy – up to 225,000 Gcal
2) $7.5 million/ 4 years
3) E
4) FS

OAO Stavropolenergo
35 ul. Universitetskaya
Pyatigorsk, Stavropol Territory, 357500
Phone: (87933) 52 195
Fax: (8793) 97 3502
E-mail: ouk2@stavre.elektra.ru
aho@stavre.elektra.ru
http://www.stavre.elktra.ru
Alexander Alexandrovich Pribytkov, CEO

CHEMICALS AND PETROCHEMICALS

39R004 ■ ● ◆

Reconstruction of production facilities for synthetic sapphire growing and stone polishing works.
Project purpose: to expand synthetic sapphire growing and processing output and increase hi-tech market share.

1) 24,480 kg a year
2) $10 million/3.5 years
3) L, E
4) BP

OAO Monokristall Synthetic Corundum Plant
4/1, pr. Kulakova, Stavropol,
Stavropol Territory, 355044
Phone: (8652) 95 6468, 56 2871, 95 6738
Fax: (8652) 95 6528
E-mail: plant@energomera.ru
monocrys@energomera.ru
Vladimir Ivanovich Polyakov, CEO

39R005 ● ◆

Reconstruction of the existing production facilities.
Project goal: to increase production of Wella and Fa products.

1) Cosmetic products – 10 million items per year
2) $6.5 million/3 years
3) L
4) BP

OAO Arnest
6, ul. Kombinatskaya, Nevinnomyssk,
Stavropol Territory, 357107
Phone: (86554) 54 105, 54 103, 66 076
Fax: (86554) 54 105, 66 076
E-mail: arnest@arnest.ru
Gennady Fedorovich Afonin, CEO

GLASS AND PORCELAIN

39R006 ● ◆

Construction of a glass factory.
Project goal: to produce glass (sheet glass, storefront glass, toned glass, armored glass, polished glass, and window glass).

1) 26 million square meters annually
2) $180 million/7 years
3) L
4) BP

OOO Agropromenergo
3, ul. Zavokzalnaya, Blagodarny,
Stavropol Territory, 356420
Phone: (86549) 23 390
Fax: (86549) 21 374
E-mail: A-Energi@mail.ru
Ivan Petrovich Sadovschikov, CEO

39R007 ● ◆

Construction and launching of a glass container manufacturing facility.
Project goal: production of glass containers.

1) Glass containers; 650 million items per year
2) $70 million/5 years
3) L
4) BP

OOO Agropromenergo
3, ul. Zavokzalnaya, Blagodarny,
Stavropol Territory, 356420
Phone: (86549) 23 390
Fax: (86549) 21 374
E-mail: A-Energi@mail.ru
Ivan Petrovich Sadovschikov, CEO

1	2	3

AGRICULTURE

39R008

Restoration of pig feeding facilities in the Blagodarnensky District. Project goal: production of meat.	1) 2,500 tons of live weight, 25,000 pigs annually 2) $10 million/1 year 3) L 4) BP	OAO Pyatigorsk Meat Plant 7, ul. Fabrichanya, Pyatigorsk, Stavropol Territory, 357500 Phone/fax: (8793) 97 3949, 97 3847 Fax: (8793) 97 3846 E-mail: pmk@megalog.ru Vyacheslav Anastasovich Marulasov, CEO

HEALTHCARE

39R009

Reconstruction of the Raduga sanatorium in Kislovodsk. Project purpose: to expand sanatorium capacity and improve quality of services.	1) Accomodation capacity increased by 124 beds 2) $11.7 million/5 years 3) E 4) BP	OAO Stavropolenergo 35 ul. Universitetskaya, Pyatigorsk, Stavropol Territory, 357500 Phone: (87933) 52 195 Fax: (8793) 97 3502 E-mail: ouk2@stavre.elektra.ru aho@stavre.elektra.ru http://www.stavre.elktra.ru Alexander Alexandrovich Pribytkov, CEO

ECOLOGY AND WASTE TREATMENT

39R010

Organization of corrugated packaging production on the basis of enhanced household and industrial waste processing. Project purpose: production of cardboard and paper.	1) 1,000 tons of cardboard monthly 2) $10 million/1 year 3) L 4) BP	PK Kavmintara 23, ul. Komsomolskaya, Mineralnyie Vody, Stavropol Territory, 357310 Phone/fax: (8792) 27 9763, 40 0620 Anatoly Vasilyevich Myagky, Chairman

III

SOUTHERN FEDERAL DISTRICT

40. ASTRAKHAN REGION [30]

ECONOMIC MAP

Volzhsky
Lake Elton
Lake Aralsor
Kapustin Yar
Akhtubinsk
Baskunchak
KAZAKHSTAN
Lake Baskunchak
Volga
Akhtuba
Lake Sarpa
Kharabali
REPUBLIC OF
KALMYKIA
Narimanov
Yashkul
ASTRAKHAN
Krasny Yar
Iki-Burul
Kamyzyak
Promyslovka
CASPIAN
Lagan
Kuma
SEA

PROCESSING INDUSTRY
- Machine engineering and metal processing
- Chemicals and petrochemicals
- Construction materials
- Food and beverages

MINING INDUSTRY
- ▲ Oil
- △ Natural gas
- Ⅲ Gypsum
- ◧ Clay
- ▭ Table salt
- ◄ Fishing ports

POWER PLANTS
- ⚡ Thermal power plants

CROPS AND LIVESTOCK BREEDING
- Melons and gourds
- Rice
- Sugar beetroot
- Orchards
- Vegetables
- Meat and dairy cattle breeding
- Sheep rearing
- Poultry farming

- 🖝 Resorts

The Astrakhan Region is said to be unique. The points on the Earth's surface where the lotus thrives are said to be the planet's energy centers, its chakras. The Astrakhan Region is an ethnological model of the Caspian Region. There is no other water body in the world that unites so many countries and ethnic groups. The poet Velimir Khlebnikov, who was born in the Region, called Astrakhan the triangle of Christ, Mohammed, and Buddha.

The unique combination of an advantageous geopolitical location, significant natural resources, and industrial, scientific, technological, and intellectual potential makes the Astrakhan Region one of the most attractive areas for investment in southern Russia.

Located at the junction of land, sea, and air routes connecting the countries of two continents, and boasting a developed transportation infrastructure and diverse economy, the Region is very well positioned to develop its economy through increased international transit flows and foreign trade activity.

The Region boasts abundant reserves of hydrocarbons, which are available to be developed through international cooperation.

The Region's agroindustrial sector is capable of supplying a large proportion of the Russian population with vegetables, both raw and processed. Today, the Caspian Basin is the most important fishing area in Russia, and the Astrakhan Region is heavily involved in sturgeon stock maintenance and reproduction.

The unique natural environment of the Volga delta attracts tourists from all over the world.

The Regional Administration is committed to enhancing the investment appeal of the Region. The regional legislation offers incentives and guarantees to investors seeking to invest in the Region.

All of the above proves that we are serious about turning our Region into a major industrial center of international significance, and making it open and lucrative for business and investment.

Anatoly Guzhvin,
HEAD OF ADMINISTRATION (GOVERNOR)
OF THE ASTRAKHAN REGION

III

SOUTHERN FEDERAL DISTRICT

1. GENERAL INFORMATION

1.1. GEOGRAPHY

The Astrakhan Region covers a total area of some 44,100 square kilometers. The Region lies in the Volgo-Akhtubinskaya valley, the Volga River Delta, and the adjacent semi-deserts of the Pre-Caspian Lowlands. To the south-west and the west, the Region borders the Republic of Kalmykia, to the north – the Volgograd Region, and to the north-east and the east – Kazakhstan.

1.2. CLIMATE

The Astrakhan Region lies in the harsh continental climatic zone with significant air temperature fluctuations. Up to 70% of the Region is desert and semi-desert. January air temperatures average –0.8°C, rising to +26.4°C in July. Annual precipitation varies between 175 mm and 244 mm. The average growing season lasts around 216 days.

The Region is covered with wormwood-saltwort semi-desert on light brown soil. The Volgo-Akhtubinskaya Valley and the Volga River Delta have alluvial soil.

1.3. POPULATION

According to preliminary 2002 census results, total population in the Region was 1,007,000 people. The average population density is 22.8 people per square kilometer. The economically active population amounts to 487,000. Official 2002 unemployment stood at 2%, while the actual rate was 11.5%.

Demographically speaking, some 61% of the population is of working age, 20.2% are below the statutory working age, and 18.8% are beyond the statutory working age.

The Astrakhan Region's major urban centers (2002 data) are Astrakhan with 506,400 inhabitants, Akhtubinsk with 46,500 inhabitants, and Znamensk with 37,000 inhabitants.

Population								TABLE 1
	1992	1997	1998	1999	2000	2001	2002
Total population, '000	1,004	1,023	1,023	1,020	1,016	1,013	1,007
Economically active population, '000	504	463	463	483	502	512	487

2. ADMINISTRATION

15, ul. Sovetskaya, Astrakhan, Astrakhan Region, 414008. Phone: (8512) 22 8519
E-mail: adm@astranet.ru; http://www1.adm.astranet.ru

NAME	POSITION	CONTACT INFORMATION
Anatoly Petrovich GUZHVIN	Head of Administration (Governor) of the Astrakhan Region	Phone: (8512) 22 8519 E-mail: adm@astranet.ru
Tatyana Nikolaevna MAKSIMOVA	Deputy Head of Administration (Governor) of the Astrakhan Region, Chairman of the Astrakhan Regional Administration Committee for Economic Development and Trade	Phone: (8512) 22 4993 Fax: (8512) 39 0955 E-mail: maxm@adm.astranet.ru
Sergei Konstantinovich TERSKOV	Deputy Head (Governor) of the Administration of the Astrakhan Region, Head of the Astrakhan Regional Administration Department for Industry, Transport, Communications, Science, and Technology	Phone/fax: (8512) 22 1814
Askar Nikolaevich KABIKEEV	Head of the Astrakhan Regional Administration Department for International Relations and Foreign Trade	Phone: (8512) 39 5173 Fax: (8512) 22 1709 E-mail: ves@mail.astrakhan.ru
Sergei Konstantinovich RYASKOV	Head of the Astrakhan Regional Administration Department for Medium and Small Enterprise Support and Tourism	Phone: (8512) 39 1018, 39 0462 E-mail: dpt@mail.astrakhan.ru
Alexander Alexandrovich GRACHEV	Head of the Astrakhan Regional Administration Department of Fishing	Phone: (8512) 22 0894
Pavel Alexandrovich BOLDYREV	Chairman of the Fuel and Natural Resource Exploration Committee of the Astrakhan Region	Phone: (8512) 39 1682, 39 2948

NAME	POSITION	CONTACT INFORMATION
Vladimir Borisovich EREMENKO	Head of the Astrakhan Regional Administration Department for Construction, Architecture, and Housing and Communal Services	Phone: (8512) 39 0247 Fax: (8512) 22 4617

3. ECONOMIC POTENTIAL

3.1. 1997–2002 GROSS REGIONAL PRODUCT (GRP). INDUSTRY BREAKDOWN

The Astrakhan Region's 2002 gross regional product amounted to $1.388 billion, up 12.6% on 2001 levels.

Since 2000, the Region's economy has steadily grown. In 2002, GRP increased by 20.7% on 2000, agriculture and forestry output grew by 32.6%, total turnover of trade and public catering companies increased by 53.7%, and transport and communication, by 25.2%. The industrial output has slightly fallen by 3.5%.

GRP trends in 1997–2002						*TABLE 2*
	1997	1998	1999	2000	2001*	2002*
GRP in current prices, $ million	1,627.8	1,136.5	731.0	1,147.3	1,233.3	1,388.4

*Estimates of the Astrakhan Regional Administration

GRP industry breakdown in 1997–2002, % of total						*TABLE 3*
	1997	1998	1999	2000	2001*	2002*
GRP	100.0	100.0	100.0	100.0	100.0	100.0
Industry	23.1	30.1	36.3	36.4	26.8	29.1
Agriculture and forestry	7.5	7.3	7.1	5.1	6.4	5.6
Construction	10.3	10.0	7.9	13.6	15.2	10.0
Transport and communications	8.9	10.0	8.8	8.2	8.1	8.5
Trade and public catering	8.6	9.1	9.4	7.7	9.4	9.8
Other	34.3	25.8	19.4	16.7	22.5	26.8
Net taxes on output	7.3	7.7	11.1	12.3	11.6	10.2

*Estimates of the Astrakhan Regional Administration

3.2. MAJOR ECONOMIC GROWTH PROJECTIONS

The main economic growth projections for the coming years are set forth in the Economic Development Projection through 2005. 2003 GRP is expected to rise by 8.5% on 2002 levels to $1.507 billion.

The projected rate of industrial development is expected to be underpinned by 23% growth in investment. The most important sectors for investment are oil and gas, energy (revamping of the Astrakhan Hydroelectric Power Station), glass (construction of the second unit of a glass factory), food (revamping of canned food and dairy plants), and construction materials.

Growth in the food industry is expected to be driven by growth in dairy and meat processing and the creation of new and revamping of existing vegetable processing facilities.

Resource conservation is set to become of paramount importance in the fishing industry, with a greater focus on deep processing technologies. Fish farming will provide an additional source of fish.

The development of the transport sector in 2003 is expected to result in an increase in freight turnover to 25.9 million tons, or 18% up on 2002. A container terminal at the port of Olya is scheduled to be completed in 2003. Work on building a rail line to the port will commence in 2003.

Gross agricultural output is expected to grow by 3.4% in 2003, with tillage expected to rise by 3.5%, and livestock output, by 3.4%. This rate of output growth is to come on the back of a 28.1% increase in investment into the sector, primarily allocated for soil fertilization, cattle bloodstock improvement, and the introduction of advanced technologies.

III

SOUTHERN FEDERAL DISTRICT

3.3. INDUSTRIAL OUTPUT IN 1997–2002 FOR MAJOR SECTORS OF ECONOMY

Industrial output in the Astrakhan Region accounts for 29.1% of GRP. The fuel industry accounts for the lion's share of the Region's industrial output. The Region also produces fish, builds and repairs ships, manufactures timber packaging materials, and produces fishing nets.

Industry breakdown of industrial output in 1997–2002, % of total						TABLE 4
	1997	1998	1999	2000	2001	2002*
Industry	100.0	100.0	100.0	100.0	100.0	100.0
Fuel	32.5	43.0	54.7	65.4	62.9	61.1
Food and beverages	23.4	20.2	21.4	14.3	13.4	12.0
Energy	17.3	15.3	8.6	6.4	8.0	9.3
Machine engineering and metal processing	12.4	11.0	7.5	6.6	7.4	9.3
Construction materials	4.6	3.5	2.6	2.6	2.9	3.0
Chemicals and petrochemicals	2.3	1.9	1.5	1.8	2.0	1.6
Flour, cereals, and mixed fodder	2.4	1.6	1.0	0.8	1.0	1.4
Light industry	1.3	1.1	0.9	0.8	0.8	0.6
Forestry, timber, and pulp and paper	1.5	0.9	0.5	0.5	0.6	0.6

*Estimates of the Astrakhan Regional Administration

Fuel. The fuel industry accounts for 61.1% of total industrial output. The largest enterprises are AO Astrakhangazprom and OAO LUKoil-Astrakhanmorneft.

Food and beverages. The food industry accounts for 12% of total industrial output. Its main sub-sectors are fishing, salt, flour and grain, butter, cheese and diary processing, fruit and vegetable processing, tobacco, and distilling.

The Region hosts 175 fishing and fish processing enterprises. The largest enterprises are OAO Kasp-Rybkholodflot, OAO Astrakhansky Rybokombinat, OAO Kaspryba, OAO Astrakhankonservprom, OAO Russkaya Ikra, and OAO Bassol.

Of the Region's 17 vegetable processing enterprises, the largest are OAO Astrakhanskiye Konservy, OAO Astrakhankonservprom, and ZAO Kamos.

Energy. Energy accounts for 9.3% of total industrial output. The largest power stations are the Astrakhan Hydroelectric Power Station, Thermal Power Station 2, and the Northern Thermal Power Station.

Machine engineering and metal processing. The machine engineering sector is represented by machine engineering and metals processing and shipbuilding and ship repair enterprises. The sector accounts for 9.3% of total industrial output in the Region. The largest enterprises are GUP Ship Repair Yard, AO Progress Machine Engineering Works, OAO Shipbuilding and Repair Yard, OAO Third International Shipbuilding and Repair Yard, OAO Krasnye Barrikady Shipyard, JV Astrakhansky Korabel, OAO Lotos Shipyard, ZAO Lenin Ship Building and Repair Plant, OAO Astrakhanskaya Shipyard, and OAO Akhtubinsk Ship Building and Repair Plant.

Agriculture. Owing to the Region's unique climate and soils, tillage plays an important role in the Region's economy. Rice, vegetables and melons are cultivated in the Region. Arable land covers some 63% of the Region's territory.

3.4. FUEL AND ENERGY BALANCE (OUTPUT AND CONSUMPTION PER RESOURCE)

Natural gas extraction is the most important industry in the fuel and energy sector of the Astrakhan Region. 2002 gas extraction amounted to 10.89 billion cubic meters, 3.5% up on 2001 levels. Production growth was achieved through intensified gas extraction, and the exploration and development of new gas fields.

3.5. TRANSPORT INFRASTRUCTURE

Roads. The Astrakhan Region has more than 3,800 kilometers of public highway. The main highways are the Astrakhan – Moscow, Astrakhan – Elista, Astrakhan – Makhachkala, and Astrakhan – Krasny Yar – Atyrau routes.

Railroads. The Astrakhan Region has some 567 kilometers of railroads. The major trunk railroad is the Privolzhskaya Railroad.

Sea and river ports. The total length of the Region's navigable inland waterway system is 1,120 kilometers. Astrakhan has an international port. The new port of Olya is being built on the Caspian sea to provide year-round transit and freight export and import services.

Some 62 inland waterway freight shipping companies operate from Astrakhan. The largest companies are OAO Astrakhansky Port, OAO Volgomost, and GUP Sea Fishing Port.

Airports. The Astrakhan international airport is used for transit flights.

Fuel and energy sector production and consumption trends, 1997–2002						TABLE 5
	1997	1998	1999	2000	2001	2002*
Electricity output, billion kWh	3.1	3.3	3.2	3.4	3.2	3.2
Oil output (including gas condensate), '000 tons	1,843.0	2,671.0	3,073.0	3,441.0	3,703.0	3,864.0
Natural gas extraction, million cubic meters	5,059.0	7,575.0	8,724.0	9,786.0	10,517.0	10,890.0
Electricity consumption, billion kWh	3.4	3.5	3.6	3.6	3.6	3.6
Natural gas consumption, million cubic meters	1,654.0	1,757.2	1,692.5	1,807.9	1,822.6	1,817.1

*Estimates of the Astrakhan Regional Administration

Oil pipelines. The Tengiz-Novorossiysk trunk oil pipeline crosses the Astrakhan Region. Plans are afoot to revamp the existing pipeline over the coming years and to build a new 250 kilometer pipeline.

3.6. MAIN NATURAL RESOURCES: RESERVES AND EXTRACTION IN 2002

The Astrakhan Region is rich in hydrocarbons, sulfur, oil, and salt. The Region possesses unique fishing resources.

Oil and natural gas. The Region's total oil and gas reserves are estimated at 8.9 million tons of oil, 572.3 million tons of gas condensate, and 3,720 billion cubic meters of natural gas. The Astrakhan Gas Condensate Field, unique in terms of reserves and content, is one of the largest in Russia. Explored deposits of natural gas total 2,631.9 billion cubic meters, and 409.8 million tons of gas condensate reserves.

Natural salts. The Astrakhan Region has unique deposits of white salt, the Baskunchakskoye and Kamenoyarskoye, the major sources of table and industrial salt in Russia.

Fisheries. The unique fish species found in the Volga River and the Caspian Sea determine to a large extent the specialization of the Region. The Region has more than 30 fish species with commercial application. The Region's population of Caspian sturgeon is unique (sturgeon, beluga, and sterlet). A considerable proportion of the black caviar sold worldwide comes from the Astrakhan Region. The biosphere resources of the Region (sazan, pike perch, catfish, bream, and Astrakhan herring) are consumed both within Russia and on the international market.

Recreational resources. The Astrakhan national park and the hunting grounds of the Volga River Delta are a favorite recreation area for hunters and sporting fishermen from all over the world. The Region has natural reserves crossed by tourist routes. The natural resources of the Region (therapeutic muds and mineral waters) make it a spa destination. The Astrakhan Region can accommodate up to 150,000 tourists annually.

4. TRADE OPPORTUNITIES IN THE REGION

4.1. MAIN GOODS PRODUCED IN THE REGION

Agriculture and fisheries. 2002 grain output was 51,100 tons, sugar beet output totaled 1,300 tons, meat and meat product output reached 700 tons, whole milk output (measured in milk equivalent) totaled 6,400 liters, and fisheries output totaled 68,800 tons.

Food. 2002 fish processing output (including canned fish) totaled 31,000 tons, bread and bakery product output reached 32,100 tons, confectionary output totaled 1,800 tons, vodka and liquors output was 905,300 decaliters, tobacco output reached 121 million items, and table salt output was 1.7 million tons.

Industrial products. In 2002, the Region's enterprises produced 47,300 cubic meters of prefabricated reinforced concrete units and components, 38.6 million conventional bricks, 2,400 cubic meters of sawn timber, and 89,200 items of knitwear.

4.2. EXPORTS, INCLUDING EXTRA-CIS

Companies in the Astrakhan Region trade with 65 countries worldwide. The Region's products are exported to 45 countries, and the Region imports goods from 55. Non-CIS exports account for 91%. The Region's main extra-CIS trading partners for exports are Iran, the UK, and Hungary. Its main CIS trading partners are Kazakhstan, Ukraine, and Azerbaijan. In 2002, the Astrakhan Region's exports totaled $233.5 million.

The bulk of the Region's exports (according to 2002 figures) consists of minerals – 69.8% (including salt and brimstone – 663,400 tons, oil and petrochemicals – 1,137,400 tons), machinery, equipment, and transport vehicles – 16% (including vessels and boats – 14,600), and food and farm feedstock – 4.5% (including fish products – 1,700 tons).

4.3. IMPORTS, INCLUDING EXTRA-CIS

2002 imports totaled $130.8 million (90% from extra-CIS countries). Machinery, equipment, and transport vehicles accounted for about 63% of imports (including vessels and boats – 34,800), food – 17.7% (including fruit – 37,100 tons, processed vegetables – 21,700 tons), metals and metal products – 6.6% (including ferrous metal products – 2,200 tons), and textiles – 4% (including ready-made textile garments – 5,700 items). The Region's main trading partners for imports

are Sweden with 38%, Norway – 16.1%, Iran – 14.1%, Germany – 8%, and Kazakhstan – 4.3%.

4.4. MAJOR REGIONAL EXPORT AND IMPORT ENTITIES

Due to the specific nature of the Region's export and import activities, export and import transactions are performed mainly by industrial enterprises.

5. INVESTMENT OPPORTUNITIES

5.1. INVESTMENTS IN 1992–2002 (BY INDUSTRY SECTOR), INCLUDING FOREIGN INVESTMENTS

The following factors determine the investment appeal of the Astrakhan Region:
- Its natural resources (hydrocarbon reserves);
- Its favorable geographical location.

5.2. CAPITAL INVESTMENT

The bulk of capital investment in 2002 went to industry (13.8%), transport (20%), and geological surveying and natural resource exploration (22.2%). The fuel sector accounted for the lion's share (79.8%) of fixed capital investments in industry.

Capital investment by industry sector, $ million						*TABLE 6*
	1997	1998	1999	2000	2001	2002*
Total capital investments	347.4	270.1	227.4	442.2	535.2	407.6
Including major industries (% of total)						
Industry	29.1	15.3	39.7	23.7	24.0	13.8
Agriculture and forestry	4.2	1.8	1.9	1.5	2.0	2.4
Construction	0.7	1.6	0.6	2.5	1.7	0.6
Transport and communications	14.8	8.6	10.6	20.2	27.7	20.0
Trade and public catering	1.5	7.7	8.6	2.7	1.8	1.5
Residential construction	32.1	37.5	29.3	17.7	18.2	24.8
Public utilities construction	5.3	10.9	1.7	1.0	3.2	1.4
Geology and natural resources exploration	4.5	8.5	4.6	26.9	17.7	22.2
Other	7.8	8.1	3.0	3.8	3.7	13.3

*Estimates of the Astrakhan Regional Administration

Fixed capital investments from all sources of financing are expected to amount to $667 million in 2003, up 23% on 2002 (in comparable prices).

In 1997–2002, foreign investments went to: industry (88%), real estate (4.9%), communications (3.1%). Cumulative foreign investment amounted to

$40.9 million at the beginning of 2003. 85.6% of this amount took the form of foreign loans issued against Russian government guarantees. The biggest investors in the Region are Germany with 86.6%, Monaco with 4.9%, the Netherlands with 3.7%, the United States with 3.1%, Cyprus with 0.9%, and Iran with 0.3%.

Foreign investment trends in 1992–2002						*TABLE 7*
	1992–1997	1998	1999	2000	2001	2002
Foreign investments, $ million	3.2	8.0	12.0	0.4	2.0	32.0
Including FDI, $ million	–	1.0	8.0	0.04	1.4	31.4

5.3. MAJOR ENTERPRISES (INCLUDING ENTERPRISES WITH FOREIGN INVESTMENT)

In 2002, the Region was home to some 201 enterprises with foreign investment, as well as branches and representative offices of foreign companies.

5.4. MOST ATTRACTIVE SECTORS FOR INVESTMENT

According to the estimates of the Astrakhan Regional Administration, oil and natural gas, transport, shipbuilding, fishing, tourism, agroindustrial sector, residential construction, and construction materials offer the greatest investment appeal.

Largest enterprises of the Astrakhan Region	*TABLE 8*
COMPANY	SECTOR
OOO Astrakhangazprom	Natural gas
OAO Bassol	Fruit and vegetables
OOO LUKoil-Astrakhanmorneft	Oil industry
OOO LUKoil-Astrakhannefteprodukt	Maintenance and logistics
OAO Svyazinform	Electric and radio communications
OOO Karon-TM	Trade and public catering
OAO Astrakhanneftegazstroi	Construction

5.5. CURRENT LEGISLATION ON INVESTOR TAX EXEMPTIONS AND PRIVILEGES

A number of laws have been adopted in the Region with a view to improving the legal base governing investment:

- On Investment Activity in the Astrakhan Region;
- On Taxes and Duties in the Territory of the Astrakhan Region;
- On the Development Budget of the Astrakhan Region.

The above Laws create provisions on the status of investment projects and the forms of state support available to investors. The laws provide tax exemptions to enterprises carrying out investment projects approved by the Regional Administration and to priority investment projects. The laws establish the regional tax component rate, grant tax exemptions, regulate investment project status, and contain provisions on the forms of state support. For enterprises carrying out priority investment projects, the regional component of profits tax is set at 12% and the regional property tax component, at 0.2%. For enterprises carrying out investment projects approved by the Regional Administration, the profit tax rate is set at 14%, and a 50% reduction is granted with respect to the property tax rate.

The following forms of state support are also available to companies investing in the Astrakhan Region:

- Participation by the Regional Administration in the charter capital of newly formed enterprises created to carry out investment projects;
- Financing of high priority investment projects carried out by enterprises incorporated with the participation of the Regional Administration;
- Budget allocations to investment projects within the framework of the regional targeted industrial development programs;
- Budget allocations to investment projects carried out by enterprises operating under leasing schemes in amounts not exceeding the initial (advance) amount of the leasing payment;
- A lower interest rate for loans to investment projects.

5.6. FEDERAL AND REGIONAL ECONOMIC AND SOCIAL DEVELOPMENT PROGRAMS FOR THE ASTRAKHAN REGION

Federal targeted programs. The federal targeted program Russia's South is currently underway in the Astrakhan Region. The program was approved by Decree No. 581 of the Russian Government on October 5, 2001, and comprises 50 regional projects aimed at developing Russia's south in line with federal interests. The program aims to create economic and social environment conductive to ongoing and non-conflict development of Russia's southern regions and ensuring strategic and geopolitical interests of Russia in these regions.

Regional programs. A number of programs are underway in the Region. These focus on industry, land relations, social welfare, and cultural heritage conservation. The priority has been accorded to the following programs: Program for State Support to Small Business in the Astrakhkan Region, 2002–2005, State Support to Companies under Restructuring in the Astrakhkan Region, Information Support to the Process of Land Management, Land and Property Relations Reform and Regulation in the Astrakhkan Region, 2003–2007, Development of the Rural Telephone Network in the Astrakhkan Region, 2002–2005, Preservation, and Revival and Development of Folk Arts in the Astrakhkan Region through 2005.

III

SOUTHERN FEDERAL DISTRICT

6. INVESTMENT PROJECTS

Industry sector and project description	1) Expected results 2) Amount and term of investment 3) Form of financing[1] 4) Documentation[2]	Contact information
1	2	3

MACHINE ENGINEERING AND METAL PROCESSING

40R001

| Upgrade and modernization of fixed assets. Project purpose: to enhance rolled metal and pipe production capacity. | 1) Annual output: rolled metals – up to 12,000 tons, pipes – up to 2,000 tons 2) $11 million/2 years 3) E, L 4) FS, BP | JV OAO Astrakhan Shipbuilder 60, ul. Admirala Nakhimova, Astrakhan, Astrakhan Region, 414018 Phone: (8512) 59 1860 Fax: (8512) 59 1866 E-mail: korabel2@astranet.ru Alexander Sergeevich Iliychev, CEO |

CONSTRUCTION MATERIALS

40R002

| Reconstruction of the Silicate Brick Works. Project goal: to expand production of facing silicate color brick and cellular concrete. | 1) Profit of $0.06 million per month 2) $1.3 million/6 months 3) L 4) FS | OOO Electric and Technology Company 47, ul. Sverdlova, Astrakhan, Astrakhan Region, 414000 Phone: (8512) 39 1671, 39 8095, 39 0462 Fax: (8512) 39 2653 E-mail: elko@mail.astrakhan.ru Vladimir Vladimirovich Kulagin, CEO, Vladimir Gennadyevich Yurlov, CTO of the Silicate Brick Works |

FOOD AND BEVERAGES

40R003

| Construction of a sturgeon breeding plant to produce delicatessen fish products out of valuable fish species. Project purpose: to access the market for ecologically pure products. | 1) Annual output: fish – 150 tons, caviar – 1 ton 2) $3.7 million/1 year 3) L 4) BP | FGUP NPC BIOS 14a, ul. Volodarskogo, Astrakhan, Astrakhan Region, 414000 Phone: (8512) 39 1126, 39 0511 Fax: (8512) 39 1129 E-mail: bios94@bk.ru Lidia Mikhailovna Vasilyeva, Director |

40R004

| Creation of fruit and vegetable preserve facilities at available premises of the Region's enterprises. Project purpose: to increase output of canned fruit and vegetable products. | 1) Daily processing of 90 tons 2) $2.1 million/6 months 3. E, L 4) BP | Department of Agriculture of the Astrakhan Regional Administration 31, ul. Sverdlova, Astrakhan, Astrakhan Region, 414000 Phone: (8512) 22 4567 Fax: (8512) 22 7701 E-mail: depagro@astranet.ru Ivan Andreyevich Nesterenko, Deputy Head of the Regional Administration, Head of Department |

[1] L – Loan, E – Equity, Leas. – Leasing, JV – Joint Venture
[2] BP – Business Plan, FS – Feasibility Study

1	2	3

AGRICULTURE

40R005 ● ◆

Implementation of industrial technologies for vegetable growing. Reconstruction of the existing and construction of new irrigation facilities for trickle sprinkling. Project purpose: to increase the vegetable-growing capacity.

1) Increasing of vegetable capacity to 90,000 kg per hectare, gross output – 157,000 tons per year
2) $1.9 million/2 years
3) L
4) BP

Department of Agriculture of the Astrakhan Regional Administration 31, ul. Sverdlova, Astrakhan, Astrakhan Region, 414000 Phone: (8512) 22 4567 Fax: (8512) 22 7701 E-mail: depagro@astranet.ru Ivan Andreyevich Nesterenko, Deputy Head of the Regional Administration, Head of Department

HOUSING CONSTRUCTION AND RETAIL

40R006 ● ▲ ◆

Construction of a residential area and mall. Project purpose: to increase residential area and enhance retail services.

1) 40,000 square meters of residential area and 22,000 square meters of retail area
2) $14.6 million/3 years
3) L
4) FS, BP

OOO Electric and Technical Company 47, ul. Sverdlova, Astrakhan, Astrakhan Region, 414000 Phone/fax: (8512) 39 1671, 39 8095 E-mail: elko@mail.astrakhan.ru Vladimir Vladimirovich Kulagin, CEO

TRANSPORT INFRASTRUCTURE

40R007 ● ◆

Construction of a container terminal at the Solyanka transit freight district. Project purpose: to increase container processing capacity.

1) Increase in container flow up to 8,300 items a year
2) $3.0 million/3.6 years
3) L
4) BP

OAO Astrakhan Port 14, ul. Chernyshevskogo, Astrakhan, Astrakhan Region, 414000 Phone: (8512) 39 4179 Fax: (8512) 22 4811 E-mail: aportt@telecomnet.ru Vladimir Timofeevich Kugashev, CEO

40R008 ■ ● ◆

Construction of a container terminal at the Olya commercial seaport. Project purpose: to increase container processing capacity.

1) Annual terminal capacity 1.25 million tons of freight (90,000 containers)
2) $34.6 million/3 years
3) E, L
4) BP

GU Marine Administration of the Port of Astrakhan 31, ul. Kapitana Krasnova, Astrakhan, Astrakhan Region, 414014 Phone: (8512) 58 4821 Fax: (8512) 58 5776 E-mail: map@astranet.ru Viktor Georgievich Paschenko, CEO

40R009 ■ ● ◆

Construction of a grain terminal at the Olya commercial seaport. Project purpose: to increase grain processing capacity.

1) Annual terminal capacity of 0.5 million tons of grain
2) $1.4 million/1 year
3) L, E
4) BP

GU Marine Administration of the Port of Astrakhan 31, ul. Kapitana Krasnova, Astrakhan, Astrakhan Region, 414014 Phone: (8512) 58 4821 Fax: (8512) 58 5776 E-mail: map@astranet.ru Viktor Georgievich Paschenko, CEO

40R010 ■ ▲

Construction of a spur-track (49 km) to the Olya commercial seaport. Project purpose: to increase freight transportation turnover.

1) Annual freight transportation turnover of 8 million tons
2) $94.4 million/3 years
3) E
4) FS

GU Marine Administration of the Port of Astrakhan 31, ul. Kapitana Krasnova, Astrakhan, Astrakhan Region, 414014 Phone: (8512) 58 4821 Fax: (8512) 58 5776 E-mail: map@astranet.ru Viktor Georgievich Paschenko, CEO

III

SOUTHERN FEDERAL DISTRICT

III

SOUTHERN FEDERAL DISTRICT

1	2	3

40R011 ● ◆

Creation of container freight processing facilities. Project purpose: to increase container processing output.	1) Container processing – up to 36,000 a year 2) $5 million/12 months 3) L 4) BP	OOO Alfa-Port 36, ul. Dzerzhinskogo, Astrakhan, Astrakhan Region, 414006 Phone: (8512) 56 3233 Fax: (8512) 56 3844 E-mail: alfaport@astranet.ru Vladimir Viktorovich Karataev, CEO

40R012 ● ◆

Construction and upgrade of cargo terminals. Project purpose: to increase cargo processing output (the North-South transport corridor).	1) Processing output of 0.6 million tons of general-purpose cargo and 0.15 million tons of container cargo 2) $10 million/1 year 3) L 4) BP	OOO Volga-Vaster 53-A, ul. Zhelyabova, Astrakhan, Astrakhan Region, 414040 Phone/fax: (8512) 39 1365, 54 0079 E-mail: askc@vast.astrakhan.ru Pavel Alexandrovich Khrapunov, CEO

HOTELS, TOURISM, AND RECREATION

40R013 ● ◆

Construction of a Congress Center on a land plot of 28,700 square meters in Astrakhan. Project purpose: to enhance services and to build a business center.	1) Total area of two buildings is 27,400 square meters 2) $13.1 million/2 years 3) L 4) BP	OOO PKF Initsiativa 53, ul. Pobedy, Astrakhan, Astrakhan Region, 414040 Phone/fax: (8512) 25 4364, 39 1399, 25 8005 E-mail: aotvs@astranet.ru Valery Ivanovich Vinokurov, Director

40R014 ● ◆

Creation of a cruise shipping company for passenger cruiser trips in the Caspian sea. Project purpose: to enhance tourism services.	1) 11,000 passengers a year 2) $3.0 million/1 year 3) L 4) BP	OOO TINTOUR Tourism Company 3, ul. Volodarskogo, Astrakhan, Astrakhan Region, 414000 Phone: (8512) 39 5665, 39 5664 Fax: (8512) 39 5315 E-mail: tintour@tintour.ru Vladimir Viktorovich Fialkin, Director

40R015 ★ ● ◆

Creation of a tourism network (motels, car camps, and inns) in the Volga-Akhtubinsk Flood-Lands and Delta of the Volga river in the Astrakhan Region. Project purpose: to enhance tourism services.	1) n/a 2) $3.5 million/5 years 3) L, Leas. 4) BP	Department of Support to Small and Medium Size Business and Tourism of the Regional Administration 20, ul. Lenina, Astrakhan, Astrakhan Region, 4140001 Phone/fax: (8512) 39 0462 E-mail: dpt@mail.astrakhan.ru Sergei Konstantinovich Ryaskov, Head of Department

41. VOLGOGRAD REGION [34]

E C O N O M I C   M A P

TAMBOV REGION

Tsna

Vorona

Rtischevo

SARATOV REGION

Volsk

Volga

Atkarsk

VORONEZH REGION

Balashov

Borisoglebsk

SARATOV

Marks

Engels

Volgogradskoe water reservoir

Zhirnovsk

Krasnoarmeysk

Urupinsk

Buzuluk

Medveditsa

Kotovo

Kamyshin

Mikhaylovka

Ilovlya

Khoper

Frolovo

Korobkovskoe

Don

Volgogradskoe water reservoir

Lake Elton

VOLGOGRAD

Volzhsky

KAZAKHSTAN

Kalach-on-Don

Volga-Don Canal

ASTRAKHAN REGION

Akhtubinsk

Lake Baskunchak

Tsimlyanskoe water reservoir

Volga

Akhtuba

Tsimlyansk

Don

REPUBLIC

Volgodonsk

KALMYKIA

Sal

Kotelnikovo

Lake Sarpa

PROCESSING INDUSTRY
- Ferrous metals
- Non-ferrous metals
- Machine engineering and metal processing
- Chemicals
- Construction materials
- Food and beverages

MINING INDUSTRY
- △ Natural gas
- ▲ Oil
- ▯ Raw cement
- ❶ Phosphorites
- ▱ Table salt
- ● Mineral water sources

CROPS AND LIVESTOCK BREEDING
- Wheat
- Sunflower
- Melons and gourds
- Mustard
- Orchards
- Potatoes
- Vegetables
- Meat and dairy cattle breeding
- Sheep rearing
- Pig breeding
- Poultry farming

POWER PLANTS
- Thermal power plants
- Hydro power plants

I am pleased to have this opportunity to introduce the Volgograd Region, which as recently as in 2001 was celebrating three anniversaries at once – the 80th anniversary of the foundation of the Tsaritsyn Province, the 65th anniversary of the Stalingrad Region, and 40th anniversary of the Volgograd Region.

In 2003, the Russian people celebrated the 60th anniversary of the Battle of Stalingrad in which the army of Nazi Germany was defeated.

Government awards have been issued to the Volgograd Region as a sign of appreciation of the Region's economic, strategic, and military potential.

The Volgograd Region was one of the initiators of the Great Volga Association for encouraging cooperation between the republics and regions of the Volga Region of the Russian Federation, and the Region became one of its founders and active members in 1991. Now, the Volgograd Region is part of the Southern Federal District, acting as an "economic bridge" of sorts between the Volga Region and North Caucasus.

Trunk railroads, highways, air routes, and waterways cross the Region, including the Lenin Volga-Don Canal. Freight is shipped via transit routes to the Baltic, White, and Caspian Seas, the Sea of Azov, and the Black Sea.

The Volga Hydroelectric Power Station is the largest hydroelectric power station in Europe.

The Volgograd Region has considerable scientific and industrial potential, diversified industry, highly developed agriculture, and a modern construction sector.

The Volgograd Region is regarded as the richest region in the south-eastern part of Russia in terms of its natural resources (oil, natural gas, bischofite, phosphorite, lime, and potassium salts). Its unique recreational resources – climate, spa and recreation areas, and mineral waters (the valleys of the Volga, Don, Khoper, Medveditsa, and Buzuluk rivers, and the therapeutic muds and brine of the Elton Lake) – make the Region all the more attractive for investment.

This potential provides a strong base for the implementation of the Program for Social and Economic Development of the Volgograd Region in 2001–2005, which sets the following regional development priorities: industrial exploration and processing of bischofite and phosphorite ore; upgrading of production facilities in the chemicals, petrochemicals, machine engineering, ferrous metals, food processing, and construction materials sectors; the development of transportation and resort and recreation areas near Lake Elton and in the Volgo-Akhtubinsk Valley; and the reproduction of valuable fish stocks.

The Volgograd Region has signed a number of loan agreements with banks to finance the Program.

The Region's insurance companies, private pension funds, and consumer credit co-operatives are expanding and attracting private investment into medium and small enterprises. The Region is continually improving its legislation.

The Volgograd Region is expanding its international economic and trade activities and has ties with many countries both in the CIS and worldwide (Italy, Greece, Germany, the US, the Netherlands, France, the UK, China, etc.).

We invite domestic and foreign investors to invest in our Region.

Nikolai Maksyuta,
HEAD OF ADMINISTRATION OF THE VOLGOGRAD REGION

1. GENERAL INFORMATION

1.1. GEOGRAPHY

Situated in the south-eastern part of European Russia, the Volgograd Region covers a total area of some 113,900 square kilometers. To the north, the Region borders the Saratov Region, to the south – the Astrakhan Region and the Republic of Kalmykia, to the west – the Rostov and Voronezh Regions, and to the east – Kazakhstan.

1.2. CLIMATE

The Volgograd Region is located within the steppe and semi-desert continental climate zone.

Air temperatures in January average −5.2°C, rising to +23.7°C in July. Annual precipitation reaches 450 mm in the north-western part of the Region, and 250 mm in the south-eastern part. The average growing season exceeds 180 days. Black earth and brown soils predominate in the Volgograd Region.

1.3. POPULATION

According to preliminary 2002 census results, the Volgograd Region's population was 2.7 million. The average population density is 23.7 people per square kilometer. The portion of economically active population is 1.3 million people. Official unemployment stood at 1% in 2002, while the actual rate was 9.8%. Demographically speaking, some 59.4% are of working age, 22.6% are beyond the statutory working age, and 18% are below the statutory working age. The major urban centers of the Volgograd Region (2002 data) are Volgograd with 1012,800 inhabitants, Volzhsky with 310,700 inhabitants, and Kamyshin with 128,100 inhabitants.

Population							_TABLE 1_
	1992	1997	1998	1999	2000	2001	2002
Total population, '000	2,642	2,702	2,700	2,693	2,677	2,658	2,703
Economically active population, '000	1,342	1,191	1,167	1,301	1,295	1,282	1,285

2. ADMINISTRATION

9, Prospekt Im. V.I. Lenina, Volgograd, Volgograd Region, 400098
Phone: (8442) 33 5203; fax: (8442) 93 6212
E-mail: glava@volganet.ru; http://www.volganet.ru

NAME	POSITION	CONTACT INFORMATION
Nikolai Kirillovich MAKSYUTA	Head of Administration of the Volgograd Region	Phone: (8442) 33 6688
Vladimir Alexandrovich KABANOV	First Deputy Head of Administration of the Volgograd Region (Economy, Industry, Transport, and Communications)	Phone: (8442) 33 5347 Fax: (8442) 33 6722
Pavel Pavlovich CHUMAKOV	First Deputy Head of Administration of the Volgograd Region (Agroindustrial Sector)	Phone: (8442) 36 2393 Fax (8442) 32 7683
Alexander Sergeevich PLOTNIKOV	Deputy Head of Administration of the Volgograd Region, Chairman of the Committee for Economy	Phone/fax: (8442) 33 5695
Valentina Nikolaevna RAKOVA	Deputy Head of Administration of the Volgograd Region, Chairman of the Volgograd Regional State Property Management Committee	Phone: (8442) 36 6495, 36 2620
Sergei Petrovich SAZONOV	Deputy Head of Administration of the Volgograd Region, Head of the Central Finance and Treasury Department	Phone: (8442) 33 5600, 33 5847

III

SOUTHERN FEDERAL DISTRICT

3. ECONOMIC POTENTIAL

3.1. 1997–2002 GROSS REGIONAL PRODUCT (GRP). INDUSTRY BREAKDOWN

The Volgograd Region's 2002 gross regional product was $3,314.3 million, 7.6% up on 2001 levels.

3.2. MAJOR ECONOMIC GROWTH PROJECTIONS

The blueprint for economic development in the Region is set forth in the Program for Social and Economic Development of the Volgograd Region in 2001–2005. The Program identifies priority scientific,

GRP trends in 1997–2002						*TABLE 2*
	1997	1998	1999	2000	2001*	2002*
GRP in current prices, $ million	5,380.7	3,237.0	1,932.5	2,626.4	3,080.9	3,314.3

*Estimates of the Volgograd Regional Administration

GRP industry breakdown in 1997–2002, % of total						*TABLE 3*
	1997	1998	1999	2000	2001*	2002*
GRP	100.0	100.0	100.0	100.0	100.0	100.0
Industry	31.0	35.0	38.1	35.0	33.7	40.2
Agriculture and forestry	13.4	11.2	14.6	13.9	16.4	15.3
Construction	8.3	6.9	5.1	11.1	10.5	5.0
Transport and communications	11.3	11.9	7.8	8.3	8.0	9.3
Trade and public catering	9.9	9.1	7.4	7.6	7.3	6.9
Other	18.3	20.6	20.2	17.6	16.8	17.8
Net taxes on output	7.8	5.3	6.8	6.5	7.3	5.5

*Estimates of the Volgograd Regional Administration

innovation, and investment projects, and is designed to spearhead the social and economic development of the region, and environmental protection.

The five-year program establishes priority comprehensive measures aimed at stabilizing and upgrading industrial enterprises in such sectors as mineral resource extraction, energy, chemicals and petrochemicals, machine engineering, ferrous metals, and construction materials. The Program focuses particularly on the food and beverages, and food processing sector.

Plans are afoot to develop deposits of magnesium chloride (bischofite) for industrial, medical, and agricultural purposes, and to extract and process phosphorites and produce phosphate fertilizers.

Other priorities established by the Program include the development of resort and recreation areas along the River Don, in the Volgo-Akhtubinsk Valley, and on the shores of Lake Elton.

The section of the Program devoted to transport infrastructure development calls for the completion of construction of a runway at OAO Volgograd International Airport, the construction of a bridge spanning the Volga, the refurbishment of the Volga–Don Canal, and the electrification of the Volga Railroad.

3.3. INDUSTRIAL OUTPUT IN 1997–2002 FOR MAJOR SECTORS OF ECONOMY

The Volgograd Region's major industrial sectors are fuel, chemicals and petrochemicals, machine engineering and metals processing, ferrous metals, energy, and food. These sectors account for a combined 85.2% of the Region's total industrial output.

Fuel. Fuel accounts for 15.6% of total industrial output. The largest enterprises are OOO LUKoil-Nizhnevolzhskneft and OOO LUKoil-Volgogradneftepererabotka.

Chemicals and petrochemicals. Chemicals and petrochemicals account for 15.2% of total industrial output. Enterprises in the sector produce hydrated sodium, pesticides, synthetic resins and plastics, and synthetic fiber and yarns. The largest enterprises are OAO Khimprom, OAO Caustic, OAO Volzhsky Orgsintez, and OAO Sibur Volzhsky.

Machine engineering and metal processing. The sector accounts for 14.9% of total industrial output. Enterprises in the sector produce tractors, ships, tower cranes, bearings, and machinery for the oil, electrical, and food industries. The Region is a major producer of drilling, transport, storage, medical, and retail equipment. The largest enter-

Industry breakdown of industrial output in 1997–2002, % of total						*TABLE 4*
	1997	1998	1999	2000	2001	2002*
Industry	100.0	100.0	100.0	100.0	100.0	100.0
Fuel	14.7	12.7	15.7	19.2	17.3	15.6
Chemicals and petrochemicals	19.9	20.3	18.3	15.7	15.3	15.2
Machine engineering and metal processing	13.9	13.7	13.6	16.2	15.6	14.9
Ferrous metals	6.5	7.0	13.1	13.0	15.4	13.8
Energy	18.9	18.3	12.1	11.6	11.7	13.4
Food	11.8	12.7	11.8	10.8	11.8	12.3
Construction materials	4.9	4.7	4.6	4.1	4.6	4.9
Non-ferrous metals	3.9	5.8	5.7	4.4	3.4	4.0
Flour, cereals, and mixed fodder	1.7	1.7	2.0	1.8	1.8	1.6
Light industry	0.7	0.7	0.6	0.8	0.8	1.2
Glass and porcelain	0.7	0.6	0.9	0.9	1.0	1.0
Forestry, timber, and pulp and paper	1.2	1.1	1.1	0.8	0.9	0.8

*Estimates of the Volgograd Regional Administration

III

SOUTHERN FEDERAL DISTRICT

prises in the sector are OAO Volgograd Tractor Plant and OAO Volgograd Bearings Plant.

Ferrous metals. Ferrous metals accounts for 13.8% of total industrial output. The largest enterprises are OAO Krasny Oktyabr Metals Plant and OAO PO Volzhsky Pipe Manufacturing Plant.

Energy. Energy accounts for 13.4% of total industrial output. The energy industry is represented by the HEP Station named in honor of the Twenty-Second Congress of the Communist Party of the USSR, six thermal power stations, and two generating plants.

Food and beverages. The food industry accounts for 12.3% of total industrial output. The largest enterprises are OAO Povolzhye, ZAO Konfil People's Enterprise, OOO Coca-Cola Volgograd Bottlers, OAO Uryupinsk Oil Extraction Plant, OAO Volgograd Diary 3, Branch of FGUP Rosspirtprom, OOO Volgogad Flour Mill, and OAO Archedinsk Bread and Bakery Products.

Agriculture. The Volgograd Region is a major agricultural region. The agricultural sector is represented by 27 state enterprises, 150 joint stock companies, 67 partnerships, 50 production cooperatives, and 12,900 farms. Some 84% of the Region's territory is given over to agricultural lands. Owing to the climatic conditions of the Region, irrigation is widely used. The Volgograd Region's agricultural output consists of wheat, sunflower seed, mustard, potato, vegetables, melons, eggs, meat, milk, wool fleece, and cotton.

3.4. FUEL AND ENERGY BALANCE (OUTPUT AND CONSUMPTION PER RESOURCE)

The Volgograd Energy System (Lower Volga Energy Area), which forms part of the integrated central energy system (ICES of the UES of Russia), fully satisfies demand for energy in the Region. 2002 electricity output amounted to 16.1 billion kWh, while energy consumption was 15.1 billion kWh.

3.5. TRANSPORT INFRASTRUCTURE

Roads. The Volgograd Region has more than 14,500 kilometers of public highway, including 8,000 kilometers of federal highway. Each year, some 250–300 kilometers of new roads are constructed in the Region. The Volgograd Region's major highways are the M-6 Caspian (Moscow – Tambov – Astrakhan, 361 kilometers of which passes through the

Fuel and energy sector production and consumption trends, 1997–2002						*TABLE 5*
	1997	1998	1999	2000	2001	2002*
Electricity output, billion kWh	16.3	17.6	17.6	15.4	17.0	16.1
Oil output (including gas condensate), '000 tons	3,735.0	3,875.0	3,603.0	3,629.0	3,470.0	3,405.0
Natural gas extraction, million cubic meters	523.0	488.0	487.0	550.0	567.0	552.0
Electricity consumption, billion kWh	15.5	15.6	16.4	16.5	16.6	15.1
Natural gas consumption, million cubic meters	6,388.8	6,789.7	6,264.0	6,644.6	7,195.0	8,367.4

*Estimates of the Volgograd Regional Administration

Region), the M-21 (Volgograd – Kamensk-Shakhtinsky, 196 kilometers within the Region), and the A-409 (Syzran – Saratov – Volgograd, 243 kilometers). A branch of the M-6 links Volgograd to Elista.

Railroads. The Volgograd Region has 1,600 kilometers of railroads. The major trunk line is the Volgograd branch of the Volga Region Railroad.

Airports. Volgograd is served by an international airport, which is managed by OAO Volgograd International Airport. The airport forms part of the North-South international air corridor.

River transport. The total length of the Region's navigable inland waterway system is 1,100 kilometers. The main navigable waterways are the Volga and Don rivers. The Volga – Don Canal connects the Black Sea and the Caspian Sea, providing the Volgograd Region with links to the industrial centers of the Volga Region, the Urals, the North Caucasus, and abroad. The largest enterprises are OAO Volgograd River Port and OAO Kalachevsk River Port.

Oil and gas pipelines. The following oil pipelines cross the Volgograd Region: Kuibyshev – Tikhoretsk (438 kilometers within the Region), Zhirnovsk – Volgograd (312 kilometers), and Kuibyshev – Lisichansk (340 kilometers).

Major gas pipelines. Soyuz, Urengoy – Novopskov, Central Asia – Center, Petrovsk – Novopskov, and Orenburg – Novopskov. All the gas pipelines are single thread. Their total length within the Region is more than 6,800 kilometers.

3.6. MAIN NATURAL RESOURCES: RESERVES AND EXTRACTION IN 2002

The Volgograd Region has more than 280 deposits of solid mineral resources. The Region boasts deposits of oil, gas, magnesium chloride (bischofite), phosphorites, table salt, sand, mineral water, and curative mud.

Oil and natural gas. The Region's oil reserves amount to more than 500 million tons, natural gas – 1.2 trillion cubic meters, and gas conden-sate – more than 450 million tons.

The Region has eight oil and gas exploration zones. High on the priority list for geological surveying are the Korobkovsko-Nizhnedobrinskaya and Caspian Depressions.

Mineral resources. The Volgograd Region is rich in mineral salts. The rock salt reserves of the Svetloyarsk deposit stand at 1.1 million tons. Potassium salt reserves are estimated at 143 million tons. Lake salt reserves amount to 3 billion tons. The Volgograd Region has unique deposits of magnesium chloride (bischofite) totaling 365.5 trillion tons. The total phosphorite reserves of the Kalachevskoye and Trekhostrovskoye deposits exceed 28.1 million tons.

Construction materials. Some 107 deposits of construction materials are found in the Region, of which 52 are explored, including 16 deposits of carbonate strata and 36 deposits of sandstone. The rock is used for the production of crushed stone and quarry stone. The total reserves of construction materials amount to 2.2 billion cubic meters.

4. TRADE OPPORTUNITIES

4.1. MAIN GOODS PRODUCED IN THE REGION

Chemicals and petrochemicals. 2002 hydrated sodium output totaled 270,300 tons, synthetic resins and plastics – 89,100 tons, man-made fibers and yarn – 17,800 tons, paints and varnishes – 7,600 tons, and automobile tires – 3 million items.

Machine engineering and metal processing. 2002 output of oil production machinery reached 7,300 tons, rolling bearings output totaled 17.8 million items, tractor output reached 3,500 items, and vacuum cleaner output totaled 7,900 items.

Ferrous metals. 2002 steel output totaled 902,600 tons, rolled steel products output totaled 239,000 tons, and steel pipe output reached 638,000 tons.

Food and beverages. 2002 processed fish product output (canned fish not included) totaled 5,460 tons, meat – 28,500 tons, dairy output (measured in milk equivalent) – 71,400 tons, butter – 2,200 tons, full fat cheese – 2,500 tons, flour – 170,100 tons, bread and bakery products – 152,000 tons, confectionery – 26,500 tons, vegetable oil – 75,600 tons, vodka and liquors – 921,000 decaliters, wine –

192,000 decaliters, beer – 15.8 million decaliters, and non-alcoholic beverages – 7.1 million decaliters.

4.2. EXPORTS, INCLUDING EXTRA-CIS

2002 extra-CIS exports totaled $961.6 million. CIS exports reached $265.8 million. The bulk of the Region's export consisted of fossil fuels, oil and petrochemicals ($636.4 million), aluminum and aluminum products ($187.3 million), organic and chemical compounds ($53.9 million), ferrous metals ($45.8 million), bread grain ($39 million), ferrous metal products ($91.6 million), inorganic compounds ($39.9 million), cotton ($11.9 million), and raw rubber and rubber products ($24.4 million).

The Region's main partners for exports are Italy (30% of exports), Greece (13%), Ukraine (9%), Kazakhstan (7%), the United States (5%), the Netherlands (3%), Belarus (2.5%), Iran (2%), and Finland (2%).

4.3. IMPORTS, INCLUDING EXTRA-CIS

Imports from extra-CIS countries amounted to $202.1 million in 2002. Imports from CIS countries totaled $103.8. The Region's imports largely consisted of equipment and accessories ($55.5 million), inorganic chemicals ($37.5 million), plastics and plastic products ($18.7 million), tobacco and tobacco substitutes ($36.5 million), paper and cardboard and paper pulp products ($16.1 million), electrical machinery and equipment ($12.8 million), cotton wool, felt and nonwoven fabric ($9 million), and organic compounds ($5 million).

The Region's main partners for imports are Germany (18% of imports), Ukraine (16%), Greece (11%), Belarus (11%), Italy (6%), France (4%), Belgium (4%), Uzbekistan (3%), and Kazakhstan (3%).

4.4. MAJOR REGIONAL EXPORT AND IMPORT ENTITIES

Owing to the specific nature of the Volgograd Region's export and import activities, export and import transactions are performed mainly by industrial enterprises.

5. INVESTMENT OPPORTUNITIES

5.1. INVESTMENTS IN 1992–2002 (BY INDUSTRY SECTOR), INCLUDING FOREIGN INVESTMENTS

The following factors determine the investment appeal of the Volgograd Region:

- Its developed transport infrastructure;
- Its considerable industrial potential;
- Its qualified workforce;
- Legislation supporting investment activity.

5.2. CAPITAL INVESTMENT

The bulk of fixed capital investment goes to transport and industrial production.

Capital investment by industry sector, $ million						TABLE 6
	1997	1998	1999	2000	2001	2002
Total capital investment	933.5	448.9	229.4	409.4	599.8	577.8
Including major industries (% of total):						
Industry	35.0	40.0	42.0	54.0	38.0	36.4
Agriculture and forestry	3.0	4.0	5.0	4.0	4.0	5.5
Construction	7.0	10.0	6.0	2.0	3.0	1.7
Transport and communications	21.0	17.0	18.0	18.0	38.0	40.7
Trade and public catering	3.0	5.0	5.0	4.0	3.0	1.6
Other	31.0	24.0	24.0	18.0	14.0	14.1

Foreign investment trends in 1995–2002					TABLE 7
	1995–1997	1998	1999	2000	2001	2002
Foreign investment, $ million	93.5	82.6	93.9	139.5	82.8	67.4
Including FDI, $ million	64.9	76.0	53.1	76.9	31.9	3.6

5.3. MAJOR ENTERPRISES (INCLUDING ENTERPRISES WITH FOREIGN INVESTMENT)

The Volgograd Region hosts some 350 joint ventures and foreign companies. The Region has investment ties with 77 foreign countries. The bulk of the Region's enterprises with foreign investment produce ferrous and non-ferrous metal products, furniture, sawn timber, and garments, and operate in the construction, installation, and scientific research sectors. Joint ventures in the service sectors include road haulage companies and motor vehicle maintenance enterprises.

5.4. MOST ATTRACTIVE SECTORS FOR INVESTMENT

According to the Volgograd Regional Administration, fuel and energy, metals, machine engineering, chemicals and petrochemicals are the most attractive industries for investment.

5.5. CURRENT LEGISLATION ON INVESTOR TAX EXEMPTIONS AND PRIVILEGES

The following legislative acts provide a framework for the support of investment activity in the Region:

- The Law of the Volgograd Region On Investment Activity in the Volgograd Region;
- The Law of the Volgograd Region On the Program for Social and Economic Development of the Volgograd Region through 2001–2005;
- The Law of the Volgograd Region On Regional Targeted Programs;
- The Law of the Volgograd Region On Economic Development Zones in the Territory of the Volgograd Region;
- The Law of the Volgograd Region On Tax Exemptions for Investors in the Volgograd Region;

Largest enterprises of the Volgograd Region	*TABLE 8*
COMPANY	SECTOR
OOO LUKoil-Volgogradneftepererabotka	Oil refining
OOO LUKoil-Nizhnevolzhskneft	Oil production
OOO Volgogradtransgaz	Pipeline transport
OAO Volgograd Aluminum	Aluminum
OAO Khimprom	Chemicals
OAO PO Volzhsky Pipe Manufacturing Plant	Pipes
OAO Volgograd Tractor Plant	Tractors and agricultural machinery
OAO Volzhsky Orgsintez	Chemicals
ZAO Krasny Oktyabr Volgograd Metals Plant	Ferrous metals
OAO Volgograd Aluminum	Primary aluminum
OAO Caustic	Chemicals
OOO Volgodeminoil, JV	Oil production
OAO Voltire	Tires
OAO Plastkard	Chemicals
OAO Volgogradneftemash	Heavy industry, power, and transportation engineering

• The Law of the Volgograd Region On Residential Mortgage Development in the Volgograd Region;

• The Decree of the Head of Volgograd Regional Administration On the Investment Fund of the Volgograd Region.

These legislative acts seek to render the Volgograd Region more attractive to investors, reduce the regional budget deficit, reform regional institutions along market economy lines, and underpin economic growth. The Regional laws provide for exemptions from regional components of profit tax, land tax, and property tax. The tax exemptions are granted to legal entities conducting investment activity in the Volgograd Region under investment projects included in the Regional Register. The exemptions include privileges for banks and other credit institutions granting loans on preferential terms to investment projects in the Volgograd Region for a term exceeding one year.

5.6. FEDERAL AND REGIONAL ECONOMIC AND SOCIAL DEVELOPMENT PROGRAMS FOR THE VOLGOGRAD REGION

Federal targeted programs. The Volgograd Region is currently participating in 22 federal targeted programs, which incorporate 25 regional projects. Major programs underway in the Region include Russia's South, 2002–2006, Soil Fertility Enhancement, 2002–2005, Federal Program for the Development of Education, 2000–2005, Program for the Creation of a Computerized State Land Cadastre and State Control of Real Estate, 2000–2007, Modernization of

Russia's Transport System, 2002–2010 (Internal Waterways sub-program), and Ecology and Natural Resources of Russia, 2002–2010 (Revival of the Volga River, Water Biosphere Resources and Aquaculture, Forests sub-programs).

Under the federal targeted programs, the Volgograd Region is a beneficiary of state support and regional budget allocations for the construction and revamping of the following enterprises: OAO Kaustic – a pilot chemicals plant producing 2.5 tons of medical substances annually; OAO Volgobiosintez – production of non-polluting protein fodder from by-products of grain processing (100,000 tons per year); OAO Khimprom – an enterprise producing the sugar substitute aspartame (50 tons per year); revamping of refrigerant production facilities at OAO Kaustic and OAO Khimprom; and reconstruction of the Volga–Don Canal.

Regional programs. In 2002, the Volgograd Regional Administration drafted and approved 32 regional targeted programs. The most important include: Exploration and Utilization of Small Oil Fields for Municipal Entities in the Volgograd Region, 2002–2006, Soil Fertility Enhancement in the Volgograd Region, 2002–2005, Research, Development, Creation and Batch Production of Drip Irrigation Systems, 2002–2006, Comprehensive Development of Transport in the Volgograd Region through 2012, Program for Upgrading Public Road Transport in the Volgograd Region, 2002–2007, and Ethnic and Social Development of the Population of the Volgograd Region, 2003–2005.

6. INVESTMENT PROJECTS

Industry sector and project description	1) Expected results 2) Amount and term of investment 3) Form of financing[1] 4) Documentation[2]	Contact information
1	2	3

CHEMICALS AND PETROCHEMICALS

41R001 ● ◆

Implementation of new technologies for the production of pollution free delayed action vulcanization accelerators at an operating enterprise.
Project goal: to diversify product mix and improve quality and environmental protection.

1) 2,000 accelerators, a profit of $0.9 million per year
2) $7 million/2 years
3) L
4) BP

OAO Volzhsky Orgsintez
Volzhsky, Volgograd Region, 404117
Phone: (8443) 22 3000
Fax: (8443) 25 7444
E-mail: zos@vlz.ru
Alexander Vladimirovich Sobolevsky, CEO

41R002 ● ◆

Creation of facilities for the production of magnesium oxide, magnesium, and bromine.
Project goal: to organize production of magnesium oxide and bromine via thermochemical treatment of magnesium chloride brine extracted from natural magnesium chloride.

1) Overall profit of $10.1 million per year
2) $30 million/n/a
3) L
4) BP

OAO Kaustic
57, ul. 40 years of VLKSM,
Volgograd, Volgograd Region, 400097
Phone: (8442) 40 6990
Fax: (8442) 40 6155
E-mail: kaustik@advent.avtlg.ru
Eldor Englenovich Azizov, CEO

41R003 ● ◆

First stage of the reconstruction and revamping of radial automobile tires facilities.
Project goal: to enhance radial automobile tire production capacity.

1) 1.8 million tires per year
2) $48 million/2 years
3) L
4) BP

OAO Voltire
3, ul. Pervomayskaya, Volzhsky,
Volgograd Region, 404103
Phone: (8443) 22 7073
Fax: (8443) 25 7852
E-mail: voltair@voltair.vlz.ru
Nikolai Vasilyevich Titov, CEO

MACHINE ENGINEERING AND METAL PROCESSING

41R004 ■ ❖ ◆

Creation of facilities for the production of wheeled tractors.
Project goal: to diversify product mix.

1) Overall profit of $1.3 million per year
2) $5 million/3.5 years
3) E ($2.5 million), JV
4) BP

OAO Volgograd Tractor Plant
pl. Dzerzhinskogo, Volgograd,
Volgograd Region, 400061
Phone: (8442) 74 6001
Fax: (8442) 74 6120
E-mail: chibf@vgtz.com
Sergei Vasilyevich Romanenko, CEO

41R005 ● ★ ◆

Creation of facilities for the production of bearings for rolling stock at an operating bearings manufacturing plant.
Project goal: to expand output and to diversify product mix.

1) 100,000 items per year
2) $15 million/3 years
3) L, Leas.
4) BP

OAO Volzhsky Bearings Plant 15
45, ul. Pushkina, Volzhsky,
Volgograd Region, 404112
Phone: (8443) 22 1600, 22 1590
Fax: (8443) 25 6996
E-mail: vpz@vpz.ru, marketing@vpz.ru
Vladimir Vasilyevich Lytov, CEO

III

SOUTHERN FEDERAL DISTRICT

---

[1] L – Loan, E – Equity, Leas. – Leasing, JV – Joint Venture
[2] BP – Business Plan, FS – Feasibility Study

1	2	3

41R006

Upgrade of facilities for the production of automated refrigerating plants at an operating enterprise.
Project goal: to diversify product mix, and quality and technology improvement.

1) Revenues of $1.5 million per year
2) $1 million/8 months
3) L
4) BP

OAO Volgogradelektronmash
1, ul. Samarskaya, Volgograd,
Volgograd Region, 400079
Phone: (8442) 42 2202
Fax (8442) 42 1878
E-mail: elmash@volgodon.ru
Igor Borisovich Abramov, CEO

41R007

Creation of facilities for the production of sprinkling machines for drip irrigation systems (acquisition of the equipment).
Project goal: to substitute imports, to diversify product mix, and to protect environment.

1) Up to 20 million pipes equipped with sprinkling machines for irrigating up to 7,000 hectares of land
2) € 1 million/1 year
3) L, JV
4) BP

AO Volgograd Irrigation Equipment Manufacturing Plant
8a, ul. Institutskaya, Volgograd,
Volgograd Region, 400002
Phone: (8442) 43 3675
Fax: (8442) 43 3650
E-mail: ortech@avtlg.ru
Leonid Davydovich Zingerman, CEO

HOUSING AND COMMUNAL SERVICES

41R008

Reconstruction and upgrade of operating water wells.
Project goal: to reduce costs through introduction of advanced technologies.

1) Daily capacity of 20,000 cubic meters of water
2) $0.6 million/2 years
3) L
4) BP

Housing and Public Utilities Committee of the Volgograd Regional Administration
21, ul. Kommunisticheskaya,
Volgograd, Volgograd Region, 400131
Phone: (8442) 93 2201, 93 2206
Fax: (8442) 97 5036
E-mail: kgkhvolg@vistcom.ru
Yury Vladimirovich Kotlyarov,
Chairman of the Committee

TRANSPORT INFRASTRUCTURE

41R009

Revamping and expansion of the Volgograd International Airport.
Project goal: to increase cargo and passenger traffic and create capacity for maintenance of new types of planes (Il 86 and Boeing 747).

1) Passenger turnover – 1,200 passengers per hour
2) $19.1 million/3 years
3) L
4) BP

OAO International Airport of Volgograd
Airport, Volgograd,
Volgograd Region, 400036
Phone: (8442) 31 7397
Fax: (8442) 31 7070
E-mail: aeroport@mav.ru
Yury Yakovlevich Dmitriyev, CEO

42. ROSTOV REGION [61]

ECONOMIC MAP

BELGOROD REGION

VORONEZH REGION

Kalach

Don

Khopyor

Medveditsa

VOLGOGRAD REGION

UKRAINE

Don

Gorlovka

Lugansk

Millerovo

Surovikino

Kalitva

Donetsk

Kamensk-
-Shakhtinsky

Gukovo

Morozovsk

Belaya Kalitva

Tsimlyanskoe
water reservoir

Zverevo
Krasny Sulin

Tsimlyansk

Novoshakhtinsk

Shakhty

Taganrog

Novocherkassk

Don

Sal

Aksay

ROSTOV-ON-DON

Volgodonsk

Azov

Bataysk

Eysk

Starominskaya

Manych

ELISTA

Salsk

Yeya

Vegorlyk

Lake
Manych-Gudilo

Primorsk-Akhtarsk

KRASNODAR
TERRITORY

Tikhoretsk

PROCESSING INDUSTRY

- Ferrous metals
- Non-ferrous metals
- Machine engineering
  and metal processing
- Chemicals and petrochemicals
- Construction materials and glass
- Light industry
- Food and beverages

MINING INDUSTRY

- Oil
- Bituminous coal

- Fishing ports

POWER PLANTS

- Thermal power plants
- Hydro power plants
- Nuclear power plants

CROPS AND LIVESTOCK BREEDING

- Wheat
- Buckwheat
- Rice
- Corn
- Melons
  and gourds
- Сады
- Sunflower
- Resorts

- Vineyards
- Vegetables
- Aromatic plants
- Soy beans
- Meat and dairy
  cattle breeding
- Sheep rearing
- Pig breeding
- Poultry farming

The Rostov Region is a major multi-profile center of industry, agriculture, science, and culture in Russia's South. Its exceptionally advantageous geographical location, mild climate, rich mineral resource base, developed transport infrastructure, and qualified workforce attract investors and businessmen to the Region. Its industrial, agricultural, and research and development potential offer broad opportunities for further cooperation.

The past three years have seen steady economic growth trends in the Region. Over the past three years, gross regional product has grown by 33.5%, industrial output has risen by 57%, agricultural output has climbed by 38%, and capital investment has increased by 64.9%. The share of investment in GRP has grown from 15% to 22%.

The strongest investment growth levels have been seen in sectors with a high return on investment and high budget efficiency: machine engineering and metals processing, light, food and beverages and food and processing industries, construction, communications, and trade.

Industrial investment growth has been driven, among other factors, by increased foreign investor interest in the Region. Over half of all investment is directed to industry.

In 2002, the Rostov International Investor Association was established with the objective of combining the efforts of Russian and foreign entrepreneurs and authorities to finance socially important projects in the Region.

The Rostov Region is the most industrially developed Region of the Russian Federation.

Our output is well known in Germany, Greece, Egypt, India, Spain, Kazakhstan, Ukraine, and other countries.

We invite potential investors to cooperate with the Rostov Region and look forward to finding reliable business partners.

Vladimir Chub,
HEAD OF ADMINISTRATION (GOVERNOR)
OF THE ROSTOV REGION

1. GENERAL INFORMATION

1.1. GEOGRAPHY

Situated in the south of the East European Plain, the Rostov Region covers a total area of 100,800 square kilometers. To the south, the Region borders the Stavropol and Krasnodar Territories, to the west and northwest – Ukraine, to the north – the Voronezh Region, to the east and north-east – the Volgograd Region, and to the south-east – the Republic of Kalmykia.

1.2. CLIMATE

The Rostov Region enjoys a temperate continental climate. Air temperatures in January average –3.7°C, rising to +24°C in July. Average annual precipitation averages 424 mm. The average growing season lasts 180 days. Some 64.2% of the Region lies under highly fertile black earth soil, with a further 26.6% covered by brown earth soil. The remaining 8% lies under alluvial and meadow-marsh soils.

1.3. POPULATION

According to preliminary 2002 census results, total population in the Region was 4,407,000 people. The average population density is 43.7 people per square kilometer. The economically active population amounts to 2,127,000 people. 2002 official unemployment stood at 0.8%, while the actual rate is 12.9%.

Demographically speaking, some 59.3% are of working age, 17.8% are below the statutory working age, and 22.9% are beyond the statutory working age.

As of 2002, the Rostov Region's major urban centers were Rostov-on-Don with 1,070,200 inhabitants, Taganrog with 282,300 inhabitants, Shakhty with 220,400 inhabitants, Novocherkassk with 170,900 inhabitants, Volgodonsk with 166,500 inhabitants, and Novoshakhtinsk with 101,200 inhabitants.

Population								*TABLE 1*
	1992	1997	1998	1999	2000	2001	2002
Total population, '000	4,346	4,404	4,387	4,368	4,341	4,317	4,407
Economically active population, '000	2,166	1,935	1,927	2,066	2,062	2,032	2,127

2. ADMINISTRATION

112, ul. Sotsialisticheskaya, Rostov-on-Don, Rostov Region, 344050
Phone: (8632) 44 1810, http://www.donland.ru

NAME	POSITION	CONTACT INFORMATION
Vladimir Fedorovich CHUB	Head of Administration (Governor) of the Rostov Region	Phone: (8632) 44 1810 Fax: (8632) 44 1559
Ivan Antonovich STANISLAVOV	First Deputy Head of Administration (Governor) of the Rostov Region	Phone: (8632) 44 1441, 40 6434 Fax: (8632) 40 5379
Viktor Vasilyevich USACHEV	First Deputy Head of Administration (Governor) of the Rostov Region	Phone: (8632) 40 5111, 40 1880 Fax: (8632) 40 3970
Viktor Yefimovich DERYABKIN	Deputy Head of Administration (Governor) of the Rostov Region, Minister of Economy, Trade, and International and External Economic Relations	Phone: (8632) 40 5257, 40 5385 Fax: (8632) 40 5480
Sergei Makarovich NAZAROV	Deputy Head of Administration (Governor) of the Rostov Region, Minister of Industry, Energy, and Natural Resources	Phone: (8632) 40 5355 Fax: (8632) 40 1124
Nina Ivanovna SVERCHKOVA	Deputy Head of Administration (Governor) of the Rostov Region, Minister of Finance	Phone: (8632) 40 6053 Fax: (8632) 40 7398
Dzhivan Khorenovich VARTANYAN	Minister of Transport, Communications, and Roads	Phone: (8632) 40 7280 Fax: (8632) 40 0091
Anna Nikolaevna PALAGINA	Deputy Minister of Economy, Head of Division of the Development of Small Enterprise and Inter-Regional Relations	Phone: (8632) 40 5949

3. ECONOMIC POTENTIAL

3.1. 1997–2002 GROSS REGIONAL PRODUCT (GRP). INDUSTRY BREAKDOWN

The 2002 gross regional product amounted to $4,895 million, which constitutes 4% growth year-on-year (in comparable prices). Per capita GRP amounted to $1,011 in 2001 and $1,112 in 2002.

3.2. MAJOR ECONOMIC GROWTH PROJECTIONS

The blueprint for economic development in the Rostov Region for forthcoming years is set forth in the Projections of the Social and Economic Development of the Rostov Region for 2003 and through 2005.

GRP trends in 1997–2002						TABLE 2
	1997	1998	1999	2000	2001*	2002*
GRP in current prices, $ million	6,147.2	4,079.7	2,778.0	3,412.8	4,361.9	4,895.0

*Estimates of the Rostov Regional Administration

GRP industry breakdown in 1997–2002, % of total						TABLE 3
	1997	1998	1999	2000	2001*	2002*
GRP	100.0	100.0	100.0	100.0	100.0	100.0
Industry	24.0	23.0	22.7	24.1	25.6	24.9
Agriculture and forestry	11.7	13.5	19.9	16.6	16.0	14.8
Construction	7.5	5.7	4.9	8.7	9.4	8.7
Transport and communications	10.0	8.3	5.6	7.5	7.8	9.1
Trade and public catering	17.2	20.7	20.3	19.5	17.5	17.7
Other	24.2	22.9	20.4	18.1	18.3	19.3
Net taxes on output	5.4	5.9	6.2	5.5	5.4	5.5

*Estimates of the Rostov Regional Administration

The Projections set forth the following main tasks: to create a favorable investment and business climate, develop financial infrastructure, encourage industrial innovation, restructure enterprises, develop transport, communications and telecommunications infrastructure, and restructure the agroindustrial sector.

3.3. INDUSTRIAL OUTPUT IN 1997–2002 FOR MAJOR SECTORS OF ECONOMY

The leading industrial sectors of the Rostov Region are energy, machine engineering and metals, and food and beverages. These account for a combined 64.9% of total industrial output.

Machine engineering and metal processing. The sector accounts for 23.7% of total industrial output and focuses on the production of electric locomotives, harvesters and other agricultural machinery, heavy lift helicopters, boilers, and equipment for nuclear and thermal power stations.

The largest companies within the sector are OAO Rostselmash, OAO Taganrog Harvester Plant, OAO Atommash, OAO Taganrog Boiler Plant Krasny Kotelschik, OAO Donpressmash, OAO Pressmash, OAO Azov Forging and Press Machinery Plant, OAO Tenth Bearing Plant, OAO Rostvertol, Federal State Unitary Company Krasny Hydropress, OAO Beriev Taganrog Aviation R&D Company, Federal State Unitary

Company Azov Optical and Mechanical Plant, OAO Gorizont, and Federal State Unitary Company Priboy.

Food and beverages. The sector accounts for 21.2% of total industrial output. Some 270 companies and 1,000 small businesses operate in the food and food processing sectors producing dairy products, meat, fish, alcoholic and non-alcoholic beverages, bread and bakery products, confectionery, macaroni, and tobacco products.

Major companies within the sector include OAO South of Russia, OAO Baltika-Rostov (a branch of OAO Baltika Brewery), OAO Don Tobacco, OOO Rostov Sausage Plant Tavr, OAO Semikarakorsky Canning Factory, OAO Millerovsky Vegetable Oil Extraction Plant, OAO Volgodonsk Dairy Plant, ZAO Milk, and OAO Rostov Flour Plant.

Energy. The sector accounts for 20% of total industrial output. The Region operates seven power stations, including a hydroelectric power station and six thermal power stations with a total installed capacity of 3,070.8 MW. Major electricity suppliers are the Novocherkasskaya Hydroelectrical Power Station, Tsimlyanskaya Power Station, and Rostovskaya Nuclear Power Station.

Ferrous metals. The sector accounts for 6.5% of total industrial output. The largest compa-

Industry breakdown of industrial output in 1997–2002, % to total

TABLE 4

	1997	1998	1999	2000	2001	2002*
Industry	100.0	100.0	100.0	100.0	100.0	100.0
Machine engineering and metal processing	21.0	20.2	23.3	23.5	27.2	23.7
Food and beverages	13.7	19.1	27.2	24.0	21.7	21.2
Energy	27.2	25.5	16.6	15.2	17.1	20.0
Ferrous metals	5.8	5.6	7.9	10.0	8.0	6.5
Fuel	13.3	12.6	6.4	5.7	6.0	5.4
Construction materials	3.8	3.9	3.7	3.7	2.9	5.1
Non-ferrous metals	3.3	4.1	4.8	3.8	3.2	4.6
Light industry	2.8	2.1	2.8	4.0	3.8	4.5
Chemicals and petrochemicals	3.2	3.4	3.6	3.6	3.5	2.9
Flour, cereals, and mixed fodder	2.6	1.9	3.3	3.4	3.2	2.7
Forestry, timber, and pulp and paper	1.0	1.4	1.5	1.7	1.7	1.8
Glass and porcelain	0.2	0.2	0.2	0.3	0.4	0.4

*Estimates of the Rostov Regional Administration

nies include OAO Taganrog Metal Works and OAO Belaya Kalitva Metal Works.

Fuel. The sector accounts for 5.4% of total industrial output. The Region hosts 40 oil processing facilities, 75 oil storage reservoirs, and 490 gasoline filling stations.

Coal extraction, which accounts for 4% of total Russian output, accounts for a large share of the Region's fuel sector. Coal companies in the Region have a total production capacity of 13.6 million tons. The largest companies are OAO Rostovugol, OAO Gukovugol, OAO Donugol, and OAO Rostovshakhtstroy.

Agriculture. Agriculture accounts for 14.8% of GRP, with tillage accounting for 62.5% of gross agricultural output. Grain cultivation is of paramount importance, with winter wheat the main grain crop. The Region is among the top three Russian wheat producing regions. Other crops cultivated in the Region include corn, rice, millet, buckwheat, and soybean.

The leading industrial crop is sunflower. The Region produces over 20% of Russia's total output of sunflower seed.

The largest companies are SZAO SKVO, SKhK Dzerzhinsky Artel, ZAO Shumilinskoye, and S.G. Shaumyan SPK.

3.4. FUEL AND ENERGY BALANCE (OUTPUT AND CONSUMPTION PER RESOURCE)

The Rostov Regional energy system is among the leading North Caucasus systems in terms of generating capacity. It fully meets local demand for electricity.

Fuel and energy sector production and consumption trends, 1997–2002

TABLE 5

	1997	1998	1999	2000	2001	2002*
Electricity output, billion kWh	13.0	10.9	11.5	10.7	15.4	18.4
Coal extraction, '000 tons	14.1	10.9	10.1	9.7	9.4	8.4
Natural gas extraction, million cubic meters	283.0	270.0	269.7	270.6	312.3	457.5
Electricity consumption, billion kWh	13.7	12.9	13.4	13.2	13.8	13.8
Coal consumption, million tons	4.9	4.2	4.4	3.9	3.5	3.2
Natural gas consumption, million cubic meters	5,450.0	5,170.0	5,028.0	5,625.0	5,871.0	6,429.0

*Estimates of the Rostov Regional Administration

3.5. TRANSPORT INFRASTRUCTURE

The Rostov Region has a developed transport infrastructure. The Regional center – Rostov-on-Don – is a major transport hub for Russia, the CIS, and Europe. Rostov-on-Don stands at the point of con-

vergence of six main railroad routes, seven arterial highways, and the River Don.

Roads. The Region has 11,500 kilometers of paved public highway. More than 450 million people are carried by road per year. The Kritsky corri-

III

SOUTHERN FEDERAL DISTRICT

dor, a major international transport artery linking St. Petersburg, Moscow, Rostov, and Novorossiysk, passes through the Region. The Don Highway crosses the Region. OAO Sovtransavto provides international road haulage services.

Railroads. The Region has 1,900 kilometers of railroads. The Region's main railroad routes are the North Caucasian railroad and the Moscow – Rostov–Caucasus route.

Sea and river ports. The Region's sea and river ports are capable of servicing river and ocean class vessels up to 5,000 tons. The Region's major international ports are the Taganrog Commercial Seaport, Azov Seaport, and Rostov river port.

Airports. The Rostov-on-Don airport services domestic and international flights, including flights to Finland, Germany, Turkey, the United Arab Emirates, the Czech Republic, Slovakia, and Bulgaria.

Oil and gas pipelines. The Region's population centers are supplied with gas from the trunk gas pipelines Stavropol – Moscow, North Cauca-

sus– Center, Orenburg – Novopskov, Novopskov – Mozdok, and Cheboksary – North Caucasus through lateral pipelines with a total length of 1,800 kilometers. Construction of a 259 kilometer oil pipeline skirting Ukraine is underway.

3.6. MAIN NATURAL RESOURCES: RESERVES AND EXTRACTION IN 2002

The Region's principle natural resources are coal, natural gas, raw building materials, and non-ore minerals used in metal processing.

Coal. The Rostov Region is the principle coal base of the North Caucasus. Proven coal reserves stand at 6.5 billion tons. Anthracite accounts for more than 90% of total coal reserves.

Oil and natural gas. Natural gas reserves are estimated at 54 billion cubic meters. The Regions has identified and explored some 20 natural gas and gas condensate fields with a total hydrocarbon reserve of some 60 billion cubic meters. Exploration of the Leonov-skoe oil field is currently underway.

4. TRADE OPPORTUNITIES

4.1. MAIN GOODS PRODUCED IN THE REGION

Machine engineering. The Region's enterprises produce 100% of Russia's electric locomotive and steam boiler output, more than half of grain harvester output, and 94% of industrial sewing machines. Heavy lift helicopters, ship navigation systems, thermal boiler and water heating equipment, and tractor cultivators manufactured in the Region are leading products in Russian industry.

In 2002, the Region produced 131 forging and press machines, 5,000 grain harvesters, 1,400 tractor cultivators, 28.3 million rolling bearings, and 78,900 electrical irons.

Agriculture. The 2002 grain crop reached 6.3 million tons, sunflower seed – 882,100 tons, and sugar beet – 50,600 tons.

Food and beverages. Vegetable oil output topped 225,000 tons in 2002, canned fruit and vegetables – 89.2 million cans, meat (including subproducts) – 36,700 tons, dairy products – 78,800 tons, bread and bakery – 24,700 tons, vodka and liquors – 667,000 decaliters, and sparkling wine – 1.1 million decaliters.

Industrial goods. In 2002, the Region produced 71,000 tons of finished rolled ferrous metals, 555,300 tons of steel, 461,000 tons of steel tube, 35,000 cubic meters of lumber, 9,300 tons of paper, 120,000 cubic meters of chipboard, 310,000 cubic meters of reinforced concrete assemblies, 22,000 tons of cement, 344 million conventional bricks of wall building

materials, 65,100 tons of paint and varnish, and 11.4 million square meters of fabric.

4.2. EXPORTS, INCLUDING EXTRA-CIS

The Rostov Region's exports to extra-CIS countries amounted to $503.4 million in 2000. Exports to the CIS totaled $205.8 million. The respective figures for 2001 were $646.7 million and $188.7 million, and $809.2 million and $203 million for 2002.

The main types of goods exported by the Region are food and raw food materials – $448.1 million, timber and pulp and paper goods – $12.6 million, metals and metal goods – $196.6 million, machinery, equipment and transport vehicles – $261.7 million, chemicals and resins – $39.6 million, leather, fur, and related goods – $0.5 million, textiles and footwear – $7.1 million, and minerals – $80.8 million. Major importers of the Region's products include Algeria, Germany, Greece, Egypt, Israel, India, Spain, Italy, Cyprus, Turkey, Kazakhstan, and Ukraine.

4.3. IMPORTS, INCLUDING EXTRA-CIS

2000 imports from extra-CIS countries amounted to $239.1 million. Imports from the CIS totaled $280.5 million. The respective figures for 2001 were $262.1 million and $385.1 million, and $376.1 million and $305.3 million for 2002.

The bulk of regional imports consists of food and raw food materials – $41.4 million, timber and pulp and paper – $47.2 million, metals and metal goods – $143.5 million, machinery, equipment, and transport vehicles – $286.7 million, chemicals and resins – $55.2 million, leather, fur and related goods – $0.7 million, minerals – $23 million, and textiles and footwear – $17.2 million. The main exporters to the Region are the UK, Germany, Greece, Italy, China, Turkey, France, and Ukraine.

4.4. MAJOR REGIONAL EXPORT AND IMPORT ENTITIES

Due to the specific features of trade in the Region, export and import operations are performed mainly by industrial companies.

5. INVESTMENT OPPORTUNITIES

5.1. INVESTMENTS IN 1992–2002 (BY INDUSTRY SECTOR), INCLUDING FOREIGN INVESTMENTS

The following factors determine the investment appeal of the Rostov Region:

- Its advantageous geographic location;
- Its developed transport infrastructure;
- Its high industrial potential and developed agriculture;
- Legislation supporting investment activities (protection of investor rights and preferential tax treatment);

- High purchasing power of its population;
- Its natural resources.

5.2. CAPITAL INVESTMENT

2002 capital investment from all sources of financing amounted to $800.3 million. Industry, transport, and communications account for the lion's share of capital investment.

Investment growth is accompanied by output growth in major sectors of the economy: energy (up 3.4%), non-ferrous metals (up 51.5%), machine engineering and metal processing (up 63.2%), construction (up 3.5%), transport (up 22.7%), and communications (up 46.6%).

Capital investment by industry sector, $ million						TABLE 6
	1997	1998	1999	2000	2001	2002
Total capital investment	1,007.1	691.2	451.6	795.0	962.6	800.3
Including major industries (% of total)						
Industry	34.7	33.5	32.2	41.3	34.7	34.2
Agriculture and forestry	4.9	4.1	6.1	5.1	5.6	10.3
Construction	1.8	2.4	1.9	2.3	1.9	2.6
Transport and communications	18.1	17.6	16.6	25.2	27.2	24.9
Trade and public catering	1.9	3.9	4.8	2.5	3.5	3.0
Other	38.6	38.5	38.4	23.6	27.1	25.0

Foreign investment trends in 1996–2002						TABLE 7
	1996–1997	1998	1999	2000	2001	2002
Foreign investment, $ million	52.0	16.8	42.1	91.1	84.0	111.8
Including FDI, $ million	37.8	2.6	12.4	40.8	20.3	52.6

5.3. MAJOR ENTERPRISES (INCLUDING ENTERPRISES WITH FOREIGN INVESTMENT)

The Region hosts more than 220 joint ventures with foreign investment from 42 countries, including the USA, the UK, Italy, Germany, Turkey, Bulgaria, and Poland. The total declared capital of joint ventures exceeds $75.5 million, including $53.5 million of foreign capital.

The largest companies with foreign investment are OOO Agroindustrial Corporation Aston, ZAO Dontelecom, OOO Don-Kassens Shipyard, OOO Belgoros, ZAO Rostov Cellular Communications, OAO Rostov Bakery, OOO F.B. KAPPA

LTD., OOO Taganrog Automobile Plant, ZAO Phamadar Carton Ltd., OAO Novocherkassky Magnet, and ZAO Beta-IR.

5.4. MOST ATTRACTIVE SECTORS FOR INVESTMENT

Investment projects in the agroindustrial sector, light industry, and building materials have been accorded priority status pursuant to the Rostov Regional Investment Program 2003.

5.5. CURRENT LEGISLATION ON INVESTOR TAX EXEMPTIONS AND PRIVILEGES

The Rostov Region has enacted legislation with a view to attracting domestic and foreign

III

SOUTHERN FEDERAL DISTRICT

		2001 SALES, $ MILLION*	2001 NET PROFIT, $ MILLION*
COMPANY	SECTOR		
OAO Don Tobacco	Tobacco	255.7	8.9
OAO Taganrog Metal Works	Ferrous metals	182.7	25.6
OAO Rostvertol	Machine engineering	177.2	19.3
OAO South of Russia	Food and beverages	127.9	36.9
OOO Agroindustrial company Aston	Wholesale	107.5	4.7
ZAO Gloria Jeans Corporation	Light industry	75.8	5.4
OAO Baltika Rostov (a branch of OAO Baltika Brewery)	Food and beverages	73.2	19.3
OAO Novocherkassky Electrode Plant	Non-ferrous metals	41.3	4.6
OOO Atlantis-Pak	Meat processing	23.6	3.8
ZAO Dontelecom	Communications	12.5	3.8
OAO Stroifarfor	Building materials	5.8	5.8

Largest enterprises of the Rostov Region — TABLE 8

*Data of the Rostov Regional Administration

investment into the Region's economy. Foreign investments enjoy full and unconditional legal protection. The following regional laws provide a legislative framework governing investment: On Support to Investment Activity in the Rostov Region (stipulates the forms of and procedures for obtaining investment support) and On the Rostov Regional Development Budget (sets forth the principles for collecting and spending the Regional budget for investment purposes).

The Regional Laws provide:
• Tax privileges to organizations engaged in investment activities, including property, profit, and land taxes at 50% of the current rate;
• A favorable regime for foreign investment;
• Rostov Region state guarantees for borrowings;
• Investment tax credits;
• Guarantees to creditors;
• Reduced interest loans;
• Interest subsidies for commercial bank loans.

Regional entities responsible for raising investment — TABLE 9

ENTITY	ADDRESS	PHONE, FAX, E-MAIL
Department of Investment and Innovation Policy of the Ministry of Economy, Trade, and International and External Economic Relations of the Rostov Region	Appt. 641, 112, ul. Sotsialisticheskaya, Rostov-on-Don, Rostov Region, 344050	Phone: (8632) 40 1579, 40 5312, 40 1427

5.6. FEDERAL AND REGIONAL ECONOMIC AND SOCIAL DEVELOPMENT PROGRAMS FOR THE ROSTOV REGION

Federal targeted programs. The Russia's South federal targeted program is a top priority program for the social and economic development of the Region. In line with the Program, the Region is constructing a trunk oil and gas export pipeline network, developing vacation, recreation and resort centers, upgrading its transport infrastructure, and safeguarding and preserving the biosphere resources of the Caspian Sea and the Sea of Azov.

The federal targeted program Electronic Russia, 2002–2010 aims to create a single data transmission and management system servicing state and local authorities, budgetary and non-budgetary funds, and organizations. The program also provides for the launching of the first leg of an electronic trading system for federal procurement purposes.

Regional programs. The Regional Administration's Investment Program for the Rostov Region 2003 aims to make effective use of investment opportunities in the Region, attract investment into the Region, enhance the competitive edge of regional companies through innovation, and facilitate the economic development of sectors that enjoy high levels of demand. The Region has allocated a $37.8 million budget for the Program.

The Region is implementing a number of targeted programs for social and economic development, including the Regional Targeted Program for Development of Long-Term Housing Financing System in the Rostov Region, 2002–2005 (with a $2.4 million budget in 2003), and the Program for Development of Small Business in the Rostov Region, 2003–2005 (with a $0.5 million funding in 2003).

6. INVESTMENT PROJECTS

Industry sector and project description	1) Expected results 2) Amount and term of investment 3) Form of financing[1] 4) Documentation[2]	Contact information
1	2	3

ENERGY

42R001

Construction of the Shakhty steam and gas power station.
Project goal: to construct a power station to supply enterprises and the residential sector with electricity and heat.

1) 569.5 million kWh of electricity per year, 452,100 Gcal of heat per year, revenue of $3.7 million per year
2) $16.9 million/2 years
3) L ($9.6 million)
4) BP, FS

OOO Energy Perspective – Southern Branch
Office 504, 114, ul. Mechnikova, Rostov-on-Don, Rostov Region, 344018
Phone: (8632) 34 2322
Fax: (8632) 99 3732
E-mail: kep_asu@aaa.net.ru
Viktor Prokhorovich Klenov, CEO

MACHINE ENGINEERING AND METAL PROCESSING

42R002

Construction of an instrument plant.
Project goal: to develop a modern industrial base to produce batteries and household and customized instruments.

1) Profit of $0.6 million per year
2) $3.6 million/5 years
3) L ($2.5 million)
4) BP

Arsenal Group of Engineering Companies
Office 601, 80, pr. Sokolova, Rostov-on-Don, Rostov Region, 344010
Phone/fax: (8632) 90 4455
E-mail: mir@bast.ru
http://www.arsenal.rostov.ru
Yakov Stanislavovich Nikitin, CEO

42R003

Development of equipment for the production of whole cans.
Project goal: to provide food companies with packaging materials in various volumes.

1) Profit of $0.3 million per year
2) $1.1 million/1 year
3) L ($0.9 million)
4) BP

OAO Azov Forging and Press Machines Plant
2, pr. Liteyny, Azov, Rostov Region, 346780
Phone/fax: (86342) 67 742, 67 797
Alexander Sergeevich Vasilyev, CEO

42R004

Production of equipment for surface pipe laying and renovation.
Project goal: to resolve the water-pipe laying problem.

1) Profit of $0.2 million per year
2) $0.8 million/1 year
3) L
4) BP

OAO Azov Forging and Press Machines Plant
2, pr. Liteyny, Azov, Rostov Region, 346780
Phone/fax: (86342) 67 742, 67 797
Alexander Sergeevich Vasilyev, CEO

42R005

Upgrading of a loader.
Project goal: to develop an advanced front loader with pneumatic wheels.

1) Profit of $2.7 million per year
2) $0.8 million/3 years
3) L ($0.6 million)
4) BP

OAO Donetsky Excavator
30, ul. Lenina, Donetsk, Rostov Region, 346338
Phone: (86368) 22575, 22828
Fax: (86368) 20 771, 23 113, 22 552
E-mail: JSC_DE@aport2000.ru
Boris Ivanovich Glushko, CEO

GLASS AND PORCELAIN

42R006

Reconstruction of glass bottle production facilities.
Project goal: to satisfy the demand for glass bottles, reduce product cost, and expand the product range.

1) Profit of $0.9 million per year
2) $4.2 million/0.8 years
3) L ($3.0 million)
4) BP

OAO Kamensky Glass Bottle Plant
58, ul. Zavodskaya, Kamensk-Shakhtinsky, Rostov Region, 347800
Phone: (86365) 53 824
Fax: (86365) 52 601
E-mail: glass@kamensk.donpac.ru
Anatoly Ivanovich Schebanov, CEO

III

SOUTHERN FEDERAL DISTRICT

[1] L – Loan, E – Equity, Leas. – Leasing, JV – Joint Venture
[2] BP – Business Plan, FS – Feasibility Study

1	2	3

FOOD AND BEVERAGES

42R007

Expansion of output of long-life dairy products. Project goal: to expand the existing markets and penetrate new segments of the regional dairy market by improving the quality and competitiveness of output.	1) 5,400 tons of dairy products per year, 5,726 tons of milk and cream per year, 811 tons of ice cream and sorbet per year, 720 tons of fruit-milk drinks per year 2) $2.7 million/7 months 3) L ($2.2 million) 4) BP in progress	OAO Novocherkassky Dairy 3, ul. 26 Bakinskikh Komissarov, Novocherkassk, Rostov Region, 346421 Phone: (86352) 45 027 Fax: (86352) 45 027 E-mail: molzavod@rambler.ru Igor Yevgenyevich Onipko, CEO

TRANSPORT INFRASTRUCTURE

42R008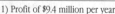

Reconstruction of the Rostov-on-Don airport. Project goal: to reconstruct the airport.	1) Profit of $0.7 million per year 2) $1.7 million/3 years 3) L 4) BP	OAO Aeroport 270/1, pr. Sholokhova, Rostov-on-Don, Rostov Region, 344066 Phone: (8632) 58 5110 Fax: (8632) 52 5462 E-mail: aeroport@rndavia.ru Gennady Fedorovich Yestafyev, CEO

42R009

Reconstruction of the airport terminal. Project goal: to reconstruct the airport terminal building, including re-engineering of facilities, reinforcing the building structure, and replacing obsolete equipment.	1) Profit of $0.6 million per year 2) $13.4 million/1.5 years 3) L 4) BP	OAO Aeroport 270/1, pr. Sholokhova, Rostov-on-Don, Rostov Region, 344066 Phone: (8632) 58 5110 Fax: (8632) 52 5462 E-mail: aeroport@rndavia.ru Gennady Fedorovich Yestafyev, CEO

HOTELS, TOURISM, AND RECREATION

42R010

Construction of an international congress center in Rostov-on-Don. Project goal: to provide hotel services and conduct business seminars and congresses.	1) Profit of $9.4 million per year 2) $150 million/7 years 3) L, Leas., E, JV 4) BP	OAO Intourist Rostov-on-Don 115, ul. Bolshaya Sadovaya, Rostov-on-Don, Rostov Region, 344622 Phone: (8632) 65 9097 Fax: (8632) 65 9007 E-mail: intourist@rostov.ru Igor Viktorovich Gorin, CEO

GENERAL COMMERCIAL MARKET SUPPORT ACTIVITIES

42R011

Provision of exhibition facilities. Project goal: to facilitate development of business links.	1) 5,000 square meters of exhibition space 2) $2.4 million/3 years 3) L ($1.9 million) 4) BP	OAO Rostvertol Trade and Exhibition Center 30, ul. M. Nagibina, Rostov-on-Don, Rostov Region, 344068 Phone/fax: (8632) 38 8688, 38 8611 Fax: (8632) 38 8610 E-mail: ETCrostvertol@jeo.ru Petr Danilovich Motrenko, CEO

IV. VOLGA FEDERAL DISTRICT

43. Republic of Bashkortostan [03]

44. Republic of Mariy El [12]

45. Republic of Mordovia [13]

46. Republic of Tatarstan [16]

47. Republic of Udmurtia [18]

48. Republic of Chuvashia [21]

49. Kirov Region [43]

50. Nizhny Novgorod Region [52]

51. Orenburg Region [56]

52. Penza Region [58]

53. Perm Region [59]

54. Samara Region [63]

55. Saratov Region [64]

56. Ulyanovsk Region [73]

57. Komi-Permyatsky

    Autonomous District [81]

REGIONS OF THE VOLGA FEDERAL DISTRICT

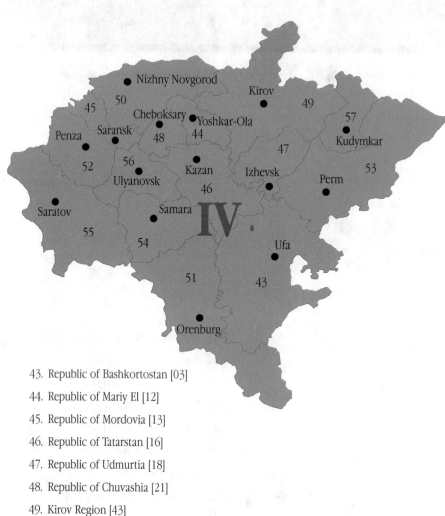

43. Republic of Bashkortostan [03]

44. Republic of Mariy El [12]

45. Republic of Mordovia [13]

46. Republic of Tatarstan [16]

47. Republic of Udmurtia [18]

48. Republic of Chuvashia [21]

49. Kirov Region [43]

50. Nizhny Novgorod Region [52]

51. Orenburg Region [56]

52. Penza Region [58]

53. Perm Region [59]

54. Samara Region [63]

55. Saratov Region [64]

56. Ulyanovsk Region [73]

57. Komi-Permyatsky
    Autonomous District [81]

43. REPUBLIC OF BASHKORTOSTAN [03]

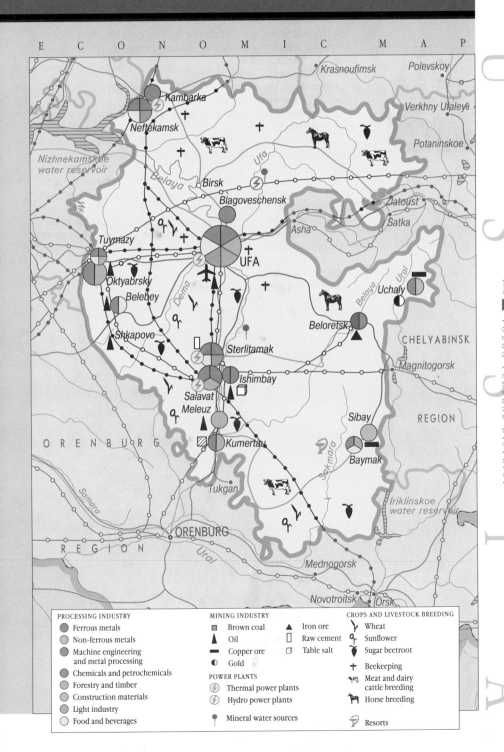

Krasnoufimsk
Polevskoy
Verkhny Ufaley
Kambarka
Neftekamsk
Potaninskoe
Nizhnekamskoe water reservoir
Belaya
Birsk
Ufa
Blagoveschensk
Zlatoust
Satka
Asha
Tuymazy
UFA
Ural
Uchaly
Oktyabrsky
Belebey
Dema
Beloretsk
CHELYABINSK
Shkapovo
Belaya
Sterlitamak
Magnitogorsk
Ishimbay
Salavat
Meleuz
Sibay
REGION
Kumertau
Baymak
ORENBURG
Sakmara
Tukgan
Iriklinskoe water reservoir
Samara
ORENBURG
REGION
Ural
Mednogorsk
Novotroitsk
Orsk

PROCESSING INDUSTRY
- Ferrous metals
- Non-ferrous metals
- Machine engineering and metal processing
- Chemicals and petrochemicals
- Forestry and timber
- Construction materials
- Light industry
- Food and beverages

MINING INDUSTRY
- Brown coal
- Oil
- Copper ore
- Gold

Iron ore
Raw cement
Table salt

POWER PLANTS
- Thermal power plants
- Hydro power plants
- Mineral water sources

CROPS AND LIVESTOCK BREEDING
- Wheat
- Sunflower
- Sugar beetroot
- Beekeeping
- Meat and dairy cattle breeding
- Horse breeding
- Resorts

The Republic of Bashkortostan has been demonstrating some of the strongest development rates in Russia. Figuring among the top ten Russian regions in terms of its gross regional product, Bashkortostan has created a favorable investment climate as borne out by its international ratings. In December 2002, Moody's Investors Service Limited raised the Republic's rating to Ba3 and the outlook to stable.

The Republic requires additional investment if it is to maintain high economic growth rates. We plan to:

- Continue upgrading the production facilities of our fuel, chemicals, machine engineering, metals, and food and beverages sectors, and to develop telecommunications;
- Upgrade our agricultural machinery;
- Improve the logistics base of our transport system; and
- Provide support to small and medium enterprise.

The Republic has carried out considerable legislative work aimed at improving the its investment appeal.

Investors now enjoy state guarantees, preferential treatment with regard to local taxation, and privileges with respect to the use of land and other natural resources.

The Republic of Bashkortostan has been steadily developing its trade and economic links with overseas countries. Our foreign trade partners include more than 90 countries worldwide.

I trust that the information in this Guide will be of use in providing additional information on the Republic's economic potential and identifying areas for effective collaboration.

Murtaza Rakhimov,
PRESIDENT OF THE REPUBLIC OF BASHKORTOSTAN

1. GENERAL INFORMATION

1.1. GEOGRAPHY

Situated in the Southern Urals, the Republic of Bashkortostan covers a total area of some 143,600 square kilometers. To the west, it borders the Republic of Tatarstan and the Republic of Udmurtia, to the north – the Perm Region and the Sverdlovsk Region, to the east – the Chelyabinsk Region, and to the south and south-west – the Orenburg Region.

1.2. CLIMATE

The Republic of Bashkortostan is located within the moderate continental climate zone.

Air temperatures in January average –8.5°C, rising to +19.4°C in July. Annual precipitation exceeds 400 mm.

1.3. POPULATION

According to preliminary 2002 census results, the population of the Republic of Bash-kortostan stood at 4,103,000 people. The average population density is 28.6 people per square kilometer. The economically active population was 1,921,000 people. In 2002, official unemployment stood at 10.7%.

Demographically speaking, some 58.8% of the population are of statutory working age, 21.7% are below the statutory working age, and 19.5% are beyond the statutory working age.

The Republic's ethnic mix is 39.3% Russian, 21.9% Bashkir, 28.4% Tatar, and 3% Chuvash.

The Republic's major urban centers (2002 data) are Ufa with 1,042,400 inhabitants, Sterlitamak with 264,400 inhabitants, Salavat with 158,500 inhabitants, Neftekamsk with 122,300 inhabitants, and Oktyabrsky with 108,700 inhabitants.

Population								TABLE 1
	1992	1997	1998	1999	2000	2001	2002
Total population, '000	4,001	4,098	4,104	4,110	4,110	4,102	4,103
Economically active population, '000	1,947	1,814	1,805	1,939	1,928	1,893	1,921

2. ADMINISTRATION

46, ul. Tukaeva, Ufa, Republic of Bashkortostan, 450101
http://www.bashkortostan.ru

NAME	POSITION	CONTACT INFORMATION
Murtaza Gubaydullovich RAKHIMOV	President of the Republic of Bashkortostan	Phone: (3472) 50 2724 Fax: (3472) 50 0281 E-mail: aprb_webmaster@kmrb.bashnet.ru
Rafael Ibragimovich BAYDAVLETOV	Prime Minister of the Government of the Republic of Bashkortostan	Phone: (3472) 50 2401
Sergei Petrovich YEFREMOV	Deputy Prime Minister of the Government of the Republic of Bashkortostan (Economic Reform, Industrial Policy, Conversion, and Communications)	Phone: (3472) 50 2386
Shamil Khusnullovich VAKHITOV	Deputy Prime Minister of the Government of the Republic of Bashkortostan (Agroindustrial Sector, Agricultural and Land Reforms, Food Policy, and Social Investment Policy in Rural Areas)	Phone: (3472) 50 2376
Ayrat Rafikovich GASKAROV	Deputy Prime Minister of the Government of the Republic of Bashkortostan (Budget, Lending, Monetary and Currency Policy, Securities, Insurance, Tax Policy, and Banking)	Phone: (3472) 50 3648 Fax: (3472) 50 3666
Valentin Alexandrovich VLASOV	Minister of Economy of the Republic of Bashkortostan	Phone: (3472) 50 4174 Fax: (3472) 50 4171
Boris Grigoryevich KOLBIN	Minister of External Relations and Trade of the Republic of Bashkortostan	Phone: (3472) 79 9625 Fax: (3472) 79 9624

3. ECONOMIC POTENTIAL

3.1. 1997–2002 GROSS REGIONAL PRODUCT (GRP). INDUSTRY BREAKDOWN

The 2002 gross regional product of the Republic Bashkortostan totaled $6,823.2 million, 6.9% up on 2001. The increase was mainly industry driven. Industry accounts for some 36.5% of total GRP. Per capita GRP equaled $1,557 in 2001, and $1,663 in 2002.

3.2. MAJOR ECONOMIC GROWTH PROJECTIONS

The blueprint for economic growth in the Republic is given in the Conceptual Framework for Social and Economic Development of the Republic of Bashkortostan through 2005, Bashkortostan – Entering the Twenty First

GRP trends in 1997–2002						*TABLE 2*
	1997	1998	1999	2000	2001*	2002*
GRP in current prices, $ million	11,186.1	6,503.4	4,522.3	5,670.0	6,385.6	6,823.2

*Estimates of the Government of the Republic of Bashkortostan

GRP industry breakdown in 1997–2002, % of total						*TABLE 3*
	1997	1998	1999	2000	2001*	2002*
GRP	100.0	100.0	100.0	100.0	100.0	100.0
Industry	34.0	33.9	38.9	44.2	36.3	36.5
Agriculture and forestry	9.3	5.8	10.8	9.1	11.2	11.4
Construction	10.0	8.5	6.0	7.7	10.1	8.7
Transport and communications	8.9	8.3	6.3	7.0	8.1	7.6
Trade and public catering	9.4	10.7	12.6	10.4	10.3	9.9
Other	17.7	20.9	13.0	12.6	14.4	17.1
Net taxes on output	10.7	11.9	12.4	9.0	9.6	8.8

*Estimates of the Government of the Republic of Bashkortostan

Century: Environment, People, Economy, and the State. The Conceptual Framework aims to:
- Create conditions conducive to enterprise reform and enhanced economic efficiency;
- Carry out structural, organizational, and institutional transformations in the economy;
- Promote innovation and investment activity in different spheres, with a focus on the real sector;
- Streamline the financial and lending sectors, pursue efficient budget and tax policies, and improve budgetary resource management;
- Reorganize the state lending system from covering budgetary deficits to long-term lending for investment purposes;
- Reform the agricultural sector and land relations;
- Improve public welfare based on the development of social infrastructure, and to stabilize real income.

3.3. INDUSTRIAL OUTPUT IN 1997–2002 FOR MAJOR SECTORS OF ECONOMY

The Republic's leading industries are fuel, machine engineering and metals processing, chemicals and petrochemicals. These account for a combined 66.3% of total industrial output.

Oil. 2002 oil output in the Republic amounted to 11.4 million tons, and 355 million cubic meters of natural gas. The largest oil production company is ANK Bashneft. In 2002, the company extracted 12 million tons of oil, with 11.2 million tons extracted within the Republic.

The oil refining industry accounts for 18% of total industrial output. In 2002, some 25.2 million tons of oil was refined. The depth of refining at oil refineries ranges from 69% to 78%. High-octane petroleum accounts for around half of total output.

Chemicals and petrochemicals. Bashkortostan's enterprises produce more than half of Russia's butyl and isobutyl spirit, soda ash, and pesticide chemicals output, half of the country's plasticizer and polystryrene output, a quarter of polyvinyl chloride output, and a fifth of caustic soda and synthetic rubber output.

Energy. In 2002, the Republic produced 23.8 billion kWh of electricity and 53.2 million Gcal of thermal energy. The installed capacity of the Republic's power stations exceeds 5 million GWh. OAO Bashkirenergo generates the bulk of both heat energy and electricity.

Machine engineering and metal processing. The Republic's machine engineering sector specializes mainly in chemical machine engineering, oil

Industry breakdown of industrial output in 1997–2002, % of total						TABLE 4
	1997	1998	1999	2000	2001	2002*
Industry	100.0	100.0	100.0	100.0	100.0	100.0
Fuel	37.6	33.0	40.0	44.6	38.8	36.1
Machine engineering and metal processing	10.7	11.7	11.9	10.4	13.8	16.0
Chemicals and petrochemicals	12.8	13.3	15.5	15.9	15.7	14.2
Energy	12.7	14.4	9.4	8.8	10.4	11.0
Food and beverages	9.6	9.9	8.2	6.6	7.5	8.7
Construction materials	3.8	4.1	2.6	2.1	2.2	2.3
Non-ferrous metals	1.6	2.2	3.5	2.6	2.1	2.3
Ferrous metals	1.9	2.2	1.7	1.9	1.9	2.0
Light industry	1.5	2.3	1.6	1.5	1.5	1.4
Forestry, timber, and pulp and paper	1.7	1.8	1.6	1.3	1.6	1.3
Glass and porcelain	0.6	0.8	0.6	0.7	0.9	1.0
Flour, cereals, and mixed fodder	3.1	2.5	1.8	1.7	1.4	0.9

*Estimates of the Government of the Bashkortostan Republic

Fuel and energy sector production and consumption trends, 1997–2002						TABLE 5
	1997	1998	1999	2000	2001	2002
Electricity output, billion kWh	24.7	24.0	24.0	24.7	24.2	23.8
Oil output (including gas condensate), million tons	13.4	12.8	12.2	11.7	11.4	11.4
Natural gas output, million cubic meters	427.0	435.0	414.0	386.0	365.0	355.0
Coal output, million tons	0.3	0.1	–	0.1	0.1	0.2
Electricity consumption, billion kWh	24.3	23.2	23.5	24.5	23.9	23.1
Oil and petroleum products consumption, million tons of fuel equivalent	n/a	7.3	6.1	5.4	5.9	5.2
Natural gas consumption, million cubic meters	12,803.5	12,538.7	13,745.3	14,769.8	14,070.7	14,327.7

*Estimates of the Government of the Bashkortostan Republic

machine engineering (oil equipment, drilling tools, and rotary pumps), and automotive (dump trucks, buses, and trolleybuses). It also produces equipment for the agroindustrial sector, metal cutting and timber processing machines, and units and parts for aircraft engines. Other emerging sub-sectors include electrical engineering, instrument manufacturing, and hardware and construction tool making.

Metals. The Republic's ferrous metals enterprises mainly specialize in the production of rolled ferrous metal products, steel strap and wire, rolled commodity metal, and metal cord. The largest metal processing enterprise is OAO Beloretsk Metals Plant.

The Republic's non-ferrous metals enterprises, namely OAO Uchalinsk Ore Dressing Plant and OAO Bashkir Copper and Sulfur Plant, specialize in the production of copper-pyrite ores, which contain copper, zinc, and precious metals.

Construction materials. The Republic produces a full spectrum of construction materials and articles: concrete, soft roofing, prefabricated ferroconcrete structures and elements, panels, and other constructions for prefabricated panel buildings, construction brick and lime, plain concrete articles, linoleum, asbestos cement articles, heat insulating materials, and porous fillers.

Agriculture. The agricultural sector accounts for 11.4% of total GRP. Major segments include grain, sugar beet, sunflower seed, meat and dairy products, and eggs, in addition to horse breeding and bee keeping.

3.4. FUEL AND ENERGY BALANCE (OUTPUT AND CONSUMPTION PER RESOURCE)

The Republic's energy sector fully covers domestic demand for electricity and heat energy.

3.5. TRANSPORT INFRASTRUCTURE

Roads. The Republic has 22,000 kilometers of paved public highway.

Railroads. The Republic has 1,476 kilometers of railroad. The Republic is linked by rail to western and central regions of Russia, the Urals, and Siberia.

Airports. Air transport services are mostly channeled through the Republic's main international airport at Ufa. The Republic's largest airline is OAO BAL (Bashkir Airlines), which services major Russian cities and the CIS.

River transport. The total length of the Republic's navigable inland waterway system is 1,018 kilometers. Over 70% of cargo is carried out of the Republic via the rivers Belaya, Kama, Volga, and Don and the Volga – Baltic Canal.

The following passenger routes are operated: Ufa – Perm – Kazan – Nizhny Novgorod – Yaroslavl– – Kostroma – Moscow, Ufa – Samara – Saratov – Volgograd – Astrakhan, and Ufa – Rostov-on-Don.

Oil and gas pipelines. Some 10,000 kilometers of trunk pipelines cross the Republic, including 4,700 kilometers of gas pipeline, 3,800 kilometers of oil pipeline, and 1,300 kilometers of petroleum product pipeline.

3.6. MAIN NATURAL RESOURCES: RESERVES AND EXTRACTION IN 2002

The Republic's principal natural resources are oil, natural gas, complex ores, ferrous and non-ferrous metal ores (copper, zinc, iron), brown coal (lignite), and mining and chemical raw materials. Bashkortostan also has significant forests reserves.

Metals. Some 47 ore and alluvial gold deposits have been explored in the Republic, plus 19 iron ore deposits with total reserves of 70 million tons. The largest of these is the Murtykty gold sulfide deposit with total reserves of 30 tons. Explored reserves of oxidized crumble ores at the Ulu-Telyak deposit total 11.3 million tons with an average manganese content of 8.5%.

Coal. The Republic is rich in high tar content lignite. Total brown coal reserves exceed 250 million tons.

Forests. The total forest area of Bashkortostan is estimated at 6.2 million hectares, with total timber reserves of 717.9 million cubic meters. Potential timber reserves for industrial use are 646.6 million cubic meters.

4. TRADE OPPORTUNITIES

4.1. MAIN GOODS PRODUCED IN THE REGION

In 2002, the Republic produced:

Energy: electricity – 23.8 billion kWh;

Oil and natural gas:

oil, including gas condensate – 11.4 million tons; natural gas – 355 million cubic meters; gasoline – 5.7 million tons; diesel fuel – 8.9 million tons; furnace fuel oil – 6.7 million tons;

Ferrous metals:

ready ferrous metals rolled stock – 439,000 tons;

Chemicals:

mineral fertilizers – 241,000 tons; polyethylene – 118,800 tons; polystyrene and co-polymers of styrene – 49,000 tons; polypropylene – 82,900 tons; polyvinyl chloride resin and co-polymers of vinyl chloride – 149,900 tons; calcinated soda 100% – 1,284,500 tons; caustic soda 100% – 245,000 tons; synthetic rubber – 186,400 tons; plasticizers – 42,900 tons;

Machine engineering:

metal cutting machines – 732 items; trolleybuses – 85 items.

4.2. EXPORTS, INCLUDING EXTRA-CIS

In 2000, extra-CIS exports amounted to $2,366.7 million and CIS exports totaled $301.9 million. The corresponding figures for 2001 were $1,891.3 million and $335.5 , and $2,202.7 million and $186.9 million for 2002.

The commodity breakdown of the Republic's 2002 exports was as follows: fuel, energy and petrochemicals (86.6%), machinery (9.1%), and metals (2%). The Republic's main export partners are the Netherlands (19.4% of total exports), China (12%), the UK (14%), Germany (7.8%), and Kazakhstan (4.2%).

4.3. IMPORTS, INCLUDING EXTRA-CIS

2000 extra-CIS imports totaled $170.1 million; CIS imports reached $71.9 million. The corresponding figures for 2001 were $222.2 million and $40.1 million, and $270.9 million and $19.1 million for 2002. The bulk of imports into the Republic (2002 data) consisted of machinery and equipment (54.2% of total imports), fuel, energy and petrochemicals (26.8%), and food and beverages (11%). The Republic's major import partners include Germany (24.2% of total imports), Kazakhstan (15.9%), China (9.3%), Italy (8.1%), and Belgium (7.3%).

5. INVESTMENT OPPORTUNITIES

5.1 INVESTMENTS
IN 1992–2002 (BY INDUSTRY
SECTOR), INCLUDING
FOREIGN INVESTMENTS

The following factors determine the investment appeal of the Republic:

- Its favorable geographic location and proximity to large markets;
- Its considerable natural resource potential;
- Its developed transport communications and production infrastructure;
- Its advanced investment legislation;
- Organizational and financial support to investment projects and business safety guarantees provided by the executive authorities;
- Its highly qualified workforce.

Capital investment by industry sector, $ million						*TABLE 6*
	1997	1998	1999	2000	2001	2002
Total capital investment	2,184	1,286	705	1,262	1,548	1,158
Including major industries (% of total):						
Industry	37.1	38.9	40.6	38.9	46.4	51.4
Agriculture and forestry	6.4	5.4	4.5	9.4	6.3	6.3
Construction	0.9	1.1	1.6	2.9	2.9	1.3
Transport and communications	14.6	20.4	18.1	16.6	11.2	14.0
Trade and public catering	0.9	0.9	3.4	1.6	1.5	1.5
Other	40.1	33.3	31.8	30.6	31.7	25.5

Foreign investment trends in 1996–2002						*TABLE 7*
	1996–1997	1998	1999	2000	2001	2002
Foreign investment, $ million	19.0	67.3	26.1	10.4	29.6	20.5
Including FDI, $ million	14.4	5.6	12.5	1.2	19.4	9.0

Largest enterprises of the Republic of Bashkortostan	*TABLE 8*
COMPANY	SECTOR
OAO Salavatnefteorgsintez	Oil refining
ANK Bashneft	Oil
OAO Ufaneftekhim	Oil refining
OAO Novoufimsky Oil Refinery	Oil refining
OAO Ufa Oil Refinery	Oil refining
ZAO Kaustik	Chemicals and petrochemicals
OAO Beloretsky Metals Plant	Metals
OAO Ufakhimprom	Chemicals and petrochemicals
ZAO Kauchuk	Chemicals and petrochemicals
ZAO Bashkir Agrochemical Company	Chemicals and petrochemicals

5.2. CAPITAL INVESTMENT

Industry accounts for the lion's share of capital investment (51.4%).

5.3. MAJOR ENTERPRISES (INCLUDING ENTERPRISES WITH FOREIGN INVESTMENT)

The largest enterprises with foreign investment are OOO Italbashkeramika (Italy), OOO SodaPro-fiStroy (Spain), OOO Agrosakhar (Germany), and OOO Termoservis (Czech Republic).

5.4. MOST ATTRACTIVE SECTORS FOR INVESTMENT

The most potentially appealing industries for investors are oil, fuel and energy, machine engineering, telecommunications, chemicals, and food sectors.

Regional entities responsible for raising investment		*TABLE 9*
ENTITY	ADDRESS	PHONE, FAX, E-MAIL
ZAO Accord Invest	25-124, Verkhnetorgovaya pl., Ufa, Republic of Bashkortostan, 450077	Phone: (3472) 51 1119
OOO Bashkir Investments	5/2, ul. Lenina, Ufa, Republic of Bashkortostan, 450077	Phone: (3472)23 5448
OOO Bashkir Securities	72, ul. Lenina, Ufa, Republic of Bashkortostan, 450077	Phone: (3472) 22 9990
OAO Social Protection Fund Berlek	27/2, ul. M. Gafuri, Ufa, Republic of Bashkortostan, 450076	Phone: (3472) 51 5203
ZAO Neftegazinvest	13-20, ul. Lenina, Ufa, Republic of Bashkortostan, 450077	Phone: (3472) 23 5626
GUP Investment Agency of the Republic of Bashkortostan	3, Verkhnetorgovaya pl., Ufa, Republic of Bashkortostan, 450077	Phone: (3472)50 3736

5.5. CURRENT LEGISLATION ON INVESTOR TAX EXEMPTIONS AND PRIVILEGES

The Republic of Bashkortostan has adopted a Law On Foreign Investment Activity in the Republic of Bashkortostan with a view to promoting investment activity in the Republic and protecting investor rights.

The Law of the Republic of Bashkortostan On the Coordination of Foreign Economic Activity in the Republic of Bashkortostan regulates issues related to the coordination of import and export activities. Pursuant to the Law, a Program for Foreign Trade Development in the Republic of Bashkortostan (2001–2002) has been drafted and successfully implemented. The Program outlines promising foreign trade segments of the Republic's economy, and provides a blueprint for the development and expansion of international, including CIS, trade and economic cooperation.

5.6. FEDERAL AND REGIONAL ECONOMIC AND SOCIAL DEVELOPMENT PROGRAMS FOR THE REPUBLIC OF BASHKORTOSTAN

Federal targeted programs. The Government of the Republic of Bashkortostan is currently implementing the Federal Targeted Program for Social and Economic Development of the Republic of Bashkortostan through 2006. The Program has been allocated a total financing of $5,411.5 million, of which $3,325.5 million is to be raised from non-budgetary sources. The Program comprises 79 investment projects and 53 comprehensive social measures.

The Program aims to:
• increase oil extraction;
• establish export-oriented facilities in the chemicals and petrochemicals sectors on the basis of OAO Ufaorgsintez, OAO Ufakhimprom, OAO Polyef, and OAO Salavatnefteorgsintez;
• introduce high-tech facilities at civilian machine engineering enterprises, including manufacturers of bypass turbofan engines, helicopters, buses, and oil flow metering instruments;
• ensure accelerated development of the forestry and timber sectors;
• create a developed transport infrastructure, including a modern airport; and reconstruct and provide technical equipment to air traffic control facilities to ensure flight safety.

Regional programs. The Republic is implementing a number of programs targeted mainly at the social sphere. The largest programs call for the extension of the rural gas supply network, residential construction, and the construction of a water reservoir at Yumaguzin.

6. INVESTMENT PROJECTS

Industry sector and project description	1) Expected results 2) Amount and term of investment 3) Form of financing[1] 4) Documentation[2]	Contact information
1	2	3

MACHINE ENGINEERING AND METAL PROCESSING

43R001 ● ◆		
Establishment of production of new generation trolleybuses. Project goal: to launch production of a new generation of comfortable, international standard trolleybuses.	1) Production of 200 trolleybuses per year 2) $2.5 million/1 year 3) L 4) BP	OAO Bashkirsky Trolleybus Factory 11, Soyedinitelnoye shosse, Ufa, Republic of Bashkortostan, 450112 Phone: (3472) 47 5330; fax: (3472) 47 9344 E-mail: bts@ufacom.ru Vladimir Fedorovich Barsukov, CEO

43R002 ● ▲		
Establishment of production of oil rig repair machines. Project goal: to expand production facilities.	1) Annual production of 60 items 2) $4.6 million/3 years 3) L ($1.6 million) 4) FS	OAO Ishimbai Engineering Plant 2, ul. B. Khmelnitskogo, Ishimbai, Republic of Bashkortostan, 453200 Phone: (34794) 22 103 Fax: (34794) 22 824 E-mail: izm@bashnet.ru Gafur Saburovich Sharafutdinov, CEO

43R003 ● ★ ◆		
Establishment of production of automobile spark plugs. Project goal: to design automobile spark plugs and develop and expand their production.	1) Annual output of 24 million 2) $1.6 million/1 year 3) L, Leas. 4) BP	FGUP Ufimskoye Agregatnoye Production Association 97, ul. Aksakova, Ufa, Republic of Bashkortostan, 450025 Phone: (3472) 22 084 Fax: (3472) 22 0843 E-mail: uapo@ufacom.ru Yury Georgiyevich Poroshin, CEO

43R004 ● ★ ◆		
Production of glow plugs. Project goal: to equip diesel automobiles with fourth-generation glow plugs.	1) Annual output of 300,000 of plugs 2) $1.3 million/18 months 3) L, Leas. 4) BP	FGUP Ufimskoye Agregatnoye Production Association 97, ul. Aksakova, Ufa, Republic of Bashkortostan, 450025 Phone: (3472) 22 0841; fax: (3472) 22 0843 E-mail: uapo@ufacom.ru Yury Georgievich Poroshin, CEO

43R005 ● ◆		
Full-scale production of Ka 226.50 helicopters. Project goal: to produce state-of-the-art machines capable of competing on the external market.	1) Annual production of 20 helicopters 2) $4.7 million/18 months 3) L 4) BP	FGUP Kumertau Aviation Plant 15a, ul. Novozarinskaya, Kumertau, Republic of Bashkortostan, 453300 Phone: (34761) 42 300 Fax: (34761) 47 624, 43 913 E-mail: kumape@bashnet.ru Boris Sergeevich Malyshev, CEO

43R006 ● ◆		
Launch of production of a light 2-person helicopter with coaxial scheme. Project goal: to provide the market with a light helicopter for the purpose of forest, gridline, and oil and gas pipeline patrolling.	1) Up to 30 helicopters a year 2) $2 million/4 years 3) L ($1 million) 4) BP	FGUP Kumertau Aviation Plant 15a, ul. Novozarinskaya, Kumertau, 453300 Phone: (34761) 42 300 Fax: (34761) 47 624, 43 913 E-mail: kumape@bashnet.ru Boris Sergeyevich Malyshev, CEO

IV

VOLGA FEDERAL DISTRICT

---

[1] L – Loan, E – Equity, Leas. – Leasing, JV – Joint Venture
[2] BP – Business Plan, FS – Feasibility Study

1	2	3
43R007 ● ◆ Development of Ka-32.10 passenger helicopter. Project goal: to develop a helicopter for various carriage and rescue operations; to sell competitive machines on the international market.	1) Up to 15 helicopters per year 2) $42.5 million/3 years 3) Loan $21 million 4) BP	FGUP Kumertau Aviation Plant 15a, ul. Novozarinskaya, Kumertau, Republic of Bashkortostan, 453300 Phone: (34761) 42 300 Fax: (34761) 47 624, 43 913 E-mail: kumape@bashnet.ru Boris Sergeevich Malyshev, CEO
43R008 ● ◆ Completion of a manufacturing complex construction. Project goal: to build facilities for the production of pipeline accessories, to replace obsolete equipment.	1) n/a 2) $8.3 million/2 years 3) L 4) BP	OAO Blagoveschensky Armaturny Zavod 1, ul. Sedova, Blagoveschensk, 453430 Republic of Bashkortostan Phone: (34766) 21 357, 22 067 Fax: (34766) 21 378 E-mail: baz@ufanet.ru Stanislav Grigoryevich Shachkov, CEO
43R009 ● ◆ ▲ Production of low-carbon heat-treated galvanized wire of 1.5–6 mm in diameter. Project goal: to purchase new equipment for annealing and galvanizing low-carbon wire.	1) Output of 24,000 tons per year, revenues of $7.2 million per year 2) $2.8 million/1 year 3) L 4) BP, FS	OAO Beloretsky Metal Works 1, ul. Bluchera, Beloretsk 453500 Phone: (34792) 40 504, 51 545 Fax: (34792) 50 376 E-mail: belmet@bmk.ufanet.ru Viktor Ivanovich Zyuzin, CEO
43R010 ● ★ ◆ Production of advanced household appliances. Project goal: to develop and manufacture advanced household appliances capable of competing on the domestic market.	1) $7.5 million per year 2) $3.0 million/2 years 3) L, Leas. 4) BP	FGUP Ufimskoye Agregatnoye Production Association 97, ul. Aksakova, Ufa 450025 Phone: (3472) 22 0841 Fax: (3472) 22 0843 E-mail: Uapo@ufacom.ru Yury Georgievich Poroshin, CEO

GLASS AND PORCELAIN

1	2	3
43R011 ■ ● ★ ▼ Production of low emission glass. Project goal: to produce low emission glass.	1) Annual output of 1,200,000 square metes, annual revenues of $10.5 million 2) $7.3 million/10 months 3) L, Leas., E 4) Investment proposal	OAO Salavatsteklo Salavat, 453253, Republic of Bashkortostan Phone: (34763) 34 960, 35 251 Fax: (34763) 35 270 E-mail: peo@salstek.ru Valentin Dmitrievich Tokarev, CEO
43R012 ■ ▼ Re-equipment of sheet glass production lines. Project goal: to produce glass using advanced Western technologies.	1) Annual output of 32 million square metes, annual revenues of $54.1 million 2) $66.6 million/1 year 3) E 4) Investment proposal	OAO Salavatsteklo Salavat, 453253, Republic of Bashkortostan Phone: (34763) 34 960, 35 251 Fax: (34763) 35 270 E-mail: peo@salstek.ru Valentin Dmitrievich Tokarev, CEO
43R013 ■ ● ★ ▼ Production of beer bottles. Project goal: to produce and sell. new high-quality products.	1) Annual output of 340 million bottles, annual revenues of $21.4 million 2) $45.5 million/1 year 3) L, Leas., E 4) Investment proposal	OAO Salavatsteklo Salavat, 453253, Republic of Bashkortostan Phone: (34763) 34 960, 35 251 Fax: (34763) 35 270 E-mail: peo@salstek.ru Valentin Dmitrievich Tokarev, CEO

1	2	3

43R014	● ◆	OAO Bashmedsteklo
Upgrading of a glass-pressing machine. Project goal: to preserve the existing facilities.	1) Output of 24.4 million glass items per year 2) $1.2 million/9 months 3) L 4) BP	4, ul. S. Yulayeva, Tuimazy 452754, Republic of Bashkortostan Phone: (34712) 73 122 Fax: (34712) 73 730 E-mail: tzms@bashnet.ru Lilia Rifkatovna Muratova, CEO

43R015	● ◆	GUP Krasnousolsky Glass Works
Construction of a second line for production of dark beer bottles. Project goal: to increase output.	1) Output of 156 million bottles per year 2) $11.0 million/2.8 years 3) Loan $7.7 million 4) BP	1, ul. Kommunisticheskaya, pos. Krasnousolsky 453050, Republic of Bashkortostan Phone: (34740) 21 058 Fax: (34740) 21 287 E-mail: ksteklo@bashnet.ru Igor Vladimirovich Mineev, CEO

IV

VOLGA FEDERAL DISTRICT

MARAT
KHAFIZOVICH
ISHMIYAROV,
CEO

Open Joint Stock Company Salavatnefte-orgsintez is the largest oil refining and petrochemicals facility in Europe. The company uses only high grade feedstocks procured in Western Siberia and Kazakhstan. The company produces more than 140 different product lines, including 76 core products, and exports

flow management system that is unique in Europe among comparable enterprises, plus a large team of highly qualified professionals. Salavatnefteorgsintez is committed to maintaining the competitiveness of our products, supporting high quality standards, and meeting the needs of our customers. Salavatnefteorgsintez has received international and Russian awards, including the European Quality Award, the 100 Best Russian Businesses Medal, the Best Russian Exporter Honorary Diploma, and the Regional Economy Leader Diploma.

to more than 20 CIS and non-CIS countries, including Finland, China, the United States, the U.K., Western Europe, the Baltic States, and elsewhere. Salavatnefteorgsintez boasts a financial

OAO SALAVATNEFTEORGSINTEZ'S MAIN PRODUCTS

- automobile gasoline
- diesel fuels
- kerosene
- heating fuel
- methylbenzene
- butyl and isobutyl spirit and plastifier
- styrol
- polyethylene, polystyrols
- silica gels and catalysts
- heavy pyrolysis tar
- anti-corrosion products, etc.

открытое акционерное общество
САЛАВАТНЕФТЕОРГСИНТЕЗ

SALAVAT, 435256, REPUBLIC OF BASHKORTOSTAN, RUSSIAN FEDERATION
TEL./FAX/SWITCHBOARD: (34763) 53 917, 53 923, 53 943
MARKETING DEPARTMENT TEL.: (34763) 52 207, 52 101, FAX: (34763) 53 752
E-MAIL: market@snos.ru; HTTP://www.snos.ru

44. REPUBLIC OF MARIY EL [12]

ECONOMIC MAP

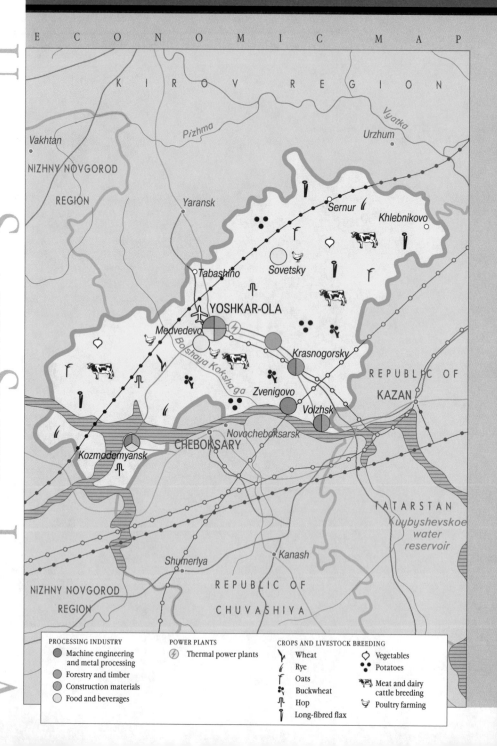

KIROV REGION

Vyatka

Vakhtan
Urzhum

NIZHNY NOVGOROD

REGION

Pizhma

Yaransk

Sernur

Khlebnikovo

Tabashino
Sovetsky

YOSHKAR-OLA

Medvedevo

Krasnogorsky

REPUBLIC OF

KAZAN

Bolshaya Kokshaga

Zvenigovo

Volzhsk

Kozmodemyansk

Novocheboksarsk

CHEBOKSARY

TATARSTAN

Kuybyshevskoe
water
reservoir

Shumerlya
Kanash

NIZHNY NOVGOROD

REGION

REPUBLIC OF

CHUVASHIYA

PROCESSING INDUSTRY	POWER PLANTS	CROPS AND LIVESTOCK BREEDING	
● Machine engineering and metal processing	⚡ Thermal power plants	Wheat	◇ Vegetables
● Forestry and timber		Rye	⁚ Potatoes
● Construction materials		Oats	
○ Food and beverages		Buckwheat	🐄 Meat and dairy cattle breeding
		Hop	🐓 Poultry farming
		Long-fibred flax	

The Republic of Mariy El enters the 21st century and the new millennium with all of the economic, political, and social conditions in place to ensure the emergence of a civilized market system. Today, the Republic is one of the most dynamically developing regions of Russia, with most economic indicators steadily rising.

The last two years have seen the Republic adopt a civilized development model based on the principles of economic liberalism in large and small enterprise, all forms of support to private initiative, and the reduction in investment risks.

The Republic of Mariy El boasts a favorable geographical location, rich natural resources, a diverse mix of manufacturing facilities, an advanced communications network, and a qualified work force, all of which contribute to accelerated economic growth in the Republic.

Stability in the Republic of Mariy El has been underpinned by the Government's consistent pursuit of a strategy aimed at supporting business owners and raising living standards through increased productivity.

Leonid Markelov,
PRESIDENT OF THE REPUBLIC OF MARIY EL,
CHAIRMAN OF THE GOVERNMENT OF THE REPUBLIC OF MARIY EL

IV

VOLGA FEDERAL DISTRICT

1. GENERAL INFORMATION

1.1. GEOGRAPHY

The total area of the Republic of Mariy El is 23,200 square kilometers. The Republic is situated at the heart of European Russia in the center of the Volga basin. To the north and north-east, the Republic borders the Kirov Region, to the south-east – the Republic of Tatarstan, to the south – the Republic of Chuvashia, and to the west – the Nizhny Novgorod Region.

1.2. CLIMATE

Spread across the forest and forest-steppe zones, the Republic of Mariy El enjoys a temperate continental climate. The average air temperature in January is –19°C, rising to +20°C in July. Approximately half of the Republic's area is covered with forests. Gray turf, loamy, mixed sandy loamy, and sandy soils prevail in the Republic.

1.3. POPULATION

According to preliminary 2002 census results, the total population in the Republic was 728,000 people. The average population density is 31.4 people per square kilometer. The economically active population amounts to 380,000 people. While official unemployment stands at 2.4%, the actual rate is 11.5%.

Demographically speaking, some 60.2% are of working age, 21.4% are below the statutory working age, and 18.4% are beyond the statutory working age. The Republic's ethnic mix is 47% Russian, 43% Mariy, 6% Tatar, and 4% other ethnic groups.

As of 2002, the Republic's major urban centers were Yoshkar-Ola with 256,800 inhabitants, Volzhsk with 60,800 inhabitants, and Kozmodemiansk with 23,800 inhabitants.

Population							TABLE 1
	1992	1997	1998	1999	2000	2001	2002
Total population, '000	762	765	763	761	759	755	728
Economically active population, '000	373	334	330	378	370	372	380

2. ADMINISTRATION

29, Leninsky pr., Yoshkar-Ola, Republic of Mariy El, 424001
Phone: (8362) 64 1525; http://gov.mari.ru

NAME	POSITION	CONTACT INFORMATION
Leonid Igorevich MARKELOV	President of the Republic of Mariy El, Chairman of the Government of the Republic of Mariy El	Phone: (8362) 63 0408 E-mail: president@gov.mari.ru
Dmitry Yevgenyevich FROLOV	Chief of the Presidential Administration, Deputy Chairman of the Government of the Republic of Mariy El	Phone: (8362) 64 1603 E-mail: frolov@gov.mari.ru
Nikolai Ivanovich KUKLIN	First Deputy Chairman of the Government of the Republic of Mariy El	Phone: (8362) 63 0019 E-mail: kuklin@gov.mari.ru
Alexander Yakovlevich YEGOSHIN	First Deputy Chairman of the Government of the Republic of Mariy El, Minister of Agriculture and Food of the Republic of Mariy El	Phone: (8362) 64 1731 E-mail: egoshin@gov.mari.ru
Dmitry Iosifovich TURCHIN	Minister of State Property of the Republic of Mariy El	Phone: (8362) 45 4975
Yevgeny Dmitrievich RYZHAKOV	Minister of Finance of the Republic of Mariy El	Phone: (8362) 12 4917
Nadezhda Vladimirovna MOMOT	Minister of Enterprise, Commerce, and Consumer Services Development of the Republic of Mariy El	Phone: (8362) 45 0344
Viktor Nikolaevich POPOV	Minister of Construction, Architecture, and Housing and Communal Services of the Republic of Mariy El	Phone: (8362) 63 0398
Ilyas Gabdraufovich YAKUPOV	Minister of Economy and Industry of the Republic of Mariy El	Phone: (8362) 64 2071

NAME	POSITION	CONTACT INFORMATION
Nikolai Alexeevich BOROUKHIN	Director of the Timber and Fuel Department of the Republic of Mariy El	Phone: (8362) 45 3201
Anatoly Alexandrovich PONOMAREV	Director of the Natural Resources and Ecological Security Department of the Republic of Mariy El	Phone: (8362) 11 6997

3. ECONOMIC POTENTIAL

3.1. 1997–2002 GROSS REGIONAL PRODUCT (GRP). INDUSTRY BREAKDOWN

In 2002, gross regional product amounted to $546.9 million, which constitutes 6.6% growth year-on-year.

The growth was achieved thanks to an increase in industrial output, which accounts for some 30% of total GRP.

3.2. MAJOR ECONOMIC GROWTH PROJECTIONS

The Government of the Republic of Mariy El has adopted the Program for Economic and Social Development of the Republic of Mariy El, 2002–2004. The Program determines main directions for economic growth in the Republic: annual GRP growth of 4.4%–4.6%, industry growth of 5% annually, priority development of production based on processing of local natural resources.

GRP trends in 1997–2002						TABLE 2
	1997	1998	1999	2000	2001*	2002*
GRP in current prices, $ million	1,056.5	657.6	403.2	421.7	513.0	546.9

*Estimates of the Government of the Republic of Mariy El

GRP industry breakdown in 1997–2002, % of total						TABLE 3
	1997	1998	1999	2000	2001*	2002*
GRP	100.0	100.0	100.0	100.0	100.0	100.0
Industry	28.1	28.3	26.7	28.4	28.2	28.9
Agriculture and forestry	16.2	17.8	23.1	20.0	22.7	21.2
Construction	5.9	6.2	5.6	5.7	5.7	5.7
Transport and communications	5.2	4.3	3.8	4.4	4.1	4.9
Trade and public catering	7.7	8.0	9.7	8.9	9.2	9.3
Other	29.4	29.5	23.8	25.5	24.4	25.5
Net taxes on output	7.5	5.9	7.3	7.1	5.7	4.5

*Estimates of the Government of the Republic of Mariy El

3.3. INDUSTRIAL OUTPUT IN 1997–2002 FOR MAJOR SECTORS OF ECONOMY

The Republic's industrial sector comprises more than 1,400 enterprises, including 150 large and medium companies. The leading industrial sectors of the Republic of Mariy El are energy, machine engineering and metal processing, forestry, timber, pulp and paper, and food and beverages. Their combined share in total industrial output is 72.5%.

Machine engineering and metal processing. The sector accounts for 22.6% of total industrial output in the Republic. Major types of products are refrigerators for the wholesale and retail sectors, equipment for the agro-industrial processing sector, retail, and public

catering; medical equipment; low yield electric motors; semiconductor instruments, and electrical connectors.

Major companies within the sector are: ZAO Ariada, OAO Potential, OAO Mariysky Machine Engineering Plant, OAO Gran, OAO Contact, OAO Kopir, OAO Semiconductor Instrument Plant, OOO PK Sovitalprodmash, OAO S.N. Butyakov Shipbuilding and Ship Repair Plant, and OAO Inreko.

Food and beverages. The share of the sector in total industrial output is 19.4%. The sector specializes in the production of meat, dairy products of various degrees of processing, bread and bakery products, and alcoholic beverages.

The sector is represented by the following major companies: ZAO Yoshkar-Ola Meat Proces-

IV

VOLGA FEDERAL DISTRICT

Industry breakdown of industrial output in 1997–2002, % of total						TABLE 4
	1997	1998	1999	2000	2001	2002*
Industry	100.0	100.0	100.0	100.0	100.0	100.0
Machine engineering and metal processing	21.6	21.7	23.4	25.1	26.2	22.6
Food and beverages	18.7	17.6	20.2	19.9	19.7	19.4
Energy	24.2	22.5	18.0	15.7	17.4	17.4
Forestry, timber, and pulp and paper	8.8	9.1	10.8	12.6	11.8	13.1
Construction materials	6.5	7.2	5.0	4.8	4.8	3.5
Flour, cereals, and mixed fodder	4.7	4.8	4.0	3.5	4.2	3.0
Light industry	3.1	3.2	3.5	3.7	3.4	3.1
Chemicals and petrochemicals	6.0	7.1	8.2	8.7	5.9	2.2
Fuel	0.2	0.7	1.0	1.0	1.8	1.1
Glass and porcelain	0.2	0.4	0.9	0.7	0.5	0.6
Ferrous metals	–	0.4	0.6	0.8	0.3	0.5
Non-ferrous metals	–	–	–	0.1	0.1	–

*Estimates of the Government of the Republic of Mariy El

sing Plant, Fokinsky Liquor Plant, a branch of FGUP Rosspirtprom, RGUP Mariysky Bread, OOO Makhaon, OAO Yoshkar-Ola Confectionery Factory, RGUP Souvenir, and OAO Our Beer.

Energy. This sector accounts for 17.4% of total industrial output. The energy sector is represented by OAO Marienergo. The installed capacity of the Yoshkar-Olinskaya TPS, OAO Mariyenergo main power generator, is 195 MW. Plans are afoot to increase the generating capacity to 70% of total energy consumption by putting into operation an additional 310 MW power unit.

Forestry, timber, and pulp and paper. The sector accounts for 13.1% of total industrial output. Local companies focus on the production of pulp, paper, and cardboard. Major companies within the sector are: OAO Mariysky Pulp and Paper Plant, ZAO Furniture Factory Zarya, ZAO Ski Plant Zarya, and OAO VDK-Mariy El.

Agriculture. The sector accounts for 21.2% of total industrial output. Agricultural companies produce grain, vegetables, potatoes, long flax, hops, meat, milk, eggs, and wool. Livestock farming prevails among agricultural companies. The Republic produces annually some 45,000 tons of meat and poultry, 300,000 tons of milk, and 200 million eggs. Agricultural products are extensively exported to other regions.

3.4. FUEL AND ENERGY BALANCE (OUTPUT AND CONSUMPTION PER RESOURCE)

The energy sector meets 46% of total electricity demand. The Republic produces neither oil nor natural gas of its own. Oil imports are processed into petrochemicals.

3.5. TRANSPORT INFRASTRUCTURE

Roads. The Republic has about 3,300 km of public highway. The main routes are: Yoshkar-Ola – Zelenodolsk (A-397), the Vyatka Highway (A-119), and part of the highway going through the Cheboksary HEP Station and linking Cheboksary and Kazan.

Railroads. The Republic of Mariy El has 202 km of railroads. The main rail corridors of the Gorkovskaya Railway are Yoshkar-Ola – Zeleny Dol and Yoshkar-Ola – Yaransk. The Republic operates the railroad routes Yoshkar-Ola – Moscow, Yoshkar-Ola – Kazan, and Yoshkar-Ola – Yaransk (the Kirov Region).

River ports. The length of shipping routes within the Republic is 335 km, including along the Volga – 230 km and the Vetluga river – 105 km. The main Volga river ports are Volzhsk, Svenigovo, Kokshaisk, Kozmodemiansk, and Yuryno. OAO Kozmodemiansk Port is the main carrier of passengers and freight.

Fuel and energy sector production and consumption trends, 1997–2002						TABLE 5
	1997	1998	1999	2000	2001	2002*
Electricity output, billion kWh	0.7	0.7	0.8	1.0	1.1	1.1
Electricity consumption, billion kWh	2.8	2.9	2.7	2.6	2.3	2.4
Natural gas consumption, million cubic meters	1,111.2	870.2	951.5	962.3	968.9	1,180.2

*Estimates of the Government of the Republic of Mariy El

Airports. The Republic operates the Yoshkar-Ola airport, which accepts small aircraft such as the An 24, Yak 40, and Tu 134.

Oil and gas pipelines. The following oil pipelines go through the Republic: Urengoi – Center, Yamburg – Yelets, and Surgut – Polotsk, as well as the Urengoi – Pomary – Uzhgorod gas pipeline.

3.6. MAIN NATURAL RESOURCES: RESERVES AND EXTRACTION IN 2002

The Republic has 63 known deposits of nine different mineral resources, 26 of which are currently being operated, two are prepared for extraction, and 35 are put in reserve.

Building materials. The Republic has proven reserves of high quality glass and molding sands and brick clay, including 39 explored and six operating deposits, and of carbonate rock, including 33 explored and nine operating deposits.

Timber. Forests cover over 1.2 million hectares, and the total timber reserve is 166.5 million cubic meters.

Organic and mineral fertilizers. The Republic has 60 sapropel healing silt deposits with a total reserve of 11 million tons. It has completed a detailed exploration of five deposits with a total reserve of 1.7 million tons.

Hydrocarbons. In 2002, the first hydrocarbon field was discovered in the Republic and high quality oil reserves were proven. Currently the dynamics, parameters, and physical characteristics of the deposits are being studied.

4. TRADE OPPORTUNITIES

4.1. MAIN GOODS PRODUCED IN THE REGION

Machine engineering. In 2002, output of low yield electrical engines increased by 75% and amounted to 119,700 units; semiconductor instrument output increased by 8% to 370,200 units; electrical connector output rose 28% to 19,712,800 units; and electrical mixer output rose 21% to 85,700 units.

Forestry, timber, and pulp and paper. Hard board output reached 6,515,500 square meters (1% growth) in 2002; paper output reached 28,100 tons (4% growth); board output reached 39,400 tons (94% growth); output of paper bags reached 3,143,700 units (13% growth); and output of industrial timber reached 300,000 cubic meters.

Construction materials. Linoleum output totaled 1,233,200 square meters in 2002, with construction lime output reaching 34,600 tons.

Light industry. In 2002, the Republic's companies produced some 136 tons of knitted fabric, 28% more that the previous year; 551,000 items of hosiery (70% increase); 46,500 items of felt footwear (17% increase); 5,391,000 square meters of leatherette (12% increase); and 175,600 items of leather footwear (20% increase).

Food and beverages. Mayonnaise output amounted to 23 tons, vodka and liquors – 763,300 decaliters (6% growth); beer – 430,000 decaliters (41% growth); sausage – 7,800 tons (28% growth); fat cheese – 6,600 tons (29% growth); dairy products (in terms of milk) – 30,700 tons (21% growth); and canned meat – 25,024,000 cans (81% growth).

4.2. EXPORTS, INCLUDING EXTRA-CIS

In 2002, the Republic of Mariy El registered exports of 436 types of locally produced goods. In 2002, some 69 countries were trading partners of the Republic of Mariy El.

The main groups of goods exported from the Republic of Mariy El are fuel (30% of total exports in revenue terms), paper and cardboard (24%), petrochemicals (11%), machinery (7%), food and beverages (7%), raw hides, furs, and fur goods (6%), timber and timber goods (6%), and clothes and footwear (1%).

Major importers of the Republic's products include Finland, Serbia and Montenegro, Poland, Ukraine, and Singapore.

4.3. IMPORTS, INCLUDING EXTRA-CIS

The structure of imports in 2002 was as follows: machinery (61% of total imports in revenue terms), petrochemicals (15%), ferrous and non-ferrous metals (11%), and food and raw materials for food processing (8%).

The main exporters to the Republic of Mariy El are Italy, Germany, Ukraine, Switzerland, and Japan.

4.4. MAJOR REGIONAL EXPORT AND IMPORT ENTITIES

In 2002, export and import transactions were performed by 199 foreign trade organizations registered in the Republic of Mariy El. Owing to the specific features of the Republic's economy, export and import operations are performed mainly by industrial companies.

IV

VOLGA FEDERAL DISTRICT

5. INVESTMENT OPPORTUNITIES

5.1 INVESTMENTS IN 1992–2002 (BY INDUSTRY SECTOR), INCLUDING FOREIGN INVESTMENTS

The main factors determining the investment appeal of the Republic of Mariy El are:

- Its high industrial potential,
- Its qualified workforce,
- Its developed construction and transport infrastructure.

Capital investment by industry sector, $ million						TABLE 6
	1997	1998	1999	2000	2001	2002*
Total capital investment	197.2	100.3	55.2	60.6	62.1	75.1
Including major industries (% of total):						
Industry	28.5	16.8	23.1	24.5	23.2	24.2
Agriculture and forestry	4.1	5.3	10.5	9.1	8.9	9.4
Construction	3.7	1.5	1.9	1.2	2.3	1.6
Transport and communications	16.2	15.0	22.4	22.8	26.2	27.9
Trade and public catering	1.2	1.5	1.3	1.8	1.8	2.2
Other	46.3	59.9	40.8	40.6	37.6	34.7

*Estimates of the Government of the Republic of Mariy El

Foreign investment trends in 1996–2002						TABLE 7
	1996–1997	1998	1999	2000	2001	2002
Foreign investment, $ million	2.5	0.4	–	0.1	–	–
Including FDI, $ million	1.4	–	–	–	–	–

5.2. MAJOR ENTERPRISES (INCLUDING ENTERPRISES WITH FOREIGN INVESTMENT)

As of the beginning of 2002, the Republic had some 80 companies, branches, and representative offices of companies with foreign investment. The Republic is implementing major investment projects in the timber sector, including the construction of a plywood plant in the village of Suslonger with a capacity of 20,000-25,000 cubic meters of plywood per year (private investment of $5 million), and the construction of a furniture factory on the basis of OAO Zarya to be launched in 2003 (investment of €5 million). Thanks to private investments, a $16 million glass packaging plant operating on local raw materials is being constructed near Yoshkar-Ola.

5.3. MOST ATTRACTIVE SECTORS FOR INVESTMENT

Building materials production is the most promising sector for investors. Given the Republic's proven reserves of glass sands, the glass sector may become an attractive sector for investors in the near future.

The timber sector also has good prospects for the future as demand for timber remains high and demand for timber products is increasing.

5.4. CURRENT LEGISLATION ON INVESTOR TAX EXEMPTIONS AND PRIVILEGES

The Republic of Mariy El has passed a number of legislative acts fostering investment:

- The Law of the Republic of Mariy El On the Attraction of Credit for Investment Purposes.
- The Law of the Republic of Mariy El On the Attraction of Investment into the Republic's Economy.

These laws provide a legal and economic framework for government support to investors registered in the Republic of Mariy El, including:

- State support of investment projects by direct credits, subsidized interest expense on bank credits up to 50%, and state guarantees;
- Support in creating business infrastructure and renting or purchasing real estate from the Republic;
- Backup of investors' applications and appeals to federal authorities and credit institutions for granting tax privileges;
- An investment credit for the regional profit tax component and regional taxes.

Tax exemptions are provided to investors in the Republic of Mariy El under the following conditions:

- Investment of no less than $50,000;
- Separate accounting of funds and property received and utilized in the investment project;

Largest enterprises of the Republic of Mariy El

TABLE 8

COMPANY	SECTOR
OAO Marienergo	Energy
OAO Mariysky Pulp and Paper Plant	Pulp and paper
OAO ICN Marbiopharm	Chemicals and pharmaceuticals
MUP Yoshkar-Ola Central Thermal Power Plant No. 1	Energy
ZAO Yoshkar-Ola Meat Processing Plant	Meat and dairy products
ZAO LUKoil-Mariy El	Fuel
OAO Martelcom	Telecommunications
GUPEP Marcommunenergo	Heating
OOO Karina	Retail
OANPO Mariholodmash	Machine engineering
OAO Mariynefteproduct	Oil
ZAO Mariyskoye	Agriculture
ZAO NP Iskozh	Leather industry
Production and Assembly Technology Company	Road vehicles

Regional entities responsible for raising investment

TABLE 9

ENTITY	ADDRESS	PHONE, FAX, E-MAIL
Ministry of Economy and Industry of the Republic of Mariy El	29, pr. Leninsky, Yoshkar-Ola, Republic of Mariy El, 424001	Phone: (8362) 64 2071 Fax: (8362) 12 6149 E-mail: mecon@gov.mari.ru
Ministry of Enterprise, Commerce, and Consumer Services Development of the Republic of Mariy El	76, ul. K. Marksa, Yoshkar-Ola, Republic of Mariy El, 424000	Phone (8362) 45 0344 Fax (8362) 45 0267
The Chamber of Industry and Commerce of the Republic of Mariy El	Offices 313, 314; 41 ul. Panfilova, Yoshkar-Ola, Republic of Mariy El 424003	Phone: (8362) 45 2327 Fax: (8362) 63 0426 E-mail: palata@mari-el.ru

IV

VOLGA FEDERAL DISTRICT

• A resolution of the Inter-Agency Commission for Investment and Economic Restructuring of the Republic of Mariy El with regard to the investment project.

5.5. FEDERAL AND REGIONAL ECONOMIC AND SOCIAL DEVELOPMENT PROGRAMS FOR THE REPUBLIC OF MARIY EL

Federal targeted programs. The major program of economic and social development of the region is the Federal Targeted Program of The Elimination of Inequalities in the Social and Economic Development of the Regions of the Russian Federation, 2002–2010 and through 2015 with a 2003 budget of $19.3 million. The program aims to reduce regional gaps in core social and economic development indicators by 2010, create conditions conducive to the development of enterprise, and improve the investment climate.

In 2001 the Republic was allocated $17.6 million from the federal budget to develop its social infrastructure, and $20.6 million in 2002, including $15.5 million under federal targeted programs.

Regional programs. The Republic has some 48 Republican targeted programs underway.

In 2001 the Republic developed and is currently implementing the Program of Economic and Social Development of the Republic of Mariy El, 2002–2004, which aims to reduce state subsidies to the region and increase the revenues of the Republic's consolidated budget.

The Program of Forestry Development and Use of Timber Resources, 2002–2005 is underway. The Program envisages organizational, economic, technical, financial, and social measures to improve the efficiency of the Republic's timber reserves.

The Republic has plans afoot to allocate a $0.06 million budget in 2003 for implementation of the Targeted Program for Small Enterprise Support, 2002–2004.

6. INVESTMENT PROJECTS

Industry sector and project description	1) Expected results 2) Amount and term of investment 3) Form of financing[1] 4) Documentation[2]	Contact information
1	2	3

IV

VOLGA FEDERAL DISTRICT

MINING

44R001 ● ◆

| Extraction of milled fuel peat. Project goal: to increase output. | 1) 20,000 tons a year 2) $1 million/n/a 3) L 4) BP | OAO Paranginskoye Turf Company 18, ul. Kommunisticheskaya, Paranga, Republic of Mariy El, 425470 Phone: (83639) 41 518, 41 656 Fax: (83639) 41 490 Valery Danilovich Dubnikov, CEO |

MACHINE ENGINEERING AND METAL PROCESSING

44R002 ● ◆

| Production of thermal electrical modules and thermal electrical portable, office, and transport refrigerators. Project goal: to introduce a new product to the market (ozone-friendly cooling thermal electrical modules and refrigerator equipment based thereon). | 1) 55,000 items a year 2) $1 million/1.5 years 3) L 4) BP | OAO Semiconductor Instrument Plant 26, ul. Suvorova, Yoshkar-Ola, Republic of Mariy El, 424003 Phone: (8362) 12 0909 Fax: (8362) 12 1339 E-mail: Zpp@nid.ru Rudolf Ivanovich Nikitin, CEO |

44R003 ● ◆

| Production of diode line transformers (split transformers) for sixth- and further generation TVs. Project goal: to introduce a new product to the market for TV equipment. | 1) 550,000 items a year 2) $0.8 million/1.5 years 3) L 4) BP | OAO Semiconductor Instrument Plant 26, ul. Suvorova, Yoshkar-Ola, Republic of Mariy El, 424003 Phone: (8362) 12 0909 Fax: (8362) 12 1339 E-mail: Zpp@nid.ru Rudolf Ivanovich Nikitin, CEO |

44R004 ● ◆

| Production of refrigerator motors. Project goal: to introduce a new product to the market. | 1) 180,000 units a year 2) $0.32 million/2 years 3) L ($0.26 million) 4) BP | OAO Krasnogorsky Electric Engine Plant 1, ul. Machinostroiteley, Krasnogorsky, Zvenigovsky District, Republic of Mariy El, 425091 Phone: (83645) 69 357, 69 141, 69 676 Fax: (83645) 69 683 E-mail: motor@mari-el.ru Eugeny Nikolaevich Kalyanov, CEO |

FOOD AND BEVERAGES

44R005 ● ★ ◆

| Production of waffles. Project goal: to introduce new products to the market. | 1) 1,500 tons a year 2) $5.1 million/3 years 3) L ($0.63 million), Leas. 4) BP | OAO Yoshkar-Ola Confectionery Factory 136, ul. Eshpaya, Yoshkar-Ola, Republic of Mariy El, 424002 Phone: (8362) 12 2096, 63 0485, 12 2170 Fax: (8362) 12 2865 E-mail: ukf@chat.ru, ukf@mailru.com Gennady Konstantinovich Timakov, CEO |

[1] L – Loan, E – Equity, Leas. – Leasing, JV – Joint Venture
[2] BP – Business Plan, FS – Feasibility Study

1	2	3

44R006

Beer production.
Project goal: to upgrade bottling operations.

1) 1 million decaliters a year
2) $0.32 million/2 years
3) L
4) BP

OAO Our Beer
24-a, ul. Chekhova, Medvedevo,
Republic of Mariy El, 425200
Phone/fax: (8362) 74 0638, 74 0689
E-mail: nashe_pivo@mari-el.ru;
Anatoly Ivanovich Polevschikov,
CEO

TOURISM

44R007

Creation of Mari Village ecological and ethnographic center.
Project goal: to develop ecological and ethnographic tourism.

1) 3,600 tourists a year
2) $0.82 million/3 years
3) L ($0.6 million)
4) BP

OOO Center of Creative Initiative Matur
Office 302, 8, ul. Krasnoarmeiskaya,
Yoshkar-Ola, Republic of Mariy El, 424000
Phone: (8362) 11 6271
Fax: (8362) 11 6382
E-mail: Matour@yoshkar-ola.ru
Galina Vasilyevna Maslyakova,
CEO

OTHER (METAL POWDERS)

44R008

Production of goods from metal powders.
Project goal: to expand product range and increase output.

1) 1,000 tons a year
   (revenue of $4 million)
2) $2.25 million/5 years
3) L
4) BP

OAO OKTB Kristall
93, ul. Stroiteley, Yoshkar-Ola,
Republic of Mariy El, 424000
Phone: (8362) 45 2007, 73 1421, 64 0352
Fax: (8362) 45 3131
E-mail: Kristall@mari-el.ru
Valery Yuryevich Izychev,
CEO

IV

VOLGA FEDERAL DISTRICT

45. REPUBLIC OF MORDOVIA [13]

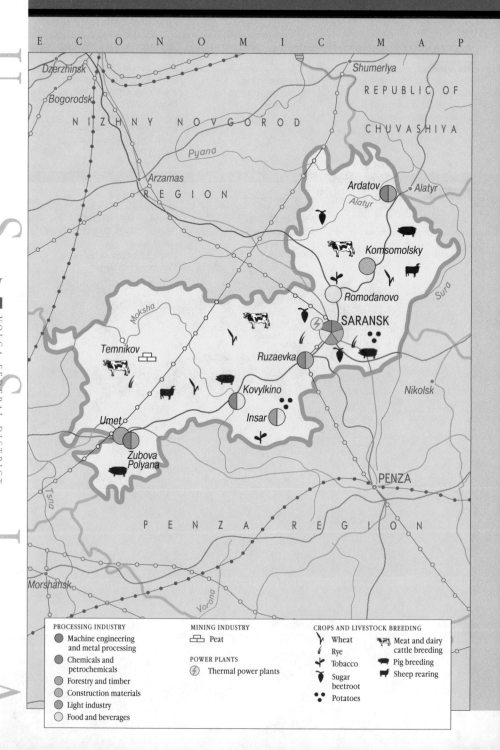

Dzerzhinsk

Bogorodsk

NIZHNY   NOVGOROD

Pyana

Arzamas

REGION

Shumerlya

REPUBLIC OF

CHUVASHIYA

Ardatov   Alatyr

Alatyr

Komsomolsky

Romodanovo

SARANSK

Moksha

Temnikov

Ruzaevka

Sura

Nikolsk

Kovylkino

Insar

Umet

Zubova
Polyana

PENZA

Tsna

PENZA   REGION

Morshansk

Vorona

PROCESSING INDUSTRY

- Machine engineering and metal processing
- Chemicals and petrochemicals
- Forestry and timber
- Construction materials
- Light industry
- Food and beverages

MINING INDUSTRY

- Peat

POWER PLANTS

- Thermal power plants

CROPS AND LIVESTOCK BREEDING

- Wheat
- Rye
- Tobacco
- Sugar beetroot
- Potatoes
- Meat and dairy cattle breeding
- Pig breeding
- Sheep rearing

The Republic of Mordovia is inhabited by nearly one million people of various nationalities and religious beliefs. The Republic received its name from its indigenous ethnic group – the Mordva, the largest ethnic group in Russia speaking the Uralic family of languages and one of the major ethnic groups in the Volga Region. The Gothic chronicler Jordan made the first historical mention of the Mordva in the sixth century A.D. The renowned Russian chronicler Nestor mentioned the Mordva in his Russian Chronicle of the twelfth century.

The economy of present day Mordovia features heavy engineering companies headed by Russian lighting equipment giant OAO Lisma. Thanks to active state support, companies in the Republic are increasingly confident in the new economic conditions and beginning to penetrate inter-regional and international markets. Today, the Republic exports electrical tools and machinery, locomotives, rubber goods, equipment, and mechanical tools. The Republic's pharmaceutical sector is highly esteemed, with pharmaceutical products exported to some 60 countries, including Germany, Italy, and Lithuania.

Mordovia has created a favorable investment climate and has attracted reliable business partners. Capital investment in 2002 amounted to $162.5 million. The bulk of investment is channeled into industry, agriculture, forestry, and construction. The Republic hosts 44 companies with foreign investment.

The Republic's authorities see the attraction of investment as one of their top priorities. Mordovia has created a legislative framework that envisages preferential taxation of investors. The Republic has published a catalog detailing 76 investment projects undertaken by 46 local companies.

Mordovia is a hospitable land whose prosperity depends on close cooperation with other peoples. Our doors and our hearts are always open to friends. Come to Mordovia and see for yourselves!

Nikolai Merkushkin,
HEAD OF THE REPUBLIC OF MORDOVIA

IV

VOLGA FEDERAL DISTRICT

1. GENERAL INFORMATION

1.1. GEOGRAPHY

The Republic of Mordovia covers a total area of some 26,200 square kilometers. The Republic lies at the center of the East European Plain in the River Volga basin. The Republic borders the Nizhny Novgorod Region to the north, the Ulyanovsk Region to the east, the Penza Region to the south, the Ryazan Region to the west and the Republic of Chuvashia to the north-east.

1.2. CLIMATE

The Republic of Mordovia is located within the temperate continental climate zone. The average temperature in the Republic is –8°C in January, rising to +21.2°C in July. Annual precipitation reaches 450–500 mm. The average growing season lasts 135 days. The Republic of Mordovia is located at the border of the forest and steppe zones.

1.3. POPULATION

According to preliminary 2002 census results, total population in the Republic of Mordovia was 889,000 people. The average population density is 33.9 people per square kilometer. The economically active population is 442,000 people. 2002 official unemployment stood at 1.9%, while the actual rate was 10.5%.

Demographically speaking, some 60% are of statutory working age, 18% are below the statutory working age, and 22% are beyond the statutory working age. The Territory's ethnic mix is 60.8% Russian, 32.5% Mordva, 4.9% Tatar, and 1.8% other ethnic groups.

The Republic's major urban centers (2002) are Saransk with 304,900 inhabitants, Ruzaevka with 49,500 inhabitants, and Kovylkino with 22,800 inhabitants.

Population								TABLE 1
	1992	1997	1998	1999	2000	2001	2002
Total population, '000	963	950	944	937	929	920	889
Economically active population, '000	474	417	409	431	445	432	442

2. ADMINISTRATION

35, ul. Sovetskaya, Saransk, Republic of Mordovia, 430002
Phone/fax: (8342) 17 9996
E-mail: kanc@whrm.moris.ru (Russian), vesrm@moris.ru (English, French, German)
http://whrm.moris.ru(Russian)
http://whrm.moris.ru/portret/vnes/mordves.htm (English, French, German)

NAME	POSITION	CONTACT INFORMATION
Nikolai Ivanovich MERKUSHIN	Governor of the Republic of Mordovia	Phone: (8342) 32 7801 Fax: (8342) 17 4526 E-mail: kanc@whrm.moris.ru
Vladimir Dmitrievich VOLKOV	Chairman of the Government of the Republic of Mordovia	Phone: (8342) 32 7469 Fax: (8342) 17 3628 E-mail: pred@whrm.moris.ru
Victor Vasilyevich AKISHEV	First Deputy Chairman of the Government of the Republic of Mordovia in charge of Industry and Energy	Phone: (8342) 32 7253 Fax: (8342) 32 7253 E-mail: przam1@whmr.moris.ru
Victor Gavrilovich PECHATKIN	First Deputy Chairman of the Government of the Republic of Mordovia, Minister of Agriculture and Provisions	Phone: (8342) 32 7795 Fax: (8342) 17 4401 E-mail: msx@whrm.moris.ru
Vladimir Fedorovich SUSHKOV	Deputy Chairman of the Government of the Republic of Mordovia in charge of Construction	Phone: (8342) 32 7596 Fax: (8342) 32 7425 E-mail: hoz@whrm.moris.ru
Sergei Mikhailovich VDOVIN	Deputy Chairman of the Government of the Republic of Mordovia, Minister of Economy	Phone: (8342) 24 2834 Fax: (8342) 17 3511 E-mail: mineco@moris.ru
Nikolai Vladimirovich PETRUSHKIN	Deputy Chairman of the Government of the Republic of Mordovia, Minister of Finance	Phone: (8342) 17 6566 Fax: (8342) 17 6592 E-mail: minfin@moris.ru

NAME	POSITION	CONTACT INFORMATION
Nikolai Nikolaevich KALINICHENKO	Minister of Foreign Economic Relations of the Republic of Mordovia	Phone: (8342) 17 6844 Fax: (8342) 17 9991 E-mail: mves@whrm.moris.ru http://whrm.moris.ru/portret/vnes/mordves.htm

3. ECONOMIC POTENTIAL

3.1. 1997–2002 GROSS
REGIONAL PRODUCT (GRP).
INDUSTRY BREAKDOWN

In 2001, the Republic's gross regional product was $833.4 million, while per capita GRP amounted to $905.

3.2. MAJOR ECONOMIC
GROWTH PROJECTIONS

Based on the existing pattern of industrial output and the Republic's main development priorities,

the industrial growth rate is projected at 8.5% in 2003, 9.8% in 2004, and 8.2% in 2005.

Machine engineering and metal processing. Output of major machine engineering products is expected to continue growing. In 2003, output in the sector is expected to grow by 11%.

Construction industry. Work will be done to promulgate advanced technologies in the sector and increase output of environmen-

GRP trends in 1997–2002						*TABLE 2*
	1997	1998	1999	2000	2001	2002
GRP in current prices, $ million	1,499.4	920.4	557.2	853.3	833.4	n/a

GRP industry breakdown in 1997–2002, % of total						*TABLE 3*
	1997	1998	1999	2000	2001	2002
GRP	100.0	100.0	100.0	100.0	100.0	100.0
Industry	26.1	26.8	26.2	23.5	29.5	n/a
Agriculture and forestry	19.0	20.5	22.9	20.7	21.4	n/a
Construction	4.7	6.3	4.2	3.9	8.1	n/a
Transport and communications	6.0	6.6	5.5	4.8	5.0	n/a
Trade and public catering	9.3	9.5	10.0	8.2	9.3	n/a
Others	34.9	30.3	31.2	38.9	26.7	n/a

tally friendly construction materials. 2003 output growth is expected to reach 11%.

The Republic plans to continue raising output of equipment used to process agricultural produce. The food and beverages and food processing sectors are set to undergo a major overhaul involving reconstruction and modernization. Meat and meat-derived food output is expected to grow by 20% in 2003, while dairy output is expected to rise by 11.8%.

3.3. INDUSTRIAL OUTPUT IN 1997–2002
FOR MAJOR SECTORS OF ECONOMY

The Republic's processing sectors are its most developed industries. Machine engineering and metals processing hold a key position. The iron foundry, chemicals, petrochemicals, light industry and food sectors are also developed.

Machine engineering and metal processing. This sector accounts for 41.6% of the Republic's total in-

dustrial output. Electrical engineering and auto manufacturing, machine tool engineering, road construction, and excavation machine manufacturing are its key sectors.

OAO Lisma is the largest enterprise in the electrical engineering sector. OAO Lisma formed the basis of the Russian Light Association, a group of Russian light bulb and light fitting manufacturers. The Electrovypryamitel Plant is a major producer of transformer devices.

The Saransk Dump Truck Plant represents the auto industry in the Republic of Mordovia. It produces tippers, auto spare parts, trailers, and haulage equipment for cars.

OAO Sareks, the largest producer of tire excavators in Russia, produces road construction and excavation machinery.

OAO Ruzaevsky Chemical Machine Engineering Plant and OAO Saransky Locomotive Repair Plant produce equipment for the chemicals, petrochemicals, gas,

Industry breakdown of industrial output in 1997–2002, % of total						TABLE 4
	1997	1998	1999	2000	2001	2002*
Industry	100.0	100.0	100.0	100.0	100.0	100.0
Machine engineering and metal processing	33.5	32.7	36.2	40.9	40.4	41.6
Food and beverages	21.5	20.5	25.4	21.0	20.9	23.6
Energy	16.5	15.7	10.5	10.5	10.0	10.8
Construction materials	7.5	9.1	8.0	8.4	8.2	9.5
Chemicals and petrochemicals	6.4	6.6	6.1	6.3	6.1	5.3
Pharmaceutical industry	7.6	8.7	7.4	7.8	6.2	4.7
Light industry	2.6	2.5	2.1	1.5	1.4	1.4
Forestry, timber, and pulp and paper	1.8	0.9	1.0	0.8	0.7	0.9
Ferrous metals	0.3	0.3	0.4	0.4	0.3	0.3

*Estimates of the Government of the Republic of Mordovia

and microbiological industries, as well as tank-wagons for the transportation of gas, oil products, and acids.

OAO Medoborudovanie is a major Russian enterprise producing disinfecting equipment and distilling apparatuses.

OAO Saransky Tool Plant specializes in instrument manufacturing for the machine engineering, chemicals, gas, and oil industries.

OAO Orbita and GP Saransky Television Plant are the base enterprises for the electronic and radio industries.

Food and beverages. The food industry accounts for 23.6% of total industrial output in the Republic of Mordovia. Five meat-processing plants, 21 dairies, a confectionery factory, seven distilleries, a sugar refinery, and a tinned food factory represent the sector.

Energy. The energy sector accounts for 10.8% of total industrial output. The Saranskaya 1, Saranskaya 2, Alekseevskaya, and Romodanovskaya Thermal Power Stations produce electricity in the Republic.

Construction materials. The construction materials industry accounts for 9.5% of total industrial output in the Republic of Mordovia. OAO Mordovtsement, Russia's largest cement producer, represents the industry.

Chemicals and petrochemicals. The chemicals and petrochemicals sector accounts for 5.3% of total

industrial output of the Republic of Mordovia. The industry is represented by OAO Saransky Rubber Equipment Plant, which produces about 15,000 types of general mechanical rubber goods used in the automotive sector.

Pharmaceuticals. The industry accounts for 4.7% of total industrial output of the Republic of Mordovia. OAO Biokhimik is one of the ten largest drug producers in Russia.

Agriculture. Agriculture accounts for 21% of the Republic's GRP. The sector specializes in cereals (wheat, rye, millet, buckwheat), potatoes, sugar beet, vegetables, and livestock rearing. Agricultural products are supplied to many regions of Russia and abroad.

3.4. FUEL AND ENERGY BALANCE (OUTPUT AND CONSUMPTION PER RESOURCE)

The Republic of Mordovia is an energy deficient territory, in which electricity consumption greatly exceeds output. The energy deficiency is made up with deliveries from the consolidated power system of the Central Volga. Major electricity consumers (2002) are industry (32.1%), residential users (17.7%), agriculture (17.2%), and transport (9.2%).

3.5. TRANSPORT INFRASTRUCTURE

Roads. The Republic of Mordovia has 4,200 kilometers of paved public highway. The Saransk –

Fuel and energy sector production and consumption trends, 1997–2002						TABLE 5
	1997	1998	1999	2000	2001	2002*
Electricity output, billion kWh	1.0	1.1	1.1	1.0	1.2	1.1
Electricity consumption, billion kWh	2.8	2.7	2.7	2.3	2.3	2.3
Natural gas consumption, million cubic meters	1,822.4	1,364.7	1,448.2	1,514.0	1,723.4	2,208.3
Coal consumption, '000 tons	147.0	n/a	148.0	58.4	32.0	20.0
Firewood consumption, '000 cubic meters	n/a	n/a	n/a	16.3	11.2	13.2

*Estimates of the Government of the Republic of Mordovia

Cheboksary, Saransk – Ryazan, Saransk – Nizhny Novgorod, and Saransk – Penza highways are the Republic's main arteries.

Railroads. The Republic of Mordovia has 500 kilometers of railroads. The Republic is crossed by the Moscow – Samara and Nizhny Novgorod – Penza railroads in the east. It also has railroad links to the west, north-west, north-east, east and south of the Russian Federation.

Gas pipelines. A number of trunk gas pipelines cross the Republic (from gas fields in the north of Western Siberia), in addition to the Saratov – Nizhny Novgorod gas pipeline.

3.6. MAIN NATURAL RESOURCES: RESERVES AND EXTRACTION IN 2002

Construction materials. The Republic of Mordovia has major deposits of marl and cretaceous minerals, and silica clays used in the production of high quality cement. The Republic also has a wide variety of clay deposits, including brick clay, fireclay, potter's clay, and faience clay. A large deposit of diatomite has been explored in the Republic, with total reserves estimated at 6 million cubic meters.

Peat deposits. The Republic of Mordovia has 530 explored peat deposits with a total area of 19,600 hectares and reserves of 35.8 million tons. This sector is promising owing to increased peat consumption as fuel and also as fertilizer. Peat also has good potential as a feedstock in the production of modern construction materials used for insulation, filters, water purification facilities, and the distillation of natural gas, oil, and other petrochemicals.

Forestry resources. The Republic has large forest reserves. Its total timber reserves are estimated at 84 million cubic meters. Annual timber reserves (for sawn timber production) are 715,000 cubic meters, with some 656,000 cubic meters fit for industrial processing.

Mineral water. The Republic of Mordovia has four underground mineral water deposits. Underground water is currently drawn from 3,600 wells. Daily output of sulfate-chloride mineral water stands at around 30 cubic meters.

4. TRADE OPPORTUNITIES

4.1. MAIN GOODS PRODUCED IN THE REGION

Food and beverages. 2002 sausage output was 9,800 tons, output of non-vegetable oil was 5,200 tons, meat output was 12,600 tons, and whole milk output reached 48,100 tons (in terms of milk equivalent).

Pharmaceuticals. 2002 pharmaceuticals output was 1,158,000 packs, and output of antibiotics was 90,073,000 vials.

Industrial output. In 2002, the Republic's industrial enterprises produced 389,827,000 electric light bulbs, 4,900 kilometers of armored cable, 7,400 kilometers of telephone cable, 18,135,000 semi-conductor devices, 712 excavators, 6,200 washing machines, 6,300 television sets, 72,700 bicycles, 17,330,000 meters of technical hosing, 2,337,000 tons of cement, 56 million bricks, 426 tons of hemp fiber, and 607,000 square meters of fabric.

4.2. EXPORTS, INCLUDING EXTRA-CIS

The Republic's 2002 foreign trade turnover was $70.3 million (up 15% on 2001).

2002 exports reached $37.7 million, including $10.3 million of extra-CIS exports. Core exports included electrical machinery and equipment (43%), railway vehicles and locomotives (39.5%), rubber goods (7%), equipment and devices (5%), and pharmaceuticals (2%).

The Republic exports to 60 countries worldwide, including Kazakhstan (49%), Germany (15%), Ukraine (8%), Turkmenistan (7%), Uzbekistan (4%), Lithuania (3%), Italy (2%), and Tajikistan (2%).

4.3. IMPORTS, INCLUDING EXTRA-CIS

2002 imports totaled $32.7 million, including $30.4 million in extra-CIS imports. This represented a 12% ($3.5 million) increase on 2001.

The Republic's main imports were: equipment and devices (48%), sugar and confectionery (26%), electrical machinery and equipment (10%), metalloceramics (6%), and land vehicles (5%). The Republic's main trading partners for imports were: Germany (16%), Brazil (11%), Cuba (11%), France (11%), Denmark (8%), Belgium (6%), and China (6%).

4.4. MAJOR REGIONAL EXPORT AND IMPORT ENTITIES

Owing to the specific nature of the Republic's export and import activities, export and import transactions are performed mainly by industrial enterprises.

IV

VOLGA FEDERAL DISTRICT

488

5. INVESTMENT OPPORTUNITIES

5.1. INVESTMENTS IN 1992–2002 (BY INDUSTRY SECTOR), INCLUDING FOREIGN INVESTMENTS

The following factors determine the investment appeal of the Republic of Mordovia:
- The emerging legal framework for economic activities in the Republic;
- The informational and organizational support offered to investors (the Republic main-

tains a catalogue of investment projects which contains information on 76 investment projects of 46 enterprises).

5.2. CAPITAL INVESTMENT

Industry, transport, communications, agriculture, and forestry account for the bulk of the capital investment. 2002 foreign investment in the Republic totaled $19.6 million. Investments were mainly in the telecommunications sector and food industry.

Capital investment by industry sector, $ million						TABLE 6
	1997	1998	1999	2000	2001	2002
Total capital investment	192.7	142.7	78.2	94.9	130.9	162.5
Including major industries (% of total):						
Industry	33.6	31.2	32.7	35.8	25.7	20.5
Agriculture and forestry	4.5	0.9	3.3	4.0	4.6	10.8
Construction	3.7	1.5	1.9	1.2	2.3	4.2
Transport and communications	21.3	42.0	34.4	30.3	38.8	33.3
Trade and public catering	3.1	0.4	0.7	0.6	1.0	0.7
Other	31.3	19.1	22.5	14.4	15.4	30.5

Foreign investment trends in 1996–2002						TABLE 7
	1996–1997	1998	1999	2000	2001	2002
Foreign investment, $ million	2.0	11.6	1.0	8.6	13.7	19.6
Including FDI, $ million	2.0	4.3	0.6	7.0	5.0	5.6

5.3. MAJOR ENTERPRISES (INCLUDING ENTERPRISES WITH FOREIGN INVESTMENT)

Some 44 enterprises with foreign investment are registered in the Republic of Mordovia. Investors from Austria, Bulgaria, China, Cyprus, Latvia, Liechtenstein, and South Korea have set up joint ventures in the Republic.

5.4. MOST ATTRACTIVE SECTORS FOR INVESTMENT

The machine engineering and metal processing, food and beverages and communications sectors are the most attractive sectors for investors.

5.5. CURRENT LEGISLATION ON INVESTOR TAX EXEMPTIONS AND PRIVILEGES

The Republic's Law On Foreign Investment in the Republic of Mordovia was enacted in 1996. The law regulates investment activities and eligibility for tax deductions (for enterprises and organizations implementing investment projects using foreign capital) with respect to the regional components of profit tax and property tax. The law has been amended

(pursuant to the latest federal legislation) with respect to the limits on tax deductions available to investors and to ensure greater eligibility.

Regulations governing the status of Especially Important Investment Projects, which qualify investors for tax exemptions, have been approved by a Decree of the Governor of the Republic of Mordovia with the aim of encouraging foreign investment in priority investment projects.

5.6. FEDERAL AND REGIONAL ECONOMIC AND SOCIAL DEVELOPMENT PROGRAMS FOR THE REPUBLIC OF MORDOVIA

Federal targeted programs. A number of federal targeted programs is underway in the Republic. The priority has been accorded to the following programs: Energy Efficient Economy, 2002–2005 and through 2010, The Elimination of Social and Economic Inequalities in the Development of the Regions of the Russian Federation, 2002–2010 and through 2015, and Increase in Sugar Output in the Russian Federation, 1997–2000 and through 2005.

Regional programs. The Republic's targeted Program for the Development of the Republic of Mordovia in 2001–2005 seeks to establish economic

Largest enterprises of the Republic of Mordovia	TABLE 8
COMPANY	SECTOR
OAO Ruzkhimmash	Machine engineering
OAO Sarek	Machine engineering
OAO Saranskkabel	Machine engineering
OAO Elektrovypryamitel	Machine engineering
OAO Saransky Rubber Equipment Plant	Rubber and asbestos
OAO Orbita	Electronics
OAO Medoborudovanie	Medical equipment
OAO Mordovtsement	Construction materials
OAO Biokhimik	Chemicals and pharmaceuticals
OAO Lato	Construction materials
OAO Lisma	Machine engineering
OAO Mordovglavsnab	Logistics
OAO Saransky Instruments Plant	Instruments
OAO Lenta	Textile
OAO Saransky Auto Repair Plant	Machine and equipment repairs
OAO Teploizolyatsiya	Construction materials
OAO Saranskinstrument	Machine tools
OAO Radiodetal	Electronics
FGUP Saransk Mechanical Plant	Defense
OAO Saransky Dump Truck Plant	Machine engineering
OAO Sura	Textiles
OAO Kovylkinsky Electrical Engineering Plant	Machine engineering
OAO Stankostroitel	Machines and tools
OAO Saranskstroyzakazchik	Construction materials
OAO Lisma-Kandoshinsky Electrical Engineering Plant	Machine engineering

and social stability in the Republic and to create conditions conducive to long-term economic and social development. Its main aims are: to develop priority industries with interconnected production processes, to raise income in the Republic, to enhance the competitiveness of the output of the Republic's enterprises, to expand markets via new products, to improve the environmental situation in the Republic, to create jobs, and to raise living standards. The program has been allocated a budget of $878.1 million (in 2000 prices), to be raised in the private sector from program participants, coupled with non-repayable federal budget allocations, commercial bank loans, and local and regional budget allocations.

IV

VOLGA FEDERAL DISTRICT

6. INVESTMENT PROJECTS

Industry sector and project description	1) Expected results 2) Amount and term of investment 3) Form of financing[1] 4) Documentation[2]	Contact information
1	2	3

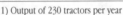

MACHINE ENGINEERING AND METAL PROCESSING

45R001

| Production of wheeled tractors with hydraulic transmission. Project goal: to market highly productive and mobile tractors with hydraulic transmission and high ergonomics. | 1) Output of 230 tractors per year 2) $0.5 million/3 years 3) L ($0.3 million) 4) BP | OAO Sareks 126a, ul. Proletarskaya, Saransk Republic of Mordovia, 430001 Phone: (8342) 24 5728 Fax: (8342) 17 3037 Gennady Ivanovich Kulebyakin, CEO |

45R002

| Production of a new type of tank railcars for light oil products. Project goal: to introduce a new product to the market. | 1) Output of 1,000 railcars per year 2) $1.3 million/10 months 3) L ($1.0 million) 4) BP | OAO Ruzkhimmash Ruzaevka-6, Republic of Mordovia, 431440 Phone: (83451) 32 645, 32 881, 20 876 Fax: (83451) 32 778, 31 318 E-mail: ruzhim@moris.ru Nikolai Vasilyevich Burmistrov, CEO |

45R003

| Production of optical fiber for fiber-optic communication cables. Project goal: to start production of domestic fiber-optic cables. | 1) Output of 1 million meters of optical fiber per year 2) $33.2 million/32 months 3) L ($20 million) 4) BP | OOO Lisma-Optica 5, sh. Svetotekhnikov, Saransk, Republic of Mordovia, 430034 Phone/fax: (8342) 17 1653 E-mail: lisma@moris.ru Vladimir Vasilyevich Lityushkin, CEO |

45R004

| Production of molybdenum wire. Project goal: to launch production of molybdenum wire. | 1) Output of 180 million meters of threaded molybdenum and 30 tons of weight molybdenum wire per year 2) $3.7 million/2 years 3) L ($0.9 million) 4) BP | OAO Lisma 5, sh. Svetotekhnikov, Saransk, Republic of Mordovia, 430034 Phone: (8342) 17 1306 Fax: (8342) 17 1380 E-mail: lisma@moris.ru Vladimir Vasilyevich Lityushkin, CEO |

45R005

| Production of a new type of converters for electric locomotives. Project goal: to introduce a new product to the market. | 1) Annual revenues of $5.8 million 2) $2.4 million/1.5 years 3) L ($1.9 million) 4) BP | OAO Elektrovypryamitel 126, ul. Proletarskaya, Saransk, Republic of Mordovia, 430001 Phone: (8342) 24 2396 Fax: (8342) 17 0288 E-mail: info@elvpr.ru Vladimir Vasilyevich Chibirkin, CEO |

45R006

| Development of production of modern electronic parts and modules in 2001–2005. Project goal: to increase output of electronic parts and modules and improve quality. | 1) Annual revenues of $9.2 million 2) $4.7 million/4 years 3) L ($4.6 million) 4) BP | OAO Orbita Yalga, Saransk, Republic of Mordovia, 430904 Phone/fax: (8342) 33 3412 Fax: (8342) 17 5070 E-mail: orbita@moris.ru Alexander Vladimirovich Garmashov, CEO |

[1] L – Loan, E – Equity, Leas. – Leasing, JV – Joint Venture
[2] BP – Business Plan, FS – Feasibility Study

1	2	3

FORESTRY, TIMBER, AND PULP AND PAPER

45R007

Introduction of equipment for timber drying. Project goal: to increase output and improve quality of parquet pieces.	1) Output of 100,000 square meters per year 2) $0.4 million/3 months 3) L 4) BP

ZAO Yelnikovskaya DSPMK
Yelniki Village, Yelnikovsky District,
Republic of Mordovia, 431370
Phone: (83444) 21 204, 21 450
Fax: (83444) 21 130
E-mail: edspmk@moris.ru
Grigory Kuzmich Smolkin,
CEO

45R008

Increase in plywood output. Project goal: to expand plywood production.	1) Annual output of 35,000 cubic meters, annual revenues of $11.6 million 2) € 2.5 million/0.5 years 3) L 4) BP, FS

ZAO LES-EXPORT
Umet Village, Zubovo-Polyansky District,
Republic of Mordovia, 431105
Phone/fax: (83458) 36 599, 36 500
E-mail: lesexport@inbox.ru
Alexei Nikolaevich Sanaev,
CEO

CONSTRUCTION MATERIALS

45R009

Production of high quality cement. Project goal: to increase output of high quality cement.	1) Output of 386,000 tons per year 2) $1.6 million/1 year 3) L ($1.3 million) 4) BP

OAO Mordovtsement
Komsomolsky Village, Chamzinsky District,
Republic of Mordovia, 431721
Phone/fax: (83437) 32 005, 31 000
E-mail: cement@moris.ru
Sergei Ivanovich Siushov,
CEO

45R010

Production of connectors for water and gas polyethylene pipes. Project goal: to introduce connectors and joiners for pipelines made of polyethylene pipes to the market.	1) Sales of $0.3 million a year 2) $0.1 million/2 years 3) L ($0.06 million) 4) BP

OAO Vismut
7, ul. Tolstogo, Ruzaevka,
Republic of Mordovia, 431444
Phone: (83451) 20 342
Fax: (83451) 20 852
E-mail: vismut@list.ru
Gennady Vasilyevich Averyushkin, CEO

FOOD AND BEVERAGES

45R011

Reconstruction of a the sugar mill and replacement of equipment. Project goal: to increase output of white sugar produced of sugar beet.	1) Annual processing of up to 300,000 tons of sugar beet and up to 100,000 tons of raw sugar 2) $7.6 million/3 years 3) L ($4.7 million) 4) BP

ZAO Romodanovsakhar
1, ul. Sakharnikov, Romodanovo, Romodanovsky
District, Republic of Mordovia, 431601
Phone: (83438) 21 122, 23 743, 21 442
Fax: (83438) 23 444
E-mail: romsugar@moris.ru
Gennady Valentinovich Mitronin, CEO

45R012

Reconstruction of athe cheese workshop. Project goal: to diversify cheese product mix and improve its quality.	1) Output of 2,000 tons per year 2) $1.2 million/5 months 3) L 4) BP

OAO Cheese Complex Ichalkovsky
2, ul. Mira, Ichalki, Ichalkovsky District,
Republic of Mordovia, 431655
Phone: (83433) 21 573
Fax: (83433) 21 673
E-mail: sircom@moris.ru
Nikolai Vasilyevich Kireev, CEO

46. REPUBLIC OF TATARSTAN [16]

ECONOMIC MAP

KIROV REGION

REPUBLIC OF UDMURTIA

REPUBLIC OF MARIY EL

YOSHKAR-OLA

IZHEVSK

Vyatka

Kama

Novocheboksarsk

Zelenodolsk

KAZAN

Mendeleevsk

Yelabuga

Menzelinsk

Naberezhnye Chelny

Sviyaga

Nizhnekamsk

Chistopol

Zay

Buinsk

Almetyevsk

Tuymazy

Bugulma

Kuybyshevskoe water reservoir

Dimitrovgrad

Bayly

ULYANOVSK

ULYANOVSK REGION

REGION

SAMARA REGION

Sok

Togliatti

Bolshaya Kinel

Buguruslan

Oktyabrsk

Syzran

SAMARA

ORENBURG REGION

Samara

PROCESSING INDUSTRY

- Machine engineering and metal processing
- Chemicals and petrochemicals
- Forestry and timber
- Construction materials
- Food and beverages

MINING INDUSTRY

- ▲ Oil

POWER PLANTS

- Thermal power plants
- Hydro power plants

- Resorts

CROPS AND LIVESTOCK BREEDING

- Wheat
- Rye
- Barley
- Rape
- Orchards
- Vegetables
- Potatoes
- Sugar beetroot
- Meat and dairy cattle breeding
- Pig breeding
- Beekeeping
- Poultry farming

The Republic of Tatarstan is conducting a consistent policy of encouraging investment in the Republic. Over the past six years, the Republic has figured among the top ten regions of Russia in terms of investment appeal thanks to positive economic and political processes in the Republic, its favorable geographical location, raw materials, large industrial sector, scientific and human resources potential, developed transport infrastructure, and other positive factors impacting the investment climate.

The Republic registered more than $1.8 billion in capital investment in 2002, most of which was invested in industry, housing and communal services, transport, communications, and construction. A significant proportion of investment went to the fuel industry, chemicals and petrochemicals, machine engineering, and the food industry. The main source of investment financing continues to be companies' own resources (profit and depreciation deductions), which account for 57% of the total.

Positive processes are underway as regards the raising of foreign investment. Joint stock companies Tatneft, Krasny Vostok, KamAZ, Nizhnekamskneftekhim, and various joint ventures, are actively working with foreign investors. Oil is extracted in Tatarstan by joint ventures such as Tatoilpetro (France-Russia), Tatoilgaz (Russia-Germany), Tatech (Russia-USA), and Ideloil (Russia-UK). Swiss investors are financing the development of beer brewing at OAO Krasny Vostok, which over the past few years has managed to increase its output several times over to become one of the largest beer breweries in Europe.

The Republic has accorded priority status to creating a legislative base regulating investment activity, and is working on bringing the Republic's statutory acts into compliance with federal law and on creating a legislative framework for the various exemptions and guarantees offered to investors by the Republic.

We are ready to engage in fruitful and mutually beneficial cooperation with all investors, be they Russian or foreign. We welcome you to our hospitable land of Tatarstan!

Mintimer Shaimiyev,
PRESIDENT OF THE REPUBLIC OF TATARSTAN

IV

VOLGA FEDERAL DISTRICT

1. GENERAL INFORMATION

1.1. GEOGRAPHY

Situated in the heartland of the Russian Federation on the East European Plain, the Republic of Tatarstan covers an area of 67,800 square kilometers. To the south, the Republic borders the Ulyanovsk, Samara, and Orenburg Regions, to the north – the Kirov Region, the Republic of Mariy-El, and the Republic of Udmurtia, to the east – the Republic of Bashkortostan, and to the west – the Republic of Chuvashia.

1.2. CLIMATE

The Republic of Tatarstan is located within the temperate continental climate zone. January air temperatures average –14°C, rising to +19°C in July. Annual precipitation averages 490 mm.

1.3. POPULATION

According to preliminary 2002 census results, the Republic of Tatarstan's total population stood at 3.780 million people. The average population density is 55.8 people per square kilometer. The economically active population amounts to 1,877,000 people. As of 2001, the official unemployment rate was 5.3%.

Demographically speaking, some 59.5% are of statutory working age, 20.5% are below the statutory working age, and 20% are beyond the statutory working age.

The Republic's ethnic mix is 48.5% Tatar, 43.3% Russian, and 3.7% Chuvash. The Republic of Tatarstan's major urban centers (2002 data) are Kazan with 1,105,300 inhabitants, Naberezhniye Chelny with 510,000 inhabitants, Nizhnekamsk with 225,500 inhabitants, and Almetyevsk with 140,500 inhabitants.

Population								TABLE 1
	1992	1997	1998	1999	2000	2001	2002	
Total population, '000	3,700	3,770	3,778	3,784	3,782	3,777	3,780	
Economically active population, '000	1,907	1,739	1,748	1,813	1,845	1,823	1,877	

2. ADMINISTRATION

President: The Kremlin, Kazan, Republic of Tatarstan, 420014
Cabinet of Ministers: 1, pl. Svobody, Kazan, Republic of Tatarstan, 420060
http://www.tatar.ru

NAME	POSITION	CONTACT INFORMATION
Mintimer Sharipovich SHAIMIYEV	President of the Republic of Tatarstan	Phone: (8432) 91 7901 http://www.tatar.ru/president
Rustam Nurgalievich MINNIKHANOV	Prime Minister of the Republic of Tatarstan	Phone: (8432) 64 7701
Ravil Fatykhovich MURATOV	First Deputy Prime Minister of the Republic of Tatarstan	Phone: (8432) 64 7733
Alexei Mikhailovich PAKHOMOV	Deputy Prime Minister of the Republic of Tatarstan, Minister of Economy and Industry	Phone: (8432) 64 4623 Fax: (8432) 64 4633 E-mail: econom@meprt.ru
Marat Gotovich AKHMETOV	Deputy Prime Minister of the Republic of Tatarstan, Minister of Agriculture and Food	Phone: (8432) 92 0382 Fax: (8432) 92 0538 E-mail: crop@bancorp.ru, mshp@kabmin.tatarstan.ru
Vladimir Alexandrovich SHVETSOV	Deputy Prime Minister of the Republic of Tatarstan, Minister of Transport and Roads	Phone: (8432) 91 9010 Fax: (8432) 91 9008
Timur Yuryevich AKULOV	State Councellor to the President of the Republic of Tatarstan for Foreign Relations	Phone: (8432) 91 7726

3. ECONOMIC POTENTIAL

3.1. 1997–2002 GROSS REGIONAL PRODUCT (GRP). INDUSTRY BREAKDOWN

The Republic of Tatarstan's 2002 gross regional product was $7,919.1 million, 4.7% up on 2001. Per capita GRP totaled $2,003 in 2001, and $2,094 in 2002.

3.2. MAJOR ECONOMIC GROWTH PROJECTIONS

The Republic of Tatarstan's main social and economic development priorities for the period 2002–2006 are as follows:

To support production of commodities for sale on the global markets (oil production, oil refining, chemicals, aircraft, automotive, instruments, and timber).

To focus on potential growth centers: Chemicals and petrochemicals; Light industry; Food and beverages; Furniture; and Construction materials.

3.3. INDUSTRIAL OUTPUT IN 1997–2002 FOR MAJOR SECTORS OF ECONOMY

Fuel (oil). The oil sector accounts for 33.8% of total industrial output. Its major products are oil,

GRP trends in 1997–2002						*TABLE 2*
	1997	1998	1999	2000	2001	2002*
GRP in current prices, $ million	11,163.9	7,190.3	4,748.9	7,207.1	7,563.5	7,919.1

*Estimates of the Cabinet of Ministers of the Republic of Tatarstan

GRP industry breakdown in 1997–2002, % of total						*TABLE 3*
	1997	1998	1999	2000	2001	2002*
GRP	100.0	100.0	100.0	100.0	100.0	100.0
Industry	35.2	42.6	44.3	50.5	44.5	44.7
Agriculture and forestry	6.9	3.6	7.7	7.2	9.4	9.1
Construction	9.6	8.9	8.6	8.7	12.2	11.8
Transport and communications	7.5	8.7	6.7	4.7	5.9	5.0
Trade and public catering	8.1	8.2	13.0	9.3	11.5	14.1
Other	19.5	20.6	12.2	11.0	14.2	15.3
Net taxes on output	13.2	7.4	7.5	8.6	2.3	–

*Estimates of the Cabinet of Ministers of the Republic of Tatarstan

Industry breakdown of industrial output in 1997–2002, % of total						*TABLE 4*
	1997	1998	1999	2000	2001	2002*
Industry	100.0	100.0	100.0	100.0	100.0	100.0
Fuel (oil)	22.7	27.7	33.8	41.9	35.6	33.8
Machine engineering and metal processing	18.5	15.0	19.4	19.7	24.3	23.5
Chemicals and petrochemicals	25.4	23.9	22.0	19.6	18.3	19.2
Food and beverages	9.7	10.0	9.5	7.0	8.5	9.3
Energy	11.2	12.2	7.1	5.3	6.3	7.4
Construction materials	3.2	3.0	1.9	1.7	1.9	2.2
Forestry, timber, and pulp and paper	1.7	1.7	1.9	1.4	1.5	1.6
Flour, cereals, and mixed fodder	3.1	2.9	1.6	1.4	1.3	0.8
Light industry	1.7	1.5	1.2	0.9	0.9	0.9
Ferrous metals	0.6	0.4	0.2	0.2	0.3	0.2

*Estimates of the Cabinet of Ministers of the Republic of Tatarstan

Fuel and energy sector production and consumption trends, 1997–2002						*TABLE 5*
	1997	1998	1999	2000	2001	2002
Electricity output, billion kWh	22.3	20.9	22.0	23.2	22.9	22.9
Oil output (including gas condensate), '000 tons	25,556.0	25,833.0	26,342.0	27,295.0	28,274.0	28,760.0
Natural gas output, million cubic meters	764.0	736.0	742.0	757.0	760.0	718.1
Energy consumption, billion kWh	22.8	22.0	22.6	23.4	23.5	23.3
Natural gas consumtion, million cubic meters	13,315.0	10,315.9	11,996.6	12,476.9	12,443.3	12,468.9

petroleum gas, heavy fuel oil, and diesel fuel. Some 26 oil companies, with OAO Tatneft the largest, operate in the Republic of Tatarstan. 2002 oil production in the Republic totaled 28.8 million tons. The Republic's oil refineries produced more than 62,000 tons of motor gasoline, 1,135,000 tons of diesel fuel, and 2,703 tons of heavy fuel oil.

Machine engineering and metal processing. Major machine engineering sectors include aircraft and automotive manufacturing. The sector's output ranges from compressor, evacuating, and refrigerating equipment to equipment for fuel and petrochemicals enterprises, shipbuilding and ship repairs, communal services, hygiene, lifting and haulage equipment, forestry equipment, construction equipment, and car and tractor repair equipment.

The automotive sector's largest manufacturers are OAO Kama Automotive Plant (KamAZ) and OAO Small Car Factory. The largest aircraft producers are OAO Kazan Helicopter Plant and Kazan Gorbunov Aircraft Plant (Tupolev).

Chemicals and petrochemicals. The sector's largest industries are synthetic resins and plastics, polyethylene, synthetic rubber and tires, plastic foil, sheet and pipes, rubber footwear, pharmaceuticals, and industrial carbon.

The sector's key manufacturers are OAO Nizhnekamsk Petrochemicals, OAO Nizhnekamsk Industrial Carbon, OAO Nizhnekamsk Tire, OAO Kazan Synthetic Rubber, and OAO Nefis Cosmetics. A deep processing (84%) sour crude refining facility is under construction in Nizhnekamsk. Installation work began in March 2000 on a middle distillate hydrotreating plant. The plant will yield around 1.2 million tons of high quality diesel fuel and 400,000 tons of aviation kerosene annually.

OAO Kazanorgsintez is one of Russia's top producers of plastics, plastic pipes for gas pipelines, synthetic refrigerating fluids, and chemical agents for oil recovery and natural gas dehydration.

Agroindustrial sector. Agricultural lands cover some 4.5 million hectares of the Republic of Tatarstan. Some 3.6 million hectares are arable lands.

Major crops include grain, potato, vegetables, and sugar beet. The Republic also hosts seed-cultivation farms and enterprises focused on the production of grain, perennial grasses, potato, sugar beet, and

fodder beet. The Republic of Tatarstan produces over 50% of Russia's total rape seed stock output.

Livestock is raised for milk, beef, and pork, and poultry for meat. Beef accounts for 51.3%, pork for 26.2%, and poultry meat for 17.4% of total meat output.

3.4. FUEL AND ENERGY BALANCE (OUTPUT AND CONSUMPTION PER RESOURCE)
The Republic's energy sector fully meets the Republic's electricity needs.

3.5. TRANSPORT INFRASTRUCTURE
Roads. The Republic has 12,600 kilometers of paved public highway. The Moscow – Nizhny Novgorod – Kazan – Ufa, Kazan – Ulyanovsk, and Kazan – Orenburg federal highways serve the Republic.

Railroads. The Republic is served by the Moscow – Kazan – Yekaterinburg, Kazan – Volgograd, and Naberezhnye Chelny – Bugulma railroads.

Airports. The Republic of Tatarstan has six airports, two of which, the Kazan Airport and the Begishevo Airport, have federal status. In 2002, the Kazan International Airport opened its second runway. In 2002, local airlines carried some 684,200 passengers for 874.6 million passenger-kilometers. Freight turnover reached 5.2 million ton-kilometers.

River transport. Passenger traffic in 2002 amounted to 12,443,000 people, or 34.1 million passenger-kilometers. Freight traffic ran to 5.7 million tons, or 11.4 million ton-kilometers.

The rivers Volga, Kama, and Vyatka are used as navigable transportation waterways. In January 2003, the Republic of Tatarstan had 342 handling units and vessels with a total carrying capacity of 190,000 tons.

River ports. The Republic operates river passenger stations at Kazan, Chistopol, Nizhnekamsk, and the district centers of Tetyushi and Bolgary. The bulk of traffic is transported via the rivers Volga and Kama.

Oil and gas pipelines. Gas pipelines running from the Urengoi and Yamburg gas fields to Western Europe cross the Republic. The total length of its oil pipelines is 2,000 kilometers.

Plans are afoot to rehabilitate the Nizhnekamsk – Almetyevsk – Nizhny Novgorod oil product pipeline and build an Andreyevka – Almetyevsk pipeline with a view to boosting traffic and improving safety standards.

3.6. MAIN NATURAL RESOURCES: RESERVES AND EXTRACTION IN 2002

The principal natural resources of the Republic of Tatarstan are oil and gas. The Republic boasts commercial reserves of limestone, dolomite, mortar sand, brick clay, building stone, gypsum, sand-gravel mix, and peat. Geological reserves of petroleum bitumen, lignite, coal, oil shale, zeolite, copper, and bauxite have been documented.

Oil. Recoverable oil reserves are estimated at 800 million tons. Each ton of oil produced is accompanied by 40 cubic meters of petroleum gas.

4. TRADE OPPORTUNITIES

4.1. MAIN GOODS PRODUCED IN THE REGION

The Republic of Tatarstan produced the following key industrial products in 2002:

Fuel and energy. Electricity – 22.9 billion kWh; oil output, including gas condensate – 28.8 million tons.

Chemicals and petrochemicals. Synthetic resin and plastics – 400,800 tons; polyethylene – 392,100 tons; synthetic rubber – 227,800 tons; tires – 9.8 million.

Automotive. Trucks – 20,200; cars – 38,700.

Machine engineering and metals. Household refrigerators and freezers – 199,300.

Timber, pulp and paper. Plywood – 89,300 cubic meters; paper – 44,000 tons; cardboard – 108,200 tons.

4.2. EXPORTS, INCLUDING EXTRA-CIS

Exports to extra-CIS countries in 2000 amounted to $2,807.4 million; exports to CIS countries totaled $182.8 million. The figures for 2001 were $2,476.2 million and $350.6 million, respectively, and $2,595.6 million and $616.6 million for 2002. The main goods exported from the Republic in 2001 included crude oil (11.7 mil- lion tons), oil products (1,384,100 tons), synthetic rubber (105,900 tons), machinery and equipment ($301.2 million), and cyclic hydrocarbons (214,800 tons). Tatarstan's chief export destinations include Switzerland, Ukraine, Finland, and Germany.

4.3. IMPORTS, INCLUDING EXTRA-CIS

Imports from extra-CIS countries in 2000 amounted to $284 million, while imports from CIS countries totaled $115.1 million. The corresponding figures for 2001 were $269 million and $77.8 million, and $212.7 million and $57.6 million for 2002.

The main goods imported by the Republic in 2001 included machinery, equipment, tools, and transportation vehicles. The Republic's main trading partners for imports are Germany, Ukraine, Uzbekistan, and the Netherlands.

Major regional export and import entities		*TABLE 6*
ENTITY	ADDRESS	PHONE, FAX, E-MAIL
Ministry of Trade and Foreign Economic Cooperation of the Republic of Tatarstan	4, ul. Ostrovskogo, Kazan, Republic of Tatarstan, 420111	Phone: (8432) 92 5082 Fax: (8432) 92 1645 E-mail: http://www.tatarmintorg.ru
Department of Foreign Relations of the President of the Republic of Tatarstan	The Kremlin, Kazan, Republic of Tatarstan, 420014	Phone: (8432) 92 1949 Fax: (8432) 92 0092, 92 0810 E-mail: secretariat@tatar.ru http://www.tatar.ru
Committee for Foreign Economic Relations of the Ministry of Trade and Foreign Economic Cooperation of the Republic of Tatarstan	2a, ul. Kremlyovskaya, Kazan, Republic of Tatarstan, 420014	Phone: (8432) 92 8196, 92 6121 Fax: (8432) 92 9672 E-mail: kvs@bancorp.ru
International Cooperation Development Agency Attached to the Cabinet of Ministers of the Republic of Tatarstan	17, ul. Kremlyovskaya, Kazan, Republic of Tatarstan, 420503	Phone: (8432) 92 7902 Fax: (8432) 92 8776 E-mail: agency@bancorp.ru
Chamber of Commerce and Industry of the Republic of Tatarstan	18, ul. Pushkina, Kazan, Republic of Tatarstan, 420503	Phone: (8432) 64 6207 Fax: (8432) 36 0966 E-mail: tpp@radiotelcom.ru

IV

VOLGA FEDERAL DISTRICT

5. INVESTMENT OPPORTUNITIES

**5.1 INVESTMENTS IN 1992–2002
(BY INDUSTRY SECTOR),
INCLUDING FOREIGN INVESTMENTS**
The following key factors determine the investment appeal of the Republic:
  • Good geographic location;
  • Raw materials and minerals;

  • Developed transport infrastructure;
  • Significant industrial potential and good scientific and research potential of the workforce;
  • Legislation supporting investment activities.
5.2. CAPITAL INVESTMENT
Industry accounts for the lion's share (47.2%) of capital investment.

Capital investment by industry sector, $ million						*TABLE 7*
	1997	1998	1999	2000	2001	2002
Total capital investment	2,442.0	1,268.2	827.3	1,589.6	1,964.6	1,816.4
Including major industries (% of total):						
Industry	37.8	37.5	47.0	49.2	48.5	47.2
Agriculture and forestry	5.8	4.5	4.1	4.2	4.6	3.7
Construction	3.4	2.4	1.9	6.5	6.2	4.6
Transport and communications	11.9	6.9	10.0	18.4	10.0	16.5
Trade and public catering	0.8	8.9	1.5	0.6	1.1	1.8
Other	40.3	39.8	35.5	21.1	29.6	26.2

Foreign investment trends in 1997–2002						*TABLE 8*
	1997	1998	1999	2000	2001	2002
Foreign investment, $ million	702.4	683.8	23.0	142.9	650.9	642.5
Including FDI, $ million	21.5	3.4	4.3	53.6	5.5	2.5

Largest enterprises of the Republic of Tatarstan			*TABLE 9*
COMPANY	SECTOR	2002 SALES, $ MILLION*	2002 NET PROFIT, $ MILLION*
OAO Tatneft	Oil	3,444.9	481.2
OAO Nizhnekamsk Petrochemicals	Chemicals and petrochemicals	659.7	79.7
KamAZ	Machine engineering	554.5	35.1
Tatenergo Energy Production Association of the Republic of Tatarstan	Energy	344.2	66.9
OAO Organic Synthesis	Chemicals and petrochemicals	226.3	28.7
OAO North-Western Oil-Trunk Pipelines	Transport	219.9	54.2
OOO Tattransgaz	Transport	188.0	31.9
OAO Krasny Vostok	Food and beverages	149.8	9.6
OAO Almetyevsk Pump Plant	Machine engineering	70.1	9.6
ZAO Naberezhniye Chelny Cardboard and Paper Plant	Timber	60.5	15.9
Gorbunov Kazan Aircraft Plant	Machine engineering	41.4	6.4
OAO Chelny Oil Products	Oil	31.9	6.4
ZAO Tatoilgaz	Oil	28.7	6.4
OAO Kamdorstroy	Construction	28.7	6.4

*Data of the Cabinet of Ministers of the Republic of Tatarstan

5.3. MAJOR ENTERPRISES (INCLUDING ENTERPRISES WITH FOREIGN INVESTMENT)

As of January 1, 2002, the Republic of Tatarstan hosted over 297 enterprises with foreign investment.

5.4. MOST ATTRACTIVE SECTORS FOR INVESTMENT

According to experts and the Cabinet of Ministers of the Republic of Tatarstan, the Republic's oil refining, chemicals and petrochemicals, chemical fertilizers, transport, telecommunications, and machine engineering sectors offer the greatest investment appeal.

5.5. CURRENT LEGISLATION ON INVESTOR TAX EXEMPTIONS AND PRIVILEGES

The following legislation regulates investment in the Republic:

The Law of the Republic of Tatarstan On Investment Activity in the Republic of Tatarstan;

The Law of the Republic of Tatarstan On Foreign Investment in the Republic of Tatarstan;

The Law of the Republic of Tatarstan On the Alabuga Free Economic Zone;

Decree of the Cabinet of Ministers of the Republic of Tatarstan On the Approval of the Regulations on the Procedure for the Provision of State Support to Enterprises and Organizations Involved in Investment Projects in the Republic of Tatarstan;

Decree of the Cabinet of Ministers of the Republic of Tatarstan On Additional Measures of State Support to Enterprises (Organizations) of the Republic of Tatarstan Involved in Investment Projects;

Decree of the Cabinet of Ministers of the Republic of Tatarstan On the Approval of the Procedure for the Provision of Subsidies from the Budget of the Republic of Tatarstan to Enterprises Raising Bank Loans for the Implementation of Investment Projects in Priority Sectors of the Economy;

Decree of the Cabinet of Ministers of the Republic of Tatarstan On State Incentives to Investment Activity of Enterprises in the Republic of Tatarstan.

Pursuant to the Decree of the Cabinet of Ministers of the Republic of Tatarstan On State Incentives to Investment Activity of Enterprises in the Republic of Tatarstan, state support in the form of targeted subsidies for a portion of the coupon yield on bond financing is available to enterprises implementing priority investment projects.

5.6. FEDERAL AND REGIONAL ECONOMIC AND SOCIAL DEVELOPMENT PROGRAMS FOR THE REPUBLIC OF TATARSTAN

Federal targeted programs: The Program for Social and Economic Development of the Republic of Tatarstan through 2006 plays a major role in the Republic's social and economic development. The program is focused on the sustainable development of the economy and reform of the social sector in the Republic of Tatarstan.

Regional entities responsible for raising investment			*TABLE 10*
ENTITY	ADDRESS	PHONE, FAX, E-MAIL
Ministry of Economy and Industry of the Republic of Tatarstan	55, ul. Kirova, Kazan, Republic of Tatarstan, 420021	Phone: (8432) 64 4623 Fax: (8432) 64 4593 E-mail: econom@meprt.ru
Ministry of Trade and Foreign Economic Cooperation of the Republic of Tatarstan	4, ul. Ostrovskogo, Kazan, Republic of Tatarstan, 420111	Phone: (8432) 92 5082 Fax: (8432) 92 1645 http://www.tatarmintorg.ru
Chamber of Commerce and Industry of the Republic of Tatarstan	18, ul. Pushkina, Kazan, Republic of Tatarstan, 420503	Phone: (8432) 64 6207 Fax: (8432) 36 0966 E-mail: tpp@radiotelcom.ru
International Cooperation Development Agency Attached to the Cabinet of Ministers of the Republic of Tatarstan	17, ul. Kremlyovskaya, Kazan, Republic of Tatarstan, 420503	Phone: (8432) 92 7902 Fax: (8432) 92 8776 E-mail: agency@bancorp.ru
Department of Small and Medium Enterprise Support and Development Attached to the Ministry of Trade and Foreign Economic Cooperation of the Republic of Tatarstan	55, ul. Kirova, Kazan, Republic of Tatarstan, 420021	Phone: (8432) 64 4512
Enterprise Development Agency of the Republic of Tatarstan	29b, ul. N. Ershova, Kazan, Republic of Tatarstan, 420045	Phone: (8432) 19 4665 Fax: (8432) 92 8776 E-mail: arprt@arprt.ru
Committee on Foreign Economic Relations of the Ministry of Trade and Foreign Economic Cooperation of the Republic of Tatarstan	2a, ul. Kremlyovskaya, Kazan, Republic of Tatarstan, 420014	Phone: (8432) 92 8196, 92 6121 Fax: (8432) 92 9672 E-mail: kvs@bancorp.ru

IV

VOLGA FEDERAL DISTRICT

Regional programs. Some 34 regional programs worth roughly $3,454.5 million are currently underway in the Republic of Tatarstan. Key regional programs include: The Program for Social and Economic Development of the Yelabuga District, 2002–2006, The Program for the Development of the Oil, Gas, Chemicals, and Petrochemicals Sectors of the Republic of Tatarstan, 1999–2003, The Program for the Encouragement of the Creation and Development of Export-Oriented and Import Replacement Production in the Republic of Tatarstan through 2003.

The following republican targeted programs are also underway in the Republic of Tatarstan: Energy Conservation in the Republic of Tatarstan, 2000–2005, Land Reform in the Republic of Tatarstan, 2000–2005, and The Commodity Market Regulation System of the Republic of Tatarstan, 1999–2005.

6. INVESTMENT PROJECTS

Industry sector and project description	1) Expected results 2) Amount and term of investment 3) Form of financing[1] 4) Documentation[2]	Contact information
1	2	3

CHEMICALS AND PETROCHEMICALS

46R001 ◆ ■		
Establishment of motor oil production using an oil company's facilities. Project goal: to introduce motor oils to the market.	1) Output of polyfine-olifine of 10,000 tons annually, annual motor oil output of 10,000 tons 2) $48.9 million/1 year 3) E 4) BP	OAO V.D. Shashin Tatneft 75, ul. Lenina, Almetyevsk, Republic of Tatarstan, 423450 Phone: (8553) 25 5856 Fax: (8553) 25 6865 E-mail: tnr@tatneft.ru Shafagat Fakhrazovich Takhautdinov, CEO
46R002 ● ◆		
Establishment of R-type car tire manufacturing at the facilities of an existing plant. Project goal: to diversify the product mix and improve product quality.	1) 2 million items per year 2) $64.5 million/2 years 3) L 4) BP	ZMSH OAO Nizhnekamsk Tire Promzona, Nizhnekamsk, Republic of Tatarstan, 423570 Phone: (8555) 37 2333, 34 8431 Fax: (8555) 34 0822 E-mail: marketing@shina-kama.ru http://www.shina-kama.ru; Radik Sabitovich Ilyasov, CEO
46R003 ● ◆		
Establishment of polyethylene production at the facilities of an existing plant. Project goal: to diversify product mix.	1) Output: 370,000 tons per year 2) $130 million/2 years 3) L 4) BP	OAO Kazanorgsintez 1, ul. Belomorskaya, Kazan, Republic of Tatarstan, 420051 Phone: (8432) 49 8990 Fax: (8432) 43 2223 Nayil Khabibovich Yusupov, CEO
46R004 ● ▲		
Establishment of polypropylene production at the facilities of an existing chemicals plant. Project goal: to increase earnings and to diversify the product mix (via deeper refining of own propylene output).	1) Output: 120,000 tons per year 2) $135 million/3 years 3) L 4) FS	OAO Nizhnekamsk Petrochemicals, Nizhnekamsk-2, Republic of Tatarstan, 423574 Phone: (8555) 37 7181 Fax: (8555) 37 9309 E-mail: nknh@nknh.ru Vladimir Mikhailovich Busygin, CEO

[1] L – Loan, E – Equity, Leas. – Leasing, JV – Joint Venture
[2] BP – Business Plan, FS – Feasibility Study

1	2	3

CHEMICALS AND PHARMACEUTICALS

46R005 ■ ● ★ ◆

Establishment of production
of ampoule intravenous solutions
at the facilities of an existing
pharmaceuticals plant.
Project goal: to increase output
and diversify the product mix.

1) Annual output of up to 30 million
   ampoules
2) $1.9 million/1 year
3) E, L, Leas.
4) BP

OAO Tatkhimfarmpreparaty
260, ul. Belomorskaya, Kazan,
Republic of Tatarstan, 420091
Phone: (8432) 71 8518, 49 9326
Fax: (8432) 71 8528, 49 9296
E-mail: talex_m@bancorp.ru
Rafik Khafizovich Gumerov,
CEO

MACHINE ENGINEERING AND METAL PROCESSING

46R006 ● ◆

Revamping of facilites for production
of 3-layer anti-corrosion coating.
Project goal: to ensure high level
of quality and competitiveness
of the pipes.

1) Annual revenues of $0.8 million
2) $456.7 million/7 months
3) L
4) BP

OAO Almetyevsk Pipes
11, Promzona, Almetyevsk,
Republic of Tatarstan, 423450
Phone: (8553) 25 9374, 25 9765
Fax: (8553) 25 9828, 25 9365
E-mail: atz@atz.ru
Alexander Mikhailovich Tokarev,
CEO

46R007 ● ◆

Production of the Tu 324 family
of aircraft.
Project goal: to introduce short-hop
high-speed aircraft to the market.

1) 2004 – 3 planes, 2005 – 5 planes,
   2006 – 8 planes, 2007 – 11 planes
2) $414.8 million/10 years
3) L
4) BP

GUP Kazan Gorbunov Aircraft Plant
1, ul. Dementyeva, Kazan,
Republic of Tatarstan, 420036
Phone: (8432) 71 3131
Fax: (8432) 71 9598
Nayil Gumerovich Khairullin,
GEO

GLASS AND PORCELAIN

46R008 ■ ◆

Renewal of fixed assets of an
existing chinaware plant.
Project goal: to increase output
and to improve product quality.

1) 15 million items per year
2) $20.5 million/30 months
3) E
4) BP

OAO Bugulma Chinaware
171, ul. Lenina, Bugulma,
Republic of Tatarstan, 423200
Phone: (85514) 47 070
Fax: (85514) 33 527
E-mail: farfor@tatais.ru;
Eldar Rashitovich Stalyakhov,
CEO

IV

VOLGA FEDERAL DISTRICT

47. REPUBLIC OF UDMURTIA [18]

ECONOMIC MAP

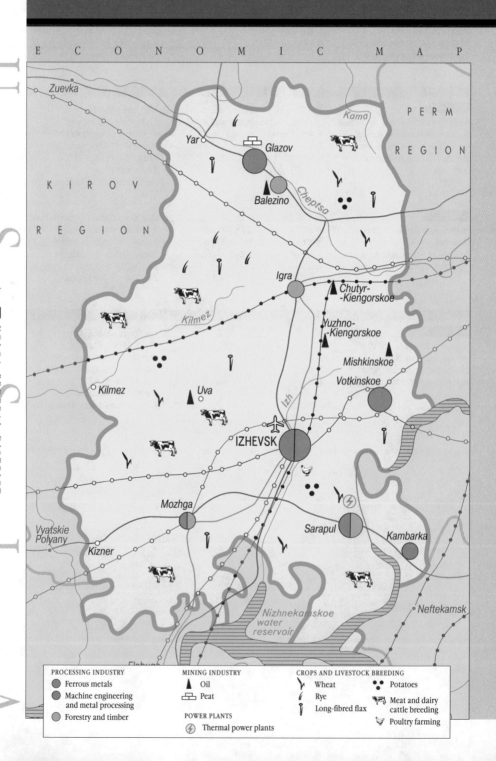

Zuevka

Kama

PERM

Yar
Glazov

REGION

KIROV

Balezino

Cheptsa

REGION

Igra
Chutyr-
-Kiengorskoe

Yuzhno-
-Kiengorskoe

Kilmez

Mishkinskoe

Votkinskoe

Kilmez

Uva

Izh

IZHEVSK

Mozhga

Sarapul
Kambarka

Vyatskie
Polyany

Kizner

*Nizhnekamskoe
water
reservoir*

Neftekamsk

PROCESSING INDUSTRY
- ● Ferrous metals
- ● Machine engineering and metal processing
- ● Forestry and timber

MINING INDUSTRY
- ▲ Oil
- ⛏ Peat

POWER PLANTS
- ⚡ Thermal power plants

CROPS AND LIVESTOCK BREEDING
- Wheat
- Rye
- Long-fibred flax
- Potatoes
- Meat and dairy cattle breeding
- Poultry farming

U dmurtia is situated in the east of the Russian Plains in the foothills of the European Urals between the Kama and Vyatka rivers. The Republic has a temperate continental climate characterized by cold snowy winters and warm summers. The Republic covers an area of more than 42,000 square km, making it bigger than European countries such as Belgium and Switzerland.

The Republic's economy is multifaceted. Its leading sectors are machine engineering, metals processing, metals, oil, forestry and timber, and cattle breeding, all of which offer strong potential for mutually beneficial cooperation.

Our Republic contributes a great deal into the industrial potential of the Russian Federation. A.F. Deryabin, the founder of the Izhevsk Arms Plant, and rifle designers M.T. Kalashnikov, E.F. Dragunov, and G.N. Nikonov have made major contributions to the development of Russia's gun industry, which is famous worldwide. The plants at Izhevsk, Votkinsk, Glazov, and Sarapul preserve this fame; their experience in weaponry enables them to produce high quality and reliable goods to world standards.

Udmurtia also makes a considerable contribution to Russia's multicultural make-up. Votkinsk, the birthplace of Petr Tchaikovsky, is home to the Tchaikovsky state museum, which hosts an annual music festival to mark the anniversary of the composer's birth. The works of Udmurtian writers such as Grigory Vereschagin, Kuzebai Gerd, and others, are internationally acknowledged. Udmurtia also counts such Olympic champions as Galina Kulakova, Tamara Tikhonova, Valery Medvedtsev, and Alexei Chizhov.

Udmurtia's diverse population preserves and enriches traditions of its ancestors – industrialists, merchants, craftsmen, and patrons of the arts. The Republic's rich natural, industrial, scientific, and cultural potential and developed infrastructure provide strong opportunities for the development of business and tourism.

Alexander Volkov,
PRESIDENT OF THE REPUBLIC OF UDMURTIA

504

1. GENERAL INFORMATION

1.1. GEOGRAPHY

The Republic of Udmurtia covers a total area of 42,100 square kilometers. The Republic is situated at the foot of the Urals between the Kama and the Vyatka rivers. To the west and north, the Republic borders the Kirov Region, to the east – the Perm Region, and to the south – the Republics of Bashkortostan and Tatarstan.

1.2. CLIMATE

The Republic of Udmurtia enjoys a temperate continental climate. The average air temperature in January is −9.9°C, rising to +20.9°C in July. Average annual precipitation reaches 450–600 mm. Turf and podzol soils prevail in the Republic.

1.3. POPULATION

According to preliminary 2002 census results, total population in the Republic was 1,571,000 people. The average population density is 37.3 people per square kilometer. The economically active population amounts to 842,000 people. While 2002 official unemployment level stood at 1.7%, the actual rate is 7.5%.

Demographically speaking, some 62.1% are of working age, 20.2% are below the statutory working age, and 17.7% are beyond the statutory working age. The Republic's ethnic mix is 58.9% Russian, 30.9% Udmurt, 6.9% Tatar, and 3.3% other ethnic groups.

As of 2002, the Republic of Udmurtia's major urban centers were Izhevsk with 632,100 inhabitants, Sarapul with 103,200 inhabitants, Glazov with 100,900 inhabitants, and Votkinsk with 101,700 inhabitants.

Population							TABLE 1
	1992	1997	1998	1999	2000	2001	2002
Total population, '000	1,634	1,633	1,633	1,633	1,629	1,624	1,571
Economically active population, '000	852	799	792	824	820	809	842

2. ADMINISTRATION

214, ul. Pushkinskaya, Izhevsk, Republic of Udmurtia, 426007
Phone: (3412) 49 7010, fax: (3412) 49 7200
E-mail: gov@udmillionet.ru; http://www.udmurt.ru

NAME	POSITION	CONTACT INFORMATION
Alexander Alexandrovich VOLKOV	President of the Republic of Udmurtia	Phone: (3412) 49 7010 Fax: (3412) 49 7200 E-mail: gov@udmillionet.ru
Yury Stepanovich PITKEVICH	Chairman of the Government of the Republic of Udmurtia	Phone: (3412) 49 7011 Fax: (3412) 49 7200 E-mail: gov@udmillionet.ru
Vladimir Vasilyevich BELTYUKOV	Deputy Chairman of the Government of the Republic of Udmurtia, Minister of Finance	Phone: (3412) 52 5251 Fax: (3412) 78 1550 E-mail: public@minfin.udm.ru
Sergei Pavlovich KASIKHIN	Deputy Chairman of the Government of the Republic of Udmurtia, Minister of Property	Phone/fax: (3412) 49 7033, 25 9061 E-mail: postmaster@gki.udm.ru postmaster@mio.udm.ru
Valery Valentinovich BOGATYREV	Acting Minister of Economy of the Republic of Udmurtia	Phone: (3412) 25 4639 Fax: (3412) 25 0030 E-mail: postmaster@econom.udm.ru econom@udmillionet.ru
Viktor Konstantinovich PRESNUKHIN	Minister of Fuel, Energy, and Communications of the Republic of Udmurtia	Phone: (3412) 25 9088 Fax: (3412) 52 5315
Andrei Anatolyevich ARMYANINOV	Minister of Industry and Transport of the Republic of Udmurtia	Phone: (3412) 51 4353 Fax: (3412) 51 4212 E-mail: postmaster@minprom.udm.ru

NAME	POSITION	CONTACT INFORMATION
Nikolai Ivanovich SOBIN	Minister of Agriculture and Food of the Republic of Udmurtia	Phone: (3412) 78 7675, 78 6377 Fax: (3412) 78 7773 E-mail: msx@msx.udmillionet.ru http://www.msx.udmillionet.ru
Valery Fedorovich ZAGAINOV	Minister of Construction, Architecture, and Housing Policy of the Republic of Udmurtia	Phone: (3412) 59 8852 Fax: (3412) 59 8797
Viktor Arkadyevich VIKULOV	Minister of International Relations of the Republic of Udmurtia	Phone: (3412) 25 9120 Fax: (3412) 78 4997 E-mail: mir@interlink.udm.ru http://mir.udmweb.ru

3. ECONOMIC POTENTIAL

3.1. 1997–2002 GROSS REGIONAL PRODUCT (GRP). INDUSTRY BREAKDOWN

The 2002 gross regional product amounted to $2,433.3 million, which constitutes 8% growth year-on-year. Per capita GRP amounted to $1,388 in 2001, rising to $1,549 in 2002.

3.2. MAJOR ECONOMIC GROWTH PROJECTIONS

The blueprint for economic development in the Republic of Udmurtia is set forth in the Program for Social and Economic Development of the Region 2001–2004. According to the Program, the 2003 gross

GRP trends in 1997–2002						*TABLE 2*
	1997	1998	1999	2000	2001*	2002*
GRP in current prices, $ million	3,418.0	2,022.3	1,499.4	1,982.4	2,252.5	2,433.3

*Estimates of the Udmurtia Republican Government

GRP industry breakdown in 1997–2002, % of total						*TABLE 3*
	1997	1998	1999	2000	2001*	2002*
GRP	100.0	100.0	100.0	100.0	100.0	100.0
Industry	39.0	37.1	46.1	52.1	44.7	44.1
Agriculture and forestry	8.1	8.9	13.0	8.7	11.0	10.0
Construction	7.0	5.9	4.2	4.8	7.3	7.1
Transport and communications	7.8	7.4	5.3	4.7	4.8	5.1
Trade and public catering	12.0	13.3	11.1	11.5	12.1	13.0
Other	22.4	22.2	13.9	13.8	14.0	14.4
Net taxes on output	3.7	5.2	6.4	4.4	6.1	6.3

*Estimates of the Udmurtia Republican Government

regional product is expected to grow by 0.9% in real terms year-on-year to reach $2,740.3 million. Machine engineering and metals processing output will amount to $912.4 million, fuel – $509.7 million, energy – $213.9 million, and ferrous metals – $110.1 million.

3.3. INDUSTRIAL OUTPUT IN 1997–2002 FOR MAJOR SECTORS OF ECONOMY

2002 industrial output was 16.2% higher than in 2001. The growth was driven mainly by the industry, energy, and machine engineering sectors.

Machine engineering and metal processing. The sector accounts for 35.5% of total 2002 indus-

trial output. The leading sub-sectors are vehicle engineering and machinery products for the fuel and energy sectors.

The largest companies within the sector are OAO Izhmash, OAO Izh-Auto, OAO NITI Progress, OAO Izhevsk Motor Plant Axion Holding, OAO Izhevsk Bearing Plant, OAO Izhevsk Radio Plant, OAO Sarapul Radio Plant Holding, State Company Kambarsky Machine Engineering Plant, and OAO Elekond.

Major producers of oil and gas equipment are OAO Izhneftemash, Federal State Unitary Company Votkin Plant, OAO Sarapul Electric Generator Plant, Federal State Unitary Company Izhevsk Mechanical

Industry breakdown of industrial output in 1997–2002, % of total						TABLE 4
	1997	1998	1999	2000	2001	2002*
Industry	100.0	100.0	100.0	100.0	100.0	100.0
Machine engineering and metal processing	30.0	38.5	37.3	44.2	35.6	35.5
Fuel	17.7	16.5	23.9	21.9	24.5	27.4
Energy	14.2	14.3	7.5	6.1	7.7	8.7
Ferrous metals	6.6	5.8	4.4	5.1	5.5	4.2
Forestry, timber, and pulp and paper	3.9	3.0	3.0	2.5	3.0	2.8
Construction materials	2.6	3.3	2.1	2.1	2.9	2.2
Light industry	0.6	0.6	0.8	0.8	0.8	0.7

*Estimates of the Government of the Republic of Udmurtia

Fuel and energy sector production and consumption trends, 1997–2002						TABLE 5
	1997	1998	1999	2000	2001	2002*
Electricity output, billion kWh	3.0	2.6	2.8	2.6	2.7	2.7
Oil output (including gas concentrate), '000 tons	8,077.0	7,937.0	7,718.0	7,680.0	7,870.0	7,789.0
Natural gas extraction, million cubic meters	62.0	62.0	60.0	58.0	54.0	54.0
Electricity consumption, billion kWh	4.3	4.2	4.0	4.4	4.7	7.4
Oil consumption, '000 tons	126.0	118.0	316.0	102.0	87.0	48.5
Natural gas consumption, million cubic meters	2,692.0	2,362.0	2,635.0	2,669.0	2,731.0	2,720.1

*Estimates of the Government of the Republic of Udmurtia

Plant, OAO Izhevsk Electric Mechanical Plant Kupol, OAO Bummash, OAO Sarapul Machine Engineering Plant, and OAO Pressure Regulator.

Federal State Unitary Company Izhevsk Mechanical Plant and OAO Izhevsk Arms Plant are the main producers of sporting and hunting rifles in Russia.

Ferrous metals. The sector accounts for 4.2% of total output. The main company within the sector is OAO Izhstal, which produces graded rolled steel, passed steel, wire, polished carbon toll steel, strip, high precision steel profiles, forges, and castings.

Agriculture. Arable lands cover a total area of 1,816,000 hectares. The Republic grows fodder grain, potatoes, vegetables, and long flax. Cattle farming accounts for 57% of total agricultural output.

3.4. FUEL AND ENERGY BALANCE (OUTPUT AND CONSUMPTION PER RESOURCE)

2002 oil output reached 7,789,000 tons. Plans are afoot to increase the oil output to 7,950,000 tons in 2003. The Republic exports 96% of its oil output. Two major oil companies are OAO Udmurtneft and OAO Belkamneft, which jointly account for some 90% of total oil extraction in the Republic.

The energy sector is represented by OAO Udmurtenergo – an automated interconnected set of three thermal power plants (the Izhevskaya TPS 1, Izhevskaya TPS 2, and Sarapulskaya TPS), an electricity grid, and the Glazovskaya TPS 1.

Local power stations satisfy 37% of the Republic's demand for electricity, with the remaining 63% supplied from the federal wholesale electricity market (FOREM). Locally produced electricity is consumed mainly by industrial enterprises.

3.5. TRANSPORT INFRASTRUCTURE

Currently, 67% of freight is transported by road, 27% – by railroad, and 6% – by water transport.

Roads. The Republic of Udmurtia has 5,700 kilometers of roads. In 2002, 23.9 million tons of freight were transported by road, 18% down on the previous year. Freight turnover fell by 11%, or 800 million ton-kilometers.

Railroads. The Republic of Udmurtia has 768.1 kilometers of railroads. The main electrified routes are Kazan – Agryz – Yekaterinburg, Kirov – Balezino – Perm, and Balezino – Izhevsk – Agryz – Alnashi.

River transport. The Republic has 179 kilometers of inland waterways; its main ports are Sarapul and Kambarka. Navigation is open for six and a half months in the year.

Airports. The airport of Izhevsk is an ICAO category one airport and provides links between Udmurtia and Moscow and six other cities of the Russian Federation.

Oil and gas pipelines. Twelve trunk gas pipelines from Siberia to Russia's central regions and five oil pipelines cross the Republic. The total length of the Republic's sections of gas pipeline is 3,800 kilometers.

3.6. MAIN NATURAL RESOURCES: RESERVES AND EXTRACTION IN 2002

Oil and natural gas. The Republic has 113 oil fields with estimated total reserves of 891.7 million tons, including 354 million tons of proven reserves.

Timber. Forests cover some 46% of the Republic's area. Nearly half of the Republic's forests are coniferous. Estimated industrial timber reserves exceed 2.3 million cubic meters.

Recreational resources. The Republic of Udmurtia is one of the most beautiful parts of Russia, with good potential for hunting, fishing, horseback trekking and hiking, and other sports, recreation, and rehabilitation.

4. TRADE OPPORTUNITIES

4.1. MAIN GOODS PRODUCED IN THE REGION

Machine engineering. In 2002, the Republic produced 78,200 cars, 17,800 motorbikes, 844 metal cutting machines, 847 rolling machines, 244,200 washing machines, and 264,100 sporting and hunting rifles.

Ferrous metals. 2002 output of steel amounted to 468,400 tons, 343,200 tons of finished roll, 5,800 tons of steel wire, and 7,600 tons of steel cold-roll strip.

Timber. In 2002, the Republic's enterprises produced 679,300 cubic meters of industrial timber, 354,300 cubic meters of lumber, 164,800 square meters of parquet board, 97,300 cubic meters of chipboard, and 7,800 cubic meters of plywood.

Agriculture. In 2002, the Republic grew 764,400 tons of grain, 553,700 tons of potatoes, 146,800 tons of vegetables, and 2,400 tons of flax fiber, and produced 602,100 tons of milk and 643.9 million eggs.

4.2. EXPORTS, INCLUDING EXTRA-CIS

The Republic's 2002 external trade turnover reached $720.2 million. 2002 exports were $630.4 million, which constitutes a 5.3% decrease year-on-year. Exports are mainly based on oil ($365.1 million, or 57.9% of total exports), ferrous and non-fer-

rous metals ($42.3 million, 6.7%), machinery and equipment ($117.8 million, 18.7%), and structural, alloyed, and stainless rolled steel, metal cutting machines, cars, motorbikes, bearings, pressure regulators, oil machinery, sporting and hunting rifles, electric motors and instruments, medical equipment, communication devices, capacitors, timber and timber goods, and non-organic chemicals, including zirconium, calcium, and casein.

Major importers of the Republic's products are Greece, India, the Netherlands, and Poland.

4.3. IMPORTS, INCLUDING EXTRA-CIS

2002 imports totaled $89.8 million, 2.2% down year-on-year. The structure of imports was as follows: petrochemicals – $37.5 million (41.7% of total imports), machinery and equipment – $29.5 million (32.9%), and ferrous and non-ferrous metals – $15.9 million (17.7%). The main exporters to the Republic of Udmurtia are Ukraine and Kazakhstan.

4.4. MAJOR REGIONAL EXPORT AND IMPORT ENTITIES

Owing to the specific features of the Republic's economy, export and import operations are performed mainly by industrial companies.

5. INVESTMENT OPPORTUNITIES

5.1 INVESTMENTS IN 1992–2002 (BY INDUSTRY SECTOR), INCLUDING FOREIGN INVESTMENTS

The following factors determine the investment appeal of the Republic of Udmurtia:

- Its advantageous geographic location (at the center of the Urals);
- Its developed industrial infrastructure;
- Its major reserves of natural resources;
- Its temperate climate and fertile soils;
- Its highly qualified industrial workforce.

5.2. CAPITAL INVESTMENT

Industry, transport, and communications account for the bulk of capital investment in the Republic.

As of January 1, 2003, France, Germany, Japan, the Czech Republic, and the USA accounted for 83%

of total foreign investment, with Germany topping the list. The capital investment of Siemens (Germany) into the charter capital of ZAO Izhtel, a switch system manufacturer, totaled $10 million. In 2002, the fuel sector attracted lending finance from France.

The largest investors into the Republic in 1990–2002 were: France – $56.4 million, Germany – $16 million, Japan – $9.6 million, the Czech Republic – $5.2 million, the USA – $4.1 million, Cyprus – $3.6 million, and Luxembourg – $3.5 million.

2002 foreign investment was channeled mainly to the oil production sector (94.3% of total foreign investment), retail and public catering (4.5%), exploration and prospecting (0.4%), public education, science and culture (0.3%), construction (0.3%), machine engineering and metals processing (0.1%), and communications (0.1%).

IV

VOLGA FEDERAL DISTRICT

Capital investment by industry sector, $ million						TABLE 6
	1997	1998	1999	2000	2001	2002
Total capital investment	767.8	327.7	259.8	319.7	458.3	326.9
Including major industries (% of total):						
Industry	35.4	41.9	67.0	61.2	47.7	47.2
Agriculture and forestry	2.9	7.0	5.7	4.2	5.0	0.1
Construction	2.8	0.3	0.3	12.1	1.3	23.7
Transport and communications	24.5	19.1	11.1	3.5	15.3	7.6
Trade and public catering	5.4	4.1	2.5	2.4	5.4	4.2
Housing	13.3	11.1	4.7	4.1	3.1	1.1
Healthcare	2.0	3.0	1.5	2.3	1.1	0.4
Education	1.8	2.6	1.5	1.3	2.4	0.6
Other	11.9	10.9	5.7	8.9	18.7	15.1

Foreign investment trends in 1993–2002						TABLE 7
	1993–1997	1998	1999	2000	2001	2002
Foreign investment, $ million	29.0	7.9	116.8	10.6	6.8	156.7
Including FDI, $ million	24.9	1.9	0.3	1.4	1.2	1.8

Largest enterprises of the Republic of Udmurtia	TABLE 8
COMPANY	SECTOR
OAO Udmurtneft	Oil
OAO Belkamneft	Oil
OAO Izhmash	Machine engineering
OAO Izhstal	Ferrous metals

5.3. MAJOR ENTERPRISES (INCLUDING ENTERPRISES WITH FOREIGN INVESTMENT)

As of January 1, 2003, the Republic of Udmurtia hosted some 183 commercial organizations with foreign investment. The largest companies as of 2002 were OAO Udmurtstalinvest ($2.3 million in foreign investment) and OAO Freight-Upak ($0.644 million).

Since 1996, the Republic has been home to three U.S.-Russian oil equipment manufacturing joint ventures with OAO Udmurtneft: ZAO Udol, ZAO Isot, and ZAO Itom, and a Russian-Canadian joint venture ZAO Izhdril.

In 2000, LUKI, Sweden, participated in the construction of the Reuster Plant producing infusion solutions. The project cost $14.3 million; the plant's capacity is 7.2 million packs per year.

5.4. MOST ATTRACTIVE SECTORS FOR INVESTMENT

According to the Udmurtia Government, the most appealing sectors for investors are oil production, ferrous metals, machine engineering and metal processing, forestry, and timber. These sec-

tors offer the best opportunities for mutually beneficial cooperation.

5.5. CURRENT LEGISLATION ON INVESTOR TAX EXEMPTIONS AND PRIVILEGES

The Government of the Republic of Udmurtia is pursuing a comprehensive policy aimed at facilitating economic stability and fostering investment activity in the Republic. As part of that policy, the State Council of the Republic of Udmurtia has passed several laws:

• On the Encouragement of Investment Activity in the Republic of Udmurtia;

• On the Development Budget of the Republic of Udmurtia;

• On the Implementation of Investment Projects at Especially Important Sites in the Republic of Udmurtia;

• On Investment Projects in the Oil Sector in the Republic of Udmurtia.

The laws provide legal guarantees and tax privileges to investors and ensure favorable conditions for investing in industrial enterprises.

In 2002, the Republic drafted laws On the State Investment Policy of the Republic of Udmurtia and

Regional entities responsible for raising investment — *TABLE 9*

ENTITY	ADDRESS	PHONE, FAX, E-MAIL
OAO Investment and Leasing Agency	268, ul. Pushkinskaya, Izhevsk, Republic of Udmurtia, 426008	Phone: (3412) 43 9067, 43 9157 Fax: (3412) 43 9419 E-mail: leasing@udm.net
Udmurtia State Small Enterprise Support Fund	P.O. Box 184, Izhevsk, Republic of Udmurtia, 426001	Phone/fax: (3412) 43 0001
ZAO Udmurtia Leasing Company	270, ul. Pushkinskaya, Izhevsk, Republic of Udmurtia, 426008	Phone: (3412) 43 0001, 43 2024
OOO Specialized Leasing Company	Office 403, 30, ul. Lenina, Izhevsk, Republic of Udmurtia, 426076	Phone: (3412) 78 3065, 51 0966
ZAO Leasing Company Paritet	69, ul. Krasnoarmeyskaya, Izhevsk, Republic of Udmurtia, 426003	Phone: (3412) 52 3458
OOO GID	6, ul. 30 let Pobedy, Izhevsk, Republic of Udmurtia, 426033	Phone: (3412) 59 7937, 59 9515 E-mail: alex@gid.udm.net
OAO Regional Securities Company Industrial Investment	219a, ul. K. Marksa, Izhevsk, Republic of Udmurtia, 426003	Phone: (3412) 51 1424, 78 0876
ZAO Financial and Industrial Company Arsenal Invest	62, ul. Rodnikovaya, Izhevsk, Republic of Udmurtia, 426000	Phone: (3412) 43 2444
ZAO KupolInvest	268, ul. Pushkinskaya, Izhevsk, Republic of Udmurtia, 426008	Phone: (3412) 43 3007, 43 0796
OOO Financial Center LigaFB	46, ul. Likhvintseva, Izhevsk, Republic of Udmurtia, 426034	Phone: (3412) 25 9167, 25 9164
OOO RenomFinance	42, building 2, ul. Molodezhnaya, Izhevsk, Republic of Udmurtia, 426072	Phone: (3412) 36 0303, 36 7196
OOO Financial and Commercial Group Saigas	61, 10th floor, per. Severny, Izhevsk, Republic of Udmurtia, 426011	Phone: (3412) 22 1201, 22 4824 E-mail: hold@saigas.udm.ru
OOO Siberian Leasing Center	7a, pl. 50-letia Oktyabrya, Izhevsk, Republic of Udmurtia, 426034	Phone: (3412) 43 5943 E-mail: kran@vpsi.udm.ru
OOO Udmurtian Leasing Company	46, ul. Azina, Sarapul, Republic of Udmurtia, 427960	Phone: (34147) 40 522 E-mail: ulc@leasing.udm.ru

On Tax Privileges to Investors. The draft laws create provisions on the major forms of state support to investment: guarantees of investor rights, budget and tax credits, tax and duty exemptions, non-financial support, and protection of investors' interests.

5.6. FEDERAL AND REGIONAL ECONOMIC AND SOCIAL DEVELOPMENT PROGRAMS FOR THE REPUBLIC OF UDMURTIA

Federal targeted programs. In 2002, the Republic was implementing 24 federal targeted programs. The total federal targeted program financing amounted to $12.2 million. The priority status was accorded to the Program of Elimination of Differences in the Social and Economic Development of the Regions of the Russian Federation (2002–2010 and through 2015).

Regional programs. In 2002, the Republic was implementing 22 republican targeted programs worth a total of $10.9 million financed by the republican budget. The main programs were The Program for Economic and Social Development of the Republic of Udmurtia, 2001–2004, The Memory of Udmurtia – Creation and Preservation of a Unified National Fund of Printed Culture Artifacts of the Republic of Udmurtia, 2001–2003, The Preservation of the Historical and Cultural Heritage of the People of Udmurtia, 2001–2003, and The Creation of an Automated Library and Information Network (RABIS) in the Republic, 2002–2004.

IV

VOLGA FEDERAL DISTRICT

6. INVESTMENT PROJECTS

Industry sector and project description	1) Expected results 2) Amount and term of investment 3) Form of financing[1] 4) Documentation[2]	Contact information
1	2	3

ENERGY

47R001 ■ ● ▲ ★

| Construction of co-generation mini thermal power plants. Project goal: to increase efficiency, and reduce heating costs. | 1) Replacement of 1,400 boilers at mini thermal power plants with a total capacity of 841 MW 2) $1,600 million/10 years 3) E, L, Leas. 4) Conceptual Framework for the Development of the Republic's Fuel and Energy Sector | Ministry of Fuel, Energy, and Communications of the Republic of Udmurtia 214, ul. Pushkinskaya, Izhevsk, Republic of Udmurtia, 426007 Phone: (3412) 25 9088 Fax: (3412) 52 5315 E-mail: mintopener@udmillionet.ru Viktor Konstantinovich Presnukhin, Minister |

CONSTRUCTION MATERIALS

47R002 ● ◆ ▲

| Production of peat wall thermal blocks. Project goal: to introduce a new product to the market. | 1) Output of 8,800 cubic meters per year, annual profit of $0.1 million 2) $0.2 million/0.5 years 3) L 4) BP, FS | OAO Uralteplokomplect 52, ul. Ordzhonikidze, Izhevsk, Republic of Udmurtia, 426063 Phone/fax: (3412) 75 1641 Alexander Alexeevich Kuksin, CEO |

FOOD AND BEVERAGES

47R003 ● ◆

| Upgrading fixed assets of a poultry-yard and dry egg powder shop. Project goal: to increase output. | 1) Net profit of $1.6 million per year 2) $6.7 million/5 years 3) L 4) BP | State Unitary Company Poultry Factory Varaksino Varaksino, Zavyalovsky District, Republic of Udmurtia, 427027 Phone: (3412) 54 5200, 54 5236 Fax: (3412) 54 5350 Vladimir Nikolaevich Zenin, Director |

TRADE

47R004 ● ▲ ◆

| Construction of an exhibition and trade center. Project goal: to expand retail facilities, set up a permanent market, and build a modern supermarket. | 1) 27,000 square meters of retail space, rent income of $7.9 million per year, supermarket of 17,000 square meters, annual sales of $13.2 million 2) $23.8 million/1.3 years 3) L 4) FS, BP | OOO Atlantida Holding Company 1a, ul. Ordzhonikidze, Izhevsk, Republic of Udmurtia, 426063 Phone: (3412) 75 8959 Fax: (3412) 75 8843 E-mail: atlantida@udm.ru, http://www.atlantida. udm.ru Yevgeny Dmitrievich Stashkov, President |

MACHINE ENGINEERING AND METAL PROCESSING

47R005 ● ◆

| Development of new medical equipment. Project goal: to increase product output. | 1) Output increase by $18.5 million per year 2) $1.1 million/2 years 3) L 4) BP | OOO Nauka 20a, ul. 30 let Pobedy, Izhevsk, Republic of Udmurtia, 426008 Phone/fax: (3412) 59 8820 Phone: (3412) 59 6176 E-mail: nauka@udmlink.ru Sergei Leonidovich Tochilov, CEO |

[1] L – Loan, E – Equity, Leas. – Leasing, JV – Joint Venture
[2] BP – Business Plan, FS – Feasibility Study

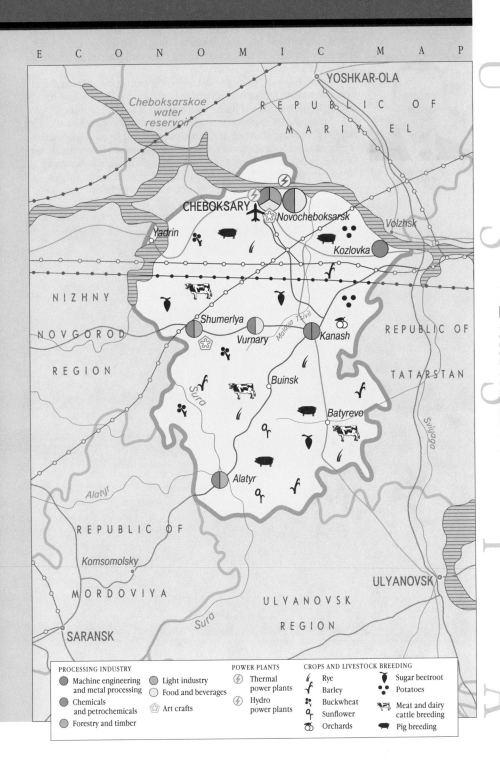

ECONOMIC MAP

YOSHKAR-OLA

Cheboksarskoe water reservoir

REPUBLIC OF MARIY EL

CHEBOKSARY

Novocheboksarsk

Yadrin

Volzhsk

Kozlovka

NIZHNY NOVGOROD REGION

Shumerlya

Vurnary

Malaya Tsivil

Kanash

REPUBLIC OF TATARSTAN

Sura

Buinsk

Batyrevo

Alatyr

Sviyaga

Komsomolsky

REPUBLIC OF MORDOVIYA

ULYANOVSK

ULYANOVSK REGION

Sura

SARANSK

Alatyr

RUSSIA

IV

VOLGA FEDERAL DISTRICT

PROCESSING INDUSTRY
- Machine engineering and metal processing
- Chemicals and petrochemicals
- Forestry and timber
- Light industry
- Food and beverages
- Art crafts

POWER PLANTS
- Thermal power plants
- Hydro power plants

CROPS AND LIVESTOCK BREEDING
- Rye
- Barley
- Buckwheat
- Sunflower
- Orchards
- Sugar beetroot
- Potatoes
- Meat and dairy cattle breeding
- Pig breeding

T he Republic of Chuvashia is one of the most stable and dynamically developing regions of Russia. Its advantageous geographic location at the center of European Russia, favorable natural environment and climate, advanced engineering and transport infrastructure, legislative and economic guarantees granted to investors, and qualified and inexpensive work force offer favorable conditions for successful business and long-term investment.

According to experts' estimates, Chuvashia is one of the leading Russian regions in terms of all social and economic development indicators for 2001 and 2002. Its infrastructure potential is fifteenth among the 89 regions of the Russian Federation. Chuvashia offers some of the best investment potential and investment appeal trends found in Russia today.

Chuvashia stands as a reliable and responsible partner in Russia and abroad. Its excellent public finance management and complete transparency have been certified by the International Bank for Reconstruction and Development.

The Republic of Chuvashia is actively pursuing a policy of innovation. It participates actively and effectively in international programs for the modernization of education, public health, finance, and housing and communal services. Having won the nationwide Electronic Russia competition, Chuvashia is implementing the Electronic Russia (2002–2010) federal targeted program as a pilot region.

Investors operating in the Republic of Chuvashia are guaranteed considerable regional and municipal tax exemptions.

Visit our Republic to see for yourself that we have created favorable conditions for successful business development.

Nikolai Fyodorov,
PRESIDENT OF THE REPUBLIC OF CHUVASHIA

1. GENERAL INFORMATION

1.1. GEOGRAPHY

The Republic of Chuvashia covers a total area of 18,300 square kilometers. The Republic is situated in the eastern part of the East European Plain on the right bank of the River Volga between its Sura and Sviyaga tributaries. To the west, the Republic borders the Nizhny Novgorod Region, to the north – the Republic of Mariy El, to the east – the Republic of Tatarstan, to the south – the Ulyanovsk Region, and to the south-west – the Republic of Mordovia.

1.2. CLIMATE

Spread across the forest and forest-steppe zones, the Republic of Chuvashia enjoys a temperate continental climate.

The average air temperature in January is −13°C, rising to +19°C in July. Average annual precipitation is 530–570 mm.

1.3. POPULATION

According to preliminary 2002 census results, total population of the Republic was 1,314,000 people. The average population density is 71.8 people per square kilometer. The economically active population amounted to 683,000 people in 2002. The 2002 official unemployment level stood at 2%. Demographically speaking, some 60.1% are of working age, 20.5%, are below the statutory working age, and 19.4% are beyond the statutory working age.

The Republic's ethnic mix is 67.8% Chuvash, 26.7% Russian, 2.7% Tatar, 1.4% Mordovian, 0.5% Ukrainian, 0.3% Mariy, and 0.1% Belarussian.

As of 2002, the Republic's major urban centers were Cheboksary with 440,800 inhabitants, Novocheboksarsk with 125,900 inhabitants, Kanash with 53,000 inhabitants, and Alatyr with 46,000 inhabitants.

Population							TABLE 1
	1992	1997	1998	1999	2000	2001	2002
Total population, '000	1,355	1,363	1,361	1,362	1,359	1,353	1,314
Economically active population, '000	653	638	618	685	686	668	683

2. ADMINISTRATION

1, pl. Respubliki, Cheboksary, Republic of Chuvashia, 428004
Fax: (8352) 62 1799; http://www.cap.ru

NAME	POSITION	CONTACT INFORMATION
Nikolai Vasilyevich FEDOROV	President of the Republic of Chuvashia	Phone: (8352) 62 4687 E-mail: president@cap.ru
Natalia Yuryevna PARTASOVA	Chairman of the Cabinet of Ministers of the Republic of Chuvashia	Phone: (8352) 62 0171 E-mail: info@cap.ru
Mikhail Alexeevich MIKHAILOVSKY	Chairman of the State Council of the Republic of Chuvashia	Phone: (8352) 62 2272 Fax: (8352) 62 2315 E-mail: gs@cap.ru
Mikhail Vasilyevich IGNATYEV	First Deputy Chairman of the Cabinet of Ministers of the Republic of Chuvashia, Minister of Agriculture	Phone: (8352) 62 0845 Fax: (8352) 62 3184 E-mail: agro@cap.ru
Alexander Viktorovich DOMANIN	Deputy Chairman of the Cabinet of Ministers of the Republic of Chuvashia, Minister of Property Relations	Phone: (8352) 42 0311 Fax: (8352) 42 0166 E-mail: gki@cap.ru
Yury Petrovich VOLOSHIN	Deputy Chairman of the Cabinet of Ministers of the Republic of Chuvashia, Minister of Industry and Transport	Phone: (8352) 62 0424 Fax: (8352) 62 0350, 62 5313 E-mail: indust@cap.ru
Nikolai Vasilyevich SMIRNOV	Deputy Chairman of the Cabinet of Ministers of the Republic of Chuvashia, Minister of Finance	Phone: (8352) 62 0015 Fax: (8352) 62 5342 E-mail: finance@cap.ru
Marina Ivanovna ILLARIONOVA	Deputy Chairman of the Cabinet of Ministers of the Republic of Chuvashia, Minister of Economic Development and Trade	Phone: (8352) 62 0965 Fax: (8352) 62 0597 E-mail: economy@cap.ru

NAME	POSITION	CONTACT INFORMATION
Vladimir Nikolaevich FILATOV	Minister of Construction, Architecture, and Roads	Phone: (8352) 62 1031 Fax: (8352) 62 2351 E-mail: construc@cap.ru
Vladimir Gennadyevich KOVALEV	Minister of Energy, Housing, and Communal Services	Phone: (8352) 62 5693 Fax: (8352) 62 2800, 62 3260 E-mail: zhkh@cap.ru

3. ECONOMIC POTENTIAL

3.1. 1997–2002 GROSS REGIONAL PRODUCT (GRP). INDUSTRY BREAKDOWN

The 2002 gross regional product amounted to $1,340 million, which constitutes 13% growth year-on-year. The growth was achieved thanks to industrial output and transport and communications, which account for a combined 37% of total GRP.

3.2. MAJOR ECONOMIC GROWTH PROJECTIONS

The Cabinet of Ministers of the Republic of Chu-vashia has endeavored to comprehensively develop the Republic's economy, and plans to increase output in all industrial sectors. The main growth drivers will be:

GRP trends in 1997–2002						TABLE 2
	1997	1998	1999	2000	2001*	2002*
GRP in current prices, $ million	1,924.7	1,229.0	732.2	895.4	1,185.9	1,340.0

*Estimates of the Cabinet of Ministers of the Republic of Chuvashia

GRP industry breakdown in 1997–2002, % of total						TABLE 3
	1997	1998	1999	2000	2001*	2002*
GRP	100.0	100.0	100.0	100.0	100.0	100.0
Industry	30.1	32.2	31.5	31.2	32.4	32.6
Agriculture and forestry	16.0	13.1	19.0	19.0	17.4	15.6
Construction	6.6	6.5	7.0	8.8	9.0	8.8
Transport and communications	4.3	3.9	2.9	4.3	4.3	4.5
Trade and public catering	12.4	11.1	10.9	10.4	10.7	9.0
Other	25.6	25.1	20.5	18.0	19.0	22.0
Net taxes on output	5.0	8.1	8.2	8.3	7.2	7.5

*Estimates of the Cabinet of Ministers of the Republic of Chuvashia

Full utilization of the potential of the Republic's machine engineering and metals processing enterprises, which constitute the core of the Republic's economy;

The creation of "industrial districts" within the Republic in conjunction with Italian companies under Russian-Italian agreements on economic, industrial, monetary, and financial cooperation;

The development, support, and implementation of investment projects in major industrial sectors.

3.3. INDUSTRIAL OUTPUT IN 1997–2002 FOR MAJOR SECTORS OF ECONOMY

The Republic's economy is industry driven. Industrial enterprises employ over 30% of the economically active population and account for over half of all fixed operating assets. The priority sectors of the Republic's industry are machine engineering and metals processing, food and beverages, energy, chemicals, and light industry. These account for a combined 88% of total industrial output.

Machine engineering and metal processing. This sector accounts for 45.2% of total industrial output. The main enterprises within the sector are OAO ChNPPP Elara, OAO Cheboksary Instrument Plant, OAO Promtractor, OAO Electronics and Mechanics Plant (ZEiM), OAO Cheboksary Electric Tools Plant, OAO Electrical Instrument, and OAO Van Plant.

Food and beverages. The food sector accounts for 13.5% of total industrial output. The sector is focused on hops cultivation (the Republic produces some 80% of Russia's gross hop yield), grain and potato cultivation, beef and dairy farming, pig rearing, poultry farming, and apiculture.

Industry breakdown of industrial output in 1997–2002, % of total						*TABLE 4*
	1997	1998	1999	2000	2001	2002*
Industry	100.0	100.0	100.0	100.0	100.0	100.0
Machine engineering and metal processing	35.7	36.1	41.2	43.4	47.3	45.2
Food and beverages	13.2	14.4	16.7	14.5	13.0	13.5
Energy	20.4	19.9	12.5	12.6	11.5	13.1
Chemicals and petrochemicals	9.4	9.2	10.1	10.2	9.5	9.5
Light industry	4.9	5.0	6.7	7.6	7.2	6.7
Construction materials	6.7	6.4	5.1	4.7	5.3	5.7
Forestry, timber, and pulp and paper	4.1	3.7	2.9	2.4	2.2	2.5
Flour, cereals, and mixed fodder	3.4	3.1	3.0	2.7	2.0	1.2
Ferrous metals	0.2	0.2	0.2	0.4	0.4	n/a

*Estimates of the Cabinet of Ministers of the Republic of Chuvashia

Fuel and energy sector production and consumption trends, 1997–2002						*TABLE 5*
	1997	1998	1999	2000	2001	2002
Electricity output, billion kWh	5.1	5.3	4.3	4.3	4.4	4.4
Electricity consumption, billion kWh	4.9	3.8	3.9	4.3	5.0	5.3
Natural gas consumption, million cubic meters	2,469.4	2,153.5	1,628.4	1,692.2	1,665.8	2,018.1

IV

The largest companies within the sector are ZAO Agricultural Company Oldeevskaya, OAO Akkond, OAO Cheboksary Brewery Chuvashia Buket, ZAO Bulgar-Khmel, OAO Cheboksary Meat Processing Plant, OAO Vurnarsky Meat Processing Plant, OAO Novocheboksarsky Macaroni Factory, Regional State Unitary Company Morgaushskaya Poultry Farm, OAO Cheboksary Municipal Milk Plant, and OAO Bread.

Energy. The sector accounts for 13.1% of total industrial output. The Republic's major power plants are the Cheboksarskaya HEPS (1,370 MW), Cheboksarskaya TPS 1 (12 MW), Cheboksarskaya TPS 2 (460 MW), and Novocheboksarskaya TPS 3 (380 MW).

Chemicals and petrochemicals. This sector's share in total industrial output is 9.5%. Among the largest companies are OAO Khimprom, OAO Vurnarsky Mixed Medicine Plant, and OAO Lakokraska.

3.4. FUEL AND ENERGY BALANCE (OUTPUT AND CONSUMPTION PER RESOURCE)

The Republic meets 88% of its energy demand internally, and imports all of its natural gas and oil product consumption. The main suppliers of oil products to the Republic are OAO Chuvashnefteproduct, OAO LUKoil-Chuvashia, and OOO Volganeftholding.

3.5. TRANSPORT INFRASTRUCTURE

The Republic has a developed transport system. Road transport accounts for the bulk of passenger and freight traffic.

Roads. The Republic of Chuvashia has 5,333 kilometers of paved public highway. Road transport accounts for some 60% of freight and 50% of passenger traffic. One of Russia's main road arteries, which links Moscow to the major industrial centers of Tatarstan, the South Urals, and Western and Eastern Siberia, passes through the Republic of Chuvashia. The highway, which passes through cities of Saratov and Volgograd, provides access to southern regions of Russia. A bridge over the Volga (along the Cheboksarskaya Hydro Electric Power Station dam) provides access to the northern and southern Urals, the Volga Region, the Kirov Region, and the Republic of Komi. Highways to Iran, Azerbaijan, the Volga Region, and the north of European Russia also pass through Cheboksary.

Railroads. The Republic of Chuvashia has 396 kilometers of railroads. The Republic's sectors of the Moscow – Kazan – Yekaterinburg and Cheboksary – Kanash – Krasny Uzel (the Republic of Mordovia) main lines link the Republic to central and southern regions, the Urals, and CIS destinations.

Airports. An international airport serves Cheboksary.

River ports. Some 20% of freight is transported by river. The Cheboksary and Novocheboksarsk river ports process large volumes of transit freight and provide freight transshipment facilities. The Republic has inland waterway links to the Black and Caspian Seas.

Oil and gas pipelines. Six trunk gas pipelines and an oil pipeline pass through the Republic.

3.6. MAIN NATURAL RESOURCES: RESERVES AND EXTRACTION IN 2002

Construction materials. The Republic of Chuvashia enjoys considerable reserves of minerals used in the production of building materials. The Republic has large explored deposits of gypsum (120 million tons), anhydride (50.9 million tons), and dolomites (12.2 million tons). The Republic has 46 registered deposits of brick clays and loam, four deposits of expanded clay aggregate with a total reserve of 9.7 million cubic meters, and eleven deposits of carbonate rock.

Oil and natural gas. The Republic is currently completing hydrocarbon field prospecting.

Land resources. The Republic has a total of 1,834,500 hectares of land, 55.1% of which is arable land, 32.6% – forests, 1.6% – populated areas, 0.4% – reserves, and 0.9% industrial land.

Mineral water. The Republic has five explored subterranean mineral water deposits.

Recreational resources. The Republic has four federal recreational areas, eight national parks, and a forest hunting reserve.

Other natural resources. The Republic has deposits of phosphorite, oil shale, tripoli, and peat. The total area of peat deposit exceeds 9,000 hectares.

4. TRADE OPPORTUNITIES

4.1. MAIN GOODS PRODUCED IN THE REGION

Machinery. Chuvashia produces high-technology energy, electrical, and technical equipment, instruments and tools, tractors, weaving looms, industrial refrigerators, cable equipment, and electrical loaders. In 2002, the Republic produced 281 bulldozers and 278 weaving looms.

Ferrous metals. 2002 steel output amounted to 122,500 tons.

Chemicals. The Republic produces caustic soda, dyes, agricultural chemicals, tanning agents, and plastic.

Light industry. 2002 output of fabric totaled 38.3 million square meters.

Food and beverages. Chuvashia produces meat and dairy products, confectionery, bread and bakery, macaroni, alcoholic and non-alcoholic beverages, beer, cereals, and mineral water. Grain output in 2002 reached 543,900 tons, potatoes – 592,000 tons, vegetables – 171,800 tons, sugar beet – 40,100 tons, vegetable oil – 260 tons, fat – 2,000 tons, and meat – 10,700 tons.

Construction materials. In 2002, the Republic produced 231 million bricks and 127,600 cubic meters of lumber. The Republic also produces reinforced concrete assemblies and components and clay aggregate.

4.2. EXPORTS, INCLUDING EXTRA-CIS

2002 external trade turnover amounted to $148.4 million, and industrial exports – $89.1 million (1.4% growth year-on-year).

The Republic maintains trade and economic relations with some 60 countries. The bulk of trade is represented by organic chemicals, machinery, including nuclear reactors, boilers, optical instruments, and transport vehicles, electrical instruments and components, and cotton thread and fabric.

The main importers of the Republic's products are China, Iraq, Germany, Luxembourg, Poland, India, Italy, France, Kazakhstan, Ukraine, Uzbekistan, and Moldova.

4.3. IMPORTS, INCLUDING EXTRA-CIS

2002 imports amounted to $59.3 million, which constitutes a 12.8% decline. The main exporters to the Republic of Chuvashia are China, the USA, France, Switzerland, Japan, Italy, Germany, Hungary, Belgium, Austria, Kazakhstan, Uzbekistan, and Ukraine. Petrochemicals and machinery account for the lion's share of imports. The Republic imports electrical and medical equipment and machinery for the food and beverages and textile sectors.

5. INVESTMENT OPPORTUNITIES

5.1 INVESTMENTS IN 1992–2002 (BY INDUSTRY SECTOR), INCLUDING FOREIGN INVESTMENTS

The following factors determine the investment appeal of the Republic of Chuvashia:

• Its developed economy (large industrial and construction sectors, a competitive agroindustrial sector, and advanced telecommunications and information infrastructure);

• Its advantageous geographical location (the Republic is situated at the center of European Russia);

• The Developed transport infrastructure;

• Organizational and financial support to investment projects, and protection of investors' rights by the Republic's executive authorities;

• Its highly qualified workforce.

5.2. MAJOR ENTERPRISES (INCLUDING ENTERPRISES WITH FOREIGN INVESTMENT)

The Republic hosts some 100 companies with foreign investment. The largest among them are OOO Joint Venture Tillev founded by OAO ZEiM and Banex, Yugoslavia, Russian-Bulgarian Joint Venture Selen (ZAO Cheboksary Ceramics and Production Construction

Capital investment by industry sector, $ million						TABLE 6
	1997	1998	1999	2000	2001	2002
Total capital investment	414.9	216.8	133.0	175.6	220.3	240.3
Including major industries (% of total):						
Industry	16.2	20.5	30.6	25.0	27.2	30.9
Agriculture and forestry	5.2	6.1	6.1	5.0	4.7	5.9
Construction	2.7	3.3	3.4	5.2	1.3	2.5
Transport and communications	27.4	21.3	12.9	17.8	16.5	21.9
Retail and public catering	1.6	3.3	3.1	3.1	3.7	2.4
Other	46.9	45.5	43.9	43.9	46.6	36.4

Foreign investment trends in 1997–2002						TABLE 7
	1997	1998	1999	2000	2001	2002
Foreign investment, $ million	1.6	2.3	2.3	1.7	35.0	4.0
Including FDI, $ million	1.6	1.8	2.1	0.9	18.0	4.0

Largest enterprises of the Republic of Chuvashia	TABLE 8
COMPANY	SECTOR
OAO Chuvashenergo	Energy
OAO ChNPPP Elara	Instrument engineering
OAO ZEiM	Instrument engineering
OAO Cheboksary Instrument Plant	Machine engineering
OAO Promtractor	Machine engineering
OAO Khimprom	Chemicals
OAO Cheboksary Cotton Factory	Textiles
OAO Cheboksary Electric Tool Plant	Electrical tools
OAO Akkond	Food and beverages

Trust, Bulgaria), ZAO Dupont-Khimprom, OOO ABB-Automation, ZAO Chuvashia-Mobile, ZAO Joint Venture Pronova, and OAO Cheboksary Cotton Factory (a joint venture with IBC GmbH, Germany).

5.3. MOST ATTRACTIVE SECTORS FOR INVESTMENT

The Republic of Chuvashia has all of the necessary prerequisites to successfully cooperate with international partners. According to the Cabinet of Ministers of the Republic of Chuvashia, the most potentially appealing sectors for investors are electrical tools, machine engineering, chemicals, textiles, leather production and processing, timber, and dairy, meat, and vegetable products.

5.4. CURRENT LEGISLATION ON INVESTOR TAX EXEMPTIONS AND PRIVILEGES

The Republic has passed a number of laws fostering investment activity:

The Law of the Republic of Chuvashia On Investment Activity in the Republic of Chuvashia provides a legal and economic framework for state support to investors, and ensures stable and equitable investor rights and equal protection thereof;

The Law of the Republic of Chuvashia On Local Tax Regulation in the Republic of Chuvashia provides for tax exemptions to investors in the Republic's economy.

An Investment Policy Council was established by decree of the President of the Republic of Chuvashia as a standing body of the Republic's Cabinet of Ministers with a brief to develop investment principles and strategies in the Republic and identify investment priorities. The Council is responsible for assessing and selecting investment projects. Investors putting their own or borrowed funds into investment projects and successfully completing competitive tenders organized by the Investment Policy Council are eligible for tax exemptions.

5.5. FEDERAL AND REGIONAL ECONOMIC AND SOCIAL DEVELOPMENT PROGRAMS FOR THE REPUBLIC OF CHUVASHIA

Federal targeted programs. The federal targeted program for The Elimination of Inequalities in

Regional entities responsible for raising investment		*TABLE 9*
ENTITY	ADDRESS	PHONE, FAX, E-MAIL
Chamber of Industry and Commerce of the Republic of Chuvashia	4/2, pr. I.Yakovleva, Cheboksary, Republic of Chuvashia, 428029	Phone: (8352) 20 0294, 20 3786 Fax: (8352) 21 0678 E-mail: tpp@tppchuvashia.ru; Igor Vladimirovich Kustarin, President

the Social and Economic Development of the Regions of the Russian Federation 2002–2010 and through 2015 plays an important role in social and economic development of the Republic. The Program aims to reduce regional gaps in core social and economic development indicators by 2010, to create conditions conducive to the development of enterprise, and to improve the investment climate.

The Presidential Program for Major Economic and Social Reform in the Republic of Chuvashia, 2005 sets forth priority areas for the Republic's development. A Plan of Action of the Cabinet of Ministers has been adopted with a view to ensuring the implementation of the Presidential program and Resolution No. 115 of the Cabinet of Ministers of the Republic of Chuvashia of April 12, 2002. The Republic has drafted a targeted republican program for social and economic development in the Republic of Chuvashia through 2005.

Regional programs. In 2002, the Republic adopted 14 republican targeted programs, the most significant of which are Mineral and Feedstock Resources of the Republic of Chuvashia, 2003–2005, Forests of Chuvashia, 2003–2010, Creation and Development of a Credit Cooperation Network in the Republic of Chuvashia, 2003–2004, Development of Rural Areas through 2010, and Prevention and Fighting of Social Diseases, 2002–2004.

6. INVESTMENT PROJECTS

Industry sector and project description	1) Expected results 2) Amount and term of investment 3) Form of financing[1] 4) Documentation[2]	Contact information
1	2	3
NON-FERROUS METALS		
48R001 ● ◆		Federal State Unitary Company Chapaev Cheboksary Manufacturing Company
Production of goods from composite aluminum and copper powder. Project goal: to increase output, expand product range, and penetrate new markets.	1) Revenue of $2.8 million per year 2) $0.4 million/2 years 3) L 4) BP	1, ul. Sotsialisticheskaya, Cheboksary, Republic of Chuvashia, 428006 Phone: (8352) 69 6210, 69 6115 Fax: (8352) 62 4223 E-mail: rti@chtts.ru Petr Konstantinovich Belousov, CEO
MACHINE ENGINEERING AND METAL PROCESSING		
48R002 ● ◆ ▲		OAO Promtraktor
Production of a new base tractor model. Project goal: to expand product range.	1) Revenue of $195.1 million per year 2) $22.7 million/5 years 3) L 4) FS, BP	101, pr. Traktorostroiteley, Cheboksary, Republic of Chuvashia, 428033 Phone: (8352) 66 2155, 62 3318 Fax: (8352) 23 0236 Semen Gennadyevich Mlodik, CEO

[1] L – Loan, E – Equity, Leas. – Leasing, JV – Joint Venture
[2] BP – Business Plan, FS – Feasibility Study

1	2	3

48R003 ● ◆ ▲

Production of industrial tractors.
Project goal: to expand product
range (to produce bulldozers
and loaders).

1) Revenue of $66.1 million per year
2) $11 million/6 years
3) L ($10.4 million)
4) FS, BP

OAO Promtraktor
101, pr. Traktorostroiteley, Cheboksary,
Republic of Chuvashia, 428033
Phone: (8352) 66 2155, 62 3318
Fax: (8352) 23 0236
Semen Gennadyevich Mlodik, CEO

48R004 ■ ● ★ ◆

Upgrading of fixed assets by
acquiring new machinery.
Project goal: to introduce new
technology at instrumental, casting,
and forging shops and to save energy.

1) Cost reduction by 10–15%
2) $14.2 million/3 years
3) L, Leas.
4) FS, BP

OAO Cheboksary Instrument Plant
1, ul. Mira, Cheboksary,
Republic of Chuvashia, 428000
Phone: (8352) 23 9544, 23 0659
Fax: (8352) 20 6486
E-mail: jawa@chaz.ru
Vladislav Ilyich Fedorov, CEO

48R005 ● ◆ ▲

Upgrading of fixed assets
by acquiring new machinery.
Project goal: to expand the product
range (matrixes and punches for complex configuration and high precision
moulds, mold slabs, castings, and
various instruments).

1) Revenue growth by $6.3 million
2) $5.9 million/4 years
3) L
4) FS, BP

OAO Cheboksary Electric Tool Plant
5, pr. I.Yakovleva, Cheboksary,
Republic of Chuvashia, 428000
Phone: (8352) 62 0461,
69 5042, 20 6551
Fax: (8352) 62 7267,
62 7324, 62 7352
E-mail: cheaz@chtts.ru
Mikhail Arkadyevich Shurdov, CEO

48R006 ● ◆ ▲

Production of pipeline valve drives.
Project goal: to expand product range
and substitute imported goods.

1) Revenue $1.9 million per year
2) $3 million/3 years
3) L ($0.3 million)
4) FS, BP

OAO Electronics and Mechanics
Plant (ZeiM)
1, pr. I.Yakovleva, Cheboksary,
Republic of Chuvashia, 428020
Phone: (8352) 21 3555, 69 5274
Fax: (8352) 20 1549
E-mail: prim@zeim.ru
Stanislav Iosifovich Lyapunov, CEO

48R007 ● ◆ ▲

Production of suspended insulated
wires and power cables with rubber
insulation.
Project goal: to increase output
and expand product range.

1) Revenue of $6.5 million per year
2) $3.3 million/5 years
3) L
4) FS, BP

ZAO RUSEL-cable (a subsidiary
of OAO ZEiM)
1, pr. I.Yakovleva, Cheboksary,
Republic of Chuvashia, 428020
Phone: (8352) 61 0958, 21 2957
Fax: (8352) 20 1549
E-mail: sol@zeim.ru
Yury Shakirovich Solovyev,
CEO

48R008 ● ◆ ▲

Production of contact free thyratron
motors for transport vehicles.
Project goal: to expand product
range and improve quality.

1) Output growth by $4.7 million per year
2) $0.9 million/3 years
3) L
4) FS, BP

OAO Cheboksary Electric Tool Plant
5, pr. I.Yakovleva, Cheboksary,
Republic of Chuvashia, 428000
Phone: (8352) 62 0461,
69 5042, 20 6551
Fax: (8352) 62 7267,
62 7324, 62 7352
E-mail: cheaz@chtts.ru
Mikhail Arkadyevich Shurdov,
CEO

48R009 ■ ● ★ ◆ ▲

Development, production,
and sales of a range of high-voltage
instruments (up to 110 kV).
Project goal: to expand product range,
improve product quality, and increase
market share.

1) Output growth by $5.7 million
   per year
2) $3 million/4 years
3) E, L, Leas.
4) FS, BP

OAO Cheboksary Electric Tool Plant
5, pr. I.Yakovleva, Cheboksary,
Republic of Chuvashia, 428000
Phone: (8352) 62 0461,
69 5042, 20 6551
Fax: (8352) 62 7267,
62 7324, 62 7352
E-mail: cheaz@chtts.ru
Mikhail Arkadyevich Shurdov, CEO

IV

VOLGA FEDERAL DISTRICT

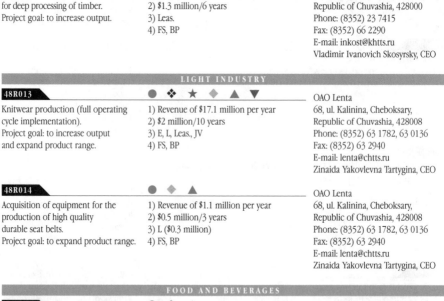

1	2	3

48R010

Production of new generation intelligent instruments.
Project goal: to introduce new products to the market.

1) Revenue of $2.4 million per year
2) $1 million/3 years
3) L
4) FS, BP

OAO Electronics and Mechanics Plant (ZeiM)
1, pr. I.Yakovleva, Cheboksary, Republic of Chuvashia, 428020
Phone: (8352) 21 3555, 69 5274
Fax: (8352) 20 1549
E-mail: prim@zeim.ru
Stanislav Iosifovich Lyapunov, CEO

48R011

Production of multi-layer printed circuit boards.
Project goal: to increase output and improve efficiency and quality.

1) 500,000 square decimeters per month
2) $10 million/3 years
3) L
4) FS, BP

OAO ChNPPP Elara
40, pr. Moskovsky, Cheboksary, Republic of Chuvashia, 428015
Phone: (8352) 45 3650, 49 1598
Fax: (8352) 42 5303
Gleb Andreevich Ilyenko, CEO

FORESTRY, TIMBER, AND PULP AND PAPER

48R012

Acquisition of machinery for deep processing of timber.
Project goal: to increase output.

1) Output of $2.3 million per year
2) $1.3 million/6 years
3) Leas.
4) FS, BP

OAO Inkost
38, Marposadskoe shosse, Cheboksary, Republic of Chuvashia, 428000
Phone: (8352) 23 7415
Fax: (8352) 66 2290
E-mail: inkost@khtts.ru
Vladimir Ivanovich Skosyrsky, CEO

LIGHT INDUSTRY

48R013

Knitwear production (full operating cycle implementation).
Project goal: to increase output and expand product range.

1) Revenue of $17.1 million per year
2) $2 million/10 years
3) E, L, Leas., JV
4) FS, BP

OAO Lenta
68, ul. Kalinina, Cheboksary, Republic of Chuvashia, 428008
Phone: (8352) 63 1782, 63 0136
Fax: (8352) 63 2940
E-mail: lenta@chtts.ru
Zinaida Yakovlevna Tartygina, CEO

48R014

Acquisition of equipment for the production of high quality durable seat belts.
Project goal: to expand product range.

1) Revenue of $1.1 million per year
2) $0.5 million/3 years
3) L ($0.3 million)
4) FS, BP

OAO Lenta
68, ul. Kalinina, Cheboksary, Republic of Chuvashia, 428008
Phone: (8352) 63 1782, 63 0136
Fax: (8352) 63 2940
E-mail: lenta@chtts.ru
Zinaida Yakovlevna Tartygina, CEO

FOOD AND BEVERAGES

48R015

Production of milk and liquid dairy products by installing a thermalisation and dairy product production and packaging line.
Project goal: to increase output and expand product range, including sterilized milk and liquid dairy products in plastic packaging with long shelf life.

1) Revenue of $7.3 million per year
2) $1 million/3 years
3) L ($0.7 million)
4) FS, BP

OAO Cheboksary Municipal Milk Plant
6, pr. Myasokombinatsky, Cheboksary, Republic of Chuvashia, 428024
Phone: (8352) 23 3950, 64 3787
Fax: (8352) 66 4348
Viktor Petrovich Bychkov, CEO

49. KIROV REGION [43]

ECONOMIC MAP

KOMI REPUBLIC

KOMI-PERMYATSKY AUTONOMOUS DISTRICT

Lalsk

Luza

Luza

Yug

Kama

Lesnoy

Rudnichny

Kirs

Oparino

Moloma

Vyatka

Murashi

Nagorsk

KOSTROMA REGION

Urya

Slobodskoy

Belaya Kholunitsa

Omutninsk

Letka

Orlov

Kirovo-Chepetsk

Cheptsa

Vetluga

KIROV

Kotelnich

Zuevka

Novovyatsk

Syava

Vakhtan

Nolinsk

Uni

REPUBLIC OF

Pizhma

Sovetsk

Urzhum

UDMURTIA

Yaransk

Vyatka

Kilmez

IZHEVSK

Malmyzh

REPUBLIC OF

YOSHKAR-OLA

Vyatskie Polyany

MARI EL

Novocheboksarsk

CHEBOKSARY

REPUBLIC OF

Volzhsk

KAZAN

TATARSTAN

Naberezhnye Chelny

PROCESSING INDUSTRY

- Ferrous metals
- Machine engineering and metal processing
- Chemicals and petrochemicals
- Forestry and timber
- Light industry
- Food and beverages
- Art crafts

MINING INDUSTRY

- Phosphorites

POWER PLANTS

- Thermal power plants

CROPS AND LIVESTOCK BREEDING

- Long-fibred flax
- Rye
- Orchards
- Meat and dairy cattle breeding

T he Kirov Region is commonly known as the Vyatka Territory. It is located between the Volga Region, the Urals, and the Russian North. The advantages of its geographical location are compounded by its developed communications system.

The Region is rich in several types of mineral resources. Its major resource is its forests. The Kirov Region is also home to the Vyatsko-Kamskoye nodular phosphorites deposit, the largest of its kind in Europe, and rich reserves of industrial peat and other minerals. The Region is also rich in mineral waters and curative muds. The Nizhneivkino health resort is well known far outside the Region.

Machine engineering, chemicals and petrochemicals, forestry, light industry, and agriculture are the main industrial sectors of the Region. What we treasure most, however, is our scientific and technological potential and highly qualified workforce. Our top-class experts enjoy the support of the Kirov city research centers.

The Kirov Region is among Russia's largest manufacturers of railway cranes, bare wires, tires for cars and trucks, and art paintbrushes. The Region has traditionally been famous for its furs and ethnic crafts: Dymkovo painted toys, wooden articles, artwork made from tree roots, straw items, pine root items, Kukarsk lace, and ceramics. The Russian basketry cottage industry is centered in the Region.

Recent years have seen Kirov-based enterprises penetrate the domestic and foreign markets extensively. The Region has developed economic and cultural relations with other Russian regions, CIS countries, and other foreign countries. The Regional Government is doing its utmost to support the establishment of new and renovation of existing production facilities and to guarantee the Region's business partners a favorable investment climate and conditions conducive to safe and profitable capital investment, including foreign capital. In a nutshell, the Region is open to constructive cooperation.

Hopefully, the investment projects offered in this Guide will help us find new business partners, open up new spheres of economic interaction, and offer scope for business activity by potential investors in the Region.

Vladimir Sergeenkov,
GOVERNOR OF THE KIROV REGION,
CHAIRMAN OF THE GOVERNMENT OF THE KIROV REGION

1. GENERAL INFORMATION

1.1. GEOGRAPHY

Located in the north-east of European Russia, the Kirov Region covers an area of some 120,800 square kilometers. To the north, the Region borders the Arkhangelsk Region and the Komi Republic, to the north-east – the Komi-Permyatsky Autonomous District and the Penza Region, to the east – the Republic of Udmurtia, to the south – the Republic of Tatarstan, to the south-west – the Republic of Mariy El, to the west – the Nizhny Novgorod Region and the Kostroma Region, and to the north-west – the Vologda Region.

1.2. CLIMATE

The Kirov Region is located in the moderate continental climate zone. Air temperatures average −14°C in January, rising to +18°C in July. Annual precipitation reaches 500–700 mm. The average growing season lasts around 165 days.

1.3. POPULATION

According to preliminary 2002 census results, the Kirov Region has a total population of 1,504,000. The average population density is 12.5 people per square kilometer. The economically active population totals 833,000. Official unemployment stood at 3.1% in 2002.

Demographically speaking, some 59.9% are of statutory working age, 18.3% are below the statutory working age, and 21.8% are above the statutory working age.

The major urban centers of the Kirov Region (2002 data) are Kirov with 457,400 inhabitants, Kirovo-Chepetsk with 90,500 inhabitants, Vyatskie Polyany with 41,900 inhabitants, Slobodskoy with 38,300 inhabitants, and Kotelnich with 29,500 inhabitants.

Population								TABLE 1
	1992	1997	1998	1999	2000	2001	2002
Total population, '000	1,658	1,625	1,613	1,603	1,590	1,576	1,504
Economically active population, '000	885	775	777	851	844	848	833

2. ADMINISTRATION

69, ul. Karla Libknekhta, Kirov, Kirov Region, 610019
Phone: (8332) 62 9564; fax: (8332) 62 8958
E-mail: region@ako.kirov.ru; http://www.ako.kirov.ru

NAME	POSITION	CONTACT INFORMATION
Vladimir Nilovich SERGEENKOV	Governor of the Kirov Region, Chairman of the Government of the Kirov Region	Phone: (8332) 62 9564
Alexei Petrovich LUGINOV	Deputy Chairman of the Government of the Kirov Region, Chairman of the Agriculture and Food Committee	Phone: (8332) 62 6857
Tatyana Alexandrovna VASILYEVA	Head of the International, Foreign Trade, and Inter-Regional Cooperation Department of the Government of the Kirov Region	Phone/fax: (8332) 62 1627 E-mail: forecon@ako.kirov.ru
Lubov Mikhailovna KUIMOVA	Head of the Economy Department of the Government of the Kirov Region	Phone: (8332) 62 1357, 38 1076 Fax: (8332) 38 1191 E-mail: econsyn@ako.kirov.ru, invest@ako.kirov.ru
Valery Alexeevich KURBATOV	Head of the Industry, and Science and Technology Department of the Government of the Kirov Region	Phone: (8332) 62 4132 E-mail: industry@ako.kirov.ru
Nikolai Vladimirovich POLYAKOV	Chairman of the Enterprise Support and Development Committee of the Government of the Kirov Region	Phone: (8332) 62 8444 Fax: (8332) 38 1471 E-mail: business@ako.kirov.ru
Leonid Nikolaevich SCHUPLETSOV	Head of the Forestry Department of the Government of the Kirov Region	Phone: (8332) 62 7851

3. ECONOMIC POTENTIAL

3.1. 1997–2002 GROSS REGIONAL PRODUCT (GRP). INDUSTRY BREAKDOWN

In 2002, the Kirov Region's gross regional product reached $1,657.1 million, 9% up on 2001. GRP per capita totaled $965 in 2001 and $1,103 in 2002.

3.2. MAJOR ECONOMIC GROWTH PROJECTIONS

The main social and economic development priorities for the coming years are set forth in the Kirov Region Social and Economic Development Conceptual Framework through 2004. The Conceptual Framework sets the tasks outlined below.

Industry: To increase industrial efficiency, optimize the production structure, produce more competitive goods, introduce advanced resource-saving technologies, intensify investment and innovation activity, and create new enterprises.

GRP trends in 1997–2002						TABLE 2
	1997	1998	1999	2000	2001*	2002*
GRP in current prices, $ million	2,909.7	1,718.9	1,104.9	1,353.2	1,520.1	1,657.1

*Estimates of the Government of the Kirov Region

GRP industry breakdown in 1997–2002, % of total						TABLE 3
	1997	1998	1999	2000	2001*	2002*
GRP	100.0	100.0	100.0	100.0	100.0	100.0
Industry	35.6	33.8	40.2	41.4	32.4	31.4
Agriculture and forestry	15.0	14.5	18.8	17.1	18.4	14.7
Construction	4.8	5.2	4.0	4.0	3.9	3.7
Transport and communications	9.4	8.4	8.0	8.6	7.7	9.9
Trade and public catering	11.6	10.6	10.9	10.1	10.5	11.2
Other sectors and net taxes on output	23.6	27.5	18.1	18.8	27.1	29.1

*Estimates of the Government of the Kirov Region

Agriculture: To increase output, introduce new scientific research based technologies, improve the financial standing of agricultural enterprises, and support individual farming.

Construction: To develop the construction sector by streamlining construction capacities based on modern construction and finishing technologies, and increase the volume of construction.

Transport: To improve the quality of transportation services, develop infrastructure, and develop air transport via the extension and renovation of the Kirov Airport's runway.

Trade: To develop the consumer market with a view to satisfying demand for goods and services.

Foreign trade: To expand cooperation with other regions of Russia and overseas, and involve the customs service in the provision of support to companies involved in foreign trade.

3.3. INDUSTRIAL OUTPUT IN 1997–2002 FOR MAJOR SECTORS OF ECONOMY

The key sectors of the Kirov Region are machine engineering, metal processing, chemicals, petrochemicals, food, and energy. These account for a combined 70.6% of total industrial output.

Machine engineering and metal processing. The sector includes aircraft, shipbuilding, electrical, machine tools, handling equipment, and railway machine engineering companies. Major enterprises include OAO AVITEC Vyatsky Machine Engineering Plant, OAO Lepse Electric Machine Engineering Plant, GUP Novovyatsky Machinery Plant 2, OAO Molot Vyatsko-Polyansky Machine Engineering Plant, OAO Kirskabel, OAO May 1 Kirov Machine Engineering Plant, and OAO Kirov Machining Tools Plant. The sector's enterprises manufacture railway cranes, non-coated wire, and washing machines.

Chemicals and petrochemicals. The largest enterprises are OAO Konstantinov Kirovo-Chepetsk Chemical Plant and OAO Kirov Tire Factory.

Food and beverages. The major enterprises are OAO Kirov Meat Processing Plant, OAO Slobodsky Meat Processing Plant, OAO Kirov Margarine Factory, ZAO Kirov Milk Processing Factory, OAO Kirov Confectionery and Macaroni Factory, OAO Bakery and Confectionery Factory, OAO Urzhumsky Distillery, OAO Slobodskoy Distillery, and OAO Vyatich.

Forestry, timber, and pulp and paper. The sector produces chipboard and fiberboard, glued plywood, parquet, skis, wooden houses, solid wood board,

Industry breakdown of industrial output in 1997–2002, % of total						TABLE 4
	1997	1998	1999	2000	2001	2002*
Industry	100.0	100.0	100.0	100.0	100.0	100.0
Machine engineering and metal processing	14.4	12.1	23.1	26.9	19.2	22.4
Chemicals and petrochemicals	19.8	20.4	17.2	17.9	20.7	18.4
Food and beverages	13.5	14.7	14.9	13.0	14.9	15.2
Energy	18.7	18.1	11.6	10.9	13.4	14.6
Forestry, timber, and pulp and paper	12.9	15.0	15.3	13.4	13.5	13.3
Ferrous metals	5.4	5.3	5.5	6.4	7.1	6.1
Light industry	4.1	3.7	4,3	4,4	3.1	3.3
Construction materials	2.9	2.5	1.7	1.6	2.0	1.8
Pharmaceuticals	1.3	1.3	1.4	1.3	1.4	1.1
Microbiology	0.2	0.8	0.9	0.7	0.7	0.3
Fuel	1.0	0.8	0.5	0.5	0.5	0.2

*Estimates of the Government of the Kirov Region

Fuel and energy sector production and consumption trends, 1997–2002						TABLE 5
	1997	1998	1999	2000	2001	2002
Electricity output, billion kWh	3.8	3.7	3.8	3.6	3.6	3.7
Oil output (including gas condensate), '000 tons	0.9	1.2	2.6	3.9	4.8	6.0
Electricity consumption, billion kWh	6.6	6.7	6.9	7.1	7.0	7.0
Natural fuel gas consumption, million cubic meters	2,471.2	2,642.4	2,336.6	2,531.4	2,725.0	2,858.5

wooden finishing materials, paper, and packaging cardboard. Major enterprises include OAO Red Anchor, OAO Novovyatsky Ski Factory, OAO Domostroitel, OAO Central Company of Vyatka-Les Invest Concern, OOO Novovyatsky Forestry Plant, OOO LPK Poleco, OAO Maiskles, and OAO Lesnoi Profil.

Ferrous metals. The largest enterprise is OAO Omutninsky Metals Plant.

Other sectors. The Region produces fur articles, traditional craft items, and art paintbrushes.

3.4. FUEL AND ENERGY BALANCE (OUTPUT AND CONSUMPTION PER RESOURCE)

The sector satisfies only 50%–60% of the regional demand for energy. The bulk of fuel is imported from other Russian regions such as the Republic of Bashkortostan, the Komi Republic, and the Perm Region.

3.5. TRANSPORT INFRASTRUCTURE

Roads. The Region has 8,915 kilometers of paved public highway, with links to adjacent regions and other parts of the Russian Federation. A section of the Northwest – Urals highway has been completed.

Railroads. The Region has some 1,098 kilometers of railways. Trunk lines passing through the Kirov Region connect Central Russia to the Urals, Siberia, the Far East, and northern regions to southern regions.

River transport. The Region has 1,800 kilometers of navigable waterways along the Vyatka River and its tributaries.

3.6. MAIN NATURAL RESOURCES: RESERVES AND EXTRACTION IN 2002

The main natural resources of the Region are minerals and raw materials, forests, water, and curative mud.

Minerals and raw materials. The Vyatsko-Kamsky Nodular Phosphorites Field (2 billion tons of recoverable reserves) and the Verkhnekamsky Phosphorite Mine are located in the Kirov Region. The Region also has around 2,000 deposits of peat (300 million tons) and explored deposits and traces of oil (583.3 million tons of inferred reserves) and bitumen shales. Fifty lake sapropel deposits explored in twelve areas of the Region contain some 420,000 tons of reserves.

Forest resources. Over 50% of the Region lies under forests. Coniferous species account for 54% of total forest reserve. The timber reserve stands at 1.1 billion cubic meters. The annual timber harvesting potential stands at 15.4 million cubic meters. The timber reserve is rising at a rate of 18 million cubic meters annually.

Water resources. Some 18 varieties of mineral water are found in the Kirov Region. Mineral water deposits with high iodine and bromine content have been explored in the Belokholunitsky District.

4. TRADE OPPORTUNITIES

4.1. MAIN GOODS
PRODUCED IN THE REGION
Energy. 2002 output: 3.7 billion kWh.

Synthetic ammonium. Output for 2002: 771,000 tons.

Synthetic resins and plastics. Output for 2002: 10,100 tons.

Tires. Output for 2002: 3.1 million items.

Timber processing machine tools. Output for 2002: 2,100 machine tools.

Washing machines. Output for 2002: 165,000 machines.

Commercial timber. Output for 2002: 4.6 million dense cubic meters.

Sawn timber. Output for 2002: 1.4 million cubic meters.

Glued plywood. Output for 2002: 74,500 cubic meters.

Footwear. 1.8 million pairs produced in 2002.

4.2. EXPORTS,
INCLUDING EXTRA-CIS
2000 extra-CIS exports amounted to $370.7 million, and CIS exports totaled $17.1 million. The corresponding figures for 2001 were $222 million and $20.5 million, and $204.7 million and $26.5 million for 2002.

The Region's main exports include petrochemicals (42.1% of total exports), timber and timber products (21.8%), machine engineering goods (5.5%), ferrous and non-ferrous metals (3%), and textiles and footwear (1.9%). The main trading partners for exports are Germany, Italy, Greece, Finland, the UK, France, Turkey, the Czech Republic, Hungary, Ukraine, Belarus, and Kazakhstan.

4.3. IMPORTS,
INCLUDING EXTRA-CIS
2000 extra-CIS imports amounted to $22 million, and CIS imports totaled $9.6 million. The corresponding figures for 2001 were $30.8 million and $7.2 million, and $32.6 million and $3.6 million for 2001.

The Region's main imports include machine engineering products, raw leather and leather goods, and food and edible raw materials. The Region's main trading partners for imports are Germany, Italy, Greece, Finland, the UK, France, Turkey, the Czech Republic, Hungary, Ukraine, Belarus, and Kazakhstan.

4.4. MAJOR REGIONAL
EXPORT AND IMPORT ENTITIES
Owing to the specific nature of the Region's export and import activities, export and import transactions are performed mainly by industrial enterprises.

5. INVESTMENT OPPORTUNITIES

5.1 INVESTMENTS IN 1992–2002
(BY INDUSTRY SECTOR),
INCLUDING FOREIGN INVESTMENTS
The following general factors determine the investment appeal of the Kirov Region:
- Its favorable geographic location (proximity to large markets and high consumer potential);
- Its well-developed transport infrastructure;
- Laws supporting investment activity (guarantees for investor rights and preferential tax treatment for investors);

- Its qualified workforce; and
- Cheap energy resources.

5.2. CAPITAL
INVESTMENT
Industry and transport account for the bulk of capital investment.

5.3. MAJOR ENTERPRISES
(INCLUDING ENTERPRISES
WITH FOREIGN INVESTMENT)
The Kirov Region hosts some 50 enterprises with foreign capital from the USA, Germany, the UK,

Capital investment by industry sector, $ million						TABLE 6
	1997	1998	1999	2000	2001	2002
Total capital investment	299.8	219.3	135.0	152.0	159.7	175.6
Including major industries (% of total):						
Industry	26.6	26.2	34.2	34.6	35.0	34.3
Agriculture and forestry	4.0	12.1	10.5	9.5	10.7	14.0
Construction	1.2	1.0	1.4	2.0	1.9	2.0
Transport and communications	17.5	12.3	15.3	15.6	15.5	18.6
Trade and public catering	1.9	2.4	1.8	5.7	4.6	1.9
Other	48.8	46.0	36.8	32.6	32.3	29.2

Foreign investment trends in 1997–2002						TABLE 7
	1997	1998	1999	2000	2001	2002
Foreign investment, $ million	0.8	0.1	2.7	14.7	3.8	2.7
Including FDI, $ million	0.8	0.1	0.5	6.7	1.8	0.6

Largest enterprises of the Kirov Region	TABLE 8
COMPANY	SECTOR
GUP Novovyatsky Machinery Plant 2	Machine engineering
OAO AVITEC Vyatsky Machine Engineering Plant	Machine engineering
OAO Konstantinov Kirovo-Chepetsk Chemical Plant	Chemicals
OAO Kirov Tire Factory	Chemicals
ZAO Kirov Dairy	Food and beverages
OAO Urzhumsky Distillery	Food and beverages

Regional entities responsible for raising investment		TABLE 9
ENTITY	ADDRESS	PHONE, FAX, E-MAIL
Basis Training and Research Center	95a, ul. Lenina, Kirov, Kirov Region, 610002	Phone: (8332) 62 4051 Phone/fax: (8332) 62 9293 Fax: (8332) 62 4051
OAO Vyatinvestfond	2, ul. Stepana Khalturina, Kirov, Kirov Region, 610000	Phone: (8332) 62 2373, 62 9506 Fax: (8332) 69 2355 E-mail: root@invest.vyatka.ru

Italy, China, Switzerland, Poland, Bulgaria, Cyprus, Ukraine, Belarus, and Uzbekistan.

5.4. MOST ATTRACTIVE SECTORS FOR INVESTMENT

According to experts and the Government of the Kirov Region, the most promising sectors for investment are machine engineering, forestry, timber and paper, light, and the agroindustrial sector.

5.5. CURRENT LEGISLATION ON INVESTOR TAX EXEMPTIONS AND PRIVILEGES

The Kirov Region has a legislative framework governing investment. The following laws have been adopted: On State Support to Private Investment Activity in the Kirov Region (basic legal provisions for investment activity in the Region, state guarantees, forms of state support, and measures to ensure protection of investor rights); On Tax Benefits Granted to Investors in the Kirov Region (lists tax benefit types and rates); On Residential Mortgages in the Kirov Region (provides a legal framework for mortgage-based purchasing of residential property in the Kirov Region).

5.6. FEDERAL AND REGIONAL ECONOMIC AND SOCIAL DEVELOPMENT PROGRAMS FOR THE KIROV REGION

Federal targeted programs. The following federal targeted programs are currently up and running in the Kirov Region: Children of Russia, 2003–2006, The Elderly, 2002–2004, the Federal Program for the Development of Education, 2001–2005, Prevention and Eradication of Social Diseases, 2002–2006, and Culture of Russia, 2001–2005.

Regional programs. The Kirov Region Investment Policy Conceptual Framework (2000–2003) and the Comprehensive Plan for its implementation were approved and adopted with a view to encouraging investment activities. The Conceptual Framework is accompanied by a comprehensive plan of actions for its implementation. The Region is implementing a regional targeted program for the Improvement of the Investment Appeal of the Kirov Region in 2002–2005. The program sets forth rules governing the regional budget subsidizing of bank interest on loans taken out by investors investing in the Region.

6. INVESTMENT PROJECTS

Industry sector and project description	1) Expected results 2) Amount and term of investment 3) Form of financing[1] 4) Documentation[2]	Contact information
1	2	3

	ENERGY	
49R001 Renewal of the main facilities of a power station (launch of a combined cycle power plant). Project goal: to increase electricity output.	1) To increase capacity by 188 MWh 2) $29.8 million/3 years 3) L ($14.1 million) 4) FS, BP	OAO Kirovenergo 51, ul. Drelevskogo, Kirov, Kirov Region, 610601 Phone: (8332) 69 1637, 62 7650 Vladimir Albertovich Lebedev, CEO

	FERROUS METALS	
49R002 Renovation of the fixed assets of the steel casting workshop of an operating metallurgy plant. Project goal: to increase output and improve product quality.	1) Capacity of 180,000 tons per year 2) $31 million/2 years 3) L ($27 million) 4) FS, BP	OAO Omutninsky Metals Plant 2, ul. Kokovikhina, Omutninsk, Kirov Region, 612740 Phone: (83352) 26 163 Alexander Dmitrievich Voloskov, CEO

	MACHINE ENGINEERING AND METAL PROCESSING	
49R003 Creation of extra facilities for electric appliance manufacturing at an operating enterprise. Project goal: to increase products output.	1) Output of 180,000 items per year 2) $25 million/3 years 3) L 4) FS, BP	GUP Novovyatsk Mechanical Plant 2 51/2, ul. Sovetskaya, Novovyatsky District, Kirov, Kirov Region, 610013 Phone: (8332) 31 8177, 31 2233 Mikhail Konstantinovich Safonov, CEO
49R004 Creation of new facilities for electric window manufacturing at an operating enterprise. Project goal: to diversify product mix.	1) Output of 500–1,000 thousand pieces per year 2) $25 million/2 years 3) L 4) BP	OAO Lepse Electric Machine Building Works 24, Oktyabrsky prospect, Kirov, Kirov Region, 610006 Phone: (8332) 23 3966, 23 2310 Gennady Alexandrovich Mamaev, CEO

	FORESTRY, TIMBER, AND PULP AND PAPER	
49R005 Creation of new facilities for tree foliage biochemical recycling at an operating enterprise. Project goal: to produce commercial products from tree foliage.	1) Product output of 40 tons per year 2) $1 million/1 year 3) L ($650 million) 4) BP	OOO Forestry Venture Company 62, ul. Truda, Kirov, Kirov Region, 610020 Phone: (8332) 35 4432 Igor Vladimirovich Belyaev, CEO
49R006 Creation of new facilities for glued timber manufacturing at an operating forestry plant. Project goal: to diversify product mix.	1) Output of 4,000 cubic meters per year 2) $0.8 million/3 months 3) L ($0.6) million 4) FS, BP	OOO Novovyatsky Forestry Plant 1, ul. Kommuny, Kirov, Kirov Region, 610013 Phone: (8332) 31 7553, 31 9090 Nikolai Nikolaevich Grukhin, CEO

[1] L – Loan, E – Equity, Leas. – Leasing, JV – Joint Venture
[2] BP – Business Plan, FS – Feasibility Study

1	2	3

49R007

● ◆ ▲

Creation of a large plywood manufacturing enterprise.
Project goal: to market plywood.

1) Output of 25,000 cubic meters per year
2) $10.6 million/8 months
3) L ($10.6 million)
4) FS, BP

OAO VyatkaLesInvest Concern
Central Company,
62, ul. Truda, Kirov, Kirov Region, 610020
Phone: (8332) 35 4432, 65 3147
Igor Nikolaevich Seleznev,
Director

49R008

● ◆ ▲

Creation of a furniture board workshop.
Project goal: to launch production and sales of articles for the furniture industry (ecological birch furniture boards produced using the heavy wood adhesion technique).

1) Output of 4,800 cubic meters per year
2) $2.2 million/6 months
3) L
4) FS, BP

OAO VyatkaLesInvest Concern
Central Company
62, ul. Truda, Kirov, Kirov Region, 610020
Phone: (8332) 35 4432, 65 3147
Igor Nikolaevich Seleznev,
Director

49R009

● ◆ ▲

Creation of new facilities for furniture board manufacturing at an operating forestry plant.
Project goal: to diversify product mix.

1) Output of 4,800 cubic meters per year
2) $2.6 million/1 year
3) L ($2.2 million)
4) FS, BP

OOO Novovyatsky Forestry Plant
1, ul. Kommuny, Kirov,
Kirov Region, 610013
Phone: (8332) 31 7553, 31 9090
Nikolai Nikolaevich Grukhin,
CEO

49R010

● ◆ ▲

Creation of new facilities for profile sawn timber and glued parts manufacturing at an operating enterprise.
Project goal: to diversify product mix.

1) Sawn timber output of 50,000 cubic meters per year
2) $1.7 million/3 years
3) L ($1.2 million)
4) FS, BP

OAO Maiskles
23, ul. Pochtovaya, pos. Bezbozhnik,
Murashinsky District,
Kirov Region, 613750
Phone: (83348) 22 855, 22 835
Zot Fomich Chernyshov,
CEO

B.P. KONSTANTINOV KIROVO-CHEPETSKY CHEMICALS COMBINE

PROFESSOR
VLADIMIR YURYEVICH
ZAKHAROV,
DOCTOR OF CHEMISTRY,
CEO

The B.P. Konstantinov Kirovo-Chepetsky Chemicals Combine (OAO KCKK) is the largest industrial enterprise in the Kirov Region. OAO KCKK produces the following chemicals:
1. Organic fluorine products: difluorochloromethane halocarbons (x-22) and 1.1.1 difluorchloroethane (x-142), octifluorcyclobutane (x-138c) and compounds thereof, ozone friendly halocarbons – octa- and heptafluorpropanes, trifluormethane (x-218, x-227, x-23), fluorinated monomers – perfluoroethylene (M-4), trifluoroethylene (M-3), vinylene fluoride (M-2), hexafluoropropylene (M-6), suspended and emulsion polytetraflouroethylene (F-4, F-4D), modified F4M and F4DM, homopolymers and copolymers (F-40, F-42, F-32, F-4MB (FEP equivalent), F-2M, F-3M, F-3) based on monomers – M-4, M-2, M-3, M-6 and on ethylene, fluorinated elastomers based on M-2 and M-3 (SKF-32) and M-6 (SKF-26), modified elastomers with a broad spectrum of resilience characteristics and vitrification temperature levels (Viton equivalent), fluoropolymer and copolymer water suspensions and latex (F-4D, F-4MD), FPR fluorinated varnish, hexafluoropropylene oxide (M-06), dimer and trimer oxides, perfluorinated oxyacids, perflourdecaline, perfluoromethylcyclohexane, perflourodimethylcyclohexane, perfluoromethyldecaline, perfluorinated oils and fluids (M-1, B-1, UPI, KST, KSK).
Inorganic fluorinated products: anhydrous hydrogen fluoride, hydrofluoric acid (40% hydrofluoric), hydrosilicofluoric acid, synthetic calcium fluoride, powder fluorocarbon, and sulphur hexafluoride (SF6 gas).
3. Inorganic products: caustic soda 40%, liquid chlorine, hydrochloric acid – synthetic, inhibited, abgaseous, nitric acid 60%, calcium chloride 32% and crystalline, synthetic and conversion calcium carbonate, sodium hypochloride, zinc chloride 40%, strontium carbonate, liquid and gaseous oxygen, liquid and gaseous nitrogen, acetylene, dihydratedicalcium phosphate, toothpaste filler.
4. Organic chemistry products: chloroform, trichloracetaldehyde, ethyl chloride.
5. Mineral fertilizers: ammonia, ammonium nitrate, nitrogen phosphate (NP) fertilizers with various component ratios, nitrogenphosphate homogenous mixes of nitrate and ammonium phosphate, nitrogen-phosphorous-potassium (NPK) fertilizers with various nutrient ratios, chlorine free nitrogen-phosphorous-potassium fertilizers with various component ratios, fertilizers with microelement additives.
6. Medical devices and articles: artificial cardiac valves, medical lint.
7. Articles from fluorine polymers and copolymers: sheet material from F-4, F-4A, F-4M, rods, disks, plugs, pipe, molded pipeline components, containers, reactors, baths, laboratory vessels from F-4 and F-4MB, pumps, valves, fixtures, seals, guided tape, film, thread reinforcement film, columnar devices, and parts.
OAO KCKK includes the following creative departments: central plant laboratory, design department, special design department for metering and automation devices, special design bureau for medical devices and articles.

7, PER. POZHARNY,
613040, KIROVO-CHEPETSK,
KIROV REGION, RUSSIA
TEL: (83361) 40 979
TEL./FAX: (8332) 62 79 21
E-MAIL: okb@kckk.ru
HTTP://www.kckk.ru

50. NIZHNY NOVGOROD REGION [52]

ECONOMIC MAP

Buy
Galich
Neya
Neya
Manturovo
Sharya
KIROV REGION

KOSTROMA REGION

Unzha

Kineshma
Gorkovskoe water reservoir
Vetluga
Vakhtan
Shakhunya

IVANOVO REGION
Shuya
Kovernino
Vetluzhsky
YOSHKAR-OLA

Chkalovsk
Gorodets
Semyonov
Cheboksarskoe water reservoir

Zavolzhiye
Balakhna
Volga
Bor
NIZHNY NOVGOROD
CHEBOKSARY

Kovrov
Dzerzhinsk
Kstovo
Lyskovo
REPUBLIC OF

Vyazniki
Bogorodsk
Oka
Pyana
Shumerlya
Kanash

VLADIMIR REGION
Murom
Pavlovo
Navashino
CHUVASHIA

Melenki
Kulebaki
Arzamas

Vyksa
Sarov
Pervomaysk
Alatyr
Alatyr

Kasimov
RYAZAN REGION

Sasovo
Moksha
REPUBLIC OF MORDOVIYA
Sura

Ruzaevka
SARANSK

PROCESSING INDUSTRY
- Ferrous metals
- Machine engineering and metal processing
- Chemicals and petrochemicals
- Forestry and timber
- Construction materials and glass
- Light industry
- Food and beverages
- Art crafts

POWER PLANTS
- Thermal power plants
- Hydro power plants

CROPS AND LIVESTOCK BREEDING
- Wheat
- Rye
- Long-fibred flax
- Orchards
- Sugar beetroot
- Potatoes
- Meat and dairy cattle breeding
- Pig breeding
- Poultry farming

The Nizhny Novgorod Region is one of the largest industrial, research and development, and trade regions of Russia. It offers enormous potential for cooperation development in business, science, education, and culture, and wide opportunities for the development of tourism and recreational facilities.

Today, we are confident that the economic situation in the Region has changed. Over the past three years, the Region has been demonstrating positive development trends – industrial growth, falling unemployment, increased trade, and rising real incomes and purchasing power.

The Region's investment appeal stems from these positive economic development trends, its advantageous geographic location, well-developed transport infrastructure, stable financial and banking system, highly qualified workforce, and modern investment legislation. The Region has a track record of successful collaboration with foreign and major Russian investors.

The Government of the Nizhny Novgorod Region accords priority status to the development of its investment climate and is continuously addressing issues related to the attraction of investment, including foreign investment, and the construction of new production facilities.

We realize that we need to ensure stable industrial growth, which can only be accomplished through investment, the introduction of advanced technologies, and the utilization of the unique research and development potential of our military industrial companies. We welcome efficient owners to our Region.

The regional authorities are also committed to creating conditions conducive to dynamic economic growth and the introduction of progressive forms of business. The success of our economic policy depends on the improvement of the Region's investment climate. Nizhny Novgorod's rising investment and international credit ratings indicate that we have improved stability and welfare in the Region.

The Nizhny Novgorod Region is open to international partnership and investment.

Gennady Khodyrev,
GOVERNOR OF THE NIZHNY NOVGOROD REGION,
CHAIRMAN OF THE GOVERNMENT OF THE NIZHNY NOVGOROD REGION

1. GENERAL INFORMATION

1.1. GEOGRAPHY

Located at the center of European Russia, the Nizhny Novgorod Region covers a total area of 76,900 square kilometers. To the north-west, it borders the Kostroma Region, to the north-east– the Kirov Region, to the east – the Republic of Mariy El and the Republic of Chuvashia, to the south – the Republic of Mordovia, to the south-west – the Ryazan Region, and to the west – the Vladimir Region and the Ivanovo Region.

1.2. CLIMATE

The Nizhny Novgorod Region enjoys a moderate continental climate. Air temperatures in January average −12°C, rising to an average of +19°C in July. Annual precipitation totals 450–600 mm. The growing season lasts around 165–175 days.

1.3. POPULATION

According to preliminary 2002 census results, the total population of the Nizhny Novgorod Region was 3,524,000 people. The average population density is 45.8 per square kilometer. The economically active population totaled 1,308,000 people. Official 2002 unemployment stood at 0.8%.

Demographically speaking, some 59.3% are of statutory working age, 16.7% are below the statutory working age, and 24% are beyond the statutory working age.

The major urban centers of the Nizhny Novgorod Region (2002 data) are Nizhny Novgorod with 1,311,200 inhabitants, Dzerzhinsk with 261,400 inhabitants, Arzamas with 109,500 inhabitants, Sarov with 86,000 inhabitants, and Kstovo with 69,000 inhabitants.

Population								TABLE 1
	1992	1997	1998	1999	2000	2001	2002	
Total population, '000	3,773	3,717	3,703	3,688	3,663	3,633	3,524	
Economically active population, '000	1,940	1,783	1,756	1,844	1,871	1,841	1,308	

2. ADMINISTRATION

1 & 2, the Kremlin, Nizhny Novgorod, Nizhny Novgorod Region, 603082
Phone: (8312) 39 0297; fax: (8312) 39 0048
E-mail: official@prav.kreml.nnov.ru; http://www.government.nnov.ru

NAME	POSITION	CONTACT INFORMATION
Gennady Maksimovich KHODYREV	Governor of the Nizhny Novgorod Region, Chairman of the Government of the Nizhny Novgorod Region	Phone: (8312) 19 7300 Fax: (8312) 39 0048
Yury Petrovich SENTYURIN	First Deputy Governor of the Nizhny Novgorod Region, Member of the Government of the Nizhny Novgorod Region	Phone: (8312) 39 0297 Fax: (8312) 39 0048
Galina Konstantinovna KUZMINA	Minister of Economy and Enterprise Development of the Nizhny Novgorod Region	Phone: (8312) 39 0662 Fax: (8312) 39 0186 E-mail: root@dep.kreml.nnov.ru
Vitaly Yevstafyevich ANTONEVICH	Minister of Industry and Innovation of the Nizhny Novgorod Region	Phone: (8312) 39 0364 Fax: (8312) 39 0323
Vadim Igorevich YERYZHENSKY	Minister of the Agroindustrial Sector of the Nizhny Novgorod Region	Phone: (8312) 39 1151, 39 1727 Fax: (8312) 39 1391
Vadim Viktorovich SOBOLEV	Minister of Finance of the Nizhny Novgorod Region	Phone: (8312) 35 5301 Fax: (8312) 35 5310
Vladimir Alexandrovich SOLOVYEV	Deputy Minister of Economy and Enterprise Development of the Nizhny Novgorod Region, Chief of the Foreign Trade Relations and Investment Department of the Ministry of the Economy and Enterprise Development of the Nizhny Novgorod Region	Phone: (8312) 39 1148, 39 0049 Fax: (8312) 39 0186 E-mail: invest@dep.kreml.nnov.ru

3. ECONOMIC POTENTIAL

3.1. 1997–2002 GROSS REGIONAL PRODUCT (GRP). INDUSTRY BREAKDOWN

The Nizhny Novgorod Region's 2002 gross regional product amounted to $6,100.9 million, 8.2% up on 2001. The industrial sector accounted for the bulk of the growth. Per capita GRP was $1,552 in 2001, and $1,730 in 2002.

3.2. MAJOR ECONOMIC GROWTH PROJECTIONS

The Social and Economic Development Projections for the Nizhny Novgorod Region for 2003 forecast output growth in all sectors of the economy. The following objectives have been set:

GRP trends in 1997–2002						TABLE 2
	1997	1998	1999	2000	2001*	2002*
GRP in current prices, $ million	8,838.1	5,236.8	3,182.1	3,707.7	5,636.5	6,100.9

*Estimates of the Nizhny Novgorod Regional Administration

GRP industry breakdown in 1997–2002, % of total						TABLE 3
	1997	1998	1999	2000	2001*	2002*
GRP	100.0	100.0	100.0	100.0	100.0	100.0
Industry	32.9	33.6	35.2	35.5	34.9	34.9
Agriculture and forestry	4.6	4.4	7.3	7.0	5.9	6.9
Construction	7.8	6.5	5.4	4.7	4.6	4.6
Transport and communications	12.6	12.0	14.4	11.2	10.1	10.5
Trade and public catering	10.4	10.5	10.5	15.5	19.9	17.3
Other	19.6	24.7	19.1	19.1	17.6	18.8
Net taxes on output	12.1	8.3	8.1	7.0	7.0	7.0

*Estimates of the Nizhny Novgorod Regional Administration

Industry: creating new and upgrading existing facilities; improving product quality; introducing new technologies and products.

Agriculture: active encouragement of resource saving technologies, streamlining of relations between land-owners and land users, maintaining public welfare in rural areas, and improving the financial standing of agricultural enterprises.

Construction: deployment of new technologies, improving produce quality, and launch of new construction sites.

3.3. INDUSTRIAL OUTPUT IN 1997–2002 FOR MAJOR SECTORS OF ECONOMY

The Nizhny Novgorod Region's major industrial sectors are machine engineering and metals processing, ferrous metals, food and beverages, energy, chemicals and petrochemicals. These account for a combined 82.4% of total industrial output.

Machine engineering and metal processing. The sector accounts for 43.2% of total industrial output, specializing in transport engineering: automotive industry (trucks, cars, buses, and automotive engines), shipbuilding (ships, vessels, and dry-cargo motor ships), diesel engineering and aircraft engineering (military and civil aircraft, hydraulic aircraft

control systems, and fastening elements for aircraft and spacecraft). The largest enterprises are OAO Gorky Automotive Plant, OAO Pavlovsky Avtobus, OAO Zavolzhsky Motor Factory, OAO Nizhny Novgorod Sokol Aircraft Engineering Plant, OAO Gidromash, OAO Normal, OAO Krasnoe Sormovo Factory, OAO Krasny Yakor, and OAO Oka Shipyard.

Ferrous metals. The sectors accounts for 11.1% of total industrial output, specializing in open-hearth operation, steelmaking, ring rolling and section rolling, and also steel pipe and railway wheels output. The largest enterprises are OAO Vyksunsky Steelworks, OAO Kulebaksky Steelworks.

Food and beverages. The sector accounts for 10.9% of total industrial output, specializing in fat-and-oil, meat, milk, and confectionery production. The largest enterprises are OAO Nizhny Novgorod Milk Plant, OAO Nizhny Novgorod Fat-and-Oil Productions, OAO Dzerzhinsky Meat Processing Plant, ZAO Sormovskaya Confectionery.

Energy. The sector accounts for 9.5% of total industrial output. The energy is produced at the Nizhegorodskaya GRES (144 MW), Igumnovskaya Thermal Power Station (87 MW), Novogorkovskaya Thermal Power Station (265 MW), Dzerzhinskaya

Industry breakdown of industrial output in 1997–2002, % of total						TABLE 4
	1997	1998	1999	2000	2001	2002*
Industry	100.0	100.0	100.0	100.0	100.0	100.0
Machine engineering and metal processing	49.1	51.9	50.2	47.0	42.6	43.2
Ferrous metals	5.9	4.6	5.3	9.4	11.1	11.1
Food and beverages	10.1	9.3	11.3	9.6	11.6	10.9
Energy	9.7	10.3	7.0	7.4	7.4	9.5
Chemicals and petrochemicals	9.8	7.8	8.6	10.5	9.2	7.7
Forestry, timber, and pulp and paper	3.0	5.1	7.6	7.2	7.1	5.5
Fuel	3.2	2.7	1.6	1.3	1.8	2.9
Glass and porcelain	1.4	1.7	1.9	1.8	2.5	2.4
Construction materials	2.1	2.0	1.6	1.4	1.7	1.6
Light industry	2.8	1.6	2.0	2.0	2.2	1.6
Flour, cereals, and mixed fodder	1.7	1.7	1.5	1.3	1.6	0.9
Non-ferrous metals	0.2	0.4	0.5	0.5	0.4	0.4

*Estimates of the Nizhny Novgorod Regional Administration

Fuel and energy sector production and consumption trends, 1997–2002						TABLE 5
	1997	1998	1999	2000	2001	2002*
Electricity output, billion kWh	11.8	12.1	11.3	10.5	10.2	9.4
Electricity consumption, billion kWh	19.6	20.7	21.2	20.9	20.8	20.9
Oil consumption, '000 tons	12,253.0	9,323.0	4,197.0	3,708.9	6,751.0	10,683.4
Natural gas consumption, million cubic meters	8,131.4	5,740.0	6,205.0	6,827.0	6,877.0	7,605.4

*Estimates of the Nizhny Novgorod Regional Administration

Thermal Power Station (435 MW), and Sormovskaya Thermal Power Station (340 MW).

Chemicals and petrochemicals. The sector accounts for 7.7% of total industrial output, specializing in producing engine fuel, lubricating oil, hydrocarbon materials for the petrochemical synthesis, ammonia, polyurethane PVC pipes, artificial corundum, plastic products, and polymer film. The largest enterprises are OAO LUKoil-Nizhegorodnefteorgsintez, OAO Plastik, and OAO Korund.

3.4. FUEL AND ENERGY BALANCE (OUTPUT AND CONSUMPTION PER RESOURCE)
The Nizhny Novgorod Region is an energy deficit region. Local power stations cover only 50% of the total demand for energy, with the Federal Wholesale Electricity and Power Market (FOREM) supplies making up the deficit.

All the natural gas consumed in the Region is supplied from outside the region.

3.5. TRANSPORT INFRASTRUCTURE
Roads. The Nizhny Novgorod Region has some 10,800 kilometers of paved public highway. The Moscow – Nizhny Novgorod – Kazan federal highway is the principal road in the Region.

Railroads. The Nizhny Novgorod Region has 1,300 kilometers of railroads. The principal railway lines are Moscow – Nizhny Novgorod – Kirov, Moscow – Arzamas – Kazan, Nizhny Novgorod – Penza, and Nizhny Novgorod – Ruzaevka.

Airports. An international airport linking the Region to Germany and the CIS countries serves the city of Nizhny Novgorod.

River transport. The total length of the Region's navigable inland waterway system is 900 km. The Region's inland waterway transportation companies use the Volga, the Oka, and the Vetluga rivers. The Volga provides a navigable waterway between the Sea of Azov, the Baltic Sea, the Black Sea, the Caspian Sea, and the White Sea.

River ports. The city of Nizhny Novgorod is served by a passenger port and a freight port. A container terminal is scheduled for construction.

Oil and gas pipelines. The Region has 946 km of oil pipelines, 3,000 km of gas pipelines, and 889 km of oil product pipelines.

The principal oil pipeline is the Almetyevsk – Nizhny Novgorod. The Region is crossed by gas pipelines, including: the Perm – Kazan – Nizhny Novgorod,

Saratov – Nizhny Novgorod – Cherepovets, and Minibayevo – Kazan – Nizhny Novgorod.

3.6. MAIN NATURAL RESOURCES: RESERVES AND EXTRACTION IN 2002

The main natural resources of the Region are non-ore minerals for construction materials, rock salt, and mineral water.

Construction materials. The Region has four molding sand deposits (the reserves exceed 138 million tons), raw clay (63 million cubic meters), raw expanded clay (46 million cubic meters), carbonate strata (325 million cubic meters), dolomite used for white cement production (3.3 million tons), and gypsum and anhydrite (400 million tons).

Forest resources. Forests cover 46.1% of the Region's territory, with the timber reserve totaling 352 million cubic meters.

Water resources. The Region counts more than 9,000 rivers and floods. The largest rivers are the Volga, the Oka, the Sura, and the Vetluga. The Region has mineral water and chloride, sodium, and bromide brine reserves.

Recreational resources. The Region has the Kerzhensky Reserve and curative mud and blue clay deposits.

Other resources. The Region has a rock-salt reserve of 2.5 billion tons, 200 peat deposits with a reserve of 232 million tons, small non-ferrous metal deposits (copper, lead, zinc), rare element (molybdenum) and rare-earth element deposits (neodymium, cerium, and ytterbium).

4. TRADE OPPORTUNITIES

4.1. MAIN GOODS PRODUCED IN THE REGION

Machine engineering. In 2002, the Region produced 16 diesel engines and diesel generator sets, 153 metal cutting machines, 208,876 cars and trucks, and 42,833 buses.

Chemicals and petrochemicals. 2002 sulfuric acid output amounted to 118,100 tons, mineral fertilizer output amounted to 11,400 tons, PVC resin and copolymers – 31,000 tons, synthetic resin and plastics – 41,700 tons, and ethylene – 153,300 tons.

Forestry, timber, and pulp and paper. 2002 sawn timber output was 250,000 cubic meters, commercial timber – 484,000 cubic meters, cardboard – 48,383,000 cubic meters, paper – 530,000 tons, and newsprint – 516,000 tons.

Construction materials. In 2002, the Region produced 31,830,000 square meters of soft roofing, 421,000 cubic meters of mineral wool, 220,000 cubic meters of precast reinforced concrete structures, and 377 million standard bricks.

Fuel. In 2002, the Region produced 2,875,000 tons of diesel fuel and 1,252,000 tons of gasoline.

4.2. EXPORTS, INCLUDING EXTRA-CIS

1999 exports to extra-CIS countries amounted to $585.8 million, while exports to CIS countries totaled $136.5 million. The corresponding figures for

2000 were $660.6 million and $201.2 million, for 2001 – $802.7 million and $251.6 million, and for 2002 – $912.3 million and $307.4 million.

The main goods exported from the Region are cars, fuel oil, bitumen, railway wheels, steel pipe, rough timber, paper, chemicals, glass, and ferrous alloys. Extra-CIS countries accounted for 74.8% of the Region's total exports in 2002. The main export partners are Germany, India, Finland, Switzerland, the USA, China, the UK, Ukraine, Kazakhstan, and Estonia.

4.3. IMPORTS, INCLUDING EXTRA-CIS

1999 extra-CIS imports amounted to $219.6 million; exports to CIS countries totaled $78.9 million. The corresponding figures for 2000 were $234.2 million and $87 million, for 2001 – $310.3 million and $86.8 million, and for 2002 – $440.2 million and $59.1 million.

The main goods imported by the Region are steel plate, car front-axle beams, diesel pump-injector units, cellulose, and food and beverages. Extra-CIS countries accounted for 88.2% of the Region's total imports in 2002. The principal import partners are Germany, Ukraine, Hungary, Spain, Latvia, Italy, France, Austria, the USA, and Finland.

4.4. MAJOR REGIONAL EXPORT AND IMPORT ENTITIES

Major regional export and import entities		*TABLE 6*
ENTITY	ADDRESS	PHONE, FAX, E-MAIL
OOO RVD Multi-Profile Company	23, ul. Marshala Golovanova, Nizhny Novgorod, Nizhny Novgorod Region, 603107	Phone: (8312) 66 1275

5. INVESTMENT OPPORTUNITIES

5.1 INVESTMENTS IN 1992–2002 (BY INDUSTRY SECTOR), INCLUDING FOREIGN INVESTMENTS

The following factors determine the investment appeal of the Nizhny Novgorod Region:

- Qualified workforce;
- Significant industrial and scientific potential (Nizhny Novgorod is the leading center of education, applied, and academic science);
- Proactive policy of the Nizhny Novgorod Regional Government for support to investment activity;
- Developed financial network;
- Positive experience in the area of raising foreign investment;
- High consumer potential;
- Well-developed transport infrastructure;
- Favorable environment for small business development;
- Historick and cultural heritage (Nizhny Novgorod is a renowned historic and cultural center of Russia).

5.2. CAPITAL INVESTMENT

Industry, transport and communications account for the bulk of capital investments.

Capital investment by industry sector, $ million						*TABLE 7*
	1997	1998	1999	2000	2001	2002
Total capital investment	1,436.7	925.5	449.2	521.0	587.5	861.3
Including major industries (% of total):						
Industry	30.9	35.9	45.4	43.4	38.5	42.3
Agriculture and forestry	2.8	4.9	4.9	4.5	5.7	5.0
Construction	6.2	2.1	1.3	1.1	1.0	1.2
Transport and communications	22.9	22.7	20.1	21.9	25.8	23.9
Trade and public catering	2.8	1.7	1.8	1.1	1.9	2.4
Other	34.4	32.7	26.5	28.0	27.1	25.2

Foreign investment trends in 1997–2002						*TABLE 8*
	1997	1998	1999	2000	2001	2002
Foreign investment, $ million	163.0	150.0	29.2	64.3	20.9	90.2
Including FDI, $ million	20.8	3.9	13.8	27.5	19.8	25.7

5.3. MAJOR ENTERPRISES (INCLUDING ENTERPRISES WITH FOREIGN INVESTMENT)

The Region hosts more than 100 enterprises with foreign investment, including ZAO Avangard Knauf (construction materials, Russia, Germany), ZAO Kapella (manufacturing of Wella products, Russia, Germany), ZAO Instrum-Rend (air tools production, Russia, USA), ZAO Volna (hotel industry, Russia, Croatia), OOO BelRoss (footwear, Russia, Belarus), OOO Coca-Cola (beverages, international), OOO McDonald's (public catering, international), ZAO Europe Foods GB (food concentrates, Spain), and OOO Tubor (starter and accumulator batteries, Spain).

5.4. MOST ATTRACTIVE SECTORS FOR INVESTMENT

According to the Regional Government, the machine engineering, chemicals and petro-chemicals, food and beverages and food processing, tourism, and agroindustrial sectors are the most attractive industries for investment.

5.5. CURRENT LEGISLATION ON INVESTOR TAX EXEMPTIONS AND PRIVILEGES

The Nizny Novgorod Region has passed the Law On State Support to Investment Activity in the Nizhny Novgorod Region, which provides for investor tax exemptions, tax credits for investments, minimal land leasing tariffs, and tax concessions for real estate leasing.

The Nizhny Novgorod Regional Government's Decree On the Procedure for the Signing, Registration, Recording and Supervision of the Implementation of Investment Agreements regulates state support of investment activity.

The Program for the Encouragement of Investment Activity in the Nizhny Novgorod Region through 2005 focuses on new tasks for the Government and enterprises seeking to raise investment.

Largest enterprises of the Nizhny Novgorod Region

TABLE 9

COMPANY	SECTOR
OAO Gorky Automobile Plant	Machine engineering
OAO Zavolzhsky Motor Plant	Machine engineering
OAO Pavlovsky Avtobus	Machine engineering
OAO Nizhny Novgorod Sokol Aircraft Construction Plant	Aviation
OAO Gidromash	Aviation
OAO Vyksunsky Steelworks	Non-ferrous metals
OAO LUKoil-Nizhegorodnefteorgsintez	Chemicals and petrochemicals
OAO Plastik	Chemicals and petrochemicals
OAO Korund	Chemicals and petrochemicals
OAO LUKoil-Volganefteprodukt	Chemicals and petrochemicals
OAO Sintez	Chemicals and petrochemicals
OAO Nizhny Novgorod Oil and Fat Plant	Food and beverages
OAO Borsky Glass Factory	Glass
OAO Nizhpharm	Chemicals and pharmaceuticals
OAO Volgatelecom	Communications

Regional entities responsible for raising investment

TABLE 10

ENTITY	ADDRESS	PHONE, FAX, E-MAIL
GUP Regional Investment Assistance Agency	Office 31, block 9, the Kremlin, Nizhny Novgorod, Nizhny Novgorod Region, 603082	Phone: (8312) 19 2511 Fax: (8312) 19 2184 E-mail: guprasi@52.ru
ZAO Regional Development Agency	1, pl. Oktyabrskaya, Nizhny Novgorod, Nizhny Novgorod Region, 603005	Phone: (8312) 19 4782 Fax: (8312) 19 9779 http://rda.nnov.ru

IV

V O L G A   F E D E R A L   D I S T R I C T

5.6. FEDERAL AND REGIONAL ECONOMIC AND SOCIAL DEVELOPMENT PROGRAMS FOR THE NIZHNY NOVGOROD REGION

Federal targeted programs. The Nizhny Novgorod Region is participating in the implementation of 21 federal targeted programs, including the program for the Modernization of Russia's Transport System, 2002–2010, Energy Efficient Economy, 2002–2005 and through 2010, The Elimination of Inequalities in the Social and Economic Development of the Regions of the Russian Federation, 2002–2010 and through 2015, The Children of Russia, 2003–2006, The Elderly, 2002–2004, and others. The programs aim to develop the Region's industry, agriculture, transportation system, construction sector, and public welfare.

Regional programs. The Nizhny Novgorod Regional Administration has developed and is implementing 18 regional targeted programs that aim to develop industry, the agroindustrial sector, public welfare, public health, and education. These include the Program for the Development of the Agroindustrial Sector of the Nizhny Novgorod Region through 2005, the Program for the Development of the Light Industry in the Nizhny Novgorod Region, 2002–2005, the Blueprint for the Develop-ment of Tourism in the Nizhny Novgorod Region, 2002–2004, Pediatric Healthcare, 2001–2005, Gifted Children, 2001–2005, Vaccination, 1999– 2000 and through 2005, Urgent Measures to Combat Tuberculosis in the Nizhny Novgorod Region, 1999–2004, Urgent Measures to Combat HIV/AIDS in the Nizhny Novgorod Region, 2002–2006 (the Anti-HIV/AIDS Program), and others.

6. INVESTMENT PROJECTS

Industry sector and project description	1) Expected results 2) Amount and term of investment 3) Form of financing[1] 4) Documentation[2]	Contact information
1	2	3

CHEMICALS AND PETROCHEMICALS

50R001 ● ▲ ■

| Reconstruction of an ethylene oxide and glycol plant. Project goal: to increase output and sales at international and domestic markets of products with high profitability. | 1) Increase in capacity to 180 tons per year 2) $10.8 million/15 months 3) L, E 4) FS | OAO Sibur-Neftekhim 63, ul. Osharskaya, Nizhny Novgorod, Nizhny Novgorod Region, 603600 Phone: (8312) 78 3322, 78 3980 Fax: (8312) 78 3961, 78 3971 E-mail: info@sibur.nnov.ru http://www.sibur.nnov.ru Petr Vladimirovich Krupnov, CEO, Valentina Dmitrievna Kolodinskaya, Deputy CEO for Development |

50R002 ● ▲ ■

| Construction of a plant for the production of polyethylenetereftalate for food packaging. Project goal: to produce and sell food packaging film on the domestic and overseas markets | 1) 200,000 tons per year 2) $87.6 million/27 months 3) L, E 4) FS | OAO Sibur-Neftekhim 63, ul. Osharskaya, Nizhny Novgorod, Nizhny Novgorod Region, 603600 Phone: (8312) 78 3322, 78 3980 Fax: (8312) 78 3961, 78 3971 E-mail: info@sibur.nnov.ru http://www.sibur.nnov.ru Petr Vladimirovich Krupnov, CEO Valentina Dmitrievna Kolodinskaya, Deputy CEO for Development |

50R003 ● ▲ ■

| Construction of new ethylenechrolhydrine facilities. Project goal: to produce and sell a highly profitable product and to dismantle the existing facility. | 1) 15,000 tons per year 2) $3.2 million/13 months 3) L, E 4) FS | OAO Sibur-Neftekhim 63, ul. Osharskaya, Nizhny Novgorod, Nizhny Novgorod Region, 603600 Phone: (8312) 78 3322, 78 3980 Fax: (8312) 78 3961, 78 3971 E-mail: info@sibur.nnov.ru http://www.sibur.nnov.ru Petr Vladimirovich Krupnov, CEO Valentina Dmitrievna Kolodinskaya, Deputy CEO for Development |

50R004 ● ▲ ■

| Construction of polyethylene facilities. Project goal: to launch production and sale of a wide range of high profitability products on the domestic and overseas markets. | 1) 120,000 tons per year 2) $102.7 million/32 months 3) L, E 4) FS | OAO Sibur-Neftekhim 63, ul. Osharskaya, Nizhny Novgorod, Nizhny Novgorod Region, 603600 Phone: (8312) 78 3322, 78 3980 Fax: (8312) 78 3961, 78 3971 E-mail: info@sibur.nnov.ru http://www.sibur.nnov.ru Petr Vladimirovich Krupnov, CEO Valentina Dmitrievna Kolodinskaya, Deputy CEO for Development |

IV

VOLGA FEDERAL DISTRICT

[1] L – Loan, E – Equity, Leas. – Leasing, JV – Joint Venture
[2] BP – Business Plan, FS – Feasibility Study

1	2	3

50R005 ■ ● ▲ ▼

Plant reconstruction for the production of pyrolysis products (ethylene, propylene, and benzyl).
Project goal: to increase output and sales and to provide raw materials for polyethylene production.

1) 360,000 tons per year
2) $33.2 million/32 months
3) L, E
4) FS, Investment proposal

OAO Sibur-Neftekhim
63, ul. Osharskaya, Nizhny Novgorod,
Nizhny Novgorod Region, 603600
Phone: (8312) 78 3322, 78 3980
Fax: (8312) 78 3961, 78 3971
E-mail: info@sibur.nnov.ru
http://www.sibur.nnov.ru
Petr Vladimirovich Krupnov, CEO
Valentina Dmitrievna Kolodinskaya,
Deputy CEO for Development

50R006 ● ◆

Launch of production of mono-methyl-aniline.
Project goal: to produce gasoline supplements to increase octane rating.

1) 6,000 tons per year, revenue of $7.9 million per year
2) $1.5 million/1 year
3) L
4) BP

State Unitary Company Y.M. Sverdlov Plant
4, pr. Sverdlova, Dzerzhinsk,
Nizhny Novgorod Region, 606002
Phone: (8313) 33 2885
Fax: (8313) 31 2418
E-mail: sverdl@sverdlova.ru
Nikolai Ivanovich Vavilov, CEO

50R007 ■ ● ❖ ◆

Construction of polymer reinforced tube facilities at the Shipbuilding Corporation.
Project goal: to produce polymer reinforced tubes.

1) 160 linear km per year, revenue of $7 million per year
2) $3 million/4 years
3) L ($1.6 million), E, JV
4) BP

OAO Shipbuilding and Repair Corporation
1, per. 1 Pozharny, Gorodets,
Nizhny Novgorod Region, 606505
Phone: (83161) 93 772
Fax: (83161) 92 818
E-mail: gsverf@sinn.ru
Nikolai Dmitrievich Kochergin,
Chief Engineer

MACHINE ENGINEERING AND METAL PROCESSING

50R008 ● ◆ ▲

Production of Cruiser-class boats with lifting underwater wings.
Project goal: to expand product range.

1) 1 vessel
2) $2 million/4 years
3) L
4) BP, FS

OAO Nizhny Novgorod Aircraft Construction Plant
1, ul. Chaadaeva, Nizhny Novgorod,
Nizhny Novgorod Region, 603035
Phone: (8312) 29 8503, 29 8501
Fax: (8312) 22 1925, 76 4604
E-mail: sokol@atnn.ru
http://www.sokolplant.ru
Vladimir Ivanovich Mikhalev,
Technical Director

50R009 ● ◆

Launch of production of caterpillar snow and moor floating carrier GAZ 3409 Bobr.
Project goal: to launch production of new generation caterpillar carriers.

1) 500 machines per year
2) $4.5 million/5 years
3) L ($3.8 million)
4) BP

OAO Zavolzhsk Caterpillar Tractor Plant
1, ul. Zheleznodorozhnaya, Zavolzhie,
Nizhny Novgorod Region, 606524
Phone: (83169) 51 128, 62 138
Fax: (83169) 32 170, 32 334
E-mail: info@zzgt.ru
http://www.zzgt.ru
Alexander Yuryevich Antipov,
Deputy CEO, Head of the Strategic Development Department

IV

VOLGA FEDERAL DISTRICT

IV

VOLGA FEDERAL DISTRICT

1	2	3

50R010

Production of SKV 20 marine passenger boats with air cavity. Project goal: to produce passenger boats.

1) 10 vessels per year, revenue of $2.5 million per year
2) $2.8 million/3 years
3) L ($1.5 million)
4) BP, FS

OAO Volga Shipbuilding Plant
51, ul. Svobody, GSP-565, Nizhny Novgorod, Nizhny Novgorod Region, 603950
Phone: (8312) 73 8320, 73 0823
Fax: (8312) 73 1372
E-mail: szvolga@nnov.sitek.net
http://www.volga-shipyard.com
Sergey Yakovlevich Rogozhkin,
Director for Marketing
and Prospective Development

50R011

Production of river-sea class bulk freight vessels with a capacity of 3500 tons. Project goal: to produce bulk freight vessels.

1) 2 vessels in 2 years
2) $6.5 million/2 years
3) L
4) BP, FS

OAO Oka Shipyard
4, ul. Proezzhaya, Navashino,
Nizhny Novgorod Region, 607100
Phone: (83175) 26 488, 23 546
Fax: (83175) 21 110, 23 101
E-mail: oka@sandy.ru
http://www.innov.ru
Alexander Gennadyevich Menshikov,
Deputy CEO for Economy

FOOD AND BEVERAGES

50R012

Launch of waffle production. Project goal: to expand product range through the acquisition of new equipment.

1) 250 tons per month, revenue of $0.4 million per month
2) $2 million/5 years
3) L
4) BP

OAO Pechersky 2 Bakery
6, Kazanskoe shosse, Nizhny Novgorod, Nizhny Novgorod Region, 603163
Phone: (8312) 60 7283, 60 7401
Fax: (8312) 60 7283
Zinaida Petrovna Nikolaeva,
Contact person
Valentin Veniaminovich Zudilov,
CEO

HOTELS, TOURISM, AND RECREATION

50R013

Third Capital sports and recreation center. Project goal: to provide recreational and entertainment services for middle class customers in a single facility.

1) Revenue of $3.4 million per year
2) $ 2.4 million/3.7 years
3) L
4) Investment proposal

ZAO Regional Development Agency
1, pl. Oktyabrskaya, Nizhny Novgorod, Nizhny Novgorod Region, 603005
Phone/fax: (8312) 31 7337, 19 4782
Sergei Dmitrievich Latyshev,
Director for Economy and Development
OOO UK Rossbel,
14b, ul. Osgarskaya, Nizhny Novgorod, Nizhny Novgorod Region, 603006
Phone: (8312) 19 6868

SCIENCE AND INNOVATION

50R014

Development and production of a Profilemer Doppler radar unit to measure high wind profile. Project goal: to produce radar units optimize flight parameters, ensure flight safety, and monitor weather.

1) Sample production, cost of $1 million
2) $1.6 million/1.5 years
3) L ($1 million), E
4) FS

State Unitary Company Nizhny Novgorod Radio Equipment R&D Institute
5, ul. Shaposhnikova, Nizhny Novgorod, Nizhny Novgorod Region, 603950
Phone: (8312) 65 0069
Fax: (8312) 64 0283
E-mail: nniirt@sandy.ru
Valery Vasilyevich Moskalenko,
Director

1	2	3

50R015

Introduction of CALS technology in the design of modern vessels. Project goal: to introduce vessel design technology.

1) 3 vessel designs prepared using the technology
2) $2 million/3 years
3) L ($01 million)
4) BP, FS

OAO Vessel Design Bureau Vympel
3, ul. Kostina, Nizhny Novgorod,
Nizhny Novgorod Region, 603600
Phone: (8312) 33 1663, 30 2170, 33 4149
Fax: (8312) 30 2096
E-mail: info@vympel.ru
http://www.vympel.ru
Vyacheslav Valentinovich Shatalov,
CEO
Yury Ivanovich Rabazov,
Technical Director

50R016

Development of production lines and small-series production facilities of pure volatile non-organic arsenic, phosphorus, silicon, and nitrogen hydrides. Project goal: to produce pure volatile non-organic arsenic, phosphorus, silicon, and nitrogen hydrides.

1) 1 ton per year, revenue of up to $2 million per year
2) $8.3 million/4 years
3) L
4) FS, BP

State Unitary Company R&D and Production Company Salyut
7, ul. Larina, Nizhny Novgorod,
Nizhny Novgorod Region, 603950
Phone: (8312) 66 8354, 66 1510, 66 1613
Fax: (8312) 66 5020
Andrei Alexandrovich Khudin,
First Deputy CEO
Sergei Anatolyevich Petrovsky,
Head of the Development and Planning Department, Project Manager

50R017

Development of a technology for the production of super-ion conductors for solid fluorine-ion batteries. Project goal: to launch serial production of super-ion conductors for solid fluorine-ion batteries for drilling equipment in deep and extra-deep wells.

1) Up to 50,000 batteries per year, up to $7.9 million per year
2) $1.6 million/2 years
3) L
4) BP, FS

Sarov State Physics and Technical Institute
6, ul. Dukhova, Sarov, Nizhny Novgorod Region, 607186
Phone/fax: (83130) 39 277, 34 809
E-mail: zvv@sarfti.sarov.ru, zorya@rol.ru
Valery Vasilyevich Zorya,
Deputy Rector for Science,
Project Manager

50R018 ● ▲

Development of a design for the construction of two-reactor nuclear power plants. Project goal: to develop technology and launch production of reliable and safe nuclear sources of energy.

1) Technology and one power plant with a 600 MW capacity
2) $18.8 million/8 years
3) L
4) FS

State Unitary Company I.I. Afrikantov Experimental Engineering Design Bureau
15, pr. Burnakovsky, Nizhny Novgorod,
Nizhny Novgorod Region, 603074
Phone: (8312) 41 7766, 75 2640, 75 4076
Fax: (8312) 41 8772
E-mail: okbm@okbm.nnov.ru
http://www.okbm.nnov.ru
Alexander Ivanovich Kiryushin, CEO
Oleg Borisovich Samoilov,
Project Manager
Yevgeny Vasilyevich Kusmartsev,
Project Coordinator

50R019

New machine production technology for Russia's fuel and energy sector aimed at improving efficiency and safety and ecological situation at mining, transportation, and processing facilities. Project goal: to start serial production of goods for the fuel and energy sector.

1) 12 types of products, revenue of $23.6 million per year
2) $12.6 million/4 years
3) L
4) FS, BP

Y.E. Sedakov R&D Institute of Measuring Systems
GSP-486, Nizhny Novgorod,
Nizhny Novgorod Region, 603950
Phone: (8312) 69 5160, 66 8760, 65 4990
Fax: (8312) 66 8752, 66 6769
E-mail: niiis@niiis.nnov.ru
http://www.niiis.nnov.ru
Valentin Yefimovich Kostyukov, CEO
Valery Viktorovich Zaitsev,
Project Manager

1	2	3

50R020 ● ◆

Production of high frequency aircraft antennas for comprehensive monitoring of ecological situation and consequences of industrial accidents. Project goal: to launch new production and expand product range.	1) 5 antennas per year 2) $0.6 million/5 years 3) L 4) BP	State Unitary Company R&D and Production Company Polet 1, pl. Komsomolskaya, GSP-462, Nizhny Novgorod, Nizhny Novgorod Region, 603950 Phone: (8312) 42 7498, 42 2104 Fax: (8312) 44 2405, 42 3157 E-mail: polyot@atnn.ru, polyot@ic.sci-nnov.ru http://www.polyot.nnov.rfnet.ru Yevgeny Leonidovich Belousov, CEO Anatoly Ivanovich Kasatkin, Project Coordinator

51. ORENBURG REGION [56]

Almetiyevsk

Chapaevsk

SAMARA

S A M A R A   R E G I O N

Tuymazy · Oktyabrsky

Buguruslan

Belebey

UFA

Ufa

Buzuluk

Belaya

Dyoma

Asha

Sorochinsko-Nikolskoe

R E P U B L I C   O F

Sterlitamak

Salavat · Ishumbay

Beloretsk

Ural

Samara

Oktyabrskoe

Кумертау

Belaya

B A S H K O R T O S T A N

Tulgan

Magnitogorsk

Aksay

Ilek

Utva

ORENBURG

Sakmara

Sol-Iletsk

Ural

K A Z A K H S T A N

Aktyubinsk

Uil

Mednogorsk

Iriklinskoe water reservoir

Novotroitsk

Gay

Orsk

Yasny

Svetly

Oktyabrsk

PROCESSING INDUSTRY	MINING INDUSTRY		CROPS AND LIVESTOCK
● Ferrous metals	▨ Brown coal	✛ Asbestos	BREEDING
● Non-ferrous metals	▲ Oil	▱ Table salt	⅄ Wheat
● Machine engineering and metal processing	△ Natural gas		⅄ Rye
● Chemicals and petrochemicals	☢ Complex ore		⅄ Barley
● Construction materials	▲ Iron ore		⅄ Sunflower
○ Food and beverages	▬ Copper ore	POWER PLANTS	⊖ Orchards
	▼ Nickel ore	⚡ Thermal power plants	🐄 Meat and dairy cattle breeding
	▲ Sulfur		

O renburg has been at the crossroads of trade routes linking Europe to Asia since ancient times. To this day the Region's inhabitants have preserved their open attitude and readiness to develop mutually beneficial collaboration with their neighbors and foreign countries.

The Region is rich in natural resources, which form the basis of a regional economy based around fuel and energy, mining and metals, and machine engineering sectors.

The Region also has a strong focus on the development of its agroindustrial sector.

Industry and agriculture enjoy considerable investment, but are still in need of additional funds.

The Orenburg Region boasts strong economic and resource potential and has the capacity to develop international and external economic ties. The Region's advantageous geopolitical location at the south-eastern border of the Russian Federation is conducive to the development of such ties.

We invite businesses from the CIS and overseas countries to mutually beneficial collaboration in our Region.

In our Region you will meet well-intentioned people and discover unique natural resources and unrivalled natural beauty.

Alexei Chernyshev,
HEAD OF ADMINISTRATION (GOVERNOR)
OF THE ORENBURG REGION,
CHAIRMAN OF THE GOVERNMENT
OF THE ORENBURG REGION

1. GENERAL INFORMATION

1.1. GEOGRAPHY

Situated at the border between Europe and Asia, the Orenburg Region covers a total area of 124,000 square kilometers. To the north, the Region borders the Republic of Tatarstan, to the north-east – the Republic of Bashkortostan, to the east – the Chelyabinsk Region, to the south and south-east – Kazakhstan, to the south-west – the Saratov Region, and to the west – the Samara Region.

1.2. CLIMATE

The Orenburg Region enjoys a continental climate. The average air temperature in January is –7°C, rising to +22°C in July. The average annual precipitation is 300–400 mm.

1.3. POPULATION

According to preliminary 2002 census results, the Region's population totaled 2,178,000 people. The average population density is 17.6 people per square kilometer. The economically active population amounts to 1,018,000 people. Official unemployment is 8.5%.

Demographically speaking, some 59.9% are of working age, 20.5% are below the statutory working age, and 19.6% are beyond the statutory working age.

As of 2002, the Orenburg Region's major urban centers were Orenburg with 548,800 inhabitants, Orsk with 250,600 inhabitants, Novotroitsk with 106,200 inhabitants, Buzuluk with 85,500 inhabitants, and Buguruslan with 54,300 inhabitants.

Population							TABLE 1
	1992	1997	1998	1999	2000	2001	2002
Total population, '000	2,171	2,223	2,225	2,225	2,220	2,212	2,178
Economically active population, '000	1,102	979	970	1,064	1,040	1,031	1,018

2. ADMINISTRATION

House of Soviets, Orenburg, Orenburg Region, 460015
Phone: (3532) 77 6931; fax: (3532) 77 3802
E-mail: office@gov.orb.ru; http://www.orb.ru

NAME	POSITION	CONTACT INFORMATION
Alexei Andreevich CHERNYSHEV	Head of Administration (Governor) of the Orenburg Region, Chairman of the Government of the Orenburg Region	Phone: (3532) 78 6010 Fax: (3532) 77 3802 E-mail: office@gov.orb.ru
Boris Vladimirovich PLOKHOTNYUK	First Deputy Head of Administration of the Orenburg Region, Head of the Department of Industry, Transport, and Natural Resources	Phone: (3532) 78 6011 Fax: (3532) 78 6113 E-mail: office02@gov.orb.ru
Valentin Matveevich BACHURIN	Deputy Head of Administration of the Orenburg Region, Head of the Finance Department	Phone: (3532) 78 6013 Fax: (3532) 78 6180 E-mail: finupr@mail.gov.ru
Sergei Georgievich GORSHENIN	Deputy Head of Administration of the Orenburg Region, Head of the International and External Economic Relations Department	Phone: (3532) 78 6017 Fax: (3532) 77 4090 E-mail: office29@gov.orb.ru
Vasily Konstantinovich YEREMENKO	Deputy Head of Administration of the Orenburg Region, Director of the Agroindustrial Sector Department	Phone: (3532) 78 6434 Fax: (3532) 77 4947 E-mail: agro@gov.orb.ru
Yury Nikolaevich KARPOV	Deputy Head of Administration of the Orenburg Region, Head of the Department of Investment in Construction, Housing and Communal Services, and Roads	Phone: (3532) 78 6014 Fax: (3532) 77 3802 E-mail: office06@gov.orb.ru
Alexei Stanislavovich PESHKOV	Deputy Head of Administration of the Orenburg Region, Director of the Economic Department	Phone: (3532) 78 6054 Fax: (3532) 77 7146, 77 6951 E-mail: office18@gov.orb.ru

3. ECONOMIC POTENTIAL

3.1. 1997–2002 GROSS REGIONAL PRODUCT (GRP). INDUSTRY BREAKDOWN

The 2002 gross regional product amounted to $2,950.9 million, which constitutes 2.3% growth year-on-year. Per capita GRP amounted to $1,302 in 2001 and $1,354 in 2002.

3.2. MAJOR ECONOMIC GROWTH PROJECTIONS

The blueprint for economic development in the Orenburg Region is set forth in the Conceptual Framework for Social and Economic Development through 2010.

3.3. INDUSTRIAL OUTPUT IN 1997–2002 FOR MAJOR SECTORS OF ECONOMY

The leading industrial sectors of the Orenburg Region are fuel, ferrous metals, and energy. Their combined share of total industrial output is 73.7%.

Fuel. The sector accounts for 49.7% of total industrial output. It is represented by OAO Orenburggazprom, OAO Orenburgneft, and ZAO Stimul.

GRP trends in 1997–2002						TABLE 2
	1997	1998	1999	2000	2001*	2002*
GRP in current prices, $ million	5,160.2	2,932.9	2,237.8	2,938.0	2,883.3	2,950.9

*Estimates of the Orenburg Regional Administration

GRP industry breakdown in 1997–2002, % of total						TABLE 3
	1997	1998	1999	2000	2001*	2002*
GRP	100.0	100.0	100.0	100.0	100.0	100.0
Industry	36.1	42.1	41.2	41.5	42.3	44.3
Agriculture and forestry	12.4	3.2	14.1	13.9	13.8	13.2
Construction	8.1	7.3	6.3	8.4	8.1	7.8
Transport and communications	6.8	9.2	5.8	7.1	7.3	7.4
Trade and public catering	7.1	10.1	11.0	9.3	9.5	9.3
Other	4.9	5.8	6.6	12.4	11.5	9.7
Net taxes on output	24.6	22.3	15.0	7.4	7.5	8.3

*Estimates of the Orenburg Regional Administration

Industry breakdown of industrial output in 1997–2002, % of total						TABLE 4
	1997	1998	1999	2000	2001	2002*
Industry	100.0	100.0	100.0	100.0	100.0	100.0
Fuel	37.4	36.1	42.5	43.6	38.7	49.7
Ferrous metals	15.0	16.4	17.1	16.2	13.8	13.1
Energy	12.7	13.6	9.8	8.6	10.2	10.9
Non-ferrous metals	5.9	5.2	5.5	7.0	9.5	8.8
Machine engineering and metal processing	12.3	9.1	8.0	9.2	9.3	6.6
Food and beverages	6.8	7.8	6.3	5.6	8.0	4.9
Construction materials	4.3	5.1	3.8	2.9	3.7	2.6
Chemicals and petrochemicals	1.1	1.6	2.2	2.1	2.1	1.5
Flour, cereals, and mixed fodder	2.2	2.3	2.0	2.6	1.8	0.9
Light industry	1.3	1.4	1.5	1.4	1.7	0.9
Forestry, timber, and pulp and paper	0.5	0.5	0.3	0.3	0.4	0.1

*Estimates of the Orenburg Regional Administration

Fuel and energy sector production and consumption trends, 1997–2002						TABLE 5
	1997	1998	1999	2000	2001	2002
Electricity output, billion kWh	17.5	17.4	18.0	17.2	15.7	14.7
Oil output (including gas concentrate), '000 tons	8,982.0	8,899.0	8,938.0	9,067.0	9,673.0	11,199.0
Natural gas extraction, million cubic meters	29,001.0	27,327.0	26,576.0	25,874.0	24,716.0	23,706.0
Coal extraction, million tons	0.8	0.3	0.4	0.1	–	–
Electricity consumption, billion kWh	13.6	13.6	13.8	14.4	11.7	11.7
Oil consumption, '000 tons	4,180.2	4,486.8	4,074.0	4,375.1	4,091.3	3,897.0
Natural gas consumption, million cubic meters	12,511.6	13,169.5	12,400.0	12,388.0	7,850.0	12,027.6

*Estimates of the Orenburg Regional Administration

Ferrous metals. The share of this sector is 13.1%. The Region's major company is OAO Nosta.

Energy. The sector accounts for 10.9% of total industrial output. Major companies within the sector are OAO Orenburgenergo, the Iriklinskaya Power Station, and the Sakmarskaya Thermal Power Station.

Non-ferrous metals. The share of the sector in total industrial output equals 8.8%. Major companies within the sector are OAO Gaisky Ore Dressing Plant, OAO Yuzhuralnickel, OAO Mednogorsky Copper and Sulphur Plant, and OAO Splav Non-Ferrous Metal Processing Plant.

3.4. FUEL AND ENERGY BALANCE (OUTPUT AND CONSUMPTION PER RESOURCE)

Thermal power stations account for the lion's share of electricity output with 99.1%. The Region's power stations are fired by natural gas (89%) and fuel oil (6.4%). In 2001, the Region exported 1.4 billion kWh to the Federal Wholesale Energy Market, and 1 billion kWh in 2002.

3.5. TRANSPORT INFRASTRUCTURE

Roads. The Region has 13,032 kilometers of paved public highway. The road network comprises several federal highways, including the Samara – Orenburg – Orsk, Bugulma – Buguruslan – Buzuluk – Uralsk, Orenburg – Ufa, and Orenburg – Aksai routes.

Railroads. The Orenburg Region has 1,652 kilometers of railroads. The Samara – Kinel – Orenburg – Iletsk line links the Volga and Urals Districts to Central Asia and Kazakhstan, and the Sergin – Ivdel – Yekaterinburg – Polevsky – Chelyabinsk – Orsk – Kimpersai – Kandagach – Guryev – Astrakhan line links the Southern and Central Urals to the Lower Volga and the Caucasus. The Orenburg – Orsk – Kartaly – Kustanai line provides access to Siberia. The Region has access to west Kazakhstan via the Iletsk – Uralsk – Urbakh line and to the Saratov Region via the Pugachev – Pogromnoye line. The Iletsk – Orenburg – Tyulpan – Ufa line provides access and transit routes to Bashkortostan. The Samara – Buguruslan – Ufa – Chelyabinsk line passes through the Region's north-western districts and links the Volga Region to the Trans-Siberian railroad.

Airports. Two international airports serve the Region: the Central Airport at Orenburg and another one at Orsk. The Region has air links to Moscow, St. Petersburg, Yekaterinburg, Khabarovsk, the CIS, Germany, Turkey, Greece, and China. 2002 passenger turnover totaled 300 million passenger-kilometers.

Oil and gas pipelines. The gas pipe network is 1,800 kilometers long. Oil pipelines run from Guryev (Kazakhstan) and Ishimbai (Bashkortostan) in the direction of Orsk. In the west of the Region, oil pipelines run from oil fields to the Samara Region.

3.6. MAIN NATURAL RESOURCES: RESERVES AND EXTRACTION IN 2002

The main natural resources of the Orenburg Region are minerals and water.

Mineral resources. The Region is rich in some 75 types of natural resources, including natural gas, oil, coal, oil shale, ferrous, non-ferrous, and rare earth metals, rock salt, limestone, asphaltite, jasper, and marble. Some 195 oil and gas fields have been discovered in the Region. Initial extracted reserves of oil amount to 1,665 million tons, natural gas – 2,712 billion cubic meters, and gas condensate – 258 million tons, including unexplored reserves of oil – 865 million tons, natural gas – 756 billion cubic meters, and gas condensate – 177 million tons. Estimated reserves of ore and placer gold amount to 1,200 tons. The Region also has reserves of potassium salt and china clay.

Water resources. The Region extracts mineral water similar by its composition to Caucasian mineral water.

4. TRADE OPPORTUNITIES

4.1. MAIN GOODS
PRODUCED IN THE REGION

The main types of industrial output as of 2002:

Energy. The Region produced 14.7 billion kWh of electricity, or 6.3% less year-on-year.

Natural gas. The Region extracted 23.7 billion cubic meters of natural gas, which constitutes 4.1% reduction year-on-year.

Finished ferrous metal roll. The Region produced 2.1 million tons of rolled metal, or 19.7% more than in 2001.

Silk fabric and non-woven textiles. The Region manufactured 34.4 million square meters of silk fabric and non-woven textiles, unchanged on 2001.

Alternating current electrical motors. 222,000 items, or 5.1% more than in 2001.

Tractor trailers and semi-trailers. 907 items, or 46.9% less than in 2001.

Forging and pressing machines. 469 items, or 2.1 times more than in 2001.

Refrigerators and freezers. 38,400 items, or 32.9% less than in 2001.

Grain. 3.5 million tons, which constitutes 4.6% growth year-on-year.

Bread and bakery. 52,200 tons, or 7.2% less than in 2001.

4.2. EXPORTS, INCLUDING EXTRA-CIS

The Orenburg Region's exports to extra-CIS countries amounted to $861.8 million in 2000. Exports to the CIS totaled $91.6 million. The corresponding figures for 2001 were $941.7 million and $110.8 million, and $1,215.1 and $136.8 million for 2002.

Major regional export and import entities		TABLE 6
ENTITY	ADDRESS	PHONE, FAX, E-MAIL
OAO Orenburgneft	2, ul. Magistralnaya, Buzuluk, Orenburg Region, 461040	Phone: (35342) 73 670 Fax: (35342) 73 630 E-mail: easablina@orneft.tnk.ru http://www.onako.ru
OAO Orsknefteorgsintez	1a, ul. Goncharova, Orsk, Orenburg Region, 462407	Phone: (3537) 29 2500 Fax: (3537) 55 0628 E-mail: mail@onos.orgus.ru
OAO Nosta	1, ul. Zavodskaya, Novotroitsk, Orenburg Region, 462352	Phone: (35376) 62 797 Fax: (35376) 62 730 E-mail: ohmk@nosta.ims.ru http://www.nosta.ru
OOO Orenburggazprom	11, ul. 60 let Oktyabrya, Orenburg, Orenburg Region, 460021	Phone: (3532) 33 2002 Fax: (3532) 41 2589 E-mail: orenburggazprom@ogp.ru
OAO Novotroitsk Chrome Compound Plant	Novotroitsk, Orenburg Region, 462353	Phone: (35376) 22 500 Fax: (35376) 20 074 E-mail: post@novochrom.dlm.ru http://www.novohrom.com
OAO Yuzhuralmash	12, pr. Mira, Orsk, Orenburg Region, 462403	Phone: (3537) 55 0984 Fax: (3537) 55 0986 E-mail: sagitov@yumz.orgus.ru http://www.ormetoyumz.ru
OAO Uralelectro-K	1, ul. Motornaya, Mednogorsk, Orenburg Region, 462275	Phone: (35379) 29 205 Fax: (35379)29 206 E-mail: mail@uralelectro.ru http://www.uralelectro.ru
OAO Yuzhuralnickel	1, ul. Prizavodskaya, Orsk, Orenburg Region, 462424	Phone: (3537) 22 0168 Fax: (3537) 22 4453 E-mail: junk@email.orgus.ru
OAO Orenburgasbest	7, ul. Lenina, Yasny, Orenburg Region, 462752	Phone: (35368) 20 160 Fax: (35368) 20 344 E-mail: orenasbest@mail.ru

The main types of goods exported by the Region are fuel and energy products, petrochemicals, metals and metal goods, and machinery. Major importers of the Region's products include Denmark, Estonia, Finland, Turkey, the Netherlands, Kazakhstan, and Ukraine.

4.3. IMPORTS, INCLUDING EXTRA-CIS

2000 imports from extra-CIS amounted to $110.4 million. Imports from the CIS totaled $368.8 million. The corresponding figures for 2001 were $65.7 and $393.4 million, and $37 million and $361.2 million for 2002.

The bulk of 2002 regional imports was represented by food and raw food materials, machinery, oil, and gas condensate. The main exporters to the Region are Germany, the USA, Sweden, Austria, Kazakhstan, and Ukraine.

5. INVESTMENT OPPORTUNITIES

5.1 INVESTMENTS IN 1992–2002 (BY INDUSTRY SECTOR), INCLUDING FOREIGN INVESTMENTS

The following factors determine the investment appeal of the Orenburg Region:

- Its advantageous geographic location, proximity to sales markets, and high consumer potential;
- Its developed transport infrastructure;
- A legislation framework conducive to investment activity (guarantees of investors' rights and preferential taxation);
- Qualified workforce;
- Cheap energy (electricity, oil, and natural gas);
- Availability of natural resources.

5.2. CAPITAL INVESTMENT

Industry and transport account for the lion's share of capital investment.

5.3. MAJOR ENTERPRISES (INCLUDING ENTERPRISES WITH FOREIGN INVESTMENT)

The Orenburg Region hosts 226 companies with foreign investment, including JV Stimul, JV Baitex, JV Uralelectro-STM, JV Uralelectro-Contactor, JV Avtoflex-Knott, JV Azimut, JV Khunor, JV Ivan Taranov Brewery, JV Ferrous, and JV Orensot.

5.4. MOST ATTRACTIVE SECTORS FOR INVESTMENT

According to experts and the Orenburg Regional Administration, the most potentially appealing sectors for investors are fuel and energy, machine engineering, food and beverages, and communications.

5.5. CURRENT LEGISLATION ON INVESTOR TAX EXEMPTIONS AND PRIVILEGES

The Orenburg Region has passed the following laws of the Orenburg Region: On the Encouragement of Foreign Investment Activities in the Orenburg Region, On Innovation and Innovation Activity in the Orenburg Region, On State Support to Small Enterprise in the Orenburg Region, On Creating Favorable Conditions for Producers of Goods and Services in the Orenburg Region, On the 2003 Regional Budget (the law envisages a reserve fund for investment guarantees), On the Provision of Guarantees from the Regional Budget, and On Encouraging Investment Projects for the Production of Import Substitutes and Goods for Exports in the Orenburg Region.

Capital investment by industry sector, $ million						*TABLE 7*
	1997	1998	1999	2000	2001	2002
Total capital investment	1,075.6	545.8	356.2	533.4	669.8	500.4
Including major industries (% of total):						
Industry	39.5	41.1	49.3	51.2	57.2	58.8
Agriculture and forestry	2.8	3.7	4.5	4.2	4.8	3.9
Construction	1.6	1.2	1.4	1.2	1.4	0.7
Transport and communications	13.1	15.7	12.7	13.9	13.6	9.7
Trade and public catering	2.7	0.6	0.7	4.3	1.4	0.5
Other	40.3	37.7	31.4	25.2	21.6	26.4

Foreign investment trends in 1996–2002						*TABLE 8*
	1996–1997	1998	1999	2000	2001	2002
Foreign investment, $ million	2.4	130.0	25.1	78.8	88.9	94.3
Including FDI, $ million	2.4	74.9	5.6	51.2	82.6	15.1

Largest enterprises of the Orenburg Region	*TABLE 9*
COMPANY	SECTOR
OOO Orenburggazprom	Natural gas
OAO Orenburgneft	Oil
OAO Nosta	Ferrous metals
OAO Orsknefteorgsintez	Oil refining
OAO Orenburgenergo	Energy
OAO Yuzhuralnickel	Non-ferrous metals
OAO Gaysky Ore Dressing Plant	Non-ferrous metals
ZAO Ivan Taranov Brewery	Food and beverages

5.6. FEDERAL AND REGIONAL ECONOMIC AND SOCIAL DEVELOPMENT PROGRAMS FOR THE ORENBURG REGION

Federal targeted programs. The Orenburg Region is implementing numerous federal targeted programs, including the following priority programs: Children of Russia, 2003–2006 (and its subprograms Disabled Children and Orphans), Social Support to the Disabled, 2000–2005, Russia's Youth, 2001–2005, Prevention and Elimination of Social Diseases, 2002–2006, Russian Culture, 2001–2005, and Housing, 2002–2010.

Regional programs. The Region is implementing a number of regional targeted programs, including Prevention of the Spread of the Human Immunodeficiency Virus, 2002–2006, Elimination of Crime in the Orenburg Region, 2001–2003, and The Preservation and Improvement of Land Fertility in the Orenburg Region, 2001–2005 under the Land Fertility Program.

6. INVESTMENT PROJECTS

Industry sector and project description	1) Expected results 2) Amount and term of investment 3) Form of financing[1] 4) Documentation[2]	Contact information
1	2	3
OIL AND NATURAL GAS		
51R001 ● ◆ ■ Development of the Rozhdestvensky oil and gas condensate field. Project goal: to penetrate the oil and gas market.	1) 47,000 tons of gas condensate per year 2) $8.4 million/2 years 3) E, L 4) BP	OOO Serviceneftegaz 64a, ul. Donguzskaya, Orenburg, Orenburg Region, 460027 Phone: (3532) 73 4063 Fax: (3532) 73 4059 E-mail: sngor@rambler.ru, sngor@newmail.ru Rustyam Midkhatovich Iskhakov, Director
51R002 ● ◆ ■ Development of the Nagumanovsky oil and gas condensate field. Project goal: to penetrate the oil and gas market.	1) 150,000 tons of oil per year 2) $43.7 million/4 years 3) E, L ($28 million) 4) BP	OOO Serviceneftegaz 64a, ul. Donguzskaya, Orenburg, Orenburg Region, 460027 Phone: (3532) 734063 Fax: (3532) 734059 E-mail: sngor@rambler.ru, sngor@newmail.ru; Rustyam Midkhatovich Iskhakov, Director

[1] L – Loan, E – Equity, Leas. – Leasing, JV – Joint Venture
[2] BP – Business Plan, FS – Feasibility Study

1	2	3

51R003

Extraction of natural gas and condensate at an operating facility.
Project goal: to increase oil
and gas supply.

1) 400,000 tons of gas condensate
   per year
2) $40 million/n/a
3) L ($30 million)
4) BP

ZAO Stimul
20, ul. Pushkinskaya, Orenburg,
Orenburg Region, 460024
Phone: (3532) 77 9117
Fax: (3532) 77 2475
E-mail: stimul@nks.ru
Valery Mikhailovich Melnikov, CEO

COAL

51R004

Construction of a brown coal
processing facility and output of electricity, mineral wax, and humic acid.
Project goal: to introduce consumer
goods from brown coal to the market.

1) 1 million tons of coal per year
2) $68 million/n/a
3) E, L
4) BP

OAO Orenburgugol
Industrial Zone, Tulgan,
Orenburg Region, 462010
Phone: (35332) 21 642
Phone/fax: (35332) 21 352, 21 951
Nikolai Nikolaevich Kolchin, CEO
Department of International and
External Economic Relations of the
Orenburg Regional Administration,
Phone: (3532) 78 6326
Fax: (3532) 77 4090
E-mail: office29@gov.orb.ru
Mars Khasanovich Bakiev,
Head of the Investment Department

MINING (EXCEPT FUEL RESOURCES)

51R005

Development of industrial deposits, and
upgrade of operating facilities with
modern metal and energy machinery.
Project goal: to increase output
of nickel and nickel alloys.

1) Increase in ore extraction
   by 1 million tons
2) $17.8 million/n/a
3) L ($9 million)
4) BP

OAO Yuzhuralnickel Plant
1, ul. Prizavodskaya, Orsk,
Orenburg Region, 462424
Phone/fax: (3537) 22 0168, 29 1130
Fax: (3537) 22 0168
E-mail: priem@unickel.ru
Anatoly Petrovich Schetinin, CEO

51R006

Development of deep layers of an
underground ore deposit.
Project goal: to increase output
of copper and zinc ore.

1) Increase in ore extraction
   by 2.3 million tons
2) $66 million/n/a
3) L ($50 million)
4) FS

OAO Gaysky Ore Dressing Plant
1, ul. Promyshlennaya, Gai,
Orenburg Region, 462630
Phone: (35362) 30 726
Fax: (35362) 30 762
E-mail: info@ggok.ru
Yury Ivanovich Starostin, CEO

51R007

Upgrading of fixed assets of an
operating ore dressing plant.
Project goal: to increase copper
concentrate output.

1) n/a
2) $22 million/n/a
3) L ($15 million)
4) FS

OAO Gaysky Ore Dressing Plant
1, ul. Promyshlennaya, Gai,
Orenburg Region, 462630
Phone: (35362) 30 726
Fax: (35362) 30 762
E-mail: info@ggok.ru;
Yury Ivanovich Starostin, CEO

51R008

Construction of a salt plant.
Project goal: to increase salt output.

1) Extraction of 1,250,000 tons per year, and
   processing of 500,000 tons per year
2) $10 million/4 years
3) L
4) BP

OAO Iletsk Salt
1, ul. Sovetskaya, Sol-Iletsk,
Orenburg Region, 461500
Phone: (35336) 21 363
Fax: (35336) 21 005
E-mail: salt@mail.esoo.ru
Irek Vilovich Abdurshin, CEO

IV

VOLGA FEDERAL DISTRICT

1	2	3

51R009 ■ ● ◆

Development of a marble deposit. Project goal: to introduce marble to the market of building materials.

1) Output increase by $5 million per year
2) $2.9 million/n/a
3) E, L
4) BP

OAO Orenburg Construction Materials
129, ul. Amurskaya, Orenburg,
Orenburg Region, 460027
Phone: (3532) 76 0782
Fax: (3532) 76 0609
Viktor Andreevich Fefelov, CEO

ENERGY

51R010 ● ◆

Upgrading and reconstruction of gas turbine units at the Iriklinskaya Power Station. Project goal: to increase output of electricity and heat, and reduce costs.

1) Electricity output increase from 2,400 MW to 2,700 MW
2) $4 million/4 years
3) L
4) BP

OAO Orenburgenergo
of RAO UES of Russia
44, ul. Marshala Zhukova, Orenburg,
Orenburg Region, 460024
Phone: (3532) 77 3182
Fax: (3532) 41 1208
E-mail: oks@orene.electro.ru
Yury Ivanovich Trofimov, CEO

FERROUS METALS

51R011 ● ▲

Reconstruction and refurbishment of an electrical steel smelting shop. Project goal: to increase output and improve the quality of castings, increase the share of castings in total output to 65%, and reduce costs.

1) Increase in steel production in electrical furnaces by 900,000 tons per year and a respective reduction in open hearth furnace steel production
2) $19 million/2 years
3) L
4) FS

OAO Nosta
1, ul. Zavodskaya, Novotroitsk,
Orenburg Region, 462352
Phone: (35376) 62 333
Fax: (35376) 62 789
E-mail: oxmk@nosta.ru
Sergei Viktorovich Filippov,
Managing Director

51R012 ● ▲

Reconstruction of thick rolled sheet production facilities. Project goal: to expand the product range and increase sales.

1) Sales of 700,000 tons per year
2) $100 million/3 years
3) L
4) FS

OAO Nosta
1, ul. Zavodskaya, Novotroitsk,
Orenburg Region, 462352
Phone: (35376) 62 333
Fax: (35376) 62 789
E-mail: oxmk@nosta.ru;
Sergei Viktorovich Filippov,
Managing Director

NON-FERROUS METALS

51R013 ● ◆

Upgrading of fixed assets of rolled metal production at an operating company. Project goal: to increase output, improve quality of rolled nonferrous metals and alloys, expand sales markets.

1) Revenue increase by $12 million
2) $3 million/n/a
3) L
4) BP

OAO Orsk Nonferrous Metal Plant
6, ul. Zavodskaya, Orsk,
Orenburg Region, 462424
Phone: (3537) 22 2604
Fax (3537) 22 1860
E-mail: ozem@email.orgus.ru
Yelena Mikhailovna Popova,
Acting CEO

CHEMICALS AND PETROCHEMICALS

51R014 ● ▲

Upgrading of fixed assets of a sulphuric acid producer. Project goal: to increase output of sulphuric acid, and improve the environmental situation.

1) Up to 200,000 tons of sulphuric acid per year
2) $16 million/3 years
3) L
4) FS

OAO Mednogorsk Copper and
Sulphur Plant
1, ul. Zavodskaya, Mednogorsk,
Orenburg Region, 462270
Phone: (35379) 31 438, 30 764
Fax: (35379) 30 766
E-mail: mmsk@cuprum.esoo.ru
Yury Sergeevich Krivonosov, CEO

1	2	3

MACHINE ENGINEERING AND METAL PROCESSING

51R015

Launching of serial production of multipurpose civilian helicopters. Project goal: to expand the product range.

1) Up to 30 helicopters per year
2) $19 million/2 years
3) L ($9 million)
4) BP

State Unitary Company Strela
26, ul. Shevchenko, Orenburg,
Orenburg Region, 460005
Phone: (3532) 65 7100, 65 7209
E-mail: strela@mail.osu.ru
Sergei Ivanovich Grachev,
CEO

51R016

Construction of new facilities for the production of low-voltage starting instruments at an operating plant. Project goal: to expand product range.

1) Increase in revenue by $2.5 million
2) $5 million/n/a
3) L ($2.5 million)
4) BP

OAO Uralelectro
1, ul. Motornaya, Mednogorsk,
Orenburg Region, 462250
Phone: (35379) 29 205
Fax: (35379) 29 206
E-mail: mail@uralelectro.ru
Vladimir Viktorovich Kiselev, CEO

LIGHT INDUSTRY

51R017

Purchasing of finishing equipment to upgrade fixed assets of an operating fabric producer. Project goal: to improve the quality of output.

1) Output of 3.5 million linear meters of fabric per year
2) $3.5 million/4 years
3) L, Leas., E
4) BP

OAO Orentex
1, Sharlykskoe shosse, Orenburg,
Orenburg Region, 460038
Phone: (3532) 36 3125
Fax: (3532) 36 4000
Andrei Anatolyevich Anikeev, CEO

FOOD AND BEVERAGES

51R018

Construction of a pectin plant. Project goal: to penetrate the pectin market.

1) 385 tons of dry pectin, 40 tons of food supplements, and 15 tons of pumpkin oil per year
2) $5 million/1.5 years
3) L
4) BP

OOO Sol-IletskPectin
68, ul. Donguzskaya, Orenburg,
Orenburg Region, 460000
Phone/fax: (3532) 76 2828,
76 2414, 53 3787, 29 0330
Gennady Fedorovich Bakiev,
CEO

ECOLOGY AND WASTE TREATMENT

51R019

Construction of a solid waste processing plant. Project goal: to increase processing of solid non-industrial waste, and improvement of the environmental situation.

1) n/a
2) $20 million/n/a
3) E, L
4) BP

Orenburg Administration
60, ul. Sovetskaya, Orenburg,
Orenburg Region, 460000
Phone: (3532) 77 5055
Fax: (3532) 77 4821
Yury Nikolaevich Mischeryakov,
Mayor of Orenburg
Lyudmila Georgievna Khludeneva,
Deputy Mayor of Orenburg
for the Economy

52. PENZA REGION [58]

ECONOMIC MAP

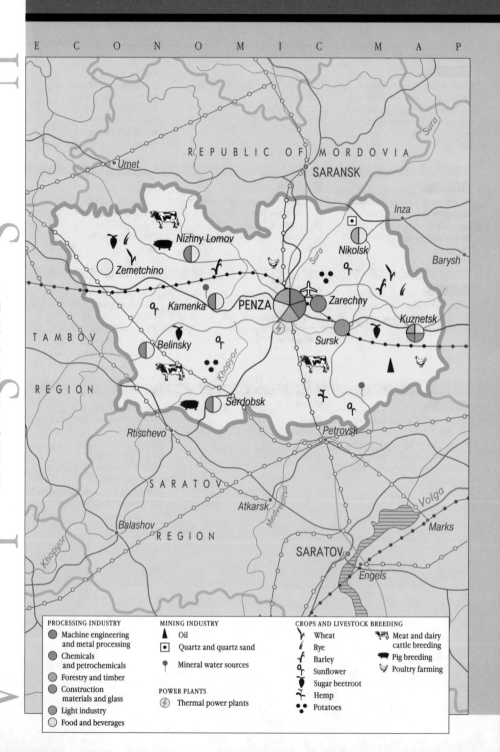

PROCESSING INDUSTRY
- ● Machine engineering and metal processing
- ● Chemicals and petrochemicals
- ● Forestry and timber
- ● Construction materials and glass
- ● Light industry
- ○ Food and beverages

MINING INDUSTRY
- ▲ Oil
- ⊡ Quartz and quartz sand
- ♦ Mineral water sources

POWER PLANTS
- ⚡ Thermal power plants

CROPS AND LIVESTOCK BREEDING
- Wheat
- Rye
- Barley
- Sunflower
- Sugar beetroot
- Hemp
- Potatoes
- Meat and dairy cattle breeding
- Pig breeding
- Poultry farming

The Penza Region is located at the center of European Russia at a distance of 620 kilometers southeast of Moscow on the crossroads of the main north-to-south and west-to-east transport routes.

The favorable geographical location of the Region and its proximity to other large industrial centers offer ample opportunity for cooperation in the area of manufacturing and distribution.

Economic growth in the Region is underpinned by liberal economic principles, with a leading role retained by the state and local government in infrastructure development, public welfare, and environmental protection.

The Regional Government has set the following economic development goals for the Region: deep integration of the regional economy with the broader Russian economy, active participation in the inter-regional and international division of labor, and active pursuit of industrial development.

We are resolved to achieve maximum transparency in order to restore trust between the state and business based on the principles of inviolable property rights, fair competition, conscientious work, and legal compliance.

Protecting fair competition and owners' rights are seen as the way forward to achieving these goals. We are resolved to create a business friendly environment and ensure financial and social stability. The Region is the second most secure region of Russia for its low level of criminal risk exposure in business.

Our Region's political stability, social consensus, and favorable legislative and tax climate for investors and trade partners offer widespread opportunity for cooperation.

We have all the necessary prerequisites for successful cooperation – considerable industrial potential, a large construction sector, bountiful agricultural resources, an advanced transport system and telecommunications network, and a highly qualified work force.

Many enterprises based in our Region are leaders in Russian industry and boast international quality certification.

Our principal machine engineering output includes chemical and oil and gas equipment, diesel engines, compressors, spinning machines, special purpose trucks, filling station equipment, and agricultural machinery.

Our Region's instrument manufacturers specialize in the design and manufacturing of radio electronics, communications, information technology, and automated control systems products.

OAO Biosintez is Russia's largest pharmaceuticals producer. OAO Surskaya Manufactura is the country's largest woolen fabric producer. OAO Mayak is the national leader in terms of decorative paper output.

The machine engineering and instrument manufacturing sectors offer widespread investment opportunities. Agriculture, food, timber, and pharmaceuticals are also promising sectors for investment.

Our Region is rich in cultural traditions and boasts a myriad of historical and architectural sites. The Region enjoys a unique natural environment, an extensive network of sanatoria and health resorts, and many picturesque areas for recreation, hunting, and fishing.

Visitors to our Region leave with unforgettable and lasting memories of our land. You are always welcome to visit, both as welcome guest and as a business partner!

Vasily Bochkarev,
GOVERNOR OF THE PENZA REGION

IV

VOLGA FEDERAL DISTRICT

1. GENERAL INFORMATION

1.1. GEOGRAPHY

Located in the East European Plain, the Penza Region covers a total area of 43,200 kilometers. Penza is situated within the Central Volga region of Russia. To the south, the Region borders the Saratov Region, to the east – the Ulyanovsk Region, to the west – the Ryazan and the Tambov Regions, and to the north – the Republic of Mordovia.

1.2. CLIMATE

The Penza Region is located within the temperate continental climate zone, at the junction of forested, steppe-forested, and native steppe zones.

Some 68% of the Region lies under highly fertile Black Earth soil.

Air temperatures in January average –7.7°C, rising to +21°C in July. Annual precipitation reaches 450–600 mm.

1.3. POPULATION

According to preliminary 2002 census results, the population of the Penza Region is 1,453,000 people. The average population density is 33.6 people per square kilometer. The economically active population is 709,000 people. Official unemployment stood at 2.1% in 2002; while the actual rate was 13.9%.

Demographically speaking, some 59.4% are of statutory working age, 17.1% are below the statutory working age, and 23.5% are beyond the statutory working age.

The Penza Region's major urban centers are Penza with 518,200 inhabitants (2002), Kuznetsk with 96,900 inhabitants, and Zarechny with 63,600 inhabitants.

Population								TABLE 1
	1992	1997	1998	1999	2000	2001	2002
Total population, '000	1,554	1,556	1,549	1,542	1,531	1,518	1,453
Economically active population, '000	764	698	707	734	768	746	709

2. ADMINISTRATION

75, ul. Moskovskaya, Penza, Penza Region, 440025.
Phone: (8412) 59 5219; fax: (8412) 55 0411
E-mail: pravobl@sura.ru; http://www.penza.ru

NAME	POSITION	CONTACT INFORMATION
Vasily Kuzmich BOCHKAREV	Governor of the Penza Region	Phone: (8412) 56 1194, 52 3304 Fax: (8412) 55 0411
Alexander Ivanovich CHERNITSOV	First Deputy Governor of the Penza Region	Phone: (8412) 55 1931, 59 5293 Fax: (8412) 52 3277
Mikhail Grigoryevich KOSOY	Deputy Governor of the Penza Region in charge of economic issues	Phone: (8412) 52 4584, 59 5139
Alexander Vladimirovich PASHKOV	Deputy Governor of the Penza Region in charge of the construction, housing and communal sector, and energy issues	Phone: (8412) 59 5695 Fax: (8412) 55 3501
Vyacheslav Alexeevich SATIN	Deputy Governor of the Penza Region, Minister of State Property	Phone: (8412) 52 1660 Fax: (8412) 52 0775
Olga Kuzminichna ATYUKOVA	Head of the Economy Division of the Government of the Penza Region	Phone: (8412) 59 5883 Fax: (8412) 56 6052
Vasily Vladimirovich KONDRATYEV	Head of the Industry, Transport and Communications Division of the Government of the Penza Region	Phone: (8412) 52 4855, 59 5596
Nina Petrovna KOMRATOVA	Chief of the International and Inter-Regional Cooperation Department of the External Relations Division of the Government of the Penza Region	Phone: (8412) 59 5112
Boris Vladimirovich YASHIN	Head of the Capital Investment Division of the Government of the Penza Region	Phone: (8412) 59 5026

3. ECONOMIC POTENTIAL

3.1. 1997–2002 GROSS REGIONAL PRODUCT (GRP). INDUSTRY BREAKDOWN

In 2002, the Penza Region's gross regional product reached $1,288.9 million, 8.2% up on 2001. Growth was mainly industry driven, as industry accounts for over 28% of GRP.

3.2. MAJOR ECONOMIC GROWTH PROJECTIONS

The blueprint for the economic development of the Region is given in the Penza Regional Government Program for Social Development and Economic Modernization, 2001–2003. The Program sets the following objectives:

Industry: a 2.5% increase in industrial output in 2003 via increased production capacity in the machine engineering, medical, light manufacturing, pulp and paper, and timber industries, retooling on an industry-wide basis, quality improvements, and increased exports.

Agriculture: 3.6% net production growth in 2003. Tillage output is expected to increase

GRP trends in 1997–2002						TABLE 2
	1997	1998	1999	2000	2001*	2002*
GRP in current prices, $ million	2,056.0	1,158.5	796.9	973.0	1,190.7	1,288.9

*Estimates of the Government of the Penza Region

GRP industry breakdown in 1997–2002, % of total						TABLE 3
	1997	1998	1999	2000	2001*	2002*
GRP	100.0	100.0	100.0	100.0	100.0	100.0
Industry	27.9	29.7	26.1	28.8	28.8	28.4
Agriculture and forestry	14.6	10.9	20.7	16.0	17.4	15.8
Construction	7.7	8.5	5.6	8.1	6.0	6.0
Transport and communications	8.6	7.9	7.3	8.1	9.7	10.7
Trade and public catering	11.5	12.3	12.7	11.3	11.6	11.8
Other	22.4	22.9	18.3	19.9	20.0	20.7
Net taxes on output	7.3	7.8	9.3	7.8	6.5	6.6

*Estimates of the Government of the Penza Region

Industry breakdown of industrial output in 1997–2002, % of total						TABLE 4
	1997	1998	1999	2000	2001	2002*
Industry	100.0	100.0	100.0	100.0	100.0	100.0
Machine engineering and metal processing	33.4	29.4	29.0	33.9	34.3	31.3
Food and beverages	18.9	20.7	26.9	24.4	24.7	24.4
Energy	18.2	23.1	14.5	12.4	12.1	15.4
Forestry, timber, and pulp and paper	5.1	5.2	7.4	8.4	8.3	9.1
Flour, cereals, and mixed fodder	2.0	1.4	1.8	1.9	3.4	3.9
Construction materials	4.9	4.6	4.0	3.5	3.9	2.9
Light industry	2.4	2.4	2.1	2.0	1.7	2.5
Fuel	–	0.1	0.1	0.3	0.8	0.8
Ferrous metals	0.6	0.5	1.1	1.2	1.1	0.7
Chemicals and petrochemicals	5.9	7.7	7.2	8.1	6.3	0.2
Glass and porcelain	0.1	0.1	0.1	–	0.1	0.2
Non-ferrous metals	–	–	0.1	0.1	0.2	0.1

*Estimates of the Government of the Penza Region

Fuel and energy sector production and consumption trends, 1997–2002						_TABLE 5_
	1997	1998	1999	2000	2001	2002
Electricity output, billion kWh	1.2	1.5	1.3	1.2	1.5	1.7
Oil output (including gas condensate), '000 tons	3	11	12	25	57	100
Electricity consumption, billion kWh	4.4	4.4	4.4	4.3	4.1	4.1
Natural gas consumption, million cubic meters	2,200	2,200	2,200	2,300	2,300	2,300

*Estimates of the Government of the Penza Region

by 1.7%, while output in the livestock sector is expected to rise by 5.4%.

3.3. INDUSTRIAL OUTPUT IN 1997–2002 FOR MAJOR SECTORS OF ECONOMY

At January 1, 2003, more than 22,000 business entities were operating in the Penza Region, or some 4.1% more than at the beginning of 2002. Some 14,600 enterprises and organizations (66.2%) are in private ownership, while more than 4,000 organizations (18.3%) are state owned.

Machine engineering and metal processing. This sector accounts for 31.3% of total GRP. Instrument enterprises specialize in designing and manufacturing products for radio electronics, communications, information technologies, and automated control systems. The city of Penza is home to Russia's aviation simulator equipment manufacturing industry. Major enterprises are FGUP Radiozavod, ZAO Foton, OAO Penzatyazhpromarmatura, OAO Penz-mash, ZAO Penzkompressormash, OAO Penzkhim-mash, OAO Penzensky Armaturny Zavod, ZAO Serdobsky Machine Building Plant AMO ZIL, OAO Penzdizelmash, GP PO Start, FGUP PPO EVT, OAO Electromekhanika, FGUP Electropribor, FGUP Radiozavod, FGUP PKBM, and OAO NPP ERA.

Food and beverages. The food industry accounts for 24.4% of GRP.

Main sub-sectors and the largest companies within the sector are: dairy, including butter and cheese production (OAO Penzensky Dairy), meat (OAO Penzensky Meat Processing Plant), brewery (OOO Vizit, OOO Samco Brewery), bread and bakery (OAO Penzensky Bakery No. 2 and OAO Penzensky Bakery No. 4), confectionery (ZAO Penzenskaya Confectionery Factory), alcohol and liquors (OAO Penzaspirtprom), and alcohol-free beverages (OAO Istok).

Energy. The energy sector accounts for 15.4% of GRP. The Penza Region's energy system is connected to Volgaenergo, the interconnected Volga District energy system. The total installed capacity of the energy system's thermal power stations is 375 MW. The total length of high-tension lines is 6,833 km.

Agriculture. Agriculture accounts for 15.8% of GRP. The sector is made up of 457 agricultural enterprises, and 1,980 farms. In 2002, gross agricultural output from all kinds of producers in the Region was $411.1 million, or 3.3% down on 2001. Tillage output

was down 5.9% at $239 million, while livestock output was down 0.3% at $172.1 million.

3.4. FUEL AND ENERGY BALANCE (OUTPUT AND CONSUMPTION PER RESOURCE)

The Penza Region is an energy deficient region. In 2002, total energy consumption was 4.4 billion kWh. Electricity production in the Region (OAO Penzaenergo) was 1.7 billion kWh, while energy imports reached 5.2 billion kWh (the Region exported 2.5 billion kWh).

3.5. TRANSPORT INFRASTRUCTURE

More than 20 million tons of freight and 415 million passengers are transported by all forms of transport in the Penza region each year. Road transport accounts for 26% of freight and 59% of passengers.

Roads. The Region has 6,200 km of paved public highway. The Region is linked to other regions of Russia by the following federal highways: Moscow – Samara, Penza – Tambov, Nizhny Novgorod – Arzamas – Saransk – Penza – Saratov. Some 5.2 million tons of freight is transported by road annually by more than 120 specialized road haulage enterprises of various forms of ownership.

Railroads. The Penza Region has 800 km of railroad. Two railroads cross the Region: the Syzran – Kuznetsk – Chaadaevka – Penza – Kamenka – Panelma – Bashmakovo line and the Rtischevo – Serdobsk – Kolyshley – Penza – Lunino – Ruzaevka line. Around 392,000 tons of freight is carried by rail each year.

Airports. The airport that serves the city of Penza provides air links to the main regions of Russia.

Oil and gas pipeline. Several trunk gas pipelines cross the Region: Saratov – Nizhny Novgorod, Chelyabinsk – Petrovsk, Central Asia – Center, Saratov – Moscow, and Urengoy – Center.

The Region is also crossed by several trunk oil pipelines: Ufa–West, Samara–Bryansk, Druzhba 1, and Druzhba 2.

3.6. MAIN NATURAL RESOURCES: RESERVES AND EXTRACTION IN 2002

The Region's principal natural resources are minerals.

Oil and gas deposits. Three oil deposits are in operation in the Penza Region. The total reserve stands at 39.8 million tons.

Construction materials mined in the Region include clay, gypsum, glass sand, marl, chalk (the largest deposit is the Surskoye), and coarse grain foundry sand (the Chaadaevskoye deposit).

4. TRADE OPPORTUNITIES

4.1. MAIN GOODS PRODUCED IN THE REGION

Machine engineering. The following types of machine engineering goods are produced annually in the Penza Region: low yield electric motors (9,000), air and gas compressors (1,000), tractor seeders (1,600), vacuum pumps and hardware (2,000), metal cutting benches and equipment for chemicals and oil industries, non-ferrous metal bodywork, car and tractor trailers, tank trucks and specialized cars, diesel vehicles and diesel generators, modular filling stations, agriculture machinery, and spinning looms. The Region also has an advanced computer hardware sector. Major consumer commodities produced in the Region include gas stoves, televisions, washing machines, bicycles, watches, tableware, and vacuum cleaners.

Paper and timber. The Region's paper and timber enterprises produce 24,200 tons of paper annually, 157,000 cubic meters of sawn timber, and 43,700 cubic meters of plywood.

Light manufacturing. The main products in this sector are tailored, knitted, and leather garments, woolen fabrics, and footwear.

Food and beverages. Processing enterprises include sugar beet processing facilities – 8,000 tons per day, canned fruit and vegetables – 30 millions standard jars per year, confectionery – 30,000 tons per year, vodka and liquors – 2.9 million decaliters per year, and non-alcoholic beverages – 3 million decaliters per year.

Construction materials. Enterprises in the Region produce prefabricated reinforced concrete units, bricks, and linoleum.

4.2. EXPORTS, INCLUDING EXTRA-CIS

Total foreign trade turnover in the Region in 2002 amounted to $109.3 million, down 32% on the previous year. In 2002, extra-CIS trade accounted for 80% of the total, with CIS trade at 20% (in 2000 – 78% and 22%, in 2001 – 47% and 53%, respectively). In 2002, total export deliveries from the Penza Region amounted to $40.3 million, 270% down on 2001. CIS exports accounted for 36% of the total in 2002, with extra-CIS exports at 64%. The Penza Region's principal export destinations in 2002 were Germany with $8.9 million, Kazakhstan – $6.9 million, Greece – $4.3 million, Ukraine – $3.8 million, the USA – $3.2 million, China – $2.1 million, and Estonia – $1.8 million. The goods breakdown of the Region's 2002 exports was as follows: machine engineering – $17.7 million, cultural and household goods – $5.6 million, timber products – $5.3 million, chemicals and petrochemicals – $4.7 million, food and food feedstock – $3.6 million, textiles and garments – $2.1 million, ferrous and non-ferrous metals and products – $0.8 million, and raw and processed mineral resources – $0.2 million.

4.3. IMPORTS, INCLUDING EXTRA-CIS

The Penza Region's 2002 imports totaled $69.0 million, up by 52% year-on-year.

The Region's major exporters were: Germany with $16.1 million, Cuba – $15.1 million, Colombia – $11.8 million, Italy – $5.9 million, Ukraine – $5.5 million, France – $3.2 million, and Guatemala – $1.9 million. The goods breakdown of the Region's 2002 imports was as follows: food and food feedstock – $35.9 million, machine engineering – $24 million, chemicals and petrochemicals – $5.8 million, textiles and garments – $1 million, and ferrous and non-ferrous metals and products – $0.9 million.

Major regional export and import entities
TABLE 6

ENTITY	ADDRESS	PHONE, FAX, E-MAIL
Penza branch of GUP Rostek (custom broker services for importers and exporters)	143, ul. Austrina, Penza, Penza Region, 440015	Phone: (8412) 57 9595 E-mail: rostek@penza.com.ru

5. INVESTMENT OPPORTUNITIES

5.1 INVESTMENTS IN 1992–2002 (BY INDUSTRY SECTOR), INCLUDING FOREIGN INVESTMENTS

The following factors determine the investment appeal of the Penza Region:
- Proximity to large industrial centers;
- A good geographical location and developed transport infrastructure providing raw material

and fuel delivery to the Region, developed cooperation links, and markets for finished products.

5.2. CAPITAL INVESTMENT

The machine engineering, transport, and industry sectors account for the lion's share of capital investment.

5.3. MAJOR ENTERPRISES (INCLUDING ENTERPRISES WITH FOREIGN INVESTMENT)

The Penza Region hosts 26 enterprises with foreign investment accounting for 2.4% of GRP.

Capital investment by industry sector, $ million						TABLE 7
	1997	1998	1999	2000	2001	2002
Total capital investment	361.2	210.3	105.2	140.6	178.5	189.7
Including major industries (% of total):						
Industry	23.4	17.6	26.8	24.9	28.2	29.5
Agriculture and forestry	5.7	11.8	12.8	9.6	11.1	9.7
Construction	13.1	2.2	2.6	2.4	1.7	1.1
Transport and communications	16.9	25.1	28.7	39.1	34.5	31.1
Trade and public catering	0.2	1.6	1.0	0.8	1.7	3.6
Other	40.7	41.7	28.1	23.2	22.8	25.0

Foreign investment trends in 1997–2002						TABLE 8
	1997	1998	1999	2000	2001	2002
Foreign investment, $ million	2.7	5.2	0.6	0.4	1.7	2.0
Including FDI, $ million	2.7	2.3	0.3	0.3	0.01	2.0

Largest enterprises of the Penza Region			TABLE 9
COMPANY	SECTOR	2002 SALES, $ MILLION*	2002 NET PROFIT, $ MILLION*
OAO Penzmash	Machine engineering	9.4	0.5
OAO Mayak	Pulp and paper	26.8	3.9
OAO Kuznetskobuv	Shoes	11.8	–1.4
OAO Biosintez	Chemicals and pharmaceuticals	28.3	0.4
ZAO Serdobsky Machine Engineering Plant	Machine engineering	0.9	–0.8
ZAO Penzakompressormash	Machine engineering	9.5	0.4
GUP Sovkhoz Progress	Agriculture	1.1	0.4
GUP Ordena Lenina Sovkhoz Bolshevik	Agriculture	1.7	0.2
SPK Kevdinsky	Agriculture	1.2	0.2

*Data of the Government of the Penza Region

5.4. MOST ATTRACTIVE SECTORS FOR INVESTMENT

The Region's Government is committed to attracting investment (including foreign) into the following core sectors of the Region's economy:
- Export-oriented and import replacing products;
- Machine engineering and processing industries;
- Manufacturing of advanced, high technology, and internationally competitive production;
- Transport and communications infrastructure;
- The services sector: creation of a chain of services firms and tourism companies, construction of international class hotels and motels, and establishment of camp sites and resort areas.

5.5. CURRENT LEGISLATION ON INVESTOR TAX EXEMPTIONS AND PRIVILEGES

The Penza Region has passed a number of legislative acts providing tax exemptions to investment projects and setting forth the legislative and economic aspects of state support to investors. These laws of the Penza Region include:
- Law On Attraction of Foreign Investment into the Penza Region;
- Law On the Penza Region Pledge Fund;
- Law On State Property Management.

These laws provide a legal and economic framework for government support to investors and tax and legal incentives to legal entities reinvesting profit in production facilities. They also provide tax and legal incentives to newly established legal entities, banks, and other credit institutions engaging in investment activity, tax exemp-

Regional entities responsible for raising investment		*TABLE 10*
ENTITY	ADDRESS	PHONE, FAX, E-MAIL
Penza-Moscow Inter-Regional Marketing Center	2, ul. Pushkina, Penza, Penza Region, 440600	Phone/fax: (8412) 56 0663, 56 0664 E-mail: center@sura.com.ru
ZAO Consulting. Leasing. Investment Financial Company	62, ul Moskovskaya, Penza, Penza Region, 440600	Phone: (8412) 56 1588 Fax: (8412) 56 1416
Business Support Agency	10, ul. Leningradskaya, Penza, Penza Region, 440035	Phone: (8412) 63 5989 Fax: (8412) 54 5281 E-mail: btc@sura.ru

tions for real estate leasing, and grandfather clause arrangements in case of legislation changes.

5.6. FEDERAL AND REGIONAL ECONOMIC AND SOCIAL DEVELOPMENT PROGRAMS FOR THE PENZA REGION

Federal targeted programs. In 2003, the following federal targeted programs for economic and social development in the Penza Region will be implemented:

Social Development of the Rural Areas through 2010; Soil Fertility Enhancement, 2002–2005; Ecology and Natural Resources of Russia, 2002–2010; and others. Some $22.9 million has been received for implementation of the program, including some $16.9 million allocated from the federal budget.

Regional programs. The Penza Region Government is currently implementing 11 regional targeted programs scheduled to run through 2008. The Program for Social and Economic Development of the Region, 2003-2008 plays an important role in the economic development of the Region. It is being implemented with the purpose of enhancing the Region's population welfare and improve output of companies and sectors of the economy, ensuring the ongoing development of the economy, and achieving economical self-sufficiency of towns, districts, and the Region as a whole.

The Program for the Development of Foreign Trade in the Penza Region and the Region's Export Potential, 2002–2005 is implemented with the purpose of improving and developing foreign trade infrastructure, enhancing the effectiveness of foreign trade activity and regional enterprises, and enhancing the financial and fiscal efficiency of export-import and investment operations.

The Program for the Development of Private Farming in the Penza Region, 2002–2005 aims to stabilize the private farming sector, increase the yields of private farms under market conditions, improve living standard in rural areas, and to secure the economic interests of private farmers.

The targeted Penza Region Soil Fertility Program, 2002–2005 aims to preserve and maintain soil fertility, to promote the rational use of natural resources, including arable land, and growth in agriculture output with a view to making the Region self-sufficient in terms of food.

6. INVESTMENT PROJECTS

Industry sector and project description	1) Expected results 2) Amount and term of investment 3) Form of financing[1] 4) Documentation[2]	Contact information
1	2	3

MACHINE ENGINEERING AND METAL PROCESSING		
52R001 ● ◆ Truck cargo trailer manufacturing: type 81651, 560 kg carrying capacity and type 83081, 6.0 tons carrying capacity. Project goal: to introduce a new product to the market.	1) 1,500 trailers annually 2) $3.2 million/2 years 3) L ($1.9 million) 4) BP	ZAO Serdobsky Machine Engineering Plant 10, ul. Vokzalnaya, Serdobsk, Penza Region, 442890 Phone: (84167) 42 357, 22 124 Fax: (84167) 22 505 Konstantin Nikolaevich Makarov, CEO

[1] L – Loan, E – Equity, Leas. – Leasing, JV – Joint Venture
[2] BP – Business Plan, FS – Feasibility Study

IV

VOLGA FEDERAL DISTRICT

1	2	3
52R002	● ◆	OAO Penzensky Fittings Plant
Ball cock manufacturing. Project goal: import replacement.	1) $33.1 million annually 2) €2.8 million/3 years 3) L ($1.5 million) 4) BP	1, ul. Transportnaya, Penza, Penza Region, 440007 Phone: (8412) 56 3503 Fax: (8412) 55 2400, 58 5051 E-mail: paz@tl.ru Alexander Ivanovich Dmitriev, CEO

FORESTRY, TIMBER, AND PULP AND PAPER

1	2	3
52R003	● ❖ ◆	ZAO Wooden Architecture
Interior door and glued timber article manufacturing from solid wood. Project goal: import replacement.	1) 240,000 doors and 30,000 square meters glued timber articles annually ($33.1 million per year) 2) $14.8 million/3 years 3) L, JV 4) BP	3a, ul. Austrina, Penza, Penza Region, 440054 Phone: (8412) 57 8733 Fax: (8412) 57 9527 E-mail: dera@sura.ru Sergei Gennadyevich Savchuk, CEO

FOOD AND BEVERAGES

1	2	3
52R004	● ❖ ◆	OAO Penzaspirtprom
Waste-free forage yeast production from afteralcohol grain. Project goal: organic substance recycling and forage yeast production.	1) 6,000 tons of yeast annually 2) $0.9 million/6 months 3) L, JV 4) BP	49, ul. Volodarskogo, Penza, Penza Region, 440600 Phone/fax: (8412) 63 1594 E-mail: spirtprom@penza.net Vitaly Vasilyevich Yeliseev, CEO

ECOLOGY

1	2	3
52R005	❖ ◆	OOO Teploservis
Recycling organic waste to produce energy. Project goal: energy production, resolution of environmental and ecologic issues.	1) Processing of 30,200 tons of wastes annually 2) $3.1 million/1 year 3) JV 4) BP	7, ul. Sobinova, Penza, Penza Region, 440060 Phone: (8412) 43 6115 Fax: (8412) 43 6211 E-mail: tservice@sura.ru Vyacheslav Leonidovich Polkovov, CEO

53. PERM REGION [59]

ECONOMIC MAP

KOMI REPUBLIC

Vesljana

Kolva

Polunochnoe

Ivdel

Gayny

Kama

Vishera

Pokrovsk--Uralsky

Rudnichny

Krasnovishersk

Krasnoturinsk

Kirs

KIROV

Byatka

Solikamsk

REGION

KUDYMKAR

Berezniki

Kizel

Kamskoe water reservoir

Gubakha

Sarany

Nizhnyaya Tura

Glazov

Cheptsa

Krasnokamsk

Gornozavodsk
Chusovoy

Kushva

Nytva

Lysva

Nizhny Tagil

Ocher

PERM

Kungur

Kirovograd

REPUBLIC OF UDMURTIA

Votkinskoe water reservoir

Osa

Votkinsk

Suksun

Pervouralsk

IZHEVSK

Revda

Chusovaya

Chaykovsky

Mozhga

Kueda

Chernushka

Krasnoufimsk

Sarapul

Sarany

PROCESSING INDUSTRY	MINING INDUSTRY	CROPS AND LIVESTOCK BREEDING
Ferrous metals	Oil	Wheat — Vegetables
Non-ferrous metals	Chromium ore	Rye — Potatoes
Machine engineering and metal processing	Potassium salt	Orchards
Chemicals and petrochemicals	Table salt	Long-fibred flax — Meat and dairy cattle breeding
Forestry and timber	Diamonds	Buckwheat — Poultry farming
Construction materials	Raw cement	Oats
Food and beverages	Limestone	
	Mineral water sources	POWER PLANTS
		Thermal power plants — Hydro power plants
		Resorts

The Perm Region is one of Russia's most economically developed regions with vast natural resources and economic potential. The Region is essentially industrial, with some 500 large and medium-sized companies in various sectors. The Region is one of the largest federal budget donors. As to its growth rates, Perm is one of the most dynamically developing regions in Russia.

Thanks to its developed economic structure, the Perm Region actively trades on the international market with 104 countries. Its major trading partners are industrially developed nations. In 2001–2002, the Region ranked third among the fifteen regions of the Volga Federal District by export and import operations volume.

According to rating entities, the Perm Region is among the top twenty Russian regions in terms of investment appeal. The Region ranks second or third in volume of investment among the Urals regions. The investment capacity of the Perm Region's companies and infrastructure facilities is estimated at $2–2.5 billion and $6.5 billion, respectively.

The lion's share of investment is channeled into the reconstruction and upgrading of industry, with a focus on certain sectors, such as oil extraction, oil and gas refining, telecommunications, and processing. These sectors account for the bulk of the Region's investment-ready enterprises, including by force of the availability of own investment resources.

Such globally recognized companies as United Technologies, Lufthansa, Siemens, Nestle, Alcatel, Shell, and others have strategic partnership arrangements with companies in the Perm Region.

The Perm Regional Administration is pursuing a long-term policy aimed at securing the legal rights of domestic and foreign investors and property owners in the Region.

One of the key requirements for WTO accession calls for industrial output to be compliant with international quality standards. In this regard, it should be noted that some thirty companies in the Perm Region have been certified by ISO-9000, TUV, and Veritas.

Many companies and firms are improving their marketing, management, and financial accounting systems, since compliance of these components with international standards is a key condition for Russia's integration into the WTO.

The Perm Region offers vast potential. We are experienced in attracting investment and creating conditions conducive to investment, and are well aware that realizing that potential will require our integration with the global community.

Yury Trutnev,
GOVERNOR OF THE PERM REGION

1. GENERAL INFORMATION

1.1. GEOGRAPHY

Situated in the north-east of the East European Plain, the Perm Region covers a total area of 160,600 square kilometers. To the north, the Region borders the Komi Republic, to the south – the Republic of Bashkortostan, to the east – the Sverdlovsk Region, and to the west – the Kirov Region and the Republic of Udmurtia.

1.2. CLIMATE

The Perm Region enjoys a temperate continental climate. The average air temperature in January is –15°C, rising to +20.1°C in July. Average annual precipitation is 450–600 mm. The Region lies under podzol and turf-podzol soils.

1.3. POPULATION

According to preliminary 2002 census results, total population in the Region was 2,824,000 people. The average population density is 17.6 people per square kilometer. The economically active population amounts to 1,478,000 people. While 2002 registered unemployment stood at 1.3%, the actual rate is 6.3%.

Demographically speaking, some 61.6% are of working age, 19.3% are below the statutory working age, and 19.1% are beyond the statutory working age.

As of 2002, the Perm Region's major urban centers are Perm with 1,000,100 inhabitants, Berezniki with 173,500 inhabitants, Solikamsk with 102,800 inhabitants, and Tchaikovsky with 90,100 inhabitants.

Population								TABLE 1
	1992	1997	1998	1999	2000	2001	2002
Total population, '000	3,044	2,989	2,977	2,970	2,956	2,941	2,824
Economically active population, '000	1,612	1,433	1,470	1,478	1,466	1,479	1,478

2. ADMINISTRATION

14, ul. Kuybysheva, Perm, Perm Region, 614006
Phone: (3422) 58 7071; fax: (3422) 90 5566
E-mail: obladm@permreg.ru; http://www.perm.ru

NAME	POSITION	CONTACT INFORMATION
Yury Petrovich TRUTNEV	Governor of the Perm Region	Phone: (3422) 58 7575 Fax: (3422) 36 0952
Anatoly Arkadyevich TEMKIN	First Deputy Governor of the Perm Region, Chairman of the Property Relations Department. In charge of the unified state policy in industry, science, and natural resources, responsible for management of state property and land resources	Phone: (3422) 58 7848 Fax: (3422) 90 1313
Arkady Borisovich KATS	Deputy Governor of the Perm Region. In charge of the unified economic, financial, and tax policy	Phone: (3422) 58 7658 Fax: (3422) 90 1616
Anatoly Grigoryevich MINAKOV	Deputy Governor of the Perm Region. In charge of the unified state policy on international and external economic relations and small and medium enterprise development	Phone: (3422) 58 7170 Fax: (3422) 90 1260
Ludmila Viktorovna KUCHINSKAYA	Head of the Perm Region Division of International and External Economic Relations	Phone: (3422) 58 7358 Fax: (3422) 90 1961 E-mail: wes@permreg.ru
Valery Nikolaevich ZAKHVATKIN	Head of the Perm Region Main Economic Division	Phone: (3422) 90 1230 Fax: (3422) 90 1971 E-mail: gue@permregion.ru
Sergei Alexandrovich DYAGILEV	Chairman of the Perm Region Department of Industry and Science	Phone: (3422) 58 7305 Fax: (3422) 90 0601 E-mail: polprom@permreg.ru

3. ECONOMIC POTENTIAL

3.1. 1997–2002 GROSS REGIONAL PRODUCT (GRP). INDUSTRY BREAKDOWN

The 2002 gross regional product amounted to $6,027.2 million, which constitutes a 4.9% decrease year-on-year. In 2002, the Perm Region won the Golden Ruble Contest and was pronounced the best Russian region in terms of the financial rehabilitation of its economy in 2000–2001.

3.2. MAJOR ECONOMIC GROWTH PROJECTIONS

The blueprint for the economic development of the Perm Region is set forth in the Conceptual Framework for Social and Economic Development, 1999–2003, which was adopted pursuant to the Law On Industrial Policy in the Perm Region.

GRP trends in 1997–2002						TABLE 2
	1997	1998	1999	2000	2001*	2002*
GRP in current prices, $ million	8,646.9	5,625.4	3,805.1	4,670.7	6,334.9	6,027.2

*Estimates of the Perm Regional Administration

GRP industry breakdown in 1997–2002, % of total						TABLE 3
	1997	1998	1999	2000	2001*	2002*
GRP	100.0	100.0	100.0	100.0	100.0	100.0
Industry	37.9	41.1	46.5	44.0	40.7	36.0
Agriculture and forestry	6.6	5.6	8.5	6.5	6.2	5.2
Construction	9.4	7.1	5.6	8.0	8.8	6.0
Transport and communications	13.5	11.8	10.4	9.9	12.5	15.0
Trade and public catering	12.9	11.1	11.8	14.1	8.8	15.1
Other	19.7	23.3	17.2	17.5	23.0	22.7

*Estimates of the Perm Regional Administration

Pursuant to the Conceptual Framework, the industrial policy goal is to create conditions conducive to developing efficient and competitive operations in the Region. In order to achieve leadership in priority areas, the Region plans to:

- Utilize its competitive advantages more rigorously and create conditions conducive to developing new competitive advantages;
- Employ its R&D potential and materials, and financial resources to the full extent;
- Provide training to foster a highly qualified industrial workforce;
- Secure the interests of producers, improve product competitiveness, and create conditions conducive to integrating the Region into the world economy on a mutually beneficial basis.

The Conceptual Framework outlines major stabilization objectives and instructs the leading industrial sectors to:

- Reinforce positive trends in the chemicals and petrochemicals and machine engineering sectors;
- Transfer non-ferrous metal companies to new raw material sources with higher useful component content;
- Utilize new effective technology to decrease costs and energy consumption;
- Focus on the production of finished goods from titanium, magnesium, and aluminum;
- Extend the product range of finished rolled ferrous metals, enhance steel quality, and utilize new environmentally friendly technology to reduce ecological charges.

3.3. INDUSTRIAL OUTPUT IN 1997–2002 FOR MAJOR SECTORS OF ECONOMY

The leading industrial sectors of the Perm Region are energy, machine engineering, chemicals and petrochemicals, fuel, forestry, timber, and pulp and paper. These account for some 76% of total industrial output.

Fuel. The sector accounts for 23.2% of total industrial output. Twelve large and medium industrial companies are represented in the sector. Major companies, which account for a combined 84% of total output, are OOO LUKoil-Perm (oil and gas extraction), ZAO LUKoil-Perm (oil and gas exploration and development, and petroleum product refining and distribution), OOO LUKoil-Permnefteorgsintez (production of gasoline, oils, and diesel fuel), OAO Perm Lubricant and Coolant Plant (production of emulsoids, lubricants, and coolants).

Industry breakdown of industrial output in 1997–2002, % of total						TABLE 4
	1997	1998	1999	2000	2001	2002*
Industry	100.0	100.0	100.0	100.0	100.0	100.0
Fuel	18.8	14.6	17.9	23.3	25.5	23.2
Chemicals and petrochemicals	16.6	19.9	22.5	19.7	18.2	17.1
Machine engineering and metal processing	13.5	12.9	11.6	12.4	13.9	14.1
Energy	18.4	18.3	11.1	10.7	10.9	13.6
Forestry, timber, and pulp and paper	6.3	7.2	8.3	8.3	7.7	8.0
Food and beverages	9.6	7.8	7.8	6.5	6.5	7.2
Non-ferrous metals	4.6	5.6	6.2	5.2	5.0	5.3
Ferrous metals	3.8	5.3	5.3	5.4	4.7	4.6
Construction materials	2.8	2.4	1.8	2.0	1.8	1.8
Light industry	2.2	1.3	1.4	1.3	1.1	1.2

*Estimates of the Perm Regional Administration

Chemicals and petrochemicals. The sector accounts for 17.1% of total industrial output. Some 27 large and medium companies operate in the sector. Major companies are OAO Uralkaliy and OAO Silvinit (potassium fertilizers), OAO Azot and OAO Mineral Fertilizers (nitrogen fertilizers), OAO Soda and OAO Bereznikovsky Soda Plant (soda ash, solid, liquid and scaled caustic potassium, liquid chlorine, liquid sodium glass, and sodium metasilicate), and OAO Sorbent (active carbon). The Region produces a variety of products of organic synthesis, namely: methanol, urotropin, polyamide (OAO Metafrax), isoprene, divynilbutadiene, benzene, liquid nitrogen (OAO Uralorgsintez); synthetic dyes (OAO Beraton), coolants, fluor-polymers (OAO Galogen), ethylene, ethyl benzene-styrene (OAO Stirol), butyl alcohol, and 2-ethylhecsanole (OAO Butyl Alcohol Plant).

Machine engineering and metal processing. The sector accounts for 14.1% of total industrial output. The aerospace sub-sector is the most promising area within the sector. The Region's companies hold leading positions in the production of aircraft and rocket engines, fuel equipment, instruments and navigation tools, gas pumping units and gas turbine plants, oil extraction machinery, and equipment for digital and fiber-optical data transmission systems. Major companies within the sector are OAO Aviadvigatel, OAO Perm Motors Plant, OAO Motovilikhinsky Plants, OAO Mashinostroitel, OAO Iskra, OAO Privod, and NPO Perm Instrumentation Development Company.

Metals. The sector is represented by ferrous, non-ferrous, and rare metals producers, in addition to powder metal companies. The Region is home to the only Russian producer of titanium sponge. The Region also processes half of Russia's magnesium output. The largest companies are OAO Avisma Titanium and Magnesium Plant, OAO Solikamskiy Magnesium Plant, OAO Chusovskoy Metal Works, OAO Nytva, and OAO Lysva Metal Plant.

Energy. The energy sector accounts for 13.6% of total industrial output. The Region is home to one of Russia's largest power stations the Permskaya GRES with a capacity of 5 GW. OAO Permenergo interconnects OAO Kamskaya Hydroelectric Power Station, OAO Votkinskaya Hydroelectric Power Station, Perm HEP stations, and a thermal power station.

Forestry, timber, and pulp and paper. The sector accounts for 8% of total industrial output. The Region's vast resources form the raw material base of the timber sector. The Region exports one third of its timber output, while another third is processed at four local pulp and paper plants, namely OAO Solikamskbumprom, State Unitary Company Kamsky Pulp and Paper Plant, OAO Kama Pulp and Paper Plant, and OAO Visherabumprom.

Agriculture. Agriculture in the Region is represented by both tillage including winter rye, spring wheat, oats, buckwheat, long flax, potato, and vegetables, and meat and dairy cattle farming. Agricultural output was up 7% year-on-year in 2002.

3.4. FUEL AND ENERGY BALANCE (OUTPUT AND CONSUMPTION PER RESOURCE)

The main fuel and energy sub-sectors are electricity and oil. The sector fully meets the regional demand for electricity. In 2002, the Region produced 25.7 billion kWh of electricity and 34.4 million GCal of heat. Annual oil output exceeds 9 million tons and natural gas output – 300 million cubic meters. The Region exports some 40% of its oil output.

3.5. TRANSPORT INFRASTRUCTURE

The Region's advantageous geographical location and developed transport infrastructure partly make up for its remoteness from international industrial centers.

Roads. The Region is continuing to expand its highway network. It currently has 6,000 km of

IV

VOLGA FEDERAL DISTRICT

Fuel and energy sector production and consumption trends, 1997–2002	1997	1998	1999	2000	2001	2002*
Electricity output, billion kWh	21.9	20.3	21.7	22.6	24.9	25.7
Oil output (including gas condensate), '000 tons	9,259	9,315	9,196	9,372	9,610	9,788
Natural gas output, million cubic meters	380	382	413	401	432	377
Coal output, '000 tons	609	250	99	19	–	–
Fuel oil output, '000 tons	2,700	1,932	2,129	1,851	1,827	2,028
Electricity consumption, billion kWh	20.8	19.6	20.6	21.6	23.8	24.5
Oil consumption, '000 tons	12,195	10,313	11,599	11,955	12,362	12,546
Natural gas consumption, million cubic meters	7,715	11,891	11,501	11,587	12,950	13,436
Coal consumption, '000 tons	1,053	720	756	1,053	850	1,215
Fuel oil consumption, '000 tons	563	654	645	643	656	611

TABLE 5

*Estimates of the Perm Regional Administration

paved public highway. Some 40 companies and over 500 private entrepreneurs operate in the road transport sector. Annual freight turnover amounts to 340 million ton-kilometers.

Railroads. The Perm Region has 2,000 km of railroads. The Trans-Siberian railroad, which links the central and north-western districts with Siberia and the Far East, crosses the Region. Construction of the shortest rail route to Arkhangelsk, a major Russian seaport, is underway.

Airports. The international airport at Bolshoye Savino has republican status and provides customs services and border passport control. It links the Region to Europe, the Middle East, and the Far East.

River transport. The Region's longest river route along the Kama river is 1,519 km long. The Kama is the main waterway in the Urals, linking the Region with the White, Baltic, Caspian and Black seas, and the Sea of Azov. Major river ports are Perm, Levshino, Berezniki, and Tchaikovsky. Annual freight turnover is 5 million ton-kilometers.

Oil and gas pipelines. Two branches of the Surgut – Polotsk oil pipeline, five main gas pipelines, and an export gas pipe Urengoy – Uzhgorod pass through the Region.

3.6. MAIN NATURAL RESOURCES: RESERVES AND EXTRACTION IN 2002

The Region's principal natural resources are oil, natural gas, coal, chrome ore, gold, diamonds, quartz, zitrin, gypsum, selenite, uvarovite, limestone, and marble.

Mineral resources. The Region extracts materials used in the production of potassium fertilizers in Russia (100% of Russia's output). The Verkhnekamskoye deposit contains 30 billion tons of potassium, magnesium, and sodium salts. The salt stratum extends as much as 514 meters. Half of Russia's rock-salt reserves are concentrated in the deposit.

Oil and gas fields. Over 200 oil and gas fields have been discovered, with 89 oil fields, 3 gas fields, and 18 oil and gas fields in operation. The most developed oil and gas fields are the Polaznenskoye, Krasnokamskoye, Kuedinskoye, Osinskoye, and Chernushenskoye.

Diamonds. Annual diamond output in the Vishera river catchment area equals 100,000 carats. The quality of the diamonds mined here is comparable with that of Namibian diamonds.

Timber. Forests cover a total of 12 million hectares in the Region, with industrial reserves amounting to 400 million cubic meters. Some 70% is coniferous, the most valuable species group from the industry point of view.

4. TRADE OPPORTUNITIES

4.1. MAIN GOODS PRODUCED IN THE REGION

Chemicals. 2002 output of mineral fertilizers totaled 5,073,000 tons, dressed carnallite – 663,800 tons, synthetic ammonia – 1,117,100 tons, synthetic resins and plastic – 81,400 tons, rectified methanol – 772,600 tons, varnish and paint materials – 6,100 tons, and detergents – 54,300 tons.

Fuel. 2002 gasoline output totaled 1,670,100 tons, diesel – 2,821,900 tons, and motor oils – 272,300 tons.

Machine engineering. In 2002, telephone equipment and subscriber units output amounted to 530,000 units, well pumps – 10,100 units, electric power cable – 13,400 km, electric saws – 104,000 units, mixers – 663,200 units, low capacity electrical engines – 101,100 units, and household electrical cookers – 62,000 units.

Pulp and paper. 571,000 tons of paper and 97,000 tons of cardboard produced in 2002.

Food and beverages. Output of bread and bakery products totaled 152,600 tons in 2002, margarine products – 13,600 tons, liquor – 2,318,500 decaliters, and beer – 7,071,000 decaliters.

Medical goods. Pharmaceutical companies in the Region produce antitoxic serums, vaccines, and dysbacteriosis treatments. Chemicals and pharmaceuticals output amounted to some $15.9 million in 2002.

4.2. EXPORTS, INCLUDING EXTRA-CIS

The Perm Region's external trade turnover stands at $2,100 million. In 2002, exports to extra-CIS amounted to $1,740 million, while exports to CIS were $140 million. The main types of goods exported by the Region (as of 2001–2002) were fossil fuels, oil, and oil products – 39% of total exports, potassium and nitrogen fertilizers – 26%, paper, cardboard, and paper goods – 6%, and organic chemicals (methanol, urotropin, polyamide, isoprene, divynilbutadiene, and benzene) – 5%.

The Region trades with 104 countries. Major importers of the Region's products include China (12%), Germany (10%), and the Netherlands (7%).

4.3. IMPORTS, INCLUDING EXTRA-CIS

In 2002, imports from extra-CIS totaled $170 million, and from CIS - $89.1 million. The main types of imported goods (as of 2001–2002) were nuclear reactors, boilers, and equipment – 40% of total imports, fossil fuels, oil, and oil products – 13%, chemicals – 8%, electrical machines and equipment – 5%, ore, slag, and ash – 5%, and locomotives – 4%.

The main exporters to the Region as of 2001–2002 were Germany (20%), Ukraine (17%), Kazakhstan (14%), and Italy (6%).

4.4. MAJOR REGIONAL EXPORT AND IMPORT ENTITIES

Due to the specific features of trade in the Region, mainly industrial companies perform export and import operations. As of 2002, some 412 regional companies were engaged in export and import.

5. INVESTMENT OPPORTUNITIES

5.1 INVESTMENTS IN 1992–2002 (BY INDUSTRY SECTOR), INCLUDING FOREIGN INVESTMENTS

The following factors determine the investment appeal of the Perm Region:
- Its unique natural resource base and developed processing industry;
- Its developed transport infrastructure and access to main roads, railroads, and waterways;
- The high scientific and technical potential of its armaments manufacturers;
- Its highly qualified workforce.

5.2. CAPITAL INVESTMENT

In 2002, companies in the Region received a total of $56 million in foreign investment.

5.3. MAJOR ENTERPRISES (INCLUDING ENTERPRISES WITH FOREIGN INVESTMENT)

The Perm Region is home to over 390 companies with foreign investment from 59 countries worldwide. Investors from Germany, the USA, and China predominate. Wholly foreign owned enterprises include OAO Permryba, OAO Kamskaya Confectionery, and ZAO Rus Lockwood.

Capital investment by industry sector, $ million						TABLE 6
	1997	1998	1999	2000	2001	2002
Total capital investment	1,195.7	629.3	612.5	980.9	1,293.4	1,183.0
Including major industries (% of total):						
Industry	37.9	50.4	44.6	46.7	46.8	35.1
Agriculture and forestry	2.6	3.5	1.7	1.7	1.6	1.8
Construction	11.2	12.6	10.7	11.2	12.9	9.2
Transport and communications	23.0	12.6	15.5	10.1	12.2	13.7
Trade and public catering	0.6	0.2	1.0	1.1	1.1	1.1
Other	24.7	20.7	26.5	29.2	25.4	39.1

Foreign investment trends in 1996–2002						TABLE 7
	1996–1997	1998	1999	2000	2001	2002
Foreign investment, $ million	52.4	42.7	42.6	96.9	97.6	56.0
Including FDI, $ million	40.7	4.3	22.3	37.1	60.9	27.4

IV

VOLGA FEDERAL DISTRICT

Largest enterprises of the Perm Region		TABLE 8
COMPANY	SECTOR	2001 NET PROFIT, $ MILLION
OAO Permenergo	Energy	46.9
OAO Permskaya Power Station	Energy	12.4
OOO LUKoil-Permneft	Fuel	45.5
OOO LUKoil-Permnefteorgsintez	Fuel	139.5
ZAO LUKoil-Perm	Fuel	133.2
ZAO Sibur-Khimprom	Chemicals and petrochemicals	10.2
OAO Solikamsky Magnesium Plant	Non-ferrous metals	8.6
OAO Avisma Titanium and Magnesium Plant	Non-ferrous metals	13.8
OAO Azot	Chemicals and petrochemicals	5.0
OAO Uralkaliy	Chemicals and petrochemicals	24.3
OAO Silvinit	Chemicals and petrochemicals	22.0
OAO Mineral Fertilizers	Chemicals and petrochemicals	5.6
OAO Metafrax	Chemicals and petrochemicals	38.1
OAO Inkar	Machine engineering	5.7
OAO Perm Motor Plant	Machine engineering	1.8
OAO Solikamskbumprom	Forestry, timber, and pulp and paper	25.4
State Company Krasnokamsky Goznak Factory	Forestry, timber, and pulp and paper	7.5
State Company Perm Goznak Printing Company	Printing	27.6

*Data of the Perm Regional Administration

5.4. MOST ATTRACTIVE SECTORS FOR INVESTMENT

According to experts and the Perm Regional Administration, the petrochemicals, chemicals, machine engineering, food and beverages, timber, transport, and communications industries are the most potentially appealing sectors for investors.

5.5. CURRENT LEGISLATION ON INVESTOR TAX EXEMPTIONS AND PRIVILEGES

Starting from 2003, Perm Region laws provide profit tax incentives to industrial companies reinvesting profits into production. The laws envisage a 2–4% reduction in the profit tax rate if at least 20–40% of profits taxable in the Region is allocated to the above purpose.

The Region also offers property tax exemptions. The tax rate is halved for newly established companies, including companies with foreign investment. A considerable reduction in the property tax rate is envisaged for newly acquired and newly commissioned fixed assets of manufacturing companies: a 75% reduction in the first year of operations, and 50% in the second and third years.

Intangible assets are property tax exempt, which is especially important to technology and knowledge based companies.

Tariff regulation, including for the whole term of the investment project, is negotiable.

5.6. FEDERAL AND REGIONAL ECONOMIC AND SOCIAL DEVELOPMENT PROGRAMS FOR THE PERM REGION

Federal targeted programs. In 2002, federal funding for the social and economic development of the Perm Region was provided for 17 federal targeted programs. The lion's share of funding was allocated for the development of transport infrastructure, industry, public welfare, and environmental rehabilitation and use of natural resources.

The federal targeted program for the Upgrade of Russia's Transport System, 2002–2010 plays an important role and aims to make the transport system more balanced and improve its efficiency and safety. The Region uses the program's funds to construct and reconstruct federal roads and the airport at Bolshoye Savino. The total transport infrastructure development budget amounted to $9.6 million in 2002.

The main objective of the federal targeted program for the Development of Civil Aviation in Russia in 2002–2010 and through 2015 is to support and develop the scientific, technical, and production potential of Russia's aviation industry. The program aims to develop the Perm Region's industry. A total of $3.4 million was allocated from the federal budget for the program.

Regional programs. The Perm Region is implementing several regional programs focusing on the development of its agroindustrial sector, healthcare, public welfare, and environmental rehabilitation worth a total of $37.8 million.

The regional targeted program for the Creation of a Computerized Land Register and State Records of Real Estate in the Perm Region, 2003–2007 aims to set up a computerized land register and state records of real estate to ensure efficient use of land and other real estate, encourage buying and selling in the sector, and stimulate investment in real estate. The program has a budget of over $3.1 million for 2003.

The program for the development of the mineral and raw material base in the Perm Region aims to meet current and future industrial, construction, and agricultural demand, and to improve the economic efficiency of mineral resource extraction. The program has a budget of over $2.3 million for 2003.

6. INVESTMENT PROJECTS

Industry sector and project description	1) Expected results 2) Amount and term of investment 3) Form of financing[1] 4) Documentation[2]	Contact information
1	2	3
FERROUS METALS		
53R001	● ◆	OAO Joint Stock Company Lysva Metal Works
1) Construction of a casting and rolling plant. Project goal: to develop local coldroll sheet facilities.	1) 340,000 tons of cold rolled metal per year 2) $440.6 million/n/a 3) L 4) BP	1, ul. Metallistov, Lysva, Perm Region, 618900 Phone: (34249) 25 543 Fax: (34249) 27 271 E-mail: voronov@aklmz.ru Vladimir Alexandrovich Ganzhin, CEO
53R002	● ◆	OAO Motovilikhinskiye Plants
Upgrade of bar production and installation of a new bar rolling machine. Project goal: production of high precision and quality bars.	1) 70,000 tons of bars a year 2) $9.4 million/6 months 3) L ($14.7 million – for steel facilities; $13.6 million – for bars production) 4) BP	35, ul. 1905, Perm, Perm Region, 614014 Phone: (3422) 60 7301 Fax: (3422) 65 6263 E-mail: zil@perm.ru Ivan Mikhailovich Kostin, CEO
53R003	● ◆	OAO Chusovskoy Metal Works
Upgrade of steel smelting operations. Project goal: to produce competitive and profitable goods to world standards.	1) Steel – 500,000 tons a year, casting sections – 487,000 tons a year, finished rolled steel – 450,000 tons a tear, finished vehicle springs – 41,000 tons a year 2) $21 million/3 years 3) L ($15,6 million), Leas. 4) BP	13, ul. Trudovaya, Chusovoy, Perm Region, 618200 Phone: (34256) 30 602, 63 121 Fax: (34256) 31 264 E-mail: adm@chmz.umn.ru, post @chmz.umn.ru Anatoly Alexandrovich Karpov, CEO
CHEMICALS AND PETROCHEMICALS		
53R004	● ▲	OAO Azot
Upgrade of ammonia still by replacing the existing catalyst with a small-bead catalyst. Project goal: to increase productivity of the ammonia unit and decrease energy consumption and waste.	1) Economic effect from installation of $0.4 million per year 2) $2.5 million/5.5 years 3) L 4) FS	75, Churtanskoye shosse, Berezniki, Perm Region, 618401 Phone: (34242) 65 390, 63 483, 98 258 Fax: (34242) 65 512, 64 872 E-mail: azot@azot.perm.ru Mikhail Adamovich Petrunyak, CEO

[1] L – Loan, E – Equity, Leas. – Leasing, JV – Joint Venture
[2] BP – Business Plan, FS – Feasibility Study

1	2	3

FORESTRY, TIMBER, AND PULP AND PAPER

53R005 ● ★ ▲

Upgrade of timber processing operations.
Project goal: to increase the product range and improve its competitiveness on domestic and international markets.

1) Processing of 15,000 cubic meters of coniferous timber per year
2) $2.0 million/5 years
3) L, Leas.
4) FS

OOO Repair and Construction Company Alexiy
84, ul. Promyshlennaya, Perm, Perm Region, 614055
Phone: (3422) 20 2177
Fax: (3422) 20 2912
E-mail: alex@nevod.ru
Mikhail Ivanovich Mukhranov, CEO

MINING

53R006 ● ★ ◆

Mining and processing of stone.
Project goal: to mine stone and produce competitive goods.

1) Mining of 2,000–3,000 cubic meters of stone per year
2) $3.0 million/4–5 years
3) L, Leas.
4) BP

OOO Permkamen
3/7, ul. Revolutsii, Perm, Perm Region, 614007
Phone: (3422) 16 4634, 16 4644
Fax: (3422) 16 4634
Andrei Sergeevich Bakhaev, Director

COMMUNICATIONS

53R007 ■ ▲

Construction of a broadband radio access system.
Project goal: to put into operation a MDMS broadband radio access system.

1) Creation of a broadband data transmission network to provide internet and telephony services and connect local networks
2) $2.2 million/3 years
3) E
4) FS

ZAO ER-Telecom
128, ul. Kirova, Perm, Perm Region, 614600
Phone: (3422) 19 5100
Fax: (3422) 19 5104
E-mail: info@ertelecom.ru
Mikhail Vladimirovich Vorobyev, CEO

SCIENCE AND INNOVATION

53R008 ■ ● ▲

Development and production of a drilling navigation unit.
Project goal: to increase efficiency of well drilling by identifying 3D well trajectory and to use effective controlled directional drilling to increase recovery at horizontal reservoirs of both onshore and offshore wells.

1) Increase in oil recovery up to 70–80%
2) $5.2 million/4.5 years
3) L, E
4) FS

OAO Perm R&D Instrument Production Company
106, ul. 25 October, GSP-590, Perm, Perm Region, 614990
Phone: (3422) 45 2336, 45 3141
Fax: (3422) 45 1219
E-mail: root@ppk.perm.ru
Alexei Guryevich Andreev, CEO

MACHINE ENGINEERING AND METAL PROCESSING

53R009 ● ◆ ❖

Launching a stainless steel pot production line.
Project goal: to establish a unit within the company structure to produce quality stainless steel saucepans with thermal diffusion bases using Italian technology and machinery.

1) 150,000 sets of five saucepans per year
2) $6.0 million/5 years
3) L, JV
4) BP

OAO Nytva
71, ul. K. Marksa, Nytva, Perm Region, 617000
Phone: (34272) 30 121
Fax: (34272) 30 929, 30 470
E-mail: ogon@permoline.ru
Rafail Zakharovich Kadyrov, CEO

54. SAMARA REGION [63]

ECONOMIC MAP

REPUBLIC OF TATARSTAN

Bugulma

Bavly

Kuybyshevskoe water reservoir

Sheshma

Svíyaga

Bolshoy Cheremshan

Shentala

ULYANOVSK

Dimitrovgrad

Sernovodsk

Bugulma

ULYANOVSK

REGION

Novoulyanovsk

Sengiley

Kondurcha

Sok

Pokhvistnevo

Bolshaya Kinel

Buguruslan

Togliatti

Zhigulyovsk

Oktyabrsk

Syzran

Novokuybyshevsk

Bezenchuk

SAMARA

Otradny

Samara

Chapaevsk

Neftegorsk

Buzuluk

Chagra

Alekseevka

Saratovskoe water reservoir

Bolshoy Irgiz

Bolshaya Glushitsa

ORENBURG

SARATOV

Bolshaya Chernigovka

REGION

Balakovo

Pugachyov

REGION

PROCESSING INDUSTRY	MINING INDUSTRY	POWER PLANTS	CROPS AND LIVESTOCK BREEDING
⬤ Non-ferrous metals	▲ Oil	⚡ Thermal power plants	⋎ Wheat
⬤ Machine engineering and metal processing	▬ Shale oil	⚡ Hydro power plants	⋏ Sunflower
⬤ Chemicals and petrochemicals	▲ Sulfur		⋎ Sugar beetroot
⬤ Construction materials	▯ Raw cement		◉ Orchards
◯ Food and beverages	▱ Table salt		🐖 Meat and dairy cattle breeding
	• Mineral water sources		🐖 Pig breeding
	℘ Resorts		🐑 Sheep rearing
			🦃 Poultry farming

The Samara Region, an industrial center of Russia, boasts a sophisticated multi-industry structure. The Region heads the list of the Volga regions in terms of total industrial output, and is among the top four regions of Russia.

The Samara Region is closely integrated into the Russian economic system and has developed trading and economic links with over 100 countries.

The Region is implementing international cooperation programs in various fields and is actively pursuing the establishment of international and inter-regional relations. We have concluded agreements with ten provinces of overseas countries envisaging cooperation between companies, the establishment of joint ventures, the implementation of advanced technology, the encouragement of investment and trade, and collaboration in the sphere of culture, education, and management practice.

The Samara Region is one of the leading Russian regions in terms of foreign investment. In 2002, General Motors, a major global producer of vehicles, established a joint venture with Russia's AvtoVAZ with an estimated output of 75,000 cars per year.

The Regional Administration is committed to creating investment conditions conducive to profitable business development in the Region. This is the number one focus area of the regional authorities' efforts.

The Region's advantageous geographic location, balanced industrial sector, high research and development and technology potential, developed market infrastructure, and highly professional and qualified workforce mean that the Region has the potential to develop any industrial sector from food and beverages and food processing to spacecraft manufacturing.

Standard & Poor's rating agency has rated the Region B+ (outlook stable), while Moody's has accorded the Region a Ba3 (outlook stable) rating. Of all Russia's regions, only Moscow and St. Petersburg enjoy higher ratings.

The Samara Region has all of the prerequisites to become a center for capital, technology, and knowledge investment, and a global trade hub.

Konstantin Titov,
GOVERNOR OF THE SAMARA REGION

1. GENERAL INFORMATION

1.1. GEOGRAPHY

Located in the south-east of the East European Plain in the middle reaches of the Volga River, the Samara Region covers an area of some 53,600 square kilometers. To the north, it borders the Republic of Tatarstan, to the west – the Ulyanovsk Region, to the east – the Orenburg Region, and to the south – the Saratov Region and Kazakhstan.

1.2. CLIMATE

The Samara Region enjoys a severe dry continental climate. Average January temperatures vary between –13°C in the west and –14°C in the east of the Region, rising to +20°C in the north-west and +22°C in the south-east in July. Annual precipitation reaches 300–450 mm. The average growing season lasts 180 days.

1.3. POPULATION

According to preliminary 2002 census results, total population in the Samara Region was 3,240,000. The average population density is 60.4 people per square kilometer. The economically active population amounts to 1,749,000. Official 2002 unemployment stood at 1.6%, while the actual rate was 5.4%.

Demographically speaking, some 61.7% are of statutory working age, 17.3% are under the statutory working age, and 21% are beyond the statutory working age.

The major urban centers of the Samara Region (2002 data) are Samara with 1,158,100 inhabitants, Togliatti with 701,900 inhabitants, Syzran with 187,800 inhabitants, and Novokuybyshevsk with 113,000 inhabitants.

Population							TABLE 1
	1992	1997	1998	1999	2000	2001	2002
Total population, '000	3,253	3,308	3,307	3,305	3,295	3,279	3,240
Economically active population, '000	1,733	1,597	1,611	1,727	1,692	1,715	1,749

2. ADMINISTRATION

210, ul. Molodogvardeyskaya, Samara, Samara Region, 443006. Phone: (8462) 32 2268; fax: (8462) 32 1340
E-mail: governor@samara.ru; http://www.adm.samara.ru

NAME	POSITION	CONTACT INFORMATION
Konstantin Alexeevich TITOV	Governor of the Samara Region	Phone: (8462) 32 2268 Fax: (8462) 32 1340 E-mail: governor@samara.ru http://www.titov.samara.ru
Victor Alexeevich KAZAKOV	Deputy Governor of the Samara Region	Phone: (8462) 32 2215 Fax: (8462) 32 1749 E-mail: governor@samara.ru
Gabibulla Rabadanovich KHASAEV	Head of the Economic Development and Investment Department of the Samara Region	Phone: (8462) 32 2744 Fax: (8462) 32 2233 E-mail: bulg@vis.infoPhone.ru, Khasaev@economy.vis.ru http://www.economy.samreg.ru
Pavel Alexandrovich IVANOV	Head of the Financial Management Department of the Samara Region	Phone: (8462) 32 1586 Fax: (8462) 32 3902 E-mail: depfin@vis.infoPhone.ru
Alexander Antonovich LATKIN	Head of the Construction, Architecture, Housing and Communal Services, and Road Department of the Samara Region	Telephone: (8462) 32 1228 Fax: (8462) 32 8486 E-mail: depart@mail.samtel.ru
Alexander Vasilyevich RUMYANTSEV	Head of the Agriculture and Food Department of the Samara Region	Phone: (8462) 32 0968 Fax: (8462) 32 1250 E-mail: aris@samtel.ru
Alexander Nikolaevich IVANOV	Head of the State Property Management Department of the Samara Region	Phone: (8462) 32 8578 Fax: (8462) 32 3700 E-mail: dugi@mail.vis.ru

NAME	POSITION	CONTACT INFORMATION
Vladimir Ivanovich DORONIN	Head of the Industry and Trade Department of the Samara Region	Phone: (8462) 42 3257 Fax: (8462) 42 3240 E-mail: prom@mail.vis.ru
Yury Alexandrovich KOPYTIN	Head of the Enterprise Development Department of the Samara Region	Phone: (8462) 32 7498 Fax: (8462) 42 3242 E-mail: dmb@sme.ru http://www.sme.ru
Petr Petrovich KOROLEV	Head of the Foreign Relations Department of the Samara Region	Phone: (8462) 32 3821 Fax: (8462) 32 7568 E-mail: RegSamara@vis.infoPhone.ru

3. ECONOMIC POTENTIAL

3.1. 1997–2002 GROSS REGIONAL PRODUCT (GRP). INDUSTRY BREAKDOWN

In 2002, the Samara Region's gross regional product was $7,756.7 million, 9.7% up on 2001. Per capita GRP amounted to $2,156 in 2001, rising to $2,393 in 2002.

3.2. MAJOR ECONOMIC GROWTH PROJECTIONS

A blueprint for economic development over the coming years is provided by the Decree of the Governor of the Samara Region, which approves social and economic development projections for the

GRP trends in 1997–2002						*TABLE 2*
	1997	1998	1999	2000	2001*	2002*
GRP in current prices, $ million	12,644.4	7,442.4	4,755.0	5,536.2	7,067.9	7,756.7

*Estimates of the Samara Regional Administration

GRP industry breakdown in 1997–2002, % of total						*TABLE 3*
	1997	1998	1999	2000	2001*	2002*
GRP	100.0	100.0	100.0	100.0	100.0	100.0
Industry	31.9	34.1	39.0	42.0	40.3	37.8
Agriculture and forestry	5.8	5.8	8.3	6.9	6.7	6.4
Construction	5.7	5.1	4.3	5.1	5.5	5.5
Transport and communications	13.3	13.5	8.9	8.6	8.4	9.7
Trade and public catering	12.4	14.9	15.7	14.1	13.2	14.6
Other	14.5	18.5	13.8	13.8	14.8	15.4
Net taxes on output	16.4	8.1	10.0	9.5	11.1	10.6

*Estimates of the Samara Regional Administration

Samara Region for 2003–2005. in order to ensure ongoing development of the Region, the Decree provides for the following key priorities and trends:

Industry: continued support to priority sectors, including the aerospace industry, the auto industry, agricultural machine engineering, chemicals and petrochemicals, and other stable and promising enterprises. The social and economic development of the Region in the coming period will largely depend upon the strategies of large business groups, both national and local.

The promotion of innovation and scientific and technical policy, the establishment of innovative infrastructure and the intensification of energy-saving activities will also be of great importance.

Agriculture: ongoing reform and the stabilization of output of major agricultural products. This will be achieved via: the development of legislation and organizational measures aimed at introducing the most effective system for the delivery of agricultural products to the markets; the encouragement of production and investment activities in the agroindustrial sector; and government financial support to promising segments of the Region's agroindustrial sector.

Industry breakdown of industrial output in 1997–2002, % of total						TABLE 4
	1997	1998	1999	2000	2001	2002*
Industry	100.0	100.0	100.0	100.0	100.0	100.0
Machine engineering and metal processing	54.1	53.1	58.9	56.5	58.9	56.5
Chemicals and petrochemicals	9.3	9.1	10.7	13.0	10.7	9.8
Fuel	9.0	7.1	6.0	6.9	8.4	8.7
Food and beverages	7.3	9.9	9.3	9.0	8.4	8.6
Energy	13.1	12.7	7.5	6.9	6.4	7.4
Non-ferrous metals	1.6	2.2	2.3	2.9	2.8	4.7
Construction materials	3.0	3.1	2.5	2.6	2.4	2.9
Forestry, timber, and pulp and paper	0.4	0.4	0.3	0.4	0.3	0.3
Light industry	0.4	0.3	0.2	0.2	0.2	0.3
Ferrous metals	0.1	0.1	0.2	0.2	0.1	0.1

*Estimates of the Samara Regional Administration

Transport: the inclusion of the Samara Region in the Europe-Asia Transportation Network; the establishment of a Samara traffic center in the context of the development of an international traffic corridor system; the continued implementation of the Aviakor Airport Project for the construction of international standard freight terminal facilities.

3.3. INDUSTRIAL OUTPUT IN 1997–2002 FOR MAJOR SECTORS OF ECONOMY

The highest rates of production growth were observed in the non-ferrous industry, food and beverages, construction materials, and chemicals and petrochemicals sector. The Region's developed industry base is made up of 415 large and medium enterprises and more than 4,000 small enterprises (employing a combined total of 410,000 people).

Machine engineering and metal processing. This sector accounts for 56.5% of total regional industrial output. Major sub-industries are: automotive, rocket and aircraft engines, electric equipment, instrumentation and tools, and machine engineering for chemicals and petrochemicals. Nearly 76% of Russian-made automobiles are produced in the Samara Region.

The largest enterprises are: OAO AvtoVAZ, OAO Elektroschit, ZAO RosLada, OAO Samara Bearings Plant, OAO Tarasov Plant, and ZAO Samara Cable Company.

Chemicals and petrochemicals. The sector accounts for 9.8% of total industrial output. Companies in the sector provide 20% of Russia's total ammonia output, 5.6% of all plant pesticides, 3.6% of all chemical fertilizers, and 4.8% of all synthetic rubber, synthetic resins, and plastics. The Region is the only Russian producer of yellow phosphorus.

The largest enterprises are: OAO Togliattiazot, ZAO Kuybyshevazot, OOO Togliattikauchuk, ZAO Novokuybyshevsk Petrochemicals Company, OAO Phosphor, OAO Plastic, OAO Samara Ethanol Factory, OAO Truboizolyatsiya, OAO Mid-Volga Chemicals

Plant, OAO Promsintez, ZAO Kraplak, OAO Uglerod, OAO Kubra, and FGUP Privolzhskaya Biofabrika.

Fuel. The industry accounts for 8.7% of total industrial output. Enterprises in the Region provide 3.1% of Russian oil output, 12.3% of gasoline output, 13.1% of diesel oil output, and 12.1% of heavy fuel oil output. According to experts, growing production volumes are facilitated by effective management and active investment policies of OAO YUKOS Oil Company.

The largest enterprises in the sector are: OAO Samaraneftegaz, OAO Kuybyshevsky Oil Refinery, OAO Novokuybyshevsky Oil Refinery, and OAO Syzransky Oil Refinery.

Food and beverages. The industry accounts for 8.6% of total industrial output. The industry is represented by six meat processing plants, 25 dairies, eight large flour milling and grain processing plants, a fat-rendering plant, yeast and oil-extraction plants, non-alcoholic beverages plants, distilleries, beer breweries, and sparkling wine and brandy production enterprises.

The largest industry enterprises are OAO Rossiya Confectionery Association, OAO Samara Spirits and Distillery Rodnik, OAO Festive Wines Production, OAO Samara Fat Rendering Plant, OAO Syzran Food Concentrates Plant, and OAO Bogatovsky Oil Extraction Plant.

Energy. Energy accounts for 7.4% of total industrial output. Samara city is the headquarters of the interregional power control company (SMUEK), which controls the energy systems of the Samara, Saratov, Ulyanovsk Regions, and the Republic of Kalmykia. The major industrial enterprise is OAO Samarenergo.

Non-ferrous metals. This industry accounts for 4.7% of total industrial output. The non-ferrous metals sector is represented by OAO Samara Metal Works – one of the largest Russian producers of aluminum rolled products, semi-finished products, and aluminum and aluminum-alloy goods.

Fuel and energy sector production and consumption trends, 1997-2002						TABLE 5
	1997	1998	1999	2000	2001	2002
Electricity output, billion kWh	23.5	25.7	25.5	24.6	24.2	24.0
Oil output (including gas condensate), '000 tons	8,540	8,160	7,690	7,930	9,725	11,50
Natural gas extraction, million cubic meters	287.0	277.0	261.0	272.0	314.0	349.3
Electricity consumption, billion kWh	21.1	20.4	20.3	21.3	21.7	21.9
Natural gas consumption, million cubic meters	12,978.7	9,654.9	9,751.7	9,601.6	10,054.4	10,209.5

*Estimates of the Samara Regional Administration

Agriculture. Over the past few years, gross agricultural output has enjoyed growth. The Samara Region has more than 500 large agricultural enterprises and more than 3,500 individual holdings. Increased allocations from the regional budget up to $50.3 million are spurring the agroindustrial sector development in 2003.

3.5. TRANSPORT INFRASTRUCTURE

The Samara Region is one of Russia's largest traffic hubs, offering the shortest routes from Central and Western Europe to Siberia, Central Asia, and Kazakhstan. The Region's transport system is made up of more than 5,000 enterprises of all forms of ownership, including 600 joint stock companies.

Roads. The Samara Region has more than 8,500 kilometers of public paved highway. The Moscow – Chelyabinsk federal highway crosses the Region, with links to Kazakhstan, Central Asia, and northern parts of Russia. The Region has an advanced shipping and forwarding transport system, the largest in the Volga District, which provides federal and regional transportation links for the North–South and West–East directions. The Samara center for freight flow consolidation continues to be formed within the framework of Europe–Asia international transport corridors.

Railroads. The Samara Region has more than 1,300 kilometers of railroad, with rail transport accorded a special role. The Kuybyshevskaya Railroad with 1,400 kilometers of track in the Samara Region is Russia's fourth or fifth largest in terms of traffic flows. Cities such as Samara, Syzran, Kinel, and Togliatti have large passenger and freight handling facilities.

Airports. The Region is served by OAO Samara Airlines, one of the leading carriers in Russia. Lufthansa commenced its operations in Samara and has carried out flights since 1996. The Kurumoch International Airport accepts all types of aircraft.

River ports. The Samara Region has some 468 kilometers of navigable inland waterways. The Samara and Togliatti river ports are capable of accepting vessels adapted to both river and sea. The Region is connected via the Volga – Don and Baltic – White Sea canals with almost all Mediterranean, Caspian and Scandinavian ports and Danube river ports. The largest shipping operator to these destinations is bulk oil shipping company OAO Volgotanker.

Oil and gas pipelines. Over 5,000 kilometers of OAO Samaratransgaz operated gas pipeline runs through the Samara Region. Other oil pipelines also cross the Region.

OAO Transammiak's ammonia line linking Togliatti to Odessa also plays significant role in the Region's transportation system.

3.6. MAIN NATURAL RESOURCES: RESERVES AND EXTRACTION IN 2002

The natural resources of the Samara Region are hydrocarbons, minerals used in construction materials, ores, and chemicals, and subsurface water.

Oil and gas fields. The principal natural resources of the region are oil and petroleum gas. The Region's approximately 400 operating oil fields contain total remaining recoverable reserves of 300 million tons. Exploration of new fields, oil extraction, and refining are important components of the Region's economic potential. Today, the key issue is the development and implementation of leading edge technologies for enhanced oil recovery.

Raw chemicals mined in the Region include phosphorites, brimstone, rock salt (the Dergunovskoye deposit's reserves are estimated at 285.7 million tons), bituminous sandstone (the Yerilkinskoye deposit's reserves are estimated at 34.8 million tons), and oil shale (the Kashpirskoye deposit). The Region has plans afoot to develop the Dergunovskoye rock salt deposit. The appeal of the unique Kashpirskoye oil shale deposit is mainly owing to the export potential of its processed products.

Construction materials. Minerals used in construction materials are spread wide across the Region: mortar sand and siliceous sand, building stone, loam and tile clay, gypsum and anhydrite, chalk, expanded clay, agloporite clays, bituminous minerals, refractory clays, and raw cement.

Subsurface water. Due to high concentrations of some components (bromine, iodine, boron, strontium, rubidium, potassium, and lithium), subsurface water can be processed using appropriate technologies to provide a source of raw hydrominerals. The Samara Region has sufficient deposits of underground waters, including treatment and table potable water and balneal water.

4. TRADE OPPORTUNITIES

4.1. MAIN GOODS
PRODUCED IN THE REGION

Cars and car components. The Region's enterprises produce various makes of VAZ cars, pick-up trucks, and vans on the basis of VAZ models, and railroad, truck and caterpillar cranes and garbage trucks on the basis of KAMAZ models. In 2002, the Region produced 746,800 cars and vehicles.

Chemicals and petrochemicals. In 2002, ammonium output stood at 2,110,000 tons, caustic soda output – 2,800 tons, phenol output – 34,000 tons, synthetic resin and plastic output – 137,000 tons, synthetic rubber output – 183,000 tons, paint and varnish output – 6,100 tons, plastic foil output – 17,000 square meters, and chemical fertilizer output– 487,000 tons.

Oil and oil products. 2002 oil output totaled 11.4 million tons, gasoline – 2.8 million tons, diesel and fuel oil – 5.3 million tons each.

Food and beverages. The 2002 grain crop reached 2,004,700 tons, dairy products (in whole milk terms) totaled 194,800 tons, bread and bakery products – 183,600 tons, meat (including category one sub-products) – 17,000 tons, and confectionery – 96,800 tons.

Construction materials. 2002 cement output reached 597,000 tons, brick production – 465 million items, and linoleum – 25.9 million square meters.

4.2. EXPORTS, INCLUDING EXTRA-CIS

2002 exports increased by 2.9% to $3,600.5 million. Core exports included cars ($285.5 million), alu-minum and aluminum products ($266.1 million), oil products ($257.1 million), anhydrous ammonia ($95.8 million), ammonium nitrate, caprolactam, synthetic rubber, and chemical fertilizers.

CIS and non-CIS exports accounted for 15% and 85%, respectively. The Region exports chiefly to Cyprus, the USA, Kazakhstan, Ukraine, the Netherlands, Finland, China, and Germany.

4.3. IMPORTS,
INCLUDING EXTRA-CIS

2002 imports increased by 22.6% to $808.4 million. The Samara Region's imports principally comprise items used in the production activities of local enterprises, including machinery and equipment ($239.2 million), aluminum and aluminum products ($33.9 million), optical appliances and devices ($31.4 million), car spare parts and equipment ($37.7 million), and cocoa beans ($51.3 million).

CIS and extra-CIS imports accounted for 17% and 83%, respectively. The Region's main trading partners for import are: Germany, Ukraine, France, Ivory Coast, Italy, the USA, Hungary, Estonia, Belgium, Slovenia, and Switzerland.

4.4. MAJOR REGIONAL EXPORT
AND IMPORT ENTITIES

Export activities in the Samara Region are mainly carried out by industrial enterprises through their trading houses.

Major regional export and import entities		_TABLE 6_
ENTITY	ADDRESS	PHONE, FAX, E-MAIL
OAO International Electrotechnical Company	19, ul. Alexeya Tolstogo, Samara, Samara Region, 443099	Phone: (8462) 32 2687
OAO Avto-Lada	6, ul. Gagarina, Togliatti, Samara Region, 445000	Phone: (8482) 22 4003
OOO JV Volgaintrans	62, ul. Nekrasovskaya, Samara, Samara Region, 443010	Phone: (8462) 32 7487, 34 6512

5. INVESTMENT OPPORTUNITIES

5.1 INVESTMENTS
IN 1992–2002 (BY INDUSTRY
SECTOR), INCLUDING
FOREIGN INVESTMENTS

The following main factors determine the investment appeal of the Samara Region:
- Developed and highly qualified labor market;
- Favorable geographical location on transportation crossroads linking European regions of Russia with the Far East and Central Asia;
- Large explored reserves of oil, gas, oil shale, and minerals used in the production of cement, brick, and keramzite;
- Investment legislation guaranteeing a stable business environment;
- A developed investment support infrastructure;
- Land laws that guarantee protection for land tenants and owners in the area of land relations, including foreign land users, and providing a framework for the land market;

IV

VOLGA FEDERAL DISTRICT

Capital investment by industry sector, $ million						TABLE 7
	1997	1998	1999	2000	2001	2002
Total capital investment	1,665.0	1,019.6	535.4	822.1	1,193.2	1,167.4
Including major industries (% of total):						
Industry	47.9	51.0	46.3	45.6	48.6	59.9
Agriculture and forestry	1.5	2.1	2.9	2.1	2.2	2.2
Construction	1.1	1.0	1.7	4.3	4.0	3.2
Transport and communications	20.4	29.6	29.0	31.5	26.1	15.7
Trade and public catering	3.0	0.8	1.6	1.1	1.3	0.9
Other (housing and communal services)	26.1	15.5	18.5	15.4	17.8	18.1

Foreign investment trends in 1992–2002						TABLE 8
	1992–1997	1998	1999	2000	2001	2002
Foreign investment, $ million	244.9	192.9	148.9	236.3	260.4	361.8
Including FDI, $ million	161.5	185.9	76.3	59.6	117.6	97.7

- High solvent demand from the local population;
- Developed communications and telecommunications systems.

5.2. CAPITAL INVESTMENT

The machine engineering, fuel, and transport sectors account for the lion's share of capital investment. With over 70% share of the total, reinvested profit continues to be the main source of capital investment financing in the Region.

The Samara Region raised $304.9 million in foreign investment in 2002 (up 17.1% on 2001).

5.3. MAJOR ENTERPRISES (INCLUDING ENTERPRISES WITH FOREIGN INVESTMENT)

The Samara Region currently hosts 83 enterprises with foreign investment from some 31 countries worldwide, including 18 from Germany and nine from the USA.

In 2001, Germany's Henkel established a joint venture, OOO Henkel Plastic Avtokomponenty, together with OAO Plastic and contributed equipment for producing plastisols. Another joint venture, ZAO Vintai Safety Belts, was started in 2001 with a capital contribution from US-based ADS Plastic and Macedonia's SIPO. In 2002, jointly with Ceramics Industry Construction Inc. a joint venture OOO Ceramic Constructions Plant was set up in Samara. The company produces brick and ceramic tile. Jointly with UEB (Spain), a joint venture for production of non-electric explosive detonation systems was registered in Chapayevsk. The bulk of direct investment is raised for the General Motors, EBRD and the AvtoVAZ joint venture to produce cars in Togliatti. This is the largest project in the Samara Region in terms of foreign capital investment, and the largest American project in Russia. The expected annual capacity of ZAO GM-AvtoVAZ joint venture is 75,000 cars.

Some other big companies with foreign investments are: ZAO Packard Electric Systems (PES/CKK), ZAO Samara Optical Cable Company, ZAO Sinko, OAO Rossiya Confectionery Association, OOO Pepsi International Bottlers (Samara), OOO Coca-Cola HBC Eurasia, and ZAO Danone Volga.

5.4. MOST ATTRACTIVE SECTORS FOR INVESTMENT

The investment strategy of the Samara Region Administration aims to provide support to the core sectors of the economy, specifically:

- Automotive
- Aviation
- Agroindustrial
- Housing construction
- Education, public health, culture, and the environment.

The main focus is on the creation of production facilities with up-to-date technologies, the development of high-tech industries, and innovation.

5.5. CURRENT LEGISLATION ON INVESTOR TAX EXEMPTIONS AND PRIVILEGES

The Samara Region Law On Investments in the Samara Region provides investors with exemptions from regional tax components (for the investment payback period up to a maximum of five years) on the following taxes:

A property tax exemption in the amount of 100% is granted for property both created or acquired, including charter capital contributions to finance investment projects;

A land tax exemption is granted for lands within duly approved limits if new construction is carried under investment projects;

A profit tax reduction of 12% on the regional tax component is granted to investors who carry

Largest enterprises of the Samara Region

TABLE 8

COMPANY	SECTOR
OAO AvtoVAZ	Automotive
OAO Samara Metal Works	Non-ferrous metals
OAO Togliattiazot	Chemicals
ZAO Kuybyshevazot	Chemicals
OOO Togliattikauchuk	Chemicals
OAO Samara Bearings Plant	Machine engineering

Regional entities responsible for raising investment

TABLE 9

ENTITY	ADDRESS	PHONE, FAX, E-MAIL
Economic Development and Investment Department of the Samara Region	210, ul. Molodogvardeyskaya, Samara, Samara Region, 443006	Phone: (8462) 32 2744, 32 2233 E-mail: bulg@vis.infotel.ru, cons@economy.vis.ru http://www.economy.samreg.ru
Foreign Relations Department of the Samara Region	210, ul. Molodogvardeyskaya, Samara, Samara Region, 443006	Phone: (8462) 32 3821, 32 7568 E-mail: RegSamara@vis.infotel.ru
Construction, Architecture, Housing and Communal Services, and Road Department of the Samara Region	146a, ul. Samarskaya, Samara, Samara Region, 443010	Phone: (8462) 32 1228, 33 3027 E-mail: depart@mail.samtel.ru
Enterprise Development Department of the Samara Region	210, ul. Molodogvardeyskaya, Samara, Samara Region, 443006	Phone: (8462) 32 7498 E-mail: dmb@sme.ru http://www.sme.ru
Chamber of Industry and Commerce of the Samara Region	6, ul. A. Tolstogo, Samara, Samara Region, 443099	Phone: (8462) 32 1159, 70 4896 E-mail: ccisr@samara.ru, dmark@transit.samara.ru http:// www.cci.samara.ru.
Center of Project Finance of the Samara Region	3a, Studenchesky per., Samara, Samara Region, 443001	Phone/fax: (8462) 32 2217, 42 0439, 42 3213 E-mail: SCPF@poria.ru
Federal Securities Market Commission, Samara Regional Office	132, ul. Galaktionovskaya, Samara, Samara Region, 443100	Phone: (8462) 42 0895, 42 2281 E-mail: samro@samara.ru
Movement for Enterprise Development of the Samara Region	Office 508, 203b, ul. Samarskaya, Samara, Samara Region, 443001	Phone: (8462) 32 6681, 42 3030 E-mail: drp@saminfo.ru
Federal Venture Fund for Small Enterprise Support in Science and Technology of the Samara Region	Office 215, 203b, ul. Samarskaya, Samara, Samara Region, 443001	Phone: (8462) 42 3574, 42 4120 E-mail: svf@saminfo.ru

out projects of $31.5 million and more within the Samara Region and have separate accounting for profits, property, and the use of assets.

Comprehensive state support is provided within the context of the Region's investment program to individual enterprises in the form of investment tax credits, guarantees, and subsidies (up to $0.5 million) for the development of the public utilities of the invested facility, for personnel training and retraining (up to 100 multiples of the minimum statutory wage), and tax reductions for investors.

5.6. FEDERAL AND REGIONAL ECONOMIC AND SOCIAL DEVELOPMENT PROGRAMS FOR THE SAMARA REGION

Federal targeted programs. The major federal targeted programs of economic and social development for the Region are The Development of Civil Aviation Engineering in Russia, 2002–2010 and through 2015, and The Reform and Development of Defense Industry Facilities, 2002–2006.

These Programs aim to strengthen the Russian Federation's position in the international market for

IV

VOLGA FEDERAL DISTRICT

aviation services and products, and affect all aerospace enterprises in the Samara Region.

Regional programs. The Samara Region is implementing several regional comprehensive targeted programs in a number of areas, including industry, agriculture, the environment, public health, culture, and public welfare. The 2003 regional budget allocates some $64.6 million for the implementation of these programs. The major programs are:

The Comprehensive Program for the Development of the Agricultural Sector in 2000–2003, which aims to restore agricultural production efficiency and solvency and increase the share of own output. The total allocation for this program amounts to $208.7 million, with the regional budget providing $62 million.

The Program for Social and Economic Development and Environmental Rehabilitation of the Town of Chapaevsk, Samara Region. The Program aims to provide a satisfactory quality of life for Chapaevsk residents on the basis of welfare programs. The total allocation for this program reaches $100.7 million, with the regional budget providing $59.8 million.

The Program for the Environmental Rehabilitation of the Town of Novokuybyshevsk, Samara Region, 2001–2005. The program aims to remedy the current disastrous environmental situation in Novokuybyshevsk by improving its environmental and living conditions. The total allocation for this program amounts to $47.2 million, with the regional budget providing $8.2 million;

The Targeted Program for Energy Saving in the Samara Region, 2000–2005. The Program aims to develop scientifically feasible technical, financial, and management energy saving policies as a basis for creating industrial, management, and financial mechanisms and measures conducive to more efficient fuel and energy utilization. The total allocation for this program amounts to $62.9 million, with the regional budget providing $1.5 million.

The Comprehensive Program for the Development and Provision of State Support to Small Enterprise in the Samara Region, 2001–2003. The Program aims to foster the effective development of local small enterprises, to increase the tax base, to promote business and investment activities, to foster competition on the market for services and goods, to stabilize the local labor market, and to achieve saturation of markets with competitive local products and services. The total allocation for this program is $1.4 million.

The Program for the Development of General Purpose Aviation (Short-Range Aircraft) in the Samara Region, 2001–2005. The program aims to create a new sector, to establish short-range aircraft operating infrastructure facilities, to establish certified aircraft and aircraft equipment manufacturing facilities, to develop the intellectual and scientific capacities of the Samara Region, to ensure the effective and stable performance of existing and newly created enterprises of all forms of ownership operating in the aviation and other sectors of the Samara Region's economy, and to encourage the production of short-range aircraft competitive both on the Russian and international markets. The total allocation for this program is $2.6 million, with the regional budget providing $0.1 million.

6. INVESTMENT PROJECTS

Industry sector and project description	1) Expected results 2) Amount and term of investment 3) Form of financing[1] 4) Documentation[2]	Contact information
1	2	3

CHEMICALS AND PETROCHEMICALS		
54R001 ● ▲		
Construction of a lime-ammonium nitrate line. Project goal: implementation of a state-of-the-art technology for the production of ammonium nitrate in special granulator units, and improvement of export capabilities.	1) Output of 316,000 tons per year 2) $3.7 million/2 years 3) L 4) FS	ZAO Kuybyshevazot 6, ul. Novozavodskaya, Togliatti, Samara Region, 445652 Phone: (8482) 29 1021 Fax: (8482) 22 5954 E-mail: office@kuazot.ru Viktor Ivanovich Gerasimenko, CEO

[1] L – Loan, E – Equity, Leas. – Leasing, JV – Joint Venture
[2] BP – Business Plan, FS – Feasibility Study

1	2	3

54R002 ● ▲

Raw benzene processing.
Project goal: to reduce the enterprise's
reliance on suppliers of scarce raw
materials needed for caprolactam
production.

1) Revenues of $23 million per year
2) $8.2 million/3 years
3) L
4) FS in progress

ZAO Kuybyshevazot
6, ul. Novozavodskaya, Togliatti,
Samara Region, 445652
Phone: (8482) 29 1021
Fax: (8482) 22 5954
E-mail: office@kuazot.ru
Viktor Ivanovich Gerasimenko, CEO

CHEMICALS AND PHARMACEUTICALS

54R003 ● ★ ◆

Production of pills.
Project goal: introduction to the market
of popular and affordable domestic
medicines, and expansion of the market
niche for nitrosorbidum production.

1) Revenues of $19.8 million per year
2) $14.6 million/3 years
3) L, Leas.
4) BP

ZAO Panda
4, ul. Komsomolskaya, Chapaevsk,
Samara Region, 446100
Phone: (84639) 20 176
Fax: (84639) 24 670
Yevgeny Vladimirovich Panov, CEO

MACHINE ENGINEERING AND METAL PROCESSING

54R004 ● ◆

Establishment of production facilities
and production of a pilot batch
of An 140 short-range aircraft.
Project goal: establishment of production
facilities for manufacturing An 140
short-range aircraft to meet rising demand
owing to the retirement of the An 24
and Yak 40 fleet, and establishment of
a sales network for the sale of core
products under leasing schemes.

1) 36 aircraft per year
2) $46.2 million/4 years
3) L
4) BP

OAO Aviakor Aviation Plant
32, ul. Pskovskaya, Samara,
Samara Region, 443052
Phone: (8462) 92 6655
Fax: (8462) 55 0707
E-mail: aviaprom@aviacor.ru
Gennady Nikolaevich Plotnikov,
CEO

54R005 ● ◆

Establishment of a certified production
line for large airframe units.
Project goal: to decrease the costs
of producing wings for regional aircraft;
enhancement of production lines with
advanced domestic and foreign
technologies, and increased production
of unified and standard parts for
production of wing units.

1) Revenues of $75.5 million per year
2) $34.2 million/3 years
3) L
4) BP

OAO Aviakor Aviation Plant
32, ul. Pskovskaya, Samara,
Samara Region, 443052
Phone: (8462) 92 6655
Fax: (8462) 55 0707
E-mail: aviaprom@aviacor.ru
Gennady Nikolaevich Plotnikov
CEO

54R006 ● ★ ▲

Revamping of car cord production
facilities.
Project goal: to maintain competitive
production prices.

1) Revenues of $7.9 million per year
2) $0.3 million/4 years
3) L, Leas.
4) FS

OOO Samaraavtozhgut BOC
11, ul. Dzerzhinskogo, Samara,
Samara Region, 443093
Phone: (8462) 66 4477, 44 3093
Fax: (8462) 60 8141
E-mail: samjgut@transit.samara.ru
Alexander Konstantinovich Dorofeev,
CEO

54R007 ● ★ ▲

Establishment of car spare parts
production for OAO AvtoVAZ with
application of advanced technologies.
Project goal: expansion of present
production of high-quality cast aluminum
to industrial scale, and introduction
of advanced technology of lost foam
and high pressure casting.

1) Revenues of $75.5 million per year
2) $0.8 million/n/a
3) L, Leas.
4) FS

OOO Production and Commercial
Company Samara Experimental
Avtodetal Plant
255, pr. Kirova, Samara,
Samara Region, 443035
Phone: (8462) 53 5027, 56 5711
Fax: (8462) 56 1974
E-mail: Avtodeteil@mail.radiant.ru
Masum Mirzaevich Khasanov,
CEO

1	2	3

FORESTRY, TIMBER, AND PULP AND PAPER

54R008 ● ▲

Creation of Novy Edem production and retail complex (a furniture manufacturer).
Project goal: output increase and total revamping of equipment.

1) Revenues of $8.2 million per year
2) $6.3 million/3 years
3) L
4) FS

Samara State Public Organization of the Disabled New Edem
101, Zavodskoye shosse, Samara, Samara Region, 443022
Phone/fax: (8462) 92 0675, 92 0744
E-mail: edem@samaramail.ru
Vyacheslav Nikolaevich Grishin, CEO

54R009 ● ▲

Revamping of production facilities.
Project goal: to improve production quality to international standards, introduce energy-saving technologies, and enhance environmental protection.

1) Revenues of $2.1 million per year
2) $1.0 million/1 year
3) L
4) FS

ZAO Syzran Furniture Factory
83, ul. Khvalynskaya, Syzran, Samara Region, 446012
Phone: (8464) 98 2945
Fax: (8464) 98 2937
Galina Semenovna Kuzmina, Director

CONSTRUCTION MATERIALS

54R010 ● ▲

Installation of a mineral wool production line.
Project goal: establishment of advanced production of basalt fiber thermal insulation, and introduction of state-of-the-art technologies.

1) Revenues of $12.3 million per year
2) $7.0 million/2 years
3) L
4) FS

OAO Termosteps-MTL
5, ul. Zavodskaya, Samara, Samara Region, 443004
Phone: (8462) 26 5145, 26 5132, 26 5133, 26 5135, 30 1616
Fax: (8462) 26 5136
E-mail: info@termostepsmtl.ru
Vyacheslav Nikolaevich Timoshin, CEO

FOOD AND BEVERAGES

54R011 ● ★ ▲

Production of sterilized long-life aseptic liquid milk.
Project goal: diversification of output.

1) Revenues of $3.8 million per year
2) $0.6 million/1 year
3) L, Leas.
4) FS

OAO Syzranmoloko
41, ul. Lokomobilnaya, Syzran, Samara Region, 446022
Phone/fax: (84643) 73 352, 73 815, 72 389
E-mail: molokomail@mail.ru
Ivan Vasilyevich Kistanov, CEO

TRANSPORT INFRASTRUCTURE

54R012 ● ★ ■

Expansion of the passenger terminal of the Samara Airport.
Project goal: to ensure high quality of passenger transportation.

1) Annual increase of traffic flow by 10%
2) $30 million/3 years
3) E, L
4) FS in progress

OAO Kurumoch International Airport
Airport, Berega, Samara, Samara Region, 443901
Phone: (8462) 29 5532, 29 5122, 29 5438, 29 5555
Fax: (8462) 29 5462
E-mail: info@siair.ru
Vyacheslav Fedorovich Chernavin, CEO

54R013 ● ◆

Construction of an automotive transportation base in Togliatti.
Project goal: expansion of service offering and market share (OAO AvtoVAZ is the key client).

1) Revenues of $15.1 million per year
2) $9.4 million/1 year
3) L
4) BP

OOO Service-Torgtrans
27, ul. Kommunalnaya, Togliatti, Samara Region, 445043
Phone: (8482) 39 0808, 39 0018, 39 1817
Fax: (8482) 39 1788
Vasily Vasilyevich Ziubenko, Director

54R014 ● ◆

Volgatransterminal as a component the Samara Region logistics system.
Project goal: construction of terminal facilities in order to provide integral storage services for industrial enterprises (warehouse – transportation – inventory control – distribution).

1) Revenues of $2.3 million per year
2) 6.5 million/1 year
3) L
4) BP

OAO Volgatransterminal
10, ul. Gagarina, Samara, Samara Region, 443079
Phone: (8462) 24 1396, 54 3463
Fax: (8462) 24 236
E-mail: office@vttlogistic.ru
Valentin Ivanovich Klinsky, CEO

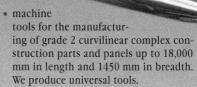

The modern day history of Samara-based OAO AVIACOR Aviation Plant is inextricably linked with that of Kuybyshev Aviation Plant (KuAZ). Our company is the successor to the best work traditions of KuAZ. Since it was founded, AVIACOR Aviation Plant has manufactured more than 22,000 aircraft, including the Il 2, Tu 4, Tu 95, Tu 114, and Tu 154.

AVIACOR Aviation Plant has manufactured various units for spacecraft, wing panels for Russia's Buran shuttle craft, and various units for the Tu 204 aircraft. Our core production facilities cover the entire spectrum of manufacturing (metallurgy, procurement, mechanical assembly, unit assembly, testing) and technologies used in aircraft and aviation unit manufacturing, in addition to all kinds of mechanical engineering goods. AVIACOR Aviation Plant has a proven track record of collaboration with international manufacturers of aviation equipment and is Russia's only supplier of parts to Boeing.

- machine tools for the manufacturing of grade 2 curvilinear complex construction parts and panels up to 18,000 mm in length and 1450 mm in breadth. We produce universal tools.
- cutting edge technologies used in pressing procedures for the manufacturing of curved pipes, connections, and other pipeline elements, and production of small parts of any level of complexity using cold pressing (maximum dimensions 400x1000x2000 mm);
- cutting edge technologies for the protective and decorative galvanization of surfaces, the manufacturing of casts from aluminum, magnesium and titanium alloys, including vacuum and clean-room casting.

The company's development prospects depend on the commencement of serial production of the An 140, which was designed to replace the An 24 passenger plane and its relatives the An 26, An 24T, An 30, and An 32.

In terms of its technical characteristics and comfort, the An 140 is comparable with the best international peers. It offers greater productivity than the An 24 and is two times better in terms of fuel efficiency.

OAO AVIACOR Aviation Plant uses automated workstations based on CAD/CAM systems, which enable the production and processing of geometric data for the construction of equipment designed using any CAD/CAM system via the exchange of graphical data in the IGES, VDA, and DXF international formats.

Our enterprise currently boasts:

- technology for the manufacturing of standard parts and fasteners, large precision pieces, and cylindrical parts up to 3,000 mm in length;

АВИАКОР *открытое акционерное общество*
авиационный завод

32, UL. PSKOVSKAYA,
SAMARA, 443052, RUSSIA
TEL.: (8462) 92 6655
FAX: (8462) 55 0707
E-MAIL: avia@aviacor.samara.ru
HTTP://www.aviacor.ru

55. SARATOV REGION [64]

E C O N O M I C   M A P

Kuybyshevskoe water reservoir

Bugiruslan

Dimitrovgrad

Sok

Buzuluk

Sura

ULYANOVSK

U L Y A N O V S K

Sengiley

Togliatti

SAMARA

Bolshaya Kinel

Samara

REPUBLIC OF

R E G I O N

Chapaevsk

S A M A R A

MORDOVIA

Inza

Syzran

R E G I O N

SARANSK

Barysh

Nikolsk

Saratovskoe water reservoir

Kuznetsk

P E N Z A

Хвалынск

Pugachyov

PENZA

Sursk

Volsk

Ozinki

R E G I O N

Balakovo

Kamenka

Khopyor

Petrovsk

Volga

Marks

SARATOV

Engels

Rtischevo

Atkarsk

Volgogradskoe water reservoir

Kalininsk

Krasnoarmeysk

Aleksandrov Gay

Balashov

Zhirnovsk

Kamyshin

K A Z A K H S T A N

Tersa

Medveditsa

Lake Aralsor

PROCESSING INDUSTRY
- Machine engineering and metal processing
- Chemicals and petrochemicals
- Construction materials and glass
- Light industry
- Food and beverages

MINING INDUSTRY
- Oil
- Shale oil
- Raw cement
- Mineral water sources

POWER PLANTS
- Thermal power plants
- Hydro power plants
- Nuclear power plants

CROPS AND LIVESTOCK BREEDING
- Wheat
- Rye
- Barley
- Orchards
- Sunflower
- Sugar beetroot
- Vegetables
- Potatoes
- Meat and dairy cattle breeding
- Pig breeding
- Sheep rearing
- Poultry farming
- Resorts

The Saratov Region boasts a well-developed economy and agricultural sector, and considerable natural resources. Saratov, a Volga port city surrounded by highly fertile land, is located at the crossroads of trade routes from Central Russia to southern and Urals regions.

The Region's machine engineering sector is represented by instrument engineering, electronic engineering, diesel motor and aircraft manufacturing, and equipment manufacturing for the energy, chemical, and oil sectors. The Region is the main supplier of trolleybuses to Russian urban transport entities.

The Saratov Region's industrial sector makes widespread use of new technologies and advanced research findings.

The Region has long been famous for its high quality wheat and major flourmills.

The Saratov land is not only rich in natural and industrial resources: it is also renowned as a major cultural and scientific center of Russia. Russia's oldest medical, sanitary, agricultural, archive, and natural science research institutions form the basis of the Region's intellectual capital.

The Saratov Region, a region of vast mineral reserves, oil and gas fields, construction material deposits, and developed industry and infrastructure, is committed to widening and strengthening mutually beneficial contacts and finding new partners.

Its advantageous geographic location, scientific and labor potential, and developed transport infrastructure guarantee the success of ventures initiated by committed individuals with an entrepreneurial spirit.

Dmitry Ayatskov,
GOVERNOR OF THE SARATOV REGION

1. GENERAL INFORMATION

1.1. GEOGRAPHY

Located in the south-eastern part of the East European Plain, in the Lower Volga region, the Saratov Region covers a total area of 100,200 square kilometers. To the north, it borders the Samara Region, the Ulyanovsk Region, and the Penza Region, to the south – the Volgograd Region, to the west – the Voronezh Region and the Tambov Region, and to the east – the Orenburg Region and Kazakhstan.

1.2. CLIMATE

The Saratov Region enjoys a moderate continental climate. Air temperatures in January average –7.4°C, rising to an average of +22.6°C in July. Annual precipitation reaches 375–580 mm.

1.3. POPULATION

According to preliminary 2002 census results, the total population of the Saratov Region was 2,669,000 people. The average population density is 26.6 per square kilometer. The economically active population totals 1,321,000. Official unemployment stood at 1.5% in 2002.

Demographically speaking, some 59.6% are of statutory working age, 18.5% are below the statutory working age, and 21.9% are beyond the statutory working age.

The major urban centers of the Saratov Region (2002 data) are Saratov with 873,500 inhabitants, Balakovo with 200,600 inhabitants, Engels with 193,900 inhabitants, Balashov with 95,600 inhabitants, and Volsk with 78,700 inhabitants.

Population								TABLE 1
	1992	1997	1998	1999	2000	2001	2002
Total population, '000	2,709	2,726	2,731	2,719	2,709	2,696	2,669
Economically active population, '000	1,380	1,259	1,271	1,327	1,321	1,309	1,321

2. ADMINISTRATION

72, ul. Moskovskaya, Saratov, Saratov Region, 410042
Phone: (8452) 27 3730; fax: (8452) 72 5254; http://www.saratov.gov.ru

NAME	POSITION	CONTACT INFORMATION
Dmitry Fedorovich AYATSKOV	Governor of the Saratov Region	Phone: (8452) 27 3730 Fax: (8452) 28 5254
Vladimir Mikhailovich MARON	Deputy Governor of the Saratov Region, First Deputy Chairman of the Government of the Saratov Region	Phone: (8452) 27 2542, 73 1728
Alexander Vasilyevich DURNOV	Deputy Chairman of the Government of the Saratov Region, Chief of Staff of the Governor of the Saratov Region	Phone: (8452) 24 1082, 73 3119, 27 9433
Yury Vladimirovich MOISEYEV	First Deputy Chairman of the Government of the Saratov Region	Phone: (8452) 27 2023, 27 9589, 24 4849
Anatoly Ivanovich SOKOLOV	Deputy Chairman of the Government of the Saratov Region, Minister of Energy and Communal Services	Phone: (8452) 24 3975, 27 2087, 27 7963
Alexander Fedorovich FOGEL	Minister of Agriculture and Food of the Saratov Region	Phone: (8452) 51 7712 Fax: (8452) 27 8981 E-mail: market@mail.saratov.ru
Alexander Alexeevich STEPANOV	Minister of Economy and Investment of the Saratov Region	Phone: (8452) 24 1746 Fax: (8452) 27 3200 E-mail: ulyanovaa@saratov.gov.ru, dobrichenkotd@saratov.gov.ru
Alexander Stepanovich LARIONOV	Minister of Finance of the Saratov Region	Phone: (8452) 24 4186 Fax: (8452) 27 3355 E-mail: minfin@saratov.gov.ru
Yury Leonidovich ZEMSKOV	Minister, Chairman of the Committee of Construction and Construction Industry of the Saratov Region	Phone: (8452) 24 3061 Fax: (8452) 24 2970

NAME	POSITION	CONTACT INFORMATION
Gevorg Dzhalalovich DZHLAVYAN	Minister of Transport and Roads of the Saratov Region	Phone: (8452) 27 3417 Fax: (8452) 27 3544
Sergei Mikhailovich LISOVSKY	Minister Chairman of the Committee of Industry, Science, and Technology of the Saratov Region	Phone: (8452) 24 0629 Fax: (8452) 27 7266 E-mail: minprom@saratov.gov.ru

3. ECONOMIC POTENTIAL

3.1. 1997–2002 GROSS REGIONAL PRODUCT (GRP). INDUSTRY BREAKDOWN

The Saratov Region's 2002 gross regional product amounted to $3,428.9 million, or 10.7% up on 2001. The energy and fuel sectors accounted for the bulk of the growth. Per capita GRP was $1,148 in 2001, and $1,284 in 2002.

3.2. MAIN ECONOMIC GROWTH PROJECTION

The blueprint for economic development in the coming years is set forth in The Middle Term Program for Social and Economic Development of the Saratov Region, 2003–2005, which sets the following economic goals: extractive industry output growth with

GRP trends in 1997–2002						*TABLE 2*
	1997	1998	1999	2000	2001*	2002*
GRP in current prices, $ million	5,229.7	2,978.9	1,941.6	2,414.1	3,096.4	3,428.9

*Estimates of the Saratov Regional Government

GRP industry breakdown in 1997–2002, % of total						*TABLE 3*
	1997	1998	1999	2000	2001*	2002*
GRP	100	100	100	100	100	100
Industry	26.8	30.4	28.2	25.6	26.8	26.7
Agriculture and forestry	14.2	7.4	14.8	17.6	17.3	15.8
Construction	8.2	7.7	6.3	7.4	6.4	6.0
Transport and communications	16.7	14.1	10.7	13.2	13.5	16.0
Trade and public catering	8.7	11.2	14.1	12.1	11.2	10.8
Other	19.5	23.5	17.4	16.3	17.4	18.5
Net taxes on output	5.9	5.7	8.5	7.8	7.4	6.2

*Estimates of the Saratov Regional Government

a steady increase in the processing sectors; the establishment of innovation infrastructure to ensure the shift to an innovative development pattern; the development and implementation of energy saving measures and investment projects.

3.3. INDUSTRIAL OUTPUT IN 1997–2002 FOR MAJOR SECTORS OF ECONOMY

The Region's major industrial sectors are fuel, energy, machine engineering (instruments, electronics, diesel engines, aircraft, energy, chemicals, and oil engineering), chemicals and petrochemicals, and food and beverages.

Fuel. The sector accounts for 25.1% of total industrial output. The largest enterprises are ZAO LUKoil-Saratov, OAO Saratovneftegaz, OAO Saratov Oil Refinery, and OAO Neft.

Energy. The sector accounts for 20.5% of total industrial output. The energy sector is represented by OAO Balakovskaya Nuclear Power Station, OAO Saratov Hydroelectric Power Station, and OAO Saratovenergo. The total installed capacity of the stations is 6.9 MW.

Machine engineering and metal processing. The sector accounts for 16.9% of total industrial output. The largest enterprises are FGUP NPP Almaz, OAO Reflektor, FGUP PO Korpus, OAO Transmash, and OAO Trolza.

Chemicals and petrochemicals. The sector accounts for 12.8% of total industrial output. The main products of the sector are synthetic fibers and filament, mineral fertilizers, and sulfuric acid. The largest enterprises are OOO

Industry breakdown of industrial output in 1997–2002, % of total						*TABLE 4*
	1997	1998	1999	2000	2001	2002*
Total	100.0	100.0	100.0	100.0	100.0	100.0
Fuel	5.6	5.6	8.5	9.4	14.2	25.1
Energy	31.9	31.6	20.5	20.5	19.0	20.5
Machine engineering and metal processing	17.2	17.7	20.1	20.7	20.9	16.9
Chemicals and petrochemicals	13.5	10.2	13.7	14.7	15.8	12.8
Food and beverages	11.0	14.2	17.5	14.8	13.4	11.6
Construction materials	7.1	7.1	5.3	5.2	4.3	3.9
Glass and porcelain	2.5	2.9	2.7	2.8	3.3	2.8
Flour, cereals, and mixed fodder	5.0	3.9	4.1	3.7	2.7	1.7
Forestry, timber and paper	1.6	1.9	2.2	1.9	1.4	1.5
Light industry	1.0	1.0	1.7	1.8	1.4	1.0
Ferrous metals	0.6	0.5	0.6	2.0	1.6	0.9
Non-ferrous metals	0.1	0.1	0.1	0.2	0.3	0.1

*Estimates of the Saratov Regional Government

Henkel-Yug, OAO Balakovskoye Khimvolokno, and OOO Saratovorgsintez.

Food and beverages. The sector accounts for 11.6% of total industrial output. The largest enterprises are OAO Saratov Bakery Production, OAO BAT-Saratov Tobacco Factory, and OOO Slavyanka.

Agriculture. The Region has 8,044,100 hectares of arable lands, with the tillage occupying 5,688,200 hectares. The principal crops in 2002 were grain – 3,721,100 tons, sunflower seed – 240,900 tons, sugar beet – 98,800 tons, potato – 442,300 tons, and vegetables – 208,100 tons.

3.4. FUEL AND ENERGY BALANCE (OUTPUT AND CONSUMPTION PER RESOURCE)

The Saratov Region produces more energy than it consumes.

Fuel and energy sector production and consumption trends, 1997–2002						*TABLE 5*
	1997	1998	1999	2000	2001	2002*
Electricity output, billion kWh	26.9	30.1	31.1	37.2	38.8	39.0
Oil output (including gas condensate), '000 tons	1,314.0	1,377.0	1,456.0	1,534.0	1,608.0	1,725.0
Natural gas extraction, million cubic meters	310.0	367.0	380.0	432.0	505.0	565.0
Electricity consumption, billion kWh	12.4	12.2	11.9	12.5	12.3	12.5
Natural gas consumption, million cubic meters	8,276.8	6,443.0	6,614.0	6,379.0	5,487.0	9,019.0

*Estimates of the Saratov Regional Government

3.5. TRANSPORT INFRASTRUCTURE

Roads. The Saratov Region has 10,231 kilometers of paved public highway. The Region has road links to Voronezh and Kursk, and federal highway links to the Penza Region, the Samara Region, and Kazakhstan.

Railroads. The Region has 2,296 kilometers of railroads. The Volga Railroad links the Region to central Russia, the Urals, Siberia, the Caucasus, and Central Asia. The principal railway lines include Moscow – Saratov – Orenburg, Volgograd – Saratov – Kazan, and Penza – Rtishchevo – Balashov – Povorino.

Airports. A federal airport serves the city of Saratov. The main air transport operator is OAO Saratov Airlines.

River transport. Waterways link the city of Saratov to the industrial center of Russia, Moscow (via the Moscow Canal), the Western Urals (via the Kama River), the Black Sea (via the Volga – Don Canal), and the Baltic States and the White Sea (the Volga – Baltic waterway). The total length of the Region's navigable inland waterway system is 715 kilometers. Passenger transport operators serve population centers situated along the Volga River.

IV

VOLGA FEDERAL DISTRICT

River ports. A specially equipped cargo port has been built to the south of Saratov.

Oil pipelines. A number of trunk oil pipelines cross the Saratov Region en route to Samara, Volgograd, and Moscow. Ammonia pipelines also cross the Region.

3.6. MAIN NATURAL RESOURCES: RESERVES AND EXTRACTION IN 2002

The Saratov Region's principal natural resources are natural gas, oil, construction materials, and oil shale.

Fuel resources. More than 40 oil and gas deposits are being developed in the Region. The largest are the Yelshansko-Kurdyumovskoye, Sokolovogorskoye, Peschano-Umetskoye, Goryuchkinskoye, Uritskoye, and Stepnovskoye. More than 100 peat deposits have been discovered in the Region. The oil shale reserve is estimated at several billions tons.

Non-ore minerals. The Region boasts deposits of phosphorites, brick clay, expanded clay, sand (glass, molding, and mortar sand), sand-and-gravel, chalk, raw cement, building stone, limestone, sandstone, mineral pigments, molding box, tripoli powder, mineral salt, zeolite, glauconite, and curative mud deposits.

Water resources. Two water reservoirs are situated on the Volga, the Saratov Reservoir (with a dam at Balakovo) and the Volgograd Reservoir. About 180 small rivers drain the Region.

Forest resources. Forests cover 560,000 hectares of the Region's territory. The total timber reserve is 52 million cubic meters. The usable reserve stands at 0.2 million cubic meters of coniferous timber, 6.1 million cubic meters of hardwood deciduous timber, and 3.9 million cubic meters of deciduous timber.

4. TRADE OPPORTUNITIES

4.1. MAIN GOODS PRODUCED IN THE REGION

The Region's output in 2002 was as follows:

Machine engineering and metals processing. 300 trolleybuses, 825 tractor trailers and semi-trailers, 142,000 household refrigerators and freezers.

Chemicals and petrochemicals. 476,600 tons of mineral fertilizers, 40,200 tons of synthetic fibers and filament.

Food and beverages. 28,200 tons of vegetable oil, 9,500 tons of laundry soap, 277,000 decaliters of ethanol from edible raw materials, 381,600 decaliters of spirits, vodka, and distilled beverages, 900 decaliters of brandy, 2,900 tons of meat, including category one by-products, 14,500 tons of butter, 32,200 tons of whole milk (in milk equivalent), 226,400 tons of flour.

Construction materials. 1,578,100 tons of cement, 68.8 million square meters of standard asbestos cement board, 297,500 cubic meters of prefabricated reinforced concrete units and components, 183.5 million standard bricks, 14.4 million square meters of window glass (physical units).

4.2. EXPORTS, INCLUDING EXTRA-CIS

The Region's 1999 extra-CIS exports totaled $152.1 million, with CIS exports totaling $26.8 million. The corresponding figures were $443 million and $41.8 million for 2000, $335.2 million and $48.5 million for 2001, and $658.9 million and $60.1 million for 2002. Main exports include: oil products and crude oil, mineral fertilizers, organic chemicals, equipment, and mechanical devices.

The principal export partners are Italy, Turkey, Belgium, Spain, Finland, and Kazakhstan.

4.3. IMPORTS, INCLUDING EXTRA-CIS

The Region's 1999 extra-CIS imports totaled $143.6 million, with imports from the CIS totaling $63.5 million. The corresponding figures were $102.6 million and $44.6 million for 2000, and $127 million and $34.9 million for 2001. According to the Saratov Regional Government, 2002 imports totaled $180.1 million. Major imported goods include equipment, devices, rubber, and rubber goods.

The major import partners are Ukraine, Uzbekistan, Italy, Germany, and Kyrghyzia.

4.4. MAJOR REGIONAL EXPORT AND IMPORT ENTITIES

Due to the specific nature of the Region's export and import activities, export and import transactions are performed mainly by industrial enterprises.

5. INVESTMENT OPPORTUNITIES

5.1 INVESTMENTS IN 1992–2002 (BY INDUSTRY SECTOR), INCLUDING FOREIGN INVESTMENTS

The following factors determine the investment appeal of the Saratov Region:

• Its favorable geographical location at the crossroads of main transport routes;

• Its mineral resources;

• Its qualified work force;

• Laws on mineral resource development guaranteeing protection of owner and user rights.

5.2. CAPITAL INVESTMENT

Industry, transport, and communications account for the lion's share of fixed capital investment.

Capital investment by industry sector, $ million						TABLE 6
	1997	1998	1999	2000	2001	2002
Total capital investments	918.2	473.5	261.2	430.9	389.4	423.9
Including major industries (% of total)						
Industry	23.8	30.5	33.6	25.1	34.1	55.5
Agriculture and forestry	6.6	4.6	7.0	4.8	5.9	4.3
Construction	2.2	2.6	1.6	1.0	1.5	1.8
Transport and communications	20.0	24.9	31.3	49.0	37.8	21.9
Trade and public catering	1.2	3.1	0.7	1.3	2.1	0.1
Other	46.2	34.3	25.8	18.8	18.6	16.4

Foreign investment trends in 1996–2002						TABLE 7
	1996–1997	1998	1999	2000	2001	2002
Foreign investments, $ million	36.3	37.3	5.7	5.5	8.9	8.2
Including FDI, $ million	22.0	4.9	3.1	4.5	1.0	4.1

5.3. MAJOR ENTERPRISES (INCLUDING ENTERPRISES WITH FOREIGN INVESTMENT)

The Saratov Region hosts more than 90 enterprises with foreign investment.

5.4. MOST ATTRACTIVE SECTORS FOR INVESTMENT

The most attractive sectors for investment are energy, fuel, and machine engineering.

5.5. CURRENT LEGISLATION ON INVESTOR TAX EXEMPTIONS AND PRIVILEGES

The Region has enacted a number of laws of the Saratov Region regulating investment activity, including the laws On Granting of Tax Exemptions in the Saratov Region (the Law aims to foster and maintain an investment friendly environment and regulate the procedure and conditions for granting tax exemptions to organizations involved in investment activities in the Saratov Region), and On Innovation and Innovative Activity.

5.6. FEDERAL AND REGIONAL ECONOMIC AND SOCIAL DEVELOPMENT PROGRAMS FOR THE SARATOV REGION

Federal targeted programs. The Saratov Region participated in the implementation of some 39 federal targeted programs in 2002. Some $134.9 million worth of work was performed within the federal targeted programs and the federal targeted investment program, with $149.4 million allocated from the federal budget. The most important federal targeted programs for the economic and social development of the Region include the following: The Children of Russia, 2003–2006, The Culture of Russia, 2001–2005, The Ecology and Natural Resources of Russia, 2002–2010, Housing, 2002–2010, The Enrichment of Russia's Soil, 2002–2005, and The Social Development of Rural Areas through 2010.

IV

VOLGA FEDERAL DISTRICT

Largest enterprises of the Saratov Region	TABLE 8
COMPANY	SECTOR
GNPP Kontakt, FGUP NPP Almaz, OAO TsNIIIA (Central Research Institute for Metering Equipment), OAO Reflektor, FGUP PO Korpus, FGUP Saratov Instrumentation Factory, FGUP Appliance Factory, OAO Transmash, OAO Trolza	Machine engineering
OAO Saratovneftegaz	Fuel
OAO Balakovskaya Nuclear Power Station, OAO Saratovskaya Hydroelectric Power Station, OAO Saratovenergo	Energy
ZAO Saratov Aircraft Plant	Aircraft engineering
OAO Balakovo Khimvolokno, OOO Saratovorgsintez	Chemicals
OAO Saratov Airlines, FGUP MPS RF Volga Railroad	Transport
OAO Saratov Bakery Productions, OAO BAT-Saratov Tobacco Factory	Food and beverages
GUP Saratov Printing Factory	Printing

Regional entities responsible for raising investment

TABLE 9

ENTITY	ADDRESS	PHONE, FAX, E-MAIL
Ministry of Economic Development and Trade of the Saratov Region	72, ul. Moskovskaya, Saratov, Saratov Region, 410042	Phone: (8452) 24 1746 Fax: (8452) 27 3200
Ministry of Construction and Housing and Communal Services of the Saratov Region	114, ul. Chelyuskintsev, Saratov, Saratov Region, 410600	Phone: (8452) 24 3061 Fax: (8452) 24 2970
Ministry of Transport and Road Construction of the Saratov Region	20, ul. Volskaya, Saratov, Saratov Region, 410600	Phone: (8452) 24 0750, 27 3417 Fax: (8452) 27 3544
Ministry of Industry, Science, and Technology of the Saratov Region	42, ul. M. Gorkogo, Saratov, Saratov Region, 410042	Phone: (8452) 24 0629 Fax: (8452) 27 7266
Saratov Regional Chamber of Industry and Commerce	30, ul. Bolshaya Kazachya, Saratov, Saratov Region, 410600	Phone: (8452) 27 7078 Fax: (8452) 27 7082
Saratov Regional Office of the Federal Commission for the Securities Market	53, ul. Gorkogo, Saratov, Saratov Region, 410042	Phone: (8452) 27 8637 Fax: (8452) 27 8659
Regional Office of the Fund for Assistance to Small Innovative Enterprises	116, of. 402, ul. Chelyuskintsev, Saratov, Saratov Region, 410600	Phone: (8452) 24 4870 Fax: (8452) 27 7266
Saratov Regional Training Center for Computer Technology in Industry	83, ul. Astrakhanskaya, Saratov, Saratov Region, 410026	Phone: (8452) 51 1521, 52 2710 Fax: (8452) 51 1521 E-mail: lab_ktu@mail.ru, kossovichLU@info.sgu.ru

Regional programs. The Region plans to allocate a total of $21.1 million from the regional budget to finance 25 regional programs in 2003. The regional programs are largely focused on public welfare, public health and education, and industrial development. The Region has underway the Governor's Program for Energy Saving in the Saratov Region, 1999–2010, to be financed to the tune of $1 million from the regional budget in 2003. The Program of Industrial Development in the Saratov Region, 2001–2005 aims to deploy scientific research work for the development and creation of advanced technologies for the production of competitive high-tech products. The Saratov Region has allocated $2.2 million in financing to fund the development of areas located on the left bank of the Volga under the Program for the Development of the Trans-Volga territories in the Saratov Region.

6. INVESTMENT PROJECTS

Industry sector and project description	1) Expected results 2) Amount and term of investment 3) Form of financing[1] 4) Documentation[2]	Contact information
1	2	3
CHEMICALS AND PETROCHEMICALS		
55R001 ● ◆		
Establishment of polymer packaging production. Project goal: to meet growing demand for packaging for bulk food, building materials, and chemicals.	1) 2003 revenue of $2.6 million 2) $2.1 million/45 months 3) L 4) BP	OAO Assembly Components Plant, Trofimovsky-II station, Saratov, Saratov Region, 410041 Phone/fax: (8452) 27 5257, 33 1645, 33 1825 Alexander Viktorovich Tarasenko, CEO

[1] L – Loan, E – Equity, Leas. – Leasing, JV – Joint Venture
[2] BP – Business Plan, FS – Feasibility Study

1	2	3

55R002 ■ ● ❖ ◆

An increase in sales of acetous anhydride.
Project goal: to export output to Western Europe.

1) Up to 1,000 tons per month
2) $1.1 million/3 months
3) L, E, JV
4) BP

OOO Pokrovskie Efiry,
1, pr. Khimikov, Engels,
Saratov Region, 413116
Phone: (84511) 29 551
Fax: (84511) 22 943
E-mail: acetatkm@engels.san.ru
Vitaly Anatolyevich Grashkin, CEO

MACHINE ENGINEERING AND METAL PROCESSING

55R003 ■ ● ★ ❖ ◆ ▲

Production of Volgar harvesting machines.
Project goal: to introduce advanced agricultural technology and create a new generation harvester.

1) Five prototypes
2) $1.9 million/2 years
3) L, Leas., E, JV
4) FS, BP

OAO Innovation Technology Center of Saratov Aviation Plant and Saratov State Technical University
1, ul. Ordzhonikidze, Saratov,
Saratov Region, 410015
Phone: (8452) 96 8646
Fax: (8452) 96 1036
E-mail: itc@forpost.ru
Alexander Mikhailovich Zakharov, Director

55R004 ● ◆ ▲

Technical upgrade of OAO Trolley Plant.
Project goal: to extend the useful life of production shops and increase output of dies.

1) 67 tons of dies per month
2) $1 million/3 years
3) L
4) FS, BP

OAO Trolley Plant
Engels, Saratov Region, 413105
Phone: (84511) 91 301
Fax (84511) 63 945, 63 890
Dmitry Nikolaevich Polulyak, CEO

55R005 ● ◆

Production of heating equipment for diesel engines of KAMAZ trucks and VTZ tractors in compliance with Euro 2 and Euro 3 standards.
Project goal: to increase output.

1) Annual revenue growth by $15.2 million
2) $20.6 million/6.4 years
3) L
4) BP

OAO Volgodieselapparat
2, 4th Liniya, Marks,
Saratov Region, 413090
Phone: (84567) 22 290, 24 980
Fax: (84567) 21 859
E-mail: vda@vda.saratov.ru
Vyacheslav Vladimirovich Pokrovsky, CEO

55R006 ● ◆ ▲

Implementation of a corporate ERP software AKHARTA.
Project goal: to accelerate data processing, increase output, expand the sales market, reduce costs, and improve the quality of the dispatch system.

1) Annual revenue growth by $0.5 million
2) $0.5 million/2 years
3) L
4) FS, BP

AZO International Bearing Concern Autoshtamp
32, ul. Barnaulskaya, Saratov,
Saratov Region, 410049
Phone: (8452) 92 8901,
92 1450, 45 5555
Fax: (8452) 92 9497, 92 9661
E-mail: avtosht@mail.saratov.ru
Sergei Vasilyevich Makarov, CEO

LIGHT INDUSTRY

55R007 ● ★ ▲

Technical development of the company.
Project goal: to expand the fabric assortment, and maintain and strengthen market position.

1) 1,200,000 linear meters
2) $2.1 million/1 year
3) L, Leas.
4) FS

OAO Balashov Textile
1, ul. Entuziastov, Balashov,
Saratov Region, 412311
Phone: (84545) 30 978
Fax: (84545) 34 366
Alexander Ivanovich Vetrov, CEO

55R008 ● ★ ◆

Launching of production of a new type of knitted linen.
Project goal: to produce highly profitable goods.

1) 117.4 tons per month
2) $1.3 million/2 years
3) L, Leas.
4) BP

OAO NitkanPorovsk
81, ul. Poligraficheskaya, Engels,
Saratov Region, 413111
Phone: (84511) 63 381
Alexander Mikhailovich Bochkov, CEO

1	2	3

FOOD AND BEVERAGES

55R009

● ◆

Launching of production
at OOO Makpo.
Project goal: to produce macaroni.

1) Processing of up to 12,000 tons
   of flour per year, output of up to
   10,000 tons of macaroni per year
2) $2.3 million/1 year
3) L
4) BP

OOO Makpo
90, ul. Chernyshevskogo, Saratov,
Saratov Region, 410017
Phone: (8452) 24 0305
Tatyana Petrovna Kovalchuk, CEO

PRINTING

55R010

★ ◆

Expansion of output of color
publications and full-color
cardboard packages.
Project goal: to increase sales.

1) Sales increase of 1.5 times;
   2003 revenue of $5.9 million
2) $4.1 million/4 years
3) Leas.
4) BP

State Unitary Company
Saratov Printing House
59, ul. Chernyshesvskogo, Saratov,
Saratov Region, 410004
Phone: (8452) 95 3309
Fax: (8452) 95 3224
E-mail: pol@overta.ru
Nikolai Mikhailovich Chukalin, CEO

TRANSPORT INFRASTRUCTURE

55R011

● ★ ◆

Development of operator
activities at ZAO Unisar-Trans.
Project goal: to improve efficiency
of transportation by railroad.

1) 2004 revenue of $0.2 million,
   2005 revenue of $0.3 million
2) $3.2 million/3 years
3) L, Leas.
4) BP

ZAO Unisar-Trans
7, ul. Severnaya, Saratov,
Saratov Region, 410031
Phone: (8452) 41 4809
Fax: (8452) 48 6435
E-mail: office@zheldor.runet.ru
Alexander Viktorovich Fedoseev,
CEO

HOTELS AND TOURISM

55R012

■ ● ★ ❖ ◆ ▲

Construction of a downhill skiing
center at Teplovka, Novoburassky
District, Saratov Region.
Project goal: to provide recreation
services.

1) Estimated revenue of $0.1 million per year
2) $4.3 million/1 year
3) L, Leas., E, JV
4) FS, BP

Ministry of Youth Policy,
Sports, and Tourism
of the Saratov Region
81, ul. Volskaya, Saratov,
Saratov Region, 410730
Phone: (8452) 73 4980
Fax: (8452) 73 4029
E-mail: minmolod@gov.saratov.ru
Sultan Raisovich Akhmerov, Minister

56. ULYANOVSK REGION [73]

ECONOMIC MAP

REPUBLIC OF CHUVASHIA

REPUBLIC OF TATARSTAN

REPUBLIC OF MORDOVIA

Surskoe

Isheevka

Cherdakly   Novochemshansk

Dimitrovgrad

ULYANOVSK

Karsun

Mayna

Novoulyanovsk

Kuybyshevskoe water reservoir

Sengiley

Tolyatti

Inza

Nikolsk

PENZA

Barysh

REGION

Oktyabrsk

Novospasskoe

Suzran

Kuznetsk

SAMARA

Nikolaevka

Chapaevsk

Novokuybyshevsk

S A M A R A

Pavlovka

R E G I O N

SARATOV

Saratovskoe water reservoir

REGION

Volsk

Balakovo   Pugachyov

PROCESSING INDUSTRY

- 🔴 Machine engineering and metal processing
- 🔵 Construction materials
- 🔵 Light industry
- ⚪ Food and beverages

MINING INDUSTRY

- ▲ Oil
- ▯ Raw cement
- ▣ Quartz and quartz sand
- Mineral water sources

POWER PLANTS

- ⚡ Thermal power plants

CROPS AND LIVESTOCK BREEDING

- Wheat
- Rye
- Barley
- Vegetables
- Potatoes
- Sunflower
- Sugar beetroot

- Meat and dairy cattle breeding
- Pig breeding
- Sheep rearing
- Resorts

The Ulyanovsk Region's favorable geographic location combined with its systemic industrial sector, high research and development and technology potential, developed market infrastructure, and qualified workforce, make it wholly feasible to establish lucrative operations in any sector from food processing to aviation.

The Region's strong investment potential, low investment risk, and favorable legislation determine its favorable investment climate and provide the prerequisites for increased investment in the Region.

The Ulyanovsk Region has strong natural resource potential and significant reserves of the main types of mineral resources, including oil, raw materials for use in the production of construction materials, filter powder, cement, glass, mineral fertilizers, dyes, chalk, brick clay, mineral water, and balneological radon water. The Tashlinskoye quartz sand deposit and Inzenskoye diatomite deposit are second to none in Europe.

The Ulyanovsk Region's industrial economy includes such sectors as machine engineering and metals processing, building materials, light industry, and food and beverages. Over a third of the economically active population is employed in these sectors. The Region's machine engineering enterprises produce all-terrain vehicles, civilian aircraft, vans, aviation instruments, machines, and building materials. We also produce a wide range of consumer goods, including knitwear, fabric, clothing, and food.

The Region's agricultural sector is represented by more than 400 large and medium-size companies and 2,000 farms. The Region is focused on grain and fodder crop cultivation. The tillage sector has vast development potential, given the fertility of the Region's soils: water meadow, black earth, turf podzol, and forest soils. Arable land is poorly utilized, however, due to a lack of financing resulting in reduced use of agricultural technology and impaired management practices. For the same reason, the Region's cattle breeding potential has not been fully harnessed.

Major air, railroad, and highway routes linking the Volga Region to Europe, Western Siberia, Central Asia, the Middle East, and China pass through the Ulyanovsk Region. The Region is served by two major airports equipped with modern radio electronic and navigation equipment, which is capable of servicing aircraft of all types based on the ICAO's first category meteorological minimum. The Region is also served by two major river ports at Ulyanovsk and Sengiley.

The Ulyanovsk Region offers strong potential for effective short-term and long-term investment in various sectors of its economy.

The Regional Administration is focused on implementing targeted and consistent measures aimed at attracting investment and fostering a favorable investment climate in the Region.

We are ready to provide investors with general information on the economic and investment prospects of our Region, information on vacant industrial sites that would be suitable for new production facilities, and the statistics and data needed to prepare business plans or feasibility studies.

Vladimir Shamanov,
HEAD OF ADMINISTRATION OF THE ULYANOVSK REGION

IV

VOLGA FEDERAL DISTRICT

1. GENERAL INFORMATION

1.1. GEOGRAPHY

The Ulyanovsk Region covers a total area of some 37,300 square kilometers. The Region is located in the central part of European Russia. To the north, the Region borders the Republic of Chuvashia and the Republic of Tatarstan, to the east – the Samara Region, to the south – the Saratov Region, and to the west – the Penza Region and the Republic of Mordovia.

1.2. CLIMATE

The Ulyanovsk Region is situated in the moderate continental climate zone.

Temperatures in January average –6.8°C, rising to +21.4°C in July. Annual precipitation averages 400 mm. The average growing period lasts 174 days.

1.3. POPULATION

According to preliminary 2002 census results, the Ulyanovsk Region has a total population of 1,382,000. The average population density is 37.1 people per square kilometer. The economically active population totals 638,000. Official unemployment was 2.2% in 2002. The actual rate was 14.2%.

Demographically speaking, some 60.9% of the population are of statutory working age, 18.4% are below the statutory working age, and 20.7% are above the statutory working age.

The major urban centers of the Ulyanovsk Region (2002 data) are Ulyanovsk with 635,600 inhabitants, Dimitrovgrad with 130,900 inhabitants, Inza with 22,600 inhabitants, and Barysh with 21,200 inhabitants.

Population							*TABLE 1*
	1992	1997	1998	1999	2000	2001	2002
Total population, '000.	1,439	1,486	1,479	1,472	1,463	1,454	1,382
Economically active population, '000.	752	703	670	734	684	687	638

2. ADMINISTRATION

IV

VOLGA FEDERAL DISTRICT

1, pl. Lenina, Ulyanovsk, Ulyanovsk Region, 432700
Phone: (8422) 41 2078; fax: (8422) 32 5244
E-mail: admobl@mv.ru; http://www.ulyanovsk-adm.ru

NAME	POSITION	CONTACT INFORMATION
Vladimir Anatolyevich SHAMANOV	Head of Administration of the Ulyanovsk Region	Phone: (8422) 41 2078, 41 2943 Fax: (8422) 41 7020
Mikhail Ivanovich SHKANOV	First Deputy Head of Administration of the Ulyanovsk Region	Phone: (8422) 41 2886
Dmitry Alexandrovich PIORUNSKY	Deputy Head of Administration of the Ulyanovsk Region for Economy	Phone/fax: (8422) 41 3151
Vladimir Pavlovich TIGIN	Deputy Head of Administration of the Ulyanovsk Region for the Agroindustrial Sector, Head of the Agriculture and Food Department	Phone: (8422) 44 2619 Fax: (8422) 41 4601
Anatoly Andreevich KRYUCHKOV	Deputy Head of Administration of the Ulyanovsk Region for Finance	Phone: (8422) 41 4024
Nikolai Petrovich POVTAREV	Deputy Head of Administration of the Ulyanovsk Region, Head of the Property Relations Department	Phone: (8422) 41 3475 Fax: (8422) 41 6343
Yevgeny Alexandrovich NIKIFOROV	Deputy Head of Administration of the Ulyanovsk Region for Industry	Phone: (8422) 41 2124 Fax: (8422) 41 3772
Alexander Yuryevich BUDARIN	Deputy Head of Administration of the Ulyanovsk Region for Capital Construction and Housing and Communal Services	Phone/fax: (8422) 41 3771
Igor Igorevich YEGOROV	Head of the Economy Department of the Administration of the Ulyanovsk Region	Phone/fax: (8422) 41 2147

NAME	POSITION	CONTACT INFORMATION
Yury Gennadyevich SHEVCHENKO	Chief of the Strategic Development Department of the Ulyanovsk Regional Administration	Phone/fax: (8422) 41 1907
Andrei Andreevich BOLGOV	Chief of the Investment Planning Department of the Ulyanovsk Regional Administration	Phone: (8422) 41 2068 Fax: (8422) 41 2147

3. ECONOMIC POTENTIAL

3.1. 1997–2002 GROSS REGIONAL PRODUCT (GRP). INDUSTRY BREAKDOWN

The 2002 gross regional product amounted to $1,563.7 million, 12% up on 2001. Per capita GRP amounted to $960 in 2001 and $1,131 in 2002.

3.2. MAIN ECONOMIC GROWTH PROJECTIONS

The Region's social and economic development priorities for the coming years are set forth in the Program of Social and Economic Development for the Ulyanovsk Region, 2002–2004, which sets the objectives outlined below.

GRP trends in 1997–2002						TABLE 2
	1997	1998	1999	2000	2001*	2002*
GRP in current prices, $ million	2,795.9	1,648.3	1,034.5	1,168.2	1,396.2	1,563.7

*Estimates of the Ulyanovsk Regional Administration

GRP industry breakdown in 1997–2002, % of total						TABLE 3
	1997	1998	1999	2000	2001*	2002*
GRP	100.0	100.0	100.0	100.0	100.0	100.0
Industry	32.4	32.9	34.0	31.6	29.6	28.9
Agriculture and forestry	10.5	3.7	12.3	13.8	16.1	17.3
Construction	4.7	6.3	4.1	4.6	4.8	4.3
Transportation and communications	6.9	7.4	9.5	11.4	9.8	8.6
Trade and public catering	8.3	11.1	14.9	11.7	12.0	11.9
Other	28.5	29.5	16.9	19.4	20.2	21.7
Net taxes on output	8.7	9.1	8.3	7.5	7.5	7.3

*Estimates of the Ulyanovsk Regional Administration

Industry: to achieve steady output growth via market expansion and increased consumer purchasing power; to boost the competitiveness of output; to expand and renovate production facilities; and to carry out efficient innovative policies.

Agriculture: to increase output and exports to other regions of Russia; and to attract investments for the creation of modern processing facilities.

Construction: to create new and rearrange existing construction facilities through the use of modern high-yield technologies in industrial and residential construction.

Transportation: to achieve growth in road transport services; to establish modern road haulage companies; to develop freight transit to other regions of the Russian Federation; and to increase air and river transport turnover.

Trade: to promote trade links with other regions of Russia and abroad.

3.3. INDUSTRIAL OUTPUT IN 1997–2002 FOR MAJOR SECTORS OF ECONOMY

The leading sectors of the Ulyanovsk Region are machine engineering (automotive, aircraft, machine tools, and instruments), energy, and food and beverages.

Machine engineering and metal processing. Major enterprises include OAO UAZ, OAO DAAZ, OAO Utes, OAO Volga Motors, OAO Dimitrovgrad-khimmash, FGUP Ulyanovsk Machine Engineering Plant, ZAO Aviastar Joint Venture, ZAO Contactor, OAO Avtodetalservice, GUP NPO Mars, OAO UZTS, OAO Gidroapparat, OAO Comet, OAO Aviastar Aviation Plant, and OAO Iskra Works. The sector's

Industry breakdown of industrial output in 1997–2002, % of total						TABLE 4
	1997	1998	1999	2000	2001	2002*
Industry	100.0	100.0	100.0	100.0	100.0	100.0
Machine engineering and metal processing	53.4	50.9	56.0	54.3	53.7	54.1
Energy	15.0	16.0	11.7	11.7	13.3	14.6
Food and beverages	12.8	12.7	13.6	9.5	14.6	14.1
Construction materials	6.7	8.3	6.2	6.0	5.9	5.7
Light industry	4.0	3.4	4.0	3.9	3.6	4.0
Fuel	1.0	1.1	3.2	5.7	3.2	2.1
Forestry, timber, and pulp and paper	1.0	1.3	1.4	2.0	2.0	2.1
Flour, cereals, and mixed fodder	1.5	1.2	1.0	0.6	0.7	0.7
Chemicals and petrochemicals	0.1	1.9	0.4	0.3	0.3	0.4
Ferrous metals	0.2	0.4	0.4	0.4	0.3	0.3
Glass and porcelain	–	–	0.3	–	0.4	0.3

*Estimates of the Ulyanovsk Regional Administration

enterprises manufacture civil aircraft, vehicles, minibuses, avionics, and unique machine tools.

Energy. The largest enterprise is OAO Ulyanovskenergo. The Ulyanovsk Regional Power System includes three thermal power stations (TPS 1, TPS 2, and TPS 3), Ulyanovsk Thermal Networks, and the Ulyanovsk, Dimitrovgrad, and Barysh power networks. The Ulyanovsk power system is connected via 110 kV and 220 kV lines to the Samara, Mordovia, Tatarstan, and Penza power systems.

Food and beverages. Its main subsectors are confectionery, cereals and macaroni, meat, dairy and vegetables, wine, and alcoholic and non-alcoholic beverages. Major companies include OAO Simbirskspirtprom Distillery, OAO Vityaz Brewery, OAO Ulyanovsksakhar, OAO Trekhsosensky Non-Alcoholic Beverages and Beer Brewery, OAO Khlebprom Bakery, OAO

Ulyanovsk Frozen Food Plant, OAO Simbirsk-Flour, OAO Ulyanovsky Meat Packing Plant, and OAO Dikom.

Construction materials. Its largest companies include OOO Inza Timber Plant, OOO Stroyplastmass Joint Venture, OAO Ulyanovskshifer Roofing Slate Works, OAO Zavod KPD 2, and OAO Dimitrovgradstroi Construction Company.

Agriculture. The Region grows various grain and fodder crops.

3.4. FUEL AND ENERGY BALANCE (OUTPUT AND CONSUMPTION PER RESOURCE)

The Ulyanovsk Region is an energy deficit region. The regional power system meets only 28% of local demand. Annual oil production exceeds 500,000 tons. The Region consumes 200,000 tons of gasoline, 300,000 tons of diesel fuel, and 700,000 tons of fuel oil annually.

Fuel and energy sector production and consumption trends in 1997–2002						TABLE 5
	1997	1998	1999	2000	2001	2002*
Electricity output, billion kWh	2.8	2.6	2.6	2.0	1.9	1.7
Oil output (including gas condensate), '000 tons	257	280	314	374	397	523
Electricity consumption, billion kWh	6.3	6.3	6.3	6.3	5.9	6.0

*Estimates of the Ulyanovsk Regional Administration

3.5. TRANSPORT INFRASTRUCTURE

Roads. The Region has 7,948 kilometers of roads. Some 20 road haulage companies offer reliable connections to other regions of the Russian Federation.

Railroads. The Region has 709 kilometers of railroads. The Ulyanovsk – Inza – Ruzaevka –

Ryazan – Moscow and Ulyanovsk – Dimitrovgrad – Novocheremshansk – Ufa – Chelyabinsk – Kurgan lines provide links to other regions of Russia.

Airports. The Region is served by two airports: the Ulyanovsk Central Airport, and the Eastern Airport (international). Some 30,000 passengers and 55,000 tons of cargo are carried by air annually. The Region's airports are equipped with

IV

VOLGA FEDERAL DISTRICT

modern radio electronic and navigational equipment that enables handling of any type of aircraft.

River transport. The Region has two river ports at Ulyanovsk and Sengiley. OAO Ulyanovsk River Port operates freight transportation. The ports are equipped with power portal cranes, escalators, specialized loaders, and conveyors with the capacity to handle thousands of tons of various cargoes. Some 17,000 passengers are carried by river annually, with freight shipments reaching 508,000 tons.

Oil and gas pipelines. The Region is crossed by the Chelyabinsk – Petrovsk, Urengoy – Novopskov, Urengoy – Petrovsk, Staraya Binaradka – Dimitrovgrad – Ulyanovsk, and Novospasskoye – Ulyanovsk trunk gas pipelines and the Druzhba oil pipeline.

3.6. MAIN NATURAL RESOURCES: RESERVES AND EXTRACTION IN 2002

The Ulyanovsk Region's main natural resources are minerals and raw materials, water, and recreational resources.

Minerals and raw materials. The Region has some 48 oil fields and 493 peat deposits with reserves of 33.2 million tons. The richest peat deposits are at the Melekessky (1.5 million tons), Inzensky (0.9 million tons), and Veshkaimsky (0.7 million tons) Districts. Oil shale deposits are found between the Volga and the Sviyaga watersheds. The Region also has reserves of minerals suitable for construction materials production at the Tashlinskoye field (100 million tons of glass sand) and the Lukyanovskoye field (quartz sand deposits). Six chalk fields with total reserves of 380 million tons have been explored in the Region.

Water resources. The Ulyanovsk Region has significant mineral water reserves with daily output of 12,000 cubic meters.

Recreational resources. The village of Undory in the Region's Ulyanovsky District hosts a large federal-level health resort. Local health resorts are situated at Beloye Ozero in the Nikolaevsky District and at Bely Yar in the Cherdaklinsky District.

4. TRADE OPPORTUNITIES

4.1. MAIN GOODS PRODUCED IN THE REGION

Automotive. In 2002, the Ulyanovsk Car Factory produced 69,000 UAZ cars and car kits.

Forestry, timber, and pulp and paper. Output for 2002: commercial timber – 72,000 cubic meters, door and window frames – 130,000 square meters.

Construction materials. Output for 2002: cement – 1.1 million tons, flexible roofing – 641,000 square meters, linoleum – 6.4 million square meters.

Light industry. Output for 2002: fabrics – 29 million square meters, including 21 million square meters of non-woven fabric; knitted fabric – 1,300 tons, knitwear – 15 million items.

Food and beverages. Output for 2002: cereals – 1,200 tons, whole-milk products – 33,400 tons, bread and bakery – 6,600 tons, meat – 5,300 tons, sausages – 8,300 tons, alcoholic beverages – 865,000 decaliters, ethyl alcohol – 1.2 million decaliters, beer – 6.1 million decaliters, confectionery – 43,600 tons.

4.2. EXPORTS, INCLUDING EXTRA-CIS

2000 exports to extra-CIS countries totaled to $150.9 million. Exports to the CIS reached $22.2 million. The corresponding figures for 2001 were

$76.8 million and $34.2 million, and $122.6 million and $43.2 million for 2002.

The Region's main exports include machine engineering goods (52.1% of total exports), petrochemicals (6%), and fuel and energy (4.6%). The main trading partners for exports are Cyprus (30% of exports) – defense systems; Egypt (13.2%) – aircraft and aircraft equipment, electrical equipment, optical equipment, timber and timber goods; and Kazakhstan (11.6%) – timber, furniture, textiles, and electrical equipment.

4.3. IMPORTS, INCLUDING EXTRA-CIS

2000 imports from outside the CIS totaled $38.4 million. CIS imports reached $14.5 million. The corresponding figures for 2001 were $36.6 million and $11.8 million, and $43.6 million and $15.5 million for 2002.

The Region's main imports include machinery and equipment, food and beverages, and petrochemicals. The Region's main trading partners for imports are Ukraine (25.3%) and Germany (17.1%).

4.4. MAJOR REGIONAL EXPORT AND IMPORT ENTITIES

Owing to the specific nature of the Region's export and import activities, export and import transactions are performed mainly by industrial enterprises.

5. INVESTMENT OPPORTUNITIES

5.1 INVESTMENTS IN 1992–2002 (BY INDUSTRY SECTOR), INCLUDING FOREIGN INVESTMENTS

• The following factors determine the investment appeal of the Region:

• Its favorable geographical location and proximity to major markets;

• Its natural resources;

• Its developed transport infrastructure;

• Legislation favoring investment activity with guaranteed investor rights and tax benefits;

• Its qualified workforce.

5.2. CAPITAL INVESTMENT

The industry and transport sectors account for the lion's share of investments in the Ulyanovsk Region.

5.3. MAJOR ENTERPRISES (INCLUDING ENTERPRISES WITH FOREIGN INVESTMENT)

Major companies with foreign capital include ZAO Volga-Dnepr Aviation Company and OOO VIS MOS (Germany).

Capital investment by industry sector, $ million						TABLE 6
	1997	1998	1999	2000	2001	2002
Total capital invested	370.3	230.9	109.9	148.8	157.3	158.6
Including major industries (% of total)						
Industry	30.5	31.3	23.1	25.6	30.7	32.3
Agriculture and forestry	5.5	8.2	7.2	6.9	5.8	4.3
Construction	1.7	0.9	3.6	2.9	10.9	11.5
Transportation and communications	9.3	7.6	24.7	31.3	29.7	30.5
Trade and public catering	2.0	0.8	0.4	1.4	1.1	1.0
Other	51.0	58.7	41.0	31.9	21.8	20.4

Foreign investment trends in 1997–2002						TABLE 7
	1997	1998	1999	2000	2001	2002
Foreign investment, $ million	2.4	0.2	1.6	1.5	2.2	17.1
Including FDI, $ million	2.4	–	0.3	–	0.1	2.1

Largest enterprises of the Ulyanovsk Region		TABLE 8
COMPANY	SECTOR	2001 REVENUE, $ MILLION*
OAO UAZ Car Factory	Machine engineering	237.7
OAO Ulyanovskenergo	Energy	109.7
OAO DAAZ	Machine engineering	98.4
ZAO Volga-Dnepr Airlines	Air freight transport	50.6
OAO Volzhanka Confectionery	Food and beverages	49.5
OAO Volga Motors	Machine engineering	46.0
OAO Ulyanovskneft	Oil	31.0
OOO VIS MOS	Construction	21.1
GNTs NIIAR	Scientific research in the field of nuclear power, and nuclear waste processing and disposal	18.8
OAO Volgatelecom	Communications	16.8
OAO Vityaz Brewery	Food and beverages	15.2
OAO Utes	Instrument engineering	14.1
ZAO Aviastar Joint Venture	Aircraft engineering	12.3
ZAO Contactor	Instrument engineering	12.2
OAO Simbirskspirtprom	Food and beverages	9.5
OAO Ulyanovsk Instrument Engineering Department	Instrument engineering	8.7
GUP NPO Mars	Instrument engineering	3.7
Vtorchermet Ulyanovsk Public Enterprise	Recycling	3.2

*Data of the Ulyanovsk Regional Administration

IV

VOLGA FEDERAL DISTRICT

5.4. MOST ATTRACTIVE SECTORS FOR INVESTMENT

According to experts and the Regional Administration, the most promising sectors for investment are food and beverages and food processing, machine engineering, aircraft engineering, radio and electronics, shipbuilding, and river transport.

5.5. CURRENT LEGISLATION ON INVESTOR TAX EXEMPTIONS AND PRIVILEGES

The Ulyanovsk Regional Administration has adopted the following laws with a view to improving the investment climate in the Region: On Investment Guarantees in the Ulyanovsk Region (contains provisions on tax relief, temporary regional tax component exemptions, and the provision of land, premises, and facilities to investors on preferential terms); On State Support to Small Business in the Ulyanovsk Region; On Simplified Taxation and Accounting for Small Businesses in the Ulyanovsk Region; On Business Agreements Between the Ulyanovsk Regional Administration and Legal Entities; On Free Economic Zones in the Ulyanovsk Region (businesses within these areas are exempt from regional components of income tax, value added tax, and road tax).

Regional entities responsible for raising investment		*TABLE 9*
ENTITY	ADDRESS	PHONE, FAX, E-MAIL
Direct Investments Institute Foundation	11a, per. 1st Khvostov, Moscow 109180	Phone: (095) 238 4763, 230 7852 Fax: (095) 777 3456 E-mail: info@ivr.ru
BINK Ulyanovsk Innovation Center	20, ul. Koryukina, Ulyanovsk, Ulyanovsk Region, 432011	Phone: (8422) 49 0216 Fax: (8422) 41 4526 E-mail: binc@mv.ru
ZAO Alfa-Intel	19, ul. Sovetskaya, Ulyanovsk, Ulyanovsk Region, 432038	Phone: (8422) 39 4095
OOO Volgoenergokomplekt	7, ul. Marata, Ulyanovsk, Ulyanovsk Region, 432001	Phone: (8422) 34 7122
ZAO Invest-Inform Stock House	4a, ul. Pushkinskaya, Ulyanovsk, Ulyanovsk Region, 432063	Phone: (8422) 32 9159
ZAO Paritet	4a, ul. Pushkinskaya, Ulyanovsk, Ulyanovsk Region, 432063	Phone: (8422) 32 9159
OAO Euro-Volga	4b, ul. Kuznetsova, Ulyanovsk, Ulyanovsk Region, 432063	Phone: (8422) 31 6527
Chamber of Commerce and Industry	19, ul. Engelsa, Ulyanovsk, Ulyanovsk Region, 432063	Phone: (8422) 31 4523
Ulyanovsk Marketing Center	12, ul. Krymova, Ulyanovsk, Ulyanovsk Region, 432001	Phone: (8422) 31 9411
ZAO Ulyanovsk Marketing Center	6, ul. Zheleznoi Divizii, Ulyanovsk, Ulyanovsk Region, 432063	Phone: (8422) 31 8756
Ulyanovsk Multi-Business Center	14a, ul. Zheleznodorozhnaya, Ulyanovsk, Ulyanovsk Region, 432063	Phone: (8422) 31 6263
Ulyanovsk-Moscow Inter-Regional Marketing Center	68, ul. Radischeva, Ulyanovsk, Ulyanovsk Region, 432071	Phone: (8422) 41 0466
Business and Investment Training Center	Room 12, 24, ul. L. Tolstogo, Ulyanovsk, Ulyanovsk Region, 432063	Phone: (8422) 31 3258
OAO Aviastar Marketing Center	1, pr. Antonova, Ulyanovsk, Ulyanovsk Region, 432072	Phone: (8422) 29 2120

5.6. FEDERAL AND REGIONAL ECONOMIC AND SOCIAL DEVELOPMENT PROGRAMS FOR THE ULYANOVSK REGION

Federal targeted programs. The Region is currently implementing the federal targeted program for the Elimination of Differences in Social and Economic Development among the Regions of the Russian Federation, which aims to diminish the gap between the major social and economic indicators by 2010, create favorable conditions for business activity, and improve the investment climate. The program has been allocated $391.1 million in funding from the federal budget, and $477 million from Russian Federation regional budgets.

Regional programs. The Region is implementing regional programs aimed at developing industry, improving the environmental situation, and improving law enforcement, health care, and public welfare. Some 12 regional programs are currently underway

with total financing to the tune of $22 million. The Region is also implementing the Program of Small Enterprise Development, 2002–2004, which aims to improve the legal, economic, and organizational conditions needed for the sustainable development of small enterprise and to consolidate funding for small enterprise in priority sectors of the regional economy.

6. INVESTMENT PROJECTS

Industry sector and project description	1) Expected results 2) Amount and term of investment 3) Form of financing[1] 4) Documentation[2]	Contact information
1	2	3
FERROUS METALS		
56R001 ● ◆ Construction of a mini metals plant based on a foundry and rolling facility. Project goal: to produce metals.	1) 70,000 tons a year 2) $9.3 million/2.5 years 3) L 4) BP	OAO Ulyanovsk Heavy Machine Tools Plant 10, ul. Gerasimova, Ulyanovsk, Ulyanovsk Region, 432042 Phone: (8422) 63 6825 Fax: (8422) 63 6917 Mikhail Ivanovich Fedotov, CEO
CHEMICALS AND PHARMACEUTICALS		
56R002 ● ◆ Radiological pharmaceuticals production startup. Project goal: to improve health care and living standards.	1) 90,000 doses a year 2) $0.9 million/7 years 3) L 4) BP	FGUP Russian State Scientific Center Nuclear Reactors Science and Research Institute Dimitrovgrad, Ulyanovsk Region, 433510 Phone: (84235) 32 727 Fax: (84235) 35 859 E-mail: gns@niiar.ru Aleksei Frolovich Grachev, CEO
MACHINE ENGINEERING AND METAL PROCESSING		
56R003 ● ◆ Startup of production of modern electronic units for the automotive sector. Project goal: to make electronic units for cars.	1) 120,000 pieces a year 2) $2.2 million/3 years 3) L 4) BP	ZAO Iskra 75, pr. Narimanova, Ulyanovsk, Ulyanovsk Region, 432030 Phone/fax: (8422) 34 1644, 34 1642 Fax: (8422) 34 4658 E-mail iskragai@mv.ru; Mark Mikhailovich Lagun, Deputy Chief Engineer

IV

VOLGA FEDERAL DISTRICT

[1] L – Loan, E – Equity, Leas. – Leasing, JV – Joint Venture
[2] BP – Business Plan, FS – Feasibility Study

1	2	3

CONSTRUCTION MATERIALS

56R004 ❖ ◆

Film materials production startup.
Project goal: to produce film materials.

1) 30 million square meters a year
2) $6.9 millionn/5 years
3) JV
4) BP

OOO Stroyplastmass-SP
Poldomasovo, Ulyanovsk District,
Ulyanovsk Region, 433319
Phone/fax: (84254) 22 442
E-mail: spms@rambler.ru
Ravil Khusainovich Nasyrov, CEO

56R005 ❖ ◆

Decorative ceramic tiles
production startup.
Project goal: to make decorative
ceramic tiles.

1) 750,000 square meters a year
2) $4.5 million/5 years
3) JV
4) BP

OOO Stroyplastmass-SP
Poldomasovo, Ulyanovsk District,
Ulyanovsk Region, 433319
Phone/fax: (84254) 22 442
E-mail: spms@rambler.ru
Ravil Khusainovich Nasyrov, CEO

56R006 ❖ ◆

Ceramic construction bricks
production startup.
Project goal: to produce construction
ceramic bricks.

1) 30 million pieces a year
2) $8.2 million/6.5 years
3) JV
4) BP

OOO Stroyplastmass-SP
Poldomasovo, Ulyanovsk District,
Ulyanovsk Region, 433319
Phone/fax: (84254) 22 442
E-mail: spms@rambler.ru
Ravil Khusainovich Nasyrov, CEO

AGRICULTURE

56R007 ● ◆

Buckwheat and sunflower
seeds processing.
Project goal: to increase
existing output.

1) 30,000 tons a year
2) $1.0 million/3 years
3) L
4) BP

OAO Ulyanovskkhleboprodukt
2, ul. Zheleznodorozhnaya,
Ulyanovsk, Ulyanovsk Region,
432063
Phone: (8422) 32 2554, 32 5604
Fax: (8422) 32 2366
Konstantin Sergeevich Zaytsev, CEO

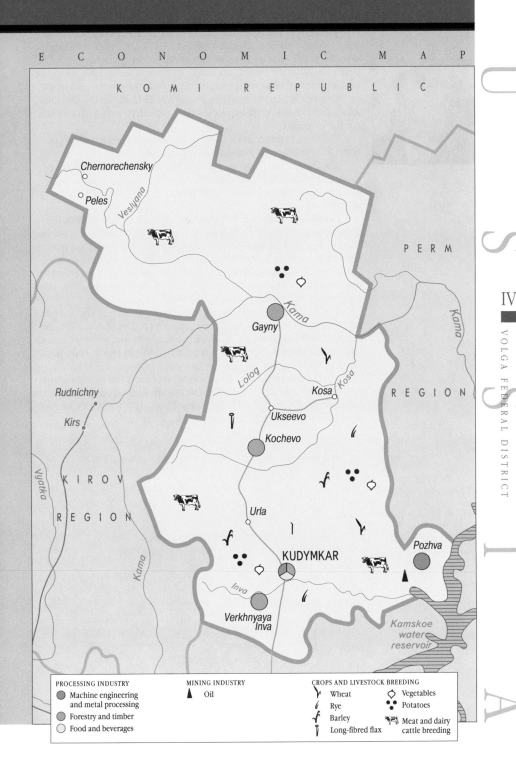

ECONOMIC MAP

KOMI REPUBLIC

PERM

Chernorechensky

Peles

Veslyana

Gayny

Kama

PERM

Kama

Rudnichny

Lolog

Kosa

Kosa

REGION

Kirs

Ukseevo

Kochevo

KIROV

Vyatka

REGION

Urla

Kama

KUDYMKAR

Pozhva

Inva

Verkhnyaya Inva

Kamskoe water reservoir

VOLGA FEDERAL DISTRICT

IV

RUSSIA

PROCESSING INDUSTRY
- ● Machine engineering and metal processing
- ● Forestry and timber
- ○ Food and beverages

MINING INDUSTRY
- ▲ Oil

CROPS AND LIVESTOCK BREEDING
- Ψ Wheat
- ι Rye
- ϟ Barley
- ϒ Long-fibred flax
- ◇ Vegetables
- ⋰ Potatoes
- 🐄 Meat and dairy cattle breeding

Established in 1925, the Komi-Permyatsky Autonomous District was the first of the national autonomous districts created in Russia. It covers an area of approximately 33,000 square kilometers and has a population of more than 135,000 people.

The traditional occupations of the District's inhabitants include timber harvesting, partial timber processing, and agriculture (mostly meat, dairy, potatoes, vegetables, and grain).

The District's 2002 consolidated budget amounted to more than $51 million, or almost twice as much as in 1998 and 1999. Budget and taxation targets were almost 100% accomplished. In what marks another positive development, more than 30% of the District's tax income comes from private businessmen and small and medium enterprises (rising to 53% in Kudymkar, the District's capital).

Despite challenging weather conditions in 2002, the rural community achieved the highest grain harvest in many years. Meat, milk, and dairy output also increased.

The District's timber sector has room for developing deep processing of timber. ZAO Lesinvest has managed to increase output by 160%.

The District also boasts good prospects for natural resource development. According to exploration geologists, the District has deposits of oil, gold, platinum, and diamonds, and considerable reserves of construction and glass-making materials.

Production infrastructure development is one of the District's social and economic development priorities. We believe that accelerating the development of the District is vital to ensuring its investment appeal. At present, new electricity transmission facilities are being built, communications are developing, and roads are being constructed. The District is participating in the Belkomur Inter-Regional Project for the design and construction of the southern sector of the Arkhangelsk – Syktyvkar – Kudymkar – Grigoryevskaya – Perm railway line.

The District is working on broadening its economic and cultural relations with the Perm Region, the Komi Republic, and other regions of Russia. The results of this cooperation are already becoming apparent, with joint economic and cultural projects underway. The District cooperates with other regions in the public health and public welfare spheres.

The District's efforts to create a production infrastructure have already partially paid off. Businesses from the Perm and Saratov Regions, Greece, Austria, and Ireland are setting up production facilities and investing in the District. We encourage this cooperation and are ready to develop it further.

Gennady Savelyev,
HEAD OF THE KOMI-PERMYATSKY AUTONOMOUS DISTRICT ADMINISTRATION

1. GENERAL INFORMATION

1.1. GEOGRAPHY

The Komi-Permyatsky Autonomous District covers a total area of some 32,800 square kilometers. The District lies in the north-east of the Perm Region. To the north, the District borders the Komi Republic, and to the west – the Kirov Region.

1.2. CLIMATE

The Komi-Permyatsky Autonomous District is located within the temperate continental climate zone. Air temperatures in January average −16°C, rising to +17°C in July. Annual precipitation reaches 480–550 mm. The District lies under infertile podzol soils.

1.3. POPULATION

According to preliminary 2002 census results, the District's population was 136,000 people. The average population density is 4.2 people per square kilometer. The economically active population is 65,000 people. Official unemployment stood at 2.7% in 2002, compared with the actual rate of 14.9%.

Demographically speaking, some 58% are of statutory working age, 23% are below the statutory working age, and 19% are beyond the statutory working age. The District's ethnic mix is 60% Komi-Permyak, 36% Russian, and 4% other ethnic groups.

The Komi-Permyatsky Autonomous District's major urban center is Kudymkar with 34,300 inhabitants.

Population							TABLE 1
	1992	1997	1998	1999	2000	2001	2002
Total population, '000	159	154	152	151	150	149	136
Economically active population, '000	75	57	60	71	66	63	65

2. ADMINISTRATION

33, ul. 50 Let Oktyabrya, Kudymkar, Komi-Permyatsky Autonomous District, 619000
Fax: (34260) 42 128; e-mail: kpao_adm1@permonline.ru

NAME	POSITION	CONTACT INFORMATION
Gennady Petrovich SAVELYEV	Head of the Komi-Permyatsky Autonomous District Administration	Phone: (34260) 45 903 Fax: (34260) 45 903
Sergei Leontyevich SIVKOV	Deputy Head of the Komi-Permyatsky Autonomous District Administration for Construction	Phone: (34260) 41 340
Marina Veniaminovna TYUSHEVA	Acting Chairman of the Komi-Permyatsky Autonomous District Administration Economic Committee	Phone: (34260) 41 723
Valentina Dmitrievna KIVILEVA	Head of the Investment Programs and Housing Projects Department of the Komi-Permyatsky Autonomous District Administration Economic Committee	Phone: (34260) 41 172
Vasily Alekseevich SHTEYNIKOV	Head of the Komi-Permyatsky Autonomous District Administration Department of Architecture, Construction, Transport, and Communications	Phone: (34260) 41 145

3. ECONOMIC POTENTIAL

3.1. 1997–2002
GROSS REGIONAL
PRODUCT (GRP).
INDUSTRY BREAKDOWN

The Komi-Permyatsky Autonomous District's 2002 gross regional product reached $91.9 million, 102.4% of the 2001 level (in comparable prices).

The leading industries are forestry and agriculture. These industries produce over 40% of GRP and employ around 30% of the economically active population.

3.2. MAJOR ECONOMIC
GROWTH PROJECTIONS

for 2002–2006 are set forth in the Social and Economic Development Program of the Komi-

IV

VOLGA FEDERAL DISTRICT

GRP trends in 1997–2002						TABLE 2
	1997	1998	1999	2000	2001*	2002*
GRP in current prices, $ million	n/a	n/a	62.9	71.7	83.7	91.9

*Estimates of the Komi-Permyatsky Autonomous District Administration

GRP industry breakdown in 1997–2002, % of total						TABLE 3
	1997	1998	1999	2000	2001*	2002*
GRP	n/a	n/a	100.0	100.0	100.0	100.0
Industry	n/a	n/a	16.8	17.0	18.7	17.8
Agriculture and forestry	n/a	n/a	42.5	41.6	40.3	40.1
Construction	n/a	n/a	5.1	4.8	4.6	5.0
Transport and communications	n/a	n/a	2.6	2.1	1.8	1.9
Trade and public catering	n/a	n/a	4.2	4.5	4.8	5.0
Other	n/a	n/a	23.5	24.4	28.1	28.3
Net taxes on output	n/a	n/a	5.3	5.6	1.7	1.9

*Estimates of the Komi-Permyatsky Autonomous District Administration

Permyatsky Autonomous District. The social and economic development program aims to:

- Diversify the timber industry;
- Increase furniture output;
- Establish industrial facilities for producing potato-derived alcohol and semi-finished foods;
- Establish enterprises (production units) for processing mushrooms and berries;
- Restore and revamp machine engineering capacities;
- Develop recreation and tourism;
- Construct new industrial infrastructure facilities;
- Increase allocations of funds to culture, scientific research, education, healthcare, and housing.

3.3. INDUSTRIAL OUTPUT IN 1997–2002 FOR MAJOR SECTORS OF ECONOMY

The leading industries of the Komi-Permyatsky Autonomous District are forestry, timber, and food and beverages, which account for 83.6% of the District's overall industrial production.

Forestry, timber, and pulp and paper. The sector accounts for 51.8% of total industrial output. Timber producing facilities include twelve forestry enterprises, one timber, and one forest rafting enterprise. The timber industry is represented by sawmills, timber processing, and construction materials production. The District processes 10% of the timber it produces.

The most prominent producers of sawn timber are ZAO Lesinvest and OAO Invenskoye KLSP, as their share in the District's timber sawing is 53%. The wood-processing sector is represented by OAO Kudymkar Furniture Factory, whith produces furniture, window and door frames, and sawn timber.

Food and beverages. The food industry's share of total GRP is 31.8%. Food processing is mainly concentrated in the District's capital – Kudymkar. The bulk of

Industry breakdown of industrial output in 1997–2002, % of total						TABLE 4
	1997	1998	1999	2000	2001	2002*
Industry	100.0	100.0	100.0	100.0	100.0	100.0
Forestry, timber, and pulp and paper	51.8	50.5	48.5	51.3	49.0	51.8
Food and beverages	26.6	33.7	32.7	25.5	26.7	31.8
Machine engineering and metal processing	10.4	3.5	2.8	4.1	6.2	7.0
Energy	9.7	8.1	7.1	6.5	7.6	6.2
Fuel	–	3.5	7.6	11.5	9.0	1.8
Printing	0.6	0.6	0.6	0.5	0.5	0.6
Light industry	–	–	–	0.1	0.4	0.6
Construction materials	0.9	0.7	0.7	0.5	0.5	0.2

*Estimates of the Komi-Permyatsky Autonomous District Administration

local output (meat processing, dairy, bakeries, fruit and vegetable processing) is consumed within the District.

Agriculture. Agriculture is dominated by cattle breeding, mainly meat-and-dairy, with more than 50% exported outside the District for processing.

Flax, rye, oats, barley, soft wheat, potatoes, and vegetables are cultivated in the District.

3.4. FUEL AND ENERGY BALANCE (OUTPUT AND CONSUMPTION PER RESOURCE)

Energy is supplied to the Komi-Permyatsky Autonomous District from the Perm energy system via local company Northern Electricity Networks (an OAO Permenergo company). Heat energy for industrial and public utilities is supplied by decentralized lower capacity facilities fired by wood, coal, and fuel oil. The District is supplied with liquefied gas from gas-filling plants in Perm.

3.5. TRANSPORT INFRASTRUCTURE

The Komi-Permyatsky Autonomous District is located at some distance from the major transport routes. Mendeleevo, the nearest railroad station to Kudymkar, is about 100 kilometers away.

Roads. The Komi-Permyatsky Autonomous District has about 5,000 kilometers of roads, some 1,400 kilometers of which are paved. Road transport is the only regular, year-round form of passenger and freight transportation.

Waterways. The Kama River flows through the north and part of the south-east of the District. The Komi-Permyatsky Autonomous District has some 300 kilometers of navigable inland waterways.

3.6. MAIN NATURAL RESOURCES: RESERVES AND EXTRACTION IN 2002

The District's natural resources include 133 deposits of minerals. These include deposits of construction materials (clay, sandy gravel), agricultural minerals (peat, marl, limestone), fuel and chemicals (peat, oil, natural gas), and hydromineral (underground water) raw materials. The District is also home to several small deposits of ore (iron, titanium, zirconium, copper, gold) and other minerals (mineral pigments, building limestone, cementing materials, glass sands). Platinum and diamond deposits have been explored.

Oil. The District has three minor explored oil fields (the Maykorskoye, Romanshorskoye, and Tukachevskoye). The only oil field in operation is the Maykorskoye field. The District's oil reserves are estimated to total some 30–70 million tons.

Forest resources. The District has considerable forest reserves totaling some 344 million cubic meters, of which 164 million cubic meters are usable.

Biosphere resources. The population of elk, brown bear, hare, squirrel, marten, and fox in the District's forests is on average higher than in other regions of Russia. The District is also home to woodgrouse, heathbird, partridge, geese, and duck. The District's considerable biosphere resources offer good potential for the development of licensed hunting, including foreign hunting tourism.

IV

VOLGA FEDERAL DISTRICT

4. TRADE OPPORTUNITIES

4.1. MAIN GOODS PRODUCED IN THE REGION

Forest, timber, pulp and paper. The District produced some 685,000 cubic meters of industrial timber in 2002, and 50,000 cubic meters of sawn timber.

Food and beverages. 2002 meat production was 1,800 tons, sausage – 1,200 tons, milk – 2,200 tons, butter – 700 tons, and non-alcoholic beverages – 141,000 decaliters.

Agricultural products. 2002 agricultural output (from all types of farms) was 45,500 tons of grain, 121,200 tons of potatoes, and 39,500 tons of vegetables.

4.2. EXPORTS, INCLUDING EXTRA-CIS

Owing to the specific nature of industrial production in the Komi-Permyatsky Autonomous District, export activities are mainly carried out by ZAO Lesinvest (a subsidiary of Greek company Gekkar Investments Limited). The District's principal export is sawn timber. 2001 exports of sawn timber amounted to 9,100 cubic meters, and in 2002 – 16,000 cubic meters. The District's main trading partners are Greece, Italy, Germany and Turkey.

Major regional export and import entities		*TABLE 5*
ENTITY	ADDRESS	PHONE, FAX, E-MAIL
ZAO Lesinvest	5, ul. Promyshlennaya, Kudymkar, 619000	Phone: (34260) 51 558 Fax: (34260) 51 796 E-mail: lesinvest@permonline.ru

5. INVESTMENT OPPORTUNITIES

5.1 INVESTMENTS IN 1992–2002 (BY INDUSTRY SECTOR), INCLUDING FOREIGN INVESTMENTS

The main factors contributing to the investment appeal of the Komi-Permyatsky Autonomous District are:

- Its natural resources: hydrocarbons and forests (potential for the development of wood-based chemical production and industrial harvesting of medicinal substances);
- High unemployment in the working age population;
- Favorable conditions for the development of tourism, including adventure sports: rich flora and fauna, national parks, historic cultural monuments, and clean environment.

5.2. CAPITAL INVESTMENT

Fixed capital investments amounted to $9.9 million in 2002, 8.8% up on the 2001 level.

The Komi-Permyatsky Autonomous District received a total of $0.2 million in foreign investments in 2002 for the development of ZAO Lesinvest.

5.3. MAJOR ENTERPRISES (INCLUDING ENTERPRISES WITH FOREIGN INVESTMENT)

ZAO Lesinvest is the largest wholly foreign-owned enterprise.

Capital investment by industry sector, $ million — TABLE 6

	1997	1998	1999	2000	2001	2002
Total investments	13.7	8.2	5.9	9.3	9.1	9.9
Including major industries (% of total)						
Industry	47.9	30.9	32.4	10.5	9.1	15.2
Agriculture and forestry	8.4	5.3	4.4	4.8	8.2	5.8
Construction	11.9	23.0	42.7	33.5	20.3	35.1
Transport and communications	2.9	15.0	1.2	17.1	4.1	10.8
Trade and public catering	0.4	0.4	0.5	6.9	1.8	0.5
Other	28.5	25.4	18.8	27.2	56.5	32.6

Foreign investment trends in 1997–2002 — TABLE 7

	1997	1998	1999	2000	2001	2002
Foreign investment, $ million	–	–	1.7	0.7	0.8	0.2

Largest enterprises of the Komi-Permyatsky Autonomous District — TABLE 8

COMPANY	SECTOR	2001 NET PROFIT, $ MILLION*
OAO Gainyles	Forestry and timber	0.08
OAO Kochevoles	Forestry and timber	0.09
OAO Myasokombinat	Food and beverages (meat)	0.11
OAO Moloko	Food and beverages (milk)	0.04
OAO Pozhvinsky Machine Engineering Plant	Machine engineering	0.08

*Data of the Komi-Permyatsky Autonomous District Administration

5.4. MOST ATTRACTIVE SECTORS FOR INVESTMENT

According to the Komi-Permyatsky Autonomous District Administration, forestry and timber are the most attractive industries for investment.

5.5. CURRENT LEGISLATION ON INVESTOR TAX EXEMPTIONS AND PRIVILEGES

The Autonomous District enacted a Law On Foreign Investments in the Komi-Permyatsky Autonomous District in 2000. The Law provides for the following exemptions from regional tax components for foreign investors and partially foreign owned enterprises:

- Additional tax and fiscal exemptions;
- A tax credit for investments;
- Allocations from the Komi-Permyatsky Autonomous District's budget for the financing of targeted investment programs involving foreign investors.

5.6. FEDERAL AND REGIONAL ECONOMIC AND SOCIAL DEVELOPMENT PROGRAMS FOR THE KOMI-PERMYATSKY AUTONOMOUS DISTRICT

Federal targeted programs. The Komi-Permyatsky Autonomous District implements a number of federal targeted programs, including the following major programs: State Housing Certificates; Revival, Construction, Revamping and Restoration of Historic Towns and Urban Centers of Russia; and Children of Russia.

Regional programs. The Komi-Permyatsky Autonomous District Administration has drafted a regional program for social and economic development in 2002–2006. The program aims to overcome the crisis in industrial production and the social sphere and create condition conducive to a gradual transition to a market system.

The program's chief goals are to:
• Increase output based on the District's own industrial potential and natural resources;

• Raise the efficiency of the District's economy through industry conversion and reconstruction, the introduction of advanced technologies, and the improvement of output quality;
• Diversify the structure of industrial output;
• Focus on social issues and improving working conditions and living standards;
• Develop industrial infrastructure, with a specific focus on transport.

A total of $290.5 million has been allocated to finance the program, including some $98.9 million from the federal budget, $41.1 million from the development budget of the Russian Federation, $63 million from private enterprise, and $87.6 million from other sources.

The Komi-Permyatsky Autonomous District is also implementing regional programs focused on healthcare, public welfare, education, environmental protection, and law enforcement.

6. INVESTMENT PROJECTS

Industry sector and project description	1) Expected results 2) Amount and term of investment 3) Form of financing[1] 4) Documentation[2]	Contact information
1	2	3
FORESTRY, TIMBER, AND PULP AND PAPER		
57R001 ■ ● ★ ◆ ▲		
Construction of a new plant to produce large-format finished birch plywood and glued timber products. Project goal: to produce high-quality timber goods.	1) Production of 60,000 cubic meters of large-format plywood and 30,000 cubic meters of glued timber products per year (sales of $63.7 million per year) 2) $67.2 million/n/a 3) E, L, Leas. 4) FS, BP	Sergei Leontyevich Sivkov, Deputy Head of the Komi-Permyatsky Autonomous District Administration Phone: (34260) 41 340
57R002 ■ ● ★ ◆ ▲		
Construction of a plant to produce glued items and templates from solid timber. Project goal: to produce high-quality timber goods.	1) Production of 30,000 cubic meters of glued timber per year 2) $16.4 million/n/a 3) E, L, Leas. 4) FS, BP	Sergei Leontyevich Sivkov, Deputy Head of the Komi-Permyatsky Autonomous District Administration Phone: (34260) 41 340
57R003 ■ ● ★ ◆ ▲		
Construction of a plant to produce glued block board and solid square log, planks, and other timber materials (in Gayny). Project goal: to produce high-quality timber goods.	1) Production of 60,000 cubic meters of timber products per year 2) $24.7 million/n/a 3) E, L, Leas. 4) FS, BP	Sergei Leontyevich Sivkov, Deputy Head of the Komi-Permyatsky Autonomous District Administration Phone: (34260) 41 340

[1] L – Loan, E – Equity, Leas. – Leasing, JV – Joint Venture
[2] BP – Business Plan, FS – Feasibility Study

IV

V. URALS FEDERAL DISTRICT

58. Kurgan Region [45]

59. Sverdlovsk Region [66]

60. Tyumen Region [72]

61. Chelyabinsk Region [74]

62. Khanty-Mansiysky Autonomous

District – Yugra [86]

63. Yamalo-Nenetsky

Autonomous District [89]

REGIONS OF THE URALS FEDERAL DISTRICT

URALS FEDERAL DISTRICT

V

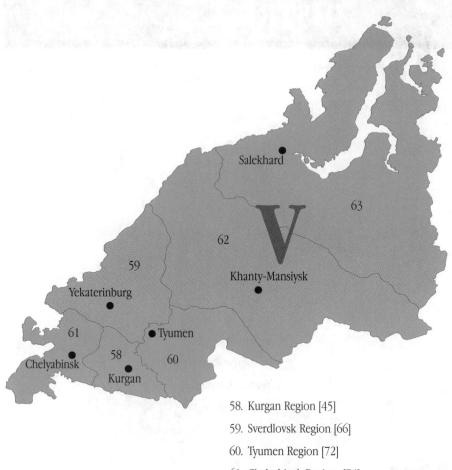

58. Kurgan Region [45]

59. Sverdlovsk Region [66]

60. Tyumen Region [72]

61. Chelyabinsk Region [74]

62. Khanty-Mansiysky Autonomous
    District – Yugra [86]

63. Yamalo-Nenetsky
    Autonomous District [89]

R U S S I A

URALS FEDERAL DISTRICT

E C O N O M I C   M A P

Tavda

Tobol

Nitsa

Irbit

Tura

SVERDLOVSK

REGION

TYUMEN

TYUMEN

REGION

Pyshma

Kamyshlov

Iset

Kataysk

Dalmatovo

Uldus

Shadrinsk

Makushino

KURGAN

Lebyazhye

Miass

Petukhovo

Shumikha

Kurtamysh

Tobol

Ishim

Ubagan

Uy

K A Z A K H S T A N

Kostanay

PROCESSING INDUSTRY	MINING INDUSTRY	CROPS AND LIVESTOCK BREEDING	
● Machine engineering and metal processing	◉ Uranium ores	Ƴ Wheat	Meat and dairy cattle breeding
● Chemicals and petrochemicals	⊞ Peat	❊ Buckwheat	Pig breeding
○ Food and beverages	● Mineral water sources	◊ Corn	Poultry farming
	POWER PLANTS		
	⚡ Thermal power plants	⚕ Resorts	

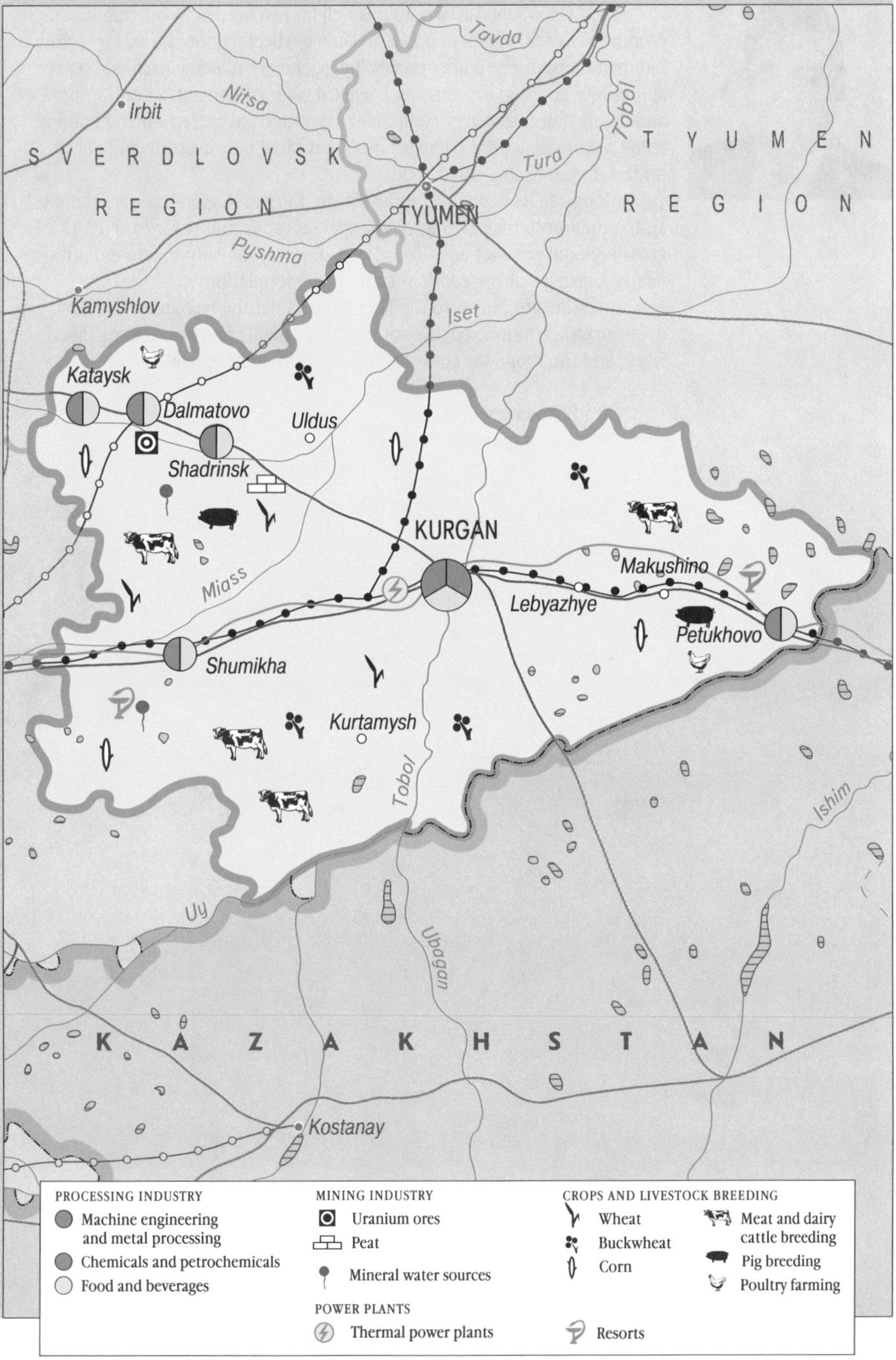

I n 2003, the Kurgan Region marked its 60th anniversary. Since its establishment in 1943, the Kurgan Region has become an industrially and agriculturally advanced and socially and politically stable region.

The arrival of the Siberian railroad, which linked Kurgan to Central Russia at the end of the 19th century, encouraged economic development and the establishment of industrial enterprises in the Region. Since then, the Kurgan Region has been known as the "Gateway to Siberia". The Region borders the Urals industrial regions of Sverdlovsk, Chelyabinsk, and Tyumen, plus Kazakhstan. This facilitates the development of internal and cross-regional relations and ensures access to Urals metals, Siberian oil and gas, Siberian and Kazakh coal, and other mineral resources.

The Region's industrial output is well known outside its borders. It comprises more than 5,000 types of goods, including wheel tractors, buses, tar spreaders, bitumen transporters, timber processing machinery, milking machines, pumps, automotive and ship instruments, chemical plant equipment, air purification and drying units, ozonizers, equipment for oil and gas extraction and refining, metal assemblies for the construction of industrial infrastructure and railway bridges, furniture, and other goods.

Alongside its developed industry, the Kurgan Region has considerable agricultural potential. The agroindustrial sector accounts for over 19.4% of gross regional product and 70% of consumer goods output, and employs nearly a quarter of the economically active population.

Investors are drawn to the Region by its natural resources, favorable production and economic conditions, readily available and low-cost qualified labor, and the scope for conversion of industrial enterprises.

Oleg Bogomolov,
GOVERNOR OF THE KURGAN REGION

1. GENERAL INFORMATION

1.1. GEOGRAPHY

The Kurgan Region covers a total area of 71,500 square kilometers. The Region is located on the border of the Urals and Siberia in the south-eastern part of the West Siberian plain. To the north and north-west, the Kurgan Region borders the Sverdlovsk Region, to the west and south-west – the Chelyabinsk Region, to the south and south-east – Kazakhstan, and to the east and north-east – the Tyumen Region.

1.2. CLIMATE

The Kurgan Region lies in the severe continental climate zone.

Air temperatures in January average –18°C, rising to +19°C in July. Average annual precipitation reaches 300–400 mm.

1.3. POPULATION

According to preliminary 2002 census results, the Kurgan Region's population totaled 1,020,000 people. The average population density is 14.3 people per square kilometer. The economically active population amounts to 503,000 people. Official unemployment stood at 12.5% in 2002.

Demographically speaking, some 59.4% of total population are of statutory working age, 19.5% are below the statutory working age, and 21.1% are beyond the statutory working age.

As of 2002, the Kurgan Region's major urban centers were Kurgan with 345,700 inhabitants and Shadrinsk with 102,000 inhabitants.

Population								_TABLE 1_
	1992	1997	1998	1999	2000	2001	2002
Total population, '000	1,114	1,106	1,104	1,102	1,096	1,087	1,020
Economically active population, '000	535	489	491	541	529	494	503

2. ADMINISTRATION

56, ul. Gogolya, Kurgan, Kurgan Region, 640024. Phone: (3522) 41 7033, fax: (3522) 41 7132
E-mail: adm044@admobl.kurgan.ru; http://www.admobl.kurgan.ru

NAME	POSITION	CONTACT INFORMATION
Oleg Alexeevich BOGOMOLOV	Governor of the Kurgan Region	Phone: (3522) 41 7033 Fax: (3522) 41 7132
Alexander Ivanovich BUKHTOYAROV	First Deputy Governor of the Kurgan Region	Phone: (3522) 41 7189 Fax: (3522) 41 7132
Nikolai Pavlovich LOGINOV	First Deputy Governor of the Kurgan Region, Director of the Agriculture and Food Department	Phone: (3522) 43 3265
Nikolai Ivanovich BOLTNEV	Deputy Governor of the Kurgan Region, Director of the Economic Development and Investment Department	Phone: (3522) 46 2321 Fax: (3522) 46 6052 E-mail: adm044@admobl.kurgan.ru
Ivan Petrovich YEVGENOV	Deputy Governor of the Kurgan Region, Director of the State Property and Industry Department	Phone: (3522) 41 7717
Valery Vladimirovich MIRONOV	Deputy Governor of the Kurgan Region, Director of the Construction, State Examination, Housing and Communal Services Department	Phone: (3522) 41 7345
Tatyana Filippovna TARASOVA	Head of the Investment and Targeted Programs Division of the Economic Development and Investment Department of the Kurgan Region	Phone: (3522) 46 2807 Fax: (3522) 46 6052 E-mail: adm044@admobl.kurgan.ru

URALS FEDERAL DISTRICT

V

3. ECONOMIC POTENTIAL

3.1. 1997–2002 GROSS REGIONAL PRODUCT (GRP). INDUSTRY BREAKDOWN

The Kurgan Region's 2002 gross regional product totaled $1,020 million, up 17.8% on 2001. Per capita GRP in 2001 was $797, rising in 2002 to $1,000.

3.2. MAJOR ECONOMIC GROWTH PROJECTIONS

The Program for the Economic and Social Development of the Kurgan Region for 2003 sets the key priorities for the Region's economic development for the coming years.

GRP trends in 1997–2002						TABLE 2
	1997	1998	1999	2000	2001*	2002*
GRP in current prices, $ million	1,546	999	621	709	866	1,020

*Estimates of the Kurgan Regional Administration

GRP industry breakdown in 1997–2002, % of total						TABLE 3
	1997	1998	1999	2000	2001*	2002*
GRP	100.0	100.0	100.0	100.0	100.0	100.0
Industry	28.0	31.7	30.8	28.8	29.8	29.0
Agriculture and forestry	20.2	6.0	17.3	14.6	19.4	16.7
Construction	6.4	5.5	3.9	4.0	3.8	4.3
Transport and communications	8.2	11.2	9.6	13.1	10.6	n/a
Trade and public catering	7.9	12.8	12.9	14.3	12.5	n/a
Other	29.3	32.8	25.5	25.2	23.9	n/a

*Estimates of the Kurgan Regional Administration

Industry: restructuring and reforming companies, increasing industrial output, expanding markets, and supporting and fostering companies producing competitive products;

Agriculture: creating the Region's own raw materials base, increasing agricultural product sales, implementing new technologies, bringing new products to markets, developing livestock breeding;

Trade: developing trade relations with other regions of Russia, the CIS, and non-CIS countries.

3.3. INDUSTRIAL OUTPUT IN 1997–2002 FOR MAJOR SECTORS OF ECONOMY

The Kurgan Region's leading industries are machine engineering and metals, energy, and food and beverages. These sectors account for a combined 83.1% of the Region's industrial output.

Industry breakdown of industrial output in 1997–2002, % of total						TABLE 4
	1997	1998	1999	2000	2001	2002*
Industry	100.0	100.0	100.0	100.0	100.0	100.0
Machine engineering and metal processing	42.8	42.6	47.0	47.6	45.2	45.7
Energy	23.0	25.7	18.6	18.2	23.8	26.4
Food and beverages	14.4	12.5	13.9	12.6	12.6	11.0
Chemicals and petrochemicals	7.7	9.2	11.7	13.9	9.1	6.9
Flour, cereals, and mixed fodder	2.3	2.2	2.9	2.5	3.7	4.6
Construction materials	3.0	2.7	1.8	1.8	1.9	1.8
Ferrous metals	0.5	0.5	0.7	0.7	1.1	0.9
Forest, timber, and pulp and paper	1.8	1.1	0.9	0.8	0.8	0.9
Light industry	1.7	1.2	0.8	0.6	0.6	0.4

*Estimates of the Kurgan Regional Administration

Machine engineering and metal processing. Major companies include OAO Kurganmash-zavod, OAO Ikar, OAO Kurgankhimmash, OAO Shadrinsk Automotive Machine Plant, and ZAO Kurganstalmost. The sector manufactures buses, wheeled haulers, auto and ship building units, air purification and drying plants, ozonizing equipment, and oil and gas extraction equipment.

Energy. The Kurganskaya Thermal Power Station (480 MW capacity) produces electricity for the Region.

Food and beverages. OAO Shadrinsk Canned Dairy Plant is the largest food and beverages company in the Kurgan Region.

Agriculture. The sector is mainly focused on tillage (winter and spring wheat, buckwheat, millet, corn) and meat and dairy products.

3.4. FUEL AND ENERGY BALANCE (OUTPUT AND CONSUMPTION PER RESOURCES)

The Kurgan Region is an energy deficient region. Its own power generation facilities meet only 30% of the Region's total energy needs. The deficit is met with energy purchased from the Federal Wholesale Energy and Power Market (FOREM). The Region imports all of its oil and gas consumption.

3.5. TRANSPORT INFRASTRUCTURE

Roads. The Kurgan Region has 7,313 kilometers of paved public highway. The Region has highway links to the neighboring regions and Kazakhstan.

Railroads. The Region has 745 kilometers of railroad. The Trans-Siberian railroad passes through the Region. In 2002, some 1,664,400 tons of freight was transported by railroad.

Oil and gas pipelines. The Kurgan Region is crossed by five oil pipelines and two gas pipelines with a total length of over 3,000 km.

3.6. MAIN NATURAL RESOURCES: RESERVES AND EXTRACTION IN 2002

The Kurgan Region's key natural resources include uranium, iron, tungsten and molybdenum ores, non-ore raw materials for construction, bentonite clays, peat, and mineral water.

Minerals and raw materials. The Kurgan Region is home to significant deposits of uranium-bearing ores (the Kurgan Region is one of Russia's leading uranium producers). The Region has iron ore fields (reserves of 2,560 million tons), tungsten and molybdenum deposits, alluvial titanium (reserves of 67,000 tons), and zirconium (reserves of 2,000 tons). The Region's rare bentonite clay reserves (27 million tons) account for one third of Russia's total reserves. The Region may also have hydrocarbon deposits.

Construction materials. The Region has fields of construction materials, including clays, sands, mineral dyes, gypsum and limestone.

Peat deposits. The Region's peat reserves total 17.7 million tons. Peat production in 2002 totaled 1,000 tons.

Water resources. The Region has over 2,500 lakes, one quarter of which contain mineralized water. The Kurgan Region's mineral water output in 2002 amounted to 64,000 cubic meters. Curative mud deposits in the Region total 17.5 million cubic meters. 2002 output was 5,000 cubic meters.

Land resources. The Kurgan Region has a total land area of 7.1 million hectares, including 4.5 million hectares (63%) of agricultural lands and 1.8 million hectares (25%) of forests.

Forest resources. The total area covered with forest is 1,766,000 hectares, including coniferous – 363,000 hectares.

Recreational resources. The Kurgan Region has a number of resorts and children's sanatoriums.

URALS FEDERAL DISTRICT

V

Fuel and energy sector production and consumption trends, 1997–2002						*TABLE 5*
	1997	1998	1999	2000	2001	2002*
Electricity output, billion kWh	1.2	1.1	0.9	1.2	1.2	1.3
Electricity consumption, billion kWh	4.6	4.6	4.6	4.8	4.5	4.4
Natural gas consumption, million cubic meters	912.0	814.1	795.0	848.5	899.7	964.7

*Estimates of the Kurgan Regional Administration

4. TRADE OPPORTUNITIES

4.1. MAIN GOODS PRODUCED IN THE REGION

Machine engineering and metal processing. In 2002, the Region produced 531 timber processing machine tools, 25,400 pumps, 1,300 buses, 31 road construction vehicles and 283 fire fighting vehicles, 25,400 centrifugal, steam, and driven pumps.

Food and beverages. In 2002, the Kurgan Region produced 6,100 tons of meat, 2,000 tons of sausage, 1,500 tons of butter, 44,900 tons of whole milk, 191,800 tons of flour, and 353,000 decaliters of liquors and vodka.

Construction materials. In 2002, the Region produced 73,200 cubic meters of timber, 57,200 cubic meters of lumber, 30.4 million con-

ventional bricks, and 42,400 cubic meters of reinforced concrete constructions and assemblies.

4.2. EXPORTS,
INCLUDING EXTRA-CIS

Exports to extra-CIS countries in 2000 amounted to $70.7 million; exports to CIS countries totaled
$113.2 million. The figures for 2001 were $38.2 million and $75 million, respectively, and for 2002 –
$31.9 million and $42.1 million, respectively.

The main goods exported from the Region are
machine engineering goods and metals (41% of total
exports): spare parts and equipment for cars ($3.2
million); cranes, valves and reinforced assemblies for
oil and gas sector ($2.3 million); tractors, cars and
trucks ($364,800); lumber ($1.3 million); food and
food feedstock ($855,800); centrifugal pumps, coal,
paper and plywood. The major importers of the
Region's goods are Kazakhstan (49% of total exports), Germany (14%), Iran (13%), Uzbekistan
(2%), and Ukraine (2%).

4.3. IMPORTS,
INCLUDING EXTRA-CIS

Imports from extra-CIS countries in 2000
reached $23.4 million; imports from the CIS totaled
$44.7 million. In 2001, the figures were, $18.8 million and $31.4 million respectively, in 2002 – $16.8
million and $14.8 million.

The Region's main imports include: pharmaceuticals ($6.5 million), rolled carbon steel ($3.4 million),
black coal ($2 million), food and food feedstock ($3.5
million), and machine engineering goods ($287,400).
Major exporters to the Kurgan Region include Kazakhstan (39% of total imports), Germany (17%), Spain
(9%), Italy (7%), the Czech Republic (4%), Sweden (4%),
Ukraine (4%), Uzbe-kistan (3%), and China (3%).

4.4. MAJOR REGIONAL
EXPORT AND IMPORT ENTITIES

Due to the specific features of exports and imports
in the Kurgan Region, export and import transactions
are mainly carried out by industrial enterprises.

5. INVESTMENT OPPORTUNITIES

5.1. INVESTMENTS
IN 1992–2002 (BY INDUSTRY
SECTOR), INCLUDING
FOREIGN INVESTMENTS

The following factors determine the investment
appeal of the Kurgan Region:

- Its good geographic location;
- Its developed transport infrastructure;
- Legislation supporting investment activities
(guarantees for investor rights, preferential tax
treatment for investors);
- Its qualified and cheap workforce;

- Cheap sources of energy;
- Significant natural resources.

5.2. CAPITAL INVESTMENT

Industry (machine engineering and metals),
transport and communications, agriculture and
forestry account for the lion's share of capital investment in the Region.

5.3. MAJOR ENTERPRISES
(INCLUDING ENTERPRISES
WITH FOREIGN INVESTMENT)

The Kurgan Region hosts numerous companies with foreign investment. Major companies

Capital investment by industry sector, $ million						TABLE 6
	1997	1998	1999	2000	2001	2002
Total capital investment	213.9	120.6	65.3	89.7	91.7	77.0
Including major industries (% of total)						
Industry	21.2	22.3	25.0	31.2	30.0	25.6
Agriculture and forestry	7.6	13.5	13.7	12.6	12.5	11.4
Construction	0.9	0.9	0.6	0.5	1.8	3.3
Transport and communications	33.4	30.5	31.7	29.3	25.0	30.6
Trade and public catering	0.3	0.5	1.9	2.6	1.2	0.7
Other	36.6	32.3	27.1	23.8	29.5	28.4

Foreign investment trends in 1997–2002						TABLE 7
	1997	1998	1999	2000	2001	2002
Foreign investment, $ million	–	0.9	0.2	0.6	0.9	0.3
Including FDI, $ million	–	0.9	–	–	0.6	–

include OOO Selena (Russian-Chinese), OOO Tavria (Russian-Ukrainian), ZAO Kodru (Russian-Moldovan), OOO Unita (Russian-Italian), OOO Tobol (Russian-Kazakh), OAO Spring (Russian-Polish), OOO Lito (Russian-Uzbek), and OOO Eurocenter (Russian-Czech).

5.4. MOST ATTRACTIVE SECTORS FOR INVESTMENT

According to the Kurgan Regional Administration, the following sectors offer the greatest investment appeal:

• Machine engineering and metals (stop valves and equipment for the oil and gas

Largest enterprises of the Kurgan Region	TABLE 8
COMPANY	SECTOR
OAO Kurganmashzavod	Machine engineering
OAO Ikar	Machine engineering
OAO Kurgankhimmash	Machine engineering
OAO Shadrinsk Automotive Unit Plant	Machine engineering
ZAO Kurganstalmost	Metal processing
OAO AKO Sintez	Chemicals and pharmaceuticals

industries of the Tyumen Region, spare parts and equipment for Russia's automotive industry, metal bridge assemblies);

• Chemicals and pharmaceuticals;

• Light manufacturing (wool and linen fabric spinning using local raw wool and flax);

• Agriculture (development of high quality bread grain production and livestock breeding, creation of agricultural companies for the production, procurement, processing, storage and sale of agricultural products and food, development of agriculture machinery maintenance infrastructure).

5.5. CURRENT LEGISLATION ON INVESTOR TAX EXEMPTIONS AND PRIVILEGES

The Kurgan Region has passed a number of laws aimed at fostering investment activities, including:

• The Law On Investment Activity in the Kurgan Region, which sets forth key principles governing investment activities and regulates issues related to investors' rights and the tax exemptions and privileges granted to investors;

• The Law On Investment Tax Credits, which establishes the terms and conditions of tax credit granted to entities implementing investment projects;

• The Law On the Development Budget of the Kurgan Region, which provides for financing on a tender basis of efficient investment projects;

• The Law On Local Economic Development Zones in the Kurgan Region, which establishes the terms of investor eligibility for tax exemptions and benefits.

Regional entities responsible for raising inestment		TABLE 9
ENTITY	ADDRESS	PHONE, FAX, E-MAIL
OAO Center for Business Cooperation	Office 306, 54, ul. Tobolnaya, Kurgan, Kurgan Region, 640020	Phone: (3522) 48 1161, 42 1261 Phone/fax: (3522) 46 6052 E-mail: cbc@list.ru

5.6. FEDERAL AND REGIONAL ECONOMIC AND SOCIAL DEVELOPMENT PROGRAMS FOR THE KURGAN REGION

The federal targeted programs. The Kurgan Region is participating in 29 federal targeted programs with a total budget of $20.8 million. The Region implements programs of social and economic development for the Kurgan Region, including The Program for the Elimination of Inequalities in the Social and Economic Development of the Regions of the Russian Federation, 2002–2010 and through 2015, Social

Support to the Disabled, 2000–2005, The Elderly, 2002–2004, and others.

Regional programs. The Kurgan Regional Administration is implementing 38 regional targeted programs focused on industry, agriculture, and public welfare, including: The Program for the Development of Pig Livestock Breeding, 2003–2005, The Program for the Development of Poultry Farming in the Kurgan Region, 2002–2005, Energy Conservation in the city of Kurgan, 2002–2005, The Program for the Development of the Education System in the Kurgan Region, 2002–2004, and others. These programs have a total budget of $14.1 million.

6. INVESTMENT PROJECTS

Industry sector and project description	1) Expected results 2) Amount and term of investment 3) Form of financing[1] 4) Documentation[2]	Contact information
1	2	3

| | ENERGY | |

58R001	● ❖ ▲	OAO Sintez
Construction of a thermal power station on the basis of gas turbine units. Project purpose: to increase production of heat and electricity.	1) 380 million kWh of electricity and 644,000 Gcal of heat annually 2) $25 million/2 years 3) L, JV 4) FS	7, pr. Konstitutsii, Kurgan, Kurgan Region, 640614 Phone: (3522) 48 8206, 48 8609 Fax: (3522) 48 8690 E-mail: market@kurgansintez.ru Viktor Georgievich Pshenichnikov, CEO
58R002	● ◆	GUP Lion Zayralyiya
Construction and launching of a gas turbine unit. Project purpose: to provide electricity for GUP Lyon Zauralya and local industrial enterprises.	1) Net profit of $0.4 million annually 2) $1 million/1 year 3) L ($0.3 million) 4) BP	33, ul. Promyshlennaya, Kurgan, Kurgan Region, 640014 Phone: (3522) 56 0998 Fax: (3522) 56 3698 E-mail: yunona10@mail.ru Anatoly Dmitrievich Sladkoshtiyev, Director

| | MACHINE ENGINEERING AND METAL PROCESSING | |

58R003	● ◆	ZAO Kataisk Pump Plant
Technical upgrade of the company. Project purpose: to increase product range.	1) 42,000 items annually 2) $3.6 million/n/a 3) L ($1.2 million) 4) BP	1, ul. Matrosova, Kataisk, Kurgan Region, 641700 Phone: (35251) 91 471, 95 392 Fax: (35251) 92 473 E-mail: knz@kataisk.zaural.ru Vyacheslav Mikhailovich Kokoteyev, CEO
58R004	● ◆	FGUP PPSO Vargashi Plant
Reconstruction of fire-fighting equipment (fire-fighting vehicles). Project purpose: to reduce production costs and improve product quality.	1) Output $6.9 million/ 320 fire-fighting vehicles 2) $2.2 million/1 year 3) L ($0.3 million) 4) BP	83, ul. Kirova, Vargashi, Kurgan Region, 641230 Phone: (35233) 91 009 Fax: (35233) 91 526 E-mail: plamya@kurgan.isp.ru Vladimir Nikolaevich Kozakov, Director

| | CONSTRUCTION MATERIALS | |

58R005	● ◆	OOO Borovlyansky Glass Plant
Creation of facilities for heat insulating materials (foamed glass) at the existing company. Project purpose: to increase product range.	1) 10,000 cubic meters annually 2) $1 million/1 year 3) L 4) BP	Glass Plant, Belozersky District, Kurgan Region, 641356 Phone/fax: (3522) 57 8261 E-mail: steklo@zaural.ru Nikolai Vladimirovich Yemelianov, Director

[1] L – Loan, E – Equity, Leas. – Leasing, JV – Joint Venture
[2] BP – Business Plan, FS – Feasibility Study

1	2	3

FOOD AND BEVERAGES

58R006   ■ ● ◆ ▲

Construction of an alcohol plant.
Project purpose: to increase
production of alcohol.

1) 3,000 decaliters daily
2) $6 million/1 year
3) E, L ($5 million)
4) FS, BP

OAO Dalspirt
31, ul. Rukmanisa, Dalmatovo,
Kurgan Region, 641730
Phone: (35252) 32 248
Fax: (35252) 31 379
E-mail: tigran@dalmatovo.ru
Boris Leonidovich Sokolov,
Executive Director

AGRICULTURE

58R007   ● ◆

Production of high quality bread grain
at Kurgan Agriculture Research
Institute model farms.
Project purpose: to increase grain output
and save resources.

1) Gross collection of cash grain
   72,000 tons a year
2) $15.5 million/1 year
3) L
4) BP

GNU Kurgan Agriculture
Research Institute
9, ul. Lenina, Sadovoye village,
Ketovsky District,
Kurgan Region, 641325
Phone/fax: (35231) 22 656
(3522) 43 3363
E-mail: kniish@ketovo.zaural.ru,
yamal@kurgan.isp.ru
Sergei Alexandrovich Pokazanyev,
Director

58R008   ● ◆

Creation of a machine and technology
stations network.
Project purpose: to increase grain output.

1) Gross collection of cash grain
   2.3 million tons a year
2) $151 million/3 years
3) L
4) BP

GNU Kurgan Agriculture
Research Institute
9, ul. Lenina, Sadovoye village,
Ketovsky District,
Kurgan Region, 641325
Phone/fax: (35231) 22 656, 22 998,
(3522) 43 3363
E-mail: kniish@ketovo.zaural.ru,
yamal@kurgan.isp.ru;
Sergei Alexandrovich Pokazanyev,
Director

HOTELS AND TOURISM

58R009   ● ◆

Construction of Blue Lakes downhill
skiing resort.
Project purpose: to expand recreation
services range.

1) 900 people a day, revenues
   $0.6 million a year
2) Up to $1 million/18 months
3) L ($0.1 million)
4) BP

OOO Kurgan-Park
19, sub-district #6, Kurgan,
Kurgan Region, 640023
Phone: (3522) 48 5783
Vladimir Afanasyevich Luzin,
CEO

URALS FEDERAL DISTRICT

V

59. SVERDLOVSK REGION [66]

E C O N O M I C   M A P

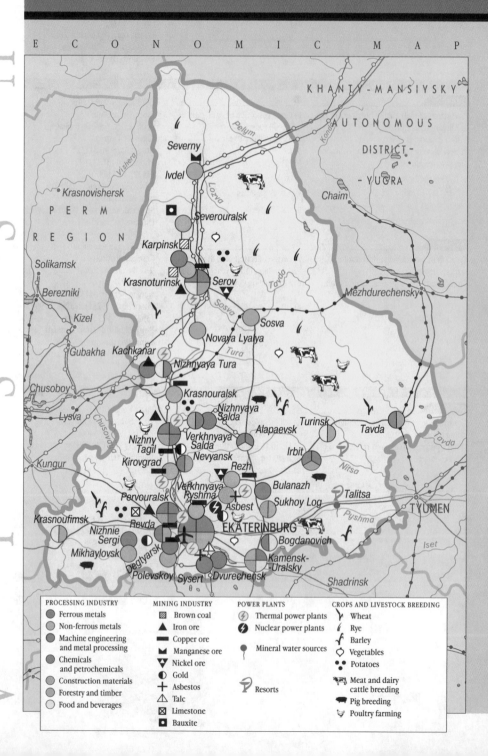

KHANTY-MANSIYSKY

AUTONOMOUS

DISTRICT-

- YUGRA

Chaim

Pelym

Konda

Severny

Ivdel

Krasnovishersk

PERM

REGION

Vishera

Severouralsk

Lozva

Karpinsk

Solikamsk

Krasnoturinsk   *Serov*

Berezniki

Sosva

Tavda

Mezhdurechensky

Kizel

Sosva

Gubakha   *Kachkanar*

Novaya Lyalya

Tura

Chusoboy

Nizhnyaya Tura

Lysva

Chusovaya

Krasnouralsk

Nizhnyaya Salda

Nizhny Tagil

Verkhnyaya Salda

Alapaevsk

Turinsk

Tavda

Tavda

Kirovgrad

Nevyansk

Irbit

Nitsa

Kungur

Rezh

Verkhnyaya Pyshma

Bulanazh

Talitsa

Pervouralsk

Asbest   *Sukhoy Log*

TYUMEN

Krasnoufimsk

Revda

EKATERINBURG

Pyshma

Nizhnie Sergi

Bogdanovich

Iset

Mikhaylovsk

Degtyarsk

Kamensk--Uralsky

Polevskoy   *Sysert*   *Dvurechensk*

Shadrinsk

PROCESSING INDUSTRY

- 🔴 Ferrous metals
- 🟡 Non-ferrous metals
- 🔴 Machine engineering and metal processing
- 🟣 Chemicals and petrochemicals
- 🔵 Construction materials
- 🟢 Forestry and timber
- ⚪ Food and beverages

MINING INDUSTRY

- ▨ Brown coal
- ▲ Iron ore
- ▬ Copper ore
- ◢ Manganese ore
- ▽ Nickel ore
- ◐ Gold
- ✛ Asbestos
- △ Talc
- ⊠ Limestone
- ▣ Bauxite

POWER PLANTS

- ⚡ Thermal power plants
- ⚡ Nuclear power plants
- 📍 Mineral water sources
- ⚕ Resorts

CROPS AND LIVESTOCK BREEDING

- Ɏ Wheat
- (Rye
- ⌇ Barley
- ◇ Vegetables
- ⁚⁚ Potatoes
- 🐄 Meat and dairy cattle breeding
- 🐖 Pig breeding
- 🦃 Poultry farming

The Sverdlovsk Region is a major industrial region with vast reserves of mineral resources. It features an advantageous geographical location, a high level of industrial development, considerable research and development and technology potential, a developed market infrastructure, and high professionalism of workforce.

The Sverdlovsk Regional authorities are striving to create investment conditions conducive to profitable and safe business development in the Region.

The Government of the Sverdlovsk Region bases its operations on the Charter for the Development and Allocation of Production Resources of the Sverdlovsk Region through 2015, the major strategic blueprint for the Region's social and economic development which aims to build an efficient, competitive, and steadily growing economy.

One of the major focuses of the Region's investment strategy is improving business conditions and coordinating the operations of all investment-related state authorities as regards the removal of administrative barriers. The Region has accorded priority status to creating conditions conducive to the intensive development of competitive economic sectors, upgrading of fixed assets, and shifting the focus of investment activity to develop production potential based on modern technology.

The Sverdlovsk Region's investment policy aims to attract internal investment resources, including the population's savings, financial institutions' funds, companies' accrued funds internally, and direct foreign investment externally.

The Region is making major efforts to ensure equal and favorable conditions for new investors through local legislation and practical steps taken by executive authorities.

A modern business infrastructure is steadily emerging in the Region: transport, communications, hotels, and exhibition facilities. We are working to improve the efficiency of the market credit and financing system.

Universities and colleges have accorded priority status to preparing qualified managers for public service and the private sector.

Information coverage of investment activity has always been a focus of our attention. The Regional Government provides potential investors with general data on economic and investment potential, and more detailed information needed to prepare business plans and feasibility studies.

An important role is accorded to organizations involved in a direct dialog with investors. These organizations include the Investment Support Fund Attached to the Sverdlovsk Regional Governor, the Investment Department of the Ministry of International and External Economic Relations of the Sverdlovsk Region, and the Department of Investment of the Ministry of the Economy and Labor of the Sverdlovsk Region.

In order to improve the efficiency of our managerial decisions, the Regional authorities invite businessmen and organizations to develop a long-term development strategy for the Region and to discuss and implement specific projects and programs.

Our Region has well-developed international links with foreign countries and their individual regions. We maintain contacts with over 100 countries, with annual trade turnover exceeding $4 billion. Among our major trading partners are the USA, the Netherlands, Germany, China, and the UK.

The Sverdlovsk Regional authorities are open to cooperation with foreign partners and are prepared to provide all the necessary conditions.

Eduard Rossel,
GOVERNOR OF THE SVERDLOVSK REGION

URALS FEDERAL DISTRICT

V

1. GENERAL INFORMATION

1.1. GEOGRAPHY

Situated in the heart of Russia at the crossroads of Europe and Asia, the Sverdlovsk Region covers a total area of 195,000 square kilometers. To the west, the Region borders the Perm Region, to the north-west – the Republic of Komi, to the north and north-east – the Khanty-Mansiysky Autonomous District – Yugra, to the east – the Tyumen Region, to the south-east – the Kurgan Region, to the south – the Chelyabinsk Region, and to the south-west – the Republic of Bashkortostan.

1.2. CLIMATE

The Sverdlovsk Region enjoys a temperate continental climate. The average air temperature in January is –15.5°C, rising to +16.9°C in July. The average annual precipitation is 500–700 mm.

1.3. POPULATION

According to preliminary 2002 census results, total population in the Region was 4,490,000 people. The average population density is 23 people per square kilometer. The economically active population totals 2,335,000 people. The 2002 official unemployment level was 1.6%.

Demographically speaking, some 58% are of working age, 28% are below the statutory working age, and 14% are beyond the statutory working age.

As of 2002, the Sverdlovsk Region's major urban centers were Yekaterinburg with 1,293,000 inhabitants, Nizhny Tagil with 390,600 inhabitants, Kamensk-Uralsky with 186,300 inhabitants, and Pervouralsk with 132,800 inhabitants.

Population								TABLE 1
	1992	1997	1998	1999	2000	2001	2002	
Total population, '000	4,765	4,660	4,646	4,631	4,603	4,573	4,490	
Economically active population, '000	2,446	2,284	2,229	2,308	2,328	2,322	2,335	

2. ADMINISTRATION

1, pl. Oktyabrskaya, Yekaterinburg, Sverdlovsk Region, 620031. Phone: (3432) 71 7642, fax: (3432) 77 1513
E-mail: so@midural.ru; http://www.rossel.ru; http://www.midural.ru

NAME	POSITION	CONTACT INFORMATION
Eduard Ergartovich ROSSEL	Governor of the Sverdlovsk Region	Phone: (3432) 70 5471 Fax: (3432) 70 5472
Alexei Petrovich VOROBIEV	Chairman of the Sverdlovsk Regional Government	Phone: (3432) 71 7920 Fax: (3432) 77 1513
Vladimir Antonovich MOLCHANOV	First Deputy Chairman of the Sverdlovsk Regional Government for Regional Business Coordination, Minister of Metallurgy	Phone: (3432) 71 7695 Fax: (3432) 77 1701
Galina Alexeevna KOVALEVA	First Deputy Chairman of the Sverdlovsk Regional Government for Economic Policy and Development, Minister of Economy and Labor	Phone: (3432) 77 1702 Fax: (3432) 77 1669
Veniamin Maxovich GOLUBITSKY	First Deputy Chairman of the Sverdlovsk Regional Government, Minister of State Property Management	Phone: (3432) 77 1706 Fax: (3432) 71 8161
Yury Valeryevich OSINTSEV	Deputy Chairman of the Sverdlovsk Regional Governmen, Minister of International and Foreign Trade Relations	Phone: (3432) 17 8672 Fax: (3432) 17 8907

3. ECONOMIC POTENTIAL

3.1. 1997–2002 GROSS REGIONAL PRODUCT (GRP). INDUSTRY BREAKDOWN

2002 gross regional product amounted to $9,350 million, which constitutes 27% growth on 2001. The growth was achieved thanks to an increase in industrial output, trade, and agriculture. Per capita GRP amounted to $1,611 in 2001, rising to $2,081 in 2002.

3.2. MAJOR ECONOMIC GROWTH PROJECTIONS

The economic potential of the Sverdlovsk Region is largely based on industry. The Region has identified its priorities up to 2015 in the following major sectors:

Energy and utilities. To upgrade existing power stations, increase the share of domestic ener-

GRP trends in 1997–2002						TABLE 2
	1997	1998	1999	2000	2001*	2002*
GRP in current prices, $ million	12,813.3	7,927.4	4,886.2	5,892.7	7,362.7	9,349.9

*Estimates of the Sverdlovsk Regional Government

GRP industry breakdown in 1997–2002, % of total						TABLE 3
	1997	1998	1999	2000	2001	2002*
GRP	100.0	100.0	100.0	100.0	100.0	100.0
Industry	37.3	41.9	46.0	46.3	42.2	46.8
Agriculture and forestry	6.5	5.8	7.2	5.9	5.9	6.2
Construction	6.6	6.2	6.9	6.6	5.9	7.6
Transport and communications	12.4	12.2	9.8	11.3	9.4	11.4
Trade and public catering	15.6	13.7	12.9	11.3	11.7	15.1
Other	21.6	20.2	17.2	18.6	24.9	12.9

*Estimates of the Sverdlovsk Regional Government

gy in the regional fuel balance, and build a fourth reactor at the Beloyarskaya Nuclear Power Station.

Metals. To enhance the raw material base, refurbish the sector with new technology, implement resource and energy saving programs, expand the product range, and increase output of competitive products.

Agriculture. To ensure food security of the Sverdlovsk Region.

Transport. To strengthen growth of the regional transport system.

3.3. INDUSTRIAL OUTPUT IN 1997–2002 FOR MAJOR SECTORS OF ECONOMY

The leading industrial sectors of the Sverdlovsk Region are ferrous and non-ferrous metals, machine engineering and metal processing, and energy. These account for 83.3% of total industrial output.

Non-ferrous and ferrous metals.
Ferrous and non-ferrous metals dominate the Region's industry structure with over 50% of the Region's total industrial output. Major companies include: OAO Nizhnetagilsky Metal Works, OAO Pervouralsky Novotrubny Plant, OAO Sinarsky Tube Plant, OAO Seversky Tube Plant, and OAO Uralelectromed.

Machine engineering and metal processing.
The sector accounts for 20.9% of total industrial output in the Region. Internationally recognized companies are OAO Uralmash, OAO Uralelectrotyazhmash, GUP Uralwagonzavod, OAO Uralkhimmash, and OAO Pnevmostroimashina. Unique automated equipment produced in the Urals is installed at numerous Russian metals, petrochemicals, and machine engineering plants.

Energy. This sector accounts for 11.4% of total industrial output. The energy sector is represented by OAO Sverdlovenergo, which is comprised of 12 thermal power plants, the largest being: the Reftinskaya Power Station with the generating capacity of 3,800 MW, Verkhnetagilskaya Power Stations – 1,500 MW, and Sredneuralskaya Power Station – 1,193 MW.

Agriculture. Demand in the Sverdlovsk Region for vegetables, potatoes, and poultry is fully covered by local production. Local output covers 70% of the Region's dairy product consumption, 55% of meat, and 25% of grain. One of the top priority agricultural areas is poultry, with the Region accounting for some 13% of Russia's total poultry output.

3.4. FUEL AND ENERGY BALANCE (OUTPUT AND CONSUMPTION PER RESOURCE)

The energy sector fully meets the regional demand for electricity and heat. The Region oper-

Industry breakdown of industrial output in 1997–2002, % to total						TABLE 4
	1997	1998	1999	2000	2001	2002*
Industry	100.0	100.0	100.0	100.0	100.0	100.0
Non-ferrous metals	17.4	23.3	32.2	29.5	26.2	27.0
Ferrous metals	25.5	19.6	20.6	24.9	25.0	24.0
Machine engineering and metal processing	18.0	17.9	15.1	16.4	19.4	20.9
Energy	15.9	15.3	11.2	10.5	10.9	11.4
Food and beverages	7.7	9.4	9.3	8.0	7.5	6.6
Construction materials	5.5	4.9	3.6	3.7	3.9	3.9
Chemicals and petrochemicals	3.3	2.8	2.6	2.2	2.6	2.3
Forestry, timber, and pulp and paper	2.2	2.1	1.9	1.8	1.6	1.5
Light industry	2.5	2.5	0.3	0.3	0.3	0.3
Fuel	0.5	0.5	0.4	0.3	0.3	0.2

*Estimates of the Sverdlovsk Regional Government

Fuel and energy sector production and consumption trends, 1997–2002						TABLE 5
	1997	1998	1999	2000	2001	2002
Electricity output, billion kWh	37.2	37.9	35.8	43.7	43.2	38.5
Electricity consumption, billion kWh	31.4	30.7	31.4	33.5	33.9	34.5
Natural gas consumption, billion cubic meters	15.1	15.1	14.5	15.7	14.9	16.6

ates 18 Power Stations with an installed capacity of 9,137 MW. The Region's utilities are interconnected to form the Sverdlovsk Regional Energy System, which covers the entire territory of the Region. The most promising energy sources are natural gas from Western Siberia and Ekibastuz coal. The Sverdlovsk Region is home to the I.V. Kurchatov Beloyarskaya Nuclear Power Station – one of the most promising sources of energy in the Region.

3.5. TRANSPORT INFRASTRUCTURE

Russia's main air, railroad, and automobile routes pass through the Sverdlovsk Region.

Roads. The Region has 10,457 km of paved public highway. Major routes are: Yekaterinburg – Perm (westbound), Yekaterinburg – Chelyabinsk (southbound), Yekaterinburg – Tyumen (eastbound), and Yekaterinburg – Serov (northbound). In 2002, over 360 million tons of freight was transported, or 0.6% more than in 2001. 2002 passenger turnover was 19.8 billion passenger-km.

Railroads. The Sverdlovsk Region has 3,569 km of railroads and is among top three railway junctions in Russia.

Airports. Yekaterinburg's international airport at Koltsovo links the Region to many other regions of Russia. Ural Airlines fly to Europe, the Middle East, and Asia. 13 international routes were launched in 2002. Lufthansa services the Frankfurt – Yekaterinburg – Novosibirsk route. A new international terminal, which increased the airport's capacity to 450 passengers/hour, was put into operation in 2002.

3.6. MAIN NATURAL RESOURCES: RESERVES AND EXTRACTION IN 2002

The Region's principle natural resources are mineral raw materials, timber, and water.

Mineral resources. The Sverdlovsk Region is the only area in Russia where high quality bauxite is produced. The Region also produces significant amounts of placer gold, platinum, gold ore, and semi-precious stones. Vanadium reserves equal 5.7 million tons, asbestos – 67 million tons, and iron ore – 7,890 million tons.

Timber. Forests cover 13.6 million hectares, or 69% of the Region's area (1.5% of Russia's total forestry reserves). Reserves of ripe timber amount to 1.4% of Russia's total, while logs amount to 5%. Industrial log reserves equal 300 million cubic meters.

Water resources. The Sverdlovsk Region has 35 water reservoirs with a total of 2,482 million cubic meters of water, 2,500 lakes with a total area of 1,100 square kilometers, and the overall length of its rivers is 68,000 km.

4. TRADE OPPORTUNITIES

4.1. MAIN GOODS
PRODUCED IN THE REGION
The Sverdlovsk Region produces 10.6% of all rolled ferrous metal produced in Russia, 34.9% of steel tubes, 12.9% of iron ore, 15% of rolled aluminum, 10% of primary aluminum, 8% of copper, and over 20% of machinery.

4.2. EXPORTS, INCLUDING EXTRA-CIS
The Sverdlovsk Region's exports to extra-CIS countries amounted to $2,495.6 million in 2000, and exports to CIS, to $284 million. The respective figures for 2001 were $2,611.9 million and $300.9 million, and 2002 – $2,763 million and $313.8 million.

The main types of goods exported by the Region in 2002 were: metal and metal goods (51.9% of total exports), chemicals (25.4%), machinery, equipment and transport vehicles (15.6%). Major importers of the Region's products include the USA (18.1% of total exports), the Netherlands (15.8%), India (11.8%), and China (8.7%).

4.3. IMPORTS, INCLUDING EXTRA-CIS
In 2000, imports from extra-CIS amounted to $317.9 million, while imports from CIS, to $260.8 million. The respective figures for 2001 were $478.1 and $269.4 million, and for 2002 – $487.9 and $283.1 million.

The bulk of 2002 regional imports was represented by chemicals and rubber (33.5% of total imports), machinery, equipment and transport vehicles (25.4 %), and mineral products (21%). The following products saw considerable growth in 2002: raw hides, furs, textile and textile goods, and footwear. The main exporters to the Region as of 2002 were: the USA (27.1% of total exports), Kazakhstan (17.8%), Germany (9.3%), and China (6.7%).

4.4. MAJOR REGIONAL EXPORT
AND IMPORT ENTITIES
Due to the specific features of trade in the Region, mainly industrial companies perform export and import operations.

5. INVESTMENT OPPORTUNITIES

5.1. INVESTMENTS
IN 1992–2002 (BY INDUSTRY SECTOR),
INCLUDING FOREIGN INVESTMENTS
The following factors determine the investment appeal of the Sverdlovsk Region:
- Its advantageous geographic location, proximity to large markets;
- Its developed transport infrastructure, and reliable communications;
- Cheap energy;
- Legislation providing support for investment activities (protection of investor rights, preferential tax treatment);
- Highly qualified workforce;
- Availability of natural resources.

5.2. CAPITAL INVESTMENT
The industry and transport sectors account for the majority of capital investment.

Capital investment by industry sector, $ million						_TABLE 6_
	1997	1998	1999	2000	2001	2002
Total capital investment	2,260.6	938.3	583.1	819.1	875.8	972.3
Including major industries (% of total)						
Industry	37.4	38.7	47.2	47.5	49.2	47.5
Agriculture and forestry	1.4	2.9	3.5	3.1	3.3	3.2
Construction	3.4	2.8	2.0	1.6	2.9	3.3
Transport and communications	28.5	16.0	15.6	15.6	23.6	21.2
Trade and public catering	2.6	2.7	1.4	1.5	1.3	1.5
Other	26.7	36.9	30.3	30.7	19.7	23.3

Foreign investment trends in 1997–2002						_TABLE 7_
	1997	1998	1999	2000	2001	2002
Foreign investment, $ million	71.0	121.0	167.0	163.0	748.0	1,354.7
Including FDI, $ million	68.4	118.9	79.2	73.6	101.6	99.7

URALS FEDERAL DISTRICT

V

5.3. MAJOR ENTERPRISES (INCLUDING ENTERPRISES WITH FOREIGN INVESTMENT)

In 2002, the Region had some 1,030 companies with foreign investment, which constitutes 15.4% growth year-on-year. The largest number of companies was established by investors from the USA, China, Germany, and the UK (National Oilwell, Duferco, Lufthansa, Coca-Cola, Pepsi, Henkel, Wrigley's, Ford, Philips, ABB), and the CIS, including Uzbekistan and Kazakhstan. The Region has registered 469 companies with 100% foreign ownership.

		2001 SALES, $ MILLION*	2001 NET PROFIT, $ MILLION*
Largest enterprises of the Sverdlovsk Region			TABLE 8
COMPANY	SECTOR		
OAO Nizhnetagilsky Metallurgical Works	Ferrous metals	727.5	31.6
OAO Siberian-Urals Aluminum Company	Non-ferrous metals	707.0	26.0
OAO Sverdlovenergo	Energy	635.4	41.1
OAO Trade House of the Sinarsky Tube Plant	Retail	322.1	0.8
OOO Uraltransgaz	Gas pipeline	288.1	145.4
OAO Uralelectromed	Non-ferrous metals	285.1	11.4
State Unitary Company Uralvagonzavod	Machine engineering	273.5	39.4
OAO Verhnesaldinskoe Metallurgical Works	Non-ferrous metals	251.8	76.1
State Unitary Company Sverdlovsk Railways	Railway	175.3	30.9
Kachkanar Ore Mining and Processing Company Vanady	Ferrous metals	173.0	7.2

*According to the Sverdlovsk Regional Government

5.4. MOST ATTRACTIVE SECTORS FOR INVESTMENT

Metals, machine engineering, and construction materials are the most potentially appealing sectors for investors.

5.5. CURRENT LEGISLATION ON INVESTOR TAX EXEMPTIONS AND PRIVILEGES

The rights of foreign investors operating in the Region are protected by legislative acts of the Russian Federation. State support to investors is provided in the form of favorable loans and tax credits. Investors participating in the Region's Targeted Investment Program (2003) enjoy a property tax exemption.

The Region has developed a program aimed at protecting the rights of investors with a focus on tax guarantees, the protection of minority shareholders' rights, regulation of natural monopoly tariffs, and guarantees of land leasing stability.

Regional entities responsible for raising investment		TABLE 9
ENTITY	ADDRESS	PHONE, FAX, E-MAIL
Sverdlovsk Regional Governor's Investment Support Fund	32g, pr. Lenina, Yekaterinburg, Sverdlovsk Region, 620151	Phone: (3432) 71 6007 Fax: (3432) 71 2103
Sverdlovsk Regional Government Ministry of International and External Economic Relations, Investment Department	1 pl. Oktyabrskaya, Yekaterinburg, Sverdlovsk Region, 620031	Phone: (3432) 17 8672 Fax: (3432) 17 8911 E-mail: r66@midural.ru

5.6. FEDERAL AND REGIONAL ECONOMIC AND SOCIAL DEVELOPMENT PROGRAMS FOR THE SVERDLOVSK REGION

Federal targeted programs. The Region accorded priority status to the following federal targeted programs: Elimination of Differences in the Social and Economic Development of the Regions of the Russian Federation 2002–2010 and Through 2015, Energy Efficient Economy 2002–2005 and Through 2010, Preservation and Development of the Architecture of Historic Towns 2002–2010, and Processing of Industrial Pollutants in the Sverdlovsk Region.

Regional programs. The Government of the Sverdlovsk Region is developing and implementing several programs focusing on the development of the industrial sector, agricultural policy, environmental rehabilitation, law enforcement, healthcare, and public welfare. Some 27 regional programs worth a total of $217 million are underway.

The Regional Government has accorded pri-ority status to programs aimed at improving the investment climate and creating a business-friendly environment:

The Regional Targeted Program for State Support to Small Enterprise in the Sverdlovsk Region 2003–2005; The Program for the Creation of a Computerized Land Register and State Accounting Records of Real Estate in the Sverdlovsk Region 2003–2007; The Program for State Property Inventory Evaluation in the Sverdlovsk Region 2003–2005; and The Program of Energy Saving in the Sverdlovsk Region for 2003.

6. INVESTMENT PROJECTS

Industry sector and project description	1) Expected results 2) Amount and term of investment 3) Form of financing[1] 4) Documentation[2]	Contact information
1	2	3
FERROUS METALS		
59R001 Construction of wide bore tube production facilities. Project goal: to extend the product range, replace imports (to supply Russia's gas and energy sectors with wide bore tube for major pipelines).	1) 600,000 tons/year 2) $690 million/3 years 3) L 4) BP	OAO Nizhnetagilsky Metallurgical Works 1 ul. Metallurgov, Nizhny Tagil, Sverdlovsk Region, 622025 Phone: (3435) 29 2385, 29 2194 Fax: (3435) 29 2694 E-mail: post@ntmk.ru Http://www.nikom.tagil.ru Sergei Konstantinovich Nosov, Managing Director
NON-FERROUS METALS		
59R002 Construction of metal powder works. Project goal: to expand the sales market.	1) 2,000 tons of powder per year 2) $3 million/2 years 3) E, L, JV, Leas. 4) BP	OOO UGMK Holding 1, ul. Lenina, V. Pyshma, Sverdlovsk Region, 624091 Phone: (34368) 49 811, 46 200 Fax: (34368) 46 051 E-mail: ugmk@elem.ru Andrei Anatolyevich Kozitsyn, CEO
59R003 Aluminum production (upgrading the existing operations). Project goal: to improve the ecological situation; increase processing of the Region's alumina.	1) 540,000 tons/year 2) $610 million/7 years 3) E, L, JV 4) FS	OAO Bogoslovsky Aluminum Plant, a subsidiary of SUAL 1 ul. K. Marksa, Krasnoturyinsk, Sverdlovsk Region, 624440 Phone: (34314) 45 005, 45 002 Fax: (34314) 45 186 E-mail: baz@baz.ru Http://www.baz.ru Anatoly Vasilyevich Sysoev, CEO
CHEMICALS AND PHARMACEUTICALS		
59R004 Production of pharmaceutical capsules. Project goal: to extend the product range.	1) 3.6 million packs/year 2) $2 million/3 years 3) E, L 4) FS, BP	OAO Yekaterinburg Pharmaceutical Factory 49 Sibirsky Tract, Yekaterinburg, Sverdlovsk Region, 620100 Phone: (3432) 24 0706 Fax: (3432) 24 0768 E-mail: bum-ff@etel.ru Alexander Nikolaevich Mehonoshin, CEO

[1] L – Loan, E – Equity, Leas. – Leasing, JV – Joint Venture
[2] BP – Business Plan, FS – Feasibility Study

URALS FEDERAL DISTRICT

V

1	2	3

MACHINE ENGINEERING AND METAL PROCESSING

59R005 ●

Production of airport ground facilities.
Project goal: to expand production
and extend the range of civil goods.

1) Revenue of $1.2 million/year
2) $0.9 million/1 year
3) L
4) Design specifications

OAO Kalinin Machine
Engineering Plant
18 ul. Kosmonavtov, Yekaterinburg,
Sverdlovsk Region, 620017
Phone: (3432) 39 5532
Fax: (3432) 34 9317
E-mail: zik@mail.ur.ru
Nikolai Vladimirovich Klein, CEO

AGRICULTURE

59R006 ●

Construction of a greenhouse.
Project goal: to increase output
and reduce costs.

1) 1,020 tons/year
2) $1.9 million/18 months
3) L
4) n/a

ZAO Teplichnoe
2 ul. Parnikovaya, Yekaterinburg,
Sverdlovsk Region, 620135
Phone: (3432) 34 9372, 34 9365
Fax: (3432) 34 0496
Vasily Fedorovich Mayorov, CEO

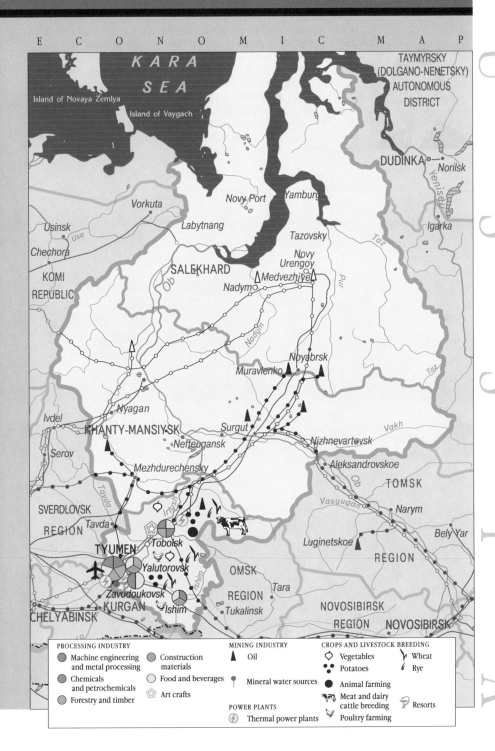

R U S S I A

URALS FEDERAL DISTRICT

PROCESSING INDUSTRY

- ⬤ Machine engineering and metal processing
- ⬤ Chemicals and petrochemicals
- ⬤ Forestry and timber
- ⬤ Construction materials
- ⬤ Food and beverages
- Art crafts

POWER PLANTS

- Thermal power plants

MINING INDUSTRY

- ▲ Oil
- Mineral water sources

CROPS AND LIVESTOCK BREEDING

- ◇ Vegetables
- Potatoes
- ⬤ Animal farming
- Meat and dairy cattle breeding
- Poultry farming
- Wheat
- Rye
- Resorts

Politicians and businessmen know the Tyumen Region as a land of vast natural resources. But the riches of our Region are not confined to oil and gas. Our Region's machine engineering, timber, processing, and food are all well known outside the Region.

Situated at the very center of Russia, the Tyumen Region traditionally tops the regional league table for major economic indices.

The Region's leading sectors are fuel, energy, and machine engineering. The Region also operates large shipbuilding, chemicals, and agricultural machinery sectors. Forestry constitutes another well-developed sector. The Region currently produces some 50% of all Coregonidae fish species output in Russia.

The Regional Administration's policy aims to realize the potential of the Region's economy, assist local producers in penetrating world markets, and create conditions conducive to joint production and sale of competitive goods.

In line with the investment opportunities offered by companies and municipalities in the Tyumen Region, the Regional Administration is committed to developing mutually beneficial business contacts, as well as research and development and cultural collaboration with foreign and domestic partners, and implementing joint projects.

Sergei Sobyanin,
GOVERNOR OF THE TYUMEN REGION

1. GENERAL INFORMATION

1.1. GEOGRAPHY

The Tyumen Region covers an area of 1,435,200 square kilometers together with the Yamalo-Nenetsky and Khanty-Mansiysky – Yugra Autonomous Districts, or 161,800 square kilometers without the Autonomous Districts. The Region is situated on the Western Siberian Plain. To the west, the Region borders the Komi Republic, to the south-west – the Sverdlovsk Region, to the south – the Kurgan Region, the Republic of Kazakhstan, and the Omsk Region, and to the east – the Tomsk Region and the Krasnoyarsk Territory.

The Tyumen Region contains two peer constituent entities of the Russian Federation – the Khanty-Mansiysky – Yugra and Yamalo-Nenetsky Autonomous Districts. This Chapter of the Guide deals only with the Tyumen Region, disregarding the Autonomous Districts. For information on the Khanty-Mansiysky – Yugra and Yamalo-Nenetsky Autonomous Districts, please refer to the relevant chapters of the Guide.

1.2. CLIMATE

The Tyumen Region is located within the temperate continental climate zone.

January air temperatures average –16.1°C, rising to +19.4°C in July. Annual precipitation averages 200–600 mm.

1.3. POPULATION

According to preliminary 2002 census results, the Tyumen Region's total population was 1,325,000 people (the Autonomous Districts excluded). The average population density is 8.2 per square kilometer (the Autonomous Districts excluded). The economically active population amounts to 645,000 people (the Autonomous Districts excluded).

Demographically speaking, some 67% are of statutory working age, 21% are below the statutory working age, and 12% are beyond the statutory working age (the Autonomous Districts included).

The major urban centers of the Tyumen Region (2002 data, the Autonomous Districts excluded) are Tyumen with 510,700 inhabitants, Tobolsk with 114,000 inhabitants, Ishim with 61,000 inhabitants, Yalutorovsk with 38,000 inhabitants, and Zavodoukovsk with 27,000 inhabitants.

Population*								TABLE 1
	1992	1997	1998	1999	2000	2001	2002
Total population, '000	1,347	1,347	1,351	1,353	1,351	1,346	1,325
Economically active population, '000	n/a	568	619	634	614	644	645

*The Autonomous Districts excluded.

2. ADMINISTRATION

45, ul. Volodarskogo, Tyumen, Tyumen Region, 625004
Fax: (3452) 24 4881. E-mail: press@adm.tyumen.ru; http://www.adm.tyumen.ru

NAME	POSITION	CONTACT INFORMATION
Sergei Semyonovich SOBYANIN	Governor of the Tyumen Region	Phone: (3452) 46 5180 Fax: (3452) 46 5542
Vladimir Vladimirovich YAKUSHEV	Deputy Governor of the Tyumen Region (Finance, Tax and Securities Department, Economics Department)	Phone: (3452) 46 3389 Fax: (3452) 46 0334
Pavel Petrovich MITROFANOV	First Deputy Governor of the Tyumen Region (Fuel and Energy Department, External Relations and Trade Department, Industry Department, Investment and Credit Policy and State Business Support Department, and Environment Department)	Phone: (3452) 46 5306 Fax: (3452) 46 3616
Vladimir Nikolaevich VASILYEV	First Deputy Governor of the Tyumen Region (Agroindustrial Department)	Phone: (3452) 46 4232
Natalya Alexandrovna SHEVCHIK	Deputy Governor of the Tyumen Region (Social Welfare, Healthcare, Education, and Science Departments)	Phone: (3452) 46 5851 Fax: (3452) 46 5040
Boris Nikolaevich PETRENKO	Deputy Governor of the Tyumen Region, Head of the Main Division for Construction	Phone: (3452) 46 3514 Fax: (3452) 46 5133

URALS FEDERAL DISTRICT

V

NAME	POSITION	CONTACT INFORMATION
Yevgeny Viktorovich KULESHOV	Deputy Governor of the Tyumen Region, Chairman of the Committee for State Property Management	Phone: (3452) 46 1788 Fax: (3452) 46 9352

3. ECONOMIC POTENTIAL

3.1. 1997–2002 GROSS REGIONAL PRODUCT (GRP). INDUSTRY BREAKDOWN

The Tyumen Region's 2002 gross regional product (the Autonomous Districts excluded) was $2,502 million, or 48% up on 2001. Per capita GRP in 2001 totaled $1,254, and $1,887 in 2002.

3.2. INDUSTRIAL OUTPUT IN 1997–2002 FOR MAJOR SECTORS OF ECONOMY

The leading industries of the Tyumen Region are fuel, energy, and machine engineering. These account for a combined 97% of total industrial output (the Autonomous Districts included).

GRP trends in 1997–2002*						TABLE 2
	1997	1998	1999	2000	2001	2002
GRP in current prices, million $	34,918	20,651	13,915	21,971	1,687	2,502

*Estimates for the Tyumen Region for 1997–2000 by the State Statistics Committee, including the Autonomous Districts. Estimates by the Tyumen Regional Administration for 2001–2002 (the Autonomous Districts excluded)

GRP industry breakdown in 1997–2002, % of total*						TABLE 3
	1997	1998	1999	2000	2001	2002
GRP	100.0	100.0	100.0	100.0	100.0	100.0
Industry	41.0	41.9	46.3	19.4	18.4	16.6
Agriculture and forestry	1.6	1.6	1.8	10.6	10.7	10.7
Construction	14.7	12.6	12.6	8.6	9.8	19.0
Transport and communications	15.7	16.0	12.7	21.7	23.1	22.8
Trade and public catering	4.2	5.1	5.3	15.5	17.1	9.5
Other	14.9	18.1	16.0	22.2	19.3	19.5
Net taxes on output	7.9	4.7	5.3	2.0	1.6	1.9

*Estimates by the Tyumen Regional Administration for 1997–1999, including the Autonomous Districts. Estimates by the Tyumen Regional Administration for 2000–2002 (the Autonomous Districts excluded)

Industry breakdown of industrial output in 1997–2002, % of total*						TABLE 4
	1997	1998	1999	2000	2001	2002
Industry	100.0	100.0	100.0	100.0	100.0	100.0
Fuel	81.9	81.8	86.8	88.5	87.1	87.9
Energy	10.6	10.9	6.8	5.1	6.1	6.0
Machine engineering and metal processing	1.8	2.2	2.2	3.3	3.3	3.1
Food and beverages	1.8	1.8	1.6	1.0	1.1	0.9
Construction materials	1.3	1.0	0.6	0.5	0.7	0.6
Forestry, timber, and pulp and paper	0.7	0.7	0.6	0.5	0.6	0.6
Chemicals and petrochemicals	0.8	0.7	0.6	0.6	0.6	0.5
Light industry	0.2	0.2	0.2	0.2	0.1	0.1
Flour, cereals, and mixed fodder	0.6	0.4	0.3	0.2	0.1	0.1

*Estimates for the Tyumen Region for 1997–2002 (for 2002 – preliminary) by the State Statistics Committee (the Autonomous Districts included)

Fuel. Output of oil and gas condensate in 2002 was 836,300 tons (the Autonomous Districts excluded). The largest companies are: OAO Tyumen Oil Company, OAO Sibnefteprovod, and OAO Zapsibgazprom.

Energy. OAO Tyumenenergo, the leading enterprise in the sector, ranks among the biggest producers of electricity and heat energy in Russia.

Machine engineering and metal processing. Major manufacturers in the sector include OAO Tyumen Accumulator Factory, OAO Tyumen Medical Equipment and Instruments, OAO Tyumen Engine Builders, OAO Neftemash, OAO Zavodoukovsky Engineering Plant, ZAO Welding Electrodes Plant, OAO Tyumenremdormash, OAO Electron Pilot Plant, OAO Tyumen Shipyard, and OAO Sibneftemash.

Agriculture. The sector's main products are grain, potato, vegetables, milk, beef and poultry meat, and eggs. The Region has 3.4 million hec-tares of agricultural lands. Annual gross output of grain ranges from 1.1 million to 1.6 million tons, vegetables – from 100,000 to 160,000 tons, and potato – from 400,000 to 600,000 tons. Extensive hayfield and pasture areas provide favorable conditions for dairy and beef husbandry. 2002 output of animal and poultry meat (live weight) was 137,000 tons, milk – 526,400 tons, and eggs – 1,102 million.

3.3. FUEL AND ENERGY BALANCE (OUTPUT AND CONSUMPTION PER RESOURCE)

Fuel and energy sector production and consumption trends, 1997–2002						*TABLE 5*
	1997	1998	1999	2000	2001	2002
Electricity output, billion kWh*	8.7	8.4	8.6	8.5	8.2	8.1
Oil output (including gas condensate), '000 tons*	305.0	499.0	495.0	556.0	592.0	836.3
Natural gas extraction, million cubic meters*	2.0	–	2.0	6.0	8.0	–
Natural gas consumption, million cubic meters**	20,454.8	27,658.9	28,167.3	23,636.5	27,168.9	28,513.7

* Data of the State Statistics Committee for the Tyumen Region (the Autonomous Districts excluded)
** Data of the State Statistics Committee for the Tyumen Region (the Autonomous Districts included)

3.4. TRANSPORT INFRASTRUCTURE

Roads. The Tyumen Region has 9,361 kilometers of paved public highways. The Region is served by federal roads connecting Tyumen to Yekaterinburg, Omsk, Kurgan, and Khanty-Mansiysk.

Railroads. The Tyumen Region has 2,451 kilometers of railroads. The Trans-Siberian Railroad crosses the Region.

Airports. An international airport serves Tyumen.

River transport. The total length of the Region's waterways is 9,844 kilometers.

River ports. The Region's major river ports are located at Tyumen and Tobolsk.

Oil and gas pipelines. Oil and gas pipelines are important elements of the regional transportation system. The Urengoy–Tobolsk product pipeline transporting light hydrocarbons to the Tobolsk Petrochemicals Plant crosses the Tyumen Region.

3.5. MAIN NATURAL RESOURCES: RESERVES AND EXTRACTION IN 2002

The Region's principal natural resources are fuel, forest, and construction materials.

Fuel resources. Oil reserves are concentrated in the south of the Region, primarily in the Uvatsky District. The nine discovered oil fields contain 122 million tons of explored reserves. Peat reserves run to 37 billion cubic meters.

Construction materials. The Region's 64 explored sand deposits contain 741 million cubic meters of sand. The Region also has 210 deposits of brick and bloating clays containing 631 million cubic meters of reserves.

Forest resources. Mature and over-mature stocks are estimated at 462 million cubic meters of the total 850 million cubic meters of deciduous and coniferous forests. Mature and over-mature coniferous stocks are estimated at 178 million cubic meters.

4. TRADE OPPORTUNITIES

4.1. MAIN GOODS PRODUCED IN THE REGION

The Tyumen Region (the Autonomous Districts not included) produced in 2002:

Fuel: Oil (including gas condensate) – 836,300 tons, primarily processed oil – 500,000 tons;

Electricity: 8.1 billion kWh;

Machine engineering: 1.7 million accumulators, 193 tractor trailers and 377 timber processing machines;

Forestry and timber: commercial timber – 2.2 million cubic meters of dense timber, sawn timber – 619,000 cubic meters, plywood – 27,800 cubic meters;

Construction materials: bricks – 146 million;

Light industry: wool fabric – 5.4 million square meters.

4.2. EXPORTS, INCLUDING EXTRA-CIS

According to the State Statistics Committee, the Tyumen Region's extra-CIS exports (the Autonomous Districts included) amounted to $14,623.5 million in 2000. Exports to CIS countries totaled $1,197.9 million. The corresponding figures for 2001 were $13,926.2 million and $1,226.9 million, and $17,461.4 million and $1,238 million for 2002.

The Region's main exports (the Autonomous Districts excluded) are oil and oil products, organic chemicals, wool yarn and fabric, accumulators, machine engineering goods, and timber and timber products.

4.3. IMPORTS, INCLUDING EXTRA-CIS

According to the State Statistics Committee, the Tyumen Region's 2000 extra-CIS imports (the Autonomous Districts included) amounted to $707.3 million. Imports from CIS countries totaled $99.7 million. The corresponding figures for 2001 were $766.1 million and $63.5 million, and $566.4 million and $173.7 million for 2002.

The main goods imported by the Region include industrial equipment (65% of total imports), transportation vehicles, and agricultural equipment.

4.4. MAJOR REGIONAL EXPORT AND IMPORT ENTITIES

Owing to the specific nature of export and import operations in the Tyumen Region, export and import transactions are carried out primarily by industrial enterprises.

5. INVESTMENT OPPORTUNITIES

5.1. INVESTMENTS IN 1992–2002 (BY INDUSTRY SECTOR), INCLUDING FOREIGN INVESTMENTS

The following key factors determine the investment appeal of the Tyumen Region:
- Its favorable geographical location and proximity to large markets;
- Its developed transport infrastructure;
- Its high industrial potential;
- Its strong solvent demand for consumer goods and services;
- Legislation supporting investment activities (guarantees for investor rights and preferential tax treatment for investors);
- Its natural resources.

5.2. CAPITAL INVESTMENT

Industry, transport, and communications account for the bulk of capital investment.

Capital investment by industry sector, $ million*						TABLE 6
	1997	1998	1999	2000	2001	2002
Total capital investment	11,288	4,862	3,419	7,112	9,654	8,135
Including major industries (% of total)						
Industry	65.4	62.2	63.3	68.6	65.7	64.1
Agriculture and forestry	0.5	0.4	0.4	0.2	0.3	0.4
Construction	1.0	3.9	1.7	2.3	1.8	1.6
Transport and communications	14.6	14.7	20.6	15.7	15.8	15.7
Trade and public catering	0.5	0.5	0.5	0.4	0.4	0.3
Other	18.0	18.3	13.5	12.8	16.0	17.9

*Estimates by the State Statistics Committee
for the Tyumen Region (the Autonomous Districts included)

Foreign investment trends in 1997–2002*						TABLE 7
	1997	1998	1999	2000	2001	2002
Foreign investment, $ million	53.9	47.5	34.3	20.1	10.2	13.4
Including FDI, $ million	42.5	47.1	31.7	20.0	10.2	12.4

*Estimates by the State Statistics Committee for the Tyumen Region
(the Autonomous Districts excluded).

5.3. MAJOR ENTERPRISES (INCLUDING ENTERPRISES WITH FOREIGN INVESTMENT)

The Region hosts some 107 enterprises with foreign capital. The largest include OAO Gazturboservis, ZAO Welding Electrodes Plant, OAO Tyumen-Diesel, ZAO Sibshvank, ZAO Sibgazpribor, JV OOO ZapsibgazOmikron, and OOO SibUnigaz.

5.4. MOST ATTRACTIVE SECTORS FOR INVESTMENT

According to experts and the Tyumen Regional Administration, the petrochemicals, timber, oil and gas machine engineering, and food and beverages sectors offer the greatest investment appeal.

Largest enterprises of the Tyumen Region*	*TABLE 8*
COMPANY	SECTOR
OAO Tyumen Oil Company	Fuel
OAO Sibnefteprovod	Fuel
OAO Zapsibgazprom	Fuel
OAO Tyumen Accumulator Factory	Machine engineering
OAO Tyumen Medical Equipment and Instruments	Machine engineering
OAO Tyumen Engine Builders	Machine engineering
OAO Neftemash	Machine engineering
OAO Crosno Tyumen Textile Corporation	Light industry
OAO Yalutorovsk Milk	Food and beverages
OAO Sibintel	Commerce, construction materials

*Data of the Tyumen Regional Administration (the Autonomous Districts excluded)

5.5. CURRENT LEGIS-LATION ON INVESTOR TAX EXEMPTIONS AND PRIVILEGES

The Law of the Tyumen Region On the Investment Activity in the Tyumen Region determines methods of state support to investors: provision of tax and levies privileges regarding property tax, profit tax, etc. to investors implementing investment projects (targeted programs) included in the investment program of the Tyumen Region; reimbursement to investors, on a payback basis, of a portion of interest (up to 50% of CB RF refinancing rate) on bank loans from the regional budget; placement of regional budget's funds for the purpose of investment projects financing on a tender, payback and term basis with interest repayment on the funds issued; and granting, on a tender basis, of state guarantees from the regional budget regarding investment projects.

5.6. FEDERAL AND REGIONAL ECONOMIC AND SOCIAL DEVELOPMENT PROGRAMS FOR THE TYUMEN REGION

Federal targeted programs. A number of federal programs are underway in the Region, including: The Upgrade of Russia's Transport System, 2002–2010, Energy Efficient Economy, 2002–2005 and through 2010.

Regional programs. The Region is implementing five industrial development programs for the period 2001–2005. For this purpose, the Tyumen Regional Administration has approved a comprehensive set of measures aimed at supporting industrial investment activity in the Region.

The main aims of the measures are: accelerated development of lending and investment mechanism for raising finance; state support to the enterprise; diversification of the regional economy; expansion of regional markets; raising living standards; job creation; encouraging the enterprise in industry; expansion of industrial and commercial links; output growth; diversification of product mix; improvement of product quality; development of industrial infrastructure; and growth in federal, regional and local tax revenues from the industrial sector.

The Tyumen Region has underway a program for state support to small businesses. The program aims to improve legal, economic and organizational conditions for small businesses development, financial support to startup businesses, assistance to the development of financial, credit and in-vestment mechanisms for small business in the Tyumen Region, assistance to municipal businesses support funds, development of a consulting network, and assistance to foreign economic activities of small businesses.

URALS FEDERAL DISTRICT

V

6. INVESTMENT PROJECTS

Industry sector and project description	1) Expected results 2) Amount and term of investment 3) Form of financing[1] 4) Documentation[2]	Contact information
1	2	3

MACHINE ENGINEERING AND METAL PROCESSING

60R001

| Production of timber processing machines. Project goal: to produce timber-processing machines. | 1) 3,479 machines by 2006
2) $7.6 million/2 years
3) L
4) BP | OAO Tyumen Machine Plant
1, ul. Stankostroiteley, Tyumen,
Tyumen Region, 625631
Phone: (3452) 44 2176
Fax: (3452) 44 2180
E-mail: stankozavod@mail.ru
Sergei Borisovich Simonyan, CEO |

60R002

| Production of trenching machines. Project goal: to produce earth-moving machinery. | 1) 8 trenching machines per year
2) $0.5 million/1 year
3) L
4) BP | ZAO Sibtechmash
81, ul. Lenina, Ishim, Tyumen Region
Phone: (34551) 21 203, 23 670
Fax: (34551) 21 660
E-mail: imz@ishim.ru
Rashit Muzagitovich Sabirov, Director |

CHEMICALS AND PETROCHEMICALS

60R003

| Completion of a polyethylene tube plant. Project goal: to produce multi-layer reinforced tubes. | 1) 1,000 tons of tubes per year
2) $5.8 million/4 years
3) L
4) BP | ZAO Sibgazapparat
P.O. Box 2836, 6 km, Velezhansky Trakt,
Tyumen, Tyumen Region, 625059
Phone: (3452) 39 7565
Fax: (3452) 39 7573
E-mail: sibgazap@rol.ru
Sergei Vladimirovich Kumyzov, CEO |

60R004

| Construction of a propylene production unit. Project goal: to produce propylene. | 1) Up to 200,000 tons per year
2) $100 million/3.5 years
3) L
4) BP | OAO Tobolsk-Neftekhim
Tobolsk, Tyumen Region, 626150
Phone: (34511) 58 410, 98 742
Fax: (34511) 98 951
Petr Alexandrovich Malkovsky, CEO |

60R005

| Production of polypropylene bags, including acquisition of equipment, assembly, and reconstruction of operating facilities. Project goal: to produce polypropylene bags. | 1) 7.5 million bags per year
2) $0.5 million/3 years
3) L ($0.5 million)
4) BP | OOO UKPTO-Tyumenavtotrans
54, ul. Zheleznodorozhnaya,
Tyumen, Tyumen Region, 625003
Phone/fax: (3452) 46 2376, 46 2271
Fax: (3452) 46 2380
E-mail: tumtrans@ttknet.ru
Alexander Samuilovich Shefer, Director
OOO Tyumen-Polymer
54, ul. Zheleznodorozhnaya,
Tyumen, Tyumen Region, 625003
Phone/fax: (3452) 46 2376, 46 2271
Fax: (3452) 46 2380
E-mail: tumtrans@ttknet.ru
Viktor Alexandrovich Belevich, Director |

URALS FEDERAL DISTRICT

V

[1] L – Loan, E – Equity, Leas. – Leasing, JV – Joint Venture
[2] BP – Business Plan, FS – Feasibility Study

1	2	3

FORESTRY, TIMBER, AND PULP AND PAPER

60R006 ● ◆ ▲

Construction of operating facilities
and purchasing of equipment for
the production of large-size plywood.
Project goal: to produce plywood and
veneer sheet.

1) 60,000 cubic meters per year
2) $20 million/1 year
3) L
4) BP, FS

OAO Tyumen Plywood Combine
109, ul. Beregovaya, Tyumen,
Tyumen Region, 625005
Phone: (3452) 46 2429
Fax: (3452) 46 2331, 46 2429
E-mail: tumfk@sibtel.ru
Almira Islamovna Karimova, CEO

60R007 ● ◆

Upgrading and technical refurbishment
of operating facilities.
Project goal: to produce furniture.

1) Revenue – $3.5 million per year
2) $1 million/5 years
3) L
4) BP

ZAO Intedi Furniture Factory
10, ul. Rusakova, Yalutorovsk,
Tyumen Region, 627016
Phone/fax: (34535) 20 445, 31 804
Pavel Petrovich Kripchun, CEO
Alexander Nikolaevich Usoltsev,
Executive Director

CONSTRUCTION MATERIALS

60R008 ● ◆

Increase in insulation wadding output.
Project goal: to produce insulation wadding.

1) 5,000 tons per year
2) $2.5 million/1.5 years
3) L
4) BP

ZAO TISMA
198, ul. Kamchatskaya, Tyumen,
Tyumen Region, 625034
Phone: (3452) 48 5190
Fax: (3452) 48 5159
Igor Valeryevich Maltsev, CEO

60R009 ● ◆

Assembly of the Tensiland production line.
Project goal: to produce reinforced
concrete goods and assemblies.

1) 53,700 cubic meters per year
2) $1.3 million/3 years
3) L
4) BP

OAO Tyumen Reinforced
Concrete Plant No. 1
249, ul. Respubliki, Tyumen,
Tyumen Region, 625014
Phone: (3452) 21 3542
Fax: (3452) 21 3442
Vladimir Vasilyevich Burlitsky, CEO

FOOD AND BEVERAGES

60R010 ● ◆

Refurbishment and upgrading of operations.
Project goal: to produce confectionery.

1) 3,187 tons of cookies, 1,050 tons
of waffles, 375 tons of chocolate
icing per year
2) $3.1 million/1 years
3) L
4) BP

ZAO Yalutorovsk Food Plant
57, ul. Lugovaya, Yalutorovsk,
Tyumen Region, 627016
Phone: (34535) 33 312, 33 227
Fax: (34535) 33 067
Yevgeny Vladimirovich Senkov, CEO

60R011 ● ◆

Construction of a fruit and berries
processing shop.
Project goal: to process and deep-freeze
agricultural produce.

1) Capacity: 15 tons per day
2) $2.2 million/1 year
3) L
4) BP

OOO Assortment
7, ul. 30 let Pobedy, Tyumen,
Tyumen Region, 625007
Phone/fax: (3452) 31 4171,
31 3200, 31 4170
E-mail: allsorts@tmn.ru
Vladislav Alexandrovich
Kolodyazhny, Director

1	2	3

60R012

	● ◆	OOO Assortment
Reconstruction of a shop for the production of canned meat, cereals, delicacies, and pet food. Project goal: to produce canned meat, cereals, delicacies, and pet food.	1) Capacity: semi-finished products, including dumplings – 2.5 tons per day, sausage – 2 tons per day, canned meat – 12,800 conventional cans per day 2) $0.9 million/6 months 3) L 4) BP	7, ul. 30 let Pobedy, Tyumen, Tyumen Region, 625007 Phone/fax: (3452) 31 4171, 31 3200, 31 4170 E-mail: allsorts@tmn.ru Vladislav Alexandrovich Kolodyazhny, Director

AGRICULTURE

60R013

	● ◆	ZAO JV Prigorodnoe
Upgrading of greenhouses. Project goal: to increase output and sales of vegetables.	1) 3,200 tons per year 2) $3.1 million/5 years 3) L 4) BP	27, ul. Odesskaya, Tyumen, Tyumen Region, 625000 Phone/fax: (3452) 41 4844 Yury Alexandrovich Demyanov, CEO

61. CHELYABINSK REGION [74]

Krasnoufimsk

Polevskoy

Kamensk-Uralsky

Shadrinsk

Verkhny Ufaley

Vishnevogorsk

Potaninskoe

Kasli

Kyshtym

Miass

Karabash

Kusa

CHELYABINSK

Kopeysk

Shumikha

Suleya

Miass

Minyar

Zlatoust

Korkino

Ust-Katav

Satka

Asha

Bakal

Chebarkul

Sim

Uruzan

Emanzhelinsk

Katav-Ivanovsk

Plast

Yuzhnouralsk

Beloretsk

Troitsk

REPUBLIC OF

Kostanay

Magnitogorsk

BASHKORTOSTAN

Kartaly

Sibay

Iriklinskoe water reservoir

K A Z A K H S T A N

Ural

Uy

Ayat

Tobol

Miass

Belaya

Sokmara

PROCESSING INDUSTRY

- Ferrous metals
- Non-ferrous metals
- Machine engineering and metal processing
- Forestry and timber
- Construction materials and glass
- Food and beverages
- Art crafts

MINING INDUSTRY

- Brown coal
- Iron ore
- Nickel ore
- Bauxite
- Copper ore
- Gold
- Micas
- Talc
- Magnesite
- Graphite
- Marble
- Raw cement

POWER PLANTS

- Thermal power plants
- Resorts

CROPS AND LIVESTOCK BREEDING

- Wheat
- Corn
- Buckwheat
- Sunflower
- Vegetables
- Meat and dairy cattle breeding
- Pig breeding
- Poultry farming

The Chelyabinsk Region is situated in the center of Russia at the crossroads of Europe and Asia. According to the estimates of the Russian Government, the Chelyabinsk Region ranks eighth in terms of social and economic development among the 89 regions of Russia. The Region boasts successful metal, machine engineering, metal processing, defense, fuel and energy, construction, and agricultural sectors. The Region's metal works produce more than a quarter of Russia's total rolled ferrous metal output and 20% of the country's steel pipe output.

The Region's investment and foreign trade appeal has led to the development of partnership trade links with foreign companies. Chelyabinsk businesses trade with companies from over 100 countries. The Region hosts 687 joint ventures and companies with foreign investment employing more than 30,000 people. The Region's total 2002 foreign trade turnover amounted to $2 billion.

Industrial companies in the Region are implementing numerous investment projects. Over the past three years, the investment inflow has increased by 35%.

Together with our foreign partners, we are ready to develop mineral deposits of titanium, magnesium, copper, nickel, gold, silver, bauxite, magnesite, and precious stones.

The Chelyabinsk Region is actively developing its consumer services and tourism sectors. Some 15 downhill skiing resorts have been built, including two world-class resorts at Abzakovo and Zavyalikha.

The Chelyabinsk Region has regional laws in place to protect the interests of foreign investors. Our guarantees are backed by budget, natural resource, and liquid stock collateral, and, of course, by our word.

Russian and foreign investors enjoy equal rights in the Region, including equal participation in investment tenders and auctions and equal access to information provided by the authorities.

I am confident that the prospects for sound business cooperation in our Region will arouse your interest. We will be happy to provide any information on the Region's investment projects and output, and will strive to provide any support you might need.

Petr Sumin,
GOVERNOR OF THE CHELYABINSK REGION,
CHAIRMAN OF THE GOVERNMENT
OF THE CHELYABINSK REGION

1. GENERAL INFORMATION

1.1. GEOGRAPHY

The Chelyabinsk Region covers a total area of 87,900 square kilometers. The Region lies in the center of Russia, on the border between its European and Asian parts. To the north the Region borders the Sverdlovsk Region, to the east – the Kurgan Region, to the south – the Orenburg Region and to the west – the Republic of Bashkortostan.

1.2. CLIMATE

The Chelyabinsk Region lies in the temperate continental climate zone. Air temperatures in January average –17°C, rising to +17.8°C in July. Annual precipitation is 700–800 mm.

1.3. POPULATION

According to preliminary 2002 census results, the Chelyabinsk Region's total population was 3,606,000 people. The average population density is 41 people per square kilometer. The economically active population amounts to 2,285,000 people. In 2002, the official unemployment level stood at 1.7%.

Demographically speaking, some 64.4% are of working age, 16.9% are below the statutory working age, and 18.7% are beyond the statutory working age.

The Region's major urban centers are Chelyabinsk with 1,078,300 inhabitants, Magnitogorsk with 419,100 inhabitants, Zlatoust with 194,800 inhabitants, Miass with 158,500 inhabitants, Troitsk with 84,300 inhabitants, and Kopeysk with 71,900 inhabitants (as of 2002).

Population							*TABLE 1*
	1992	1997	1998	1999	2000	2001	2002
Total population, '000	3,707	3,673	3,676	3,678	3,667	3,651	3,606
Economically active population, '000	1,870	1,735	1,737	1,822	1,817	1,711	2,285

2. ADMINISTRATION

27, ul. Tsvillinga, Chelyabinsk, Chelyabinsk Region, 454089
Phone: (3512) 63 9241; fax: (3512) 63 1283; e-mail: gubernator@chel.surnet.ru; http://www.ural-chel.ru

NAME	POSITION	CONTACT INFORMATION
Petr Ivanovich SUMIN	Governor of the Chelyabinsk Region, Chairman of the Government of the Chelyabinsk Region	Phone: (3512) 63 9241 Fax: (3512) 63 1283
Victor Anatolyevich TIMASHOV	First Deputy Governor of the Chelyabinsk Region for Industrial Policy and State Property	Phone: (3512) 63 3003 Fax: (3512) 63 7251 E-mail: timashov@reginf.urc.ac.ru
Andrei Nikolaevich KOSILOV	First Deputy Governor of the Chelyabinsk Region for Social Policy and Agro-Industry	Phone: (3512) 63 9321 Fax: (3512) 63 1283
Vladimir Nikolaevich DIATLOV	First Deputy Governor of the Chelyabinsk Region for Economy, Construction, and Infrastructure	Phone: (3512) 63 9765 Fax: (3512) 63 1283
Victoria Georgievna GOLUBTSOVA	Deputy Governor of the Chelyabinsk Region for Budget Policy, Head of the Finance Administration	Phone: (3512) 66 2151 Fax: (3512) 66 2109
Nikolai Mikhailovich RYAZANOV	Deputy Governor of the Chelyabinsk Region, Chief of Staff of the Govenment of the Chelyabinsk Region	Phone: (3512) 63 4181 Fax: (3512) 63 1283
Konstantin Nikolaevich BOCHKAREV	Deputy Governor of the Chelyabinsk Region, Head of Administration	Phone: (3512) 63 3585
Gennady Nikolaevich PODTESOV	Deputy Governor of the Chelyabinsk Region, Head of the Central Administration Office for Radiation Security and Environmental Safety	Phone: (3512) 64 6680 Fax: (3512) 36 5932

NAME	POSITION	CONTACT INFORMATION
Valentin Ivanovich BURAVLEV	Deputy Governor of the Chelyabinsk Region for Trade, Services and Liaison with Law Enforcement Agencies	Phone: (3512) 63 5881 Fax: (3512) 63 4462

3. ECONOMIC POTENTIAL

3.1. 1997–2002 GROSS REGIONAL PRODUCT (GRP). INDUSTRY BREAKDOWN

In 2002, the Chelyabinsk Region's gross regional product reached $5,491 million, or 5.7% up on 2001 in comparable prices. Per capita GRP totaled $1,422 in 2001, rising to $1,523 in 2002.

3.2. MAJOR ECONOMIC GROWTH PROJECTIONS

The social and economic policy of the Chelyabinsk Regional Administration for 2003 sets the following objectives:

Creating conditions conducive to expanding internal demand, increasing wages in line with indus-

GRP trends in 1997–2002						TABLE 2
	1997	1998	1999	2000	2001*	2002*
GRP in current prices, $ million	8,972.1	4,738.3	3,387.7	4,836.9	5,193.7	5,490.9

*Estimates of the Chelyabinsk Regional Government

GRP industry breakdown in 1997–2002, % of total						TABLE 3
	1997	1998	1999	2000	2001*	2002*
GRP	100.0	100.0	100.0	100.0	100.0	100.0
Industry	39.4	43.2	48.4	46.9	44.1	42.7
Agriculture and forestry	5.6	2.8	6.5	4.2	5.3	5.1
Construction	8.4	7.4	6.5	7.5	7.1	7.3
Transport and communications	6.6	7.2	6.7	6.8	6.9	7.1
Trade and public catering	9.4	10.7	9.6	8.3	10.3	11.4
Other industries	30.6	28.7	22.3	26.3	26.3	26.4

*Estimates of the Chelyabinsk Regional Government

trial output growth, maintaining high level of employment, ensuring investment growth through internal sources of investment financing, and implementing monetary policies aimed at control of inflation. The following objectives were determined for 2003:

Industry. Output is expected to increase by 2%. Ferrous and non-ferrous metals output is expected to develop, with exports rising and output of import-replacement goods increasing.

Agriculture. The Region plans to raise productivity through the implementation of energy saving technologies, the deployment of new high yield crops and soil fertilizers, improved bloodstock, and better professional training for managers at agricultural enterprises.

Trade. Retail trade is expected to increase by 6%. The Region plans to continue fostering trade relations with other regions of Russia and abroad.

Investment. Investment in the Region is expected to increase, mainly thanks to capital expenditure by companies in the Region.

3.3. INDUSTRIAL OUTPUT IN 1997–2002 FOR MAJOR SECTORS OF ECONOMY

The Chelyabinsk Region's core industrial sectors are ferrous metals, machine engineering and metal processing, energy and non-ferrous metals. The Region is home to some 830 major and medium-sized enterprises, which together account for a combined total of some 96.7% of the Region's industrial output.

Ferrous metals. This sector accounts for 54.5% of total GRP. Major enterprises include OAO Magnitogorsk Metals Combine, OAO Mechel, OAO Chelyabinsk Pipe Plant, OAO Chelyabinsk Electrometallurgical Combine, and OAO Magnesit Combine.

Machine engineering and metal processing. This sector accounts for 16.7% of total regional industrial output. Major enterprises include OAO Urals Motor Plant, OOO ChTZ-Uraltruck, OAO Forge & Press Plant, OAO Trubodetal, and OAO Kopeysk Machine Engineering Plant.

Industry breakdown of industrial output in 1997-2002, % of total						_TABLE 4_
	1997	1998	1999	2000	2001	2002*
Industry	100.0	100.0	100.0	100.0	100.0	100.0
Ferrous metals	43.4	46.7	51.6	55.6	51.3	54.5
Machine engineering and metal processing	19.5	17.2	15.9	15.9	18.7	16.7
Energy	13.6	14.5	9.0	7.2	7.9	8.6
Non-ferrous metals	3.9	4.7	8.6	8.8	7.4	7.1
Food and beverages	4.6	5.5	5.0	4.3	5.3	4.0
Construction materials	7.1	4.4	3.0	2.8	3.4	3.1
Flour, cereals, and mixed fodder	0.2	1.6	2.1	1.9	2.1	2.4
Fuel	2.1	1.9	1.4	0.8	0.7	0.8
Forestry, timber, and pulp and paper	0.9	1.0	1.0	0.9	1.0	0.7
Chemicals and petrochemicals	0.9	0.7	1.1	0.4	0.7	0.6
Light industry	0.5	0.5	0.5	0.6	0.5	0.6
Glass and porcelain	0.2	0.1	0.1	0.2	0.2	0.2

*Estimates of the Chelyabinsk Regional Government

Energy. The energy sector accounts for 8.6% of total industrial output. Major enterprises include OAO Chelyabenergo and OAO Troitsk GRES, whose output in 2002 totaled some 8.5 and 5.5 billion kWh, respectively.

Non-ferrous metals. The sector accounts for 7.1% of total industrial output. Major enterprises include OAO Chelyabinsk Zinc Electrolysis Plant, ZAO Kyshtym Copper Electrolysis Plant, and OAO Ufaleynikel.

Agriculture. Tillage accounts for 44.7% of the output in this sector and livestock for 55.3%. A total of 1,882,100 hectares was under tillage in 2002, or 2,600 hectares more than in 2001. 1,351,500 tons of crops were harvested in 2002. In livestock farming, pig stock grew by 7.9%, while poultry stock grew by 4.3%.

3.4. FUEL AND ENERGY BALANCE (OUTPUT AND CONSUMPTION PER RESOURCE)

The Chelyabinsk Region is an energy deficient region. In 2002, energy imports exceeded exports by 9.3 billion kWh. The Region also has a negative fuel balance: in 2002, the Chelyabinsk Region imported 1.6 million tons of oil products and more than 4 million tons of coal.

Fuel and energy sector production and consumption trends, 1997-2002						_TABLE 5_
	1997	1998	1999	2000	2001	2002*
Electricity output, billion kWh	22.2	21.5	17.8	20.4	20.6	20.8
Coal output, million tons	5.7	4.8	4.7	4.4	3.3	3.2
Electricity consumption, billion kWh	28.6	28.3	29.8	31.5	31.0	30.1
Coal consumption, million tons	17.5	16.0	14.5	7.7	6.9	7.0
Natural gas consumption, billion cubic meters	n/a	12.3	12.3	12.7	13.1	13.5

*Estimates of the Chelyabinsk Regional Government

3.5. TRANSPORT INFRASTRUCTURE

Roads. The Chelyabinsk Region has 8,158 kilometers of paved public highway. The Moscow–Chelyabinsk and Kazakhstan – Yekaterinburg federal highways cross the Region. Some 7 million tons of freight is transported by road, with freight turnover amounting to 230 million ton-kilometers.

Railroads. The Chelyabinsk Region has 1,793 kilometers of railroads. The Southern Urals Railroad, which crosses the European and Asian continents, runs through the Chelyabinsk Region.

Airports. The Chelyabinsk Region has two airports – at Chelyabinsk and Magnitogorsk, with passenger traffic averaging 190,000 annually and

URALS FEDERAL DISTRICT

V

freight turnover averaging 1,100 tons. Chelyabinsk International Airport operates regular flights to Germany and charter flights to many European and Asian countries.

3.6. MAIN NATURAL RESOURCES: RESERVES AND EXTRACTION IN 2002.

The main natural resources of the Chelyabinsk Region are mineral, water and forest.

Mineral resources. The main mineral resource deposits of the Urals are concentrated in the Chelyabinsk Region. These include ferrous and non-ferrous (titanium and magnesium, copper, and nickel ores), coal, chemical feedstock, construction materials, gems, gold, silver, bauxites, and magnesite. More than 300 commercial deposits have been explored, more than 20 of which contain iron ore (with total reserves of 1.3 billion tons). Deposits of high quality marble (over 10 million cubic meters), fluxes and dolomites (1.5 billion tons) and over 50 graphite fields have also been discovered in the Region.

Water. The Chelyabinsk Region is located at the triple watershed of the Volga, Ural, and Tobol Rivers. The Region has 378 water reservoirs with a total volume of 3.2 cubic kilometers.

Forestry. 2,650,000 hectares of the Region's territory lies under forest cover, with 728,700 hectares of coniferous forest and 1,584,500 hectares of deciduous. Logging is permitted in 2,350,100 hectares of forest. Birch accounts for 53% of merchantable timber, followed by aspen with 8%, pine with 25%, and spruce with 4%.

4. TRADE OPPORTUNITIES

4.1. MAIN GOODS PRODUCED IN THE REGION

Ferrous metals. In 2002, the Region produced 1.8 million tons of iron ore, 12.3 million tons of cast iron, 16 million tons of steel, and 0.6 million tons of refractory materials. The Chelyabinsk Region tops the Urals league table in terms of rolled ferrous metals output.

Machine engineering. In 2002, the Region produced 447,700 low yield motors, 439 metal cutting machine tools, 9,138 trucks, 1,683 tractors, 1,359 bulldozers, 75 excavating machines, and 370 motor graders.

Chemicals and petrochemicals. In 2002, the Region produced 3,909 tons of paint and varnish materials, 1,235 tons of polymeric film, and 5,017 tons of plastic articles.

Food and beverages. In 2002, the output of bread and bakery products reached 194,500 tons, pasta – 113,900 tons, and confectionery – 46,400 tons. Meat and dairy products output increased by 18.8%. Flour output totaled 538,200 tons, and cereals output totaled 27,900 tons.

4.2. EXPORTS, INCLUDING EXTRA-CIS

In 2000, non-CIS exports amounted to $1,648 million, while export to the CIS countries reached $213 million. The corresponding figures for 2001 were $1,449.5 million and $271.8 million, and $1,851.2 million and $259.5 million respectively for 2002.

Core exports include ferrous and non-ferrous metals (83.9% of total exports), and machine engineering products and equipment (9.7%). Major importers include China (20%), Iran (9.8%), Turkey (6.6%), the Netherlands (6.3%), Italy (5.2%), Kazakhstan (7%), and Ukraine (2.9%).

4.3. IMPORTS, INCLUDING EXTRA-CIS

In 2000, imports from outside the CIS totaled $142.9 million, with CIS imports amounting to $444 million. The corresponding figures for 2001 were $234.9 million and $457.1 million, and $207.2 million and $427.7 million respectively for 2002.

Core imports include mineral resources (56.7% of total imports), equipment (20%), ferrous and non-ferrous metals (7.2%), and food (6.4%).

4.4. MAJOR REGIONAL EXPORT AND IMPORT ENTITIES

Due to the specific nature of export and import activities in the Chelyabinsk Region, export and import activities are mainly carried out by industrial enterprises.

5. INVESTMENTS OPPORTUNITIES

5.1. INVESTMENTS IN 1992–2002 (BY INDUSTRY SECTOR), INCLUDING FOREIGN INVESTMENTS

The following main factors determine the investment appeal of the Chelyabinsk Region:
• Its favorable geographical location;
• Its developed transport infrastructure;
• Its significant industrial potential;
• Legislation supporting investment activities;
• Its highly qualified low cost workforce;
• The availability of natural resources.

5.2. CAPITAL INVESTMENT

Transport and industry accounted for the bulk of capital investment in 2002.

Capital investment by industry sector, $ million						*TABLE 6*
	1997	1998	1999	2000	2001	2002
Total capital investment	1,445.0	654.1	406.5	697.0	910.9	765.4
Including major industries (% of total)						
Industry	41.6	47.1	51.9	50.5	52.0	59.2
Agriculture and forestry	1.3	2.7	2.7	2.1	2.0	3.3
Construction	4.1	0.9	1.3	1.1	1.9	1.5
Transport and communications	16.1	17.2	14.9	15.4	21.1	14.7
Retail and public catering	3.1	1.0	0.5	1.3	1.4	0.7
Other	33.8	31.1	28.7	29.6	21.6	20.6

Foreign investment trends in 1996–2002						*TABLE 7*
	1996–1997	1998	1999	2000	2001	2002
Foreign investment, $ million	49.4	22.7	434.9	559.3	765.9	798.7
Including FDI, $ million	35.1	16.2	34.3	4.4	16.2	0.9

5.3. MAJOR ENTERPRISES (INCLUDING ENTERPRISES WITH FOREIGN INVESTMENT)

Major enterprises with foreign investment in the Chelyabinsk Region include JV Primula Mode International Fashion House (USA), JV OOO Hotel Victoria (Switzerland), OOO Chelyabinsk Cellular Network (USA), ICN Polypharm (USA), ZAO Autograph (USA), ZAO Paritet (USA), and ZAO Kamella Rassvet Dairy Products (Ireland).

Largest enterprises of the Chelyabinsk Region	*TABLE 8*
COMPANY	SECTOR
OAO Magnitogorsk Metals Plant	Ferrous metals
OAO Mechel	Ferrous metals
OAO Chelyabinsk Pipe Plant	Ferrous metals
OAO Chelyabinsk Electrometallurgical Plant	Ferrous metals
OAO Chelyabinsk Zinc Electrolysis Plant	Non-ferrous metals
ZAO Kyshtym Copper Electrolysis Plant	Non-ferrous metals
OAO Ufaleynikel	Non-ferrous metals
OAO Chelyabenergo	Energy
OAO Troitskaya GRES	Energy
OAO Ural Automotive Plant	Machine engineering
OOO ChTZ-UralTruck	Machine engineering

5.4. MOST ATTRACTIVE SECTORS FOR INVESTMENT

According to the regional administration, ferrous and non-ferrous metals, machine engineering and metal processing are the most appealing sectors for investors. The food and beverages sector is also beginning to attract investment.

5.5. CURRENT LEGISLATION ON INVESTOR TAX EXEMPTIONS AND PRIVILEGES

With a view to creating a favorable investment climate in the Region, the Chelyabinsk Region has passed a law On State Support to Investment Activity in the Chelyabinsk Region (the law provides for tax exemptions for foreign investors); a Decree of the Governor of the Chelyabinsk Region On the Procedure for the Provision of Government Guarantees from the Regional Budget on a Competitive Basis; a Decree of the Governor of the Chelyabinsk Region On the Procedure for the Provision in 2002 of Tax Credits and Investment Related Tax Credits with Respect to Taxes, Levies and Penalties Payable to the Regional Budget; and a Decree of the Governor of the Chelyabinsk Region On the Partial Reimbursement of Bank Interest on Commercial Bank Loans to Parties Involved in Investment Projects.

URALS FEDERAL DISTRICT

V

Regional entities responsible for raising investment		*TABLE 9*
ENTITY	ADDRESS	PHONE, FAX, E-MAIL
OOO Milkom-Invest	P.O. Box 1796, 9, ul. Gagarina, Chelyabinsk, Chelyabinsk Region, 454010	Phone: (3512) 51 2677, 51 2956 Fax: (3512) 52 9762
OOO Region-F	Office 12, 16A, ul. Entuziastov, Chelyabinsk, Chelyabinsk Region, 454091	Phone: (3512) 65 5719 Fax:(3512) 65 5715

5.6. FEDERAL AND REGIONAL ECONOMIC AND SOCIAL DEVELOPMENT PROGRAMS FOR THE CHELYABINSK REGION

Federal targeted programs. The Program for the Economic and Social Development of the Chelyabinsk Region, 1999–2005 (with three sub-programs) plays a major role for the economic and social development of the Chelyabinsk Region (these sub-programs include: Development of the Ferrous Metals Industry, Development of Machine Engineering, Improvement of the Environment). Ecology and Natural Resources of Russia (2002–2010); Overcoming the Consequences of Radiation Accidents (through to 2010); Prevention and Elimination of Social Illnesses (2002–2006); Federal Program for the Development of the Education System (2002–2006); Development of Russia's Judicial System (2002–2006); Modernization of Russia's Transport System (2002–2010).

Regional programs. In 2002, the Chelyabinsk Regional Administration adopted 14 regional programs focusing on public health and welfare, agriculture, natural resources, and forming and developing the telecommunications information system. The priority programs include: The Program for Increasing Soil Fertility in the Chelyabinsk Region, 2002–2005, The Program of State Support and Development of Small Businesses in the Chelyabinsk Region 2003–2005, Housing, 2002–2010, The Program for the Creation of a Regional Television Channel and Improvement of Municipal TV Broadcasting in the Chelyabinsk Region, 2002–2004.

6. INVESTMENT PROJECTS

Industry sector and project description	1) Expected results 2) Amount and term of investment 3) Form of financing[1] 4) Documentation[2]	Contact information
1	2	3
MINING		
61R001	● ◆	ZAO Uralgraphit
Reconstruction of the Tayginsky graphite open-pit mine. Project goal: to increase output and raise quality.	1) Annual revenue: $0.9 million 2) $9.4 million/10 years 3) L 4) BP	1a, ul. Mira, Taiginka Village, Kyshtym, Chelyabinsk Region, 456862 Phone: (35151) 33 181 Fax: (35151) 33 181, 32 351 Vasily Pavlovich Tereschenko, CEO
FERROUS METALS		
61R002	● ★ ◆	OAO Magnitogorsk Metering Plant
Technical revamping of a calibrating workshop and a line for ∅4.0–35.0 mm coil metal processing. Project goal: to increase and raise quality of output.	1) Annual revenue: $1.6 million 2) $5 million/18 months 3) L, Leas. 4) BP	3, ul. 9 Maya, Magnitogorsk, Chelyabinsk Region, 455007 Phone: (3519) 24 2829 Fax: (3519) 24 7028 E-mail: hromova@kalibr.mgn.chel.ru Yevgeny Veniaminovich Karpov, CEO

[1] L – Loan, E – Equity, Leas. – Leasing, JV – Joint Venture
[2] BP – Business Plan, FS – Feasibility Study

| 1 | 2 | 3 |

MACHINE ENGINEERING AND METAL PROCESSING

61R003

Production of 30kW wind Power Stations.
Project goal: to establish new facilities
and implement alternative energy sources.

1) 50 items per year
2) $1 million/2 years
3) L
4) Pilot samples, project
documentation, BP

Makeev State Rocket Center
1, Turgoyakskoye Shosse, Miass,
Chelyabinsk Region, 456000
Phone: (35135) 26 333, 26 370
Fax: (35135) 66 191
E-mail: src@makeyev.ru,
veter@makeyev.ru
Vladimir Grigoryevich Degtyar, CEO

61R004

Manufacture of equipment for enterprises in the fuel and energy sector.
Project goal: to increase output
and diversify product mix.

1) Annual revenue: $18.3 million
2) $4.7 million/3 years
3) JV, L
4) BP

OAO FNPTs Stankomash
Chelyabinsk,
Chelyabinsk Region, 454010
Phone: (3512) 52 8492
Fax: (3512) 52 9112
E-mail: fnpc@mail.ru
Anatoly Ignatyevich Tarasov,
Acting CEO

61R005

Manufacture of special hydraulic
hoisting equipment.
Project goal: to expand business
by establishing a multiproduct enterprise
for developing, manufacturing, marketing
and servicing hydraulic hoisting equipment.

1) 1,200 items per year
2) $7 million/3 years
3) E, L
4) BP

ZAO NK Uralterminalmash
66, pr. Oktyabria, Miass,
Chelyabinsk Region, 456018
Phone: (35135) 27 068
Fax: (35135) 46 646
E-mail: utm@miass.ru
Alexander Boleslavovich Okonsky, CEO

61R006

Production of competitive fuel equipment
for diesel engines.
Project goal: to expand sales market,
improve quality of fuel equipment, comply
with international standards.

1) Annual revenue: $20.5 million
2) €7.5 million/5 years
3) L, Leas.
4) BP

OOO ChTZ UralTruck
3, ul. Lenina, Chelyabinsk,
Chelyabinsk Region, 454007
Phone: (3512) 75 1760
Fax: (3512) 72 9583
E-mail: tractor@chtz.chel.ru
Valery Mikhailovich Platonov, CEO

61R007

Production of high-precision
and semi-finished castings.
Project goal: to improve quality of casting,
provide opportunities to expand sales
market via cooperation, including exports.

1) 5,000 tons per year
2) €1.5 million/3 years
3) L, Leas.
4) FS

OOO ChTZ UralTruck
3, ul. Lenina, Chelyabinsk,
Chelyabinsk Region, 454007
Phone: (3512) 75 1760
Fax: (3512) 72 9583
E-mail: tractor@chtz.chel.ru
Valery Mikhailovich Platonov, CEO

61R008

Creation of a new type of tram-cars with
ultra-low floor level.
Project goal: to diversify product mix
(new type of tram-cars).

1) 450 trams
2) $1.3 million/5 years
3) L
4) FS, BP

Kirov Ust-Katav Coach Works
Federal State Unitary Enterprise
1, Zavodskaya, Ust-Katav,
Chelyabinsk Region, 456040
Phone: (35167) 26 541
Fax: (35167) 25 548
E-mail: ukvz@chel.surnet.ru
Pavel Viktorovich Abramov, CEO

61R009

Production of functional medical beds, and
neonatal functional beds, including sales
and servicing.
Project goal: to diversify product mix.

1) Up to 600 functional medical beds
per year, up to 400 neonatal
beds per year
2) $1 million/1 year
3) L
4) BP

FGUP Zlatoust Machine
Engineering Plant
1, Parkovy Proezd, Zlatoust,
Chelyabinsk Region, 456208
Phone: (35136) 39 101, 39 162,
37 506, 39 310
Fax: (35136) 37 507
E-mail: mechta@chel.surnet.ru
Gennady Pavlovich Starikov, CEO;
Dmitry Ivanovich Popov,
Marketing Director

62. KHANTY-MANSIYSKY AUTONOMOUS DISTRICT – YUGRA [86]

E C O N O M I C M A P

KOMI REPUBLIC
Usinsk
Usa
Pechora
Vorkuta
YAMALO-
-NENETSKY
Labytnangi
SALEKHARD
Novy Port
Severnaya Sosva
Berezovo
Igrim
Oktyabrsky
Nadym
Tazovsky
Novy Urengoy
Ivdel
Sovetsky
Nyagan
A U T O N O M O U S
Nadym
Pur
Tarko-Sale
Shaim
Uray
KHANTY-MANSIYSK
Kogalym
Noyabrsk
D I S T R I C T
Mezhdurechensky
Nefteugansk
Surgut
Raduzhny
Langepas
Megion
Demyanskoe
Tavda
Irtysh
Tobolsk
Tobol
Nizhnevartovsk
Vakh
Ishim
Ishim
OMSK REGION
Vasugan
TOMSK
Narym
Tukalinsk
Tara
Luginetskoe
Kolpashevo

PROCESSING INDUSTRY
- Forestry and timber
- Construction materials
- Food and beverages

MINING INDUSTRY
- Oil
- Natural gas

POWER PLANTS
- Thermal power plants

CROPS AND LIVESTOCK BREEDING
- Vegetables
- Potatoes
- Animal farming
- Meat and dairy cattle breeding
- Reindeer breeding

The history of Yugra – the land of the Khanty and Mansi peoples – goes back to prehistoric times. Yugra moved into a bright new chapter of its history when in September 1953, a natural gas fountain welled up near the village of Berezovo, thus announcing the discovery of Russia's largest reserve of oil and gas. This marked the beginning of industrial development of the lands of the Middle Ob. Over the past 50 years, more than 7.5 billion tons of oil have been extracted from Yugra. Samotlor, Fiodorovskoye and Priobskoye oil and gas fields are renowned worldwide. In the midst of taiga and marshes, pioneers built modern cities, constructed thousands of kilometers of roads, and developed a social infrastructure.

Today the Khanty-Mansiysky Autonomous District – Yugra is steadily developing its fuel and energy sector, which provides the lion's share of Russia's oil, gas, and electricity output. The District accounts for over 30% of Russia's total federal budget revenues. 2002 industrial output amounted to $15.4 billion, topping the league table of Russian regions.

In 2002, Khanty-Mansiysky – Yugra taxpayers paid $8 billion to Russia's consolidated budget, which constitutes 43.1% growth year-on-year (the second highest growth rate in Russia).

In December 2002, Standard & Poor's rating agency raised the District's long-term foreign currency credit rating from B+ to BB-. At the same time, the District was awarded the ruAA rate on the Russian credit rating scale.

Oil extraction is our main industry, with more than 86% of total industrial output. 2002 oil output in the District amounted to 209.9 million tons, which constitutes 8.1% growth year-on-year. The District provides the highest oil extraction volume in Russia.

The Khanty-Mansiysky Autonomous District – Yugra's energy sector is one of the largest in the country. The two Surgut Thermal Power Stations and Nizhnevartovsk Thermal Power Station are fueled using petroleum gas. Electricity output in 2002 totaled 55.9 billion kWh, or 108.1% to the previous year's figure, which is the second highest output rate in Russia.

The Autonomous District's authorities are pursuing a policy with a strong focus on the social sphere. The District allocates a quarter of its consolidated budget to social needs and has implemented more than 40 targeted programs. As a result, living standards in the District are among the highest in Russia. 2002 per capita earnings increased 11% year-on-year. Wages in the District average $480 per month.

The District attracts major Russian and international sports competitions in volleyball, mini-football, martial arts, judo, boxing, northern national multiathlon, and tennis. Since 1997, the Khanty-Mansiysk Ski Center has been hosting international biathlon competitions. In March 2003, the District hosted the first world biathlon championship held in Russia.

The District enjoys good prospects for the development of tourism. Our land is one of beautiful forests, rivers, and lakes. The District boasts excellent hunting and fishing sites and opportunities for exotic tourist routes to the Northern and Arctic Urals.

We invite you to engage in mutually beneficial collaboration with our District!

Alexander Filipenko,
GOVERNOR OF THE KHANTY-MANSIYSKY AUTONOMOUS
DISTRICT – YUGRA, CHAIRMAN OF THE GOVERNMENT
OF THE KHANTY-MANSIYSKY AUTONOMOUS DISTRICT – YUGRA

1. GENERAL INFORMATION

1.1. GEOGRAPHY

Located in the central part of the West Siberian Plain, the Khanty-Mansiysky Autonomous District – Yugra covers a total area of 534,800 square kilometers. To the west it borders the Komi Republic and the Sverdlovsk Region, to the east – the Krasnoyarsk Territory, and to the southeast – the Tomsk Region.

1.2. CLIMATE

The District enjoys a severe continental climate. Air temperatures in January average −24.2°C, rising to an average of +18.4°C in July. Annual precipitation totals 400–550 mm.

1.3. POPULATION

According to preliminary 2002 census results, the total population of the District was 1,433,000 people. The average population density is 2.7 people per square kilometer. The economically active population totals 793,000 people. Official unemployment stood at 1.7% in 2002.

Demographically speaking, some 67.8% are of statutory working age, 25.2% are below the statutory working age, and 7% are beyond the statutory working age.

The ethnic mix of the District is 0.9% Khanty, 0.5% Mansi, 66.3% Russian, 11.6% Ukrainian, 7.6% Tatar, and 2.4% Bashkir, and 10.7% other nationalities.

The major urban centers of the District (2002 data) are Surgut with 285,500 inhabitants, Nizhnevartovsk with 239,000 inhabitants, Nefteyugansk with 107,800 inhabitants, and Nyagan with 68,000 inhabitants.

Population							TABLE 1
	1992	1997	1998	1999	2000	2001	2002
Total population, '000	1,319	1,350	1,372	1,384	1,382	1,402	1,433
Economically active population, '000	n/a	744	679	789	771	785	793

2. ADMINISTRATION

5, ul. Mira, Khanty-Mansiysk, Khanty-Mansiysky Autonomous District – Yugra, 628011. Phone: (34671) 32 095; fax: (34671) 32 683; e-mail: press-service@hmansy.wsnet.ru; http://www.hmao.wsnet.ru

NAME	POSITION	CONTACT INFORMATION
Alexander Vasilyevich FILIPENKO	Governor of the Khanty-Mansiysky Autonomous District – Yugra, Chairman of the Government of the Khanty-Mansiysky Autonomous District – Yugra	Phone: (34671) 92 000, 32 095 Fax: (34671) 32 683
Vyacheslav Fyodorovich NOVITSKY	First Deputy Chairman of the Government of the Khanty-Mansiysky Autonomous District – Yugra	Phone: (34671) 92 026, 92 018 Fax: (34671) 31 913
Oleg Leonidovich CHEMEZOV	First Deputy Chairman of the Government of the Khanty-Mansiysky Autonomous District – Yugra	Phone: (34671) 92 027, 92 021 Fax: (34671) 33 075
Vladimir Ivanovich KARASYOV	Deputy Chairman of the Government of the Khanty-Mansiysky Autonomous District – Yugra for Subsoil Resources and Fuel and Energy Sector	Phone: (34671) 92 030, 30 164 Fax: (34671) 21 556
Yury Yevgenyevich PECHENOV	Deputy Chairman of the Government of the Khanty-Mansiysky Autonomous District – Yugra for the Construction Sector	Phone: (34671) 92 046, 92 434 Fax: (34671) 92 046
Valery Timofeevich BOBYLYOV	Deputy Chairman of the Government of the Khanty-Mansiysky Autonomous District – Yugra for the Agroindustrial Sector, Forestry and Ecology	Phone: (34671) 92 028, 92 161 Fax: (34671) 92 028
Sergei Mikhailovich SARYCHEV	Deputy Chairman of the Government of the Khanty-Mansiysky Autonomous District, Chief of the Government Staff	Phone: (34671) 92 029, 92 153 Fax: (34671) 92 153
Gadzhi Amirovich AMIROV	Deputy Chairman of the Government of the Khanty-Mansiysky Autonomous District – Yugra, Chief of the State Property Department of the Khanty-Mansiysky Autonomous District – Yugra	Phone: (34671) 92 032, 92 055 Fax: (34671) 30 903

NAME	POSITION	CONTACT INFORMATION
Vera Arkadyevna DYUDINA	Deputy of the Chairman of the Government of the Khanty-Mansiysky Autonomous District – Yugra, Chief of the Finance Department of the Khanty-Mansiysky Autonomous District – Yugra	Phone: (34671) 92 034 Fax: (34671) 31 589

3. ECONOMIC POTENTIAL

3.1. 1997–2002 GROSS REGIONAL PRODUCT (GRP). INDUSTRY BREAKDOWN

The District's 2002 gross regional product amounted to $20,321 million, or 5% up on 2001. Industrial output, transport and communications accounted for the bulk of the growth. Per capita GRP was $13,801 in 2001 and $14,181 in 2002.

3.2. MAIN ECONOMIC GROWTH PROJECTIONS

In 2003, industrial output is expected to grow through oil and gas output and production drilling output growth, totaling $17,933.3 million.

3.3. INDUSTRIAL OUTPUT 1997–2002 FOR THE MAJOR SECTORS OF ECONOMY

The District's major industrial sectors are fuel and energy, accounting for a combined 95.6% of total industrial output.

Fuel. The sector accounts for 89.3% of the total industrial output. The 2002 oil output was up 0.2% on 2001, natural gas output was up 0.7% on 2001, and oil refinery product output was up 0.03% on 2001. Some 55 oil and gas producers operated in the District in 2002, 15 of which were

GRP trends in 1997–2002						TABLE 2
	1997	1998	1999	2000	2001*	2002*
GRP in current prices, $ million	20,095	11,949	9,611	15,281	19,351	20,321

*Estimates of the Khanty-Mansiysky Autonomous District – Yugra Government

GRP industry breakdown in 1997–2002, % of total						TABLE 3
	1997	1998	1999	2000	2001*	2002*
GRP	100.0	100.0	100.0	100.0	100.0	100.0
Industry	48.1	45.3	52.0	61.2	59.7	59.3
Agriculture and forestry	0.5	0.4	0.4	0.3	0.3	0.3
Construction	11.4	10.8	6.1	8.2	8.5	8.3
Transport and communications	17.7	17.5	12.1	7.9	7.7	8.4
Trade and public catering	4.8	3.4	3.1	2.6	2.8	2.5
Other	17.5	22.6	26.3	19.8	21.0	21.2

*Estimates of the Khanty-Mansiysky Autonomous District – Yugra Government

Industry breakdown of industrial output in 1997–2002, % of total						TABLE 4
	1997	1998	1999	2000	2001	2002*
Industry	100.0	100.0	100.0	100.0	100.0	100.0
Fuel	84.3	84.0	90.8	91.4	89.8	89.3
Energy	12.5	11.9	6.5	4.7	5.5	6.3
Machine engineering and metal processing	0.9	1.7	1.2	2.6	3.3	3.0
Forestry, timber, and pulp and paper	0.6	0.6	0.5	0.4	0.4	0.5
Construction	0.8	0.6	0.3	0.3	0.4	0.5

*Estimates of the Khanty-Mansiysky Autonomous District – Yugra Government

enterprises with foreign investment. The largest enterprises are OOO LUKoil-Western Siberia (45.7 million tons of oil produced in 2002), OAO Surgutneftegaz (49.1 million tons of oil produced in 2002), OAO YUKOS Oil Company (42.9 million tons of oil produced by OAO Yuganskneftegaz, the Company's regional production outfit, in 2002), and OAO Tyumen Oil Company.

Energy. The sector accounts for 6.3% of total industrial output. The total installed capacity of the District's power stations amounts to 9.5 GW. The largest enterprises are OAO Nizhnevartovs-

kaya GRES, OAO Surgutskaya GRES-1, and OAO Surgutskaya GRES-2.

Forestry, timber, and pulp and paper. The sector accounts for 0.5% of total industrial output. The largest enterprises are OOO Sovetsklesprom, OOO Sovetskles, OAO Khantymansiyskles, OAO Koda-Les, and OAO Surgutles.

3.4. FUEL AND ENERGY BALANCE (OUTPUT AND CONSUMPTION PER RESOURCE)

The District's electricity output was the second highest among Russia's regions in 2002.

Fuel and energy sector production and consumption trends, 1997–2002						TABLE 5
	1997	1998	1999	2000	2001	2002*
Electricity output, billion kWh	50.6	50.7	55.0	53.5	51.7	55.9
Oil output (including gas condensate), million tons	168.4	166.6	169.9	180.9	194.2	209.9
Natural gas extraction, million cubic meters	18,714	18,749	19,798	20,587	20,865	20,826
Electricity consumption, billion kWh	24.3	24.7	30.9	33.0	34.9	n/a
Natural gas consumption, million cubic meters	18,714	18,749	19,798	20,587	20,865	20,826

*Estimates of the Khanty-Mansiysky Autonomous District – Yugra Government

3.5. TRANSPORT INFRASTRUCTURE

Roads. The District has some 18,023 kilometers of roads. The Tyumen – Khanty-Mansiysk federal highway is the main link between roads under construction in the District.

Railroads. The District has 1,106 kilometers of railroad. The principal trunk railways are Tyumen – Nizhnevartovsk, Yekaterinburg – Priobye, and Yekaterinburg – Mezhdurechensky.

Airports. The District is served by 13 airports, three of which (Surgut, Kogalym, and Raduzhny) have international status. The District operates flights to more than 50 cities in Russia and abroad.

River transport. The Ob and the Irtysh are the District's principal navigable rivers. The Khanty-Mansiysky Autonomous District – Yugra has some 4,799 kilometers of navigable inland waterways. The Ob and the Irtysh rivers link the District's population centers to the large cities of Siberia: Omsk, Tobolsk, Salekhard, Tomsk and Novosibirsk. Navigation on the Region's waterways is open for five and a half months in the year.

Oil and gas pipelines. Several oil pipelines pass through the District, forming a large regional network. These include the Nizhnevartovsk – Anzhero-Sudzhensk – Irkutsk, Surgut – Polotsk, Nizhne-vartovsk – Samara, and Ust-Balyk – Omsk lines. The Urengoy – Pomary – Uzhgorod, and Urengoy – Chelyabinsk gas pipelines also cross the District's territory. The District has some 6,283 kilometers of trunk oil pipelines and 19,500 kilometers of trunk gas pipelines.

3.6. MAIN NATURAL RESOURCES: RESERVES AND EXTRACTION IN 2002

Fuel resources. The District is the main oil and gas bearing region of the Russian Federation. Some 395 oil and gas-and-oil deposits have been discovered in the District, with total reserves amounting to around 20 billion tons. More than 180 hydrocarbon deposits are being developed in the District. The Khanty-Mansiysky Autonomous District – Yugra has Russia's second largest natural gas reserves (after the Yamalo-Nenetsky Autonomous District). The largest oil and gas deposits in the District are at the Samotlorskoye, Fedorovskoye, Mamontovskoye and Priobskoye.

Ores. The District boasts large reserves of various mineral resources. Potential reserves of gold bearing ore exceed 216 tons. Iron ore reserves and traces of bauxites, copper, zinc, lead, niobium, tantalum and other minerals have been discovered.

Non-metal resources. Lode quartz, rock crystal and piezoquartz deposits have been in operation in the District since the 1930s, with output grade among the highest in the world. Black coal and lignite deposits have been discovered in the District.

Forest reserves. Forests cover 48.6 million hectares of the District's territory. Commercial timber potential output amounts to 25 million cubic meters.

Biosphere resources. The District's reindeer breeding, hunting and fur farming (black silver fox, blue fox, and mink) sectors are well developed.

4. TRADE OPPORTUNITIES

4.1. MAIN GOODS
PRODUCED IN THE REGION

Total 2002 industrial output of the District (core activities) amounted to $15.4 billion. In 2002, the Region produced:

Energy: Electricity – 55.9 billion kWh, heat energy – 23.6 million Gcal;

Fuel: Oil output (including gas condensate) – 209.9 million tons, gas – 20,826 million cubic meters, primary oil processing – 5.1 million tons;

Forestry, timber pulp and paper: commercial timber – 1.87 million cubic meters, sawn timber – 0.47 million cubic meters.

4.2. EXPORTS, INCLUDING EXTRA-CIS

Total 1999 exports amounted to $3,226 million, corresponding figures for 2000 and 2001 were $6,330.8 million and $10,833 million respectively. 2002 exports to extra-CIS countries totaled $14,627.7 million, with CIS exports coming in at $1,166.8 million.

The bulk of the Region's exports consist of crude oil (99% of the total exports), oil prod-ucts, and commercial timber. The District's main export partners are Ukraine, Kazakhstan, Poland, France and Germany.

4.3. IMPORTS, INCLUDING EXTRA-CIS

Total 1999 imports amounted to $333 million, while corresponding figures for 2000 and 2001 were $530.1 million and $586 million, respectively. 2002 imports from outside the CIS totaled $369.3 million, with CIS imports at $40.6 million. The bulk of the Region's imports is constituted by high-tech fuel and energy equipment, ferrous metal products, telecommunications and computer equipment, and transport facilities. The main import partners are the USA, Germany, Ukraine, the Czech Republic, and Japan.

4.4. MAJOR REGIONAL
EXPORT AND IMPORT ENTITIES

Due to the specific nature of the Khanty-Mansiysky Autonomous District – Yugra's export and import activities, export and import transactions are performed mainly by industrial enterprises.

Major regional export and import entities		*TABLE 6*
ENTITY	ADDRESS	PHONE, FAX, E-MAIL
OOO LUKoil-Western Siberia	20, ul. Pribaltiyskaya, Kogalym, Khanty-Mansiysk Autonomous District, 628481	Phone: (34667) 22 000 Fax: (34667) 29 800 E-mail: lws@ws.lukoil.com http://www.lukoil.ru
OAO Tyumenenergo	31, ul. Mayakovskogo, Surgut-6, Khanty-Mansiysk Autonomous District, 628406	Phone: (3462) 77 6677 Fax: (3462) 77 6360 http://www.te.ru
OAO Surgutneftegaz	1, ul. Kukuyevitskogo, Surgut-15, Khanty-Mansiysk Autonomous District, 628400	Phone: (3462) 42 6937 Fax: (3462) 42 6531 E-mail: secret_b@surgutneftegas.ru http://www.surgutneftegas.ru
OAO YUKOS Oil Company	26, Ulansky per., Moscow, 103045	Phone: (095) 232 3161 Fax: (095) 232 3160 http://www.yukos.ru
OAO Tyumen Oil Company	18/2, ul. Shchipok, Moscow, 113092	Phone: (095) 905 7280 Fax: (095) 959 7294 http:// www.tnk.ru

5. INVESTMENT OPPORTUNITIES

5.1. INVESTMENTS IN 1992–2002
(BY INDUSTRY SECTOR),
INCLUDING FOREIGN INVESTMENTS

The following factors determine the investment appeal of the Khanty-Mansiysky Autonomous District – Yugra:

• Its enormous mineral resources;

• Laws supporting investment activity (guarantees for investor rights, and preferential tax treatment for investors).

5.2. CAPITAL
INVESTMENT

Industry accounts for the lion's share of capital investments.

URALS FEDERAL DISTRICT

V

Capital investment by industry sector, $ million

TABLE 7

	1997	1998	1999	2000	2001	2002
Total capital investment	5,878	2,453	1,620	3,726	5,137	4,129
Including major industries (% of total)						
Industry	65.9	68.4	72.0	73.7	67.9	63.8
Geology and mineral exploration	1.9	2.2	2.0	2.8	3.0	1.8
Construction	0.7	1.7	1.9	1.4	2.6	1.8
Transport and communications	12.3	11.0	12.2	10.0	8.3	10.3
Trade and public catering	0.5	0.3	0.3	0.4	0.3	0.4
Housing	6.9	5.1	3.4	3.1	6.2	8.0
Communal services	4.3	2.8	2.2	2.2	2.8	0.4
Other	7.5	8.5	6.0	6.4	8.9	13.5

Foreign investment trends in 1997–2002

TABLE 8

	1997	1998	1999	2000	2001	2002
Foreign investment, $ million	130.5	106.6	89.0	61.3	201.0	232.7
Including FDI, $ million	22.5	32.4	47.1	25.1	26.9	22.7

Largest enterprises of the Khanty-Mansiysky AD – Yugra

TABLE 9

COMPANY	SECTOR
OOO LUKoil–Western Siberia, OAO Surgutneftegaz, OAO YUKOS Oil Company, OAO Tyumen Oil Company, Sidanko Oil Company, Slavneft Oil Company	Oil and natural gas
OAO Nizhnevartovskaya GRES, OAO Surgutskaya GRES-1, OAO Surgutskaya GRES-2	Energy
OOO Sovetsklesprom, OAO Sovetskles, OAO Khantymansiyskles, OOO Voskhod, OAO Kodales, OOO Surgutmebel, OAO Yukondrev	Forestry and timber

5.3. MOST ATTRACTIVE SECTORS FOR INVESTMENT

Oil production and geology and mineral exploration sectors offer the greatest investment appeal.

5.4. CURRENT LEGISLATION ON INVESTOR TAX EXEMPTIONS AND PRIVILEGES

The District's investment legislation is based on the District's Law On Support to Investment Activities by the Government Bodies of the Khanty-Mansiysky Autonomous District – Yugra. The law aims to promote investment activity in the District, and to deploy both domestic and foreign material and financial resources and advanced technologies.

The Khanty-Mansiysky Autonomous District – Yugra's Law On the Development Budget of the Khanty-Mansiysky Autonomous District – Yugra sets forth the legislative and organizational framework for the formation and expenditure of the District's budget for the provision of state support to investors in the form of state guarantees or interest-bearing, repayable, fixed term funding.

The District's Law On State Support to Leasing Organizations (Companies, Firms) in the Khanty-Mansiysky Autonomous District – Yugra was adopted with a view to developing leasing in the District as a form of investment activity.

Regional entities responsible for raising investment

TABLE 10

ENTITY	ADDRESS	PHONE, FAX, E-MAIL
The Investment, Science and Technology Department of the Khanty-Mansiysky Autonomous District – Yugra	5, ul. Mira, Khanty-Mansiysk, Khanty-Mansiysky Autonomous District – Yugra, 682006	Phone: (34671) 92 193, 92 049 Fax: (34671) 92 102 E-mail: Markovev@admhmao.ru http://www.hmao.wsnet.ru

5.5. FEDERAL AND REGIONAL ECONOMIC AND SOCIAL DEVELOPMENT PROGRAMS FOR THE KHANTY-MANSIYSKY AUTONOMOUS DISTRICT – YUGRA

Federal targeted programs. Several federal targeted programs are underway in the District, including Energy Efficient Economy (2002–2005 and through 2010), which aims to revamp boiler plants, and The Elimination of Inequalities in the Social and Economic Development of the Regions of the Russian Federation 2002–2010 and Through 2015, which aims to create a business friendly environment, improve the investment climate, and raise the efficiency of state support to Russia's regions.

Regional programs. The District's Government is implementing programs aimed at improving public healthcare, law enforcement and public welfare provision. Programs for the environmental rehabilitation of the District and the proper utilization of mineral resources that are currently underway include the Khanty-Mansiysky Autonomous District – Yugra Government Program for the Development and Restructuring of the District's Forestry and Timber Sector, which seeks to devise and implement a number of measures aimed at ensuring stabilization and development of the forestry and timber sector, to restore the existing timber and paper production facilities, and to create new facilities to meet demand in the District and supply products to Russian and foreign markets.

6. INVESTMENT PROJECTS

Industry sector and project description	1) Expected results 2) Amount and term of investment 3) Form of financing[1] 4) Documentation[2]	Contact information
1	2	3

OIL

62R001

Regional prospecting and estimation of oil and gas fields in the east and north-west of the Autonomous District. Project goal: to increase oil reserves.

1) n/a
2) $620 million/7 years
3) L, E, JV
4) FS

Department for Oil, Gas, and Mineral Resources of the Khanty-Mansiysky Autonomous District – Yugra 2, ul. Studencheskaya, Khanty-Mansiysk, Khanty-Mansiysky Autonomous District – Yugra, 628007 Phone: (34671) 26 303 Fax: (34671) 26 303 E-mail: kng@kng.hmao.ru Veniamin Fedorovich Panov, Director

62R002

Construction of an oil refinery. Project goal: to refine oil.

1) Processing capacity of 500,000 tons
2) $17 million/4 years
3) L, E, JV
4) Investment proposal

Department for Oil, Gas, and Mineral Resources of the Khanty-Mansiysky Autonomous District – Yugra 2, ul. Studencheskaya, Khanty-Mansiysk, Khanty-Mansiysky Autonomous District – Yugra, 628007 Phone: (34671) 26 303, Fax: (34671) 26 303 E-mail: kng@kng.hmao.ru Veniamin Fedorovich Panov, Director

COAL

62R003

Development of brown coal deposits in the Berezovsky District and construction of module thermal Power Stations to supply populated areas of the Berezovsky District with electricity and heat. Project goal: to supply the District's populated areas with electricity and heat.

1) 100,000 tons per year
2) $9.4 million/5.4 years
3) L, JV
4) FS

OAO Berezovskoe REP 4, ul. Kaluzhskaya, Obninsk, Kaluga Region, 249039 Phone/fax: (08439) 97 065 Fax: (08439) 97 066 E-mail: geolog@obninsk.com Nikolay Filippovich Bochkarev, CEO

[1] L – Loan, E – Equity, Leas. – Leasing, JV – Joint Venture
[2] BP – Business Plan, FS – Feasibility Study

1	2	3

ENERGY

62R004

● ◆ ▲

Construction of a second unit of the Nizhnevartovsk Thermal Power Station. Project goal: to increase electricity output.

1) 800 MW
2) $56.6 million/2 years
3) L
4) FS, BP

OAO Tyumenenergo
4, ul. Universitetskaya, Surgut, Khanty-Mansiysky Autonomous District – Yugra, 628400
Phone: (3462) 77 6350, 77 6456, (095) 775 0710
Fax: (3462) 77 6360, 77 6677
Artem Elbrusovich Bikov, CEO
Vasily Alexandrovich Kornev, Deputy CEO

62R005

● ▲

Reconstruction of the Surgut Thermal Power Station-1. Project goal: to produce electricity.

1) 720 MW
2) $177.7 million/2 years
3) L
4) FS

OAO Tyumenenergo
4, ul. Universitetskaya, Surgut, Khanty-Mansiysky Autonomous District – Yugra, 628400
Phone: (3462) 77 6350, 77 6456, (095) 775 0710
Fax: (3462) 77 6360, 77 6677
Artem Elbrusovich Bikov, CEO,
Vasily Alexandrovich Kornev, Deputy CEO

CHEMICALS AND PETROCHEMICALS

62R006

■ ● ❖ ▼

Development of the petrochemical and gas chemical sector in the Autonomous District. Project goal: to launch high added value facilities.

1) Gasoline – up to 300,000 tons per year, polyethylene – 90,000 tons per year
2) $6.9 billion/4 years
3) L, E, JV
4) Investment proposal

Department for Oil, Gas, and Mineral Resources of the Khanty-Mansiysky Autonomous District – Yugra
2, ul. Studencheskaya, Khanty-Mansiysk, Khanty-Mansiysky Autonomous District – Yugra, 628007
Phone: (34671) 26 303
Fax: (34671) 26 303
E-mail: kng@kng.hmao.ru
Veniamin Fedorovich Panov, Director

FORESTRY, TIMBER, AND PULP AND PAPER

62R007

 ■ ● ❖ ▲

Construction of a pulp and paper plant. Project goal: to produce paper.

1) 320,000 tons per year
2) $1 billion/8 years
3) L, E, JV
4) FS

Department of Investment, Science, and Technology
5, ul. Mira, Khanty-Mansiysk, Khanty-Mansiysky Autonomous District, 628006
Phone/fax: (34671) 92 049, 92 193, 92 102
E-mail: hugintf@adm.hmao.ru
Timur Faritovich Khuzhin, Deputy CEO
Yevgeny Vladimirovich Markov, Director

62R008

 ■ ● ★ ▼

Construction of a chipboard manufacturing plant in Nizhnevartovsk. Project goal: to produce chipboard.

1) 150,000 cubic meters per year
2) $30 million/2.5 years
3) L, E, Leas.
4) Investment proposal

Executive Directorate of the Generation Fund of the Khanty-Mansiysky Autonomous District – Yugra
30, ul. Komsomolskaya, Khanty-Mansiysk, Khanty-Mansiysky Autonomous District – Yugra, 628012
Phone: (34671) 32 029
Fax: (34671) 34 857
E-mail: gosfond@hmansi.vsnet.ru
Alexander Ivanovich Kondyrev, CEO

1	2	3

62R009   ■ ● ★ ▼

Construction of a chipboard manufacturing plant in Salym.
Project goal: to produce chipboard.

1) 240,000 cubic meters per year
2) $30 million/2 years
3) L, E, Leas.
4) Investment proposal

Executive Directorate of the Generation Fund of the Khanty-Mansiysky Autonomous District – Yugra
30, ul. Komsomolskaya, Khanty-Mansiysk, Khanty-Mansiysky Autonomous District – Yugra, 628012
Phone: (34671) 32 029
Fax: (34671) 34 857
E-mail: gosfond@hmansi.vsnet.ru
Alexander Ivanovich Kondyrev, CEO

62R010   ■ ● ❖ ▲

Construction of a chipboard and fibreboard manufacturing plant.
Project goal: to produce chipboard and fibreboard.

1) Up to 600,000 cubic meters per year
2) $80 million/5 years
3) L, E, JV
4) FS

OAO Sovetsky DOK
10, ul. Lenina, Sovetsky,
Tyumen Region, 628240
Phone/fax:(34675) 34 432, 36 633, ext. 199
E-mail: paivinhmao@mail.ru
Alexei Viktorovich Paivin
Head of Economic Planning Department
Viktor Vasilyevich Paivin, CEO

GLASS AND PORCELAIN

62R011   ■ ● ❖ ▲

Construction of a sheet glass manufacturing plant.
Project goal: to produce sheet glass.

1) 150,000 tons per year
2) $120 million/2 years
3) L, E, JV
4) FS in progress

Department of Investment, Science, and Technology
5, ul. Mira, Khanty-Mansiysk, Khanty-Mansiysky AD – Yugra, 628006
Phone/fax: (34671) 92 049, 92 193, 92 102
E-mail: hugintf@adm.hmao.ru
Timur Faritovich Khuzhin, Deputy CEO
Yevgeny Vladimirovich Markov, Director

TRANSPORT INFRASTRUCTURE

62R012   ● ❖ ▲

Construction of trunk oil pipelines Yugansk Depression–Mamontovo, Priobskoe Field–Chaprovskoe Field, and Severo-Seliyarovskoe Field–Krasnoleninsky TsTP.
Project goal: to transport crude oil.

1) Total length of oil pipelines – 450 km
2) $223.4 million/8 years
3) L, JV
4) FS

Department for Oil, Gas, and Mineral Resources of the Khanty-Mansiysky Autonomous District – Yugra
2, ul. Studencheskaya, Khanty-Mansiysk, Khanty-Mansiysky Autonomous District – Yugra, 628007
Phone: (34671) 26 303
Fax: (34671) 26 303
E-mail: kng@kng.hmao.ru
Veniamin Fedorovich Panov, Director

62R013   ● ★ ◆

Further development of the Tyumen-Tobolsk-Surgut railway.
Project goal: to increase passenger and freight turnover.

1) Up to 6 billion passenger-km per year.
2) $4.7 million/8 years
3) L, Leas.
4) BP

OAO Surguttransstroi
5, pr. Lokomotivny, Surgut, Khanty-Mansiysky Autonomous District – Yugra, 628414
Phone: (3462) 53 0264
Fax: (3462) 36 2046
E-mail: sts@surgut.ru
Ilya Yefimovich Kreindel, CEO

62R014   ● ▼

Construction and reconstruction of the Perm – Serov – Khanty-Mansiysk –Nefteyugansk – Surgut – Nizhnevartovsk – Tomsk highway.
Project goal: to extend the route linking Western Siberia to the Urals.

1) Two-fold increase of passenger flow
2) $1.3 billion/10 years
3) L
4) Investment proposal

Road Department of the Khanty-Mansiysk Autonomous District – Yugra
52, ul. Lenina, Khanty-Mansiysk, Khanty-Mansiysky Autonomous District – Yugra, 628012
Phone: (34671) 31 632
Fax: (34671) 31 981
E-mail: office@roaddep.ru
Viktor Alexandrovich Bets, Director

URALS FEDERAL DISTRICT

V

1	2	3

62R0015 ● ▼

Construction and reconstruction of the Tyumen–Surgut–Novy Urengoi –Nadym–Salekhard highway. Project goal: to provide direct transport route linking northern territories of the Yamalo-Nenetsky Autonomous District, Khanty-Mansiysky Autonomous District – Yugra, and the Tyumen Region with access to federal highways.

1) Passenger flow increase by 60%
2) $131.4 million/2 years
3) L
4) Investment proposal

Road Department of the Khanty-Mansiysk Autonomous District – Yugra 52, ul. Lenina, Khanty-Mansiysk, Khanty-Mansiysky Autonomous District – Yugra, 628012
Phone: (34671) 31 632
Fax: (34671) 31 981
E-mail: office@roaddep.ru
Viktor Alexandrovich Bets, Director

COMMUNICATIONS

62R0016 ● ★ ▲

Implementation of a program for rural telephone communications with access to long-distance lines and the Internet. Project goal: to develop rural telephone communications.

1) Refurbishment of 10,000 rural telephone network lines
2) $15.4 million/4 years
3) L, Leas.
4) FS

Branch of OAO Uralsvyazinform 3, ul. Kominterna, Khanty-Mansiysk, Khanty-Mansiysky Autonomous District – Yugra, 628011
Phone: (34671) 91 003, 56 071
Fax (34671) 22 583
Eduard Vasilyevich Lebedev, Director

URALS FEDERAL DISTRICT

V

63. YAMALO-NENETSKY AUTONOMOUS DISTRICT [89]

ECONOMIC MAP

KARA SEA

Islands of Novaya Zemlya

Dikson

TAYMYRSKY

(DOLGANO-NENETSKY)

AUTONOMOUS

DISTRICT

Drovyanoy

Island of Vaygach

DUDINKA · Norilsk

Yamburg

KOMI
Vorkuta

REPUBLIC

Novy Port

Tazovsky

Igarka

Labytnangi

SALEKHARD

Novy Urengoy

Urengoy

Medvezhe

Ob

Nadym

Gubkinsky

Tarko-Sale

Berezovo

Muravlenko

Noyabrsk

Priobiye

KHANTY-MANSIYSKY

AUTONOMOUS DISTRICT

KHANTY-MANSIYSK

Surgut

Nizhnevartovsk

Vakh

Ob

Yenisey

Taz

Pur

Nadym

Taz

PROCESSING INDUSTRY
- 🔵 Forestry and timber
- 🔵 Construction materials
- ⚪ Food and beverages

MINING INDUSTRY
- ▲ Oil
- △ Natural gas
- 🐟 Fishing ports

POWER PLANTS
- ⚡ Thermal power plants

CROPS AND LIVESTOCK BREEDING
- 🦌 Reindeer breeding
- ⚫ Animal farming

The Yamalo-Nenetsky Autonomous District contains as much as a third of the world's natural gas reserves. For the past 20 years, the "End of the Earth" (the meaning of the word "Yamal" in the Nenets language) has been Russia's number one gas extraction region. The District accounts for some 90% of Russia's total output of the "blue fuel". We are confident that the District has a prosperous future in store. The District has excellent prospects for the development of its natural resources, since in addition to gas our land harbors billions of tons of oil and non-ferrous, rare, and precious metals. The Arctic Urals region's deposits of gold, lead, phosphorus, heavy spar, and unique varieties of marble remain virtually untouched.

Apart from its vast reserves of minerals, the District is especially proud of its ecologically pure and delicious reindeer meat. The Yamal land is also rich in furs. In addition, the Ob and the 48,000 other rivers that flow through the District contain one third of the world's total reserves of valuable species of fresh water fish.

Many businesses already appreciate the development potential and stability of the Yamal District, one of Russia's donor regions. Investors from 26 countries, including Germany, the USA, the UK, China, and Finland, have become partners in companies with foreign capital and joint ventures operating in the District.

The District boasts a developed legislative base providing considerable tax privileges to foreign companies, guaranteeing protection of investor rights, and extending state support to investment activity.

We are committed to expanding mutually beneficial cooperation. Political stability, promising prospects, and favorable conditions for partnership, are all the distinguishing characteristics of the Yamalo-Nenetsky Autonomous District.

Yury Neelov,
GOVERNOR OF THE YAMALO-NENETSKY
AUTONOMOUS DISTRICT

1. GENERAL INFORMATION

1.1. GEOGRAPHY

Situated in the north of Western Siberia, the Yamalo-Nenetsky Autonomous District covers a total area of 750,300 square kilometers. To the east it borders the Krasnoyarsk Territory, and to the west the Komi Republic and the Arkhangelsk Region. To the north lies the Kara Sea.

1.2. CLIMATE

The District is located within the severe continental climatic zone. January air temperatures average –24°C, rising to +9°C in July. Annual precipitation reaches 200-400 mm.

1.3. POPULATION

According to preliminary 2002 census results, the population of the Yamalo-Nenetsky Autonomous District stood at 507,000 people.

The average population density is 0.7 people per square kilometer. The economically active population amounts to 329,000 people. Official 2002 unemployment stood at 2.7%.

Demographically speaking, some 70.6% of population are of statutory working age, 22.9% are below the statutory working age, and 6.5% are beyond the statutory working age.

The District's ethnic mix is 4.2% Nenets, 59.2% Russian, 17.2% Ukrainian, 5.3% Tatar, and 14.1% other.

The District's major urban centers (2002 data) are Salekhard with 34,100 inhabitants, Noyabrsk with 108,100 inhabitants, Novy Urengoy with 100,100 inhabitants, Nadym with 44,300 inhabitants, and Muravlenko with 36,800 inhabitants.

Population								TABLE 1
	1992	1997	1998	1999	2000	2001	2002
Total population, '000	488	501	506	507	504	505	507
Economically active population, '000	n/a	323	306	305	303	305	329

2. ADMINISTRATION

72, ul. Respubliki, Salekhard, Yamalo-Nenetsky Autonomous District, 629008
Phone: (34922) 44 602; Fax (34922) 47 999, 45 289; e-mail: admokr@gov.yamal.ru

NAME	POSITION	CONTACT INFORMATION
Yury Vasilyevich NEELOV	Governor of the Yamalo-Nenetsky Autonomous District	Phone: (34922) 44 602
Iosif Lipatyevich LEVINSOHN	Deputy Governor of the Yamalo-Nenetsky Autonomous District	Phone: (34922) 45 024 Fax: (34922) 41 751
Alexei Vladimirovich ARTEEV	Deputy Governor of the Yamalo-Nenetsky Autonomous District	Phone: (34922) 40 836
Nikolai Andreevich BABIN	Deputy Governor of the Yamalo-Nenetsky Autonomous District, Head of the Department for Agroindustrial Sector Development	Phone: (34922) 41 045
Oleg Vasilyevich DEMCHENKO	Deputy Governor of the Yamalo-Nenetsky Autonomous District for Transport, Communications, and Life Sustenance Systems	Phone: (34922) 45 135
Igor Anatolyevich ISHMAEV	Deputy Governor of the Yamalo-Nenetsky Autonomous District, Chief of the State Property Management Committee	Phone: (34922) 44 358 Fax: (34922) 46 049
Albina Petrovna SVINTSOVA	Deputy Governor of the Yamalo-Nenetsky Autonomous District, Chief of the Financial Department of the Yamalo-Nenets Autonomous District Administration	Phone: (34922) 31 249, 31 171
Alexander Mikhailovich KIM	Deputy Governor of the Yamalo-Nenetsky Autonomous District, Chief of the Economy and Investment Policy Department of the Yamalo-Nenetsky Autonomous District Administration	Phone: (34922) 45 031 Fax: (34922) 35 608

NAME	POSITION	CONTACT INFORMATION
Lyudmila Dmitrievna VOLKOVA	Deputy Governor of the Yamalo-Nenetsky Autonomous District, Chief of Staff of the Yamalo-Nenetsky Autonomous District Governor	Phone: (34922) 31 935
Vitaly Leonidovich TERENTYEV	Deputy Governor of the Yamalo-Nenetsky Autonomous District for Construction	Phone: (34922) 46 667 Fax: (34922) 31 043

3. ECONOMIC POTENTIAL

3.1. 1997–2002 GROSS REGIONAL PRODUCT (GRP). INDUSTRY BREAKDOWN

The Yamalo-Nenetsky Autonomous District's 2002 gross regional product amounted to $9,012 million, or 27.7% up on 2001. Growth was mainly industry driven: industry accounts for over 60% of GRP.

3.2. MAJOR ECONOMIC GROWTH PROJECTIONS

2003 industrial output is expected to rise by 13.4% on 2002 levels (in comparable prices). Capital investment in the fuel industry from all sources of financing is expected to rise by 8.8%. Capital investment in oil production, including gas condensate, is expected to rise by 31.6%, and investment in gas production is expected to rise 8%.

3.3. INDUSTRIAL OUTPUT IN 1997–2002 FOR MAJOR SECTORS OF ECONOMY

The Yamalo-Nenetsky Autonomous District's major industrial sector is the fuel industry.

GRP trends in 1997–2002						TABLE 2
	1997	1998	1999	2000	2001*	2002*
GRP in current prices, $ million	n/a	5,049	3,055	4,950	7,057	9,012

*Estimates of the Yamalo-Nenetsky Autonomous District Administration

GRP industry breakdown in 1997–2002, % of total						TABLE 3
	1997	1998	1999	2000	2001*	2002*
GRP	100.0	100.0	100.0	100.0	100.0	100.0
Industry	n/a	63.7	50.2	49.9	54.5	60.3
Agriculture and forestry	n/a	0.3	0.1	0.1	–	–
Construction	n/a	13.6	24.0	32.2	31.5	28.3
Transport and communications	n/a	3.9	3.9	2.6	2.0	2.4
Trade and public catering	n/a	3.9	4.4	4.2	3.9	3.5
Other	n/a	14.6	17.4	11.0	8.1	5.5

*Estimates of the Yamalo-Nenetsky Autonomous District Administration

Industry breakdown of industrial output in 1997–2002, % of total						TABLE 4
	1997	1998	1999	2000	2001	2002*
Industry	100.0	100.0	100.0	100.0	100.0	100.0
Fuel	96.4	92.3	92.4	93.8	96.5	95.8
Energy	0.7	5.4	4.9	3.9	1.4	2.8
Machine engineering and metal processing	0.4	0.2	0.6	0.6	0.7	0.5
Food and beverages	0.9	0.9	1.0	0.7	0.6	0.4
Construction materials	1.2	1.0	0.7	0.6	0.5	0.3
Forestry, timber, and pulp and paper	0.2	0.1	0.2	0.1	0.1	0.1
Light industry	0.1	0.1	0.1	0.1	0.1	0.1

*Preliminary data of the State Statistics Committee of Russia

Fuel. The fuel industry accounts for 95.8% of total industrial output. The District provides 90% of Russia's natural gas output, and 10% of total oil output. The largest enterprises are OOO Yamburggazdobycha, OOO Urengoygazprom, OOO Noyabrskgazdobycha, OOO Nadymgaz-prom, OAO Sibneft-Noyabrsk-neftegaz, and OAO Rosneft-Purneftegas.

Machine engineering and metal processing. The sector accounts for 0.5% of total industrial output. The largest enterprise is OAO Yamal-neftegazzhelezobeton.

3.4. FUEL AND ENERGY BALANCE (OUTPUT AND CONSUMPTION PER RESOURCE)

2002 natural gas extraction amounted to 523.5 billion cubic meters, oil extraction amounted to 43 million tons, and electricity production amounted to 1,465 million kWh.

3.5. TRANSPORT INFRASTRUCTURE

Roads. The Yamalo-Nenetsky Autonomous District has 830 kilometers of paved public highway. One of the District's priority goals is the construction of the Salekhard-Nadym-Novy Urengoy and Karachaevo-Purovsk roads. 2002 passenger turnover amounted to 32.5 million people.

Railroads. The Yamalo-Nenetsky Autonomous District has 495 kilometers of railroads. Two sections (in the western and central parts of District) provide railroad links to Tyumen and north-eastern regions of Russia.

Airports. The District is served by major airports in Salekhard, Novy Urengoy, Noyabrsk and Nadym.

River ports. Food and fuel are shipped to remote areas of the District via the Ob, Nadym, Pur, and Taz rivers during the summer months. 2002 passenger turnover amounted to 25,300 people, and freight turnover reached 361,400 tons.

3.6. MAIN NATURAL RESOURCES: RESERVES AND EXTRACTION IN 2002

The Yamalo-Nenetsky Autonomous District's principal natural resources are mineral raw materials and water resources.

Minerals resources. The District has the country's largest gas fields. Other deposits include oil, precious metals (gold), lead, phosphate, barite, marble, bauxites, copper, chrome-molybdenum and copper-zinc ores.

Water resources. The District has 300,000 lakes and 48,000 rivers. The District's rivers contain unique species of fish. The Ob River's annual fisheries output amounts to 30,000–40,000 tons.

Fuel and energy sector production and consumption trends, 1997–2002						*TABLE 5*
	1997	1998	1999	2000	2001	2002*
Electricity output, billion kWh	1.4	1.4	1.3	1.4	1.4	1.5
Oil output (including gas condensate), million tons	33.8	32.2	30.2	31.9	35.8	43.0
Natural gas extraction, million cubic meters	504,036.0	523,200.0	523,395.8	510,587.6	506,550.8	523,527.9
Electricity consumption, billion kWh	n/a	n/a	5.8	5.5	6.1	6.5
Natural gas consumption, million cubic meters	n/a	4,969.0	5,010.4	3,735.5	3,482.8	3,596.8

*Estimates of the Yamalo-Nenetsky Autonomous District Administration

4. TRADE OPPORTUNITIES

4.1. MAIN GOOD PRODUCED IN THE REGION

In 2002, the Yamalo-Nenetsky Autonomous District produced:

Energy: 1,465 million kWh.
Natural gas: 523.5 billion cubic meters.
Commercial timber: 20,100 cubic meters.
Sawn timber: 18,800 cubic meters.
Bread and bakery products: 23,000 tons.

4.2. EXPORTS, INCLUDING EXTRA-CIS

In 2002, the District's extra-CIS exports totaled $22.2 million. CIS exports reached $1.9 million.

Fuel products, equipment and mechanical engineering goods constitute the bulk of the District's

export. Main importers of the District's products include Germany, the UK, Finland, and Poland.

4.3. IMPORTS, INCLUDING EXTRA-CIS

In 2002, the District's extra-CIS imports totaled $147.3 million. CIS imports reached $112.4 million.

Equipment and mechanical engineering products and ferrous metal goods constitute the bulk of the District's import. Main exporters to the District include Ukraine, the USA, and Germany.

4.4. MAIN REGIONAL EXPORT AND IMPORT ENTITIES

Owing to the specific nature of the Region's export and import activities, export and import transactions are performed mainly by industrial enterprises.

5. INVESTMENT OPPORTUNITIES

5.1. INVESTMENTS IN 1992–2002 (BY INDUSTRY SECTOR), INCLUDING FOREIGN INVESTMENTS

The following key factors determine the investment appeal of the Yamalo-Nenetsky Autonomous District:
- Legislation supporting investment activity;
- Qualified work force;
- Natural resources (largest natural gas resources in Russia).

5.2. CAPITAL INVESTMENT

Industry and transport account for the lion's share of capital investment.

Capital investment by industry sector, $ million						TABLE 6
	1997	1998	1999	2000	2001	2002
Total capital investments	4,435.9	1,668.9	1,479.6	2,931.4	3,697.5	3,170.8
Including major industries (% of total)						
Industry	74.4	59.6	61.4	67.4	66.5	69.9
Agriculture and forestry	0.1	0.1	0.1	–	–	–
Construction	1.3	5.2	1.5	3.1	1.1	1.2
Transport and communications	11.3	16.6	25.7	20.6	21.5	18.2
Trade and public catering	0.3	0.4	0.2	0.4	0.2	0.2
Other	12.6	18.1	11.1	8.5	10.7	10.5

Foreign investment trends in 1997–2002						TABLE 7
	1997	1998	1999	2000	2001	2002
Foreign investments, $ million	38.1	28.2	53.5	102.9	73.2	111.4
Including FDI, $ million	0.4	11.2	28.6	102.9	73.2	111.4

5.3. MAJOR ENTERPRISES (INCLUDING ENTERPRISES WITH FOREIGN INVESTMENT)

The Yamalo-Nenetsky Autonomous District hosts some 78 enterprises with foreign investment from Germany, the USA, Cyprus, the UK, Finland, Bulgaria, China, Belarus, etc.

5.4. MOST ATTRACTIVE SECTORS FOR INVESTMENT

According to experts and the District's Administration, the most attractive sectors for investment include oil refining and natural gas processing, extraction, transportation and processing of low-pressure gas, energy, and agriculture.

Largest enterprises of the Yamalo-Nenetsky Autonomous District	TABLE 8
COMPANY	INDUSTRY, SECTOR
OOO Urengoygazprom	Natural gas
OOO Yamburggazdobycha	Natural gas
OOO Nadymgazprom	Natural gas
OOO Noyabrskgazdobycha	Natural gas
OAO Sibneft-Noyarbskneftegaz	Oil
OAO Rosneft-Purneftegaz	Oil

5.5. CURRENT LEGISLATION ON INVESTOR TAX EXEMPTIONS AND PRIVILEGES

The Yamalo-Nenetsky Autonomous District has enacted several laws with a view to fostering a favorable investment climate: On Investments; On Innovation Activity; On the State Insurance Pledge Fund; On Investment Tax Exemptions in the Territory of the Yamalo-Nenetsky Autonomous District.

Regional entities responsible for raising investment		*TABLE 9*
ENTITY	ADDRESS	PHONE, FAX, E-MAIL
Yamalo-Nenetsky Autonomous District Administration Department for the Economy and Investment Activity	72a, ul.Respubliki, Salekhard, Yamalo-Nenetsky Autonomous District, 629008	Phone: (34922) 45 031 Fax: (34922) 45 608

5.6. FEDERAL AND REGIONAL ECONOMIC AND SOCIAL DEVELOPMENT PROGRAMS FOR THE YAMALO-NENETSKY AUTONOMOUS DISTRICT

Federal targeted programs. The Yamalo-Nenets Autonomous District government is implementing a number of federal targeted programs, with priority given to the program for the Economic and Social Development of the Small Indigenous Peoples of the North, through 2011; Children of Russia (2003–2006); Housing (2002–2010 – sub-program: Provision of Housing to Participants in Elimination of Radiation Accidents and Disasters Results).

Regional programs. The District is implementing the following programs: Development of Fishing Industry of the Yamalo-Nenetsky Auto- nomous District, 2002–2005 (goal – to increase fisheries output, increase the quality of fish products); Preservation of Deer Farming in the Yamalo-Nenetsky Autonomous District, 2002–2005 (goal – to create conditions conducive to the preservation of deer farming); Preservation of the Selkup People and Job Creation for the Indigenous Peoples of the North in the Krasnoselkupsky District, 2002–2003 (goal – to provide jobs to the indigenous population of the Ksrasnoselkupsky District); Protection of Deer Pastures in the Yamalo-Nenetsky Autonomous District From Forest and Tundra Fires, 2002–2005 (goal – to improve the protection of deer pastures from fires); Provision of Housing to Indigenous Peoples of the North, 2002–2005 (goal – to improve the living conditions of the indigenous peoples of the North).

URALS FEDERAL DISTRICT

V

VI. SIBERIAN FEDERAL DISTRICT

64. Republic of Altai [02]

65. Republic of Buryatia [04]

66. Republic of Tyva [17]

67. Republic of Khakassia [19]

68. Altai Territory [22]

69. Krasnoyarsk Territory [24]

70. Irkutsk Region [38]

71. Kemerovo Region [42]

72. Novosibirsk Region [54]

73. Omsk Region [55]

74. Tomsk Region [70]

75. Chita Region [75]

76. Aginsky Buryatsky
    Autonomous District [80]

77. Taimyrsky (Dolgano-Nenetsky)
    Autonomous District [84]

78. Ust-Ordynsky Buryatsky
    Autonomous District [85]

79. Evenkiysky Autonomous
    District [88]

64. Republic of Altai [02]
65. Republic of Buryatia [04]
66. Republic of Tyva [17]
67. Republic of Khakassia [19]
68. Altai Territory [22]
69. Krasnoyarsk Territory [24]
70. Irkutsk Region [38]
71. Kemerovo Region [42]
72. Novosibirsk Region [54]
73. Omsk Region [55]

74. Tomsk Region [70]
75. Chita Region [75]
76. Aginsky Buryatsky
    Autonomous District [80]
77. Taimyrsky (Dolgano-Nenetsky)
    Autonomous District [84]
78. Ust-Ordynsky Buryatsky
    Autonomous District [85]
79. Evenkiysky Autonomous
    District [88]

64. REPUBLIC OF ALTAI [02]

ECONOMIC MAP

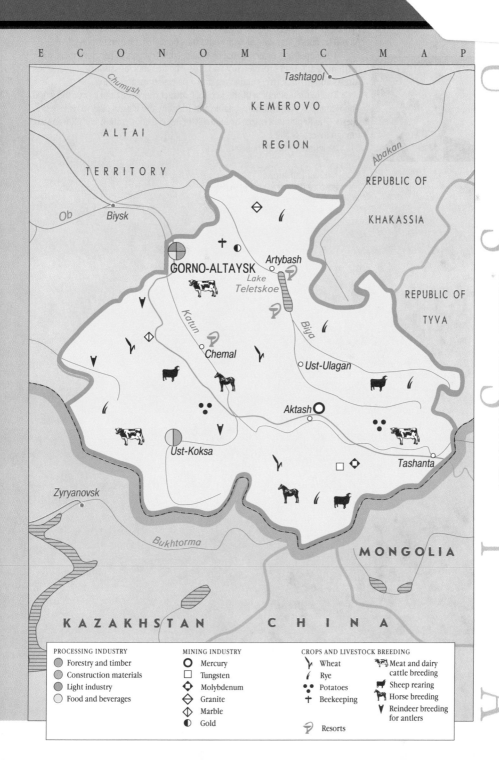

Tashtagol

KEMEROVO

REGION

ALTAI

TERRITORY

Chumysh

Ob Biysk

Abakan

REPUBLIC OF

KHAKASSIA

GORNO-ALTAYSK

Artybash

Lake
Teletskoe

Katun

Chemal

Biya

Ust-Ulagan

REPUBLIC OF

TYVA

Aktash

Ust-Koksa

Tashanta

Zyryanovsk

Bukhtorma

MONGOLIA

KAZAKHSTAN   CHINA

PROCESSING INDUSTRY
- ⬤ Forestry and timber
- ⬤ Construction materials
- ⬤ Light industry
- ⬤ Food and beverages

MINING INDUSTRY
- ⬭ Mercury
- ☐ Tungsten
- ⬥ Molybdenum
- ⬥ Granite
- ⬥ Marble
- ◖ Gold

CROPS AND LIVESTOCK BREEDING
- Ⅴ Wheat
- ⌇ Rye
- ⁂ Potatoes
- ✝ Beekeeping

- Meat and dairy cattle breeding
- Sheep rearing
- Horse breeding
- Reindeer breeding for antlers

- ℱ Resorts

L ocated at the exact center of Eurasia, the Republic of Altai borders three foreign countries (Mongolia, China and Kazakhstan), and four Russian regions: the Altai Territory, the Republic of Tyva, the Republic of Khakassia and the Kemerovo Region.

The Republic of Altai boasts several world heritage sites: Mount Belukha, the highest mountain in the Asian part of Russia, the world-famous Teletskoye Lake, the Ukok Plateau with its fantastic historical relics, and the Katun Reserve. Two major Siberian rivers, the Katun and the Biya, rise from sources in the Republic of Altai. The entire Republic of Altai could thus be called a natural reserve.

The Republic's subsoil contains incalculable reserves of precious metals, rare earth minerals, iron ore, mercury and coal. The Republic boasts an abundance of forests and pristine rivers and lakes, and a diverse flora and fauna.

The natural wonders of the Republic attract tourists from all over the world. The Republic's people are hospitable and friendly, and always glad to receive guests. The Republic is open for mutually beneficial cooperation with Russian and foreign investors alike.

Welcome to the Republic of Altai!

Mikhail Lapshin,
HEAD OF THE REPUBLIC OF ALTAI,
CHAIRMAN OF THE GOVERNMENT
OF THE REPUBLIC OF ALTAI

1. GENERAL INFORMATION

1.1. GEOGRAPHY

Situated in the Asian part of Russia, the Republic of Altai covers a total area of 92,900 square kilometers. To the north, the Republic borders the Altai Territory, to the north-west – the Kemerovo Region, to the north-east – the Republic of Khakassia, to the east – the Republic of Tyva, to the south-west – Kazakhstan, and to the south-east – Mongolia and China.

1.2. CLIMATE

The Republic of Altai enjoys a temperate continental climate. The average air temperature in January is –17°C, rising to +14°C in July. The average annual precipitation is 500–600 mm.

1.3. POPULATION

According to preliminary 2002 census results, the population of the Republic of Altai totaled 203,000 people. The average population density is 2.2 people per square kilometer. The economically active population amounts to 87,400 people. 2002 official unemployment was 9.8%.

Demographically speaking, some 59% are of working age, 26.2% are below the statutory working age, and 14.8% are beyond the statutory working age.

The Republic's ethnic mix is 31% Altai, 60.4% Russian, 5.6% Kazakh, and 3% other ethnic groups.

As of 2002, the Republic's major urban center is Gorno-Altaisk with 53,500 inhabitants.

Population								TABLE 1
	1992	1997	1998	1999	2000	2001	2002
Total population, '000	196	201	202	203	204	205	203
Economically active population, '000	86	88	84	80	91	90	87

2. ADMINISTRATION

24, ul. Chaptynova, Gorno-Altaisk, Republic of Altai, 649000
Phone: (38822) 23 132, 22 607; fax: (38822) 95 121; e-mail: root@apra.gorny.ru

NAME	POSITION	CONTACT INFORMATION
Mikhail Ivanovich LAPSHIN	Head of the Republic of Altai, Chairman of the Government of the Republic of Altai	Phone: (38822) 22 630
Nikolai Mikhailovich TAITAKOV	First Deputy Chairman of the Government of the Republic of Altai	Phone: (38822) 22 615; 22 607
Nikolai Mikhailovich MOSKALEV	Deputy Chairman of the Government of the Republic of Altai, Minister of Industry, Construction, and Residential and Communal Services	Phone: (38822) 22 547; 22 776
Alexander Alexandrovich KULAGIN	Deputy Chairman of the Government of the Republic of Altai, Minister of Agriculture	Phone: (38822) 24 349, 25 676
Viktor Vasilyevich ROMASHKIN	Deputy Chairman of the Government of the Republic of Altai, Minister of Property Relations	Phone: (38822) 25 253
Yury Vasilyevich ANTARADONOV	Deputy Chairman of the Government of the Republic of Altai, Chairman of the Investment Policy Committee	Phone: (38822) 21 425 Fax: (38822) 41 770
Grigory Barzynovich CHEKURASHEV	Minister of Economic Development, Trade and Business of the Republic of Altai	Phone: (38822) 22 019

3. ECONOMIC POTENTIAL

3.1. 1997–2002 GROSS REGIONAL PRODUCT (GRP). INDUSTRY BREAKDOWN

2002 gross regional product amounted to $241 million, which constitutes 28.2% growth year-on-year. The growth was achieved thanks to an increase in the provision of services.

3.2. MAJOR ECONOMIC GROWTH PROJECTIONS

The Government of the Republic of Altai has identified the focus areas of social and economic development as development of agricultural and industrial production infrastructure, maintenance and development of natural and

GRP trends in 1997–2002						TABLE 2
	1997	1998	1999	2000	2001*	2002*
GRP in current prices, $ million	246	165	104	143	188	241

*Estimates of the Government of the Republic of Altai

GRP industry breakdown in 1997–2002, % of total						TABLE 3
	1997	1998	1999	2000	2001*	2002*
GRP	100.0	100.0	100.0	100.0	100.0	100.0
Industry	6.6	4.5	5.5	5.0	6.1	5.2
Agriculture and forestry	25.6	25.5	27.8	21.3	27.5	24.7
Construction	6.7	11.3	5.8	6.9	6.7	5.9
Transport and communications	4.4	3.4	2.2	1.8	1.8	1.6
Trade and public catering	16.8	9.9	10.1	9.0	8.6	7.2
Other	31.6	39.2	33.8	56.0	28.3	24.4
Net taxes on output	8.3	6.2	14.8	-	21.0	31.0

*Estimates of the Government of the Republic of Altai

energy resources, creation of favorable investment and business environment.

3.3. INDUSTRIAL OUTPUT IN 1997–2002 FOR MAJOR SECTORS OF ECONOMY

The leading industrial sectors of the Republic of Altai are construction materials, non-ferrous metals, food and beverages, and timber. Their combined share of total industrial output is 86.9%.

Construction materials. This sector accounts for 29% of total industrial output. The major company within the sector is OAO Gorno-Altaisk Plant of Reinforced Concrete Goods.

Non-ferrous metals. Metals account for 27.5% of total industrial output. Major companies are Federal State Unitary Company Mine Vesioly and OOO Stone-Cutters of Altai.

Food and beverages. The share of this sector is 24%. The food and beverage companies produce dairy products, meat, confectionery, bread and bakery, vodka and liquor, fish, cereals, macaroni, and yeast. Among the major companies are OAO Altai Food Company, OOO Maima Milk, ZAO Ust-Koksinsk Butter and Cheese Plant, ZAO Cherginsk Butter and Cheese Plant, OOO Alp, and OAO Sinegorie and Co..

Agriculture. The Republic is home to 93 agricultural, 14 processing, and 12 servicing companies, and 1,239 farms. Producers have 3.2 million hectares of land at their disposal. Cattle farming accounts for 81% of agricultural products and plant growing – for 19%. Cattle farming focuses on sheep-breeding, goat-breeding, horse-breeding, and meat and dairy cattle breeding. Apiculture is well developed. Reindeer breeding for antlers is of paramount importance as it provides a unique product, which has an unbeatable competitive advantage of quality and has no analogue in the world. The major companies within the sector are Agricultural Company Abaisky, State Unitary Agricultural Company Tenginsky, State Unitary Agricultural Company Gorno-Altaisky, State Unitary Company Shirgaita, OOO Merkit, and State Unitary Farm Zarechny.

Recreation and resorts. Nature and climate provide wide opportunities to develop virtually all types of tourism, including fishing, hunting, mountain hiking, horseback hiking, and mountaineering.

3.4. FUEL AND ENERGY BALANCE (OUTPUT AND CONSUMPTION PER RESOURCE)

The fuel and energy sector of the Republic of Altai is not well developed. The Republic is connected to OAO Altaienergo energy system, while its own ener-

Industry breakdown of industrial output in 1997–2002, % of total						TABLE 4
	1997	1998	1999	2000	2001	2002*
Industry	100.0	100.0	100.0	100.0	100.0	100.0
Construction materials	13.4	18.7	11.5	21.6	34.2	29.0
Non-ferrous metals	16.5	17.1	26.8	24.6	19.9	27.5
Food and beverages	35.7	30.5	34.3	31.5	24.5	24.0
Forestry, timber, and pulp and paper	6.8	8.1	6.3	6.5	6.7	6.4
Machine engineering and metal processing	13.5	9.2	6.3	5.4	5.0	4.7
Light industry	9.9	7.0	5.4	5.8	4.9	3.8
Printing	1.4	2.8	2.3	2.1	1.9	2.4
Flour, cereals, and mixed fodder	0.2	0.8	0.9	1.7	1.3	1.0

*Estimates of the Government of the Republic of Altai

Fuel and energy sector production and consumption trends, 1997–2002						TABLE 5
	1997	1998	1999	2000	2001	2002*
Electricity output, billion kWh	0.4	0.3	0.3	0.9	1.7	1.7
Electricity consumption, billion kWh	0.4	0.4	0.5	0.5	0.4	0.4
Liquefied natural gas consumption, million cubic meters	n/a	3.4	3.4	3.1	2.6	2.8

*Estimates of the Government of the Republic of Altai

gy system is represented by small-capacity hydroelectric and diesel power stations supplying electricity to remote and difficult to access areas.

3.5. TRANSPORT INFRASTRUCTURE

Roads. The Republic has some 2,700 km of paved public highway. Roads account for over 90% of all transport system. Federal Chuisky highway of 541 km, which goes from Biysk to the Mongolian border, crosses the Republic from north to south east. Freight turnover of road transport amounted to 130.5 million tons-km in 2002.

Airports. The sector is represented by Gorny Altai Airlines. The Republic of Altai has three airports servicing local routes.

3.6. MAIN NATURAL RESOURCES: RESERVES AND EXTRACTION IN 2002

The main natural resources of the Republic of Altai are minerals, water, and forests.

Mineral resources. The Republic extracts gold, molybdenum, tungsten, decorative stone,

and building materials. There are deposits of iron res, coal, mercury, and rare metals.

Water resources. The Republic's hydro re-source network comprises over 20,000 rivers and streams with a total length of over 60,000 km and some 7,000 lakes with a total area of over 700 square kilometers. The Telets Lake alone has high quality fresh water reserves in excess of 40 cubic kilometers. Total recorded ice volume of Altai glaciers reaches 52 cubic kilometers. The largest glaciers are Taldurinensky – 35 square km, Mensu – 21 square km, and Sofiysky – 17 square km. The Republic accounts for 30% of gross hydro-electricity potential of West Siberia. Potential capacity of the Katun river hydro resources reaches 4 GW.

Forest resources. The Republic of Altai is famous for its Alpine meadows thriving medicinal herbs of exceptional quality comparable with the Alps' herbs. The Republic is home to over 40 various bactericidal fruit and berries rich in vitamins. The Republic's forests total 42,000 square kilometers, including 600 million cubic meters of coniferous trees.

4. TRADE OPPORTUNITIES

4.1. MAIN GOODS PRODUCED IN THE REGION

Agriculture. In 2002, the Republic produced 22,500 tons of grain and beans, 24,000 tons of potatoes, 11,000 tons of vegetables, 60,000 tons of whole

milk, 14.5 million of eggs, 247 tons of wool, 4.6 tons of down, 27.9 tons of Siberian deer and reindeer antlers.

Industry. In 2002, the Republic produced 32,600 tons of industrial timber, 24,500 cubic meters of sawn timber, 175,000 square meters of fabric,

39,100 decaliters of wine and vodka, 1,400 tons of meat, 1,300 tons of cheese, 1,400 tons of flour.

4.2. EXPORTS, INCLUDING EXTRA-CIS

The Republic of Altai's exports to extra-CIS countries amounted to $19.4 million in 2000, and exports to CIS, to $1.4 million. The respective figures for 2001 were $15.4 million and $1.5 million, and for 2002, $17.4 million and $0.8 million.

The main types of goods exported by the Republic of Altai are wheat flour, antlers of young Siberian stag, road vehicles, and pharmaceutical products. Major importers of the Republic's products are: Mongolia (36.6% of total exports), South Korea (20.8%), Ukraine (3.4%), and Kazakhstan (0.9%).

4.3. IMPORTS, INCLUDING EXTRA-CIS

2000 imports from extra-CIS amounted to $0.9 million, and imports from CIS, to $0.1 million. The respective figures for 2001 were $1.1 million and $0.2 million. In 2002, imports from extra-CIS were $1.9 million, while there were no imports from CIS countries.

Some 89.3% of imports are food. The main import partners are Mongolia and Kazakhstan.

Major regional export and import entities		TABLE 6
ENTITY	ADDRESS	PHONE, FAX, E-MAIL
External Economic Relations Company ASOKHRA	8, ul. Severnaya, Gorno-Altaisk, Republic of Altai, 649000	Phone: (38822) 24 436
OAO GornoAltaivneshtorg	6, ul. Lenina, Gorno-Altaisk, Republic of Altai, 649000	Phone/fax: (38822) 42 428
Industrial Company Abaisky	Village of Talda, Ust-Koksinsky District, Republic of Altai, 649483	Phone: (38848) 26 319, 22 190
OOO Ayula	Village of Karagai, Ust-Koksinsky District, Republic of Altai, 649497	Phone: (38848) 26 535, 26 519
ZAO Nadezhda	2, ul. Pervomaiskaya, Ust-Kansky District, Republic of Altai, 649450	Phone: (38847) 22 340

5. INVESTMENT OPPORTUNITIES

5.1. INVESTMENTS IN 1992–2002 (BY INDUSTRY SECTOR), INCLUDING FOREIGN INVESTMENTS

The following factors determine the investment appeal of the Republic of Altai:
- Its advantageous geographic location;
- Legislation framework conducive to investment activity (guarantees of investors' rights and preferential taxation);
- Qualified workforce;
- Natural resources.

5.2. CAPITAL INVESTMENT

Transport and agriculture accounted for the lion's share of capital investment in 2001.

5.3. MAJOR ENTERPRISES (INCLUDING ENTERPRISES WITH FOREIGN INVESTMENT)

OOO Agaiyn and Co. (Mongolia), OAO United Sugar Company (Cyprus), OOO Tyungur (Cyprus), OOO Faist (South Korea), and OOO Brand Management (Germany).

Capital investment by industry sector, $ million						TABLE 7
	1997	1998	1999	2000	2001	2002
Total capital investment	26.9	16.8	10.1	21.9	38.7	35.6
Including major industries (% of total)						
Industry	4.7	5.9	1.6	3.6	2.3	4.3
Agriculture and forestry	25.3	5.2	8.5	13.1	5.8	11.1
Construction	4.3	1.1	1.7	5.7	3.5	5.7
Transport and communications	19.3	19.9	38.6	38.1	33.3	37.8
Trade and public catering	4.3	0.2	0.1	0.2	0.2	0.4
Other	42.1	67.7	49.5	39.3	54.9	40.7

Largest enterprises of the Republic of Altai

TABLE 8

COMPANY	SECTOR
FGUP Mine Vesioly	Metals
State Unitary Company Taiga	Forestry and timber
OAO Weaving Mill	Light industry
OAO Gorno-Altaisk Reinforced Concrete Goods Plant	Construction materials
State Unitary Company Gorno-Altaisk Republican Printing House	Printing
OAO Farm-Plant Podgorny	Food and beverages
OAO Sinegorie and Co.	Food and beverages
ZAO Terek	Food and beverages
OAO Altai Food Company	Food and beverages
ZAO Cherginsky Butter and Cheese Plant	Food and beverages
OOO Republican Apiculture Center	Food and beverages

5.4. MOST ATTRACTIVE SECTORS FOR INVESTMENT

According to expert estimates of the Republican Government, the most appealing sectors for investors are building materials, metals, food and food processing industries.

5.5. CURRENT LEGISLATION ON INVESTOR TAX EXEMPTIONS AND PRIVILEGES

In order to create favorable investment climate in the Republic, the Republic of Altai has passed the following laws: On Investment Activity in the Republic of Altai, On Tax Privileges to Investors in Social Sector of the Republic of Altai, and On Transport Tax in the Republic of Altai.

5.6. FEDERAL AND REGIONAL ECONOMIC AND SOCIAL DEVELOPMENT PROGRAMS FOR THE REPUBLIC OF ALTAI

Federal targeted programs. The federal targeted program The Elimination of Inequalities in the Social and Economic Development of the Regions of the Russian Federation 2002–2010 and through 2015 plays an important role in social and economic development of the Republic. The Program is focused on creation of favorable environment for business development and improvement of investment climate in the Republic.

The Republic is implementing the Energy Efficient Economy, 2002–2005 Program, which provides for construction of energy facilities, including micro TPP's of 2 MW capacity.

Regional programs. The Republican Government develops and implements programs aimed to improve the situation in industry, energy, agriculture, education, culture, healthcare, and social welfare. The major programs include: Development of Forestry and its Liaison with the Timber Industry of the Republic of Altai, 2002-2010, Human Resources for the Agroindustrial Complex, 2000–2005, Exploration of Underground Resources and Reproduction of the Mineral and Feedstock Base in the Republic of Altai, 2003, and Preventing and Fighting Social Diseases, 2002–2006.

S I B E R I A N   F E D E R A L   D I S T R I C T

VI

Regional entities responsible for raising investment

TABLE 9

ENTITY	ADDRESS	PHONE, FAX, E-MAIL
OOO Amikom	68, pr. Kommunistichesky, Gorno-Altaisk, Republic of Altai, 649000	Phone/fax: (38822) 23 772, 23 626 E-mail: amicom@mail.gorny.ru
OOO Altai	57/1 ul. Choros-Gurkina, Gorno-Altaisk, Republic of Altai, 649000	Phone: (38822) 25 422 Fax: (38822) 26 417 E-mail: fk_altay@mail.gorny.ru
OOO Veritas	53, pr. Kommunistichesky, Gorno-Altaisk, Republic of Altai, 649000	Phone: (38822) 41 529 Fax: (38822) 41 537
OOO Councellor	29, ul. Choros-Gurkina, Gorno-Altaisk, Republic of Altai, 649000	Phone: (38822) 41 278 Fax: (38822) 41 165
ZAO Management Company Altai	13, ul. Komsomolskaya, Gorno-Altaisk, Republic of Altai, 649000	Phone: (38822) 41 008 Fax: (38822) 41 134, 42 133 E-mail: mc@mail.gorny.ru

6. INVESTMENT PROJECTS

Industry sector and project description	1) Expected results 2) Amount and term of investment 3) Form of financing[1] 4) Documentation[2]	Contact information
1	2	3

HOTELS, TOURISM, AND RECREATION

64R001 ■ ● ❖ ◆ ▲		
Construction of a downhill ski resort at the Sinyukha mountain. Project goal: to build a modern tourist center to world standards.	1) Cable-way capacity 1,200 people per hour 2) $2.8 million/4 years 3) L, E, JV 4) BP, FS	Tourism and Recreation Development Center of the Republic of Altai 3, ul. Promyshlennaya, Gorno-Altaisk, Republic of Altai, 649000 Phone: (38822) 62 532 Fax: (38822) 22 012 E-mail: eko@region.gorny.ru Mikhail Petrovich Lepetov, Director
64R002 ■ ● ❖ ◆ ▲		
Construction of a tourist center at the Teletskoye lake. Project goal: to build a modern tourist center to world standards.	1) Center capacity: 160 rooms 2) $2.8 million/2 years 3) L, E, JV 4) BP, FS	Tourism and Recreation Development Center of the Republic of Altai 3, ul. Promyshlennaya, Gorno-Altaisk, Republic of Altai, 649000 Phone: (38822) 62 532 Fax: (38822) 22 012 E-mail: eko@region.gorny.ru Mikhail Petrovich Lepetov, Director
64R003 ■ ● ❖ ◆ ▲		
Construction of a tourist center at the Aya lake. Project goal: to build a modern tourist center to world standards.	1) Capacity: 80 people 2) $0.8 million/1.5 years 3) L, E, JV 4) BP, FS	Tourism and Recreation Center of the Republic of Altai 3, ul. Promyshlennaya, Gorno-Altaisk, Republic of Altai, 649000 Phone. (38822) 62 532 Fax: (38822) 22 012 E-mail: eko@region.gorny.ru Mikhail Petrovich Lepetov, Director
64R004 ■ ● ❖ ◆ ▲		
Construction of a chain of tourism and health facilities based on existing and brand new reindeer-breeding farms. Project goal: to build a modern tourist complex to world standards.	1) Capacity: 80 to 100 people 2) $1 million/3 years 3) L, E, JV 4) BP, FS	Tourism and Recreation Center of the Republic of Altai 3, ul. Promyshlennaya, Gorno-Altaisk, Republic of Altai, 649000 Phone: (38822) 62 532 Fax: (38822) 22 012 E-mail: eko@region.gorny.ru Mikhail Petrovich Lepetov, Director

[1] L – Loan, E – Equity, Leas. – Leasing, JV – Joint Venture
[2] BP – Business Plan, FS – Feasibility Study

65. REPUBLIC OF BURYATIA [04]

Nizhnyaya Tunguska

Bodaybo
Nerpo
Vitim
Nelyaty
Kalakan

Ichyora

Taksimo

I R K U T S K
Kirensk

Kumora
Bagdarin

Vitim

Ust-Kut

Nizhneangarsk
Verkhnyaya Angara

Rudnogorsk
Severobaykalsk

Kurumkan

Barguzin
Ust-Barguzin

CHITA

Bratsk

R E G I O N
Zhigalovo
Lena

Goryachinsk

Bratskoe
water
reservoir

Kachug

Uda

ULAN-UDE

Tulun

Selenginsk
UST-ORDYNSKY

Sibirskoe
Angara
Kamensk

Yamarovka
Chikoy

Angarsk
IRKUTSK

Petrovsk-
Zabaykalsky

Gusinoozersk
Chikoy

Baikalsk

Kyakhta

Botogaliye
Oka

Dzhida

M O N G O L I A

Lake
Khubsugul
(Khuvsgel-Nuur)

ULAN-BATOR

LEGEND

PROCESSING INDUSTRY
- Machine engineering and metal processing
- Forestry and timber
- Construction materials and glass
- Light industry
- Food and beverages

MINING INDUSTRY
- Brown coal
- Bituminous coal
- Tungsten
- Molybdenum
- Gold
- Raw cement
- Graphite
- Mineral water sources

POWER PLANTS
- Thermal power plants
- Resorts
- Fishing ports

CROPS AND LIVESTOCK BREEDING
- Wheat
- Long-fibred flax
- Barley
- Oats
- Sugar beetroot
- Meat and dairy cattle breeding
- Sheep rearing

T he Republic of Buryatia is Russia's eastern gateway, the storehouse of a great culture born on the shores of the unique world heritage site of Lake Baikal.

Drawn from more than 100 national groups, the hard-working and highly educated people of the Republic are of European and Asian stock. They live together in peace and harmony, working constructively in the severe Siberian climate.

The Republic is an agroindustrial region with great industrial and raw material potential. In the Republic we have striven to create a business-friendly environment, ensuring all of the necessary conditions for foreign business and trade relation development, including appropriate legislation.

Buryatia looks forward to the 21st century with confidence. As one of Siberia's leading regions in terms of industrial output growth (despite rigid environmental protection regulations), the Republic has reached a new stage of its development.

The Republic understands that preserving for future generations Buryatia's biosphere with its inimitable landscapes and at its heart Lake Baikal, the world's greatest freshwater reserve, is crucial for the sustainable development of the entire Baikal region.

The principal goal of Buryatia's government is to create the economic basis for shifting the Republic to sustainable development of its economic potential based on vigorous principles of self-development, economic modernization, enhanced production efficiency, and competitiveness.

Buryatia's people work well and are not work shy. The Republic is open for investors.

Leonid Potapov,
PRESIDENT OF THE REPUBLIC OF BURYATIA,
CHAIRMAN OF THE GOVERNMENT
OF THE REPUBLIC OF BURYATIA

1. GENERAL INFORMATION

1.1. GEOGRAPHY

Located in eastern Siberia, the Republic of Buryatia covers an area of some 351,400 square kilometers. To the south, it borders Mongolia, to the south-east, the Republic of Tuva, to the north and north-west, the Irkutsk Region, and to the west, the Chita Region. Administratively speaking, the Republic is divided into 21 districts. It has six cities, 29 urban settlements, and 614 settlements.

1.2. CLIMATE

The Republic of Buryatia enjoys a severe continental climate. The January air temperature averages −30°C, rising to +17 °C in July. Annual precipitation reaches 300–400 mm.

1.3. POPULATION

According to preliminary 2002 census results, the total population in the Republic of Buryatia was 981,000 people. The average population density is 2.8 per square kilometer. The economically active population is 469,000. Official unemployment in 2002 stood at 15.4%.

Demographically speaking, some 61% are of statutory working age, 24% are below the statutory working age, and 15% are beyond the statutory working age.

The Republic's ethnic mix is 24% Buryat, 70% Russian, 2.2% Ukrainian, and 3.8% other nationalities.

The Republic's major urban centers are Ulan-Ude with 359,400 inhabitants, Gusinoozersk with 29,000 inhabitants, and Severobaikalsk with 28,000 inhabitants.

Population								TABLE 1
	1992	1997	1998	1999	2000	2001	2002
Total population, '000	1,057	1,048	1,043	1,038	1,032	1,026	981
Economically active population, '000	508	443	430	489	491	456	469

2. ADMINISTRATION

The Government House, 54, ul. Lenina, Ulan-Ude, Republic of Buryatia, 670001
Phone/fax: (3012) 21 0251; e-mail: buryatia@icm.buryatia.ru; http://www.buryatia.ru

NAME	POSITION	CONTACT INFORMATION
Leonid Vasilyevich POTAPOV	President of the Republic of Buryatia, Chairman of the Government of the Republic of Buryatia	Phone: (3012) 21 5186 Fax: (3012) 21 2822
Vladimir Ottovich GEINDEBRECHT	First Deputy Chairman of the Government of the Republic of Buryatia	Phone: (3012) 21 4703
Leonid Dasheevich TURBYANOV	Deputy Chairman of the Government of the Republic of Buryatia for the Agroindustrial Complex	Phone: (3012) 21 3902
Yevgeny Mikhailovich PALTSEV	Deputy Chairman of the Government of the Republic of Buryatia, Chairman of State Committee for Property Relations in the Republic of Buryatia	Phone: (3012) 21 2237
Vladimir Vasilyevich PERELYAEV	Deputy Chairman of the Government of the Republic of Buryatia, Minister of Industry, Production Infrastructure, and Technology of the Republic of Buryatia	Phone: (3012) 21 0684
Nikolai Innokentyevich BYKOV	Deputy Chairman of the Government of the Republic of Buryatia, Minister of Construction, Architecture, of the Republic of Buryatia and Housing and Communal Services of the Republic of Buryatia	Phone: (3012) 21 1440
Bair Gvibalovich BALZHIROV	Deputy Chairman of the Government of the Republic of Buryatia, Chief of the Official Representative Office of the Republic of Buryatia to the President of the Russian Federation	Phone: (095) 925 9500 Fax: (095) 923 6046

SIBERIAN FEDERAL DISTRICT

VI

3. ECONOMIC POTENTIAL

3.1. 1997–2002 GROSS REGIONAL PRODUCT (GRP). INDUSTRY BREAKDOWN

The 2002 gross regional product of the Republic of Buryatia reached $1,258 million, 18.2% up on 2001. The growth was mainly industry driven.

3.2. MAJOR ECONOMIC GROWTH PROJECTIONS

The Republic plans to implement a number of social and economic reforms in the near future aimed at securing stable economic growth and promoting business development with a focus on the

GRP trends in 1997–2002						*TABLE 2*
	1997	1998	1999	2000	2001*	2002*
GRP in current prices, $ million	1,947	1,150	689	799	1,065	1,258

*Estimates of the Government of the Republic of Buryatia

GRP industry breakdown in 1997–2002, % of total						*TABLE 3*
	1997	1998	1999	2000	2001*	2002*
GRP	100.0	100.0	100.0	100.0	100.0	100.0
Industry	25.8	24.8	22.8	24.4	24.5	25.6
Agriculture and forestry	15.1	14.5	14.6	13.3	11.3	10.8
Construction	8.9	7.8	5.6	6.7	8.3	6.8
Transport and communication	10.2	12.3	17.2	17.7	20.6	19.5
Trade and public catering	12.4	12.9	14.7	13.8	12.8	11.4
Other	24.3	25.9	20.0	23.6	21.6	25.0
Net taxes on output	3.3	1.8	5.1	0.5	0.9	0.9

*Estimates of the Government of the Republic of Buryatia

development of the machine engineering, instrument manufacturing, and electrical engineering industries. The Republic plans to establish a number of enterprises for the processing of local raw materials. The purpose of the reforms is to introduce the Republic's products to the international market.

3.3. INDUSTRIAL OUTPUT IN 1997–2002 FOR MAJOR SECTORS OF ECONOMY

The Republic's key industries are: machine engineering and metal processing, energy, non-ferrous metals, and food and beverages, which together account for 84% of total industrial output.

Machine engineering and metal processing. Machine engineering and metal processing account for the lion's share of the Republic's industrial output (30.9%). Major enterprises include OAO Ulan-Ude Aviation Plant, ZAO Ulan-Udestalmost, OAO Electrical Machinery Plant, GUP Ulan-Ude Locomotive Plant, OAO Electromashina, and ZAO Bely Lebed.

Energy. Energy sector enterprises account for 30.5% of total industrial output. Buryatia's energy system is based on the Gusinoozerskaya Hydroelectric Power Station (UES of Russia-owned) and the Ulan-Ude Thermal Power Station 1, an OAO Buryatenergo subsidiary.

Non-ferrous metals. Non-ferrous metals account for 13% of total industrial output. Total

gold output in 2001 amounted to 2,000 kilograms. The Republic is home to goldfields with abundant supplies of high-grade placer gold. The Republic's top gold producer is OAO Buryatzoloto's Irokinda.

Fuel (coal) industry. The coal industry, the source of raw materials for the Republic's energy facilities, is represented by open-pit mine Tugnuisky (OAO Vostsibugol) with 90% of total coal output, three minor open-pit mines, the Okino-Klyuchevskoi, Daban-Gorkhonsky (OAO Buryatlestoprom), and Khara-Khurzhinsky (OAO Zakamenskaya PMK), and open-pit mine Orkhon-1.

Agriculture. Meat and milk cattle rearing, sheep rearing, tillage and vegetables are the mainstays of the Republic's agricultural sector. The Republic produces the following grain crops: spring wheat, barley, oats, sugar beet and fiber flax. The Republic has some 521,700 hectares of tillage land with grain crops covering 321,200 hectares. Arable lands cover 38.2%, and hayfields, 30%. The largest enterprises are OAO Buryatmyasoprom and OAO Ulan-Ude Macaroni Plant.

Sanatorium and spa facilities. Buryatia is home to the following balneotherapeutic resorts: the Arshan Resort in the Sayany foothills (mineral waters) and the Goryachinsk Resort (radon thermal springs on the shores of Lake Baikal). The Republic's natural environment is conducive to the promotion of tourism.

Industry breakdown of industrial output in 1997–2002, % of total

	1997	1998	1999	2000	2001	2002*
Industry	100.0	100.0	100.0	100.0	100.0	100.0
Machine engineering and metal processing	16.7	12.0	14.8	22.3	29.5	30.9
Energy	39.0	45.9	32.1	27.0	29.3	30.5
Non-ferrous metals	4.9	6.8	12.7	14.8	11.7	13.0
Food and beverages	9.6	9.0	10.9	9.9	9.0	9.6
Forestry, timber, and pulp and paper	7.0	7.0	11.2	9.9	7.3	7.0
Fuel	11.6	9.2	6.6	5.7	5.2	3.5
Light industry	2.5	2.3	3.1	3.1	2.6	2.2
Construction materials	4.0	3.6	2.8	3.4	2.6	2.0
Chemicals and petrochemicals	0.1	0.2	0.5	0.7	0.2	1.3
Flour, cereals, and mixed fodder	2.1	1.8	3.4	1.8	1.3	1.0

*Estimates of the Government of the Republic of Buryatia

3.4. FUEL AND ENERGY BALANCE (OUTPUT AND CONSUMPTION PER RESOURCE)

The Republic's fuel and energy sector is represented by the fuel industry and the electricity and thermal power supply sector. The Republic's energy output completely covers demand.

3.5. TRANSPORT INFRASTRUCTURE

Roads. The Republic has 6,226 kilometers of paved public highway. The main federal highways are: Irkutsk – Ulan-Ude and Ulan-Ude – Chita. Total road freight in 2001 amounted to 296 million kilometer-tons, with passenger bus traffic totaling 146 million passenger-kilometers.

Fuel and energy sector production and consumption trends, 1997–2002

	1997	1998	1999	2000	2001	2002*
Electricity output, billion kWh	4.3	3.8	3.3	3.1	3.5	4.6
Coal output, million tons	3.9	3.4	3.8	3.9	3.9	3.7
Electrical energy consumption, billion kWh	3.2	2.9	3.1	3.2	3.2	3.3
Oil product consumption, '000 tons	373.1	342.3	251.2	618.2	286.6	307.1
Natural gas consumption, tons of conventional fuel	10.0	20.0	800.0	700.0	500.0	1,547.0
Coal consumption, million tons	4.4	4.3	3.8	4.1	4.2	4.2

*Estimates of the Government of the Republic of Buryatia

Railroads. The Republic has 1,199 kilometers of railroads. Buryatia has very favorable geographic location at the crossroads of the Trans-Siberian and the Baikal – Amur, which connect the central regions of the Russian Federation with the Far East and East Asia: China, North Korea, and Mongolia.

Airports. Air transport is represented by OAO Buryat Airlines, which provides air links both within the Republic and to other destinations in Russia. The Ulan-Ude International Airport serves Moscow, St. Petersburg, Vladivostok, Khabarovsk, Yakutsk, Yuzhno-Sakhalinsk, Chita, Irkutsk, Bratsk, Tomsk, Krasnoyarsk, Novosibirsk, and Omsk.

River transport. The Republic has a well-developed inland waterway transportation sector, with main routes running along the Selenga River and through Lake Baikal. The Republic has some 282 kilometers of navigable waterways. The main goods transported by inland waterway are timber products, sandy gravel, and oil products.

River ports. Major ports on Lake Baikal are Ust-Barguzinsk, Nizhneangarsk, and Severobaikalsk. Ulan-Ude also has a large river port.

3.6. MAIN NATURAL RESOURCES: RESERVES AND EXTRACTION IN 2002

The Republic's principle natural resources are: minerals, water, and forest resources.

Mineral resources. The Republic is home to six explored molybdenum deposits, five complex ore deposits (48% of nationwide zinc reserves and 24% of nationwide lead reserves), ten fluor spar deposits (reserves over 10 million tons), major uranium-ore deposits, and around 300 auriferous fields. One tin deposit, three beryllium deposits, and three chrysotile asbestos deposits are in production. The Republic's Cheremshanskoye deposit contains over 40 million tons of quartz sandstone, and seven deposits of grainy quartz have been explored in the Severobaikalsk District.

Water resources. The Republic's largest reservoir is Lake Baikal (total reserves of 24,000 cubic kilo-

meters). The Republic also has 53 rivers with a total length of 1,200 kilometers, and 176 artesian wells.

Forest resources. Forests are one of the Republic's principal natural resources, with forest coverage totaling some 27.2 million hectares. The Republic's forests are exclusively upland. Hardwood (65%), pine (21%), and dark softwood (10%) prevail.

4. TRADE OPPORTUNITIES

4.1. MAIN GOODS PRODUCED
IN THE REGION

Energy. In 2002, the Republic produced 4.6 billion kWh of electricity.

Coal. In 2002, the Republic produced 3.7 million of coal.

Electric motors. In 2002, the Republic produced 914 AC motors.

Industrial timber. In 2002, the Republic produced 556,000 cubic meters of industrial timber.

Vacuum cleaners. In 2002, the Republic produced 16,900 vacuum cleaners.

4.2. EXPORTS,
INCLUDING EXTRA-CIS

In 2000, extra-CIS exports amounted to $113.3 million, and CIS exports reached $3.2 million. The figures for 2001 were $139.7 and $2.1 million respectively, and for 2002 – $202.1 million and $10.3 million.

The main goods exported from the Region are industrial timber, machinery, and fuel and energy products. The Republic's main export destinations are China (64% of exports – timber, machinery, ferrous and non-ferrous metals), Mongolia (12% – food, fuel and energy products,

and machinery), Iran (11% – machinery), and Japan (7% – coal). CIS countries account for 5% of exports: Kazakhstan imports paper and paperboard, while Ukraine imports woolen fabrics.

4.3. IMPORTS, INCLUDING EXTRA-CIS

In 2000, extra-CIS imports amounted to $24.5 million, and CIS imports reached $5.2 million. The figures for 2001 were $21 million and $9.2 million, respectively, and for 2002 – $24.6 million and $13.9 million.

The Republic's main imports are food and machinery. Its main trading partners for imports are Mongolia (26% of total imports – beef), the USA (14% – rice, flour, beans, buckwheat, and vegetable oil); China (13% – fruit), Italy (5% – drilling machinery), and Germany (4% – meat and poultry processing equipment). CIS imports account for over 36% of the total, including Ukraine (28% – turboprop engines for civilian aircraft) and Uzbekistan (7.3% – vegetables, fruit and wool).

4.4. MAJOR REGIONAL EXPORT
AND IMPORT ENTITIES

Owing to the specific nature of export and import transactions in the Republic of Buryatia, export and import activities are carried out mainly by industrial enterprises.

5. INVESTMENT OPPORTUNITIES

5.1. INVESTMENTS IN 1992–2002
(BY INDUSTRY SECTOR),
INCLUDING FOREIGN INVESTMENTS

The key factors determining the investment appeal of the Republic are:

• Its developed transport infrastructure;

• Legislation supporting investment activity (guarantees of investor rights and preferential tax treatment for investors);

• Its highly qualified workforce;

• Cheap energy resources (electricity, coal);

• Natural resources (minerals deposits).

5.2. CAPITAL INVESTMENT

In 2002, industrial enterprises and transportation companies accounted for the lion's share of capital investment.

5.3. MAJOR ENTERPRISES
(INCLUDING ENTERPRISES
WITH FOREIGN INVESTMENT)

The Republic hosts 258 large and medium-sized enterprises, including 65 with foreign investments.

5.4. MOST ATTRACTIVE SECTORS
FOR INVESTMENT

According to the estimates of the Republic's Government, the most attractive sectors for investors are energy, non-ferrous metals, timber, transport, communications, and the food industry.

5.5. CURRENT LEGISLATION ON INVESTOR
TAX EXEMPTIONS AND PRIVILEGES

With a view to creating a favorable investment environment, the Republic of Buryatia has adopted the following laws: On Mechanisms for

Capital investment by industry sector, $ million

TABLE 6

	1997	1998	1999	2000	2001	2002
Total capital investment	309.9	171.3	96.2	116.8	173.2	146.6
Including major industries (% of total):						
Industry	33.8	25.9	25.4	31.8	20.8	37.8
Agriculture and forestry	2.6	1.7	2.1	3.1	1.6	2.0
Construction	2.0	1.4	2.1	3.0	3.6	0.7
Transport and communications	36.6	50.8	52.0	45.6	59.8	43.3
Trade and public catering	0.9	2.3	3.9	2.0	0.4	1.0
Other	24.1	17.9	14.5	14.5	13.8	15.2

Foreign investment trends in 1997–2002

TABLE 7

	1997	1998	1999	2000	2001	2002*
Foreign investment, $ million	0.2	13.0	0.8	0.2	–	9.2
Including FDI, $ million	0.2	2.1	0.1	0.1	–	0.1

Raising Investments in the Republic's Economy (establishes the main requirements with respect to investments projects implemented with state support), On Investment Activities in the Republic of Buryatia (establishes the major principles governing investment activity, its forms and methods and provides for investor tax exemptions and credits), On the Encouragement of Foreign Investments in the Economy of the Republic of Buryatia (provides a favorable investment environment for foreign investors and tax exemptions), and the Decree of the Government if the Republic of Buryatia On the Strategy for the Transition of the Republic of Buryatia to Sustainable Development, 2002–2010 (aims to ensure sustainable development, to preserve the Lake Baikal's ecosystem, and to ensure full utilization of resources).

Largest enterprises of the Republic of Buryatia

TABLE 8

COMPANY	SECTOR
OAO Buryatenergo	Energy
OAO Ulan-Ude Aviation Plant	Machine engineering
OAO Ulan-Ude Instrument Production Association	Machine engineering
ZAO Ulan-Ude Fine Fabrics Plant	Light industry
OAO Ulan-Ude Amta Confectionery	Food industry
OAO Buryatzoloto	Jewelry
OAO Ulan-Ude Macaroni Factory	Food industry
OAO Ulan-Udestalmost	Machine engineering and metals processing

5.6. FEDERAL AND REGIONAL ECONOMIC AND SOCIAL DEVELOPMENT PROGRAMS FOR THE REPUBLIC OF BURYATIA

Federal targeted programs. The Republic is implementing a significant number of federal targeted programs for economic and social development of the Republic of Buryatia, including:

• Economic and Social Development of the Far East and the Trans-Baikal Region (1996-2005 and through 2010);

• The Economic and Social Development of Indigenous Peoples of the North (through 2011);
• Culture of Russia (2001-2005);
• Disabled Persons Welfare (2000-2005);
• Housing (2002-2010);
• The Children of Russia, The Youth of Russia (2001-2005);
• Ecology and Natural Resources of Russia (2002–2010).

SIBERIAN FEDERAL DISTRICT

VI

Regional programs. In 2002, the Republican Government adopted 16 regional targeted programs focused on industry, the energy sector, agriculture, education, culture, and public health and welfare. The most important programs are The development of the Retail market in the Republic of Buryatia, 2002-2006,

Reforming and upgrade of the construction and construction materials industries of the Republic of Buryatia, 2002-2010, Creation and development of the educational information environment, 2002-2005, Modernization of economic relations in the education system of Ulan-Ude, 2002-2005.

Regional entities responsible for raising investment		*TABLE 9*
ENTITY	ADDRESS	PHONE, FAX, E-MAIL
Fund for the Implementation of the Federal Program for the Social and Economic Development of the Republic of Buryatia	54, ul. Lenina, Ulan-Ude, 670001	Phone: (3012) 21 1057, 21 1659 Fax: (3012) 21 1057
The Chamber of Commerce and Industry of the Republic of Buryatia	1a, ul. Komsomolskaya, Ulan-Ude, 670002	Phone: (3012) 27 2048, 27 2047 Fax: (3012) 27 2048
The Republic of Buryatia's Union of Industrialists and Entrepreneurs	1a, ul. Komsomolskaya, Ulan-Ude, 670002	Phone: (3012) 44 3535, 45 3151 Fax: (3012) 26 6129 E-mail: spprb@burnet.ru
Directorate of the Republic of Buryatia's Securities and Stock Market Commission	55, ul. Lenina, Ulan-Ude 670001	Phone: (3012) 21 5429 Fax: (3012) 21 5429 E-mail: kom_cb@burnet.ru

6. INVESTMENT PROJECTS

Industry sector and project description	1) Expected results 2) Amount and term of investment 3) Form of financing[1] 4) Documentation[2]	Contact information
1	2	3
MINING		
65R001		
Establishment of a new ore mining and processing enterprise for quartz extraction and dressing. Project goal: to introduce marketable products based on chemically pure quartz.	1) Annual quartz output 200,000 tons; piezo-quartz monocrystal output 15 tons, highly dressed quartz - 200 tons; semiconductor silicon - 200 tons. 2) $22 million/1 year 3) L 4) BP	OAO Sakhayur Commercial Quartz Apt. 61, 15, ul. Geologicheskaya, Ulan-Ude, Republic of Buryatia, 670031 Phone: (3012) 23 3709 Fax (3012) 21 1416 (Government of the Republic of Buryatia) E-mail: alexx@ofpsrv.bsc.buryatia.ru Vladimir Dugarovich Bazarov, CEO
65R002		
Establishment of a new ore-mining and processing enterprise for complex ore extraction and dressing (the Ozernoye Deposit). Project goal: to market zinc and other polymetals.	1) 6 million tons annually 2) $40 million/5 years 3) L 4) FS	Main Division of the Ministry of Natural Resources of the Russian Federation for the Republic of Buryatia 57, ul. Lenina, Ulan-Ude, Republic of Buryatia, 670000 Phone: (3012) 21 1534, 21 4746 Fax: (3012) 21 5206, 21 1917 E-mail: gupr@burnet.ru Vladimir Ivanovich Bakhtin, Head

[1] L – Loan, E – Equity, Leas. – Leasing, JV – Joint Venture
[2] BP – Business Plan, FS – Feasibility Study

1	2	3

ENERGY

65R003 ● ▲

Renewal of fixed assets and heating networks of the Ulan-Ude Thermal Power Station 1. Project goal: to increase power supply output.

1) Increase of power supply output by 30%, thermal power output by 40%
2) $41.5 million/5 years
3) L
4) FS

OAO Buryatenergo
13, prospekt 50-letiya Oktyabrya,
Ulan-Ude, Republic of Buryatia, 670034
Phone/fax: (3012) 45 3065, 45 3073
E-mail: root@burene.elektra.ru
Sergei Vladimirovich Lystsev, CEO

65R004 ▲

Construction of new power generating facilities (Moksky Hydroelectric Power Station). Project goal: to increase output, expand export opportunities.

1) 1,410MW capacity
2) $2.700 billion/n/a
3) Concession financing
4) FS

OAO Buryatenergo
13, prospekt 50-letiya Oktyabrya,
Ulan-Ude, Republic of Buryatia, 670034
Phone/fax: (3012) 45 3065, 45 3073
E-mail: root@burene.elektra.ru
Sergei Vladimirovich Lystsev, CEO

MACHINE ENGINEERING AND METAL PROCESSING

65R005 ● ★ ◆

Production of a new brand of helicopter (medium-size). Project goal: to diversify product mix (to market a new helicopter model.

1) Up to 60 units a year
2) $47.5 million/3 years
3) L, Leas.
4) BP

OAO Ulan-Ude Aviation Factory
1, ul. Khorinskaya, Ulan-Ude,
Republic of Buryatia, 670009
Phone: (3012) 25 3386
Fax: (3012) 25 2147
E-mail: uuaz@uuaz.ru
Leonid Yakovlevich Belykh, CEO

LIGHT INDUSTRY

65R006 ■ ● ★ ◆

Reconstruction of yarn spinning facilities for finished garment production. Project goal: expansion of production output, improvement of quality.

1) Revenues of $15.1 million annually
2) $13.8 million/1.5 years
3) L, Leas., E
4) BP

ZAO Ulan-Ude Fine Fabric Plant
9, ul. Sakhzynovoy, Ulan-Ude,
Republic of Buryatia, 670042
Phone: (3012) 43 6075
Fax: (3012) 43 6275
E-mail: tcm@burnet.ru
Klavdiya Pavlovna Altsman, CEO

SIBERIAN FEDERAL DISTRICT

VI

66. REPUBLIC OF TYVA [17]

ECONOMIC MAP

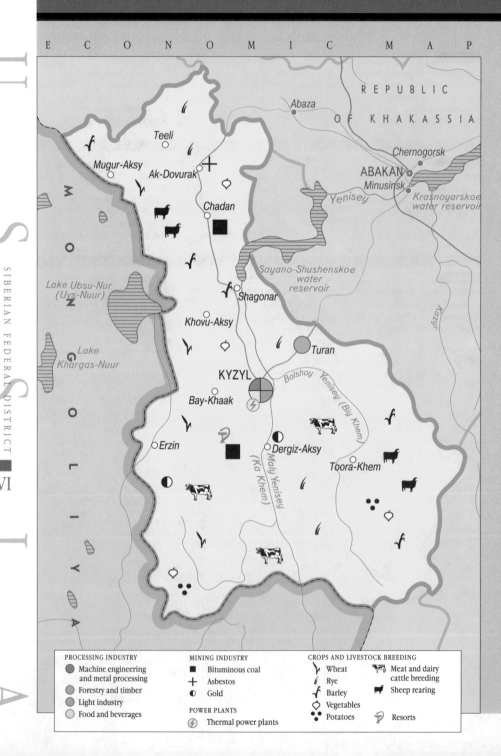

PROCESSING INDUSTRY
- ● Machine engineering and metal processing
- ● Forestry and timber
- ● Light industry
- ○ Food and beverages

MINING INDUSTRY
- ■ Bituminous coal
- ✛ Asbestos
- ◑ Gold

POWER PLANTS
- ⚡ Thermal power plants

CROPS AND LIVESTOCK BREEDING
- 🌾 Wheat
- Rye
- Barley
- ◇ Vegetables
- ⦙ Potatoes
- 🐄 Meat and dairy cattle breeding
- 🐑 Sheep rearing
- Resorts

L ocated at the heart of Eurasia, the Republic of Tyva borders Mongolia, the Republics of Altai, Khakassia and Buryatia, the Krasnoyarsk Territory, and the Irkutsk Region. While the Republic of Tyva could easily be called a natural reserve, it also possesses enormous natural resources that have the potential to yield immense benefit provided they are invested and developed rationally.

Boasting considerable resource and cultural potential, the Republic's investment appeal is unique in Russia inasmuch as the opportunities for the attraction and utilization of investment compensate for the potental investment risk.

Projects in the timber industry, agricultural produce processing, mining, construction materials, and tourism account for the bulk of the Republic's investment and foreign trade potential.

The Government of the Republic of Tyva is actively striving to improve the investment climate and raise foreign investment. A legislative base regulating investment activities is currently being developed. Amendments introducing tax benefits for investors in the real sector of the Republic's economy are being added to Law No. 284 of the Republic of Tyva On Investment Activity in the Republic of Tyva adopted on July 26, 1999.

A portfolio of innovation and investment projects is being formed. The Republic's administration encourages local enterprises to participate in exhibitions and venture fairs across Russia.

Last but not least, the Republic's natural beauty attracts tourists from all over the world. We are happy to welcome guests. The Republic of Tyva is open to mutually beneficial cooperation with Russian and foreign business circles.

Sherig-ool Oorzhak,
CHAIRMAN OF THE GOVERNMENT
OF THE REPUBLIC OF TYVA

1. GENERAL INFORMATION

1.1. GEOGRAPHY

Situated in the south of Eastern Siberia, the Republic of Tyva covers a total area of 170,500 square kilometers. To the north, the Republic borders the Krasnoyarsk Territory, to the east and north-east – the Irkutsk Region, to the south and south-east – Mongolia, to the west – the Republic of Altai, and to the north-west – the Republic of Khakassia.

1.2. CLIMATE

The Republic of Tyva enjoys a continental climate.

The average air temperature in January is –28°C, rising to +18°C in July. The average annual precipitation in lowland areas is 150–400 mm and in upland areas, 400–1,000 mm.

1.3. POPULATION

According to preliminary 2002 census results, the Republic's total population was 306,000 people. The average population density is 1.8 people per square km. The economically active population amounts to 129,000 people. Official unemployment in 2002 was 10.1%. Demographically speaking, some 54.6% are of working age, 31.3% are below the statutory working age, and 14.1% are beyond the statutory working age.

The Republic's ethnic mix is: Tyvan – 64.3%, Russian – 32%, other – 3.7%.

As of 2002, the Republic of Tyva's major urban centers were Kyzyl with 104,100 inhabitants, Ak-Dovurak with 13,200 inhabitants, and Chadan with 8,100 inhabitants.

Population							TABLE 1
	1992	1997	1998	1999	2000	2001	2002
Total population, '000	306	310	310	311	311	310	306
Economically active population, '000	143	122	115	124	115	120	129

2. ADMINISTRATION

18, ul. Chuldum, Kyzyl, Republic of Tyva, 667000
Fax of the Government of the Republic of Tyva: (39422) 11 346
Fax of the Chancellery of the Government of the Republic of Tyva: (39422) 11 354
E-mail: gov@tuva.ru; http://www.gov.tuva.ru

NAME	POSITION	CONTACT INFORMATION
Sherig-ool Dizizhikovich OORZHAK	Chairman of the Government of the Republic of Tyva	Phone: (39422) 36 948
Alexandr Vladimirovich BROKERT	Acting First Deputy Chairman of the Government of the Republic of Tyva, Minister of Innovation, Investment Policy, and External Economic Relations	Phone: (39422) 11 605, 11 294 E-mail: minnaz@tuva.ru
Sergei Viktorovich NIKONOV	Acting Deputy Chairman of the Government of the Republic of Tyva, Minister of Energy, Transport, and Communications	Phone: (39422) 37 188
Alexandr Borisovich SVINTSOV	Acting Deputy Chairman of the Government of the Republic of Tyva, Minister of Construction	Phone: (39422) 11 828
Radislav Sanaevich BAYAN	Acting Deputy Chairman of the Government of the Republic of Tyva, Minister of Finance	Phone: (39422) 10 426
Svetlana Nikolaevna SAPOVA	Acting Minister of Economy of the Republic of Tyva	Phone: (39422) 13 455, 32 556 Fax: (39422) 11 767 E-mail: mineconom@tuva.ru
Ezher Vasilyevich CHELOKOV	First Deputy Minister of Innovation, Investment Policy, and External Economic Relations of the Republic of Tyva	Phone: (39422) 11 163 E-mail: minnaz@tuva.ru

3. ECONOMIC POTENTIAL

3.1. 1997–2002 GROSS REGIONAL PRODUCT (GRP). INDUSTRY BREAKDOWN

The 2002 gross regional product of the Republic of Tyva amounted to $179 million, which constitutes 9.2% growth year-on-year. Per capita GRP totaled $531 in 2001 and $586 in 2002.

3.2. MAJOR ECONOMIC GROWTH PROJECTIONS

The Republic's future economic development priorities are set forth in the State Conceptual Framework for the Development of the Republic of Tyva through 2010. The strategic goal is to stimulate the comprehensive development of the economy through output increases in all industrial spheres:

Industry: Industrial output growth through an increase in labor productivity, capacity utilization, and improved labor force training. Growth will be secured through innovation, improved quality of goods and services, and new market development and penetration.

GRP trends in 1997–2002						TABLE 2
	1997	1998	1999	2000	2001*	2002*
GRP in current prices, $ million	284	187	108	134	164	179

*Estimates of the Government of the Republic of Tyva

GRP industry breakdown in 1997–2002, % of total						TABLE 3
	1997	1998	1999	2000	2001*	2002*
GRP	100.0	100.0	100.0	100.0	100.0	100.0
Industry	12.6	12.7	14.4	10.2	10.8	10.6
Agriculture and forestry	12.4	12.5	21.3	19.5	22.9	18.6
Construction	4.4	4.7	3.6	3.0	6.5	5.4
Transport and communications	8.2	5.1	3.7	3.3	3.0	2.6
Trade and public catering	21.4	16.5	14.7	12.1	13.1	12.2
Other	50.4	54.7	42.0	51.3	45.2	50.6
Net taxes on output	−9.4	−6.2	0.3	0.6	−1.5	–

*Estimates of the Government of the Republic of Tyva

Agriculture: Output growth and an increase in gross product by upgrading and expanding operations, attracting investments, and constructing new agricultural facilities.

Construction: Maintenance and increase in resource efficiency and higher operations mobility.

3.3. INDUSTRIAL OUTPUT IN 1997–2002 FOR MAJOR SECTORS OF ECONOMY

The leading industrial sectors of the Republic of Tyva are non-ferrous metals (cobalt and gold mining), energy, and food and beverages. These account for some 72.5% of total industrial output. Industry is raw material focused and represented by small and medium enterprises.

Non-ferrous metals. This sector accounts for 25.5% of total industrial output in the Republic. Non-ferrous metals mining in the Republic is currently limited to gold. Digger outfits are the main type of gold mining companies.

Energy. Energy accounts for 26.8% of total industrial output. The sector is represented by the Kyzyl Thermal Power Station, diesel power plants, and a low capacity hydroelectric power station.

Food and beverages. This sector accounts for 20.2% of total industrial output. The Republic produces bread and bakery products, confectionery, pasta products, sausage, liquor, and meat products. The largest food and beverage companies are OAO Kyzyl Bakery and OAO Sayan-Alko.

Fuel. The fuel industry accounts for 13.2% of total industrial output. Open cast coal mining for the fuel industry is conducted at the Kaa-Khemsky and Chadansky open cast pits of the Ulug-Khemsky and Chadansky coalfields.

Forestry, timber, and pulp and paper. The sector accounts for 3.2% of total industrial output. A total of 36,500 cubic meters of timber was felled in 2002. The main companies in the sector are OOO Tyva-Timber, OAO Tyva Furniture, and State Unitary Company Turanlesprom.

Agriculture. The sector is represented mainly by transhumance cattle farming and grain growing, and accounts for 18.6% of the Republic's GRP.

SIBERIAN FEDERAL DISTRICT

VI

Industry breakdown of industrial output in 1997–2002, % of total						TABLE 4
	1997	1998	1999	2000	2001	2002*
Industry	100.0	100.0	100.0	100.0	100.0	100.0
Non-ferrous metals	12.0	25.2	36.4	36.8	29.2	25.5
Energy	29.1	25.4	23.3	24.2	30.1	26.8
Food and beverages	18.8	13.3	10.7	11.0	9.9	20.2
Fuel	18.4	14.0	10.8	11.6	13.3	13.2
Forestry, timber, and pulp and paper	2.3	2.3	1.8	3.0	4.0	3.2
Construction materials	6.5	6.8	4.3	3.5	4.0	3.0
Flour, cereals, and mixed fodder	5.7	4.7	5.5	2.4	2.2	2.8
Light industry	1.7	1.4	1.6	3.0	3.3	2.3
Machine engineering and metal processing	2.5	1.6	1.3	1.3	1.2	1.0

*Estimates of the Government of the Republic of Tyva

3.4. FUEL AND ENERGY BALANCE (OUTPUT AND CONSUMPTION PER RESOURCE)

The Republic of Tyva is an energy deficit region. OAO Tyvaenergo produced 44.9 million kWh of energy, or 7% of consumption in 2002. RAO UES supplied 606 million kWh of energy in 2002, 1.8% more than in 2001.

The Republic's 2002 output of heat was 1.2 million Gcal.

Fuel and energy sector production and consumption trends, 1997–2002						TABLE 5
	1997	1998	1999	2000	2001	2002*
Electricity output, million kWh	36.3	41.6	36.6	39.5	42.8	44.9
Coal output, '000 tons	554.0	489.0	547.0	523.0	575.0	522.0
Electricity consumption, million kWh	571.4	598.6	623.5	640.6	637.9	650.9
Coal consumption, '000 tons	554.0	489.0	547.0	523.0	575.0	522.0

*Estimates of the Government of the Republic of Tyva

3.5. TRANSPORT INFRASTRUCTURE

Roads. The Republic has 2,321 km of paved public highway. Main routes linking the Republic to neighboring regions are: State Frontier – Kyzyl – Abakan – Krasnoyarsk (the bulk of freight flow is registered on the Abakan – Kyzyl section) and Ak-Dovurak – Abaza – Abakan (used mainly to transport raw materials for the asbestos plant). Roads transportation accounts for 99.8% of freight and 99% of passenger transport. In 2002, some 1,033,000 tons of freight was transported by road.

Airports. A new modern airport building with an international terminal is being constructed in Kyzyl.

River transport. Goods and passengers are transported by the Great and Lesser Yenisei Rivers. Navigation is open for 150 days from June to October. In 2002, some 1,100 tons of freight was transported by water.

3.6. MAIN NATURAL RESOURCES: RESERVES AND EXTRACTION IN 2002

The Republic's principle natural resources are non-ferrous, rare earth, and precious metals, coal, ferrous metals, non-metal construction materials, and fresh and mineral water.

Mineral resources. The Republic of Tyva is rich in silver, gold, bismuth, copper, nickel, and cobalt ores. The Republic has the prerequisites to start profitable deep processing of ore concentrates at the Tardan gold ore deposit, Ulug-Tanzeksky tantalum-niobium deposit, Terlighainsky mercury deposit, Tastygsky lithium deposit, Kyzyl-Tashtygsky lead and zinc deposit, and other deposits of rare earth metals. The Republic's estimated gold reserves amount to 500 tons, including 200 tons of placer gold.

Reserves of coking and fuel coal amount to 20.2 billion tons, 84% of which is high-grade coal. 2002 output totaled 522,000 tons.

The Republic operates a major chrysotile asbestos deposit at Ak-Dovuak. 2002 output of high-grade asbestos amounted to 1,300 tons.

Construction materials. Nine deposits of brick clay with a total reserve of 13.8 million cubic meters have been explored and prepared for extraction in the Republic, alongside three deposits of sand and gravel mix, and deposits of construction sand, marble lime, and marble. Some 20 deposits of various construction materials have been explored in the Republic.

Timber. Forests cover some 50% of the Republic's area. Total timber reserves amount to 1,050.1 million cubic meters. The most valuable tree species found in the Republic are Siberian larch, cedar, pine, and spruce.

Land resources. Agricultural lands cover 50,000 square kilometers, or 29% of the Republic's area, including 3,901,000 hectares of pastures, 121,000 hectares of hayfields, and 585,000 hectares of arable land.

Water resources. The Republic of Tyva is home to the Sayano-Shushenskoe water reservoir and 34 mineral water springs. The Republic is drained by the Great Yenisei, Lesser Yenisei, and Upper Yenisei rivers.

Biological resources. Water reservoirs in the Republic contain valuable fish species such as Hucho taimen (Salmonidae), grayling, sturgeon, Coregonus peled, and other Coregonidae. The estimated annual catch is some 400-500 tons per year. Hunting reserves account for over 60% of the Republic's total area. Valuable species of fauna found in the Republic include sable, Sayan squirrel, lynx, wolverine, ermine, bear, Siberian stag, mountain goat, and musk deer.

4. TRADE OPPORTUNITIES

4.1. MAIN GOODS PRODUCED
IN THE REGION

Fuel. In 2002, the Republic produced some 522,000 tons of coal, which represents a fall of 9% year-on-year.

Construction materials. As of 2002, asbestos output totaled 1,300 tons; 2002 sawn timber output was 14,700 cubic meters, and wall materials, 0.6 million brick equivalents. The Republic manufactures prefabricated concrete assemblies and components.

Agricultural products. The 2002 gross grain yield amounted to 24,700 tons, the potato yield was 24,400 tons, and the vegetable yield totaled 7,700 tons. In 2002, the Republic produced 26,200 tons of meat and poultry (live weight), 43,200 tons of milk, and 4.6 million eggs.

Food and beverages. In 2002, the Republic of Tyva produced some 12,900 tons of bread and bakery

products, 200 decaliters of liquor, 46 tons of meat, and 850 tons of dairy products.

4.2. EXPORTS, INCLUDING EXTRA-CIS

The Republic of Tyva's foreign trade totaled some $5.7 million in 2001 and $8.5 million in 2002.

2001 exports amounted to $4.6 million and 2002 exports totaled $6.9 million.

The main product exported by the Republic is food. The Republic's main importer is Mongolia, which accounts for 99% of total foreign trade turnover.

4.3 IMPORTS, INCLUDING EXTRA-CIS

2001 imports totaled $1.1 million and 2002 imports, $1.6 million. The bulk of imports was represented by meat, cattle hide, sheep fleece, and car tires.

4.4. MAJOR REGIONAL EXPORT
AND IMPORT ENTITIES

Major regional export and import entities		*TABLE 6*
ENTITY	ADDRESS	PHONE, FAX, E-MAIL
OOO Atsbo	14-4b, ul. Kalinina, Kyzyl, Republic of Tyva, 667003	Phone: (39422) 53 918
OOO Mongol-Tyva	62, ul. Internatsionalnaya, Kyzyl, Republic of Tyva, 667004	Phone: (39422) 56 884

5. INVESTMENT OPPORTUNITIES

5.1. INVESTMENTS IN 1992–2002
(BY INDUSTRY SECTOR),
INCLUDING FOREIGN INVESTMENTS

The following factors determine the investment appeal of the Republic of Tyva:

• The availability of vast reserves of natural resources suitable for the development of highly profitable mining and metal processing industries;

• Cheap energy (considerable reserves of coking and fuel coals);

• A qualified and relatively cheap workforce;

• Its advantageous geographical location;

• Unique environmental conditions for recreation, tourism, and recuperation;

• Organizational and financial support for investment projects and business protection guarantees provided by the Republic's executive authority.

5.2. CAPITAL INVESTMENT

Energy, construction materials, and machine engineering account for the lion's share of capital investment.

Capital investment by industry sector, $ million						TABLE 7
	1997	1998	1999	2000	2001	2002
Total capital investment	24.7	20.1	11.5	10.0	21.8	22.1
Including major industries (% of total):						
Industry	32.5	28.9	34.8	20.1	13.6	12.4
Agriculture and forestry	10.0	6.0	9.1	7.4	2.7	2.2
Construction	0.1	–	0.2	–	–	–
Transport and communications	18.1	27.4	31.3	25.0	10.9	6.8
Trade and public catering	–	–	1.6	0.5	–	–
Other	39.3	37.7	23.0	47.0	72.8	78.6

Foreign investment trends in 1996–2002						TABLE 8
	1996–1997	1998	1999	2000	2001	2002
Foreign investment, $ million	–	2.0	–	0.4	–	–
Including FDI, $ million	–	2.0	–	–	–	–

5.3. MAJOR ENTERPRISES (INCLUDING ENTERPRISES WITH FOREIGN INVESTMENT)

The Republic of Tyva has registered several companies with foreign investment, including Russian-British OOO Ekonika-Kyzyl, OOO Mongol-Tyva, and OOO Atsbo (Tyva-Mongolia).

5.4. MOST ATTRACTIVE SECTORS FOR INVESTMENT

According to the Ministry of Innovation, Investment Policy, and External Economic Relations of the Republic of Tyva, the mining, timber, food and beverages, and tourism and rehabilitation industries are the most appealing sectors for investors.

Largest enterprises of the Republic of Tyva	TABLE 9
COMPANY	SECTOR
FGUP Kaa-Khemsky Open Cast Pit	Coal
GUP Tyvaasbestos Plant	Construction materials
GUP Tyva Carpets	Light industry
GUP Garment and Knitwear Factory	Light industry
OAO Kyzyl Bakery	Food and beverages
OAO Sayan-Alko	Food and beverages

5.5. CURRENT LEGISLATION ON INVESTOR TAX EXEMPTIONS AND PRIVILEGES

The Republic of Tyva has passed Law No. 284 On Investment Activity in the Republic of Tyva dated July 26, 1999, which outlines a number of privileges for investors. Currently, the law is undergoing additions with regard to tax privileges to investors in the real sector of the Republic's economy.

The Law provides a legal and economic framework for government support to investors, guarantees equitable protection of rights, and provides tax exemptions to investors in the Republic. Investors with projects that have been accorded the status of Particularly Important Investment Project (projects that will accelerate the development of priority areas of the Republic's econo-

my) and who have entered into an investment agreement with the Government of the Republic of Tyva enjoy full tax exemptions or reduction in certain taxes.

With a view to channeling investment into the Republic's economy and initiating innovation, the Republic's Government has announced an annual competition for the best innovation project. The Republic uses the results of the competition to form a portfolio of innovation and investment projects, which are then presented at Russia's investment fairs and exhibitions. Competition winners receive awards.

5.6. REGIONAL ENTITIES RESPONSIBLE FOR RAISING INVESTMENT

The Government of the Republic of Tyva undertakes to raise investment in the Republic.

5.7. FEDERAL AND REGIONAL ECONOMIC AND SOCIAL DEVELOPMENT PROGRAMS FOR THE REPUBLIC OF TYVA

Federal targeted programs. The Republic of Tyva participates in 34 federal targeted programs worth a total of $9.0 million, including $2.1 million from the Republic's budget. The priority status was accorded to the following programs for the economic and social development of the Republic of Tyva:

The program for the Elimination of Inequalities in the Social and Economic Development of the Regions of the Russian Federation, 2002-2010 and through 2015, which aims to reduce regional gaps in core social and economic development indicators by 2010, create conditions conducive to the development of enterprise, and improve the investment climate. A budget of $3.1 million has been allocated to this program from the federal budget to complement the $0.4 million allocated from the Republic's budget.

The Republic has also underway a program for the Economic and Social Development of Minor Indigenous Peoples of the North through 2011, which aims to create conditions conducive to the development of agricultural processing and traditional crafts of the peoples of the North, the creation of employment, and the development of industrial and social infrastructure. A budget of $0.2 million was allocated to the program from the federal budget in 2002.

Regional programs. The Government of the Republic of Tyva is developing and implementing over 50 programs focused on industrial development, agricultural policy, environmental rehabilitation, law enforcement, healthcare, public welfare, and culture. In 2002, the Republic allocated $1.3 million to implement 44 republican targeted programs. Top priority programs focus on improving the investment climate, creating conditions conducive to the development of enterprise, and supporting small enterprise.

The State Conceptual Framework for the Development of the Republic of Tyva through 2010 aims to improve the Republic's investment appeal, increase the efficiency of the Republic's business, and develop internal and external transport systems. The implementation of the program will create over 10,000 jobs.

6. INVESTMENT PROJECTS

Industry sector and project description	1) Expected results 2) Amount and term of investment 3) Form of financing[1] 4) Documentation[2]	Contact information
1	2	3
NON-FERROUS METALS		
66R001 ● ◆		OAO Tyvacobalt
Upgrading and launch of the Tyvacobalt Plant. Project goal: to restore production of cobalt for export.	1) 709 tons of cobalt per year, 948 tons of nickel per year, 1,140 tons of silver per year, and 153 tons of copper per year 2) $29 million/7 years 3) L 4) BP	Ministry of Industry of the Republic of Tyva 11, ul. Kalinina, Kyzyl, Republic of Tyva, 667010 Phone: (39422) 51 557 Fax: (39422) 51 573 Vasily Dorzhuevich Ondar, Chief of the Investment Dept
MINING		
66R002 ● ◆		OAO Tyva Lead
Development of the Kyzyl-Tashtygsky pyrites and polymetal deposit. Project goal: to produce concentrated polymetals with subsequent transition to pure metal extraction.	1) 600,000 tons of ore per year 2) $59.7 million/5 years 3) L 4) BP	Tyva R&D Institute of Comprehensive Development of Natural Resources of the RF Academy of Sciences 117a, ul. Internatsionalnaya, Kyzyl, Republic of Tyva, 667007 Phone: (39422) 11 753, 11 853 Fax: (39422) 11 753 E-mail: tikopr@tuva.ru Vladimir Ilyich Lebedev, Director

SIBERIAN FEDERAL DISTRICT

VI

[1] L – Loan, E – Equity, Leas. – Leasing, JV – Joint Venture
[2] BP – Business Plan, FS – Feasibility Study

1	2	3

LIGHT INDUSTRY

66R003

Launch of tanning operations at vacant facilities at a fur plant.
Project goal: to introduce new products.

1) 18,038,000 square decimeters of footwear leather uppers per year; 16,539,000 square decimeters of split leather per year, and 1,962,000 square decimeters of clothing leather per year
2) $3 million/2 years
3) L
4) BP

GUP Tannery Company
144b, ul. Kalinina, Kyzyl,
Republic of Tyva, 667000
Phone: (39422) 53 914
Fax: (39422) 51 573
Danil Bolat-oolovich Chymba, CEO

67. REPUBLIC OF KHAKASSIA [19]

ECONOMIC MAP

KEMEROVO

Tsentralny

Belogorsk

Tom

K E M E R O V O

Chistogorsky

R E G I O N

Novokuznetsk

Mezhdurechensk

Tashtagol

K R A S N O Y A R S K

Uzhur

T E R R I T O R Y

Chulym

Sarala

Kopevo

Ius

Dzhirim

Kommunar

Shira

Krasnoyarskoe water reservoir

Sorsk

Chernogorsk

Ust-Abakan

Charkov

Minusinsk

Zeleny Bor

ABAKAN

Birikchul

Tom

Mrassu

Sayanogorsk

Sizaya

Anchul

Abakan

Abaza

Arbaty

K R A S N O Y A R S K   T E R R I T O R Y

Sayano-Shushenskoe water reservoir

R E P U B L I C   O F   A L T A Y

R E P U B L I C   O F   T Y V A

(Ka Khem) Maly Yenisey

PROCESSING INDUSTRY

- Ferrous metals
- Non-ferrous metals
- Machine engineering and metal processing
- Forestry and timber
- Construction materials
- Light industry
- Food and beverages

MINING INDUSTRY

- Bituminous coal
- Iron ore
- Gold
- Marble
- Molybdenum
- Mineral water sources

POWER PLANTS

- Thermal power plants
- Hydro power plants

CROPS AND LIVESTOCK BREEDING

- Wheat
- Potatoes
- Meat and dairy cattle breeding
- Sheep rearing
- Resorts

The Republic of Khakassia, where I have been head of government for six years now, is one of the most economically advanced regions of Siberia. It ranks sixth in terms of economic development among Russia's regions, and second only to Yakutia among the Siberian regions.

Our industrial potential is based on the energy sector, with the gigantic Sayano-Shushenskaya hydroelectric power station located in the Republic. A reasonable tariff policy and efforts to balance the interests of the Republic and the federal center have enabled us to produce the cheapest energy in the country and thus develop modern energy intensive production facilities, including aluminum production. Khakassia is home to the most advanced aluminum plant in Russia, a Russian Aluminum Group company, which manufactures a wide range of products for various applications.

The Republic offers vast potential for the development of the light industry. The Republic hosts OAO Sitex, a major Russian textile manufacturer with the capacity to launch production of fabrics with different wool content at short notice using raw materials from Southern Siberia and neighboring Mongolia.

Our subsoil contains nearly all of the elements of the periodic table, and our mineral resource sector is well developed. The most attractive sectors are high quality coal, gold, iron ore, and molybdenum. Khakassia is a monopoly producer of molybdenum.

The Republic boasts a well-developed transport infrastructure, including roads and railroads. The Republic's airport has international status, acting as a hub for trade with China, and is capable of servicing shipments to any destination. Khakassia boasts the warmest airport in Siberia, and our mild winters with little snow mean it is open for the longest period of the year.

Khakassia is an excellent place for tourism. Our Republic is blessed with a diverse landscape varying from wide steppe and innumerable salty and freshwater lakes to mountain peaks and boundless taiga.

Lately, the Republican Government has been putting considerable effort into the construction of vacation and recreation centers and downhill ski resorts.

The stable inter-ethnic situation, hospitality of our people, and relatively cheap labor compared to European and especially American standards, make our Republic an attractive partner for international business cooperation.

Alexei Lebed,
CHAIRMAN OF THE GOVERNMENT
OF THE REPUBLIC OF KHAKASSIA

1. GENERAL INFORMATION

1.1. GEOGRAPHY

Located in the south-west of Eastern Siberia, the Republic of Khakassia covers a total area of 61,900 square kilometers. To the north and north-east, the Republic borders the Krasnoyarsk Territory, to the south-east – the Republic of Tyva, to the south-west – the Republic of Altai, and to the west – the Kemerovo Region.

1.2. CLIMATE

The Republic of Khakassia lies in the harsh continental climate zone.

Air temperatures in January average –17.5°C, rising to +18.5°C in July. Annual precipitation reaches 300–700 mm.

1.3. POPULATION

According to preliminary 2002 census results, the Republic's total population was 546,000 peo-ple. The average population density is 8.8 people per square kilometer. The economically active population amounts to 268,200 people. The official unemployment rate in 2002 was 3.3%.

Demographically speaking, some 62.5% are of the statutory working age, 20.3% are below the statutory working age, and 17.2% are beyond the statutory working age.

The Republic's ethnic mix is 11.1% Khakas, 79.5% Russian, 2.3% Ukrainian, 2.0% German, and 5.1% other ethnic groups.

The Republic's major urban centers are Abakan with 165,200 inhabitants, Chernogorsk with 79,600 inhabitants, and Sayanogorsk with 75,800 inhabitants (2002 data).

Population							TABLE 1
	1992	1997	1998	1999	2000	2001	2002
Total population, '000	579	583	582	581	579	578	546
Economically active population, '000	286	276	246	267	267	269	268

2. ADMINISTRATION

67, pr. Lenina, Abakan, Republic of Khakassia, 655019
Fax: (39022) 65 096; e-mail: inform@khakasnet.ru; http://www.gov.khakasnet.ru

NAME	POSITION	CONTACT INFORMATION
Alexei Ivanovich LEBED	Chairman of the Government of the Republic of Khakassia	Phone: (39022) 63 322 Fax: (39022) 65 096
Vasily Ivanovich TSYGANOK	First Deputy Chairman of the Government of the Republic of Khakassia	Phone: (39022) 51 515, 99 114
Nina Alexandrovna PILIUGINA	Deputy Chairman of the Government of the Republic of Khakassia	Phone: (39022) 63 633, 99 115
Gennady Mikhailovich CHANKIN	Deputy Chairman of the Government of the Republic of Khakassia	Phone: (39022) 99 119, 99 182
Alexei Moiseevich IVANOV	Minister of Economy and Finance of the Republic of Khakassia	Phone: (39022) 99 120
Alexander Ivanovich TREIZE	Minister of Agriculture of the Republic of Khakassia	Phone: (39022) 66 437
Petr Nikolaevich VOLKOV	Minister of Transport and Roads of the Republic of Khakassia	Phone: (39022) 62 380
Irina Vladimirovna DUNAEVA	Chairman of the State Property Management Committee of the Republic of Khakassia	Phone: (39022) 99 122
Ivan Ivanovich VISHNEVETSKY	Chairman of the State Environment Protection and Use Committee of the Republic of Khakassia	Phone: (39022) 66 547

SIBERIAN FEDERAL DISTRICT

VI

3. ECONOMIC POTENTIAL

3.1. 1997–2002 GROSS REGIONAL PRODUCT (GRP). INDUSTRY BREAKDOWN

The 2002 gross regional product of the Republic of Khakassia amounted to $691 million, 7.7% up on 2001. Per capita GRP in 2001 reached $1,110 and in 2002, $1,265.

3.2. MAJOR ECONOMIC GROWTH PROJECTIONS

The Economic and Social Development Program of the Republic of Khakassia (2003-2005) sets forth the blueprint for the Republic's economic development for the coming years. The Program sets the following objectives:

GRP trends in 1997–2002						*TABLE 2*
	1997	1998	1999	2000	2001*	2002*
GRP in current prices, $ million	1,360	836	541	620	641	691

*Estimates of the Government of the Republic of Khakassia

GRP industry breakdown in 1997–2002, % of total						*TABLE 3*
	1997	1998	1999	2000	2001*	2002*
GRP	100.0	100.0	100.0	100.0	100.0	100.0
Industry	39.9	43.0	50.3	48.1	42.1	37.5
Agriculture and forestry	10.6	8.0	8.7	12.1	11.8	10.8
Construction	6.8	7.5	5.6	4.2	7.9	7.0
Transport and communications	13.3	10.5	6.7	7.2	7.7	7.4
Trade and public catering	10.6	10.1	11.4	12.6	13.5	14.6
Other	18.8	20.9	17.3	15.8	17.0	22.7

*Estimates of the Government of the Republic of Khakassia

To enhance the competitiveness of the Republic's output and the technical level of its industrial infrastructure, to secure access for the Republic's products to domestic and external markets, and to ensure sustainable industrial growth;

To increase machine engineering output for the Republic's domestic market;

To provide state support to the timber industry in the form of state guarantees on loans raised and partial subsidies of bank loan interest;

To develop and strengthen inter-regional relations in the ferrous and non-ferrous metals sectors;

To consolidate the Republic's unified economic territory and to reduce economic and social development gaps between different re-gions of the Republic;

To increase output and improve the quality of consumer goods (the food and beverages and light industries);

To increase the share of processing industries in total output in order to offset raw materials industry development trends;

To boost Russia's gold reserves by putting new and promising gold fields into operation;

To produce common construction materials using new technologies and raw materials found in the Republic for supply to the Republic's construction sector;

To maintain the stability of the Republic's food supplies by improving the material and technical basis of the Republic's agricultural enterprises, creat-

ing a strong forage reserve, improving the efficiency of livestock breeding, increasing the food product range, and improving food quality and output at food processing companies.

3.3. INDUSTRIAL OUTPUT IN 1997–2002 FOR MAJOR SECTORS OF ECONOMY

The leading industries of the Republic of Khakassia are non-ferrous metals, energy, and food and beverages sectors. Together these account for 77.1% of the Republic's total industrial output.

Non-ferrous metals. The sector accounts for 46.5% of the Republic's total industrial output. The largest companies are OAO Sayanogorsk Aluminum Plant and OOO Sayany Foil.

Energy. The energy sector accounts for 21.7% of the Republic's total industrial output. The Republic's energy system includes the Sayano-Shushenskaya HEP Station, Mainskaya HEP Station, and three electric power plants with total capacity of 7,016 MW.

Food and beverages is one of the fastest growing sectors in the Republic of Khakassia. In 2002, it accounted for 8.9% of the Republic's total industrial output. Output growth is driven by the pasta, confectionery, meat, and brewery sectors. Private investment with a focus on quality improvement and product range expansion is also growing.

Machine engineering and metal processing. The sector accounts for 2.7% of the Republic's

Industry breakdown of industrial output in 1997–2002, % of total						_TABLE 4_
	1997	1998	1999	2000	2001	2002*
Industry	100.0	100.0	100.0	100.0	100.0	100.0
Non-ferrous metals	29.7	44.3	56.4	53.7	45.7	46.5
Energy	25.0	21.0	16.1	14.9	21.4	21.7
Food and beverages	7.9	7.2	5.9	10.8	7.6	8.9
Fuel	13.7	9.1	4.9	4.6	10.0	8.0
Ferrous metals	3.1	1.9	1.9	1.4	1.8	3.2
Light industry	3.4	2.8	2.5	3.1	2.8	2.9
Machine engineering and metal processing	5.2	4.3	5.7	4.1	2.9	2.7
Construction materials	4.4	2.8	1.6	2.8	2.8	2.4
Forestry, timber, and pulp and paper	1.1	1.0	0.9	0.9	1.7	1.9
Flour, cereals, and mixed fodder	1.4	1.1	0.9	0.8	1.3	0.6
Chemicals and petrochemicals	2.2	1.7	0.3	0.4	–	–

*Estimates of the Government of the Republic of Khakassia

total industrial output. The sector's largest company is OAO Abakanvagonmash (large freight containers and flat railroad wagons).

3.4. FUEL AND ENERGY BALANCE (OUTPUT AND CONSUMPTION PER RESOURCE)

The Republic has a powerful energy system. About two thirds of total energy output is supplied to the Siberian energy system. Coal output is partially used for the Republic's own needs and partially exported, including to non-CIS countries.

3.5. TRANSPORT INFRASTRUCTURE

Roads. The Republic of Khakassia has 2,498 kilometers of paved public highway. The M-54 Yenisei and Abakan – Kyzyl – Ak-Dovurak federal highways cross the territory of the Republic, linking it to the Krasnoyarsk Territory, the Republic of Tyva, and other Russian areas of Eastern and Western Siberia. Construction of the Abakan – Bolshoi Orton – Mezhdurechensk – Tashtagol highway is one of the Republic's top priorities.

Railroads. The Republic of Khakassia has 781 kilometers of railroad. The Abakan – Taishet, Abakan – Achinsk, and Abakan – Novokuznetsk

railroads link the Republic to the Trans-Siberian railroad and the Kuzbass industrial areas.

Airports. The international airports at Abakan and Sayanogorsk provide regular services to Moscow, Novosibirsk, Krasnoyarsk, Irkutsk, and Blagoveschensk .

3.6. MAIN NATURAL RESOURCES: RESERVES AND EXTRACTION IN 2002

Mineral, water and forest resources are the main natural resources of the Republic of Khakassia.

Mineral resources. The Republic of Khakassia contains explored and developed deposits of coal, iron, molybdenum, gold, barite, bentonite, gems, and facing stones. The four coalfields of the Minusinsk coal basin contain total reserves of 5.3 billion tons. The Minusinsk basin also includes eight magnetite fields.

Water resources. The Republic enjoys significant reserves of fresh subterranean and surface waters (the Shirinskoye mineral water deposit and the Dikooziorskoye radon water deposit). More than 320 rivers, including the Yenisei, drain the Republic.

Forest resources. Forests cover 61% of the Republic's total area. Valuable cedar species account for 31% of the Republic's forests.

SIBERIAN FEDERAL DISTRICT

VI

Fuel and energy sector production and consumption trends, 1997–2002						_TABLE 5_
	1997	1998	1999	2000	2001	2002*
Electricity output, billion kWh	25.5	20.1	21.4	25.7	27.6	19.5
Coal output, million tons	6.6	5.1	5.1	5.4	6.8	5.9
Electricity consumption, billion kWh	6.6	6.8	7.5	7.9	7.9	7.9
Coal consumption, million tons	n/a	n/a	n/a	2.4	2.5	2.5

*Estimates of the Government of the Republic of Khakassia

4. TRADE OPPORTUNITIES

4.1. MAIN GOODS PRODUCED
IN THE REGION

Coal. 2002 coal output was 5,858,000 tons, down 13.9% on 2001.

Iron ore. 2002 iron ore output was 1,712,000 tons, down 1.4% on 2001.

Non-ferrous metals. 2002 primary aluminum output was up 1.2 % on 2001, rolled aluminum output rose 10.2% compared to 2001, aluminum foil output was up 17.4% compared to 2001, and concentrated molybdenum output fell 6% on 2001.

Containers. In 2002, the Republic produced 4,312 containers, down 39.4% on 2001.

Industrial timber. In 2002, the Republic produced 87,700 cubic meters of industrial timber, down 24.8% on 2001.

Natural facing stone (marble). In 2002, output of facing stone goods amounted to 114,700 conventional square meters compared to 2001 figures.

Mineral water. In 2002, the Republic produced 23 million liters of mineral water, an 83% increase compared to 2001.

4.2. MAIN EXPORTS, INCLUDING EXTRA-CIS

In 2000, the Republic's exports to extra-CIS countries amounted to $377 million; exports to the CIS totaled $3 million. The corresponding figures for 2001 were $353.9 million and $6.9 million, respectively, and $337.9 million and $7.2 million for 2002.

The Republic's main exports in 2002 included aluminum and aluminum goods (over 80% of total exports), molybdenum concentrate (5.7%), coal (3.5%), timber (2.2%), and machine engineering goods (0.2%). The Republic's major export destinations include the USA, Turkey, Japan, China, Germany, and the Netherlands.

4.3. MAIN IMPORTS, INCLUDING EXTRA-CIS

In 2000, the Republic's imports from extra-CIS countries reached $74.3 million, while imports from the CIS totaled $112.9 million. The corresponding figures for 2000 were $51.9 million and $117.7 million, and $32.9 million and $128 million for 2002.

In 2002, the main goods imported to the Republic included alumina (83% of total imports), coke (9%), and machine engineering goods (2.5%). The main exporters to the Republic are Kazakhstan and Ukraine (over 79% of total imports), China, Germany, Italy, the Netherlands, and Japan.

4.4. MAJOR REGIONAL EXPORT
AND IMPORT ENTITIES

Owing to the specific features of export and import operations in the Republic of Khakassia, export and import transactions are performed mainly by industrial companies.

5. INVESTMENT OPPORTUNITIES

5.1. INVESTMENTS IN 1992–2002
(BY INDUSTRY SECTOR), INCLUDING
FOREIGN INVESTMENTS

The following main factors determine the investment appeal of the Republic of Khakassia:
- Its favorable geographical location;
- Its developed transport infrastructure;
- Legislation supporting investment activities (protection of investor rights, preferential tax treatment);
- Its qualified workforce;
- Cheap sources of energy (electricity, oil, gas);
- Its natural resource potential.

5.2. CAPITAL INVESTMENT

The bulk of capital investment in 2002 went to industry, transport and communications.

5.3. MAJOR ENTERPRISES (INCLUDING
ENTERPRISES WITH FOREIGN INVESTMENT)
5.4. MOST ATTRACTIVE
SECTORS FOR INVESTMENT

According to the Government of the Republic of Khakassia, non-ferrous metals, energy, fuel, machine engineering and metals processing, construction materials, agriculture, and tourism are the Republic's most potentially appealing sectors for investors.

Capital investment by industry sector, $ million						TABLE 6
	1997	1998	1999	2000	2001	2002
Total capital investment	179.6	147.4	77.2	64.4	84.0	53.8
Including major industries (% of total):						
Industry	32.9	33.3	48.1	40.7	43.9	66.0
Agriculture and forestry	4.3	3.6	3.1	3.3	2.5	2.3
Construction	22.2	6.4	4.4	4.1	5.0	0.5
Transport and communications	24.9	22.5	24.7	30.2	27.7	12.7
Other	15.7	34.2	19.7	21.7	20.9	18.5

Largest enterprises of the Republic of Khakassia	TABLE 7
COMPANY	SECTOR
OAO Sayanogorsk Aluminum Plant	Non-ferrous metals
OAO Khakasenergo	Energy
OAO P. S. Neporozhny Sayano-Shushenskaya HEP Station	Energy
OOO Sorsky Ore Mining and Processing Plant	Non-ferrous metals
OAO Sayany Foil	Non-ferrous metals
OAO AYAN	Brewery
OOO Abakan Ore Mining Management Office	Ferrous metals
ZAO Stepnoy Open Pit Mine	Coal
OOO Construction Office for Main Installations	Construction
OOO Chernogorsk Coal Company	Coal
OAO Elektrosvyaz of the Republic of Khakassia	Transport and communications
ZAO Golden Star Gold Mining Company	Non-ferrous metals
OOO Sayansoyuzservice	Coal
OAO Kommunarovsky Mine	Non-ferrous metals

5.5. CURRENT LEGISLATION ON INVESTOR TAX EXEMPTIONS AND PRIVILEGES

In order to create a favorable investment climate, the Republic of Khakassia has passed laws On State Support to Investment Activities in the Republic of Khakassia (the law seeks to encourage investment by business entities), On the Development Budget of the Republic of Khakassia (regulates the legal and economic conditions for raising and spending the development budget), and On the Collateral Fund of the Republic of Khakassia (provides guarantees to Russian and foreign investors).

5.6. FEDERAL AND REGIONAL ECONOMIC AND SOCIAL DEVELOPMENT PROGRAMS FOR THE REPUBLIC OF KHAKASSIA

Federal targeted programs. A number of federal targeted programs of economic and social development of the Republic of Khakassia is underway in the Republic. The priority has been accorded to The Program for the Elimination of Differences in the Social and Economic Development of the Regions of the Russian Federation, 2002–2010 and through 2015. The Program's main objectives are to diminish the gap in terms of major social and economic development indicators by 2010, to create a favorable environment for business, and to improve the investment climate.

Regional programs. The Republican Government develops and implements targeted programs, most of which are socially focused. These include:

• The Program for the Economic and Social Development of the Republic of Khakassia (2003-2005). The Program's goal is to create a favorable social climate and improve living standards in the Republic;

• The Program of State Support to Small Enterprise in the Republic of Khakassia (2003). The Program's objectives include improving the legal, economic, and organizational conditions to ensure the sustainable development of small enterprise and to ensure funding to priority areas of business.

The Development of Tourism in the Republic of Khakassia (2000-2005) Program is also underway.

Regional entities responsible for raising investment		TABLE 8
ENTITY	ADDRESS	PHONE, FAX, E-MAIL
Ministry of Finance and Economy of the Republic of Khakassia	67, pr. Lenina, Abakan, Republic of Khakassia, 655019	Phone: (39022) 99 120, 66 037 Fax: (39022) 55 555, 99 253 E-mail: minfinrx@khakasnet.ru
State Committee for Industry and Enterprise of the Republic of Khakassia	18, ul. Schetinkina, Abakan, Republic of Khakassia, 655019	Phone: (39022) 62 076, 39 352 Fax: (39022) 39 572 E-mail: gkprom@khakasnet.ru
Tourism Committee of the Government of the Republic of Khakassia	67, pr. Lenina, Abakan, Republic of Khakassia, 655019	Phone/fax: (39022) 68 651, 51 709 E-mail: komtour@khakasnet.ru

6. INVESTMENT PROJECTS

Industry sector and project description	1) Expected results 2) Amount and term of investment 3) Form of financing[1] 4) Documentation[2]	Contact information
1	2	3

MINING

67R001

Integrated facilities reconstruction project at OOO Abakan Ore Mining Management Office.
Project goal: to reconstruct existing facilities to enable deeper processing of ore deposits from the Abakan ore field with a view to maintaining annual processing capacity at 3.5 million tons of raw ore (OOO Abakan Ore Mining Management Office).

1) Stage 1: preparation for extraction of 18.5 million tons of explored ore. Stage 2: by 2016 year-end, extraction of 45.7 million tons of explored ore ($4.7 million a year)
2) $76.2 million/14 years
3) L
4) BP, FS

OOO Abakan Ore Mining Management Office
35a, ul. Lenina, Abaza, Tashtypsky District, Republic of Khakassia, 655750
Phone: (39047) 23 584
Fax: (39047) 23 651
Nikolai Ivanovich Baiborodov, CEO

FERROUS METALS

67R002

Launch of steel casting production facilities.
Project goal: to launch production facilities at an unfinished production site (OAO Abakan Steel Plant) for the production of cast steel for railroad cars.

1) Cast steel for railroad cars – 62,000 tons a year ($2.7 million a year)
2) $14.2 million/3 years
3) E, L
4) BP, FS

State Committee for Industry and Enterprise of the Republic of Khakassia
P.O. Box 705, 18, ul. Schetinkina, Abakan, Republic of Khakassia, 655019
Phone: (39022) 62 076
Fax: (39022) 39 572
E-mail: gkprom@khakasnet.ru
Vasily Ivanovich Molchanov, Chairman of the State Committee, Yury Fedorovich Ustinov, Deputy Chairman of the State Committee

67R003

Production of rolled steel.
Project goal: to acquire and assemble equipment for production of rolled and reinforcing 2-13 mm diameter steel at casting and rolled steel facilities with an annual capacity of 100,000 tons (OAO Abakan Steel Plant).

1) Rolled steel – 100,000 tons a year ($0.7 million a year)
2) $1.9 million/3 years
3) E, L
4) BP, FS

State Committee for Industry and Enterprise of the Republic of Khakassia
P.O. Box 705, 18, ul. Schetinkina, Abakan, Republic of Khakassia, 655019
Phone: (39022) 62 076
Fax: (39022) 39 572
E-mail: gkprom@khakasnet.ru
Vasily Ivanovich Molchanov, Chairman of the State Committee, Yury Fedorovich Ustinov, Deputy Chairman of the State Committee

CHEMICALS AND PETROCHEMICALS

67R004

Production of activated charcoal.
Project goal: to produce activated decolorizing charcoal.

1) Activated decolorizing charcoal – 2,100 tons a year
2) $2.1 million/2 years
3) L
4) BP, FS

State Committee for Industry and Enterprise of the Republic of Khakassia
P.O. Box 705, 18, ul. Schetinkina, Abakan, Republic of Khakassia, 655019
Phone: (39022) 62 076
Fax: (39022) 39 572
E-mail: gkprom@khakasnet.ru
Vasily Ivanovich Molchanov, Chairman of the State Committee, Yury Fedorovich Ustinov, Deputy Chairman of the State Committee

[1] L – Loan, E – Equity, Leas. – Leasing, JV – Joint Venture
[2] BP – Business Plan, FS – Feasibility Study

1	2	3

FORESTRY, TIMBER, AND PULP AND PAPER

67R005 ● ◆ ▲

Timber production for export purposes.
Project goal: to launch a timber processing line for timber production using band saw equipment (ZAO Tekhincom).

1) 5,800 cubic meters of timber a year ($0.2 million a year)
2) $0.07 million/1 year
3.) L
4) BP, FS

ZAO Tekhincom
10, ul. Marshala Zhukova, Abakan, Republic of Khakassia, 655012
Phone/fax: (39022) 44 933, 52 611, 91 531; e-mail: dokfuomz@dimetra.ru
Vladimir Vladimirovich Kryukov, CEO

67R006 ● ◆ ▲

Launch of semi-finished goods assembly facilities.
Project goal: to acquire and assemble equipment (OOO Abazlestorg).

1) 10,000 cubic meters of lumber a year ($0.07 million a year)
2) $0.5 million/1 year
3) L
4) BP, FS

OOO Abazlestorg
6, ul. Promyshlennaya, Abaza, Tyshtypsky District,
Republic of Khakassia, 655750
Phone: (39047) 23 336
Vladimir Dmitrievich Nadelyayev, CEO

CONSTRUCTION MATERIALS

67R007 ■ ● ◆ ▲

Production of double-glazed plastic windows with heat reflection coating.
Project goal: to produce double-glazed plastic windows with heat reflection coating.

1) 388,800 square meters of double-glazed plastic windows with heat reflection coating
2) $2.0 million/18 months
3) E, L
4) BP, FS

State Committee for Industry and Enterprise of the Republic of Khakassia
18, ul. Schetinkina, Abakan, Republic of Khakassia, 655019
Phone: (39022) 62 076
Fax: (39022) 39 572
E-mail: gkprom@khakasnet.ru
Vasily Ivanovich Molchanov, Chairman of the State Committee,
Yury Fedorovich Ustinov, Deputy Chairman of the State Committee

LIGHT INDUSTRY

67R008 ● ◆ ▲

Sheepskin processing facilities for producing fur coats and sheepskins.
Project goal: to install and launch sheepskin processing equipment, expand the sewing workshop, and acquire equipment for production of a new product range (ZAO Chernogorsk Primary Wool Processing Plant).

1) Sheepskin coats– 4,260 a year, short fur coats –3,600 a year ($0.2 million a year)
2) $0.6 million/2 years
3) L
4) BP, FS

ZAO Chernogorsk Primary Wool Processing Plant
1, ul. Energetikov, P.O. Box 33, Chernogorsk-8,
Republic of Khakassia, 655158
Phone: (39031) 23 115
Fax: (39031) 24 042, 24 021
Yury Sergeevich Sitnikov, CEO

COMMUNICATIONS

67R009 ■ ● ◆

Regional targeted program Electronic Khakassia, part of the Electronic Russia (2002-2010) federal targeted program.
Project goal: to create trunk communications systems for the Republic of Khakassia connecting the local government authorities to the general communications network.

1) $0.4 million a year
2) $12.0 million/3 years
3) E, L
4) BP

State Committee for Industry and Enterprise of the Republic of Khakassia
P.O. Box 705, 18, ul. Schetinkina, Abakan, Republic of Khakassia, 655019
Phone: (39022) 62 076
Fax: (39022) 39 572
E-mail: gkprom@khakasnet.ru
Vasily Ivanovich Molchanov, Chairman of the State Committee,
Yury Fedorovich Ustinov, Deputy Chairman of the State Committee

HOTELS, TOURISM, AND RECREATION

67R010 ■ ● ◆ ▲

Development of the Gladenkaya alpine skiing resort.
Project goal: to create modern infrastructure at the alpine skiing resort (OOO Gladenkaya).

1) $2.0 million a year
2) $18.0 million/3 years
3) E, L
4) BP, FS

Tourism Committee of the Government of the Republic of Khakassia
67, pr. Lenina, P.O. Box 706, Abakan, Republic of Khakassia, 655019
Phone: (39022) 68 651, 51 709
Fax: (39022) 68 651, 51 709
E-mail: komtour@khakasnet.ru
Valery Stepanovich Sidorchuk, Chairman of the Committee

68. ALTAI TERRITORY [22]

ECONOMIC MAP

TOMSK REGION

TOMSK

Yaya

Anzhero-Sudzhensk

NOVOSIBIRSK REGION

Kuybyshev

KEMEROVO

Chulym NOVOSIBIRSK

KEMEROVO REGION

Barabinsk

Iskitim

Leninsk-Kuznetsky

Belovo

Lake Chany

Gurievsk

Prokopevsk

Zarinsk

Novo-Kuznetsk

Kamen-on-Obi

BARNAUL *Novoaltaysk*

Slavgorod

Lake Kulundinskoe

Aleysk

Aley

Ob

Biysk

Pavlodar

Kulunda

e

Belokurikha GORNO-ALTAYSK

Rubtsovsk

Charysh

Katun

REPUBLIC OF

Gornyak

ALTAI

Semipalatinsk

Ust-Kamenogorsk

Zyryanovsk

KAZAKHSTAN

PROCESSING INDUSTRY

- Machine engineering and metal processing
- Chemicals and petrochemicals
- Construction materials
- Light industry
- Food and beverages

MINING INDUSTRY

- Complex ore
- Table salt
- Glauber's salt
- Mineral water sources

POWER PLANTS

- Thermal power plants

CROPS AND LIVESTOCK BREEDING

- Wheat
- Rye
- Orchards
- Crown flax
- Sunflower
- Sugar beetroot
- Beekeeping
- Meat and dairy cattle breeding
- Sheep rearing
- Poultry farming
- Resorts

T he Altai Territory enjoys an advantageous geographical location on the border with Kazakhstan, Mongolia, and China. Its transport infrastructure, which provides cargo transport links to neighboring Russian regions and Asian countries, has been developing quite rapidly. The Territory's highway density exceeds Russia's average by 2.7 times.

To reduce its electricity costs, the Territory is constructing the Barnaul – Biysk – Altaisk natural gas pipeline with a pipe link to Belokurikha. This has already made it possible to supply some populated areas with natural gas. One of the priority development tasks is to introduce energy saving technology.

Leasing services provided by the Territory's Leasing Fund for a total of $4.4 million in 2002 facilitated the upgrading of fixed assets of the Territory's companies, including agricultural producers. The most successful leasing company is OAO Altaiagropromsnab.

The Territory's financial infrastructure is represented by ten commercial banks and branches of 14 banks from other regions. Telecommunications infrastructure is experiencing a fast-pace growth. The coverage area for GSM cellular networks is increasing steadily.

To ensure unlimited access to information about the Altai Territory for potential investors, the Altai Territory has posted its official website in the Internet. The website contains information on investment opportunities and conditions in the Territory.

Projects in timber processing could be of interest for investors. We have developed a program for the technical upgrading of 18 timber cutting and processing companies. The program envisages the attraction of $7.1 million in investments.

The Territory's strong research and development and educational base helps maintain a highly qualified workforce. The Territory is characterized by long-established social stability. Since 2000, the Altai Territory has been among the regions with minimum political risk.

The Territory accords an important role to external economic activities in solving its social and economic development tasks. Over the past few years, companies in the Territory have developed economic links with over 70 foreign countries. The blueprint for external economic development is set forth in the Comprehensive Program for the Development of External Economic Activity, 1998–2005.

The Altai Territory Administration is creating a favorable investment climate, which will be improved through the implementation of the following investment policy guidelines: improvement of the local taxation system, acceleration of the transfer of savings into investment by providing guarantees and developing the insurance system, state support to investment activity in the form of federal program funding, budget lending, state participation in investment programs of commercial organizations, a system of economic and organizational state support in the form of privileged operating regime in territorial operating zones and preferential tax treatment in free enterprise zones, and the development of the legislative base to facilitate investment activity and ensure reliable protection of investments.

Alexander Surikov,
HEAD OF THE ALTAI TERRITORY ADMINISTRATION

SIBERIAN FEDERAL DISTRICT

VI

1. GENERAL INFORMATION

1.1. GEOGRAPHY

Located in the south-west of Western Siberia, the Altai Territory covers a total area of 169,100 square kilometers. To the north and north-west, the Territory borders the Novosibirsk Region, to the north-east – the Kemerovo Region, to the east and southeast – the Republic of Altai, and to the south and south-west – the Republic of Kazakhstan.

1.2. CLIMATE

The Altai Territory lies in the continental climate zone. Air temperatures in January average –17.6°C, rising to +18.4°C in July. Annual precipitation reaches 250–350 mm. The average growing season lasts 120 days.

1.3. POPULATION

According to preliminary 2002 census results, total population in the Territory was 2,607,000. The average population density is 15.4 people per square kilometer. The economically active population is some 1,260,000 people (2001), while registered unemployment stands at 3.2% (2002).

Demographically speaking, some 61.6% are of working age, 18.3% are below working age, and 20.1% are beyond the statutory working age.

The Altai Territory's major urban centers are Barnaul with 603,500 inhabitants, Biysk with 218,600 inhabitants, and Rubtsovsk with 163,100 inhabitants (2002).

Population								TABLE 1
	1992	1997	1998	1999	2000	2001	2002
Total population, '000	2,667	2,679	2,672	2,665	2,654	2,643	2,607
Economically active population, '000	1,312	1,208	1,123	1,273	1,260	1,237	1,260

2. ADMINISTRATION

59, pr. Lenina, Barnaul, Altai Territory, 656035. Phone: (3852) 35 6935
fax: (3852) 36 3863; teletype (3852) 23 3252 Krai; e-mail: glava@alregn.ru; http://www.altairegion.ru

NAME	POSITION	CONTACT INFORMATION
Alexander Alexandrovich SURIKOV	Head of the Altai Territory Administration	Phone: (3852) 35 6935, 36 3805, 35 6958 E-mail: press@alregn.ru
Alexander Alexeevich KUFAEV	First Deputy Head of the Altai Territory Administration, Head of the Main Division of the Agriculture of the Altai Territory Administration	80, pr. Komsomolsky, Barnaul, Altai Territory, 656035 Phone: (3852) 35 6964, 36 3166 Fax: (3852) 24 3379 E-mail: admin@agro.altai.ru
Nikolai Alexandrovich CHERTOV	First Deputy Head of the Altai Territory Administration for Finance, Economy, Construction, and Business	Phone: (3852) 36 3518, 36 3566, 35 6968
Semen Petrovich BAYKALOV	Deputy Head of the Altai Territory Administration for Industry, Energy, Housing, Natural Gas, and Inter-Regional Relations	Phone: (3852) 36 3687, 36 3745, 35 8995
Nikolai Gavrilovich ZAYGANOV	Deputy Head of the Altai Territory Administration for Transport, Roads, Communications, Retail Markets, and Foreign Economic Relations	Phone: (3852) 35 8801, 36 3592, 38 0204
Alexander Fedorovich ZHILIN	Director of the Foreign Relations Department of the Altai Territory Administration	41, pr. Lenina, Barnaul, Altai Territory, 656099 Phone: (3852) 36 9048 Fax: (83852) 26 2360 E-mail: dved@altgate.altai.ru
Vladimir Ivanovich PSAREV	Deputy Head of the Altai Territory Administration, Head of the Main Division of Economy and Investment	59, pr. Lenina, Barnaul, Altai Territory, 656035 Phone: (3852) 36 3377, 35 6834 Fax: (3852) 35 4813 E-mail: econom@alregn.ru

NAME	POSITION	CONTACT INFORMATION
Raissa Kondratyevna SOLODOVNIKOVA	Head of the Investment Department, Deputy Head of the Main Division for Economy and Investment	118, pr. Komsomolsky, Barnaul, Altai Territory, 656038 Phone: (3852) 35 4819

3. ECONOMIC POTENTIAL

3.1. 1997–2002 GROSS REGIONAL PRODUCT (GRP). INDUSTRY BREAKDOWN

The 2002 gross regional product in the Altai Territory reached $2,500 million, a 11.6% increase on 2001 levels. The growth was mainly transport and communications driven. Per capita GRP amounted to $848 in 2001, rising to $959 in 2002.

3.2. MAJOR ECONOMIC GROWTH PROJECTIONS

The blueprint for economic development over the coming years is provided by The Altai Territory Social and Economic Development Plan 1998–2000 and through 2005. The Plan sets forth the following objectives:

Industry: to ensure positive industry growth trends, stabilize and increase industrial output, raise product competitiveness, and promote efficient industrial management;

Agriculture and forestry: to maintain current levels and ensure sustainable growth in agricultural output. Plans are afoot to create complex processing facilities for the processing of raw agriculture produce to ensure maximum profits;

GRP trends in 1997–2002						*TABLE 2*
	1997	1998	1999	2000	2001*	2002*
GRP in current prices, $ million	3,595	2,242	1,365	1,731	2,240	2,500

*Estimates of the Altai Territory Administration

GRP industry breakdown in 1997–2002, % of total						*TABLE 3*
	1997	1998	1999	2000	2001*	2002*
GRP	100.0	100.0	100.0	100.0	100.0	100.0
Industry	28.6	25.2	28.1	21.2	21.2	22.0
Agriculture and forestry	11.5	17.4	20.1	27.3	26.1	23.8
Construction	5.9	5.5	4.2	5.2	5.0	5.2
Transport and communications	12.5	9.6	8.5	8.6	7.9	8.2
Trade and public catering	9.3	13.2	13.6	12.3	13.0	14.0
Other	27.6	26.2	21.9	21.2	24.4	23.8
Net taxes on output	4.6	2.9	3.6	4.2	2.4	3.0

*Estimates of the Altai Territory Administration

Construction: to install and launch new technologies at OAO EDSK Novoaltaisky Plant, and diversify part of the reinforced concrete production facilities to low-rise construction. Revival of brick making facilities in rural areas;

Transport: to maintain the road network, accelerate road repair works, and improve the technical characteristics and carrying capacity of trunk roads. To develop air carriers.

3.3. INDUSTRIAL OUTPUT IN 1997–2002 FOR MAJOR SECTORS OF ECONOMY

The Altai Territory's major industries include: food and beverages, machine engineering and metals, energy, and ferrous metals. Together they account for 73.2% of total industrial output.

Food and beverages. The sector accounts for 24.2% of the Territory's output. The sector meets all of the Territory's food requirements. The sector has the capacity to process up to 2 million tons of grain, 1.6 million tons of whole milk, 0.4 million tons of sunflower seeds, and 0.3 million tons of meat and poultry annually.

Machine engineering and metal processing. The sector accounts for some 20.3% of the Territory's total output. It produces row-crop caterpillars, engines for tractors and combines, steam boilers of various capacity (operating on liquid, solid, and gaseous fuel), cargo railroad cars, drilling machinery, automobile and tractor generators, and agriculture vehicles. The sector's largest enterprises

SIBERIAN FEDERAL DISTRICT

VI

Industry breakdown of industrial output in 1997–2002, % of total						TABLE 4
	1997	1998	1999	2000	2001	2002
Industry	100.0	100.0	100.0	100.0	100.0	100.0
Food and beverages	16.2	17.3	19.7	18.8	18.7	24.2
Machine engineering and metal processing	25.6	23.2	24.9	24.4	24.1	20.3
Energy	22.9	25.2	15.6	15.4	17.0	18.8
Ferrous metals	4.6	6.5	11.2	8.2	7.1	9.9
Flour, cereals, and mixed fodder	6.3	6.2	9.9	10.6	13.0	9.7
Chemicals and petrochemicals	11.5	9.8	9.3	12.9	11.2	7.2
Construction materials	2.8	3.6	3.2	3.5	2.9	3.0
Forestry, timber, and pulp and paper	2.1	2.2	2.2	2.3	2.2	2.0
Light industry	2.2	1.2	0.9	0.9	0.8	0.9

*Estimates of the Altai Territory Administration

include OAO Altai Tractor Plant, OAO Rubtsovsk Machine Engineering Plant, OAO Sibenergomash, and OAO Biyskenergomash.

Energy. The energy sector accounts for 18.8% of the Territory's total industrial output. The Territory's energy system is incorporated into the unified Siberian energy system, which includes the largest Siberian GRES power stations.

Chemicals and petrochemicals. The sector accounts for some 7.2% of the Territory's total industrial output. Companies within the sector manufacture automobile tires, chemical fertilizers, chemical fibers and threads, and varnish and paint products. Major enterprises include OAO Barnaul Tire Plant, OAO Kauchuksulfat, OAO Altaikhimprom, and OAO Altai-Koks.

Agriculture. The sector is focused on the following areas: tillage, cattle breeding, forage crops,

and beekeeping. The Territory's agricultural lands total 11 million hectares. The Territory has a diverse agricultural system composed of 5,882 individual farm holdings, 183 open and closed joint stock companies, 81 state enterprises, 29 limited liability companies, 41 collective farms, 11 state farms, and 394 agricultural cooperatives. The sector employs 23% of the Altai Territory's economically active population.

3.4. FUEL AND ENERGY BALANCE (OUTPUT AND CONSUMPTION PER RESOURCE)

The Altai Territory is an energy deficit region. The Territory's energy system includes eight thermal power stations, which cover only 50% of the Territory's needs. The Territory's energy sector is currently transitioning from coal and fuel oil to natural gas. Annual gas requirements are estimated at 10.8 billion cubic meters.

Fuel and energy sector production and consumption trends, 1997–2002						TABLE 5
	1997	1998	1999	2000	2001	2002
Electricity output, billion kWh	4.2	4.4	4.7	5.0	5.3	5.3
Electricity consumption, billion kWh	9.6	10.1	10.2	10.6	10.4	9.6

3.5. TRANSPORT INFRASTRUCTURE

The Altai Territory is served by road, rail, air, river and pipeline transportation systems.

Roads. The Territory has 14,441 kilometers of paved public highway. Federal trunk roads crossing the Altai Territory include the A-349 which links Barnaul – Rubtsovsk – Semipalatinsk, and the M-52, which links Novosibirsk – Barnaul – Biysk – Tashanta – Mongolia.

Railroads. The Altai Territory has 1,803 kilometers of railroad. The Southern Siberian trunk railroad crosses the Territory along the east-west route.

The main trunk railroad Novosibirsk – Barnaul – Semipalatinsk links the Territory to the rest of Siberia and Central Asia.

Airports. The Barnaul International Airport operates regular flights to the major cities of Russia, the CIS, Germany, Turkey, the United Arab Emirates, and China. The Barnaul Airport is a separate territory of the Altai Free Economic Zone.

River transport. The Territory's navigable waterways are the Ob, Biya, Katun, Charysh, and Chumysh rivers. The total length of the Territory's navigable inland waterways is 781 kilometers. The Territory has two river ports at Barnaul and

Biysk, and three river stations. River transportation provides cost-effective links to the Novosibirsk and Tomsk Regions and northern areas of the Ob river basin (Nizhnevartovsk, Salekhard, Surgut, and Khanty-Mansiysk).

Oil and gas pipelines. The Altai Territory has an operational trunk gas pipeline with an annual carrying capacity of 1.7 billion cubic meters.

3.5. MAIN NATURAL RESOURCES: RESERVES AND EXTRACTION IN 2002

Minerals, water, and forest resources represent the Altai Territory's main natural resources.

Minerals and raw materials. The Altai Territory has deposits of complex metal ores, table salt, soda, coal, nickel, cobalt, iron ore, and precious metals. Complex metal ores are concentrated in eight fields with a total reserve capacity of 50 million tons of ore.

Two magnetite fields with a total reserve capacity of 500 million tons represent the mineral and raw materials basis for the Territory's ferrous metals industry. Black coal reserves are estimated at 1,750 million tons, while brown coal reserves stand at 1,650 million tons.

Forest resources. The Altai Territory has 6 million hectares of forests. Timber reserves are estimated at 600 million cubic meters. In the southeast of the Territory, coniferous species predominate, including Siberian fir, cedar, pine, and spruce. The Territory has over forty bactericidal and vitamin rich berry species.

Water resources. The Biya and the Katun are the largest rivers of the Altai Territory. The Territory has some 13,000 lakes, of which more than half contain fresh water. Kulundinskoye Lake is the Territory's largest (728 square kilometers).

4. TRADE OPPORTUNITIES

4.1. MAIN GOODS PRODUCED IN THE REGION

Energy. 2002 energy output amounted to 5.3 billion KWh, a 0.7% increase on 2001.

Coke. 2002 coke production was 3,030,000 tons, 300 tons up on 2001.

Tractors. In 2002, 867 tractors were produced, 1,347 less than in 2001.

Cargo railroad cars. In 2002, 2,237 cargo railroad cars were produced, 1,035 up on 2001.

Tires. In 2002, 724,900 tires were produced in the Territory, 50% less than in 2001.

Chemical fertilizers. In 2002, chemical fertilizers output amounted to 15,200 tons, an 8% increase compared to 2001 figures.

Food and beverages. In 2002, production of grain was 4,750,300 tons; whole milk – 1,355,200 tons; and flour – 1,093,000 tons, cereals – 158,000 tons.

4.2. EXPORTS, INCLUDING EXTRA-CIS

Exports to non-CIS countries amounted to $51.4 million in 2000, while exports to CIS countries totaled $155.2 million. The figures for 2001 were $60.6 million and $214.3 million, respectively, and for 2002 – $71.9 million and $190.9 million, respectively.

In 2002, the Territory's main exports included coke (43% of total exports), flour and cereals (4.5%), machine engineering goods (3.8%), and rubber tires (2.4%). Main export destinations include Mongolia, Japan, China, Kazakhstan, Ukraine, and Uzbekistan.

4.3. IMPORTS, INCLUDING EXTRA-CIS

Imports from non-CIS countries totaled $47.6 million in 2000, while imports from CIS countries amounted to $66.4 million. The respective figures for 2001 were $58.2 million and $85.8 million, and for 2002 – $70.1 million and $45.9 million.

Main imports in 2002 included food (fruit, vegetables, fish), machinery, food and grain processing equipment, metals and metal goods, transport vehicles, petrochemicals products, tobacco, and alcohol. Major import partners include Italy, Germany, Turkey, China, Kazakhstan, Ukraine, and Uzbekistan.

4.4. MAJOR REGIONAL EXPORT AND IMPORT ENTITIES

Owing to the specifics of the Altai Territory's economy, export and import activities are mainly conducted by industrial enterprises.

5. INVESTMENT OPPORTUNITIES

5.1. INVESTMENTS IN 1992–2002 (BY INDUSTRY SECTOR), INCLUDING FOREIGN INVESTMENTS

The following factors determine the investment appeal of the Altai Territory:

• Its favorable economic position (in proximity to large natural resource deposits);

• Its unique natural resources (manganese, chrome, titanium, nickel, and lead);

• Its well developed transport infrastructure providing freight access to South-East and Central Asia;

• Its highly qualified and cheap labor;

• Legislation guaranteeing investors' rights and supporting ongoing investment activities.

5.2. CAPITAL INVESTMENT

Capital investments in 2002 were focused on industrial enterprises, transport, and agriculture.

SIBERIAN FEDERAL DISTRICT

VI

Capital investment by industry sector, $ million						*TABLE 6*
	1997	1998	1999	2000	2001	2002
Total capital investment	473.1	340.1	204.3	239.3	235.3	305.4
Including major industries (% of total)						
Industry	26.0	21.5	17.2	22.7	20.7	23.3
Agriculture and forestry	5.5	10.3	12.1	14.2	18.0	16.6
Construction	1.3	2.5	8.4	1.3	2.5	2.2
Transport and communications	11.6	14.5	21.2	32.0	17.0	15.6
Trade and public catering	2.0	1.7	3.7	2.4	4.2	4.4
Other	53.6	49.5	37.4	27.4	37.6	37.9

Foreign investment trends in 1996–2002						*TABLE 7*
	1996–1997	1998	1999	2000	2001	2002
Foreign investment, $ million	65.1	5.9	11.3	6.6	1.5	1.0
Including FDI, $ million	64.4	5.9	8.4	6.6	1.5	1.0

5.3. MAJOR ENTERPRISES (INCLUDING ENTERPRISES WITH FOREIGN INVESTMENT)

The Altai Territory hosts over 1,360 enterprises, including 115 dairies, 140 meat companies, 387 grain processing enterprises, and five distilleries.

5.4. MOST ATTRACTIVE SECTORS FOR INVESTMENT

According to experts and the Altai Territory Administration, timber processing, food and food processing, pharmaceuticals, housing, and transport and communications offer the strongest investment appeal.

5.5. CURRENT LEGISLATION ON INVESTOR TAX EXEMPTIONS AND PRIVILEGES

Investment activities in the Territory are regulated by the following Laws of the Altai Territory: On Industrial Policy, On the Procedure for Granting Additional Exemptions on Taxes and Levies Charged to the Territory's Budget, On Investment Activities in the Altai Territory, and On State Support to Innovative Activities in the Agroindustrial Sector of the Altai Territory. These laws provide state guarantees of investors' rights and a stable environment for investor activities.

Largest enterprises of the Altai Territory	*TABLE 8*
COMPANY	SECTOR
OAO Altai Tractor Plant	Machine engineering and metal processing
OAO Rubtsovsky Machine Engineering Plant	Machine engineering and metal processing
OAO Sibenergomash	Machine engineering and metal processing
OAO Biyskenergomash	Machine engineering and metal processing
OAO Kauchuksulfat	Chemicals and petrochemicals
OAO Barnaul Tire Plant	Chemicals and petrochemicals
OAO Altai-Koks	Chemicals and petrochemicals

5.6. FEDERAL AND REGIONAL ECONOMIC AND SOCIAL DEVELOPMENT PROGRAMS FOR THE ALTAI TERRITORY

Federal targeted programs. The priority has been accorded to the following programs for the economic and social development of the Altai Territory:

The Elimination of Social and Economic Inequalities in the Development of the Regions of the Russian Federation 2002-2010 and through 2015. Objective: to create conditions conducive to the development of regions where the social and economic development levels are below the nationwide average, and to improve the investment climate. The Program will be financed in 2003 to the tune of $4.1 million from the federal budget and $2.4 million from the regional budget.

Upgrade of the Russian Transport System 2002-2010. Objective: to build and upgrade roads and bridges, enhance safety, and improve environmental protection. The Program will be financed in 2003 to

Regional entities responsible for raising investment		*TABLE 9*
ENTITY	ADDRESS	PHONE, FAX, E-MAIL
Foreign Economic Department of the Altai Territory Administration	41, pr. Lenina, Barnaul, Altai Territory, 656099	Phone: (3852) 23 4369 Fax: (3852) 26 2360 E-mail: dved@ab.ru
Division of Economy and Investment of the Altai Territory Administration	118, pr. Komsomolsky, Barnaul, Altai Territory, 656038	Phone: (3852) 66 9495 Fax: (3852) 35 4813 E-mail: econom@alregn.ru
The Altai Territory Fund for Small Business Support	36, pr. Krasnoarmeysky, Barnaul, Altai Territory, 656049	Phone/fax: (3852) 35 3752, 35 3763

the tune of $17.2 million from the federal budget and $2.2 million from the regional budget.

Regional programs. The Altai Territory Administration has developed and is implementing a number of regional programs in industry, agriculture, environmental protection, law and order, healthcare, and social welfare. Some 44 programs are currently being implemented in the Territory.

The priority has been accorded to the following programs: The Program for Development and Reproduction of Hunting Reserves of the Altai territory, 2003–2006, Prevention and Fighting the Social Deseases, 2002–2006, Social Protection of the Disabled People of the Altai Territory, 2002–2004, and Protection of Maternity and Childhood in the Altai Territory, 2002–2005.

6. INVESTMENT PROJECTS

Industry sector and project description	1) Expected results 2) Amount and term of investment 3) Form of financing[1] 4) Documentation[2]	Contact information
1	2	3
CHEMICALS AND PETROCHEMICALS		
68R001 ● ◆		OAO Altai-Koks
To continue construction of a coke batteries launch facility. Project goal: to increase production (launch of an additional coke battery).	1) 2.1 million tons of coke a year 2) $56.6 million/2 years 3) L 4) BP	Zarinsk-7, Altai Territory, 659107 Phone: (38595) 53 180, 52 017 Fax:(38595) 79 201 E-mail rimma@altai-koks.ru Sergei Viktorovich Mochalnikov, CEO
68R002 ■ ● ★ ❖ ◆		OAO Polieks
Production of carboxylmethylcellulose for use in drilling fluids for oil and/or natural gas extraction and production of synthetic detergents. Project goal: to increase production, extend product range, and implement new technologies.	1) 7,500 tons a year 2) $1.4 million/1 year 3) L, Leas., E, JV 4) BP	Biysk, Altai Territory, 659315 Phone: (3854) 23 6010, 23 1502, 23 1500 Fax: (3854) 23 4385, 25 2537 E-mail: sktb.dunin@rambler.ru. Andrei Ivanovich Chernyavsky, CEO

[1] L – Loan, E – Equity, Leas. – Leasing, JV – Joint Venture
[2] BP – Business Plan, FS – Feasibility Study

1	2	3
68R003	● ◆	FGUP Biysk Oleum Plant
Establishment of facilities for dry sulphonol production (used in synthetic washing liquids and powders). Project goal: to extend product range.	1) 1,500 tons a year 2) $0.6 million/8 months 3) L 4) BP	Biysk, Altai Territory, 659315 Phone: (3854) 23 1349, 23 1300 Fax: (3854) 23 4370 E-mail: root@boz.biysk.ru Anatoly Andreevich Ananyin, Director

CHEMICALS AND PHARMACEUTICALS

1	2	3
68R004	● ◆	ZAO Altaivitaminy
Production and sales of intravenous solutions in ampoules. Project goal: to increase production, and extend product range.	1) 57.7 million ampoules a year 2) $2.8 million/1.9 year 3) L 4) BP	69, ul. Zavodskaya, Biysk, Altai Territory, 659325 Phone: (3854) 32 8609 Fax: (3854) 32 7153 E-mail: office@mx.altayvitamin.biysk.ru http://www.altayvitamin.ru Yury Antonovich Koshelev, CEO

FORESTRY, TIMBER, AND PULP AND PAPER

1	2	3
68R005	● ◆	OOO Inco-Trade
Creation of facilities for the closed cycle production of gummed straps using equipment manufactured by Weinig. Project goal: to increase output and extend product range.	1) 9,000 cubic meters a year 2) $1.7 million/4 months 3) L 4) BP	18a, ul. Mamontova, Biysk, Altai Territory 659300 Phone: (3854) 32 4797, 33 0616 Fax: (3854) 32 4797 E-mail: intrade@mail.biysk.ru Vyacheslav Alexandrovich Batischev, Director

FOOD AND BEVERAGES

1	2	3
68R006	● ◆	OOO PFK Biysk Wine Plant
To create facilities for the production of food supplements (cedar oil, protein powder, and chlorella). Project goal: to increase output and extend product range.	1) 554 tons a year 2) $1 million/1 year 3) L 4) BP	59, ul. Revolutsiyi, Biysk, Altai Territory 659325 Phone: (3854) 32 7954 Fax: (3854) 32 9087 E-mail: lemm@mail.biysk.ru Mikhail Sergeevich Korolev, Director

69. KRASNOYARSK TERRITORY [24]

ECONOMIC MAP

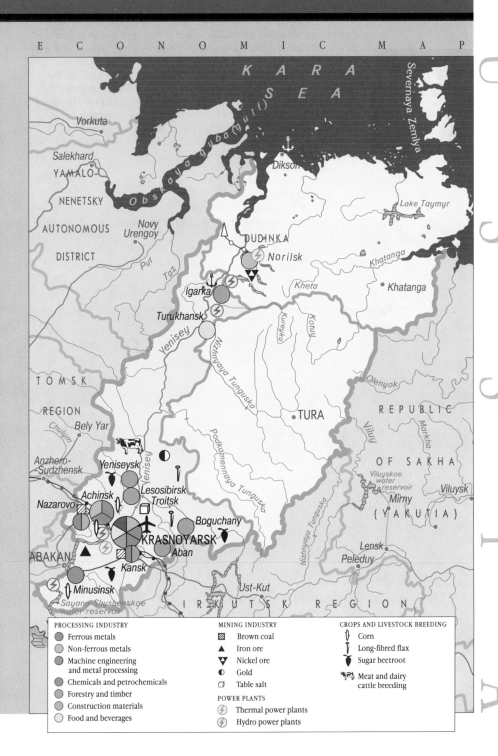

KARA SEA

Severnaya Zemlya

Vorkuta

Salekhard

YAMALO-NENETSKY

AUTONOMOUS

DISTRICT

Obskaya guba (gulf)

Dikson

Lake Taymyr

Novy Urengoy

DUDINKA

Norilsk

Khatanga

Khatanga

Pur

Taz

Igarka

Kheta

Kheta

Turukhansk

Yenisey

Nizhnyaya Tunguska

Kureyka

Kotuy

TOMSK

REGION

Chulym

Bely Yar

TURA

REPUBLIC

Olenyok

Viluy

Markha

Anzhero-Sudzhensk

Yeniseysk

Lesosibirsk

Troitsk

Podkamennaya Tunguska

OF SAKHA

Viluyskoe water reservoir

Viluysk

Achinsk

Nazarovo

Boguchany

Mirny

(YAKUTIA)

KRASNOYARSK

Aban

Nizhnyaya Tunguska

Lensk

Peleduy

ABAKAN

Kansk

Ust-Kut

Minusinsk

Sayano-Shushenskoe water reservoir

IRKUTSK REGION

PROCESSING INDUSTRY	MINING INDUSTRY	CROPS AND LIVESTOCK BREEDING
Ferrous metals	Brown coal	Corn
Non-ferrous metals	Iron ore	Long-fibred flax
Machine engineering and metal processing	Nickel ore	Sugar beetroot
Chemicals and petrochemicals	Gold	Meat and dairy cattle breeding
Forestry and timber	Table salt	
Construction materials	POWER PLANTS	
Food and beverages	Thermal power plants	
	Hydro power plants	

The Krasnoyarsk Territory is a traditional exporter of metals to the international market. Non-ferrous metals account for some 80% of the Territory's total exports. The Territory's largest non-ferrous metal companies are the Krasnoyarsk Aluminum Plant and Mining and Metal Company Norilsk Nickel. These companies are famous throughout the world and need no special presentation.

These industrial giants, however, are not the only competitive companies in the Krasnoyarsk Territory. Our Territory also hosts other less famous manufacturers of world-class products. Notably, the share of exports of companies in the fuel and energy, chemicals, timber, and machine engineering sectors is steadily increasing. These companies offer enormous potential for expanding trade and economic links.

We are committed to cooperating with investors in all sectors seeking to introduce new advanced technologies and launch new operations. The Krasnoyarsk Territory's Administration is pursuing an investment policy that calls for maximum consideration of the interest of all parties based on guarantees of stable operations for Russian and foreign investors alike.

I am confident that this Investment Guide will become a valuable tool in developing mutually beneficial cooperation, and help you identify areas for cooperation and reliable business partners.

Good luck in your work!

Alexander Khloponin,
GOVERNOR OF THE KRASNOYARSK TERRITORY,
CHAIRMAN OF THE KRASNOYARSK TERRITORY ADMINISTRATION COUNCIL

1. GENERAL INFORMATION

1.1 GEOGRAPHY

Located in Eastern Siberia, the Krasnoyarsk Territory covers a total area of some 2,339,700 square kilometers. To the north, the Territory is washed by the Kara and Laptev Seas, to the east it borders the Republic of Sakha (Yakutia), to the south-east – the Irkutsk Region and the Republic of Tyva, to the south – the Republic of Khakassia, to the south-west – the Kemerovo Region, and to the west – the Tomsk and Tyumen Regions.

1.2. CLIMATE

The Krasnoyarsk Territory is located within the extreme continental climate zone.

January air temperatures average −27°C, rising to +15°C in July. Annual precipitation reaches 300–350 mm.

1.3. POPULATION

According to preliminary 2002 census results, the Krasnoyarsk Territory's total population stood at 2,966,000 people. The average population density is 1.3 people per square kilometer. The economically active population amounts to 1,546,000 people. Official 2002 unemployment stood at 7.7%.

Demographically speaking, some 63.2% of population are of statutory working age, 19.6% are below the statutory working age, and 17.2% are beyond the statutory working age.

The Krasnoyarsk Territory's largest cities in 2002 were Krasnoyarsk with 911,700 inhabitants, Norilsk with 135,100 inhabitants, Achinsk with 118,700 inhabitants, Kansk with 103,100 inhabitants, and Zheleznogorsk with 95,300 inhabitants.

Population							*TABLE 1*
	1992	1997	1998	1999	2000	2001	2002
Total population, '000	3,173	3,107	3,092	3,076	3,051	3,032	2,966
Economically active population, '000	1,587	1,545	1,514	1,511	1,631	1,565	1,546

2. ADMINISTRATION

110, pr. Mira, Krasnoyarsk, Krasnoyarsk Territory, 660009
Phone: (3912) 49 3026; fax: (3912) 22 1178, 49 3302; e-mail: public@krskstate.ru

NAME	POSITION	CONTACT INFORMATION
Alexander Gennadyevich KHLOPONIN	Governor of the Krasnoyarsk Territory, Chairman of the Krasnoyarsk Territory Administration Council	Phone: (3912) 49 3363
Lev Vladimirovich KUZNETSOV	First Deputy Governor of the Krasnoyarsk Territory	Phone: (3912) 49 3111
Yury Pavlovich OLEINIKOV	Deputy Governor of the Krasnoyarsk Territory for Foreign Economic Activity	Phone: (3912) 49 3353
Sergei Mikhailovich SOKOL	Deputy Governor of the Krasnoyarsk Territory	Phone: (3912) 49 3416
Edkham Shukrievich AKBULATOV	Deputy Governor of the Krasnoyarsk Territory, Head of the Central Department for Economic Development and Planning of the Krasnoyarsk Territory Administration	Phone: (3912) 49 3491 Fax: (3912) 49 3670 E-mail: saraev@krskstate.ru
Vadim Viktorovich MEDVEDEV	Deputy Governor of the Krasnoyarsk Territory	Phone: (3912) 21 5227
Andrei Alekseevich GNEZDILOV	Head of the Krasnoyarsk Territory Administration Department for Industry, Fuel, and Energy	Phone: (3912) 49 3331
Sergei Alekseevich KACHEROV	Head of the Krasnoyarsk Territory Administration Department for Foreign Relations	Phone: (3912) 49 3232 Fax: (3912) 21 7039 E-mail: uvs@krasmail.ru

SIBERIAN FEDERAL DISTRICT

VI

3. ECONOMIC POTENTIAL

3.1. 1997–2002 GROSS REGIONAL PRODUCT (GRP). INDUSTRY BREAKDOWN

The Krasnoyarsk Territory's 2002 gross regional product amounted to $7,084 million, or 5.1% down on 2001. Per capita GRP totaled $2,461 in 2001 and $2,387 in 2002.

3.2. INDUSTRIAL OUTPUT IN 1997–2002 FOR MAJOR SECTORS OF ECONOMY

The Krasnoyarsk Territory's major industrial sectors are non-ferrous metals, energy, machine engineering, and metals processing, which together account for a combined 83.5% of total industrial output.

Non-ferrous metals. Non-ferrous metals account for 68.2% of the Krasnoyarsk Territory's total industrial output. The largest enterprises are OAO GMK Norilsk Nickel, OAO Gulidov Krasnoyarsk Non-Ferrous Metals Plant, OAO Krasnoyarsk Aluminum Plant, OAO Achinsk Alumina Plant, and OAO Kras-noyarsk Metals Plant.

Energy. Energy accounts for 9.4% of total industrial output. The Territory hosts 17 power stations, including four hydroelectric power stations (the Krasnoyarskaya, Ust-Khantaiskaya, Kureiskaya HEPS, and North Yeniseiskaya Mine GRES), three condensation power stations (the Nazarovskaya GRES, Krasnoyarskaya GRES 2, and Berezovskaya GRES 1),

GRP trends in 1997–2002						TABLE 2
	1997	1998	1999	2000	2001*	2002*
GRP in current prices, $ million	10,899.6	7,366.8	5,176.1	7,724.6	7,464.0	7,084.1

*Estimates of the Krasnoyarsk Territory Administration

GRP industry breakdown in 1997–2002, % of total						TABLE 3
	1997	1998	1999	2000	2001*	2002*
GRP	100.0	100.0	100.0	100.0	100.0	100.0
Industry	45.1	61.6	62.4	66.9	58.0	55.8
Agriculture and forestry	7.8	3.9	10.4	8.9	7.9	6.8
Construction	7.4	6.7	3.9	4.5	5.4	4.8
Transport and communications	8.3	2.9	2.9	2.6	3.1	3.7
Trade and public catering	6.4	19.0	15.0	12.2	19.8	22.9
Other	25.0	5.9	5.4	4.9	5.8	6.0

*Estimates of the Krasnoyarsk Territory Administration

Industry breakdown of industrial output in 1997–2002, % of total						TABLE 4
	1997	1998	1999	2000	2001	2002*
Industry	100.0	100.0	100.0	100.0	100.0	100.0
Non-ferrous metals	42.9	56.7	70.1	78.9	72.8	68.2
Energy	13.1	11.7	6.9	5.3	6.9	9.4
Machine engineering and metal processing	5.9	4.4	3.4	3.7	5.2	5.9
Food and beverages	8.3	6.1	4.2	3.1	4.1	4.5
Forestry, timber, and pulp and paper	5.6	4.5	3.8	3.3	3.6	3.7
Fuel	8.6	4.8	2.2	2.0	3.0	3.2
Construction materials	3.3	2.0	1.2	0.9	1.3	1.2
Chemicals and petrochemicals	8.6	7.4	5.5	0.8	0.7	1.0
Ferrous metals	1.0	0,5	0.3	0.2	0.4	0.4
Light industry	0.8	0.5	0.3	0.2	0.2	0.2

*Estimates of the Krasnoyarsk Territory Administration

and ten thermal power stations (TPS) (the Norilskaya TPS 1, TPS 2, and TPS 3, Krasnoyarskaya TPS 1, TPS 2, and TPS 3, Kanskaya TPS, Kansk Biochemicals Plant TPS, Achinck Alumina Plant TPS, and Minusisnskaya TPS), with a total combined capacity of 14 GW.

Machine engineering and metal processing. The sector accounts for 5.9% of total industrial output. The largest enterprises are FGUP NPO Electrochemicals Plant, FGUP NPO Applied Mechanics, FGUP Krasnoyarsk Machine Engineering Plant, OAO PO Krasnoyarsk Combine Plant, OAO Siberian Heavy Engineering Plant, and OAO Krasnoyarsk Refrigerator Plant Biryusa.

Food and beverages. The sector accounts for 4.5% of total industrial output. The largest enterprises are OAO Krasnoyarsk Bread, OAO Yenisei Bakery, ZAO Kraskon, OAO Filimonovsky MKK, OAO Nazarovskoye Moloko, OOO Milko, OAO Miaso, OAO Zubr, MUP Uyarsky Meat Plant, OAO Pikra, and OAO Yarich.

Forestry, timber, and pulp and paper. The sector accounts for 3.7% of total industrial output.

The largest enterprises are OAO Lesosibirsky LDK 1, ZAO Novoyeniseisky LHK, OOO TTS-LES, OAO Sibirsky CBK, AK Yeniseiles, OAO Krasnoyarsky Timber Processing Plant, OAO Maklakovsky LDK, and OAO Lesosibirsky Colophony Extraction Plant.

3.3. FUEL AND ENERGY BALANCE (OUTPUT AND CONSUMPTION PER RESOURCE)

The Krasnoyarsk Territory's fuel and energy sector fully meets local demand for electricity. The main electricity producer is OAO Krasnoyarskenergo.

The Krasnoyarsk Territory produces about 52 million tons of brown coal annually. The Territory has sufficient oil reserves to maintain output at a level of 40-45 million tons per year. As new oil deposits are developed, the Territory may begin exporting oil to the countries of the Asian-Pacific region.

Gas company OAO Norilskgazprom's activities range from well drilling and the production and transportation of natural gas to gas condensate extraction, transportation, and processing.

Fuel and energy sector production and consumption trends, 1997-2002						TABLE 5
	1997	1998	1999	2000	2001	2002*
Electricity output, billion kWh	48.6	48.6	46.5	49.9	49.9	47.8
Heat energy output, '000 Gcal	n/a	54.4	53.2	52.8	51.8	49.7
Electricity consumption, billion kWh	47.6	47.8	48.0	48.7	49.0	46.3

*Estimates of the Krasnoyarsk Territory Administration

3.4. TRANSPORT INFRASTRUCTURE

Roads. The Krasnoyarsk Territory has 12,842 kilometers of paved public highway. Two federal highways, the Novosibirsk – Krasnoyarsk – Irkutsk and Krasnoyarsk – Kyzyl routes, cross the Krasnoyarsk Territory. The Territory's road haulage enterprises provide freight services to China, Mongolia, and Western Europe.

Railroads. The Krasnoyarsk Territory has 2,068 kilometers of railroads. The Trans-Siberian and South-Siberian Railroads cross the Territory from west to east. The central part of the Krasnoyarsk Territory has rail links to other regions of the Russian Federation. Norilsk has a rail link to the port of Dudinka.

Airports. The Territory is served by AO AK Krasnoyarsk Airlines. The Territory has an air transport network based around 24 airports located in the Territory. The Territory's airspace and the Krasnoyarsk airport are used for trans-polar flights.

River transport. The total length of the Territory's navigable waterways linking its northern and eastern parts with Krasnoyarsk is 6,000 kilometers. Shipping company OAO Yenisei River Navigation operates all classes of river vessels along the Yenisei River.

River ports. The Krasnoyarsk and Lesosibirsk river ports provide river-to-rail transshipment services. The river delta ports in the north of the Territory can handle ocean-going vessels.

3.5. MAIN NATURAL RESOURCES: RESERVES AND EXTRACTION IN 2002

The Krasnoyarsk Territory's main natural resources are minerals and raw materials, timber, and water resources.

Minerals and raw materials. The Territory has the richest deposits of platinum, platinoid, and copper-nickel ores in Russia. It also boasts considerable reserves of cobalt, zinc (at the Gorevskoye lead-zinc deposit), cadmium, chromium, molybdenum, wolfram, mercury, tin, stibium, metal alkali, phosphates, graphite, manganese ores, talc, helium, and building stone. The Norilsk copper ore area has over 10 developed deposits of complex ores.

The Krasnoyarsk Territory's iron ore reserves amount to 2.3 billion tons, 56% of which are classed as easily dressed. Explored bauxite reserves between the Angara and Podkamennaya Tunguska rivers amount to 100 million tons. Black iron ore reserves in the Angara area amount to 500 million tons. Alluvial gold reserves are sufficient to increase and maintain an annual output level of 4.5–5 tons.

Some 25 oil and gas fields have been explored in the Territory. Oil reserves are estimated at 600 million tons, and natural gas and gas condensate reserves, at 1,000 billion cubic meters and 50 million tons, respectively. The largest coal reserves (112 billion tons) are concentrated in the Kansko-Achinsky coalfield.

Forest resources. The Krasnoyarsk Territory's forest resources include northern taiga (marshy arctic forests), central taiga (dark coniferous forests with cedar, larch, and fir species prevailing), and southern deciduous forests. The Territory is home to over 450 plant species.

Water resources. The River Yenisei flows from south to north through the Territory. The Territory has 323,000 lakes, including a group of lakes rich in mineral water and therapeutic muds located in the south of the Krasnoyarsk Territory.

4. TRADE OPPORTUNITIES

4.1. MAIN GOODS PRODUCED IN THE REGION

Electricity. 2002 electricity output amounted to 47.8 billion kWh, 4.2% down on 2001; heat output totaled 49.7 million Gcal, 11.1% down on 2001.

Fuel. In 2002, the Territory's oil refinery output was 3% up on 2001, motor gasoline output rose by 6.5% on 2001, disel fuel output increased by 2.3% on 2001, and coal output amounted to 33.1 million tons, 14.6% down on 2001.

Chemicals and petrochemicals. 2002 sulfuric acid output stood at 58,400 tons, 8.9% down on 2001, soda ash output reached 518,800 tons, 4.5% up on 2001, and mineral fertilizer output fell 10.5% year-on-year to 21,600 tons.

4.2. EXPORTS, INCLUDING EXTRA-CIS

In 1999, the Territory's extra-CIS exports totaled $2,891.6 million, with CIS exports totaling $39.3 million. The corresponding figures were $3,550.2 million and $82.7 million for 2000, $2,755.5 million and $104 million for 2001, and $2,904.8 million and $213.4 million for 2002.

The bulk of the Territory's exports consists of ferrous and non-ferrous metals and products, oil products (gasoline, diesel fuel, fuel oil), timber and timber products, and machinery and equipment. The Territory's major export partners are the UK, the USA, the Netherlands, Japan, China, France, Germany, Egypt, and Kazakhstan.

4.3. IMPORTS, INCLUDING EXTRA-CIS

In 1999, imports from outside the CIS totaled $408.1 million, with CIS imports coming to $81.6 million. The corresponding figures were $472.6 million and $177 million for 2000, $378.2 million and $232.3 million for 2001, and $421.5 million and $119.8 million for 2002.

The bulk of the Territory's imports consists of chemicals, foodstuffs, machinery and equipment, and fuel and energy products. Major import partners are France, Finland, Germany, Canada, Sweden, Brazil, China, Ukraine, Tajikistan, Uzbekistan, Moldova, and Kazakhstan.

4.4. MAJOR REGIONAL EXPORT AND IMPORT ENTITIES

Due to the specific nature of import and export operations in the Krasnoyarsk Territory, export and import transactions are mainly carried out by industrial enterprises.

5. INVESTMENT OPPORTUNITIES

5.1. INVESTMENTS IN 1992–2002 (BY INDUSTRY SECTOR), INCLUDING FOREIGN INVESTMENT

The following factors determine the investment appeal of the Krasnoyarsk Territory:

• Its favorable geographical location (direct link to the Territory via the Northern Sea Route);
• Its enormous industrial potential;
• Its developed transport infrastructure;
• Its considerable reserves of natural resources;
• Legislation supporting investment activities (guarantees for investor rights and preferential tax treatment for investors);
• Its qualified workforce;
• Cheap energy resources (electricity, oil, and gas).

5.2. CAPITAL INVESTMENT

The bulk of fixed capital investment goes to industrial production and transport.

5.3. MAJOR ENTERPRISES (INCLUDING ENTERPRISES WITH FOREIGN INVESTMENT)

The Krasnoyarsk Territory hosts 50 enterprises with foreign investment from the USA, North Korea, China, Cyprus, Lithuania, and other countries.

5.4. MOST ATTRACTIVE SECTORS FOR INVESTMENT

According to experts and the Krasnoyarsk Territory Administration, the most promising sectors for investment are forestry, food, natural resources, and transport.

Capital investment by industry sector, $ million

TABLE 6

	1997	1998	1999	2000	2001	2002
Total capital investment	1,856.2	355.9	235.7	763.3	1,044.7	823.0
Including major industries (% of total)						
Industry	55.1	53.1	59.4	56.1	55.8	58.8
Agriculture and forestry	2.3	3.4	3.4	2.3	1.8	2.4
Construction	7.3	0.5	1.2	8.8	5.2	5.4
Transport and communications	12.2	18.3	15.6	17.5	22.8	12.1
Trade and public catering	0.1	0.1	0.1	0.1	0.1	0.1
Other	23.0	24.6	20.3	15.2	14.3	21.2

Foreign investment trends in 1997–2002

TABLE 7

	1997	1998	1999	2000	2001	2002
Foreign investment, $ million	380.0	7.6	195.2	64.3	30.1	364.1
Including FDI, $ million	33.5	7.6	5.6	14.6	0.8	1.9

Largest enterprises of the Krasnoyarsk Territory

TABLE 8

COMPANY	SECTOR
OAO GMK Norilsk Nickel	Non-ferrous metals
OAO Gulidov Krasnoyarsk Non-Ferrous Metals Plant	Non-ferrous metals
OAO Krasnoyarsk Aluminum Plant	Non-ferrous metals
OAO Achinsk Alumina Plant	Non-ferrous metals
OAO Krasnoyarsk Metals Plant	Non-ferrous metals
OAO Krasnoyarsk Synthetic Rubber Plant	Chemicals
OAO Krasnoyarsk Industrial Rubber Products Factory	Chemicals
OAO Yenisei Chemicals Plant	Chemicals
FGUP Electrochemical Plant	Machine engineering
FGUP NPO Applied Mechanics	Machine engineering
FGUP Krasnoyarsk Machine Engineering Plant	Machine engineering
ZAO Novoyeniseisky LHK	Timber
OAO Sibirsky CBK (Paper Mill)	Timber
OAO Krasnoyarsk Bread	Food and beverages
ZAO Kraskon	Food and beverages
OAO Pikra	Food and beverages

SIBERIAN FEDERAL DISTRICT

VI

5.5. CURRENT LEGISLATION ON INVESTOR TAX EXEMPTIONS AND PRIVILEGES

Regional legislative acts regulating investments in the Krasnoyarsk Territory include the Laws On the Territorial Targeted Program for the Promotion of Innovation Activities in the Krasnoyarsk Territory; On Investment Activities in the Krasnoyarsk Territory; On the Territorial Targeted Program of State Support to Small Enterprise in the Krasnoyarsk Territory, 2001–2002; The Krasnoyarsk Territory Administrative Regulation On the Organization and Conduct of Small Business Investment Project Tenders; The Krasnoyarsk Territory Administrative Regulation On the Adoption of the Krasnoyarsk Territory Development Concept through 2010; The Krasnoyarsk Territory Administrative Council Regulation On State Support to Enterprises in the Territory Conducting Investment Projects within the Krasnoyarsk Territory.

5.6. FEDERAL AND REGIONAL ECONOMIC AND SOCIAL DEVELOPMENT PROGRAMS FOR THE KRASNOYARSK TERRITORY

Federal targeted programs. The following federal programs are currently underway in the Territory: Energy Efficient Economy 2002–2005 and through 2010, and Defense Industry Reorganization and Development 2002–2006.

Regional programs. The Territory's regional targeted programs seek to develop the transport infrastructure, increase industrial output, and advance the social sphere. The most important programs are: Krasnoyarsk Territory Roads 2002–2005 ($39 million allocated from the Territory's budget);

Geological Exploration and the Development of Mineral Resources in the Krasnoyarsk Territory, 2003–2005 ($4.7 million allocated from the Territory's budget); Stabilization and Development of the Agroindustrial Sector in the Krasnoyarsk Territory, 2001–2005 ($1.7 million allocated from the Territory's budget); The Territory's Targeted Program for Forest Regeneration, 2000–2004 ($0.8 million allocated from the Territory's budget); Stabilization and Development of the Public Health Service in the Krasnoyarsk Territory, 2002–2004 ($2.1 million allocated from the Territory's budget); Computerization of Education: Information Technologies in General Education, 2001–2004 ($0.9 million allocated from the Territory's budget).

Regional entities responsible for raising investment		*TABLE 9*
ENTITY	ADDRESS	PHONE, FAX, E-MAIL
Central Department for Economic Development and Planning of the Krasnoyarsk Territory Administration	123, ul. Lenina, Krasnoyarsk, Krasnoyarsk Territory, 660009	Phone: (3912) 23 6731 Fax: (3912) 23 2369 E-mail: vasilenko@econ.krasnoyarsk.su
Foreign Relations Department of the Krasnoyarsk Territory Administration	125, ul. Lenina, Krasnoyarsk, Krasnoyarsk Territory, 660009	Phone: (3912) 49 3718 Fax: (3912) 21 7031 E-mail: oiuvs@mail.ru

6. INVESTMENT PROJECTS

Industry sector and project description	1) Expected results 2) Amount and term of investment 3) Form of financing[1] 4) Documentation[2]	Contact information
1	2	3

MACHINE ENGINEERING AND METAL PROCESSING		
69R001	● ❖ ◆ ▲	
Metal product corrosion protection. Project goal: to prevent corrosion of metal products, ship structures, and municipal utility infrastructure, to create jobs, and increase tax payments.	1) Output capacity of 5,000 tons annually, sales of $3.2 million annually 2) $4.2 million/36 months 3) JV, L 4) BP, FS	Foreign Relations Department of the Krasnoyarsk Territory Administration, Foreign Investments Division 110, pr. Mira, Krasnoyarsk, Krasnoyarsk Territory, 660009 Phone: (3912) 49 3718, 49 3716 Fax: (3912) 21 7039 E-mail: oiuvs@mail.ru, uvs@krasmail.ru Oleg Vladimirovich Ivanov, Division Head

[1] L – Loan, E – Equity, Leas. – Leasing, JV – Joint Venture
[2] BP – Business Plan, FS – Feasibility Study

1	2	3

FORESTRY, TIMBER, AND PULP AND PAPER

69R002

■ ● ▼

Cardboard packaging for liquid products.
Project goal: to set up and develop cardboard
packaging production for liquid products.

1) Brick cartons output of 45.6 million
units annually; triple-layered
cartons – 5.4 million units annually,
triple-layered house type cartons –
57.6 million units annually, triple-
layered longitudinal brick cartons –
1.92 million units annually,
sales of $9.1 million annually.
2) $2.8 million/12 months
3) L, E
4) Investment proposal

Foreign Relations Department
of the Krasnoyarsk Territory Administ-
ration, Foreign Investments Division
110, pr. Mira, Krasnoyarsk,
Krasnoyarsk Territory, 660009
Phone: (3912) 49 3718, 49 3716
Fax: (3912) 21 7039
E-mail: oiuvs@mail.ru,
uvs@krasmail.ru
Oleg Vladimirovich Ivanov,
Division Head

GLASS AND PORCELAIN

69R003

● ★ ◆ ▲

Launch of a new glass container
manufacturing facility.
Project goal: to produce high-
quality glass containers.

1) Up to 60 million bottles annually
2) $4.4 million/44 months
3) L ($3.7 million), Leas.
4) BP, FS

Foreign Relations Department
of the Krasnoyarsk Territory Administ-
ration, Foreign Investments Division
110, pr. Mira, Krasnoyarsk,
Krasnoyarsk Territory, 660009
Phone: (3912) 49 3718, 49 3716
Fax: (3912) 21 7039
E-mail: oiuvs@mail.ru, uvs@krasmail.ru
Oleg Vladimirovich Ivanov,
Division Head

FOOD AND BEVERAGES

69R004

● ◆ ▲

Revamping of OAO Kansk Tobacco Plant.
Project goal: to produce higher quality
tobacco goods through improved tobacco
preparation technologies and increased
capacity of production lines.

1) Up to 2,500 kg of cut tobacco per hour
2) $2.1 million/24 months
3) L ($1.6 million)
4) BP, FS

Foreign Relations Department
of the Krasnoyarsk Territory Administ-
ration, Foreign Investments Division
110, pr. Mira, Krasnoyarsk,
Krasnoyarsk Territory, 660009
Phone: (3912) 49 3718, 49 3716
Fax: (3912) 21 7039
E-mail: oiuvs@mail.ru, uvs@krasmail.ru
Oleg Vladimirovich Ivanov,
Division Head

AGRICULTURE

69R005

● ★ ◆ ▲

Industrial production of pork
and processing into meat products
at the Pervomansky pork factory.
Project goal: to create a resource base
for the meat processing sector
in the Krasnoyarsk Territory, and restoration
of the Pervomansky pork factory.

1) 54,000 heads annually
2) $1.0 million/20 months
3) L, Leas.
4) BP, FS

Foreign Relations Department
of the Krasnoyarsk Territory Administ-
ration, Foreign Investments Division
110, pr. Mira, Krasnoyarsk,
Krasnoyarsk Territory, 660009
Phone: (3912) 49 3718, 49 3716
Fax: (3912) 21 7039
E-mail: oiuvs@mail.ru, uvs@krasmail.ru
Oleg Vladimirovich Ivanov,
Division Head

69R006

● ★ ◆ ▲

Construction of an oil and soy cake
production plant.
Project goal: to produce soy oil and cake.

1) 3,600 tons monthly
2) $4.7 million/42 months
3) L, Leas.
4) BP, FS

Foreign Relations Department
of the Krasnoyarsk Territory Administ-
ration, Foreign Investments Division
110, pr. Mira, Krasnoyarsk,
Krasnoyarsk Territory, 660009
Phone: (3912) 49 3718, 49 3716
Fax: (3912) 21 7039
E-mail: oiuvs@mail.ru, uvs@krasmail.ru
Oleg Vladimirovich Ivanov,
Division Head

1	2	3

LIGHT INDUSTRY

69R007 ● ◆ ▲

Creation of a multifunctional enterprise in Sharypovo.
Project goal: to produce garments and knitwear, to construct a shop (selling goods manufactured by the enterprise), a cafe-bar with billiards, dry cleaners, and a hair-dressing saloon.

1) Garments and knitwear production – 628,000 units annually, sales of €0.363 million annually
2) $2.1 million/39 months
3) L
4) BP, FS

Foreign Relations Department of the Krasnoyarsk Territory Administration, Foreign Investments Division
110, pr. Mira, Krasnoyarsk, Krasnoyarsk Territory, 660009
Phone: (3912) 49 3718, 49 3716
Fax: (3912) 21 7039
E-mail: oiuvs@mail.ru, uvs@krasmail.ru
Oleg Vladimirovich Ivanov, Division Head

70. IRKUTSK REGION [38]

ECONOMIC MAP

Viluysk

TURA

EVENKIYSKY

Viluyskoe water reservoir

REPUBLIC OF SAKHA

Chernyshevsky

Mirny

(YAKUTIA)

AUTONOMOU

Olyokminsk

DISTRICT

Podkamennaya Tunguska

Lensk

Nizhnyaya Tunguska

Peleduy

Angara

Boguchany

Ust-Ilimsk

Kirensk

Vitimsky

Mama

Bodaybo

Mamakan

Ust-Kut

Bratsk

Nizhneangarsk

Tayshet

REPUBLIC

Birusinsk
Nizhneudinsk

Zhigalovo

Tulun

Kachug

Sayansk

Lena

Zima

OF BURYATIA

Cheremkhovo

Ust-Barguzin

Svirsk

UST-ORDYNSKY

Lake Baikal

CHITA

Mishelevka

IRKUTSK

Usole-Sibirskoe

ULAN-UDE

AGINSKOE

Angarsk
Shelekhov

Sludyanka

Baykalsk

Petrovsk-
Zabaykalsky

REPUBLIC

OF TYVA

MONGOLIA

KRASNOYARSK TERRITORY

PROCESSING INDUSTRY	MINING INDUSTRY	CROPS AND LIVESTOCK BREEDING	
● Non-ferrous metals	■ Bituminous coal	Wheat	Meat and dairy cattle breeding
● Machine engineering and metal processing	▨ Brown coal	Barley	
● Chemicals and petrochemicals	▲ Iron ore	Long-fibred flax	Pig breeding
● Forestry and timber	◗ Gold	Sugar beetroot	Sheep rearing
● Construction materials	⬚ Shale oil		Poultry farming
● Food and beverages	⬓ Table salt		

POWER PLANTS

⚡ Thermal power plants   ⚡ Hydro power plants   Resorts

T he Irkutsk Region's history dates back as far as three centuries. The Region enjoys a favorable economic and geographical location at the center of Asian Russia on the crossroads of trade routes linking Central Russia to the Pacific Rim countries.

The Irkutsk Region is an acknowledged leader among Russia's regions in terms of the sheer wealth and variety of its resources. It has 11% of Russia's total reserves of timber and large explored deposits of gold, rare earth metals, easily dressed iron ore, mica, magnesite, talc, calcium and rock salt, and semi-precious stones. We are one of the few Russian regions with adequate reserves of all types of fuel and energy resources – more than 7% of total nationwide reserves of coal, oil, and natural gas, and 10% of the nation's hydro resources. The Region is home to the Kovyktinskoe gas condensate deposit, the largest deposit of its kind in the East of Russia, the major Sukholozhskoe gold ore deposit, the Sayany rare earth metal province, the largest of its kind worldwide, and others. The Irkutsk Region is also a likely location for the discovery of industrial deposits of diamonds.

The Irkutsk Region has the country's largest fuel and energy, mining, timber, and petrochemicals sectors. Machine engineering and non-ferrous metals are also developing rapidly.

The Irkutsk Region's electricity system boasts a generation capacity of 75 billion kWh. The Region's considerable hydroelectric resources mean electricity costs are among the lowest in the country.

While the Region's population accounts for only 1.9% of the total population of Russia, the Region produces 85% of Russia's total mica output, 53% of its synthetic resins and plastic output, 53% of its pulp output, 50% of its nitrate fertilizers and caustic soda output, more than a third of total aluminum output, 10% of the country's gold output, 9% of its petrochemicals output, 7% of its electricity, 6% of its coal, and 5% of its iron ore.

The Regions ranks thirteenth in terms of industrial output, eighth in per capita output, and fifth in terms of volume of exports.

The Irkutsk Region enjoys a developed infrastructure. Its transport infrastructure includes the Trans-Siberian and Baikal – Amur railroads, which link the Irkutsk Region to European Russia and the Pacific Rim states, two international airports at Irkutsk and Bratsk, and a developed highway network that enables the shipment of goods to and from the Region quickly and effectively.

The Region is also the home of Lake Baikal – the largest fresh water lake on earth. Baikal concentrates 80% of Russia's total surface fresh water reserves and 20% of the world's reserves of surface fresh water. The Baikal area offers unique opportunities for the development of tourism and leisure.

The strong investment appeal of the Irkutsk Region is determined by its extensive resource, energy, research and development, and educational potential. According to Expert rating agency, in 2002 the Irkutsk Region showed the sharpest drop in investment risk. Its investment appeal is now rated 2B (medium potential – moderate risk). In 2002, Standard & Poor's raised the Region's long-term foreign currency credit rating from CCC+ to B- (outlook positive).

The Irkutsk Region invites business partners to collaborate on a mutually beneficial basis with the Region. The Regional Administration is committed to providing investors with the most favorable conditions for conducting business.

Boris Govorin,
GOVERNOR OF THE IRKUTSK REGION

1. GENERAL INFORMATION

1.1. GEOGRAPHY

Located in the southern part of Eastern Siberia in the upper reaches of the Lower Tunguska, Angara, and Lena Rivers, the Irkutsk Region covers a total area of 775,000 square kilometers. To the north-east it borders the Republic of Sakha (Yakutia), to the east and south – the Chita Region and the Republic of Buryatia, to the west – the Krasnoyarsk Territory, and to the south-west – the Republic of Tyva.

1.2. CLIMATE

The Irkutsk Region enjoys a continental climate. Air temperatures in January average −28.5°C, rising to an average of +16.4°C in July. Annual precipitation reaches 400 mm (in the northern and mountainous areas of the Region). The growing season lasts around 80–125 days.

1.3. POPULATION

According to preliminary 2002 census results, total population of the Irkutsk Region was 2,582,000 people. The average population density is 3.3 people per square kilometer. The economically active population totals 1,346,000. Official unemployment stood at 2% in 2002, while the actual rate was 10.9%.

Demographically speaking, some 62.2% are of statutory working age, 21.1% are below the statutory working age, and 16.7% are beyond the statutory working age.

The major urban centers of the Irkutsk Region (2002 data) are Irkutsk with 593,400 inhabitants, Bratsk with 259,200 inhabitants, Angarsk with 247,100 inhabitants, Ust-Ilimsk with 100,600 inhabitants, and Usolye-Sibirskoye with 103,300 inhabitants.

Population		1992	1997	1998	1999	2000	2001	2002
Total population, '000		2,816	2,780	2,768	2,758	2,742	2,729	2,582
Economically active population, '000		1,481	1,293	1,240	1,355	1,406	1,359	1,346

TABLE 1

2. ADMINISTRATION

1a, ul. Lenina, Irkutsk, Irkutsk Region, 664027
Phone: (3952) 24 1773, fax: (3952) 24 3340; http://www.admirk.ru

NAME	POSITION	CONTACT INFORMATION
Boris Alexandrovich GOVORIN	Governor of the Irkutsk Region	Phone: (3952) 20 0015
Tatyana Ivanovna RYUTINA	Deputy Head of the Irkutsk Regional Administration, Chief of Staff of the Governor of the Irkutsk Region	Phone: (3952) 25 6016
Dmitry Zakaryevich BAYMASHEV	Deputy Head of the Irkutsk Regional Administration for the Agroindustrial Sector and Consumer Market	Phone: (3952) 20 0082
Anatoly Alekseevich KOZLOV	Deputy Head of the Irkutsk Regional Administration, Director of the Central Finance Department	Phone: (3952) 25 6315
Irina Ivanovna DUMOVA	Deputy Head of the Irkutsk Regional Administration for the Economic Policy	Phone: (3952) 25 6062
Larisa Innokentyevna ZABRODSKAYA	Deputy Head of the Irkutsk Regional Administration for Economic Development and Resource Management	Phone: (3952) 33 2661
Alexei Ivanovich SOBOL	Deputy Head of the Irkutsk Regional Administration for Regional Infrastructure Development	Phone: (3952) 24 1531

SIBERIAN FEDERAL DISTRICT

VI

3. ECONOMIC POTENTIAL

3.1. 1997–2002 GROSS REGIONAL PRODUCT (GRP). INDUSTRY BREAKDOWN

The Irkutsk Region's 2002 gross regional product amounted to $4,963 million, 10.0% up on 2001. Per capita GRP was $1,655 in 2001, and $1,922 in 2002.

3.2. MAJOR ECONOMIC GROWTH PROJECTIONS

The blueprint for the social and economic development of the Irkutsk Region (2003–2005) forecasts GRP growth at 14.1% in comparable prices, bringing GRP up to $6,254 million in current prices by 2005.

GRP trends in 1997–2002						TABLE 2
	1997	1998	1999	2000	2001*	2002*
GRP in current prices, $ million	9,326	5,352	3,298	3,801	4,513	4,963

*Estimates of the Irkutsk Regional Administration

GRP industry breakdown in 1997–2002, % of total						TABLE 3
	1997	1998	1999	2000	2001*	2002*
GRP	100.0	100.0	100.0	100.0	100.0	100.0
Industry	28.6	32.4	43.6	41.1	40.0	39.5
Agriculture and forestry	7.0	6.6	7.9	6.2	6.8	6.3
Construction	0.3	0.3	0.2	0.3	0.3	0.3
Transport and communications	7.3	7.0	8.1	6.4	7.1	6.5
Trade and public catering	5.3	6.5	3.7	4.4	4.6	4.7
Other	51.5	47.2	36.5	41.6	41.2	42.7

*Estimates of the Irkutsk Regional Administration

Industrial output is expected to increase by 19% by 2005. The strongest growth is expected in construction materials (30%), machine engineering and metal processing (24%), and non-ferrous metals (23%). By 2005, growth is expected to reach 13–16% in the coal, petrochemicals, ferrous metals, and energy sectors.

The Region plans to develop its non-ferrous metals industry, with a special focus on aluminum. A new aluminum plant is slated to be built.

Agroindustrial output is expected to increase by 1.7% by 2005, reaching $505 million in current prices.

The Regional Administration expects fixed capital investments to grow by 14.5% to $721 million. Foreign investment is expected to rise by 54% to $189.2 million.

3.3. INDUSTRIAL OUTPUT IN 1997–2002 FOR MAJOR SECTORS OF ECONOMY

The Irkutsk Region's major industrial sectors are non-ferrous metals, forestry, machine engineering, and energy. These account for a combined 74.3% of total industrial output.

Non-ferrous metals. The sector accounts for 25.2% of total industrial output. The aluminum industry accounts for the lion's share of the sector's output. The largest enterprises in the sector are OAO Siberian and Urals Aluminum Company and OAO Bratsk Aluminum Plant. These companies produce aluminum,

alumina, and fluorides, accounting for one-third of total Russian and 4% of worldwide aluminum output.

Gold mining companies in the Irkutsk Region are developing new deposits. Gold ore output grew by 67% in 2002.

Forestry, timber, and pulp and paper. The sector accounts for 20.7% of total industrial output. Enterprises in the sector specialize in commercial timber, sawn timber, glued plywood, chipboard and fiberboard, cellulose, and paper and cardboard. The largest enterprises in the sector are OAO Irkutsklesprom, ZAO Sibexportles, OAO PO Ust-Ilimsk Timber Processing Plant, OAO Ust-Ilimsk Sawmill and Timber Processing Plant, and OAO Baikal Pulp and Paper Mill.

Machine engineering and metal processing. The sector accounts for 15.7% of total industrial output. The leading enterprises in the sector are OAO IRKUT Scientific Production Corporation (producing Su 27 and Su 30 military aircraft and Be 200 and Yak 112 civilian planes) and OAO Irkutskkabel.

Energy. The energy sector accounts for 12.7% of total industrial output. The Region's energy sector is represented by one of the largest energy systems in the Russian Federation, OAO Irkutskenergo. OAO Irkutskenergo's subsidiaries include three hydroelectric power stations, twelve thermal power stations, and electricity grids. The Bratsk Hydroelectric Power Station

Industry breakdown of industrial output in 1997–2002, % of total						TABLE 4
	1997	1998	1999	2000	2001	2002*
Industry	100.0	100.0	100.0	100.0	100.0	100.0
Non-ferrous metals	20.2	25.3	25.3	27.4	27.4	25.2
Forestry, timber, and pulp and paper	15.4	16.9	17.4	22.5	21.5	20.7
Machine engineering and metal processing	12.2	7.7	15.0	11.5	13.1	15.7
Energy	17.5	20.2	12.9	10.7	10.9	12.7
Chemicals and petrochemicals	5.1	4.9	6.9	9.8	6.9	7.5
Food and beverages	9.4	8.9	7.0	6.6	7.1	7.0
Fuel	12.3	9.3	9.0	5.0	6.6	6.3
Construction materials	3.2	2.8	1.5	1.6	1.6	1.6
Ferrous metals	2.3	1.9	2.7	2.7	2.4	1.5
Flour, cereals, and mixed fodder	0.9	0.7	0.4	0.5	0.5	1.1
Light industry	0.5	0.3	0.2	0.3	0.3	0.3
Glass and porcelain	0.2	0.2	0.1	0.1	–	0.1

*Estimates of the Irkutsk Regional Administration

is the largest generator, accounting for more than 40% of total energy output in the Irkutsk Energy System.

Chemicals. The sector accounts for 7.5% of total industrial output. Enter-prises in the sector specialize in organic chemicals (PVC, plastics, synthetic resin), non-organic chemicals (caustic, sulfuric acid) nitrogen fertilizers, and medicines and technical substances. The largest enterprises in the sector are OAO Sayanskkhimprom, OAO Usolyekhimprom, and OAO Tulunsky Hydrolysis Plant.

3.4. FUEL AND ENERGY BALANCE (OUTPUT AND CONSUMPTION PER RESOURCE)

The Region's energy system has an electricity generation capacity of over 70 billion KWh and a heat energy capacity of up to 46 million Gcal. The Region produces more energy than it consumes. The installed capacity of the Irkutsk Energy System is 12.9 GW. The bulk of energy is consumed by industry: aluminum, chemicals and petrochemicals, forestry, paper, and the railroad.

Fuel and energy sector production and consumption trends, 1997–2002						TABLE 5
	1997	1998	1999	2000	2001	2002*
Electricity output, billion kWh	49.0	52.4	54.6	53.9	55.3	57.4
Oil output (including gas condensate), '000 tons	–	11.0	14.0	26.0	44.0	45.9
Natural gas output, million cubic meters	–	–	–	6.0	23.0	25.0
Coal output, '000 tons	12,396	14,491	14,031	14,894	15,294	11,996
Electricity consumption, billion kWh	32.4	33.8	34.4	35.6	36.2	34.7

*Estimates of the Irkutsk Regional Administration

3.5. TRANSPORT INFRASTRUCTURE

Roads. Several federal highways pass through the Region. These include the Novosibirsk – Irkutsk, Irkutsk – Chita, and Kultuk – Mondy. The federal Irkutsk – Mondy road and 20 regional main roads also form part of the Region's road network. The Irkutsk Region has 11,700 kilometers of public highway, 10,100 kilometers of which is paved. In 2002, some 5.1 million tons of freight was transported by road.

Railroads. The Trans-Siberian Railway and the Baikal – Amur Railroad pass through the Irkutsk

Region. The Region has 2,481 kilometers of railroads. Rail transport accounts for 70% of freight carriage and one-third of passenger carriage in the Region.

Airports. Three large airports located at Irkutsk, Bratsk, and Ust-Ilimsk serve the Region. Two of the airports (Irkutsk and Bratsk) have international status.

3.6. MAIN NATURAL RESOURCES: RESERVES AND EXTRACTION IN 2002

The Region has considerable mineral reserves. The Mamsko-Chuyskaya Mica Province, the Angarskaya Iron Ore Province, the East Sayan Rare Metal Province, the

Irkutsk Coal Basin, and the East Siberian Salt Basin, the largest salt deposit of its kind anywhere in the world, are all situated in the Region. Iron ore reserves are concentrated in the Angarsk District. The Savinskoe magnesite deposit is the largest in Russia. The Igirminskoe molding quartz sand deposit has been explored. The Region is a major mica supplier. Significant reserves of potassium and rock salt, talcum, and decorative stone are located in the Region. Gold deposits are an important component of the Region's mineral resources.

Oil and gas. Eleven oil and gas deposits have been discovered and explored in the Region. The Region is home to the Kovyktinskoye gas condensate deposit. Reserves are estimated at 2 trillion cubic meters of natural gas and 115 million tons of liquid gas condensate.

Coal. Potential coal reserves stand at 8.2 billion tons. Output totals 12 million tons. The Region accounts for 5.6% of total coal output of Russia. The largest coal deposits are at the Cheremkhovskoye and Voznesenskoye.

Iron ore. The potential reserve amounts to 1.9 billion tons. Output stands at 9.5 million tons. The Region accounts for 11.5% of total iron ore output in Russia.

Gold. Output stands at 16 tons. The Sukholozhskoye gold deposit is one of the largest in the world. The industrial development of the deposit will enable annual output of 20 tons of gold or more.

Diamonds. The Irkutsk Region is likely to contain deposits of diamonds, and commercial diamond deposits are quite likely to be discovered in the Region.

Rare metals. The unique Sayan Rare Metal Province offers substantial investment interest. Eleven rare metal deposits have been discovered in the Province, including deposits of tantalum, niobium, cesium, rubidium, and lithium. The largest deposits are at the Beloziminskoye, Bolshetagninskoye, Vishnyakovskoye, and Goltsovskoye.

Water resources. Lake Baikal, the deepest freshwater lake in the world, is located in the south-eastern part of the Region. The Lake contains 23,000 cubic kilometers of fresh water constituting 80% of Russia's fresh surface water reserve and 20% of the global reserve.

The Irkutsk Region's potential hydroelectric power resources are estimated at 200–250 billion kWh per year. The usable resource stands at 190 billion kWh per year (10% of Russia's hydroelectric power resources). The hydroelectric power sector is currently operating at one-third of its capacity.

4. TRADE OPPORTUNITIES

4.1. MAIN GOODS PRODUCED IN THE REGION

Non-ferrous metals. The Region's 2002 gold output amounted to 16 tons, a record output level for the Region. 2002 primary aluminum output was 1,194,600 tons.

Chemicals. The Irkutsk Region is the third largest producer of synthetic resin and plastics in Russia with 326,000 tons output in 2002.

Timber. The Region is a leading Russian timber producer with 13.4 million cubic meters of dense commercial timber output, 1.8 million cubic meters of sawn timber, 127,000 cubic meters of glued plywood, and 1.2 million tons of cellulose (2002 data).

Agriculture. The 2002 grain harvest was 519,900 tons. The vegetable crop totaled 207,700 tons.

4.2. EXPORTS, INCLUDING EXTRA-CIS

The Region's 2002 exports totaled more than $3,200 million. Non-CIS exports accounted for 98.9%. The Region exported 85.9% of its total industrial output in 2002, including 73.1% of aluminum output, more than 71% of cellulose output, 86.5% of PVC output, 52.8% of sawn timber output, and more than 35% of petrochemicals output.

In 2002, the Region's products were exported to 66 countries. Major 2002 export partners were China (34.3% of the total), Japan (21.8%), India (12.8%), the USA (10.7%), Ireland (3.5%), Mongolia (3.3%), the Netherlands (2.8%), Singapore (1.7%), Turkey (1.3%), and South Korea (1.2%). Machinery and equipment, cellulose, cardboard, plastics, PVC resin, ethylene and other chemicals and round timber are exported to China; aluminum, timber and coal – to Japan; machine engineering products, timber and paper – to India; aluminum and chemicals – to the USA; cellulose, processed timber, and glued plywood – to Ireland; petrochemicals, ferrous metals, machinery and equipment – to Mongolia; and chemicals and aluminum – to the Netherlands.

4.3. IMPORTS, INCLUDING EXTRA-CIS

2002 imports totaled more than $400 million (67.3% from extra-CIS countries).

The Region imports raw material for the aluminum industry (about 64% of total imports), machine engineering products (industrial equipment, equipment for agricultural product processing, machines, and automobiles), petrochemicals, food and pharmaceuticals, and consumer goods.

In 2002, the Region imported products from 64 countries, with industrially developed countries accounting for 24.1% of the total imports, developing countries accounting for 28.1%, China – for 12.2%, and CIS countries – for 32.7%.

The Region's main trading partners for imports are Kazakhstan (20.4% of the total imports), India (19.7%), China (12.2%), Ukraine (10.7%), Australia (8.6%), Guinea (5%), and Germany (4.2%).

Aluminum ore, lead and minerals are imported from Kazakhstan; alumina, pharmaceuticals, and consumer goods – from India; oil coke, pitch and pitch coke, food, equipment, and consumer goods – from China; and aluminum ore and machinery and equipment – from Ukraine and Australia.

4.4. MAJOR REGIONAL
EXPORT AND IMPORT ENTITIES

Owing to the specific nature of the Region's export and import activities, export and import transactions are performed mainly by industrial enterprises.

These include OAO Ust-Ilimsk Timber Processing Plant, OAO Irkutsklesprom, OAO Bratskkomplekskholding, OAO Baikal Pulp and Paper Mill, OAO Sayanskkhimplast, and others.

5. INVESTMENT OPPORTUNITIES

5.1. INVESTMENTS
IN 1992–2002
(BY INDUSTRY SECTOR),
INCLUDING FOREIGN
INVESTMENTS

The following factors determine the investment appeal of the Irkutsk Region:

- Its favorable geographical location (a transport hub);
- Its well-developed transport infrastructure (the Trans-Siberian Railway and the Baikal – Amur Railroad pass through the Region);

- Legislation supporting investment activity (guarantees for investor rights and preferential tax treatment for investors);
- Its qualified work force;
- Cheap energy resources (the Region has one of the largest energy systems of the Russian Federation);
- Its considerable natural resources.

5.2. CAPITAL INVESTMENT

Industry accounts for the lion's share of fixed capital investments (42.7%), with transport and communications accounting for 27.4%.

Capital investment by industry sector, $ million						TABLE 6
	1997	1998	1999	2000	2001	2002
Total capital investments	859.6	526.8	334.1	377.9	430.9	387.0
Including major industries (% of total)						
Industry	37.8	43.1	45.1	44.2	50.8	42.7
Agriculture and forestry	2.2	2.8	2.6	3.0	2.0	2.3
Construction	5.2	0.7	0.9	1.4	0.9	1.9
Transport and communications	21.6	18.3	30.8	29.6	25.0	27.4
Trade and public catering	5.2	1.1	0.2	0.4	0.3	9.6
Other	28.0	34.0	20.4	21.4	21.0	16.1

Foreign investment trends in 1996–2002					TABLE 7
	1996–1997	1998	1999	2000	2001	2002
Foreign investment, $ million	74.3	135.2	86.0	82.3	101.1	82.2
Including FDI, $ million	12.5	51.9	15.6	18.7	12.4	18.1

5.3. MAJOR ENTERPRISES
(INCLUDING ENTERPRISES
WITH FOREIGN INVESTMENT)

The Irkutsk Region is home to 23 major enterprises with foreign investment, including OAO RUSIA Petroleum, OOO Wagner Sibir Equipment, OOO SP Igirma-Tayriku, and OOO JV Baikal.

5.4. MOST ATTRACTIVE
SECTORS FOR INVESTMENT

The Irkutsk Regional Administration and experts name non-ferrous metals, transport, energy, construction, and trade as the most attractive sectors for investors.

5.5. CURRENT LEGISLATION ON INVESTOR
TAX EXEMPTIONS AND PRIVILEGES

The Region enacted the Law of the Irkutsk Region On Regional Investment Policy and the Encouragement of Investment Activities. The Law provides for the following:

Investors implementing investment projects included into the schedule of priority investment programs, and investors carrying out targeted programs, are granted an investment tax credit for the regional tax components in accordance with the tax legislation;

Guaranteed protection of investments (no investment in the Region can be nationalized, except for specific cases regulated by federal law);

Largest enterprises of the Irkutsk Region

TABLE 8

COMPANY	SECTOR
OAO Irkutskenergo	Energy
OAO Angarskaya Petrochemical Company	Petrochemicals
OAO Korshunovsky Ore Dressing Plant	Metals
OAO Bratsk Aluminum Plant	Metals
OAO Sayanskkhimplast	Chemicals
OAO IRKUT Scientific Production Corporation	Machine engineering
OAO Irkutskkabel	Machine engineering
OAO Ust-Ilimsky Timber Processing Plant	Forestry, timber, and pulp and paper

Any loss, including lost profits, arising as a result of unlawful actions on the part of government bodies, must be compensated in accordance with the above Law;

Government bodies are prohibited from interfering in investors' activities and must guarantee equitable protection of rights to all investors and their partners.

5.6. FEDERAL AND REGIONAL ECONOMIC AND SOCIAL DEVELOPMENT PROGRAMS FOR THE IRKUTSK REGION

Federal targeted programs. The Federal Targeted Program for the Economic and Social Development of the Far East and the Trans-Baikal Region 1996-2005 and through 2010 plays a key

Regional entities responsible for raising investment

TABLE 9

ENTITY	ADDRESS	PHONE, FAX, E-MAIL
ZAO Angarsky Investment House	25, pr. Karla Marksa, Angarsk, Irkutsk Region, 665835	Phone: (3951) 52 6193 E-mail: fda@fonda.irkutsk.ru
ZAO Baikal Investment House	6, ul. Lenina, Irkutsk, Irkutsk Region, 664000	Phone: (3952) 25 8005
OOO Bratsk Investment House	8, ul. Kosmonavtov, Bratsk, Irkutsk Region, 665729	Phone: (3953) 43 9073 E-mail: bfd@mail.ru
OAO East Siberian Investment Company	17, ul. Rossiyskaya, Irkutsk, Irkutsk Region, 664000	Phone: (3952) 34 7500 Fax: (3952) 34 6340
ZAO East Siberian Investment Company VSG-Invest	109, ul. Sovetskaya, Irkutsk, Irkutsk Region, 664009	Phone/fax: (3952) 27 0314
OOO Irkutsk Investment Agency	P. O. Box 64, GSP, Irkutsk, Irkutsk Region, 664000	Phone: (3952) 34 0430 E-mail: info@isa.esib.ru
ZAO Priangarye Plus	3, ul. Sovetskaya, Irkutsk, Irkutsk Region, 664047	Phone: (3952) 25 1048 Fax: (3952) 25 1048 E-mail: plus@radin.irkutsk.ru
ZAO Rossiya-Vostok	6, ul. Lenina, Irkutsk, Irkutsk Region, 664000	Phone: (3952) 24 2302
OAO SibTrust	P. O. Box 184, Irkutsk, Irkutsk Region, 664003	Phone: (3952) 33 5168 Fax: (3952): 33 5168
ZAO Siver	55, ul. Sovetskaya, Irkutsk, Irkutsk Region, 664000	Phone: (3952) 24 1080 Fax: (3952) 25 8225 E-mail: siver@angara.ru
ZAO Energiya-Invest Management Company	6, ul. Lenina, Irkutsk, Irkutsk Region, 664000	Phone: (3952) 24 0137
ZAO Finance & Management	18, ul. Lenina, Irkutsk, Irkutsk Region, 664000	Phone: (3952) 33 4482 Fax: (3952) 25 8031 E-mail: root@finmail.irkutsk.ru

part in the social and economic development of the Region. The Program provides for the reform of the regional natural gas transport system in Eastern Siberia based on the Irkutsk Region – China – Korean Peninsula trunk gas pipeline.

Road construction is underway in newly developed areas in the north of the Region under the Federal Targeted Program for the Modernization of Russia's Transport System (2002-2010).

The Federal Targeted Program for Energy Efficient Economy (2002–2005 and through 2010) provides for the development of the Kovyktinskoye natural gas deposit in the Irkutsk

Region, with output of up to 20 billion cubic meters expected by 2010.

Regional programs. The Region has drafted a program for social and economic development through 2005 with a view to raising living standards in the Region. In order to achieve this goal, the Regional Administration is adopting measures aimed at creating an investment friendly environment for regional insurance companies, banks, and use of enterprises' funds and outside financing. The program will require a budget of $1,498 million in 2002 to $2,190 million in 2005.

6. INVESTMENT PROJECTS

Industry sector and project description	1) Expected results 2) Amount and term of investment 3) Form of financing[1] 4) Documentation[2]	Contact information
1	2	3

	MINING	
70R001 ◼ Development of a gold deposit. Project goal: to extract gold.	1) 30 tons per year 2) $1.7 billion/n/a 3) E 4) Reserve estimation	Irkutsk Regional Administration 1a, ul. Lenina, Irkutsk, Irkutsk Region, 664027 Phone: (3952) 33 2661 Fax: (3952) 24 1751, 24 3340 E-mail: alexr@admirk.ru Alexander Adamovich Rudik, Deputy Head of the Regional Administration

	CHEMICALS AND PETROCHEMICALS	
70R002 ● ▲ ◆ Introduction of new caustic soda production technology. Project goal: to increase output and improve ecological situation.	1) Output of 230,000 tons of chlorine per year (the first unit – 150,000 tons) 2) $60 million/3 years 3) L 4) FS, BP	OAO Sayanskkhimplast P. O. Box 17, Sayansk-1, Irkutsk Region, 666301 Phone/fax: (3952) 25 8371, (39513) 45 006, 45 540 E-mail: mail@scpsayansk.ru Viktor Kuzmich Kruglov, CEO

SIBERIAN FEDERAL DISTRICT

VI

[1] L – Loan, E – Equity, Leas. – Leasing, JV – Joint Venture
[2] BP – Business Plan, FS – Feasibility Study

1	2	3

CHEMICALS AND PHARMACEUTICALS

70R003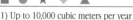

Production of medicine.
Project goal: to introduce
new medicine to the market.

1) Revenue of $1.4 million per year
2) $0.8 million/1 year
3) L
4) Investment proposal

Irkutsk Chemical R&D Institute
of the Siberian Branch
of the Russian Academy of Sciences
1, ul. Favorskogo, Irkutsk,
Irkutsk Region, 664033
Phone: (3952) 46 2400; fax: (3952) 39 6046
E-mail: voronkov@irioch.irk.ru
Mikhail Grigoryevich Voroonkov,
Academician, Counsellor
of the Academy of Sciences
OAO Usolye-Sibirskoye Chemical
and Pharmaceutical Plant
Usolye-Sibirskoye, Irkutsk Region, 665462
Phone: (39543) 46 711; fax: (39543) 45 493
E-mail: himfarm@usolsib.ru
Anton Iosifovich Orlov,
Director for Strategic Development

FORESTRY, TIMBER, AND PULP AND PAPER

70R004

Construction of a timber
processing plant
Project goal: to penetrate
the timber market.

1) Output of 100,000 cubic meters
   of product (revenue
   of $11.7 million) per year
2) $5 million/1 year
3) L
4) BP

OAO Avgustsib
1a, ul. Zavodskaya, Smolenschina Village,
Irkutsk Region, 664519
Phone: (3952) 36 5778; fax (3952) 36 5785
E-mail: avgustsib@irmail.ru
Vasily Vladimirovich Golubev,
CEO

CONSTRUCTION MATERIALS

70R005

Production of construction units
from foam concrete.
Project goal: to introduce building
materials with advanced consumer
features to the market.

1) Up to 10,000 cubic meters per year
2) $2.2 million/1.5 years
3) L, JV, Leas., E
4) FS, BP

ZAO Academstroyinvest
Office 116, 10, ul. Deputatskaya,
Irkutsk, Irkutsk Region, 664047
Phone: (3952) 27 1723
E-mail: iktus@rol.ru
Igor Alexandrovich Pelmenev, CEO

FOOD AND BEVERAGES

70R006

Construction of alcohol production
facilities at an operating hydrolysis plant.
Project goal: to expand
the product range.

1) Output of 2 million
   decaliters per year
2) $0.9 million/1 years
3) L
4) BP

OAO Tulun Hydrolysis Plant
1, ul. Gidroliznaya, Tulun-15,
Irkutsk Region, 665210
Phone: (39530) 24 271; fax: (3952) 43 6695
E-mail: Kedr@tgz.irtel.ru
Vladimir Alexandrovich Khamataev, CEO

TRANSPORT INFRASTRUCTURE

70R007

Construction of a runway
at the Irkutsk Airport.
Project goal: to increase passenger
and freight turnover.

1) n/a
2) $139.5 million/6 years
3) L
4) Preliminary project documents

FGUP Irkutsk Airport
13, ul. Shiryamova, Irkutsk,
Irkutsk Region, 664009
Phone: (3952) 54 4369, 26 6625, 54 4351
Fax: (3952) 54 4369, 54 4351
E-mail: iktoffice@angara.ru
Alexei Ivanovich Kulikov, CEO

HOTELS, TOURISM, AND RECREATION

70R008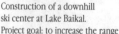

Construction of a downhill
ski center at Lake Baikal.
Project goal: to increase the range
and quality of tourist services.

1) 10,000 people per day
2) $19.5 million/5 years
3) L, JV
4) BP, FS

OOO Snow Land
6, ul. Gorkogo, Listvyanka,
Irkutsk Region
Phone: (3952) 33 3906, 33 3908, 24 4285
Fax: (3952) 33 3904
E-mail: plutonyi38@hotbox.ru
Yury Yevgenyevich Korenev, CEO

1	2	3

70R009 ■ ● ▲

| Construction of Baikal-Mongol Asia historical and eco-tourist tourism center. Project goal: to provide ethnographic tourism services. | 1) 150,000 people per year
2) $6 million/8 years
3) E, L
4) Preliminary FS | Non-State Organization Inter-Baikal Social and Ecological Expedition Office 4, 33, ul. Chkalova, Irkutsk, Irkutsk Region, 664000 Phone: (3952) 36 2507, fax: (3952) 36 2507 E-mail: expedition@interbaikal.irkutsk.ru Vladimir Viktorovich Berezhnykh, Director |

ECOLOGY AND WASTE TREATMENT

70R010 ■ ● ▲ ◆

| Construction of a solid waste processing plant with output of humus. Project goal: to improve environmental situation in the city. | 1) Processing capacity of 70,000 tons per year
2) $4 million/2 years
3) E, L ($2.5 million)
4) FS, BS | OOO Korall-K R&D and Production Company Office 415, 3, ul. Sovetskaya, Irkutsk, Irkutsk Region, 664047 Phone/fax: (3952) 20 7540 E-mail: Koral@irk.ru, soldatov@irnet.ru Dmitry Lvovich Ananyin, Director; Sergey Vladimirovich Soldatov, Director for Research and Development, Project Manager |

SCIENCE AND INNOVATION

70R011 ❖ ◆

| Production of organic and mineral fertilizers through hydrolysis of lignin. Project goal: to implement an R&D finding in commercial production. | 1) Output of 500,000 tons per year
2) $0.9 million/3–4 years
3) JV
4) BP | A. E. Favorsky Irkutsk Research and Development Chemistry Institute of the Russian Academy of Sciences 1, ul. Favorskogo, Irkutsk, Irkutsk Region, 664033 Phone: (3952) 51 1431; fax: (3952) 39 6046 E-mail: admin@irioch.irk.ru Academician Boris Alexandrovich Trofimov, Director of the Institute |

70R012 ❖ ▼

| Construction of a company for the production of polymer food packaging materials. Project goal: to implement R&D in commercial production. | 1) Revenue of over $10 million per year
2) $2.9 million/4 years
3) JV
4) Investment proposal | A. E. Favorsky Irkutsk Research and Development Chemistry Institute of the Russian Academy of Sciences 1, ul. Favorskogo, Irkutsk, Irkutsk Region, 664033 Phone: (3952) 51 1431; fax: (3952) 39 6046 E-mail: admin@irioch.irk.ru Academician Boris Alexandrovich Trofimov, Director of the Institute |

70R013 ❖ ▼

| Construction of a company for the production of polyvinyl-chloride plastic filled with local natural materials. Project goal: to implement R&D in commercial production. | 1) 195,000 tons per year
2) $9.6 million/0.5 year
3) JV
4) Investment proposal | A. E. Favorsky Irkutsk Research and Development Chemistry Institute of the Russian Academy of Sciences 1, ul. Favorskogo, Irkutsk, Irkutsk Region, 664033 Phone: (3952) 51 1431; fax: (3952) 39 6046 E-mail: admin@irioch.irk.ru Academician Boris Alexandrovich Trofimov, Director of the Institute |

GENERAL COMMERCIAL MARKET ACTIVITIES

70R014 ■ ● ◆

| Creation and development of a business and innovation incubator in Irkutsk. Project goal: to support small enterprise in innovation fields. | 1) Extension of small enterprise
2) $1.3 million/1.5 years
3) E, L
4) BP | Irkutsk Business Development Agency 7-B, ul. Proletarskaya, Irkutsk, Irkutsk Region, 664011 Phone: (3952) 33 6272, 34 0599 Fax: (3952) 34 3037 E-mail: info@irbp.ru Vladimir Ivanovich Snegirev, Director |

SIBERIAN FEDERAL DISTRICT

VI

71. KEMEROVO REGION [42]

ECONOMIC MAP

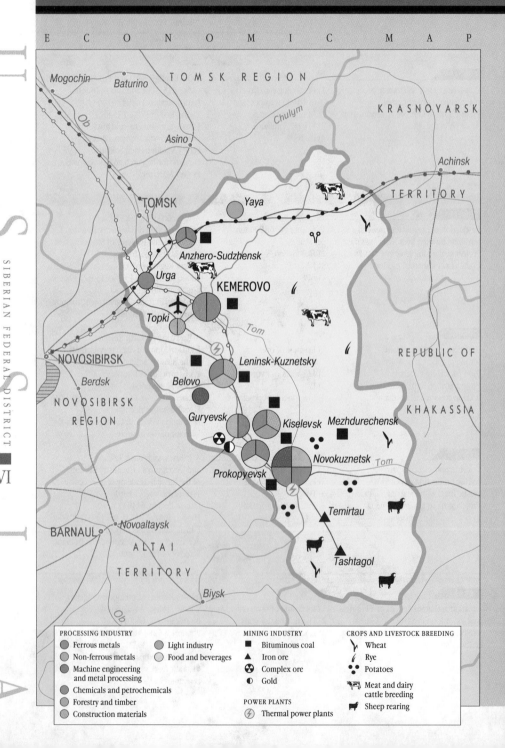

PROCESSING INDUSTRY
- ● Ferrous metals
- ○ Non-ferrous metals
- ● Machine engineering and metal processing
- ● Chemicals and petrochemicals
- ● Forestry and timber
- ● Construction materials
- ● Light industry
- ○ Food and beverages

MINING INDUSTRY
- ■ Bituminous coal
- ▲ Iron ore
- ☢ Complex ore
- ◑ Gold

POWER PLANTS
- ⚡ Thermal power plants

CROPS AND LIVESTOCK BREEDING
- 𝔶 Wheat
- 𝔶 Rye
- ⁝ Potatoes
- 🐄 Meat and dairy cattle breeding
- 🐑 Sheep rearing

The Kuzbass, as the Kemerovo Region is commonly known, is rightfully considered to be the heart of Russia's industry. It accounts for nearly half of total power generation coal output, 80% of coking coal output, and over half of ferrosilicium output. The Kuzbass ranks a nationwide third in steel melting and fourth in rolled steel production, and is the country's only producer of railway track.

The high quality of the Region's products has secured export customers for the Region's companies in some 58 countries worldwide, including Germany, the UK, China, Japan, Finland, and the USA.

The Kemerovo Region is a nationwide leader in enterprise development and investment appeal.

Priority sectors for capital investment include the development of new mineral deposits, the construction of mines and open cast pits using advanced technologies, the construction of deep coal processing facilities, the technological revamping of such sectors as metals processing, chemicals and machine engineering, consumer goods manufacturing, and food, the production of building materials using local minerals, and the development of tourism. The Region has already made significant inroads in these areas.

Over the past four years, the Region's coal sector has launched some 15 mining enterprises with a total capacity exceeding 22 million tons and three dressing plants with a total capacity of 6.2 million tons of concentrate. In 2003, the Region plans to launch eight new coal mining facilities.

West Siberian Metal Works has launched a continuous casting machine that is one of only five in the world, while Kuznetsk Ferroalloy Plant has launched the only micro-silica machine in Russia.

The reorganization of Kuznetsk Metal Works has been one of the Region's most progressive achievements. The company was divided into nine companies focused on the production of competitive products.

The Region hosts two of the flagships of the domestic chemicals sector, OAO Azot and OAO Khimvoloko AMTEL-Kuzbass.

The strategic economic policy goal of the Kemerovo Regional Administration is to build up steady internal revenue sources and gradually relinquish federal subsidies through the development of small enterprise. Small enterprise already employs 170,000 people, or 10% of the Region's population, and provides 11% of local tax revenues.

Priority areas for small enterprise growth include roadside services on major transportation routes and the development of tourism at the Shoria Mountains national park.

The Kuzbass is ever ready and available for active cooperation and mutually beneficial partnership.

Aman Tuleev,
GOVERNOR OF THE KEMEROVO REGION

SIBERIAN FEDERAL DISTRICT

VI

1. GENERAL INFORMATION

1.1. GEOGRAPHY

The Kemerovo Region covers an area of some 95,700 square kilometers. The Region is located in the south of Western Siberia. To the south it borders the Altai Republic, to the southwest – the Altai Territory, to the west – the Novosibirsk Region, to the north – the Tomsk Region, to the north-east – the Krasnoyarsk Territory, and to the east – the Republic of Khakassia.

1.2. CLIMATE

The Kemerovo Region enjoys a severe continental climate. January air temperatures average −20.5°C, rising to +16.3°C in June. Average precipitation reaches 300–500 mm.

1.3. POPULATION

According to preliminary 2002 census results, the Kemerovo Region had a total population of 2.9 million. The average population density is 30.3 per square kilometer. The economically active population is 1.3 million. In 2002, official unemployment stood at 3.5%; the actual rate was 10.1%.

Demographically speaking, some 61% of population are of statutory working age, 19% are below the statutory working age, and 20% are beyond the statutory working age.

The Region's major urban centers are Novokuznetsk (550,100 inhabitants in 2002), Kemerovo (485,000), Prokopyevsk (224,600), Leninsk-Kuznetsky (112,300), Kiselevsk (106,400), and Mezhdurechensk (102,000).

Population		1992	1997	1998	1999	2000	2001	2002
Total population, '000		3,101	3,037	3,017	3,002	2,982	2,962	2,900
Economically active population, '000		1,602	1,477	1,444	1,476	1,475	1,439	1,339

TABLE 1

2. ADMINISTRATION

62, Sovetsky prospekt, Kemerovo, Kemerovo Region, 650099
Phone: (3842) 36 3409, fax: (3842) 58 3156
E-mail: postmaster@ako.kemerovo.su; http://www.kemerovo.su

NAME	POSITION	CONTACT INFORMATION
Aman Gumirovich TULEEV	Governor of the Kemerovo Region	Phone: (3842) 36 4333 Fax: (3842) 36 3409 E-mail: postmaster@ako.kemerovo.su
Vladimir Grigoryevich VODOPYANOV	Deputy of the Governor of the Kemerovo Region for Business Development and Foreign Economic Relations	Phone: (3842) 36 4521 Fax: (3842) 36 4638 E-mail: ved@ako.kemerovo.su
Igor Andreevich KOROBETSKY	Head of the Department for Investment and Technical Policy	Phone: (3842) 58 4307 Fax: (3842) 58 4441 E-mail: Korobetski-Igor@ako.kemerovo.su
Yekaterina Alexeevna TARABRINA	Deputy Head of the Department for Foreign Economic Relations and Tourism of the Kemerovo Regional Administration	Phone: (3842) 36 7546 Fax: (3842) 36 4638 E-mail: ved@ako.kemerovo.su

3. ECONOMIC POTENTIAL

3.1. 1997–2002 GROSS REGIONAL PRODUCT (GRP). INDUSTRY BREAKDOWN

The Kemerovo Region's 2002 gross regional product was $4,156 million, 5.9% up on 2001. The growth was mainly due to the expansion of the services sector (transport, communications, retail and public catering), which accounts for approximately 27% of GRP, and to industry growth. Per capita GRP in 2001 reached $1,326, and $1,434 in 2002.

3.2. MAJOR ECONOMIC GROWTH PROJECTIONS

The blueprint and goals for medium-term (through 2010) social and economic develop-

GRP trends in 1997–2002						TABLE 2
	1997	1998	1999	2000	2001*	2002*
GRP in current prices, $ million	7,872	4,677	2,735	3,329	3,924	4,156

*Estimates of the Kemerovo Regional Administration

GRP industry breakdown in 1997–2002, % of total						TABLE 3
	1997	1998	1999	2000	2001*	2002*
Total GRP	100.0	100.0	100.0	100.0	100.0	100.0
Industry	36.2	37.5	42.2	44.4	42.4	41.1
Agriculture	5.3	3.8	6.8	5.8	5.2	5.0
Construction	8.0	5.6	6.1	5.9	4.9	4.8
Transport and communications	12.7	11.1	10.3	10.8	11.9	12.0
Trade and public catering	12.1	14.5	13.4	11.9	14.4	15.2
Other	20.3	20.4	16.8	15.6	16.5	17.5
Net taxes on output	5.4	7.1	4.4	5.6	4.7	4.4

*Estimates of the Kemerovo Regional Administration

Industry breakdown of industrial output in 1997–2002, % of total						TABLE 4
	1997	1998	1999	2000	2001	2002*
Industry	100.0	100.0	100.0	100.0	100.0	100.0
Ferrous metals	27.0	25.6	31.8	32.4	31.0	33.7
Fuel (including coal)	32.5	33.7	27.9	26.8	32.3	31.4
Energy	13.4	12.8	10.6	11.1	12.6	14.0
Chemicals and petrochemicals	5.0	3.5	5.6	6.2	5.5	5.4
Machine engineering and metal processing	6.6	6.6	5.6	5.3	5.7	4.6
Food and beverages (including flour, cereals, and mixed fodder)	6.1	6.1	6.9	5.7	5.3	4.3
Non-ferrous metals	3.3	5.9	7.2	9.0	3.8	3.3
Construction materials	2.9	2.7	2.1	1.7	1.9	1.9
Forestry, timber, and pulp and paper	1.3	1.1	0.8	0.5	0.4	0.4
Light industry	0.7	0.6	0.5	0.5	0.5	0.4

*Estimates of the Kemerovo Regional Administration

ment in the Kemerovo Region are set forth in the Conceptual Framework for the Strategic Development of the Kemerovo Region (2001). The leading role in the Kemerovo Region's economic development is assigned to the fuel and energy industries, which together with ferrous metals account for approximately 80% of its total industrial output. The Kemerovo Region plans to make the coal industry profitable, to restructure the steel industry using advanced technologies, and to redesign machine engineering production lines.

3.3. INDUSTRIAL OUTPUT IN 1997–2002 FOR MAJOR SECTORS OF ECONOMY

The Region holds the twelfth position in terms of industrial output in Russia and second position in the Siberian Federal District rating.

Metals (ferrous and non-ferrous). The sector accounts for 37% of total industrial output. Its major enterprises are located in the city of No-vokuznetsk. These include OAO West-Siberian Metals Plant, OAO Kuznetsky Metals Plant, and the Novokuznetsky Aluminum Plant. Over the past five years, output of steel, rolled products, and cast iron has risen by 28–36%.

Coal. Coal accounts for 31.4% of total industrial output. The sector consists of 98 functioning coal-mining enterprises. The Region supplies coal to all areas of the Russian Federation and to CIS and non-CIS countries. The Raspadskaya, Pervo-maiskaya, and Zyryanovskaya mines in the Kuzbass make extensive use of modern mechanized mining processes. The Region's largest coal-mining companies are OAO HK Kuzbass-razrezugol, OAO UK Kuzbassugol, OAO UK Yuzh-kuzbassugol, OAO UK Yuzhny Kuzbass, and OAO UK Mezhdurechenskugol.

Energy. Energy accounts for 14% of the Region's total industrial output. Energy facilities include 10 power stations with a total annual capacity of approximately 28 billion kWh. OAO Kuzbassenergo is one of the largest companies within the UES of Russia holding.

Chemicals. The sector accounts for 5.4% of total industrial output in the Region. The Region produces over 600 different chemical products.

The largest enterprises in the sector include OAO Azot (Kemerovo), a major Russian producer of organic fertilizers.

Over the past five years, chemicals output in the Region has almost doubled.

Machine engineering and metal processing. The machine engineering sector is concentrated in Kemerovo, Yurga, and Anzhero-Sudzhensk. The largest enterprise is OAO Yurginsky Machine Engineering Plant. The Region's machine engineering plants produce subterranean mining equipment and electrical equipment.

Agriculture. Agriculture accounts for approximately 5% of total GRP. The Region hosts 274 agricultural enterprises and 74 processing companies. Agricultural lands cover an area of some 1.9 million hectares, including 1.5 million hectares of arable lands.

3.4. FUEL AND ENERGY BALANCE (OUTPUT AND CONSUMPTION PER RESOURCE)

The Kuzbass power supply system is Russia's sixth largest in terms of power output and fifth in terms of supply. OAO Kuzbassenergo accounts for more than 30% of the Integrated Siberian Power Supply Grid's balance. The Region satisfies 94% of its own energy needs (2002 data).

Fuel and energy sector production and consumption trends in 1997–2002						TABLE 5
	1997	1998	1999	2000	2001	2002*
Electricity output, billion kWh	22.7	25.6	27.5	27.2	27.1	27.9
Coal output, million tons	93.9	98.2	108.8	114.9	127.7	131.7
Electricity consumption, billion kWh	29.3	29.4	30.7	31.9	32.3	31.7
Coal consumption, million tons	n/a	42.6	48.1	51.4	52.9	53.0
Natural gas consumption, billion cubic meters	2.9	2.6	3.0	3.4	3.8	3.3

*Estimates of the Kemerovo Regional Administration

3.5. TRANSPORT INFRASTRUCTURE

Roads. The Region has more than 5,635 kilometers of paved public highway.

Railroads. The Kemerovo Region has 1,728 kilometers of railroad. The Region lies between two branches of the Trans-Siberian Railway (the south and north branches) and has direct railroad connections with all regions of Russia.

Airports. Kemerovo is served by an international airport. Novokuznetsk and Tashtagola are also served by airports.

3.6. MAIN NATURAL RESOURCES: RESERVES AND EXTRACTION IN 2002

Coal. The Kuznetsky coalfield is one of the largest coalfields in the world. Coal reserves extend to a depth of up to 1,200 meters and exceed 540 billion tons. Coking coal reserves total 42.8 billion tons (75% of Russia's total reserves).

Non-metal minerals. The Region has around two dozen explored deposits of fluxing limestone, dolomites, quartzites, fire clay, and molding sand.

The Region has deposits of vermiculite, asbestos, talcum, tremolite, basalt, and peat (230 deposits with total reserves of around 200 million tons).

Forestry. Coniferous forests cover an area of some 2.5 million hectares; deciduous forests cover 1.8 million hectares (forests cover 65% of the Region). The most common species are pine, fir, spruce, cedar, aspen, and birch.

Water resources. The Region is drained by tributaries of the Ob. The largest river is the Tom. The hydroelectric potential of the Region is estimated at 24.9 billion kWh annually (12.5% of Western Siberia's hydroelectric potential).

Estimated accessible reserves of subterranean water amount to 1.7 million cubic meters per day, including 911,700 cubic meters per day suitable for industrial use.

4. TRADE OPPORTUNITIES

4.1. MAIN GOODS PRODUCED IN THE REGION

Kemerovo accounts for 54% of Russia's total coal output (including 78% of coking coal output), 16% of total steel and cast iron output, 23% of graded rolled product output, more than 11% of aluminium output, 17% of coke output, and approximately 60% of ferroselite output.

Energy. 2002 electricity output amounted to 27.9 billion kWh.

Fuel. 2002 coal output amounted to 131.7 million tons, 3.1 % up on 2001.

Metals. In 2002, the Region's metals enterprises produced some 6.8 million tons of cast iron and 8.3 million tons of steel. The Kemerovo Region accounts for 80% of Russian railroad rail output and 100% of Russian tram rail output. 2002 output of ferrous rolled products reached 6.8 million tons. Steel pipes output was 17,400 tons.

Chemicals. 2002 chemicals output increased by 9.7% on 2001 to $239.5 million. The Region produced synthetic ammonia – 818,000 tons, organic fertilizers – 570,000 tons, chemical fibers and threads – 17,200 tons, and synthetic resins and plastics – 116,000 tons.

Forestry and timber. In 2002 the Region logged 115,000 cubic meters of commercial timber, and 130,000 cubic meters of sawn timber.

4.2. EXPORTS, INCLUDING EXTRA-CIS

Exports to extra-CIS countries in 2001 reached $1,920.8 million (89.9%); exports to CIS countries totaled $215.3 million (10.1%). The corresponding figures for 2002 were $1,596.2 million (90%) and $177.2 million (10%).

The main goods exported from the Region are coal, coke, ferrous and non-ferrous metals, fertilizers, and machinery. The fuel and energy sector and metal industry account for 91% of exports. The Region's main trading partners for exports are the UK, Germany, Japan, Slovakia, Greece, China, and Spain.

4.3. IMPORTS, INCLUDING EXTRA-CIS

Imports from extra-CIS countries in 2001 reached $67.6 million (37.4%); imports from CIS countries totaled $113.4 million (62.6%). The corresponding figures for 2002 were $69.7 million (47.1%) and $78.2 million (52.9%). Synthetic chemicals account for more than 50% of the Region's imports ($90.2 million in 2001, mainly from Kazakhstan).

Together with chemicals, subterranean mining equipment, boilers, machinery, and mechanical rubber items account for a significant portion of the Region's imports.

The Region's main trading partners for imports are Kazakhstan, Germany, Italy, the UK, the USA, Poland, and Ukraine.

Major regional import and export entities

TABLE 6

ENTITY	ADDRESS	PHONE, FAX, E-MAIL
OAO West-Siberian Metals Plant	16, Kosmicheskoye shosse, Novokuznetsk, Kemerovo Region, 654080	Phone: (3843) 59 5904, (095) 232 1360
OAO Novokuznetsky Aluminum Plant	Kuznetzky District, Novokuznetsk, Kemerovo Region, 654034	Phone: (3843) 39 7322
OOO KMK Steel	1, pl. Pobedy, Novokuznetsk, Kemerovo Region, 654000	Phone: (3843) 79 1567
OAO Azot	Predzavodskoy Village, Kemerovo, Kemerovo Region 650099	Phone: (3842) 28 4387
OAO Razrez Bachatsky	19-a, ul. Komsomolskaya, Belovo, Kemerovo Region, 652642	Phone: (3842) 52 3800
OAO Sokolovskaya Investment Company	15, ul. Aleyskaya, Kiselevsk, Kemerovo Region, 652701	Phone: (38464) 53 704
ZAO Chernigovets	Berezovsky, Kemerovo Region, 652420	Phone: (38445) 96 213, 96 212 Fax: (38445) 96 390

5. INVESTMENT OPPORTUNITIES

5.1. INVESTMENTS IN 1992–2002 (BY INDUSTRY SECTOR), INCLUDING FOREIGN INVESTMENTS

The following main factors determine the investment appeal of the Kemerovo Region:
- Its developed industry (coal, ferrous metals);
- Its significant mineral reserves and raw material resources (coal, iron ore);
- Legislation supporting investment activities;
- Its developed transport infrastructure.

5.2. CAPITAL INVESTMENT

Capital investment in the Region has been intensifying since 2000. In 2001, capital investments increased by a factor of 1.4 on 2001 levels to reach $48.3 million. On the whole, for the past two years investment increased by a factor of more than nine. Ferrous metals and telecommunications account for the lion's share of capital investments.

5.3. MAJOR ENTERPRISES (INCLUDING ENTERPRISES WITH FOREIGN INVESTMENT)

The Kemerovo Region hosts 205 legal entities with foreign capital, including 56 100% foreign-owned. The principal investor countries are Germany, Austria, the Czech Republic, Italy, Greece, and the UK.

5.4. MOST ATTRACTIVE SECTORS FOR INVESTMENT

According to the Regional Administration, the most attractive sectors for investments are participa-

Capital investments by industry sector, $ million						TABLE 7
	1997	1998	1999	2000	2001	2002
Total capital investment	1,672.9	848.1	473.7	617.8	684.6	691.8
Including major industries (% of total):						
Industry	59.5	61.1	59.6	59.1	61.1	53.2
Agriculture	1.8	2.8	3.1	2.3	2.3	2.0
Construction	4.9	0.8	1.0	1.5	3.0	0.5
Transport and communications	10.6	11.1	12.6	16.8	11.2	8.2
Trade and public catering	0.7	0.5	0.6	0.6	1.9	1.3
Other	22.5	23.7	23.1	19.7	20.5	34.8

Foreign investment trends in 1996–2002						TABLE 8
	1996-1997	1998	1999	2000	2001	2002
Foreign investment, $ million	64.9	8.1	3.3	5.1	33.9	48.3
Including FDI, $ million	2.7	0.2	2.4	2.4	3.4	0.3

Largest enterprises of the Kemerovo Region	TABLE 9
COMPANY	SECTOR
OAO HK Kuzbassrazrezugol	Coal
OAO UK Kuzbassugol	Coal
OAO UK Yuzhkuzbassugol	Coal
OAO UK Yuzhny Kuzbass	Coal
OAO UK Mezhdurechenskugol	Coal
OAO West-Siberian Metals Plant	Metals
OAO Kuznetsky Metals Plant	Metals
OAO Novokuznetsky Aluminum Plant	Metals
OAO Kuzbassenergo	Energy
OAO Yurginsky Machine Engineering Plant	Machine engineering and metal processing
OAO Azot	Chemicals

tion in the technical revamping of metals, chemicals and machine engineering enterprises, development of new natural resource deposits, construction of mines and open-cast pits using modern technology, establishment of deep coal processing plants, consumer goods and food production companies, production of construction materials using local raw materials, and tourism.

5.5. CURRENT LEGISLATION ON INVESTOR TAX EXEMPTIONS AND PRIVILEGES

The Kemerovo Region has passed a Law On the Provision of Tax Privileges to Investors in the Kemerovo Region (2001). The Law provides for exemptions on the regional component of profits tax and property tax.

Under the current tax legislation, municipal and local authorities are entitled to grant exemptions for local tax components and levies.

5.6. FEDERAL AND REGIONAL ECONOMIC AND SOCIAL DEVELOPMENT PROGRAMS FOR THE KEMEROVO REGION

Federal targeted programs. In 2002, the Kemerovo Region implemented some 16 federal targeted programs, including the priority programs focusing on the improvement in the transport infrastructure, social welfare, and general and specialized education standards. In 2002, the federal budget allocated some $26.7 million for the implementation of these federal targeted programs.

Regional programs. The Region is carrying out 23 regional targeted programs and six territorial social and economic development programs, including the following priority programs: Ecology and Natural Resources of the Kemerovo Region, 2002–2004, Energy Saving, 2001–2003, and the Program of Support to Small Businesses in Kemerovo, 2002–2003. These programs are focused on the development of natural resources and environmental protection, development of education, raising living standards, and social and economic development of urban areas.

In 2002, the regional budget allocated some $31.9 million for the implementation of these regional targeted programs.

Regional entities responsible for raising investments		*TABLE 10*
ENTITY	ADDRESS	PHONE, FAX, E-MAIL
OAO Sokolovskaya Investment Company	15, ul. Aleyskaya, Kiselevsk, Kemerovo Region, 652700	Phone: (38464) 53 703 Fax: (38464) 53 711 E-mail: sokolovskaya@mtu-net.ru
OAO Alpari Investment Company	28, prospect Kirova, Leninsk-Kuznetsky, Kemerovo Region, 652515	Phone/fax: (38456) 51 345 E-mail: ikalpari@lnk.kuzbass.net
OOO Primula Company	50 a, ul. Krasnoarmeyskaya, Kemerovo, Kemerovo Region, 650010	Phone: (3842) 25 7533 Fax: (3842) 25 8878

6. INVESTMENT PROJECTS

Industry sector and project description	1) Expected results 2) Amount and term of investment 3) Form of financing[1] 4) Documentation[2]	Contact information
1	2	3

COAL		
71R001 ● ★ ◆		OOO Kolmogorovskaya 2 Mine
Construction of a coal mine and production of high class coal (reserves to be developed – 38.8 million tons). Project goal: to introduce high class coal to the market (ash content 7.8%, low sulfur content).	1) 2 million tons per year 2) $20 million/2.5 years 3) L ($20 million), Leas. 4) BP	12, ul. Lenina, Belovo, Kemerovo Region, 652600 Phone: (38452) 21 121, 22 953 Fax: (38452) 62 074 E-mail: sibug@hotmail.ru Vladimir Dmitrievich Khramchenko, CEO

[1] L – Loan, E – Equity, Leas. – Leasing, JV – Joint Venture
[2] BP – Business Plan, FS – Feasibility Study

1	2	3

71R002

Construction of a mine and coking coal production.
Project goal: to expand coking coal output.

1) Up to 2 million tons per year
2) $58 million/2 years
3) L, Leas. ($55.9 million)
4) BP

ZAO Kostromovskaya Mine
1, ul. Vasilyeva, Leninsk-Kuznetsky,
Kemerovo Region, 652507
Phone: (38456) 31 226
Fax: (38456) 31 225
Victor Ivanovich Grubnikov,
CEO

CHEMICALS AND PETROCHEMICALS

71R003

Setting up facilities for polymeric waste recycling.
Project goal: recycling of plastics waste, production of marketable goods (combined and composed materials for construction and for electrical purposes).

1) Recycling of 56,600 tons of waste annually for $28 million annual sales
2) $44 million/1.5-2 years
3) L
4) BP

OAO Polymer
1, ul. Narodnaya, Kemerovo,
Kemerovo Region, 650068
Phone: (3842) 61 0007
Fax: (3842) 61 0200
E-mail: polimer@kmr.ru
Victor Alexeevich Chabanenko,
CEO

71R004

Purchasing equipment for the production of fine textile threads.
Project goal: increase in and diversification of output.

1) $6.3 million of marginal income annually
2) €1.1 million/0.5 years
3) L
4) BP

OOO Khimvolokno AMTEL-KUZBASS
39, ul. Tereshkovoi, Kemerovo,
Kemerovo Region, 650036
Phone: (3842) 31 2067
Fax: (3842) 31 2993
E-mail: khmarketing@mail.ru
Victor Fedorovich Anisimov, CEO

71R005

Purchasing of lithium bromide absorption refrigerators.
Project goal: energy conservation.

1) $0.2 million annually in energy savings
2) $1 million/1 year
3) L
4) BP

OOO Khimvolokno AMTEL-KUZBASS
39, ul. Tereshkovoi, Kemerovo,
Kemerovo Region, 650036
Phone: (3842) 31 2067
Fax: (3842) 31 2993
E-mail: khmarketing@mail.ru
Victor Fedorovich Anisimov, CEO

71R006

Equipment revamping.
Project goal: to improve quality and reduce raw materials consumption.

1) Materials savings of $0.4 million annually
2) $0.65 million/1 year
3) L
4) BP

OOO Khimvolokno AMTEL-KUZBASS
39, ul. Tereshkovoi, Kemerovo,
Kemerovo Region, 650036
Phone: (3842) 31 2067
Fax: (3842) 31 2993
E-mail: khmarketing@mail.ru
Victor Fedorovich Anisimov, CEO

CHEMICALS AND PHARMACEUTICALS

71R007

Production of solid medicines at an existing enterprise.
Project goal: to increase and diversify output and replace imports.

1) 1,500 million pills annually
2) $16.5 million/3 years
3) E, L $13 million
4) BP

OAO Organika
3, Kuznetskoye shosse, Novokuznetsk,
Kemerovo Region, 654034
Phone: (3843) 37 0575
Fax: (3843) 37 2496
E-mail: root@organika.kemerovo.su
Yevgeny Anatolyevich Vinogradov, CEO

MACHINE ENGINEERING AND METAL PROCESSING

71R008

Development, production, testing, and mass manufacturing of explosion-proof induction motors and low-voltage appliances at an existing enterprise.
Project goal: to supply domestic equipment to Russian industries that use explosion-proof electrical equipment (underground mining equipment, petro-chemicals machinery and equipment).

1) 480 kits a year; $7.9 million
2) $0.92 million/2.5 years
3) L
4) BP

OAO NIIVEM
8, pr. Sovetsky, Kemerovo,
Kemerovo Region, 650099
Phone: (3842) 25 3244
Fax: (3842) 36 7421
E-mail: niivem@kemnet.ru
Valery Grigorevich Vlasov, CEO
Mikhail Andreevich Vsyakikh,
Investment Project Supervisor

1	2	3

71R009

	● ◆	
Manufacturing of new efficient coal miner for underground coal production (for mines with gas and dust hazards) at an existing enterprise. Project goal: to diversify output and replace imports.	1) Machines producing 25 tons/min 2) $0.27 million/9 months 3) L 4) BP	OAO Yurginsky Machine Engineering Plant 3, ul. Shosseinaya, Yurga, Kemerovo Region, 652050 Phone: (38451) 74 499, 74 100, 74 005 E-mail: yumz@yurmash.ru Igor Vasilyevich Kalievsky, Executive Director

71R010

	■ ● ◆	
Mass production of machine-based mining facilities for underground coal production at an existing enterprise. Project goal: diversification of output.	1) $2.8 million net profit annually 2) $4.7 million/1.5 years 3) E, L ($3.8 million) 4) BP	OAO Yurginsky Machine Engineering Plant 3, ul. Shosseinaya, Yurga, Kemerovo Region, 652050 Phone: (38451) 74 499, 74 100, 74 005 Fax: (38451) 74 499 E-mail: yumz@yurmash.ru Igor Vasilyevich Kalievsky Executive Director

CONSTRUCTION MATERIALS

71R011

	● ◆	
Construction of a brick plant. Project goal: to meet the Region's needs for high-quality brick.	1) 36 million bricks annually 2) $5.8 million/0.5 year 3) L 4) BP	OOO Kuzbass Promyshlennost Torgovlya 4a, ul. Leonova, office 101, Yurga, Kemerovo Region, 652050 Phone: (38451) 54 071 Fax: (38451) 54 072 E-mail: KPT@yrg.kuzbass.net Igor Anatolyevich Kolesnikov, CEO

GLASS AND PORCELAIN

71R012

	● ◆	
Setting up production of container glass. Project goal: to introduce new products to the market.	1) 1 million pieces annually 2) $10 million/1.5 years 3) L 4) BP	OOO Sibirskaya Management Company Office 1, 57, ul . Kirova, 650099 Phone/fax: (3842) 25 9072 Nikolai Vladimirovich Sukhoverkhov, CEO Stanislav Nikolaevich Semenenkov, Executive Director

LIGHT INDUSTRY

71R013

	● ★ ◆	
Production of overcoats for children and adults (equipment purchasing). Project goal: to increase output.	1) Additional production for $0.02 million annually 2) $1.1 million/3 years 3) L ($0.56 million), Leas 4) BP	OOO Gornyachka 9, ul. Shishkina, Prokopyevsk, Kemerovo Region, 653004 Phone/fax:(38466) 32 596 Victor Vasilyevich Kudashov, CEO

AGRICULTURE

71R014

	● ★ ◆	
Setting up facilities for industrial production of mushrooms (a first in Siberia and the Far East). Project goal: to introduce mushrooms into the market.	1) Up to 1,000 tons annually 2) $4 million/1.5 years 3) L ($0.9 million), Leas ($1.8 million) 4) BP	OOO Sibirsky Champignon 73, blv. Stroitelei, Kemerovo, Kemerovo Region, 650517 Phone: (3842) 51 0329 Fax: (3842) 51 3355 E-mail: denisd@kemtel.ru Nilolai Ivanovich Fedorov, Director

SIBERIAN FEDERAL DISTRICT

VI

| 1 | 2 | 3 |

ECOLOGY

71R015 ● ◆

| | | OAO IK Sokolovskaya |
| Construction of facilities for recycling of industrial and domestic carbonic waste into liquid fuel. Project goal: disposal of waste and production of marketable items (fuel or electricity). | 1) Recycling of 86,500 tons of waste 2) $14.5 million/3 years 3) L ($13 million) 4) BP | 15, ul. Aleiskaya, Kiselevsk, Kemerovo Region, 652700 Phone: (38464) 53 703 Fax: (38464) 53 711 E-mail: finance@sokolovskay.ru Moscow Representative Office 5a, ul. Pryanichkova, Moscow, 127550 Phone: (095) 502 9492 Fax: (095) 502 9494, 502 9495 Alexander Mikhailovich Dramichnikov, President Vladimir Vasilyevich Dobrydin, Vice President |

HOTELS, TOURISM, AND RECREATION

71R016 ● ◆

| | | Kemerovo Regional Administration |
| Construction of a family recreation area. Project goal: to provide tourism services. | 1) Revenues of $0,2 million annually 2) $0.6 million/3 years 3) L 4) BP | Department of Foreign Economic Relations and Tourism 62, pr. Sovetsky, Kemerovo, Kemerovo Region, 650099 Phone: (3842) 36 4806 Fax: (3842) 36 4638 E-mail: ved@ako.kemerovo.su Irina Zakharovna Lebedeva, Deputy Chief of the Tourism Dept. |

72. NOVOSIBIRSK REGION [54]

ECONOMIC MAP

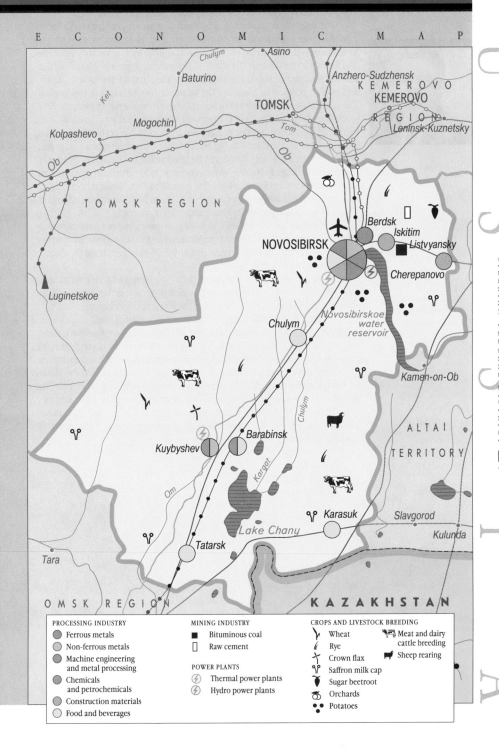

PROCESSING INDUSTRY
- 🔴 Ferrous metals
- 🟡 Non-ferrous metals
- 🔵 Machine engineering and metal processing
- 🔵 Chemicals and petrochemicals
- 🔵 Construction materials
- ⚪ Food and beverages

MINING INDUSTRY
- ◼ Bituminous coal
- ▢ Raw cement

POWER PLANTS
- ⚡ Thermal power plants
- ⚡ Hydro power plants

CROPS AND LIVESTOCK BREEDING
- Wheat
- Rye
- Crown flax
- Saffron milk cap
- Sugar beetroot
- Orchards
- Potatoes
- Meat and dairy cattle breeding
- Sheep rearing

I nwards investment and successful sales of manufactured goods are the keystones of dynamic economic development. We in the Novosibirsk Region are deeply concerned with promoting active investment in our economy and with enhancing the trade and economic relations of the Region. Clearly, investment cannot be forthcoming unless appropriate political, economic and infrastructure conditions are created. Investor and trade partners look for financial transparency, clear economic perspectives, and unequivocal legislation. The Novosibirsk Region, on the whole, meets these conditions.

The Region's economy has been displaying steady positive trends for the past three years. We are in the process of creating an environment in which investment will bear dividends. Our financial, insurance, telecommunications, and service sectors are on the rise. The Novosibirsk Region holds one of the leading positions in Russia for its communication and telephony infrastructure, and twelfth position in Russia for the number of active banks in the Region. The Region also offers promising scientific and manufacturing projects.

One of the chief goals of the Regional Administration is to create an investment-friendly climate. A modern legislative framework has been formulated and enacted. More effective use is being made of state-owned enterprises, state guarantees for bank loans are offered, and budget funding is allocated to finance interest repayments. Promising investment projects are granted regional tax privileges. The timeframes for securing rights to construction sites and obtaining approval for construction projects have been shortened. The rights and responsibilities of respective parties are clearly regulated in contracts.

The Region has worked hard to attract customers and potential clients, to establish reliable partnerships with major customers, other regions, and foreign countries. Last year, the Region registered $1 billion in foreign trade turnover, with exports twice as high as imports.

At present, the Region hosts more than 700 enterprises with foreign investment. We have implemented a number of joint projects together with the World Bank and the European Bank for Reconstruction and Development.

In 2003, the Novosibirsk Region will launch a number of major economic and social development programs that aim, first and foremost, to improve living standards in the Region. We need investors to buy into the economy of our Region. We are ready and willing to develop trade relations with foreign and Russian partners.

A number of countries maintain consulates in Novosibirsk, and the Ministry of Foreign Affairs of the Russian Federation has a representative office here. These factors contribute to the development of international contacts in the Region.

The political situation in the Novosibirsk Region is stable. As for business safety, the Region enjoys a business friendly atmosphere thanks to the efforts of the local authorities.

Viktor Tolokonsky,
HEAD OF ADMINISTRATION
OF THE NOVOSIBIRSK REGION

1. GENERAL INFORMATION

1.1. GEOGRAPHY

Located in the south-east of the Western Siberian Plain and, partially, in the foothills of the Salair mountain range, the Novosibirsk Region covers a total area of 178,200 square kilometers. The Region extends from the west to the east for over 600 km, and from the south to the north for over 400 km. To the north, the Region borders the Tomsk Region, to the south – the Altai Territory and Kazakhstan, to the west – the Omsk Region, and to the east – the Kemerovo Region.

1.2. CLIMATE

The Novosibirsk Region lies in the severe continental climate zone.

Average multi year air temperature in January is –19.1°C, rising to +18.8°C in July. Annual precipitation reaches 300–500 mm.

1.3. POPULATION

According to preliminary 2002 census results, the Novosibirsk Region's total population was 2,692,000 people. The average population density was 15.1 people per square kilometer. The economically active population amounts to 1,338,000 million people. Official unemployment 2002 was 1.4%; the actual rate is 12%.

Demographically speaking, some 60.3% are of the statutory working age, 18.5% are below the statutory working age, and 21.2% are beyond the statutory working age.

The Novosibirsk Region's major urban centers are Novosibirsk with 1,425,600 inhabitants, Berdsk with 87,100 inhabitants, Iskitim with 68,400 inhabitants, Kuibyshev with 51,500 inhabitants, Barabinsk with 34,600 inhabitants, Tatarsk with 28,000 inhabitants, and Ob with 24,900 inhabitants (2002 data).

Population								TABLE 1
	1992	1997	1998	1999	2000	2001	2002
Total population, '000	2,755	2,743	2,746	2,748	2,740	2,731	2,692
Economically active population, '000	1,434	1,251	1,294	1,381	1,380	1,308	1,338

2. ADMINISTRATION

18, Krasny prospekt, Novosibirsk, Novosibirsk Region, 630011
Phone: (3832) 23 0862; fax: (3832) 23 5700
E-mail: pochta@obladm.nso.ru; http://www.adm.nso.ru

NAME	POSITION	CONTACT INFORMATION
Viktor Alexandrovich TOLOKONSKY	Head of Administration of the Novosibirsk Region	Phone: (3832) 23 2995 Fax: (3832) 23 5700
Viktor Semenovich KOSOUROV	First Deputy Head of Administration of the Novosibirsk Region	Phone: (3832) 23 0725 Fax: (3832) 23 6359
Vadim Leonidovich FEDOROV	Deputy Head of Administration of the Novosibirsk Region, Head of the Economic Development and Industry Department	Phone: (3832) 23 4563 Fax: (3832) 23 8663
Dmitry Benediktovich VERKHOVOD	Deputy Head of Administration of the Novosibirsk Region, Head of the Property and Land Department	Phone: (3832) 23 9526 Fax: (3832) 10 3663
Viktor Alexandrovich GERGERT	Deputy Head of Administration of the Novosibirsk Region, Head of the Agroindustrial Complex Department	Phone: (3832) 23 5959 Fax: (3832) 23 0701
Afanasy Stepanovich FRANTSEV	Deputy Head of Administration of the Novosibirsk Region, Head of the Construction, Architecture and Roads Department	Phone: (3832) 23 0606 Fax: (3832) 23 6972
Valentin Ivanovich SHATALOV	Deputy Head of Administration of the Novosibirsk Region, Head of the Energy and Housing Department	Phone (3832) 23 1890 Fax: (3832) 18 1575
Gennady Alexeevich SAPOZHNIKOV	Deputy Head of Administration of the Novosibirsk Region, Head of the Science, Higher and Secondary Professional Education, and Technology Department	Phone: (3832) 23 8259 Fax: (3832) 23 9826

SIBERIAN FEDERAL DISTRICT

VI

NAME	POSITION	CONTACT INFORMATION
Nikolai Andreevich TITENKO	Deputy Head of Administration of the Novosibirsk Region in charge of Economic Relations	Phone: (3832) 23 0394 Fax: (3832) 23 5245

3. ECONOMIC POTENTIAL

3.1. 1997–2002 GROSS REGIONAL PRODUCT (GRP). INDUSTRY BREAKDOWN

The 2002 gross regional product of the Novosibirsk Region reached $4,114 million, 13.7% up on 2001. Per capita GRP in 2001 was $1,325 and $1,528 in 2002.

3.2. MAJOR ECONOMIC GROWTH PROJECTIONS

Forecasts for the coming years are as follows:

Industry: increased competitiveness of output, development and upgrading of production facilities using borrowed funds and direct investments, development of innovative businesses on the basis of industrial estates, reducing current production costs;

GRP trends in 1997–2002						TABLE 2
	1997	1998	1999	2000	2001*	2002*
GRP in current prices, $ million	6,331.5	3,620.5	2,226.8	2,735.4	3,617.7	4,114.4

*Estimates of the Novosibirsk Regional Administration

GRP industry breakdown in 1997–2002, % of total						TABLE 3
	1997	1998	1999	2000	2001*	2002*
GRP	100.0	100.0	100.0	100.0	100.0	100.0
Industry	22.1	23.9	24.8	23.2	21.2	20.2
Agriculture and forestry	8.3	10.0	18.1	18.8	15.4	13.0
Construction	6.1	4.4	3.5	3.8	4.0	3.4
Transport and communications	12.8	12.7	11.2	12.1	11.4	13.7
Trade and public catering	12.8	16.7	16.4	13.3	14.0	14.6
Other	31.6	28.6	22.0	23.7	23.3	26.6
Net tax on output	6.3	3.7	4.0	5.1	10.7	8.5

*Estimates of the Novosibirsk Regional Administration

Agriculture: increased agriculture output, increased profitability in the sector, growth in sales markets;

Construction: growth in output and structural overhaul of production facilities in the sector based on modern and efficient technologies.

3.3. INDUSTRIAL OUTPUT IN 1997–2002 FOR MAJOR SECTORS OF ECONOMY

The Novosibirsk Region's major industries include food and beverages, machine engineering and metal processing, energy, non-ferrous metals, and construction materials. Together these sectors accounted for 79.7% of total industrial output in 2002.

Food and beverages. In 2002, the sector accounted for 23.3% of total industrial output in the Region. The sector is focused on the production of cereals and pasta, meat, whole milk and vegetable products of various degrees of processing, and alcoholic and non-alcoholic beverages. The major companies of the sector are: OAO Siberian Milk, OAO Karasuk Milk, and OAO Karasuk Meat Processing Plant.

Machine engineering and metal processing. In 2002, the sector accounted for 21.9% of the Region's total output. Major companies include GUP Electric Locomotive Repair Plant, OAO Elsib, FGUP Novosibirsk PO Sibselmash, OAO Tyazhstankogidropress, OAO Novosibirsk Instruments Plant, OOO Novosibirsk Elektrosignal Plant Corporation, OAO Siblitmash, OAO Zavod Trud, and OAO Soyuz Novosibirsk Electric Vacuum Plant Holding Company.

Energy. In 2002, the energy sector accounted for 17.1% of the Region's total industrial output. The Region's energy system produced 11,242 million kWh of electricity in 2002 (4.5% up on 2001), and 11.4 million Gcal of heat energy (6% down on 2001 output).

Non-ferrous metals. In 2002, the sector accounted for 10.2% of the Region's total industrial output. The

Industry breakdown of industrial output in 1997–2002, % of total						*TABLE 4*
	1997	1998	1999	2000	2001	2002
Industry	100.0	100.0	100.0	100.0	100.0	100.0
Food and beverages	21.3	24.5	23.7	22.7	22.8	23.3
Machine engineering and metal processing	30.1	26.3	31.9	25.9	27.3	21.9
Energy	21.3	22.9	14.7	13,7	16.0	17.1
Non-ferrous metals	2.8	3.2	5.2	14.2	10.1	10.2
Construction materials	7.8	7.0	5.8	5.7	6.3	7.2
Flour, cereals, and mixed fodder	4.3	3.7	4.0	3.1	3.4	3.6
Light industry	2.3	2.3	3.2	2.4	2.7	2.7
Ferrous metals	0.9	0.4	0.8	1.1	1.2	2.5
Medical goods and pharmaceuticals	1.6	2.3	2.1	2.5	2.7	2.5
Chemicals and petrochemicals	2.7	2.2	3.0	2.7	2.1	2.4
Forestry, timber, and pulp and paper	2.1	2.2	2.3	2.9	2.2	2.4
Printing	0.6	0.9	0.8	0.9	1.2	1.6
Fuel	0.3	0.2	0.5	0.7	0.8	1.5

largest companies in the sector are OAO Novosibirsk Electrode Plant and OAO Novosibirsk Tin Plant.

Construction materials. In 2002, the construction materials industry accounted for 7.2% of the Region's total output. Its largest companies include OAO Cherepanovsky Construction Materials Plant, OAO Iskitimtsement, and GP SpetsZhelezoBeton.

3.4. FUEL AND ENERGY BALANCE (OUTPUT AND CONSUMPTION PER RESOURCE)

The Novosibirsk Region's power generation sector plays the leading role in the Region's fuel and energy complex. The Region's thermal power stations and the Novosibirskaya hydroelectric power plant satisfy all of the Region's electricity needs. The TPS 5 (heat energy capacity 2,590 Gcal/hour, electricity generation capacity 900 MW) is the largest power generator in the Region. The Novosibirskaya HEPS has a capacity of 450 MW. During the summer season, the Novosibirskaya HEPS covers 30% of the total electricity needs of the Region.

3.5. TRANSPORT INFRASTRUCTURE

The Novosibirsk Region boasts a well-developed transport system.

Roads. The Region has 16,924 kilometers of roads, 74.4% of which are paved. In 2002, haulage companies in the Region carried some 5.2 million tons of freight. Freight turnover in 2002 reached 613.7 million ton-kilometers; passenger turnover was 2.1 million passenger-kilometers.

Railroads. The Region has 1,530 kilometers of general use railroads. Main lines include a portion of the Trans-Siberian Railroad, the Novosibirsk – Kuzbass railroad, the Novosibirsk – Barnaul railroad, the Tatarsk – Karasuk – Kulunda railroad, and the Karasuk – Kamen-on-Ob railroad.

Airports. The Novosibirsk Region is served by five airports, including two federal airports, one at Tolmachevo (with an international terminal), and one at Novosibirsk. The Novosibirsk Airport services domestic and local airlines. The Tolmachevo Airport is the largest airport in Siberia. Well located geographically, the Tolmachevo Airport provides transit stop-overs for technical and commercial landings of planes and services flights along the Trans-Siberian route. In 2002, total passenger turnover reached 7.6 billion passenger-kilometers.

Subway. In 1985, the first subway in Siberia was opened in Novosibirsk with total length of 13.2

SIBERIAN FEDERAL DISTRICT

VI

Fuel and energy sector production and consumption trends, 1997–2002						*TABLE 5*
	1997	1998	1999	2000	2001	2002
Electricity output, billion kWh	9.2	10.8	11.3	12.3	10.8	11.2
Oil output (including gas condensate), '000 tons	25.9	32.6	33.5	38.2	84.6	238.5
Coal output, '000 tons	260.0	156.0	314.0	450.0	508.0	570.0
Electricity consumption, billion KWh	12.0	12.2	12.2	13.1	12.9	12.8

kilometers. The Novosibirsk subway has eleven stations and in terms of passenger turnover occupies the third place in the Russian Federation after Moscow and St. Petersburg. The Novosibirsk subway project provides for the construction of 16 stations and up to 21,5 kilometers of track through 2015.

River ports. OAO Novosibirsk River Port services river transportation along the Ob.

Oil and gas pipelines. The Novosibirsk Region is crossed by an oil pipeline (900 km length) and a gas pipeline (1,160 km length).

3.6. MAIN NATURAL RESOURCES: RESERVES AND EXTRACTION IN 2002

The Novosibirsk Region boasts 523 mineral resource fields, including oil, gas, gas condensate, coal, peat, gold, bauxites, mineral construction materials, subterranean mineral water, and sapropel. Some 83 fields are currently operational.

Oil and natural gas. The bulk of oil and gas reserves are located in the north of the Region. Oil reserves stand at 514.5 million tons, while natural gas reserves total 110 billion cubic meters.

Mineral water. The Novosibirsk Region has significant reserves of potable, medical, and therapeutic mineral water. The renowned mineral water sources of Karachinskaya, Dovolenskaya and Duplinskaya are situated near Lake Chany.

Daily mineral water reserves in the Region stand at 471,800 decaliters, while daily bottling output is only 140,700 decaliters.

Ferrous, non-ferrous, and rare earth metals. The Region has deposits of zirconium dioxide and titanium dioxide totaling 7.2 million tons and 1.7 million tons, respectively. It also has two bauxite fields. The south-eastern part of the Region has one gold ore field and 24 alluvial gold fields.

Coal and peat. The bulk of the Region's coal reserves is concentrated in three coal basins located in the east of the Region. The Region produces high quality anthracite, which is used as a feedstock by the Novosibirsk Electrode Plant. Projected anthracite reserves are estimated at 5,527 million tons, while long-flame coal and coke reserves stand at 2,720 million tons. Large peat fields (7.6 billion tons) are located in the north of the Region.

Construction materials. The Region has deposits of fireproof clay, raw materials for concrete production, and facing marble. The Region also has deposits of sand, clay, and gravel for use in construction.

Recreational resources. The Novosibirsk Region has 17 health centers and 31 spa resorts. The Region's recreational and health complex offers medical water and mud treatment programs and can accommodate over 3,500 people.

4. TRADE OPPORTUNITIES

4.1. MAIN GOODS PRODUCED IN THE REGION

Fuel and energy sector. In 2002, coal output amounted to 570,000 tons; oil output was 238,500 tons.

Chemicals. In 2002, polymeric film output was 5,600 tons, flexible PVC output reached 3,600 tons, plastic goods – 5,400 tons, and plasticizers – 4,000 tons.

Ferrous metals. In 2002, steel pipe output increased by 8.4% on 2001 levels to 154,900 tons. Finished ferrous metals goods output reached 220,100 tons.

Non-ferrous metals. In 2002, graphite electrode output reached 14,200 tons, carbon electrode output topped 4,500 tons, cathode output was 18,100 tons, and anode paste output was 14,500 tons.

Machine engineering and metal processing. In 2002, six generators were produced in the Region for steam, gas and hydraulic turbines. The Region also produced 84 mobile electric power stations, 235 large electric machines, 453 direct current electric machines, 3.7 million semiconductors, 5,500 tractor-dri-ven seeders, 15.1 million electric detonators, 100.4 million meters of demolition cord, and 4.5 million of non-electric detonation systems.

Construction materials. In 2002, construction materials output amounted to $133.8 million. The bulk of construction materials produced in the Region consists of brick (65 million brick equivalents), concrete – 651,000 tons, and precast concrete – 210,000 cubic meters.

Food and beverages. Total grain production in 2002 reached 2.6 million tons, whole milk output was 203,800 tons, bread and bakery output reached 173,700 tons, meat output topped 49,900 tons, pasta output was 11,800 tons, mineral water output reached 1.8 million decaliters, and vodka and liquors output was 1.6 million decaliters.

Medical goods and pharmaceuticals. In 2002, total output amounted to $45.9 million, a 10.9% increase compared to 2001 figures. The sector's main products include ampoule medication – 187.5 million ampoules, medical plaster – 21.1 million packs, and bactericidal plaster – 21.8 million strips.

4.2. MAIN EXPORTS, INCLUDING EXTRA-CIS

1999 exports to extra-CIS countries reached $147.4 million, while exports to CIS countries totaled $162.1 million. The corresponding figures for 2000 were $163.6 million and $300.2 million, respectively, and $170.5 million and $331.8 million for 2001. In 2002, the Novosibirsk Region's exports to extra-CIS countries totaled $243.3 million, and exports to CIS countries reached $342.9 million.

The machine engineering sector accounts for the bulk of the Region's exports with 65.7% of the total. The sector produces fuel elements (exports to Bulgaria, Ukraine), electric magnets (exports to the USA, Switzerland, Germany, Italy), railroad and tram equipment (exports to Kazakhstan, Ukraine), electric machinery and engines (exports to South Korea, France, Germany, Ukraine, Iraq, Italy, and China), and aircraft (exports to Algeria, Angola, Libya, and Malaysia).

In 2002, the chemicals sector accounted for 7.3% of total exports (export destinations included Austria, Belgium, the UK, Ghana, Germany, India, Italy, Kazakhstan, Canada, Kyrghyzia, China, Macedonia, Mongolia, the USA, Uzbekistan, France, the Czech Republic, Switzerland, Japan, France, and Cuba), metals and metal goods accounted for 5.0% of total exports (Azerbaijan, Afghanistan, Belgium, Germany, Italy, Kazakhstan, Kyrghyzia, Mongolia, Norway, Uzbekistan, France, and Switzerland), and timber

exports accounted for 2.4% of the total (Austria, Afghanistan, the UK, Germany, Greece, Denmark, Egypt, Spain, Italy, Kazakhstan, Kirghizia, China, South Korea, Syria, the USA, Tajikistan, Uzbekistan, Ukraine, the Czech Republic, and Estonia).

4.3. MAIN IMPORTS, INCLUDING EXTRA-CIS
2000 imports from extra-CIS countries reached $111.5 million, while imports from the CIS totaled $150.7 million. The respective figures for 2001 were $164.8 million and $162 million, and $209.1 million and $147.2 million for 2002.

Chemicals (56%) and machine engineering (22.9%) account for the bulk of imports.

Major regional export and import entities

TABLE 6

ENTITY	ADDRESS	PHONE, FAX, E-MAIL
OAO Novosibirsk Chemicals Plant	94, ul. B. Khmelnitskogo, Novosibirsk, Novosibirsk Region, 630110	Phone: (3832) 74 8346, 74 8154 Fax: (3832) 74 2397, 74 8472
FGUP NAPO Im. Chkalova	15, ul. Polzunova, Novosibirsk-51, Novosibirsk Region, 630051	Phone: (3832) 79 8501 Fax: (3832) 77 1035 E-mail: napavc@mail.cis.ru
Budker Nuclear Physics Institute of the Russian Academy of Sciences	11, pr. Akademika Lavrentyeva, Novosibirsk-90, Novosibirsk Region, 630090	Phone: (3832) 39 4498, 39 4791, 39 4730, 39 4721; fax: (3832) 34 2163 E-mail: G.N.Kulipanov@inp.nsk.su, V.V.Shary@inp.nsk.su

5. INVESTMENT OPPORTUNITIES

5.1. INVESTMENTS IN 1992–2002 (BY INDUSTRY SECTOR), INCLUDING FOREIGN INVESTMENTS
The following factors determine the investment appeal of the Novosibirsk Region:
• Its favorable geographical location. (The Region is located at the crossroad of air routes, railroads, waterways, and highways linking European Russia with eastern areas of the country);
• Its developed transport infrastructure;

• Its developed industrial infrastructure;
• Legislation providing tax incentives to investors and encouraging investment activities;
• Its highly qualified workforce;
• Favorable conditions for recreational activities, tourism, and medical treatment.
5.2. CAPITAL INVESTMENT
Industry, agriculture and forestry, housing, transport, and communications account for the bulk of capital investment in the Region.

VI

Capital investment by industry sector, $ million

TABLE 7

	1997	1998	1999	2000	2001	2002
Total capital investment *Including major industries* (% of total):	865.8	465.3	244.6	384.1	484.9	518.0
Industry	22.1	23.0	24.7	24.0	23.1	46.0
Agriculture and forestry	2.7	8.8	9.6	7.1	10.6	10.8
Construction	9.8	0.9	1.1	1.1	1.9	1.6
Transport and communications	26.5	31.7	38.1	41.9	37.0	23.4
Trade and public catering	5.0	1.9	2.1	2.1	2.6	3.3
Housing and communal services	26.6	20.0	14.7	12.2	10.5	12.0
Other	7.3	13.7	9.7	11.6	14.3	2.9

Foreign investment trends in 1996–2002 | TABLE 8

	1996–1997	1998	1999	2000	2001	2002
Foreign investment, $ million	155.6	186.2	139.1	157.2	103.9	8.4
Including FDI, $ million	71.5	159.1	131.0	151.8	89.1	0.8

5.3. MAJOR ENTERPRISES (INCLUDING ENTERPRISES WITH FOREIGN INVESTMENT)

The Novosibirsk Region hosts more than 700 companies with foreign investment. The Region's largest companies include: OAO Elsib (China and the USA), and OAO Novosibirsk Tin Plant (the UK).

5.4. MOST ATTRACTIVE SECTORS FOR INVESTMENT

According to specialists and the Regional Administration, food and beverages, construction materials, communications, retail, and services are the most attractive sectors for investors.

Largest enterprises of the Novosibirsk Region | TABLE 9

COMPANY	SECTOR	2001 SALES, $ MILLION*
OAO Novosibirsk Chemicals Plant	Chemicals and petrochemicals	104.04
OAO Novosibirsk Electrode Plant	Non-ferrous metals	44.96
OAO VINAP	Food and beverages	35.06
OAO Novosibirsk Tin Plant	Non-ferrous metals	33.93
OAO Siberian Milk	Food and beverages	27.35
FGUP Iskra Novosibirsk Mechanical Plant	Machine engineering and metal processing	24.74
GUP Novosibirsk Electric Locomotive Repair Plant	Machine engineering and metal processing	22.62
FGUP Novosibirsk PO Sibselmash	Machine engineering and metal processing	22.28
OAO Novosibirsk Kuzmin Metal Plant	Ferrous metals	17.20
OAO Elsib	Machine engineering and metal processing	15.70
OAO Novosibkhimpharm	Medicals and pharmaceuticals	12.03
OAO SIBIAR	Chemicals	10.93
OAO Sinar	Light industry	9.77
OAO Tyazhstankogidropress	Machine engineering and metal processing	8.57
OAO Novosibirsk Instrument Plant	Machine engineering and metal processing	8.19
OAO Soyuz Novosibirsk Electric Vacuum Plant Holding Company	Machine engineering and metal processing	7.78
OOO Elektrosignal Novosibirsk Plant Corporation	Machine engineering and metal processing	7.75
OAO Karasuk Meat Processing Plant	Food and beverages	7.71
OAO Karasuk Milk	Food and beverages	6.75

*Data of Novosibirsk Region's enterprises

5.5. CURRENT LEGISLATION ON INVESTOR TAX EXEMPTIONS AND PRIVILEGES

The Novosibirsk Region passed a number of legislative acts in 2002 providing for tax benefits with respect to investment activities in the Novosibirsk Region. The principal law is the Law On State Support to Investment Activity in the Novosibirsk Region.

This Law establishes the legal and economic aspects of state support to investors. Investors are eligible for tax exemptions if they invest own or borrowed funds into investment projects or if they win tenders.

The Novosibirsk Region provides the following support to investors:

• Variable tax rates and exemptions for the regional tax components;
• Deferrals on regional taxes and levies and investment tax credits;
• Discounted lease charges on property owned by the Region and leased to investors for investment purposes;
• Regional budget loans to investors;
• Regional guarantees for investor obligations arising in the course of investment projects;
• Provision of collateral for investor liabilities arising in the course of investment projects;
• Investment funding from the regional budget;

- Regional budget subsidies for portions of bank interest on loans issued to investors for business development purposes within the Novosibirsk Region.

Bodies of local self governance in the Region provide exemptions on local taxes and charges to entities involved in investment activities, as well as other forms of investment support.

Regional entities responsible for raising investment		*TABLE 10*
ENTITY	ADDRESS	PHONE, FAX, E-MAIL
OOO BrokerCreditService	37, ul. Sovetskaya, Novosibirsk, Novosibirsk Region, 630099	Phone: (3832) 11 9090 Fax: (3832) 10 3032 E-mail: info@bcs.ru
ZAO TIK LAND	276, ul. D. Kovalchuk, Novosibirsk, Novosibirsk Region, 630049	Phone: (3832) 12 5743 Fax: (3832) 12 5743 E-mail: land@ticland.com
ZAO IFK Alemar	20, pr. K. Marksa, Novosibirsk, Novosibirsk Region, 630092	Phone: (3832) 46 0697 Fax: (3832) 46 0231 E-mail: alemar@alemar.ru
ZAO FK InterspreadInvest Company	30, pr. K. Marksa, Novosibirsk, Novosibirsk Region, 630087	Phone: (3832) 11 9070 Fax: (3832) 11 9070 E-mail: ispr@ispr.nsk.su
Novosibirsk Branch of OAO Alfa-Bank	1, pr. Dimitrova, Novosibirsk, Novosibirsk Region, 630004	Phone: (3832) 23 9739 Fax: (3832) 23 9739 E-mail: novosibirsk@alfabank.ru
ANO Koltsovo Innovation Center	12, Koltsovo, Novosibirsk Region, 630559	Phone: (3832) 36 6345 Fax: (3832) 36 6345 E-mail: kateshova@kolzovo.ru

5.6. FEDERAL AND REGIONAL ECONOMIC AND SOCIAL DEVELOPMENT PROGRAMS FOR THE NOVOSIBIRSK REGION

Federal targeted programs. The Novosibirsk Region is carrying out some 24 federal targeted programs, of which 18 programs are focused on social issues. Total financing allocated for the federal programs for the whole period of validity is $129 million. In 2002, the financing reached $16.6 million, including: $11.9 million from the federal budget, $3.5 million from the regional budget, and $1.2 million from non-budgetary sources.

The largest federal targeted program of economic and social development for the Novosibirsk Region is the Program for the Elimination of Economic and Social Development Differences Between the Regions of the Russian Federation 2002–2010, and through 2015. The program's main objective is to mitigate social and economic differences between the Novosibirsk Region and other areas and territories of the Russian Federation, to reduce the gap in principal social and economic development indicators, to create a favorable environment for investment activities, to increase state-funded construction of social and communications infrastructure, and to promote economic independence in the Region. In 2002, $2.6 million in funding was allocated to the Program, including $1.6 million from the federal budget, $0.9 million from the regional budget, and

$0.1 million from non-budgetary sources. The total budget of the Program for its validity period is $22 million.

Regional programs. The Novosibirsk Region has some 16 regional targeted programs underway with a focus on industry development, investment, small business support, health and environmental protection, job creation, and social welfare. According to the Regional Administration, some $9.1 million was allocated to these programs from the regional budget in 2002. The bulk of the funds went to the following social programs:

The Novosibirsk Region has accorded priority status to the Program of State Support to Industrial Investment Activity in the Novosibirsk Region (2000-2003). Based on the results of the 2000-2001 round of tenders, some 38 investment projects in 14 industries were approved for state support, with 1,990 jobs created as a result. Some $0.8 million was allocated from the regional budget in 2002 to finance state support to industrial investment projects.

Nine small business projects have received a total financing of $0.2 million under the Program of State Support to Small Enterprise in the Novosibirsk Region (2001–2003), with 519 new jobs created. Eleven small business investment projects have received a total funding of $0.2 million from the regional budget and $0.3 million from the Novosibirsk Regional Fund for Small Business Support on a tender basis in 2002.

6. INVESTMENT PROJECTS

Industry sector and project description	1) Expected results 2) Amount and term of investment 3) Form of financing[1] 4) Documentation[2]	Contact information
1	2	3

CHEMICALS AND PHARMACEUTICALS

72R001 ● ★ ◆

Creation of a regional center for deep donor blood processing.
Project goal: Donor blood plasma processing.

1) Up to 150 tons a year
2) $35 million/2 years
3) L, Leas.
4) BP

DGUEPP Vector-Bialgam
P.O. Box 149, Koltsovo,
Novosibirsk Region, 630599
Phone/fax: (3832) 36 7501
E-mail: kousliy@vector.nsc.ru
Leonid Georgievich Nikulin,
Director

MACHINE ENGINEERING AND METAL PROCESSING

72R002 ● ▲

Helicopter repairs.
Project goal: to repair the fleet of Mi 8 helicopters.

1) 7 Mi 8 MTV helicopters; 15 Mi 8T helicopters
2) $4.1 million/1 year
3) L
4) FS

OAO Novosibirsk Aircraft Repair Plant
2/4 Airport, Novosibirsk,
Novosibirsk Region, 630123
Phone: (3832) 28 9650
Fax: (3832) 28 9694
E-mail: murasev@nars.gcom.ru
Vladimir Viktorovich Kostin,
CEO

72R003 ● ▲

Construction of a ventilation equipment plant.
Project goal: to produce ventilation equipment.

1) Revenues of $2.1 million a year
2) $0.9 million/8 months
3) L ($0.8 million)
4) FS

ZAO Lazurit
6a, Vokzalnaya magistral, Novosibirsk,
Novosibirsk Region, 630004
Phone: (3832) 18 3950
Fax: (3832) 17 7656
E-mail: lazurit@cns.ru
Vyacheslav Yegorovich Pikalov,
CEO

72R004 ● ▲

Creation of facilities for laser equipment components production.
Project goal: to satisfy market demand for laser equipment components.

1) Revenues of $1 million a year
2) $3.4 million/2 years
3) L
4) FS

ZAO Sibirsky Monokristall-EKSMA
43, ul. Russkaya, Novosibirsk,
Novosibirsk Region, 630058
Phone/fax: (3832) 33 3759
E-mail: yurkin@ssc.nsib.ru
Alexander Mikhailovich Yurkin,
CEO

FORESTRY, TIMBER, AND PULP AND PAPER

72R005 ● ■ ◆

Launch of a packaging production line.
Project goal: to produce packaging materials.

1) Revenues of $13 million a year
2) $4.5 million/n/a
3) L, E
4) BP

OAO Kharmens
18, Mochischenskoye shosse, Novosibirsk,
Novosibirsk Region, 630123
Phone/fax: (3832) 90 9010, 90 9020, 90 9030, 90 9040
E-mail: vereschagin@harmens.ru;
Yury Anatolyevich Vereschaghin,
CEO

[1] L – Loan, E – Equity, Leas. – Leasing, JV – Joint Venture
[2] BP – Business Plan, FS – Feasibility Study

1	2	3

GLASS AND PORCELAIN

71R006 ● ◆ ▲

Construction of a glass plant.
Project goal: to satisfy regional demand
for glass containers.

1) 750 million bottles a year
2) $45 million/3 years
3) L
4) FS, BP

OAO Novosibirsk Plant EKRAN
8a, ul. Dargomyzhskogo, Novosibirsk,
Novosibirsk Region, 630047
Phone: (3832) 28 6310
Fax: (3832) 25 8498
E-mail: kanun@online.sinor.ru
Sergei Nikolaevich Vasyukov,
CEO

LIGHT INDUSTRY

71R007 ● ◆

Creation of facilities for wet flax spinning.
Project goal: to produce a new
competitive product range.

1) 775 tons a year
2) $5.4 million/1.5 years
3) L
4) BP

ZAO Novosibirsk Cotton
and Linen Company
1, ul. Prigranichnaya, Novosibirsk,
Novosibirsk Region, 630068
Phone: (3832) 58 1084
Fax: (3832) 38 3835
E-mail: nxbk@online.nsk.su
Gennady Romanovich Petrov,
CEO

TRANSPORT INFRASTRUCTURE

71R008 ● ▲

Reconstruction of the domestic
airport terminal.
Project goal: to provide stable
flight services.

1) 1,000 passengers an hour
2) $15 million/4 years
3) L ($10 million)
4) FS

OAO Tolmachevo Airport
Ob-4, Novosibirsk Region, 633104
Phone: (3832) 16 9230
Fax: (3832) 16 9433
E-mail: ops@tolmachevo.ru
Vyacheslav Mikhailovich Shatalin,
CEO

COMMUNICATIONS

71R009 ● ▲

Construction of a multi-protocol
multimedia communications network.
Project goal: to provide communication
services.

1) 315,000 subscribers
2) $27.2 million/3 years
3) L ($20 million)
4) FS

OAO Sibirtelecom
53, ul. M. Gorkogo, Novosibirsk
Novosibirsk Region, 630099
Phone: (3832) 19 1167, 19 1106
Fax: (3832) 19 1207
E-mail: const@sibnet.ru
Anatoly Ivanovich Nikulin, CEO

OTHER

71R010 ● ★ ▲

Facilities upgrade for paint brush production.
Project goal: to produce paint
brushes using modern technologies.

1) 63.5 million brushes a year
2) $1.8 million/1 year
3) L, Leas ($1.4 million)
4) FS

OOO Akor NGOOI SIN
18, ul. Petrozavodskaya, Novosibirsk,
Novosibirsk Region, 630040
Phone: (3832) 90 6957, 90 5165
Fax: (3832) 905165
E-mail: akor@akor.ru
Alexander Alexandrovich Kolesnichenko,
Director

SIBERIAN FEDERAL DISTRICT

VI

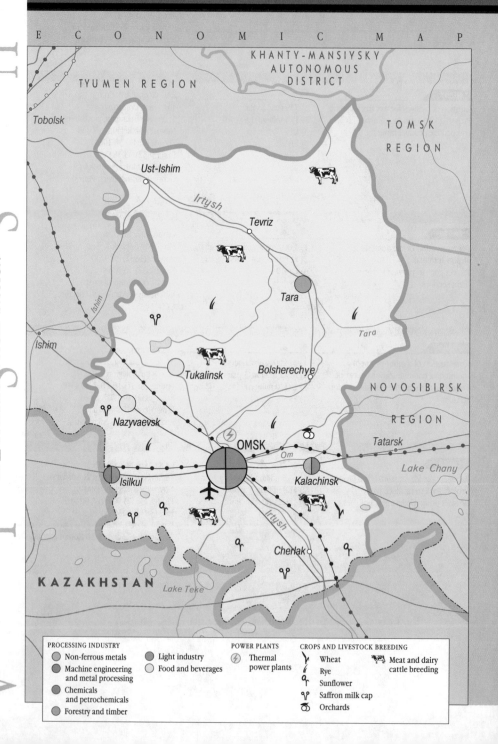

73. OMSK REGION [55]

E C O N O M I C   M A P

KHANTY-MANSIYSKY
AUTONOMOUS
DISTRICT

TYUMEN REGION

Tobolsk

TOMSK
REGION

Ust-Ishim

Irtysh

Tevriz

Tara

Ishim

Tara

Tukalinsk

Bolsherechye

NOVOSIBIRSK

REGION

Nazyvaevsk

OMSK

Om

Tatarsk

Lake Chany

Isilkul

Kalachinsk

Irtysh

Chenak

KAZAKHSTAN   Lake Teke

PROCESSING INDUSTRY
- Non-ferrous metals
- Machine engineering and metal processing
- Chemicals and petrochemicals
- Forestry and timber
- Light industry
- Food and beverages

POWER PLANTS
- Thermal power plants

CROPS AND LIVESTOCK BREEDING
- Wheat
- Rye
- Sunflower
- Saffron milk cap
- Orchards
- Meat and dairy cattle breeding

T he first two years of the new century have demonstrated that the Omsk Region is progressing steadily toward its set goal of building a stable and competitive real sector.

Reforms imply not only tactical objectives, but a strategic approach as well. The idea of sustainable development has gained common currency both in the developed world and in transition economies. The experience of many countries shows that rather than leading to social and economic stability, market driven economic growth tends to widen the gap between rich and poor. We view sustainable development as the most suitable growth model for our Region.

One component of this approach involves creating optimal conditions for international cooperation in both the economic and humanitarian spheres. The Omsk Region offers good potential for the development of business, including businesses backed by foreign capital. Our Region is characterized by political, social, and economic stability, a constructive relationship between the representative and executive bodies, broad partnership links with other regions of Russia, and an attractive investment climate.

The products of our oil refining and petrochemicals, defense and food sectors are well known and in demand both within Russia and abroad. This is the result of our regional economic policies, which are focused on creating conditions conducive to sustainable economic development.

Leonid Polezhaev,
GOVERNOR OF THE OMSK REGION

SIBERIAN FEDERAL DISTRICT

VI

1. GENERAL INFORMATION

1.1. GEOGRAPHY

The Omsk Region covers a total area of 141,100 square kilometers. The Region is situated in the southern part of the West Siberian Plain. To the south, the Region borders Kazakhstan, to the west and north – the Tyumen Region, and to the east – the Tomsk and Novosibirsk Regions.

1.2. CLIMATE

The Omsk Region has a continental climate.

The average air temperature in January is –20.8°C, rising to +17°C in July. Average annual precipitation exceeds 300–400 mm. The growing season lasts for some 153–162 days.

1.3. POPULATION

According to preliminary 2002 census results, total population in the Region was 2,079,000 people. The average population density is 14.7 people per square kilometer. The economically active population amounts to 1,080,000 people. The 2002 official unemployment level was 1.8%.

Demographically speaking, some 61% are of the statutory working age, 20% are below the statutory working age, and 19% are beyond the statutory working age.

As of 2002, the Omsk Region's major urban centers are Omsk with 1,133,900 inhabitants, Isilkul with 27,800 inhabitants, Tara with 26,900 inhabitants, and Kalachinsk with 25,100 inhabitants.

Population							TABLE 1
	1992	1997	1998	1999	2000	2001	2002
Total population, '000	2,171	2,175	2,180	2,180	2,164	2,147	2,079
Economically active population, '000	1,087	984	976	1,032	1,040	979	1,080

2. ADMINISTRATION

1, ul. Krasny Put, Omsk, Omsk Region, 644002. Phone: (3812) 24 1415, 24 4011, fax: (3812) 24 2372
E-mail: teleomsk@echo.ru; http://www.omskportal.ru

NAME	POSITION	CONTACT INFORMATION
Leonid Konstantinovich POLEZHAEV	Governor of the Omsk Region	Phone: (3812) 24 1415 Fax: (3812) 24 2372
Valentin Alexandrovich TRETYAKOV	First Deputy Governor of the Omsk Region in charge of Law Enforcement and Healthcare	Phone: (3812) 24 2570, 24 4155
Yevgeny Mikhailovich VDOVIN	First Deputy Governor of the Omsk Region in charge of Social and Economic Development	Phone: (3812) 24 3255, 24 1912
Alexander Mikhailovich LUPPOV	Deputy Governor of the Omsk Region	Phone: (3812) 24 0105, 23 1890
Viktor Yakovlevich BELEVKIN	Deputy Governor of the Omsk Region, Head of the Agricultural Department	Phone: (3812) 24 1256, 23 1612
Natalia Konstantinovna FROLOVA	Deputy Governor of the Omsk Region, Chairman of the Finance and Control Committee	Phone: (3812) 23 4770, 23 1934
Vladimir Vladimirovich RADUL	Deputy Governor of the Omsk Region in charge of Information and Analytical Support to the Administration	Phone: (3812) 23 2201, 23 6123
Vladimir Mikhailovich BOGDANOV	Deputy Governor of the Omsk Region, Chairman of the Property Management Committee	Phone: (3812) 23 2263, 23 2563
Sergei Viktorovich YEVSEENKO	Chairman of the Economic Committee of the Omsk Region	Phone: (3812) 24 1470, 24 8749 Fax: (3812) 24 8839
Viktor Stepanovich BAZHENOV	Chairman of the Committee for External and Inter-Regional Economic Relations of the Omsk Region	Phone: (3812) 24 6379

3. ECONOMIC POTENTIAL

3.1. 1997–2002 GROSS REGIONAL PRODUCT (GRP). INDUSTRY BREAKDOWN

The 2000 gross regional product amounted to $2,549 million, which constitutes 7.8% growth year-on-year in comparable prices. Per capita GRP amounted to $1,100 in 2001 and $1,227 in 2002.

3.2. MAJOR ECONOMIC GROWTH PROJECTIONS

The blueprint for economic development in the Omsk Region is set forth in the Conceptual Framework for the Development of External Economic Relations of the Omsk Region 2005, adopt-

GRP trends in 1997–2002						TABLE 2
	1997	1998	1999	2000	2001*	2002*
GRP in current prices, $ million	5,556.0	2,998.5	1,510.9	1,731.4	2,364.6	2,549.4

*Estimates of the Omsk Regional Administration

GRP industry breakdown in 1997–2002, % of total						TABLE 3
	1997	1998	1999	2000	2001*	2002*
GRP	100.0	100.0	100.0	100.0	100.0	100.0
Industry	27.4	24.4	20.4	21.2	19.8	n/a
Agriculture and forestry	9.4	9.5	16.1	18.5	20.8	n/a
Construction	5.1	4.5	3.6	3.8	4.8	n/a
Transport and communications**	13.4	10.4	9.0	10.6	12.4	n/a
Trade and public catering	12.9	16.2	21.2	20.2	15.2	n/a
Other	19.1	25.7	20.3	20.7	20.0	n/a
Net taxes on output	12.7	9.3	9.4	5.0	7.0	n/a

*Estimates of the Omsk Regional Administration
**Data on the transport sector only

ed in 2002, which envisages considerable growth in external trade, improvement of the export structure through an increased share of machinery exports, geographical expansion of external trade to European countries, expansion of the exported range of services, strengthening of inter-regional cooperation, and an increase in foreign investment in the Region.

Currently, the Regional Administration is developing and approving the Program for Social and Economic Development and Financial Stabilization of the Omsk Region, 2002-2005.

3.3. INDUSTRIAL OUTPUT IN 1997–2002 FOR MAJOR SECTORS OF ECONOMY

The leading industrial sectors of the Omsk Region are food and beverages, chemicals and petrochemicals, energy, and machine engineering. These account for a combined 77.9% of total industrial output. The Region is among Russia's top ten regions in terms of output of grain, milk, and meat.

Food and beverages. The sector accounts for 27% of total industrial output. In 2001, the Omsk Region was Russia's second region in terms of meat output (including category one subproducts), fifteenth in terms of butter output, and seventeenth for dairy output (in terms of milk). The Region's major

companies within the sector are OAO Omsk Bacon, OAO Omsk Meat Yard-Sausage Plant, ZAO Omsky Meat Processing Plant, and OOO Omkhleb.

Chemicals and petrochemicals. The sector accounts for 20.5% of total industrial output. The top company in the sector is OAO Omsk Oil Refinery, a modern plant producing all kinds of fuel, lubricants, additives, and high-quality aromatic hydrocarbons. The refinery's output is forwarded to petrochemical plants owned by OAO Omsk Tire, OAO Omskkhimprom, OAO Omsk Resin, OAO Omsk Industrial Carbon Plant, and ZAO Plastmass-Service.

Machine engineering and metal processing. The industry accounts for 14.3% of total industrial output. The Region's defense enterprises account for a large share of the machine engineering sector's output. Enterprises in the sector produce An 74 aircraft, tractors, aircraft engines, communications devices, medical equipment, agricultural and oil and gas equipment, refrigerator and freezer compressor motors, cryogen, navigation, and hydraulic equipment, and tires. The major defense enterprises within the sector are FGUP PO Polet, GUP Omsk Transport Machinery Plant, OAO Sibcryotechnika, FGUP Baranov Mechanical

Industry breakdown of industrial output in 1997–2002, % of total						TABLE 4
	1997	1998	1999	2000	2001	2002
Industry	100.0	100.0	100.0	100.0	100.0	100.0
Food and beverages	12.4	21.3	28.3	29.0	26.6	27.0
Chemicals and petrochemicals	6.3	10.3	13.0	17.1	20.9	20.5
Energy	13.8	23.7	17.9	17.0	16.1	16.1
Machine engineering and metal processing	9.7	12.1	13.6	14.5	15.0	14.3
Fuel	48.2	15.6	11.3	11.8	11.0	11.0
Construction materials	4.0	4.9	3.4	3.8	4.8	3.6
Flour, cereals, and mixed fodder	2.4	4.0	3.6	3.4	3.0	2.4
Light industry	1.0	1.4	1.7	1.2	0.9	0.5
Forestry, timber, and pulp and paper	1.1	1.6	1.1	0.9	0.7	0.5
Ferrous metals	0.1	0.2	0.3	0.5	0.1	0.1
Non-ferrous metals	–	0.1	0.2	0.2	0.1	0.1

Engineering Plant, FGUP Siberian Instruments and Systems, OAO Relero, GUP Omsk Irtysh Company, OAO Omskgidroprivod, and OAO Omsk Instrument Plant.

Agriculture. The total area of arable lands in the Region is about 7 million hectares, including over 4 million hectares of ploughed lands, with chernozem (black earth) as the core land, and roughly 1 million hectares are hayfields.

3.4. FUEL AND ENERGY BALANCE (OUTPUT AND CONSUMPTION PER RESOURCE)

The Region's generating capacities meet 70% of local energy demand. Kazakhstan is the major energy exporter to the Region.

Fuel and energy sector production and consumption trends, 1997–2002						TABLE 5
	1997	1998	1999	2000	2001	2002
Electricity output, billion kWh	6.7	6.8	5.9	6.2	6.0	6.2
Oil output (including gas condensate), '000 tons	–	0.4	1.3	0.8	0.2	61.5
Natural gas extraction, million cubic meters	–	1.0	1.6	3.2	9.0	12.3
Electricity consumption, billion kWh	9.2	9.2	8.9	9.2	9.4	9.4
Natural gas consumption, million cubic meters	896.3	1,434.9	1,487.4	1,851.9	2,016.3	2,070.8

3.5. TRANSPORT INFRASTRUCTURE

Roads. The Region has 19,100 kilometers of paved public highway. The Region is crossed by the Chelyabinsk – Kurgan – Petropavlovsk – Omsk – Novosibirsk, Omsk – Tyumen – Yekaterinburg, and Omsk – Pavlodar federal highways.

Railroads. The Omsk Region has 775 kilometers of railroads. The Trans-Siberian railroad passes through the Region.

Airports. Omsk is served by an international airport.

River transport. Passengers and freight are transported along the Irtysh river, which links Omsk to eastern Kazakhstan and provides access to the Northern Sea Route.

Oil and gas pipelines. The Region has 580 kilometers of oil and oil product pipelines.

3.6. MAIN NATURAL RESOURCES: RESERVES AND EXTRACTION IN 2002

The Region is rich in over 17 types of mineral resources, including fuel raw materials, mineral salts, and curative mud.

Fuel resources. The Region has four oil fields with a total reserve of 22.5 million tons and a gas field with a reserve of 0.6 billion cubic meters. Estimated oil reserves are 216 million tons and gas reserves 22.5 billion cubic meters.

Non-ore mineral resources. Some 350 deposits of peat with a total reserve of 5.2 billion tons are located in the northern part of the Omsk Region, including 28 deposits ready for commercial development. Mineral resources are also represented by deposits of brick and ceramic clay, sand, sapropel, bentonite clay (the second largest deposit in Siberia with a total reserve of 20 million tons), mineral salts and curative mud, and thermal and mineral water.

Water resources. The Region's main water resource is the Irtysh river and its tributaries, plus minor rivers and subterranean waters. The largest reserves of fresh subterranean water are concentrated in the northern part of the Region. The Region has three explored mineral water fields with a total reserve of 18,500 cubic meters per day.

Land and forests. Highly fertile soils, including a zone of common and leached black earth soil in the south and turf-meadow and gray forest soil in the center and north of the Region, account for the Region's focus on grain cultivation and cattle farming.

Forests cover a total area of 5,878,500 hectares. The most common species are fir, silver fir, cedar, pine, birch, and ash.

4. TRADE OPPORTUNITIES

4.1. MAIN GOODS
PRODUCED IN THE REGION

Food and agriculture products. 2002 grain output fell by 30% year-on-year to 2,645,300 tons, potato output reached 917,100 tons (2.3% growth), vegetables – 296,900 tons (4.3% growth), meat and poultry – 219,300 tons (8.9% growth), milk – 945,600 tons (10.4% growth), eggs – 716.8 million (13.3% growth), and flour – 210,800 tons.

Oil and gas products. 2002 oil output totaled 61,500 tons, while primary refining output amounted to 13.3 million tons. The Region produced 4.6 million tons of diesel fuel and 3.1 million tons of gasoline in 2002.

Natural gas output was 12.3 million cubic meters in 2002.

Petrochemicals. In 2002, the Region produced 6.5 million tires, which constitutes 14% growth year-on-year, and 73,100 tons of synthetic rubber.

Timber. 2002 output of timber amounted to 959,000 cubic meters.

4.2. EXPORTS, INCLUDING EXTRA-CIS

The Omsk Region's exports totaled $826.3 million in 2001, with extra-CIS and CIS exports accounting for 72.2% and 27.8%, respectively. Exports in 2002 totaled $881.1 million, with extra-CIS exports accounting for 78.5% and CIS exports for 21.5%.

The main types of goods exported by the Region in 2002 were fuel and energy – $631.9

million, rubber ($182.6 million), machinery, equipment, and transport vehicles – $25.9 million (exports were halved in 2002), food and agricultural raw materials ($28.7 million), metal and metal goods ($5.3 million), and timber and pulp and paper goods ($3.7 million). Major importers of the Region's products include Germany, the Netherlands, Finland, China, Kazakhstan, Iran, Italy, Kyrghyzia, and Uzbekistan.

4.3. IMPORTS, INCLUDING EXTRA-CIS

2001 imports totaled $176.8 million, with extra-CIS imports accounting for 31.7% and CIS imports for 68.3%. Imports in 2002 totaled $178.8 million, with extra-CIS imports accounting for 38.7% and CIS imports for 61.3%.

The bulk of 2002 imports consisted of food and agricultural raw materials ($30.0 million), fuel and energy ($30.2 million), chemicals ($11.6 million), metals and metal goods ($14.5 million), and machinery, equipment, and transport vehicles ($73.9 million). The main exporters to the Region include France, Germany, the USA, Italy, Kazakhstan, and Ukraine.

4.4. MAJOR REGIONAL EXPORT
AND IMPORT ENTITIES

Due to the specific features of trade in the Region, mainly industrial companies perform export and import operations.

SIBERIAN FEDERAL DISTRICT

VI

5. INVESTMENT OPPORTUNITIES

5.1. INVESTMENTS IN 1992–2002
(BY INDUSTRY SECTOR),
INCLUDING FOREIGN INVESTMENTS

The following factors determine the investment appeal of the Omsk Region:

• Its developed transport infrastructure;
• Its developed industrial infrastructure;
• Legislation providing support for investment activities;
• Its natural resources.

5.2. CAPITAL INVESTMENT

Industry, transport, and communicationS account for over 50% of capital investment.

5.3. MAJOR ENTERPRISES
(INCLUDING ENTERPRISES
WITH FOREIGN INVESTMENT)

Major companies with foreign investment include ZAO Rosar (Sun-Interbrew holding), OAO Omsk Bacon, OOO JV Siberian-Scandinavian Bus Company (Volvo), ZAO Matador-Omsk Tire, and JV Polet-Fris.

Capital investment by industry sector, $ million						TABLE 6
	1997	1998	1999	2000	2001	2002
Total capital investment	647.5	366.6	188.7	183.4	298.6	317.9
Including major industries (% of total)						
Industry	29.8	29.6	36.2	34.3	43.6	40.5
Agriculture and forestry	5.7	7.7	9.3	11.9	10.3	11.7
Construction	1.8	1.2	0.7	1.3	3.0	5.3
Transport and communications	25.3	15.7	23.8	22.6	19.1	17.2
Trade and public catering	0.9	0.9	2.2	3.2	4.7	5.4
Other	36.5	44.9	27.8	26.7	19.3	19.9

Foreign investment trends in 1992–2002						TABLE 7
	1997	1998	1999	2000	2001	2002
Foreign investment, $ million	365.4	452.2	884.1	791.8	952.2	2,401.5
Including FDI, $ million	3.3	12.1	1.5	2.1	4.9	2.7

Largest enterprises of the Omsk Region	TABLE 8
COMPANY	SECTOR
OAO Omsk Tire	Petrochemicals
OAO Omsk Refinery	Oil refining
OAO Omsk Bacon	Food

5.4. MOST ATTRACTIVE SECTORS FOR INVESTMENT

According to the Omsk Regional Administration, the most appealing sectors for investors are chemicals, petrochemicals, oil refining, transport and agricultural machine engineering, and the agroindustrial sector.

5.5. CURRENT LEGISLATION ON INVESTOR TAX EXEMPTIONS AND PRIVILEGES

The Omsk Region has in effect the Law On State Support to Investment Projects in the Omsk Region.

In 2002, the Omsk Region passed a Law On Corporate Profit Tax Reductions, which envisages preferential taxation for organizations involved in investment activity.

5.6. FEDERAL AND REGIONAL ECONOMIC AND SOCIAL DEVELOPMENT PROGRAMS FOR THE OMSK REGION

Federal targeted programs. The Omsk Region is implementing some 35 federal targeted programs with the aim of upgrading its transport system, providing social protection, rehabilitating the environment, and improving public healthcare. The program for The Elimination of Inequalities in the Social and Economic Development of the Regions of the Russian Federation 2002-2010 and through 2015 provides funding for the construction of social facilities in the Region.

Regional programs. The Regional Administration has developed programs focused on the development of healthcare, reinforcement of law and order, and social welfare. The Key Development and Modernization Directions for Life Supporting Industries of the Omsk Region, 2001-2010 are being implemented in the Region. These directions provide for financial stabilization, improvement of life supporting industries of the Omsk Region, implementation of investment policies, improvement of management systems, anti-monopoly measures, enhancement of competition in the life-supporting industries, and strengthening of welfare.

Regional entities responsible for raising investment		TABLE 9
ENTITY	ADDRESS	PHONE, FAX, E-MAIL
Committee for External and Inter-Regional Economic Relations of the OmskRegion	5, ul. Krasny Put, Omsk, Omsk Region, 644002	Phone: (3812) 24 6379 Fax: (3812) 23 2765
West Siberian Investment Center	Office 9, 5, ul. Krasny Put, Omsk, Omsk Region, 644002	Phone: (3812) 24 9049 E-mail: wsic@omsknet.ru

6. INVESTMENT PROJECTS

Industry sector and project description	1) Expected results 2) Amount and term of investment 3) Form of financing[1] 4) Documentation[2]	Contact information
1	2	3

ENERGY

73R001

Construction of an autonomous rotary wind power plant. Project goal: to produce electricity.

● ▲ ◆
1) 15 units a year
2) $1.5 million/4 years
3) L
4) FS, BP

State Unitary Company PO Polet
226, ul. B. Khmelnitskogo, Omsk,
Omsk Region, 644021
Phone/fax: (3812) 51 0087, 57 7021
E-mail: polyot@polyot.omsk.ru
Oleg Petrovich Dorofeev,
CEO

73R002

Transfer of TPS 4 second unit's boilers to natural gas. Project goal: to reduce pollution, ash storage, and waste dumping into local water reservoirs.

● ◆
1) Transfer of 4 boilers to gas
2) $7 million/1year
3) L
4) BP

OAO AK Omskenergo
10, ul. Partizanskaya, Omsk,
Omsk Region, 644037
Phone/fax: (3812) 24 0862, 23 3569, 25 0749
Alexander Vladimirovich Antropenko,
CEO

CHEMICALS AND PETROCHEMICALS

73R003

Construction of an experimental industrial zinc oxide production unit. Project goal: to produce feedstocks for paint, medicine, perfume, and rubber goods.

● ▲
1) n/a
2) $1.2 million/1 year
3) L
4) FS

OOO Zinc Whitewash of Russia
Krutaya Gorka, Omsk Region, 644092
Phone/fax: (3812) 30 8993, 91 1593
Anatoly Viktorovich Polukhin, CEO

73R004

Construction of sapropel processing facilities Based on the Omsk Region's deposits. Project goal: production of sapropel fertilizers, fodder additions, veterinary medicines, and Sibsorbent-I hydrophobic sorbent for oil and oil product collection on any type of surface.

● ▲ ◆
1) 44,000 tons a year
2) $ 4.5 million/3 years
3) L
4) FS, BP

ZANPO Vega-2000-Siberian Organics
Office 12, 26, pr. Koroliova, Omsk,
Omsk Region, 644012
Phone/fax: (3812) 24 1510, 24 6575, 24 0990
E-mail: sapropel@siborganics.com
Alexander Georgievich Tretiakov,
CEO

MACHINE ENGINEERING AND METAL PROCESSING

73R005

Launch of commercial production of a multi-fuel gas turbine TPS. Project goal: to generate electricity and heat from autonomous sources operating on economical and ecologically friendly fuel (natural and associated gas).

● ▲
1) Unit capacity 20 MW
2) $10 million/1 year
3) L
4) FS

Unitary Company Mechanical Engineering Plant, a subsidiary of State Unitary Company Baranov Mechanical Engineering Plant
283, ul. B. Khmelnitskogo, Omsk,
Omsk Region, 644021
Phone/fax: (3812) 39 3474, 36 0793
E-mail: mz@omo.omskcity.com
Yury Alexandrovich Shipitsin,
Director

SIBERIAN FEDERAL DISTRICT

VI

[1] L – Loan, E – Equity, Leas. – Leasing, JV – Joint Venture
[2] BP – Business Plan, FS – Feasibility Study

1	2	3
73R006 ● ▲		Unitary Company Mechanical Engineering Plant, Subsidiary of State Unitary Company Baranov Mechanical Engineering Plant
Launch of commercial production of a mobile gas turbine unit. Project goal: to create a mobile source of electricity and heat for the Ministry of Emergency Situations, housing services and oil companies.	1) Unit capacity 4 MW 2) $10 million/1 year 3) L 4) FS	283, ul. B. Khmelnitskogo, Omsk, Omsk Region, 644021 Phone/fax: (3812) 39 3474, 36 0793 E-mail: mz@omo.omskcity.com Yury Alexandrovich Shipitsin, Director
73R007 ● ◆ ▲		ZAO Avers Production Environmental Association
Construction of biological energy plants. Project goal: to develop and launch production of biological energy generation units for the production of alternative fuels (biogas) and organic fertilizers and for waste utilization.	1) n/a 2) $1.5 million/1.5 years 3) L 4) FS, BP	13a, ul. Dobrovolskogo, Omsk, Omsk Region, 644099 Phone/fax: (3812) 25 2478, 23 3201 E-mail: avers@omsktown.ru Ivan Ivanovich Logvinov, CEO
73R008 ● ▲		Unitary Company Mechanical Engineering Plant, a subsidiary of State Unitary Company Baranov Mechanical Engineering Plant
Launch of commercial output of the Tornado compressor plant based on an aircraft turbojet engine. Project goal: to manufacture compressor plants for construction, operation, and repair of trunk oil, gas, and condensate pipelines.	1) n/a 2) $4.0 million/1 year 3) L 4) FS	283, ul. B. Khmelnitskogo, Omsk, Omsk Region, 644021 Phone/fax: (3812) 39 3474, 36 0793 E-mail: mz@omo.omskcity.com Yury Alexandrovich Shipitsin Director
73R009 ● ▲		Unitary Company Omsk Plant of Oil Refining Equipment, Subsidiary of State Unitary Company PO Polet
Launch of commercial output of mobile multipurpose modular units to intensify oil production and reduce costs. Project goal: to reduce oil extraction costs and prevent accidents at oil fields.	1) n/a 2) $4.3 million/1 year 3) L 4) FS	226, ul. B. Khmelnitskogo, Omsk, Omsk Region, 644021 Phone/fax: (3812) 57 7087, 57 9000, 57 7021 Sergei Vasilyevich Krasyuk, Director
73R010 ● ▲		State Unitary Company PO Polet
Launch of commercial output of several types of An 3T aircraft. Project goal: to develop competitive products from mainly domestic components.	1) up to 30 items per year 2) $1.4 million/0.5 year 3) L 4) FS	226, ul. B. Khmelnitskogo, Omsk, Omsk Region, 644021 Phone/fax: (3812) 51 0087, 57 7021 E-mail: polyot@polyot.omsk.ru Oleg Petrovich Dorofeev, CEO

FORESTRY, TIMBER, AND PULP AND PAPER

1	2	3
73R011 ● ▲		OOO Timber Plant
Production of lumber. Project goal: to produce lumber.	1) 60,000 cubic meters per year 2) $1.5 million/1 year 3) L 4) FS	P.O. Box 9314, 69, pr. Mira, Omsk, Omsk Region, 644029 Phone: (3812) 64 2777 Fax: (3812) 64 5065, 64 7318 E-mail: dok@omskmail.ru Alexei Yuryevich Kondyurin, CEO

1	2	3

73R012 ● ❖ ◆ ▲

Production of Tetra-Brick-Aseptic packaging.
Project goal: to increase output.

1) 700 tons a month
 (sales of $2 million annually)
2) $20 million/1 year
3) L, JV
4) FS, BP

OAO Polipax, Omsk Laminated Paper Plant
31, ul. 2 Solnechnaya, Omsk-73,
Omsk Region, 644073
Phone/fax: (3812) 13 1688, 13 2913
Fax: (3812) 13 1866
E-mail: polypack@polypack.omsk.su
Igor Trofimovich Falkovich,
CEO

TRANSPORT INFRASTRUCTURE

73R013 ● ▲

Omsk-Fedorovka Airport facilities.
Project goal: to increase the passenger flow.

1) Capacity increase to 1,650
 passengers an hour
2) $119.6 million/42 months
3) L
4) FS

OAO Airport Omsk-Fedorovka
1, ul. Inzhenernaya, Omsk,
Omsk Region, 644031
Phone/fax: (3812) 55 6397
Phone: (3812) 53 1384, 53 2390, 31 0517
Fax (3812) 31 7536
Oleg Nikolaevich Romanyuk,
CEO

COMMUNICATIONS

73R014 ● ◆

Construction of a digital communication
network in Omsk.
Project goal: to provide quality
communication services.

1) minimum 50,000 subscribers
2) $11.0 million/5 years
3) L
4) BP

OAO Omsk Telephone Company
P.O. Box 2098, Omsk-29,
Omsk Retion, 644029
Phone: (3812) 41 3933
Phone/fax: (3812) 41 9030
E-mail: otk@echo.ru
Gennady Nikolaevich Kulichenko,
CEO

ECOLOGY AND WASTE TREATMENT

73R015 ● ▲

Construction of a production
and household waste processing plant.
Project goal: to release land, decrease
epidemic threat, and utilize waste.

1) n/a
2) $20.3 million/1.5 years
3) L
4) FS

Omsk Branch of Glushko Production
Company Energomash, Chemical Plant 3
Krutaya Gorka, Omsk Region, 644092
Phone: (3812) 91 5100
Anatoly Viktorovich Polukhin,
Director

SCIENCE AND INNOVATION

73R016 ● ▲ ◆

Upgrading of the Cosmos carrier rocket.
Project goal: to upgrade the Cosmos
carrier rocket.

1) 4 launches a year
2) $14.8 million/2.5 years
3) L
4) FS, BP

State Unitary Company PO Polet
226, ul. B. Khmelnitskogo, Omsk,
Omsk Region, 644021
Phone/fax: (3812) 51 0087, 57 7021
E-mail: polyot@polyot.omsk.ru
Oleg Petrovich Dorofeev,
Director

SIBERIAN FEDERAL DISTRICT

VI

74. TOMSK REGION [70]

ECONOMIC MAP

YAMALO-NENETSKY
AUTONOMOUS DISTRICT

Noyabrsk
Vyngapuroyskoe

Taz

KRASNOYARSK

KHANTY-MANSIYSKY

Varyeganskoe

AUTONOMOUS

Vakh

DISTRICT

TERRITORY

Yenisey

Nizhnevartovsk

Strezhevoy
Aleksandrovskoe

Ob

Tym

Vasyugan

Narym

Kargasok

Ket

Myldzhino

Kolpashevo

Bely Yar

Luginetskoe

Mogochin

Baturino

Chulym

Bakchar

Asino

Seversk

TOMSK

Yaya

Anzhero-Sudzhensk

NOVOSIBIRSK

Kuybyshev

KEMEROVO

Tатарск

Chulym

NOVOSIBIRSK

KEMEROVO

Barabinsk

Iskitim

Leninsk-Kuznetsky

REGION

Lake Chany

REGION

PROCESSING INDUSTRY
- Non-ferrous metals
- Machine engineering and metal processing
- Chemicals and petrochemicals
- Forestry and timber
- Food and beverages

MINING INDUSTRY
- Oil
- Natural gas
- Iron ore

POWER PLANTS
- Thermal power plants

CROPS AND LIVESTOCK BREEDING
- Rye
- Saffron milk cap
- Meat and dairy cattle breeding

For almost half a century, the Tomsk Region with its numerous defense and nuclear facilities was closed to outside world. This corner of Siberia still draws a blank for many. Today, the lack of comprehensive and objective information is probably the main obstacle to investment in the Region.

In 2002, the Region's industrial growth rate and per capita investments placed the Tomsk Region near the top of the league table in the Siberian Federal District.

Russian fuel majors such as OAO Gazprom and NK YUKOS extract oil and gas in our Region. Russian petrochemicals giant Tomsk Petrochemicals Plant also operates in the Region. These companies are actively seeking and finding partners in South East Asia, which is clearly set to become the number one market of the 21st century. The Tomsk Region is actively seeking investors to develop its natural resources (a second oil and gas province is slated to be established in the Region) and forestry sector, with its potential annual timber yield of 10 million cubic meters. We hold the number one position in Russia in terms of lignite reserves, and second position in terms of peat reserves. The Region has rich deposits of iron ore, titanium, and zirconium. Half of Siberia's geothermal springs are located in the Region.

And yet the most valuable resource of our Region is the intellectual potential of our people. More than one hundred years ago, Asian Russia's first university was opened in the Tomsk, followed by an institute of technology. Today, one in five residents of the city of Tomsk is a student. Departments dedicated to the commercial evaluation of scientific research and student business centers have been opened at Tomsk's universities and research institutes. Research by Tomsk based scientists in the fields of new materials synthesis, information technology, biotechnology, and chemistry have won the acclaim of EU Tacis experts. The commercial potential of local science projects is estimated at around $1 billion by international experts.

Among the long-term investment projects worth mentioning are a project for the construction of a gas storage reservoir and pipeline to the Tomsk Petrochemicals Plant, and a project for the construction of a gas liquefaction plant. A project for the construction of a new paper mill in the Region is currently being drafted.

The Tomsk Region is free of political risks. The Region's stable political elite, the consensus between the various branches of power, and the regional legislation's liberal slant mean that for the third consecutive year, the Region has seen growth rates double the national average. This is in large part thanks to consistent and steady increases in exports. The Tomsk Region has a past to be proud of, work to do in the present, and confidence in its future.

Viktor Kress,
HEAD OF ADMINISTRATION (GOVERNOR) OF THE TOMSK REGION

SIBERIAN FEDERAL DISTRICT

VI

1. GENERAL INFORMATION

1.1. GEOGRAPHY
Situated in the south-eastern part of the Western Siberian Plain, the Tomsk Region covers a total area of 314,400 square kilometers. The Region borders the Tyumen, Omsk, Novosibirsk, and Kemerovo Regions and the Krasnoyarsk Territory.

1.2. CLIMATE
The Tomsk Region lies in the moderately continental climate zone. Air temperatures in January average –19.2°C, rising to +18.1°C in July. Annual precipitation reaches 450–590 mm.

1.3. POPULATION
According to preliminary 2002 census results, the population of the Tomsk Region is 1,046,000 people. The average population density is 3.3 people per square kilometer. The economically active population amounts to 555,000 people. The official unemployment rate in 2002 was 3.7%; the actual unemployment rate is 13.5%.

Demographically speaking, some 64.7% are of working age, 18.4% are below the statutory working age, and 16.9% are beyond the statutory working age.

The Tomsk Region's major urban centers are Tomsk with 487,700 inhabitants, Seversk with 115,700 inhabitants, and Storozhevoy with 43,500 inhabitants.

Population							TABLE 1
	1992	1997	1998	1999	2000	2001	2002
Total population, '000	1,086	1,075	1,074	1,072	1,068	1,065	1,046
Economically active population, '000	511	497	513	531	532	534	555

2. ADMINISTRATION

6, ul. Lenina, Tomsk, Tomsk Region, 634050
Phone: (3822) 51 0505, 51 0686, (reception 51 0001); fax: (3822) 51 0323, 51 0730
E-mail: ato@tomsk.gov.ru; http://www.tomsk.gov.ru

NAME	POSITION	CONTACT INFORMATION
Viktor Melkhiorovich KRESS	Head of Administration (Governor) of the Tomsk Region	Phone: (3822) 51 0686, 51 0813 Fax: (3822) 51 0730
Viacheslav Vladimirovich NAGOVITSIN	First Deputy Head of the Tomsk Regional Administration, Chairman of the Tomsk Region Government	Phone: (3822) 51 0990 Fax: (3822) 51 0394
Oksana Vitalyevna KOZLOVSKAYA	Deputy Head of the Tomsk Regional Administration for Economy, Investment, and State Property Management, Deputy Chairman of the Tomsk Region Government	Phone: (3822) 51 0564 Phone/fax: (3822) 51 0526
Vladislav Yuganovich BROK	Deputy Head of the Tomsk Regional Administration Head of the Department of Social and Economic Development of Rural Areas	Phone: (3822) 51 0714, 51 0150 Fax: (3822) 51 0714
Vladislav Ivanovich ZINCHENKO	Deputy Head of the Tomsk Regional Administration, Head of the Department of Science and Technology and Higher and Secondary Professional Education of the Tomsk Regional Administration	Phone/fax: (3822) 51 0619, 51 0818
Vladimir Vasilyevich GONCHAR	Deputy Head of the Tomsk Regional Administration for Construction, Housing and Communal Services, Energy, Communications, and Transport of the Tomsk Regional Administration	Phone: (3822) 51 0376 Fax: (3822) 51 0662
Andrei Alexandrovich TRUBITSIN	Acting Deputy Head of the Tomsk Regional Administration, Head of the Department of Industry and Timber of the Tomsk Regional Administration	Phone/fax: (3822) 51 0867

NAME	POSITION	CONTACT INFORMATION
Alexander Nikolaevich CHEREVKO	Head of the Tomsk Region's Representative Office to the Government of the Russian Federation	38, bld.1, ul. Dolgorukovskaya, Moscow 103030 Phone: (095) 973 2538/39, 200 3980, 299 3795 Fax: (095) 299 3795
Viktor Konstantinovich SHISHKIN	Chairman of the Committee for External Relations of the Tomsk Regional Administration	Phone: (3822) 51 0624 Fax: (3822) 51 2753
Inna Valeryevna DEMIDENKO	Chairman of the Committee for Investment Policy of the Tomsk Regional Administration	Phone: (3822) 51 0409

3. ECONOMIC POTENTIAL

3.1. 1997–2002 GROSS REGIONAL PRODUCT (GRP). INDUSTRY BREAKDOWN

2002 GRP came to $2,492.7 million, a 15.9% increase compared to 2001. Per capita GRP in 2001 was $2,019, rising to $2,384 in 2002.

3.2. MAJOR ECONOMIC GROWTH PROJECTIONS

Relatively rapid growth is expected in the coming years for the oil, non-ferrous metals, chemicals, and petrochemicals industries.

GRP trends in 1997–2002						TABLE 2
	1997	1998	1999	2000	2001*	2002*
GRP in current prices, $ million	3,526.4	2,151.3	1,173.0	1,555.8	2,150.9	2,492.7

*Estimates of the Tomsk Regional Administration

GRP industry breakdown in 1997–2002, % of total						TABLE 3
	1997	1998	1999	2000	2001*	2002*
GRP	100.0	100.0	100.0	100.0	100.0	100.0
Industry	34.2	38.4	31.4	36.8	37.8	38.1
Agriculture and forestry	6.8	7.2	8.1	7.2	5.7	4.7
Construction	8.1	9.5	6.6	6.9	7.9	8.1
Transport and communications	12.0	8.2	11.0	11.4	9.4	11.0
Trade and public catering	8.9	9.5	13.1	11.5	11.9	12.7
Other	30.0	27.2	29.8	26.2	27.3	25.4

*Estimates of the Tomsk Regional Administration

The **fuel industry** is set to develop due to increased oil and gas production at existing fields, the launching of new fields, and the restart of idle wells at existig fields.

Chemicals and petrochemicals are expected to expand by around 140%-150% on 2001 levels by 2005, when OAO Tomsk Petrochemicals Plant becomes fully operational.

The forestry and timber sector is expected to practically double industrial timber output to 5.5–7.0 million cubic meters annually by 2010.

The Tomsk Region's Innovation Strategy sets the following priority economic development objectives: new materials development technologies, biotechnologies, information technologies, and chemical technologies.

3.3. INDUSTRIAL OUTPUT IN 1997–2002 FOR MAJOR SECTORS OF ECONOMY

The Region's leading industries include: fuel, non-ferrous metals, chemicals and petrochemicals, machinery and metal processing, energy, forestry and timber, and food and beverages. The fuel and non-ferrous sectors account for over 50% of total output.

Oil. Two companies form the basis for the Region's oil industry: OAO VNK Tomskneft (a subsidiary of YUKOS) and OAO Vostokgazprom (a subsidiary of OAO Gazprom).

Industry breakdown of industrial output, 1997–2002, % of total						TABLE 4
	1997	1998	1999	2000	2001	2002*
Industry	100.0	100.0	100.0	100.0	100.0	100.0
Fuel	31.4	29.0	25.0	12.9	28.9	37.4
Non-ferrous metals	–	0.1	28.3	40.3	17.5	17.5
Machine engineering and metal processing	9.0	7.1	10.1	4.4	15.3	13.4
Chemicals and petrochemicals	25.2	33.4	7.9	0.1	13.1	8.3
Energy	13.9	12.8	10.5	25.7	9.0	9.4
Food and beverages	6.5	6.0	7.0	7.2	7.7	6.7
Construction materials	5.2	4.0	3.0	2.4	2.5	2.4
Forestry, timber, and pulp and paper	5.6	2.8	2.6	1.9	2.4	2.2
Flour, cereals, and mixed fodder	2.2	1.4	2.5	2.2	1.9	1.2
Light industry	0.4	0.3	0.3	0.3	0.3	0.3
Ferrous metals	0.2	0.2	0.2	0.7	0.2	0.1
Glass and porcelain	0.1	0.1	0.1	–	–	–

*Estimates of the Tomsk Regional Administration

Non-ferrous metals. The industry is represented by FGUP Siberian Chemical Plant, one of the largest nuclear centers in the world. The Plant focuses on the production of enriched uranium and uranium products. It also produces hi-tech products, including ultra-dispersing metal oxide powders, piezoceramics, and powerful magnets.

Machine engineering and metal processing. This sector produces general industrial products including mining equipment, electric motors, cable and wire, electric bulbs, bearings, metal cutting equipment, manometers, and semiconductors.

Chemicals and petrochemicals. The sector is represented by OAO Tomsk Chemicals Plant, one of the largest companies in Western Siberia, ZAO Methanol, one of the world's major methanol producers, and OAO Tomsk Rubber Footwear Plant.

Energy. OAO Tomskenergo forms the basis of the Region's energy sector. It includes thermal power stations and heating plants with a total capacity of 421 MW.

Forestry and timber processing. This industry also plays a significant role in the Region, despite its relatively small share of total output (2.2% in 2002 compared with 12.0% in 1990). The sector exports 26.2% of its total output.

3.4. FUEL AND ENERGY BALANCE (OUTPUT AND CONSUMPTION PER RESOURCE)

The Region imported around 50% of its energy consumption in 2001.

Fuel and energy sector production and consumption trends, 1997–2002						TABLE 5
	1997	1998	1999	2000	2001	2002
Electricity output, billion kWh	5.8	5.1	4.6	4.7	4.8	4.6
Oil output (including gas condensate), '000 tons	6,528.0	6,185.0	6,108.0	6,903.0	7,754.0	10,104.1
Gas extraction, million cubic meters	153.0	152.0	707.0	2,595.0	3,720.0	4,431.1
Electricity consumption, billion kWh	6.4	6.9	6.9	7.2	7.4	7.4
Natural gas consumption, million cubic meters	1,404.0	2,221.2	1,414.9	1,918.9	2,141.2	2,384.8

3.5. TRANSPORT INFRASTRUCTURE

Roads. The Region has 4,500 kilometers of public roads, including 3,500 kilometers of paved highway. The Northern Latitude Highway linking Perm – Khanty-Mansiysk – Surgut – Nizhnevartovsk – Tomsk is currently under construction. This road will join the northern oil and gas provinces of Western Siberia with southern regions and provide links to western and eastern regions of the country.

Railroads. The Tomsk Region has 404 kilometers of railroads. The Bely Yar – Tomsk – Taiga mainline links the Region to the Trans-Siberian railroad.

Airports. The Tomsk Region has three airports: the Tomsk, Strezhevoy, and Kolpashevo. Annual passenger turnover is around 800,000 people. The Tomsk airport is currently under reconstruction.

River transport. The Region's main naviga-ble waterways are the rivers Ob, Tom, Ket, Chulym, Vasyugan, and Parabel. Navigation is open for 170–180 days in the year.

3.6. MAIN NATURAL RESOURCES: RESERVES AND EXTRACTION IN 2002.

Fuel and energy resources. Potential (extrapo-lated) reserves of hydrocarbons are estimated at 5.5 bil-lion tons, peat – 28.7 billion tons (Russia's No. 2 region in terms of peat reserves), and brown coal – 74.7 billion tons (Russia's No. 1 region in terms of coal reserves). Recoverable reserves of oil are 1,449 million tons, and 632 billion cubic meters of natural gas.

The Region is home to 101 hydrocarbon fields, including 82 oil fields, 13 oil and gas condensate fields, and six gas condensate fields. For the purpose of hydrocarbon exploration and extraction, 83 fields have been assigned under natural resources utiliza-tion agreements. Of those, some 46 fields are cur-rently in production. The Region's oil and gas compa-nies have more than 20 years worth of reserves.

Ore deposits. The Region has large fields of iron and titanium ores. The projected reserves of the Bach-kayarskoye iron ore field are estimated at 110 billion tons.

Titanium ores have been explored in the Tugans-koye and Georgievskoye gravel deposits. Zirconium reserves stand at 1,380,000 tons, ilmenite – 3,400,000 tons, and leucoxene and rutile – 600,000 tons.

Water reserves. The Region has 573 rivers and 35 lakes. The Ob is the Region's largest river. Sturgeon and white-fish spawn sites are found in the upper Ob.

The Tomsk Region produces mineral water under the Chazhemto and Omega brands. The Region is also home to hot hydrogen sulphide sources.

Forest resources. The Tomsk Region is home to multiple varieties of forests with total forest cover ex-ceeding 29.2 million hectares. Total timber reserves stand at 2.6 billion cubic meters, including conifers at 1.6 billion cubic meters. The Region has a potential total annual timber output of 28.6 million cubic meters, including conifers of 8.4 million cubic meters. Currently, the Region produces over 2 million cubic meters of timber a year.

4. TRADE OPPORTUNITIES

4.1. MAIN GOODS PRODUCED IN THE REGION

Oil and natural gas. 2002 oil output increa-sed by 30% on 2001 to 10.1 million tons. 2002 pro-duction of natural gas fuel rose 19% compared to the previous year to 4,431 million cubic meters.

Chemicals. 2002 methanol production was 566,000 tons; polyethylene and polypropylene output was 149,300 tons and 98,800 tons, respectively.

Machinery. In 2002, the Region produced 22.2 million bearings, 109.9 million bulbs, and 80,300 alter-nating current electric motors. In 2002, the Region pro-duced some 4,426 kilometers of telephone cable.

Timber. In 2002, the Region produced 807,100 cubic meters of industrial lumber and 192,800 cubic meters of sawn timber.

4.2. MAIN EXPORTS, INCLUDING EXTRA-CIS

The Region's export decreased by 9.6% year-on-year in 2002. The Region exported a total of

$592.7 million worth of goods, with CIS exports accounting for 6.4% of the total and extra-CIS exports accounting for 93.6%.

The bulk of the Region's exports is represent-ed by chemicals and petrochemicals (polypropy-lene, polyethylene, methanol), machinery (metering instruments, bearings, cable and wire, and other goods), wood and timber goods, and crude oil.

Major importers of the Region's goods (2002) include the USA (34.2%), China (13.1%), South Korea (8.2%), and Finland (6.8%).

4.3. MAIN IMPORTS, INCLUDING EXTRA-CIS

The Region imported some $40.9 million worth of goods in 2002. The bulk of the Region's imports was represented by machinery, equipment, transport vehi-cles (61.5 %), chemical products (23.7 %), metals and metal goods (5.3 %), and food and beverages (2.7 %).

Major exporters to the Region include the USA, Germany, the UK, Hungary, Kazakhstan, South Korea, Uzbekistan, and Italy.

SIBERIAN FEDERAL DISTRICT

VI

Major export and import entities		TABLE 6
ENTITY	ADDRESS	PHONE, FAX, E-MAIL
OOO PFK Astra	46, ul. Pushkina, Tomsk, Tomsk Region, 634003	Phone (3822) 21 3355, 21 2702 Fax: (3822) 21 4803
ZAO Sibenergoresurs	65/1, ul. Pushkina, Tomsk, Tomsk Region, 634006	Phone/fax: (3822) 65 9556, 65 9566, 77 9783 E-mail: ser@mail.tomsknet.ru
ZAO Rosenergokomplekt	13/1, ul. Nakhimova Tomsk, Tomsk Region, 634034	Phone/fax: (3822) 42 3333, 42 5585 E-mail: reckom@mail.tomsknet.ru Http://www.rek.tomsk.ru

5. INVESTMENT OPPORTUNITIES

5.1. INVESTMENTS IN 1992–2002 (BY INDUSTRY SECTOR), INCLUDING FOREIGN INVESTMENT

The following factors determine the investment appeal of the Tomsk Region:

- Tax benefits for investors;
- Its natural resources and raw materials (fuel and energy, timber);
- Its advanced high-tech sector;
- Its highly qualified population.

5.2. CAPITAL INVESTMENT

The Region's industry accounts for the bulk of capital investments in the Region.

Capital investment by industry sector, $ million						TABLE 7
	1997	1998	1999	2000	2001	2002
Total capital investment, $ million	784.1	536.9	245.5	330.8	490.5	454.3
Including major industries (% of total):						
Industry	63.8	74.2	73.2	67.4	71.5	70.8
Agriculture and forestry*	1.4	1.6	1.7	1.5	1.0	1.4
Construction	1.1	1.1	0.5	1.3	1.1	1.1
Transport and communications	12.5	9.5	10.9	10.7	15.7	17.2
Trade and public catering	0.2	0.3	0.1	0.5	0.2	0.1
Other	21.0	13.3	13.6	18.6	10.5	9.4

*Data for the agriculture sector only

Foreign investment trends in 1995–2002						TABLE 8
	1995*–1997	1998	1999	2000	2001	2002
Foreign investment, $ million	202.1	97.0	18.5	25.1	24.6	28.6
Including FDI, $ million	3.7	0.02	1.7	0.6	12.8	16.3

*Statistical data gathered since 1995

5.3. MAJOR ENTERPRISES (INCLUDING ENTERPRISES WITH FOREIGN INVESTMENT)

The Tomsk Region is home to more than 250 companies with foreign investment

5.4. MOST ATTRACTIVE SECTORS FOR INVESTMENT

Oil and gas is the most attractive industry for investment. In 2002, capital investment in the sector reached 57% of total investments in the Region's economy.

5.5. CURRENT LEGISLATION ON INVESTOR TAX EXEMPTIONS AND PRIVILEGES

The Tomsk Region has passed the laws encouraging investment activity in the Region, including:

- On State Support to Investment Activity in the Tomsk Region;
- On the Procedure for Granting Additional Exemptions from Regional Taxes and Fiscal Payments;
- On the Development Budget of the Tomsk Region;

Largest enterprises of the Tomsk Region	TABLE 9
COMPANY	SECTOR
OAO Tomskneft VNK (NK YUKOS)	Oil and gas
OAO Vostokgazprom	Natural gas
FGUP Siberian Chemical Plant	Non-ferrous metals, chemicals
OAO Tomsk Petrochemical Plant	Petrochemicals
ZAO Methanol	Petrochemicals
OAO Tomskenergo	Energy

• On Investment Tax Credit in the Tomsk Region.

Investors engaged in investment projects that are crucial to the social and economic development of the Region are granted:

• Tax exemptions on regional tax components;
• Investment tax credits;
• Government guarantees for loans, or preferential financing.

Separate tax exemptions are provided to entities with foreign investment and leasing companies.

5.6. FEDERAL AND REGIONAL ECONOMIC AND SOCIAL DEVELOPMENT PROGRAMS FOR THE TOMSK REGION

Federal targeted programs. In 2002, the Region implemented 25 federal targeted programs, of which the most important were: Children of Russia, 2003–2006, Older Generation, 2002–2004, Energy Saving Economy, 2002–2005 and through 2010 and

Elimination of Differences in the Social and Economic Development of regions of the Russian Federation, 2002–2010 and through 2015.

Regional programs. The comprehensive targeted Tomsk Region Program for Social and Economic Development through 2005 plays an important role in the social and economic development of the Region. The Program's objective is to develop the Region's strengths and advantages and modernize and restructure the Region's economy with a focus on sectors ensuring its competitiveness.

The Region is also implementing a comprehensive targeted Tomsk Region Timber Industry Development Program through 2010 aimed at increasing timber output and raising investments for the construction of a plant near Asino for the production of chemical and thermo-mechanical pulp from low-grade conifer timber, and the Tomsk Region Comprehensive Small Business Support Program, 2001–2003.

Regional entities responsible for raising investment		*TABLE 10*
ENTITY	ADDRESS	PHONE, FAX, E-MAIL
Direct Investment Institute Fund	Office 306, 11, 1st Khvostov per., Moscow, 109180	Phone: (095) 238 4763, 230 7852, 777 3456 Fax: (095) 238 4763 E-mail: info@ivr.ru
OOO Diapazonfinservice	Office 301, 53, ul. Belinskogo, Tomsk, Tomsk Region, 634034	Phone: (3822) 55 5038 Fax: (3822) 55 7840 E-mail: dfs@dfs.ru; http://www.dfs.ru
OAO Tomsk Investment and Industrial Company	Office 90, 55, pr. Lenina, Tomsk, Tomsk Region, 634050	Phone: (3822) 53 0450, 52 6430 E-mail: timc@timc.tomsk.ru

6. INVESTMENT PROJECTS

Industry sector and project description	1) Expected results 2) Amount and term of investment 3) Form of financing[1] 4) Documentation[2]	Contact information
1	2	3

MINING		
74R001 ■ ● ◆		OOO Tomsk Mining Company
Development of the Kamenskoye marmorized limestone field. Project goal: to introduce local construction materials to the market (concrete, ground limestone, facing tile, and crushed stone).	1) 1,000,000 tons a year 2) $2.2 million/3.1 years 3) E, L 4) BP	232, pr. Frunze, Tomsk, Tomsk Region, 634021 Phone: (3822) 24 4164, 24 4412 Fax: (3822) 24 4164 E-mail: TomGDK@narod.ru Http://www.tomgdk.narod.ru Mikhail Stepanovich Parovinchak, CEO

[1] L – Loan, E – Equity, Leas. – Leasing, JV – Joint Venture
[2] BP – Business Plan, FS – Feasibility Study

1	2	3

74R002 ■ ● ▲

Development of the Barantsevskoye facing stone field.
Project goal: to introduce local construction materials to the market (facing stone, construction stone, facing tile, and crushed stone).

1) 500,000 tons
2) $2.5 million/2.8 years
3) E, L
4) FS

OOO Tomsk Mining Company
232, pr. Frunze, Tomsk,
Tomsk Region, 634021
Phone: (3822) 24 4164, 24 4412
Fax: (3822) 24 4164
E-mail: TomGDK@narod.ru
Http://www.tomgdk.narod.ru
Mikhail Stepanovich Parovinchak,
CEO

ENERGY

74R003 ● ◆

Construction and operation of a gas turbine power plant on the basis of the Silginsky gas condensate deposits.
Project goal: to set up new generating capacity.

1) 100 MW
2) $89.9 million/n/a
3) L, JV
4) BP

OAO Tomskenergo
36, pr. Kirova, Tomsk,
Tomsk Region, 634041
Phone: (3822) 55 4645
Fax: (3822) 53 6647
E-mail: adm@tomske.elektra.ru
Nikolai Alexandrovich Vyatkin, CEO

FERROUS METALS

74R004 ● ◆

Production of nitrogen based alloy fusions.
Project goal: to introduce new products to the market (nitro-chrome, nitrogenized manganese, nitrogenized ferro-niobium, nitrogenized ferrovanadium, and nitrogenized ferrosilicum).

1) 600 tons a year
2) $2.5 million/2 years
3) L ($0.2 million)
4) BP

Tomsk Research Center of Siberian
Branch of the Russian Academy
of Sciences, Structural Macrokinetics Dept
10/3, pr. Akademichesky, Tomsk,
Tomsk Region, 634021
Phone: (3822) 25 9702, 25 9471
Fax: (3822) 25 9838
E-mail: Maks@fisman.tomsk.ru
Yury Mikhailovich Maksimov,
Head of Department

CONSTRUCTION MATERIALS

74R005 ● ◆

Foamed glass production.
Project goal: to increase production and improve quality through upgrade of heat insulation facilities.

1) 9,000 cubic meters a year
2) $0.2 million/0.6 years
3) L
4) BP

OAO Tomsk Housing Company
79/1, ul. Yelizarovykh, Tomsk,
Tomsk Region, 634021
Phone: (3822) 24 2611, 24 2603
Fax: (3822) 24 2603
E-mail: Dsk@Post.Tomica.ru
Alexander Karlovich Shpeter,
CEO

SCIENCE AND INNOVATION

74R006 ■ ● ◆

Production of new generation cellular ceramic tube.
Project goal: to market a new product for the petrochemicals, natural gas, chemicals, and metals industries.

1) 3 million pieces a year
2) $2.5 million/2 years
3) E, L
4) BP

Tomsk Research Center of Siberian
Branch of the Russian Academy
of Science, Structural Macrokinetics Dept
10/3, pr. Akademichesky, Tomsk,
Tomsk Region, 634021
Phone: (3822) 25 9702
Fax: (3822) 25 9838
E-mail: Maks@fisman.tomsk.ru
Yury Mikhailovich Maksimov,
Department Head

1	2	3

74R007

| Production of solar quality silicon and solar energy devices. Project goal: to introduce new products to the market. | 1) 500 tons a year/annual production of 1 MW
 2) $1.6 million/2.3 years
 3) L ($1.3 million)
 4) BP | FGUP Semiconductors Research and Development Institute
 99 a, ul. Krasnoarmeyskaya, Tomsk,
 Tomsk Region, 634034
 Phone: (3822) 48 8118, 48 8135
 Fax: (3822) 55 5089
 E-mail: Reaper2@mail.ru
 Eduard Fedorovich Yauk,
 Director |

MACHINE ENGINEERING AND METAL PROCESSING

74R008

| Production of long-distance radiolocation systems. Project goal: to launch a new product. | 1) 400 units a year
 2) $0.6 million/1 year
 3) E, L ($0.08 million)
 4) BP | OAO Tomsk Metering Instruments Plant
 51, Ul. Voykova, Tomsk,
 Tomsk Region, 634009
 Phone: (3822) 72 2476, 72 2350
 Fax: (3822) 72 2476
 E-mail: tzia@tomsk.ru
 Vasily Nikolaevich Zharzhevsky,
 CEO |

SIBERIAN FEDERAL DISTRICT

VI

75. CHITA REGION [75]

ECONOMIC MAP

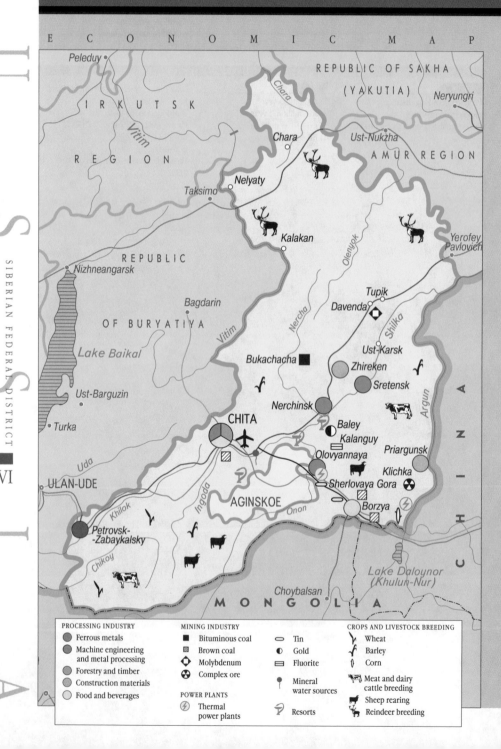

REPUBLIC OF SAKHA (YAKUTIA)

Neryungri

IRKUTSK

REGION

AMUR REGION

Peleduy

Chara

Ust-Nukzha

Nelyaty

Taksimo

Yerofey Pavlovich

Kalakan

Olenyok

Nercha

Nizhneangarsk

REPUBLIC

Bagdarin

Tupik

Davenda

Shilka

OF BURYATIYA

Vitim

Ust-Karsk

Lake Baikal

Bukachacha

Zhireken

Sretensk

Ust-Barguzin

Nerchinsk

Argun

Turka

CHITA

Baley

Kalanguy

CHINA

Olovyannaya

Priargunsk

Uda

Klichka

ULAN-UDE

Sherlovaya Gora

Khilok

AGINSKOE

Borzya

Ingoda

Onon

Petrovsk-Zabaykalsky

Chikoy

Lake Daloynor (Khulun-Nur)

Choybalsan

MONGOLIA

PROCESSING INDUSTRY	MINING INDUSTRY		CROPS AND LIVESTOCK BREEDING
● Ferrous metals	■ Bituminous coal	⬭ Tin	Wheat
● Machine engineering and metal processing	▨ Brown coal	◐ Gold	Barley
● Forestry and timber	◈ Molybdenum	⊟ Fluorite	Corn
● Construction materials	☢ Complex ore		Meat and dairy cattle breeding
● Food and beverages		● Mineral water sources	Sheep rearing
	POWER PLANTS		Reindeer breeding
	⚡ Thermal power plants	⚲ Resorts	

Everything in the Trans-Baikal region is immense and grand in scale: abundant natural resources, the green ocean of the taiga, boundless steppe, mighty and full-flowing rivers, lofty mountains, rosemary clad hills...

The development and colonization of these vast lands has historically been inextricably linked with the protection of Russia's frontiers, the building of the famous Trans-Siberian Railway, and the exploration of natural resources. Of special interest is the development of mining in the area.

Dozens of placer and rock deposits of gold, copper, zinc, and lead, in addition to coal, zeolite, and magnesite fields have been explored in the Region. We supply almost all of Russia's uranium and tungsten, two thirds of the country's tantalum output, and one third of total fluor-spar and molybdenum output. The vast Chineisky, Udokansky, Katuginsky, Apsatsky, and Golevsky fields alone serve as a basis for industrial conglomerates within the Region. National and local authorities at all levels understand and recognize that the development of the natural resources of the Chita Region will have profound effect on the Russian economy. Russian businesses are already showing interest in the riches of the Trans-Baikal region, and joint inter-regional projects are beginning to see the light of day.

Our Region's geopolitical location is also highly important. The Chita Region has about 2,000 kilometers of international frontier with two countries, China and Mongolia. This offers favorable conditions for trade and economic cooperation in border areas. Major transport throughways cross the Chita Region towards the Russian Far East. In the future, these may be used to ship Russian goods to Asia-Pacific countries, and primarily China and Mongolia.

Most cargo shipments between Russia and China pass via Zabaikalsk, the largest international road and railroad border checkpoint in Eastern Russia. Today Zabaikalsk is becoming a unique place for capital investment and inter-regional and international cooperation. A bridge border-crossing over the Amur River was opened last year, connecting Russia to China. Another bridge over the Amur at Pokrovka (Russia) and Loguhue (China) is slated to be opened in the future. The Zabaikalsk – Manchuria border crossing provides the shortest route for shipments to Europe. Very soon, oil and gas will flow through Zabaikalsk from Siberia to China, and onwards to Asia-Pacific countries.

All of this makes our Region one of the most promising regions in Russia for investment.

We in the Chita Region strive also to preserve the historical and natural riches of our Region, to make it attractive to visit not only for future investors, but also for tourists. Both will be surprised to find here an ecologically clean environment, a diverse biosphere, and exotic, and occasionally unique, landscapes. We have everything needed for adventure tourism and memorable vacations: the deserts of Charsky Sands, the Kodar Glaciers, the Udokan volcanos, and myriad thermal and mineral springs.

Ravil Geniatulin,
HEAD OF ADMINISTRATION (GOVERNOR) OF THE CHITA REGION

1. GENERAL INFORMATION

1.1. GEOGRAPHY
The Chita Region is located in south-eastern Siberia and covers a total area of 431,500 square kilometers. To the north the Region borders the Irkutsk and Amur Regions and the Republic of Sakha (Yakutia), to the west – the Republic of Buryatia, and to the south – Mongolia and China.

1.2. CLIMATE
The Chita Region enjoys a severe continental climate. The average air temperature in January is –32°C, rising to +18.8°C in July. The average annual precipitation exceeds 700 mm.

1.3. POPULATION
According to preliminary 2002 census results, the Region's population totaled 1,156,000 people.

The average population density is 2.7 people per square kilometer. The economically active population amounts to 518,000 people. While 2002 official unemployment level stood at 4.8%, the actual rate is 14.4 %.

Demographically speaking, some 62.5% are of statutory working age, 22.5% are below the statutory working age, and 15% are beyond the statutory working age.

As of 2002, the Chita Region's major urban centers were Chita with 317,800 inhabitants, Krasnokamensk with 60,200 inhabitants, Borzya with 31,400 inhabitants, and Petrovsk-Zabaikalsky with 23,400 inhabitants.

Population							TABLE 1	
	1992	1997	1998	1999	2000	2001	2002	
Total population, '000	1,326	1,284	1,274	1,266	1,256	1,247	1,156	
Economically active population, '000	680	592	569	566	565	543	518	

2. ADMINISTRATION

**8, ul. Tchaikovskogo, Chita, Chita Region, 672021. Phone: (3022) 35 2184, 35 2096; fax: (3022) 35 8251
E-mail: adobl@mail.chita.ru; http://www.adm.chita.ru**

NAME	POSITION	CONTACT INFORMATION
Ravil Faritovich GENIATULIN	Head of Administration (Governor) of the Chita Region	Phone: (3022) 35 3493 Fax: (3022) 35 8248
Vladimir Viktorovich OKUNEV	First Deputy Head of the Chita Regional Administration	Phone: (3022) 32 5279 E-mail: adobl@mail.chita.ru
Bolot Vandanovich AYUSHIEV	Deputy Head of the Chita Regional Administration, Head of the Financial Department	Phone: (3022) 23 6021
Nikolai Illarionovich GANTIMUROV	Deputy Head of the Chita Regional Administration for Agriculture and Food	Phone: (3022) 23 3872
Tatyana Ivanovna MAIZLINGER	Deputy Head of the Chita Regional Administration for Economy	Phone: (3022) 26 8979, 23 2625
Vyacheslav Mikhailovich PETUKHOV	Deputy Head of the Chita Regional Administration for Fuel, Energy, and Mining	Phone: (3022) 35 4658
Nikolai Innokentyevich SEMENOV	Deputy Head of the Chita Regional Administration for Industry, Transport, Roads, and Housing and Communal Services	Phone: (3022) 35 5278
Nadezhda Innokentyevna YELUKHINA	Acting Chairman of the State Property Management Committee of the Chita Region	Phone: (3022) 32 4419

NAME	POSITION	CONTACT INFORMATION
Viktor Mikhailovich STOLYAROV	Deputy Head of the Chita Regional Administration, Head of the Representative Office of the Chita Regional Administration at the RF Government in Moscow	Phone: (095) 203 3328 Fax: (095) 203 4539
Alexander Nikolaevich NOVOSELTSEV	Department of International Cooperation and External Economic Relations and Tourism of the Chita Region	Phone: (3022) 23 8154 Fax: (3022) 35 8149 E-mail: crafed@mail.chita.ru

3. ECONOMIC POTENTIAL

3.1. 1997–2002 GROSS REGIONAL PRODUCT (GRP). INDUSTRY BREAKDOWN

2002 gross regional product amounted to $1,293 million, which constitutes 5.4% growth year-on-year. The growth was achieved thanks to transport and communications, which accounted for 33.9% of GRP, and industrial output (18.2% of total GRP). Per capita GRP amounted to $984 in 2001 and $1,119 in 2002.

GRP trends in 1997–2002						TABLE 2
	1997	1998	1999	2000	2001*	2002*
GRP in comparable prices, $ million	2,177.0	1,324.4	858.8	1,121.5	1,227.2	1,292.9

*Estimates of the Chita Regional Administration

GRP industry breakdown in 1997–2002, % of total						TABLE 3
	1997	1998	1999	2000	2001*	2002*
GRP	100.0	100.0	100.0	100.0	100.0	100.0
Industry	23.9	22.6	22.0	16.8	17.8	18.2
Agriculture and forestry	11.9	9.4	12.5	12.0	10.7	11.0
Construction	7.3	6.5	6.2	12.4	10.8	8.2
Transport and communications	23.0	25.1	30.8	32.6	30.6	33.9
Trade and public catering	8.5	7.7	6.1	5.3	6.4	7.4
Other	25.4	27.1	20.5	20.4	21.1	19.4
Net taxes on output	–	1.6	1.9	0.5	2.6	1.9

*Estimates of the Chita Regional Administration.

3.2. MAJOR ECONOMIC GROWTH PROJECTIONS

The Program for the Social and Economic Development of the Chita Region, 2003–2005 sets forth the following major development objectives: streamlining industrial structure, improving competitiveness of industrial and agricultural output, creating a favorable investment climate in the Region, improving transport efficiency and safety, and supporting local producers.

3.3. INDUSTRIAL OUTPUT IN 1997–2002 FOR MAJOR SECTORS OF ECONOMY

The leading industrial sectors of the Chita Region are non-ferrous metals, energy, and food and beverages. These account for a combined 82.4% of total industrial output.

Non-ferrous metals. The sector accounts for 39.7% of total industrial output. Major companies within the sector are OAO Priargunskoe Production Mining and Chemical Company, OAO Zabaikalsky Ore Dressing Plant, OAO Zhirekensky Ore Dressing Plant, and OOO Kvarts Gold Prospectors. The Region is home to over 40 gold-mining companies.

Energy. This sector accounts for 33.8% of total industrial output. The main companies within the sector are OAO Chitaenergo, Kharanorskaya HEP Station, and the Atomic Energy Ministry's Krasnokamennaya Power Station.

Food and beverages. This sector accounts for 8.9% of total industrial output. The main focus areas are meat and dairy products of various degrees of processing, beer, alcoholic beverages, and confectionery. Among the largest companies are ZAO Zabaikalagrobusiness, ZAO Chita Springs, OAO Chita Dairy Plant, OAO Extra, and OAO Kenon.

SIBERIAN FEDERAL DISTRICT

VI

Industry breakdown of industrial output in 1997–2002, % of total						TABLE 4
	1997	1998	1999	2000	2001	2002*
Industry	100.0	100.0	100.0	100.0	100.0	100.0
Non-ferrous metals	18.8	24.2	39.0	40.3	36.9	39.7
Energy	38.6	37.2	26.4	25.7	28.3	33.8
Food and beverages	6.8	7.3	7.3	7.2	7.8	8.9
Coal	16.1	14.6	13.0	12.9	13.6	7.3
Machine engineering and metal processing	5.0	4.4	4.1	4.4	6.2	3.8
Forestry, timber, and pulp and paper	2.4	1.9	1.4	1.9	1.7	2.8
Construction materials	3.7	3.0	2.2	2.4	1.2	1.3
Flour, cereals, and mixed fodder	2.9	2.6	3.3	2.2	1.7	1.2
Light industry	0.7	0.4	0.6	0.3	0.4	0.5
Ferrous metals	2.3	1.9	0.7	0.7	1.7	0.2

*Estimates of the Chita Regional Administration

Coal. The sector accounts for 7.3% of total industrial output. Annual coal extraction amounts to 12-14 million tons. The Kharanorsky open cast pit produces over 50% of all the coal mined in the Region.

3.4. FUEL AND ENERGY BALANCE (OUTPUT AND CONSUMPTION PER RESOURCE)

The fuel and energy sector is represented by the electricity and coal sub-sectors. The Chita Region is an energy deficit region. As of 2002, local output satisfied 87.5% of demand.

3.5. TRANSPORT INFRASTRUCTURE

Roads. The Region has 9,700 kilometers of paved public highway. Most roads cross the central and south-eastern parts of the Region, providing access to the Trans-Siberian railroad. Construction work on the Amur highway linking Chita and Khabarovsk is soon to be completed.

Railroads. The Chita Region has 2,400 kilometers of railroads. The railway network consists of the Trans-Baikal section of the Trans-Siberian and Baikal – Amur railroads.

Fuel and energy sector production and consumption trends, 1997–2002						TABLE 5
	1997	1998	1999	2000	2001	2002*
Electricity output, billion kWh	5.0	5.2	5.9	5.9	5.3	5.6
Coal extraction, million tons	11.7	9.3	12.4	13.2	14.3	10.5
Electricity consumption, billion kWh	6.5	6.0	6.4	6.6	6.7	6.4
Coal consumption, million tons	9.5	9.3	10.2	10.0	8.5	7.0

*Estimates of the Chita Regional Administration

Airports. Chita is served by an international airport. The Region is crossed by trans-polar air routes (above the Arctic Ocean).

River transport. During the navigable period, freight and passengers are transported along the Shilka river.

3.6. MAIN NATURAL RESOURCES: RESERVES AND EXTRACTION IN 2002

The Region is rich in coal, ferrous metals (estimated reserves are 38 billion tons and proven reserves are two billion tons), non-ferrous metals, precious (gold) and rare earth (zeolite, magnesite, and tantalum) metals, uranium (200,000 tons), raw chemical materials, gems and semi-precious

stones, and building materials. The Region has vast forest reserves of 32 million hectares.

Coal. The Chita Region has registered 24 industrial coal deposits and several dozen potential coal deposits with 6.9 billion tons of reserves. Total reserves of black coal amount to 2 billion tons and brown coal – 2.2 billion tons (the Kharanorskoye, Tataurovskoye, and Urtuiskoye deposits). The Apsatskoye and Chitkandinskoye coal deposits are rich in natural gas. Total methane reserves concentrated in coal deposits reach 63–65 billion cubic meters.

Non-ferrous metals. The largest copper deposit is Udokanskoye with 20 million tons of reserves. The Region has discovered promising deposits of lead and zinc ores (2 million tons), molybdenum (1.5 million tons), tungsten (300,000 tons), and ore tin.

Gems and semi-precious stones. The Region has over 400 deposits of some 50 types of raw gemstones: beryl (25 tons), colored tourmaline (115 tons), topaz (12.7 tons), and rock crystal (146.9 tons). The Region has explored potential deposits of chrysolite, corundum, spinel, andalusite, spodumene, nephrite, rhodonite, fire opal, jasper, and other semi-precious stones.

4. TRADE OPPORTUNITIES

4.1. MAIN GOODS
PRODUCED IN THE REGION
Energy. 2002 electricity output grew 3.7% year-on-year to 5,560.1 million kWh.

Coal. The Region extracted 10.5 million tons of coal in 2002 (26.6% decrease year-on-year).

Construction materials. Wall building material output totaled 31.3 million bricks (16.8% growth) and 25,600 cubic meters of reinforced concrete assemblies and goods (4.1% decrease).

Machine engineering and metal processing. 2002 output of refrigeration units totaled 21 (40% decrease), 523 air and gas compressors (37.7% decrease), 40 mining loading trucks (360% increase), and 161 electrical bridge cranes (0.6% decrease).

Forestry and timber. Industrial timber output totaled 276,700 cubic meters in 2002 (12.4% increase), and lumber output reached 87,400 cubic meters (24.9% increase).

Food and beverages. 2002 output totaled: 4,000 tons of sausage (240% increase), 8,400 tons of milk (no change), 39,400 tons of bread and bakery (6.9% decrease), 2,600 tons of confectionery (8.3% increase), and 738,000 decaliters of non-alcoholic beverages (19.8% increase).

4.2. EXPORTS, INCLUDING EXTRA-CIS
The Chita Region's 2002 exports amounted to $87.5 million. Extra-CIS and CIS exports accounted for 99% and 1%, respectively. The Region's main trade partners are China (82%), France (10%), and Mongolia (2%).

The main types of goods exported by the Region are timber (74%) and chemicals (15%).

4.3. IMPORTS, INCLUDING EXTRA-CIS
2002 imports totaled $47.1 million. The main types of imported goods are food and agricultural raw materials (74%) and machinery, equipment, and transportation vehicles (8%). In 2002, food imports increased significantly: meat and meat products (600%), fruit and vegetables (doubled). Machinery and equipment imports rose by 180%.

4.4. MAJOR REGIONAL EXPORT
AND IMPORT ENTITIES
Due to the specific features of trade in the Region, export and import operations are performed mainly by industrial companies.

Major regional export and import entities		*TABLE 6*
ENTITY	ADDRESS	PHONE, FAX, E-MAIL
OAO Priargunskoye Production Mining and Chemical Company	Krasnokamensk, Chita Region, 674665	Phone: (30243) 25 110, 25 000 Fax: (30243) 25 141
State Unitary Company Chita Food	13, ul. Amurskaya, Chita, Chita Region, 672010	Phone/fax: (3022) 26 4813
ZAO Chita Springs	1, ul. Promyshlennaya, Chita, Chita Region, 672020	Phone: (3022) 32 6487, 32 2183 Fax: (3022) 32 6493
OOO Furniture Company Rassvet	5, ul. Sovetskaya, Novopavlovka, Petrovsk-Zabaikalsky District, Chita Region, 673120	Phone: (30236) 22 619

5. INVESTMENT OPPORTUNITIES

5.1. INVESTMENTS IN 1992–2002
(BY INDUSTRY SECTOR),
INCLUDING FOREIGN INVESTMENTS
The following factors determine the investment appeal of the Chita Region:

• Its advantageous geographic location (proximity to Pacific Rim markets, and convenient location for developing trade and economic links with China and Mongolia);

• Its unique mineral resource base;

• Legislation providing for protection of investor rights and preferential taxation.

5.2. CAPITAL INVESTMENT

Transport and communications, energy, and non-ferrous metals account for the lion's share of capital investment.

5.3. MAJOR ENTERPRISES (INCLUDING ENTERPRISES WITH FOREIGN INVESTMENT)

As of January 1, 2003, the Chita Region hosted some 175 companies with foreign investment.

Capital investment by industry sector, $ million						TABLE 7
	1997	1998	1999	2000	2001	2002
Total capital investment	337.5	180.2	129.2	242.1	309.1	170.7
Including major industries (% of total)						
Industry	42.9	28.4	26.1	19.1	28.4	22.9
Agriculture and forestry	1.7	2.0	1.6	0.8	0.7	1.7
Construction	2.0	0.7	0.2	0.1	0.3	0.2
Transport and communications	19.4	47.0	57.9	70.6	60.5	51.2
Trade and public catering	2.0	0.1	0.1	0.1	0.3	–
Other	32.0	21.8	14.1	9.3	9.8	24.0

Foreign investment trends in 1996–2002					TABLE 8
	1996–1997	1998	1999	2000	2001	2002
Foreign investment, $ million	0.9	12.5	–	0.4	6.0	0.2
Including FDI, $ million	0.9	–	–	0.3	0.1	0.2

Largest enterprises of the Chita Region	TABLE 9
COMPANY	SECTOR
Kharanorskaya HEPS (a RAO UES of Russia subsidiary)	Energy
OAO Chitaugol	Coal
OAO Mining Equipment Plant	Machine engineering
OAO Priargunskoye Production Mining and Chemical Company	Non-ferrous metals
OAO Zabaikalsky Ore Dressing Plant	Non-ferrous metals
OAO Zhirekensky Ore Dressing Plant	Non-ferrous metals
OOO Furniture Company Rassvet	Forestry and timber
OAO Dauria ChMDK	Furniture
ZAO Chita Springs	Food and beverages
ZAO Zabaikalagrobusiness	Food and beverages

5.4. MOST ATTRACTIVE SECTORS FOR INVESTMENT

According to the Chita Regional Administration, the most potentially appealing sectors for investors are non-ferrous metals, forestry and timber, machine engineering, energy, coal, and food and beverages.

5.5. CURRENT LEGISLATION ON INVESTOR TAX EXEMPTIONS AND PRIVILEGES

The Chita Region has passed the following laws and regulatory acts with a view to improving its investment appeal:

• On State Support to Investment Activity in the Chita Region (2001); and

• On the Attraction of Foreign Investment into the Regional Economy (2001).

In addition to these laws, the Governor of the Chita Region passed several resolutions in 2001-2002 guaranteeing protection of investor rights, providing privileged tax treatment and preferential loan interest, and setting forth provisions on investment tenders.

5.6. FEDERAL AND REGIONAL ECONOMIC AND SOCIAL DEVELOPMENT PROGRAMS FOR THE CHITA REGION

Federal targeted programs. The Program for the Economic and Social Development of the Far East and Trans-Baikal Region, 1996-2005 and through 2010 has a total budget of $783.4 million and aims to create conditions conducive to stable economic growth in the Region, including its priority sectors, a favorable investment climate, and social welfare.

Regional entities responsible for raising investment		TABLE 10
ENTITY	ADDRESS	PHONE, FAX, E-MAIL
ZAO Zabaikalinvestservice	37, ul. 9 Yanvarya, Chita, Chita Region, 672010	Phone: (3022) 26 6795
OAO Zabaikalskaya Investment Company	7, ul. Promyshlennaya, Chita, Chita Region, 672020	Phone: (3022) 32 9701
OAO PickInvest	Office 309, 9, ul. 9 Yanvarya, Chita, Chita Region, 672010	Phone: (3022) 26 0551

Regional programs. The Chita Region is implementing some 55 regional programs focused on the development of its agroindustrial complex, healthcare, education, public welfare, environmental rehabilitation, and law enforcement. The Region has accorded priority status to the following programs:

• The Regional Program for State Support for Small Enterprise in the Chita Region, 2003–2004, which aims to create the prerequisites for the development of small enterprise in market economy conditions.

• The Program for Social and Economic Development of the Chita Region in 2003–2005, which aims to improve living standards through sustainable economic growth.

• The Program for the Stabilization and Development of Agroindustrial Production in the Chita Region through 2005 has a budget of $210.8 million, including $28.3 million from the regional budget.

6. INVESTMENT PROJECTS

Industry sector and project description	1) Expected results 2) Amount and term of investment 3) Form of financing[1] 4) Documentation[2]	Contact information
1	2	3
MINING		
75R001 Reconstruction of gold mining facilities at the Klyuchevskoye gold field. Project goal: to extract gold.	1) Processing of 1 million tons of ore per year 2) $15 million/4 years 3) L 4) BP	OAO Klyuchi Mine 12, ul. Kalinina, Klyuchevsky, Mogochinsky District, Chita Region, 673811 Mikhail Ivanovich Petrov, Executive Director Fuel, Energy and Natural Resources Department of the Chita Region Phone: (3022) 32 5277 Fax: (3022) 32 5156 E-mail: obladm@chiten.elektra.ru Leonid Nikolaevich Voita, Department Head

[1] L – Loan, E – Equity, Leas. – Leasing, JV – Joint Venture
[2] BP – Business Plan, FS – Feasibility Study

1	2	3
75R002 ● ◆		OAO Ksenievsky Goldfield
Development of the Itakinskoye field. Project goal: geological prospecting and extraction of gold.	1) Processing of 900,000 tons of ore annually 2) $30 million/3 years 3) L 4) BP	1, ul. Zolotaya, Ksenievka, Mogochisky District, Chita Region, 673750 Phone: (3022) 26 3761 (Chita office), (095) 276 0553 (Moscow office) Fuel, Energy and Natural Resources Department of the Chita Region Phone: (3022) 32 5277 Fax: (3022) 32 5156 E-mail: obladm@chiten.elektra.ru Leonid Nikolaevich Voita, Department Head
75R003		Head Office of the Natural Resources and Environmental Protection
Development of the Ukoninskoye field. Project goal: geological prospecting and extraction of gold.	1) 300,000 tons of ore annually 2) $50 million/n/a 3) n/a 4) n/a	Department of the Ministry of Natural Resources of Russia for the Chita Region P.O. Box 159, 91/15, ul. Amurskaya, Chita, Chita Region, 672000 Phone: (3022) 23 4646 E-mail: kpr@geo.chita.ru Khapis Suleimanovich Bakhramov, Department Head
75R004		OAO Priargunsky Mining and Chemicals Plant
Creation of energotechnological facilities for processing germanium bearing coals. Project goal: to process germanium bearing coal.	1) 38.2 ton annually 2) $5.1 million/n/a 3) n/a 4) n/a	Krasnokamensk, Chita Region, 674673 Phone: (30245) 25 192 Fax: (30245) 46 911, 25 034 E-mail: uprav@kr.chita.ru Valery Fedorovich Golovin, Director
75R005 ■ ❖		OAO Zabaikalsky Mining and Ore Dressing Plant
Production facilities for tantalum and niobium concentrates processing. Project goal: to produce and dress ore.	1) Annual production: tin in 20% tin concentrate – 133 tons of ore; tantalum in potassium fluorotantalate – 74 tons, and niobium in pentaxide – 101 tons 2) $2 million/n/a 3) E, JV 4) n/a	18, ul. Mira, Pervomaysky, Chita Region, 673390 Phone: (30262) 42 389, 42 303 Fax: (30262) 41 010, 42 303 E-mail: Pgok@megalink.ru Gennady Mikhailovich Adosik, CEO
75R006 ■ ❖ ◆		OAO Zabaikalstalinvest Mining and Metal Company
Construction of the first unit of the Mining and Ore Dressing Plant at the Chineiskoye titanium and magnetite field. Project goal: to produce ore and concentrated ore.	1) 10 million tons of ore annually 2) $150 million/5 years 3) JV, E 4) BP	20a/4, ul. Magistralnaya, Novaya Chara, Kalarsky District, Chita Region, 674159 Fuel, Energy and Natural Resources Department of the Chita Region Phone: (3022) 32 5277 Fax: (3022) 32 5156 E-mail: obladm@chiten.elektra.ru Leonid Nikolaevich Voita, Department Head

1	2	3

ENERGY

75R007 ● ▲

Construction of the 3rd energy unit of the Kharanorskaya GRES. Project goal: to increase power production.	1) 225 MW annually 2) $106.2 million/3 years 3) L 4) FS	OAO Kharanorskaya GRES Yasnogorsk, Olovianninsky District, Chita Region, 674520 Phone: (3022) 26 8583, 23 7032 Fax: (3022) 32 5122, 26 1561 (Chita Representative office) E-mail: root@xar.megalink.ru Sergei Ivanovich Vasilchuk, CEO

75R008 ● ▲

Reconstruction of equipment at thermal power stations. Project goal: to increase power output and improve the city's environmental situation.	1) 466 MW 2) $3.9 million/5 years 3) L 4) FS	OAO Chitaenergo 23, ul. Profsoyuznaya, Chita, Chita Region, 672090 Phone: (3022) 23 6120 Fax: (3022) 32 3101 E-mail: delo@chiten.elektra.ru Sergei Borisovich Tikhonov, CEO

MACHINE ENGINEERING AND METAL PROCESSING

75R009 ■ ❖ ▲

Construction of resource saving facilities for production of spare parts and nodes with improved wear resistance. Project goal: to decrease costs and enhance wear resistance of restored parts vs. brand new parts by 3–4 times.	1) Spare parts acquisition and production cost reduction by 80%–85% 2) $4.4 million/2 years 3) E, JV 4) FS	OAO Prospective Technologies Siberian Scientific and Production Center 1, ul. Tobolskogo, Chita, Chita Region, 672026 Phone: (3022) 21 3256 Fax: (3022) 21 3256 Mikhail Nikolaevich Toropov, CEO

75R010 ● ▲

Construction of a modernized freight vessel. Project goal: to satisfy the demand for freight vessels.	1) Construction of a 1,100 ton displacement vessel with a 500 ton carrying capacity 2) $1.8 million/1.5 years 3) L 4) FS	OOO Sretensky Vessel Construction Plant 9, ul. Zavodskaya, Kokuy, Sretensky District, Chita Region, 673530 Phone: (30246) 91 553 Phone/fax: (30246) 91 688 E-mail: sretensk@mail.chita.ru Petr Petrovich Pokhitonov, Director

75R011 ● ◆

Construction of fishing vessels. Project goal: to satisfy demand for fishing vessels.	1) 10 vessels annually 2) $7.8 million/3 years 3) L 4) BP	OOO Sretensky Vessel Construction Plant 9, ul. Zavodskaya, Kokuy, Sretensky District, Chita Region, 673530 Phone: (30246) 91 553 Phone/fax: (30246) 91 688 E-mail: sretensk@mail.chita.ru Petr Petrovich Pokhitonov, Director

TRANSPORT INFRASTRUCTURE

75R012 ● ▲

Electrification of a section of the Karymskaya – Zabaikalsk railroad, improvement of railroad tracks, and repair of railroad stations. Project goal: to transfer the railroad section to electric power.	1) 365.6 km of railroad 2) $181 million/2 years 3) L 4) FS	FGUP Zabaikalskaya Railroad 34, ul. Leningradskaya, Chita, Chita Region, 672092 Phone: (3022) 97 4316, 97 4400 Fax (3022) 26 0573 Viktor Fedorovich Sekhin, Department Head

SIBERIAN FEDERAL DISTRICT

VI

1	2	3

75R013 ● ▲

Extension of a landing strip.
Project goal: to accept all
types of aircraft.

1) Up to 3,000 planes annually
2) $7.5 million/3 years
3) L
4) FS

OAO Chitaavia
Airport, Chita, Chita Region, 678018
Phone: (3022) 33 8392
Phone: (3022) 33 8395
E-mail: avia@mail.chita.ru
Alexander Gennadyevich Popov,
Executive Director

75R014 ● ★ ▲

Construction of a cargo terminal
at the Chita airport.
Project goal: to build a free
customs warehouse terminal.

1) Up to 200 tons of freight a day
2) $44.3 million/3 years
3) L, Leas.
4) FS

OAO Chitaavia
Airport, Chita, Chita Region, 678018
Phone: (3022) 33 8392
Fax: (3022) 33 8395
E-mail: avia@mail.chita.ru
Alexander Gennadyevich Popov,
Executive Director

COMMUNICATIONS

75R015 ● ★ ◆

Reconstruction of the city
telephone network.
Project goal: to provide modern
and quality communication services.

1) Capacity expansion
   to 18,000 subscribers
2) $3.9 million/n/a
3) L, Leas.
4) BP

OAO Elektrosvyaz
107, ul. Lenina, Chita,
Chita Region, 672076
Phone: (3022) 23 2906
Fax: (3022) 26 5550
E-mail: root@telecom.chita.ru
Alexei Sergeevich Sukontsev,
CEO

TRADE

75R016 ❖

Establishment of the Zabaikalsk Border
Trade Zone within the Russian-Chinese
Zabaikalsk (Chita Region) – Manchuria
(China) Trade Complex.
Project goal: to create a Russian-
Chinese trade and industry complex
incorporating two border zones linked
by a border crossing.

1) Revenues – from $60 million,
   BTZ capacity
   of 1,000 people a day
2) $35 million/n/a
3) JV
4) n/a

GUP Chita Region Development
Corporation, 15, ul. Leningradskaya,
Chita, Chita Region, 672090
Phone: (3022) 23 0784
Phone/fax: (3022) 23 4572
Nikolai Nikolaevich Vorobiov, CEO

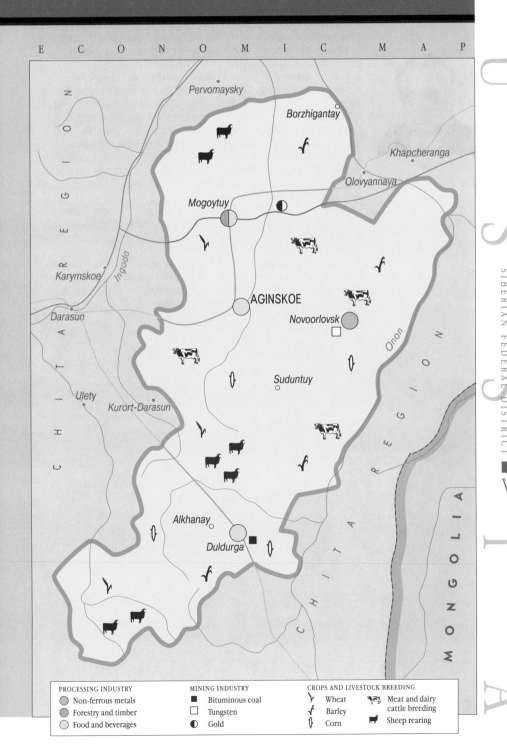

ECONOMIC MAP

RUSSIA

SIBERIAN FEDERAL DISTRICT

VI

PROCESSING INDUSTRY
- 🔴 Non-ferrous metals
- 🔴 Forestry and timber
- ⚪ Food and beverages

MINING INDUSTRY
- ⬛ Bituminous coal
- ⬜ Tungsten
- ◐ Gold

CROPS AND LIVESTOCK BREEDING
- Wheat
- Barley
- Corn
- Meat and dairy cattle breeding
- Sheep rearing

The Aginsky Buryatsky Autonomous District is located in the Eastern Trans-Baikal region – a wonderful land characterized by the legends of its nomadic tribes, the wide-open beauty of its steppes, the purity of its air and rivers and lakes, the diversity of its livestock, its hard-working herders coming from a long line of ancestors carrying on the same occupation from generation to generation, and the millions of tons of mineral resources stored in its subsoil.

Today, the District is home to many ethnic groups, yet it has never experienced inter-ethnic strife. The District's output includes dozens of items of environmentally pure agricultural and industrial products and foods. The challenges of the time, which include maintaining and developing the education system, public health, public welfare, and culture, are successfully met.

The recovery of the national economy, to which the District is linked by hundreds of financial and industrial ties, is pushing up demand for the District's mineral resources. Those include dozens of deposits of placer gold and gold ore, tantalum and tungsten, bismuth and tin, stibium and manganese, black coal, basalt, building and facing stone, mineral water, and many others. The future of the District lies in the exploration and industrial development of those resources.

With this in mind, the District Administration has accorded priority to supporting investors and encouraging investment activity. The District has enacted a number of laws that aim to provide optimal tax, organizational, and other conditions for domestic and foreign investment.

One of the positive factors impacting the District's investment appeal is its proximity to China, which is in the throes of all-out industrial expansion, and to Mongolia, which enjoys vast natural resources. Both countries have rail and highway links to the District.

We believe that the time is coming when demand for our land's natural resources will skyrocket. We are eager to establish mutually beneficial partnerships in all spheres of economy. We are committed to providing organizational support to investors and to protecting their property and their business.

Bair Zhamsuev,
HEAD OF THE AGINSKY BURYATSKY
AUTONOMOUS DISTRICT ADMINISTRATION

1. GENERAL INFORMATION

1.1. GEOGRAPHY

The Aginsky Buryatsky Autonomous District covers a total area of some 19,600 square kilometers. The District lies in the southwestern part of the Eastern Trans-Baikal region wholly within the Chita Region. It does not border any other region of Russia.

1.2. CLIMATE

The Aginsky Buryatsky Autonomous District has a severe continental climate. Air temperatures in January average −27°C, rising to an average of +20°C in July. Annual precipitation reaches 250–350 mm.

1.3. POPULATION

According to preliminary 2002 census results, the District's total population stood at 72,000 peo-

ple. The average population density is 3.7 people per square kilometer. The economically active population amounted to 31,000 people, while the official unemployment rate was 6%.

Demographically speaking, some 58.1% are of working age, 29.7% are below the statutory working age, and 12.2% are beyond the statutory working age.

The District's ethnic mix is 55% Buryat, 41% Russian, 1% Ukrainian, and 3% other ethnic groups.

The District's administrative center is Aginskoye (9,500 inhabitants).

Population		1992	1997	1998	1999	2000	2001	2002
Total population, '000		79	79	79	79	79	79	72
Economically active population, '000		42	27	31	29	32	32	31

TABLE 1

2. ADMINISTRATION

92, ul. Bazara Rinchino, Aginskoye, Aginsky Buryatsky Autonomous District, 678000
Phone: (30239) 34 152; fax: (30239) 34 540; e-mail: admabao@agatel.ru

NAME	POSITION	CONTACT INFORMATION
Bair Bayaskhalanovich ZHAMSUEV	Head of the Aginsky Buryatsky Autonomous District Administration	Phone: (30239) 34 152
Zhargal Sungrupovich ZHIGZHITZHAPOV	First Deputy Head of the Aginsky Buryatsky Autonomous District Administration, Chairman of the Committee for Finance, Chairman of the Property Management Committee	Phone: (30239) 34 367
Bair Galsanovich GALSANOV	First Deputy Head of the Aginsky Buryatsky Autonomous District Administration, Chairman of the Committee for Economic Development and Enterprise	Phone: (30239) 34 244
Vladimir Tsedashievich TSEDASHIYEV	Deputy Head of the Aginsky Buryatsky Autonomous District Administration, Chairman of the Committee for Agriculture	Phone: (30239) 34 649
Viktor Ivanovich SMOLIN	Deputy Head of the Aginsky Buryatsky Autonomous District Administration, Chairman of the Committee for Industry, Transport, Communications, and Energy	Phone: (30239) 34 691
Svetlana Tsyrenzhapovna ZAYAKHANOVA	Deputy of the Head of the Aginsky Buryatsky Autonomous District Administration for Social Issues	Phone: (30239) 34 183

3. ECONOMIC POTENTIAL

3.1. 1997–2002 GROSS REGIONAL
PRODUCT (GRP). INDUSTRY BREAKDOWN
The Aginsky Buryatsky Autonomous District's 2002 gross regional product amounted to $51 million, 15.9% up on 2001. Per capita GRP totaled $557 in 2001, rising to $708 in 2002.

3.2. MAJOR ECONOMIC
GROWTH PROJECTIONS
The District Administration has identified the District's social and economic development priorities for 2003 for the principal sectors of the District's economy, as follows:

GRP trends in 1997–2002						TABLE 2
		1998	1999	2000	2001	2002*
GRP in current prices, $ million	n/a	38.3	23.7	36.5	44.0	51.0

*Estimates of the Aginsky Buryatsky Autonomous District Administration

GRP industry breakdown in 1997–2002, % of total						TABLE 3
	1997	1998	1999	2000	2001	2002*
GRP	100.0	100.0	100.0	100.0	100.0	100.0
Industry	n/a	9.3	11.4	10.2	6.7	7.3
Agriculture and forestry	n/a	36.2	33.9	32.9	28.5	28.5
Construction	n/a	5.0	4.4	8.9	6.0	6.1
Transport and communications	n/a	0.1	0.1	0.1	0.4	0.5
Trade and public catering	n/a	6.7	7.7	6.0	7.6	7.4
Other	n/a	42.7	42.5	41.9	50.8	50.2

*Estimates of the Aginsky Buryatsky Autonomous District Administration

Agriculture: improving technical maintenance and service systems, forming a stable finance and credit system, maintaining output growth rates, and increasing deliveries of the District's produce to the domestic market and to other regions of the Russian Federation.

Industry: maintaining output growth rates in the metals mining industry through state support to existing enterprises and the creation of new enterprises, enhancing product competitiveness, expansion and renewal of production capacity through borrowing and direct investment, active pursuit of innovation, curtailment of production costs, and active encouragement of resource saving technologies.

Construction: creation of new and restructuring of existing construction capacity using modern high-yield technologies;

Trade: development of trade relations with other regions of Russia and expanding cross-border trade with China and Mongolia;

Transport: growth in the road haulage sector, creation of modern road haulage organizations and encouragement of transit traffic.

3.2. INDUSTRIAL OUTPUT
IN 1997–2002 FOR MAJOR
SECTORS OF ECONOMY
The Aginsky Buryatsky Autonomous District's major industrial sectors are non-ferrous metals, energy, food and fuel. These account for 84.1% of total industrial output.

Non-ferrous metals. Non-ferrous metals dominate the District's industry, accounting for 38.5% of total industrial output. The largest enterprise is ZAO Novoorlovsky Ore Dressing Plant.

Food and beverages. The sector accounts for 15.2% of total industrial output and is spread across six branches: dairy, meat, flour, bakery, distillery, and fruit and vegetables. The largest enterprises are OOO Mogoytuy Food Company, GUP Aginsky Meat Processing Plant, and ZAO Mogoytuy Meat Processing Plant.

Agriculture. The agriculture sector is represented by 31 collective farms, 312 individual farm holdings, and 13,000 private market gardening allotments. The total area of arable lands is 986,700 hectares. The principal line of activity is stockbreeding.

Industry breakdown of industrial output in 1997–2002, % of total						_TABLE 4_
	1997	1998	1999	2000	2001	2002*
Industry	100.0	100.0	100.0	100.0	100.0	100.0
Non-ferrous metals	53.8	73.7	71.1	80.6	39.3	38.5
Energy	5.0	3.8	–	–	0.8	17.3
Food and beverages	8.5	3.8	6.8	5.7	8.8	15.2
Fuel	–	–	0.4	0.1	10.7	13.1
Flour, cereals, and mixed fodder	3.7	1.3	1.6	0.6	0.6	7.8
Machine engineering and metal processing	4.6	3.3	5.7	3.2	4.2	4.9
Printing	2.6	1.3	0.8	1.0	2.4	1.9
Forestry, timber, and pulp and paper	7.1	1.1	3.6	1.4	6.4	1.2
Light industry	–	–	–	–	0.1	0.1
Construction materials	14.7	11.7	9.4	7.4	26.7	–

*Estimates of the Aginsky Buryatsky Autonomous District Administration

Fuel and energy sector production and consumption trends, 1997–2002						_TABLE 5_
	1997	1998	1999	2000	2001	2002
Oil output (including gas condensate), '000 tons	10.0	4.0	2.0	–	10.0	–
Electricity consumption, billion kWh	0.2	0.2	0.2	0.1	0.1	0.1
Natural gas consumption, million cubic meters	0.1	0.1.	0.1	0.1	0.1	0.1

3.3. FUEL AND ENERGY BALANCE (OUTPUT AND CONSUMPTION PER RESOURCE)

The Aginsky Buryatsky Autonomous District is an electricity deficit region with no active power plants.

3.4. TRANSPORT INFRASTRUCTURE

Roads. The Aginsky Buryatsky Autonomous District has more than 900 kilometers of roads, with a number of road haulage companies assuring freight and passenger carriage. The road network links the District to other regions of the Russian Federation and to cross-border destinations in China and Mongolia.

Railroads. The District has 71 kilometers of railroads. A railway line passes through the District (Mogoytuy station), providing a link to other regions of Russia, China and Mongolia.

Oil and gas pipelines. The Angarsk – Datsin (China) oil pipeline passing through the Chita Region and the Aginsky Buryatsky Autonomous District is slated for construction in the near future.

3.5. MAIN NATURAL RESOURCES: RESERVES AND EXTRACTION IN 2002

The Region's principal natural resources are mineral resources, mineral water, gold, silver, bismuth, tantalum, tungsten, antimony, copper, manganese, and coal.

Mineral resources. The Territory has considerable deposits of minerals used in the production of construction materials (clay, sand, limestone, gravel, and basalt).

Water resources. The Territory's mineral water reserves can support a production rate of 1,000 cubic meters a day. The mineral water bottling sector is currently operating at 3% of its potential capacity.

Recreational resources. The District has several spa and recreational facilities close to mineral water springs. The largest of them are Ugsakhay, Zymka, and Novoorlovsky Village.

4. TRADE OPPORTUNITIES

4.1. MAIN GOODS PRODUCED IN THE REGION

Food. The grain harvest was 32,300 tons in 2002, milk output reached 40,100 tons, meat output was 5,200 tons, and output of eggs topped 2,769,000. 2002 saw an increase in alcoholic beverages output to 100,000 decaliters.

Agricultural feedstock. 570 tons of wool was produced in the District in 2002.

SIBERIAN FEDERAL DISTRICT

VI

4.2. EXPORTS, INCLUDING EXTRA-CIS

The District's 2002 exports to extra-CIS countries amounted to $4.2 million, while exports to CIS
countries totaled $0.2 million.

4.3. IMPORTS, INCLUDING EXTRA-CIS

The District's 2000 imports from extra-CIS
countries amounted to $160.6 million, and imports
from CIS countries totaled $0.2 million.

4.4. MAJOR REGIONAL EXPORT AND IMPORT ENTITIES

Due to the specific nature of the District's
export and import activities, export and import
transactions are performed mainly by industrial
enterprises.

5. INVESTMENT OPPORTUNITIES

5.1. INVESTMENTS IN 1992–2002 (BY INDUSTRY SECTOR), INCLUDING FOREIGN INVESTMENTS

The following factors determine the investment appeal of the Aginsky Buryatsky Autonomous District:

* Its favorable geographical location in close
proximity to China with its developing
industrial sector and Mongolia with its rich
natural resources;
* Its developed industrial infrastructure;
* Legislation providing support for investment
projects (guarantees of investor rights and the
provision of tax incentives to investors);
* Organizational and financial support for
investment projects and government guarantees
of a safe business environment;

* Convenient conditions for recreation,
tourism, and convalescence.

5.2. CAPITAL INVESTMENT

The transport and industry sectors accounted
for the lion's share of capital investment.

5.3. MAJOR ENTERPRISES (INCLUDING ENTERPRISES WITH FOREIGN INVESTMENT)

The Aginsky Buryatsky Autonomous District
is home to 2,035 enterprises of various forms
of ownership.

5.4. MOST ATTRACTIVE SECTORS FOR INVESTMENT

According to the District Administration,
mining, agricultural processing, and tourism are
the most attractive industries for investors.

Capital investment by industry sector, $ million						_TABLE 6_
	1997	1998	1999	2000	2001	2002
Total capital investment	8.2	3.5	2.4	3.0	5.0	8.0
Including major industries (% of total)						
Industry	43.8	35.1	7.6	4.9	25.3	4.5
Agriculture and forestry	6.2	11.2	2.3	3.9	9.0	11.2
Construction	–	–	–	–	0.2	0.4
Transport	7.9	24.2	66.0	69.2	26.7	1.0
Trade and public catering	1.9	2.3	1.3	0.1	0.2	0.2
Other	40.2	27.2	22.8	21.9	38.6	82.7

Largest enterprises of the Aginsky Buryatsky Autonomous District	_TABLE 7_
COMPANY	SECTOR
ZAO Novoorlovsky Ore Dressing Plant	Mining
SP Brickyard	Machine engineering
ZAO Agroeliks	Agriculture
OOO Mogoytuy Food Company	Food and beverages
GUP Aginsky Meat Processing Plant	Food and beverages
ZAO Mogoytuy Meat Processing Plant	Food and beverages

5.5. CURRENT LEGISLATION ON INVESTOR TAX EXEMPTIONS AND PRIVILEGES

The Aginsky Buryatsky Autonomous District passed a number of legislative acts in 2002 providing tax exemptions on investment projects carried out in the District, regulating state support of investors, guaranteeing equitable protection of rights, and facilitating investor access to government bodies. These included the Law On State Support to Investment Activity in the Aginsky Buryatsky Autonomous District and the Law On Amendments to the Autonomous District Law On Simplified Taxation, Records and Accounting System for Small Enterprises in the Aginsky Buryatsky Autonomous District (providing for exemptions for leased assets, deferral of regional tax components, and profit and property tax and local tax reductions).

Regional entities responsible for raising investment		*TABLE 8*
ENTITY	ADDRESS	PHONE, FAX, E-MAIL
ZAO Aginskoye Regional Small and Medium Business Support Agency	105, ul. Bazara Rinchino, Aginskoye, Aginsky Buryatsky Autonomous District, Chita Region, 678000	Phone: (30239) 35 164 Fax: (30239) 34 560 E-mail: fpmp@aginsk.chita.ru

5.6. FEDERAL AND REGIONAL ECONOMIC AND SOCIAL DEVELOPMENT PROGRAMS FOR THE AGINSKY BURYATSKY AUTONOMOUS DISTRICT

Federal targeted programs. Several federal targeted programs for economic and social development are underway in the Aginsky Buryatsky Autonomous District. These include the The Federal Targeted Program for the Economic and Social Development of the Far East and Trans-Baikal Region, 1996–2005 and through 2010; Children of Russia, 2003–2006 with its sub-programs Physically Disabled Children and Orphans; The Elderly, 2002–2004; Prevention and Treatment of Social Diseases, 2002–2006 with its sub-programs HIV(AIDS) Prevention, Vaccination, Urgent Tuberculosis Prevention Measures, and Diabetes Mellitus, and The Development of Family and Child Social Services. In all, eleven programs are currently underway in the District. A budget of $2.8 million is to be allocated for these programs in 2003.

Regional programs. The Aginsky Buryatsky Autonomous District Administration has devised and is implementing a number of programs targeting industry development, agriculture and food policy, environmental rehabilitation, law enforcement, public health, and public welfare. In all, 18 regional programs are currently underway. The District's Administration has accorded priority status to the Aginsky Buryatsky Autonomous District Small Enterprise Support and Development Program (2002–2005), which aims to improve the legal, economic, and organizational environment with a view to fostering sustainable small enterprise development, and to consolidate financing for priority sectors of small enterprise. Some $0.3 million was allocated from the District's budget to finance the program in 2002.

6. INVESTMENT PROJECTS

Industry sector and project description	1) Expected results 2) Amount and term of investment 3) Form of financing[1] 4) Documentation[2]	Contact information
1	2	3
COAL		
76R001	● ◆	OAO Ureysky Coal Pit
Open-pit coal mining at the Ureysky coal pit. Project goal: to increase coal output.	1) Coal output: 30,000 tons per year 2) $0.9 million/1 year 3) L 4) BP	4, ul. Kirova, Village of Duldurga, Aginsky Buryatsky Autonomous District, Chita Region, 687200 Phone/fax: (30256) 34 295; 34 362 E-mail: ureiu@duldurga.chita.ru Sergei Vladislavovich Pertsev, CEO

[1] L – Loan, E – Equity, Leas. – Leasing, JV – Joint Venture
[2] BP – Business Plan, FS – Feasibility Study

1	2	3

FORESTRY, TIMBER, AND PULP AND PAPER

76R002

Establishing a timber processing enterprise on the basis of existing facilities in Mogoytuy Village. Project goal: to produce sawn and dried timber, glued cant, and furniture panels.

1) Processing of 50,000 cubic meters per year
2) $3.2 million/2 years
3) L
4) BP

Small Enterprise Support Fund
105, ul. Bazara Rinchino, Aginskoye,
Aginsky Buryatsky Autonomous District,
Chita Region, 678000
Phone/fax: (30239) 34 560
E-mail: fpmp@aginsk.chita.ru
Bair Dashievich Shirabon,
Executive Director

77. TAIMYRSKY (DOLGANO-NENETSKY) AUTONOMOUS DISTRICT [84]

ECONOMIC MAP

KARA SEA

Severnaya Zemlya

Dikson

Pyasina

Lake Taymyr

Verkhnyaya Taymyr

Ust-Port

DUDINKA

Norilsk

Khatanga

Khatanga

Kheta

Yenisey

Igarka

Turukhansk

Nizhnyaya Tunguska

Kureyka

Kotuy

Tembenchi

Kochechum

Vivi

EVENKISKY

AUTONOMOUS

DISTRICT

TURA

REPUBLIC

OF SAKHA

(YAKUTIA)

Olenyok

Viluy

Markha

PROCESSING INDUSTRY
- Non-ferrous metals
- Food and beverages

MINING INDUSTRY
- Bituminous coal
- Natural gas
- Nickel ore

POWER PLANTS
- Thermal power plants
- Hydro power plants

CROPS AND LIVESTOCK BREEDING
- Reindeer breeding

The Taimyrsky Autonomous District is the only region in Russia that lies entirely beyond the Arctic Circle. It is not without reason that it is commonly known as the Treasure Peninsula. The District is among the top five regions for reserves of platinum, gold, diamonds, nickel, copper, rhodium, niobium, and coal. The District has explored oil, natural gas, and gas condensate fields. It is developing deposits of non-ferrous and precious metals, coal, natural gas, and gas condensate. The District hosts the world's largest producer of non-ferrous and precious metals, Mining and Metal Processing Company Norilsk Nickel.

Taimyr enjoys unique geographic location: it is a key link in the Northern Sea Route connecting Taimyr to Russia and the world.

The Taimyrsky Autonomous District Administration has a strong focus on projects that aim to improve the District's social and economic situation. These include social programs and programs for the preservation of the culture and folk arts and crafts of the native peoples of Taimyr. Several targeted programs for the development of natural resources, processing industries, and small and medium enterprise are currently underway. The District is engaged in active agricultural, education, and healthcare reforms. The District Administration is faced with the task of maximizing the utilization of the District's potential for the benefit of its people and the nation.

The people of the Taimyr Peninsula are another of its unique attractions, who living in a severe northern climate surprise by their courage, stamina, warmth, and internal qualities. Once you have come here, you will never want to leave. Visitors to Taimyr value the generosity of the harsh land and the spiritual wealth of its people.

Oleg Budargin,
GOVERNOR OF THE TAIMYRSKY
(DOLGANO-NENETSKY) AUTONOMOUS DISTRICT

1. GENERAL INFORMATION

1.1. GEOGRAPHY

The Taimyrsky (Dolgano-Nenetsky) Autonomous District covers a total area of some 904,600 square kilometers. The District lies in the northernmost part of Siberia, on the Taimyr Peninsula, and is washed by the Kara Sea and the Laptev Sea from the north.

1.2. CLIMATE

The District enjoys a severe continental climate. Air temperatures in January average −32°C, rising to an average of +5°C in July. Annual precipitation reaches 200–300 mm.

1.3. POPULATION

According to preliminary 2002 census results, the District's total population stood at 40,000 people. The average population density is 0.04 people per square kilometer. The economically active population amounts to 27,000 people, while the official unemployment rate was 7.6% as of 2002.

Demographically speaking, some 68.1% are of statutory working age, 22.4% are below the statutory working age, and 9.5% are beyond the statutory working age.

The District's ethnic mix is 8.8% Dolgan, 67.1% Russian, 4.4% Nenets, 8.6% Ukrainian, and 11.1% other ethnic groups.

The District's major urban center is Dudinka with 26,700 inhabitants (2002 data).

Population						TABLE 1
	1997	1998	1999	2000	2001	2002
Total population, '000	46	45	44	44	44	40
Economically active population, '000	18	26	26	27	26	27

2. ADMINISTRATION

35, ul. Sovetskaya, Dudinka, Taimyrsky (Dolgano-Nenetsky) Autonomous District, 647000
Phone: (39111) 23 317; fax: (39111) 58 207

NAME	POSITION	CONTACT INFORMATION
Oleg Mikhailovich BUDARGIN	Governor of the Taimyrsky (Dolgano-Nenetsky) Autonomous District	Phone: (39111) 21 160
Sergei Gennadyevich TARASOV	Deputy Governor of the Taimyrsky (Dolgano-Nenetsky) Autonomous District for Finance and Economy	Phone: (39111) 25 374
Alexander Ivanovich RYABOV	Deputy Governor of the Taimyrsky (Dolgano-Nenetsky) Autonomous District	Phone: (39111) 58 305
Longin Andreevich KHAN	Deputy Governor of the Taimyrsky (Dolgano-Nenetsky) Autonomous District for Infrastructure Development	Phone: (39111) 58 565
Yury Kazbekovich ZAFESOV	Head of the Department for Government Orders and Consumer Market of the Administration of the Taimyrsky (Dolgano-Nenetsky) Autonomous District	Phone: (39111) 57 090

3. ECONOMIC POTENTIAL

3.1. 1997–2002 GROSS REGIONAL PRODUCT (GRP). INDUSTRY BREAKDOWN

The District's 2002 gross regional product amounted to $142 million, 7.8% down on 2001. Per capita GRP in 2001 amounted to $3,499 and in 2002, $3,547.

3.2. INDUSTRIAL OUTPUT IN 1997–2002 FOR MAJOR SECTORS OF ECONOMY

The Taimyrsky (Dolgano-Nenetsky) Autonomous District's major industrial sectors are food and beverages, fuel, and energy. They account for 96.4% of total industrial output.

GRP trends in 1997–2002 — TABLE 2

	1997	1998	1999	2000	2001*	2002*
GRP in current prices, $ million	n/a	n/a	n/a	77	154	142

*Estimates of the Taimyrsky (Dolgano-Nenetsky) Autonomous District Administration

GRP industry breakdown in 1997–2002, % of total — TABLE 3

	1997	1998	1999	2000	2001*	2002*
GRP	100.0	100.0	100.0	100.0	100.0	100.0
Industry	n/a	n/a	n/a	4.3	1.9	1.5
Agriculture and forestry	n/a	n/a	n/a	1.5	0.3	0.3
Construction	n/a	n/a	n/a	42.0	19.0	17.6
Transport and communications	n/a	n/a	n/a	6.2	4.2	4.7
Trade and public catering	n/a	n/a	n/a	4.0	8.2	8.4
Other	n/a	n/a	n/a	42.0	46.4	46.4
Net taxes on output	n/a	n/a	n/a	–	20.0	21.1

*Estimates of the Taimyrsky (Dolgano-Nenetsky) Autonomous District Administration

Industry breakdown of industrial output in 1997–2002, % of total — TABLE 4

	1997	1998	1999	2000	2001	2002*
Total	100.0	100.0	100.0	100.0	100.0	100.0
Food and beverages	54.0	37.4	45.2	70.5	61.3	46.1
Fuel	22.8	35.0	30.1	14.1	27.7	40.3
Energy	8.4	13.2	14.3	8.3	7.5	10.0
Printing	n/a	n/a	n/a	2.0	2.6	3.6
Construction materials	3.0	3.2	2.3	1.1	–	–

*Estimates of the Taimyrsky (Dolgano-Nenetsky) Autonomous District Administration

Food and beverages. The sector accounts for 46.1% of total industrial output.

Fuel. The sector accounts for 40.3% of total industrial output. The largest enterprise is OAO Kotuy Mine.

Energy. The sector accounts for 10% of total industrial output.

Agriculture. The District's 18 state-owned unitary farms and 159 private farms represent the agriculture sector. Reindeer breeding is well developed in the District.

3.3. FUEL AND ENERGY BALANCE (OUTPUT AND CONSUMPTION PER RESOURCE)

The Taimyrsky (Dolgano-Nenetsky) Autonomous District consumes energy supplied by power stations located in the Norilsk Industrial Area.

Fuel and energy sector production and consumption trends, 1997–2002 — TABLE 5

	1997	1998	1999	2000	2001	2002*
Natural gas output, billion cubic meters	4.3	4.0	3.8	3.7	3.7	4.0
Electricity consumption, billion kWh	0.1	0.1	0.1	0.1	0.1	0.1
Natural gas consumption, billion cubic meters	3.7	3.7	3.8	3.7	3.4	4.0

*Estimates of the Taimyrsky (Dolgano-Nenetsky) Autonomous District Administration

3.4. TRANSPORT INFRASTRUCTURE

Sea transport is the most common transportation means in the District. The District has links to other regions of the Russian Federation and overseas via the Yenisei River and the Northern Sea Route.

Roads. The District has some 262 kilometers of paved public highway.

Railroads. The District has 110 kilometers of railroad linking the seaport of Dudinka to Norilsk.

Seaports. The principal ports are Dudinka, Khatanga, and Dikson.

The Dudinka seaport is vital for the entire District and the Norilsk Industrial Area. It is the main gateway for the District's exports, with freight vessels led by icebreakers. The port of Dudinka has freight handling facilities of 25,000 tons a day and 706.5 hectares of berthing facilities and warehouses.

FGUP Khatanga Commercial Seaport, which is situated on the right bank of the Khatanga River, specializes in freight handling and carriage.

The Dikson seaport is a support center for arctic expeditions and polar stations. The port's deepwater (15 meters) berthing facilities can handle vessels of up to 50,000 tons.

3.5. MAIN NATURAL RESOURCES: RESERVES AND EXTRACTION IN 2002

The Taimyrsky (Dolgano-Nenetsky) District's principal natural resources are minerals and water.

Mineral resources. The District has copper and nickel ore deposits (the Talnakhskoye and Oktyabrskoye) and industrial diamond deposits (the Udarnoye and Skalistoye). The estimated reserve of black and brown coal is between 500 and 700 billion tons. The total reserve of titaniferous magnetite ore is estimated at 800 million tons.

More than 30 oil and gas deposits have been discovered in the District, the largest being the Messoyakhskoye, Pelyatkinskoye, Suzunskoye, Tagulskoye, Payakhskoye, and Vankorskoye. The District's principal gold reserves are situated in the Taimyro-Severozemelskaya gold province, which occupies the northern part of the Taimyr Peninsula. Lead and zinc ore is found in two complex ore deposits. Apatite and apatite and magnetite ores have been discovered in the Maymecha-Kotuyskaya province.

Water resources. Household and industrial water is pumped from three subterranean fresh water deposits and used in the Norilsk Industrial Region. Mineral water is used for medical and industrial purposes and as a source of potable water.

4. TRADE OPPORTUNITIES

4.1. MAIN GOODS PRODUCED IN THE REGION

Coal. Coal output in 2002 amounted to 27,000 tons.

Bread and bakery. Bakery output in 2002 amounted to 1,200 tons.

Meat. Meat output in 2002 amounted to 235 tons.

5. INVESTMENT OPPORTUNITIES

5.1. INVESTMENTS IN 1992–2002 (BY INDUSTRY SECTOR), INCLUDING FOREIGN INVESTMENTS

The following factors determine the investment appeal of the District:

• Its favorable geographical location along the Northern Sea Route;

• Its qualified work force;
• Cheap energy feedstock (electricity, oil, and natural gas);
• Rich natural resources.

5.2. CAPITAL INVESTMENT

Industry accounts for the lion's share of capital investment.

Capital investment by industry sector, $ million						_TABLE 6_
	1997	1998	1999	2000	2001	2002
Total capital investment _Including major industries_ (% of total)	11.9	4.2	3.2	61.3	53.8	85.9
Industry	–	–	–	27.8	82.5	85.3
Agriculture and forestry	3.0	1.0	4.4	0.1	–	–
Construction	–	–	–	1.1	0.2	0.1
Transport and communications	0.1	–	–	0.1	0.7	3.2
Trade and public catering	–	–	–	–	0.7	0.1
Other	96.9	99.0	95.6	70.9	15.9	11.3

5.3. MAJOR ENTERPRISES (INCLUDING ENTERPRISES WITH FOREIGN INVESTMENT)

Largest enterprises of the Taimyrsky (Dolgano-Nenetsky) Autonomous District	TABLE 7
COMPANY	SECTOR
OAO Kotuy Mine	Fuel
FGUP Khatanga Trade Seaport	Transport
Taimyr Publishing Complex	Printing

5.4. CURRENT LEGISLATION ON INVESTOR TAX EXEMPTIONS AND PRIVILEGES

The current tax legislation of the Taimyrsky (Dolgano-Nenetsky) Autonomous District does not provide specifically for any investor tax exemptions or privileges.

5.5. FEDERAL AND REGIONAL ECONOMIC AND SOCIAL DEVELOPMENT PROGRAMS FOR THE TAIMYRSKY (DOLGANO-NENETSKY) AUTONOMOUS DISTRICT

Federal Targeted Programs. The Conceptual Framework for the Social and Economic Development of the Taimyrsky (Dolgano-Nenetsky) Autonomous District, 2003–2008 is currently being implemented.

Regional Programs. In 2003, the Taimyrsky (Dolgano-Nenetsky) Autonomous District Administ-ration is implementing regional programs for education, public health, public welfare, geology, and transport and communications. In all, some 38 programs with a total budget of $6.5 million are being implemented in the District.

The District Administration has accorded priority to the geological exploration of the District and the replenishment of its mineral reserves. A budget of $2.2 million is to be allocated for the purpose.

78. UST-ORDYNSKY BURYATSKY AUTONOMOUS DISTRICT [85]

E C O N O M I C   M A P

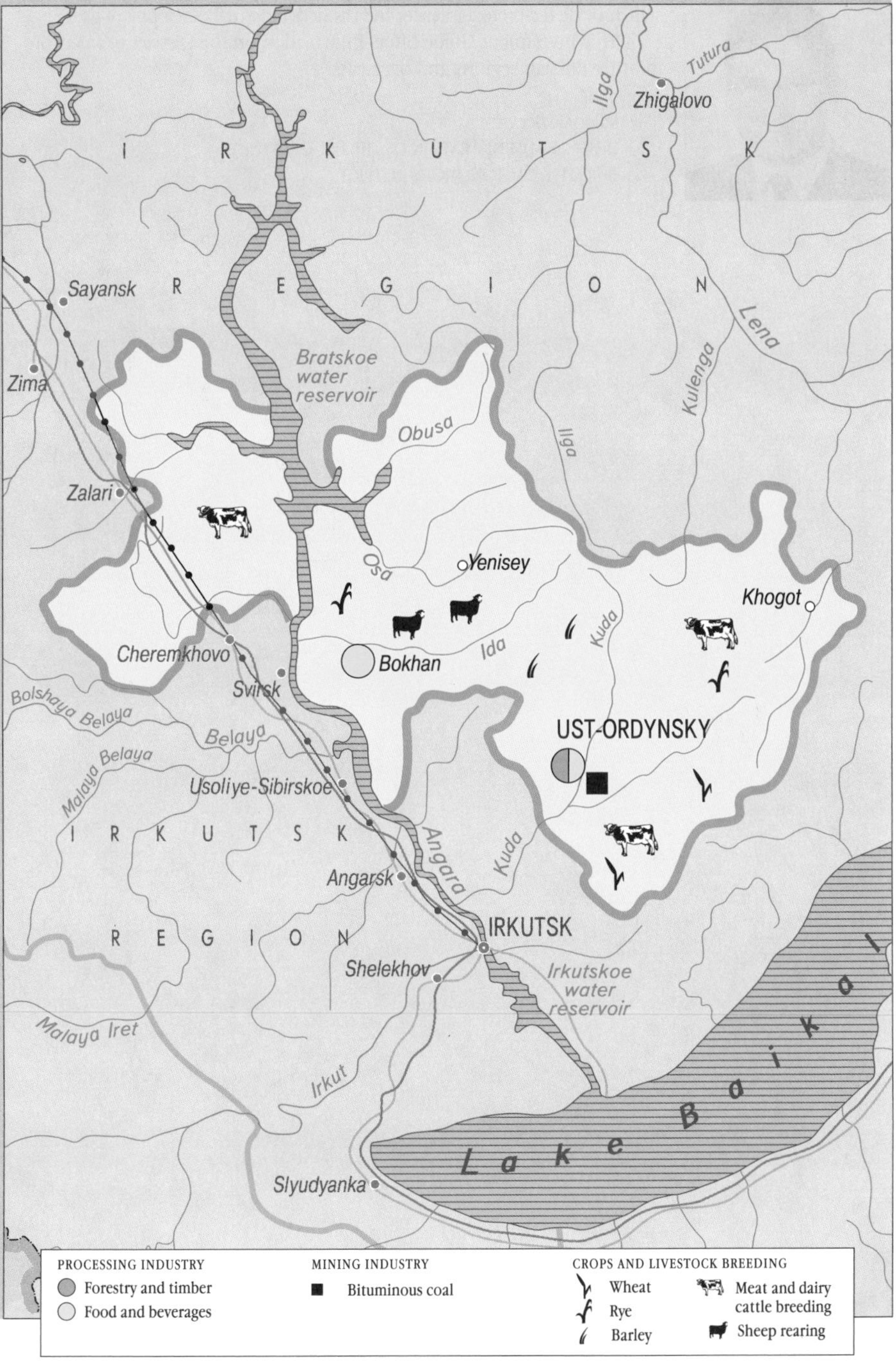

Tutura

Ilga

Zhigalovo

I R K U T S K

R E G I O N

Sayansk

Lena

Zima

Bratskoe water reservoir

Obusa

Kulenga

Ilga

Zalari

Osa

Yenisey

Khogot

Kuda

Cheremkhovo

Bokhan

Ida

UST-ORDYNSKY

Svirsk

Bolshaya Belaya

Belaya

Usoliye-Sibirskoe

Malaya Belaya

I R K U T S K

Kuda

R E G I O N

Angarsk

Angara

IRKUTSK

Malaya Iret

Shelekhov

Irkutskoe water reservoir

Irkut

L a k e   B a i k a l

Slyudyanka

PROCESSING INDUSTRY	MINING INDUSTRY	CROPS AND LIVESTOCK BREEDING	
⬤ Forestry and timber	◼ Bituminous coal	Wheat	Meat and dairy cattle breeding
◯ Food and beverages		Rye	Sheep rearing
		Barley	

The Ust-Ordynsky Buryatsky Autonomous District is not a large industrial region with a high population density. Its economy is primarily agricultural, with grain cultivation and cattle breeding the predominant activities. The District produces wheat, oats, barley, potato, vegetables, corn, and sugar beet, and breeds cattle, sheep, and goats.

Agriculture determines the specific features of the District's infrastructure. While the difficulties provoked by the systemic changes that took place in the late 1990s inevitably affected the District's economy, we have managed nonetheless to maintain and even increase output in many sectors of the economy. The District's natural resources, including oil, natural gas and gas condensate, coal, clay, and gypsum, provide the prerequisites for the District's industrial development goals.

This Investment Guide offers information on the District to investors in other Russian regions and overseas.

Valery Maleev,
HEAD OF ADMINISTRATION OF THE UST-ORDYNSKY
BURYATSKY AUTONOMOUS DISTRICT

SIBERIAN FEDERAL DISTRICT

VI

1. GENERAL INFORMATION

1.1. GEOGRAPHY

Situated in the north-east of Russia, the Ust-Ordynsky Buryatsky Autonomous District covers a total area of 22,400 square kilometers. The District forms part of the Irkutsk Region.

1.2. CLIMATE

The District has a temperate continental climate. The average air temperature in January is −24°C, rising to +18°C in July. The average annual precipitation is 160 mm. The growing season lasts for some 110–120 days.

1.3. POPULATION

According to preliminary 2002 census results, the District's population totaled 135,000 people.

The average population density is 6 people per square kilometer. The economically active population amounts to 62,000 people. The 2002 official unemployment level stood at 1.1%.

Demographically speaking, some 54.7% are of working age, 29.6% are below the statutory working age, and 15.7% are beyond the statutory working age.

The District's ethnic mix is 56.5% Russian, 36.3% Buryat, 3.2% Tatar, 1.7% Ukrainian, and 2.3% other ethnic groups.

The Ust-Ordynsky Buryatsky Autonomous District has no cities, and the District center is the Ust-Ordynsky settlement with 13,200 inhabitants.

Population							TABLE 1
	1992	1997	1998	1999	2000	2001	2002
Total population, '000	140	143	143	143	143	143	135
Economically active population, '000	–	62	52	63	67	61	62

2. ADMINISTRATION

18, ul. Lenina, Ust-Ordynsky, Ust-Ordynsky Buryatsky Autonomous District, 669001
Phone: (39541) 21 062; fax: (39541) 22 593

NAME	POSITION	CONTACT INFORMATION
Valery Gennadyevich MALEEV	Head of Administration of the Ust-Ordynsky Buryatsky Autonomous District	Phone: (39541) 21 062 Fax: (39541) 22 593
Vyacheslav Nikolaevich PAVLOV	First Deputy Head of Administration of the Ust-Ordynsky Buryatsky Autonomous District	Phone: (39541) 21 766
Oleg Alexandrovich ADUKHAEV	Deputy Head of Administration of the Ust-Ordynsky Buryatsky Autonomous District for Construction	Phone: (39541) 22 097
Igor Viktorovich SHPAKOV	Deputy Head of Administration of the Ust-Ordynsky Buryatsky Autonomous District, Chairman of the Property Management Committee	Phone: (39541) 22 072

3. ECONOMIC POTENTIAL

3.1. 1997–2002 GROSS REGIONAL PRODUCT (GRP). INDUSTRY BREAKDOWN

The 2002 gross regional product amounted to $114.6 million, a 5.5% increase on 2001 levels. Per capita GRP equaled $759 in 2001, and $848 in 2002.

3.2. INDUSTRIAL OUTPUT IN 1997–2002 FOR MAJOR SECTORS OF ECONOMY

The leading industrial sectors of the Ust-Ordynsky Buryatsky Autonomous District are forestry, timber, pulp and paper, food and beverages, energy, and fuel. Their combined share in total industrial output is 86.4%.

Forestry, timber, and pulp and paper. The sector accounts for 30.1% of total industrial output. The largest enterprises are OAO Primorsk and OAO Buryat-Yangutsky Timber Company.

Fuel. The share of this sector in total industrial output is 24.2%. The largest company in the sector is OAO Kharanutsky Open Cast Pit.

Food and beverages. The sector accounts for 16% of total industrial output. Major companies within the sector are OAO Angara, OAO Bokhansky Butter Plant, and OAO Ust-Ordynsky Food Company.

GRP trends in 1997–2002 — TABLE 2

	1997	1998	1999	2000	2001	2002*
GRP in current prices, $ million	n/a	142.1	86.3	75.5	108.6	114.6

*Estimates of the Ust-Ordynsky Buryatsky Autonomous District Administration

GRP industry breakdown in 1997–2002, % of total — TABLE 3

	1997	1998	1999	2000	2001*	2002*
GRP	100.0	100.0	100.0	100.0	100.0	100.0
Industry	–	6.7	8.2	8.4	6.4	6.3
Agriculture and forestry	–	56.4	70.0	65.0	68.5	66.8
Construction	–	3.9	2.0	3.1	2.6	3.5
Transport and communications	–	–	–	0.1	0.1	0.1
Trade and public catering	–	3.2	3.1	3.8	3.5	3.6
Other	–	29.8	15.8	18.2	17.5	17.8
Net taxes on output	–	–	0.9	1.4	1.4	1.9

*Estimates of the Ust-Ordynsky Buryatsky Autonomous District Administration

Industry breakdown of industrial output in 1997–2002, % of total — TABLE 4

	1997	1998	1999	2000	2001	2002
Industry	100.0	100.0	100.0	100.0	100.0	100.0
Forestry, timber, and pulp and paper	n/a	22.5	30.6	31.6	27.0	30.1
Fuel	n/a	7.9	4.9	5.7	9.9	24.2
Energy	n/a	3.9	3.8	3.9	5.3	16.1
Food and beverages	n/a	15.6	16.6	22.1	20.9	16.0
Construction materials	n/a	8.9	8.5	4.8	6.2	6.2
Light industry	n/a	2.0	1.7	1.8	2.2	6.1
Machine engineering and metal processing	n/a	11.8	7.8	5.5	5.6	0.3
Flour, cereals, and mixed fodder	n/a	19.1	17.6	18.2	22.2	–

3.3. FUEL AND ENERGY BALANCE (OUTPUT AND CONSUMPTION PER RESOURCE)

Fuel and energy sector production and consumption trends, 1997–2002 — TABLE 5

	1997	1998	1999	2000	2001	2002
Coal output, '000 tons	100	130	97	126	105	97

3.4. TRANSPORT INFRASTRUCTURE

Roads. The District has 1,980 kilometers of paved public highway.

Railroads. A 30-kilometer section of Trans-Siberian railway passes through the District.

Sea and river transport. The District's navigable waterway is the Angara river.

3.5. MAIN NATURAL RESOURCES: RESERVES AND EXTRACTION IN 2002

The District is rich in oil, natural gas and gas condensate, coal, and non-metal building materials (clay and gypsum).

Coal. Estimated coal reserves amount to 301 million tons. The main deposits are the Zabitui-Zalarinskoye with 192 million tons of reserves, the Golovinskoye with 2.5 million tons, the Tyretskoye with 9 million tons, and the Kharanutskoye with 93.3 million tons.

Fuel reserves. The District's natural gas reserves amount to 35 billion cubic meters, oil – 24 million tons, and coal – 310 million tons.

Non-metal building materials. The District's gypsum reserves total 38 million tons. The largest gypsum deposit is Zalarinsky.

4. TRADE OPPORTUNITIES

4.1. MAIN GOODS PRODUCED IN THE REGION

The main types of industrial output as of 2002:
Fuel: 97,000 tons of coal;
Forestry, timber, and pulp and paper: industrial timber – 77,900 cubic meters and lumber – 30,100 cubic meters;

Food and beverages: 91 tons of meat, including category one sub-products, 44 tons of butter, and 2,200 tons of dairy products.

4.2. MAJOR REGIONAL EXPORT AND IMPORT ENTITIES

Owing to the specific features of trade in the District, export and import operations are performed mainly by industrial companies.

5. INVESTMENT OPPORTUNITIES

5.1. INVESTMENT IN 1992–2002 (BY INDUSTRY SECTOR), INCLUDING FOREIGN INVESTMENT

The following factors determine the investment appeal of the District:
• Its developed transport infrastructure;

• Legislation providing support to investment activity;
• Cheap energy (coal and oil);
• Qualified workforce.

5.2. CAPITAL INVESTMENT

Agriculture and forestry account for a considerable share of investment.

Capital investment by industry sector, $ million						TABLE 6
	1997	1998	1999	2000	2001	2002
Total capital investment	16.6	6.7	3.7	6.2	6.4	5.8
Including major industries (% of total)						
Industry	32.5	12.1	19.3	14.1	15.2	12.6
Agriculture and forestry	20.3	28.3	35.2	16.5	14.8	14.0
Construction	–	–	–	0.3	0.3	–
Transport and communications	11.9	1.1	10.0	3.7	1.1	0.9
Trade and public catering	0.5	–	–	8.6	8.2	–
Other	34.8	58.5	35.5	56.8	60.4	72.5

Foreign investment trends in 1996–2002						TABLE 7
	1996–1997	1998	1999	2000	2001	2002
Foreign investment, $ million	–	–	–	2.0	–	–
Including FDI, $ million	–	–	–	2.0	–	–

5.3. MAJOR ENTERPRISES (INCLUDING ENTERPRISES WITH FOREIGN INVESTMENT)

Industry in the Ust-Ordynsky Buryatsky Autonomous District is represented by 26 enterprises.

5.4. MOST ATTRACTIVE SECTORS FOR INVESTMENT

According to the Ust-Ordynsky Buryatsky Autonomous District Administration, the most potentially appealing sectors for investors are food and beverages, forestry, timber, pulp, and paper, and fuel.

SIBERIAN FEDERAL DISTRICT

VI

Largest enterprises of the Ust-Ordynsky Buryatsky Autonomous District	*TABLE 8*
COMPANY	SECTOR
OAO Alarsky Open Cast Pit	Coal
OAO Kharanutsky Open Cast Pit	Coal
OAO Nukutsky Gypsum Pit	Construction
OAO Primorsk	Forestry
OAO Buryat-Yangutsky Timber Company	Forestry
OAO Angara	Food and beverages
OAO Bokhansky Butter Plant	Food and beverages

5.5. CURRENT LEGISLATION ON INVESTOR TAX EXEMPTIONS AND PRIVILEGES

The District has passed a Law On State Support to Small Enterprise in the Ust-Ordynsky Buryatsky Autonomous District. Pursuant to the Law, investors performing investment activity in the District are eligible for preferential loans with compensation for the difference to credit organizations by the Small Enterprise Support Fund.

Regional entities responsible for raising investment		*TABLE 9*
ENTITY	ADDRESS	PHONE, FAX, E-MAIL
Administration of the Ust-Ordynsky Buryatsky Autonomous District	18, ul. Lenina, Ust-Ordynsky, Ust-Ordynsky Buryatsky Autonomous District, 669001	Phone: (39541) 22 629

5.6. FEDERAL AND REGIONAL ECONOMIC AND SOCIAL DEVELOPMENT PROGRAMS FOR THE UST-ORDYNSKY BURYATSKY AUTONOMOUS DISTRICT

Federal targeted programs. The Autonomous District has accorded priority status to the federal targeted program for The Elimination of Inequalities in the Social and Economic Development of the Regions of the Russian Federation, 2002–2010 and through to 2015.

79. EVENKIYSKY AUTONOMOUS DISTRICT [88]

ECONOMIC MAP

PROCESSING INDUSTRY
- ● Forestry and timber
- ○ Food and beverages

MINING INDUSTRY
- ▲ Oil
- ▲ Graphite

CROPS AND LIVESTOCK BREEDING
- ● Animal farming
- 🐄 Meat and dairy cattle breeding
- 🐖 Pig breeding
- 🦌 Reindeer breeding

E venkia is a wonderful land, a virgin land untouched by modern industry. With vast natural resource potential, enormous reserves of almost all known minerals, and expansive forests, the District has all of the necessary pre-requisites for fast economic growth. The development of Evenkia's wealth will make the Far North self-sustaining and bring huge profits to Russia.

Forward-looking Russian corporations that are seeking to expand their resource bases are supporting human habitation in Russia's northern territories in the knowledge that Evenkia has strong prospects for becoming a new oil and gas province and coal extraction area based at the Tunguss coal deposit, a large part of which is located in the District. Explored reserves account for as little as 8% of the District's total hydrocarbon reserve.

We understand that the exploration and exploitation of the District's reserves will require greater financing. Foreign investors are ready to provide the required investment. This is borne out by the interest expressed in joint investment projects for the construction of a gas refinery, hydrometal works, and timber production facilities at the Sixth Annual Russian-American Investment Symposium Investment in Russia: New Opportunities, which took place in Boston in late 2002.

The District has great investment potential for the creation of infrastructure for international adventure tourism. Evenkia is an incredibly beautiful land with an abundance of rare species of fish, and its taiga forests abound in wild game and fur animals.

The District Administration is striving to preserve the traditional lifestyle and culture of the Evenk, a small and ancient people of the North. We view this task as the social responsibility of the authorities and business, one which, if neglected, renders all other initiatives pointless.

Evenkia not only extracts oil and coal, builds plants and produces timber; more importantly, it provides normal civilized living conditions for its people. Ultimately, all investment is investment in the development of this vigorous, rich, and beautiful land and its people.

Boris Zolotarev,
GOVERNOR OF THE EVENKIYSKY AUTONOMOUS DISTRICT

1. GENERAL INFORMATION

1.1. GEOGRAPHY

Located in Eastern Siberia, the Evenkiysky Autonomous District covers a total area of 767,600 square kilometers. To the south and south-east it borders the Irkutsk Region, to the north – the Taimyrsky (Dolgano-Nenetsky) Autonomous District, to the east – the Republic of Sakha (Yakutia), and to the west and south-west – the Krasnoyarsk Territory.

1.2. CLIMATE

The Evenkiysky Autonomous District is located within the severe continental climate zone. Air temperatures in January average –36°C, rising to +15°C in July. Annual precipitation is 400 mm. Part of the District's territory lies within the permafrost zone.

1.3. POPULATION

According to preliminary 2002 census results, the District has a total population of 18,000. The average population density is 0.02 people per square kilometer. The economically active population totals 9,000. In 2002, official unemployment was 4.1%.

Demographically speaking, some 62% of the population are of statutory working age, 26.4% are below the statutory working age, and 11.6% are above the statutory working age.

The ethnic mix is 59.3% Russian, 21.1% Evenk, 5.2% Yakut, 4.6% Even, 3% Ukrainian, and 6.8 % other ethnic groups.

The major urban centers of the District (2002 data) are Tura with 6,000 inhabitants, Baikit with 4,500 inhabitants, and Vanavara with 3,400 inhabitants.

Population							TABLE 1
	1992	1997	1998	1999	2000	2001	2002
Total population, '000	25	20	20	20	19	18	18
Economically active population, '000	n/a	11	10	11	11	11	9

2. ADMINISTRATION

2, ul. Sovetskaya, Tura, Evenkiysky Autonomous District, 648000
Phone: (39113) 22 135, (3912) 63 6355, 63 6353, (095) 789 3126, 789 3127; fax: (3912) 63 6356, (095) 207 7594
http://www.evenkya.ru

NAME	POSITION	CONTACT INFORMATION
Boris Nikolaevich ZOLOTAREV	Governor of the Evenkiysky Autonomous District	Phone: (39113) 22 135, (3912) 63 6355, 63 6353 Fax: (3912) 63 6356
Valentina Ivanovna BOKOVA	First Deputy Governor of the Evenk Autonomous District	Phone: (3912) 63 6353, (39113) 22 778
Eldar Vagifovich VERDIEV	Deputy Governor of the Evenkiysky Autonomous District (in charge of Foreign Relations)	Phone: (095) 789 9818
Gennady Nikolaevich YASCHENKO	Deputy Governor of the Evenkiysky Autonomous District, Head of the State Property Management Committee	Phone: (3912) 63 6374, (39113) 22 434
Ivan Alekseevich BAKHTIN	Deputy Governor of the Evenkiysky Autonomous District, Head of the Logistics Department	Phone: (3912) 63 6300, 63 6301

3. ECONOMIC POTENTIAL

3.1. 1997–2002 GROSS REGIONAL PRODUCT (GRP). INDUSTRY BREAKDOWN

GRP of the Evenkiysky Autonomous District amounted to $21.1 million in 2000 and to $32.5 million in 2001.

3.2. MAJOR ECONOMIC GROWTH PROJECTIONS

The following is an outline of the main goals set by the Evenkiysky Autonomous District Administration for the coming years:

SIBERIAN FEDERAL DISTRICT

VI

814

Industry: to further develop the oil and gas industry, build a major gas processing plant, create new hydrometals facilities, and establish a forestry and timber industry.

Agriculture: to stabilize and reform the production of the most important agricultural commodities and develop reindeer farming.

Communications: to develop the telecommunications infrastructure, provide public telephone communications and data transmission services, bring national TV and radio channels to the District, and provide Internet access to every community.

3.3. INDUSTRIAL OUTPUT IN 1997–2002 FOR MAJOR SECTORS OF ECONOMY

The leading sectors of the Evenkiysky Autonomous District are fuel, energy, and food and beverages. These account for a combined 97.3% of industrial output.

GRP industry breakdown in 1997–2002, % of total						TABLE 2
	1997	1998	1999	2000	2001	2002
GRP	100.0	100.0	100.0	100.0	100.0	100.0
Industry	n/a	n/a	n/a	16.7	12.2	n/a
Agriculture and forestry	n/a	n/a	n/a	6.4	5.4	n/a
Construction	n/a	n/a	n/a	2.3	8.3	n/a
Transportation and communications	n/a	n/a	n/a	6.6	5.9	n/a
Trade and public catering	n/a	n/a	n/a	1.3	6.3	n/a
Other	n/a	n/a	n/a	8.4	54.9	n/a
Net taxes on output	n/a	n/a	n/a	n/a	n/a	n/a

Industry breakdown of industrial output in 1997–2002, % of total						TABLE 3
	1997	1998	1999	2000	2001	2002*
Industry	100.0	100.0	100.0	100.0	100.0	100.0
Fuel	5.5	11.0	12.5	77.5	79.4	52.5
Energy	23.4	26.9	20.6	10.4	10.5	25.2
Food and beverages	15.0	18.3	34.4	9.8	8.0	19.6
Forestry, timber, and pulp and paper	11.7	15.6	22.4	2.2	2.0	2.3
Machine engineering and metal processing	0.4	0.5	0.2	–	–	–
Construction materials	6.5	14.8	–	–	–	–

*Estimates of the Evenkiysky Autonomous District Administration

SIBERIAN FEDERAL DISTRICT

VI

Fuel. The sector accounts for 52.5% of industrial output, with a main focus on oil and gas. The major enterprises are OAO NK YUKOS, OAO Yenisei Oil and Gas, and OAO Krasnoyarskgazprom.

Energy. The sector accounts for 25.2% of industrial output. Power is supplied by GUP Vanavaraenergo, GUP Baikitsky Communal Services and Production Enterprise, and OGUP Ilimpiysky Power Grid. The District's power stations are diesel fired.

Food and beverages. The sector accounts for 19.6% of industrial output, with a main focus on bakery products.

Agriculture and forestry. The sector specializes mainly in reindeer farming (herds grew by 17.5% in 2002), fur farming, trapping (sable hunting), dairy farming, and pig breeding. The major enterprises are GUP Traditional Farming of the North and GUP Suridinsky Reindeer Stud Farm.

3.4. FUEL AND ENERGY BALANCE (OUTPUT AND CONSUMPTION PER RESOURCE)

Fuel and energy sector production and consumption trends, 1997–2002						TABLE 4
	1997	1998	1999	2000	2001	2002*
Electricity output, billion kWh	80.0	80.0	70.0	70.0	70.0	62.9
Oil output (including gas condensate), '000 tons	15.0	12.0	22.0	52.0	45.0	47.8

*Estimates of the Evenkiysky Autonomous District Administration

3.5. TRANSPORT INFRASTRUCTURE

Airports. The District is served by the Gorny Airport at Tura. The main carrier is GUP Turinsky Air Company.

River transport. The bulk of freight is shipped by OAO Yeniseisky River Company along the Nizhnyaya Tunguska and Podkamennaya Tunguska rivers. Freight traffic is seasonal. During the navigation period, some 80,000-110,000 tons of cargo is delivered to the District.

Oil and gas pipelines. Plans are afoot to build an oil pipeline in the District.

3.6. MAIN NATURAL RESOURCES:
RESERVES AND EXTRACTION IN 2002

The main natural resources found in the Evenkiysky Autonomous District are hydrocarbons, diamonds, coal, graphite, gold and platinoids, optical calcite, phosphate minerals, rare metals, rare earth elements, and semiprecious stones. The District contains promising deposits of copper, nickel and iron ores, abrasives, and mineral dyes.

Minerals and raw materials. The District has five explored oil and gas fields with proven reserves of 1.1 billion tons: the Yurubcheno-Tokhomskoye, Kuyum-binskoye, Sobinskoye, Omorinskoye, and Paiginskoye. The District has four coal fields: the Noginskoye, Yukta-kon, Chopko, and Korablik, plus further promising deposits of coal at the Verkhnemoerinskoye, Srednepelyatkinskoye, Vodopadninskoye, Bugariktinskoye, and Chirindinskoye. A large part of the barely explored Tungussky Coal Field with inferred reserves of 109 billion tons lies within the District.

Bedrock deposits of diamond have been discovered in the Maimecha-Kotuisky locality in the Kharamaisky Kimberlite Field with inferred reserves of 20 million carats. Several potentially diamondiferous areas such as the Maimecha-Kotuisky, Ilimpiysky, Velminsky, Katangsky, and Tychansky have also been explored.

Traces of gold have been found in the Chernorechensky (reserves of 3,740 kilograms), Ilimpiysky, and Vanavarsky localities. All known Russian deposits of optical calcite are located in the Evenk Autonomous District. Some 26 fields of Iceland spar have been found in the District. The Noginsky Graphite Mine is involved in graphite extraction.

Forests. Some 80% of the District lies under larch taiga, with pine and cedar the predominant species. A total of 33,915,000 hectares lies under forest cover. Timber reserves stand at 3,657 million cubic meters.

Water resources. The hydropower potential of the Podkamennaya Tunguska river stands at 20.6 billion kWh, while that of the Nizhnyaya Tunguska reaches 60.7 billion kWh.

Biosphere resources. The most common fauna species found in the District are sable, squirrel, ermine, muskrat, glutton, lynx, Arctic fox, North American mink, brown bear, Siberian and Arctic wolf, elk, and wild reindeer.

Recreational resources. The Putoransky and Tungussky national parks are located within the District.

4. TRADE OPPORTUNITIES

4.1. MAIN GOODS
PRODUCED IN THE REGION

Fuel. Oil output in 2002: 47,800 tons.
Agriculture. Output in 2002: potatoes – 900 tons

Major regional export and import entities		*TABLE 5*
ENTITY	ADDRESS	PHONE, FAX, E-MAIL
District State Unitary Enterprise Evenkianefteprodukt	Neftebaza, Tura, Evenkiysky Autonomous District, 648000	Phone/fax: (3912) 63 6359 E-mail: tkalenkovg@tura.evenkya.ru Vladimir Georgievich Tkalenko, CEO
Logistics Department (UMTS) of the Evenkiysky Autonomous District Administration	2, ul. Sovetskaya, Tura, Evenkiysky Autonomous District, 648000	Phone: (3912) 63 6300 Phone/fax: (3912) 63 6316 E-mail: bahtinia@krasn.evenkya.ru Ivan Alekseevich Bakhtin, Deputy Governor of Evenkiysky Autonomous District, Head of the Logistics Dept.

SIBERIAN FEDERAL DISTRICT

VI

5. INVESTMENT OPPORTUNITIES

5.1. INVESTMENTS IN 1992–2002 (BY INDUSTRY SECTOR), INCLUDING FOREIGN INVESTMENTS

The following general factors determine the investment appeal of the District:

- Legislation favoring investment activity;
- Rich natural resources.

5.2. CAPITAL INVESTMENT

Industry, transportation, and communications account for the lion's share of fixed capital investments.

Capital investments by industry sector, $ million						TABLE 6
	1997	1998	1999	2000	2001	2002*
Total capital investment	4.1	2.9	1.6	1.4	5.7	36.5
Including major industries (% of total)						
Industry	–	17.7	0.6	9.2	18.0	0.9
Agriculture and forestry	21.4	24.2	–	28.2	0.7	3.7
Construction	0.9	–	–	–	1.9	0.8
Transportation and communications	19.7	10.8	3.3	32.5	11.7	26.2
Trade and public catering	–	–	–	–	–	0.4
Other	58.0	47.3	96.1	30.1	67.7	68.0

*Estimates of the Evenkiysky Autonomous District Administration

Largest enterprises of the Evenkiysky Autonomous District	TABLE 7
COMPANY	SECTOR
GUP Turinsky Air Company	Transportation
OAO Eniseineftegaz	Fuel
OAO NK YUKOS	Fuel
OAO Krasnoyarskgazprom	Fuel
GUP Baikitsky Communal Services and Production Enterprise	Energy
GUP Vanavaraenergo	Energy
OGUP Ilimpiysky Power Grid	Energy
OGUP Ilimsky Power Grid	Energy

5.3. MOST ATTRACTIVE SECTORS FOR INVESTMENT

According to experts and the District Administration, the most promising sectors for investment are oil, timber, mining, and tourism.

5.4. CURRENT LEGISLATION ON INVESTOR TAX EXEMPTIONS AND PRIVILEGES

The Evenkiysky Autonomous District Law On Specific Aspects of Taxation in the District aims to improve the investment climate in the District and attract investment from other regions of the Russian Federation and overseas.

5.5. REGIONAL ENTITIES RESPONSIBLE FOR RAISING INVESTMENT

The District Administration is responsible for investment raising activities.

5.6. FEDERAL AND REGIONAL ECONOMIC AND SOCIAL DEVELOPMENT PROGRAMS FOR THE EVENKIYSKY AUTONOMOUS DISTRICT

Federal targeted programs. The District is participating in several federal targeted programs which aim to develop the transportation system, industry, and agriculture, and to improve public welfare, including: Modernization of Russia's Transportation System, 2002–2010, Energy Efficient Economy, 2002–2005 and through 2010, The Elimination of Differences in the Social and Economic Development of the Regions of Russian Federation, 2002–2010 and through 2015, and Ecology and Natural Resources of Russia, 2002–2010.

Regional programs. The District Administration is currently implementing some 21 regional targeted programs, most of which are socially focused.

6. INVESTMENT PROJECTS

Industry sector and project description	1) Expected results 2) Amount and term of investment 3) Form of financing[1] 4) Documentation[2]	Contact information
1	2	3

COAL		
79R001 ● ▲ Coal mining at the Noginsky Graphite Field, Ilimpiysky locality.	1) $0.5 million a year 2) $1.8 million/1 year 3) L 4) FS	Natural Resources Department of the Evenkiysky Autonomous District 20, ul. Krasnoyarskaya, Tura, Evenkiysky Autonomous District, 648000 Phone: (31113) 22 164 Fax: (3912) 63 6378 E-mail: upr@tura.evenkya.ru Nikolai Grigoryevich Oskin, Deputy Head of the Natural Resources Department, Head of the Environmental Protection Service

MINING		
79R002 ● ▲ Graphite mining at the Noginsky Graphite Field, Ilimpiysky locality.	1) $1.7 million a year 2) $0.5 million/1 year 3) L 4) FS	Natural Resources Department of the Evenkiysky Autonomous District 20, ul. Krasnoyarskaya, Tura, Evenkiysky Autonomous District, 648000 Phone: (31113) 22 164 Fax: (3912) 63 6378 E-mail: upr@tura.evenkya.ru Nikolai Grigoryevich Oskin, Deputy Head of the Natural Resources Department, Head of the Environmental Protection Service
79R003 ● ▲ Exploration followed by the recovery of gold ore at the Burny Field, Baikitsky locality.	1) $9.4 million a year 2) $3.9 million/12 years 3) L 4) FS	Natural Resources Department of the Evenkiysky Autonomous District 20, ul. Krasnoyarskaya, Tura, Evenkiysky Autonomous District, 648000 Phone: (31113) 22 164 Fax: (3912) 63 6378 E-mail: upr@tura.evenkya.ru Nikolai Grigoryevich Oskin, Deputy Head of the Natural Resources Department, Head of the Environmental Protection Service
79R004 ● Exploration followed by the recovery of strontium and barium at the Uvakinsky deposits of the Chunya-Ilimpiysky ore basin.	1) $1.4 million a year 2) $3.2 million/15 years 3) L 4) n/a	Natural Resources Department of the Evenkiysky Autonomous District 20, ul. Krasnoyarskaya, Tura, Evenkiysky Autonomous District, 648000 Phone: (31113) 22 164 Fax: (3912) 63 6378 E-mail: upr@tura.evenkya.ru Nikolai Grigoryevich Oskin Deputy Head of the Natural Resources Department, Head of the Environmental Protection Service

SIBERIAN FEDERAL DISTRICT

VI

[1] L – Loan, E – Equity, Leas. – Leasing, JV – Joint Venture
[2] BP – Business Plan, FS – Feasibility Study

1	2	3

79R005

Launch of production and processing of brines for lithium, magnesium, bromine, and calcium recovery, and of commercial sodium chloride (table salt) brine at the Noginsky Deposit, Ilimpiysky locality.

1) $56.9 million a year
2) $28.5 million/5 years
3) L
4) BP

OOO Evenk Lithium Company
20, ul. Krasnoyarskaya, Tura,
Evenkiysky Autonomous District, 648000
Phone: (31113) 22 164, 36 7263
Fax: (3912) 36 7841
Ylena Vasilyevna Izarova, CEO

FORESTRY, TIMBER, AND PULP AND PAPER

79R006

Logging operations at the Chemdalsky Site of the Tungussky-Chunsky forest.

1) Expected revenue of
   $10.7 million a year
2) $5.2 million/5 years
3) L
4) FS

Natural Resources Department
of the Evenkiysky Autonomous District
13, ul. Krasnoyarskaya, Tura,
Evenkiysky Autonomous District, 648000
Phone: (31113) 22 932
Fax: (3912) 63 6378
E-mail: upr@tura.evenkya.ru
Vladimir Alexandrovich Sel,
Deputy Head of the Natural Resources
Department, Head of the Forestry Service

79R007

Logging operations at the Osharovsky Site of the Baikitsky forest.

1) Expected revenue of
   $2.8 million a year
2) $3.0 million/5 years
3) L
4) FS

Natural Resources Department
of the Evenkiysky Autonomous District
13, ul. Krasnoyarskaya, Tura,
Evenkiysky Autonomous District, 648000
Phone: (31113) 22 932
Fax: (3912) 63 6378
E-mail: upr@tura.evenkya.ru
Vladimir Alexandrovich Sel,
Deputy Head of the Natural Resources
Department, Head of the Forestry Service

79R008

Logging operations at the Sulomaisky Site of the Baikitsky forest.

1) Expected revenue of
   $1.6 million a year
2) $2.9 million/5 years
3) L
4) FS

Natural Resources Department
of the Evenkiysky Autonomous District
13, ul. Krasnoyarskaya, Tura,
Evenkiysky Autonomous District, 648000
Phone: (31113) 22 932
Fax: (3912) 63 6378
E-mail: upr@tura.evenkya.ru
Vladimir Alexandrovich Sel,
Deputy Head of the Natural
Resources Department
Head of the Forestry Service

VII. FAR EASTERN FEDERAL DISTRICT

80. Republic of Sakha (Yakutia) [14]

81. Maritime Territory [25]

82. Khabarovsk Territory [27]

83. Amur Region [28]

84. Kamchatka Region [41]

85. Magadan Region [49]

86. Sakhalin Region [65]

87. Jewish Autonomous Region [79]

88. Koryaksky Autonomous District [82]

89. Chukotsky Autonomous District [87]

REGIONS OF THE FAR EASTERN FEDERAL DISTRICT

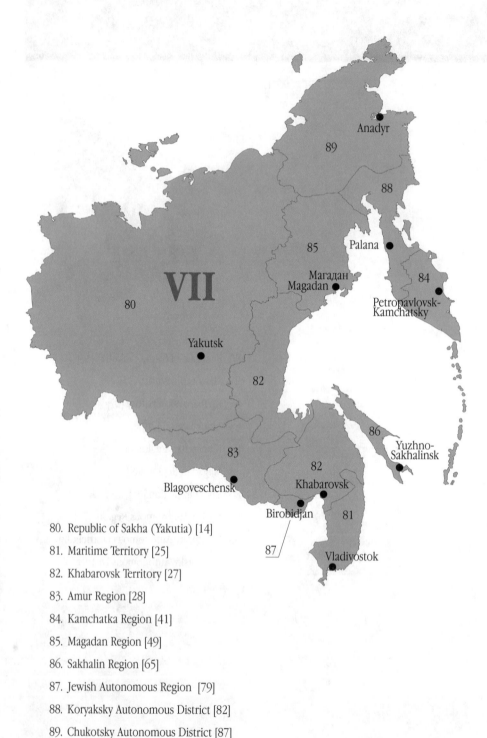

Anadyr

89

88

85 Palana

VII

Магадан
Magadan

Petropavlovsk-
Kamchatsky

84

80

Yakutsk

82

86

Yuzhno-
Sakhalinsk

83

82

Blagoveschensk

Khabarovsk

81

Birobidjan

87

Vladivostok

80. REPUBLIC OF SAKHA (YAKUTIA) [14]

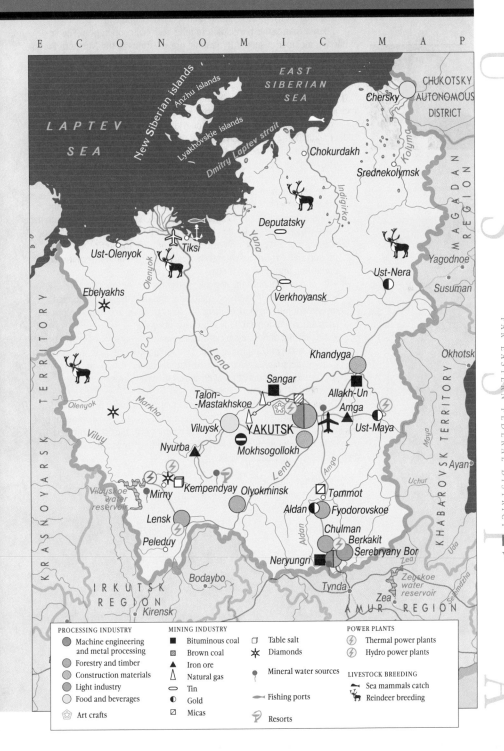

ECONOMIC MAP

PROCESSING INDUSTRY
- Machine engineering and metal processing
- Forestry and timber
- Construction materials
- Light industry
- Food and beverages
- Art crafts

MINING INDUSTRY
- Bituminous coal
- Brown coal
- Iron ore
- Natural gas
- Tin
- Gold
- Micas
- Table salt
- Diamonds
- Mineral water sources

Fishing ports

Resorts

POWER PLANTS
- Thermal power plants
- Hydro power plants

LIVESTOCK BREEDING
- Sea mammals catch
- Reindeer breeding

The Republic of Sakha (Yakutia) is one of the most attractive regions of the Far East Federal District in terms of investment appeal. The Republic possesses unique natural resources and high industrial and agricultural potential.

The year 2002 saw considerable structural changes in the Republic that resulted in the reform of the legislature and executive, the harmonization of Republican laws with the federal legislation, and the renewal of contracts with the federal authorities. The Republic has developed and adopted several important programs for its future economic and social development.

Yakutia is an active participant in inter-regional cooperation. The Republic is a member of such international organizations as the Northern Forum, the International Association for North-East Asian Regional Authorities, and the Russia-ASEAN Cooperation Fund. Over the past ten years, the Republic has established trade and economic links with more than 50 countries.

The Government of Sakha (Yakutia) is striving to create conditions conducive to the development of enterprise and foreign investment. The Republic is implementing a targeted program for the realization of the export potential of Sakha (Yakutia) in 2003-2006. The aim of the program is to achieve international market penetration for the Republic's output and increase its exports.

The program for the realization of the Republic's export potential envisages the following:

- the improvement of the legislative base governing investment guarantees, the development of a system of export guarantees and insurance, and the inclusion of the Republic's export-oriented mineral resource deposits into the list of deposits eligible for development under Product Sharing Agreements;
- comprehensive research into the competitive market position of prospective export goods and the search for potential international marketing and sales partners;
- the improvement of the Republic's customs service infrastructure;
- the acquisition of advanced equipment and the attraction of foreign investment into the development of export oriented and import replacing production and foreign trade infrastructure; and
- the drafting of business plans and investment proposals for export oriented companies in compliance with the international standards, participation in investment fairs, assistance in the international certification of exported goods, and the introduction of advanced management systems at exporting companies.

The deployment of the political, intellectual and financial potential of Russia and overseas countries to facilitate the implementation of major investment projects in the Republic of Sakha (Yakutia) will contribute to the economic, social, and political development of the Republic and the country as a whole and strengthen their international links.

Vyacheslav Shtyrov,
PRESIDENT OF THE REPUBLIC OF SAKHA (YAKUTIA)

1. GENERAL INFORMATION

1.1. GEOGRAPHY

Located in the northeast of the Asian part of Russia, the Republic of Sakha (Yakutia) covers a total area of 3,103,200 square kilometers. To the south it borders the Amur Region and the Khabarovsk Territory, to the east the Magadan Region and the Chukotsky Autonomous District, to the south-west and the Irkutsk Region, and to the west the Krasnoyarsk Territory. The Laptev Sea and the Eastern Siberian Sea wash the northern shores of the Republic.

1.2. CLIMATE

The Republic of Sakha (Yakutia) is located within the severe continental climatic zone.

January air temperatures descend to −43.2°C on average, rising to +18.7°C in July. Annual precipitation reaches 240 mm.

1.3. POPULATION

According to preliminary 2002 census results, the population of the Republic of Sakha (Yakutia) stood at 948,000 people. The average population density is 0.3 per square kilometer. The economically active population amounts to 484,400 people. Official 2002 unemployment stood at 1.2%, actual unemployment was 7.8%.

Demographically speaking, some 63.5% of the population are of the statutory working age, 25.8% are below the statutory working age, and 10.7% are beyond the statutory working age.

The Republic's ethnic mix is 45.5% Russian, 39.6% Sakha (Yakut), 4.4% Ukrainian, and 3.5% Evenk.

The major urban centers of the Republic of Sakha (Yakutia) are (2002 data): Yakutsk with 209,500 inhabitants, Neryungri with 74,300 inhabitants, and Mirny with 36,900 inhabitants.

Population								*TABLE 1*
	1992	1997	1998	1999	2000	2001	2002
Total population, '000	1,105	1,028	1,016	1,001	989	986	948
Economically active population, '000	601	508	504	503	497	489	484

2. ADMINISTRATION

11, ul. Kirova, Yakutsk, Republic of Sakha (Yakutia), 677022. Fax: (4112) 43 5557, 43 5055, (095) 925 5281
E-mail: gov_staff@first.sakhanet.ru; info@gov.sakha.ru; http://www.sakha.gov.ru

NAME	POSITION	CONTACT INFORMATION
Vyacheslav Anatolyevich SHTYROV	President of the Republic of Sakha (Yakutia)	Phone: (4112) 43 5050
Alexander Konstantinovich AKIMOV	Vice President of the Republic of Sakha (Yakutia)	Phone: (4112) 43 5566
Yegor Afanasyevich BORISOV	Head of the Government of the Republic of Sakha (Yakutia)	Phone: (4112) 43 5555
Gennady Fedorovich ALEKSEEV	First Deputy Head of the Government of the Republic of Sakha (Yakutia)	Phone: (4112) 43 5199
Artur Nikolaevich ALEKSEEV	Deputy Head of the Government of the Republic of Sakha (Yakutia) for Transport Infrastructure	Phone: (4112) 42 2334
Vasily Borisovich GRABTSEVICH	Deputy Head of the Government of the Republic of Sakha (Yakutia) for Housing and Communal Services, Energy and Construction	Phone: (4112) 43 5656
Alexander Vasilyevich VLASOV	Deputy Head of the Government of the Republic of Sakha (Yakutia)	Phone: (4112) 42 0804
Vladimir Danilovich DANILOV	Minister of Economic Development of the Republic of Sakha (Yakutia)	Phone: (4112) 42 0310 Fax: (4112) 42 1089 E-mail: minekon@optilink.ru http://www.invest.ykt.ru/

FAR EASTERN FEDERAL DISTRICT

VII

NAME	POSITION	CONTACT INFORMATION
Alexander Vasilyevich MIGALKIN	Minister of External Affairs of the Republic of Sakha (Yakutia)	Phone: (4112) 24 2451 Fax: (4112) 24 1939 E-mail: mvs@sakhanet.ru

3. ECONOMIC POTENTIAL

3.1. 1997–2002 GROSS REGIONAL PRODUCT (GRP). INDUSTRY BREAKDOWN

The Republic of Sakha's (Yakutia) 2002 gross regional product amounted to $4,330 million, or 10.3% up on 2001. Per capita GRP amounted to $3,982 in 2001, and $4,567 in 2002.

3.2. MAIN ECONOMIC GROWTH PROJECTIONS.

The blueprint for economic growth is set forth in the targeted program of Economic and Social Development in the Republic of Sakha (Yakutia)

Through 2007 (approved on April 22, 2002), and in the following programs: The Extension of the Urban Gas Network of the Republic of Sakha (Yakutia), The Development of the Gold Mining Industry and Non-Ferrous Metals Deposits in the Republic of Sakha (Yakutia), The Development of the Diamond Processing Industry of the Republic of Sakha (Yakutia), The Development of Jewelry and Stone Cutting Industries of the Republic of Sakha (Yakutia), The Development of the Timber Industry of the Republic of Sakha (Yakutia), and The Deployment of the Export Potential of the Republic of Sakha (Yakutia).

GRP trends in 1997–2002						TABLE 2
	1997	1998	1999	2000	2001*	2002*
GRP in current prices, $ million	5,213	3,397	2,499	2,912	3,925	4,330

*Estimates of the Republic of Sakha (Yakutia) Government

GRP industry breakdown in 1997–2002, % of total						TABLE 3
	1997	1998	1999	2000	2001*	2002*
GRP	100.0	100.0	100.0	100.0	100.0	100.0
Industry	31.2	41.1	55.6	49.7	48.1	41.4
Agriculture and forestry	3.9	2.7	2.5	2.7	4.3	4.1
Construction	8.6	6.6	4.3	7.1	7.6	6.7
Transport and communications	10.5	6.8	4.5	4.4	4.6	4.5
Trade and public catering	5.0	8.4	7.5	5.9	4.5	4.9
Other	39.4	34.7	27.4	31.0	31.1	39.2
Net taxes on output	1.4	−0.3	−1.8	−0.8	−0.2	−0.8

*Estimates of the Republic of Sakha (Yakutia) Government

The programs seek to accomplish the following goals:

• to develop the diamond industry by opening the mines at Aikhal and Mir, the proven kimberlite pipe deposits at Komsomolskaya, and the Nyurbinsky and Botuobinsky open pit mines;

• to develop the diamond cutting industry through technical revamping and modernization;

• to develop gold mining by opening the Kuranakhskoye ore field and implementing investment projects for the Nezhdaninskoye, Kuranakhskoye, Kuchusskoye, and Nizhne-Yakokitskoye deposits;

• to satisfy the Republic's demand for oil through putting into operation of an oil extraction and

refinery enterprise at Srednetuobinskoye oil and gas condensate field, an oil extraction and refinery enterprise in Western Yakutia at the Irelyakhskoye oil and gas condensate field, opening the Talakanskoye gas field, and developing the Chayandinskoye gas field; and

• to develop the coal mining industry through the expansion of the Yuzhno-Yakutsky open pit coal mine; opening of the Elginskoye deposit; completion of reconstruction works at OAO Yakutia Coal Ore Dressing Mill, technical revamping of the Neryungrinsky open pit mine and the Gebariki-Khaya mine; and the construction and expansion of the Chulmakanskaya mine.

Industry breakdown of industrial output in 1997–2002, % of total						TABLE 4
	1997	1998	1999	2000	2001	2002*
Industry	100.0	100.0	100.0	100.0	100.0	100.0
Non-ferrous metals	51.9	65.8	77.4	78.0	75.8	72.7
Fuel	17.4	13.6	10.3	9.9	9.6	11.2
Energy	14.6	12.8	7.4	7.1	7.2	11.0
Food and beverages	6.9	4.0	2.2	2.2	3.1	2.0
Construction materials	3.5	0.8	0.6	0.8	0.9	0.9
Forestry, timber, and pulp and paper	1.3	0.7	0.7	0.7	2.0	0.8
Machine engineering and metal processing	1.7	0.8	0.4	0.3	0.3	0.3
Light industry	0.6	0.2	0.2	0.2	0.1	0.2

*Estimates of the Republic of Sakha (Yakutia) Government

3.3. INDUSTRIAL OUTPUT IN 1997–2002 FOR MAJOR SECTORS OF ECONOMY

The Republic of Sakha's (Yakutia) major industrial sectors are non-ferrous metals (diamond mining, diamond cutting, and gold mining), energy, fuel, and food and beverages, which account for 96.9% of total industrial output.

Non-ferrous metals (diamond mining and processing, gold mining). The sector accounts for 72.7% of total industrial output.

The diamond mining industry grew by 2.6% year-on-year in 2002 (in real terms). The sector accounts for 62.8% of total industrial output. AK ALROSA accounts for the bulk of output. Other enterprises in the sector include OAO Alrosa-Nyurba, OAO Nizhne-Lenskoye and OOO Anabar Diamonds.

The diamond cutting sector accounts for 2.7% of total industrial output. The largest enterprises are OAO Tuymaada Diamond, OOO NPK EPL-Diamond, OAO Sapi-Diam, and ZAO SABE.

The gold mining sector accounts for 6.9% of total industrial output. Gold mining output increased by 10.7% in 2002. The largest enterprises are OAO Indigirzoloto, OAO Aldanzoloto, PK Zolotinka, Zapadnaya Cooperative, OOO Gold Prospectors Artel, Seligdar Cooperative, OOO Nirungan, and ZAO Yursky Mine.

Fuel. The fuel sector accounts for 11.2% of total industrial output.

The leading coal producer is OAO Yakut Coal, a major exporter of coal to the Asia-Pacific region.

Oil is produced at the Srednetuobinskoye and Irelyakhskoye oilfields. The major oil producer in the Republic is OAO Lena Oil and Gas (with more than 77% of total output).

The major gas producer in the Republic is OAO Yakutgazprom (86%).

Energy. Energy accounts for 11% of the total industrial output. The Republic's energy system includes 106 power stations, 97 of which are

diesel fired. The major stations are: Vilyuisk unified hydroelectric system (two HPS with a total installed capacity of 680 MW, a third 80 MW HPS to be launched in the fourth quarter of 2003), Neryungrinskaya HPS (570 MW), and Yakutskaya HPS (240 MW).

Forestry, timber, and pulp and paper. The sector accounts for 0.8% of total industrial output. Major enterprises include OAO Sakhales, ALROSA-Lesprom, OAO Aldanlesprom, OOO Mass, OAO Tabaginskaya Forestry Company, and OAO DOP Yakutuglestroy.

3.4. FUEL AND ENERGY BALANCE (OUTPUT AND CONSUMPRION PER RESOURCE)

The Republic's fuel resources and the support provided by the state have predetermined the emergence of an advanced fuel sector in Yakutia, one of the largest in the Far East of Russia. The Republic accounts for 32.1% of the coal output, 51.6% of the natural gas output, and 20.3% of the energy output of the Far East Federal District, or 40% of its combined primary fuel output.

Electricity and coal account for the lion's share of the Republic's fuel and energy sector.

The Republic's energy consumption amounts to 7 billion kWh per year. The Republic supplies surplus energy output (some 1 billion kWh) to adjacent energy systems. Over 60% of the Republic's total coal output is exported.

The ongoing development of the fuel and energy sector will depend on the development of the Yuzhno-Yakutsky coalfield deposits and small open pit coal mines, and the opening of the Chayandinsky and Srednevilyuisky gas condensate fields and the Talakansky and Srednebotuobinsky oil and gas condensate fields. This will enable the Republic to lessen its dependence on fuel imports and increase its revenues from the export of fuel to other regions of the Russian Federation and the Asia-Pacific region.

FAR EASTERN FEDERAL DISTRICT

VII

Fuel and energy sector production and consumption trends, 1997–2002						TABLE 5
	1997	1998	1999	2000	2001	2002*
Electricity output, billion kWh	7.3	7.1	7.4	7.6	8.1	7.9
Oil output (including gas condensate), '000 tons	229.5	239.1	304.5	418.9	436.2	415.0
Natural gas output, million cubic meters	1,577.0	1,552.0	1,602.0	1,628.0	1,623.0	1,591.8
Coal extraction, million tons	10.5	9.6	10.0	10.1	9.7	9.9
Electricity consumption, billion kWh	6.6	6.1	6.8	6.8	6.8	6.4
Oil consumption (including gas condensate), '000 tons.	219.3	229.2	248.9	348.1	404.2	278.9
Natural gas consumption, million cubic meters	1,579.6	1,552.9	1,601.2	1,621.0	1,624.6	1,388.1
Coal consumption, million tons	3.4	2.5	3.1	2.8	2.9	3.0

*Estimates of the Republic of Sakha (Yakutia) Government

3.5. TRANSPORT INFRASTRUCTURE

Roads. The Republic of Sakha (Yakutia) has 7,242 kilometers of paved public highway. The main highways are Neryungri – Yakutsk – Khandyga – Magadan, and Yakutsk – Nyurba – Mirny.

Railroads. The Republic of Sakha (Yakutia) has 165 kilometers of public railroads. A railroad is under construction to link Berkakit–Tommot–Yakutsk. The new line will considerably reduce freight transportation expenses for transport of goods to Yakutsk.

Airports. The Republic of Sakha (Yakutia) has 33 operational airports, two of which are federal (Yakutsk and Tiksi). Average annual passenger turnover amounts to 600,000 passengers. After the reconstruction and modernization of the air traffic control system, the Republic's airports will be capable of accepting all types of aircraft. In 2002, some 33,800 tons of freight was transported by air.

River transport. The Republic of Sakha (Yakutia) has 16,108 kilometers of navigable waterways. The main navigable waterways are the rivers Lena, Vilyui, Aldan, Kolyma, Indigirka, and Yana. Sea shipping companies use the Northern Route ports of Tiksi, Nizhneyansk, and Bykovsky. Navigation on the River Lena is open from May to October, and from June to October on the rivers Indigirka, Yana, and Kolyma.

Sea and river ports. The Republic of Sakha (Yakutia) has six river ports (Yakutsky, Nizhneyansky, Belogorsky, Lensky, Olekminsky, and Khandygsky) and two seaports (Tiksi and Zelenomyssky).

Oil and gas pipelines. The Republic of Sakha (Yakutia) has 1,818 kilometers of pipelines. In 2002, 1,247,400 tons of gas and 295,600 tons of oil were transported by pipeline.

3.6. MAIN NATURAL RESOURCES: RESERVES AND EXTRACTION IN 2002

The Republic's principal natural resources are diamonds, oil and gas, coal, gold, tin, and stibium.

Diamonds. Yakutia accounts for over 90% of Russia's total diamond output. Its major deposits are the Udachnaya, Mir, Aikhad, and Yubileynaya diamond pipes. Exploration work at the Botuobinskaya and Nyurbinskaya pipes has confirmed good prospects for the development of new kimberlite pipes.

Oil and natural gas. The highest concentration of hydrocarbon resources is found at the Vilyuiskaya, Nepsko-Botuobinskaya, and Predpatomskaya oil and gas fields. Major natural gas fields include the Srednevilyuiskoye, Srednebotuobinskoye, Srednetyungskoye, Verkhnevilyuchanskoye, and Chayandinskoye fields. All explored fields are located within the Nepsko-Botuobinskaya oil and gas area. The Srednebotuobinskoye (reserves estimated at 54,700,000 tons) and Irelyakhskoye (reserves estimated at 12,100,000 tons) fields are under pilot development, as well as the Talakanskoye field with deposit reserves of 114,400,000 tons.

Coal. The Republic of Sakha (Yakutia) has over 40% of Russia's total coal reserves, with 44 explored deposits. The Republic's coal fields include the Yuzhno-Yakutsky, Zyryansky, Lensky, and Tungussky fields. One of the most promising coal fields in the Republic at Elginskoye contains high quality coking coal reserves. The total coal reserve is estimated at 9.6 billion tons.

Gold. The Republic of Sakha (Yakutia) has over 20% of Russia's total gold reserves. Major gold extraction fields are located in the eastern and southern parts of Yakutia, for the most part in the basins of the Indigirka, Yana, and Aldan rivers.

Tin. The Republic has gigantic reserves of tin (50% of total Russian reserves), and accounts for 40% of Russia's total tin output.

Stibium. The Republic's stibium reserves are estimated at over 90% of Russia's total. Stibium deposits in the Republic include the large Sarylakhsky deposit, the suspended Sentachansky deposit, small gold and stibium deposits at Maltansky, Kimovsky, and Tansky with low content of associated stibium. The Sarylakhskoye and Sentachasnkoye deposits are estimated to contain 210,000 tons of stibium.

4. TRADE OPPORTUNITIES

4.1. MAIN GOODS
PRODUCED IN THE REGION

In 2002 the Republic of Sakha (Yakutia) produced:

Non-ferrous metals: Rock diamonds – $1,705.0 million; cut diamonds – $166.2 million; gold – $188.6 million; jewelry – $15.9 million.

Coal: 9,869,000 tons.

Hydrocarbons: natural gas – 1,591,800 cubic meters, gas condensate – 75,600 tons.

Timber: sawn timber – 16,670 cubic meters.

Construction materials: cement – 236,000 tons, non-metal construction materials – 843,100 cubic meters.

Food and beverages: whole milk products – 20,800 tons; bread and bakery products – 48,800 tons; meat – 1,600 tons; fish – 2,600 tons; butter – 2,400 tons; flour – 5,900 tons; non-alcoholic beverages –1,000 decaliters.

4.2. EXPORTS,
INCLUDING EXTRA-CIS.

In 2000, the Republic's extra-CIS exports totaled $1,089 million, with CIS exports $0.5 million. The corresponding figures for 2001 were $1,282.8 million and $15.5 million, and $943.9 million and $13.5 million for 2002.

Jewelry diamonds (66.7%), brilliants (17.7%), and coal (13.7%) constitute the bulk of the Republic's export. Main importers of the Republic's products include the UK (62.4% of total 2002 exports), Israel (11.5%), Japan (10.3%), and the USA (6.5%).

4.3. IMPORTS, INCLUDING EXTRA-CIS

In 2000, the Republic's extra-CIS imports totaled $25 million; CIS imports totaled $4 million. The corresponding figures for 2001 were $29.9 million and $1.9 million, and $31.6 million and $5.9 million for 2002.

Machinery and equipment (39.1%), trucks (13.4%), car spare parts (13.7%), and rubber and rubber items (13.6%) constitute the bulk of the Republic's import. Main exporters to the Republic include the USA (37.8% of total 2002 imports), Japan (18.4%), Sweden (12.4%), and Finland (12.2%).

Major regional export and import entities		*TABLE 6*
ENTITY	ADDRESS	PHONE, FAX, E-MAIL
ZAO AK ALROSA	6, ul. Lenina, Mirny, Republic of Sakha (Yakutia), 678170	Phone: (41136) 90 021 Fax: (41136) 30 451, 90 162, (095) 745 8061 E-mail: AHO@centr.alrosa-mir.ru
ZAO Sarylakh-Stibium	2, ul.Lenina, p. Ust-Nera, Oymyakonsky Ulus, Republic of Sakha (Yakutia), 678730	Phone: (41154) 21 783, 22 629, 20 122
OAO Yakut Coal	3/1, ul. Lenina, Neryungri, Republic of Sakha (Yakutia), 678960	Phone: (41147) 43 874, 96 125 Fax: (41147) 42 024 E-mail: post@yakutugol.ru
OAO Sakhales	Offices 201-206, 208, 22, pr. Lenina, Yakutsk, Republic of Sakha (Yakutia), 677018	Phone: (4112) 24 3624 Fax: (4112) 24 3629 E-mail: oliwikko@yakutia.ru
OOO Sakha Jewelry	Office 505, 1, ul. Oktyabrskaya, Yakutsk, Republic of Sakha (Yakutia), 677000	Phone/fax: (4112) 44 6199, 44 6708
OAO Tuymaada Diamond	22/1, pr. Lenina, Yakutsk, Republic of Sakha (Yakutia), 677000	Phone: (4112) 32 0041 Fax: (4112) 32 1617 E-mail: TDiamond@sakhanet.ru, tdiam314@sakha.com
GUP Sakhabult	3, ul. 50 let Sovetskoy Armii, Yakutsk, Republic of Sakha (Yakutia), 677001	Phone: (4112) 45 6186, 46 3227, 46 1000 Fax: (4112) 45 6186, 46 3562, 43 5641

FAR EASTERN FEDERAL DISTRICT

VII

5. INVESTMENT OPPORTUNITIES

5.1. INVESTMENTS IN 1992–2002 (BY INDUSTRY SECTOR), INCLUDING FOREIGN INVESTMENTS

The following main factors determine the investment appeal of the Republic of Sakha (Yakutia):
- Its favorable geographical location and proximity to the Asia-Pacific markets;
- Its considerable raw materials (diamonds, gold) and energy resources;
- The willingness of state and local administration bodies to negotiate with investors on investment and investment capital guarantees.

5.2. CAPITAL INVESTMENT

Industry and construction account for the lion's share of capital investment.

5.3. MAJOR ENTERPRISES (INCLUDING ENTERPRISES WITH FOREIGN INVESTMENT)

The Republic's enterprises with foreign investment operate mostly in the diamond cutting industry (OOO Sakha-Deutsche Diamant, OAO Sapi-Diam, ZAO Sakha-Belgian AK Sabe, OOO Choron Diamond) and the coal-mining industry (OOO Erchim Tkhan, OOO Erel Ltd).

5.4. MOST ATTRACTIVE SECTORS FOR INVESTMENT

According to experts and the Government of the Republic of Sakha (Yakutia), the most attractive sectors for investment are the gold mining industry and fuel and energy sectors (oil and gas, coal mining, and energy).

Capital investment by industry sector, $ million						*TABLE 7*
	1997	1998	1999	2000	2001	2002
Total capital investment	993.5	430.9	367.3	569.9	727.0	711.5
Including major industries (% of total)						
Industry	38.2	52.1	59.4	61.0	54.2	71.5
Agriculture and forestry	3.1	1.3	1.3	2.1	2.9	0.2
Construction	1.7	3.5	1.5	1.2	10.5	21.6
Transport and communications	11.8	10.4	8.4	9.1	3.6	2.7
Trade and public catering	2.2	2.0	0.7	1.8	1.1	0.4
Other	43.0	30.7	28.7	24.8	27.7	3.6

Foreign investment trends in 1997–2002						*TABLE 8*
	1997	1998	1999	2000	2001	2002
Foreign investments, $ million	14.1	196.6	85.6	159.6	144.6	291.3
Including FDI, $ million	9.8	0.9	0.4	0.6	4.0	9.9

Largest enterprises of the Republic of Sakha (Yakutia)		*TABLE 9*
COMPANY	INDUSTRY	2001 NET PROFIT, $ MILLION*
ZAO AK ALROSA	Non-ferrous metals	416.3
ZAO Sarylakh-Stibium	Non-ferrous metals	0.2
OAO AK Yakutskenergo	Energy	-2.2
OAO Yakutgazprom	Natural gas	5.2
OAO Yakut Coal	Coal	29.0
OOO SP Erel-Ltd	Coal	0.5
GUP Sakhalekom	Telecommunications	10.9
GUP FAPK Yakutia	Food and beverages	0.09
OAO Sapi-Diam	Diamond cutting	0.3
OAO APUK Yakutia Gold	Jewelry	0.7

*Estimates of the Republic of Sakha (Yakutia) Government

5.5. CURRENT LEGISLATION ON INVESTOR TAX EXEMPTIONS AND PRIVILEGES

Investor tax privileges are granted under the federal legislation. Regional tax privileges are approved under the Law of the Republic of Sakha (Yakutia) On the Tax Policy of the Republic of Sakha (Yakutia).

The Law of the Republic of Sakha (Yakutia) On Foreign Investment in the Republic of Sakha (Yakutia) regulates foreign investment activity in the Republic.

The Government of the Republic of Sakha (Yakutia) also drafts (within its authority) legislative acts regulating international and foreign tra-de relations. The Law of the Republic of Sakha (Yakutia) On International and Foreign Trade Relations of the Republic of Sakha (Yakutia), which was drafted in 2002, provides a procedure for the drafting, coordination, signing and ratification of the Republic's foreign trade agreements and reg-

ulates the activities of foreign representative offices of the Republic of Sakha (Yakutia).

Direct relations are gradually being established with administrative bodies in overseas countries. The Republic has drafted and is coordinating agreements on trade, scientific and technical and cultural cooperation between the Government of the Republic of Sakha (Yakutia), on the one hand, and the Government of the Province of Heilongjiang, China, and the Administration of the Almaty Region of Kazakhstan, on the other hand.

The State Customs Committee of the Russian Federation and the Government of the Republic of Sakha (Yakutia) have agreed to establish a customs post at Yakutsk. This will enable the enterprises registered in the Yakutsk customs jurisdiction to obtain export clearance in a reduced timeframe, thus boosting the Republic's diamond producing, diamond cutting and jewelry sectors.

Regional entities responsible for raising investments

TABLE 10

ENTITY	ADDRESS	PHONE, FAX, E-MAIL
OAO Republican Investment Company Sakhacapital	22, pr. Lenina, Yakutsk, the Republic of Sakha (Yakutia), 677000	Phone: (4112) 24 3152, 24 3134 Fax: (4112) 24 3152 E-mail: sc@sakha.ru; http://www.sc.sakha.ru
OAO Investment Group ALROSA	6/1, per. Posledny, Moscow 107045 33, ul. Merzlotnaya, Yakutsk, the Republic of Sakha (Yakutia), 677010	Phone: (095) 748 2080 Fax: (095) 748 2064 E-mail: Prokhorenko@alrosa-inv.ru Phone: (4112) 33 4595 Fax: (4112) 33 4890
ZAO Investment Company VostokCapital	Building 6, 3, Shlyuzovaya Naberezhnaya, Moscow, 113114; Office 41, 18, ul. Ammosova, Yakutsk, the Republic of Sakha (Yakutia), 677000	Phone: (095) 232 3445 Fax: (095) 238 1519 Phone/fax: (4112) 24 1467
OAO Investment Company Sakhainvest	3/1, per. Pryamoy, Moscow, 121099; 20, ul. Tolstogo, Yakutsk, the Republic of Sakha (Yakutia), 677000	Phone: (095) 241 8515 E-mail: sis@sakhainvest.ru http://www.sakhainvest.ru Phone: (4112) 42 0610 Fax: (4112) 42 0556

5.6. FEDERAL AND REGIONAL ECONOMIC AND SOCIAL DEVELOPMENT PROGRAMS FOR THE REPUBLIC OF SAKHA (YAKUTIA)

Federal targeted programs. The major federal targeted program for the Republic is the program for the Economic and Social Development of the Far East and Trans-Baikal Region, 1996–2005 and through 2010, which aims to create economic conditions conducive to sustainable economic development taking into account the geo-strategic interests and security of the country, to develop infrastructure and foster a favorable investment climate for the development of priority industries, to encourage cooperation with overseas and adjacent countries, and to develop the social sphere. The program financing amounts to $1,576.3 million from all sources.

The program for the Modernization of Russia's Transport System, 2002–2010 seeks to improve the coordination, efficiency, and safety of the national transport system, and support the vital national interests of Russia.

Regional programs. The program for the Development of Enterprise and Non-Food Mar-kets in the Republic of Sakha (Yakutia), 2003– 2006 aims to improve the system of state support and foster small enterprise, to develop local production, create jobs, improve utilities services, public catering, and tourism, and promote better home economics education. The program is expected to result in increased output of goods and services and the creation of new jobs. A total of $10 million in financing was allocated from the Republic's budget in 2003.

The Program for the Social and Economic Development of Rural Areas in the Republic of Sakha (Yakutia), 2002–2006 aims to improve living standards in rural areas using material, technical, financial, and labor resources, and to create conditions conducive to rural social and economic development and agricultural output growth. A total of $90.3 million in financing was allocated from the Republic's budget in 2003.

FAR EASTERN FEDERAL DISTRICT

VII

6. INVESTMENT PROJECTS

Industry sector and project description	1) Expected results 2) Amount and term of investment 3) Form of financing[1] 4) Documentation[2]	Contact information
1	2	3

OIL

80R001

| Creation of an oil extraction, transportation and processing plant at Talakanskoye gas and oil field.
Project goal: to supply consumers in the Republic of Sakha (Yakutia) with oil products, to export oil. | 1) 4.5 million tons of oil per year
2) $871 million/8.3 years
3) L
4) Investment proposal | Ministry of Industry of the Republic of Sakha (Yakutia)
12, ul. Kirova, Yakutsk, Republic of Sakha (Yakutia), 677000
Phone: (4112) 42 0269
Fax: (4112) 42 0283, 42 3525
E-mail: minprom@ykt.ru
Larisa Mikhailovna Alekseeva, Head of the Department of Investment and Targeted Programs
Alexander Anatolyevich Ogly, Minister of Industry of the Republic of Sakha (Yakutia) |

OIL AND NATURAL GAS

80R002

| Development of the Chayandinskoye oil and gas condensate field.
Project goal: to supply consumers in the Far East District of Russia with gas and oil and to export gas and oil to the northern-eastern provinces of China. | 1) 20 billion cubic meters of gas per year, 1.9 million tons of oil per year
2) $2,800 million/10.5 years
3) L
4) FS | Ministry of Industry of the Republic of Sakha (Yakutia)
12, ul. Kirova, Yakutsk, Republic of Sakha (Yakutia), 677000
Phone: (4112) 42 0269
Fax: (4112) 42 0283, 42 3525
E-mail: minprom@ykt.ru
Larisa Mikhailovna Alekseeva, Head of the Department of Investment and Targeted Programs
Alexander Anatolyevich Ogly, Minister of Industry of the Republic of Sakha (Yakutia) |

80R003

| Development of a gas processing plant at Srednevilyuyskoye field.
Project goal: to increase output of processed gas condensate. | 1) Up to 4 billion cubic meters per year
2) $624 million/13.2 years
3) L
4) BP | OAO NNGK Sakhaneftegaz
4/1, ul. Khalturina, Yakutsk, Republic of Sakha (Yakutia), 677000
Phone/fax: (4112) 45 5235, 45 5126
Ruslan Yuryevich Shipkov, President |

COAL

80R004

| Development of Elginskoye coal field.
Project goal: to develop and sell coal. | 1) Sales of $600 million per year
2) $500 million/8 years
3) L, E
4) Investment proposal | OAO Elgaugol
5, ul. Severnaya, Neryungri, Republic of Sakha (Yakutia), 678922
Moscow representative office:
5, Khruschevsky per., Moscow, 119034
Phone: (095) 201 2788; Fax: (095) 201 4288
E-mail: elgaugol@mail.ru
Anatoly Vasilyevich Baulin, Executive Director
Alexander Alexandrovich Kulakovsky, Chairman of the Board of Directors |

[1] L – Loan, E – Equity, Leas. – Leasing, JV – Joint Venture
[2] BP – Business Plan, FS – Feasibility Study

1	2	3

MINING

80R005

Development of Aykhal underground mine.
Project goal: to produce rock diamonds.

● ◆ ▲

1) 0.5 million tons of ore output per year; sales of $45.6 million per year
2) $40 million/5.5 years
3) L
4) FS, BP

ZAO AK ALROSA
6, ul. Lenina, Mirny, Republic
of Sakha (Yakutia), 678170
Phone: (41136) 90 021
Fax (41136) 30 451, 90 162, (095) 745 8061
E-mail: AHO@centr.alrosa-mir.ru
Alexei Timofeevich Vedin,
Director of Yakutniproalmaz Institute
Vladimir Tikhonovich Kalitin, President

80R006

Development of Mir underground mine.
Project goal: to produce rock diamonds.

● ◆ ▲

1) Sales of $209.2 million per year
2) $200 million/5 years
3) L
4) FS, BP

ZAO AK ALROSA
6, ul. Lenina, Mirny, Republic
of Sakha (Yakutia), 678170
Phone: (41136) 90 021
Fax (41136) 30 451, 90 162, (095) 745 8061
E-mail: AHO@centr.alrosa-mir.ru
Alexei Timofeevich Vedin,
Director of Yakutniproalmaz Institute
Vladimir Tikhonovich Kalitin, President

80R007

Development of deep reserves
at the Udachnaya pipe.
Project goal: to produce rock diamonds.

● ◆ ▲

1) Up to 4 million tons of ore per year, sales of $262.9 million per year
2) $650 million/6.4 years
3) L
4) FS, BP

ZAO AK ALROSA
6, ul. Lenina, Mirny, Republic
of Sakha (Yakutia), 678170
Phone: (41136) 90 021
Fax (41136) 30 451, 90 162, (095) 745 8061
E-mail: AHO@centr.alrosa-mir.ru
Alexei Timofeevich Vedin,
Director of Yakutniproalmaz Institute
Vladimir Tikhonovich Kalitin, President

80R008

Industrial development of Kyuchus gold
mine: development of deposit and construction of an ore-dressing plant.
Project goal: to produce ore.

■ ● ★ ❖ ▲

1) Sales of $113.4 million per year
2) $241.2 million/6 years
3) JV, E, L, Leas.
4) FS

Ministry of Industry of the Republic
of Sakha (Yakutia)
12, ul. Kirova, Yakutsk, Republic
of Sakha (Yakutia), 677000
Phone: (4112) 42 0269
Fax: (4112) 42 0283, 42 3525
E-mail: minprom@ykt.ru
Larisa Mikhailovna Alekseeva,
Head of the Department of Investment
and Targeted Programs
Alexander Anatolyevich Ogly, Minister of
Industry of the Republic of Sakha (Yakutia)

80R009

Construction of a gold-mining center
at Kuranakhskoye ore field.
Project goal: to create a modern
gold-mining center.

● ◆

1) 4 million tons of ore per year
2) $83 million/7.5 years
3) L
4) BP

OAO Aldanzoloto
14, ul. Stroitelnaya, pos. Nizhny Kuranakh,
Aldansky ulus, Republic of Sakha
(Yakutia), 678940
Phone/fax: (41145) 62 500, 21 882,
62 714, 21 882
Mikhail Lvovich Bruk, Director

80R010

Construction of the first stage
of the a new production center
at Nezhdaninskoye gold field.
Project goal: to produce gold.

● ▲

1) Up to 5 tons per year
2) $121 million/8 years
3) L
4) FS

ZAO Yuzhno-Verkhoyanskaya
Mining Company
33, ul. Merzlotnaya, Yakutsk,
Republic of Sakha (Yakutia), 677010
Phone: (4112) 33 4595; fax: (4112) 33 4890
E-mail: svmcinfo@sakha.ru
Gennady Fedorovich Piven, CEO
Grigory Nikolaevich Ivanov,
Executive Director

FAR EASTERN FEDERAL DISTRICT

VII

1	2	3
80R011 ● ◆		Gold Prospectors Artel Cooperative Seligdar
Construction of an ore-mining center for gold extraction at Nizhneyakitskoye ore field. Project goal: to extract gold.	1) 4.8 tons of commercial gold per year 2) $18.4 million/1.8 years 3) L 4) BP	12, 25-th Piket, Aldan, Republic of Sakha (Yakutia), 678900 Phone/fax: (41145) 21 815, 21 625 E-mail: office@seligdar.ru Http://www.seligdar.ru Anatoly Nikitich Labun, Head of Artel
80R012 ● ◆		OOO Gold Prospectors Artel Drazhnik
Creation of a golden ore dressing plant at Zaderzhninskoye field. Project goal: to produce ore.	1) 20,000 tons of ore per year 2) $3 million/2.8 years 3) L 4) BP	4, ul. Drazhnikov, pos. Zvezdochka, Ust-Maysky District, Republic of Sakha (Yakutia), 678627 Phone: (41140) 25 542; fax: (41140) 21 149 Vasily Pavlovich Stepanov, CEO

ENERGY

1	2	3
80R013 ● ◆ ▲		OAO AK Yakutskenergo
Construction of high-tension line Mirny-Suntar-Nyurba. Project goal: to reduce electricity losses in electricity supply networks.	1) 373.4 kilometers of lines 2) $48.9 million/5 years 3) L 4) FS, BP	14, ul. F. Popova, Yakutsk, Republic of Sakha (Yakutia), 677000 Phone: (4112) 46 1350, 46 1351 Phone/fax: (4112) 46 1355 E-mail: inform@yakut.electra.ru Konstantin Konstantinovich Ilkovsky, CEO
80R014 ● ▲		OAO AK Yakutskenergo
Construction of high-tension line Khandyga-Gebariki-Khaya. Project goal: to reduce electricity losses in electricity supply networks.	1) Total budget savings of $1.6 million 2) $6.43 million/2 years 3) L 4) FS	14, ul. F. Popova, Yakutsk, Republic of Sakha (Yakutia), 677000 Phone: (4112) 46 1350, 46 1351 Phone/fax: (4112) 46 1355 E-mail: inform@yakut.electra.ru Konstantin Konstantinovich Ilkovsky, CEO

TRANSPORT INFRASTRUCTURE

1	2	3
80R015 ● ◆ ▲		OAO AK Yakutia Railroads
Completion of Berkakit-Tommot-Yakutsk railroad construction. Project goal: to improve transport service, to increase freight turnover.	1) Freight turnover of up to 1,716.5 million tons-kilometers per year, cargo volume of up to 5.2 million tons per year 2) $988 million/6 years 3) L 4) FS, BP	14, ul. Mayakovskogo, Aldan, Republic of Sakha (Yakutia), 677890 Phone/fax: (41145) 22 3070 Alexander Nikolaevich Dudnikov, CEO

HOTELS AND TOURISM

1	2	3
80R016 ● ▲		Science and Technology Park of YSU
Creation of "Pole of Cold" inter-regional education and research center for the development of adventure tourism. Project goal: to increase the tourist inflow into the Republic.	1) 710 tourists in the first year; sales of $0.5 million for the first year 2) $1.2 million/5 years 3) L 4) FS	Office 607, 48, ul. Kulakovskogo, Yakutsk, Republic of Sakha (Yakutia), 677016 Phone: (4112) 25 3590 Fax: (4112) 25 3593 E-mail: YBTI@sitc.ru Alexander Nikolaevich Myarin, Director

OTHER (JEWELRY)

1	2	3
80R017 ● ◆		OAO Aldanzoloto
Modernization of Kuranakhsky jewelry plant. Project goal: to increase output and diversify product mix.	1) Sales of up to $31.5 million per year 2) $15.5 million/5.5 years 3) L 4) BP	14, ul. Stroitelnaya, Nizhny Kuranakh, Aldansky ulus, Republic of Sakha (Yakutia), 678940 Phone/fax: (41145) 62 500, 21 882, 62 714 Mikhail Lvovich Bruk, Director

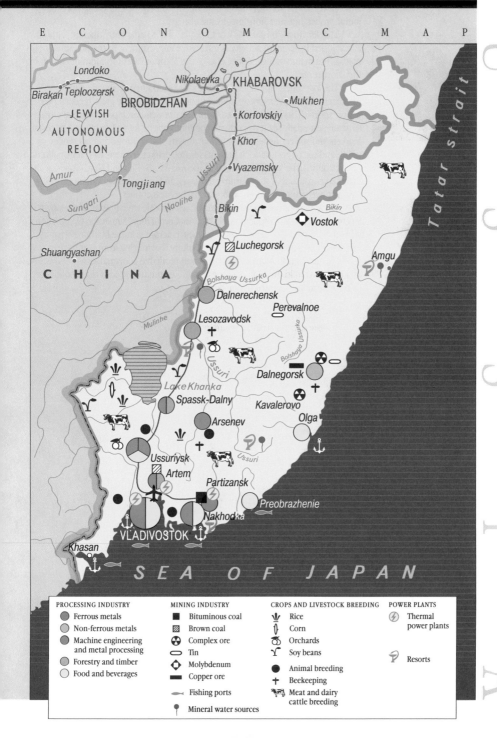

ECONOMICMAP

Londoko
Birakan Teploozersk
NIKOLAEVKA KHABAROVSK
BIROBIDZHAN
JEWISH
AUTONOMOUS
REGION
Mukhen
Korfovskiy
Khor
Vyazemsky
Amur
Tongjiang
Sungari
Naolihe
Ussuri
Bikin
Bikin
Vostok
Shuangyashan
Luchegorsk
Amgu
CHINA
Bolshaya Ussurka
Dalnerechensk
Mulinhe
Perevalnoe
Lesozavodsk
Bolshaya Ussurka
Dalnegorsk
Ussuri
Lake Khanka
Spassk-Dalny
Kavalerovo
Arsenev
Olga
Ussuri
Ussuriysk
Artem
Partizansk
Preobrazhenie
Nakhodka
VLADIVOSTOK
Khasan

S E A   O F   J A P A N

Tatar strait

PROCESSING INDUSTRY	MINING INDUSTRY	CROPS AND LIVESTOCK BREEDING	POWER PLANTS
Ferrous metals	Bituminous coal	Rice	Thermal power plants
Non-ferrous metals	Brown coal	Corn	
Machine engineering and metal processing	Complex ore	Orchards	Resorts
Forestry and timber	Tin	Soy beans	
Food and beverages	Molybdenum	Animal breeding	
	Copper ore	Beekeeping	
	Fishing ports	Meat and dairy cattle breeding	
	Mineral water sources		

Located in the southern part of Russia's Far East, the Maritime Territory is one of the fastest growing economies among Russian regions. The fishing industry, constituting one third of the Territory's total industrial output, forms the basis of the Territory's economy. The Territory produces fish in the seas of the Far East and in the Pacific and Indian oceans. Fish species include: salmon, herring, rockfish, flounder, halibut, pollack, tuna fish, saury, mackerel, and sardine. The Territory also catches crab, shrimp, trepang, mussels, queens and seaweed. The Territory has a developed industry: machine engineering, metal processing, and non-ferrous metals.

The Territory's businesses would not be able to efficiently operate without a developed investment activity. A qualitative improvement in the investment climate is the main strategic policy goal of the Maritime Territory Administration in the short-term.

The investment appeal of the Territory is determined by: its rare natural resources with strong export potential (more than 30% of the gross regional product is exported); its highly qualified workforce; its well-developed industrial infrastructure, especially sea transport and communications; its well-developed financial markets and solvent demand; its efficient system of state protection of owners' rights; and the opportunities it presents for free market relations with regional economic entities (the leading countries of the Asia-Pacific Rim and North America all maintain consulates in the Maritime Territory); and its legal environment providing basis for free market relations with regional business entities.

World famous companies, including Coca-Cola Hellenic Bottling Company, LG Electronics, Hyundai Corporation, Nissho Iwai Corporation, Sumitomo Corporation and others, are developing successful business enterprises in the Maritime Territory. Investment by Russian businesses in the Territory is increasing from year to year.

We are open to mutually beneficial and profitable cooperation with investors and business circles from all countries. We are committed to fostering confidence in the enormous potential of our Territory.

Sergei Darkin,
GOVERNOR OF THE MARITIME TERRITORY

1. GENERAL INFORMATION

1.1. GEOGRAPHY

The Maritime Territory covers an area of 165,900 square kilometers. To the north, the Territory borders the Khabarovsk Territory, and to the west and southwest – China and North Korea. The Territory is washed by the Sea of Japan in the east and south.

1.2. CLIMATE

The Maritime Territory enjoys a monsoon climate. Winters are frosty, with little snow. Monsoon rains are typical for the region. Typhoons and flooding are not uncommon at the end of summer and in the fall. January temperatures average around −18.4°C, rising to +18.8°C in July. Annual precipitation of 500–900 mm makes the Maritime Territory a relatively damp region.

1.3. POPULATION

According to preliminary 2002 census results, total population in the Maritime Territory was 2,068,000 people. The average population density is 12.5 people per square kilometer.

The economically active population amounted to 1,120,000. Official unemployment in 2002 was 8.9%; the actual rate was 12%.

Demographically speaking, some 64.2% are of statutory working age, 19% are below the statutory working age, and 16.8% are beyond the statutory working age.

The major urban centers of the Maritime Territory (2002 data) are Vladivostok with 591,800 inhabitants, Ussuriysk with 157,800 inhabitants, and Nakhodka with 149,300 inhabitants.

Population								TABLE 1
	1992	1997	1998	1999	2000	2001	2002
Total population, '000	2,307	2,234	2,214	2,194	2,172	2,155	2,068
Economically active population, '000	1,247	1,106	1,118	1,127	1,166	1,142	1,120

2. ADMINISTRATION

22, ul. Svetlanskaya, Vladivostok, Maritime Territory, 690110
Phone: (4232) 22 3800; fax (4232) 22 1769; e-mail: webmaster@primorsky.ru; http://www.primorsky.ru

NAME	POSITION	CONTACT INFORMATION
Sergei Mikhailovich DARKIN	Governor of the Maritime Territory	Phone: (4232) 22 3800 Fax: (4232) 22 1769 E-mail: gubernator@primorsky.ru
Igor Vladimirovich IVANOV	First Vice Governor of the Maritime Territory for International Relations	Phone: (4232) 22 2785 E-mail: ivanov@primorsky.ru
Alexander Ivanovich KOSTENKO	First Vice Governor of the Maritime Territory for Economy and Finance	Phone: (4232) 22 3793 Fax: (4232) 22 7225 E-mail: kostenko@primorsky.ru
Fedor Timofeevich NOVIKOV	First Vice Governor of the Maritime Territory for Fishing and Defense Industry	Phone: (4232) 22 2631 E-mail: novikov@primorsky.ru
Yury Ivanovich POPOV	Vice Governor of the Maritime Territory for Agriculture and Food	Phone: (4232) 22 5755 Fax: (4232) 22 9867 E-mail: pip77@primorsky.ru
Yury Ivanovich LIKHOYDA	Vice Governor of the Maritime Territory for Fuel and Energy	Phone: (4232) 22 2402 Fax: (4232) 22 0543 E-mail: lihoyda@primorsky.ru
Victor Vasilyevich GORCHAKOV	Vice Governor of the Maritime Territory for Foreign Economic Activity	Phone: (4232) 22 1019 E-mail: gorchakov@primorsky.ru

FAR EASTERN FEDERAL DISTRICT

VII

3. ECONOMIC POTENTIAL

3.1. 1997–2002 GROSS REGIONAL PRODUCT (GRP). INDUSTRY BREAKDOWN

The Territory's 2002 GRP was $2,881 million, or 13% up on 2001. Per capita GRP was $1,186 in 2001, and $1,393 in 2002.

3.2. MAJOR ECONOMIC GROWTH PROJECTIONS

The blueprint for economic development in the Territory is provided in the Framework for Social and Economic Development in the Maritime Territory Through 2005. The Framework sets the following priority targets for industrial reforms: to improve the competitiveness and technical quality of the Territory's output; to secure access for the Territory's innovative and high-tech products to domestic and foreign markets; and to encourage the production of import substitution products. The Framework also calls for greater diversification of industrial output.

GRP trends in 1997–2002						TABLE 2
	1997	1998	1999	2000	2001*	2002*
GRP in current prices, $ million	4,897	3,193	2,224	2,358	2,554	2,881

*Estimates of the Maritime Territory Administration

GRP industry breakdown in 1997–2002, % of total						TABLE 3
	1997	1998	1999	2000	2001*	2002*
GRP	100.0	100.0	100.0	100.0	100.0	100.0
Industry	30.5	32.3	30.3	29.6	26.9	24.3
Agriculture and forestry	3.6	5.0	4.1	4.6	5.8	4.9
Construction	5.3	4.9	3.8	4.1	4.5	4.2
Transport and communications	19.7	17.6	21.7	20.7	20.4	21.8
Trade and public catering	11.2	12.4	15.3	15.1	15.7	16.1
Other	31.1	27.4	21.9	23.0	25.8	26.8
Net taxes on output	−1.4	0.4	2.9	2.9	0.9	1.9

*Estimates of the Maritime Territory Administration

3.3. INDUSTRIAL OUTPUT IN 1997–2002 FOR MAJOR SECTORS OF ECONOMY

The Territory's leading industries are energy, light industry and food and beverages (including fishing), machine engineering, coal, forestry and timber.

Food and beverages. The sector accounts for 35.8% of total industrial output. Fish output and fish and seafood processing account for about 25% of Russia's total fisheries output and 40% of the country's fish meal fodder output. Annual output amounts to nearly 1 million tons of fish and seafood.

The industry is represented by more than 500 enterprises and organizations. Major enterprises include OAO Nakhodka Active Marine Fisheries, OAO Dalmoreproduct Holding Company, OAO Preobrazhensk Trawler Fleet, OAO TURNIF, ZAO DMP – Trawlers, and Primorsky Krairybakolkhozsoyuz.

Energy. The Territory's largest energy company is OAO Dalenergo, one of the largest energy systems in the east of Russia. It comprises 18 branches, including three electric power stations, four power grid enterprises, and heating network facilities. Electric power stations are currently under construction in Ussuriysk and Nakhodka. The total installed capacity of the Territory's power stations amounts to 2,669 MW, the available capacity is 1,997 MW.

Machine engineering and metal processing. Major industries: ship repair and shipbuilding (OAO Slavyansky Ship Repair Works, OAO Vladivostok Ship Repair Works, OAO Nakhodka Ship Repair Works, OAO Eastern Shipyard, GUP Zvezda Far East Plant, OAO Dalzavod Holding Company); machine engineering and instrument manufacturing (Ussuriisk Locomotive Repair Plant, OAO Era Vladivistok Electric and Radio Equipment Company, OAO Izumrud, OAO Radiopribor, OAO Dalpribor); aircraft engineering (OAO Progress Arsenyev Aircraft Company).

Forestry, timber, and pulp and paper. The Territory's forestry and timber sector accounts for a considerable share of Russia's total exports of timber and output of lumber, pulp, paper and chipboard. The Territory is home to a number of new plywood, matches and furniture plants. The sector is experiencing growth in lumber and timber operations. Major enterprises include OAO

Industry breakdown of industrial output in 1997–2002, % of total						TABLE 4
	1997	1998	1999	2000	2001	2002
Industry	100.0	100.0	100.0	100.0	100.0	100.0
Food and beverages	38.3	46.4	54.5	46.7	40.6	35.8
Energy	29.4	25.7	18.0	16.4	25.0	28.5
Machine engineering and metal processing	8.4	7.3	8.5	16.3	10.6	10.3
Forestry, timber, and pulp and paper	4.1	5.2	6.1	6.8	8.0	7.6
Fuel	9.4	3.4	2.3	2.1	3.0	3.6
Non-ferrous metals	1.4	1.8	3.0	3.7	4.0	3.4
Construction materials	3.2	4.2	2.0	2.5	3.1	2.8
Chemicals and petrochemicals	1.7	1.7	1.2	1.0	2.2	2.7
Light industry	0.5	0.6	0.7	1.3	1.4	1.7
Flour, cereals, and mixed fodder	1.5	1.3	1.4	0.9	0.4	0.3
Ferrous metals	0.2	0.2	0.2	0.2	0.1	–

Terneyles (a holding company of nine enterprises) and OAO Primorsklesprom (36 enterprises). These account for 70% of total output in the sector.

Non-ferrous metals. The major enterprise is OAO GMK Dalpolimetal, which mainly produces lead and zinc concentrates. Large companies also are: ZAO Dalpolimetal Lead Plant, OAO Yaroslavsky Mining and Dressing Plant, OAO Primorsky Mining and Dressing Plant, OAO Lermontovskaya Mining Company.

Mining. The mining sector produces boron, tungsten, lead, zinc, bismuth, fluorite, tin and copper.

Coal industry. 10.7 million tons of coal were excavated in 2002. Demand is estimated at 13.8 million tons. Major coal producers include ZAO LuTEK (over 60%) and OAO Primorskugol (about 30%).

3.4. FUEL AND ENERGY BALANCE (OUTPUT AND CONSUMPTION PER RESOURCE)

The Maritime Territory is an energy deficit region. In 2002, the deficit reached around 0.4 billion kWh. Some 10 million tons of coal are excavated within the Territory annually, while 3–4 million tons are supplied from Southern Yakutia, Irkutsk and the Kemerovo Region.

The following power stations in the Territory are coal-fired: Primorskaya Thermal Power Station in the town of Luchegorsk, and thermal power stations in the cities of Artem, Partizansk and Vladivostok.

Liquid fuel is supplied from Khabarovsk, Komsomolsk-on-Amur and Angarsk.

Fuel and energy sector production and consumption trends, 1997–2002						TABLE 5
	1997	1998	1999	2000	2001	2002*
Electricity output, billion kWh	7.8	7.9	8.6	8.1	8.6	9.2
Coal output, million tons	11.3	9.4	11.3	10.4	9.0	10.7
Electricity consumption, billion kWh	8.6	8.3	9.2	9.5	9.6	9.6

*Estimates of the Maritime Territory Administration

3.5. TRANSPORT INFRASTRUCTURE

The Maritime Territory has a well-developed transport network, including sea, rail, road and air transport. Sea and rail transport play a major role in the regional transport infrastructure.

Roads. The Maritime Territory has 7,003 kilometers of paved public highways, including 557 kilometers of federal highways.

Railroads. The Vladivostok Branch of the Far East Railroad has 2,306 kilometers of railroad with 1,564 kilometers of track in use. The Trans-Siberian Railroad

crosses the Maritime Territory. The Territory's rail system handles up to 20 million tons of freight annually.

Airports. The Maritime Territory is served by Vladivostok International Airport. The largest airline operating from Vladivostok is OAO Vladivostok-Avia.

Sea transport. The largest shipping companies in the Territory are OAO Far East Shipping Company (Vladivostok) and OAO Maritime Shipping Company (Nakhodka).

Seaports. The largest seaports of the Maritime Territory are OAO Vladivostok Commercial Seaport

FAR EASTERN FEDERAL DISTRICT

VII

(Vladmortorgport), OAO Nakhodka Commercial Seaport, OAO Nakhodka Oil Port (Nefteport), and OAO Vostochny Port. Almost all of the Maritime Territory's fishing ports have outlets to the Trans-Siberian Railroad.

3.6. MAIN NATURAL RESOURCES: RESERVES AND EXTRACTION IN 2002

The Maritime Territory has substantial reserves of fuel, energy and natural resources. Its unique geographical situation, relief and climate provide conditions for efficient use of its water, hydroelectric power, forests, and recreational resources.

Coal. The Territory has more than 100 coalfields with reserves totaling 2.4 billion tons. Brown coal is mined at the Bikinskoye, Pavlovskoye, Shkotovskoye and Artemovskoye fields, and rock coal is mined at the Partizanskoye and Razdolnenskoye fields. Some of the deposits are deep and costly to operate, although more than 70% are suitable for open-pit mining.

Tin and complex ores. Around 30 tin deposits have been discovered in the Maritime Territory. The largest deposits are located in the Kavalerovsky, Dalnegorsky and Krasnoarmeysky districts of the Sikhote Alin mountains, which also have 15 deposits of complex ores containing lead and zinc with some copper, silver, bismuth and some other rare metal content. The Territory's tin and complex ore deposits are located at great depths, and only appear on the surface in certain river valley areas.

Tungsten. A number of tungsten deposits are found in the Krasnoarmeysky and Pozharsky districts of the Maritime Territory. The tungsten ores are found deep in the Earth's crust. Besides tungsten, the deposits contain copper, silver, gold, bismuth and other rare metals.

Gold. More than 50 gold deposits have been discovered in the north and south of the Territory. About 60% of the Territory's gold reserves are found in stream gravel along the valleys of the rivers Pogranichnaya, Fadeyevka, Malaya Nesterovka, Sobolinaya Pad and Izyubrinnaya.

Boron. One of Russia's largest open pit boron deposits is situated in the Dalnegorsk area. The field depletion period is estimated at 50 years.

Fluorite, used in the metals industry, is produced at the Voznesenskoye and Pogranichnoye fields of the Khorolsk district. Besides fluorite, the ores contain such rare metals as lithium, beryllium, tantalum and niobium.

Mineral resources. The Territory has more than 100 deposits of minerals used for construction materials spread throughout almost all of its districts. Limestone is produced at major deposits near Spassk. Many of the deposits contain large reserves of high quality materials and are accessible by transport.

Oil. By various estimates, the Territory's oil fields contain total recoverable reserves of 10–150 million tons of oil.

Forestry. Forests cover 13,012.2 million hectares, or 77% of the Maritime Territory. Total timber resources amount to 1,755.8 million cubic meters. The most common species are pine, oak, ash, larch, cedar, fir, birch, elm, walnut, and beech.

4. TRADE OPPORTUNITIES

4.1. MAIN GOODS PRODUCED IN THE REGION

Industrial goods: In 2002, the Territory's enterprises produced: sulfuric acid in monohydrate 209,000 tons, 9,700 electricity meters, 9,000 bathroom mixers, 2.1 million cubic meters of dense industrial timber, 167,000 cubic meters of lumber, 475,000 tons of cement, 120,000 cubic meters of assembled reinforced concrete installations and goods, 21.2 million conventional bricks, and 20.3 million garments.

Food and beverages: In 2002, the Territory produced 84,800 tons of bread and bakery, 8,600 tons of vegetable oil, 1.4 million decaliters of vodka and liquors, 27,100 decaliters of brandy, 3,100 tons of meat (including category 1 subproducts), 476 tons of butter, 52,100 tons of dairy products (in terms of whole milk), 576,000 tons of fish and seafood, and 554,000 tons of commercial edible fish products (including canned fish).

4.2. EXPORTS, INCLUDING EXTRA-CIS

2000 exports to extra-CIS countries reached $608.8 million, while export to the CIS totaled $3.6 million. The corresponding figures were $1,145 million and $1.1 million for 2001 and $788.6 million and $1 million for 2002.

The bulk of the Maritime Territory's exports consists of (2001): mining machinery and equipment ($373 million), fish and seafood ($361 million), timber ($116 million) and bituminous coal ($90 million). Major export destinations include Japan (20.4%, 2001), South Korea (16%) and Singapore (27%).

4.3. IMPORTS, INCLUDING EXTRA-CIS

2000 imports from extra-CIS countries totaled $318.8 million, while CIS imports totaled $10.5 million. The corresponding figures were $452.1 million and $14 million for 2001, and $754.7 million and $4.1 million for 2002.

The bulk of the Maritime Territory's imports consists of (2001): polyethylene ($68.1 million), knitted fabrics ($52 million), bunker fuel ($52 million) and equipment and mechanical devices ($43.6 million). The Territory's major import partners in 2001 included South Korea (32.8%, 2001), China (22.3%) and Japan (9.4%).

Major regional export and import entities

TABLE 6

ENTITY	ADDRESS	PHONE, FAX, E-MAIL
Maritime Chamber of Commerce and Industry	13a, Okeansky pr., Vladivostok, Maritime Territory, 690600	Phone: (4232) 22 9630 Fax: (4232) 22 7226 E-mail: palata@online.vladivostok.ru http://www.ptpp.ru
VO Dalintorg	16a, Nakhodkinsky pr., Nakhodka, Maritime Territory, 692900	Phone: (266) 44 970 Fax: (266) 44 893 E-mail: general@dalintorg.ru http://www.dalintorg.ru
OAO Primsnabcontract	3, ul. Sukhanova, Vladivostok, Maritime Territory, 690091	Phone: (4232) 22 7803 Fax: (4232) 22 5803 E-mail: info@primsnab.ru http://www.primsnab.ru
Maritime Territory Consumers Association	3, ul. Mordovtseva, Vladivostok, Maritime Territory, 690000	Phone: (4232) 22 5370 Fax: (4232) 22 2560
Maritime Territory Fisheries Consumer Association	3, ul. Mordovtseva, Vladivostok, Maritime Territory, 690000	Phone: (4232) 26 8995 Fax: (4232) 26 9235

5. INVESTMENT OPPORTUNITIES

5.1. INVESTMENTS IN 1992–2002 (BY INDUSTRY SECTOR), INCLUDING FOREIGN INVESTMENTS

The Maritime Territory is of strategic importance to Russia. This has led to the development of its role as a link to the rest of the world and to the establishment of free economic and free trade zones in the Territory.

The following factors determine the investment appeal of the Maritime Territory:

• Its favorable geographical location, climate, and high natural resource potential;

• Its developed transport infrastructure (the Commercial Port of Vladivostok, Russia's main gateway to north-east Asia, is located in the Maritime Territory);

• Its diverse industrial base.

5.2. CAPITAL INVESTMENT

The investment policy of the Maritime Territory is aimed at creating conditions conducive to foreign investment. Investment programs are developed pursuant to the Law On Investment Activity in the Maritime Territory.

5.3. MAJOR ENTERPRISES (INCLUDING ENTERPRISES WITH FOREIGN INVESTMENT)

In 2003, some 1,416 organizations with foreign investment were registered in the Maritime Territory. The largest companies with foreign investment are: ZAO Coca-Cola Vladivostok Bottlers (USA), OAO Holding Company Dalmoreproduct (USA, South Korea, France, Japan, Panama), OAO Ussuriysky Dairy Plant (UK, Japan), ZAO Vostoktelecom (Japan), and OAO New Telephone Company (South Korea).

Capital investment by industry sector, $ million

TABLE 7

	1997	1998	1999	2000	2001	2002
Total capital investment *Including major industries* (% of total)	629.9	336.6	226.2	260.7	328.1	325.4
Industry	33.0	28.0	24.0	29.7	24.5	26,2
Agriculture and forestry	2.0	3.0	3.0	1.9	2.1	1.6
Construction	1.0	1.0	1.0	0.6	0.6	0.4
Transport and communication	24.0	24.0	38.0	40.5	70.7	53.0
Trade and public catering	3.0	4.0	3.0	0.4	0.5	0.6
Other	37.0	40.0	31.0	26.9	1.6	18.2

Foreign investment trends in 1996–2002						TABLE 8
	1996–1997	1998	1999	2000	2001	2002
Foreign investment, $ million	191.0	84.6	54.0	78.1	108.6	57.3
Including FDI, $ million	126.4	46.1	19.9	30.5	65.8	25.8

Largest enterprises of the Maritime Territory			TABLE 9
COMPANY	SECTOR	2001 SALES, $ MILLION*	2001 NET PROFIT, $ MILLION*
OAO Nakhodka Active Marine Fisheries	Fishing	85.4	4.8
OAO Preobrazhenskaya Trawler Fleet Base	Fishing	62.1	0.4
OAO Bor	Chemicals	37.0	1.1
OAO Primorskugol	Coal industry	35.9	0.01
OAO TURNIF	Fishing	30.6	0.2
OAO Terneyles	Forestry and timber	30.5	0.8
OAO SpasskCement	Construction	23.5	0.008

*Data of the Maritime Territory Administration

5.4. MOST ATTRACTIVE SECTORS FOR INVESTMENT

According to experts and the Territory Administration, transport and communications, fishing, forestry and timber, fuel and energy, and tourism offer the greatest investment appeal.

5.5. CURRENT LEGISLATION ON INVESTOR TAX EXEMPTIONS AND PRIVILEGES

The Maritime Territory has passed a number of regional laws on foreign investment. These include the laws: On Investment Activity in the Maritime Territory; and On Investment Tax Credit in the Maritime Territory.

According to the regional legislation, enterprises with foreign investments (more than 30% foreign capital, not less than $0.1 million) incorporated after January 1, 1997, registered and conducting business activities (including businesses delivering public services) in the Maritime Territory, are eligible for the following arrangements with respect to the regional component of property and profit taxes: a 100% exemption on the taxes for the first two years of operations provided that revenue from manufacturing exceeds 70% of the total revenue from sales of products (works, services). In the third and fourth years of operations, respectively, the investor is liable for 25% and 50% of the basic rate of the stated taxes, provided revenue from manufacturing exceeds 90% of the total revenue from the sale of products (works, services).

Businesses with foreign investments exceeding 30% and situated in the Nakhodka Free Economic Zone (FEZ) are eligible for the following tax exemptions and pay the following taxes:

- A 7% profit tax paid to superordinate budgets;
- Local Nakhodka and the Partizansk district profit tax – not more than 3%;
- Federal budget profit expatriation tax – 7%; local Nakhodka and the Partizansk district profit expatriation tax – not more than 3%
- A full 5-year profit tax and profit expatriation tax exemption for five years following the first declared profit;
- Exemption from taxation of profits reinvested into the social sector of the Nakhodka Free Economic Zone and into its infrastructure projects.

The Law of the Maritime Territory On Investment and Tax Credits sets forth the terms of eligibility for investment tax credits on regional taxes.

5.6. FEDERAL AND REGIONAL ECONOMIC AND SOCIAL DEVELOPMENT PROGRAMS FOR THE MARITIME TERRITORY

Federal targeted programs. Some 35 federal targeted programs worth a total of roughly $157.3 million per year are in place in the Territory. The major federal targeted programs for the economic and social development of the Region are:

- Economic and Social Development of the Far East and Trans-Baikal Region, 1996–2005 and Through 2010;
- Modernization of Russia's Transportation System 2002–2010;
- Energy Efficient Economy, 2002–2005, and Through 2010;
- Elimination of Inequalities in the Social and Economic Development of the Regions of the Russian Federation, 2002–2005 and Through 2015;
- The Ecology and Natural Resources of Russia, 2002–2010;
- The Social Development of Rural Areas Through 2010;
- The Program for Economic and Social Development of the Far East and Trans-Baikal

Region, 1996–2005 and Through 2010, which was approved by Government Decree No. 169 of March 19, 2002, covers a number of investment projects, including the conversion of OAO Dalzavod and OAO Dalpribor, the reconstruction of OAO GMK Dalpolimetal, and the reconstruction and development of the ports of Vladivostok, Nakhodka and Vostochny.

Regional Programs. The Maritime Territory is implementing numerous regional programs, including programs for the development of the

Territory's energy sector, the regional fishing and agro-industrial infrastructure, communications and computerization, engineering infrastructure, and welfare. The priority status was accorded to the following programs: Improvement of the Accounting for Heat and Energy Savings at the Municipal Enterprises and Establishments of Vladivostok, 2003–2005, General Physician (Family) Practice, 2003–2006, Vaccine Treatment, 2002–2005, and Improvement of Labor Conditions and Protection in the Maritime Territory, 2001–2005.

6. INVESTMENT PROJECTS

Industry sector and project description	1) Expected results 2) Amount and term of investment 3) Form of financing[1] 4) Documentation[2]	Contact information
1	2	3
OIL		
81R001 ● ◆ Construction of the Nadezhda industrial facility. Project goal: field exploration of the Sakhalin shelf.	1) n/a 2) $27.5 million/10 years 3) L ($27.2 million) 4) BP	GUP Zvezda Far East Plant 1, ul. Lebedeva, Bolshoi Kamen, Maritime Territory, 692809 Phone: (42335) 51 140 extension 121 Fax: (42335) 42 585 E-mail: zvezda57@mail.ru, Admin_zato@mail.primorye.ru Yury Petrovich Shulgan, Director
COAL		
81R002 ● ★ ◆ Construction of the Severo-Zapadny site. Project goal: to develop the Rakovsky coal cut.	1) 1.5 million tons of coal per year 2) $20 million/3 years 3) L ($17 million), Leas. 4) BP	ZAO Energiya Vostoka Far East Industrial and Investment Company 32–23, ul. Utkunskaya, Vladivostok, Maritime Territory, 690091 Phone/fax: (4232) 22 3128 E-mail: saveliev@mail.primorye.ru Stanislav Borisovich Priemenko, CEO
81R003 ● ★ ◆ Development and revamping of production facilities at the Luchegorsky-2 coal cut. Project goal: to increase the coal cut's capacity.	1) 1.5 million tons per year 2) $51.6 million/3 years 3) L ($9.1 million), Leas. 4) BP	ZAO Luchegorsky Fuel and Energy Complex Luchegorsk, Maritime Territory, 692001 Phone: (42357) 21 350, 21 915 Fax: (42357) 21 686, 21 350 E-mail: office@prima.elektra.ru Oleg Nikolaevich Serebrennikov, Deputy CEO

[1] L – Loan, E – Equity, Leas. – Leasing, JV – Joint Venture
[2] BP – Business Plan, FS – Feasibility Study

1	2	3

MINING

81R004 ● ★ ◆

Development of OAO GMK Dalpolimetal.
Project goal: to increase ore output
and domestic and external sales
of non-ferrous metals (lead, zinc, bismuth).

1) n/a
2) $45 million/4 years
3) JV, L ($40.6 million), Leas.
4) BP

Management Company GMK
Dalpolimetal
3, ul. Mordovtseva, Vladivostok,
Maritime Territory, 690950
Phone/fax: (4232) 26 6775,
26 6740, 26 8400
Fax: (4232) 26 8020
E-mail: femco@trunk.vtc.ru
Vasily Ivanovich Usoltsev, President

81R005 ● ◆

Establishment of production facilities
and production of marketable fluorite
concentrate briquettes.
Project goal: to launch a briquetting line
at OAO Yaroslavsky Ore Dressing Plant.

1) n/a
2) $3 million/7 months
3) L ($2.5 million)
4) BP

OAO Yaroslavsky Ore-Dressing Plant
66, ul. Yubileynaya, Yaroslavsky,
Khorolsky District,
Maritime Territory, 692272
Phone: (42347) 35 335
Fax: (42347) 21 701
E-mail: ecgok@hotmail.com
Viktor Vladimirovich Korshunov,
Arbitration Manager

81R006 ● ◆

Reconstruction of an ore dressing plant.
Project goal: to develop fluoride
concentrate production.

1) 350,000 tons of ore per year
2) $13.8 million/7 months
3) L ($10 million)
4) BP

OAO Yaroslavsky Ore Dressing Plant
66, ul.Yubileynaya, Yaroslavsky,
Khorolsky district,
Maritime Territory, 692272
Phone: (42347) 35 335
Fax: (42347) 21 701
E-mail: yarogok@primorye.ru,
ecgok@hotmail.com
Viktor Vladimirovich Korshunov,
Arbitration Manager

ENERGY

81R007 ■ ● ◆

Construction of a modular
waste-incineration plant.
Project goal: to use surplus energy
for electric power production.

1) n/a
2) $5.6 million/2 years
3) L ($5.1 million), E
4) BP

Artem Municipality
48, ul. Kirova, Artem,
Maritime Territory, 692800
Phone: (4232) 43 2317, 22 6412
Vladimir Mikhailovich Novikov,
Head of Artem Municipality
Alexander Pavlovich Latkin,
Project Manager

CHEMICALS AND PETROCHEMICALS

81R008 ● ★ ◆

Construction of manufacturing
infrastructure for liquid detergents.
Project goal: to complete construction.

1) n/a
2) $35.7 million/2 years
3) L ($10.4 million), JV, Leas.
4) BP

OAO Slavda, OOO JV Skit
100, ul. Dneprovskaya, Vladivostok,
Maritime Territory, 690089
Phone: (4232) 34 3416, 34 3544
E-mail: slavda@mail.ru
Yury Mikhailovich Serebryakov,
Chairman

MACHINE ENGINEERING AND METAL PROCESSING

81R009 ● ◆

Building of fishing vessels.
Project goal: to build medium-sized
refrigerator trawlers and small fishing boats.

1) 2003 – 3 vessels; 2004 – 4 vessels;
   2005 – 4 vessels
2) $20.6 million/3 years
3) L ($3.5 million)
4) BP

Zvezda Far East Plant State
Unitary Enterprise
1, ul. Lebedeva, Bolshoi Kamen,
Maritime Territory, 692809
Phone: (42335) 51 140 extn. 121
Fax: (42335) 42 585
E-mail: zvezda57@mail.ru,
Admin_zato@mail.primorye.ru
Yury Petrovich Shulgan, Director

1	2	3

81R010 ● ◆

Construction of small vessels.
Project goal: to provide offshore fisheries with vessels.

1) n/a
2) $4.2 million/1 year
3) L ($3.6 million)
4) BP

OOO Poseidon Fishing
Industrial Company
32, ul. Naberezhnaya, Livadia,
Nakhodka, Maritime Territory, 692900
Phone: (42366) 52 456
Fax: (42366) 52 902
Vasily Vasilyevich Vasilyev, CEO

81R011 ● ◆

Construction of Yak 112 aircraft
Project goal: to produce the four-seater multipurpose Yak 112 aircraft.

1) n/a
2) $2.5 million/2 years
3) L ($1.8 million)
4) BP

OAO Sazykin Progress Arsenyev
Aviation Company
5, pl. Lenina, Arsenyev,
Maritime Territory, 692335
Phone: (42361) 25 232, 26 130
Fax: (42361) 23 584
Viktor Ivanovich Pechenkin, CEO

81R012 ● ★ ◆

Construction of a household refrigerator manufacturing plant.
Project goal: to commercialize six new models of refrigerators.

1) 10,000 refrigerators per month
2) $10 million/4 years
3) L ($7 million), Leas.
4) BP

V-Lazer Company Group
2, ul. Nekrasova, Ussuriysk,
Maritime Territory, 692500
Phone: (42341) 44 855, 47 187, 47 798
Fax: (42341) 47 187
E-mail: penka@v-lazer.com
Boris Vladimirovich Postovalov, CEO

FORESTRY, TIMBER, AND PULP AND PAPER

81R013 ◆

Construction of a timber plant in Dalnerechensk.
Project goal: wood processing.

1) Annually: soft wood 60-100,000 m³, hard wood 30,000-50,000 m³
2) $15 million/1 year
3) JV (foreign partner's contribution $11.3 million)
4) BP

OAO Primorsklesprom
3, ul. Sukhanova, Vladivostok, 690091
Phone: (4232) 26 7572, 26 7711
Pipvvo@mail.primorye.ru
Viktor Alexandrovich Doroshenko, CEO

81R014 ◆

Construction of a timber-processing plant.
Project goal: to launch sawn-timber and glued timber production using Siberian raw materials; export deliveries by OOO Okeaninterbusiness vessels.

1) 40,000 m³ of sawn timber per year
2) $5.4 million/1.5 years
3) JV (foreign partner's contribution $2.7 million)
4) BP

OOO Okeaninterbusiness
35, ul. Vladivostokskaya,
Nakhodka, 692900
Phone: (42366) 58 314, 58 055, 58 077
Fax: (4236) 62 5834
E-mail: info@oib.ru,
oib@nhk.infosys.ru
Viktor Alexandrovich Klyus, CEO

CONSTRUCTION MATERIALS

81R015 ◆

Construction of ash dump processing plant.
Project goal: to process Vladivostok Thermal Power Plant-2's waste into construction materials.

1) production of all-purpose ash blocks – 20,000 m³ per year; wall blocks and gas (foamed) ash concrete – 20,000 m³ per year, cement-and-sand roof tiles – 350,000 pieces/year
2) $5.5 million/27 months
3) JV (foreign partner's contribution $1.7 million)
4) BP

OAO Dalenergo
19, ul. Tigrovaya, Vladivostok, 690600
Phone: (4232) 41 2070, 41 0525
Fax: (4232) 41 0508
E-mail: post@dale.elektra.ru
Oleg Alexandrovich Onishenko, CEO

1	2	3
FOOD AND BEVERAGES		
81R016 ● ★ ❖		OAO Vladivostok Fishing Plant
Reconstruction of a factory workshop. Project goal: to produce canned baby food.	1) 2,100 tons per year 2) $10 million/1 year 3) Leas., JV, L ($4 million) 4) n/a	1, ul. Tatarskaya, Vladivostok, Maritime Territory, 690950 Phone: (4232) 31 1657 Fax: (4232) 31 1622 Yury Mikhailovich Loginov, CEO
81R017 ● ◆		OAO Slavda, Joint-venture OOO Skit
Construction of an iced tea and beverages production plant. Project goal: to produce iced tea and beverages.	1) n/a 2) $98 million/2 years 3) L ($98 million) 4) BP	100, ul. Dneprovskaya, Vladivostok, Maritime Territory, 690089 Phone: (4232) 34 3416, 34 3544 E-mail: slavda@mail.ru Yury Mikhailovich Serebryakov, Chairman
TRANSPORT INFRASTRUCTURE		
81R018 ● ❖ ◆		The Road Committee of the Maritime
Reconstruction of the Vladivostok-Nakhodka highway. Project goal: to develop the Vladivostok-Nakhodka highway.	1) highway length –114.2 km 2) $252.8 million/5 years 3) L ($123.9 million), JV 4) BP	Territory Administration 12, ul. Borodinskaya, Vladivostok, 690049 Phone: (4232) 33 2841 Vladimir Vladimirovich Rosenberg, Chairman
81R019 ❖ ◆		OAO Industrial Port of Vladivostok
Construction of transshipment units. Project goal: to launch transshipment units.	1) n/a 2) $273 million/6 years 3) JV (foreign partner's contribution $200 million) 4) BP	3B, ul. Strelnikova, Vladivostok, 690950 Phone/fax: (4232) 49 1720 Anatoly Yevgenyevich Lyubenko, CEO
81R020 ❖ ◆		OAO Yuzhny Maritime Terminal
Construction of freight handling terminal at the port. Project goal: to launch the terminal.	1) n/a 2) $18.4 million/2 years 3) JV (foreign partner's contribution $16.6 million) 4) BP	3B, ul. Strelnikova, Vladivostok, Maritime Territory, 690950 Phone/fax: (4232) 49 1720, 49 5874 Anatoly Yevgenyevich Lyubenko, CEO
81R021 ● ◆		OAO Commercial Seaport
Reconstruction of a container terminal. Project goal: to increase the terminal's handling capacity.	1) 130,000 tons 2) $7.8 million/1 year 3) L ($5.4 million) 4) BP	of Vladivostok 9, ul. Strelnikova, Vladivostok, Maritime Territory, 690600 Phone: (4232) 22 4074, 49 5222 Fax: (4232) 22 2364, 49 7356 E-mail: market@vmtp.ru Mikhail Fedorovich Robkanov, President
HOTELS AND TOURISM		
81R022 ● ❖ ◆		OAO Slavda
Construction of a de-luxe class hotel. Project goal: hotel services.	1) n/a 2) $100 million/3 years 3) JV, L ($70 million) 4) BP	100, ul. Dneprovskaya, Vladivostok, Maritime Territory, 690089 Phone: (4232) 34 3416, 34 3544 E-mail: slavda@mail.ru Yury Mikhailovich Serebryakov, Chairman

1	2	3

81R023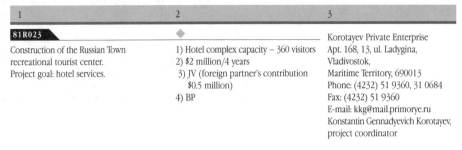

		Korotayev Private Enterprise
Construction of the Russian Town recreational tourist center. Project goal: hotel services.	1) Hotel complex capacity – 360 visitors 2) $2 million/4 years 3) JV (foreign partner's contribution $0.5 million) 4) BP	Apt. 168, 13, ul. Ladygina, Vladivostok, Maritime Territory, 690013 Phone: (4232) 51 9360, 31 0684 Fax: (4232) 51 9360 E-mail: kkg@mail.primorye.ru Konstantin Gennadyevich Korotayev, project coordinator

COMMUNICATIONS AND TV AND RADIO BROADCASTING

81R024

		ZAO Trunking Information Systems
Launching of digital TV broadcasting in Vladivostok and the adjacent regions. Project goal: to provide Vladivostok and the adjacent regions with digital TV.	1) n/a 2) $2.7 million/1 year 3) E, Leas., L ($1.8 million) 4) BP	5th floor, 3, ul. Mordovtseva, Vladivostok, Maritime Territory, 690950 Phone: (4232) 26 7637, 22 4422, 26 7252 Fax: (4232) 26 8020 Alexander Fedorovich Lomakin, Deputy CEO

FAR EASTERN FEDERAL DISTRICT

VII

82. KHABAROVSK TERRITORY [27]

ECONOMIC MAP

Aldan

Khandyga

REPUBLIC

YAKUTSK OF SAKHA

Pokrovsk (YAKUTIA)

Mokhsogollokh

Ust-Maya

Maya

Aldan

Uchur

Moymakan

Maya

Ayan

Shantar islands

MAGADAN
REGION

Stekolny

MAGADAN

Okhotsk

SEA OF

OKHOTSK

Okha

Mago

Nikolaevsk-
-on-Amur

Island of Sakhalin

Nogliki

Zeya

Uda

Zeyskoe
water
reservoir

Zeya

Amgun

Amur

Aleksandrovsk-
-Sakhalinsky

AMUR REGION

Komsomolsk-
-on-Amur

Shimanovsk

Chegdomyg

Svobodny

Solnechny

Belogorsk

Amursk

Vanino

Poronaysk

Litovko

Sovetskaya
Gavan

BLAGOVESCHENSK

Raychikhino

KHABAROVSK

YUZHNO-
SAKHALISK

Kholmsk

BIROBIDZHAN

Khor

Nevelsk

Amur

Vyazemsky

Svetlaya

Hegan

Bikin

CHINA

PROCESSING INDUSTRY	MINING INDUSTRY	POWER PLANTS	CROPS AND LIVESTOCK BREEDING
Machine engineering and metal processing	Bituminous coal	Thermal power plants	Corn
Chemicals and petrochemicals	Tin		Orchards
Forestry and timber	Mineral water sources		Meat and dairy cattle breeding
Construction materials	Fishing ports		Sea mammals catch
Food and beverages	Resorts		

The Khabarovsk Territory is rightfully known as the heart of Russia's Far East. The Territory boasts an advantageous geographical location, a unique natural environment, bountiful natural resources, considerable industrial and scientific potential, and a qualified workforce.

Unlike other areas of the Far East, the Khabarovsk Territory enjoys a diversified industrial base in which processing sectors account for the lion's share of total output. The Khabarovsk Territory has a strong machine engineering sector. Machine engineering companies in the Territory manufacture advanced Sukhoi military aircraft, civilian aircraft, ocean and river vessels of various classes and purposes, metal cutting machinery, diesel engines and generators, casting equipment, and consumer goods, including modern household appliances.

The Khabarovsk Territory ranks first among the Far Eastern regions in terms of industrial timber output and is among the top three Russian gold mining regions.

The Territory's location on the border with China, its seaports, its international airport, which is the largest in the Far East, and access to the Trans-Siberian and Baikal-Amur Railroads, make the Khabarovsk Territory an important player in Russia's integration with the rest of the Pacific Rim.

The Territory's economy stands to benefit from foreign and Russian capital investment, advanced technology, and managerial experience. Priority areas for investment include mineral resource extraction and processing, launching and revamping of production of new types of machinery and consumer goods, and development of transport infrastructure and communications, tourism, and consumer services. The Territory has vast potential for the development of trade, scientific, and cultural links with overseas countries and other Russian regions.

We invite you to invest in the Khabarovsk Territory and are confident that you will find committed and responsible partners here.

Victor Ishaev,
GOVERNOR OF THE KHABAROVSK TERRITORY,
CHAIRMAN OF THE KHABAROVSK
TERRITORY GOVERNMENT

FAR EASTERN FEDERAL DISTRICT

VII

1. GENERAL INFORMATION

1.1. GEOGRAPHY

The Khabarovsk Territory covers a total area of 788,600 square kilometers. The Territory lies in the central part of the Far East. It borders China, the Maritime Territory, the Amur and Magadan Regions, the Jewish Autonomous Region, and the Republic of Sakha (Yakutia).

1.2. CLIMATE

The Khabarovsk Territory is located in the monsoon climate zone.

Air temperatures in January average –24.1°C, rising to +16.9°C in July. Annual precipitation is 500–800 mm.

1.3. POPULATION

According to preliminary 2002 census results, the population of the Khabarovsk Territory was 1,435,000 people. The average population density is 1.8 people per square kilometer. The economically active population amounts to 774,000 people. 2002 official unemployment stood at 2.6%, while the actual rate was 7.8%.

Demographically speaking, some 64.8% are of statutory working age, 18.8% are below the statutory working age, and 16.4% are beyond the statutory working age.

The Territory's major urban centers are Khabarovsk with 582,700 inhabitants and Komsomolsk-on-Amur with 281,000 inhabitants.

Population							*TABLE 1*
	1992	1997	1998	1999	2000	2001	2002
Total population, '000	1,623	1,546	1,535	1,523	1,506	1,496	1,435
Economically active population, '000	870	772	744	781	792	776	774

2. ADMINISTRATION

56, ul. K. Marxa, Khabarovsk, Khabarovsk Territory, 680000
Phone: (4212) 32 5121; fax: (4212) 32 8756; e-mail: econ@adm.khv.ru; http://www.adm.khv.ru

NAME	POSITION	CONTACT INFORMATION
Victor Ivanovich ISHAEV	Governor of the Khabarovsk Territory, Chairman of the Khabarovsk Territory Government	Phone: (4212) 32 5121 Fax: (4212) 32 8756 E-mail: econ@adm.khv.ru
Vladimir Alexandrovich POPOV	First Deputy Chairman of the Khabarovsk Territory Government for the Construction and Fuel and Energy Industries	Phone: (4212) 32 5073 E-mail: energy@adm.khv.ru
Andrei Borisovich CHIRKIN	First Deputy Chairman of the Khabarovsk Territory Government, Chief of the Khabarovsk Territory's Representation to the Government of the Russian Federation	Phone: (095) 203 4128 Fax: (095) 203 3411
Vladimir Ivanovich SYRKIN	Acting First Deputy Chairman of the Khabarovsk Territory Government for Economy, Deputy Chairman of the Territory's Government, Chief of the Khabarovsk Territory Government's Strategic Planning Center	Phone: (4212) 32 5471 Fax: (4212) 32 2253 E-mail: svi@adm.khv.ru
Alexander Stanislavovich KATSUBA	Deputy Chairman of the Khabarovsk Territory Government, Minister of Finance of the Khabarovsk Territory	Phone: (4212) 32 7388 Fax: (4212) 32 4047 E-mail: priem@krfd.khv.ru
Alexander Borisovich LEVINTAL	Deputy Chairman of the Khabarovsk Territory Government, Minister of Economic Development and Foreign Relations of the Khabarovsk Territory	Phone: (4212) 32 5544 Fax: (4212) 32 2253 E-mail: econ@adm.khv.ru

3. ECONOMIC POTENTIAL

3.1. 1997–2002 GROSS REGIONAL PRODUCT (GRP). INDUSTRY BREAKDOWN

In 2002, the Khabarovsk Territory's gross regional product reached $3,213 million, or 14.5% up on 2001. The growth was mainly driven by the industry, transport and communications. Per capita GRP to-taled $1,876 in 2001 and $2,240 in 2002

3.2. MAJOR ECONOMIC GROWTH PROJECTIONS

The Territory's economic prospects strongly depend on the development of its own fuel base, improvement of the fuel and energy balance, and reconstruction of power generating facilities. The Territory has plans afoot to increase coal output to 6 million tons by 2010, and to increase gas fuel component in the energy sector. Upgrade of oil refineries will enable the Territory to enhance oil refinery output and increase high quality oil product output.

Machine engineering. The Territory will develop its civil aircraft building and shipbuilding sectors. Plans are afoot to significantly increase production of television sets, consumer electric appliances with gradual development of spare parts and components production. The Territory will develop powder metal-based production of cutting tools, and production of electric devices and industrial equipment.

Non-ferrous metals. The Territory is implementing a program for the development of a number of gold fields, which will ensure that by 2005 the Territory's annual gold output will total 23 tons. Forestry development prospects are based on a future increase in timber output to 8–9 million cubic meters and the development

of timber processing facilities, including pulp, newsprint, plywood, veneer sheet and furniture production.

Communications and transport infrastructure, including roads and port terminals, will be growing faster than average.

3.3. INDUSTRIAL OUTPUT IN 1997–2002 FOR MAJOR SECTORS OF ECONOMY

The leading industries of the Khabarovsk Territory are machine engineering and metal processing, energy, Forestry, timber, pulp and paper, non-ferrous metals, and food and beverages.

Machine engineering and metal processing. This industry accounts for 42.7% of total industrial output. Principal sub-sectors include military and civil ship and aircraft building, electric cables, machinery and diesel engineering, cast metals equipment, lifting and carriage transport equipment, and energy equipment. OAO Amur Shipyard, FGUP Khabarovsk Shipyard, and OAO Nikolaevsk Shipyard are the Territory's major shipbuilding outfits. OAO Komsomolsk-on-Amur Aircraft Production Association is the Territory's major aircraft manufacturer.

Energy. The energy sector accounts for 12.9% of the industrial output. OAO Khabarovskenergo is the major supplier of electricity and heat.

Forestry, timber, and pulp and paper. This industry accounts for 11.2% of total industrial output. 2002 timber exports reached 7.1 million cubic meters. The Territory manufactures sawn timber, railroad ties, chipboard, pulp chips, and furniture. Plans are afoot to commence production of pulp, newsprint, veneer sheet, plywood, and laminated plate. The bulk of the Territory's timber is exported to Japan, China, and South Korea.

GRP trends in 1997–2002						TABLE 2
	1997	1998	1999	2000	2001*	2002*
GRP in current prices, $ million	5,331	3,027	1,694	2,442	2,807	3,213

*Estimates of the Khabarovsk Territory Ministry of Economic Development and Foreign Relations

GRP industry breakdown in 1997–2002, % of total						TABLE 3
	1997	1998	1999	2000	2001*	2002*
GRP	100.0	100.0	100.0	100.0	100.0	100.0
Industry	24.9	31.9	36.1	45.9	44.1	42.7
Agriculture and forestry	3.6	5.5	4.2	3.6	4.4	3.9
Construction	5.9	4.7	6.1	5.6	7.0	6.7
Transport and communications	30.6	24.1	16.2	14.4	14.7	16.4
Trade and public catering	6.7	7.5	12.8	8.6	8.3	10.3
Other	25.7	24.4	21.1	17.5	19.0	17.5
Net taxes on output	2.6	1.9	3.5	4.4	2.5	2.5

*Estimates of the Khabarovsk Territory Ministry of Economic Development and Foreign Relations

Industry breakdown of industrial output in 1997–2002, % of total						TABLE 4
	1997	1998	1999	2000	2001	2002
Industry	100.0	100.0	100.0	100.0	100.0	100.0
Machine engineering and metal processing	12.8	33.7	23.5	50.4	47.2	42.7
Energy	34.2	23.4	14.1	8.5	9.6	12.9
Forestry, timber, and pulp and paper	6.5	4.8	10.6	8.0	9.7	11.2
Food	12.6	12.7	13.9	8.5	9.3	10.3
Non-ferrous metals	4.7	4.4	11.8	8.4	9.8	9.6
Fuel	19.0	10.0	15.0	7.9	6.4	5.6
Ferrous metals	0.6	3.0	3.7	3.3	2.7	4.1
Construction materials	1.5	2.6	1.9	1.3	1.9	1.3
Light industry	0.3	0.4	0.4	0.3	0.3	0.3
Chemicals and petrochemicals	0.8	0.2	0.2	0.1	0.1	0.1

Food and beverages. This industry accounts for 10.3% of total industrial output. The fishing industry's annual catch amounts to some 140,000 tons of fish and various seafood species.

Non-ferrous metals. This industry accounts for 9.6% of total industrial output. The Khabarovsk Territory is one of the three major gold mining regions of Russia. In addition to gold, significant amounts of platinum and silver are mined alongside tin and copper concentrates. The largest entities are ZAO Amur Prospectors Cooperative and ZAO Mnogovershinnoye.

3.4. FUEL AND ENERGY BALANCE (OUTPUT AND CONSUMPTION PER RESOURCE)

The Territory's energy sector fully covers the Territory's energy needs. Surplus energy is sold on the Far East's energy market.

The two oil refineries at Khabarovsk and Komsomolsk-on-Amur supply oil products to the whole Far East region and abroad. The main products are gasoline, aviation and diesel fuel, and heavy fuel oil. Aggregate crude oil processing capacity amounts to some 10 million tons per year.

Fuel and energy sector production and consumption trends, 1997–2002						TABLE 5
	1997	1998	1999	2000	2001	2002
Electricity output, million kWh	7,792.8	7,498.8	8,122.8	8,497.5	8,417.6	8,320.0
Primary oil refining, '000 tons	4,076.4	3,635.6	5,155.0	6,220.4	6,592.8	7,285.7
Coal extraction, '000 tons	1,633.0	1,306.0	1,896.0	2,030.0	2,295.0	2,638.0
Coal consumption, '000 tons	7,478.5	7,786.1	6,654.8	6,994.2	6,336.7	5,983.2
Electricity consumption, million kWh	6,652.8	6,477.4	6,948.0	7,399.0	7,362.8	7,277.4
Natural gas consumption, million cubic meters	972.5	963.9	867.5	962.2	948.7	899.7

3.5. TRANSPORT INFRASTRUCTURE

Roads. The Khabarovsk Territory has 4,600 kilometers of paved public highway. The roads network is mainly restricted to the southern sector of the Territory. Local roads have been under construction in the Territory in recent years, including roads in the northern regions. The Khabarovsk–Komsomolsk-on-Amur and Lidoga–Vanino highways are now open to traffic, the latter connecting the Far East's road network with the Pacific port of Vanino.

In 1999, the fisrt portion of reconstructed combined automotive road and railroad bridge over the Amur river near Khabarovsk was launched.

Railroads. The Khabarovsk Territory has some 2,300 kilometers of railroads. Two mainline routes pass through the Territory, the Trans-Siberian and Baikal-Amur Railroads. Some 80% of the freight to and from other regions of Russia and 72% of freight within the Territory is carried by rail.

Airports. Khabarovsk International Airport is the major international airport for the Far East of Russia.

Sea and river ports. Vanino, the Territory's major seaport, handles over 10 million tons of freight annually and is the third largest of Russia's Far-East seaports. The Territory's major river ports are located at Khabarovsk and Komsomolsk-on-Amur.

Oil and gas pipelines. Oil and gas are transported by pipeline from the Sakhalin fields to the Komsomolsk-on-Amur industrial hub. In recent years, over 200 kilometers of main and distribution pipelines have been put into operation. The construction of the 462 kilometer Komsomolsk-on-Amur–Khabarovsk trunk pipeline began in 2001.

3.6. MAIN NATURAL RESOURCES: RESERVES AND EXTRACTION IN 2002

The main natural resources of the Khabarovsk Territory are mineral deposits, forests and water reserves.

Mineral resources. The Khabarovsk Territory has gold, platinum and silver fields. Precious metals reserves in the core fields enable the Territory to ensure steady output in the future. The Territory has seven areas rich with tin ores. Tin ores are extracted and dressed in Komsomolsky and Khingano-Olonoysky areas. The fields contain complex ores with industrial copper, silver, tungsten and bismuth.

Inferred reserves of black and brown coal are, respectively, 1.4 and 7 billion tons. Inferred reserves of oil and gas in the Territory are 500 million tons. Iron ore reserves are concentrated in two areas: Jujursky (6.6 billion tons) and Udsko-Selemjinsky (1.6 billion tons) districts. Deposits of manganese, apatite, alunite, chromite, and other ores have been discovered in the Territory. Any one of these may contain associated elements, such as iron, titanium, copper, silver, vanadium, bismuth, tungsten, and indium.

Water. The aggregate length of the Territory's major rivers (confluents of the Amur) exceeds 1,000 kilometers. Major lakes such as Udyl, Orel, Bolon, and Chukagir, also lie in the Amur basin.

Several mineral and drinking water sources have been explored and developed.

4. TRADE OPPORTUNITIES

4.1. MAIN GOODS PRODUCED IN THE REGION

Electricity. In 2002, 8.3 billion kWh was generated.

Fuel. 2002 coal output amounted to 2.6 million tons.

Oil refinery. In 2002, primary oil refinery output exceeded 7 million tons, gasoline output totaled 484,900 tons, diesel fuel – 1,355,100 tons, and furnace fuel topped 2,747,400 tons.

Metal processing. In 2002, 398,200 tons of ferrous roll were produced.

Machine engineering. In 2002, the Territory manufactured 107,000 accumulators and storage batteries, 59 diesel engines, 34 electric bridge cranes, and 180,600 television-sets.

Forestry and timber. In 2002, the Khabarovsk Territory produced 7.1 million cubic meters of timber and 321,300 cubic meters of lumber.

Food and beverages. In 2002, 80,700 tons of bread and bakery products, 4,500 tons of meat (including category 1 by-products), 47,300 tons of milk, and 5,452,000 decaliters of beer were produced. Output of fish and seafood was 139,100 tons.

4.2. MAIN EXPORTS, INCLUDING EXTRA-CIS

2001 exports totaled $2,053 million, compared with $1,397.8 million in 2002.

The Territory's main exports are machine engineering articles, $354.5 million ($1,200 million in 2001, the main importer is China); round timber, 6.3 million cubic meters, or $312.6 million (main importers: Japan and China); oil products, 3,339,200 tons, or $497.7 million (importers: Singapore, Switzerland, China); ferrous metals, 300,000 tons, or $53.4 million (main importer: Austria); and fish and crustaceans, 58,400 tons or $57.4 million.

The main export destinations are China (44.6%), Singapore (14.3%), Japan (11.6%), Switzerland (9.6%), and South Korea (5.4%).

4.3. MAIN IMPORTS, INCLUDING EXTRA-CIS

The Territory's 2002 imports totaled $233.9 million (39% up on 2001).

The bulk of the Territory's imports constitute machinery, equipment, and transport vehicles (49% of the total), primarily electrical machinery and equipment ($33.1 million). The main machinery suppliers are China (28%), Japan (23.7%), South Korea (8.23%), the USA (7%), and Sweden (4.6%).

The Territory also imports polymer materials ($4.4 million) and food ($19.9 million). China is the main supplier of food and agricultural feedstock (72% of total imports in this group of goods).

The Territory's major import partners are China (27%), Japan (24%), South Korea (9%), the USA (7%), and the UK (3.6%).

4.4. MAJOR REGIONAL EXPORT AND IMPORT ENTITIES

Due to the specific nature of the Khabarovsk Territory's exports and imports, most export and import transactions are carried out by industrial enterprises. The major industrial enterprises are:

FAR EASTERN FEDERAL DISTRICT

VII

Major regional export and import entities		TABLE 6
ENTITY	ADDRESS	PHONE, FAX, E-MAIL
OAO Komsomolsk-on-Amur Aircraft Production Association	3, ul. Sovietskaya, Komsomolsk-on-Amur, Khabarovsk Territory, 681018	Phone: (42172) 76 589, 76 428 Fax: (42172) 29 851, 76 451 E-mail: knaapo@kmscom.ru
OAO Amur Shipyard	1, Alleya Truda, Komsomolsk-on-Amur, Khabarovsk Territory, 681000	Phone: (42172) 42 830 Fax: (095) 960 2641 E-mail: market@amurshipyard.ru
OAO Amurmetall	30 ul. Vagonnaya, Komsomolsk-on-Amur, Khabarovsk Territory, 681000	Phone: (42172) 44 423, 45 316 Fax: (42172) 45 103, 46 145 E-mail: amurmetal@amur.rosnet.ru
OAO Amurlitmash	1, ul. Kulturnaya, Komsomolsk-on-Amur, Khabarovsk Territory, 681008	Phone: (42172) 28 777, 56 641, 56 076 Fax: (42172) 45 586, 40 269
OOO Vostokrybprom	12, per. Topografichesky, Khabarovsk, Khabarovsk Territory, 680030	Phone: (4212) 22 7285 Fax: (4212) 22 7364 E-mail: vrp@pop.redcom.ru
OAO Dallesprom	23-A, ul. Pushkina, Khabarovsk, Khabarovsk Territory, 680000	Phone: (4212) 32 7103, 32 4769 Fax: (4212) 32 4769, 32 4811 E-mail: dallesprom@gin.ru
OAO Komsomolsk-on-Amur Refinery – Rosneft	7, ul. Leningradskaya, Komsomolsk-on-Amur, Khabarovsk Territory, 681007	Phone (42172) 22 991, 27 025 Fax: (42172) 22 988, 22 891 E-mail: knpz@rosneft.ru

5. INVESTMENT OPPORTUNITIES

5.1. INVESTMENTS IN 1992–2002 (BY INDUSTRY SECTOR), INCLUDING FOREIGN INVESTMENTS

The main factors contributing to the investment appeal of the Khabarovsk Territory are:

- Its advantageous geographical position (close to markets, high consumption potential);
- Its highly developed infrastructure;
- Significant natural resources (fish);
- Laws supporting investment (guarantees of investors' rights, preferential tax treatment).

5.2. CAPITAL INVESTMENTS

The major share of investments goes to the energy, fuel, food and beverages, machine engineering and metals sectors.

Capital investment by industry sector, $ million						TABLE 7
	1997	1998	1999	2000	2001*	2002*
Total investments	543.6	319.0	234.9	412.5	499.8	570.4
Including major industries (% of total):						
Industry	21.9	18.6	36.8	36.8	36.1	46.0
Agriculture and forestry	2.2	2.2	2.9	1.4	1.4	1.1
Construction	1.2	2.8	2.1	1.2	4.0	2.0
Transport and communications	39.5	43.4	33.5	41.0	35.8	28.0
Trade and public catering	2.4	2.0	1.3	1.0	1.5	1.5
Other	32.8	31.0	23.4	18.6	21.2	20.3

*Investments after 2001 shown net of VAT

Foreign investment trends in 1996–2002						_TABLE 8_
	1996–1997	1998	1999	2000	2001	2002
Foreign investment, $ million	90.8	40.1	33.2	27.2	19.9	31.2
Including FDI, $ million	89.5	14.8	24.7	18.0	8.9	2.4

Largest enterprises of the Khabarovsk Territory	_TABLE 9_
COMPANY	SECTOR
OAO Khabarovskenergo	Electricity
OAO Urgalugol	Coal
OAO Northern Urgal	Coal
OAO Alliance Khabarovsk Refinery	Oil processing
OAO Rosneft Komsomolsk Refinery	Oil processing
OAO Komsomolsk-on-Amur Aircraft Production Association	Machine engineering
OAO Amur Shipyard	Machine engineering
ZAO Amur Prospectors Cooperative	Non-ferrous metals
OAO Far-East Resources Prospectors	Non-ferrous metals
OAO Dallesprom	Forestry, timber, and pulp and paper
FGUP Far-East Railroad	Transport

5.3. MOST ATTRACTIVE SECTORS FOR INVESTMENT

According to the Khabarovsk Territory Ministry of Economic Development and Foreign Relations, the oil processing, Forestry, timber, and pulp and paper sector, non-ferrous metals, machine engineering, food (including fish), transport, and communications industries are the most attractive ones for investment.

5.4. CURRENT LEGISLATION ON INVESTOR TAX EXEMPTIONS AND PRIVILEGES

The Khabarovsk Territory passed the Law On Investment Activity in the Khabarovsk Territory in 2000. The Law provides for the protection of investors' rights, governmental support, and tax privileges for investors in the Territory.

The Khabarovsk Territory's Laws On Investment Activity in the Khabarovsk Territory and On Taxes and Duties in the Khabarovsk Territory provide for profit tax, property tax, and land tax deductions to entities involved in investment and innovation activities.

The Khabarovsk Territory's Law On the Budget System of the Khabarovsk Territory for 2003 provides for an exemption on the regional component of land lease charges to entities involved in investment activities, and implementing investment projects for creating new production facilities, provided such projects are agreed upon with the Territory Government, and to real sector companies providing capital investments into social, culture and sports projects included in the territorial order list to the extent of land allocated for the above projects.

The Khabarovsk Territory passed the Law On the Khabarovsk Territory Pledge Fund (and a Pledge Fund was created) with a view to promoting Russian and foreign investment in order to finance investment projects in the priority sectors of the Territory's economy.

5.5. FEDERAL AND REGIONAL ECONOMIC AND SOCIAL DEVELOPMENT PROGRAMS FOR THE KHABAROVSK TERRITORY

Federal targeted programs. The top priority program in terms of economic and social devel-

Regional entities responsible for raising investment		_TABLE 10_
ENTITY	ADDRESS	PHONE, FAX, E-MAIL
The Khabarovsk Territory Foreign Investment Promotion Agency (offers support to investors at all stages of investment projects)	72, ul. Frunze, Khabarovsk, 680002	Phone: (4212) 32 4362 Fax: (4212) 32 4121 E-mail: vnesh@adm.khv.ru http://www.fipa.khv.ru

opment of the Khabarovsk Territory is The Economic and Social Development for the Far East and Trans-Baikal Region, 1996–2005 and through 2010. Program goal: to solve the problems of the Far East regions and coordinate the implementation of federal targeted programs in the Far East.

The Territory also has the following federal targeted programs underway: Energy Efficient Economy, 2002–2005 and through 2010; Modernization of Russia's Transport System, 2002–2010; Ecology and Natural Resources of Russia, 2002–2010.

The Territory is also implementing public health programs (infectious decease control), child education and health improvement, and support to the elderly), educational and cultural programs, and public utilities programs (The Housing, 2002–2010 federal targeted program).

Regional programs. The Khabarovsk Territory's investment po-licy is based around The Khabarovsk Territory Investment Program for 1998–2005, which aims to create a favorable investment climate for raising Russian and foreign investments.

6. INVESTMENT PROJECTS

Industry sector and project description	1) Expected results 2) Amount and term of investment 3) Form of financing[1] 4) Documentation[2]	Contact information
1	2	3

COAL		
82R001	● ◆ ▲	OAO Urgalugol
Construction of the Bureinsky open-pit coal mine. Project goal: to increase coal mining output.	1) Mining of 1 million tons of coal per year 2) $8.4 million/2 years 3) L ($6.4 million) 4) FS, BP	2, ul. Magistralnaya, Chegdomyn, Verkhnebureinsky District, Khabarovsk Territory, 682030 Phone: (42149) 51 768, 51 587 Gennady Alexandrovich Solovyev, CEO

MINING		
82R002	● ◆	OOO Georos Ore Mining Company
Development of the Algaminskoye zirconium ore deposit (new full cycle production). Project goal: to bring the product to the market.	1) 0.6 million tons of reserves to be developed 2) $20 million/2 years 3) L ($10 million) 4) BP	15, ul. Balashovskaya, Khabarovsk, Khabarovsk Territory, 680041 Phone: (4212) 55 7744, 55 7762 E-mail: adm@geoph.khv.ru Vladimir Vasilyevich Shatlov, CEO

ENERGY		
82R003	● ▲	OAO Khabarovskenergo
Construction of a second block at the Khabarovsk Thermal Power Station-3 (two power plants). Project goal: to increase energy output, improve the reliability of electricity supply.	1) Combined capacity: 770 MW of electricity, 1,880 Gcal/h of heat 2) $52 million/2.5 years 3) L ($30 million) 4) FS	49, ul. Frunze, Khabarovsk, Khabarovsk Territory, 680000 Phone: (4212) 30 5308 Fax: (4212) 21 3087 E-mail: hab@khaben.elektra.ru Valery Moiseevich Levit, CEO

82R004	● ★ ▲	OAO Khabarovskenergo
Construction of a combined cycle power plant at the Amur Thermal Power Station-1. Project goal: to increase output, reduce CO_2 emissions.	1) 210 MW capacity 2) $211 million/1.5 years 3) L ($151 million), Leas. 4) FS	49, ul. Frunze, Khabarovsk, 680000 Phone: (4212) 30 5308 Fax: (4212) 21 3087 E-mail: hab@khaben.elektra.ru Valery Moiseevich Levit, CEO

[1] L – Loan, E – Equity, Leas. – Leasing, JV – Joint Venture
[2] BP – Business Plan, FS – Feasibility Study

1	2	3

MACHINE ENGINEERING AND METALS PROCESSING

82R005

	● ◆ ▲	OAO Komsomolsk-on-Amur
Manufacture of C-80 lightweight multi-purpose passenger and cargo aircraft for local and regional airlines. Project goal: to launch the C-80 aircraft.	1) Output: 258 aircraft per year 2) $94.5 million/2 years 3) L ($12.8 million) 4) FS, BP	Aircraft Production Association 1, ul. Sovetskaya, Komsomolsk-on-Amur, Khabarovsk Territory, 681018 Phone: (42172) 63 200, 63 230 Fax: (42172) 63 451, 29 851 E-mail: knaapo@kmscom.ru Viktor Ivanovich Merkulov, CEO

82R006

	● ◆ ▲	OAO Komsomolsk-on-Amur
Manufacture of Be-103 lightweight multi-purpose amphibious aircraft. Project goal: to launch the Be-103 aircraft.	1) Output: 366 aircraft per year 2) $9.3 million/1 year 3) L ($2.7 million) 4) FS, BP	Aircraft Production Association 1, ul. Sovetskaya, Komsomolsk-on-Amur, Khabarovsk Territory, 681018 Phone: (42172) 63 200, 63 230 Fax: (42172) 63 451, 29 851 E-mail: knaapo@kmscom.ru Viktor Ivanovich Merkulov, CEO

82R007

	● ◆	OAO Amur Shipyard
Building of small-sized fishing vessels. Project goal: to satisfy the needs of the Far East fishing fleet.	1) 5 vessels 2) $6 million/1 year 3) L 4) BP	1, Alleya Truda, Komsomolsk-on-Amur, Khabarovsk Territory, 681000 Phone: (42172) 43 019, 43 224, (095) 784 7899 Fax: (42172) 45 026 E-mail: shipper@kmscom.ru Nikolai Grigoryevich Povzyk, CEO

82R008

	● ★ ◆	KGUP Amurkabel
Organization of manufacture of telephone cable containing 10 to 600 pairs of wires. Project goal: to increase output, expand product range, and improve quality.	1) Output: 5000 km per year 2) $11.7 million/2 years 3) L ($10.5 million), Leas. 4) BP	87, ul. Artemovskaya, Khabarovsk, Khabarovsk Territory, 680001 Phone: (4212) 55 2327 Fax: (4212) 55 2148 E-mail: amurkab@mail.khv.ru Nikolai Korneevich Kostiuchenko, CEO

82R009

	● ★ ▲	KGUP Amurkabel
Organization of optic cable production. Project goal: to expand product range, improve quality, launch the manufacturing of a product with high operational characteristics.	1) Output: 5000 km per year 2) $12.0 million/2 years 3) L ($9.5 million), Leas. 4) FS	87, ul. Artemovskaya, Khabarovsk Khabarovsk Territory, 680001 Phone: (4212) 55 2327 Fax: (4212) 55 2148 E-mail: amurkab@mail.khv.ru Nikolai Korneevich Kostyuchenko, CEO

FORESTRY, TIMBER, AND PULP AND PAPER

82R010

	■ ● ◆	OAO Khorsky Biochemical Plant
Manufacture of cellulose and chlorine-free newsprint. Project goal: to introduce high quality newsprint to the market, recycle paper waste, protect the environment.	1) Production of 100,000 tons of newsprint per year 2) $80.6 million/2.6 years 3) E, L 4) BP	21, ul. Mendeleeva, Sergeya Lazo District, Khor, Khabarovsk Territory, 682922 Phone: (42154) 15 577, 15 459, 15 237 E-mail: biochem@mail.kht.ru http://www.khorbiz.khv.ru Nikolai Ivanovich Lipatkin, Manager

FAR EASTERN FEDERAL DISTRICT

VII

1	2	3

82R011 ■ ● ▲

Creation of pulp and paper production at PO Amurmash facilities.
Project goal: to increase output.

1) Production of 200,000 tons of pulp and 100,000 tons of boxboard per year
2) $480 million/2 years
3) E, L
4) FS

FGUP Amurmash
Zapadnoye shosse, Amursk,
Khabarovsk Territory, 682640
Phone: (42142) 20 404
Yury Viktorovich Barsukov, CEO

82R012 ■ ● ◆

Creation of new timber sawing facilities.
Project goal: to produce sawn timber.

1) Output: 75,000 cubic meters per year
2) $19.5 million/1 year
3) E, L
4) BS

OOO Business Marketing
78-A, per. Oblachny Khabarovsk,
Khabarovsk Territory, 680030
Phone: (4212) 23 2866, 23 3324, 23 3439
E-mail: postmaster@bm.kht.ru
Alexander Kaleevich Pudovkin, CEO

HOUSING AND COMMUNAL SERVICES

82R013 ● ◆ ▲

Construction of a new underground water intake.
Project goal: to provide the Khabarovsk population with drinking water.

1) 100,000 cubic meters of water per day
2) $41.4 million/5 years
3) L ($29 million)
4) FS, BP

MUP Vodokanal
12, per. Topografichesky, Khabarovsk,
Khabarovsk Territory, 680000
Phone: (4212) 30 4982
Fax: (4212) 30 6305
E-mail: adm@warter.khv.ru
Vladimir Ivanovich Steblevsky, CEO

TRANSPORT INFRASTRUCTURE

82R014 ■ ● ▲

Construction of Sakhalin–Komsomolsk-on-Amur–Khabarovsk gas pipeline.
Project goal: to supply natural gas to Khabarovsk Territory consumers from Sakhalin Island's offshore fields.

1) Outputs of units 1, 2 and 3: 3.3, 3.9 and 4.5 billion cubic meters per year, respectively
2) $281.7 million/3.8 years
3) E, L
4) FS

OAO Daltransgaz
71, ul. Frunze, Khabarovsk,
Khabarovsk Territory, 680000
Phone: (4212) 31 2904, 33 3473
Nikolai Fedorovich Chuykov, CEO

82R015 ■ ▲

Construction of a coal terminal at the port of Vanino.
Project goal: to create new coal handling facilities.

1) Cargo turnover of units 1 and 2: 6 and 10 million tons of coal per year, respectively
2) $115 million/3.5 years
3) E
4) FS

Marine Administration of Vanino and Sovietskaya Gavan Seaports
2, ul. Zheleznodorozhnaya,
Vanino, Khabarovsk Territory, 682860
Phone: (42137) 24 590
Anatoly Georgievich Klimov, Director

COMMUNICATIONS

82R016 ● ★ ◆ ▲

Creation of an integrated radio and TV broadcasting network in the Far East Federal District.
Project goal: to expand communication services including the existing regional satellite network.

1) Launch of three digital federal channels
2) $55.9 million/1.5 years
3) L ($32.9 million), Leas.
4) FS, BP

ZAO VostokInfoCosmos
61, ul. Kalinina, Khabarovsk,
Khabarovsk Territory, 680000
Phone: (4212) 30 6371
Fax: (4212) 21 7661
E-mail: post@vic.ru
Vladimir Alexandrovich Astafyev, CEO

KNAAPO

VIKTOR IVANOVICH
MERKULOV,
GENERAL DIRECTOR

F ew aviation manufacturers in the East of Russia or indeed the entire Asia-Pacific region compare in terms of technological advancement or scale of operations with Yury Gagarin Komsomolsk-on-Amur Aviation Manufacturing Conglomerate (KNAAPO), one of Russia's recognized aviation manufacturing sector leaders. In the 65 years since its inception, KNAAPO has built hundreds of civilian and thousands of military aircraft with the broadest possible range of applications: from the very first surveillance and intelligence gathering aircraft, to the modern Su 27 fighter plane. KNAAPO is one of Russia's leading exporters of fighter aircraft. The Su 27 fighter plane and its various modifications are a staple feature at airshows the world over. Today, Su 27 class fighter planes manufactured by KNAAPO are found in the air forces

KNAAPO has been an open joint stock company since December 2002. While the way in which the company is run may have changed, its objectives have remained the same: to develop new versions of its renowned aircraft, to remain true to its commitments, and to respect its customers. KNAAPO is today an enterprise of vital importance to its home city, and indeed region. It is a research and industrial center of federal importance. And it is a maker of fifth generation aircraft. KNAAPO is headed by Viktor Merkulov, a modest man with an aversion to the camera lens. Viktor Merkulov has a PhD in technical sciences, is author of numerous articles and scientific works, and laureate of the State Prize, the Peter the Great National Prize, and the Order of Peter the Great under the nomination "Best Enterprise Leader". The sheer elegance of an airborne Su is his dream for the greatness of the Motherland, a dream he has been serving all his life.

of Russia and numerous Asian and CIS countries. KNAAPO, in cooperation with Sukhoi Design Bureau, is constantly upgrading its aircraft to meet the constantly changing market environment and the needs of our potential clients. Alongside our core military output, the conglomerate is also successfully carrying out a number of civilian projects. KNAAPO is currently testing new aircraft developed in conjunction with Sukhoi and Beriev Design Bureaus: the Su 80 aircraft for local airlines and the SA 20P seaplane. The Be 103 seaplane is already available on the international market. KNAAPO also maintains its own research foundation, with an engineering center equipped to international standards. Viktor Merkulov is confident that KNAAPO has no rivals in Russia in terms of the quality of its production facilities, its production capacity, and the talent of its people.

КНААПО

OAO YURY GAGARIN KOMSOMOLSK-ON-AMUR
AVIATION MANUFACTURING CONGLOMERATE

1 UL. SOVETSKAYA, KOMSOMOLSK-ON-AMUR, 681018, RUSSIA
PHONE: (42172) 76 200, 28 525; FAX (42172) 76 451, 29 851
E-MAIL: knaapo@kmscom.ru

MOSCOW OFFICE:
5 UL. SKAKOVAYA, MOSCOW, 125040, RUSSIA
PHONE: (095) 933 5814, 933 5815; FAX (095) 933 5816
E-MAIL: mpknaapo@co.ru

83. AMUR REGION [28]

E C O N O M I C   M A P

Yukatali

Neryungri

REPUBLIC OF SAKHA
(YAKUTIA)

Aldan

CHITA

REGION

Tynda

Solovyovsk

Skovorodino

Gonzha

Gulian

Mangui

Ovsyanka

Zea

Zeyskoe
water
reservoir

Zea

Uchir

Uda

Shimanovsk

Selemdzhinsk

Tokur

Zlatoustovsk

Selemdzha

Svobodny

Heihe

BLAGOVESHCHENSK

Belogorsk

KHABAROVSK

Chegdomyn

Amur

Nen Jiang

Zavitinsk

Poyarkovo

Raychikhinsk

Bureya

TERRITORY

Bej'an

CHINA

BIROBIDZHAN

PROCESSING INDUSTRY
- 🔴 Machine engineering and metal processing
- 🟢 Forestry and timber
- 🟢 Construction materials
- 🔴 Light industry
- ⚪ Food and beverages

MINING INDUSTRY
- ▨ Brown coal
- ◐ Gold
- • Mineral water sources

POWER PLANTS
- ⚡ Thermal power plants
- ⚡ Hydro power plants

CROPS AND LIVESTOCK BREEDING
- Υ Wheat
- ⌐ Rye
- f Barley
- ◊ Corn
- Υ Soy beans
- ⬮ Orchards
- ✝ Beekeeping
- 🦌 Meat and dairy cattle breeding
- 🦌 Reindeer breeding
- ⚘ Resorts

T he Amur Region is one of the largest regions in Russia's Far East. The Region has some 54% of the total arable land of the Far East, 64% of its area is covered with forests, and the hydroelectric potential of the Amur, Zeya, and Bureya rivers accounts for two thirds of the economically effective hydro resources of the Far East. The Region's proven reserves of mineral resources are worth $400 billion.

The Amur Region is known as Russia's largest soybean producer, accounting for up to 60% of this valuable protein crop, which is in high demand in Russia and abroad. Our soybean yield potential, however, is constrained by insufficient investment in machinery and production technology.

The Region plays a leading role in satisfying the Far East's demand for fuel and energy. Zeyskaya Hydroelectric Power Station, the largest power plant in Russia's East, generates up to 5 billion kWh of the cheapest electricity per year. In 2003, the first units of the twice as powerful Bureyskaya hydroelectric power station will be put into operation. The further development of the fuel and energy sector will be assured by the construction of the Nizhnebureyskaya and other HEP stations, the reconstruction of thermal power plants, and the development of new coal deposits with a total reserve in excess of 70 billion tons.

The Amur Region has been mining gold for more than a century now. Its gold reserves rank third in the country. The sector has advanced in recent years thanks to investment in high-technology projects. The introduction of precious metal grouped leaching technology for use in cold winter conditions at Pokrovsky Ore Dressing Plant attracted considerable direct foreign investment to the company. Several other projects are underway for the development of the unique titanium, magnum, and gold-bearing deposits of Great Seim, Kuranakh, and other fields.

The Amur Region's investment potential is continuously increasing as its transport and communications infrastructure expands. The Region is located at the crossroads of the main transport corridors linking Russia to the Pacific Rim states. The total length of the Trans-Siberian and the Baikal-Amur mainline railroads in the Region exceeds 3,000 kilometers. In 2005, construction work on the Amur highway from Chita to Khabarovsk will be completed. Our four river ports on the Amur and Zeya rivers have an annual freight handling capacity of 6-7 million tons. The further development of the transport infrastructure is closely linked to the implementation of investment projects aimed at servicing foreign trade, primarily with China, given the 1,200 kilometer international frontier between the Region and China. The frontier has several customs and border crossing points, with Blagoveschensk situated at the opposite bank of the Amur river from the Chinese town of Heihe. Considerable funds were allocated to the reconstruction of Blagoveschensk international airport and the construction of modern terminal facilities in 2003. Design and research work is underway for the construction of an international bridge across the Amur river linking Blagoveschensk to Heihe pursuant to a bilateral agreement between the Governments of Russia and China.

The investment appeal of the Amur Region is determined by many other factors, including its advanced construction sector which emerged in the course of the construction of the Baikal-Amur railroad and Zeyskaya HEPS. The construction sector has received added impetus thanks to the construction of the Bureyskaya HEPS, Chita-Khabarovsk highway, and Ulak-Elga road. Annual capital investment amounts to $376–441 million.

The Amur Region boasts a fully-fledged financial sector consisting of five regional banks, nine commercial branches of other regions' banks, correspondent accounts at international banks, and twelve insurance companies, including five that are based in the Region.

The Amur Regional Administration accords top priority to the task of fostering a favorable investment climate and conditions conducive to the implementation of major federal and small enterprise investment projects.

Leonid Korotkov,
GOVERNOR OF THE AMUR REGION

1. GENERAL INFORMATION

1.1. GEOGRAPHY

The Amur Region covers a total area of 361,900 square kilometers. The Region is situated in the south east of the Asian part of Russia. To the south, the Region borders China, to the west – the Chita Region, to the north – the Republic of Sakha (Yakutia), and to the east – the Khabarovsk Territory.

1.2. CLIMATE

The Amur Region has a continental monsoon climate.

The average air temperature in January is –29.6°C, rising to +20°C in July. The average annual precipitation exceeds 600 mm. The growing season lasts for some 120 days.

1.3. POPULATION

According to preliminary 2002 census results, total population in the Region was 903,000 people. The average population density is 2.5 people/square km. The economically active population amounts to 487,400 people. While 2002 official unemployment level stands at 2.5%, the actual rate is 11.8 %.

Demographically speaking, some 64.4% are of working age, 20.2% are below the statutory working age, and 15.4% are beyond the statutory working age.

As of 2002, the Amur Region's major urban centers are Blagoveschensk with 218,800 inhabitants, Belogorsk with 74,200 inhabitants, Raichikhinsk with 75,400 inhabitants, Svobodny with 69,200 inhabitants, and Tynda with 45,500 inhabitants.

Population								_TABLE 1_
	1992	1997	1998	1999	2000	2001	2002
Total population, '000	1,055	1,024	1,016	1,008	998	990	903
Economically active population, '000	564	511	508	517	520	486	487

2. ADMINISTRATION

135, ul. Lenina, Blagoveschensk, Amur Region, 675023. Phone: (4162) 37 2703; phone/fax: (4162) 44 6201

NAME	POSITION	CONTACT INFORMATION
Leonid Viktorovich KOROTKOV	Governor of the Amur Region	Phone: (4162) 44 0322, 37 2703
Vladimir Vladimirovich TEREKHOV	Deputy Governor of the Amur Region, Chairman of the State Property Management Committee of the Amur Regional Administration	Phone: (4162) 44 3214
Viktor Yevgenyevich MITR	Deputy Governor of the Amur Region, in charge of Industry, Transport, Communications, Use of Natural Resources, and Mining	Phone: (4162) 44 3838
Valery Nikolaevich GLADILOV	Deputy Governor of the Amur Region for Housing and Communal Services, Architecture, and Construction	Phone: (4162) 44 9260
Valery Anatolyevich YEFREMOV	Deputy Governor of the Amur Region, Head of the Financial Department	Phone: (4162) 37 2715
Nikolai Lvovich SAVIN	Deputy Governor of the Amur Region	Phone: (4162) 44 3652
Alexander Anatolyevich MIGULYA	Deputy Governor of the Amur Region in charge of Economy and Prices, Chairman of the Regional Energy Commission	Phone: (4162) 37 3944
Nikolai Grigoryevich KULESHOV	Deputy Governor of the Amur Region for Agroindustrial Complex	Phone: (4162) 37 2644
Vladimir Ilyich CHEKULAEV	Chairman of the Committee on the Economy of the Amur Regional Administration	Phone: (4162) 44 1948 Fax: (4162) 44 1966 E-mail: ecocom@amur.net
Valentina Grigoryevna GNILOUKHOVA	Chairman of the Architecture and Construction Committee of the Amur Regional Administration	Phone: (4162) 44 3629 Fax: (4162) 44 3629

3. ECONOMIC POTENTIAL

3.1. 1997–2002 GROSS REGIONAL PRODUCT (GRP). INDUSTRY BREAKDOWN

2002 gross regional product amounted to $1,346 million, which constitutes 3.4% growth year-on-year. Per capita GRP amounted to $1,316 in 2001 and $1,491 in 2002.

3.2. MAJOR ECONOMIC GROWTH PROJECTIONS

The blueprint for economic development in the Amur Region is set forth in the Conceptual Framework for Social and Economic Development 2001–2005. Among the Region's priority

GRP trends in 1997–2002						TABLE 2
	1997	1998	1999	2000	2001*	2002
GRP in current prices, $ million	2,658	1,492	855	958	1,303	1,346

*Estimates of the Amur Regional Administration

GRP industry breakdown in 1997–2002, % of total						TABLE 3
	1997	1998	1999	2000	2001*	2002*
GRP	100.0	100.0	100.0	100.0	100.0	100.0
Industry	19.1	18.7	16.3	16.5	14.9	16.2
Agriculture and forestry	9.1	9.5	15.3	16.2	14.2	14.9
Construction	7.3	5.0	3.6	5.4	17.7	9.2
Transport and communications	23.8	19.8	27.1	24.9	21.4	22.8
Trade and public catering	12.3	13.8	14.8	14.6	12.2	12.7
Other	28.0	31.2	21.1	21.4	20.6	23.3
Net taxes on output	0.4	2.0	1.8	1.0	-1.0	0.9

*Estimates of the Amur Regional Administration

sectors are: fuel, energy, mining, forestry, transport infrastructure, and agriculture.

3.3. INDUSTRIAL OUTPUT IN 1997–2002 FOR MAJOR SECTORS OF ECONOMY

The leading industrial sectors of the Amur Region are energy, non-ferrous metals, food and beverages, machine engineering and metal processing, forestry, timber, and pulp and paper, and fuel. Raw materials account for the lion's share (over 60%) of total industrial output.

Energy. This sector accounts for 35.3% of total industrial output. It is represented by OAO Amurenergo, OAO Zeyskaya Hydroelectric Power Station, and OAO Bureyskaya Hydroelectric Power Station. the Zeyskaya HEPS, Blagoveschenskaya Thermal Power Plant, and Raichikhinskaya Power Plant, with respective installed capacities of 1,330 MW, 280 MW, and 227 MW, have the largest potential.

Gold mining. The Region is among Russia's top three regions for gold mining, which is the second most important sector in the Region's industrial structure after energy. Zeya, the Regional gold mining center, is located 120 km away from the Trans-Siberian railroad.

Machine engineering and metal processing. Machine engineering is represented by producers of mining and ore processing machinery, lifting and transport vehicles, tractors and other agricultural machinery, metal assemblies and goods, electrical appliances, and electrical machines and tools. The largest engineering company is the Blagoveschensk Shipbuilding Plant.

Coal sector. The sector accounts for 5% of total industrial output. The Amur Region's coal industry is represented by three brown coal deposits developed by OAO Dalvostugol.

Food and beverages. The region is home to some 60 food and beverage companies producing butter, oil, cheese, sausages, canned meat, fruit and vegetables, beer, soft drinks, pasta, flour, and cereals. Most output is consumed locally.

Forestry, timber, and pulp and paper. The sector comprises large and medium lumber companies, including OAO Zeysky Lumber and Trans-portation Plant, OAO Tyndales Timber Plant, and OAO Taldansky Forestry.

Agriculture. The Region grows vegetables and potatoes, and has a developed dairy and meat cattle farming sector. Some two thirds of the grain and 50% of soybean yield of all the Far East regions is produced in the Amur Region.

3.4. FUEL AND ENERGY BALANCE (OUTPUT AND CONSUMPTION PER RESOURCE)

The Amur Region is an energy deficit region. The launch of a 2,320MW dam at the Bureyskaya hydroelectric power station, and the launch of the Gilyuiskaya and Sorokoverstnaya hydroelectric

Industry breakdown of industrial output in 1997–2002, % of total						
	1997	1998	1999	2000	2001	2002
Industry	100.0	100.0	100.0	100.0	100.0	100.0
Energy	45.9	45.2	34.7	34.2	33.3	35.3
Non-ferrous metals (gold mining)	11.0	13.1	26.2	29.6	22.0	21.8
Food and beverages	10.8	10.8	13.7	10.2	10.6	13.4
Forestry, timber, and pulp and paper	4.2	4.6	6.4	5.7	6.7	8.1
Construction materials	4.1	4.8	3.2	3.3	5.9	7.0
Machine engineering and metal processing	5.2	4.7	4.5	6.3	7.4	5.1
Fuel (coal)	13.3	11.2	5.5	4.7	7.0	5.0
Flour, cereals, and mixed fodder	3.8	2.9	4.0	4.2	5.4	3.0
Light industry	0.1	0.1	0.1	0.3	0.3	0.4
Ferrous metals	0.1	0.2	0.5	0.7	0.5	0.4
Chemicals and petrochemicals	–	0.1	–	0.1	0.2	–
Glass and porcelain	0.4	1.2	0.3	0.1	–	–

TABLE 4

power stations will solve the energy problem and enable the Region to export electricity.

3.5. TRANSPORT INFRASTRUCTURE

Roads. The Region has 10,152 km of paved public highway. The road network is comprised of several federal highways, including the Amur highway (Chita-Khabarovsk) – part of Moscow-Vladivostok main route. Its length within the Amur Region is 1,017 km.

Railroads. The Amur Region has 3,295 km of railroads. Trans-Siberian railroad goes through the Region and provides access to the Maritime Territory's seaports of Nakhodka, Vostochny, and Vladivostok. A section of the Far-East Railroad (Baikal-Amur Railroad) also goes through the Region and links it to the Khabarovsk Territory's seaports of Vanino and Sovetskaya Bay.

Airports. GUP Blagoveschensk Airport is the Region's main international airport with annual throughput of some 100,000 passengers. The airport links the Region to regions in central Russia by transit and direct routes, and to eastern regions through Khabarovsk airport. The regional centers of Tynda, Zeya, and Ekimchan have municipal airports servicing local routes.

River transport. The Region has 2,595 km of navigable sections of the Amur and Zeya rivers. During the navigable period, some 500,000–600,000 tons of goods and over 150,000 passengers are transported. Tourist routes to China account for some 60% of passenger flow.

River ports. The Region is home to four river freight and passenger ports: ZAO Blagoveschensk Trade Port, ZAO Svobodny Trade Port, ZAO Poyarkovo Trade Port, and ZAO Zeya Trade Port. Blagoveschensk's passenger port AmurAsso specializes in international routes.

3.6. MAIN NATURAL RESOURCES: RESERVES AND EXTRACTION IN 2002

The Region is rich in over 60 types of mineral resources, including gold, silver, platinum, graphite, kaolin, titanium, magnesium, copper, apatite, black and brown coal, semi-precious stones, and rare earth elements, including uranium and diamonds. Proven reserves of mineral resources amount to $400 billion.

Gold. The Region tops Russia's list of estimated reserves of placer gold and holds third position in the world. Over 3,000 deposits of placer gold have been registered in the Region. Currently, the Pokrovskoye

FAR EASTERN FEDERAL DISTRICT

VII

Fuel and energy sector production and consumption trends, 1997–2002						
	1997	1998	1999	2000	2001	2002*
Electricity output, billion kWh	5.6	5.2	5.7	6.9	6.1	5.4
Coal extraction, '000 tons	5,386	4,099	2,801	2,144	2,700	2,503
Electricity consumption, billion kWh	4.0	5.1	5.7	5.7	5.9	5.6
Coal consumption, '000 tons	8,329	6,754	6,117	5,187	5,484	5,640

TABLE 5

*Estimates of the Amur Regional Administration

ore gold deposit with estimated reserves of 60 tons is being prepared for commercial development. Similar reserves have been discovered in the Berezit deposit of the Tynda district of the Amur Region.

Coal. Coal is the second valuable resource. Estimated reserves of bituminous and brown coal are 71 billion tons. Some 90 coal deposits have been discovered in the Region so far. The largest of them are: the Raichik-hinskoye deposit with balance reserves of 35.9 million tons, including 26.3 million tons of industrial reserves, the Arkharo-Boguchanskoye deposit with balance reserves of 74.5 million tons, including 56.8 million tons of indust-rial reserves, and the Erkovets-

koye deposit with balance reserves of 1.3 billion tons. The Region has commissioned operations at the Gerbikano-Ogodzhinky coal deposit with 1 billion tons of total reserves. In the future it plans to develop the Ogodzhinky, Svobodny, Sergeevsky, and the Erkovetsky deposits by attracting foreign investment.

Iron ore. Among prospective deposits is the Garinsky iron ore deposit with 388.8 million tons of reserves. Ore contains nearly 55% of iron, requires no dressing, and is suitable for non-coke metal processing.

Forestry. Forests cover 21.8 million hectares, 73% of the Region's area. The main kinds of forest trees are Siberian larch, fir, silver-fir, pine, oak, birch, and ash-tree.

4. TRADE OPPORTUNITIES

4.1. MAIN GOODS PRODUCED IN THE REGION

The main types of industrial output in 2002:

Fuel and energy: energy – 5.4 billion kWh (88.5% of 2001 levels), heat – 4.2 million Gcal (11.9%), coal – 2.5 million tons (92.7%).

Machine engineering: 22 electric bridge cranes (53.7%), 4 automotive cranes (44%);

Forestry and timber: lumber – 41,500 cubic meters (189.5%); fiberboards – 8.8 million conventional square meters (204%), furniture – $0.7 million (140%);

Ferrous metals: steel – 812 tons (58.9%)

Food and beverages: sausage – 3,400 tons (122.3%), butter – 920 tons (114.2%), commercial fish products – 61.9 tons (158.7%), meat – 7,500 tons (148.2%), dairy products – 17,600 tons (115.3%);

Agriculture products: soybeans – 523,900 tons (106.6%), potatoes – 523,900 tons (106.7%), vegetables – 111,600 tons (99.6%).

4.2. EXPORTS, INCLUDING EXTRA-CIS

The Amur Region's exports to extra-CIS countries amounted to $58.3 million in 2000, exports to CIS countries – $0.1 million. The respective figures for 2001

were $96.4 million and $0.1 million, and 2002 – $70.7 million, while there were no exports to the CIS.

The main types of goods exported by the Region are: soybeans (7,500 tons to China in 2001), raw timber (708,400 cubic meters to China, North Korea, South Korea, and Japan), processed timber (4,500 tons to China), and fiber board (4,711,900 square meters to China, North Korea, and Japan during the first nine months of 2002).

4.3. IMPORTS, INCLUDING EXTRA-CIS

2000 imports from extra-CIS countries amounted to $15.8 million, and imports from CIS countries – $1.3 million. The respective figures for 2001 were $20 million and $1.6 million, and for 2002 – $23.8 million and $0.5 million.

The bulk of 2002 regional imports was represented by meat and meat products (214.5 tons from Vietnam and China in 2001), vegetables (14,134.9 tons from Kazakhstan, Uzbekistan, and China), fruit (14,067 tons from Azerbaijan, Tajikistan, Uzbekistan, China, and the Philippines), knitwear (15,738 tons from China), and machinery and equipment ($5.3million from Ukraine, Finland, and Japan).

Major regional export and import entities		TABLE 6
ENTITY	ADDRESS	PHONE, FAX, E-MAIL
OAO Tyndales Timber Plant	7, ul. Profsoyuznaya, Tynda, Amur Region, 676080	Phone: (41656) 32 473 Fax (41656) 22 900 E-mail: tyndales@amur.ru
OOO Amurlesexport	Office 9, 156, ul. Amurskaya, Blagoveschensk, Amur Region, 675000	Тел. (4162) 53 1155 Fax (4162) 53 2100 E-mail: victory@tsl.ru
ZAO Blagoveschensk Trade Port	1, ul. Lazo, Blagoveschensk, Amur Region, 675002	Phone (4162) 44 2865 Fax (4162) 44 4818 E-mail: rechport@amur.ru
OAO Amurlesprom Timber Holding Company	3, per. Relochny, Blagoveschensk, Amur Region, 675002	Phone (4162) 42 4645 Fax (4162) 42 8834 E-mail: lesprom@tsl.ru

5. INVESTMENT OPPORTUNITIES

5.1. INVESTMENTS IN 1992–2002 (BY INDUSTRY SECTOR), INCLUDING FOREIGN INVESTMENTS

The following factors determine the investment appeal of the Amur Region:

• Its advantageous geographic location, and proximity to markets (primarily China);
• Its developed transport infrastructure (developed railroads and river transport);
• Cheap energy (developed hydro-energy);
• Availability of large reserves of natural resources (gold, coal).

Foreign investment trends in 1997–2002						TABLE 7
	1997	1998	1999	2000	2001	2002
Foreign investment, $ million	0.5	0.4	2.3	4.5	0.2	0.2
Including FDI, $ million	0.3	0.4	2.3	4.5	0.2	0.2

Capital investment by industry sector, $ million						TABLE 8
	1997	1998	1999	2000	2001	2002
Total capital investment	409.8	205.2	84.1	164.3	542.1	390.8
Including major industries (% of total)						
Industry	36.0	36.7	27.2	42.1	25.0	48.9
Agriculture and forestry	1.3	1.0	1.6	1.7	0.5	1.1
Construction	3.5	1.2	1.7	1.2	0.4	2.6
Transport and communications	26.8	32.4	47.0	37.3	67.3	34.1
Trade and public catering	3.3	1.1	0.7	0.8	0.7	1.0
Other	29.1	27.6	21.8	16.9	6.1	12.3

5.2. MAJOR ENTERPRISES (INCLUDING ENTERPRISES WITH FOREIGN INVESTMENT)

The Amur Region has registered over 14,000 companies. As of January 1, 2003, the Region was home to 154 companies with foreign investment, including 126 companies established by investors from China. The largest companies with foreign investment are: OAO Pokrovsky Mine (gold mining), OOO KSK Khuafu (housing construction), a branch of OAO Dal Telecom International (communications).

Largest enterprises of the Amur Region	TABLE 9
COMPANY	INDUSTRY, SECTOR
OAO Zeysky Lumber and Transportation Plant	Forestry
OAO Tyndales Timber Plant	Forestry
OAO Taldansky Forestry	Forestry
OAO Blagoveschensk October Revolution Shipbuilding Plant	Machine engineering
OAO Blagoveschensk Electrical Tool Plant	Machine engineering
OAO Svobodny Electrical Tool Plant	Machine engineering
OAO Amurdormash	Machine engineering
OAO Bureya-Kran	Machine engineering
OAO Amurenergo	Energy
OAO Zeyskaya Hydroelectric Power Station	Energy
OAO Blagoveschensk Plant of Construction Materials	Construction

5.3. MOST ATTRACTIVE
SECTORS FOR INVESTMENT

According to the Amur Regional Administration, the most potentially appealing sectors for investors are energy, agriculture and food processing, exploration, mining and processing of raw metals, machine engineering, deep timber processing, recycling, production of consumer goods, and innovation.

One potential area for western investment is the development of deep timber processing. The Region has good prospects for profitable investment in the upgrading of existing and construction of new lumber and timber processing facilities with short payback period.

5.4. CURRENT LEGISLATION ON INVESTOR
TAX EXEMPTIONS AND PRIVILEGES

The Amur Region has passed the following regional laws:

• On Investment Activity in the Amur Region. The law guarantees protection of investor rights and provides tax privileges to domestic and foreign investors;

• On Small Enterprise in the Amur Region.

The Region has established a Production Development Fund and an Enterprise Support Fund.

The following provisions of the law On Investment Activity in the Amur Region aim to support sectors of the Region's economy and attract investment: On Investment Tax Credit in the Amur Region, On Guarantees of the Amur Regional Administration Against Loans and Credits, On the Approval of Credit Provision to Legal Entities from the Regional Budget (State and Municipal Unitary Companies Excluded), and On Production Development Fund in the Amur Region.

Pursuant to the current law, companies that attract investment and use their own funds to expand, upgrade, diversify, or launch new operations, enjoy the following privileges on local taxes:

A decrease in profit tax rate by no more than 4%;
An exemption from property tax.

Privileges apply to the tax base resulting from the implementation of investment projects during the total payback period up to a maximum of three years.

5.5. FEDERAL AND REGIONAL
ECONOMIC AND SOCIAL DEVELOPMENT
PROGRAMS FOR THE AMUR REGION

Federal targeted programs. The major federal targeted program underway in the Amur Region is The Program for Economic and Social Development of the Far East and Trans-Baikal Territories, 1996-2005 and through 2010. The Program has been developed with the purpose to create transport corridors, enhance external economic relationships and reinforce the Russian Federation's standing in terms of global transport system, modernization of structure and development of key economy sectors, transport and fishery industries, and create favorable climate for small and medium business development.

Regional programs. In 2002, the Region passed a number of legislative acts regarding 21 regional targeted programs, including the priority programs: Restoration of Forest Reproduction, 2002–2005; Restoration and Protection of Water Resources of the Amur Region, 2002; Development of Minerals and Feedstock Basis of the Amur Region, 2003–2005; Improvement of Labor Conditions and Safety in the Amur Region, 2002–2005.

6. INVESTMENT PROJECTS

Industry sector and project description	1) Expected results 2) Amount and term of investment 3) Form of financing[1] 4) Documentation[2]	Contact information
1	2	3
MINING		
83R001	● ▲	Natural Resources and Mining
Development of the Garin iron ore deposit. Project goal: to construct an ore dressing plant to produce iron ore pellets for domestic and foreign market.	1) 2.8 million tons of iron ore pellets per year 2) $120 million/6 years 3) L 4) FS	Industry Committee 24, ul. Shevchenko, Blagoveschensk, Amur Region, 675000 Phone: (4162) 53 2225 Fax: (4162) 42 7376 E-mail: kpp@ascnet.ru

[1] L – Loan, E – Equity, Leas. – Leasing, JV – Joint Venture
[2] BP – Business Plan, FS – Feasibility Study

1	2	3

83R002

Development of Chalganivsky deposit of kaolin containing sands.
Project goal: to launch pit extraction and processing of kaolin.

1) n/a
2) $5.5 million/3 years
3) L
4) FS

Amur Research and Development Center
1, per. Relochny, Blagoveschensk, Amur Region, 675000
Phone: (4162) 42 7232
Fax (4162) 42 5931
E-mail: aurum@amur.su
Valentin Grigoryevich Moiseenko, Chairman of the Academy

CONSTRUCTION MATERIALS

83R003

Launching production of basalt reinforced tubes.
Project goal: to reconstruct production facilities, produce rigging, acquire required equipment, and increase working capital.

1) 160 kilometers of tubes per year; 1,200 tons of materials from basalt fiber per year
2) $2.2 million/ n/a
3) L
4) BP

OAO October Revolution Shipbuilding Plant
189, ul. Pushkina, Blagoveschensk, Amur Region, 675003
Phone: (4162) 42 3609
Vyacheslav Stepanovich Popov, CEO

FORESTRY, TIMBER, AND PULP AND PAPER

83R004

Development of timber storage and deep processing operations.
Project goal: to increase timber output and expand processed timber product range.

1) Annual output of 1 million cubic meters of industrial timber, 32,000 cubic meters of 8 mm plywood, 10,000 cubic meters of 16–32 mm plywood, and 55,000 cubic meters of timber per year
2) $23.8 million/1 year
3) L ($18.5 million)
4) BP

OAO Tyndales Timber Plant
7, ul. Profsoyuznaya, Tynda, Amur Region, 676080
Phone: (41656) 32 473
Fax: (41656) 22 000
Nikolay Sergeevich Sarnavsky, CEO

FOOD AND BEVERAGES

83R005

Construction of an extraction soy bean processing plant.
Project goal: to construct the soybean processing plant at a former construction machinery repair plant.

1) Deodorized soy bean oil – 13,600 tons per year, margarine – 7,500 tons per year, mayonnaise – 5,000 tons per year, and sprats – 75,700 tons per year
2) $25.1 million/4.5 years
3) L, JV
4) BP

OAO Amur Soya
24, ul. Shevchenko, Blagoveschensk, Amur Region, 675000
Phone: (4162) 44 4801
Yury Alexandrovich Pugachev, President

83R006

Brewery reconstruction.
Project goal: to construct new brewing and fermenting shops.

1) Output expansion to 3 million decaliters per year
2) $5.3 million/3 years
3) L
4) BP

ZAO Far East Food Company
17, ul. Pervomayskaya, Blagoveschensk, Amur Region, 675000
Phone: (4162) 44 1988
Fax: (4162) 44 6649
E-mail: dpk@amur.ru
Sergey Gennadyevich Shashev, CEO

HEALTHCARE

83R007

Construction of a rehabilitation center at the Byssinsky thermal mineral water springs.
Project goal: to provide recreational services.

1) Utilization of up to 560 cubic meters of thermal mineral water per day and up to 800 cubic meters of fresh cold water per day.
2) $2.5 million/3 years
3) L, E, JV
4) Investment proposal

Public Health Committee of the Amur Regional Administration,
Blagoveschensk, Amur Region, 675023
Phone: (4162) 44 3682, 44 1948
Regional Administration
Village of Ekimchan, Selemdzhunsky District, Amur Region, 676560
Phone: (41646) 21 460, 21 665

84. KAMCHATKA REGION [41]

ECONOMIC MAP

CHUKOTSKY AUTONOMOUS DISTRICT

Penzhina

Pakhachi

KORYAKSKY

Vyvenka

AUTONOMOUS

DISTRICT

Penzhinskaya guba (gulf)

MAGADAN

REGION

Evensk

B E R I N G

S E A

Shelikhov

Gulf

PALANA

Ust-Kamchatsk

Karaginsky Island

Komandor Islands

Yamsk

MAGADAN

Ust-Khayruzovo

Kamchatka

Klyuchi

Milkovo

PETROPAVLOVSK-KAMCHATSKY

Krutogorovsky

S E A   O F

O K H O T S K

Kirovsky

Yelizovo

Paratunka

Oktyabrsky

Ozernovsky

PROCESSING INDUSTRY
- Machine engineering and metal processing
- Forestry and timber
- Construction materials
- Food and beverages

- Fishing ports
- Mineral water sources
- Resorts

POWER PLANTS
- Thermal power plants

LIVESTOCK BREEDING
- Meat and dairy cattle breeding
- Animal breeding
- Sea mammals catch

For a long time, the Kamchatka Region was closed to the outside world. That situation has changed, however, and now the Region is actively developing its economic links. Our Region is certainly attractive for tourists, who now have the opportunity to visit our unique and spectacularly beautiful peninsula, but also for Russian and foreign businessmen, who have expressed interest in the Region's energy, fisheries, transport, and timber sectors.

Kamchatka is a wonderful place. Its volcanoes, geysers, lakes, rivers, and forests cannot fail to impress. Our Region is rich in mineral resources, its seas are rich in fish and seafood, and its rivers are renowned spawning grounds for valuable species of salmon. Kamchatka is a land of contrast and unlimited opportunity.

Owing to Kamchatka's geographical location, air and sea transport play major roles in sustaining life on the peninsula.

Yelizovo International Airport, 30 kilometers outside Petropavlovsk-Kamchatsky, can accept aircraft of any freight capacity. Reconstruction work was completed at the airport at the beginning of 2003. The result has been increased throughput capacity and added comfort for passengers. The Region is developing and revamping its transport infrastructure to service international flights in view of the increased passenger and freight traffic in the Northern Pacific Rim. The airport is ideally situated for the development of international tourism.

The port of Petropavlovsk-Kamchatsky, the northernmost year-round seaport in the Far East, handles 99.9% of Kamchatka's freight. The port services cargo routes to many Pacific Rim destinations.

The Region is implementing a number of important economic development projects, including the construction of a trunk gas pipeline from a gas condensate field in the Sea of Okhotsk to Petropavlovsk-Kamchatsky, construction of the Mutnovsky geothermal power plant, and construction of low-yield hydroelectric power stations on the Tolmacheva River.

Other projects worth serious consideration are being conducted in the fisheries, forestry, mining and metals processing, and tourism sectors.

Investments are needed to accelerate the implementation of many of these projects and facilitate cooperation with the Far East regions.

We will do everything in our power to ensure that investments in our Region provide good returns and that our Region maintains a favorable investment climate.

Mikhail Mashkovtsev,
GOVERNOR OF THE KAMCHATKA REGION

FAR EASTERN FEDERAL DISTRICT

VII

1. GENERAL INFORMATION

1.1. GEOGRAPHY

The Kamchatka Region covers a total area of 170,800 square kilometers. The Region is located in the north-east of Russia in the southern part of the Kamchatka Peninsula and the Komandorskie Islands. To the south the Region borders the Kuril Islands. On its eastern coast, the Peninsula is washed by the Pacific Ocean, on its north-eastern coast by the Bering Sea, and in the west by the Sea of Okhotsk. This section contains information regarding the Kamchatka Region only, excluding the Koryaksky Autonomous District.

1.2. CLIMATE

The Kamchatka Region has a temperate monsoon climate. Its central parts enjoy a temperate continental climate.

The average air temperature in January is −16.4°C, rising to +13.0°C in July. Average annual precipitation reaches 1,000 mm.

1.3. POPULATION

According to preliminary 2002 census results, a total population in the Region was 359,000 people. The average population density is 2.1 people per square kilometer. The economically active population amounted to 225,000 people as of 2001. 2002 official unemployment level was 11.6%.

Demographically speaking, some 69.9% are of working age, 18.2% are below the statutory working age, and 11.9% are beyond the statutory working age.

As of 2002, the Kamchatka Region's major urban centers were Petropavlovsk-Kamchatsky with 198,200 inhabitants, Elizovo with 36,400 inhabitants, and Vilyuchinsk with 33,200 inhabitants.

Population							TABLE 1
	1992	1997	1998	1999	2000	2001	2002
Total population, '000	424	377	370	365	359	355	359
Economically active population, '000	273	211	200	214	209	215	225

2. ADMINISTRATION

1, pl. Lenina, Petropavlovsk-Kamchatsky, Kamchatka Region, 683040
Phone: (4152) 11 2091; fax: (41522) 73 843
E-mail: kra@svjaz.kamchatka.ru

NAME	POSITION	CONTACT INFORMATION
Mikhail Borisovich MASHKOVTSEV	Governor of the Kamchatka Region	Phone: (4152) 11 2096 Fax: (4152) 11 2091
Vladislav Vasilyevich GRIBKOV	First Deputy Governor of the Kamchatka Region for Economic Development and Industry	Phone: (4152) 11 2130 Fax: (4152) 27 3843 E-mail: kra@svjaz.kamchatka.ru
Natalia Lvovna PARKHOMENKO	First Deputy Governor of the Kamchatka Region	Phone: (4152) 11 2274 Fax: (4152) 11 2091 E-mail: kra@svjaz.kamchatka.ru
Gennady Panteleevich SEREBRENNIKOV	Deputy Governor of the Kamchatka Region, Chairman of the Committee for Agriculture, Food, and Trade	Phone: (4152) 11 8000 Fax: (4152) 11 8203 E-mail: kra@svjaz.kamchatka.ru
Vladimir Ivanovich OBUKHOV	Head of Industrial Policy, Enterprise Development, and Investment Department	Phone: (4152) 11 2635 Fax: (4152) 12 3734 E-mail: kra@svjaz.kamchatka.ru

3. ECONOMIC POTENTIAL

3.1. 1997–2002 GROSS REGIONAL PRODUCT (GRP). INDUSTRY BREAKDOWN

The 2002 gross regional product of the Kamchatka Region amounted to $813 million, which constitutes 7.2% growth year-on-year. Per capita GRP amounted to $2,133 in 2001 and $2,263 in 2002.

3.2. MAJOR ECONOMIC GROWTH PROJECTIONS

According to the forecasts of the Kamchatka Regional Administration, 2003 industrial output will amount to $767.7 million, rising to $930.0 million in 2004, and $974.6 million in 2005.

The 2003 fish and seafood catch is expected to reach 550,000 tons. Estimated 2003 commercial edible fish output, including canned fish, is expect-ed to reach 425,000 tons, provided the Kamchatka Region is allocated the required quotas. Deep processed products, such as dressed fish, fish fillet, fish stuffing, balyk, and various kinds of processed herring, account for an increasingly growing share in the structure of edible fish output.

In the energy sector, plans are afoot to increase coal output from 45,000 tons in 2002 to 55,000 tons in 2005. Electricity output in 2003 is expected to reach 1,675 million kWh (100.3% of the 2002 level), rising to 1,690 million kWh in 2004, and 2% growth per year thereafter. The proportion of electricity produced by hydroelectric and geothermal power stations will increase. 2003 heat output will grow 1% year-on-year, and 2% a year thereafter.

GRP trends in 1997–2002						TABLE 2
	1997	1998	1999	2000	2001*	2002*
GRP in current prices, $ million	1,377	1,146	599	652	757	813

*Estimates of the Kamchatka Regional Administration

GRP industry breakdown in 1997–2002, % of total						TABLE 3
	1997	1998	1999	2000	2001	2002*
GRP	100.0	100.0	100.0	100.0	100.0	100.0
Industry	36.8	47.6	52.2	46.2	49.7	46.2
Agriculture and forestry	9.8	7.5	4.8	5.8	4.6	4.7
Construction	5.9	7.4	2.5	6.2	6.5	6.5
Transport and communications	7.4	6.2	5.3	6.3	5.4	5.5
Trade and public catering	11.6	8.0	9.3	9.5	9.8	9.7
Other	28.5	23.3	25.9	26.0	24.0	27.4

*Estimates of the Kamchatka Regional Administration

3.3. INDUSTRIAL OUTPUT IN 1997–2002 FOR MAJOR SECTORS OF ECONOMY

The leading industrial sectors of the Kamchatka Region are food (fishery), energy, and non-ferrous metals.

Food sector (fisheries). The sector accounts for 59.7% of total industrial output. This is the priority industry of the Kamchatka Region. The Region engages in whaling and crab catching. Most fishing companies are situated in Petropavlovsk-Kamchatsky.

Agriculture. The Region grows vegetables, potatoes, and breeds cattle. Vegetables are grown in greenhouses heated by hot thermal springs. Large areas are set aside for fodder crops and perennial herbs fed to cattle. Reindeer breeding is popular in the north, where vast pastures are located.

3.4. FUEL AND ENERGY BALANCE (OUTPUT AND CONSUMPTION PER RESOURCE)
3.5. TRANSPORT INFRASTRUCTURE

The Region employs mainly sea, air, and road transport. Products are exported and imported either by sea or by air. The Region has no railroads.

Seaports. The largest commercial seaport in the Region is at Petropavlovsk-Kamchatsky. Other ports include the port of Ust-Kamsk and small fishing ports. The Region has sea links to South Korea, Japan, China, Hong Kong, the USA, and Canada.

Airports. The main civilian airport is located at Yelizovo. The Region also has 32 local airports, including four state-owned airports, with the rest owned by seven private companies. Kamchatka's airports host regular direct flights to North America, South Korea, and South-East Asia.

Industry breakdown of industrial output in 1997–2002, % of total						TABLE 4
	1997	1998	1999	2000	2001	2002*
Industry	100.0	100.0	100.0	100.0	100.0	100.0
Food and beverages (including fishery)	63.0	48.8	66.1	63.3	61.9	59.7
Energy	19.8	24.8	17.1	20.1	21.2	22.5
Machine engineering and metal processing	8.3	4.4	3.3	4.0	4.4	5.7
Construction materials	2.0	1.2	0.9	0.9	0.7	0.7
Forestry, timber, and pulp and paper	1.3	0.9	0.6	0.6	0.5	0.5
Flour, cereals, and mixed fodder	1.4	0.2	0.2	0.5	0.3	0.3
Light industry	0.5	0.2	0.2	0.2	0.2	0.2
Fuel	0.3	0.4	0.2	0.3	0.3	0.4
Ferrous metals	0.0	0.1	0.0	0.1	0.1	0.0
Chemicals and petrochemicals	0.2	0.0	0.0	0.1	0.1	0.1

*Estimates of the Kamchatka Regional Administration

Fuel and energy sector production and consumption trends, 1997–2002						TABLE 5
	1997	1998	1999	2000	2001	2002*
Electricity output, billion kWh	1.6	1.5	1.5	1.6	1.6	1.7
Natural gas extraction, million cubic meters	–	–	–	7.4	7.9	8.5
Electricity consumption, billion kWh	1.4	1.4	1.3	1.4	1.4	1.6

*Estimates of the Kamchatka Regional Administration

Oil and gas pipelines. Pursuant to the program for the transition to electricity and heat generation in the Kamchatka Region using non-traditional renewable energy sources and local fuel, the Region is constructing a natural gas pipeline from a gas condensate field to the Regional center. The pipe-line is due to be completed in 2004.

3.6. MAIN NATURAL RESOURCES: RESERVES AND EXTRACTION IN 2002

The Region's principle natural resources are natural gas, coal, native sulphur, thermal waters, gold, and silver.

Gold. The Region has over 400 explored gold ore deposits and mineralization points. Some eleven tons of gold has been extracted in the Region since production began, while the total reserve is estimated to exceed 200 tons.

Construction materials. The Region has some 64 deposits of volcano slag and pumice-stone.

Forests. Forests cover a total of 43.9 million hectares, or 95% of the Region' area. The most common tree species are Kamchatka larch, Kyander larch, fir, birch, ash, poplar, Chosenia arbutifolia, Sakhalin willow, cedar, and alder.

4. TRADE OPPORTUNITIES

4.1. MAIN GOODS PRODUCED IN THE REGION

Main types of industrial output in 2002:
Electricity – 1.7 billion kWh;
Fish and seafood – 522,000 tons.

4.2. EXPORTS, INCLUDING EXTRA-CIS

The Kamchatka Region's exports amounted to $386.8 million in 2001, and to $143 million in 2002.

The main types of goods exported by the Region in 2001 were: food and raw food (fish, crayfish, and shellfish – $376.3 million), machinery, equipment, and vehicles ($7.6 million), and metals and metal goods ($2.9 million). Major importers of the Region's products include China, South Korea, Japan, Hong Kong, the USA, Germany, and the UK.

4.3. IMPORTS, INCLUDING EXTRA-CIS

2001 imports amounted to $83.8 million, and in 2002 this figure was $23 million. The bulk of 2001 regional imports was represented by: machinery, equipment, and vehicles ($34.1 million), fuel ($31.1 million), metals and metal goods ($1.9 million), chemicals ($2.7 million), food and raw food ($1.9 million), and clothes and footwear ($1.5 million). The main exporters to the Region are: the USA, Germany, South Korea, Japan, China, Poland, Canada, Hong Kong, Ireland, Ukraine, and the UK.

5. INVESTMENT OPPORTUNITIES

5.1. INVESTMENTS IN 1992–2002 (BY INDUSTRY SECTOR), INCLUDING FOREIGN INVESTMENTS

The following factors determine the investment appeal of the Kamchatka Region:
- Its unique geographic location;
- Rich natural resources (estimated potential natural resource value is over $20 billion);
- Extensive reserves of biosphere resources.

5.2. MAJOR ENTERPRISES (INCLUDING ENTERPRISES WITH FOREIGN INVESTMENT)

As of 2001 the Region was home to some 9,295 companies with foreign investment.

5.3. CURRENT LEGISLATION ON INVESTOR TAX EXEMPTIONS AND PRIVILEGES

In 2001, the Kamchatka Regional Administration passed Regulations for Industry, Business and Investment Management focused on creating an environment to ensure increasing investment appeal of the Kam-chatka Region, development of priority industries and real economy sectors, business and investment process, identifying principal directions, measures and mechanisms for implementation of the Kamchatka Regional Administration's investment and industrial policies, assistance to development and increased efficiency of business entities' external economic relations,

Capital investment by industry sector, $ million						*TABLE 6*
	1997	1998	1999	2000	2001	2002
Total capital investment	180.3	91.7	41.2	126.1	100.8	150.8
Including major industries (% of total)						
Industry	45.0	47.3	41.9	30.0	27.4	48.6
Agriculture and forestry	2.7	0.7	2.0	6.2	7.6	4.3
Construction	0.1	0.4	1.1	0.2	0.6	–
Transport and communications	13.3	14.2	32.2	50.1	49.0	30.0
Trade and public catering	3.6	2.0	1.9	0.6	0.2	0.1
Other	35.3	35.4	20.9	12.9	15.2	17.0

Foreign investment trends in 1997–2002						*TABLE 7*
	1997	1998	1999	2000	2001	2002
Foreign investment, $ million	32.6	35.8	8.7	29.1	74.1	42.7
Including FDI, $ million	0.5	0.04	0.04	0.1	0.8	0.01

an establishing and carrying out business relationships with Russian and foreign investors, investment funds and other financial institutions regarding social and economic development of the Kamchatka Region.

5.4. FEDERAL AND REGIONAL ECONOMIC AND SOCIAL DEVELOPMENT PROGRAMS FOR THE KAMCHATKA REGION

Federal targeted programs. The major federal targeted programs underway in the Region include: Social and Economic Development of the Far East and Trans-Baikal Territories through 2010, Ecology and Natural Resources of Russia, 2002– 2010, Energy Efficient Economy, 2002–2005 and through 2010, Elimination of Differences in the Social and Economic Development of Regions of the Russian federation, 2002–2010 and through 2015, and Children of Russia, 2003–2006.

Regional programs. A number of regional targeted programs is underway in the Kamchatka Region, with the priority accorded to the following programs: Enhancement of Soil Fertility in the Kamchatka Region, 2002–2005, Improvement of Human Resource Potential of the Agroindustrial Sector of the Kam-chatka Region, 2002–2005, Youth of Kamchatka, 2002–2004, and Culture of Kamchatka, 2002–2004.

Largest enterprises of the Kamchatka Region		TABLE 8
COMPANY	SECTOR	
OAO Kamchatenergo	Energy	
OAO Kamchatcement	Construction materials	
OAO Oceanrybflot	Fishery	
OAO Kamchatrybprom	Fishery	
OAO Koryba	Fishery	
ZAO Yanin Kutkh	Fishery	
OOO Ustkamchatryba	Fishery	
OAO Kamchatalko	Food and beverages	
OAO Kampivo	Food and beverages	

6. INVESTMENT PROJECTS

Industry sector and project description	1) Expected results 2) Amount and term of investment 3) Form of financing[1] 4) Documentation[2]	Contact information
1	2	3

MINING

84R001

| Construction of a modular ore dressing plant to process titanium and magnesium sand from the Khalaktyrsky deposit. Project goal: to introduce iron-titanium and aluminum-silicon alloys, titanium and magnesium concentrates, cement, liquid glass, and insulation goods produced from basalt fiber to the market. | 1) Revenue of $11.4 million per year 2) $50.0 million/3 years 3) L 4) BP | OOO Ecomet 50, ul. Stepnaya, Petropavlovsk-Kamchatsky, Kamchatka Region, 683008 Phone: (41522) 76 635, 76 777 Fax: (41522) 11 8017 E-mail: oks@tec2.kamchataten.elektra.ru Vladimir Andreevich Semchev, Director |

84R002

| Commercial development of the Yagodinsky deposit of natural zeolite. Project goal: to introduce zeolite products to the market. | 1) 50,000 tons 2) $1.0 million/2.5 years 3) L 4) Design and budget documentation | OOO Zeolite 19, ul. Pogranichnaya, Petropavlovsk-Kamchatsky, Kamchatka Region, 683032 Phone: (4152) 12 6705 Fax: (4152) 12 5241 Vladimir Dmitrievich Shevchuk, Director |

[1] L – Loan, E – Equity, Leas. – Leasing, JV – Joint Venture
[2] BP – Business Plan, FS – Feasibility Study

1	2	3

FOOD AND BEVERAGES

83R003

Production (cultivation) of brown seaweed (Laminaria and Alaria marginata), shellfish (mussel, scallop, and crab) and salmon farming (Coho salmon and stone loach). Project goal: to extend the product range.

1) 220 tons of commercial product per year
2) $1.0 million/6 years
3) L ($0.7 million)
4) Design documentation

Fishing Artel Pacific Market
96, ul. Primorskaya,
Petropavlovsk-Kamchatsky,
Kamchatka Region, 683901
Phone: (4152) 16 8819
Fax: (4152) 16 8817
E-mail: tral@mail.kamchatka.ru
Vladimir Gennadyevich Rezvanov
Chairman
Oleg Yuryevich Kozyrsky,
Deputy Chairman

83R004

Utilization of underground fresh water reservoirs of Russkaya Bay. Project goal: to increase product output.

1) 15,000 cubic meters per day
2) $7.0 million/3 years
3) L
4) BP

OOO Russian Water
38, ul. Leninskaya,
Petropavlovsk-Kamchatsky,
Kamchatka Region, 683000
Phone/fax: (4152) 12 3591
Alexander Yevgenyevich Gorbunov,
CEO

HOTELS AND TOURISM

83R005

Construction of a tourist hotel near Petropavlovsk-Kamchatsky. Project goal: to develop leisure and business tourism.

1) 50 rooms
2) $0.5 million/2 years
3) L
4) BP

OOO Sampotour
6, pr. Pobedy,
Petropavlovsk-Kamchatsky,
Kamchatka Region, 683000
Phone: (41522) 94 949
Fax: (41522) 52 280
E-mail: sampotur@mail.kamchatka.ru
Vladimir Vladimirovich Yevstratov,
CEO

83R006

Construction of a year-round tourist center on the basis of a children's camp. Project goal: to extend services and improve service quality.

1) 12,000–16,000 people per year
2) $25.0 million/2 years
3) L
4) BP

OOO Children's Camp Aliye Parusa
Village of Paratunki,
Yelizovsky District,
Kamchatka Region, 683034
Nikolai Ivanovich Vorobyev,
Director

83R007

Construction of a rehabilitation and recreation center. Project goal: to improve the quality of service and promote tourism.

1) 100 rooms
2) $0.6 million/1 year
3) Credit $0.5 million
4) BP

OOO Dixon
Village of Paratunki,
Yelizovsky District,
Kamchatka Region, 683034
Phone: (41531) 93 281
E-mail: sails@intercom.kamchatka.ru
Http://sails.vulcan.ru
Alexander Leontyevich Dozhdev,
CEO

85. MAGADAN REGION [49]

ECONOMIC MAP

CHUKOTSKY AUTONOMOUS DISTRICT

KORYAKSKY AUTONOMOUS DISTRICT

Omolon
Oloy
Omolon

REPUBLIC OF SAKHA (YAKUTIA)

Kolyma

Evensk

Dukat   Galimy
Omsukchan
Sugoy

Shelikhov

Gulf

Penzhinskaya guba (gulf)

Orotukan

Yagodnoe
Kolymskoe
Arkagala   Susuman
Karamken

Indigirka
Stekolny

Kolyma
MAGADAN

KHABAROVSK

SEA   OF

OKHOTSK

REGION

Udomo

PROCESSING INDUSTRY
- ● Machine engineering and metal processing
- ● Construction materials
- ○ Food and beverages

MINING INDUSTRY
- ■ Bituminous coal
- ◯ Tin
- ◑ Gold
- 🐟 Fishing ports

POWER PLANTS
- ⚡ Thermal power plants
- ⚡ Hydro power plants

LIVESTOCK BREEDING
- ● Animal farming
- 🦭 Sea mammals catch
- 🐄 Meat and dairy cattle breeding
- 🦌 Reindeer breeding

The Magadan Region, also called Golden Kolyma, is one of the most wonderful places in Russia. Everything is unique in this land - its history, natural environment, resources, and most importantly, its people and the relations between them predetermined by our rigorous climate and bountiful land.

Over the 50 years of its existence as an administrative entity, the Region has accumulated vast economic potential. The Kolyma Refining Plant, Explosives Plant, and mechanical repair plants service dozens of large and small gold mining companies. Gold mining is expanding from year to year and new facilities are continuously being put into operation. In 2002, operations were launched at the Juliet deposit with a capacity of 2.5 tons of gold per year, and gold processing plants are operating at the Lunnoe, Shkolnoe, and Vetrenskoe deposits. In 2003, the ore dressing plant at Dukat, the third largest silver and gold deposit in the world, will reach its operating capacity. The Region's gold ore reserves are estimated to be worth $36.4 billion. Magadan accounts for 25% of Russia's total gold output.

In recent years, the Magadan Region has constructed and launched several specialized fish processing plants. Fish products account for over 60% of the Region's exports. The food and construction sectors are also flourishing.

A project for the construction of an oil refinery with an annual refining capacity of 600,000–800,000 tons of crude oil also presents considerable investor interest. The project has a payback period of five years at a cost of $50–70 million. The total oil reserves of the Magadan shelf amount to 1.4–2.5 billion tons, with gas reserves clocking in at 2.7–4.5 trillion cubic meters.

The Magadan Region has created conditions conducive to economic development. Since 1999, a Special Economic Zone in the Region has provided participants with extensive tax and customs privileges. This has improved the Re-gion's investment appeal and given new zest to the Region's industrial development, which has already been facilitated by investors from the UK, Canada, Germany, and the USA. Russian investors are also showing a healthy interest in gold mining projects, as it was they who invested the lion's share of funds into gold prospecting and mining in 2002.

We shall be happy to discuss with foreign and Russian investors their participation in the proposed investment projects.

Nikolai Dudov,
GOVERNOR OF THE MAGADAN REGION

FAR EASTERN FEDERAL DISTRICT

VII

1. GENERAL INFORMATION

1.1. GEOGRAPHY

The Magadan Region covers a total area of 461,400 square kilometers. A large part of the Region is located on the Kolyma plateau. The main river – the Kolyma – flows through Magadan.

To the west the Region borders the Koryaksky Autonomous District, to the north-east – the Chukotsky Autonomous District, to the north-west – the Republic of Sakha (Yakutia), to the south-west – the Khabarovsk Territory, and to the south and south-east the Region is washed by the Sea of Okhotsk.

1.2. CLIMATE

The Magadan Region has a sub-arctic continental climate. The average air temperature in January is –29.4°C, rising to +14.4°C in July. The average annual precipitation is 396 mm.

1.3. POPULATION

According to preliminary 2002 census results, total population of the Region was 183,000 people. The average population density is 0.4 people/square km. The economically active population amounts to 138,000 people (as of 2002). The 2002 official unemployment level is 4.3%.

Demographically speaking, some 70.5% are of working age, 17.8% are below the statutory working age, and 11.7% are beyond the statutory working age.

As of 2002, the Magadan Region's major urban centers are Magadan with 120,600 inhabitants and Susuman with 8,700 inhabitants.

Population								TABLE 1
	1992	1997	1998	1999	2000	2001	2002
Total population, '000	370	257	252	246	239	234	183
Economically active population, '000	193	136	142	146	144	138	138

2. ADMINISTRATION

6, pl. Gorkogo, Magadan, Magadan Region, 685000
Phone: (841322) 97 686; fax: (41322) 97 807, 97 161; teletype: 145343 Sovet
E-mail: postmast@regadm.magadan.ru; http://www.magadan.ru

NAME	POSITION	CONTACT INFORMATION
Nikolai Nikolaevich DUDOV	Governor of the Magadan Region	Phone: (41322) 23 134 Fax: (41322) 97 807
Vyacheslav Alexandrovich MOSKVICHEV	Acting First Deputy Governor	Phone: (41322) 99 404
Konstantin Viktorovich CHALOV	Deputy Governor (Fuel and Energy, Construction, Transport, and Communications)	Phone: (41322) 99 401 Fax: (41322) 27 491
Alexander Vladimirovich POLYAKOV	Deputy Governor (Economy and Industry)	Phone: (41322) 25 005
Tatiana Mikhailovna MALINOVSKAYA	Deputy Governor, Chief of the Administration Apparatus	Phone: (41322) 23 261
Yevgeny Ivanovich ANTOSCHENKOV	Acting Deputy Governor, Chairman of the State Property Committee of the Magadan Region	Phone: (41322) 23 122 Fax: (41322) 99 607
Irina Stanislavovna PENIEVSKAYA	Chairwoman of the Economics Committee of the Magadan Regional Administration	Phone: (41322) 97 715 Fax: (41322) 26 208
Valentina Andreevna MOISEEVA	Head of the Financial Department of the Magadan Regional Administration	Phone: (41322) 20 939 Fax: (41322) 20 792

3. ECONOMIC POTENTIAL

3.1. 1997–2002 GRP (INDUSTRY BREAKDOWN). MAJOR ECONOMIC GROWTH PROJECTIONS

2002 gross regional product amounted to $608 million, which constitutes 10.4% growth year-on-year. The growth was achieved mainly thanks to an increase in mining and food and beverages sectors. Per capita GRP totaled $2,358 in 2001, and $3,327 in 2002.

3.2. INDUSTRIAL OUTPUT IN 1997–2002 FOR MAJOR SECTORS OF ECONOMY

The Region's industry is focused on the extraction of mineral resources. The leading industrial sectors are mining (gold, silver, tin, tungsten, and coal) and fisheries. These accounted for 77% of total 2002 industrial output. Machine engineering and metal processing are also well developed.

GRP trends in 1997–2002						TABLE 2
	1997	1998	1999	2000	2001*	2002*
GRP in current prices, $ million	1,077	630	420	454	552	608

*Estimates of the Magadan Regional Administration

GRP industry breakdown in 1997–2002, % of total						TABLE 3
	1997	1998	1999	2000	2001*	2002*
GRP	100.0	100.0	100.0	100.0	100.0	100.0
Industry	25.6	40.0	51.7	52.5	58.1	58.1
Agriculture and forestry	−0.5	1.0	1.1	1.5	1.4	1.7
Construction	16.0	8.3	4.6	6.1	6.6	7.7
Transport and communications	11.6	8.9	7.1	6.4	6.1	6.1
Trade and public catering	13.8	10.8	9.4	11.2	9.5	9.5
Other	44.6	35.1	26.3	25.8	27.5	26.1
Net taxes on output	−11.1	−4.1	−0.2	−3.5	−9.2	−9.2

*Estimates of the Magadan Regional Administration

The Magadan Region is a major gold mining area. The annual mining capacity of the Region's companies is 12-15 tons of placer gold, 15-18 tons of ore gold, and several hundred tons of silver.

Mining. Mining, the Region's leading industry, accounts for over 50% of total industrial output.

The Region operates a unified gold turnover system from licensing extraction and gold mining to

Industry breakdown of industrial output in 1997–2002, % of total						TABLE 4
	1997	1998	1999	2000	2001	2002*
Industry	100.0	100.0	100.0	100.0	100.0	100.0
Mining	40.5	56.6	70.9	66.4	57.2	60.0
Food and beverages (including fishery)	7.1	10.1	10.1	14.0	14.9	21.7
Energy	43.4	26.7	14.9	15.3	23.3	15.1
Fuel	3.1	2.7	1.1	1.1	1.3	1.2
Machine engineering and metal processing	2.6	1.9	1.4	1.5	1.8	1.0
Construction materials	1.5	0.9	0.6	0.9	0.7	0.5
Forestry, timber, and pulp and paper	0.7	0.2	0.3	0.3	0.1	0.2
Chemicals and petrochemicals	–	–	–	–	–	0.1
Light industry	0.4	0.1	0.1	0.1	0.1	–

*Estimates of the Magadan Regional Administration

gold processing. With the commissioning of the Kolyma Refining Plant, the Region has become capable of processing all the extracted gold and associated silver into bars. Gold mining is centered around the towns of Susuman and Yagodnoe.

The Region also has copper and coal deposits (Arkagala and Galimy).

Food and beverages (including fishing).
A fleet of 80 vessels and the associated operating infrastructure owned by some 30 companies and organizations represents the fishing sector. Operating capacity of fishing companies amounts to 70,000 tons of fish, including canned fish, and nearly 2,000 tons of auxiliary fish products such as fish fodder and fish powder.

Energy. The Magadan Regional Energy System is local and isolated from the Unified Energy System of Russia. The Region's utilities form a single energy center with the generating capacity of 797 MW, which covers the entire territory of the Region with the exception of the North-Evensky District.

Agriculture. This sector is the least developed. The Region relies mainly on imported food. Internally produced food meets only 50% of the local demand. The main agricultural sectors are tillage, dairy cattle and poultry farming, and sectors specific to the Region such as reindeer herding, fur farming, and indigenous hunting and fishing.

3.3. FUEL AND ENERGY BALANCE (OUTPUT AND CONSUMPTION PER RESOURCE)
The refineries at Komsomolsk-on-Amur, Khabarovsk, Omsk, and Achinsk, as well as the Angarsk Petrochemicals Company supply oil products to the Magadan Region. Oil product imports account for some 25% of regional energy consumption. Actual demand for refined oil amounts to 600,000 tons per annum, but annual supplies of 300,000-400,000 tons limit consumption. The Region is attempting to solve its fuel problem by delivering coal from Sakhalin. Another 600,000 tons of coal are brought from the Khabarovsk Territory and Kuzbass.

Fuel and energy sector production and consumption trends, 1997–2002						TABLE 5
	1997	1998	1999	2000	2001	2002*
Electricity output, billion kWh	2.6	2.8	2.8	2.8	2.8	2.8
Coal output, million tons	0.9	0.8	0.5	0.7	0.6	0.6
Electricity consumption, billion kWh2.6	2.6	2.6	2.6	2.6	2.6	2.6

*Estimates of the Magadan Regional Administration

3.4. TRANSPORT INFRASTRUCTURE
The Magadan Region is linked with Russia's other regions by sea, air, and roads (with the Republic of Sakha (Yakutia)). The Region has no railroads.

Seaports. Stretching across 18,000 hectares in the Nagaevo Bay of the Tauisky inlet on the north coast of the Sea of Okhotsk, the Port of Magadan services a large fishing fleet and operates all year round. The port accepts most of the freight for Magadan and the Region.

Roads. The Region has 2,546 km of paved highway. Magadan is the starting point of the northeast federal road Yakutsk-Magadan, also known as Kolyma. The 1,400 km long Kolyma highway is the main freight delivery route to various districts of the Region.

Airports. Magadan's international airport accepts all types of passenger and transport aircraft. The shortest air routes linking the northern states of the USA and Canada with the Pacific Rim countries and Australia go through Magadan.

3.5. MAIN NATURAL RESOURCES: RESERVES AND EXTRACTION IN 2002
The main mineral resources of the Magadan Region are: gold, silver, tungsten, copper, molybdenum, poly-metal ore, facing stone, oil, peat, timber, and gas concentrate.

Silver. The Region has some 48 deposits of ore silver. Dukat is the largest deposit with 14,800 tons of silver. The total estimated silver reserves exceed 80,000 tons, which accounts for some 50% of Russia's total explored reserves.

Gold. The Magadan Region has some 2,000 deposits of placer gold and about 100 deposits of ore gold. The total estimated gold reserves in the Region are 4,000 tons, or 11% of Russia's proven placer gold reserves and 15% of its total ore gold reserves. The largest deposit is Natalka with over 250 tons of proven reserves.

Oil and gas. Some 29 zones of potential oil and gas accumulation have been identified under the Sea of Okhotsk, with a total estimated reserve of 3.5 billion tons of fuel equivalent, including 1.2 billion tons of oil and 1.5 billion cubic meter of gas.

Fishery. The Region's main species of marketable fish are pollack, herring, cod, flat fish, plaice, and salmon. The Region also produces crab, squid, and shrimp. The northern sector of the Sea of Okhotsk is considered to be one of the richest fisheries in the world. Its proven reserves account for over 20% of Russia's total fish and seafood reserves. The main fisheries of the Magadan Region's fishing industry are the North Okhotsk, West Bering, and West Kamchatka sub-zones with potential reserves of over one million tons.

4. TRADE OPPORTUNITIES

4.1. MAIN GOODS
PRODUCED IN THE REGION

In 2002, the Magadan Region produced:

Electricity and heat: electricity – 2,770 million kWh (down by 1.1% on 2001); heat – 2.98 million Gcal (+0.3%);

Mining industry: gold – 33 tons (+8.5%);

Food and beverages: fish output – 76,600 tons (–15%), commercial fish products, including canned fish – 48,300 tons (–15.7%); seafood – 4,400 tons (–16.8%); frozen fish – 33,400 tons (–53.1%); meat, including category 1 sub-products – 122 tons (–45.5%); convenience meat – 185 tons (+120%); sausage – 308 tons (+5.8%); dairy products in terms of milk – 4,900 tons (–3.9%); bread and bakery – 7,500 tons (–11.6%); confectionary products – 211 tons (+93.8%); pasta – 103 tons (–5.5%); alcohol-free beverages – 280,000 decaliters (+4.9%); beer – 607,000 decaliters (+35.8%); vodka and liquors – 277,400 decaliters (–11%); ethyl alcohol made of edible raw materials – 130,000 decaliters (+5.2%);

Construction materials: precast concrete– 4,200 cubic meters (–14.3); wall materials – 0.7 million of conventional brick (–66.7%); concrete – 15,800 tons (+9.7%);

Forestry, timber, and pulp and paper: sawn timber – 900 cubic meters (-35.7%);

Ferrous metals: steel – 1.5 million tons (-32.5%).

4.2. EXPORTS, INCLUDING EXTRA-CIS

The Magadan Region's exports to extra-CIS countries amounted to $33.7 million in 2000, and exports to CIS countries to $0.1 million. The respective figures for 2001 were $2.8 million to extra-CIS countries and zero exports to CIS countries, and for 2002 – $6.3 million to extra-CIS countries and $0.1 million to CIS countries.

Fish and seafood take up the largest share of exports. Pollack and high value crustacean and shellfish products dominate fish and seafood exports. These products are exported primarily to Japan, South Korea, and USA, which jointly account for over 90% of total exports.

4.3. IMPORTS, INCLUDING EXTRA-CIS

2000 imports from extra-CIS countries amounted to $39.8 million, and imports from CIS to $0.5 million. The respective figures for 2001 were $55.3 million and $0.1 million, and for 2002 – $47.8 million and $0.1 million.

Imports are dominated by machinery, equipment, and transport vehicles. The Region also imports food, such as meat and meat products, sausage, fish, vegetables, fruit, potatoes, pasta products, flour, and canned food. The main exporters to the Region are the USA, Canada, Brazil, and South Korea.

5. INVESTMENT OPPORTUNITIES

5.1. INVESTMENTS IN 1992–2002
(BY INDUSTRY SECTOR),
INCLUDING FOREIGN INVESTMENTS

The following factors determine the investment appeal of the Magadan Region:

• The establishment of a Special Economic Zone in the Region in 1999 (residents enjoy exemptions from all federal taxes and customs duties);

• Its unique mineral and raw material base (the Region leads Russia's gold industry);

• The diversity and relative abundance of water biological resources;

• The potential for oil extraction in the northern sector of the Sea of Okhotsk;

• Energy (a potential to improve the electricity balance due to the construction of the Ust-Srednekanskaya Hydroelectric Power Station to be commissioned in 2006);

• The availability of an international airport;

• The availability of a commercial seaport.

5.2. CAPITAL INVESTMENT

Industry accounts for the lion's share of capital investment (66.5%).

5.3. MOST ATTRACTIVE
SECTORS FOR INVESTMENT

According to the Magadan Regional Administration, the Region's mining and fishing industries are the most appealing ones for investors.

5.4. CURRENT
LEGISLATION ON
INVESTOR TAX EXEMPTIONS
AND PRIVILEGES

Pursuant to the Magadan Regional Law On State Support to Investment Activity in the Special Economic Zone in the Magadan Region, investors are entitled to the following support from the regional authorities:

• The Regional Administration's assistance in developing and implementing targeted programs and investment projects;

• The provision of grants, state subsidies, and budget and non-budgetary loans to develop business;

• The allocation of funds on a repayable, fixed-date, and interest basis on terms and conditions specified in the Regional Budget Law and investment agreements;

FAR EASTERN FEDERAL DISTRICT

VII

Capital investment by industry sector, $ million						*TABLE 6*
	1997	1998	1999	2000	2001	2002
Total capital investment	238.2	152.1	53.8	76.0	85.4	83.3
Including major industries (% of total)						
Industry	80.9	76.7	55.1	68.0	68.0	66.5
Agriculture and forestry	2.4	2.7	2.7	0.5	1.4	0.7
Construction	0.6	0.1	1.0	0.2	2.2	0.4
Transport and communications	5.0	9.9	26.0	21.0	19.6	22.6
Trade and public catering	6.1	2.0	5.7	1.7	1.3	0.3
Other	5.0	8.6	9.5	8.6	7.5	9.5

Foreign investment trends in 1995–2002						*TABLE 7*
	1995–1997	1998	1999	2000	2001	2002
Foreign investment, $ million	225.9	49.8	30.1	27.7	26.4	4.6
Including FDI, $ million	120.6	44.8	26.9	4.8	4.1	0.5

- The provision of guarantees by the Regional Governor;
- Temporary local tax exemptions;
- Bond issues to finance projects of paramount importance to the Region.

The above Law stipulates investor guarantees with regard to changes in the legal framework, political situation, and illegal actions by state authorities and officials.

The Law also states that investors placing their own or borrowed funds into investment projects are eligible for local tax exemptions in the amount of up to 100% of the taxes. Moreover, banks, insurance, leasing, and other companies, which invest no less than 30% of the estimated cost of an investment project, are entitled to an exemption from the local component of the profit tax on profit received from investment activities.

5.5. FEDERAL AND REGIONAL ECONOMIC AND SOCIAL DEVELOPMENT PROGRAMS FOR THE MAGADAN REGION

Federal targeted programs. Some 14 federal targeted programs focused on the economic

Largest enterprises of the Magadan Region	*TABLE 8*
COMPANY	SECTOR
OAO Magadanenergo, OAO Kolymaenergo	Energy
OAO Kolyma Coal Company, OAO Omsukchansky Open Mine, a branch of OAO Kolyma Coal Company, OAO Kadykchansky Open Mine, a branch of OAO Kolyma Coal, OAO SeveroVostokugol Company	Fuel
OAO Omolon Gold Company, JV ZAO Omsukchansk Mining Company, ZAO Silver of the Territory, ZAO Silver of Magadan, OAO Matrosov Mine, ZAO Nelkobazoloto, OAO Susumanzoloto Susuman Ore Dressing Plant, OAO Berelekh Mining Company, OAO Kolyma Refining Plant, OAO NPK Kolymavzryvprom, OAO Magadan Mechanical Plant	Non-ferrous metals
OAO Magadan Group, OOO Pacific Fish Industrial Company, OOO Mag-Sea International, RPZ Tandem, OOO TRK, OOO Arzhan, ZAO Dalrybflot, OOO Magadanryba, OAO Magadan Pasta Factory, OOO Magadan Sausages, OAO Magadan Liquors, OAO Magadansky Alcohol Plant, PK Magadansky Bread Factory, OAO Magadansky City Dairy Plant	Food and beverages
OOO Magadan Narodno-Khudozhestvennyie Promysly	Light industry
UMSKhP Novaya Arman, UMSKhP Khasynskoye, KKh Seimchan State Farm, KFKh Magadanptitsa, UMSKhP Energetik, UMSKhP Prosperity of the North	Agriculture
FGUP Magadan Airport, OAO Magadan Commercial Seaport, GU Maritime Administration of the Port of Magadan	Transport and communications

and social development of the Region are currently being implemented. Federal grants have been allocated for the construction and reconstruction of social and cultural facilities and the construction of such major industrial facilities as the Ust-Srednekanskaya Hydroelectric Power Station (under the Federal Targeted Program Energy Efficient Economy, 2002–2005 and through 2010) and the reconstruction of the Magadan airport

(under the Federal Targeted Program Upgrading of Russia's Transport System, 2002–2010).

Regional programs. The Magadan Regional Administration has developed and is implementing regional targeted programs focused on social and welfare development of the Region. The priority was accorded to The Magadan Region's Program for Protection of Consumer's Rights, 2002–2004 and The Program for Development of Magadan's Culture, 2001–2005.

6. INVESTMENT PROJECTS

Industry sector and project description	1) Expected results 2) Amount and term of investment 3) Form of financing[1] 4) Documentation[2]	Contact information
1	2	3
MINING		
85R001 ● ▲		
Reconstruction of the Matrosov Mine at the Natalka gold deposit. Project goal: to increase gold production.	1) 10 tons of gold per year 2) $210 million/3 years 3) L 4) FS	OAO Matrosov Mine Matrosov, Tenkinsky District, Magadan Region, 686071 Fax: (41344) 24 414 Alexander Anatolyevich Karlash, CEO
85R002 ● ❖ ◆		
License acquisition, geological prospecting, identification of conditional reserves and development of the gold deposit at Degdekan. Project goal: to develop a new gold deposit to a commercial level.	1) Gold reserves of 800 tons, average gold content: 2.6 grams/ton. Annual ore processing capacity of 11.8 million tons 2) $185 million/5 years 3) L, JV 4) BP	Magadan Regional Natural Resource Department 11, ul. Proletarskaya, Magadan, Magadan Region, 685000 Phone: (41322) 99 610, 99 618 Fax:(41322) 22 090 E-mail: geolcom@online.magadan.su Vyacheslav Ivanovich Kobets, Department Chief Vladimir Nikolaevich Makurgin, Division Chief
85R003 ● ❖ ◆		
License acquisition and commercial development of the gold and silver deposit at Sopka Kvartsevaya. Project goal: to develop a new gold and silver deposit to a commercial level.	1) 2,750 tons of gold equivalent per year 2) $50.7 million/9 years 3) L, JV 4) BP	Magadan Regional Natural Resource Department 11, ul. Proletarskaya, Magadan, Magadan Region, 685000 Phone: (41322) 99 610, 99 618 Fax: (41322) 22 090 E-mail: geolcom@online.magadan.su Vyacheslav Ivanovich Kobets, Department Chief Vladimir Nikolaevich Makurgin, Division Chief
85R004 ● ◆		
Development of tailings at the Belov Ore Dressing Plant. Project goal: to introduce combined leaching and sorption of dissolved gold from pulp using activated carbon.	1) Gold reserves of 1,500 tons, average contents gold content: 2.7 grams/ton. Gold extraction of up to 80% 2) $0.8 million/2 months 3) L 4) BP	OOO Gold Miners Artel Tsiklon Appt. 69, 13, ul. Mira, Ust-Omchug, Tenkensky District, Magadan Region, 686053 Phone: (41322) 21 295, 22 484 Boris Ivanovich Babushkin, Director

[1] L – Loan, E – Equity, Leas. – Leasing, JV – Joint Venture
[2] BP – Business Plan, FS – Feasibility Study

1	2	3

FOOD AND BEVERAGES

85R005 ● ◆

Acquisition of three vessels equipped with fishing and processing facilities for squid jigging and long-line catching and netting of ground fish.
Project goal: to expand output and product range.

1) 3,500 tons of seafood per year (for the three vessels)
2) $13.6 million/1 year
3) L
4) BP

State Unitary Company Magadan Seafood Processing Plant
1, ul. Marchekanskaya, Magadan, Magadan Region, 685000
Phone: (41322) 36 263, 36 070
Fax: (41322) 36 546
Vladimir Valentinovich Vologzhin, Director

85R006 ● ◆

Acquisition of three vessels (BATM type) equipped with fishing facilities.
Project goal: to expand output and product range.

1) 64,500 tons of seafood per year (for the three vessels)
2) $15.6 million/3 years
3) L
4) BP

State Unitary Company Magadan Seafood Processing Plant
1, ul. Marchekanskaya, Magadan, Magadan Region, 685000
Phone: (41322) 36 263, 36 070
Fax: (41322) 36 546
Vladimir Valentinovich Vologzhin, Director

85R007 ● ◆

Acquisition of a specialized ice-class hunting and fishing vessel equipped with machinery for deep catch processing.
Project goal: to expand output and product range.

1) Catch of 12,000 seals, processing of 100,000 tons of herring and salmon per year
2) $22.5 million/3 years
3) L
4) BP

State Unitary Company Magadan Seafood Processing Plant
1, ul. Marchekanskaya, Magadan, Magadan Region, 685000
Phone: (41322) 36 263, 36 070
Fax: (41322) 36 546
Vladimir Valentinovich Vologzhin, Director

85R008 ● ◆

Acquisition of two vessels equipped with fishing and processing facilities for squid jigging and long-line catching of Nototheniidae species of fish.
Project goal: to expand output and product range.

1) 3,200 tons of seafood per year (for the two vessels)
2) $7.5 million/1 year
3) L
4) BP

State Unitary Company Magadan Seafood Processing Plant
1, ul. Marchekanskaya, Magadan, Magadan Region, 685000
Phone: (41322) 36 263, 36 070
Fax: (41322) 36 546
Vladimir Valentinovich Vologzhin, Director

85R009 ● ◆

Acquisition of two vessels for coastal fishing equipped with fishing and processing equipment.
Project goal: to expand output and product range.

1) 3,300 tons of food per year
2) $9.0 million/1 year
3) L
4) BP

State Unitary Company Magadan Seafood Processing Plant
1, ul. Marchekanskaya, Magadan, Magadan Region, 685000
Phone: (41322) 36 263, 36 070
Fax: (41322) 36 546
Vladimir Valentinovich Vologzhin, Director

85R010 ● ◆

Acquisition of five processing trawlers equipped with fishing and processing equipment.
Project goal: to expand output and product range.

1) 65,000 tons of seafood per year (for the five vessels)
2) $77.9 million/5 years
3) L
4) BP

State Unitary Company Magadan Seafood Processing Plant
1, ul. Marchekanskaya, Magadan, Magadan Region, 685000
Phone: (41322) 36 263, 36 070
Fax: (41322) 36 546
Vladimir Valentinovich Vologzhin, Director

SCIENCE AND INNOVATION

85R011 ● ◆

Development of deep placer gold mining methods.
Project goal: to improve mining machinery, develop new technology, and identify reserves.

1) 100–150 kg per year
2) $0.8 million/0.5 year
3) L
4) BP

OAO East Research and Development Institute of Gold and Rare Metals (VNII-1)
12, ul. Gagarina, Magadan, Magadan Region, 685000
Phone: (41322) 25 739, 25 741
Fax: (41322) 25 741
Nikolai Platonovich Lavrov, CEO

MAVIAL MAGADAN AIRLINES

ALEXANDER
PETROVICH
SHUVAEV,
CEO

Federal State Unitary Enterprise Magadan Airlines is Russia's only domestic and international carrier operating in the North-Eastern region. Magadan Airlines operates flights linking Magadan to Moscow and St. Petersburg, the major cities of Siberia, the Urals and the Far East, and to Krasnodar, the capital of Kuban. Magadan Airlines has been operating international services to the United States since 1989. The airline uses eight Tu 154 aircraft and one Il 62n, piloted by top class crews qualified to fly in the ICAO's highest category meteorological minima. The airline's highly qualified pilots are licensed to fly in any country worldwide, and the airline's maintenance division is capable of servicing any type of aircraft flown in Russia.

The airline's production capacities enable it to carry out double the number of flying hours and five times more in terms of cargo operations. Each year, the airline carries 90,000 passengers and 3,300 tons of mail and cargo. According to a report on the financial and economic state

of the airline, "Magadan Airlines has the capacity to maintain independently the requisite level of financial stability and solvency, and to keep its operations going stable."

Magadan Airlines was the first airline in the Far East to install the Sirena 3 ticket reservation and sales system, which is linked via satellite to a center in Moscow. Sirena 3 shortens the time needed to buy an airline ticket and enables tickets to be bought for connecting flights on any domestic and international routes. Sirena is also used to select in-flight meals, book hotels, and order taxis. Magadan Airlines has offices in all

of the cities it flies to in order to better serve our passengers. Our relatively low fares, excellent service standards, and experienced and knowledgeable crews enable us to raise our customer service standards even higher. In 2001, Magadan Airlines won the Russian Wings prize, was awarded a gold medal For Excellent Business Reputation, and the international Gold Ingot award for its business dynamism.

SOKOL, MAGADAN-18, 685018, MAGADAN, RUSSIA
TEL: (41 322) 93 970, 93 644; FAX (41 322) 93 060; E-MAIL: ak_ml@tch.ru; HTTP://www.mavial.magtrk.ru

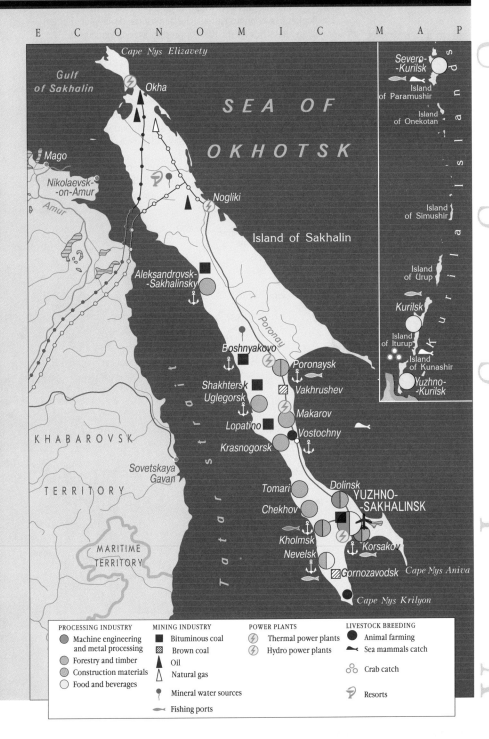

ECONOMIC MAP

R U S S I A

FAR EASTERN FEDERAL DISTRICT

VII

Cape Mys Elizavety

Gulf of Sakhalin

Okha

SEA OF OKHOTSK

Mago

Nikolaevsk-on-Amur

Amur

Nogliki

Island of Sakhalin

Aleksandrovsk-Sakhalinsky

Poronau

Boshnyakovo

Poronaysk

Shakhtersk
Uglegorsk

Vakhrushev

Makarov

Lopatino

Vostochny

Krasnogorsk

KHABAROVSK

Sovetskaya Gavan

TERRITORY

Tomari

Dolinsk

YUZHNO-SAKHALINSK

Chekhov

MARITIME
TERRITORY

Kholmsk

Nevelsk

Korsakov

Gornozavodsk

Cape Mys Aniva

Cape Mys Krilyon

Severo-Kurilsk

Island of Paramushir

Island of Onekotan

Island of Simushir

Island of Urup

Kurilsk

Island of Iturup

Island of Kunashir

Yuzhno-Kurilsk

Kuril Islands

Tatar Strait

PROCESSING INDUSTRY
- ⬤ Machine engineering and metal processing
- ⬤ Forestry and timber
- ⬤ Construction materials
- ◯ Food and beverages

MINING INDUSTRY
- ▪ Bituminous coal
- ▨ Brown coal
- ▲ Oil
- △ Natural gas
- ● Mineral water sources
- ⚓ Fishing ports

POWER PLANTS
- Thermal power plants
- Hydro power plants

LIVESTOCK BREEDING
- ● Animal farming
- Sea mammals catch
- Crab catch
- Resorts

L ocated in Russia's Far East, the Sakhalin Region is a dynamic area that offers immense opportunities for mutually beneficial cooperation. In terms of its natural resource potential, Sakhalin is one of the richest regions in Russia and East Asia. Large reserves of oil, gas, coal, fish, seafood, and timber resources, combined with a qualified workforce, advantageous geographical location, proximity to international commercial transport hubs, a stable political and social situation, and other factors, are driving growth in the Region's economy and the development of international links with over 80 countries worldwide.

The Region has won international acclaim for the development of its offshore oil and gas fields on the basis of product sharing agreements. The Region has commenced large scale construction of infrastructure facilities for the Sakhalin-1 and Sakhalin-2 projects, which are bound to change its social and economic situation profoundly. The implementation of these projects and launch of other similar projects in the near future will make Sakhalin a leading supplier of energy resources to the Pacific Rim.

The Region has accorded priority status to the development of its fisheries, timber, food, coal, and construction sectors and its transport infrastructure. These sectors have seen stable growth in recent years and provide an economic base for ongoing sustainable development.

We are committed to strengthening these positive trends and achieving steady progress. For that reason, we accord priority to the creation of a favorable investment climate and conditions conducive to business development.

Igor Farkhutdinov,
GOVERNOR OF THE SAKHALIN REGION

1. GENERAL INFORMATION

1.1. GEOGRAPHY

The Sakhalin Region covers a total area of 87,100 square kilometers. The Region is located off the Pacific coast of Russia on the islands of Sakhalin (76,600 square kilometers), Moneron and Tyuleny, and the Kuril Islands.

1.2. CLIMATE

The Sakhalin Region lies in the monsoon climate zone.

Air temperatures in January average −11.7°C, rising to +13.3°C in July. Average annual precipitation reaches some 600 mm.

1.3. POPULATION

According to preliminary 2002 census results, the Region's population totaled 547,000 people.

The average population density is 6.3 people per square kilometer. The economically active population totals 323,000 people. 2002 official unemployment rate stood at 2%, while the actual unemployment level was 12.4%.

Demographically speaking, some 66.9% are of statutory working age, 18.7% are below the statutory working age, and 14.4% are beyond the statutory working age.

As of 2002, the Sakhalin Region's major urban centers were Yuzhno-Sakhalinsk with 174,700 inhabitants, Kholmsk with 38,500 inhabitants.

Population								TABLE 1
	1992	1997	1998	1999	2000	2001	2002
Total population, '000	719	634	620	609	599	591	547
Economically active population, '000	410	334	296	313	324	323	323

2. ADMINISTRATION

39, Kommunistichesky prospect, Yuzhno-Sakhalinsk, Sakhalin Region, 693011
Phone: (4242) 72 1902; fax: (4242) 72 1801; http://www.adm.sakhalin.ru, http://www.sakhipa.ru

NAME	POSITION	CONTACT INFORMATION
Igor Pavlovich FARKHUTDINOV	Governor of the Sakhalin Region	Phone: (4242) 72 1902 Fax: (4242) 72 1801
Ivan Pavlovich MALAKHOV	First Deputy Governor of the Sakhalin Region, Chairman of the Sakhalin Regional Committee for Economy	Phone: (4242) 72 2978 Fax: (4242) 72 3942 E-mail: dp_pro@adm.sakhalin.ru
Vitaly Yevgenyevich GOMILEVSKY	Deputy Governor of the Sakhalin Region, Chief of the Apparatus of the Sakhalin Regional Administration in Charge of the Agroindustrial Complex	Phone: (4242) 74 2841 Fax: (4242) 72 1801
Sergei Gennadyevich DEGTERIOV	Deputy Governor of the Sakhalin Region in Charge of Fuel and Energy, Transport and Communications, Housing and Communal Sectors	Phone: (4242) 74 2842, 42 1446 Fax: (4242) 74 4517
Sergei Anatolyevich PODOLIAN	Deputy Governor of the Sakhalin Region in Charge of Fishing and Forestry	Phone: (4242) 42 1380 Fax: (4242) 74 1572
Sergei Petrovich BELOZERSKIKH	Deputy Governor of the Sakhalin Region in Charge of the Construction Industry	Phone: (4242) 72 2522 Fax: (4242) 74 4517
Natalia Mikhailovna NOVIKOVA	Deputy Governor of the Sakhalin Region, Chief of the Financial Department	Phone: (4242) 42 4581 Fax: (4242) 42 9074 E-mail: fu_agtr_no@adm.sakhalin.ru
Vladislav Vladimirovich RUKAVETS	Chairman of the Committee for International, Foreign Economic and Inter-Regional Relations of the Sakhalin Region	Phone: (4242) 72 7494 Fax: (4242) 72 7493 E-mail: up_forecon@adm.sakhalin.ru
Georgy Alexandrovich KARLOV	Chairman of the Committee for Industry and Trade of the Sakhalin Region	Phone: (4242) 74 2828 Fax: (4242) 72 3903 E-mail: dr_trade@adm.sakhalin.ru

NAME	POSITION	CONTACT INFORMATION
Sergei Alexandrovich KARPENKO	Deputy Chief of the Investment Department of the Sakhalin Regional Committee for Economy	Phone: (4242) 42 2686 Fax: (4242) 72 3942 E-mail: ipa@invest.adm.sakhalin.ru

3. ECONOMIC POTENTIAL

3.1. 1997–2002 GROSS REGIONAL PRODUCT (GRP). INDUSTRY BREAKDOWN

The Sakhalin Region's gross regional product in 2002 amounted to $1,772 million, or 7.4% up on 2001 levels. The growth was mainly driven by construction (27.7% of total GRP). Per capita GRP in 2001 was $2,793, rising to $3,238 in 2002.

3.2. MAJOR ECONOMIC GROWTH PROJECTIONS.

The following sectors are expected to grow in 2003–2005:

• Fuel: a 30.1% increase in oil output on 2002 levels by 2005;

• Energy: energy output will increase by 2004–2005 with the commissioning of the second unit of the Mendeleevskaya Geothermal Power Station on the island of Kunashir and the third unit of a mini hydroelectric power station on the island of Paramushir;

• Timber, pulp and paper: industrial timber output up 8.8–10.7% on 2002 levels by 2005, lumber output up 45.8–52.8%;

• Fishing: output growth by 3.4–15.5% on 2002 by 2005.

3.3. INDUSTRIAL OUTPUT IN 1997–2002 FOR MAJOR SECTORS OF ECONOMY

The Sakhalin Region's leading industries are oil and gas, food and beverages (fishing), timber, and pulp and paper. Together they account for a combined 86% of total industrial output of the Region.

GRP trends in 1997–2002						TABLE 2
	1997	1998	1999	2000	2001*	2002*
GRP in current prices, $ million	2,054	1,326	1,107	1,259	1,650	1,772

*Estimates of the Sakhalin Regional Administration

GRP industry breakdown in 1997–2002, % of total						TABLE 3
	1997	1998	1999	2000	2001*	2002*
GRP	100.0	100.0	100.0	100.0	100.0	100.0
Industry	25.1	26.0	28.7	51.3	41.7	33.4
Agriculture and forestry	4.3	5.1	2.8	3.1	4.1	3.2
Construction	20.4	19.7	33.8	10.6	20.6	27.7
Transport and communications	13.7	10.2	5.8	7.4	6.3	6.7
Trade and public catering	8.6	8.5	7.1	8.2	7.4	8.4
Other	25.8	24.9	18.1	17.6	17.9	18.4
Net taxes on output	2.1	5.6	3.7	1.8	2.0	2.2

*Estimates of the Sakhalin Regional Administration

Fuel. The sector accounts for 52.2% of the Region's total industrial output. The northern part of the Region produces oil and gas. The oil and gas sector accounts for 92% of the Region's total fuel output. The largest companies are OAO Rosneft-Sakhalinmorneftegaz and ZAO Petrosakh. The coal industry is the main fuel supplier for the energy sector and accounts for some 8% of the total fuel output. The largest companies in the coal sector are ZAO Solntsevskoye (incorporated into OAO SUEK), ZAO Poronayskugol, and OAO Boshnyakovsky Colliery (incorporated into ZAO Vostok-Inkom).

Food and beverages (fishing). The sector accounts for 31.2% of total industrial output. Fishing accounts for over 82% of the total output of the food industry. The largest companies are BINOM Fishing and Industrial Group, ZAO Sisafico, OAO Pilenga, ZAO Gidrostroy, ZAO Sakhalin Leasing Fleet, OOO Tunaycha Company, and ZAO Ekarma-Sakhalin.

Energy. The sector accounts for 10.4% of the Region's total industrial output. The overall capacity of all power stations in the Region amounts to 901.9 MW. In 2002, electricity output reached 2.7 billion kWh;

Industry breakdown of industrial output in 1997–2002, % of total						_TABLE 4_
	1997	1998	1999	2000	2001	2002*
Industry	100.0	100.0	100.0	100.0	100.0	100.0
Fuel	34.6	31.1	35.9	60.6	54.2	52.2
Food and beverages (including fishing)	30.0	40.5	44.1	27.4	31.6	31.2
Energy	21.7	19.3	9.7	6.0	8.4	10.4
Forestry, timber, and pulp and paper	6.5	4.2	4.9	3.2	2.9	2.6
Construction materials	1.5	1.1	2.0	0.8	0.8	1.4
Machine engineering and metal processing	4,5	2,6	1,6	1,2	1,2	1,0
Non-ferrous metals	0.2	0.4	0.3	0.2	0.2	–
Ferrous metals	0.1	–	0.2	0.1	0.1	0.1
Chemicals and petrochemicals	–	0.1	–	0.1	0.1	0.2
Light industry	0.3	0.1	0.2	0.1	0.1	0,1
Flour, cereals, and mixed fodder	0.1	0.1	0.2	0.1	0.1	n/a

*Estimates of the Sakhalin Regional Administration

heating output was 5.3 million Gcal. The largest companies include OAO Sakhalinenergo (Yuzhno-Sakhalinskaya Thermal Power Station-1, Sakhalinskaya GRES, Okhinskaya Thermal Power Station) and OAO Noglikskaya Hydroelectric Power Station. The Kuril Islands energy sector focuses on local alternative power sources, and geothermal sources first and foremost.

Forestry, timber, and pulp and paper. The sector accounts for 2.6% of the Sakhalin Region's total industrial output. The largest companies are GUP Sakhalin Timber Company, OAO Tymovskaya Timber Industrial Company, ZAO Sakhinterlesprom, and OOO Uglegorsk Paper Mill.

3.4. FUEL AND ENERGY BALANCE (OUTPUT AND CONSUMPTION PER RESOURCE)
The Sakhalin Region has sufficient fuel reserves to satisfy its energy needs. Fuel used within the Region includes coal, natural gas, fuel oil and diesel fuel. Coal (62%) and natural gas (31%) account for the bulk of the Region's energy and fuel consumption. Currently, some 80% of oil and 50% of natural gas produced in the Region is exported to other regions of Russia.

Fuel and energy sector production and consumption trends, 1997–2002						_TABLE 5_
	1997	1998	1999	2000	2001	2002*
Electricity output, billion kWh	2.5	2.4	2.4	2.7	2.7	2.7
Oil output (including gas condensate), '000 tons	1,720.0	1,696.0	1,836.0	3,362.0	3,767.0	3,252.0
Natural gas extraction, million cubic meters	1,844.0	1,863.0	1,763.0	1,860.0	1,895.0	1,852.0
Coal output, million tons	2.4	2.3	2.5	2.7	3.3	3.0
Electricity consumption, billion kWh	2.5	2.4	2.4	2.7	2.7	2.7
Oil consumption, '000 tons	n/a	32.0	63.0	43.0	30.0	30.0
Natural gas consumption, million cubic meters	840	798	791	872	903	1,005

*Estimates of the Sakhalin Regional Administration

3.5. TRANSPORT INFRASTRUCTURE
Roads. The Sakhalin Region has 2,754 kilometers of paved public highway. The Region's main highways are the Yuzhno-Sakhalinsk – Korsakov and Yuzhno-Sakhalinsk – Kholmsk routes.

Railroads. The Region has 957.2 kilometers of railroad. The Sakhalin railroad links the town of Korsakov in the south to the settlement of Nogliki in the north. The 312 kilometer railroad owned by OAO Rosneft-Sakhalinmorneftegaz links the port of Moskalvo and town of Okha to the settlement of Nogliki. The Vanino-Kholmsk ferry links the Sakhalin railroad network to the railroads of the mainland Russian Federation.

Airports. The Region's largest airport at Yuzhno-Sakhalinsk offers regular flights to Moscow, St. Petersburg, Novosibirsk, Omsk, Krasnoyarsk, Irkutsk, Khabarovsk, Vladivostok, and Blagoveschensk,

FAR EASTERN FEDERAL DISTRICT

VII

and international flights to Hakodate, Niigata, Tokyo and Sapporo in Japan, Seoul and Pusan in South Korea, and Dalang, Harbin, and Shanghai in China. GUP Sakhalin Airlines Company is the largest passenger and freight carrier in the Region.

Sea transport. Some 2,141,500 tons of freight, or 49.7% of total freight traffic, was transported by sea in 2002. Freight is carried both in cargo ships and in railroad cars by ferry between Vanino and Kholmsk. The largest private shipping company is OAO Sakhalin Shipping Company.

Seaports. The Region has eleven seaports, including eight commercial ports, two fishing ports and the port of Moskalvo, which is owned by OAO Rosneft-Sakhalinmorneftegaz. The ports of Korsakov and Kholmsk are the Region's largest ice-free ports and account for the bulk of freight transported in and out of the Region.

Oil and gas pipelines. The Region pumps oil and gas to Komsomolsk-on-Amur via trunk oil and gas pipelines. The overall length of pipelines (to the Khabarovsk Territory's border) is 1,300 kilometers.

3.6. MAIN NATURAL RESOURCES: RESERVES AND EXTRACTION IN 2002

The Sakhalin Region's key natural resources are: oil, natural gas, coal, fish and sea food, and timber.

Oil and natural gas. The Region has 112 explored oil and gas fields (including 17 offshore deposits), plus further 25 promising oil and gas basins. The Region's reserves of oil total 896.2 million tons, gas – 671 billion cubic meters, and gas condensate – 69.3 million tons. The Sakhalin Region's largest oil and gas fields are the Chaivo, Piltun-Astokhskoye, Odoptu, and Lunskoye (gas condensate).

Coal. The Region has over 60 coalfields and promising coal basins. Coal reserves in the Region are estimated at some 20 billion tons at 52 coal-fields and basins, including 8 billion tons of brown coal, 12 billion tons of black coal and 1.9 billion tons of coke. The Region's coal industry has an annual capacity of 3.3 billion tons, including 2.5 billion tons extracted in opencast mining.

Forests. Forests in the Sakhalin Region cover a total area of over 69,000 square kilometers, or 79% of the Region's territory. The Region's total timber reserves exceed 600 million cubic meters. The estimated annual timber harvest is 3.5 million cubic meters. 2002 timber exports from the Region amounted to 918,100 cubic meters.

Marine biosphere reserves. The total biomass of edible fish in the Region's seas exceeds 6.3 million tons. The annual fishing quota is more than 1 million tons, including more than 800,000 tons of fish, and 285,000 tons of invertebrates. The most valuable species are the Pacific salmon, which reproduces in rivers of Sakhalin and the Kuril Islands. The Region's fishing sector focuses mainly on herring, flounder, hunchback, Siberian salmon, mackerel, cod, navaga, rasp, plaice, crab, squid, fur seal, eared seal, seal, shrimp, and shellfish. Laminaria and alfencia (seaweed) are produced in industrial amounts of up to 2 million tons annually with no impact on reproduction. Total reserves are estimated at 9.8 million tons. The sector's 2002 catch totaled 373,000 tons of fish and sea food.

Non-ferrous metal ores and rare metals. Total gold reserves in the Kuril Islands are estimated at 1,867 tons, silver at 9,284 tons, titanium at 39.7 million tons, and iron at 273 million tons. The Region also has deposits of complex ores.

Thermal water sources. The Kuril Islands and some areas in the Sakhalin have geothermal water and steam sources with a potential for use in the energy sector.

4. TRADE OPPORTUNITIES

4.1. MAIN GOODS PRODUCED IN THE REGION

In 2002 the Sakhalin Region produced:

Fuel industry:

Oil, including gas condensate – 3,252,000 tons; Gas condensate– 1,852.2 million cubic meters; Coal – 3,014,000 tons.

Forestry, timber, and pulp and paper sectors:

Industrial timber – 822,000 cubic meters; lumber – 752,200 cubic meters; paper – 4,600 tons; pulp – 4,600 tons.

Food industry:

Fish and seafood – 373 thousand tons;

Canned and preserved fish and seafood – 45.3 million conventional cans.

4.2. EXPORTS, INCLUDING EXTRA-CIS

In 1999, exports to extra-CIS countries totaled $219 million, while exports within the CIS reached $3.6 million. The figures for 2000 were $423.8 million and $1.5 million, respectively; $330.3 million and $0.9 million for 2001, and $636.2 million and $0.1 million for 2002. The Region's main trading partners are Japan, South Korea, China, Singapore, and the USA.

4.3. IMPORTS, INCLUDING EXTRA-CIS

Imports from extra-CIS countries in 1999 reached $143.9 million, while imports from the CIS totaled $14.9 million. The figures for 2000 were $77.7 million and $7.4 million, respectively; $164.9 million and $3.8 million for 2001, and $232.8 million and $0.6 million for 2002.

Major regional export and import entities		*TABLE 6*
ENTITY	ADDRESS	PHONE, FAX, E-MAIL
Sakhalin Energy Investment Company Ltd., Yuzhno-Sakhalinsk Branch	35, ul. Dzerzhinskogo, Yuzhno-Sakhalinsk, Sakhalin Region, 693000	Phone: (4242) 73 2000 Fax: (4242) 73 2012
OAO Rosneft-Sakhalinmorneftegaz	17, ul. Khabarovskaya, Yuzhno-Sakhalinsk, Sakhalin Region, 693000	Phone: (4242) 72 1490 Fax: (4242) 72 1466
OOO Sakhalin-Troika	1, ul. Admirala Makarova, Kholmsk, Sakhalin Region, 694620	Phone: (42422) 55 966 Fax: (42422) 57 984
OOO Sakhalin Timber Manufacturers Association	246-a, ul. Lenina, Yuzhno-Sakhalinsk, Sakhalin Region, 693000	Phone: (4242) 72 5851 Fax: (4242) 72 1503
OAO Pilenga	1, ul. Pogranichnaya, Yuzhno-Sakhalinsk, Sakhalin Region, 693000	Phone/fax: (4242) 55 3695
ZAO Gidrostroy	53, ul. Kryukova, Yuzhno-Sakhalinsk, Sakhalin Region, 693000	Phone: (4242) 72 2937 Fax: (4242) 46 2493
ZAO Sisafico	15, per. Altaisky, Yuzhno-Sakhalinsk, Sakhalin Region, 693000	Phone/fax: (4242) 72 7371

5. INVESTMENT OPPORTUNITIES

5.1. INVESTMENTS IN 1992–2002 (BY INDUSTRY SECTOR), INCLUDING FOREIGN INVESTMENTS

The following key factors determine the investment appeal of the Sakhalin Region:
• Its good geographic location and proximity to high capacity markets (Asia-Pacific);
• Its abundant biosphere and mineral resources;
• Its favorable investment and tax legislation (development of oil and gas fields on a Production Sharing Agreement basis).

5.2. CAPITAL INVESTMENT

Industry represents the bulk of capital investment in the Region (87.5%)

Capital investment by industry sector, $ million						*TABLE 7*
	1997	1998	1999	2000	2001	2002
Total capital investment	395.4	517.0	647.4	288.5	575.7	750.2
Including major industries (% of total):						
Industry	45.6	64.0	77.1	50.8	72.1	87.5
Agriculture and forestry	0.7	1.8	1.1	2.7	1.4	1.2
Construction	3.7	0.3	0.1	0.5	0.1	0.4
Transport and communications	8.9	7.8	4.6	16.4	5.9	6.7
Trade and public catering	0.7	–	–	0.1	0.1	0.1
Other	40.4	26.1	17.1	29.5	20.4	4.1

Foreign investment trends in 1997–2002						*TABLE 8*
	1997	1998	1999	2000	2001	2002
Foreign investment, $ million	52.7	136.1	1,042.7	250.5	388.9	706.7
Including FDI, $ million	49.0	131.9	1,038.6	246.1	374.6	679.8

5.3. MAJOR ENTERPRISES (INCLUDING ENTERPRISES WITH FOREIGN INVESTMENT)

As of January 1, 2003, the Sakhalin Region hosted some 544 companies with foreign investment, including companies from Japan, the USA, South Korea, China, the UK, Australia and Canada. The Region hosts representative offices of major international companies such as Mitsui Co. Ltd.,

Mitsubishi Corporation, and SO DECO, which are involved in the Sakhalin-1 and Sakhalin-2 projects on a Production Sharing Agreement basis. The largest companies with foreign investment (including wholly foreign-owned companies) are OOO Krilion, OOO Marinika, OOO Nord-Union, OOO Pilenga-Godo, OOO Sakhalin Marine Services, ZAO Sisafico, OOO Energen Insurance Company, OOO Sfera-Ayoka, OOO Ecoshelf, and others.

Largest enterprises of the Sakhalin Region			*TABLE 9*
COMPANY	INDUSTRY	2000 SALES, $ MILLION*	2000 NET PROFIT, $ MILLION*
ZAO Petrosakh	Fuel	33.6	3.3
ZAO Gidrostroy	Fishing	25.3	10.0
OAO Sakhalinmorneftemontazh	Fuel	16.0	0.04
GUP Sakhalin Airlines Company	Transport	15.7	n/a
OAO Rosneft-Sakhalinmorneftegaz	Fuel	13.0	3.0
OAO Yuzhno-Sakhalinsk Katsev Bread Plant	Food and beverages	6.2	0.4
ZAO Korsakov Preserve Plant	Food and beverages	1.7	n/a
OAO Sakhalinenergo	Energy	1.5	n/a
OAO Sakhalin Shipping Company	Transport	0.7	0.5
OAO Yuzhno-Sakhalinsky Dairy	Food and beverages	0.2	0.001
OAO Kholmsk Marine Commercial Port	Transport	0.09	0.001
OAO Sakhincenter International Business Cooperation Center	Services	0.09	0.02
OAO Sakhalinsky Food Factory	Food and beverages	0.05	0.002

*Estimates of the Sakhalin Regional Administration

5.4. MOST ATTRACTIVE SECTORS FOR INVESTMENT

According to the Sakhalin Regional Administration, the following sectors offer the greatest investment appeal: fuel, fishing, construction, communications, trade and public catering, and timber.

5.5. CURRENT LEGISLATION ON INVESTOR TAX EXEMPTIONS AND PRIVILEGES

The Governor of the Sakhalin Region has issued a Decree On Granting Tax Exemptions to Companies with Foreign Investments Engaged in Manufacturing in the Sakhalin Region. The Decree

Regional entities responsible for raising investment			*TABLE 10*
ENTITY	ADDRESS	PHONE, FAX, E-MAIL	
The Sakhalin Agency for Raising Investment	Office 426, 39, Kommunistichesky pr., Yuzhno-Sakhalinsk, Sakhalin Region, 693011	Phone: (4242) 42 2686, 42 2692 Fax: (4242) 72 3942 E-mail: ipa@invest.adm.sakhalin.ru http://www.sakhipa.ru	
The Sakhalin Regional Fund for Business Support	Office 139, ul. Dzerzhinskogo, Yuzhno-Sakhalinsk, Sakhalin Region, 693000	Phone: (4242) 72 8484, 72 8292	
ZAO Sakhalin Leasing Company	119-A, pr. Mira, Yuzhno-Sakhalinsk, Sakhalin Region	Phone: (4242) 72 6622, 72 6623 E-mail: salco@sakhalin.ru, http://www.salco.ru	
ZAO Delta-Lease – Far East	Office 206, 20, ul. Karla Marksa, Yuzhno-Sakhalinsk, Sakhalin Region	Phone/fax: (4242) 74 4074 E-mail: arybkin@dsc.ru	

establishes the terms and conditions for the provision of a five year exemption on the regional profits tax component to foreign investors engaged in manufacturing activities, provided the profit generated is reinvested into manufacturing. The exemption is not available to fuel and energy companies.

5.6. FEDERAL AND REGIONAL ECONOMIC AND SOCIAL DEVELOPMENT PROGRAMS FOR THE SAKHALIN REGION

Federal targeted programs. The Region is implementing The Program for the Social and Economic Development of the Kuril Islands, Sakhalin Region, 1994–2005. The aim of the Program is to ensure comprehensive economic development of the Kuril Islands on the basis of balanced use of modern technologies and marine biosphere resources with a focus on energy, transport and fishing. The Program's budget is $262.7 million.

The Sakhalin Region is implementing The Program for the Economic and Social Development of the Far East and Trans-Baikal Territories, 1996–2005 and Through 2010. The aim of the Program is to create an economic environment conducive to sustainable development of the Far East and Trans-Baikal territories with a view to safeguarding the Russian Federation's geostrategic interests and national security. The Program's budget is $612.3 million.

Regional programs. The Regional Administration has drafted and is implementing The Program of State Support to Small Enterprise in the Sakhalin Region, 2001–2003. The Program seeks to foster small enterprise in the manufacturing, innovation and other sectors of the Region's economy. The Program's budget is $0.8 million.

The purpose of The Reproduction of Forests in the Sakhalin Region, 2001–2005 is to ensure timely reproduction of forest stock, enhance productivity in the forestry sector, and improve the species mix and the quality of forestry output. The Program's budget is $4.9 million.

The Program for the Economic and Social Development of the Indigenous Peoples of the North, 2001–2004 is underway in the Region.

6. INVESTMENT PROJECTS

Industry sector and project description	1) Expected results 2) Amount and term of investment 3) Form of financing[1] 4) Documentation[2]	Contact information
1	2	3
CHEMICALS AND PETROCHEMICALS		
86R001		OOO Eureka-2
Production of packaging using modern polymer technologies. Project goal: to produce packaging to meet demand in the food industry, and the fishing sector in particular.	1) Annual revenues $2.5 million 2) $2.3 million/3 years 3) E 4) BP	1, per. Solnechny, Yuzhno-Sakhalinsk, Sakhalin Region, 693008 Phone: (4242) 72 3581 Fax: (4242) 72 6132 E-mail: eureka2002@yandex.ru Anatoly Grigoryevich Zhukov, Director
FORESTRY, TIMBER, AND PULP AND PAPER		
86R002		The Timber Industry Department of the Sakhalin Region
Establishment of new timber facilities. Project goal: to produce timber.	1) 150,000 cubic meters 2) $8.5 million/5 years 3) E 4) BP	Office 411, 39, Kommunistichesky prospekt, Yuzhno-Sakhalinsk, Sakhalin Region, 693000 Phone: (4242) 42 2690 Fax: (4242) 42 4865 Miron Maximovich Kremin, Department Head

[1] L – Loan, E – Equity, Leas. – Leasing, JV – Joint Venture
[2] BP – Business Plan, FS – Feasibility Study

1	2	3

FOOD AND BEVERAGES

86R003 ■ ● ◆

Reconstruction of the Korsakov Agar Plant, agar production.
Project goal: agar production.

1) Annual output 64 tons, revenues – $2.6 million a year
2) $2.1 million/4 years
3) L, E
4) BP

OAO Binom-Center
7, ul. Militseyskaya,
Yuzhno-Sakhalinsk,
Sakhalin Region, 693000
Phone: (4242) 42 8119
Fax: (4242) 72 6031
E-mail: binom@binom.info
Alexander Matveevich Popov ,
Director

86R004 ■ ● ◆

Construction of a fish farm on the Nituy river.
Project goal: farming of hunchback salmon.

1) Annual output up to 30 million fish
2) $3.4 million/18 months
3) L, E
4) BP

OOO Turovka
Novoye, Makarovsky district,
Sakhalin Region, 693000
Phone: (4242) 42 3710, 77 2617
Igor Viktorovich Smirnov,
Director

86R005 ■ ● ◆

Construction of a modern brewery.
Project goal: production of beer.

1) Annual 13 million liters
2) $6.3 million/6 years
3) L, E
4. BP

ZAO Northern Star
39, ul. Purkaeva,
Yuzhno-Sakhalinsk,
Sakhalin Region, 693000
Phone/fax: (4242) 77 3000, 77 3030
Viktor Sergeevich Levandovsky,
Director

HOTELS AND TOURISM

86R006 ● ◆

Organization of inland trips
to the island of Moneron.
Project goal: to provide tourism services.

1) 600 tourists a year
2) $1.2 million/10 years
3) L
4) BP

Nevelsk Administration
115, ul. Rybatskaya, Nevelsk,
Sakhalin Region, 694740
Phone: (42436) 61 301
Fax: (42436) 60 202
Angelika Anatolyevna Markova,
Director

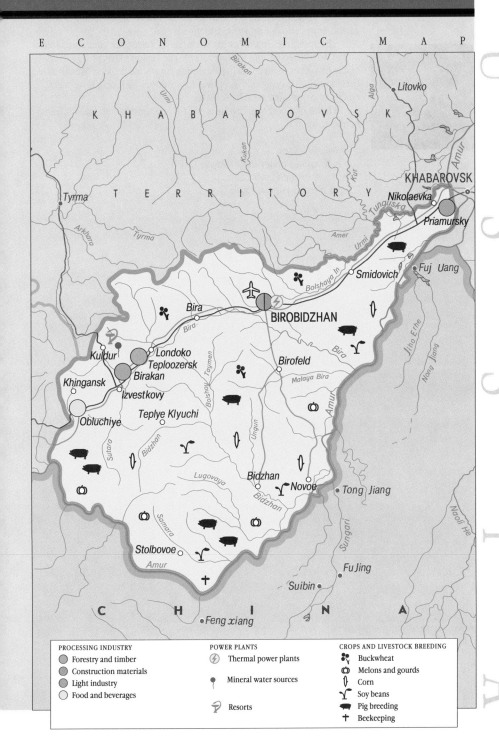

ECONOMIC MAP

R U S S I A

FAR EASTERN FEDERAL DISTRICT

VII

KHABAROVSK

Litovko

KHABAROVSK

Tyrma

TERRITORY

Nikolaevka

Priamursky

Fuj Uang

Smidovich

Bira

BIROBIDZHAN

Londoko
Teploozersk

Kuldur

Birakan

Birofeld

Khingansk

Izvestkovy

Obluchiye

Teplye Klyuchi

Bidzhan

Novoe

Tong Jiang

Stolbovoe

Fu Jing

Suibin

Feng xiang

C H I N A

PROCESSING INDUSTRY
- Forestry and timber
- Construction materials
- Light industry
- Food and beverages

POWER PLANTS
- Thermal power plants
- Mineral water sources
- Resorts

CROPS AND LIVESTOCK BREEDING
- Buckwheat
- Melons and gourds
- Corn
- Soy beans
- Pig breeding
- Beekeeping

I n spite of its small size, the Jewish Autonomous Region is a potentially interesting partner for trading, economic, and investment cooperation due to its advantageous geographic location at the Chinese border and its well-developed transport links.

The Region lincs its economic development prospects primarily with the agroindustrial sector, which is focused on soybean and other crop cultivation and processing.

Our Region's subsoil is rich in a variety of minerals, including manganese, iron ore, tin, magnesite, and brown coal.

The authorities in the Jewish Autonomous Region are committed to creating favorable conditions for investment. The Region's laws provide considerable privileges to investors implementing large-scale projects. We are also developing other economic incentives for investors, including investment credits to cover interest on bank loans.

I hope that potential investors will find the investment projects listed herein of interest.

Nikolai Volkov,
GOVERNOR OF THE JEWISH AUTONOMOUS REGION,
CHAIRMAN OF THE GOVERNMENT
OF THE JEWISH AUTONOMOUS REGION

1. GENERAL INFORMATION

1.1. GEOGRAPHY

Located in the south of the Russia's Far East and drained by the Amur River, the Jewish Autonomous Region covers a total area of some 36,000 square kilometers. To the north-west, the Region borders the Amur Region, to the north, north-east and east, the Khabarovsk Territory, and to the south and west, China.

1.2. CLIMATE

The Region lies in the temperate monsoon climate zone.

Air temperatures in January average −24.1°C, rising to +16.9°C in July. Annual precipitation averages 500–800 mm. The average growing season lasts 170–175 days.

1.3. POPULATION

According to preliminary 2002 census results, total population of the Region was 191,000 people. The average population density is 5.3 people per square kilometer. The economically active population amounts to 83,000 people. The registered unemployment rate in 2002 was 1.8%, while the actual rate stood at 15.1%.

Demographically speaking, some 62.6% are of working age, 21.1% are below the statutory working age, and 16.3% are beyond the statutory working age.

The Region's ethnic mix is 4.2% Jewish, 83.2% Russian, 7.4% Ukrainian, and 5.2% other.

As of 2002, the Region's major urban centers were Birobidjan with 78,400 inhabitants and Obluchie with 11,200 inhabitants.

Population								TABLE 1
	1992	1997	1998	1999	2000	2001	2002
Total population, 000'	220	206	203	201	197	196	191
Economically active population, 000'.	114	95	91	99	94	94	83

2. ADMINISTRATION

18, pr. 60-letiya SSSR, Birobidjan, Jewish Autonomous Region, 679016
Fax: (42622) 60 725; e-mail: gov@eao.ru; http://www.eao.ru

NAME	POSITION	CONTACT INFORMATION
Nikolai Mikhailovich VOLKOV	Governor of the Jewish Autonomous Region, Chairman of the Government of the Jewish Autonomous Region	Phone: (42622) 60 242 Fax: (42622) 40 725
Gennady Alexeevich ANTONOV	Deputy Governor of the Jewish Autonomous Region	Phone: (42622) 40 730 Fax: (42622) 40 684 E-mail: antonov@eao.ru
Viktor Spiridonovich GOZHY	First Deputy Chairman of the Government of the Jewish Autonomous Region	Phone: (42622) 60 322
Valery Petrovich SHULYANIKOV	First Deputy Chairman of the Government of the Jewish Autonomous Region	Phone: (42622) 62 691 E-mail: shulatnikov@eao.ru
Valery Solomonovich GUREVICH	Deputy Chairman of the Government of the Jewish Autonomous Region	Phone: (42622) 62 672 E-mail: gurevich@eao.ru
Maria Makarovna ZHIRDETSKAYA	Deputy Chairman of the Government of the Jewish Autonomous Region	Phone: (42622) 62 692 E-mail: socifl@eao.ru
Anatoly Spiridonovich KIYASHKO	Deputy Chairman of the Government of the Jewish Autonomous Region	Phone: (42622) 64 871 E-mail: selo@eao.ru
Yakov Borisovich SHERMAN	Deputy Chairman of the Government of the Jewish Autonomous Region, Chairman of the Regional State Property Committee of the Jewish Autonomous Region	Phone: (42622) 69 738 E-mail: kugi@on-line-jar.ru

3. ECONOMIC POTENTIAL

3.1. 1997–2002 GRP (INDUSTRY BREAKDOWN). MAJOR ECONOMIC GROWTH PROJECTIONS

The 2002 Gross Regional Product of the Jewish Autonomous Region totaled $215 million, up 19.8% on 2001. Per capita GRP was $918 in 2001 and $1,128 in 2002.

3.2. INDUSTRIAL OUTPUT IN 1997–2002 FOR MAJOR SECTORS OF ECONOMY

The leading industrial sectors of the Jewish Autonomous Region are construction materials, energy, machine engineering and metals, timber, pulp and paper, light, and food and beverages. Together they account for 92% of total industrial output of the Region.

GRP trends in 1997–2002						*TABLE 2*
	1997	1998	1999	2000	2001*	2002*
GRP in current prices, $ million	290	156	120	136	180	215

*Estimates of the Jewish Autonomous Region Government

GRP industry breakdown in 1997–2002, % of total						*TABLE 3*
	1997	1998	1999	2000	2001*	2002*
GRP	100.0	100.0	100.0	100.0	100.0	100.0
Industry	10.6	15.4	16.3	14.6	13.2	14.2
Agriculture and forestry	3.6	13.5	13.0	9.9	13.1	12.5
Construction	14.8	15.1	6.7	4.9	3.8	3.4
Transport and communications	3.6	4.6	22.6	29.5	39.0	36.6
Trade and public catering	37.8	15.9	15.9	16.1	11.3	10.6
Other	30.6	34.3	27.6	27.6	23.1	24.9
Net taxes on output	-1.0	1.2	-2.1	-2.6	-3.5	-2.2

*Estimates of the Jewish Autonomous Region Government

Construction materials. The sector accounts for 30.4% of the Region's total industrial output. The leading company in the sector is Teplooziorsky Concrete Plant, one of Russia's concrete majors.

Energy. The energy industry accounts for 17.9% of the Region's total industrial output. Birobidjan Thermal Power Station, a subsidiary of OAO Khabarovskenergo, is the largest company in the fuel and energy sector.

Machine engineering and metal processing. The sector accounts for 13.3% of the Region's total industrial output. The largest companies are OAO Dalselmash and OAO Birobidjan Power Transformer Electrical Engineering Plant.

Agriculture. The Region's agricultural lands cover a total area of 391,100 hectares, including 136,100 hectares of arable land, 129,900 hectares of hayfields, and 104,600 hectares of pastures. Fallow lands cover a total area of 20,400 hectares. Most of the Region's agriculture is given over to tillage (70% of total agriculture output). Crops include corn, buckwheat, soya beans and melons. Livestock breeding (pigs and poultry) is also well established.

Recreation and resorts. The Region is home to the Kuldur resort (Kuldur thermo-mineral source).

3.3. FUEL AND ENERGY BALANCE (OUTPUT AND CONSUMPTION PER RESOURCE)

The Birobidjan Thermal Power Station, a subsidiary of OAO Khabarovskenergo, produces heat energy for the Region only. Annual electricity supplies to the Region are 0.6–0.7 billion kWh. The Region's coal needs (700,000 tons per year) are fully satisfied by supplies of brown coal. The Region has plans to develop its own limited fuel infrastructure based on small coal pits.

3.4. TRANSPORT INFRASTRUCTURE

The Jewish Autonomous Region has a well-developed transport infrastructure. The Amur River links the Region to the Pacific ocean. The Trans-Siberian railroad also crosses the Region.

Roads. The Jewish Autonomous Region has 1,640 kilometers of public highway. The Region's main artery is the Khabarovsk – Birobidjan – Obluchie – Amur Region highway, with a ferry over the Amur river. The Region has international road links over the Amur River to the Chinese towns of Tongjiang, Mingshang and Jiayin.

Industry breakdown of industrial output in 1997–2002, % to total						*TABLE 4*
	1997	1998	1999	2000	2001	2002*
Industry	100.0	100.0	100.0	100.0	100.0	100.0
Construction materials	29.9	27.9	22.8	23.3	27.9	30.4
Energy	20.1	23.9	23.8	13.5	17.6	17.9
Machine engineering and metal processing	15.0	12.4	16.8	25.4	20.0	13.3
Forestry, timber, and pulp and paper	8.3	7.0	4.7	5.5	8.7	12.8
Light industry	7.7	5.4	10.7	10.5	10.8	10.4
Food and beverages	11.5	16.3	10.9	13.3	8.0	7.2
Non-ferrous metals	0.9	2.4	3.9	4.7	2.5	2.7
Fuel (coal)	0.4	0.2	0.6	0.2	0.8	1.9
Flour, cereals, and mixed fodder	1.6	1.7	0.8	0.4	0.7	0.7
Ferrous metals	1.5	1.4	1.5	1.0	0.7	0.6
Chemicals and petrochemicals	0.1	0.2	0.1	0.5	0.2	0.0

*Estimates of the Jewish Autonomous Region Government

Fuel and energy sector production and consumption trends, 1997–2002						*TABLE 5*
	1997	1998	1999	2000	2001	2002*
Coal output, '000 tons	4.0	8.0	34.0	15.0	51.7	124.1
Energy consumption, billion kWh	0.6	0.6	0.6	0.7	0.7	0.7

*Estimates of the Jewish Autonomous Region Government

Railroads. The Jewish Autonomous Region has 310 kilometers of railroad. The Trans-Siberian railroad links the Region to the rest of Russia.

Airports. The Region's airport at Zhiolty Yar links Birobidjan with Khabarovsk and remote urban centers. The Region also plans to start international flights between Birobidjan and Jiamusi (China).

River transport. The total length of the Region's waterways (Amur and Tunguska rivers) is 600 kilometers. Navigation is open on the Amur River for 180 days on average.

3.5. MAIN NATURAL RESOURCES: RESERVES AND EXTRACTION IN 2002

Mineral resources. The Region is home to the Khinganskoe, Karadubskoye, Bidjanskoye and Yuzhno-Khinganskoye tin deposits. In addition to tin, these deposits also contain silver, molybdenum, gold, copper, lead, zinc, arsenic, bismuth, and antimony ores. There are manganese and iron ore deposits. Gold is extracted at Maly Khingan and in the basin of the Sutara River. Large deposits of magnesite (11 fields) and brucite (the Kuldurskoye, Tsentralnoye, Savkinskoye and

Taragayskoye fields) have been discovered in the Region. The Jewish Autonomous Region has the second largest brucite deposits in the world.

A talc field has been discovered in the vicinity of the settlement of Birakan. Graphite deposits are found at the Soyuznenskoye field, the world's largest deposit of graphite. Coal deposits are found at the Ushumunskoye (brown coal) and Birskoye (black coal) coalfields. The Region has 55 peat deposits and 114 deposits of construction materials (various clays, claydite, sand, gravels, concrete, and facing stones).

Forest resources. The Region is home to valuable forestry species, with rare cedar forest covering 170,000 hectares, coniferous forest covering 223,000 hectares, and larch, oak and birch forest covering 145,000 hectares.

Flora and fauna. The Region has over 200 species of nectariferous plants and about 300 herbs with curative properties. The Region's fauna includes 59 mammal species (brown bear and Himalayan bear, Nepal marten, fox, mink, sable, wild boar, moose, Siberian deer), and 73 species of fish. The Jewish Autonomous Region has five national forest reserves.

FAR EASTERN FEDERAL DISTRICT

VII

898

4. TRADE OPPORTUNITIES

4.1. MAIN GOODS PRODUCED IN THE REGION

Machine engineering: The Region produced 930,000 kWh worth of power transformers in 2002.

Construction materials: In 2002, the Region produced 360,000 tons of cement and 464,000 cubic meters of non-ore construction materials.

4.2. EXPORTS, INCLUDING EXTRA-CIS

Exports to extra-CIS countries in 2000 amounted to $3.8 million, and $0.1 million to CIS countries. 2001 exports to extra-CIS countries reached $16.7 million. 2002 exports to extra-CIS countries reached $8.1 million.

4.3. IMPORTS, INCLUDING EXTRA-CIS

Imports from extra-CIS countries in 2000 totaled $4.2 million, and $0.4 million from CIS countries. The respective figures for 2001 were $3.6 million and $0.4 million; 2002 imports were $4.0 million and $0.1 million, respectively.

Major regional export and import entities		TABLE 6
ENTITY	ADDRESS	PHONE, FAX, E-MAIL
OAO Birobidjan Power Transformer Plant	1, ul. Transformatornaya, Birobidjan, 679000	Phone: (42622) 62 296 Fax: (42622) 68 814
OAO Elegant	44, ul. Sholom-Aleikhema, Birobidjan, 679000	Phone: (42622) 68 455 Fax: (42622) 68 426
OAO Typlooziorsky Concrete Plant	Tyoploe Ozero, Obluchensky District, Jewish Autonomous Region, 679110	Phone: (42666) 31 415 Fax: (42666) 32 203
Office Furniture Factory, Private Co. S.V. Abramov	72-e, ul. Sovetskaya, Birobidjan, 679000	Phone: (42622) 40 125, (42622) 41 280
OOO Far East Medical Systems	14, ul. Lenina, Birobidjan, 679000	Phone: (42622) 68 824 Fax: (42622) 20 504
ZAO Zolotaya Sutara	1, ul. Verkhnyaya, Obluchie, Jewish Autonomous Region, 679100	Phone/fax: (42666) 42 504
ZAO Kuldursky Brucite Mine	1, ul. Zheleznodorozhnaya, Izvestkovy, Obluchensky District, Jewish Autonomous Region, 679125	Phone: (42666) 21 744 Fax: (42666) 43 340
OOO SengHe – Timber Industry	154, ul. Gagarina, Amurzet, Oktyabrsky District, Jewish Autonomous Region, 679230	Phone: (42665) 22 547

5. INVESTMENT OPPORTUNITIES

5.1. INVESTMENTS IN 1992–2002 (BY INDUSTRY SECTOR), INCLUDING FOREIGN INVESTMENTS

The following factors determine the investment appeal of the Jewish Autonomous Region:

• Its good geographical location (direct access to the Pacific via the Amur River) and proximity to markets (China);

• Its developed transport infrastructure (the Region is bisected by the Trans-Siberian railroad);

• Legislation providing support for investment activities.

5.2. CAPITAL INVESTMENT

The transport and communications sector accounts for the majority of capital investment in the Region.

5.3. MAJOR ENTERPRISES (INCLUDING ENTERPRISES WITH FOREIGN INVESTMENT)
5.4. MOST ATTRACTIVE SECTORS FOR INVESTMENT

According to the Regional Government, the sectors offering the greatest investment appeal are natural resource extraction and processing, agriculture processing, and consumer goods manufacturing.

5.5. CURRENT LEGISLATION ON INVESTOR TAX EXEMPTIONS AND PRIVILEGES

The Jewish Autonomous Region has passed a number of legislative acts on tax exemption and privileges for investors, including:

• The Jewish Autonomous Region Government Resolution On the Investment Program of the Jewish Autonomous Region, 1999–2005;

Capital investment by industry sector, $ million   TABLE 7

	1997	1998	1999	2000	2001	2002
Total capital investment	75.3	22.4	13.0	12.1	13.6	18.1
Including major industries (% of total)						
Industry	6.6	21.6	5.4	9.7	18.0	10.9
Agriculture and forestry	1.0	0.6	1.9	3.4	6.4	6.4
Construction	0.2	0.3	1.4	11.4	18.4	8.4
Transport and communications	65.3	62.9	81.0	56.7	28.5	40.0
Trade and public catering	0.3	0.4	1.4	1.1	0.1	0.1
Other	26.6	14.2	8.9	17.7	28.6	34.2

Foreign investment trends in 1996–2002   TABLE 8

	1996–1997	1998	1999	2000	2001	2002
Foreign investment, $ million	0.8	–	0.1	0.2	–	0.4
Including FDI, $ million	0.8	–	0.1	0.2	–	0.4

Largest enterprises of the Jewish Autonomous Region   TABLE 9

COMPANY	SECTOR	2002 NET PROFIT, $ MILLION*
OAO Teplooziorsky Concrete Plant	Construction materials	0.777
ZAO Vostok Holding	Light	0.351
GUP Railroad Machine Station	Construction	0.348
OAO Viktoria	Light	0.319
GUP DRSU-1	Construction	0.124
OAO Elegant	Light	0.083
ZAO Raddovskoye	Agriculture	0.044

*Estimates of the Jewish Autonomous Region Government

• The Jewish Autonomous Region Law On Creation of Economic Environment for Raising Investment in the Jewish Auto-nomous Region;
• Resolution of the Governor of the Jewish Auto-nomous Region On State Support to Investment Projects in the Jewish Autonomous Region;
• Decree of the Governor of the Jewish Autono-mous Region On the Creation of Investment Council of the Jewish Autonomous Region;
• Decree of the Head of the Jewish Autonomous Region Administration On Proactive Measures Aimed at Raising Domestic and Foreign Investment in the Jewish Autonomous Region.

The investment program of the Jewish Auto-nomous Region provides measures required to cre-ate favorable conditions for economic growth in the Region and the attraction of investment to the Region. Investors implementing investment proj-ects are eligible for full or partial exemptions on the regional property tax component with respect to newly created or acquired property. They are also eligible to investment credits for investment

projects approved by the Investment Council of the Jewish Autonomous Region.

5.6. FEDERAL AND REGIONAL ECONOMIC AND SOCIAL DEVELOPMENT PROGRAMS FOR THE JEWISH AUTONOMOUS REGION

Federal targeted programs. The Region is implementing the federal targeted program for the Economic and Social Development of the Far East and Trans-Baikal Regions, 1996–2005 and through 2010. The Program includes twelve projects of sig-nificance for the Region. Oil and gas exploration and prospecting with subsequent extraction are an important component of the Program.

Regional programs. The Government of the Jewish Autonomous Region is developing and imple-menting a number of programs focused on the development of industry, agriculture, food policy, environmental protection, law enforcement, health care, and public welfare. In 2002, the Re-gion carried out some 22 programs with a total budget of $2.5 million. In 2003, the Region has plans to implement 27 programs with a total budget of $4.6 million.

6. INVESTMENT PROJECTS

Industry sector and project description	1) Expected results 2) Amount and term of investment 3) Form of financing[1] 4) Documentation[2]	Contact information
1	2	3

OIL AND NATURAL GAS

87R001   ■ ● ❖ ▲

| Exploration and prospecting. Project goal: to explore, prospect and develop oil and gas fields. | 1) n/a 2) $200 million/n/a 3) L, JV, E 4) FS | The Natural Resources and Environmental Protection Department of the Russian Natural Resources Ministry for the JAR 111, ul. Sovetskaya, Birobidjan, JAR, 679016 Phone/fax: (42622) 46 729 Yury Arkadyevich Nedorezov, Head of Department |

COAL

87R002   ■ ● ❖ ◆

| Development of the Ushumunsky coalfield. Project goal: coal production. | 1) 300,000 tons of coal annually 2) $28.9 million/n/a 3) L, E, JV 4) BP | OAO Ushumunsky Open Pit Coal Mine Office 15, 8, ul. Mirnaya, Ptichnik, JAR, 679510 Phone: (42622) 75 801 Valery Vasilyevich Kasyanov, Director |

MINING (FUEL RESOURCES)

87R003   ■ ● ❖ ▲

| Construction of a mining and ore processing plant at the Birakan talc deposit. Project goal: talc extraction and enrichment. | 1) 2.0 million tons of ore and 80,000 tons of talc powder annually 2) $15 million/n/a 3) L, E, JV 4) FS | Natural Resources and Environmental Protection Department of the Russian Natural Resources Ministry for the JAR 111, ul. Sovetskaya, Birobidjan, JAR, 679016 Phone/fax: (42622) 46 729 Yury Arkadyevich Nedorezov, Head of Department |

87R004   ■ ● ❖ ▲

| Development of the Soyuzny graphite deposit. Project goal: graphite production. | 1) Stage I – up to 30,000 tons annually, Stage II – 75,000 tons annually 2) $30 million/n/a. 3) L, E, JV 4) FS | Natural Resources and Environmental Protection Department of the Russian Natural Resources Ministry for the JAR 111, ul. Sovetskaya, Birobidjan, JAR, 679016 Phone/fax: (42622) 46 729 Yury Arkadyevich Nedorezov, Head of Department |

87R005   ■ ● ❖ ▲

| Construction of a mining and ore processing plant and development of the Yuzhno-Khinganskoye manganese ore field. Project goal: production of concentrated manganese. | 1) Up to 200,000 tons of ore and 60,000 tons of concentrated manganese annually 2) $40 million/n/a 3) L, E, JV 4) FS | Natural Resources and Environmental Protection Department of the Russian Natural Resources Ministry for the JAR 111, ul. Sovetskaya, Birobidjan, JAR, 679016 Phone/fax: (42622) 46 729 Yury Arkadyevich Nedorezov, Head of Department |

[1] L – Loan, E – Equity, Leas. – Leasing, JV – Joint Venture
[2] BP – Business Plan, FS – Feasibility Study

1	2	3

87R006 ■ ● ❖ ▲

Construction of a mining and ore processing plant and development of the Kimkanskoye and Sutarskoye iron ore fields. Project goal: production of concentrated iron ore.	1) Annual open pit output of 16.5 million tons, annual rock output of 20 million cubic meters, annual processing plant output of 5,573,000 tons of concentrated ore 2) $983.5 million/n/a 3) L, E, JV 4) FS	Natural Resources and Environmental Protection Department of the Russian Natural Resources Ministry for the JAR 111, ul. Sovetskaya, Birobidjan, JAR, 679016 Phone/fax: (42622) 46 729 Yury Arkadyevich Nedorezov, Head of Department

87R007 ■ ● ▲

Preparation, extraction and processing of tin ores extracted at the Khinganskoye field. Project goal: production of concentrated tin ore.	1) Up to 1,446 tons of concentrated tin ore annually 2) $11.2 million/n/a 3) L, E 4) FS	OAO Khingan Tin 1, per. Shkolny, Khingansk, Obluchensky district, JAR, 679141 Phone: (42666) 21 744 Fax: (42666) 21 544 Viktor Nikolaevich Rabota, CEO

LIGHT INDUSTRY

87R008 ■ ● ★ ◆

Partial upgrade of underwear and hosiery production facilities. Project goal: production of underwear and hosiery.	1) Annual output of 62 million items, revenues $2.98 million. 2) $1.3 million/n/a 3) E, L, Leas. 4) BP	OAO Viktoria 62, ul. Pionerskaya, Birobidjan, JAR, 679000 Phone: (42622) 64 589 Fax: (42622) 61 878 Yelena Nikolaevna Samoilenko, CEO

88. KORYAKSKY AUTONOMOUS DISTRICT [82]

ECONOMIC MAP

CHUKOTSKY AUTONOMOUS

DISTRICT

Mayn

Velikaya

Penzhina

Pakhachi

Kamenskoe

Vyvenka

Korf

Penzhinskaya

Rekinniki

MAGADAN

Ilpyrskoe

BERING

REGION

Evensk

SEA

gulf

Karaginsky Island

Ossora

Shelikhov

PALANA

Gulf

Voyampolka

Ust-Kamchatsk

Kamchatka

Klyuchi

Yamsk

Sedanka

MAGADAN

Ust-Khayruzovo

Ola

KAMCHATKA

SEA OF

REGION

OKHOTSK

PROCESSING INDUSTRY	MINING INDUSTRY	LIVESTOCK BREEDING
● Forestry and timber	▨ Brown coal	🦌 Reindeer breeding
● Food and beverages		Crab catch

The Koryaksky Autonomous District is a region with considerable economic potential. It is a unique area due to its geographical and ethnic features and natural resources contained in its seas, continental shelf, and land. Its principal natural resources include seafood, fuel (oil, gas and coal), and precious and rare metals (gold, platinum, etc.).

The erstwhile government policy which saw the northern regions of Russia treated as feedstock producing appendages without any real indigenous economic development has now passed into history. The legacy of that policy, however, is that these regions now lag behind in terms of industrial and economic development, with under-developed energy facilities, processing industries, transport and communications.

The District's Administration has devised a program for the social and economic development of the District, the creation of a local fuel and energy sector, energy producing facilities and on-shore fish processing plants, and the expansion of a road network.

The Koryaksky Autonomous District's investment legislation enables us to invite investors and trading partners to participate in the development of the District's abundant natural resources. The Administration is committed to minimizing risks, providing an investment friendly environment, and encouraging investment activity in the District.

The Koryaksky Autonomous District Administration is eager to talk to all partners interested in investing in the District and to consider proposals for participation in the implementation of the District's programs and projects. Numerous forms of involvement are possible. We invite you to invest in our District on mutually beneficial terms.

Vladimir Loginov,
GOVERNOR OF THE KORYAKSKY AUTONOMOUS DISTRICT

1. GENERAL INFORMATION

1.1. GEOGRAPHY

Located in the extreme north-east of Russia, the Koryaksky Autonomous District occupies the northern part of the Kamchatka peninsula, the adjacent part of the continent and the Karaginsky Island. The District covers a total area of 301,500 square kilometers and is washed by the Sea of Okhotsk (to the west) and the Bering Sea (to the east). The District borders the Chukotsky Autonomous District.

1.2. CLIMATE

The Koryaksky Autonomous District lies within the sub-arctic climate zone. Air temperatures in January average −17°C, rising to +14°C in July. Annual precipitation averages 300–700 mm.

1.3. POPULATION

According to preliminary 2002 census results, the District's total population was 25,000 inhabitants, of whom 17,000 were economically active. The average population density was 0.1 people per square kilometer. Official unemployment stood at 8%.

Demographically speaking, some 60% are of statutory working age, 18% are below the statutory working age, and 22% are beyond the statutory working age.

The District's largest urban centers are Palana, with 4,000 inhabitants at January 1, 2002, and Ossora with 3,400 inhabitants.

Population		1992	1997	1998	1999	2000	2001	2002
Total population, '000		40	33	32	31	30	29	25
Economically active population, '000		24	20	18	18	17	17	17

TABLE 1

2. ADMINISTRATION

22, ul. Porotova, Palana, Kamchatka Region, Koryaksky Autonomous District, 688000
Fax: (41543) 31 370; e-mail: akar@mail.kamchatka.ru

NAME	POSITION	CONTACT INFORMATION
Vladimir Alexandrovich LOGINOV	Governor of the Koryaksky Autonomous District	Phone: (41543) 31 380 Reception: (41543) 31 560
Vasily Andreevich MYSHLYAEV	Deputy Governor of the Koryaksky Autonomous District	Phone: (41543) 31 807
Vladimir Ivanovich GRAZHDANKIN	Deputy Governor of the Koryaksky Autonomous District	Phone: (41543) 32 339
Nikolai Nikolaevich LAPCHENKO	Deputy Governor of the Koryaksky Autonomous District	Phone: (41543) 32 683, 31 588
Ludmila Ivanovna SAVCHENKO	Head of the Economic Development and Trade Department of the Koryaksky Autonomous District	Phone: (41543) 31 823
Sergei Vladimirovich LEBEDEV	Deputy Head of the Economic Development and Trade Department of the Koryaksky Autonomous District, in Charge of Industry, Investment and Business Development	Phone: (41543) 32 031
Vladimir Nikolaevich MIZININ	Acting Chairman of the State Property Management Committee of the Koryaksky Autonomous District	Phone: (41543) 32 777
Lev Stanislavovich ALYKHIN	Head of the Fishing and Hunting Department of the Koryaksky Autonomous District	Phone: (41543) 31 588
Andrei Alexeevich SEMIKOLENNYKH	Head of the Mineral Resources and Raw Materials Department of the Koryaksky Autonomous District	Phone: (41543) 31 851

NAME	POSITION	CONTACT INFORMATION
Yury Vasilyevich BURMISTROV	Deputy Head of the Mineral Resources and Raw Materials Department of the Koryaksky Autonomous District	Phone: (41543) 31 851
Pavel Ivanovich KRAPOVITSKY	Head of the Agriculture and Food Department of the Koryaksky Autonomous District	Phone: (41543) 32 083

3. ECONOMIC POTENTIAL

3.1. 1997–2002 GROSS REGIONAL PRODUCT (GRP). INDUSTRY BREAKDOWN

The Koryaksky Autonomous District's 2002 gross regional product was $237 million, up 9.4% on 2001 figures. Per capita GRP totaled $7,495 in 2001, and $9,506 in 2002.

3.2. MAJOR ECONOMIC GROWTH PROJECTIONS

The Koryaksky Autonomous District's economic and social development Program for 2003–2008 contains projections for the District's development in the forthcoming years and determines the following goals and objectives:

GRP trends in 1997–2002						TABLE 2
	1997	1998	1999	2000	2001*	2002*
GRP in current prices, $ million	119	190	107	189	217	237

*Estimates of the Koryaksky Autonomous District Administration

GRP industry breakdown in 1997–2002, % of total						TABLE 3
	1997	1998	1999	2000	2001*	2002*
GRP	100.0	100.0	100.0	100.0	100.0	100.0
Industry	n/a	n/a	n/a	57.7	65.9	65.9
Agriculture and forestry	n/a	n/a	n/a	1.2	1.2	1.2
Construction	n/a	n/a	n/a	0.6	1.4	1.8
Transport and communications	n/a	n/a	n/a	3.4	3.1	3.2
Trade and public catering	n/a	n/a	n/a	4.5	2.3	2.3
Other	n/a	n/a	n/a	30.6	25.0	24.5
Net taxes on output	n/a	n/a	n/a	2.0	1.1	1.1

*Estimates of the Koryaksky Autonomous District Administration

Industry: maintaining growth by enhancing customer solvency, extending and upgrading production facilities, and decreasing current production costs. The Program specifically focuses on the fishing sector, including: extending and developing fish processing facilities, job creation at coastal settlements, and the development of coastal production facilities;

Agriculture: increasing reindeer livestock;

Construction: increasing growth by creating new production facilities.

3.3. INDUSTRIAL OUTPUT IN 1997–2002 FOR MAJOR SECTORS OF ECONOMY

Fishing and mining represent the District's leading industries. In 1998–2002, together they accounted for over 90% of total output in the District.

Food and beverages. This sector, mainly based around the fishing industry, accounts for some 50% of the District's total industrial output. Major companies include: ZAO Koryakryba, ZAO Evening Star, OOO Pollux, OOO Koryakmoreproduct, Udarnik Collective Fishing Cooperative, and Bekkereva Collective Fishing Cooperative.

Mining. This sector (gold and platinum extraction) accounts for 41.5% of total industrial output. The largest company is ZAO Koryakgeologodobycha.

Energy and fuel. The energy sector accounts for 5.7% of total industrial output, and fuel for 1.3%. Coal is the only fuel produced in the District.

3.4. FUEL AND ENERGY BALANCE OF THE REGION (OUTPUT AND CONSUMPTION PER RESOURCE)

Energy is supplied to the District by seven diesel power stations owned by OAO Kamchatskenergo, 19 diesel power plants run by the District's housing sector, and ten power plants owned by various District authorities. All plants operate on imported fuel.

FAR EASTERN FEDERAL DISTRICT

VII

Industry breakdown of industrial output in 1997–2002, % of total						TABLE 4
	1997	1998	1999	2000	2001	2002*
Industry	100.0	100.0	100.0	100.0	100.0	100.0
Food and beverages	55.9	28.1	44.2	52.2	54.5	51.4
Mining	19.1	65.8	50.2	40.9	38.6	41.5
Energy	20.2	4.2	4.0	5.6	5.7	5.7
Fuel (coal)	2.2	1.6	1.3	1.0	0.9	1.3
Printing	0.4	0.1	0.1	0.1	0.1	0.1
Forestry, timber, and pulp and paper	1.5	0.1	0.1	0.1	0.1	–

*Estimates of the Koryaksky Autonomous District Administration

Fuel and energy sector production and consumption trends in 1997–2002						TABLE 5
	1997	1998	1999	2000	2001	2002*
Energy output, billion kWh	0.1	0.1	0.1	0.1	0.1	0.1
Coal output, '000 tons	30.0	30.0	40.0	40.0	40.0	50.0

*Estimates of the Koryaksky Autonomous District Administration

3.5. TRANSPORT INFRASTRUCTURE

Roads. The District has 555 kilometers of paved public highways, in addition to 497 kilometers of winter roads. Currently, three new paved roads with a total length 504 kilometers are under construction.

Airports. Flights are operated to and from the only airport serving the district at Petropavlovsk-Kamchatsky. FGUP Koryak Airlines Company operates practically all cargo and passenger flights within the District.

Sea transport. Sea transport accounts for the bulk of freight transportation. The following items constitute the majority of goods shipped in the District: oil products, coal, food, construction materials and equipment. Goods are transported by sea during the summer months only.

Seaports. Goods are mainly shipped in and out of the District via the port of Petropavlovsk-Kamchatsky.

3.6. MAIN NATURAL RESOURCES: RESERVES AND EXTRACTION IN 2002

The District's principal natural resources include oil, natural gas, coal, gold, platinum, silver, sulfur, nickel, copper, tin, zinc, mercury, and biosphere resources.

Gold, mercury, and sulfur reserves. Explored reserves of gold amount to over 40 tons, mercury – 2,100 tons. The District's sulfur fields at Maletoivayamskoye and Vetrovayamskoye are the largest in the Far East. The District also has about one hundred smaller sulfur fields. Total sulfur reserves are estimated at 16.2 million tons.

Coal reserves. Explored coal reserves amount to 14.8 million tons; prospected reserves are estimated at 6,162.2 million tons.

Biosphere resources. Principal fauna include: various species of fish, marine mammals (walrus, seal, sea-otter), reindeer, wild animals and birds. Principal flora includes red cowberries, cranberries, crowberries, honeysuckle, great bilberries, cloudberries, mushrooms, herbs, and damsons (wild garlic).

Thermal sources. The Koryaksky Autonomous District has plenty of thermomineral sources, which are used as a heat, energy, and rare mineral source, and a valuable recreational resource.

4. TRADE OPPORTUNITIES

4.1. MAIN GOODS PRODUCED IN THE REGION

The main goods produced in the Koryaksky Autonomous District include fish products, coal, gold and platinum.

Fish products. In 2002, fish products output (including canned fish) totaled 89,100 tons. Almost all fish products are shipped out of the District.

Coal. In 2002, coal output was 50,000 tons. All extracted coal is used within the District.

4.2. MAIN EXPORTS, INCLUDING EXTRA-CIS

Exports to extra-CIS countries in 2002 were at $34.4 million; there were no exports to CIS countries in 2002.

Fish products represent the District's core export, including assorted frozen fish, frozen herring, frozen liver and caviar, crab, and ground fish meal. Fish product exports amounted to 28,500 tons in 2002. Principal export destinations include Japan, South Korea, China, the USA, Canada, and Cyprus.

4.3. MAIN IMPORTS, INCLUDING EXTRA-CIS

Imports from extra-CIS countries in 2002 were practically unchanged on 2001 levels at $1.1 million; there was no imports from CIS countries in 2002.

The District imports bunker fuel and ship fuel only. In 2002, imports totaled 4,300 tons. Major importers to the district include: China, Japan, South Korea, the USA, and Cyprus.

5. INVESTMENT OPPORTUNITIES

5.1. INVESTMENTS IN 1992–2002 (BY INDUSTRY SECTOR), INCLUDING FOREIGN INVESTMENTS

The following main factors determine the investment appeal of the Koryaksky Autonomous District:
- Its favorable geographical location (potential for development of economic relations with Asia-Pacific countries);

- Legislation supporting investment activities (guarantees of investors' rights and tax benefits for investors);
- Natural resource potential, including extensive biosphere reserves.

5.2. CAPITAL INVESTMENT

The transport, communications, and industry sectors together account for the bulk of capital investment.

Capital investment by industry sector, $ million						TABLE 6
	1997	1998	1999	2000	2001	2002
Total capital investment	6.6	0.9	1.9	9.5	9.6	4.8
Including major industries (% of total):						
Industry	79.0	66.3	85.3	40.6	53.1	40.2
Agriculture and forestry	–	–	–	5.2	2.8	0.1
Construction	–	–	–	–	–	–
Transport and communications	9.7	–	–	12.0	29.0	36.8
Trade and public catering	3.1	–	–	5.2	–	–
Other	8.2	33.7	14.7	37.0	15.1	22.9

Foreign investment trends in 1997–2002						TABLE 7
	1997	1998	1999	2000	2001	2002
Foreign investment, $ million	1.4	7.1	17.3	0.3	4.3	–
Including FDI, $ million	1.4	7.1	–	–	–	–

5.3. MAJOR ENTERPRISES (INCLUDING ENTERPRISES WITH FOREIGN INVESTMENT)

The largest companies are ZAO Koryakryba, the Udarnik Collective Fishing Cooperative, the Bekkereva Collective Fishing Cooperative, OOO Koryakmoreprodukt, ZAO Evening Star, OOO Pollux, FGUP Koryak Airlines Company, and ZAO Koryakgeologodobycha.

5.4. MOST ATTRACTIVE SECTORS FOR INVESTMENT

According to the Koryaksky Autonomous District Administration, the fishing and mining sectors, and energy, transport and tourism are the most attractive industries for investors.

5.5. CURRENT LEGISLATION ON INVESTOR TAX EXEMPTIONS AND PRIVILEGES

The Koryaksky Autonomous District has passed a number of legislative acts regulating investment activities. These include:
- The Koryaksky Autonomous District Law On Investment Activities in the Koryaksky Autonomous District;
- The Koryaksky Autonomous District Law On Investment Activities Supported by the District Authorities in the Koryaksky Autonomous District;
- The Koryaksky Autonomous District Law On Tourism in the Koryaksky Autonomous District. These laws establish the legal aspects of state sup-

port to investors and ensure equal investor rights in terms of investment activities conducted in the District. Foreign investors may be eligible for additional benefits with regard to taxes charged to the regional budget.

5.6. FEDERAL AND REGIONAL ECONOMIC AND SOCIAL DEVELOPMENT PROGRAMS FOR THE KORYAKSKY AUTONOMOUS DISTRICT

Federal targeted programs. A major role in social and economic development for the Koryaksky Autonomous District is played by:

• The Program for the Economic and Social Development of Far East and Trans-Baikal Region 1996–2005 and Through 2010. The Program was developed with the aim of creating conditions conducive to the economic development of the Far East and Trans-Baikal Regions. The objective of the Program is to create a fuel and energy industry based around local natural resources (including the construction of several mini Thermal Power Stations; building work on two TPSs began in 2002); develop the Region's road network; build a landing strip near the District's main urban center, and develop the social infrastructure. The Program

provides for $56.9 million in financing for these projects within the District.

• The District is implementing the Program of Economic and Social Development of the Indigenous Peoples of the North Through 2011. The Program aims to create conditions conducive to sustainable and comprehensive development along self-sufficiency lines of the indigenous peoples of the North with a focus on local traditional activities, their resource base, and their spiritual and cultural advancement. The Program's core objective is to raise living standards among the indigenous peoples of the North. The Program provides for $9.1 million in financing for these projects within the District.

Regional programs. The Autonomous District is currently implementing some 30 targeted programs with total financing of $944 million, including: the District's Targeted Small Enterprise Support and Development Program, the Program for Development of Coastal Fishing and On-Shore Fish Processing Facilities, the Program for the Support, Preservation and Development of Social and Economic Facilities at Coastal Settlements, and the Program for the Development of Sustainable Agriculture.

6. INVESTMENT PROJECTS

Industry sector and project description	1) Expected results 2) Amount and term of investment 3) Form of financing[1] 4) Documentation[2]	Contact information
1	2	3
ENERGY		
88R001	■ ● ▲	Koryaksky Autonomous District Administration
Construction of a mini thermal power station in Palana. Project goal: to transfer the District's power plants to local coal.	1) Annual energy output – 13 million kWh, heating – 75,000 Gcal 2) $3.6 million/2 years 3) E, L ($1.5 million) 4) FS	22, ul. Porotova, Palana, KAD, Kamchatka Region, 688000 Phone: (41543) 31 380 Reception (41543) 31 560 Fax: (41543) 31 370 E-mail: akar@mail.kamchatka.ru Vladimir Alexandrovich Loginov, Governor
88R002	■ ● ▲	Koryaksky Autonomous District Administration
Construction of mini thermal power station in Korf. Project goal: to transfer the District's power plants to local coal.	1) Annual energy output – 22 million kWh, heating – 85,000 Gcal 2) $7.6 million/2 years 3) E, L ($6.1 million) 4) FS	22, ul. Porotova, Palana, KAD, Kamchatka Region, 688000 Phone: (41543) 31 380 Reception (41543) 31 560 Fax: (41543) 31 370 E-mail: akar@mail.kamchatka.ru Vladimir Alexandrovich Loginov, Governor

[1] L – Loan, E – Equity, Leas. – Leasing, JV – Joint Venture
[2] BP – Business Plan, FS – Feasibility Study

1	2	3

TRANSPORT INFRASTRUCTURE

88R003

Reconstruction of the Palana airport landing strip.
Project goal: to improve transport links within the Koryaksky Autonomous District and with other regions of Russia.

■ ● ▲
1) 234,000 square meters
2) $32.5 million/3 years
3) E, L ($30.7 million)
4) FS

FGUP Koryak Airlines Company (FGUP KAC)
19, ul. Pilota, Korf,
Oliutorsky District, KAD,
Kamchatka Region, 688811
Phone: (41544) 52 703, 58 980
Alexei Vasilyevich Dyadechkin, CEO

88R004

Construction of the Palana – Anavgai winter road.
Project goal: to create a unified core road network within the Peninsula.

■ ● ▲
1) 435 kilometers
2) $64.2 million/8 years
3) E, L ($61.7 million)
4) FS

GU Territorial Road Fund of the Koryaksky Autonomous District
2v, ul. Obukhova, Palana, KAD
Kamchatka Region, 688000
Phone: (41543) 32 899
Fax: (41543) 32 463
E-mail: tdfkao@palana.ru
Yury Ivanovich Ivintaksyan, CEO

FAR EASTERN FEDERAL DISTRICT

VII

89. CHUKOTSKY AUTONOMOUS DISTRICT [87]

E C O N O M I C M A P

Bering Strait
Cape of Dezhnev
Uelen
Lavrentiya

CHUKCHI

SEA

Provid")

Provideniya

Vrangel Island

Cape of Chukotka

EAST
SIBERIAN
SEA

Iulgin

Egvekinot

Gulf
Anadyr

Amguema

Cape Mys Navarin

Krasnoarmeyskoe
Komsomolsky

Shakhtersky

Beringovsky

Pevek

ANADYR

Ust-Belaya

Velikaya

Bilibino

Khatyrka

Chersky

Anuysk

Bolshoy Anuy

Lamutskoe

Chuvanskoe

Markovo

Anadyr

B
E
R
I
N
G

S
E
A

Kolyma

Oloy

Penzhina

KORYAKSKY AUTONOMOUS

Pakhachi

Omolon

DISTRICT

REPUBLIC OF SAKHA (YAKUTIA)

Omolon

Kedon

Korf

MAGADAN

Penzhinskaya guba (gulf)

Kolyma

REGION

Evensk

Zyryanka

PROCESSING INDUSTRY	MINING INDUSTRY	POWER PLANTS	LIVESTOCK BREEDING
Food and beverages	Bituminous coal	Thermal power plants	Reindeer breeding
Art crafts	Brown coal	Nuclear power plants	Sea mammals catch
	Tin		

Chukotka is a region of high geopolitical importance and strong economic potential. Located in the far north-east of Eurasia, the Chukotsky Autonomous District is isolated from the country's industrial and transport centers. Its Arctic climate, lack of railroad infrastructure, and limited navigation period are inevitably reflected in the population's lifestyle and the economic life of the Region. And yet, thanks to considerable direct investment into the District, over the past few years Chukotka has been demonstrating steady economic growth.

2002 gross regional product increased by 28.5%. The fisheries and fuel and energy sectors underwent extensive growth, the construction sector expanded, and trade and commercial services increased. The District communicates with the rest of Russia and the world via satellite.

Gold is one of the main natural resources of Chukotka. Priority status has been accorded to the development of the major ore deposits at Maiskoye (estimated output of six tons per year), Valunistoye, Kupol, and Klen.

In addition to gold mining, fishing and fish processing, including marine hunting, is yet another prospective area for investment.

Foreign investors may also be interested in developing the District's numerous mineral resources. According to geological surveys, the District has extensive deposits of hydrocarbons located mainly offshore.

We believe that the District's political and social stability and proximity to the Pacific Rim countries and North America, as well as the District Government's commitment to international business norms will contribute to the formation of a favorable investment climate and attract investors' attention. Chukotka is open for cooperation and is ready to develop trade and economic partnerships.

Roman Abramovich,
GOVERNOR OF THE
CHUKOTSKY AUTONOMOUS
DISTRICT, CHAIRMAN
OF THE GOVERNMENT
OF THE CHUKOTSKY
AUTONOMOUS DISTRICT

FAR EASTERN FEDERAL DISTRICT

VII

1. GENERAL INFORMATION

1.1. GEOGRAPHY

The Chukotsky Autonomous District covers a total area of 737,700 square kilometers. The District is situated in the north-east of the Russian Federation on the Chukotka Peninsula and the adjoining mainland. To the west, the District borders the Republic of Sakha (Yakutia) and to the south – the Magadan Region and the Koryaksky Autonomous District. The Chukotsky Autonomous District is washed by the Chukchi Sea, East Siberian Sea, and Bering Sea.

1.2. CLIMATE

The District has a harsh continental climate. The average air temperature in January is −29.2°C, rising to +9.4°C in July. The average annual precipitation is 300 mm.

1.3. POPULATION

According to preliminary 2002 census results, the Chukotsky Autonomous District's total population amounted to 54,000 people. The average population density is 0.1 people per square kilometer. The economically active population amounts to 47,000 people. 2002 official unemployment level stood at 1%.

Demographically speaking, some 70.2% are of working age, 19.7% are below the statutory working age, and 10.1% are beyond the statutory working age.

The District's ethnic mix is 66.1% Russian, 16.8% Ukrainian, 7.3% Chukchi, and 9.8% other ethnic groups.

As of 2002, the Autonomous District's major urban centers were Anadyr with 12,000 inhabitants, Bilibino with 8,000 inhabitants, and Pevek with 5,400 inhabitants.

Population								TABLE 1
	1992	1997	1998	1999	2000	2001	2002
Total population, '000	152	92	87	83	79	75	54
Economically active population, '000	82	58	46	50	48	44	47

2. ADMINISTRATION

2, ul. Beringa, Anadyr, Chukotsky Autonomous District, 689000
Phone: (42722) 29 013; fax: (42722) 22 919; e-mail: admin87chao@mail.ru; http://www.chukotka.org

NAME	POSITION	CONTACT INFORMATION
Roman Arkadyevich ABRAMOVICH	Governor of the Chukotsky Autonomous District, Chairman of the Government of the Chukotsky Autonomous District	Phone: (42722) 29 000, 29 040 Fax: (42722) 29 043, 22 725 E-mail: goubernator@chukotka.sibneft.ru
Andrei Viktorovich GORODILOV	First Deputy Governor of the Chukotsky Autonomous District, First Deputy Chairman of the Government of the Chukotsky Autonomous District, Head of the Industrial and Agricultural Policy Department	Phone: (42722) 24 755, 29 059 Fax: (42722) 20 426
Irina Alexandrovna PANCHENKO	Deputy Governor of the Chukotsky Autonomous District, Deputy Chairman of the Government of the Chukotsky Autonomous District for Finance, Economy, and Property Relations, Head of the Financial, Economic, and Property Management Department	Phone: (42722) 24 755, 29 059 Fax: (42722) 20 426

3. ECONOMIC POTENTIAL

3.1. 1997–2002 GROSS REGIONAL PRODUCT (GRP). INDUSTRY BREAKDOWN

2002 Gross Regional Product amounted to $275 million, which constitutes 28.5% growth year-on-year. Per capita GRP amounted to $2,858 in 2001 and $5,105 in 2002.

3.2. MAJOR ECONOMIC GROWTH PROJECTIONS

The blueprint for economic development in the Autonomous District in the near future is set in the Governor's Address to the Deputies of the District Duma and the Social and Economic Development Forecast of the Chukotsky Autonomous District in 2003–2005.

GRP trends in 1997–2002						*TABLE 2*
	1997	1998	1999	2000	2001*	2002*
GRP in current prices, $ million	362	254	120	147	214	275

*Estimates of the Chukotsky Autonomous District Government

GRP industry breakdown in 1997–2002, % of total						*TABLE 3*
	1997	1998	1999	2000	2001*	2002*
GRP	100.0	100.0	100.0	100.0	100.0	100.0
Industry	42.7	36.7	42.6	36.7	32.9	37.7
Agriculture and forestry	2.4	0.2	2.6	1.2	1.4	1.4
Construction	5.7	5.5	3.6	7.2	15.5	16.3
Transport and communications	17.5	12.9	12.0	11.5	10.9	10.8
Trade and public catering	9.8	6.6	6.6	8.7	11.4	16.7
Other	n/a	43.3	36.8	33.0	25.7	13.7
Net taxes on output	n/a	−5.2	−4.2	1.7	2.2	3.4

*Estimates of the Chukotsky Autonomous District Government

The mid-term development forecast focuses on expanding manufacturing and services and developing trade links with other Russian regions. The District intends

- In non-ferrous metals – to develop promising new deposits of precious metals;
- In food and beverages – to increase fishery output and develop fishing infrastructure;
- In transport – to build new highways, increase freight transportation from seaports to populated areas and precious metal deposit sites, and

increase transportation of coal extracted in the District, including transportation to seaports for export. The Chukotsky Autonomous District plans to expand air transportation by overhauling its airports and landing strips.

3.3. INDUSTRIAL OUTPUT IN 1997–2002 FOR MAJOR SECTORS OF ECONOMY

The leading industrial sectors of the Chukotsky Autonomous District are non-ferrous metals, energy, and food and beverages. These account for a combined 93.5% of total industrial output.

Industry breakdown of industrial output in 1997–2002, % of total						*TABLE 4*
	1997	1998	1999	2000	2001	2002
Industry	100.0	100.0	100.0	100.0	100.0	100.0
Non-ferrous metals	41.3	40.6	61.1	63.8	56.3	56.3
Energy	40.0	45.1	27.0	24.3	25.7	25.7
Food and beverages	3.2	3.5	4.1	4.1	11.5	11.5
Fuel	14.5	9.7	7.2	7.3	6.2	6.2
Machine engineering and metal processing	0.2	0.3	0.2	0.1	0.1	0.1
Light industry	0.2	0.2	–	0.1	0.1	0.1
Forestry, timber, and pulp and paper	0.2	0.2	0.1	0.1	–	–
Construction materials	0.1	0.1	–	–	–	–

Non-ferrous metals (gold). The sector accounts for 56.3% of total industrial output. The District extracts placer and ore gold. Its largest deposits are the Valunistoe, Kupol, and Maiskoe.

Energy. This sector accounts for 25.7% of total industrial output. The local energy system consists of OAO Chukotenergo and State Company Bilibino Nuclear

Power Station. Autonomous low-yield diesel power plants and boilers supply energy to remote rural areas. The residential housing energy system is connected into the centrally managed State Unitary Company Chukotcommunkhoz, with the exception of the Bilibino district.

Food and beverages. The share of this sector is 11.5% of total industrial output. The District focuses on fisheries, which account for 80% of all produced food, while bread, bakery, meat, dairy products, and beer account for the remaining 20%.

Fuel (coal). The sector accounts for 6.2% of total industrial output. The sector is represented by two mines producing high quality brown and black coal. Some 0.5 million tons of coal was extracted in 2002, 21% up on 2001.

3.4. FUEL AND ENERGY BALANCE (OUTPUT AND CONSUMPTION PER RESOURCE)

OAO Chukotenergo and State Company Bilibino Nuclear Power Station together with the Residential Housing Energy System fully meet the District's demand for electricity. The District energy system provides electricity only to local companies, organizations, and residential sector and is autonomous from the energy systems of other Russian regions.

The District's coal reserves exceed the demand for coal of its industrial base, enabling the District to export the mineral.

3.5. TRANSPORT INFRASTRUCTURE

Roads. The District has 1,279 kilometers of paved public highway.

To improve cross-regional links, the District is upgrading the Bilibino–Anyuisk winter road to the Republic of Sakha (Yakutia) border, and is preparing design and budget documentation for the construction of an access road to the port of Zeleny Mys in

the Republic of Sakha (Yakutia). To develop local links, the District is constructing access roads to its seaports and precious metal deposits being developed.

Airports. FGUP ChukotAVIA owns ten airports, including two federal airports in Anadyr and Pevek. The District has two international airports at Anadyr and Providenie. Chukotka's airports link the District to Moscow, Khabarovsk, Bratsk, Omsk, and Magadan, while local routes link populated areas to regional centers and villages.

Sea and river transport. Sea and river routes function during a navigation season that lasts several month. Deliveries to the District take place during the navigation season. Freight is shipped to populated areas by river.

Seaports. The District has five seaports at Pevek, Providenie, Egvekinot, Anadyr, and Beringovsky.

3.6. MAIN NATURAL RESOURCES: RESERVES AND EXTRACTION IN 2002

The District's principle natural resources are gold, black and brown coal, tin, mercury, and natural gas.

Hydro resources. The largest rivers flowing through the District are the Anadyr with its tributaries the Mein, Belaya, and Tanyurer, and the Velikaya, Amguema, Omolon, and Bolshoi and Maly Anyui rivers. The largest lakes are Krasnoye, Elgygytkhyn, and Pekulneyskoye.

Fuel and energy sector production and consumption trends, 1997–2002						*TABLE 5*
	1997	1998	1999	2000	2001	2002*
Electricity output, billion kWh	0.6	0.6	0.6	0.6	0.6	0.6
Coal extraction, million tons	0.5	0.3	0.3	0.3	0.4	0.5
Electricity consumption, billion kWh	0.6	0.6	0.6	0.6	0.6	0.6

*Estimates of the Chukotsky Autonomous District Government

4. TRADE OPPORTUNITIES

4.1. MAIN GOODS PRODUCED IN THE REGION

Energy. 2002 electricity output amounted to 549 million kWh. Heat output totaled 1,018,000 GCal.

Coal. The District produced 0.5 million tons of coal in 2002, or 21% up year-on-year.

Food and beverages. In 2002, the District's food companies produced 22,900 tons of commercial edible fish products (570% growth year-on-year), 2,271 tons of bread and bakery products (11% decrease), 698.7 tons of reindeer and cattle meat and poultry – live weight (30% decrease), and 2,710,700 eggs (370% growth).

4.2. EXPORTS, INCLUDING EXTRA-CIS

The Chukotsky Autonomous District's exports to extra-CIS countries amounted to

$0.31 million in 2000, $0.05 million in 2001, and $0.13 million in 2002.

The District exports mainly food and agricultural raw materials. Major importers of the District's products are Cyprus, China, Japan, and South Korea.

4.3. IMPORTS, INCLUDING EXTRA-CIS

2000 imports from extra-CIS countries amounted to $1.8 million, $14.5 million in 2001, and $14.1 million in 2002. Imports from CIS countries totaled $0.3 million.

The main types of goods imported by the District are machinery, food, agricultural raw materials, metals and metal goods. The main exporters to the District are Canada, Poland, the USA, Turkey, Switzerland, and Germany.

5. INVESTMENT OPPORTUNITIES

5.1. INVESTMENTS IN 1992–2002 (BY INDUSTRY SECTOR), INCLUDING FOREIGN INVESTMENTS

The following factors determine the investment appeal of the Chukotsky Autonomous District:

- Its advantageous geographic location (proximity to the US and East Asian markets);

- The availability of natural resources (black and brown coal, gold, tin, and mercury).

5.2. CAPITAL INVESTMENT

Transport and communications account for the lion's share of capital investment.

5.3. MAJOR ENTERPRISES (INCLUDING ENTERPRISES WITH FOREIGN INVESTMENT)

Capital investment by industry sector, $ million						*TABLE 6*
	1996	1998	1999	2000	2001	2002
Total capital investment	32.4	18.3	9.1	24.9	58.6	149.0
Including major industries (% of total)						
Industry	50.0	2.0	27.9	15.2	12.6	6.0
Agriculture and forestry	–	1.1	0.2	–	–	–
Construction	–	–	–	–	–	–
Transport and communications	10.1	65.0	42.7	13.9	27.0	38.7
Trade and public catering	–	–	–	37.4	14.1	–
Other	39.9	31.9	29.2	33.5	46.3	55.3

Largest enterprises of the Chukotsky Autonomous District	*TABLE 7*
COMPANY	SECTOR
FGUP ChukotAVIA	Aviation
OAO North Gold	Non-ferrous metals
ZAO Baranikha	Non-ferrous metals
ZAO Chukotka Trade Company	Trade and public catering
OAO Chukotenergo	Energy
State Company Bilibino Nuclear Power Station	Energy
ZAO Chukotka Fishing Fleet	Fishery
State Unitary Company Chukotcommunkhoz	Energy

5.4. MOST ATTRACTIVE SECTORS FOR INVESTMENT

The most potentially appealing sectors for investors are non-ferrous metals and fishery.

5.5. FEDERAL AND REGIONAL ECONOMIC AND SOCIAL DEVELOPMENT PROGRAMS FOR THE CHUKOTSKY AUTONOMOUS DISTRICT

Federal targeted programs. The Program for Economic and Social Development of the Far East and the Trans-Baikal Regions 1996–2005 and through 2010 aims to create the economic prerequisites for stable growth of the Far East and Trans-Baikal regions in line with Russia's geopolitical and defense interests. The Program seeks to reduce the gap between the economic develop-ment of the Far East and Trans-Baikal and the average level of economic development in Russia, to foster financial self-sufficiency, to raise living standards, and to reduce social tensions in the District. The Program for social and economic development has a total budget of $115.8 million, including $24.2 million in federal funding.

Regional programs. The Government of the Chukotsky Autonomous District is developing and implementing a portfolio of programs focusing on the agroindustrial sector, environmental rehabilitation, education, healthcare, and public welfare. The District allocates funds to the projects from the local budget on an annual basis and uses non-budgetary sources of financing. Currently, some 15 regional programs worth a total of $47.2 million are in progress.

6. INVESTMENT PROJECTS

Industry sector and project description	1) Expected results 2) Amount and term of investment 3) Form of financing[1] 4) Documentation[2]	Contact information
1	2	3

MINING

89R001

■ ● ▲

| Development of the Maysky gold deposit. Project goal: to extract gold. | 1) Up to 6 tons per year with revenue of up to $56 million per year 2) $114 million/5 years 3) L, E 4) FS | Representative Office of the Governor of the Chukotsky Autonomous District 4, per. Kursovoy, Moscow, 119034 Phone: (095) 937 6591, 502 9730 Fax: (095) 937 6580 E-mail: predstavitelstvo@chao.sibneft.ru Mikhail Valeryevich Khokhlov, Project Coordinator |

---

[1] L – Loan, E – Equity, Leas. – Leasing, JV – Joint Venture
[2] BP – Business Plan, FS – Feasibility Study

APPENDICES
INDEXES AND REFERENCES

RUSSIAN FEDERATION ECONOMIC DEVELOPMENT REVIEW, JANUARY–JUNE 2003

The Russian economy has been following a stable upwards trajectory since 1999 despite a sometimes unfavorable global and domestic environment. This points to the effectiveness of the market reforms, the optimal approach to securing stable economic development, and the successful resolution of serious social problems. Russia's economic performance figures for the first half of 2003 clearly demonstrate the reality of this trend.

INVESTMENT
ACTIVITY GROWTH

The first half of 2003 saw the unfolding of a series of events of vital importance to the Russian economy. International rating agency Fitch upgraded its sovereign rating for Russia by two notches to BB+, just one notch short of an investment rating. The Organization for Economic Cooperation and Development (OECD) moved Russia from fifth to fourth credit rating category. According to the OECD rating, as of July 1, Russia was on par with oil-rich Algeria and Iran. The signing of a massive deal worth $2.4 billion between British Petroleum (BP) and Tyumen Oil Company (TNK) was the clearest sign of the "vote of confidence" in the new political and economic stability in Russia. That deal, in which BP bought a stake in TNK, was followed by a series of agreements and deals between Russian corporations and major foreign investors. In May 2003, France's Groupe Louis Dreyfus, a major supplier of grain, bought Volgogradsky Elevator. In the same month news emerged of the establishment of a joint venture by two of the largest international producers of titanium: Russian holding company VSMPO-Avisma and U.S. company Allegheny Technologies. Numerous overseas companies are now looking into the possibility of direct investment in Russia. U.S. agricultural producer Cargill has announced plans to build a sunflower seed oil plant in the Voronezh Region. American tire major Goodyear plans to set up manufacturing facilities in Russia through the creation of collective capacities. In June 2003, an international consortium composed of Royal Dutch Shell and Mitsui & Co Ltd. gave the go-ahead for the investment of $10 billion in the creation of Russia's first ever condensed natural gas plant on Sakhalin. In June 2003, the U.S.-based Overseas Private Investment Corporation announced plans to invest up to $700 million in Russia in 2003 for the creation of a range of joint ventures.

According to the State Statistics Committee, foreign investment in the first half of 2003 totaled $12.7 billion, or one and a half times up on the same period of last year. Direct foreign investment rose 35.3% to $2.5 billion, while other investment, largely composed of loans from overseas enterprises and banks, rose by 60.2% to $10.1 billion.

Chart 1. **Trends in foreign investment in the first half of 2002–2003 ($ million)**

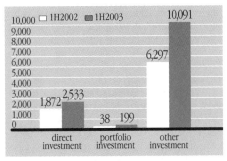

Source: State Statistics Committee

The increase in foreign investment in the Russian economy in the first half of 2003 came on foot of increased foreign investor confidence in Russia, reduced investment risks, and the new-found political and social stability in Russia.

The increase in foreign investment is mirrored by a revival in domestic investment. In the first half of 2003, capital investment rose 11.9% compared with the 2.6% increase seen in the first half of 2002.

Chart 2. **Capital investment growth in January–June 2001–2003, % year-on-year**

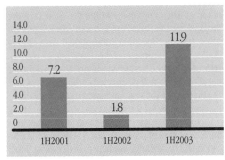

Source: State Statistics Committee

The following factors contributed to the upturn in investment activity in corporate Russia in the first half of 2003:

• High fuel and non-ferrous metals prices on the world markets, leading to greater profit margins in export-oriented industries and increased capital expenditure;

• The improved financial situation in the real sector. The first half of 2003 saw a 76.2% increase in the combined profits of Russian corporations, enabling enterprises to increase capital expenditure financed from own resources.

APPENDICES

POLITICAL AND
SOCIAL STABILITY

Political and social stability combined with improved economic fundamentals saw a marked improvement in the investment climate in Russia in the first half of 2003. The course of actions adopted by Russian President Vladimir Putin with a view to improving the political and economic situation within the country has found widespread support among the international community and within Russia. According to the results of a survey conducted by the All-Russian Center for Public Opinion Research, the Russian President enjoys the support of 77% of Russians.

The first half of 2003 saw an all-out drive to improve the efficiency of the federal executive power system. The Presidential Decree On Administrative Reform Measures, 2003–2004 seeks to eliminate unnecessary state regulation, to eradicate duplication of functions and powers among federal executive bodies, and to complete the process of segregation of authority between the federal and regional executive bodies.

The first half of 2003 also saw changes for the better in the social situation: industrial action was down despite an increase in trade union activity, and pensions and the statutory minimum wage were gradually rising. Real income was also on the rise: during the first half of 2003, real disposable income rose by 14.7% compared with 10.1% in the first half of 2002. Some 700,000 new jobs were created, bringing the active population up to 65.9 million. The number of unemployed fell by 550,000 in the first half of the year, bringing real unemployment down to 8.5% of the economically active population.

The first half of 2003 saw successful implementation of federal programs within the context of the Program for the Social and Economic Development of the Russian Federation in the Middle Term (2003–2005). Work continued on the development and reform of healthcare and education. The total financing allocated to federal targeted social programs in the first half of the year amounted to 40.7% of the maximum limit for the year.

Increased real income combined with the active implementation of programs aimed at developing education and healthcare contribute to better social stability, which translates into an improved economic situation and investment appeal.

ECONOMIC DEVELOPMENT
GDP TRENDS

In terms of its GDP growth rates for the past number of years, Russia is one of the fastest growing economies in the world. According to the Ministry of Economic Development and Trade, Russia's GDP rose by 7.2% in the first half of 2003 compared with 3.8% in the same period of last year. The fastest growing sectors were construction, transport, retail and catering, and industry. Growth in retail and catering was driven by increased real income, while industry growth was

driven chiefly by the favorable price situation on the metals and energy markets and the transformation of external demand into internal (consumer and investment) demand. The upturn in investment activity among Russian corporations fueled growth in the transport and construction sectors.

Chart 3. **GDP growth rate in January–June 2000–2003, % year-on-year**

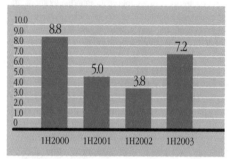

Source: State Statistics Committee, Estimates of the Ministry of Economic Development and Trade of Russia

In his address to the Federal Assembly of the Russian Federation in May 2003, President Vladimir Putin set the goal of doubling GDP by 2010. While this goal is realistic, the economic growth rates recorded in 2001–2003 mean that its accomplishment will require Russia's GDP to grow by at least 8.2% a year between now and 2010. The achievement of that level of growth will depend on the implementation of a range of structural and economic reforms in banking, pensions, the reduction of red tape, and the ongoing reduction of the tax burden. Accelerated GDP growth will also depend on the development of high added value sectors such as machine engineering and metal processing, electronics, and high-tech industries. Combined with effective economic reforms, this should alleviate Russia's dependency on world oil prices and bring GDP growth up to the required level.

GDP BREAKDOWN

In January–June 2003, **industrial output** rose by 6.8% compared with 3.0% in the first half of last year. The first half of 2003 was marked by the development of high added value sectors, with continued growth in the fuel and ferrous and non-ferrous metals sectors driven by the favorable export environment.

Retail sales rose by 8.9%, in line with the growth rate observed a year earlier. Retail supply was in line with solvent demand: real income in the first half of the year rose by 14.7%.

Agricultural output fell by 0.5% in the first half of 2003 compared with 4.8% growth in the first half of 2002. This downturn came on foot of the disparity in prices and income between the agricultural sector and other sectors of the economy. In the context of economic liberalization, the agricultural sector proved defenseless in the face of monopolized industry sectors. Rural deindustrialization also contributed to the downturn in the agricultural sector: in the first half of 2003, fixed asset disposals in the country's agricultural machinery and tractor fleet exceeded new acquisitions by a factor of 11.

Commercial cargo transport (excluding pipelines) expanded by 8.5% in the first half of 2003 compared with 2.8% in the same period of 2002. Railway cargo transportation rose by 13%, pipeline transportation was up 6.5%, and road transportation grew by 1%. The increase in cargo transportation was accompanied by increased investment in the transport sector: capital investment in the first quarter of 2003 rose by 10.6% to 15.1% of total capital investment in Russia.

INDUSTRIAL OUTPUT

Industrial output rose by 6.8% in the first half of 2003. The fuel sector accounted for around 42% of the growth, with raw materials sectors accounting for 27%, and manufacturing sectors, including machine engineering and metal processing, accounting for 30%. The sector breakdown of industrial output growth underwent positive changes in the first half of 2003 thanks to the increasing share of high added value industries.

Energy. Electricity output rose by 7.1% year-on-year in January–June 2003. Growth in the sector was spurred by increased demand for electricity and heat energy from enterprises in the ferrous metals, machine engineering and metal processing, and transport and housing and communal services sectors. Electricity output was also driven upwards by the colder winter conditions than the year before. Output at nuclear power stations rose by 6.7%, while thermal stations recorded a 9.4% increase in output.

Fuel. The first half of 2003 saw output in the sector rise by 10% year-on-year, the highest growth figure in any industry. High world oil prices were the main driving force behind growth in the fuel sector. The reasons behind this sensitivity to the world energy market environment is no mystery: in the first half of 2003, some 67% of Russia's oil output was exported.

Oil output in the first half of 2003 rose by 11.3% to 196 million tons, while output in the oil processing sector rose by 4.7%. Stable growth in oil output was underpinned by growing domestic demand for certain oil products, including gasoline and lubricants, output of which rose by 4.5% and 12.4%, respectively. Gas industry output rose by 4.9% in the first half of the year, while coal output was up 12.5%.

Chart 4. **Industrial output breakdown for the first half of 2003**

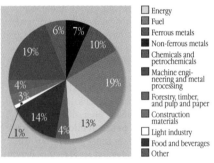

Source: State Statistics Committee

Ferrous metals. Output in the sector in the first half of 2003 rose by 9.5%. Ore output rose by 13.3%, ferrous metals output was up 8.7%, and pipe output increased by 11.7%. Growth in the sector was

Growth rates in the main industry sectors, January–June 2002–2003, % year-on-year	JANUARY–JUNE 2002	JANUARY–JUNE 2003
INDUSTRY	3.2	6.8
Energy	- 2.2	7.1
Fuel	5.6	10.0
Ferrous metals	0.6	9.5
Non-ferrous metals	9.7	6.5
Chemicals and petrochemicals	1.9	4.6
Machine engineering and metal processing	0.9	7.6
Forestry, timber, and pulp and paper	1.9	3.2
Construction materials	4.9	5.6
Light industry	0.3	-0.8
Food and beverages	8.2	4.3

TABLE 1

Source: State Statistics Committee

driven by the improved financial situation of enterprises: in the first half of the year, the own resources balance at enterprises in the metals sector stood at 13% compared with 8% throughout industry as a whole. Growth in the sector was also fueled by increased domestic demand for ferrous metals products from enterprises in the machine engineering and metal processing, transport, and construction sectors.

Non-ferrous metals. Non-ferrous metals output was up 6.5% in the first half of 2003, bringing the sector up to third position behind the fuel and ferrous metals sectors. The growth was mainly driven by increased output of nickel and tungsten: output in the nickel-cobalt subsector rose by 13.1% year-on-year in the first half of 2003, while output in the tungsten-molybdenum subsector rose by 30.2%. Other non-ferrous metals subsectors saw slower growth rates, with aluminum output up 3.2% and output of lead and zinc up 5.1%.

The main factor driving growth in the sector was the favorable environment on the global market for non-ferrous metals. Increased sales margins led to an improvement in the financial situation of enterprises in the sector, which registered a combined profit of $710 million in January–May 2003, or 2.3 times higher than in the same period of 2002. The improved financial situation enabled enterprises to increase capital expenditure on restructuring.

Chemicals and petrochemicals. Output in this sector rose by 4.6% in January–June 2003. The sector lagged behind other industrial sectors in terms of output growth owing to lower profit margins: sales margins in the chemicals and petrochemicals sector in the first half of the year stood at 8.9% compared with 14.5% for industry as a whole.

Machine engineering and metal processing. Growth rates in the sector in the first half of the year outstripped growth in industry output as a whole at 7.6%. Growth in the sector was driven by increased demand for machine engineering and metal processing goods sparked by the upturn in investment by industrial enterprises. Machine engineering output for the metals sector increased by 11.9% in the first half of the year on foot of growth in the ferrous and non-ferrous metals sectors thanks to the improved financial condition of enterprises in those sectors. Machine engineering output for the chemicals and oil sector fell by 10.6% however. The fast growth rates seen in the fuel sector failed to translate into growth in output of machine engineering products for the sector owing to the major role played by imports in satisfying demand for oil production equipment. Imports rose by 20.7% year-on-year in the first half of 2003 to $32.7 billion, with the share of machinery and equipment in the import structure rising from 37.5% to 38.1%.

Growth in this sector is of vital importance both to industrial output and the economy as a whole, as it points to increased investment activity at the enterprise level and, accordingly, represents an indicator of future economic growth.

Light industry. This is the only sector to have registered a downturn in output in the first half of 2003 (output in the first half of 2003 stood at 99.2% of the figure recorded in the first half of 2002). The sector's main problem is the stiff competition posed by imported products. In January–April 2003, enterprises in the sector registered a net loss of $26.5 million.

Food and beverages. Output in January–June 2003 rose by 4.3%, which was lower than the output growth rate for industry as a whole (6.8%). The output growth rate in the sector was down by a factor of two year-on-year owing to increased imports of certain types of food products, notably meat and meat products, poultry, milk, and dairy products.

DEVELOPMENT OF THE FINANCIAL SYSTEM

Russia's financial system continued to improve in the first half of 2003. Increased export revenues saw the country's gold and currency reserves rise by 34.8% to $64.4 billion at the end of June 2003. Rouble liquidity rose as a result: money supply rose by 22.9% in nominal terms over the period compared with the 9.3% increase registered in January–June 2003. Despite excess rouble liquidity, the rouble strengthened significantly in real terms against the dollar, thereby increasing the investment appeal of rouble assets.

REDUCED INFLATION

Curbing inflation is one of the government's priority objectives. The results of the first half of the year show that progress has already been achieved in that area. The Consumer Price Index (CPI) rose by 7.9% in January–June 2003 compared with 9.0% in the same period of last year. Inflation was reined in thanks to additional demand for cash created by economic growth. The introduction of Central Bank monetary policy tools, including transactions on the government securities market and deposits at the Central Bank, also proved effective in the fight against inflation in the first half of the year.

Food price inflation in the period in question clocked in at 7.4%, compared with 4.6% for non-food products, and 15.6% for communal services.

Chart 5. **CPI inflation and CPI inflation breakdown, January–June 2002–2003, %**

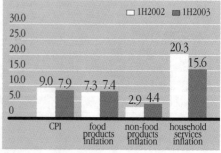

Source: State Statistics Committee

BUDGET EXECUTION RESULTS

The budget for 2003 provides for expenditure at $75.6 billion, or 18% of projected GDP ($421.4 billion), and revenue at $78.4 billion, or 18.5% of GDP, resulting in a budget surplus of 0.55% of GDP.

The budget was executed in the first half of 2003 in line with the budget parameters for the year: budget revenue clocked in at $39.8 billion, with expenditure at $33.9 billion resulting in a surplus of $5.9 billion, or 2.9% of GDP. The surplus was fueled by increased tax collections from industry thanks to the favorable situation on the world oil and metals markets.

In the first half of 2003, tax collections including the unified social tax (UST) rose to 77.8% of total budget revenue.

The federal budget's main expenditure item is financial assistance to regional and local budgets, which accounted for 23.4% of total budget expenditure in the first half of 2003. The share of debt servicing expense in federal budget expenditure fell from 17% to 13.4%.

TAX POLICY AND TAX REFORM

The first half of 2003 saw numerous changes to the tax legislation with a view to reducing the tax burden. Federal laws adopted in the first half of the year will see the value added tax rate reduced from 20% to 18% as of January 1, 2004, and the abolition of sales tax. During its spring 2003 session, the State Duma adopted in the first reading a draft law on the reduction of the unified social tax base rate. Federal Law No. 110-FZ dated July 7, 2003 increased the limit on social deductions for education and healthcare expenditure.

BANKING SECTOR
DEVELOPMENT AND REFORM

The first half of 2003 saw further strides in the development of the Russian banking sector. According to the Central Bank of the Russian Federation, total assets of the banking sector rose by 16% in January–May 2003, bank equity rose by 23%, and client deposits rose by 14.8%, including private deposits, which rose by 17.9%.

The growth in the main indicators of the country's banking system in the first half of 2003 was overshadowed by the continued high lending risk factor. Excess rouble liquidity spurred lending to the real sector on the one hand, but the increase in corporate equity and increased foreign borrowing held back growth in loan demand on the part of the most financially sound borrowers. This led to a 30.4% increase in overdue loans in the lending portfolios of banks in January–May 2003.

In the first half of 2003, the State Duma continued actively discussing draft laws on the reform of the banking system (on private deposit insurance, on credit institutions bankruptcy, and on mortgage securities). A consensus has yet to be reached with respect to certain issues, most notably the draft law on private deposit insurance. This is largely due to the position of the Savings Bank of the Russian Federation (Sberbank) within the deposit insurance system. Sberbank holds a monopoly in the private deposits market, and as such would effectively assume the entire risk inherent in the banking system if compelled to join the deposit insurance system.

The banking legislation package is expected to be adopted by the State Duma during its fall 2003 session.

STOCK MARKET GROWTH

The Russian stock market went from strength to strength in the first half of 2003: the Russian Trading System (RTS) Index yield was 40% for the period compared with 38% for the whole of 2002. On June 25, the RTS Index pierced the 500 points mark. High oil prices were once again the reason behind the growth in the Russian stock market. The share of oil companies in the total capitalization of the Russian stock market now stands at around 70%. Excess rouble liquidity was another growth factor, leading to reduced interest rates on the debt market and a partial reassignment of investments from the bond market to the stock market. The seasonal factor also weighed in: the first half of the year, and April–May in particular, are traditionally good months for the Russian market. This is the time when Russian companies announce their dividend payments on the previous year's results and close their shareholder records. The first half of 2003 was no exception: in April–May alone, the RTS index gained 30%.

The first half of the year saw no major changes in the capitalization structure of the Russian stock market. The market is represented by a small number of industries, the largest of which are oil (70%), power (11%), telecommunications (6.5%), and metals and machine engineering (8%). Poor corporate governance and transparency combined with the underdeveloped nature of the stock market as a whole mean that public listing remains a pipe dream for the majority of Russian enterprises at present.

Chart 6. **RTS Index in 2002 and 1H2003**

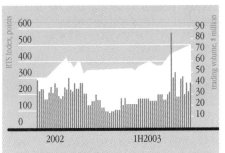

Source: Russian Trading System

FOREIGN TRADE
TRADE BALANCE

The first half of 2003 saw ongoing fast growth in foreign trade between Russia and the CIS and beyond. Russia's foreign trade turnover rose by 27.3% in the period to $95.2 billion, with a positive trade balance of $28.8 billion. Growth in exports outstripped growth in imports, largely thanks to growth in world prices for commodities. Imports continued growing at a fast pace owing to the increased investment activity of industrial enterprises and the increase in real income.

Chart 7. **Core foreign trade indicators, January–June 2001–2003 ($ billion)**

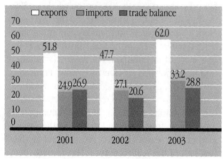

Source: State Statistics Committee

Exports. Exports grew by 29.8% year-on-year to $62 billion in the first half of 2003. Extra-CIS exports grew by 29.1% to $52.5 billion, while CIS exports rose 33.8% to $9.4 billion. The war in Iraq led to reduced supplies of oil to the world markets, keeping fuel prices high. Oil exports rose by 16% year-on-year in the first half of 2003 to 106 million tons. Increased prices for non-ferrous metals, and nickel in particular, led to increased exports among enterprises in the metals sector.

However, the increase in exports was not accompanied by an improvement in their structure, resulting in a further increase in the fuel and raw materials component. Fuel accounted for 61.2% of total exports in the first half of 2003 compared with 56.5% in the same period of last year. Metals accounted for 14.4%, chemicals accounted for 6.8%, and timber and pulp and paper products clocked in at 4.6%. The share of high added value products (machinery and equipment, transport vehicles) in total exports fell in the first half of the year from 7.4% to 5.7%.

Imports. Russia's imports totaled $33.2 billion in the first half of 2003, up 22.8% on the same period of last year. Imports from non-CIS countries rose by 23.4% to $26.7 billion, and imports from the CIS rose by 20.1% to $6.6 billion.

Machinery and equipment accounted for the bulk of imports in the period, accounting for 38.7% of total imports in cost terms, or 1.3 percentage points higher than in January–July 2002. The growth in equipment

Chart 8. **Extra-CIS export breakdown, January–May 2003**

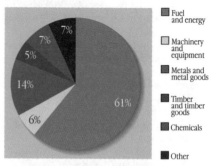

Source: Ministry of Economic Development and Trade of the Russian Federation

imports has both positive and negative implications: on the one hand, increased procurement of equipment on foot of increased investment activity means the renewal of plant at industrial enterprises. On the other hand, equipment import growth is holding back growth in the domestic machine engineering sector, which by numerous parameters is still not capable of offering any real competition in the face of imported products.

The share of chemicals imports in the import total rose by 0.4% to 18.1%. The share of food and beverages and feedstock fell by 2.3% to 23.7%, the share of textiles rose by 1% to 4.7%, and the share of timber and pulp and paper products rose by 0.1% to 4.6%.

Chart 9. **Extra-CIS import breakdown, Junuary–May 2003**

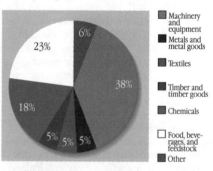

Source: Ministry of Economic Development and Trade of the Russian Federation

GLOBAL ECONOMIC INTEGRATION

The first half of 2003 saw the continuation of efforts aimed at developing cooperation between the Russian Federation and international trade and economic organizations and foreign countries.

Negotiations continued with the member countries of the working group on Russia's accession to the World Trade Organization (WTO). According to the Ministry of Economic Development and Trade, the report on the terms of Russia's WTO accession is 85% finalized. Nevertheless, quite a number of issues remain outstanding for agreement, including the reduction of tariffs for fuel, and natural gas in particular, and measures to protect the domestic market. The gradual resolution of outstanding issues is the best approach for Russia, as such an approach will enable accession on the best possible terms.

Work is continuing on the creation of a common economic area (CEA) between Russia, Ukraine, Kazakhstan, and Belarus with a view to opening up new trade cooperation possibilities between the member countries. The first half of the year saw the development of the basic principles governing economic cooperation between these countries. The agreement on the creation of the CEA is expected to be ready by the time the CIS heads of state meet in September 2003.

In addition to work on integrating Russia into the world economy, the first half of the year saw far-reaching work aimed at improving the legislation governing foreign economic activity. Import quotas were introduced for beef and pork, raw sugar, confectionery, and certain chemicals products with a view to realizing protective measures with regard to foreign trade with non-CIS countries.

June 2003 saw the signing of the new Customs Code, which provides for a liberalized customs regime. The new Customs Code significantly reduces the powers of the customs authorities by providing procedures for all export and import customs formalities, thus rendering the customs regime more transparent and predictable. The new Customs Code will simplify foreign trade activity and reduce administrative costs, which is of vital importance to Russia in the light of its forthcoming accession to the WTO.

NEW LEGISLATION

The first half of 2003 saw the continuation of efforts to improve the Russian legislation with a view to creating favorable conditions for business, improving the tax and financial systems, and regulating foreign trade activity.

Improving the financial system. In the first half of 2003, a draft law On Insuring the Deposits of Private Individuals at Banks in the Russian Federation was submitted to the State Duma. The purpose of the law is to increase the resource base of banks. The first half of the year also saw the signing of the Federal Law On Currency Regulation and Currency Control, which provides for liberalization of the rules governing the import and export of foreign currency.

Supporting domestic industry and regulating foreign economic activity. In the first half of 2003, the State Duma adopted in the first reading a draft law On the Fundamentals of State Regulation of Foreign Trade Activity; and the State Duma adopted in the second reading a draft law On Special Protective, Anti-Dumping and Compensatory Measures Regarding

the Import of Goods, which simplifies the procedures followed in anti-dumping investigations.

Social protection. The State Duma adopted in the third reading a Federal Law On the Minimum Statutory Wage; and the law On the Fundamentals of Federal Housing Policy was signed.

Improving the tax system. In the first half of 2003, a Federal Law On the Introduction of Amendments and Additions into Part Two of the Tax Code was signed.

SOCIAL AND ECONOMIC DEVELOPMENT FORECAST FOR RUSSIA IN 2003[1]

Russia's economic development indicators for the first half of 2003 suggest that 2003 is going to be a better year for the Russian economy than last year. The Ministry of Economic Development and Trade expects 2003 GDP to hit 5.9% compared with 4.3% in 2002. In 2003, industrial output growth is also expected to coincide with GDP growth at 5.9% thanks to the rapid development of the transport and retail sectors. In industry, the fuel sector is expected to become the growth leader, with output growth in the sector expected to reach 7.9%. Ferrous metals output is expected to grow by 7% thanks to growing demand both within Russia and overseas. Machine engineering and metal processing output is expected to rise by 6% in the course of the year.

The foreign economic environment is expected to remain favorable for Russian exporters in the second half of 2003. 2003 exports will rise by 16.4% year-on-year to $124.9 billion, while imports will rise by 16.4% to $71 billion.

Chart 10. **Core foreign trade indicators, 2001–2003 ($ billion)**

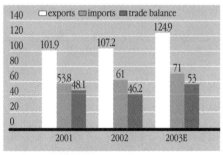

Source: State Statistics Committee, Ministry of Economic Development and Trade estimates

Fixed capital investment growth rates are expected to decline in the second half of 2003, with capital investment expected to rise by 9.3% for the year as a whole. Direct foreign investment will rise by 62.5% year-on-year to $6.5 billion.

[1] Source: Ministry of Economic Development and Trade estimates, estimates of the Russian Academy of Sciences Institute of Economics

APPENDICES

Growth rates by industry sector, 2001–2003			TABLE 2
	2001	2002	2003E
INDUSTRIAL OUTPUT	4.9	3.7	5.9
Energy	1.6	-0.7	4.4
Fuel	6.1	7.0	7.9
Ferrous metals	-0.2	3.0	7.0
Non-ferrous metals	4.9	6.0	5.5
Chemicals and petrochemicals	6.5	1.6	4.6
Machine engineering and metal processing	7.2	2.0	6.0
Forestry, timber, and pulp and paper	2.6	2.4	4.0
Construction materials	5.5	3.0	6.5
Light industry	5.0	-3.4	0.0
Food and beverages	8.4	6.5	4.4

Source: State Statistics Committee, Ministry of Economic Development and Trade

Chart 11. **Capital investment growth rates in 2001–2003, %**

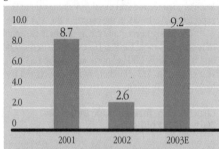

Source: State Statistics Committee, Ministry of Economic Development and Trade estimates

Chart 12. **Inflation in 2001–2003, %**

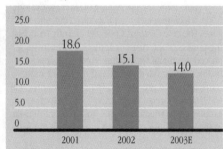

Source: State Statistics Committee, Ministry of Economic Development and Trade estimates

Despite the government's active policy of combating inflation, it remains arguable whether or not inflation for the year will exceed the 10–12% built into the budget. The government is proceeding on the basis that the budget target is attainable, although the results of the first half of the year show that attaining that target may turn out to be difficult. The fall and winter months traditionally see an inflationary spike as budget funded organizations go on a spending spree. Inflation is also driven upwards by the increa-

sed money supply, which tends to have a 3–6 month lag effect. According to the Russian Academy of Sciences Institute of Economics, 2003 inflation may reach 14% compared with 15.1% in 2002.

The budget execution results for the first half of 2003 make it possible to forecast with confidence that the year-end budget surplus will be significantly in excess of the surplus built into the budget (0.6% of GDP). The extra treasury income from high oil prices should push the 2003 budget surplus up to 1.4% of GDP.

THE TAX SYSTEM OF THE RUSSIAN FEDERATION (AS AT SEPTEMBER 1, 2003)

GENERAL

Russia's tax system has undergone major changes since the country first began to lay the basis of a modern tax system back in 1991. January 1, 1999, marked the introduction into force of Part I of the RF Tax Code, which establishes the general principles, rules and procedures to be followed by the tax authorities and taxpayers.

Certain sections of Part 2 of the RF Tax Code have already taken effect. The chapters on value added tax, excise tax, personal income tax and the unified social tax took effect on January 1, 2001. The chapters on profit tax and mineral resource extraction tax took effect on January 1, 2002. The section of the RF Tax Code governing special tax regimes took effect on January 1, 2003. This section provides for a simplified tax regime, a unified tax on imputed income for certain forms of activity and the taxation of agricultural producers, and includes a section governing local tax procedures.

Another positive result of the evolution of Russia's tax system has been the recognition of Russia's international tax responsibilities by the Russian tax authorities and the expansion of the number of double taxation avoidance treaties signed by Russia. Russia is currently party to 56 such treaties, including those concluded by the former Soviet Union and honored by the Russian Federation. A further thirty are at various stages of the negotiations and ratification process.

Russia's State Duma is due to review in 2003 a swathe of new tax laws introduced by the Russian Government. These laws are aimed at improving the country's tax system and reducing the overall tax burden, including via a liberalized tax regime for small enterprises, a reduction in the unified social tax rate, and the improvement of the simplified tax system. Other legislation due to take effect includes laws governing tax aspects of property relations and the use of natural resources.

TAX SYSTEM STRUCTURE

The structure of Russia's tax system provides for tax revenues for three budgetary tiers: federal, regional, and local. Legislation introducing, amending and abolishing taxes, setting rates and providing exemptions is enacted at the federal level. With respect to regional and local taxes, however, regional and local governments have the power to establish rates within the limits provided by federal law, to establish settlement procedures and deadlines, to determine reporting procedures, and to grant exemptions to certain categories of taxpayer.

The following is a summary of the major taxes and levies payable by businesses and individuals in the Russian Federation.

Federal taxes
- Profit tax
- Value added tax (VAT)
- Excise taxes on certain goods (services) and certain types of minerals.
- Personal income tax
- Unified social tax
- Customs duty and levies
- Government duty
- Mineral resource extraction tax

Regional taxes
- Property tax
- Sales tax
- Tax on gambling
- Transport tax

Local taxes
- Advertising tax
- Land tax
- Inheritance tax or gift tax

Moreover, the RF Tax Code allows for federal, regional, and local licensing duties.

CERTAIN ASPECTS OF THE LEGISLATIVE FRAMEWORK

The introduction into force on January 1, 1999, of Part I of the RF Tax Code led to a substantial curtailment in the number of tax laws on the statute books. Most articles of the Law on the Fundamentals of the Tax System of the Russian Federation lost effect. The introduction into force of certain sections of Part II of the RF Tax Code of the Russian Federation effectively made redundant those sections of the federal laws and instructions of the Ministry for Taxes and Duties that dealt with the taxes in question. At September 1, 2003, Russia's legislation on taxes and duties comprised the RF Tax Code of the Russian Federation and federal, regional and local laws passed in pursuance thereof. Some tax issues are governed by Methodological Recommendations and Letters issued by the Ministry for Taxes and Duties.

ANTI-AVOIDANCE LEGISLATION

Russia's anti-avoidance legislation is mainly based around the transfer pricing regulations, which took effect on January 1, 1999, with the entry into force of Part I of the RF Tax Code. Under these regulations, the tax authorities have the right to adjust the price of transactions between related parties, barter transactions, foreign trade transactions, and in relation to goods sold where the prices varied by more than 20% of the prices set by the taxpayer for similar (homogenous) goods within a short period of time. In the above event, the tax authorities have the right to issue a substantiated ruling adjusting the transaction price for tax purposes to the market price level and levy a penalty.

APPENDICES

TAX PENALTIES

The penalty regime underwent substantial changes with the introduction of the RF Tax Code in 1999, and has generally become more liberal. The RF Tax Code stipulates a variety of tax violations with various penalties for each violation. Underpayment of taxes, for example, entails a penalty of 20–40% of the underpaid tax amount. Late filing of a tax return carries a penalty of 5–10% per month of the unpaid tax. Failure to withhold tax entails a penalty of 20% of the tax for the tax agent.

Other penalties are provided for late registration and for failure to provide information requested by the tax authorities in accordance with the law, etc.

Interest for late payment of taxes is charged at 1/300 of the refinancing rate of the Central Bank of Russia (November 4, 2000, through April 8, 2002 – 25%, April 9, 2002, through August 6, 2002 – 23%, since August 7, 2002 – 21%, since February 17, 2003 – 18%, and since June 21, 2003 – 16%) per day.

Underpaid tax and interest can be collected by the tax authorities without the agreement of the taxpayer and without a court order. However, penalties can only be collected on the basis of a court order.

TAX REFUNDS

The law allows taxpayers to apply for refunds of overpaid tax. Refunds are made within one month of the approval of the refund by the tax authority.

TAX ADMINISTRATION

Tax administration is carried out by the tax authorities and other bodies authorized to administer taxes within their respective competencies, such as customs bodies and non-budgetary funds with respect to tax and duty payers and tax agents.

TAX ADMINISTRATION BODIES

The Ministry for Taxes and Duties and its local branches is the tax authority of the Russian Federation.

In certain cases stipulated by the RF Tax Code, customs bodies and non-budgetary funds are authorized to perform taxation functions.

The Tax Police set up in 1993 was dissolved as of July 1, 2003, and its functions were transferred to the Ministry of Internal Affairs. Pursuant to the amendments to the RF Tax Code, police may participate in field tax audits carried out by tax authorities. Moreover, if tax authorities find criminal tax violations they must inform the police in order to institute criminal charges.

CORPORATE TAXPAYERS

Registration requirements

The RF Tax Code requires every legal entity to register with the tax authorities at its place of location and in every region in which it has a branch, representative office, other separate sub-division, real property, or vehicles subject to registration.

A foreign legal entity is required to register with the tax authorities in each region in which it carries out entrepreneurial activities for more than 30 days

in any one calendar year, or where it has real property or vehicles. A simplified registration procedure is open to foreign legal entities that are not engaged in activity in the Russian Federation but that have property in Russia or wish to open a rouble account at a Russian bank. A foreign legal entity must notify the tax authorities in each region in which it has a source of income. Notification must also be sent to the tax inspectorate responsible for the location in which the foreign legal entity has movable property.

Tax returns and assessments

Companies are obliged to file monthly or quarterly returns depending on the tax and the company's business activity. Taxes are paid monthly or quarterly, and final settlement is made on the basis of the annual tax return.

Tax audits

The RF Tax Code specifies two types of tax audit: in-chamber and field. The tax audit may cover only a three-year period of taxpayer's activity prior to the year of audit. During in-chamber audits the tax officer verifies the tax computations contained in the tax return and other tax documentation submitted by the taxpayer.

The tax authorities may also perform field audits of companies, which involve a thorough investigation of the accounting, tax and other documentation underlying the tax computations. Field audits may not last for more than two months (in certain cases, three months) or cover more than three years prior to the year of audit. The tax authorities are not allowed to audit the same period twice, except in certain restricted situations.

INDIVIDUAL TAXPAYERS

Individuals are deemed resident in Russia for tax purposes if present in the Russian Federation for at least 183 days in the calendar year. Resident individuals are taxed on their worldwide income. Non-resident individuals are taxed on income received from sources in the Russian Federation only.

Employer withholding obligations

Personal income tax is withheld at source by employers, acting as tax agents, on all forms of compensation paid to the individual (employees and contractors, except for contractors who are duly registered as individual entrepreneurs). According to the current legislation, responsibility for acting as a tax agent lies with Russian legal entities, individual entrepreneurs, and permanent representations of foreign legal entities doing business in Russia and paying compensation to individuals. In addition to withholding obligations, employers are obliged to notify the tax authorities of the amount of compensation paid and the amount of tax withheld and transferred, and of instances whereby taxes cannot be withheld.

Tax returns

Pursuant to the current legislation, special categories of taxpayers are required to file tax returns by April 30 of the year following the tax year and pay personal income tax. These are:

- Self-employed individuals who have not formed a legal entity, and are engaged in private practice;
- Individuals who are in receipt of income paid by other individuals who are not deemed to be tax agents;
- Resident individuals in receipt of income from overseas;
- Individuals whose income was not taxed at source by a tax agent.

Personal income tax withheld by a tax agent is deducted from the final tax liability for the year.

Taxation of foreign individuals

Pursuant to the current legislation, the procedure for the assessment and payment of personal income tax for foreign individuals is identical to that applicable to Russian nationals, except where the foreign individual is not a resident in Russia for tax purposes or has been seconded to Russia, and in instances whereby a double taxation avoidance treaty applies.

TAXATION OF CORPORATIONS
PROFIT TAX
Tax base. Highlights

Corporate profits are subject to profit tax. Expenses incurred in connection with the generation of income from the sale of goods, work, services, and material rights, in addition to non-operating income, are deducted from the income to arrive at the taxable income.

Russian legal entities are taxed on their worldwide income. Foreign legal entities are taxed on their income from sources in Russia.

All Russian legal entities are obliged to maintain accounting records pursuant to the accounting regulations. Effective January 1, 2002, Russian legal entities are required to maintain a tax accounting system in parallel with their Russian accounting system for the purpose of determining the profit tax base.

Effective January 1, 2002, income and expenditure are recognized using the accrual method for profit tax purposes, i.e. income and expenditure are recognized in the period in which they arise, regardless of when the transaction is actually settled. An exception is made for a small group of taxpayers, who are still entitled to use the cash method. The tax year coincides with the calendar year.

Until January 1, 1999, branches of Russian legal entities having their own bank accounts and maintaining their own separate balance sheet were deemed separate taxpayers. Since Part 1 of the RF Tax Code took effect, branches and other separate divisions are no longer deemed to be separate taxpayers, and are now responsible only for paying the parent organization's tax liabilities to the budget of the tax district in which they are situated.

Profit tax rate

Profit tax is levied at 24% on all taxpayers. Tax on dividends received from Russian companies by Russian companies and individuals resident for tax purposes is levied at 6%. Dividends received by foreign organizations from Russian organizations and vice-versa are taxed at a rate of 15%. The rate of tax on dividends received by foreign shareholders may be reduced or cancelled completely pursuant to the Russian Federation's double tax avoidance treaties.

In accordance with the current legislation, profit tax is remitted to the three tiers of the budget in the following proportions:

- Federal budget – 6%;
- Regional budget – up to 16% (not less than 12%);
- Local budget – 2%.

Deductible expenses

Until the adoption of Part II of the RF Tax Code, expenses were only deductible if specifically listed in the relevant legislation. An expense had to be properly documented in order to be allowable, and insufficient documentation was often a reason for disallowance of an expense for tax purposes.

The Profit Tax chapter of the RF Tax Code represents a major step forwards in improving the rules on deductibility for tax purposes. The new rules significantly expand the list of deductible expenses. Effective January 1, 2002, organizations are allowed to deduct economically justified and documented expenses incurred for the purpose of carrying out activities aimed at deriving a profit. The supporting documents must be executed in accordance with the Russian legislation. The RF Tax Code provides a list of non-deductible expenses and expenses with limited deductibility. There are some restrictions on the deductibility of some expenses, including the following:

- Insurance expenses are deductible within certain limits; not all types of voluntary insurance are deductible;
- Certain types of advertising expenses are deductible up to a limit established as a percentage of turnover;
- Loan interest may be deductible under certain conditions up to an established limit;
- Business trip expenses are only deductible within established limits;
- Entertainment expenses are only deductible up to a limit expressed as a percentage of payroll.

Depreciation for tax purposes

On January 1, 2002, a new procedure for the calculation of depreciation expense allowing for tax deductions came into effect. Depreciable property consists of fixed and intangible assets owned by an organization, used for the generation of income, and having a useful service life of more than 12 months and a historic cost of more than RUR 10,000 ($331.5). The new rules provide for the possibility of using either the straight line or reducing balance method. Depreciable property is classified into ten groups depending on service life in accordance with the Fixed Assets Classifier approved by the Government of the Russian Federation.

APPENDICES

Intangible assets are amortized over the life of the asset. If the life of the asset cannot be determined with an adequate degree of certainty, it is fixed at ten years for tax purposes.

Tax depreciation is accrued on a monthly basis starting with the month following the date at which the asset was put into service until the first date of the month following the month of full depreciation or disposal of the asset.

Timing of profit tax payments

Profit tax is paid on a cumulative basis with monthly advance payments calculated either based on the previous quarter's profit tax or the actual profit received year to the end of the corresponding month. Companies are allowed to select the procedure for paying the monthly advance payments. Advance payments are made on the 28th day of the month following the reporting month. Under the monthly payments system, tax returns based on actual profits are submitted within the same deadlines. Under the quarterly system of payments based on the estimated profit of the company for the previous quarter, a quarterly report must be filed by the 28th day of the month following the end of the quarter. The annual tax return is filed by March 28 of the year following the reporting year, and the final tax payment must be made within the same deadline.

As of September 1, 2003, foreign legal entities operating in the Russian Federation via permanent establishment are required to follow the schedule for tax payments and returns established for Russian legal entities.

Losses carried forward

Currently, organizations are allowed to carry forward losses for tax purposes for 10 years following the loss year. However, a loss carried forward may not exceed 30% of the tax base of the tax period to which it is carried. In the event of reorganization, the losses of the "old" company may be carried forward by its successor to future periods.

Profit tax exemptions

The profit tax exemptions provided under the previous legislation were abolished effective January 1, 2002. The rights of the regional and local authorities to grant profit tax exemptions on the portion of the tax allocated to their budgets have also been restricted. Exemptions may only be established with respect to the "regional" rate, which cannot be reduced by more than four percentage points (from 16% to 12%).

Special provisions

Certain types of businesses, gambling for example, are taxed under special rules and are not subject to the general profit tax provisions. Regional authorities are entitled to introduce a tax on imputed income within their jurisdictions for legal entities and individual entrepreneurs carrying out activities in certain sectors, including retailing, public catering, household services, transportation, renovation services, and car servicing and washing,

provided that the enterprise does not employ more than a certain number of employees and provided certain other criteria are met. Imputed income is determined on the basis of a basic earnings formula provided by law for various forms of activity and physical indicators characterizing the nature of the business environment. The rate of tax is established at 15% of imputed income. Payers of the unified tax on imputed income are relieved of the obligation to pay value added tax, sales tax, profit tax (personal income tax for entrepreneurs), property tax, and the unified social tax in regard to activities subject to the unified tax on imputed income.

Enterprises and entrepreneurs that meet certain requirements as regards employee numbers, total annual income, and value of fixed assets, may apply to be placed under the simplified tax system. The five taxes listed above are replaced by a unified tax on income or income less expenses. At January 1, 2003, the unified tax rate was established at 6% on income or 15% on income less expenses.

Taxation of foreign legal entities

Tax registration requirements

A foreign legal entity carrying out or intending to carry out a business activity in Russia for more than thirty days in a single calendar year is obliged to register with the tax authorities at its place of business regardless of whether or not the activity is taxable. Moreover, if a foreign legal entity has business activities in several regions throughout Russia, the entity must register in each region individually.

Taxation of income received in the Russian Federation via a permanent establishment

Foreign legal entities (their representative offices and branches) are taxed on income received from sources in the Russian Federation. In general, taxation of profits is limited to those attributable to a permanent establishment (PE). A PE is defined by law as a "branch, sub-division, office, bureau, agency or any other place through which a foreign legal entity regularly carries out its business activity in the Russian Federation", which relates to certain activities listed in the RF Tax Code.

A foreign legal entity is deemed in accordance with the current tax legislation to have set up a PE if it conducts business in Russia via a representative. A representative is defined as a Russian legal entity or individual who represents the interests of the foreign legal entity in the Russian Federation on the basis of a contract, acts on behalf of the foreign legal entity, and has authority to conclude contracts on behalf of the foreign legal entity or to negotiate significant terms of contracts.

Establishments and branches of foreign legal entities are subject to substantially the same profit tax regime as Russian legal entities. In cases where it is not possible to calculate profit directly, an indirect method may be used. Pursuant to the RF Tax Code, an indirect method may only be used to calculate taxable profit if a foreign legal entity provides preparatory and/or ancillary services without charge to a third party, resulting in the setting up of a PE. In such cases, the taxable profit is deemed to be 20% of the expense incurred by the PE in connection with the performance of such activities.

PEs are entitled to deduct their expenses from their income. Deductible expenses for profit tax purposes are determined in accordance with the procedures applicable to Russian legal entities.

The requirement to maintain tax accounting records applicable to Russian legal entities also applies to PEs and branches of foreign legal entities.

Taxation of income of foreign legal entities received other than via a PE

Withholding tax rates where a foreign legal entity has no PE in Russia and is not protected by a double taxation avoidance treaty are as follows:

- 10% in relation to income from the leasing or sub-letting of ships and aircraft and/or transportation vehicles and international shipping containers, and income from international freight services.
- 15% in relation to dividends and income from participation in enterprises with foreign investment, and income on interest-bearing state and municipal securities;
- 20% in relation to income in the form of profit or property allocated to a foreign organization, income on other debentures issued by Russian organizations, royalties on the use of intellectual property rights in the Russian Federation, income from the leasing or sub-letting of property in the Russian Federation, including income on leasing transactions and other similar income;

These rates may be reduced under the terms of a relevant double taxation avoidance treaty. Treaty protection may be claimed without obtaining advance permission from the Russian tax authorities if evidence is provided to the tax agent that the foreign legal entity is permanently resident in a jurisdiction with which Russia has signed such a treaty.

Taxation of shareholders

Domestic corporate shareholders

All dividends paid to a Russian legal entity by its Russian subsidiary are taxed at 6%. The tax is withheld at source. Dividends received in the current period by the tax agent paying the dividends are deductible from the tax base for dividends payable to domestic shareholders.

Foreign shareholders

All dividends paid to a foreign legal entity are taxed at 15% except where double taxation avoidance treaty protection is available, in which case the tax may be substantially reduced or cancelled.

VALUE ADDED TAX

General principles

Sales of goods and services within Russia and imports of goods into Russia are subject to value added tax (VAT). Exports of goods and certain services are exempt from VAT.

The current legislation provides special procedures for determining the place of sale of work and services in order to determine whether they are subject to VAT or not. For example, purchasers of services of a consultancy nature, or services related to patent, license or similar rights, rendered to an entity which has the Russian Federation as its place of economic activity, are subject to VAT. Work and services performed with respect to immovable property located in the Russian Federation are also subject to VAT. Work and services involving movable property are subject to VAT if rendered in the Russian Federation.

Under the current legislation, branches are not independent VAT taxpayers, since they only carry out the parent organization's tax liabilities.

Rates and taxable base

Exports of goods from Russia are subject to VAT at 0%.

Certain foodstuffs, children's goods, medicines and medical devices, and educational, scientific and cultural periodicals and books, are subject to VAT at a rate of 10%.

All other goods, work and services are subject to VAT at 20%. Pursuant to Law No. 117-FZ of July 7, 2003, effective January 1, 2004, the base VAT rate will be reduced to 18%. Depending on the transaction type, VAT is calculated on the following tax bases:

Imports

VAT is charged on the value applied for customs purposes (including delivery, insurance and other expenses linked with cross-border shipment) plus customs duty and excise taxes. Certain medical goods, as well as equipment, components and spare parts imported as a charter capital contribution, are VAT-exempt.

Manufacturing, wholesale trade, retail, and service operations

VAT collected from purchasers is paid to the tax authorities net of input VAT paid to suppliers of goods, materials, services, etc. Input VAT is only credited if the goods and services are actually received and the relevant VAT, including import VAT, has been paid. For a limited number of transactions, VAT is charged at 20/120% (or 10/110%) on the gross-VAT tax base. Examples include the sale of fixed assets and imported goods exempted at acquisition or import.

Loan interest

Interest on cash loan finance is exempt from VAT.

However, interest (discount) on promissory notes, interest on bonds received in consideration for goods and services sold, and interest on commercial credits are subject to VAT to the extent that the interest in question exceeds the RF Central Bank's refinancing rate.

VAT to suppliers and contractors

VAT paid to suppliers and contractors for inventories, work and services acquired in connection with

APPENDICES

the performance of a VATable activity may be credited. Input VAT in relation to business trip expenses may be credited subject to the same limitations as apply in the case of profit tax. Input VAT corresponding to VAT exempt sales is not credited, but rather charged to the cost of the goods, work or services acquired. VAT paid to construction firms in relation to construction projects may be credited once the constructed object has been put into service.

General exemptions

Apart from the import transactions described above, VAT exemptions also apply to banking and insurance transactions with certain exclusions, the circulation of securities, medical services (per the established list), the leasing of premises to foreign nationals and representative offices of overseas companies accredited in the Russian Federation provided that their country of origin provides reciprocal arrangements for Russian nationals and firms, etc. No input VAT credit is normally available in these cases, and the VAT is charged to the cost of acquisition. VAT exemption with respect to transactions subject to licensing is available provided the relevant license has been obtained.

The taxpayer has the right to waive certain VAT exemptions.

Tax returns and timing of tax payments

VAT is paid on a monthly or quarterly basis depending on the taxpayer's quarterly sales figures. Tax returns are filed before the 20th day of the month following the expired tax period. The tax is paid by the same deadline.

EXCISE TAXES

Excise taxes are levied on a variety of consumer goods (including alcoholic beverages, beer, tobacco, cars and motorcycles, etc.), and oil products (gasoline, lubricants) and natural gas.

Excise taxes apply to the sale of excisable goods produced or processed in Russia (with some exceptions), imports of excisable goods, contributions of excisable goods to the charter capital of organizations, use of excisable goods for the internal needs of the manufacturer, and some other operations. The transfer of excisable goods between sub-divisions of an organization for use as a raw material in the manufacturing of other excisable goods is not an excisable transaction.

Effective January 1, 2003, the production and acquisition of oil products is excisable.

Export sales of excisable goods are exempt from excise with the exception of natural gas exports.

For most excisable goods (including imported excisable goods), the excise tax rate is set as a fixed ruble amount per unit of measurement (fixed rate).

On July 7, 2003, the Federation Council approved a law, which, inter alia, establishes the indexing of excise tax rates for certain excisable goods and abolishes excises for natural gas while simultaneously by increasing natural gas production tax rate and natural gas export duties effective January 1, 2004.

SALES TAX

The current legislation provides regional authorities with the right to establish a sales tax. Sales tax has been introduced in numerous regions, including St. Petersburg and Moscow. Sales tax is levied on the sales price (including VAT and excise) of goods, work and services sold to individuals for cash or credit/debit card settlement. The tax rate can be set by the regional authority up to a maximum rate of 5%. Sales tax is not levied on banking or insurance services, securities, real estate property, children's goods, bread, milk, medicines, and certain other essential goods and services as defined by the RF Tax Code.

The sales tax has been abolished effective as of January 1, 2004.

CUSTOMS DUTY

Customs duty rates vary from 5% to 30% of the customs value of goods liable to customs duty. Customs duty is paid before or at the moment of customs clearance. The base rates provided by the legislation apply to countries that have been granted Most Favored Nation status. Certain goods from developing countries and least developed countries are liable to customs duty at 75% of the base rate and 0%, respectively. Goods imported from other countries and goods for which the country of origin cannot be determined are subject to customs duty at twice the base rate. The classification of customs codes corresponds to the worldwide system of tariff headings.

Foreign nationals are entitled to duty-free temporary import of goods for their personal use. Such goods cannot be used for production or commercial purposes, and must be re-exported. Cars may be imported duty free for up to one year.

Goods (equipment) may be imported temporarily (usually for up to two years), in which case periodic customs payments are charged at 3% per month of the total duty that would be payable if the goods were imported for free circulation. Periodic customs payments are not refunded once the goods are re-exported. In the case of goods originally imported under the temporary regime which are then declared as for free circulation, the periodic customs payments may be credited against the final customs liability.

An exemption from customs duty applies to foreign investors' in-kind contributions of fixed assets of a production designation to the charter capital of a Russian company with foreign investment during the formation of the charter capital.

UNIFIED SOCIAL TAX

Effective January 1, 2001, a unified social tax was introduced. The tax is levied on compensation paid by employers to employees on a regressive scale starting at a rate of 35.6% (for income less than RUR 100,000 ($3,551.1)) sliding to 2% (for income exceeding RUR 600,000 ($21,306.8)). For the regressive scale to be applicable, the accumulated average year-to-date taxable base per employee at the moment of payment of the tax for the expired month must be not less than

RUR 2,500 ($88.8). The tax is shared by the Federal Budget, the federal and territorial compulsory medical insurance funds, and the compulsory Social Security Fund of the Russian Federation. An exemption for the compulsory Social Security Fund portion of the tax is provided in relation to fees paid to individuals working on contract and under copyright and license agreements.

Compulsory Pension Fund contribution accruals are credited against the Federal Budget's portion of the Unified Social Tax for the same period. Compulsory Pension Fund contributions are collected on the basis of a regressive scale of rates sliding from 14%.

In its spring 2003 session, the State Duma approved in the first reading a bill on reducing the base rates of Unified Social Tax and changing its regressive scale effective January 1, 2005. Thus, annual income of up to RUR 50,000 ($1,647.5) is proposed to be taxed at a rate of 30%, while income in excess of RUR 600,000 ($19,769.4) per year would attract a rate of 5%. The State Duma will continue discussing the bill in its fall 2003 session.

OTHER TAXES

Property tax

Russian legal entities, foreign legal entities, their representative offices, branches and other separate subdivisions are liable for property tax. Foreign entities are liable for property tax on the value of their property held in Russia, including property located on Russia's continental shelf and in exclusive economic zone.

Property tax is levied on fixed assets, intangible assets, inventories, and expenses carried on the taxpayer's balance sheet. The scope of the tax also covers capital investments into construction in progress and acquisitions of fixed assets and intangible assets in progress once the timeframe for construction (assembly) provided in the project documentation has expired. Taxpayers compute the tax on the basis of the average annual value of their property. The rate is established by the regional authorities up to a maximum of 2%. In its spring 2003 session, the State Duma approved in the second reading a bill on increasing the maximum property tax rate to 2.2% effective January 1, 2004. The State Duma will continue discussing the bill in its fall 2003 session.

The tax is paid to the authorities in the regions where the parent enterprise and its separate sub-divisions are located. The amount of the tax payable to the authorities at the place of location of a separate sub-division is determined with reference to the value of the fixed assets, materials, and goods pertaining to that sub-division.

Tax on mineral resource extraction

Tax on mineral resource extraction is levied on legal entities and individual entrepreneurs deemed to be subsoil users pursuant to the legislation of the Russian Federation.

The tax is levied on the extraction of mineral resources from the subsoil and from extraction waste. For the purposes of this tax, mineral resources are deemed to be coal, peat, crude hydrocarbons (oil, nat-

ural gas, gas condensate), ferrous, non-ferrous and rare earth metal ores, mined chemicals and non-metallic raw materials, some construction materials, etc.

The tax is levied on the value of the extracted mineral resources, which is computed as the quantity produced multiplied by the sales price realized in the tax period. In certain cases, an estimated value equivalent to the sum of the cost of extracting the mineral resources may be used for the purposes of computing the tax.

Tax on mineral resource extraction is levied at variable rates ranging from 3.8% for potassium salts to 16.5% for crude hydrocarbons.

Transport tax

Transport tax is levied on legal entities and individuals registering taxable transportation vehicles (e.g., cars and trucks, motorcycles, buses, yachts, motor launches, aircraft, etc.). The tax rate is established as a fixed rouble amount per unit of horsepower for the various vehicles. Rates are differentiated depending on the power of the vehicle's motor. For certain categories of transportation vehicle, the tax is levied on the vehicle as a unit.

TAXATION OF INDIVIDUALS
PERSONAL INCOME TAX

Tax residency criteria

An individual is deemed resident in the Russian Federation for tax purposes if physically present in Russia for 183 days in a calendar year.

Resident individuals are taxed on their worldwide and Russian-sourced income in the calendar year. Non-resident individuals are taxed on their Russian-sourced income.

Tax administration

Effective January 1, 2001, personal income tax is levied at a flat rate of 13%. A rate of 6% applies to income received by individuals in the form of dividends on equity stakes in Russian entities. A rate of 30% applies to all Russian-sourced income received by non-residents. Certain types of income received by individuals are taxed at a rate of 35%, including interest on bank deposits bearing interest at a rate exceeding the Central Bank's refinancing rate in roubles or 9% in foreign currency, in addition to insurance compensation on long-term voluntary insurance policies (upwards of five years) in amounts exceeding the total premium contributions multiplied by the Central Bank's refinancing rate.

Income received in-kind, including the provision of a car for personal use, is taxable on the basis of the market value of the goods, work or services received.

Tax deductions

The following categories of deductions from taxable income are allowed:

Standard deductions: a monthly deduction of RUR 400 ($14.2) is available to taxpayers whose income does not exceed RUR 20,000 ($710.2). A similar deduction in the amount of RUR 300 ($10.7) is available for his/her dependants;

APPENDICES

Social deductions: charitable donations and educational and medical expenses are deductible within certain limits. For example, expenses incurred with respect to the education of a taxpayer and/or his/her children and medical care expenses may be deducted up to a limit of RUR 38,000 ($1,195.7) (RUR 25,000 ($786.7) prior to January 1, 2003);

Property deductions: expenses incurred with respect to the acquisition or construction of housing (plus interest on bank loans taken out to finance such transactions) may be deducted up to a maximum of RUR 1 million ($31,466.3) (RUR 600,000 ($18,879.8) prior to January 1, 2003) once in a lifetime. Proceeds of the sale of personal residential property are exempt from personal income tax up to a maximum of RUR 1 million ($31,466.3), or RUR 125,000 ($3,933.3) for other property, provided that the property has been in the taxpayer's possession for up to five and three years, respectively. If the property has been in the possession of the taxpayer for more than five and three years, respectively, the proceeds of a sale are entirely exempt from personal income tax. The taxpayer may apply to avail of deductions for the actual cost of acquiring the property rather than the deduction described above.

INCOME EXEMPT FROM PERSONAL INCOME TAX

- State pensions;
- Compensation for workplace accidents, within certain limits;
- Statutory redundancy payments;
- Unemployment benefits;
- Stipends;
- Disbursals and compensation for health spa and curative treatment funded from social security or corporate net profit;
- Interest on bank deposits up to the refinancing rate for rouble deposits and 9% for foreign currency deposits;
- Certain other forms of income.

Personal income tax on foreign currency income

Foreign currency income is converted into roubles using the exchange rate at the date of receipt for personal income tax computation purposes.

TAX TREATIES

Policy

Russia honors tax treaties concluded by the USSR until replaced by new tax treaties, and is pursuing a policy of renewing existing and concluding new treaties. All of these follow the guidelines of the tax convention model of the Organization for Economic Cooperation and Development (OECD), although the UN model convention for developing countries has had an influence as well.

Withholding taxes

Unless otherwise provided by a tax treaty, a non-resident foreign legal entity is taxed at a rate of 15% on Russian-sourced dividend income, and a 20% tax on income received from copyright, licenses, and services provided in Russia, and certain other forms of income, unless the services in question are connected with the establishment of a PE. Income from freight is taxed at 10%.

When applying to avail of treaty protection, a foreign legal entity must provide the tax agent with confirmation of permanent residency in a treaty country, endorsed by the competent authority of that treaty country. If the confirmation is provided in advance of the receipt of the income, the income may be exempted from withholding tax or the withholding tax rate reduced.

Otherwise the tax is withheld at source and refund procedures must be followed. Refunds are obtained subject to the provision of a declaration of place of residency and a copy of the contract under which the income was paid.

Permanent establishments

Russia's tax treaties provide the following definition of a permanent establishment: "a fixed place of business through which the business of a resident of another country is permanently or periodically carried out". In the absence of a double taxation avoidance treaty, the permanent establishment definition given in the RF Tax Code is applied.

Personal services

Most income received by freelance workers is not taxable in Russia if the beneficiary is a treaty country national, spends less than 183 days in Russia in a calendar year, and/or is not in receipt of a fixed and regular Russia-sourced income. Employment income is taxable except in cases whereby the beneficiary spends less than 183 days in Russia in a calendar year (i.e. is non-resident for tax purposes) and if the activity of the foreign legal entity bearing the remuneration is not connected with a permanent establishment of that employer in the Russian Federation.

Elimination of double taxation

Elimination generally takes the form of a credit for taxes paid to other jurisdictions. Effective January 1, 2001, such credit is only granted for personal income tax if a treaty containing relevant provision is in place.

FOREIGN INVESTMENT LAWS OF THE RUSSIAN FEDERATION (AS AT SEPTEMBER 1, 2003)

Over the past few years, Russia's investment laws have undergone considerable liberalization. The liberalization process has been extended to cover corporate and anti-monopoly legislation as well. The list of activities subject to licensing has been significantly reduced. New legislative and regulatory acts in the fields of tax, arbitration procedural, civil procedural, and land law have been enacted, in addition to a new Law on (Insolvency) Bankruptcy No. 127-FZ of October 26, 2002. These new legislative and regulatory acts are to all intents and purposes free of discrimination against foreign investment and, more importantly, create general conditions conducive to more transparent business in Russia.

1. INVESTMENT LAWS

Investor activities in the Russian Federation are regulated by legislative and regulatory acts that can be classified as follows:

Group A. Legislative acts that regulate Russia's investment climate in general. These include:
- Civil Code of the Russian Federation (Part 1) No. 51-FZ of November 30, 1994;
- Tax Code of the Russian Federation (Part 1) No. 146-FZ of July 31, 1998;
- Law No. 1488-1 of the Russian Soviet Federative Socialist Republic of June 26, 1991, On Investment in the RSFSR;
- Federal Law No. 39-FZ of February 25, 1999, On Investment Activities in the Form of Capital Investments in the Russian Federation;
- Federal Law No. 160-FZ of July 9, 1999, On Foreign Investments in the Russian Federation;
- Law of the Russian Federation No. 948-1 of March 22, 1991, On Competition and the Restriction of Monopolies Operating in the Commodities Markets;
- Federal Law No. 117-FZ of June 23, 1999, On the Protection of Competition in the Financial Services Markets;
- Federal Law No. 13-FZ of January 22, 1996, On the Kaliningrad Region Special Economic Zone;
- Federal Law No. 104-FZ of May 31, 1999, On the Magadan Region Special Economic Zone.

Group B. Legislative acts that regulate specific investment activities, such as:
- Tax Code of the Russian Federation (Part 2) No. 117-FZ of August 5, 2000, Section VIII.1. Special Tax Regimes;
- Federal Law No. 164-FZ of October 29, 1998, On Financial Lease (Leasing);
- Federal Law No. 225-FZ of December 30, 1995, On Production Sharing Agreements;
- Federal Law No. 2395-1 of February 21, 1992,On Subsoil Resources;
- Federal Law No. 39-FZ of April 22, 1996, On the Securities Market;
- Federal Law No. 46-FZ of March 5, 1999, On the Protection of Investor Rights and Lawful Interests in the Securities Market.

Group C. International treaties, including:
- Treaties designed to protect foreign investments. These include treaties on mutual guarantees and the protection of investment, and multilateral conventions. Russia is party to around 50 bilateral treaties on mutual guarantees and the protection of investment, and is a signatory of the Seoul Convention[1].
- Treaties binding participant states to regulate foreign investment. Pursuant to the Agreement on Partnership and Cooperation made between the European Union, the European Union member states, and the Russian Federation[2], Russia has undertaken to observe the international trade rules, including rules on foreign investment regulation, included in the GATT/WTO agreements.

Group D. Legislative acts of the Russian Federation's constituent entities regarding the coordination of actions undertaken by the Federal constituent entities with regard to foreign investment regulation in accordance with the Russian Federation's policies on foreign trade.

Notably, these legislative and regulatory acts do not cover relations with regard to foreign investment in the banking, other credit institutions, and insurance sectors, which are regulated by laws on banks and banking activities and laws on insurance, respectively. Nor do these legislative acts apply to investments into non-commercial institutions, such as educational establishments, charitable institutions, and scientific or religious organizations, which are governed by the laws on non-commercial organizations of the Russian Federation.

Below is a summary of the Federal laws. The purpose of the summary is to demonstrate main approaches to regulation of investment activities in the Russian Federation.

2. LEGAL ENVIRONMENT AND PRINCIPAL GUARANTEES FOR FOREIGN INVESTORS IN THE RUSSIAN FEDERATION

The legal environment in which foreign investors operate has been declared national, i.e. it must not be

APPENDICES

---

[1] Russia ratified the Convention on December 22, 1992.

[2] The Agreement was signed in Corfu in 1993 and Russia ratified it in 1996.

less favorable than the regime applicable to Russian investors, with exceptions as specified in federal law.

Federal law may establish exceptions of a restrictive nature for foreign investors only insofar as this may be necessary in order to protect the fundamentals of the constitutional order, public morality and health, the rights and lawful interests of other persons, and the security and defense of the State. Currently, exceptions of a restrictive nature are established by the Law on Currency Regulation and Currency Control, the Land Code, the Tax and Customs Codes, the Mass Media Law, and other legislative and regulatory acts. However, the trend within the area of currency regulation is towards greater liberalization. At present, business entities with foreign participation are registered on a general, rather than special regime, basis, and foreign investors no longer require a Bank of Russia permit to pay their charter capital contribution.

Broadly speaking, foreign investors now enjoy equal legal status with their Russian peers. Foreign investors[3] in the Russian Federation are afforded full and unconditional protection of their rights and interests as provided by the norms and regulations of Russian civil law. The Russian Federation guarantees that:

- The property of a foreign investor or business entity with foreign investments in its charter capital shall not be requisitioned by force, including nationalization or confiscation, except where such requisition by force is carried out on the basis of a Russian federal law or an international treaty concluded by the Russian Federation.
- A foreign investor is entitled to indemnification for any damages incurred thereto as a result of the illegal actions (inactions) of government bodies, bodies of local self-governance, and officers of such bodies.
- A foreign investor may assign claims and transfer debts by contract in accordance with Russian Federation civil law.
- A foreign investor may invoke a grandfather clause in the event of new federal laws or legislative acts coming into effect that are unfavorable for the foreign investor.
- Disputes involving foreign investors arising in connection with the performance of investment and business activities in the Russian Federation by foreign investors are settled in accordance with the international treaties of

the Russian Federation and federal law in a court or arbitration court, or in an international court of arbitration (court of mediation).

- Foreign investors are entitled to freely dispose without hindrance in the Russian Federation through reinvestment or export of all and any revenue, profit, and other foreign currency amounts[4] legally earned in the Russian Federation from investments previously made by the investor.

At the same time, the guarantees and advantages offered by the Russian legislation, as well as the restrictions placed upon business activities conducted within the Russian Federation, depend on whether the investments qualify as foreign investments.

A foreign investment is an investment of foreign capital into a business entity within the Russian Federation in the form of an object of civil law owned by the foreign investor, unless such object of civil law is prohibited or restricted in the Russian Federation.

The forms a foreign investment may take are defined in keeping with international practice such as: investors' stake at the establishment of a company; the acquisition of a stake, equity, stocks or other securities in an existing company; the registration of a branch of a foreign company; the acquisition of title to land and natural resources; the acquisition of other property rights, and other exclusive title to intellectual property rights expressed in monetary terms, including the results of intellectual activity, services, and information.

Government guarantees are mainly granted to participants in priority investment projects and owners of direct investments. The term "portfolio investment" is not defined separately.

Direct foreign investment includes:

- The acquisition by a foreign investor of at least a 10% stake in the charter capital of a business entity which has been or is being registered in the Russian Federation as a joint stock or limited liability company;
- The investment of funds into fixed assets of a branch of a foreign legal entity being registered in the Russian Federation;
- The leasing out by a foreign investor of any equipment listed in sections XVI and XVII of The Nomenclature of Goods in Foreign Trade Activity having a customs value of at least one million rubles[5].

Priority investment projects include projects that are economically feasible in terms

[3] A foreign investor may be a foreign legal entity, a foreign non-incorporated organization, a foreign national, a stateless person, a foreign state, or an international organization. The nationality of a foreign investor is determined in accordance with the incorporation principal. Russian legal entities controlled by foreign entities, but incorporated under Russian law, do not qualify for foreign investor status.

[4] Other amounts: dividends, interest, liabilities settlement, indemnification resulting from liquidation, and compensation for losses incurred.

[5] Section XVI. Machinery and Mechanical Appliances, Electrical Equipment and Parts, Audio and Video Recording and Reproduction Equipment, and Spare Parts and Accessories.
Section XVII. Vehicles, Aircrafts, Vessels, and Transport Related Devices and Equipment.

of the amount and terms of the direct foreign investment. These include:

- Investment projects for a total amount of foreign investment of at least RUR 1 billion (or the equivalent amount in a foreign currency at the exchange rate quoted by the Central Bank of the Russian Federation at the date of adoption of the law: USD 41,017,227 at July 14,1999);
- Investment projects in which the minimum share (stake) of foreign investors in the charter capital of a business entity with foreign investment is at least RUR 100 million (or the equivalent amount in a foreign currency at the exchange rate quoted by the Central Bank of the Russian Federation at the date of adoption of the law: USD 4,101,722);
- Any other projects included in the List of Priority Investment Projects approved by the Government of the Russian Federation.

The fact that the Russian Government has implemented economical feasibility assessment criteria for foreign investment project evaluation based on priority means that the Government has effectively introduced a foreign investment clearance (registration) procedure (Article 9.5 of the Law On Foreign Investments in the Russian Federation). However, the Russian Government has not yet approved the registration procedure. Therefore, priority is not taken into consideration as regards the granting of various benefits. Accordingly, the grandfather clause does not apply to investment projects that, although covered by the term priority investment project, have not undergone the economic feasibility evaluation procedure.

Since the grandfather clause is one of the best guarantees offered to foreign investors, below we included a detailed analysis of how it can be applied:

Apart from priority investment projects, the grandfather clause is applicable to business entities with foreign investment if the share of foreign investors in the charter capital exceeds 25%.

The grandfather clause may be exercised in the event of any of the following:

- Changes to import customs duties (except for customs duties resulting from actions undertaken to protect the economic interests of the Russian Federation); federal taxes (except excise taxes and VAT on goods manufactured within the Russian Federation); and contributions to state non-budgetary funds (except contributions to the Pension Fund of the Russian Federation);
- An increase in the overall tax burden on a foreign investor or a business entity with foreign investment engaged in a priority investment project;

- The introduction of a prohibition or restrictions with respect to foreign investment in the Russian Federation.

If a foreign investor or a business entity with foreign investment fails to adhere to the terms of the grandfather clause, the benefits granted are terminated. Amounts for which exemptions were granted under the clause must then be repaid.

A grandfather clause is valid until such time as the investment project reaches break-even point, up to a maximum of seven years, provided that goods shipped into the customs territory of the Russian Federation are used as specified for the priority investment project in question. The Government of the Russian Federation may, exceptionally, decide to extend a grandfather clause if the priority investment project concerns manufacturing or creation of transport or other infrastructure, when the total amount of foreign investment exceeds RUR 1 billion and the project is not expected to reach break-even point within a seven year period.

The grandfather clause does not apply to legislative amendments adopted with a view to protecting the constitutional order, public morality and health, the rights and lawful interests of other persons, or the security and defense of the State.

Until such time as the Russian Government approves a priority investment project registration procedure, the stability of the tax regime is guaranteed only to those business entities whose foreign investment share exceeds 25% of the charter capital.

3. SPECIFIC INVESTMENTS IN VARIOUS INDUSTRY SECTORS (SPECIFIC ASPECTS OF FOREIGN INVESTOR ACTIVITIES)

Leasing. The Russian Federation legislation on financial lease (leasing) has been substantially revised and harmonized with the norms of the UNIDROIT[6] Convention of May 28, 1988.

Non-residents may be any parties to leasing transactions, as well as founders of leasing companies. Leasing companies are no longer subject to licensing requirements.

Any non-consumable property, including companies and other property complexes, buildings, installations, equipment, transport vehicles and any other movable and non-movable property that can be used for business purposes, except plots of land and any other natural resource, may be leased.

Title to property leased and/or leasing agreement are subject to state registration provided the types of property to be leased (real estate, aircraft machinery, vessels, etc.) are subject to state registration pursuant to RF law.

APPENDICES

---

[6] lInternational Institute for the Unification of Private Law (UNIDROIT).

Any individual or legal entity, except for non-commercial entities that are not entitled to lease fixed assets, can be a lessee.

Any individual or legal entity that, at its own expense and/or using borrowed funds, purchases any property and leases such property out to a lessee for a certain fee for a certain period of time and under certain terms for temporary ownership and use with or without transfer of the title to such property, may be a lessor.

The lessor's guarantees: The proprietary right to the leased property is vested in the lessor. The lessor alone is entitled to collateralize the property and to assign part or all of the lessor's rights arising from the lease agreement to third parties. The lessor is entitled unilaterally to collect leasing payments from the lessee's bank account should the lessee default on the lease payments per the leasing agreement on more than two consecutive occasions. Title to leased property may transfer to the lessee following the expiration of the lease agreement only if specific provision to that effect is made between the lessor and the lessee in the lease agreement.

The lessee's obligations: The lessee bears all proprietary risks arising from the acceptance of the leased property. The lessee is obliged to insure against liability arising from any damage to third parties' life, health or property resulting from use of the leased property. The lessee may also insure against liabilities arising with respect to any violation of the lease agreement. Third parties cannot file claims on leased property with respect to the lessee's obligations, even if the leased property is registered in the lessee's name.

For accounting purposes, leased property may be listed on the lessor or lessee's balance sheet, depending on the agreement between the parties. The party which lists the leased property on its balance sheet is entitled to apply a special depreciation ratio of not more than three (accelerated depreciation) to the principal depreciation rate. Any other property is depreciated at a ratio of not more than two in accordance with the Russian legislation.

The lessee is entitled to classify lease payments, less depreciation charged, as profit tax deductible business expenses.

Banking. Bank of Russia clearance must be obtained for foreign investor participation in the following events: establishing credit institutions with foreign investments; increasing charter capital via contributions from non-residents; and assigning shares (contributions) to non-residents.

When considering whether or not to approve a transaction, the Bank of Russia takes into consideration the following: the extent to which the Russian banking system's foreign investment quota has been used; the financial standing and business reputation of the prospective non-resident shareholders; and the application filing sequence.

The Bank of Russia is entitled, with the approval of the Russian Government, to set reciprocal limitations on banking operations for credit institutions with foreign investments and branches of foreign banks if the corresponding foreign countries have set limitations on the establishment and operations of banks with Russian investments and branches of Russian banks.

The Bank of Russia is entitled to set additional requirements for credit institutions with foreign investments and branches of foreign banks with regard to statutory norms and regulations, reporting procedures, management approval and banking operations and services, as well as minimum size of the charter capital for credit institutions with foreign investments and branches of foreign banks. Currently, the minimum charter capital requirement for any foreign bank's subsidiary credit institution is equivalent to €5 million.

Insurance. Subsidiaries of foreign insurance companies or insurance companies with more than 49 per cent foreign ownership are prohibited from providing the following services within the Russian Federation: life insurance, compulsory insurance, statutory insurance, property insurance with regard to government procurement contracts, and property insurance for government and municipal organizations.

Once foreign investment participation in the insurance industry exceeds the 15 per cent of total capitalization quota, insurance licenses are no longer issued.

Insurance companies with foreign investments are required to obtain an advance permission from the Ministry of Finance of the Russian Federation (the authority which supervises insurance activities) for the following activities:

• Increasing charter capital by raising funds from foreign investors and/or subsidiaries;
• Assigning shares to a foreign investor (including selling such shares to foreign investors);
• Open branches within the Russian Federation.

Foreign investors may only pay for their shares in insurance companies in the cash form in the currency of the Russian Federation.

Individuals holding the position of CEO or CFO at an insurance company with foreign investment must be Russian Federation nationals.

A subsidiary insurance company is entitled to carry out insurance activities within the Russian Federation only if its holding company has carried out insurance activities for at least 15 years in full compliance with the laws of its country of residence and participated in insurance companies registered in the Russian Federation for at least two years.

Securities. Limitations may be introduced under Russian law on total foreign investor participation in the charter capital of some Russian issuers, first and foremost conversion organizations continuing to conduct scientific and/or production activities involving federal national defense and security. Should a foreign investor purchase such issuers' shares, the parties to the agreement must notify the federal executive authority responsible for the securities market.

Currently, there are limitations with regard to:
- RAO Gazprom – total foreign share at 14 per cent[7].
- RAO UES – total share at 25 per cent of all types of shares[8].

Subsoil resources. Subsoil resources located within the territory of the Russian Federation are Russian state property. Issues of the ownership, use and disposal of natural resources fall under the joint jurisdiction of the Russian Federation and its constituent entities. Subsoil allotments are transferred for use only, and may be alienated or transferred from one entity to another only insofar as federal laws permit such transfer. Foreign business entities are eligible to use natural resources. The use of certain subsoil allotments may be limited or prohibited in the interests of national security and environmental protection.

Subsoil allotments are granted for the purpose of mineral resources extraction for the resource extraction term as determined on the basis of a feasibility study for field extraction conducted to ensure that the subsoil resources are properly used and protected. Subsoil allotments are obtained on the basis of:
- A Russian Government resolution issued on the basis of a tender or auction: for the purpose of mineral resource exploration and extraction from deposits under the Russian Federation's inland seas, territorial waters and continental shelf; and for the purpose of deep burial of radioactive waste and toxic substances, and other hazardous waste materials ensuring localization of such waste;
- A joint resolution of a federal authority or its local subdivision governing the state subsoil resource fund and an executive authority of the relevant Russian Federation constituent entity, issued on the basis of a tender or auction: for the purpose of subsoil resource exploration and extraction within the constituent entity in question; and for the purpose of construction and operation of deep oil and gas reservoirs, and industrial and communal waste disposal;
- An effective Production Sharing Agreement concluded pursuant to the Federal Law On Production Sharing Agreements.

Mineral resource utilization permits are granted in the form of a license.

Title to use of subsoil allotments transfers to another business entity in the event of the following:

- Reorganization of an entity holding a subsoil allotment license;
- Establishment of a new legal entity by an entity holding a subsoil allotment license to conduct the same activities within the granted allotment;
- The acquisition of a bankrupt company's (allotment holder's) properties in accordance with the bankruptcy legislation.

The license is reissued if the title to a subsoil allotment is transferred.

A foreign entity utilizing underground natural resources is deemed to be operating via a permanent establishment, which is deemed to have been registered either at the date of the license (permit) or at the date of actual start-up of operations.

Production Sharing Agreements.
Entering into a Production Sharing Agreement (hereinafter – PS Agreement) made by the Russian Government with a foreign investor forms a basis for obtaining title to use subsoil allotments. The Law On Foreign Investments is not therefore applicable to such investments, provided that the investor enters into a direct agreement with the Government. Below, we review the main provisions of this legislation.

The legislation on Production Sharing Agreements covers the relations arising from Russian and foreign investors' investments into mineral resource prospecting, exploration and extraction within the Russian Federation, on the Russian Federation's continental shelf, and/or within the exclusive economic zone of the Russian Federation.

A PS Agreement is a contract whereby the Russian Federation (represented by the Government or a constituent entity) grants the investor, on a compensatory basis and for a specified term, exclusive rights to prospect, explore and extract mineral resources within the subsoil allotment[9] specified in the agreement, and to conduct all related work. The investor undertakes to conduct the work in question at the investor's own expense and risk.

A PS Agreement is concluded by the Government with a party interested in developing the allotment under the PS Agreement upon a failure of the auction to grant the title to develop the allotment on terms other than PS Agreement, due to the lack of biddens. The Agreement is concluded within one year of the announcement of the results of the tender or auction. The license to the allotment is issued to the investor on production sharing terms within 30 days of signing the PS Agreement.

---

[7] Presidential Decree No. 529 of May 28, 1997, On Trading in RAO Gazprom Shares for the Duration of Federal Ownership of RAO Gazprom. Presidential Decree No. 943 of August 10, 1998, On the Terms of Sale of RAO Gazprom Shares.

[8] Federal Law No. 74-FZ of May 7,1998 On Specific Aspects of Management of RAO UES Shares.
[9] The federal legislation specifies subsoil allotments that may be granted under a Product Sharing Agreement as follows: a subsoil allotment is

included in the list of allotments to be developed under PS Agreement if there is no other possibility to prospect, explore, and extract natural resources from this allotment.

The project output is divided between the Government and the investor in accordance with the PS Agreement terms, which define the following: the total output and the value of the products; the share of compensatory product to be transferred to the investor[10]; and the procedure for dividing surplus product between the State and the investor.

Throughout the period of validity of the agreement, the investor pays only the profits tax and mineral resource royalties. The tax payments comply with the general principles set out for these taxes with the exceptions specified for certain types of products.

Amounts of other taxes and levies paid by the investor, namely value-added and unified social tax, lump-sum payments for the use of mineral and water resources, stamp and customs duties, land tax, excise, and payments for damage to the environment paid by investors are subject to reimbursement.

Investors are exempt from regional and local taxes and duties, and property tax in regard to fixed and intangible assets, inventories and costs on their balance sheets used solely for PS Agreement-related purposes. Investors' means of transport (cars excluded) are exempt from transport tax if used solely for PS Agreement-related purposes.

Goods imported to the RF for PS Agreement-related work specified in work schedules and budgets and duly approved, as well as output produced in compliance with PS Agreements and exported from the RF, are exempt from customs duties.

Raw mineral resources transferred to the investor may be exported from the customs territory of the Russian Federation without quantity export restrictions. Any property created or acquired by the investor and used by the investor to conduct work under the agreement is the property of the investor. Title to such property may be transferred from the investor to the state at the date at which the cost of such property has been fully recovered or at the date of termination of the agreement.

The investor, as well as legal entities (agreement operators, contractors, suppliers, transporters, and other entities) participating in work performed under the agreement on the basis of agreements (contracts) with the investor are not subject to the requirements regarding the mandatory conversion of a portion of foreign currency proceeds from work performed under the agreement.

Investors are entitled to wholly or partially transfer their rights and obligations under agreement to any legal entity or any citizen (individual), subject to the consent of the Government.

The terms of an agreement remain effective throughout the term of its validity (grandfather clause). Changes to the agreement are allowed only with the consent of both parties or at the request of one of the parties in the event of substantial changes in circumstances.

Land. Foreign investors are allowed to own plots of land on a freehold or leasehold basis within the Russian Federation, except for plots of land located in the vicinity of the Russian Federation's international frontiers and in other specified areas of the Russian Federation.

In addition, neither foreign nor Russian investors are permitted to execute transactions involving land plots if such plots of land are:

- Withdrawn from circulation (as state-owned natural reserves and national parks, sites of technical constructions, installations, and communications lines erected for the purpose of securing the international frontiers of the Russian Federation, etc.)
- Limited in circulation (forest reserves, water reserves, sites of cultural monuments, lands allocated for transport needs, including sea and river ports, railroad stations, aerodromes and airports, air traffic control constructions and installations, etc.).

Plots of land are granted to foreign investors as properties for a consideration of a statutory fee.

Foreign investors and legal entities with more than 50 per cent foreign ownership may own agricultural land (plots of land) on a leasehold basis only.

Title to land (plots of land) is acquired on the basis of purchase and sale agreements or leasing agreements and is subject to mandatory state registration in compliance with the Law On the State Registration of Title to Immovable Property and Transactions Therewith.

In addition, the legislation provides for the allocation through auction of federal and municipal land (plots of land) for construction purposes, and for the leasing of such land on the basis of resolutions of federal or local executive bodies.

4. FOREIGN INVESTMENTS AND SPECIAL ECONOMIC ZONES

Russia currently has two special economic zones that offer special beneficial tax treatment to businesses. This special treatment also applies to foreign trade and investment activities.

Kaliningrad Region Special Economic Zone. The Special Economic Zone in the Kaliningrad Region (hereinafter the KSEZ) covers the whole territory of the Kaliningrad Region, except for defense sites that are of high strategic and defense importance for the Russian Federation.

---

[10] The maximum share of compensatory product shall not exceed 75 percent (90 percent of extraction from the continental shelf of the Russian Federation) of total output.

The development of the KSEZ is based on the Federal Targeted Program for Development of the Kaliningrad Region through 2010 approved by the Russian Government. No date has been fixed for the liquidation of the KSEZ. Its status may only be changed on the basis of a special law on the liquidation of the KSEZ. The terms and conditions applicable to investor activities shall survive the enactment of a KSEZ liquidation law for a period of three years.

The KSEZ attracts investment on a contractual basis. The KSEZ's Administration, taking guidance from the Federal Targeted Program for the Development of the KSEZ, considers applications submitted by Russian and foreign investors with regard to regional investment projects and enters into relevant agreements with them.

The Administration is entitled to conduct auctions, and in special cases whereby unique technologies and equipment are offered by the investor, to conduct direct negotiations with specific Russian and foreign investors and businesses with a view to concluding agreements and implementing regional investment projects.

Representative offices and branches of foreign legal entities may be set up within the KSEZ with clearance from the Administration subject to statutory requirements.

Land tenure is granted within the KSEZ to foreign legal entities and individuals and international organizations with the participation of Russian and foreign legal entities and individuals exclusively on the basis of lease agreements (without the right of redemption). Lease agreements are concluded on the basis of free market land leasing tariffs.

With respect to customs duties and other payments (including taxes) payable on imported and exported goods at customs, the KSEZ is treated as a free customs area.

Goods produced within the KSEZ (as confirmed by the certificate of origin) and exported overseas are exempt from customs duties and other payments normally charged at customs (except customs charges).

Goods imported from overseas into the KSEZ are exempt from import customs duties and other payments normally charged at customs (except customs charges, VAT, and excise charged on excisable goods). Certain goods and services may be subject to economic policy restrictions, including quotas. Quotas are imposed on the import of food staples (wheat flour, meat and dairy, canned meat), liquors, tobacco, dragnets and certain construction materials.

Goods are deemed produced within the KSEZ if the processing added value is at least 30 per cent, while hi-tech electronic goods and electrical appliances are deemed produced within the KSEZ if the processing added value is at least 15 per cent, and processing has entailed a change in the customs classification code.

Magadan Region Special Economic Zone.
The Special Economic Zone is located within the city limits of Magadan (hereinafter the MSEZ). A special legal business regime applies within the zone from May 31, 1999, through December 31, 2014.

Individuals and legal entities registered within the Magadan city limits and having proper registration certificates, carrying out their principal business activities and having at least 75 per cent of their fixed assets in the Magadan Region are treated as participants of the MSEZ.

Through December 31, 2005, MSEZ participants are exempt from tax payments to the federal budget (except contributions to the Russian Pension Fund, and excise taxes and VAT on imported excisable goods) when conducting business within the MSEZ and the Magadan city limits. From January 1, 2006, through December 31, 2014, MSEZ participants shall be exempt from profit tax on profits invested in business development and the social sphere within the Magadan Region.

Russian and foreign goods imported by MSEZ participants into the territory of the MSEZ are imported into, disposed of, utilized, and shipped out of the MSEZ in accordance with terms and procedures set for free customs zones.

Foreign goods purchased by MSEZ participants for their own industrial purposes and used in the Magadan Region are exempt from import customs duties and other payments (except customs charges, excise taxes and VAT on excisable goods) when shipped from the MSEZ to other locations within the Magadan Region.

Goods manufactured within the MSEZ and shipped out of the MSEZ to other locations within the Russian Federation or overseas are exempt from customs duties and other payments (except customs charges) charged at customs.

Goods are treated as manufactured within the MSEZ if they were fully manufactured within the MSEZ or processed to a sufficient extent in accordance with the following criteria:

• A change has been made to the product's classification code per The Nomenclature of Goods in Foreign Trade Activity at any of the first four digit levels as a result of the processing of the goods;
• The performance of any industrial or technical operations sufficient or insufficient for treating the goods as originating within the MSEZ;
• A change in the value of the goods, if the processing added value amounts to at least 30 per cent of the initial value of the delivered goods (for electronics or technical appliances – at least 15 per cent).

5. TERMS AND CONDITIONS FOR FOREIGN INVESTORS

Registration of a business entity with foreign investments. Legal entities with foreign investments are subject to state registration pursuant to the Federal Law On State Registration of Legal

Entities. Currently, the said law provides for a uniform registration procedure for domestic legal entities and entities with foreign investments.

The following documents are submitted to the state registration authority for the purpose of obtaining state registration: an application for state registration drafted per the approved form and signed by the applicant; a resolution on the establishment of a legal entity in the form of an agreement, minutes, or any other document; founding documents of the legal entity; an excerpt from the relevant country's register of legal entities or other equivalent legal proof of the legal status of the founding party; and documentary evidence of the payment of stamp duty.

Anti-monopoly laws. Foreign investors are obliged to comply with the anti-monopoly legislation of the Russian Federation and to refrain from unfair competition and restrictive business practices.

Unfair competition and restrictive business practices include: the creation within the Russian Federation of a business entity with foreign investment or branch of a foreign legal entity for the purpose of producing goods in high demand, with subsequent self-liquidation for the purpose of promoting similar goods of foreign origin in the Russian market. Unfair competition practices may result in legal consequences, which, as the case may be, may include the issuance of a resolution by a relevant authority banning or restricting the activities of the foreign investor within the Russian Federation, restoring the rights of domestic producers, and other steps and measures taken with a view to restoring fair competition within the Russian market. In addition, the anti-monopoly authority may intervene in cases whereby a transaction causes more than one third of a specific market to fall under control of a single entity. Transactions with corporate securities amounting to over 20% of the charter capital of a company require prior consent of the anti-monopoly authority.

Property insurance. Any business entity with foreign investments may obtain insurance against loss, impairment or damage to property, in addition to civil liability or business risk insurance, at its own discretion, unless otherwise established by Russian law.

The Russian legislation provides for compulsory insurance for entities engaged in high risk activities: transport vehicle owners, notaries public, medical and pharmaceutical professionals, auditors (as regards statutory audits of companies with state participation), pawn shops and banks (for deposit repayment), arbitration managers, attorneys (as of 2007), surveyors, non-state pension funds, and lessees.

Trends in the development of foreign investment legislation. Broadly speaking, the legislative authorities have demonstrated intention to complete reforming the legislative base governing business activities. The Russian Government's policy aimed at enhancing the investment appeal of the country is focused on stabilizing the existing business regulations.

However, in certain areas the Russian legislation is not yet fully harmonized with international law and practices, indeed this process is now at its peak.

The currency regulation law has been amended. The compulsory currency conversion norm was reduced from 50% to 25%, and the abolition of this requirement in 2007 is being discussed. July 2003 was marked by the adoption of a special chapter of the RF Tax Code governing the tax treatment of product sharing agreements.

January 1, 2004 will see the enactment of a new Customs Code of the Russian Federation that will cover changes of the past few years in the Russian and international legislation. The Code's provisions comply with the International resolution of the Kyoto convention of May 18, 1973 on simplifying and harmonizing customs procedures. Thus, the Code reduces customs declaration and other document and goods processing from 10 to 3 days, sets rigid rules as to the composition and contents of customs documentation, and allows exporters and importers to independently choose a customs clearance location.

Currently, the draft law On Concession Agreements with Russian and Foreign Investors is being prepared; the law has passed the second reading in the State Duma. In addition to the mineral resource sector, the concessions system will also apply to infrastructure industries such as housing and road construction.

The Russian Government has plans afoot to introduce a new version of the Federal Law On Special Economic Zone in the Kaliningrad Region to the State Duma in October 2003. The new version of the Law envisages preservation of the existing privileges and brings this law in conformity with new provisions of the Tax and Customs Codes of the Russian Federation.

Russia's Federal Securities Market Commission has developed a concept of draft federal law On Amendments and Additions to the Federal Laws On Joint Stock Companies and On the Securities Market. The Amendments aim to protect shareholder rights in the event of acquisition of 25% and more of the company's voting shares by a third-party investor(s). It is envisaged to strictly regulate the takeover mechanism and introduce a pre-approved offer form and procedure for its discussion and adoption by all shareholders, as well as mechanisms for share purchase, price setting, offer adjustment options, and putting forward a counter share-purchase offer. These innovations will safeguard the interests of both the existing and potential shareholders.

REGIONAL BANKS OF THE RUSSIAN FEDERATION[1]

Bank	Contact information
1	2

CENTRAL FEDERAL DISTRICT

BELGOROD REGION

ZAO BelDorBank

34a, ul. Pushkina, Belgorod, 308800
Phone/fax: (0722) 32 0238
E-mail: beldorbank@senergy.ru
Emanuil Isakovich Shein, Chairman of the Board

OAO Belgorodpromstroybank

79, ul. Narodnaya, Belgorod, 308800
Phone/fax: (0722) 32 1363
E-mail: bank@bpsb.ru
Sergei Petrovich Kuksov, Chairman of the Board

ZAO UKB Belgorodsotsbank

73, ul. Litvinova, Belgorod, 308800
Phone: (0722) 32 2208; fax: (0722) 33 6352
E-mail: mail@belsocbank.ru
Tatyana Grigoryevna Yevstigneeva, Chairman of the Board

BRYANSK REGION

OAO KB Bryansk People's Bank

1, ul. Lyubeznogo, Bryansk, 241011
Phone: (0832) 74 2102; fax: (0832) 74 3829
E-mail: root@bnbank.debryansk.ru
Valentina Afanasyevna Sigaeva, Chairman of the Bank

Commercial Joint Stock Bank Bezhitsa-Bank

1a, ul. Bryanskoy Proletarskoy Divizii, Bryansk, 241035
Phone: (0832) 56 2766; fax: (0832) 56 8604, 56 2714
E-mail: root@bbank.bryansk.ru
Nikolai Petrovich Burdel, Chairman of the Board

VLADIMIR REGION

ZAO AKB Alexcombank

14, ul. Oktyabrskaya, Alexandrov, Vladimir Region, 601650
Phone/fax: (09244) 20 647, 23 436
E-mail: alkb@mail.ru
Lyudmila Stepanovna Dyatchina, Chairman of the Board

ZAO Vladbusinessbank

35, pr. Lenina, Vladimir, 600015
Phone: (0922) 24 1865; fax: (0922) 24 1984
E-mail: vbb@vbb.elcom.ru
Tatyana Yuryevna Sinyakova, Chairman of the Board

OOO Vladimir Industrial Bank

17, pr. Suzdalsky, Vladimir, 600027
Phone/fax: (0922) 21 6207
E-mail: bank@vpb.vinfo.ru
Valery Anatolyevich Sorokin, Chairman of the Board

VORONEZH REGION

OAO KB Agroimpuls

3, pl. Lenina, Voronezh, 394018
Phone/fax: (0732) 77 4434, 52 4604
E-mail: mail@agroimpuls.vrn.ru
Alexander Vladimirovich Koshevarov, Chairman of the Board

APPENDICES

---

[1] According to the Bank of Russia, as of June 1, 2003, Russia had 1,332 credit institutions. This list is not exhaustive.

1	2
OAO Inter-Regional Joint Stock South-East Bank	24, ul. Studencheskaya, Voronezh, 394000 Phone: (0732) 52 1442; fax: (0732) 77 7702 E-mail: root@sebank.vrn.ru Lyudmila Grigoryevna Boyarina, Chairman of the Board
OAO Voronezhprombank	25, ul. Ordzhonikidze, Voronezh, 394000 Phone: (0732) 39 0390; fax: (0732) 55 5970 E-mail: postmaster@ptr1.vrn.ru Gennady Nikolaevich Markin, CEO
IVANOVO REGION	
OAO Commercial Investment Bank Euroalliance	13, ul. Stanko, Ivanovo, 153000 Phone: (0932) 41 7857; fax: (0932) 41 2238 E-mail: ramb@indi.ru Margarita Vladimirovna Suglobova, Chairman of the Board
OOO Ivanovo Regional Bank	33, ul. Bagaeva, Ivanovo, 153000 Phone/fax: (0932) 32 7524 E-mail: iobank@mail.ru Olga Viktorovna Borodina, Chairman of the Board
Joint Stock Commercial Bank Kranbank	53, pr. F. Engelsa, Ivanovo, 153000 Phone: (0932) 30 0481; fax: (0932) 32 7756 E-mail: kb@interline.ru Vasily Ivanovich Davydov, Chairman of the Board
KALUGA REGION	
OAO Kaluga Gas and Energy Joint Stock Bank	4, ul. Plekhanova, Kaluga, 248030 Phone: (0842) 53 1394; fax: (0842) 53 1395 E-mail: gebank@kaluga.ru Anatoly Alexandrovich Ivanov, Chairman of the Board
ZAO Obninsk Joint Stock Investment Bank INVESKO-BANK	41, ul. Kurchatova, Obninsk, Kaluga Region, 249032 Phone: (08439) 65 881, 65 225, 91 212 Fax: (08439) 65 756 E-mail: invesco@obninsk.ru Anton Ivanovich Kudryavtsev, President
OAO Zembank	38, ul. Ryleeva, Kaluga, 248600 Phone: (0842) 56 2747; fax: (0842) 57 3550 E-mail: zembank@zembank.com Igor Ivanovich Gorskikh, Chairman of the Board
KOSTROMA REGION	
OOO KB Kostromabusinessbank	21, pr. Mira, Kostroma, 156000 Phone: (0942) 51 6300; fax: (0942) 51 6311 E-mail: bizbank@kmtn.ru Tatyana Vladimirovna Ayazova, Chairman of the Board
OOO Kostromaselkhozbank	6b, pr. Mira, Kostroma, 156605 Phone: (0942) 51 4954; fax: (0942) 35 0251 E-mail: selkbank@kosnet.ru Lidia Arkadyevna Zhenodarova, Chairman of the Board
OOO KB Nerekhtacombank	15, ul. Krasnoarmeyskaya, Nerekhta, Kostroma Region, 157800 Phone: (09431) 75 395, 75 442; fax: (09431) 75 324 E-mail: mkb2002@mail.ru Galina Nikolaevna Danilova, Chairman of the Board

1	2

OAO Kursk Industrial Bank	13, ul. Lenina, Kursk, 305000 Phone: (0712) 56 6147, 56 7613; fax: (0712) 56 7532 E-mail: Kpb@kurskprombank.ru Fedor Grigoryevich Khandurin, Chairman of the Board

OAO Lipetskcombank	8, ul. Internatsionalnaya, Lipetsk, 398600 Phone: (0742) 72 5955; fax: (0742) 72 0831 E-mail: office@kombank.lipetsk.ru Olga Nikolaevna Mitrokhina, CEO
OAO Lipetsk Regional Bank	1, pl. Plekhanova, Lipetsk, 398050 Phone: (0742) 77 5352; fax: (0742) 48 5887 E-mail: konst@oblbank.lipetsk.ru Alexei Alexandrovich Kiselev, CEO

OOO KB Agropromcredit	Bldg. 2, 13, 5th district, Lytkarino, Moscow Region, 140061 Phone: (095) 236 5004, 933 1130 Andrei Nikolaevich Shishkin, Chairman of the Board
OOO GAZENERGOPROMBANK	Village of Gazoprovod, p/o Kommunarka, Leninsky District, Moscow Region, 142770 Phone: (095) 428 8324, 428 8420 Larisa Ivanovna Ivanova, Chairman of the Board
ZAO AKB KHOVANSKY	25, ul. 2 Dombrovskaya, Pushkino, Moscow Region, 142200 Phone: (095) 287 9752, 287 9942 Fax: (095) 287 9983, 971 2082 Vasily Valeryevich Tsepkov, Chairman of the Board

ZAO Oryol Social Bank	70, nab. Dubrovinskogo, Oryol, 302030 Phone/fax: (08622) 51 056, 51 988, 56 648 E-mail: oskb@valley.ru Viktor Vladimirovich Perelygin, CEO
ZAO AIKB Zenit Business Bank	29, ul. Moskovskaya, Oryol 302030 Phone: (08622) 51 477, 55 158, 58 615 Fax: (0862) 43 0442 Vladimir Vladimirovich Stroev, CEO

OAO Prio-Vneshtorg-Bank	82/26, ul. Yesenina, Ryazan 390023 Phone: (0912) 24 4900, 24 4901, 24 4914 Fax: (0912) 24 4917 E-mail: post@priovtb.com Nikolay Mikhailovich Larionov, Chairman of the Board
OOO Sergei Zhivago MKB	64, ul. Pochtovaya, Ryazan, 390000 Phone: (0912) 28 9525; fax: (0912) 27 5242 E-mail: bank@jivago.ryazan.ru Alexei Anatolyevich Kosyanin, Chairman of the Board
OAO AKB Vyatich	110, ul. Vvedenskaya, Ryazan, 390046 Phone/fax: (0912) 21 9407, 21 9409 E-mail: stt@vyatich.ryazan.su Viktor Andreevich Katunin, Chairman of the Board

1	2
SMOLENSK REGION	
OAO Roslavl Joint Stock Commercial Bank Smolevich	47, ul. Proletarskaya, Roslavl, Smolensk Region, 216500 Phone/fax: (08134) 41 085, 42 469 E-mail: smolevich@smolensk.mtsmail.ru Lyudmila Avgustovna Maretskaya, Chairman of the Board
OAO SKA-Bank	13a, ul. Lenina, Smolensk, 214000 Phone: (08122) 32 528; fax: (0812) 64 6986 E-mail: ska@sci.smolensk.ru Vladimir Ivanovich Ivanov, President
OOO KB Smolensk Bank	5, pr. Gagarina, Smolensk, 214000 Phone: (08122) 91 584; fax: (08122) 91 581 E-mail: smolensk@smolbank.ru Anatoly Andreevich Danilov, Chairman of the Board
TAMBOV REGION	
OAO Joint Stock Social Bank Bastion	125, ul. Sovetskaya, Tambov, 392000 Phone: (0752) 53 4726, 53 0716, 53 5654 Fax: (0752) 53 9032 Valery Valentinovich Ten, President
OAO AKB Tambovkreditprombank	118, ul. Sovetskaya, Tambov, 392000 Phone: (0752) 72 0508; fax: (0752) 72 2664 E-mail: postmaster@tkpb.tambov.ru Galina Veniaminovna Haustova, CEO
TVER REGION	
OAO KB Torzhokuniversalbank Branch:	3, pl. Ananyina, Torzhok, Tver Region, 172002 Phone: (08251) 51 730; fax: (08251) 52 921 12, ul. Musorgskogo, Tver Phone/fax: (0822) 31 0089 Galena Viktorovna Utkina, Chairman of the Board
OAO Tver City Bank	Bldg. 2, 1, pr. Tchaikovskogo, Tver, 170000 Phone/fax: (0822) 33 4576 E-mail: tcbank@tcbank.ru Valentina Ivanovna Potapova, Chairman of the Board
OAO Tveruniversalbank	34, ul. Volodarskogo, Tver, 170000 Phone: (0822) 33 3136; fax: (0822) 32 1718 E-mail: po@tub.tver.ru Alexandra Mikhailovna Kozyreva, President
TULA REGION	
OAO AKB Express-Tula	1, ul. Puteyskaya, Tula, 300041 Phone/fax: (0872) 30 7484 E-mail: info@express.tula.net Sergei Valeryevich Khudyakov, Chairman of the Board
OAO AKB Priupskbank	10, nab. Dreira, Tula, 300002 Phone: (0872) 34 1473, 34 1273 Fax: (0872) 34 3224, 39 3329 E-mail: pbank@tula.net Lev Mikhailovich Obukhov, President
OAO AKB Spiritbank	85a, pr. Lenina, Tula, 300012 Phone: (0872) 33 1576; fax: (0872) 33 2874 E-mail: spiritb@tula.net Viktor Mikhailovich Alexashin, Chairman of the Board

1	2
OOO Tula Industrialist Commercial Investment Industrial Bank	18b, ul. Smidovich, Tula, 300028 Phone: (0872) 33 2630, 33 3012, 33 3034 Fax: (0872) 33 2652 E-mail: info@tulaprombank.ru Rushan Abdulkadyrovich Khisyametdinov, Chairman of the Board

YAROSLAVL REGION

OOO Investment Commercial Bank for Development Yarinterbank	30, ul. Sobinova, Yaroslavl, 150000 Phone/fax: (0852) 32 8658, 72 5553 E-mail: root@yarinterbank.ru Lidia Sergeevna Bulygina, Chairman of the Board
OAO Yaroslavich Commercial Bank	31/6, ul. Sobinova, Yaroslavl, 150000 Phone/fax: (0852) 30 2646 E-mail: gertsev@yaroslavl.ru Tatyana Vasilyevna Schegoleva, President
OAO Yaroslavl Commercial Bank for Social Development Yarsotsbank	14, ul. Pobedy, Yaroslavl, 150003 Phone: (0852) 30 3124; fax: (0852) 30 2326 E-mail: sov@osb.ru Igor Gennadyevich Zakharov, Chairman of the Board

MOSCOW

OAO Alfa-Bank	9, ul. Mashi Poryvaevoy, Moscow, 107078 Phone/fax: (095) 974 2515, 755 5830, 207 0059, 207 6001 E-mail: mail@alfabank.ru Leonard Berngardovich Vid, Chairman of the Board
Foreign Trade Bank (OAO Vneshtorgbank)	16, ul. Kuznetsky most, Moscow, 103031 Phone: (095) 101 1880; fax: (095) 258 4781 Yury Valentinovich Ponomarev, President, Chairman of the Board
ZAO AB Gazprombank	Bldg. 1, 16, ul. Nametkina, Moscow, 117420 Phone: (095) 719 1763; fax: (095) 913 7319 E-mail: mailbox@gazprombank.ru Andrei Igorevich Akimov, Chairman of the Board
RF Joint Stock Commercial Savings Bank (OAO Sberbank of Russia)	19, ul. Vavilova, Moscow, 117997 Phone: (095) 957 5862; fax: (095) 957 5731 E-mail: sbrf@sbrf.ru Andrei Ilyich Kazmin, President
OAO Joint Stock Moscow Municipal Commercial Bank, Bank of Moscow	Bldg. 3, 8/15, ul. Rozhdestvenka, Moscow, 107996 Phone: (095) 105 8000, 745 8000; fax: (095) 795 2600 E-mail: info@mmbank.ru Andrei Fridrikhovich Borodin, President
OAO MDM-Bank	Bldg. 1, 33, Kotelnicheskaya nab., Moscow, 115172 Phone: (095) 797 9500; fax: (095) 797 9501 E-mail: info@mdmbank.ru Andrei Igorevich Melnichenko, Chairman of the Board
OAO Sobinbank	Bldg. 56, 15, ul. Rochdelskaya, Moscow, 123022 Phone/fax: (095) 725 2525 http://www.sobinbank.ru Sergei Anatolyevich Kirilenko, Chairman of the Board

APPENDICES

1	2

NORTH-WESTERN FEDERAL DISTRICT

REPUBLIC OF KARELIA

OAO Petrozavodsk Municipal
Commercial Bank Onego

6a, ul. Chapaeva, Petrozavodsk, 185002
Phone/fax: (8142) 72 2051
E-mail: bank@onego.ru
Sergei Yevgenyevich Savinsky, President

KOMI REPUBLIC

OOO Bank for Savings and Development

19, ul. Babushkina, Syktyvkar, Komi Republic, 167000
Phone/fax: (8212) 29 1088, 24 9535
Vitaly Nikolaevich Kostrikov, President

OAO Komiregionbank Ukhtabank

14, ul. Oktyabrskaya, Ukhta, Komi Republic, 169300
Phone: (82147) 62 042, 62 488; fax: (82147) 63 783
E-mail: uhbank@uhb.parma.ru
Dmitry Valeryevich Orlov, Chairman of the Board

OAO AKB Northern People's Bank

68, ul. Pervomayskaya, Syktyvkar, 167000
Phone: (8212) 44 5364; fax: (8212) 44 5417
E-mail: snbank@online.ru
Sergei Vyacheslavovich Serditov, Chairman of the Board

ARKHANGELSK REGION

ZAO AZHKB

Bldg. 1, 10, ul. 23 Gvardeyskoy Divizii, Arkhangelsk, 163060
Phone: (8182) 23 6631; fax: (8182) 23 6636
E-mail: root@jinkb.sts.ru
Sergei Fedorovich Andreev, Chairman of the Board

ZAO First Shipping Bank

49, ul. Pomorskaya, Arkhangelsk, 163000
Phone: (8182) 65 6394; fax: (8182) 65 0947
E-mail: postmaster@fs-bank.ru
Sergei Valentinovich Poludnitsyn, CEO

ZAO North Clearing Chamber

8, ul. Voskresenskaya, Arkhangelsk, 163000
Phone/fax: (8182) 65 2345, 65 3675
E-mail: nch@atnet.ru
Alexander Nikolaevich Preminin, CEO

VOLOGDA REGION

OAO Metal Commercial Bank

57, ul. Krasnodontsev, Cherepovets, 162623
Phone/fax: (8202) 53 5330, 23 9074
E-mail: metcombank@metcombank.ru
Pavel Yuryevich Kosolapkov, CEO

OAO Promenergobank

12, ul. Batyushkina, Vologda, 160001
Phone: (8172) 72 7030; fax: (8172) 72 2183
E-mail: mail@promenergobank.ru
Sergei Stanislavovich Tugarin, Chairman of the Board

OAO KB Severgazbank

3, ul. Blagoveschenskaya, Vologda, 160001
Phone: (8172) 78 3783; fax: (8172) 78 3701
E-mail: sgbank@severgazbank.ru
Alexei Valentinovich Zhelezov, Chairman of the Board

KALININGRAD REGION

ZAO KB Energotransbank

83a, ul. Klinicheskaya, Kaliningrad, 236016
Phone/fax: (0112) 45 1938
E-mail: mail@energotransbank.com
Igor Dmitryevich Ivanov, Chairman of the Board

1	2
OAO Investbank	28, pr. Leninsky, Kaliningrad, 236040 Phone: (0112) 35 1440, 43 1101 Fax: (0112) 35 1315, 43 1103 E-mail: bank@investbank.ru, postmaster@investbank.ru Yury Andreevich Matveev, President
ZAO Network Oil Bank	57, ul. B. Khmelnitskogo, Kalinigrad, 236039 Phone: (0112) 44 5533, 35 2001; fax: (0112) 35 2041 E-mail: info@netoil.ru Yelena Tikhonovna Osenchugova, Chairman of the Board

LENINGRAD REGION

ZAO Constance-Bank	55-A, ul. B. Morskaya, St. Petersburg, 190000 Phone: (812) 315 0884; fax: (812) 325 7679 E-mail: mail@constbank.spb.ru Irina Vladimirovna Vakatova, Chairman of the Board
OAO Petroenergobank	11, ul. Mikhailova, St. Petersburg, 195009 Phone: (812) 542 8812; fax: (812) 541 8417 E-mail: peb@mail.metrocom.ru Sergei Viktorovich Amelfin, Chairman of the Board
OAO Vyborg-Bank	2, ul. Pionerskaya, Vyborg, Leningrad Region, 188800 Phone: (81278) 25 293, 24 886; fax: (81278) 25 480 E-mail: info@wyborgbank.spb.ru Alla Vladimirovna Tuchina, Chairman of the Board

MURMANSK REGION

OOO KB Barentsbank	26, ul. Marata, Murmansk, 183010 Phone: (8152) 25 1305; fax: (8152) 23 3957 E-mail: barencb@com.mels.ru Ivan Vladimirovich Studentsov, Chairman of the Board
OAO Monchebank	14, pr. Lenina, Murmansk, 183032 Phone: (8152) 40 5301, 40 5340; fax: (8152) 40 5325 E-mail: mailbox@monb.com Alla Vasilyevna Bochman, Chairman of the Board
OAO Murmansk Social Commercial Bank (OAO MSKB)	12, pr. Lenina, Murmansk, 183032 Phone/fax: (8152) 23 0334; fax: (8152) 23 0334, 23 0340 Andrei Vladimirovich Atamas, Chairman of the Board

NOVGOROD REGION

ZAO Novgorod Commercial Bank Slavyanbank	12, ul. Cheremnova-Konyukhova, Veliky Novgorod, 173004 Phone: (8162) 66 5301; fax: (8162) 66 5247 E-mail: leo@novgorod.net Viktor Ivanovich Titov, Chairman of the Board
OOO Universal Commercial Bank Novobank	11, nab. Gzen, Veliky Novgorod, 173003 Phone/fax: (8162) 13 2077, 11 5111; (81664) 23 332 E-mail: postmaster@novobank.natm.ru Galina Nikolaevna Salagina, Chairman of the Board

PSKOV REGION

OAO Commercial Joint Stock Bank Pskovbank	40b, pr. Rizhsky, Pskov, 180016 Phone: (8112) 46 3743; Fax: (8112) 46 1551 E-mail: info@pskovbank.ru Lyudmila Vasilyevna Martynenko, Chairman of the Board

1	2
OAO KB Russian Regional Bank	50a, pr. Oktyabrsky, Pskov, 180004 Phone/fax: (8112) 72 2664, (8122) 28 698, 22 859 E-mail: post@rrb.psc.ru Elena Vladimirovna Schagina, Chairman of the Board
OAO KB Velikiye Luki	27a, ul. Komsomolskaya, Velikiye Luki, Pskov Region, 182100 Phone: (81153) 52 918, 53 736; fax: (81153) 57 129 E-mail:vlb@mart.ru Galina Nikolaevna Timofeeva, Chairman of the Board
ST. PETERSBURG	
ZAO Baltyisky Bank	34, ul. Sadovaya, St. Petersburg, 191023 Phone: (812) 312 8789; fax: (812) 310 9274 E-mail: info@baltbank.ru Oleg Anatolyevich Shigaev, Chairman of the Board
OAO Bank Menatep St. Petersburg	1, prospekt Nevsky, St. Petersburg, 191186 Phone: (812) 326 3901, 326 3939; fax: (812) 326 3940 E-mail: entrance@menatepspb.com Dmitry Alexeevich Lebedev, Chairman of the Board
OAO Industrial and Construction Bank	17/18, per. Kovensky, St. Petersburg, 191014 Phone: (812) 329 8329, 329 8321; fax: (812) 310 6173 E-mail: lider@isb.spb.ru Alexander Vladimirovich Pustovalov, Chairman of the Board
OAO International Bank of St. Petersburg	5, per. Krapivny, St. Petersburg, 194044 Phone: (812) 541 8217, 327 1107; fax: (812) 541 8393 E-mail: mail@ibsp.ru Sergei Viktorovich Bazhanov, President
OAO St. Petersburg Bank	178, prospekt Nevsky, St. Petersburg, 193167 Phone: (812) 329 5855, 312 1240; fax: (812) 325 5082 E-mail: bank_spb@bspb.ru Alexander Vasilyevich Savelyev, Chairman of the Board

SOUTHERN FEDERAL DISTRICT

REPUBLIC OF ADYGEYA	
ZAO AKB Galabank	91, ul. Chapaeva, Krasnogvardeyskoe, Republic of Adygeya, 385300 Phone: (87778) 52 495, 52 748; fax: (87778) 53 035 E-mail: galabank@radnet.ru Galina Ivanovna Pinkalo, Chairman of the Board
ZAO AKB Maikopbank	276, ul. Pionerskaya, Maikop, 385000 Phone: (87722) 25 630; fax: (87722) 25 788 E-mail: mbank@radnet.ru Yury Vladimirovich Ovsepiants, Chairman of the Board
OAO AKB Novatsiya	Bldg. 1, 4, ul. Dimitrova, Maikop, 385011 Phone/fax: (87722) 30 078, 30 079 E-mail: office@novabank.ru Yekaterina Andreevna Mescheryakova, Chairman of the Board
REPUBLIC OF DAGESTAN	
OAO AKB Elbin	56, ul. Batyraya, Makhachkala, 367025 Phone: (8722) 64 2160; fax: (8722) 64 4085 E-mail: elbin@dinet.ru Magomed Amirovich Omarov, Chairman of the Board

1	2
OOO AKB Irdagbank	92, ul. Abubakarova, Makhachkala, 367020 Phone/fax: (8722) 64 6183, 64 4347 E-mail: irdag@sinol.ru Sultan Omarovich Umakhanov, Chairman of the Board
OOO IKB Mesed	70, ul. Gagarina, Makhachkala, 367010 Phone: (8722) 68 2560, 62 3445, 62 2560; fax: (8722) 62 3445 Shamsiyat Abdulkadyrovna Radzhabova, Chairman of the Board

REPUBLIC OF INGUSHETIA

OAO Sunzha Bank	32, ul. Oskanova, Ordzhonikidzevskaya, Sunzhensky District, Republic of Ingushetia, 366700 Phone/fax: (87341) 22 412 Aslambek Idrisovich Sagov, Chairman of the Board

REPUBLIC OF KABARDINO-BALKARIA

ZAO Eurostandard	66, ul. Kabardinskaya, Nalchik, 360051 Phone: (8662) 44 3799; fax: (8662) 44 3799 E-mail: eurostd@rambler.ru Zalim Khasenovich Urusmambetov, Chairman of the Board
OAO KBRR	16, ul. Shogentsugova, Nalchik, 360051 Phone: (8662) 42 1453, 44 2776; fax: (8662) 40 1212 E-mail: kbank@kbrnet.ru Oleg Ibragimovich Kushkhov, Chairman of the Board
OOO Nalchik Bank	77, ul. Tolstogo, Nalchik, 360051 Phone: (8662) 42 2846; fax: (8662) 42 1565 E-mail: bnalchik@digsys.ru Boris Aubekirovich Endreev, Chairman of the Board

REPUBLIC OF KALMYKIA

OAO Kalmykia KB Creditbank	3a, ul. Neiman, Elista, 358000 Phone: (84722) 52 336, 52 425; fax: (84722) 54 563 Nikolai Dmitrievich Pompaev, CEO
OOO KB National Clearing Bank	243, ul. Lenina, Elista 358000 Phone: (84722) 50 601; fax: (095) 797 61 54, 232 15 45 E-mail: ncb@bumba.ru Viktor Sandzhyevich Sharapov, Chairman of the Board

REPUBLIC OF KARACHAYEVO-CHERKESSIA

AKB Kavkaz-Gelios	82, ul. Pushkinskaya, Cherkessk, 369000 Phone/fax: (87822) 50 278, 50 289 E-mail: kgb@mail.svchr.ru Sergei Ivanovich Golovin, Chairman of the Board
OAO Kavkazpromstroibank	84, ul. Pushkinskaya, Cherkessk, 369000 Phone: (87822) 51 907, 51 465; fax: (87822) 58 930 Vasily Petrovich Redkin, Chairman of the Board
OOO KB Razvitye	64, ul. Krasnoarmeyskaya, Cherkessk, 369000 Phone: (87822) 56 778, 62 223; fax: (87822) 51 590 Dzhambut Pakovich Khapsirokov, Chairman of the Board

REPUBLIC OF NORTH OSSETIA – ALANIA

OAO AKB ADAMON Bank	9, ul. Stanislavskogo, Vladikavkaz, 362040 Phone: (8672) 74 1355; fax: (8672) 54 0081 E-mail: adamon@mail.ru Alan Sultanovich Gatagov, Chairman of the Board

APPENDICES

1	2
OAO AKB Bank for Regional Development	8a, ul. Shmulevicha, Vladikavkaz, 362019 Phone: (8672) 54 0989, 54 0929; fax: (8672) 54 5309 E-mail: akbbrr@yandex.ru Gennady Yuryevich Beroev, Chairman of the Board
OOO Commercial Bank Art-Bank	93, pr. Kosta, Vladikavkaz, 362008 Phone: (8672) 75 7205; fax: (8672) 51 7195 E-mail: artbank@alanianet.ru Rimma Mukhtarovna Dzitsoeva, Chairman of the Board
KRASNODAR TERRITORY	
OAO Promfinservisbank	6, ul. Isaeva, Novorossiysk, Krasnodar Territory, 353905 Phone/fax: (8617) 25 1075, 25 9304 Nadezhda Nikolaevna Moskovtseva, Chairman of the Board
OAO Yugbank	52, ul. Krasnaya, Krasnodar, 350016 Phone: (8612) 62 3420; fax: (8612) 62 1121 E-mail: alik@ugbank.ru Vladimir Petrovich Guryanov, CEO
OAO Yug-Investbank	113, ul. Krasnaya, Krasnodar, 350000 Phone: (8612) 59 6656; fax: (8612) 59 52 52 Email: invb@mail.kubtelecom.ru Sergei Vladimirovich Oblogin, Chairman of the Board
STAVROPOL TERRITORY	
OAO Joint Stock Investment Commercial Industrial and Construction Bank Stavropolye	88a, ul. Krasnoflotskaya, Stavropol, 355041 Phone: (8652) 32 7730, 35 9255; fax: (8652) 94 5230 E-mail: scib@scib.ru; admin@psbst.ru, http://www.scib.ru Anatoly Ivanovich Buiny, Chairman of the Board
ZAO AKB Pyatigorsk	28, ul. Kozlova, Pyatigorsk, Stavropol Territory 357500 Phone/fax: (87933) 79 201, 79 578 Valentina Davydovna Ponomarenko, President
OAO Sevkavinvestbank	58a, ul. 40 let Oktyabrya, Pyatigorsk, Stavropol Territory, 357500 Phone/fax: (87933) 35 017, 41 375 E-mail: skib@skib.ru Boris Sergeevich Burakov, Chairman of the Board
ASTRAKHAN REGION	
OAO Agroindustrial Investment Commercial Bank	37, ul. Krasnaya Naberezhnaya, Astrakhan, 414040 Phone: (8512) 22 9774, 22 7041; fax: (8512) 22 3888 E-mail: agroinko@teonet.ru Nikita Seitovich Iskakov, Chairman of the Board
OAO Euroasian Trade and Industrial Commercial Bank	3, ul. Nogina, Astrakhan, 414000 Phone: (8512) 22 7223 Phone/fax: (8512) 39 0226 E-mail: post@eatpbank.ru Lyudmila Yuryevna Tsareva, President
OAO Volga-Caspian Joint Stock Bank	20, ul. Lenina, Astrakhan, 414000 Phone: (8512) 22 1698; fax: (8512) 22 9709 E-mail: vka@mail.astrakhan.ru Vladimir Pavlovich Sukhorukov, President
VOLGOGRAD REGION	
OAO AKB KOR	3, ul. Nevskaya, Volgograd, 400087 Phone: (8442) 37 1630, 37 8747; fax: (8442) 37 1688 E-mail: moneta2@list.ru, bcor@mail.ru Roman Sergeevich Bekov, Chairman of the Board

1	2
OAO AKB Volgoprombank	24a, ul. Mira, Volgograd, 400131 Phone: (8442) 33 5022; fax: (8442) 36 6479 E-mail: vpb@volgopro.ru Arkady Alexandrovich Makarov, CEO

ROSTOV REGION

OAO KB Center-Invest	62, pr. Sokolova, Rostov-on-Don, 344010 Phone: (8632) 67 5376, 64 5416; fax: (8632) 67 0006 E-mail: welcome@centrinvest.ru, press@centrinvest.ru, http://www.centrinvest.ru Anatoly Yakovlevich Cherenkov, Chairman of the Board
OOO KB DONINVEST	99, per. Khalturinsky, Rostov-on-Don, 344011 Phone: (8632) 67 8022, 67 95 44; fax: (8632) 6781 05 E-mail: doninvest@mail.ru Alla Vitalyevna Malakhova, Chairman of the Board
OAO Rostpromstroybank	36, ul. Bolshaya Sadovaya, Rostov-on-Don, 344002 Phone: (8632) 40 6935; fax: (8632) 40 1296 E-mail: rkl@psb.rost.ru, http://www.rostpromstroybank.ru Igor Nikolaevich Pyatigorets, Chairman of the Board
OAO AKB Selmashbank	102, pr. Selmash, Rostov-on-Don, 344029 Phone: (8632) 54 4788; fax: (8632) 52 8566 E-mail: smbku@aaanet.ru Vadim Mikhailovich Khlus, Chairman of the Board

VOLGA FEDERAL DISTRICT

REPUBLIC OF BASHKORTOSTAN

OAO Bashkortostan Industrial Bank	11, ul. Zhukova, Ufa, 450099 Phone: (3472) 36 0902; fax: (3472) 36 1001 Vladimir Sergeevich Yakovlev, Chairman of the Board
OAO Sotsinvestbank	42, ul. Frunze, Ufa, 450002 Phone/fax: (3472) 50 6395; fax: (3472) 50 1731 E-mail: post@sibank.ru, http://www.sibank.ru Dmitry Nikolaevich Neverov, CEO
OAO Uralsib	41, ul. Revolyutsionnaya, Ufa, 450000 Phone: (3472) 51 9555/30; fax: (3472) 23 5835 E-mail: ufa@uralsibbank.ru Azat Talgatovich Kurmanaev, President

REPUBLIC OF MARIY EL

OAO Yoshkar-Ola Bank	110, ul. K. Marksa, Yoshkar-Ola, 424000 Phone: (8362) 11 0822; fax: (8362) 12 9793 E-mail: postmaster@mkb.mari.ru Olga Gennadyevna Kulalaeva, President

REPUBLIC OF MORDOVIA

OAO Aktiv Bank	52, ul. Kommunisticheskaya, Saransk, 430000 Phone: (8342) 17 5270; fax: (8342) 17 52 70 E-mail: aktivkb@moris.ru Nikolai Nikolaevich Nikolaev, President
OAO Joint Stock Commercial Credit Insurance Bank KS-bank	52, ul. Kommunisticheskaya, Saransk, 430000 Phone: (8342) 32 7600; fax: (8342) 32 7600 E-mail: ksbank@saransk-com.ru Vladimir Ivanovich Gribanov, President

APPENDICES

1	2
OAO AKB Mordovpromstroybank	36a, ul. B. Khmelnitskogo, Saransk, 430000 Phone: (8342) 32 7705; fax: (8342) 17 7416 E-mail: mpsb@mpsb.ru Alexander Nikolaevich Lavrentyev, Chairman of the Board

REPUBLIC OF TATARSTAN

1	2
Bank Tatarstan Branch No. 8610 of Sberbank of Russia	44, ul. Butlerova, Kazan, 420012 Phone: (8432) 64 4900; fax: (8432) 64 4700 E-mail: sbtat@sb.tatarstan.ru Gennady Nikolaevich Zakharov, Manager
OAO AK Bars Bank	1, ul. Dekabristov, Kazan, 420066 Phone: (8432) 19 3870, 19 3900, 19 3910; Fax: (8432) 19 3975; E-mail: kanc@akbars.ru Robert Khalitovich Minnegaliev, Chairman of the Board
OAO AB Devon-Credit	77, ul. Lenina, Almetyevsk, Republic of Tatarstan, 423450 Phone: (8553) 31 7513; Fax: (8553) 25 8835, (095) 174 2613 E-mail: office@devonkredit.ru Zufar Masgutovich Nasybullin, President
National Bank of the Republic of Tatarstan	37, ul. Baumana, Kazan, 420013 Phone: (8432) 36 6082; fax: (8432) 36 63 48 Email: nbrt@nb.kazan.ru Yevgeny Borisovich Bogachev, Chairman
OAO Tatecobank	47, ul. Bratyev Kasimovykh, Kazan, 420101 Phone: (8432) 34 1151, 35 3443, 35 8938 Fax: (8432) 35 0516 Evelina Arkadyevna Filina, Chairman of the Board
OAO AIKB Tatfondbank	2/43, ul. Ukhtomskogo, Kazan, 420111 Phone: (8432) 91 9800; fax: (8432) 91 9845, 91 9804 E-mail: tfb@tfb.ru Ildus Anvarovich Minzagetdinov, Chairman of the Board

REPUBLIC OF UDMURTIA

1	2
OAO Eurasian Bank for Economic Development	182a, ul. Krasnoarmeyskaya, Izhevsk, 426057 Phone: (3412) 51 0329, 51 1307, 78 0735 Fax: (3412) 52 6236 E-mail: office@eabank.udmnet.ru Aidar Sabirovich Zubairov, Chairman of the Board
OOO KB Pervomaysky	44a, ul. Lenina, Izhevsk, 426076 Phone: (3412) 78 5777; fax: (3412) 51 8398 E-mail: pervomay@udm.net Gulyusa Gilemovna Kolesnik, Chairman of the Board
OAO Ural Trust Bank	268, ul. Pushkinskaya, Izhevsk, 426008 Phone: (3412) 51 0244, 43 9175; fax: (3412) 43 9340 E-mail: contacts@utb.udm.ru Oirat Dzangir ogly Guseinov, Chairman of the Board

REPUBLIC OF CHUVASHIA

1	2
AKB Chuvashkreditprombank	3, pr. Moskovsky, Cheboksary, 428000 Phone: (8352) 62 0108, 42 6897; fax: 42 1919 E-mail: kredbank@chtts.ru Vladimir Vasilyevich Guryev, President

1	2
OOO KB Megapolis	22, ul. K. Marksa, Cheboksary, 428032 Phone: (8352) 66 1255; fax: (8352) 66 1244 E-mail: mega@chbd.ru Vadim Alexeevich Spirin, Chairman of the Board
OOO KB United Bank of the Republic	3, pr. Kabelny, Cheboksary, 428022 Phone/fax: (8352) 63 2476, 63 5623 E-mail: obr@cbx.ru Vladimir Petrovich Ilivanov, Chairman of the Board
KIROV REGION	
OAO Commercial Bank Khlynov	40, ul. Uritskogo, Kirov, 610002 Phone/fax: (8332) 67 3810, 67 3311 E-mail: oabt@bank-hlynov.kirov.ru Nikolay Vasilyevich Popov, Chairman of the Board
ZAO First Joint Stock Commercial Road and Transport Bank	24, pr. Oktyabrsky, Kirov, 610006 Phone/fax: (8332) 24 3326 E-mail: dtb1@dtb1.kirov.ru Vladimir Valeryevich Sablin, Chairman of the Board
OAO AKB Vyatka-Bank	4, ul. Engelsa, Kirov, 610000 Phone: (8332) 65 0282, 65 1084; fax: (8332) 65 1485 E-mail: secretary@vtkbank.ru Genrietta Nikolaevna Karelina, President
NIZHNY NOVGOROD REGION	
OAO AKB Avtogazbank	Bldg. 1, 100, pr. Lenina, Nizhny Novgorod, 603004 Phone: (8312) 96 2651; fax: (8312) 92 3167 E-mail: post@agbank.nnov.ru Olga Yuryevna Scheglova, Chairman of the Board
OAO NBD-Bank	6, pl. Gorkogo, Nizhny Novgorod, 603950 Phone: (8312) 30 8061; fax: (8312) 34 3948 E-mail: info@nbdbank.ru Alexander Georgievich Sharonov, Chairman of the Board
ZAO Nizhegorodpromstroybank	21, ul. Gruzinskaya, Nizhny Novgorod, 603950 Phone: (8312) 33 9544; fax: (8312) 33 3747, 33 4311 E-mail: npsb@kis.ru Egor Leontyevich Kaloshin, Chairman of the Board
OAO GB Nizhny Novgorod	31, ul. Nesterova, Nizhny Novgorod, 603005 Phone: (8312) 37 6011; fax: (8312) 19 7972 E-mail: root@gab.nnov.su Vyacheslav Yevgenyevich Rasskazov, President
ZAO AKB SAROVBUSINESSBANK	13, ul. Silkina, Sarov, Nizhny Novgorod Region, 607189 Phone: (83130) 33 640, 40 778, 42 989; Fax: (83130) 43 395 E-mail: secret@sbb.sar.ru Valery Dmitrievich Dimitrov, Chairman of the Board
ORENBURG REGION	
ZAO AKB Forshtadt	7, per. Rybny, Orenburg, 460000 Phone: (3532) 77 6494, 77 4326; fax: (3532) 77 6270 E-mail: bank@forshtadt.ru Zoya Vasilyevna Muzyka, Chairman of the Board
OAO Niko-Bank	5, per. Alexeevsky, Orenburg, 460000 Phone: (3532) 72 3853, 72 4421; fax: (3532) 72 3382 E-mail: niko@mail.iso.ru Nina Petrovna Yakovleva, Chairman of the Board

APPENDICES

1	2
OAO Orenburg Bank	25, ul. Marshala Zhukova, Orenburg, 460024 Phone: (3532) 77 9522; fax: (3532) 41 1411 E-mail: info@orbank.ru Yury Vladimirovich Samoilov, Chairman of the Board
Orenburg Mortgage KB Rus	7, per. Shevchenko, Orenburg, 460000 Phone/fax: (3532) 77 9351, 77 9984 E-mail: bnkrus@mail.esoo.ru Vladimir Nikolaevich Kidanov, President
OAO AKB Orskindustriabank	75a, pr. Lenina, Orsk, Orenburg Region, 462431 Phone: (3537) 21 6273, 21 6741; fax: (3537) 21 6462 Olga Pavlovna Dmitrieva, Chairman of the Board
ZAO AKB Sol-Iletsk	12, ul. Pushkina, Sol-Iletsk, Orenburg Region, 461500 Phone/fax: (35336) 22 104 Tatyana Borisovna Kovaleva, Director
OAO KB Sputnik	103, ul. Frunze, Buguruslan, Orenburg Region, 461630 Phone/fax: (35352) 23 361, 27 268 E-mail: sputnik@buguruslan.ru Anatoly Alexandrovich Yegorov, Chairman of the Board
PENZA REGION	
OOO Kuznetsky Bank	39, ul. Vokzalnaya, Kuznetsk, Penza Region, 442530 Phone: (257) 44 564; fax: (257) 45 332 Nina Dmitrievna Sokrustova, Chairman of the Board
Penza GB Tarkhany	14, ul. Kuybysheva, Penza, 440052 Phone: (8412) 55 0863, 55 0979; fax: (8412) 55 0799 E-mail: aea@tarkhanebank.ru Senik Varshamovich Saakyan, Chairman of the Board
PERM REGION	
OAO Dzershinsky Commercial Bank	43, ul. Kirova, Perm, 614990 Phone: (3422) 12 5614, 20 3200; fax: (3422) 20 3206 E-mail: dzerbank@dzerbank.perm.ru Mikhail Borisovich Kogman, Chairman of the Board
OAO AKB Perm	10, ul. Kuybysheva, Perm, 614000 Phone: (3422) 90 1607, 90 1140; fax: (3422) 91 0310 E-mail: akbperm@perm.su, info@bankperm.ru Lyudmila Vasilyevna Saranskaya, Chairman of the Board
OAO Permkredit Bank	43, ul. Ordzhonikidze, Perm, 614000 Phone: (3422) 19 8228, 12 1768; fax: (3422) 19 8209 E-mail: permkredit@permonline.ru Andrei Borisovich Shurygin, Chairman of the Board
OAO Prikamye Commercial Bank	104, ul. Sovetskaya, GSP, Perm, 614990 Phone: (3422) 36 1718, 37 3674; fax: (3422) 37 3233 E-mail: prikamye@permonline.ru Anna Pavlovna Gryaznova, Chairman of the Board
OAO AKB Ural Financial House	64, ul. Lenina, Perm, 614990 Phone: (3422) 40 1001, 40 1016, 33 5011 Fax: (3422) 40 1069 E-mail: main@uralfd.perm.su Andrei Rudolfovich Konogorov, Chairman of the Board

1	2

SAMARA REGION

ZAO AKB Gazbank	70, ul. Agibalova, Samara, 443041 Phone: (8462) 41 7447; fax: (8462) 41 1054 E-mail: gazbank@gazbank.ru Alexander Viktorovich Bondarenko, Chairman of the Board
OAO Industrial Commercial Bank AVTOVAZBANK	26a, ul. Golosova, Togliatti, Samara Region, 445021 Phone: (8482) 22 1556; fax: (8482) 22 1447 E-mail: avbmbox@gin.ru Vera Vladimirovna Prokopenko, President
OAO Inter-Regional Volga-Kama Bank for Reconstruction and Development	14, ul. Garazhnaya, Samara, 443099 Phone/fax: (8462) 32 1201, 41 8860 Vladimir Viktorovich Yudin, President
OAO KB Solidarnost	90, ul. Kuybysheva, Samara, 443099 Phone: (8462) 33 6385, 32 8516 Fax: (8462) 32 6130, 32 6001, 70 3350 E-mail: general@solid.ru Oleg Yuryevich Sinitsyn, President
ZAO AKB Togliattikhimbank	96, ul. Gorkogo, Togliatti, Samara Region, 445009 Phone: (8482) 20 8285; fax: (8482) 48 0933 Alexander Yevgenyevich Popov, Chairman of the Board

SARATOV REGION

ZAO Econombank	28, ul. Radischeva, Saratov, 410031 Phone: (8452) 24 0613; fax: (8452) 27 7507 E-mail: root@ecobank.sar.ru Alexander Viktorovich Suslov, Chairman of the Board
ZAO AKB Express-Volga	4, per. Mirny, Saratov, 410600 Phone/fax: (8452) 50 6116, 50 9120 E-mail: bank@volgaex.ru Yevgeny Gennadyevich Zubakov, Chairman of the Board
OAO KB Sinergiya	27, ul. Rabochaya, Saratov, 410028 Phone: (8452) 22 3501, 26 7789; fax: (8452) 22 3117 E-mail: info@sinergia.shere.ru Yury Mikhailovich Kolesnikov, Chairman of the Board

ULYANOVSK REGION

ZAO Bank Venets	19, ul. Marata, Ulyanovsk, 432071 Phone/fax: (8422) 32 6284 E-mail: venets@mv.ru Vladimir Alexeevich Yendovitsky, Chairman of the Board
ZAO AKB Regionalny	6, ul. Samarskaya, Dimitrovgrad, Ulyanovsk Region, 433508 Phone: (84235) 27 144; fax: (84235) 58 127 E-mail: night@comp-net.ru Andrei Alexeevich Sbitnev, Chairman of the Board
Volga Regional Joint Stock Bank ZAO UlyanovskVneshtorgbank	1, ul. K. Marksa, Ulyanovsk, 432600 Phone: (8422) 31 7450; fax: (8422) 31 7400 E-mail: vtb@mail.uln.ru Mikhail Nikolaevich Melnikov, Chairman of the Board

APPENDICES

1	2

URALS FEDERAL DISTRICT

KURGAN REGION

OAO AKIB Kurgan

78, ul. Gogolya, Kurgan, 640000
Phone: (3522) 46 1265, 46 4290; fax: (3522) 46 6076
E-mail: kbkurgan@zaural.ru
Larisa Ivanovna Baron, Chairman

AKB Kurganprombank

23, ul. Savelyeva, Kurgan, 640000
Phone/fax: (3522) 53 1324, 41 2067, 41 2355, 42 2155
E-mail: kpb@kpb.ru
Igor Nikolaevich Vedernikov, Chairman

ZASKB Nadezhnost

37a, ul. Gogolya, Kurgan, 640000
Phone: (3522) 43 2550; fax: (3522) 43 3431
E-mail: nadega@zaural.ru
Viktor Fedorovich Terentyev, Chairman

SVERDLOVSK REGION

OAO Bank Yekaterinburg

13, ul. 8 Marta, Yekaterinburg, 620014
Phone: (3432) 71 3585, 77 6717, 77 6611
Fax: (3432) 66 4745
E-mail: bank@emb.ru
Mikhail Mikhailovich Sitnikov, President

OAO Bank Severnaya Kazna

17, ul. Gorkogo, Yekaterinburg, 620051
Phone: (3432) 59 2707; fax: (3432) 59 2734
E-mail: kazna@kazna.ru
Andrei Valeryevich Volchik, Chairman of the Board

ZAO KB Dragotsennosti Urala

14, ul. Gagarina, Yekaterinburg, 620062
Phone: (3432) 49 5940; fax: (3432) 49 5984
E-mail: nist-ap@kbdu.ru
Oleg Yevgenyevich Merkuryev, Chairman of the Board

ZAO MDM-BANK-URAL

68, ul. Vostochnaya, Yekaterinburg, 620075
Phone: (3432)50 2010, 24 3467; fax: (3432) 72 8783
E-mail: reception@mdmbank.com
Andrei Valeryevich Zyuzin, Chairman of the Board

ZAO Sverdlovsk Provincial Bank

35, ul. Uralskikh Rabochikh, Yekaterinburg, 620012
Phone: (3432) 37 8972, 32 6959; fax: (3432) 37 8972
E-mail: sgbank@sgbank.ru
Alexander Vladimirovich Ivanov, Chairman of the Board

OAO Ural Commercial Foreign Trade Bank

4, Liter B, ul. Chebysheva, Yekaterinburg, 620062
Phone: (3432) 17 8178; fax: (3432) 75 8298
E-mail: mybanker@uvtb.ru
Valerian Vladimirovich Popkov, President

OAO Uralpromstroybank

6, ul. Marshala Zhukova, Yekaterinburg, 620219
Phone: (3432) 71 2188; fax: (3432) 79 6623
E-mail: mail@upsb.ru
Lyudmila Germanovna Mezentseva, President

OOO Urals Bank for Reconstruction
and Development

95, ul. Kuybysheva, Yekaterinburg, 620026
Phone: (3432) 64 5580, 64 5560, 61 5702
Fax: (3432) 62 4422
E-mail: bank@ubrr.ru
Sergei Vitalyevich Dymshakov, President

1	2

Joint Stock West-Siberian Commercial Bank OAO Zapsibcombank	17a, ul. Podshibyakina, Salekhard, Tyumen Region, Yamalo-Nenetsky Autonomous District, 629008 Phone: (34922) 44 539; fax: (34922) 44 539 (Salekhard), Phone: (3452) 24 0984; fax: (3452) 24 0519 (Tyumen) E-mail: rut@wscb.salekhard.ru, http://www.wscb.ru Dmitry Yuryevich Goritsky, Chairman of the Board
OAO Khanty-Mansiysk Bank	13, ul. Mira, Khanty-Mansiysk, Tyumen Region, Khanty-Mansiysky Autonomous District, 628012 Phone: (34671) 30 210, 90 600; fax: (34671) 30 219 E-mail: hmbank@khmb.ru Dmitry Alexandrovich Mizgulin, President
Nefteyugansk Branch of OAO Menatep Bank	24, 2nd Micro District, Nefteyugansk, Khanty-Mansiysky Autonomous District, 628309 Phone: (34612) 37 801; fax: (34612) 29 680 E-mail: bank@unbank.ru Yevgenia Vasilyevna Osipova, Branch Manager
OAO Sibneftbank	39, ul. Pervomayskaya, Tyumen, 625000 Phone: (3452) 79 9200, 79 9299; fax: (3452) 79 9300 E-mail: siboil@snb.ru Vladimir Valentinovich Kozhevnikov, President
ZAO Surgutneftegazbank	19, ul. Kukuevitskogo, Surgut, Tyumen Region, 628400 Phone: (3462) 39 8717, 34 8700 Fax: (3462) 39 8711, 39 8708 E-mail: telex@sngb.ru Yevgenia Viktorovna Nepomnyaschikh, Chairman of the Board
OAO AKB Tyumen City Bank	28, ul. Profsoyuznaya, Tyumen, 625002 Phone: (3452) 24 4243; fax: (3452) 24 3621 E-mail: info@tgb.tmn.ru Viktor Leonidovich Demin, Chairman of the Board
ZAO Tyumenagroprombank	33, ul. Odesskaya, Tyumen, 625023 Phone: (3452) 32 2772; fax: (3452) 41 5815 E-mail: department@tmapb.ru, http://www.tmapb.ru Alexandra Pavlovna Bezgodova, Director

OAO Bank Snezhinsky	26, ul. Engelsa, Chelyabinsk, 454080 Phone: (3512) 66 6857; fax: (3512) 65 7069 E-mail: bank@snbank.ru Vladislav Borisovich Yegorov, Chairman of the Board
OAO Chelindbank	80, ul. K. Marksa, Chelyabinsk, 454091 Phone: (3512) 64 7682; fax: (3512) 65 1754 E-mail: mail@chelindbank.ru Mikhail Ivanovich Bratishkin, CEO
OAO Credit Ural Bank	17, ul. Gagarina, Magnitogorsk, Chelyabinsk Region, 455044 Phone: (3519) 24 8910; fax: (3519) 24 8930 E-mail: office@creditural.ru, http://www.creditural.ru Alexander Eduardovich Grabovsky, Chairman of the Board
OAO Joint Stock Chelyabinsk Investment Bank Chelyabinvestbank	8, pl. Revolutsii, Chelyabinsk, 454113 Phone: (3512) 63 8444; fax: (3512) 65 1754 E-mail: bank@chelinvest.ru Vyacheslav Grigoryevich Nazarets, Chairman of the Board

1	2

SIBERIAN FEDERAL DISTRICT

REPUBLIC OF ALTAI

OOO KB Altaienergobank

53/1, ul. Choros-Gurkina, Gorno-Altaisk, 649000
Phone: (38822) 25 545, 22 161; fax: (38822) 95 104
E-mail: alten@mail.gorny.ru
Raisa Ilyinichna Ivanova, Chairman of the Board

OOO KB El Bank

3, ul. Sotsialisticheskaya, Gorno-Altaisk, 649000
Phone: (38822) 22 109; fax: (38822) 95 030
E-mail: info@elf.gorny.ru
Alexander Nikolaevich Alchubaev, Chairman of the Board

ZAO AKB Sibir Energy Bank

6, pr. Kommunistichesky, Gorno-Altaisk, 649002
Phone: (38822) 41 516; fax: (38822) 95 148
Igor Semenovich Proskudin, Chairman of the Board

REPUBLIC OF BURYATIA

OAO AK Baikalbank

28, ul. Krasnoarmeyskaya, Ulan-Ude, 670034
Phone: (3012) 44 1194, 44 0591; fax: (3012) 44 0529
E-mail: post@bbank.burnet.ru
Vadim Nikolaevich Yegorov, Chairman of the Board

OAO KB Sibirskoye OVK

3b, ul. Tereshkovoy, Ulan-Ude, 670031
Phone: (3012) 43 5959, 23 0055; fax: (3012) 23 0338
E-mail: bikom@rex.ru, www.sibovk.ru
Alexander Viktorovich Devyashin, Chairman of the Board

REPUBLIC OF TYVA

OAO AKB Arat Commercial Farmers' Land Bank

12, ul. Agnii Barto, Kaa-Khem, Kyzyl District,
Republic of Tyva, 668070
Phone: (39422) 58 715, 97 004, 91 200
Vera Petrovna Popova, Chairman of the Board

OAO Bank Tuvacredit

40a, ul. Chulduma, Kyzyl, 667000
Phone: (39422) 36 579, 36 569
Fax: (39422) 30 739, 36 800
E-mail: tv-kredit@tyva.ru
Alexander Nikolaevich Shulepov, Chairman of the Board

OAO AB People's Bank of the Republic of Tyva

18, ul. Tuvinskikh Dobrovoltsev, Kyzyl, 667000
Phone: (39422) 35 389, 36 153; fax: (39422) 35 389
E-mail: pb@tyva.ru
Karolina Vladimirovna Kara-Sal, Chairman of the Board

REPUBLIC OF KHAKASSIA

OOO KB Central Asian

69, ul. Sovetskaya, Abakan, 655017
Phone: (39022) 40 400; fax: (39022) 49 505
Natalia Alexeevna Shulbaeva, Chairman of the Board

OAO AKB Khakassia Bank

67, ul. Pushkina, Abakan, 655012
Phone: (39022) 46 357, 53 949; fax: (39022) 53 949
http://www.resbank.khakasnet.ru
Alexei Ivanovich Kormilkin, Chairman of the Board

OOO KB Khakassia Municipal Bank

73, ul. Khakasskaya, Abakan, 655017
Phone: (39022) 54 443; fax: (39022) 54 443
E-mail: kbhmb@khakasnet.ru
Alexander Vladimirovich Koval, Chairman of the Board

1	2

ALTAI TERRITORY

OOO KB Altaicapitalbank	38a, ul. L. Tolstogo, Barnaul, 656043 Phone: (3852) 23 6214; fax: (3852) 23 6214 E-mail: capital@ab.ru Igor Vladimirovich Germanenko, President
OAO KB ForBank	39, ul. M. Gorkogo, Barnaul, 656056 Phone: (3852) 23 2474; fax: (3852) 23 7959 E-mail: forbank@forbank.alt.ru Andrei Ivanovich Makulov, Chairman of the Board
ZAO AKB Zernobank	6, ul. Anatolia, Barnaul, 656056 Phone: (3852) 26 1425; fax: (3852) 24 9490 E-mail: office@GoldenGrain.ru Nikolai Nikolaevich Nikolaev, President

KRASNOYARSK TERRITORY

ZAO AIKB Yenisey United Bank	62, ul. K. Marksa, Krasnoyarsk, 660132 Phone: (3912) 59 1105, 66 0592; fax: (3912) 66 0588 E-mail: bank@united.ru Assia Valyevna Belonogova, President
OOO KB Kansky	1, ul. Vlast Sovetov, Kansk, Krasnoyarsk Territory, 663600 Phone: (39161) 22 468; fax: (39161) 23 462 E-mail: pub00281@krasmail.ru Valentina Alexandrovna Sutko, Chairman of the Board
ZAO KB Kedr	33, ul. Vokzalnaya, Krasnoyarsk, 660021 Phone: (3912) 65 0937; fax: (3912) 65 0923 E-mail: petrova@kedr.kts.ru Igor Yakovlevich Sternin, Chairman of the Board
OOO Provincial Bank Taimyr	14, ul. Sovetskaya, Dudinka, Krasnoyarsk Territory, 663210 Phone: (39111) 25 742, 21 106; fax: (39111) 25 742 E-mail: bank.taim@norcom.ru Anna Nikolaevna Stupina, Chairman of the Board
KB Stromcombank	33, ul. Parizhskoy Kommuny, Krasnoyarsk, 660049 Phone: (3912) 23 7386; fax: 22 7430 E-mail: erm@strc.ru Valery Mikhailovich Gorodilov, Chairman of the Board

IRKUTSK REGION

OAO KB BaikalROSBANK	5, ul. Oktyabrskoy Revolutsii, Irkutsk, 664007 Phone: (3952) 25 8800; fax: (3952) 24 3160 E-mail: mailbox@baikalrosbank.ru Alexander Viktorovich Vedernikov, Chairman of the Board
OAO Joint Stock East Siberian Transport Commercial Bank (OAO VostSibtranscombank)	7, ul. K. Marksa, Irkutsk, 664003 Phone: (3952) 64 4035; fax: (3952) 33 0878 E-mail: post@vstbank.ru Igor Ilyich Rumyantsev, Chairman of the Board
OAO SIBREGIONBANK	6, ul. Lenina, Irkutsk, 664000 Phone: (3952) 21 8551, 21 8700; fax: (3952) 21 8552 E-mail: corsar@akbbgs.ru Gennady Vasilyevich Gatsukov, Chairman of the Board

APPENDICES

1	2
KEMEROVO REGION	
OAO Kemerovo Social Innovation Bank (OAO KEMSOTSINBANK)	31, ul. Kuzbasskaya, Kemerovo, 650099 Phone: (3842) 36 9090; fax: 36 7416 E-mail: root@ksib.ru, http://www.ksib.ru Oleg Igorevich Belikov, CEO
OOO Kuzbass Provincial Bank	56, pr. Sovetsky, Kemerovo, 650000 Phone: (3842) 36 3293; fax: (3842) 58 5391 E-mail: kgb-bk@kem.ru Yulia Yuryevna Dolgova, Chairman of the Board
OAO AKB Kuzbasskhimbank	12, ul. Y. Dvuzhilnogo, Kemerovo, 650024 Phone: (3842) 30 5079; fax: (3842) 30 1190 E-mail: pto@mail.kuzbass.net Sergei Vasilyevich Bolshakov, Chairman of the Board
OAO AKB Kuzbassugolbank	2, pr. Oktyabrsky, Kemerovo, 650059 Phone: (3842) 52 3859; fax: (3842) 52 2865 E-mail: oper@cbank.ru Alexander Nikolaevich Kolobov, Chairman of the Board
OAO AB Kuznetskbusinessbank	89a, ul. Kirova, Novokuznetsk, Kemerovo Region, 654080 Phone: (3843) 46 3240; fax: (3843) 46 6091 E-mail: kbb@kbb.ru Yury Nikolaevich Bulanov, Chairman of the Board
OOO KB Taidon	5, pr. Molodezhny, Kemerovo, 650070 Phone: (3842) 31 9437; fax: (3842) 31 3319 Andrei Leonidovich Kornienko, CEO
NOVOSIBIRSK REGION	
OAO KB Accept	53, ul. M. Gorkogo, Novosibirsk, 630099 Phone: (3832) 27 1021, 27 1022; fax: (3832) 27 1023 E-mail: postmaster@accept.nsk.ru, http://www.akcept.ru Igor Viktorovich Astafyev, CEO
OAO Bank Alemar	37, ul. Serebrennikovskaya, Novosibirsk, 630099 Phone: (3832) 22 1530; fax: (3832) 20 4881 E-mail: root@alemar.nsk.su Irina Vasilyevna Stefanenko, Chairman of the Board
OAO Novosibirsk Commercial Municipal Bank	14, ul. Derzhavina, Novosibirsk, 630091 Phone: (3832) 18 4144; fax: (3832) 18 4199 E-mail: info@nmb.ru Vladimir Gavrilovich Zhenov, CEO
Novosibirsk Social KB Levoberezhny	25/1, ul. Plakhotnogo, Novosibirsk, 630054 Phone/fax: (3832) 10 7650 E-mail: root@kbl.nsk.su Nadezhda Pavlovna Ivaschenko, CEO
ZAO KRAB Novosibirskvneshtorgbank	44, ul. Kirova, Novosibirsk, 630102 Phone: (3832) 10 2089; fax: 10 3024 E-mail: nvtb@nvtb.ru Nadezhda Tikhonovna Streltsova, President
OAO ROSINBANK-SIBIR	8a, Vokzalnaya magistral, Novosibirsk, 630004 Phone: (3832) 18 1508; fax: (3822) 18 1548 E-mail: info@seb.ru Vasily Petrovich Ozheredov, President

1	2
OAO Sibacadembank	18, ul. Lenina, Novosibirsk, 630004 Phone: (3832) 10 0224, 23 9810; fax: (3832) 22 3010, 22 2470 E-mail: secret@sibacadem.ru Andrei Alexandrovich Bekarev, CEO

OMSK REGION

OAO AKB International Trade Bank (OAO AKB IT-Bank)	43, pr. Mira, Omsk, 644029 Phone: (3812) 69 3063; fax: (3812) 69 3420 Oleg Alexandrovich Silnyagin, Chairman of the Board
OAO Omsk Bank	6, per. Gazetny, Omsk, 644099 Phone: (3812) 25 1496; fax: (3812) 25 1496 E-mail: root@omskbank.ru; http://www.omb.omsk.ru Alexei Mikhailovich Chernin, Chairman of the Board
OAO Omskpromstroybank	3a, ul. Ordzhonikidze, Omsk, 644099 Phone: (3812) 28 9507; fax: (3812) 23 7822 E-mail: info@opsb.ru, http://www.opsb.ru Valery Nikolaevich Stepanov, President

TOMSK REGION

OOO KB Dvizhenie	2, per. Kooperativny, Tomsk, 634009 Phone: (3822) 51 0623; fax: (3822) 51 0672 E-mail: info@dvizhenie.tomsknet.ru Vladimir Nikolaevich Durnev, Chairman of the Board
OAO Joint Stock Social Bank Tomsk-Reserve	112, pr. Frunze, Tomsk, 634021 Phone: (3822) 26 0421; fax: (3822) 26 0421 E-mail: office@rezerv.tspace.ru Olga Vladimirovna Pankova, Chairman of the Board
OAO Tomsk Joint Stock Investment Commercial Industrial and Construction Bank	90, pr. Frunze, Tomsk, 634061 Phone: (3822) 26 6302, 26 5931, 26 5994 Fax: (3822) 26 6818 E-mail: tspbank@tspb.com.ru Anatoly Ivanovich Ozerov, Chairman of the Board

CHITA REGION

OAO Chitapromstroybank	37, ul. Petrovskaya, Chita, 672088 Phone: (3022) 23 1540, 23 2858, 23 5251, 23 5640, 26 6455 Fax: (3022) 26 6801 E-mail: root@psb.chita.ru Svetlana Vladimirovna Zatynatskaya, Acting President
OAO Zabaikalsky Bank	41, ul. Amurskaya, Chita, 672010 Phone: (3022) 23 9706; fax: (3022) 23 6394 E-mail: root@zabl.chita.ru Tamara Georgievna Stromilova, Chairman of the Board

FAR EASTERN FEDERAL DISTRICT

REPUBLIC OF SAKHA (YAKUTIA)

KB Almazergienbank	28/1, ul. Kirova, Yakutsk, 677021 Phone: (4112) 42 9290, 42 9369; fax: (4112) 42 9928 E-mail: alergb@yacc.yakutia.su Aisen Sergeevich Nikolaev, Chairman of the Board
Neryungri Commercial Bank Neryungribank	29/4, pr. Druzhby Narodov, Neryungri, Republic of Sakha (Yakutia), 678922 Phone: (41147) 43 232, 40 707 E-mail: nrgbnk@ramir.yakutugol.ru Olga Alexeevna Dmitrieva, Chairman of the Board

APPENDICES

1	2
Republican Investment and Credit Bank Sakhakreditbank	1, prospekt Lenina, Yakutsk, 677000 Phone: (4112) 42 1931, 42 2403; fax: (4112) 42 5425 E-mail: skb757@mail.ru Alexander Stepanovich Mironov, Chairman of the Board
OOO KB SakhaDiamondBank	12, ul. Kirova, Yakutsk, 677000 Phone: (4112) 42 0047; fax: (4112) 42 0047 E-mail: sdbf@mail.sakha.ru Yegor Yegorovich Maksimov, Branch Director Bldg. 1, 9, per. Kolpachny, Moscow 101000 Phone: (095) 923 4435, 923 8231 Tatyana Yuryevna Pakhomova, Chairman of the Board
OAO AB Sir	20, ul. Dzerzhinskogo, Yakutsk, 677000 Phone: (4112) 45 2782, 45 3813; fax: (4112) 45-3650 E-mail: sir@first.sakhanet.ru Viktor Nikolaevich Grigoryev, Chairman of the Board
MARITIME TERRITORY	
OAO Far Eastern Bank	27a, ul. Verkhneportovaya, Vladivostok, 690950 Phone: (4232) 51 6400; fax: (4232) 51 6444 E-mail: post@dvbank.ru Yadviga Mikhailovna Dobryanskaya, President
ZAO Joint Stock Commercial Bank Primorye	47, ul. Svetlanskaya, Vladivostok, 690990 Phone: (4232) 22 6875; fax: (4232) 43 1400 E-mail: mail@primbank.ru Valery Alexeevich Aleshin, CEO
OAO Maritime Social Commercial Bank Primsotsbank	44, pr. Partizansky, Vladivostok, 690106 Phone: (4232) 42 1407; fax: (4232) 42 2076 E-mail: bank@pskb.com Dmitry Borisovich Yarovoi, Chairman of the Board
KHABAROVSK TERRITORY	
OAO Far Eastern Commercial Bank Dalcombank	27, ul. Gogolya, Khabarovsk, 680000 Phone: (4212) 30 6696; fax: (4212) 74 7720 E-mail: dcb@dalcombank.com Andrei Zakharovich Shlyakhovoi, President
Bank Far Eastern OVK	26, ul. Kim Yu Chena, Khabarovsk, 680000 Phone: (4212)) 32 6958; fax: (4212) 32 7092 E-mail: referent@dvovk.ru Sergei Nikolaevich Vlasov, Chairman of the Board
ZAO Joint Stock Commercial Bank for Regional Development Regiobank	18, b-r Amursky, Khabarovsk, 680000 Phone: (4212) 32 4794; fax: (4212) 32 8708 E-mail: admin@regiobank.ru Sergei Grigoryevich Grebenyuk, President
AMUR REGION	
ZAO Amur Joint Stock Investment Commercial Industrial and Construction Bank Amurpromstroybank	225, ul. Amurskaya, Blagoveschensk, 675000 Phone: (4162) 44 5717; fax: (4162) 39 1128 E-mail: apsb@tsl.ru Valery Kuzmich Fedorov, Chairman
AKB Dalcombank	173a, ul. Zeyskaya, Blagoveschensk, 675000 Phone: (4162) 44 0465, 44 6801; fax: (4162) 44 0465 E-mail: dkb@dalcombank.ru Valentina Nikolaevna Timoshenko, Chairman of the Board

1	2

KAMCHATKA REGION

Joint Stock Kamchatka Commercial Agroindustrial Bank Kamchatcomagroprombank	5, pr. 50 let Oktyabrya, Petropavlovsk-Kamchatsky, 683024 Phone: (41522) 60 270; fax: (41522) 31 643 Dmitry Markovich Povzner, President
OAO Kamchatprombank	14, ul. Sovetskaya, Petropavlovsk-Kamchatsky, 683000 Phone/fax: (4152) 12 5783, 11 2361 Vladimir Ivanovich Ablamonov, President
ZAO AKB Municipal Kamchatprofitbank	19, ul. Pogranichnaya, Petropavlovsk-Kamchatsky, 683032 Phone: (4152) 16 9209; fax: (4152) 11 1164 E-mail: secr@profit.siks.ru Igor Alexeevich Polunin, Chairman of the Board, CEO

MAGADAN REGION

OAO Import-Export IMPEXbank, Magadan Branch	48a, ul. Yakutskaya, Magadan, 685000 Phone: (41322) 50 858; fax: (41322) 97 140 E-mail: impex@kolyma.ru Marina Vadimovna Androsova, Acting Director
OAO Kolyma-Bank	17, ul. Proletarskaya, Magadan, 685000 Phone: (41322) 97 264; fax: (41322) 28 041 E-mail: main@kolymabank.magadan.su Vladimir Leonidovich Fel, President
OAO AKB Nadezhny Bank	17, ul. Proletarskaya, Magadan, 685000 Phone: (41322) 21 065; fax: (41322) 21 065 E-mail: nadb@sferacom.ru Leonid Mikhailovich Krasner, Chairman of the Board

SAKHALIN REGION

ZAO KB Dolinsk	119a, pr. Mira, Yuzhno-Sakhalinsk, 693007 Phone: (4242) 72 3683; fax: (4242) 72 3683 E-mail: office@bankdolinsk.ru Dmitry Vladimirovich Nesterov, Chairman of the Board
OAO MABES Sakhalin-West	24, pr. Pobedy, Yuzhno-Sakhalinsk, 693007 Phone: (4242) 74 1050; fax: 55 1692 E-mail: sw@sw.sakhalin.ru Anatoly Ivanovich Mokhov, Chairman of the Board

INTERNATIONAL AND FOREIGN FINANCIAL INSTITUTIONS IN THE RUSSIAN FEDERATION

Financial institutions	Contact information
1	2

1. INTERNATIONAL AND REGIONAL INSTITUTIONS

European Bank for Reconstrution and Development (EBRD)	Bldg. 1, 36, ul. B. Molchanovka, Moscow, 121069 Phone: (095) 787 1111; fax: (095) 787 1122
International Bank for Recostrution and Development (IBRD)	Bldg. 1, 36, ul. B. Molchanovka, Moscow, 121069 Phone: (095) 745 7000; fax: (501) 745 7002, 967 1209
International Financial Corporation (IFC)	Bldg. 2, house 5, 7, ul. B. Dmitrovka, Moscow, 103009 Phone: (095) 755 8818; fax: (501) 755 8296
International Monetary Fund (IMF)	11, Gogolevsky blvd., Moscow, 119019 Phone: (095) 705 9200; fax: (095) 705 9136
The Multilateral Investment Guarantee Agency (MIGA)	Bldg. 1, 36, ul. B. Molchanovka, Moscow, 121069 Phone: (095) 745 7000, 9673167; fax: (095) 745 7002, 967 1209

2. GOVERNMENT EXPORT PROMOTION ORGANIZATIONS

Foreign Commercial Service (USA)	23/38, ul. B. Molchanovka, Moscow, 121069 Phone: (095) 737 5030, 737 5029; fax: (095) 7375033 E-mail: Moscow.Office.Box@mail.doc.gov; Oganes.Sarkisov@mail.doc.gov
Japan Bank for International Cooperation (Japan)	Office 905, International Trade Center, 12, Krasnopresnenskaya nab., Moscow, 123610 Phone: (095) 258 1832, 258 1835, 258 1836; fax: (095) 258 1858

3. FOREIGN BANKS AND REPRESENTATIVE OFFICES[1]

ARMENIA	
OOO Anelik Bank (Branch)	19, ul. 1st Yamskogo Polya, Moscow, 125124 Phone: (095) 251 1919, 251 2408; fax: (095) 251 1427 E-mail: anelik@arminco.com

AUSTRIA	
Donau-Bank AG (Representative office)	Office 5, 17/1, ul. Petrovka, Moscow, 103031 Phone: (095) 921 4221; fax: (095) 935 8533 E-mail: donauag.repoffice@public.mtu.ru
Raiffeisen Zentral Bank Oesterreich AG (Representative office)	Bldg. 1, 14, Prechistensky per., Moscow, 119034 Phone: (095) 721 9903; fax: (095) 721 9907
ZAO Raiffeisenbank – Austria	Bldg. 1, 17, ul. Troitskaya, Moscow, 129090 Phone: (095) 721 9900; fax: (095) 721 9901 E-mail: common@raiffeisen.ru

APPENDICES

---

[1] The list includes existing 100% non-resident owned banks and banks with non-resident stakes of over 50% of the charter capital.

1	2
AZERBAIJAN	
OOO International Bank of Azerbaijan – Moscow	Bldg. 2, 6, ul. Tverskaya, Moscow, 125009 Phone: (095) 937 7727; fax: (095) 937 7719 E-mail: iba-moscow@ibamoscow.ru
BELARUS	
Belarusbank Savings Bank (Representative office)	Office 423, 69/75, ul. Vavilova, Moscow, 117997 Phone: (095) 938 2344; fax: (095) 938 2345 E-mail: belbank@orc.ru
Belpromstroybank (Representative office)	22, B. Tishinsky per., Moscow, 123557 Phone: (095) 253 6702; fax: (095) 253 7868
Belvneshekonombank (Representative office)	7, ul. Mashi Poryvayevoy, Moscow, 107078 Phone/fax: (095) 204 9302
CHINA	
ZAO Bank of China (Elos), Joint Stock Commercial Bank	72, pr. Mira, Moscow, 129110 Phone: (095) 795 0462, 795 0451; fax (095) 795 0454 E-mail: bocru@online.ru
CYPRUS	
Bank of Cyprus (Representative office)	6th floor, bldg. 1, 33, pr. Mira, Moscow, 129110 Phone: (095) 797 5808; fax: (095) 797 5810 E-mail: bankofcyprus@deol.com
Cyprus Popular Bank (Representative office)	1005a, 12, Krasnopresnenskaya nab., Moscow, 123610 Phone: (095) 967 0185; fax: (095) 967 0186 E-mail: popularbank@wtt.ru
Hellenic Bank Ltd. (Representative office)	15, Savvinskaya nab., Moscow, 119435 Phone: (095) 792 9988; fax: (095) 792 9985 E-mail: hellenicbank@sovintel.ru
ZAO Investment Bank of Kuban	113, ul. Krasnaya, Krasnodar, 350620 Phone (8612) 699 879; fax: (8612) 696 878 E-mail: ibk@kuban.net
CZECH REPUBLIC	
OOO Home Credit and Finance Bank	4, ul. Baumanskaya, Moscow, 105005 Phone: (095) 534 1449, 785 8210; fax: (095) 785 8218 E-mail: info@homecredit.ru
FINLAND	
Nordea Bank (Representative office)	Office 758, Smolensky Passage, 3, Smolenskaya pl., Moscow, 121099 Phone: (095) 721 1646; fax: (095) 721 1647
FRANCE	
ZAO AKB Bank Societe Generale Vostok	Golutvinsky Dvor Business Center 2, Yakimanskaya nab., Moscow, 119180 Phone: (095) 720 6700, 720 6701, 720 6702; fax: (095) 720 6749
Banque Commerciale pour l'Europe du Nord – Eurobank (Representative office)	29, ul. Novy Arbat, Moscow, 123001 Phone: (095) 956 4450; fax: (095) 967 8173
ZAO BNP Paribas Bank	Samsung Business Center Bldg. 2, B. Gnezdnikovsky per., Moscow, 125009 Phone: (095) 785 6070; fax: (095) 785 6071

APPENDICES

1	2
ZAO Commercial Bank Credit Lyonnais Rusbank	12, Nevsky pr., St. Petersburg, 191186 Phone (812) 449 1100; fax: (812) 449 1190
Credit Agricole Indosuez (Representative office)	23, ul. 1st Tverskaya-Yamskaya, Moscow, 125047 Phone: (095) 258 0415; fax: (095) 258 0418
ZAO Natexis Banque Populair	Bldg. 1, 23, ul. 1st Tverskaya-Yamskaya, Moscow, 125047 Phone: (095) 787 1700; fax: (095) 787 1718 E-mail: natexis@nxbp.ru
GERMANY	
Bankgesellschaft Berlin AG (Representative office)	5/2, 1st Kazachy per., Moscow, 119017 Phone: (095) 956 9802; fax: (095) 956 9803 E-mail: bb_moskau@col.ru
Bayerische Hypovereinsbank AG (Representative office)	Bldg.1, 14, Prechistensky per., Moscow, 119034 Phone: (095) 937 1897; fax: (095) 937 1898
Bayerische Landesbank (Representative office)	7, 1st Kazachy per., Moscow, 119017 Phone: (095) 234 4958; fax: (095) 234 4988 E-mail: jylia.gorbatschova@bayernlb.ru
ZAO Westdeutsche Landesbank Vostok	Bldg. 4, 23, ul. Povarskaya, Moscow, 121069 Phone: (095) 258 6100, 258 6102; fax: (095) 258 6148
ZAO Commerzbank (Eurasia)	14/2, Kadashevskaya nab., Moscow, 119017 Phone: (095) 797 4800; fax: (095) 797 4827
Commerzbank (Representative office)	14/2, Kadashevskaya nab., Moscow, 119017 Phone: (095) 797 4848; fax: (095) 797 4849 E-mail: rep.moskau@commerzbank.com
OOO Deutsche Bank	4, ul. Schepkina, Moscow, 129090 Phone: (095) 797 5000; fax: (095) 797 5017 E-mail: db.moscow@db.com
ZAO Dresdner Bank	30, Podsosensky per., Moscow, 105062 Phone: (095) 737 3450, 737 3464, 737 7667; fax: (095) 737 3451 E-mail: zao@dresdner.com
ZAO International Moscow Bank	9, Prechistenskaya nab., Moscow, 119034 Phone: (095) 258 72 58; fax: (095) 258 7272 E-mail: imbank@imbank.ru
Ost-West Handelsbank AG (Representative office)	5th floor, bldg. 1, 14, Prechistensky per., Moscow, 119034 Phone: (095) 783 6068; fax: (095) 783 6070 E-mail: service@owh.de
INDIA	
State Bank of India (Representative office)	Offices 24 and 25, 14, ul. B. Dorogomilovskaya, Moscow, 121059 Phone: (095) 974 8138, 974 8137; fax: (095) 974 8136
IRAN	
ZAO Bank Melli Iran	9/1, ul. Mashkova, Moscow, 105064 Phone: (095) 207 0075, 207 14 59; fax: (095) 928 6286 E-mail: mellimos@rex400.ru
ITALY	
Banca di Roma (Representative office)	Office 8, 4, Mamonovsky per., Moscow, 123001 Phone: (095) 209 6625, 209 6501; fax: (095) 200 0233 E-mail: bdrmo@co.ru

1	2
Banca Monte dei Paschi di Siena SpA (Representative office)	12, Krasnopresnenskaya nab., Moscow, 123610 Phone: (095) 967 0475; fax: (095) 967 0477 E-mail: montepaschi@mavica.ru
Banca Nazionale del Lavoro (Representative office)	Bldg.1, 8, M. Znamensky per., Moscow, 119019 Phone: (095) 203 0326, 202 7657, 203 0395; fax: (095) 202 9983 E-mail: bnlmosca@cityline.ru
San Paolo IMI (Representative office)	16, ul. Marksistskaya, Moscow, 109147 Phone: (095) 232 6740; fax: (095) 232 6741 E-mail: cispaolo@rol.ru
Sella Corporate Finance (Representative office)	Office 318, bldg. 2, 3/8, Lavrushinsky per., Moscow, 119017 Phone/fax: (095) 951 6972 E-mail: marello@online.ru
	JAPAN
Bank of Tokyo, Mitsubishi (Representative office)	6th floor, Trubhaya ul., Moscow, 107045 Phone: (095) 797 4501; fax: (095) 797 4500 E-mail: btm-moscow@mtu-net.ru
ZAO AKB Michinoku Bank (Moscow)	Bldg. 4, 37/1, ul. B. Ordynka, Moscow, 119017 Phone: (095) 729 5858; fax: (095) 729 58 98 E-mail: michin@dol.ru
	LATVIA
Multibanka (Representative office)	7/10, ul. B. Polyanka, Moscow, 119180 Phone: (095) 950 8326, 950 8327; fax: (095) 950 8131 E-mail: info@multibanka.com
	THE NETHERLANDS
ZAO ABN AMRO Bank A.O.	Bldg.1, 17, ul. B. Nikitskaya, Moscow, 125009 Phone: (095) 931 91 41; fax: (095) 931 9140
ZAO ING Bank (Eurasia)	31, ul. Krasnaya Presnya, Moscow, 123022 Phone: (095) 755 5400, 937 7900; fax: (095) 755 5499
Rabobank Nederland (Representative office)	3rd floor, 10, Novaya pl., Moscow, 109012 Phone: (095) 721 1984; fax: (095) 721 1985
	POLAND
Bank Gospodarki Zywnosciowej S.A. (Representative office)	9, Milyutinsky per., Moscow, 101000 Phone: (095) 937 5908; fax: (095) 222 4072 E-mail: bgzsa@mail.ru
	SERBIA AND MONTENEGRO
ZAO AKB EuroAxis Bank	Bldg. 1, 17, Spiridonyevsky per., Moscow, 123104 Phone: (095) 200 6215; fax: (095) 200 2334
	SLOVENIA
Nova Ljubljanska Banka (Representative office)	Office 608, 7, ul. Mashi Poryvayevoy, Moscow, 107078 Phone: (095) 230 6666; fax: (095) 956 3196 E-mail: nlbmos@dol.ru
	SWEDEN
Svenska Handelsbanken (Representative office)	19a, Khlebny per., Moscow 121069 Phone: (095) 291 6811; fax: (095) 230 6256

APPENDICES

1	2
SWITZERLAND	
ZAO Bank Credit Swiss First Boston AO	5, Nikitsky per., Moscow, 103009 Phone: (095) 967 8200, 967 8888; fax: (095) 967 8210
ZAO AKB Creditsoyuzcombank	23, B. Golovin per., Moscow, 107045 Phone: (095) 737 5885; fax: (095) 737 5887
S. G. Warburg & Co Ltd. (Representative office)	11th floor, 2/2, Paveletskaya pl., Moscow, 113054 Phone: (095) 726 5700; fax: (095) 726 5701
SLB Commercial Bank (Representative office)	35, ul. Myasnitskaya, Moscow, 101000 Phone: (095) 933 1615; fax: (095) 9331616
TAJIKISTAN	
Orienbank (Tajikistan Industrial and Construction Bank – Representative office)	19, Skatertny per., Moscow, 121069 Phone/fax: (095) 202 0152
TURKEY	
ZAO AKB Finansbank (Moscow)	Bldg. 2, 2, Paveletskaya pl., Moscow, 113054 Phone: (095) 725 4040; fax: (095) 725 4041
ZAO KB Garanti Bank-Moscow	5th floor, bldg. 1, 52, Kosmodamianskaya nab., Moscow, 113035 Phone: (095) 961 2500; fax: (095) 961 2502, 961 2503 E-mail: postmaster@gbm.ru
ZAO Iktisat Bank (Moscow)	Bldg. 1, 2, ul. Sadovnicheskaya, Moscow, 115035 Phone: (095) 725 1020; fax: (095) 725 1025 E-mail: postoffice@iktisatbank
ZAO AKB Yapi Kredi Bank Moscow	Bldg. 2, 1, Goncharnaya nab., Moscow, 115172 Phone: (095) 234 9889; fax: (095) 956 1972 E-mail: yap@online.ru
ZAO Ziraat Bank (Moscow),	16, ul. Marksitskaya, Moscow, 109147 Phone: (095) 232 6737; fax: (095) 232 6736 E-mail: admin@ziraatbank.rmt.ru
UNITED KINGDOM	
ZAO Alef-Bank Joint Stock Comercial Bank	20, ul. Dmitriya Ulyanova, Moscow, 119333 Phone/fax: (095) 411 7747 E-mail: alefbank@alefbank.ru
ZAO Bank for Small Business Lending (KMB-Bank)	Bldg. 2, 3, Yelokhovsky pr., Moscow, 107066 Phone: (095) 967 3060; fax (095) 789 6827
HSBC Bank (RR), OOO	9, Dmitrovsky per., Moscow, 107031 Phone: (095) 721 1515; fax: (095) 258 3154 E-mail: hsbc.moscow@hsbc.com
ZAO Industrial Export and Import Bank, Joint Stock Bank	Bldg. 3, Sretensky blvd., Moscow, 103045 Phone: (095) 924 6579; fax: (095) 262 5188 E-mail: info@pbank.ru
ZAO Investment Bank of Kuban	113, ul. Krasnaya, Krasnodar, 350620 Phone: (8612) 699 879; fax: (8612) 696 878 E-mail: ibk@kuban.net
Moscow Narodny Bank Ltd. (Representative office)	Bldg. 1, 13, 1st Kadashevsky per., Moscow, 115035 Phone: (095) 792 3060; fax: (095) 792 3062

1	2
Mosnarbank Commercial Bank, ZAO	Bldg. 5, 12, 1st Troitsky per., Moscow, 129090 Phone/fax: (095) 785 2000, 785 5000
Standard Bank London Ltd. (Representative office)	Bldg. 2, 4/7, ul. Vozdvizhenka, Moscow, 125009 Phone: (095) 721 3800; fax: (095) 721 3801

UNITED STATES

American Express Bank Ltd. (Representative office)	Bldg. 1, 33, ul. Usacheva, Moscow, 119048 Phone: (095) 933 8448; fax: (095) 933 8449
ZAO Bank for Small Business Lending (KMB-Bank)	Bldg. 2, 3, Yelokhovsky pr., Moscow, 107066 Phone: (095) 967 3060; fax (095) 789 6827
ZAO KB Citibank	8/10, ul. Gasheka, Moscow, 125047 Phone: (095) 725 1000; fax: (095) 725 6700
ZAO KB DeltaCredit	Bldg. 2, 4/7, ul. Vozdvizhenka, Moscow, 125009 Phone: (095) 230 6060; fax: (095) 260 3162 E-mail: deltacredit@deltacredit.ru
ZAO Deltabank	Bldg. 1, 11, per. Kamennaya Sloboda, Moscow, 121099 Phone: (095) 721 3870, 258 0400; fax: (095) 244 8949 E-mail: banking@deltabank.ru
J.P. Morgan Bank International, KB, OOO	Bldg.1, 2, Paveletskaya pl., Moscow, 115054 Phone: (095) 937 7300; fax: (095) 937 7334
Morgan Stanley (Representative office)	7, ul. Gasheka, Moscow, 123056 Phone: (095) 785 2200; fax: (095) 785 2229
OOO Western Union DP Vostok Non-Banking Credit Institution	Bldg. 2, 4, ul. Sivashskaya, Moscow, 113149 Phone: (095) 797 2189; fax: (095) 797 2188

UZBEKISTAN

ZAO AKB Asia-Invest Bank	11/2, 1st Kazachy per., Moscow, 119017 Phone/fax: (095) 363 3702, 230 7009 E-mail: main@asiainvestbank.ru

4. INSURANCE COMPANIES

ZAO SK AIG Russia (USA)	16/2, ul. Tverskaya, Moscow, 125009 Phone: (095) 935 8950; fax: (095) 935 8952
ZAO SK Ost-West-Allianz, (Germany)	3, 3rd Samotechny per., Moscow, 127473 Phone: (095) 937 6996; fax: (095) 937 6980 E-mail: allianz@allianz.ru
ZAO SK Zurich-Rus (Switzerland)	26, Denisovsky per., Moscow, 105005 Phone: (095) 933 5141; fax: (095) 933 5142 E-mail: info@zurich.ru

5. LEASING COMPANIES

ZAO Delta Leasing (USA)	4th floor, M. Sukharevskaya pl., Moscow, 127051 Phone (095) 960 2243; fax (095) 960 2240 E-mail: moscow@deltaleasing.ru
ZAO DeltaLeas – Far East (USA)	10/12, pr. Okeansky, Vladivostok, 690000 Phone: (4232) 491 221; fax: (4232) 491 220 E-mail: info@dlfe.ru

APPENDICES

1	2
OOO Karkade (Poland)	Bldg. 1, 24/7, ul. Myasnitskaya, Moscow, 111000 Phone/fax: (095) 933 8816
ZAO KMB-Leasing (UK, USA)	15/7, 1st Neopalimovsky per., Moscow, 119121 Phone: (095) 967 6707; fax: (095) 967 3062 E-mail: leasing@kmb.ru
OOO Raiffeisen Leasing (Austria)	17/1, ul. Troitskaya, Moscow, 129090 Phone: (095) 721 9900; fax: (095) 721 9901 E-mail: leasing@raiffeisen.ru

6. INVESTMENT FUNDS
6.1 DIRECT EQUITY FUNDS AND VENTURE FUNDS

Agribusiness Management Company LLC	Bldg. 2, 1, B. Gnezdnikovsky per., Moscow, 121069 Phone: (095) 792 3450; fax: (095) 792 3451
AIG Brunswick Millennium Fund	9th floor, 52/3, Kosmodamianskaya nab., Moscow, 113035 Phone: (095) 961 2000; fax: (095) 961 2001
Baring Vostok Private Equity Fund; First NIS Regional Fund; Sector Capital Fund	Baring Vostok Capital Partners Management Company Office 750, 7, ul. Gasheka, Moscow, 123056 Phone: (095) 967 1307; fax: (095) 967 1308 E-mail: webmaster@bvcp.ru
Berkeley Capital Partners	Office 232, 11, ul. Musy Jalilya, Novosibirsk, 630055 Phone: (3832) 397 915; fax: (3832) 397 913 E-mail: wsvf@online.ru Office 316, 9, Spiridoniyevsky per., Moscow, 103104 Phone: (095) 202 5559; fax: (095) 937 5684 E-mail: wsvf@online.ru
Brunswick Russian Growth Fund, Brunswick Russian Directional Fund	Management Company Brunswick Asset Management Research Ltd. 2/2, Paveletskaya pl., Moscow, 113054 Phone: (095) 961 2040; fax: (095) 258 5293
Commercial Capital	Bldg. 6, 33/2, ul. Usacheva, Moscow, 119048 Phone: (095) 933 3178; fax: (095) 933 3179 E-mail: rep@comcap.ru
Daiwa Far East and Eastern Siberia Investment Fund	7, ul. Moskovskaya, Khabarovsk, 680000 Phone: (4212) 227 243; fax: (4212) 336 287 E-mail: rif@daiwa.khv.ru
Delta Capital Management	2/3, Paveletskaya pl., Moscow, 113054 Phone: (095) 960 3131; fax: (095) 960 3132 E-mail: reception@deltacap.ru
Eagle Black Earth Fund	38, ul. Stepana Razina, Voronezh, 394000 Phone: (0732) 713 180; 719 441; 713 291; 573 886 Fax: (0732) 712 303 E-mail: eagle@rabo.vrn.ru
Eagle Urals Fund	Office 514, 15a, ul. Antona Valeka, Yekaterinburg, 620014 Phone: (3432) 787 174; fax: (3432) 787 175 E-mail: eagle@evp.bcforum.ru
Eagle Venture Partners BV	7, ul. Novy Arbat, Moscow, 129019 Phone: (095) 234 4217; fax: (095) 234 4218 E-mail: info@evp.ru

1	2
Eurasia Fund	Bldg. 1, 4/6, 3rd Monetchikovsky per., Moscow, 115054 Phone: (095) 970 1567; fax: (095) 970 1568 E-mail: efmoscow@eurasia.msk.ru
Framlington Russian Investment Fund	Office 8, bldg. 1, 13/3, ul. Sadovaya-Chernogryazskaya, Moscow, 105064 Phone: (095) 937 5933; fax: (095) 937 4845
Lower Volga Regional Venture Fund	Regional Partners Management Company: 14, Stoleshnikov per., Moscow, 103031 Phone: (095) 234 3095; fax: (095) 234 3099
North-West and West of Russia Regional Venture Fund	3, Kaluzhsky per., St. Petersburg, 193015 Phone: (812) 320 0404; fax: (812) 320 0405
OOO Bridge Investments	Bldg. 3, 47, Lenigradsky pr., Moscow, 125167 Phone: (095) 787 0535; fax: (095) 787 0535 E-mail: info@bimc.ru
OOO Equity and Management Quadriga Capital Russia	Office 3.14, 30, Nevsky pr., St. Petersburg, 191011 Phone: (812) 325 8474; fax: (812) 325 8477 E-mail: info@quadriga-capital.ru
Pio Global Asset Management	5, Gazetny per., Moscow, 125993 Phone: (095) 956 6056; fax: (095) 202 3945
Ros-Venture Management	6th floor, 10, ul. Beregovaya, Rostov-on-Don, 344007 Phone: (8632) 673 128, 673 422; fax: (8632) 670 407 E-mail: rosvm@rostov.ru
Russian Fund for Small Business Support of the European Bank for Reconstruction and Development	36, ul. B. Molchanovka, Moscow, 121069 Phone: (095) 799 5577; fax: (095) 799 5588 E-mail: main@ebrd-rsbf.ru
Russian Technology Fund	Bldg. 12v, 27, prosp. Engelsa, St. Petersburg, 194156 Phone: (812) 244 2506, 554 9384; fax: (812) 326 6191 E-mail: rtf@fi.ru

6.2 PORTFOLIO FUNDS

Brunswick Asset Management Research Limited	2/2, Paveletskaya pl., Moscow, 113054 Phone: (095) 961 2040; fax: (095) 258 5293
Hermitage Capital Management Limited	9, Dmitrovsky per., Moscow, 103031 Phone: (501) 258 3160; fax: (501) 258 3161 E-mail: info@hermitagefund.com
Russia Growth Fund	Bldg. 2, 7, prosp. Mira, Moscow, 129090 Phone: (095) 956 7950; fax: (095) 956 7951 E-mail: rgf@mailru.com
Templeton Eastern European Fund; Emerging Markets Fund; Emerging Markets Bond Fund; Templeton Russia Fund	Management Company Templeton Asset Management 5th floor, bldg. 1, 16/2, ul. Tverskaya, Moscow, 125009 Phone: (095) 935 8368; fax (095) 937 5464 E-mail: vsemend@templeton.com
The Russian Prosperity Fund; Prosperity Cub Fund; Prosperity Quest Fund; Prosperity Quest Telecom; Pros- perity Quest Power; Seligson Prosperity Russia Fund	Management Company Prosperity Capital Management Ltd. 52/3, Kosmodamianskaya nab., Moscow, 113035 Phone: (095) 961 2810; fax: (095) 961 2816

APPENDICES

Moscow Bar In Jure is made up of legal specialists with many years of practical experience. The Bar specializes in providing legal and contractual support to companies, case defense, creating corporate legal security systems, tax optimization, and legal support to corporations operating abroad. The Bar is staffed by authoritative experts in various areas of law. The Bar keeps up to date with the practices of law enforcement agencies and bodies. We offer the following services:

- Representation and defense in court, arbitration court, the International Commercial Arbitration Court Attached to the Chamber of Commerce and Industry of the Russian Federation, and other tribunals;
- Preparation of claims and out-of-court settlement;
- Enforcement of rulings of the International Commercial Arbitration Court Attached to the Chamber of Commerce and Industry of the Russian Federation;
- Comprehensive services with respect to the financial and business activities of legal entities in Russia, including land law, real estate purchasing, sale and leasing, foreign trade, customs regulation, and taxation;
- Receipt of permits for the opening of branches and representative offices of Russian legal entities abroad, and for the opening of branches and representative offices of foreign legal entities in Russia, including translation of the relevant documents into and from Russian;
- Drafting of foundation documents for social and religious associations and companies, including companies with foreign investment, branches and representative offices of foreign firms, and the urgent registration/accreditation of organizations with the appropriate bodies;
- Agreement drafting, including: purchase/sale (real estate, goods, services), leasing, loan, agency, investment agreements, etc.

The Bar's working languages are English, French, German, and Arabic. In Jure looks forward to servicing your company's legal department and discussing issues of interest to your company.

IN JURE

RUSSIA OFFICE: BUILDING 6, 10, GOLUTVINSKY PER., 119180, MOSCOW
TEL.: (095) 792 3474; FAX: (095) 792 3473; E-MAIL: mail@injure.ru; HTTP://www.injure.ru

SWITZERLAND OFFICE: 15, RUE DU CENDRIER, 1201 GENEVE, SWITZERLAND
TEL.: (41 22) 716 3133, (41 22) 716 3111; FAX: (41 22) 716 3140

GERMANY OFFICE: 108, LITTENSTRASSE 10179 BERLIN, GERMANY
TEL.: (030) 243 13 90; FAX: (030) 243 13 99; E-MAIL: mail@arzinger.de

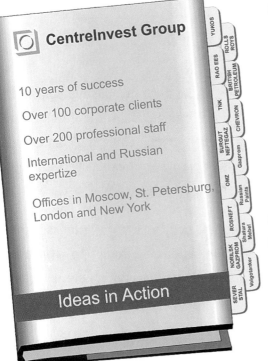

UNITED NATIONS
DEVELOPMENT PROGRAMME (UNDP)

United Nations Development Programme (UNDP)
is the UN's global development network, advocating for change
and connecting countries to knowledge, experience and resources to help
people build a better life. We are on the ground in 166 countries.

UNDP areas of activity

- Democratic Governance
- Poverty Reduction (Social and Economic Development)
- Information and Communications Technology
- HIV/AIDS
- Energy and Environment
- Crisis Prevention and Recovery

UNDP in Russia

United Nations Development Programme
has been operating in Russia since 1993, the year in which the UNDP
treaty was signed with the Russian government.
UNDP opened its permanent representation in Russia in 1997.

**UNDP has carried out or is in the process of carrying
out some 53 projects in Russia in the following areas:**

- **Improvement of the system of state governance**
- **Raising investment into social and economic development**
- **Environmental protection and energy efficiency**

United Nations
Development Programme
Permanent representation in Russia
28, ul. Ostozhenka, 119034, Moscow

Tel.: +7 (095) 787 2100
Fax: +7 (095) 787 2101
E-mail: info@undp.ru
http://www.undp.ru

ICC – THE WORLD BUSINESS ORGANIZATION IN RUSSIA

TANYA MONAGHAN,
SECRETARY GENERAL
ICC RUSSIA

The International Chamber of Commerce – The World Business Organization (ICC) is an influential international independent non-profit organization based in Paris. Established in 1919 on the initiative of the most famous representatives of the world business, ICC is a global association of thousands of businesses, unions and companies all over the world.

ICC works in close contact and in co-operation with such organizations as the United Nations, WTO, World Bank, EBRD, G8 and others acting as a collective consultative body expressing the interests of the world business;

ICC is a rule-making organization — unlike local chambers it is being involved in rule-making activities. ICC sets unified rules and standards for international business, reviews the best international practices of doing business, and takes an active part in the process of changing the national legislation to reflect the interests of business, trade and investments.

The ICC's main objective is to promote the best international business practices. Its activities are aimed at solving the most urgent issues confronting the world business.

On May 6 2000, the ICC World Council unanimously admitted Russia to the World Business Organization and approved the establishment of The Russian National Committee (ICC Russia). This initiative is important to the world business community and to the Russian business as well. It demonstrates the importance the international business community attaches to integrating Russia into the world economic system.

ICC RUSSIA'S MAIN LINES OF ACTIVITIES

ICC Russia will focus on the following priority activities. We will

- contribute our members' business expertise to the Russian Government's and the Russian Parliament's activities in the field of legislation;
- hold seminars and conferences on the key business issues and organize presentations to introduce ICC most significant products, such as Incoterms 2000, UCP 500, unified rules and standard contracts;
- hold regular meetings of the Russian entrepreneurs-ICC Russia members with the members of the Russian Government and the Parliament; with entrepreneurs and political leaders from other countries; with such world organizations as the World Bank, OSCD, EBRD and others, including private banks and funds;
- develop co-operation and partnership relations with governmental organizations in other countries, with the most active and influential ICC national committees in other countries, with investment banks, funds, companies;
- take measures to increase the number of ICC Russia members;
- work an on-going advertising campaign in mass media;
- attract ICC Russia member companies to the work of the ICC commissions following the main objectives outlined in ICC Action Plan;
- promote ICC World Congresses in Russia.

ICC Russia

OFFICE 342, 17, KOTELNICHESKAYA NAB., 109240, MOSCOW, RUSSIA
PHONE: (+7 095) 720 5080; FAX: (+7 095) 720 5081; E-MAIL: iccadmin@iccwbo.ru; HTTP://www.iccwbo.ru

The Russian Children's
Welfare Society (RCWS)

The Russian Children's Welfare Society (RCWS) was established in New York City in 1926 to improve the lives of needy children of Russian descent around the world. Since the breakup of the Soviet Union in 1991, Russia has experienced a grave social crisis, placing millions of children at risk

• Medical Programs;
• Rehabilitation Centers for Disabled Children
• Scholarship and Educational Programs.

Actively following and contributing to the latest research in children's development, RCWS works to assist children throughout the world. In 2003,

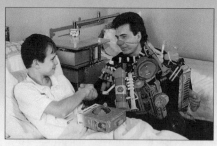

Given such great need, the Society now directs 90% of its yearly aid to programs in Russia. The Society provides assistance to organizations in Russia that support children in four main program areas:
• Orphanages and Homeless Shelters;

RCWS is initiating a new project to assist children suffering from the Fragile X Syndrome, which is the single most common inherited cause of mental impairment. Currently, 80-90% of people with fragile X are not correctly diagnosed. With this project we hope that our efforts will benefit children globally.

The Russian Children's Welfare Society is a US based nonprofit organization with 501 (c) 3 status. To learn more about us, please contact us in our New York office at 888-732-RCWS 212-473-6263 fax 212-473-6301 or visit our website www.rcws.org.

Full contact information:
200 Park Avenue South, Suite 1617, New York, NY 10003.

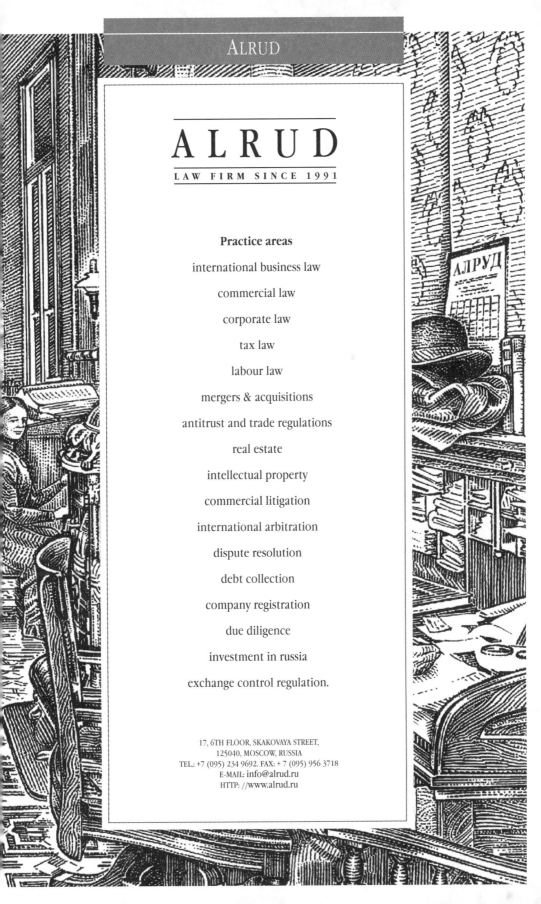

A L R U D
LAW FIRM SINCE 1991

Practice areas

international business law

commercial law

corporate law

tax law

labour law

mergers & acquisitions

antitrust and trade regulations

real estate

intellectual property

commercial litigation

international arbitration

dispute resolution

debt collection

company registration

due diligence

investment in russia

exchange control regulation.

17, 6TH FLOOR, SKAKOVAYA STREET,
125040, MOSCOW, RUSSIA
TEL.: +7 (095) 234 9692. FAX: + 7 (095) 956 3718
E-MAIL: info@alrud.ru
HTTP: //www.alrud.ru

INDEXES
AND REFERENCES

* Page number
** Section number
*** Table number

INDEXES AND REFERENCES

IND

IND

INDEXES AND REFERENCES

FUEL

COAL AND PEAT

Komi Republic
238 (3.3)
Pskov Region
312 (3.6)
Republic of Dagestan
350 (3.6)
Rostov Region
453 (3.3)
Kurgan Region
619 (3.6)
Republic of Buryatia
684 (3.3)
Republic of Tyva
693 (3.3)
Republic of Khakassia
703 (3.6)
Krasnoyarsk Territory
721 (3.3)
Irkutsk Region
732 (3.6)
Kemerovo Region
742 (3.3)
Novosibirsk Region
754 (3.6)
Chita Region
784 (3.3)
Taymyrsky
(Dolgano-Nenetsky)
Autonomous District
802 (3.2)
Ust-Ordynsky Buryatsky
Autonomous District
809 (3.5)
Republic of Sakha
(Yakutia)
825 (3.3)
Maritime Territory
837 (3.3)
Amur Region
860 (3.3)
Magadan Region
878 (3.2)
Sakhalin Region
886 (3.3)
Koryaksky Autonomous
District
905 (3.3)
Chukotsky
Autonomous District
914 (3.3)

FUEL
(NO SPECIFICATION)

Vladimir Region
55 (Tbl4)
Ivanovo Region
73 (Tbl4)
Moscow Region
123 (Tbl4)
Ryazan Region
151 (Tbl4)
Tver Region
179 (Tbl4)
Yaroslavl Region
200 (Tbl4)

Murmansk Region
294 (Tbl4)
Novgorod Region
303 (Tbl4)
Republic of Adygeya
340 (Tbl4)
Republic
of Kabardino-
Balkaria
367 (Tbl4)
Republic of Mariy El
476 (Tbl4)
Republic
of Udmurtia
506 (Tbl4)
Kirov Region
525 (Tbl4)
Nizhny Novgorod
Region
534 (Tbl4)
Ulyanovsk Region
599 (Tbl4)
Sverdlovsk Region
628 (Tbl4)
Chelyabinsk Region
647 (Tbl4)
Omsk Region
764 (Tbl4)
Aginsky Buryatsky
Autonomous District
795 (Tbl4)
Khabarovsk Territory
850 (Tbl4)
Kamchatka Region
870 (Tbl4)
Jewish Autonomous
Region
897 (Tbl4)

NATURAL GAS

Komi Republic
238 (3.3)
Nenetsky Autonomous
District
329 (3.3)
Republic
of Dagestan
349 (3.3)
Republic of Kalmykia
377 (3.3)
Chechen Republic
403 (3.5)
Krasnodar Territory
410 (3.6)
Stavropol Territory
421 (3.3)
Astrakhan Region
432 (3.3)
Volgograd Region
444 (3.6)
Republic
of Bashkortostan
464 (3.3)
Orenburg Region
546 (3.3)

Perm Region
566 (3.3)
Saratov Region
588 (3.3)
Tyumen Region
637 (3.2)
Khanty-Mansiysky
Autonomous
District – Yugra
655 (3.3)
Yamalo-Nenetsky
Autonomous District
667 (3.3)
Tomsk Region
773 (3.3)
Republic of Sakha
(Yakutia)
825 (3.3)
Sakhalin Region
886 (3.3)

NUCLEAR FUEL

Kurgan Region
619 (3.6)
Tomsk Region
774 (3.3)

OIL

• **Oil processing**
Moscow
213 (3.3)
Komi Republic
238 (3.3)
Leningrad Region
281 (3.3)
Krasnodar Territory
409 (3.3)
Stavropol Territory
421 (3.3)
Volgograd Region
442 (3.3)
Republic of
Bashkortostan
464 (3.3)
Republic of Tatarstan
496 (3.3)
Perm Region
566 (3.3)
Samara Region
577 (3.3)
Saratov Region
588 (3.3)
Khanty-Mansiysky
Autonomous
District – Yugra
655 (3.3)
• **Oil extraction**
Komi Republic
238 (3.3)
Kaliningrad Region
270 (3.3)
Nenetsky Autonomous
District
329 (3.3)

Republic of Dagestan
349 (3.3)
Republic of Ingushetia
357 (3.3)
Republic of Kalmykia
377 (3.3)
Chechen Republic
402 (3.3)
Krasnodar Territory
410 (3.6)
Stavropol Territory
421 (3.3)
Astrakhan Region
432 (3.3)
Volgograd Region
442 (3.3)
Republic of
Bashkortostan
464 (3.3)
Republic of Tatarstan
495 (3.3)
Orenburg Region
546 (3.3)
Penza Region
558 (3.6)
Perm Region
566 (3.3)
Samara Region
577 (3.3)
Saratov Region
588 (3.3)
Komi-Permyatsky
Autonomous District
609 (3.6)
Tyumen Region
637 (3.2)
Khanty-Mansiysky
Autonomous
District – Yugra
655 (3.3)
Yamalo-Nenetsky
Autonomous District
667 (3.3)
Tomsk Region
773 (3.3)
Evenkiysky
Autonomous District
814 (3.2)
Republic of Sakha
(Yakutia)
825 (3.3)
Sakhalin Region
886 (3.3)

**GLASS AND
PORCELAIN**

Vladimir Region
54 (3.3)
Leningrad Region
282 (3.3)
Bryansk Region
44 (Tbl4)
Kursk Region
103 (Tbl4)

Oryol Region
140 (Tbl4)
Tver Region
179 (Tbl4)
Vologda Region
259 (Tbl4)
Novgorod Region
303 (Tbl4)
Pskov Region
312 (Tbl4)
Republic of North
Ossetia – Alania
393 (Tbl4)
Krasnodar Territory
409 (Tbl4)
Volgograd Region
443 (Tbl4)
Rostov Region
453 (Tbl4)
Republic of
Bashkortostan
465 (Tbl4)
Republic of Mariy El
476 (Tbl4)
Nizhny Novgorod
Region
534 (Tbl4)
Penza Region
557 (Tbl4)
Saratov Region
589 (3.6)
Ulyanovsk Region
599 (Tbl4)
Chelyabinsk Region
647 (Tbl4)
Irkutsk Region
731 (Tbl4)

JEWELRY

Smolensk Region
160 (3.3)
Republic of Sakha
(Yakutia)
825 (3.3)

LIGHT INDUSTRY

Vladimir Region
55 (3.3)
Ivanovo Region
73 (3.3)
Kostroma Region
93 (3.3)
Moscow Region
123 (3.3)
Ryazan Region
152 (3.2)
Tambov Region
171 (3.3)
Tver Region
179 (3.2)
Moscow
213 (3.3)

Bryansk Region
44 (Tbl4)
Vladimir Region
55 (Tbl4)
Moscow Region
123 (Tbl4)
Oryol Region
140 (Tbl4)
Ryazan Region
151 (Tbl4)
Tula Region
190 (Tbl4)
Moscow
212 (Tbl4)
Republic
of Karelia
229 (Tbl4)
Komi Republic
238 (Tbl4)
Arkhangelsk Region
249 (Tbl4)
Vologda Region
259 (Tbl4)
Pskov Region
312 (Tbl4)
Republic
of Karachayevo-
Cherkessia
386 (Tbl4)
Volgograd Region
443 (Tbl4)
Rostov Region
453 (Tbl4)
Nizhny Novgorod
Region
534 (Tbl4)
Penza Region
557 (Tbl4)

Saratov Region
589 (Tbl4)
Omsk Region
764 (Tbl4)
Jewish Autonomous
Region
897 (Tbl4)

MINING AND
QUARRYING *

METAL ORE MINING

Belgorod Region
35 (3.3)
Kursk Region
103 (3.6)
Arkhangelsk Region
250 (3.5)
Murmansk Region
293 (3.3)
Republic of Dagestan
350 (3.6)
Republic
of Kabardino-
Balkaria
367 (3.3)
Sverdlovsk Region
628 (3.6)
Republic of Altai
677 (3.6)
Republic of Buryatia
685 (3.6)
Republic of Tyva
693 (3.3)
Republic of Khakassia
703 (3.6)

Krasnoyarsk Territory
721 (3.5)
Irkutsk Region
730 (3.3)
Chita Region
784 (3.3)
Republic of Sakha
(Yakutia)
825 (3.3)
Maritime Territory
837 (3.3)
Khabarovsk
Territory
851 (3.6)
Amur Region
860 (3.3)
Kamchatka Region
870 (3.6)
Magadan Region
877 (3.2)
Jewish Autonomous
Region
897 (3.5)
Koryaksky
Autonomous
District
905 (3.3)
Chukotsky
Autonomous
District
913 (3.3)

QUARRYING

Vladimir Region
56 (3.6)
Kostroma Region
103 (3.6)

Lipetsk Region
112 (3.6)
Moscow Region
126 (3.6)
Leningrad Region
283 (3.6)
Pskov Region
312 (3.6)
Republic
of Dagestan
350 (3.6)
Republic
of Mariy El
477 (3.6)
Republic
of Mordovia
487 (3.6)
Republic of Altai
677 (3.6)
Republic
of Khakassia
703 (3.6)
Novosibirsk Region
754 (3.6)
Maritime Territory
838 (3.6)

OTHER MINING
AND QUARRYING

Kaliningrad Region
271 (3.6)
Leningrad Region
283 (3.6)
Murmansk Region
294 (3.6)
Stavropol Territory
422 (3.5)

Astrakhan Region
433 (3.6)
Volgograd Region
444 (3.3)
Republic of Mordovia
487 (3.6)
Perm Region
568 (3.6)
Sverdlovsk Region
628 (3.6)
Khanty-Mansiysky
Autonomous
District – Yugra
656 3.6)
Republic
of Buryatia
686 (3.6)
Republic of Tyva
694 (3.6)
Republic
of Khakassia
703 (3.6)
Irkutsk Region
732 (3.6)
Evenkiysky
Autonomous
District
815 (3.5)
Republic
of Sakha
(Yakutia)
826 (3.3)
Maritime Territory
838 (3.3)
Koryaksky
Autonomous
District
906 (3.6)

---

*Excluding fuel
and energy resources

INDEXES AND REFERENCES

IND

INDEXES AND REFERENCES

IND

*Excluding food and beverages and energy sectors

INDEXES AND REFERENCES

IND

INDEXES AND REFERENCES

IND

---

*Excluding fuel
and energy resources

*Excluding food and beverages and energy sectors

INDEXES AND REFERENCES

IND

INDEXES AND REFERENCES

IND

---

* Excluding fuel and energy resource extraction

INDEXES AND REFERENCES

IND

Novosibirsk Region 754 (3.6)

Chita Region 784 (3.6)

Aginsky Buryatsky Autonomous District 795 (3.5)

Taymyrsky (Dolgano-Nenetsky) Autonomous District 803 (3.5)

Evenkiysky Autonomous District 815 (3.6)

Republic of Sakha (Yakutia) 826 (3.6)

Maritime Territory 838 (3.6)

Khabarovsk Territory 851 (3.6)

Amur Region 861 (3.6)

Kamchatka Region 870 (3.6)

Magadan Region 878 (3.5)

Sakhalin Region 888 (3.6)

Jewish Autonomous Region 897 (3.5)

Koryaksky Autonomous District 906 (3.6)

Chukotsky Autonomous District 914 (3.6)

• **Rare earth metals (tantalum, niobium, vanadium, cerium, zirconium, ytterbium, etc.)**

Bryansk Region 45 (3.5)

Republic of Karelia 230 (3.6)

Murmansk Region 294 (3.6)

Stavropol Territory 422 (3.6)

Nizhny Novgorod Region 535 (3.6)

Orenburg Region 547 (3.6)

Komi-Permyatsky Autonomous District 609 (3.6)

Kurgan Region 619 (3.6)

Sverdlovsk Region 628 (3.6)

Khanty-Mansiysky Autonomous District – Yugra 656 (3.6)

Republic of Altai 677 (3.6)

Republic of Buryatia 685 (3.6)

Republic of Tyva 694 (3.6)

Irkutsk Region 732 (3.6)

Novosibirsk Region 754 (3.6)

Chita Region 784 (3.6)

Aginsky Buryatsky Autonomous District 795 (3.5)

Evenkiysky Autonomous District 815 (3.6)

Maritime Territory 838 (3.6)

• **Stibium ore**

Krasnoyarsk Territory 721 (3.5)

Aginsky Buryatsky Autonomous District 795 (3.5)

Republic of Sakha (Yakutia) 826 (3.6)

• **Tin ore**

Republic of Buryatia 685 (3.6)

Krasnoyarsk Territory 721 (3.5)

Chita Region 785 (3.6)

Republic of Sakha (Yakutia) 826 (3.6)

Maritime Territory 838 (3.6)

Khabarovsk Territory 851 (3.6)

Magadan Region 878 (3.5)

Jewish Autonomous Region 897 (3.5)

Koryaksky Autonomous District 906 (3.6)

Chukotsky Autonomous District 914 (3.6)

• **Titanium ore (including ilmenite and leucoxene)**

Bryansk Region 45 (3.5)

Republic of Karelia 230 (3.6)

Komi Republic 238 (3.6)

Murmansk Region 294 (3.6)

Stavropol Territory 422 (3.6)

Komi-Permyatsky Autonomous District 609 (3.6)

Kurgan Region 619 (3.6)

Chelyabinsk Region 648 (3.6)

Novosibirsk Region 754 (3.6)

Tomsk Region 775 (3.6)

Taymyrsky (Dolgano-Nenetsky) Autonomous District 803 (3.5)

Amur Region 861 (3.6)

• **Tungsten ore**

Republic of Kabardino-Balkaria 368 (3.6)

Republic of Karachayevo-Cherkessia 386 (3.6)

Kurgan Region 619 (3.6)

Republic of Altai 677 (3.6)

Krasnoyarsk Territory 721 (3.6)

Chita Region 785 (3.6)

Aginsky Buryatsky Autonomous District 795 (3.5)

Maritime Territory 838 (3.6)

Magadan Region 878 (3.5)

RAW MINERALS FOR CHEMICALS AND FERTILIZERS PRODUCTION FACILITIES

ALUNITE

Khabarovsk Territory 851 (3.6)

APATITE

Republic of Karelia 230 (3.6)

Krasnodar Territory 410 (3.6)

Taymyrsky (Dolgano-Nenetsky) Autonomous District 803 (3.5)

Khabarovsk Territory 851 (3.6)

Amur Region 861 (3.6)

BARIUM SULFATE (BARITE)

Komi Republic 238 (3.6)

Yamalo-Nenetsky Autonomous District 667 (3.6)

Republic of Khakassia 703 (3.6)

FLUOR-SPAR (FLUORITE)

Nenetsky Autonomous District 330 (3.6)

Republic of Buryatia 685 (3.6)

Maritime Territory 838 (3.6)

MINERAL DYES

Oryol Region 140 (3.6)

Ryazan Region 152 (3.5)

Yaroslavl Region 201 (3.6)

Novgorod Region 303 (3.6)

Pskov Region 312 (3.6)

Saratov Region 590 (3.6)

Komi-Permyatsky Autonomous District 609 (3.6)

Kurgan Region 619 (3.6)

Evenkiysky Autonomous District 815 (3.6)

MINERAL SALT (EXCLUDING TABLE SALT)

Stavropol Territory 422 (3.6)

Volgograd Region 444 (3.6)

Orenburg Region 547 (3.6)

Perm Region 568 (3.6)

Saratov Region 590 (3.6)

Irkutsk Region 732 (3.6)

Omsk Region 765 (3.6)

NATURAL BORATES

Maritime Territory 838 (3.6)

PHOSPHORITES

Bryansk Region 45 (3.5)

Voronezh Region 65 (3.6)

Kaluga Region 83 (3.6)

Kursk Region 103 (3.6)

Lipetsk Region 112 (3.6)

Moscow Region 125 (3.6)

Oryol Region 140 (3.6)

Ryazan Region 152 (3.5)

Tambov Region 171 (3.6)

Leningrad Region 283 (3.6)

Murmansk Region 294 (3.6)

Volgograd Region 444 (3.6)

Republic of Chuvashia 516 (3.6)

Kirov Region 525 (3.6)

Samara Region 578 (3.6)

Saratov Region 590 (3.6)

Yamalo-Nenetsky Autonomous District 667 (3.6)

Krasnoyarsk Territory 721 (3.5)

Evenkiysky Autonomous District 815 (3.6)

SAPROPEL

Ivanovo Region 74 (3.6)

Kostroma Region 94 (3.6)

Moscow Region 125 (3.6)

Smolensk Region 161 (3.6)

INDEXES AND REFERENCES

IND

INDEXES AND REFERENCES

IND

- *Silver*
Republic of Tyva
697 (66R001)
- **Non-ferrous metal goods**
- *Aluminum and aluminum-alloy goods*
Moscow Region
130 (10R001)
Komi Republic
243 (20R008)
- *Composite aluminum goods*
Republic of Chuvashia
518 (48R001)
- *Molybdenum wire*
Republic of Mordovia
490 (45R004)
- *Rolled non-ferrous metals*
Orenburg Region
552 (51R013)
- **Other non-ferrous metals related goods**
- *Alumina*
Komi Republic
243 (20R008)

MINING* AND QUARRYING

STONE, CLAY AND SAND QUARRYING

- **Building stone (marble, granite, sandstone and other building and facing stones)**
Republic of Karelia
233 (19R001)
Orenburg Region
552 (51R009)
Perm Region
572 (53R006)
Tomsk Region
777 (74R001),
778 (74R002)
- **Clay and kaolin**
Kaluga Region
86 (06R001),
87 (06R004)
Amur Region
865 (83R002)
- **Gravel, sand, and crashed stone**
Kaluga Region
86 (06R003)
Moscow Region
133 (10R020)

*Excluding fuel and energy resource extraction

Tver Region
186 (15R023)
Leningrad Region
287 (24R001)
Stavropol Territory
425 (39R001)
- **Limestone, dolomite, gypsum, and chalk**
Kaluga Region
86 (06R001)
Republic of Ingushetia
361 (32R002)

IRON ORES EXTRACTION

- **Concentrated iron ore**
Jewish Autonomous Region
901 (87R006)
- **Iron ore**
Republic of Khakassia
706 (67R001)
- **Pellets**
Amur Region
864 (83R001)
Tula Region
194 (16R001)

METAL ORES EXTRACTION (NO SPECIFICATION)

- **Ore (no specification)**
Murmansk Region
297 (25R001)

NON-FERROUS ORES

- **Alkaline and alkaline-earth metals ores and concentrated ores (barium, lithium, stronzium, etc.)**
Evenkiysky Autonomous District
817 (79R004),
818 (79R005)
- **Complex ores (including: copper, lead and zinc ore)**
Orenburg Region
551 (51R006)
Republic of Buryatia
688 (65R002)
Republic of Tyva
697 (66R002)

Maritime Territory
842 (81R004)
- **Concentrated copper ore**
Orenburg Region
551 (51R007)
- **Concentrated manganese ore**
Jewish Autonomous Region
900 (87R005)
Komi Republic
242 (20R005)
- **Concentrated molybdenum ore**
Republic of Kabardino-Balkaria
371 (33R001)
- **Concentrated tin ore**
Jewish Autonomous Region
901 (87R007)
- **Concentrated titanium and manganese ore**
Kamchatka Region
872 (84R001)
- **Concentrated tungsten ore**
Republic of Kabardino-Balkaria
371 (33R001)
- **Gold ores and placer gold**
Irkutsk Region
735 (70R001)
Chita Region
787 (75R001),
788 (75R002),
788 (75R003)
Evenkiysky Autonomous District
817 (79R003)
Republic of Sakha (Yakutia)
831 (80R008),
831 (80R009),
831 (80R010),
886 (80R011),
832 (80R012)
Magadan Region
881 (85R001),
881 (85R002),
881 (85R003),
881 (85R004),
882 (85R011)
Chukotka Autonomous District
916 (89R001)
- **Nickel ore**
Orenburg Region
551 (51R005)

- **Rare metal ores (berillium, niobium, tantalum, zirconium)**
Tambov Region
173 (14R001)
Chita Region
788 (75R004),
788 (75R005),
788 (75R006)
Khabarovsk Territory
854 (82R002)
- **Titanium ore**
Komi Republic
243 (20R006)

OTHER MINING AND QUARRYING

- **Raw minerals for chemicals and fertilizers production facilities**
- *Barium sulfate barite)*
Komi Republic
242 (20R004)
- *Fluor-spar*
Maritime Territory
842 (81R005),
842 (81R006)
- *Zeolite*
Kamchatka Region
872 (84R002)
- **Other subsoil natural resources**
- *Graphite*
Chelyabinsk Region
650 (61R001)
Evenkiysky Autonomous District
817 (79R002)
Jewish Autonomous Region
900 (87R004)
- *Quartz*
Republic of Buryatia
688 (65R001)
- *Raw diamonds*
Republic of Sakha (Yakutia)
831 (80R005),
831 (80R006),
831 (80R007)
- *Salt*
Komi Republic
243 (20R007)
Orenburg Region
551 (51R008)
- *Talc*
Jewish Autonomous Region
900 (87R003)

- *Tripoli*
Kaluga Region
87 (06R005)

PRINTING INDUSTRY

PRINTED MATTER

Yaroslavl Region
206 (17R009)
Saratov Region
594 (55R010)

OTHER INDUSTRIES

ECOLOGY AND WASTE PROCESSING

- **Automobile and household appliance processing facility for production of briquetted ferrous and non-ferrous metals**
Moscow Region
133 (10R018),
133 (10R023)
- **Automotive tire and rubber waste processing products**
Moscow Region
133 (10R019),
134 (10R025)
- **Construction and reinforced concrete waste processing facility for production of building materials**
Moscow Region
133 (10R020)
- **Corrugated packaging production on the basis of enhanced household and industrial waste processing**
Stavropol Territory
427 (39R010)
- **Elimination of filtration dumping into the Moskva river and combustible facility products into the air**
Moscow Region
134 (10R024)

- **Development of the design for the construction of two-reactor nuclear power plants**
Nizhny Novgorod Region
541 (50R018)
- **Elaboration of deep placer gold mining methods**
Magadan Region
882 (85R011)
- **Implementation of technology for heat insulating materials production**
Oryol Region
147 (11R029)
- **Introduction of a Perfocor medical unit into medical practice**
Moscow Region
135 (10R029)
- **Introduction of CALS technology for the design of modern vessels**
Nizhny Novgorod Region
541 (50R015)
- **Production of cellular ceramic tube**
Tomsk Region
778 (74R006)
- **Production of high frequency aircraft antennas**
Nizhny Novgorod Region
542 (50R020)
- **Production of long-distance radiolocation systems**
Tomsk Region
779 (74R008)
- **Production of organic and mineral fertilizers**
Irkutsk Region
737 (70R011)
- **Production of polymer food packaging materials**
Irkutsk Region
737 (70R012)

- **Production of polyvinyl-chloride plastic filled with local natural materials**
Irkutsk Region
737 (70R013)
- **Production of «solar quality» silicon and solar energy devices**
Tomsk Region
779 (74R007)
- **Research and certification of materials used in energy equipment**
Moscow Region
135 (10R030)
- **Technology for production of automation systems for fuel and energy sector**
Nizhny Novgorod Region
579 (50R019)
- **Upgrading of Cosmos carrier rocket**
Omsk Region
769 (73R016)

TRADE

- **Construction of an interregional wholesale market**
Tver Region
186 (15R024)
- **Expanding of trade and office areas**
Tver Region
186 (15R025)
Astrakhan Region
438 (40R013)
Republic of Udmurtia
510 (47R004)
- **Providing services to the public (car service center, consumer household s ervices, catering)**
Yaroslavl Region
206 (17R013)
- **Renting out sales space**
Moscow
221 (18R009),
221 (18R010),
221 (18R011)

- **Services provided by an international trade and industry complex**
Chita Region
790 (75R016)
- **Updating product mix (improving retail trade services**
Oryol Region
147 (11R028)
Yaroslavl Region
206 (17R012)
Vologda Region
265 (22R012)
Astrakhan Region
437 (40R006)
Krasnoyarsk Territory
726 (69R007)

TRANSPORT AND COMMUNICATIONS

- **Cellular communication networks and Internet services**
Oryol Region
147 (11R027)
Yaroslavl Region
206 (17R011)
- **Communication services**
Khanty-Mansiysky Autonomous District – Yugra
662 (62R016)
Chita Region
790 (75R015)
- **Construction of a broadband radio access system**
Perm Region
572 (53R007)
- **Construction of a digital communication network**
Republic of Khakassia
707 (67R009)
Novosibirsk Region
759 (72R009)
Omsk Region
769 (73R014)
- **High-speed transport system**
Moscow
220 (18R008)
- **Integrated radio and TV broadcasting network**
Khabarovsk Territory
856 (82R016)

- **International freight road haulage services**
Voronezh Region
69 (04R009)
- **Launching of digital TV broadcasting**
Maritime Territory
845 (81R024)
- **On-surface services for aircraft**
Moscow Region
132 (10R013)
- **Optical fiber communication line services**
Komi Republic
244 (20R013)
- **Passenger and freight traffic by air**
Ivanovo Region
78 (05R005)
Yaroslavl Region
206 (17R010)
Arkhangelsk Region
254 (21R013),
254 (21R014)
Kaliningrad Region
275 (23R015)
Republic of Adygeya
344 (30R005)
Republic of Dagestan
353 (31R009)
Republic of Kalmykia
381 (34R009)
Volgograd Region
448 (41R009)
Rostov Region
458 (42R008),
458 (42R009)
Samara Region
584 (54R012)
Irkutsk Region
736 (70R007)
Novosibirsk Region
759 (72R008)
Omsk Region
769 (73R013)
Chita Region
790 (75R013)
Koryaksky Autonomous District
909 (88R003)
- **Passenger and freight traffic by motor transport**
Kostroma Region
98 (07R004)
Smolensk Region
166 (13R016)
Tver Region
185 (15R022)

Tver Region
186 (15R023)
Kaliningrad Region
276 (23R018)
Nenetsky Autonomous District
333 (29R004)
Samara Region
584 (54R013)
Khanty-Mansiysky Autonomous District – Yugra
661 (62R014),
662 (62R015)
Maritime Territory
844 (81R018)
Koryaksky Autonomous District
909 (88R004)
- **Passenger and freight traffic by railroad transport**
Komi Republic
244 (20R012)
Arkhangelsk Region
254 (21R015)
Astrakhan Region
437 (40R010)
Saratov Region
594 (55R011)
Khanty-Mansiysky Autonomous District – Yugra
661 (62R013)
Chita Region
789 (75R012)
Republic of Sakha (Yakutia)
832 (80R015)
- **Passenger and freight traffic by sea transport**
Kaliningrad Region
276 (23R016),
276 (23R017)
Leningrad Region
289 (24R011)
Murmansk Region
298 (25R007)
Nenetsky Autonomous District
333 (29R003)
Republic of Dagestan
353 (31R008)
Republic of Kalmykia
381 (34R008)
- **Taxi services**
St. Petersburg
325 (28R007)

- **Training
  of business
  class aviation
  professionals**
Moscow Region
  132 (10R013)
- **Transport pro-
  cessing
  of cargoes**
Moscow Region
  132 (10R013)
Murmansk Region
  298 (25R006)

Krasnodar
  Territory
  415 (38R012),
  415 (38R013),
  415 (38R014),
  415 (38R015)
Astrakhan
  Region
  437 (40R007),
  437 (40R008),
  437 (40R009),
  438 (40R011),
  438 (40R012)

Maritime Territory
  844 (81R020),
  844 (81R021)
Khabarovsk Territory
  856 (82R015)
- **Transportation
  of gas via pipelines**
Arkhangelsk Region
  254 (21R012)
Kaliningrad Region
  275 (23R014)
Khabarovsk Territory
  856 (82R014)

- **Transportation
  of oil via pipelines**
Khanty- Mansiysky
  Autonomous
  District – Yugra
  661 (62R012)
- **Transshipment
  port services**
Leningrad Region
  288 (24R008),
  289 (24R009),
  289 (24R010),
  289 (24R012),

  289 (24R013),
  289 (24R014)
Murmansk Region
  298 (25R005)
Maritime Territory
  844 (81R019)
- **Warehouse
  terminal
  services**
Samara Region
  584 (54R014)
Chita Region
  790 (75R014)

CONTENTS

SPONSORS AND ADVERTISERS OF THE GUIDE

COMPANIES

Access Industries
Delta Air Lines
John Deere
KV Partners
SwissFone

ALRUD Law Firm
Aviacor Aviation Plant, OAO
Avtoban Road Construction
  Company, OAO
Baltimor
B.P. Konstantinov Kirovo-
  Chepetsky Chemicals
  Combine, OAO
CentreInvest Group
Expocentr, ZAO
Gazkomplektimpeks-Patterani,
  Joint Venture, ZAO
In Jure Moscow Bar
KaliningradGazkomplektimpex
Marka Publishing and Trading
  Centre, FGUP

Mavial Magadan Airlines, FGUP
Moscow Training &
  Manufacturing Enterprise No.
  11 VOS, OOO
Non-state Pension
  Fund Opeka
President Publishing
  Center, OOO
Plaza Gruppa
Remtyazhmash, ZAO
  Roseximbank
Salavatnefteorgsintez, OAO
St. Petersburg Brand
Svoboda Cosmetics
  Association, OAO
Talosto
Technolux
Togliattikauchuk, OOO
Yakor Insurance
  Company, OAO
Yury Gagarin Komsomolsk-on-
  Amur Aviation Manufacturing
  Conglomerate (KNAAPO), OAO
Vnesheconombank

ORGANIZATIONS

Council for Trade
  and Economic Cooperation
  Russia–USA (CTEC)
Russian Children's Welfare
  Society (RCWS)
Russian Union of Industrialists
  and Entrepreneurs
  (Employers)
St. Petersburg Jewelers
  Assembly The International
  Chamber of Commerce –
  The World Business
  Organization (ICC)
United Nations Development
  Programme (UNDP)
USA-Russia Business Council

PERIODICAL PUBLICATIONS

Diplomat Magazine
The Moscow Times

HYDROGRAPHY AND RELIEF

Sea

River, lake

BARENTS SEA   Names of seas

Lake Seliger   Volga   Names of lakes, rivers

Dolgy island   Names of islands, peninsulas

Cape of Kanin Nos   Names of capes

COUNTRIES, REGIONS, AND TOWNS

FINLAND   Names of countries

TAMBOV REGION   Names of Territories, Regions

PSKOV   Names of regional centers

Plussa   Names of other towns

ROADS

———————   Railroad

———————   Road

PIPELINES

Oil pipelines

Gas pipelines

PORTS

⚓   Seaports

🐟   Fishing ports

✈   International airports

✈   Interregional airports

ECONOMY

INDUSTRY

MINING
INDUSTRY

- Oil
- Natural gas
- Combustible shale
- Raw cement
- Bituminous coal
- Brown coal
- Iron ore
- Gold
- Mica
- Table salt
- Marble
- Phosphorites
- Tin
- Tungsten
- Molybdenum
- Graphite
- Chrome
- Copper
- Manganese
- Nickel
- Complex ore
- Sulfur
- Asbestos
- Potassium salt
- Talc
- Fluorite
- Bauxite
- Diamonds
- Magnesite
- Apatite
- Amber
- Mercury
- Uranium
- Quartz
- Peat
- Clay
- Chalk
- Limestone
- Granite
- Dolomite
- Gypsum
- Construction stone
- Barite
- Marl
- Glauber's salt
- Mineral
  water
  sources

PROCESSING
INDUSTRY

- Ferrous metals
- Non-ferrous metals
- Machine engineering
  and metal processing
- Chemicals
  and petrochemicals
- Forestry and timber
- Construction materials/
  construction
  materials and glass
- Light industry
- Food and beverages
- Art crafts

AGRICULTURE

CROPS

- Wheat
- Rye
- Barley
- Sunflower
- Melons and gourds
- Rice
- Sugar beetroot
- Orchards
- Mustard
- Long-fibred flax
- Crown flax
- Vineyards
- Aromatic plants
- Corn
- Tobacco
- Buckwheat
- Soybeans
- Saffron milk cap
- Vegetables
- Hemp
- Hop
- Oats
- Potatoes
- Tea
- Rape

LIVESTOCK BREEDING

- Meat and dairy
  cattle breeding
- Pig breeding
- Sheep rearing
- Reindeer breeding
- Reindeer breeding for antlers
- Poultry farming

- Horse breeding
- Beekeeping
- Animal farming

SEA ANIMAL
CATCH

- Sea animal catch
- Crab catch

POWER PLANTS

- Thermal power plants
- Hydro power plants
- Nuclear power plants
- Coordinated
  hydroelectric system

- Resorts

INVESTMENT
PROJECT
CONVENTIONAL
SYMBOLS

- Loan
- Equity
- Leasing
- Joint venture
- Business plan
- Feasibility study
- Investment proposal
- Project documentation

US-RUSSIA COUNCIL FOR TRADE & ECONOMIC COOPERATION (CTEC)

Established in 1992 in Moscow as a Russian non-commercial partnership, the US-Russia Council for Trade & Economic Cooperation (CTEC) is a public association of businesses from the US and Russia. In terms of its charter aims and sphere of activities, the CTEC is the successor to US-USSR Trade and Economic Council (ASTEC). The CTEC aims to develop the full spectrum of trade, economic and investment collaboration between Russia and the US at the corporate level. In collaboration with other business associations in the US, the Council hosts various events including conferences, seminars, exhibitions, etc.
Major areas of activity include information and advisory services, visa and passport support, and organizing business programs both within Russia and abroad. The Council has a special mission to identify opportunities for the organization of collaboration between individual companies on trade and investment projects. Publishing is another one of the Council's activities; the Council initiated the publication of this Guide. The Council works in close collaboration with the Russian Union of Industrialists and Entrepreneurs.

NAB. T. SHEVCHENKO 3, MOSCOW 121248
TEL.: (095) 243 54 70, 243 54 94; FAX (095) 258 83 80
E-MAIL: ctec@sovintel.ru; http://www.ctec.ru

K.C. HENNESSEY ASSOCIATES LLC

K.C. Hennessey Associates LLC, Investors and Advisors in Eastern Europe and Russia. Founded in 1998 by Kevin C. Hennessey, after 25 years in Global Investment Banking as Head of Emerging Markets and Chairman of the Ethics Committee of one of the world's leading investment banks. Together with its affiliated organizations, K.C. Hennessey Associates LLC has a wide range of assignments and philanthropic interests from Nuclear Non Proliferation to Asset Management.

10, ROCKEFELLER PLAZA, SUITE 1007
NEW YORK, NEW YORK 10020
TEL.: 212 332 2969
FAX: 212 332 2998
E-MAIL: kvhennessey@kvpartnersllc.com

CentreInvest Group

Founded in 1992, CentreInvest Group is Russia's leading independent financial and advisory firm. CentreInvest Group has several divisions: Aksion Consulting provides financial and management advisory services to Russian corporate and private clients in most industry sectors, as well as international corporations and government organizations.

The company has won several tenders organized by international organizations, including tenders for advisory projects in Russia organized by the World Bank and the European Union Tacis Programme. CentreInvest Group also Russian brokerage firm CentreInvest Securities and information technology and corporate information system developer CentreInvest Soft. The Group's international financial transactions are looked after by CentreInvest Inc. (USA), which holds SEC and NASD licenses to perform all types of securities transactions in the US. CentreInvest Group employs more than 200 professionals at its offices in Moscow, St. Petersburg, New York and London. CentreInvest Group is proud to have prepared for print the Russia: All 89 Regions. Trade & Investment Guide.

CentreInvest Group

10 years of success

Over 100 corporate clients

Over 200 professional staff

International and Russian expertize

Offices in Moscow, St. Petersburg, London and New York

YUKOS · ROLLS ROYS · BRITISH PETROLEUM · RAO EES · TNK · CHEVRON · SURGUT NEFTEGAZ · Gazprom · OMZ · Russian Paints · ROSNEFT · Shatura Mebel · NORILSK GAZPROM · Volgabanker · SEVER STAL

Ideas in Action

UL. VRUBELYA 12, MOSCOW 125080
TEL: (095) 797 80 50
FAX: (095) 797 80 51
E-MAIL: info@centreinvest.com
http://www.centreinvest.com

President Publishing Center

Established in 1997, President Publishing Center specializes in the publication of social and economic directories and journals created by the federal bodies of state governance of the Russian Federation.
President Publishing Center collaborates closely on publishing and other projects with the Federation Council, Ministry of Transport of Russia, Ministry of Agriculture of Russia, and Government of Moscow.

ПРЕЗИДЕНТ®
ИЗДАТЕЛЬСКИЙ ЦЕНТР

UL. MYASNITSKAYA 24/7 BUILDING 4, MOSCOW 101000
TEL: (095) 923 61 64, 923 09 15
E-MAIL: design@president-press.org

How to buy the Guide

The publisher, CTEC PUBLISHING LLC, offers individual and corporate users and book traders a broad range of options for long-term and mutually beneficial collaboration in purchasing and distributing this publication, including its bi-annual main volumes, additional interim editions, and electronic versions.

The publisher will introduce a discount system and special offers for permanent subscribers, and will apply a customized approach to users of the Guide and our potential partners.

CTEC PUBLISHING LLC is available to discuss all suggestions and initiatives aimed at enhancing the distribution of this Guide with a view to developing the trade, economic, and investment links between Russia's regions and the international business community, enhancing Russia's image, and promoting its economic achievements to potential partners.

Russia:
All 89 Regions.
Trade
and Investment
Guide

For more information
on distribution, sales,
subscription,
and on how to advertise
in the Guide,
please contact:

THE PRESIDENT PUBLISHING CENTER
WORKS IN COOPERATION WITH
THE STATE LEGISLATIVE AND EXECUTIVE
AGENCIES, ORGANIZATIONS
AND ESTABLISHMENTS, INCLUDING:

THE COUNCIL OF FEDERATION OF THE FEDERAL ASSEMBLY
OF THE RUSSIAN FEDERATION
MINISTRY OF TRANSPORT OF THE RUSSIAN FEDERATION
MINISTRY OF COMMUNICATIONS OF THE RUSSIAN FEDERATION
MINISTRY OF HEALTHCARE OF THE RUSSIAN FEDERATION
MINISTRY OF EDUCATION OF THE RUSSIAN FEDERATION
MINISTRY OF AGRICULTURE OF THE RUSSIAN FEDERATION
GOVERNMENT OF MOSCOW CITY
CITY COUNCIL OF ST. PETERSBURG
RUSSIAN UNION OF INDUSTRIALISTS
AND ENTREPRENEURS (EMPLOYERS)
RUSSIA – USA CTEC
CENTREINVEST GROUP
KHRUNICHEV SPACE CENTER
MOSCOW CITY SANITARY AND EPIDEMIC CONTROL CENTER
FEDERAL DIRECTORY PUBLICATION
RUSSIA'S ECONOMY: 21ST CENTURY MAGAZINE
WORLD TEA FESTIVAL
NATIONAL HEALTH LEAGUE

ПРЕЗИДЕНТ®

ИЗДАТЕЛЬСКИЙ ЦЕНТР

THE PRESIDENT PUBLISHING CENTER MEANS
WORKING IN OUR RUSSIA AND FOR RUSSIA.
IT MEANS SERVING THE STATE.

The PRESIDENT Publishing Center means working for the President.
It means creation of a respectable, fine, discrete and always
beautiful style, reflecting a strict balance between a form and content.
The President and the Government, the State Duma
and the Council of Federation, Federal ministries
and large companies – in their work all of them need publications
created in line with their status. It is our concern to produce
presentation books, business brochures, illustrated albums, annual reports,
and calendars of immaculate design and high printing quality.

BY HAVING ENTRUSTED YOUR ORDER
TO US YOU MAY BE SURE THAT WE
WILL DO OUR WORK TO QUALITY
STANDARDS AND DEADLINES.

PRESIDENT

PUBLISHING CENTER

BLDG. 4, 24/7, UL. MYASNITSKAYA, MOSCOW, RUSSIA, 101000
TEL: +7 095 923 6164, 923 0915; FAX: +7 095 923 6327
E-MAIL: DESIGN@PRESIDENT-PRESS.ORG

ПРЕЗИДЕНТ®
ИЗДАТЕЛЬСКИЙ ЦЕНТР

PRESIDENT PUBLISHING CENTER
General Director
VLADIMIR PANKOV
Chief Designer
YURY MEDOVIKOV
Project Designer
YURY BUTOV
Advertisement design by
YEVGENIA BUBER, OLGA KOZHANOVA,
INNA SELIVERSTOVA, YELENA SHUTOVA
Computer page layout by
YEVGENIA BUBER, INNA SELIVERSTOVA,
ALEXEI SHISHKIN
Maps by
NATALIA KOUZINA
Prepress managers
MARIA MALINKINA, IRINA SOBOLEVA
Scanning and illustration processing by
OLEG TSUPRIKOV
Proof by
GALINA GADZHIYEVA, RIDIA MERKULOVA,
LYUDMILA NAUMOVA, ANTONINA PANTSOVA
Technical support by
ANDREI CHULICHKOV
English translation and editing
BRIAN KEEGAN, VSEVOLOD DEMIDOV,
YURY KUNITSKY

Russia:
ALL 89 REGIONS

TRADE

AND INVESTMENT

GUIDE

Offset printing
Paper WF OFFSET 70 g/m^2
Garniture Garamond Narrow
Circulation 6,800 copies

Design, page layout and makeup,
and technical support by
PRESIDENT PUBLISHING CENTER
License ID #04248 of March 12, 2001
BLDG. 4, 24/7, ul. Myasnitskaya,
Moscow, Russia, 101000
Telephones: +7 095 923 0915, 923 6164
Fax: +7 095 923 6327
E-mail: design@president-press.org
www.president.mediatext.ru
Printed in Porvoo, Finland by
WS BOOKWELL OY